# Canada

## THE ROUGH GUIDE

**Other available Rough Guides**
Amsterdam • Andalucia • Australia • Barcelona • Berlin • Brazil
Brittany & Normandy • Bulgaria • California • Corsica • Crete • Cyprus
Czech & Slovak Republics • Egypt • England • Europe • Florida • France
Germany • Greece • Guatemala & Belize • Holland, Belgium & Luxembourg
Hong Kong • Hungary • Ireland • Italy • Kenya • Mediterranean Wildlife
Mexico • Morocco • Nepal • New York • Nothing Ventured
Pacific Northwest • Paris • Peru • Poland • Portugal • Prague • Provence
Pyrenees • St Petersburg • San Francisco • Scandinavia • Scotland
Sicily • Spain • Thailand • Tunisia • Turkey • Tuscany & Umbria • USA
Venice • Wales • West Africa • Women Travel • Zimbabwe & Botswana

**Forthcoming**
India • Malaysia & Singapore • Classical Music • World Music

## Rough Guide to Canada credits

Editor: Jonathan Buckley
Assistant editor: David Reed
Production: Susanne Hillen and Vivien Antwi
Proofreading: Margaret Doyle
Typesetting: Andy Hilliard and Gail Jammy
Series editor: Mark Ellingham

The authors and editor would like to thank Mary Watson for all her work on the Rockies, Jan Johnston for her assistance in the early stages of this project, and Mary Ellen Collins, her successor at Canada House, for subsequent help. Individually, the authors would like to thank:

**Tim** – the staff at Alberta House and British Columbia House in London; *Greyhound*; Simon Reeve; Su; Mandy Wheelwright; Madeleine Tucker; and very special thanks to James and Vicky Ballantyne.

**Phil** – for their generous support, special thanks to Kelly Russell of Pigeon Inlet Productions and Kay Coxworthy of Newfoundland and Labrador Tourism; Lynda Hanscome of PEI Tourism; Catherine McNab and John Hamilton of Metropolitan Toronto Visitors' Association; Mike and Teri Gartner of Winnipeg; Jim Crone and Richard Wilson of the Manitoba Parks Department; Colette Fontaine and especially Joyce Meyer of Travel Manitoba; Karen Weild of Tourism Regina; and Gerard Makuch of Tourism Saskatchewan. Also thanks to Cathy Rees for her patience, Emma Rees for her company, and Ruth Rigby for the phrases.

**Tania** – Liz Fauteaux in Ottawa; Paul Les Fleurs and all at the Nicholas Gaol Hostel; Geneviève Beauvais at Québec House; the Labrier clan in Montréal; the Québec City posse – François, Marie-Claude, Michel and Valerie; Jean-Michel and the Tadoussac hostel; Alison Walsh; Henley and Penny Smith; Jim Mawdsley; Charlotte Bouchier; and special cheers to JB for the masses of help.

The publishers and authors have done their best to ensure the accuracy and currency of all information in *The Rough Guide to Canada*; however, they can accept no responsibility for any loss, injury, or inconvenience sustained by any traveller as a result of information or advice contained in the guide.

First published 1992, reprinted 1993 and April 1994 by Rough Guides Ltd, 1 Mercer Street, London WC2H 9QJ.

Distributed by the Penguin Group:

Penguin Books Ltd, 27 Wrights Lane, London W8 5TZ
Penguin Books USA Inc., 375 Hudson Street, New York 10014, USA
Penguin Books Australia Ltd, 487 Maroondah Highway, PO Box 257, Ringwood, Victoria 3134, Australia
Penguin Books Canada Ltd, 10 Alcorn Avenue, Toronto, Ontario, Canada M4V 1E4
Penguin Books (NZ) Ltd, 182–190 Wairau Road, Auckland 10, New Zealand

Previously published in the United States and Canada as *The Real Guide Canada*.

Typeset in Linotron Univers and Century Old Style to an original design by Andrew Oliver.
Printed in the United Kingdom by Cox and Wyman Ltd (Reading).
Maps by Micromap, 1 Nursery Gardens, Romsey, Hampshire SO51 8UU.
Illustrations in Part One and Part Three by Edward Briant.
Illustrations on p.1 and p.609 by Henry Iles.

672pp. Includes index.

A catalogue record for this book is available from the British Library.

ISBN 1-85828-001-X

# Canada

## THE ROUGH GUIDE

Written and researched by
**Tim Jepson, Phil Lee
and Tania Smith**

With contributions from
David Robson, Roger Spalding
and Steve & Kathi Quinn

THE ROUGH GUIDES

# CONTENTS

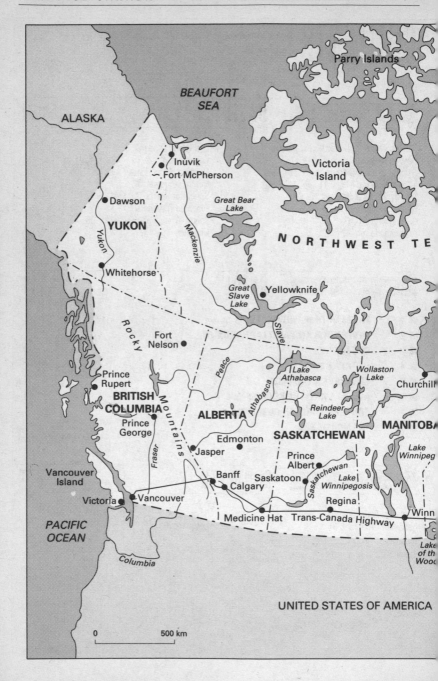

Parry Islands

BEAUFORT SEA

ALASKA

Inuvik
Fort McPherson

Dawson

YUKON

Victoria Island

Great Bear Lake

NORTHWEST TE

Mackenzie

Whitehorse

Great Slave Lake

Yellowknife

ROCKY

Fort Nelson

Slave

Peace

Lake Athabasca

Wollaston Lake

Churchill

Prince Rupert

BRITISH COLUMBIA

Mountains

Athabasca

Reindeer Lake

Prince George

Fraser

ALBERTA

SASKATCHEWAN

MANITOBA

Edmonton

Jasper

Prince Albert

Saskatchewan

Lake Winnipeg

Vancouver Island

Banff
Calgary

Saskatoon

Lake Winnipegosis

Victoria

Vancouver

Regina

Winn

PACIFIC OCEAN

Medicine Hat

Trans-Canada Highway

Lake of th Wood

Columbia

UNITED STATES OF AMERICA

0        500 km

# INTRODUCTION

S tretching from Atlantic to Pacific and from the latitude of Rome to beyond the Magnetic North Pole, Canada is almost unimaginably vast. Its archetypal scenes are the Rocky Mountain lakes and peaks, the endless forests and the prairie wheatfields, but Canada holds landscapes that defy expectations: rainforest and desert lie close together in the southwest corner of the country, while in the east a short drive can take you from fjords to lush orchards. What's more, great tracts of Canada are completely unspoiled – ninety percent of the country's 26 million population lives within 150 kilometres of the US border.

Like its intimidating neighbour, Canada is a spectrum of cultures, a hotch-potch of immigrant groups who supplanted the continent's native peoples. There's a crucial difference, though. Whereas citizens of the United States are encouraged to perceive themselves as Americans above all else, Canada's concertedly multicultural approach has done more to acknowledge the origins of its people, creating an ethnic mosaic as opposed to America's "melting-pot". Alongside the French and British majorities live a host of communities who maintain the traditions of their homelands – Chinese, Ukrainians, Portuguese, Indians, Pakistanis, Dutch, Polish, Greek, Spanish and Yugoslavs, to name just the most numerous. For the visitor, the mix that results from the country's exemplary tolerance is an exhilarating experience, offering such widely differing environments as Vancouver's huge Chinatown and the austere religious enclaves of Manitoba. Canadians themselves, however, are often troubled by the lack of a clear self-image, tending to emphasise the ways in which they are different from the US as a means of self-description. The question "What is a Canadian?" has acquired a new immediacy with the sometimes acrimonious movement of Québec towards independence, but ultimately there can be no simple characterisation of a people whose country is not so much a single nation as a committee on a continental scale. Pierre Berton, one of Canada's finest writers, wisely ducked the issue; Canadians, he explained, are "people who know how to make love in a canoe".

The typical Canadian might be an elusive concept, but there's a distinctive feel to any visit. Some towns might seem a touch too well-regulated and unspontaneous, but against this there's the overwhelming sense of Canadian pride in their history and pleasure in the beauty of their land. Canada embraces its own clichés with an energy that's irresistible, promoting everything from the Calgary Stampede to maple syrup festivals and lumberjacking contests with an extraordinary zeal and openness. As John Buchan said, "You have to know a man awfully well in Canada to know his surname".

## Where to go
The time and expense involved in covering Canada's immense distances means that most visitors confine their explorations to the area around one of the main cities – usually Toronto, Montréal, Vancouver or Calgary for arrivals by air. The attractions of these centres vary widely, but they have one thing in common with each other and all other Canadian towns – they are within easy reach of the great outdoors.

Canada's most southerly region, southwest **Ontario**, contains not only the manufacturing heart of the country and its largest city, **Toronto**, but also **Niagara Falls**, Canada's premier tourist sight. North of Toronto there's the far less packaged scenic attraction of **Georgian Bay**, an elegiac waterscape of pine-studded islets set against crystal blue waters. Like the forested Algonquin park, the bay is also accessible from the capital city of **Ottawa**, not as dynamic a place as Toronto, but still well worth a stay for its art galleries and museums, and for the nightlife over the Ottawa river in Hull.

**Québec**, set apart from the rest of the continent by the profundity of its French tradition, is a more party-loving place than its Anglophone neighbour, and its biggest city, **Montréal**, is for many people the most vibrant place in the country, a fascinating mix of old-world style and commercial dynamism. The pace of life is more relaxed in the historic provincial capital, **Québec City**, and more easy-going still in the villages dotted along the St Lawrence lowlands, where glittering spires attest to the enduring influence of the Catholic Church. For something more bracing, you could continue north to **Tadoussac**, where whales can be seen near the mouth of the splendid **Saguenay** fjord – and if you're really prepared for the wilds, forge on through to **Labrador**, as inhospitable a zone as you'll find in the east.

Across the mouth of the St Lawrence, the pastoral **Gaspé** peninsula – the easternmost part of Québec – borders **New Brunswick**, a mild-mannered introduction to the **Maritime Provinces**, a region whose people have long been dependent on timber and the sea for their livelihood. The tiny fishing villages of the Maritimes are at their most beautiful near **Halifax**, the bustling capital of **Nova Scotia**, and along the starker shores of **Cape Breton Island**, whose rugged topography anticipates that of the island of **Newfoundland** to the north. Newfoundland's isolation has spawned a distinctive culture that's at its most lively in **St John's**, where the local folk music scene is the country's best. The island also boasts some of the Atlantic seaboard's finest landscapes, the flat-topped peaks and glacier-gouged lakes of **Gros Morne National Park**.

Back on the mainland, separating Ontario from the Rockies, the so-called prairie provinces of **Manitoba** and **Saskatchewan** have a reputation for dullness that's somewhat unfair: even in the flat southern parts there's the diversion of **Winnipeg**, whose traces of its early days make it a good place to break a trans-Canadian journey. To the north, the myriad lakes and gigantic forests of the provinces' wilderness regions offer magnificent canoeing and hiking, especially within **Prince Albert National Park**. Up in the far north, beside Hudson Bay, the settlement of **Churchill** – remote but accessible by train – is famous for its polar bears, who gather near town from the end of June waiting to move out over the ice as soon as the bay freezes.

Moving west, **Alberta**'s wheatfields ripple into ranching country on the approach to the **Canadian Rockies**, whose awesome reputation is more than borne out by the reality. The provincial capital, **Edmonton**, is overshadowed by **Calgary**, a brash place grown fat on the region's oil and gas fields, and the most useful springboard for a venture into the mountains. **British Columbia** embodies the popular picture of Canada to perfection: a land of snow-capped summits, rivers and forests, pioneer villages, gold-rush ghost towns, and some of the greatest hiking, skiing, fishing and canoeing opportunities in the world. Its urban focus, **Vancouver**, is the country's third city, known for its spectacular natural setting and a laid-back West Coast hedonism. Off the coast lies **Vancouver Island**, a microcosm of the province's immense natural riches, and home to **Victoria**, a devotedly Anglophile little city.

North of British Columbia, wedged alongside Alaska, is the **Yukon Territory**, half grandiose mountains, half sub-arctic tundra, and full of evocative echoes of the Klondike gold rush. **Whitehorse**, its capital, and **Dawson City**, a gold-rush relic, are virtually the only towns here, each accessed by dramatic frontier highways. The **Northwest Territories**, arching over the provinces of Alberta, Saskatchewan and Manitoba, are an immensity of stunted forest, lakes, tundra and ice, the realm of Dene and Inuit native groups whose traditional way of life is being threatened as oil and gas exploration reaches up in to the Arctic. Roads are virtually non-existent in the deep north, and only **Yellowknife**, a bizarre frontier city, plus a handful of ramshackle villages, offer the air links and resources necessary to explore this wilderness.

## When to go

Obviously Canada's **climate** is varied and changeable, but it's a safe generalisation to say that the areas near the coast or the Great Lakes have milder winters and cooler summers than the interior. **July and August** are reliably warm throughout the country, even in the far north, making these the best but also the busiest months to visit. **November to March**, by contrast, is an ordeal of sub-zero temperatures almost everywhere but the west coast, though winter days in many areas are clear and dry, and all large Canadian towns are geared to the challenge of winter, with covered walkways and indoor malls protecting their inhabitants from the worst of the weather.

More specifically, the **Maritimes and eastern Canada** have four distinct seasons: chill, snowy winters; short, mild springs; warm summers (which are shorter and colder in northern and inland regions); and long crisp autumns. Summer is the key season in the resorts, though late September and October, particularly in New Brunswick, are also popular for the autumn colours. Coasts year-round can be blanketed in mist or fog.

In **Ontario and Québec** the seasons are also marked and the extremes intense, with cold, damp and grey winters in southern Ontario (drier and colder in Québec) and a long temperate spring from about April to June. Summers can be hot, but often uncomfortably humid, with the cities often empty of locals but full of visitors. The long autumn can be the best time to visit, with equable temperatures and few crowds.

The **central provinces** of Manitoba, Saskatchewan and Alberta experience the country's wildest climatic extremes, suffering the longest, harshest winters, but also some of the finest, clearest summers. Winter skiing brings a lot of people to the **Rockies**, but summer is still the busiest, especially in the mountains, where July and August offer the best walking weather. Although precipitation is low it is dramatic, often falling as summer thunderstorms or raging winter blizzards.

The **southwestern parts of British Columbia** enjoy some of Canada's best weather: the extremes are less marked and the overall temperatures generally milder than elsewhere. Much of the province, though, bears the brunt of Pacific depressions, so this is one of the country's damper regions – visiting between late spring and early autumn offers the best chance of missing the rain.

Across the **Yukon and Northwest Territories** winters are bitterly cold, with temperatures rarely above freezing for months on end, though precipitation year-round is among the country's lowest. Summers, by contrast, are short but surprisingly warm, and spring – though late – can produce outstanding displays of wild flowers across the tundra.

### CANADIAN DISTANCE CHART

The figures shown on this chart represent total distances in kilometres on the shortest available route by road, rather than straight lines drawn on a map.

| | St. John's | Halifax | Montréal | Ottawa | Toronto | Winnipeg | Regina | Edmonton | Calgary | Vancouver | Whitehorse |
|---|---|---|---|---|---|---|---|---|---|---|---|
| Halifax | 1349 | | | | | | | | | | |
| Montréal | 2448 | 1318 | | | | | | | | | |
| Ottawa | 2638 | 1508 | 190 | | | | | | | | |
| Toronto | 2987 | 1857 | 539 | 399 | | | | | | | |
| Winnipeg | 4855 | 3726 | 2408 | 2218 | 2099 | | | | | | |
| Regina | 5427 | 4297 | 2979 | 2789 | 2670 | 571 | | | | | |
| Edmonton | 6212 | 5082 | 3764 | 3574 | 3455 | 1357 | 785 | | | | |
| Calgary | 6183 | 5042 | 3743 | 3553 | 3434 | 1336 | 764 | 299 | | | |
| Vancouver | 7248 | 6119 | 4801 | 4611 | 4492 | 2393 | 1822 | 1244 | 1057 | | |
| Whitehorse | 8298 | 7168 | 5850 | 5660 | 5528 | 3524 | 2871 | 2086 | 2385 | 2697 | |
| Yellowknife | 7723 | 6593 | 5275 | 5086 | 4966 | 2868 | 2297 | 1511 | 1811 | 2411 | 2704 |

## CLIMATE: TEMPERATURE AND SNOWFALL

| | Average daily max. temperatures in degrees Celsius | | | | Annual snowfall (cm) | Duration of cover (days) |
|---|---|---|---|---|---|---|
| | **Jan** | **April** | **July** | **Oct** | | |
| **Banff** | -7 | 8 | 22 | 10 | 251 | 149 |
| **Calgary** | -6 | 9 | 23 | 12 | 153 | 116 |
| **Charlottetown** | -3 | 7 | 23 | 12 | 275 | 122 |
| **Edmonton** | -17 | 9 | 22 | 11 | 136 | 133 |
| **Goose Bay** | -12 | 3 | 21 | 7 | 445 | 188 |
| **Halifax** | -1 | 9 | 23 | 14 | 217 | 99 |
| **Inuvik** | -25 | -8 | 19 | -5 | 177 | 232 |
| **Montréal** | -6 | 11 | 26 | 13 | 243 | 116 |
| **Ottawa** | -6 | 11 | 26 | 13 | 206 | 121 |
| **Regina** | -13 | 9 | 26 | 12 | 87 | 134 |
| **Thunder Bay** | -9 | 8 | 24 | 11 | 213 | 132 |
| **Saint John** | -3 | 8 | 22 | 12 | 224 | 104 |
| **St John's** | 0 | 5 | 21 | 11 | 322 | 109 |
| **Vancouver** | 5 | 13 | 22 | 14 | 51 | 11 |
| **Whitehorse** | -16 | 6 | 20 | 4 | 78 | 170 |
| **Winnipeg** | -14 | 9 | 26 | 12 | 126 | 135 |
| **Yellowknife** | -25 | -1 | 21 | 1 | 135 | 210 |

# PART ONE

# THE
# BASICS

## GETTING TO CANADA FROM THE UK AND IRELAND

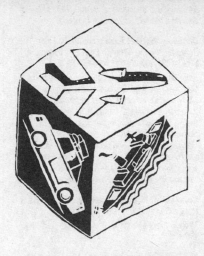

The only economical way to get to Canada **from the UK** is to fly. The main gateways into the country are Montréal and Toronto, but there are also **scheduled non-stop** flights from the UK to Calgary, Edmonton, Halifax, Ottawa, St John's and Vancouver and **direct** services (which may land once or twice on the way, but keep the same flight number throughout the journey) to a number of other destinations. You can fly to Canada from Heathrow, Gatwick, Stanstead, Birmingham, Newcastle, Manchester, Edinburgh, Glasgow, Dublin and Belfast (see box overleaf) but you will find that there are fewer choices as regards non-stop flights from airports outside London.

Competition between the big two Canadian carriers, *Air Canada* and *Canadian Airlines*, keeps scheduled rates reasonable, and **charter flights** to the more popular destinations, especially Toronto and Montréal, throw up even more low-cost options. It may also be worth considering a cheap flight **to the US**, as the greater competition between airlines on the US routes can produce fares to New York as low as £100 return; from the US it's easy to get into Canada cheaply by bus or train (see "Getting there from the US").

For a precise picture of all the available options at any given time, contact an **agent** specialising in low-cost flights (see box overleaf) who may – especially if you are under 26 or a student – be able to undercut the regular Apex fares. These agents also offer cut-price seats on charter flights, though these tend to be of limited availability during the summer. Package operators can also be a source of cheap one-off flights, as they sell off any unsold seats at the last moment. Finally, be sure to check the travel ads in the Sunday papers, and, in London, in *Time Out*, *City Limits*, the *Evening Standard* and giveaway magazines aimed at young travellers, like *TNT*.

### FARES

Generally the most **expensive** time to fly is between early July and mid-September and around Christmas. Mid-May to early July and mid-September to mid-October – the "shoulder" seasons – are slightly less pricey, leaving the rest of the year as low season. Make sure of the exact season dates observed by your operator or airline, as you might be able to make major savings by shifting your departure by as little as a day. Whatever time of year you fly, midweek flights tend to cost around £20 more than weekend ones, and an airport tax of £10 is usually added to the quoted price. Return flights from regional airports cost around £70 more than flights from London.

A variety of **Apex** fares are offered by the majors. *Air Canada's* "Maple Leaf" fares have to be booked fourteen days in advance with a minimum stay of seven nights and a maximum of three months. *Canadian Airlines* offers Apex deals with seven- and fourteen-day advance booking, both with a minimum stay of seven nights, maximum two months. **Seat sale** fares, which cost about the same as 21-day Apex deals, are available on both Canadian majors for flights returning before June and must be completely paid for within forty-eight hours or before thirty days prior to departure. Generally these require a minimum stay of a week and a maximum of four weeks. *British Airways* has seven-, fourteen- and twenty-one-day advance booking with minimum stays of seven nights and maximum of six months', three months' and three weeks' stay respectively.

## MAJOR AIRLINES FROM THE UK TO CANADA

**Air Canada** 7–8 Conduit St, London W1R 9TG (☎081/759 2636 or ☎0800/181313); 4 Westmoreland St, Dublin (☎01/771 488).

*Non-stop services from Heathrow to Calgary (4 weekly), Edmonton (3 weekly), Halifax (3 weekly), Montréal (daily), Ottawa (2 weekly), St John's (3 weekly), Toronto (daily) and Vancouver (daily). Connections are available to London (Ontario), Regina, Saskatoon, Thunder Bay, Windsor and Winnipeg from Toronto; to Charlottetown, Deer Lake, Fredericton, Moncton, Saint John and Sydney from Halifax; and to Victoria from Vancouver. They also fly from Manchester to Calgary (1 weekly), Edmonton (1 weekly), Montréal (3 weekly), Ottawa (1 weekly), Toronto (5 weekly), Vancouver (1 weekly) and Winnipeg (1 weekly). From Glasgow non-stop flights serve Halifax (2 weekly) and Toronto (6 weekly). From Birmingham, Edinburgh, Dublin and Belfast there are daily flights to Toronto via London.*

**Air India** 17–18 New Bond St, London W1Y 0BD (☎071/491 7979).

*Three weekly non-stop flights to Toronto from Heathrow.*

**American Airlines** 15 Berkeley St, London W1 (☎081/572 5555 or ☎0800/010151).

*Various destinations in Canada via New York from Heathrow, Gatwick and Stanstead (by the end of 1992).*

**British Airways** 156 Regent St, London W1A 5TA (☎081/897 4000 from London, ☎041/332 9666 from Glasgow or ☎061/228 6311 from Manchester); 9 Fountain Centre, College St, Belfast (☎0345/222 111).

*From Heathrow daily non-stop flights to Toronto and Montréal. Four non-stop flights a week to Vancouver. Via London there are daily flights from Birmingham, Edinburgh, Glasgow, Manchester and Newcastle to Toronto,*

*Montréal and Vancouver and from Belfast to Montréal (daily) and Toronto (1 weekly).*

**Canadian Airlines International** 1st Floor, Rothschild House, Whitgift Centre, Croydon CR9 3HN (☎081/667 0666 or ☎0345/616 767).

*From Gatwick there are non-stop flights to Calgary (3 weekly), Edmonton (2 weekly), Toronto (daily) and Vancouver (2 weekly). Flights to Halifax (6 weekly), London, Ontario (daily), Montréal (daily), Ottawa (daily), Regina (2 weekly), Saskatoon (6 weekly), Thunder Bay (daily), Windsor (6 weekly) and Winnipeg (6 weekly) all go via Toronto. Flights to Québec City (6 weekly) touch down at Toronto and Montréal and those to Victoria (2 weekly) stop at Vancouver.*

**Continental Airlines** Beulah Court, Albert Rd, Horley, Surrey RH6 7HZ (☎0293/776464).

*Weekly flight to Vancouver via Denver from Gatwick.*

**KLM** KLM Building, 8 Hanover St, London W1R (☎081/750 9000).

*Direct flights to Halifax, Ottawa, Toronto, Montréal, Calgary and Vancouver via Amsterdam from Heathrow, Manchester, Birmingham, Cardiff, Bristol and Southampton.*

**Northwest Airlines,** Northwest House, Tinsley Lane, Crawley, W Sussex RH10 2TP (☎0345/747800).

*Direct flights to Edmonton, Toronto, Montréal and Winnipeg via the US from Gatwick.*

**United Airlines** 193 Piccadilly, London W1 (☎081/990 9900 or ☎0800/888555).

*Direct flights to Vancouver, Calgary and Toronto via the US from Heathrow.*

**US Air** Piccadilly House, Regent St, London SW1 (☎0800/777333).

*Daily flight to Charlottetown from Gatwick.*

---

Most agents offer **"open-jaw"** deals that enable you to fly into one Canadian city and back from another – a useful idea if you want to make your way across the country; fares are calculated by halving the return fares to each destination and adding the two figures together.

Typical **midweek 14-day Apex return fares** from London in **low season** are: to Toronto, Montréal or Halifax – £349 (£299 seat sale or 21-day Apex); to Vancouver – £469 (£439); to Winnipeg – £499 (£379). In **high season**: to Toronto, Montréal or Halifax – £479 (£449 seat sale); to Vancouver – £599 (£519); to Winnipeg – £579 (£499).

The **standard return** fares are double these prices.

## FLIGHT AGENTS IN THE UK

### LOW-COST SPECIALISTS

**Campus Travel** 52 Grosvenor Gardens, London SW1W 0AG (☎071/730 8111).

**Council Travel** 28a Poland St, London W1V 3DB (☎071/437 7767).

**CTS Travel** 44 Goodge St, London W1P 2AD (☎071/323 5130).

**Flightfile** 49 Tottenham Court Rd, London W1P 9RE (☎071/323 4340).

**STA Travel** 74 Old Brompton Rd, London SW7 3LH (☎071/937 9971).

**Touropa** 52 Grosvenor Gardens, London SW1W 0NP (☎071/730 2101).

**Trailfinders** 42–50 Earl's Court Rd, London W8 6EJ (☎071/937 5400).

**Travel Cuts** 295 Regent St, London W1R 7YA (☎071/637 3161). Main Canadian student travel organisation with offices throughout Canada.

**USIT** Aston Quay, O'Connell Bridge, Dublin 2 (☎01/778 117); 13b College Street, Belfast BT1 6ET (☎0232/324 073).

### CANADA SPECIALISTS

**Albany Travel** Central Buildings, 211 Deansgate, Manchester M3 3NW (☎0703/812 535).

**Canada Air Holidays** 50 Sauchiehall St, Glasgow, Strathclyde G2 3AG (☎041/332 1511).

**Globespan** 236 Atlantic House, Gatwick Airport, W Sussex RH6 0NP (☎0293/562 690).

**Sussex Travel** 12/14 Terminus Rd, Eastbourne, East Sussex BN21 3LP (☎0323/ 411 500).

**Unijet** *Sandrocks*, Rocky Lane, Haywards Heath, W Sussex (☎0444/459 100).

## PACKAGES

**Package holidays** – whether fly-drive, flight-accommodation, flight-guided tours or a combination of all three – can work out cheaper than arranging the same trip yourself, though they do have drawbacks: chiefly loss of flexibility and the fact that you'll probably be made to stay in fairly expensive hotels.

Short-stay **city packages** start from around £500 per person for a transatlantic return flight and accommodation in a downtown Toronto hotel for three nights. **Fly-drive** deals, which give cut-rate car rental when buying a transatlantic ticket from an airline or tour operator, are always cheaper than renting on the spot and give great value if you intend to do a lot of driving: a return flight to Vancouver and a fortnight's car rental might cost as little as £475 per person. A typical **flight-guided tour** might comprise a 14-day trans-Canadian holiday taking in Toronto, Niagara Falls, Ottawa, Montréal, Calgary, the Rockies and Vancouver, including an outbound flight to Toronto, a domestic flight, coach trips, middle-range hotel accommodation and some sightseeing tours, at a cost of around £1300.

To see a chunk of Canada's great outdoors without being hassled by too many practical considerations, you could take a specialist **touring** or **adventure package**, which usually includes transport in Canada, accommodation, food and a guide – but not a flight to and from the country. Some of the more adventurous carry small groups around on minibuses and use a combination of budget hotels and camping, providing all equipment. These deals are not cheap, however – a typical package of five days' hiking in the Yukon will cost around £500, and prices are far higher in areas that require detailed planning and outfitting. Operators offering a range of Canadian adventure holidays are listed in the box overleaf; companies specialising in the more extreme locations – for example, Labrador – are given in the appropriate sections of the guide.

## COURIER FLIGHTS

**Courier flights**, which give the customer a cheap ticket in return for delivering a parcel, can be a good option for those on a tight budget, but you'll be given tight restrictions on dates and will be limited to hand luggage only. Furthermore, few companies operate a courier service to Canada. At the time of writing, *Polo Express* (☎081/759 5383) were one of very few firms with

## SPECIALIST HOLIDAY OPERATORS IN THE UK

### GENERAL

**All Canada Travel & Holidays** All Canada House, 90 High St, Lowestoft, Suffolk NR32 1XN (☎0502/585 825).

**American Connections** 7 York Way, Lancaster Rd, High Wycombe, Buckinghamshire HP12 3PY (☎0494/473 173).

**AmeriCanada Travel** St Andrews Court, Exchange St, Bolton, Lancashire BL1 1LD (☎0204/397 367).

**ASAT** ASAT House, 11 Oakdene Rd, Redhill, Surrey RH1 6BT (☎0737/778 560).

**Capture Canada**, 56–58 High St, Ewell, Surrey KT17 1RW (☎081/393 0127).

**National Holidays** Clarendon House, Clarendon Rd, Eccles, Greater Manchester M30 9AA (☎061/707 4403).

**Premier Holidays** Premier Travel Centre, Westbrook, Milton Rd, Cambridge, Cambridgeshire CB4 1YQ (☎0222/322 634).

**Shirespeed Canada Holidays** 30 Brittania Pavillion, Albert Dock, Liverpool, Merseyside L3 4AA (☎0800/262 522).

**Thomson Tour Operations Ltd** Greater London House, Hampstead Rd, London NW1 7SD (☎071/387 9321).

**Travelpack** 39–41 Alfreton Rd, Nottingham, Nottinghamshire NG7 3JE (☎0602/424 424).

### ADVENTURE HOLIDAYS

**Accessible Isolation Holidays** Midhurst Walk, West St, Midhurst, W Sussex (☎0730/812 535).

**AmeriCan Adventures** 45 High St, Tunbridge Wells, Kent TN1 1XL (☎0892/511 894).

**American Pioneers** PO Box 229, Westlea, Swindon, Wiltshire SN5 7HJ (☎0793/881882).

**American Round-Up** PO Box 126, Hemel Hempstead, Hertfordshire HP3 0AZ (☎0442/214 621).

**Arctic Experience** 29 Nork Way, Banstead, Surrey SM7 1PB (☎0737/362 361).

**Exodus Expeditions** 9 Weir Rd, London SW12 0LT (☎081/675 5550).

**Greyhound World Travel Ltd** Sussex House, London Rd, East Grinstead, W Sussex RH19 1LD (☎0342/317317).

**International Adventure** 7 Melbourn St, Royston, Hertfordshire SG8 7BP (☎0763/242867).

**Trek America** Trek House, The Bullring, Deddington, Oxford, Oxfordshire OX5 4TT (☎0869 38777).

**Worldwide Journies** 146 Gloucester Rd, London SW7 4SZ (☎071/370 5032).

regular courier flights: their one- or two-week return flights to Toronto cost from £99 in March to £299 from June to September; one-week returns to Montréal are £299 all year; and two-week returns to Vancouver vary from £210 in April to £325 in summer. It is worth checking the major courier firms who have the occasional one-off to Canada: *DHL* (☎081/890 9393) and *CTS* (☎071/351 0300) are among the biggest; check the Yellow Pages for others.

## GETTING TO CANADA FROM THE US

Crossing the longest undefended border in the world is straightforward. Many visitors from the northern US just drive, as the major Canadian cities – Montréal and Toronto in the east, Winnipeg and Calgary in the middle, and Vancouver in the west – are all within an hour's drive of the border. However, if you're coming from Florida or southern California, or want to go from New York to British Columbia, flying is obviously going to be a lot quicker. Travelling by train is another alternative, best for those who aren't in a hurry and want to see something of the landscapes along the way, and there are a few bus and ferry options too.

### BY CAR

The US highway system leads into Canada at thirteen points along the border, the busiest corridors being Detroit–Windsor and at Niagara Falls. You may encounter traffic jams there, but these are the only problems on the otherwise smooth transition between the countries. At customs you will probably be asked to declare your citizenship, place of residence and proposed length of stay – and that's it. Vehicle insurance, with minimum liability coverage of $200,000, is compulsory and it is also advisable to obtain a **Canadian Non-Resident Inter-Provincial Motor Vehicle Liability Card** from your insurance company before you go. If you are renting a car in the US you should mention that you intend to travel to Canada, though this is rarely a problem. Fill the car with gas before going, as US prices are about half those over the border.

### BY BUS

The **Greyhound** bus network extends into Canada from three points on the East Coast and one each from the West and middle America. They run from **New York to Montréal** (6 daily; 7hr–8hr 30min; US$60 one-way); from **Buffalo to Toronto** (5 daily; 2hr 45min; US$23 one-way); from **Burlington** (Vermont) **to Montréal** (3 daily; 2hr 50min; US$27 one-way); from **Seattle to Vancouver** (4 daily; 4hr; US$28 one-way); and from **Fargo (**North Dakota) **to Winnipeg** (1 daily; 6hr; US$41 one-way). For information on cross-border services call ☎212/635-0800 in New York, ☎716/855-7531 in Buffalo, ☎802/864-6811 in Burlington, ☎206/628-5526 in Seattle and ☎701/293-1222 in Fargo.

### BY AIR

As well as *Air Canada* and *Canadian Airlines*, most US airlines offer regular flights between the US and Canada: Montréal, Toronto and Vancouver are the most common destinations, but there are also services to Halifax, Calgary and Edmonton. Non-stop service is offered from over twenty US cities, and connecting flights within Canada serve some 75 additional places. **Apex** fares on all major airlines are usually pretty much the same price: if you buy your ticket 21 days before departure you should be able to find round-trip flights between Boston or New York and Toronto or Montréal for around US$300. Similarly, a midweek, round-trip flight between Los Angeles and Vancouver costs around US$250. In addition to regular Apex fares, many airlines offer special one-off deals, and when one airline offers a cheap fare all the others follow suit.

Long-haul **domestic flights** wholly within the US or Canada generally cost somewhat less than flights between the two countries, so you may make considerable savings by crossing the border before or after your flight. This is especially true of flights to the West Coast: a transcontinental flight from New York to Seattle can be as much as US$200 cheaper than a similar flight to

## AIRLINES AND FLIGHT AGENTS IN THE US

### MAJOR AIRLINES

**American Airlines**, PO Box 619616, Dallas/Fort Worth International Airport, Dallas, TX 75261 (☎817/267-1151 or 800/433-7300).

**Air Canada**, 300 N State St, Room 1100, Marina City Office Bldg, Chicago, IL (☎800/776-3000).

**British Airways**, 530 Fifth Ave, New York, NY 10017 (☎800/247-9297).

**Canadian Airlines**, Logan International Airport, Terminal East, Boston, MA (☎800/426-7000).

**Continental Airlines**, 2929 Allen Parkway, Houston, TX 77019 (☎713/821-2100 or ☎800/231-0856).

**Delta Airlines**, Hartsfield Atlanta International Airport, Atlanta, GA 30320 (☎404/765-5000 or ☎800/241-4141).

**Northwest Airlines**, Minneapolis/St Paul International Airport, St Paul, MN 55111 (☎612/726-1234 or ☎800/225-2525).

**Trans World Airlines**, 100 South Bedford Rd, Mount Kisco, NY 10549 (☎212/290-2141 or ☎800/892-4141).

**United Airlines**, PO Box 66100, Chicago, IL 60666 (☎708/952-4000 or ☎800/241-6522).

**US Air**, Crystal Park Four, 2345 Crystal Drive, Arlington, VA 22227 (☎703/418-7000 or ☎800/622-1015).

### DISCOUNT FLIGHT AGENTS, TRAVEL CLUBS AND CONSOLIDATORS

**Access International**, 101 West 31st St, Suite 104, New York, NY 10001 (☎800/TAKE-OFF). Consolidator with good East Coast and central US deals.

**Airkit**, 1125 W 6th St, Los Angeles, CA 90017 (☎213/957-9304). West Coast consolidator with seats from San Francisco and LA.

**Council Travel**, 205 E 42nd St, New York, NY 10017 (☎212/661-1450). Head office of the nationwide US student travel organisation. Branches in San Francisco, LA, Washington, New Orleans, Chicago, Seattle, Portland, Minneapolis, Boston, Atlanta and Dallas, to name only the larger ones.

**Discount Club of America**, 61-33 Woodhaven Blvd, Rego Park, NY 11374 (☎718/335-9612). East Coast discount travel club.

**Discount Travel International**, Ives Bldg, 114 Forrest Ave, Suite 205, Narbeth, PA 19072 (☎215/668-2182 or 800/221-8139). Good deals from the East Coast.

**Encore Short Notice**, 4501 Forbes Blvd, Lanham, MD 20706 (☎301/459-8020 or 800/638-0830). East Coast travel club.

**Interworld**, 3400 Coral Way, Miami, FL 33145 (☎305/443-4929). Southeastern US consolidator.

**Last-Minute Travel Club**, 132 Brookline Ave, Boston, MA 02215 (☎617/267-9800 or 800/LAST-MIN).

**Moment's Notice**, 425 Madison Ave, New York, NY 10017 (☎212/486-0503). Travel club that's good for last-minute deals.

**Nouvelles Frontières**, 12 E 33rd St, New York, NY 10016 (☎212/779-0600). Main US branch of the French discount travel outfit.

**STA Travel**, 17 E 45th St, Suite 805, New York, NY 10017 (☎212/986-9470); 166 Geary St, Suite 702, San Francisco, CA 94108 (☎415/391-8407). Main US branches of the originally Australian and now worldwide specialist in independent and student travel. Other offices in LA, Boston and Honolulu.

**Stand Buys**, 311 W Superior St, Chicago, IL 60610 (☎800/331-0257). Good Midwestern travel club.

**TFI Tours**, 34 W 32nd St, New York, NY 10001 (☎212/736-1149 or ☎800/825-3834). The best East Coast deals.

**Travel Brokers**, 50 Broad St, New York, NY 10004 (☎800/999-8748). New York travel club.

**Travelers Advantage**, 49 Music Square, Nashville, TN 37203 (☎800/548-1116). Reliable travel club.

**Travac**, 1177 N Warson Rd, St Louis, MO 63132 (☎800/872-8800). Good central US consolidator.

**Travel Avenue**, 180 N Jefferson, Chicago, IL 60606 (☎312/876-1116 or 800/333-3335). Discount travel agent.

**Unitravel**, 1177 N Warson Rd, St Louis, MO 63132 (☎800/325-2222). Reliable consolidator.

**Worldwide Discount Travel Club**, 1674 Meridian Ave, Miami Beach, FL 33139 (☎305/534-2082).

Vancouver, only a hundred miles from Seattle. If your main destination is somewhere in the outback you can often save money by buying a separate, domestic flight from the nearest major Canadian destination, rather than treating that leg of the journey as part of an international itinerary.

For full-time students and those under 26 the best sources of cheap flights are agencies like *STA* or *Council Travel*; for others, there are numerous travel clubs and consolidators who might be able to beat the standard Apex fares, but bear in mind that most of these specialise in transatlantic and around-the-world flights.

### BY TRAIN

Four *Amtrak* routes from the northeastern US have direct connections with *VIA rail*: the *Maple Leaf* from **New York to Toronto** via Buffalo and Niagara Falls (1 daily; 12hr; US$96 one-way); the *Adirondak* from **New York to Montréal** via Albany and Plattsburgh (1 daily; 10hr; US$67 one-way); the *Erie* and the *Mohawk* from **Chicago to Toronto** via Detriot (both daily; 14hr; US$88); and the *Montrealer* from **Washington DC to Montréal** via Atlantic City and New York (1 daily; 19hr; US$98 one-way). Amtrak information and reservations are available on ☎1-800/USA-RAIL.

### BY FERRY

There are four US–Canada ferry services, two on each coast. The *Victoria Clipper* catamaran runs between **Seattle** and **Victoria** on Vancouver Island, three times daily from mid-June to mid-September, twice daily in spring and autumn (2hr 30min; US$42 one-way; reservations ☎206/448-5000). Further north a *Sealinks* ferry links **Skagway** in Alaska to **Prince Rupert** on alternate days from May to late September (3hr; US$118 one-way, cars US$278; reservations ☎1-800-642-0066).

In the east, from early May to mid-October a nightly car ferry runs from **Portland** in Maine to **Yarmouth** in Nova Scotia (9hr; US$68 one-way, cars US$93; reservations ☎1-800-482-0955 in Maine, ☎1-800-341-7540 elsewhere). Finally, a *Marine Atlantic* ferry runs from **Bar Harbour** in Maine to **Yarmouth** daily from late June to late September, three times weekly from the rest of the year except late April to late May, when there's no service (6hr; US$38 one-way, cars US$70; reservations ☎1-800-432-7344 from Maine, ☎1-800-341-7981 elsewhere).

### PACKAGES

Many US companies offer all-inclusive packages combining plane tickets, bus or train travel, hotel accommodation, meals and sightseeing tours and other organised activities. Even if the "pre-packaged" aspect isn't a thrill, this is one way of saving money and hassle, as the operators buy in bulk and have taken loads of people on similar tours many times before. Local travel agents will have details of a vast range of possibilities; the box below lists the major package companies in the US.

---

### TOUR OPERATORS IN THE US

**American Express Vacations** Box 5014, Atlanta, Georgia 30302 (☎1-800-556-5454 in Georgia, ☎1-800-241-1700 from elsewhere).

**Contiki Holidays** 1432 East Katella Ave, California 92805 (☎714/937-0611).

**Cosmos/Globus Gateway** 150 S Los Robles Ave, Suite 860, Pasadena, California (☎818/449-0919 or ☎1-800-556-5454).

**Four Winds Travel** 175 5th Ave, New York, New York 10010 (☎212/777-0261).

**Maupintour** 1515 St Andrews Drive, Lawrence, Kansas 66046 (☎913/843-1211 or ☎1-800/255-4266).

**Suntrek Tours America** PO Box 1190, Rohnert Park, California 94928 (☎1-800/292-9696).

**Trek America** PO Box 1338, Gardena, California (☎1-800/221-0596).

## GETTING TO CANADA FROM AUSTRALASIA

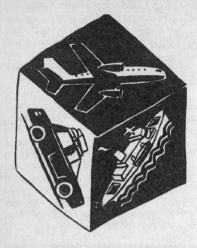

Australia and New Zealand there are daily flights **to Vancouver**, the cheapest option, and three weekly flights to Toronto. Return fares from Sydney or Melbourne to Vancouver vary from Aus$1349 in low season to Aus$1599 in high season; flights to Toronto cost from Aus$1549 to Aus$1993. From Auckland, returns cost NZ$1979–2179 to Vancouver, and NZ$2531–2731 to Toronto. Discounted flights for students and under-26s are sold by *STA* in Australia and in New Zealand (see box below).

> ### AIRLINES AND AGENTS IN AUSTRALIA AND NEW ZEALAND
>
> **STA** 1a Lee St, Railway Square, Sydney 2000 (☎02/519-9866); 222–224 Faraday St, Carlton 3053 (☎03/347-4711); 64 High St, Auckland (☎09/309-0458).
>
> **Canadian Airlines** 1st Level, 30 Clarence St, Sydney (☎02/299-7843); 500 Collins St, Melbourne (☎03/629-6731); 15th Level, Jetset Centre, 44–48 Emily Place, Auckland (☎09/309-0735 or ☎0800-802-245).

Apex deals from Australia and New Zealand to Canada are available from *Canadian Airlines*, whose aircraft link up in Honolulu with *Qantas* carriers from Sydney and Melbourne and with *Air New Zealand* flights from Auckland. From both

## RED TAPE AND VISAS

of identification: a current driving licence, birth certificate, or passport are all accepted.

All visitors to Canada have to complete a **waiver form**, which you'll be given on the plane or at the US-Canada border. On the form you'll have to give details of where you intend to stay during your trip. If you don't know, write "touring", but be prepared to give an idea of your schedule and destinations to the immigration officer.

At the point of entry, the Canadian **immigration** officer decides the length of stay permitted up to a **maximum of six months**, but not usually more than three. The officers rarely refuse entry, but they may ask you to show them how much **money** you have: a credit card or $250 cash per week of the proposed visit is usually considered sufficient. They may also ask to see documentary evidence establishing you are able to return home or continue your journey out of Canada: a return or onward transportation ticket will suffice. If they

Citizens of the EC, Scandinavia and most British Commonwealth countries travelling to Canada do not need an entry visa: all that is required is a full valid passport (not a one-year British Visitor's Passport). United States citizens need some form ask you where you're staying and you give the name and address of friends, don't be surprised if they check. Officers at the more obscure entry points on the US-Canada border can be real sticklers, so expect to be delayed.

For visits of more than six months, study trips and stints of temporary employment, contact the nearest Canadian Embassy, Consulate or High Commission for authorisation prior to departure (see below). Inside Canada, if an extension of stay is desired, written application must be made to the nearest **Canada Immigration Centre** well before the expiry of the authorized visit.

The **duty-free** allowance if you're over nineteen (eighteen in Alberta, Manitoba and Québec) is two hundred cigarettes and fifty cigars, plus one litre of liquor or twenty-four 355ml-sized bottles of beer.

## CANADIAN HIGH COMMISSIONS, CONSULATES & EMBASSIES

### UNITED STATES

**Atlanta** Suite 400, South Tower, One CNN Center, Atlanta, GA 30303-2705 (☎404/577-6810).

**Boston** 3 Copley Place, Suite 400, Boston, MA 02116 (☎617/262-3760).

**Chicago** Suite 1200, 310 South Michigan Ave, Chicago, IL 60604-4295 (☎312/427-1031).

**Dallas** St Paul Place, Suite 1700, 750 North St Paul, Dallas, TX 75201 (☎214/922-9806).

**Detroit** Suite 1100, 600 Renaissance Center, Detroit, MI 48243-1704 (☎313/567-2340).

**Los Angeles** 10th Floor, Suite 1000, California Plaza, 300 Grand Ave, Los Angeles, CA 90071 (☎213/687-7432).

**New York** 1251 Avenue of the Americas, New York, NY 10020-1175 (☎212/768-2400).

**San Francisco** 50 Fremont St, Suite 2100, San Francisco, CA 94105 (☎415/495-6021).

**Washington** 501 Pennsylvania Ave NW, Washington DC 20001 (☎202/682-1740).

### AUSTRALIA AND NEW ZEALAND

**Canberra** Commonwealth Ave, Canberra, ACT 2600 (☎062/733-844).

**Melbourne** 6th Floor, One Collins St, Melbourne, Victoria, 3000 (☎03/654-1433).

**Sydney** AMP Centre, 8th Floor, 50 Bridge St, Sydney, NSW 2000 (☎02/231-6522).

**Wellington** ICI Building, Molesworth St, Wellington (☎739 577).

**Auckland** Princes Court, 2 Princes St, Auckland (☎393-516).

### EUROPE

**Ireland**
65 St Stephen's Green, Dublin 2 (☎01/781-988).

**Netherlands**
Sophialaan 7, The Hague (☎070/614111).

**United Kingdom**
Macdonald House, 1 Grosvenor Square, London W1X0AB (☎071/629 9492).

## INFORMATION AND MAPS

No country on earth can match the sheer volume of tourist information handed out by the Canadians. The most useful sources of information are various **provincial tourist departments** in Canada. The box overleaf provides their addresses; if you contact them well in advance of your departure and are as specific as possible about your intentions, they'll be able to provide you with everything you need to know. Outside of Canada, the consulates, embassies and high commissions (see above) usually have tourist departments, though these cannot match the specific detailed advice dispensed in Canada and some Canadian provinces maintain tourist offices in London (see overleaf), though these serve mainly as clearing-houses for free publicity material. Most of Canada's provinces have at least one **toll-free** visitor information number for use within mainland North America. The toll-free numbers are staffed by tourist office employees trained to answer all manner of queries and advise on room reservations.

## PROVINCIAL TOURIST OFFICES IN CANADA

**Alberta**
Alberta Tourism, PO Box 2500, Edmonton, Alberta T5J 2Z4 (☎403/427-4321).
Toll-free: within Alberta ☎1-800-222-6501; within Canada and mainland USA ☎1-800-661-8888.

**British Columbia**
Tourism British Columbia, Parliament Buildings, Victoria, BC V8V 1X4 (☎604/387-1642).
Toll-free: Vancouver ☎1-800-888-8835; within mainland USA ☎1-800-663-6000.

**Manitoba**
Travel Manitoba, 7th Floor, 155 Carlton St, Winnipeg, Manitoba R3C 3H8 (☎204/945-3777).
Toll-free: within Canada and mainland USA ☎1-800-665-0040.

**New Brunswick**
New Brunswick Dept of Tourism, PO Box 12345, Fredericton, New Brunswick E3B 5C3 (☎506/453-2444).
Toll-free: within New Brunswick ☎1-800-442-4422; within Canada and mainland USA ☎1-800-561-0123.

**Newfoundland and Labrador**
Newfoundland and Labrador Dept of Tourism, PO Box 8730, St John's, Newfoundland A1B 4J6 (☎709/729-2830).
Toll free: within Canada and mainland USA ☎1-800-563-6353.

**Northwest Territories**
Northwest Territories Dept of Tourism, Yellowknife, Northwest Territories X1A 2L9 (☎403/873-7200).
Toll-free: within Canada and mainland USA ☎1-800-661-0788.

**Nova Scotia**
Nova Scotia Tourism and Culture, PO Box 456, Halifax, Nova Scotia B3J 2R5 (☎902/424-4207).
Toll-free: within Canada ☎1-800-565-0000; within mainland USA ☎1-800-341-6096.

**Ontario**
Ontario Travel, Queen's Park, Toronto, Ontario M7A 2R9 (☎416/965-4008).
Toll-free: Toronto ☎1-800-363-1990; within Canada and mainland USA ☎1-800-268-3735.

**Prince Edward Island**
Prince Edward Island Dept of Tourism, PO Box 940, Charlottetown, PEI C1A 7M5 (☎902/368-5555).
Toll-free: within the Maritimes ☎1-800-565-7421; within Canada and mainland USA ☎1-800-565-0267.

**Québec**
Tourisme Québec, PO Box 20000, Québec, Québec G1K 7X2 (☎514/873-2015).
Toll-free: within Canada and mainland USA ☎1-800-363-7777.

**Saskatchewan**
Tourism Saskatchewan, 1919 Saskatchewan Drive, Regina, Saskatchewan S4P 3V7 (☎306/787-9685).
Toll-free: Saskatchewan ☎1-800-667-7538; within Canada and mainland USA ☎1-800-667-7191.

**Yukon**
Tourism Yukon, PO Box 2703, Whitehorse, Yukon Y1A 2C6 (☎403/667-5340).
Toll-free: within Canada and mainland USA ☎1-800-661-0788.

## PROVINCIAL GOVERNMENT OFFICES IN LONDON

**Alberta** 1 Mount St, London W1Y 5AA (☎071/491 3430).
**British Columbia** British Columbia House, 1 Regent St, London SW1Y 4NS (☎071/930 6857).
**Nova Scotia** Crusade House, 14 Pall Mall, London SW1X 7LY (☎071/930 6864).

**Ontario** 21 Knightsbridge, London SW1X 7LY (☎071/245 1222).
**Québec** 59 Pall Mall, London SW1Y 5JH (☎071/930 8314).

In Canada, there are seasonal **provincial tourist information centres** along the main highways, especially at provincial boundaries and along the US border. These dispense all sorts of glossy material and, most usefully, have details of local provincial and national parks. The parks themselves (see "Outdoor Pursuits") have offices that give help on the specifics of hiking, canoeing, wildlife watching and so forth. At the country's airports general information is harder to come by, though there's usually a **city tourist desk** which will help arrange accommodation. All of Canada's large cities have their own tourist bureaux, with the services of the main branch complemented by summertime booths, kiosks and offices. Smaller towns nearly always have a seasonal **tourist office** or **visitor centre**, frequently operated by the municipal chamber of commerce, holding local maps and information. In the larger towns a **free newspaper** or broadsheet is often available, carrying local reviews and entertainment listings.

## MAPS

The **free maps** issued by each province are excellent for general driving and route planning, especially as they provide the broad details of ferry connections. The maps are available at all the outlets mentioned above. The best of the commercially produced maps are those published by *Rand McNally*, bound together in their *Rand McNally Road Atlas* (£9.95). In the case of **hiking** and **canoe** routes, all of the national and provincial parks have **visitors' centres** which provide free parkland maps indicating hiking and canoe trails. Many of them also sell proper local survey maps as do lots of outfitters and some of the provincial parks' departments, whose details are given in the guide or can be obtained through the toll-free numbers. If you want to be absolutely sure of getting the maps you need for independent wilderness travel, contact the **Canada Map Office**, 615 Booth St, Ottawa, Ontario K1A OE9 (☎613/952-7000). They supply map indexes, which will identify the map you need, produce two useful brochures entitled *How to Use a Map* and *Maps and Wilderness Canoeing*, and publish two main series of maps, 1:250,000 and 1:50,000.

In the UK you could also try a specialist stockist such as *Stanfords*, 12–14 Long Acre, London WC2 (☎071/836 1321). Bear in mind, too, that if you're a member of the AA, RAC or AAA, you can get free road maps from the *Canadian Automobile Association*; they are based at 1775 Courtwood Crescent, Ottawa, Ontario (☎613/226-7631), and have offices in every major city.

# MONEY, BANKS AND COSTS

Canadian currency is based on the dollar ($), with 100 cents (¢) to the dollar. Coins are issued in 5¢, 10¢, 25¢ and $1 denominations (the $1 coin is known as a "loonie" after the bird on one face); paper currency comes in $2, $5, $10, $50, $100, $500 and $1000 denominations. Although US dollars are widely accepted, it's on a one-for-one basis, and as the US dollar is usually worth slightly more than its Canadian counterpart, it makes sense to exchange US currency. There's no limit to the amount of money you can take in to or out of Canada.

## CHEQUES, CREDIT CARDS AND BANKS

While it's a good idea to have some Canadian cash from the outset, the best way to carry the bulk of funds is in **travellers' cheques**, available from banks and building societies, usually with a one percent commission on the amount ordered. Buy cheques in Canadian dollars and try to take *American Express* or *Visa* cheques, which are accepted in virtually every shop, garage, restaurant and bar throughout Canada. Using travellers' cheques in this way is a better option than trying to cash them in a bank – a surprising number of major banks in Canada will not change travellers' cheques, and when they do you'll usually have to pay a commission.

It's wise to have at least one **credit card** to pre-pay for hotels or car hire, where otherwise you're likely to be asked for a big cash deposit: *Visa*, *Access/Mastercard*, *American Express* and *Diners* are widely accepted, as are most other credit cards, state bank cards and ATM cards, though it's as well to check with your bank before leaving home. You can also get cash advances from selected banks and bureaux de change on credit cards, but there will invariably be a minimum amount you can draw.

If you run out of money abroad, or there is some kind of emergency, the quickest way to get **money sent out** is to contact your bank at home and have them wire the cash to the nearest bank. You can do the same thing through *Thomas Cook* or *American Express* if there is a branch nearby, and can also have cash sent out through *Western Union* (FREEFONE 100 in UK; ☎1-800-325-6000 in US) to a bank, post office or local agent – a process which takes just minutes but will cost a ten percent commission.

General **banking hours** are Mon–Thurs 10am–3pm, and until 6pm on Fridays; the trend is increasingly to longer hours and Saturday morning opening – but don't rely on finding a bank open outside these weekday hours. The main nationwide banks include the Toronto Dominion, the Royal Bank of Canada, the National Bank of Canada, the Bank of Montréal, and the Canadian Western Bank.

## AVERAGE COSTS

Most **basic** things cost less than in Britain and about the same as they do in the US: cheap Canadian breakfasts are the stuff of legend, dishing up coffee, bacon, eggs and toast for around $6 or less, and healthier snacks like soups and salads from about $3. **Buses** are reasonable, the eighteen-hour journey from Vancouver to Calgary, for instance, costing about $65. **Trains** cost a good deal more – $150 for the same journey – but much less than internal flights. **Room rates** start at around $10 for a hostel dorm, and about $25 for a double in the grottier hotels. In most parts of the country, you should find perfectly

good motel rooms for $35. Basic town **campgrounds** are never expensive, and provincial and national sites start from as little as $5; in fully serviced commercial places it's rare to pay more than $15. Accommodation prices are higher from June to early September, and throughout the more remote areas of the north, particularly the Yukon and NWT.

Generally, if you're sticking to a very **tight budget** – hitching, camping and buying food from shops – you could squeeze through on **$20–25 a day**. A more comfortable **average daily budget**, covering a motel room, bus travel, a museum or two and a restaurant meal would work out at around **$50–60**.

## TIPS AND TAXES

There are several hidden costs to take into account when travelling round Canada. **Tips** and service are generally not added to restaurant bills; it's usual to leave fifteen percent, even after the cheapest meals. All provinces except Alberta, the Yukon and NWT levy a **provincial sales tax** of five to seven percent on most goods and services; visitors to Ontario, Nova Scotia and Newfoundland can apply for a rebate – claim forms are supplied by tourist offices. Most provinces also have a **hotel rooms' tax** of between five and ten percent. Finally, the **Goods and Services Tax** (GST) is a nationwide seven percent charge levied on most goods and services, including hotel and restaurant bills.

Visitors can claim a **rebate** of GST on certain goods over the value of $7 if they're for use outside Canada and removed from the country within sixty days. More significantly, a GST rebate is available for **accommodation expenditure** over $100 during a maximum period of one month. Claim forms are available at many hotels, shops or from any Canadian embassy. Return them, with **all receipts**, to Revenue Canada, Customs and Excise, Visitors Rebate Program, Ottawa, Canada K1A 1J5.

---

Unless stated otherwise, all **accommodation prices** in this book are for high-season doubles, not including taxes; all **entry charges** are the full adult ticket price – the great majority of museums and similar attractions give at least fifty percent **discounts** for children and seniors, as well as **student reductions**.

## HEALTH AND INSURANCE

It is vital to take out travel insurance against potential medical expenses. Canada has an excellent health service, but it costs non-residents anything between $50 to $1000 a day to use. There is no free treatment, and in some provinces doctors and hospitals add a surcharge to treatment meted out to foreigners. If you have an accident, medical services will get to you quickly and charge you later.

**Doctors** can be found listed in the *Yellow Pages*, and ambulance services are usually displayed on the inside cover. If you are bringing medicine prescribed by your doctor, bring a copy of the **prescription**; first to avoid problems at customs and immigration, and second for renewing medication with Canadian doctors. **Pharmacies** are often well equipped to advise on minor ailments and to distinguish between unfamiliar brand names. Most larger towns and cities should have one open 24 hours, and many drugstores stay open late as a matter of course.

### HEALTH PROBLEMS

Canada requires no specific vaccinations, but problems can start when you're walking or camping in the backcountry. Tap water is generally safe to drink, though at campgrounds water is sometimes good for washing only – ask if in doubt. You should always boil **backcountry water** for at least ten minutes to protect against the *Giardi lamblia* parasite (or "beaver fever"), which thrives in warm water, so be careful about swimming in **hot springs** – if possible keep

nose, eyes and mouth above water. Symptoms are intestinal cramps, flatulence and vomiting, which can appear up to a week after infection. If left untreated more unpleasant complications can arise, so see a doctor.

**Blackfly and mosquitoes** are notorious for the problems they cause walkers and campers, and are especially bad in areas near water and throughout most of northern Canada. April to June is the blackfly season, and the mosquito season is from July until about October. Before you go, take three times the recommended daily dosage of Vitamin B complex for two weeks, and take the recommended dosage while you're in Canada – this cuts down bites by up to 75 percent. Once you're there, repellent creams and sprays may help: the best repellents are those containing **DEET** – the ointment version of *Deep-Woods Off* is the best brand, with 95 percent DEET. If you're camping or picnicking you'll find that burning coils or candles containing allethrin or citronella can help. If you're walking in an area that's rife with pests, it's well worth taking a gauze mask to protect your head and neck; wearing white clothes and no perfumed products also makes you less attractive. Once bitten, an **antihistamine** cream like phenergan is the best antidote. On no account go anywhere near an area marked as a blackfly mating ground – people have died from bites sustained when the monsters are on heat.

If you develop a large rash and flu-like symptoms, you may have been bitten by a tick carrying **lyme borreliosis** (or "lyme tick disease"). This is easily curable, so see a doctor, but if left can lead to nasty complications. It's spreading in Canada, especially in the more southerly and wooded parts of the country. Check on its prevalence with the local tourist authority – it may be advisable to buy a strong tick repellent and to wear long socks, trousers and sleeved shirts when walking.

In backcountry areas look out for **poison ivy**, which grows in most places, but particularly in a

---

The nationwide number for police, fire or ambulance is ☎911, but in some remoter areas you will still have to call ☎0 for the operator.

belt across southern Ontario and Québec; poison ivy ointment is widely available. It causes itchy open blisters and lumpy sores up to ten days after contact. Also keep an eye open for **snakes** in certain western areas: pharmacists and wilderness outfitters can advise on snakebite kits, and park wardens can give useful preventive advice. Should you get bitten without an antidote on you, get a good look at the culprit so that the doctor can identify the species and administer the right medicine.

Also be aware of the dangers posed by **bears**. Most people blow a whistle while walking in bear country to warn them off. If confronted don't run, make loud noises or sudden movements, all of which are likely to provoke an attack. Leave the animal an escape route and back off slowly. If you have a pack, leave it as a distraction. If attacked, climbing a tree or playing dead may save you from a grizzly, but not from black bears. Fighting back only increases the ferocity of an attack. For more on bears (see p.442).

If walking or climbing go properly equipped and be prepared for sudden changes of weather. Watch out for signs of **exposure** – mild delirium, exhaustion, inability to get warm – and on snow or in high country during summer take a good **sun-block**. Finally, of course, take the same precautions against **HIV** infection as you would back home – have safe sex, use a condom and don't share needles.

## TRAVEL INSURANCE

It's essential to have **travel insurance** to cover loss of possessions and money as well as the cost of all medical and dental treatment. Many bank and charge accounts include some form of travel cover, and insurance is also sometimes included if you pay for your trip with a credit card. Among **British** insurers, *Endsleigh* are about the cheapest, offering a month's cover for around £20. Their policies are available from most youth/ student travel specialists or direct from their offices at 97–107 Southampton Row, London WC1 (☎071/436 4451). You must make sure you keep all medical bills, and, if you have anything stolen, get a copy of the police report when you report the incident – otherwise you won't be able to claim.

Travellers from the **US** should carefully check the insurance policies you already have before taking out a new one. You may discover that you're covered already for medical and other losses while abroad. Holders of **ISIC** cards are entitled to be reimbursed for $3000-worth of accident coverage and 60 days of in-patient benefits up to $100 a day for the period the card is valid – though this isn't going to go far in the event of a serious setback. If you do want a specific travel insurance policy, there are numerous kinds to choose from: short-term combination policies covering everything from baggage loss to broken legs are the best bet and cost around $25 for ten days, plus $1 a day for trips of 75 days or more. One thing to bear in mind is that none of the currently available policies covers theft; they only cover loss while in the custody of an identifiable person – though even then you must make a report to the police and get their written statement. Two companies you might try are *Travel Guard*, 110 Centrepoint Drive, Steven Point, WI 54480 (☎715/345-0505 or ☎1-800-826-1300), or *Access America International*, 600 Third Ave, New York, NY 10163 (☎212/949-5960 or ☎1-800-284-8300).

# GETTING AROUND

Distances in Canada are so huge that it's essential to plan carefully how you'll get around. With *VIA rail* services becoming more skeletal each year, province-wide bus companies provide the main links between major cities, though in isolated areas you may be thrown back on more sporadic local services. Flying is of course more expensive, but competition in the skies can lead to some decent bargains. On most forms of public transport there are cheaper fares for children under 12, for youths between 13 and 21, and over-60s. It has to be said, however, that things are always easier if you have a car: even if a bus can take you to the general vicinity of a provincial park, for example, it can prove impossible to explore the interior without your own vehicle.

## BY BUS

If you're travelling on your own, **buses** are by far the cheapest way to get around, bar hitching. *Greyhound Canada* runs a service along the Trans-Canada Highway from Toronto to Vancouver and the major centres in the rest of the country are served by a network of smaller lines. **Long-distance** buses run to a fairly full timetable (at least daily), stopping only for meal breaks and driver change-overs. Nearly all are non-smoking and are less uncomfortable than you might expect – it's feasible to save on a night's accommodation by sleeping on the bus, though you may not feel up to much the next day. Any sizeable community will have a main bus station, but in smaller places the petrol station doubles as the bus stop and ticket office. Seats can be reserved but this is rarely necessary: only those

services between nearby cities like Montréal and Québec are likely to get booked out, and even then you'll only have to wait an hour or so for the next departure. Out in the less populated areas, buses are fairly scarce, sometimes only appearing once or twice a week, and here you'll need to plot your route with care.

**Fares** are pretty standard from company to company: as an example, Toronto to Winnipeg, a distance of 2099km, costs $113 one way. The free *Official Canadian Bus Guide* containing all Canadian bus **timetables** is produced bimonthly but is not made readily available to travellers. It is pretty hefty anyway so you are better off picking up free individual timetables from the major bus stations. Always double-check routes and times by phoning the local terminal (we've included telephone numbers for most towns), or the companies (see box below).

### PASSES

Non-North American travellers intending to explore Canada by bus can save a lot by purchasing one of two **passes** before leaving home. The **Greyhound Canada Pass** allows unlimited travel within a fixed time limit on all *Greyhound*

## CANADA'S BUS COMPANIES

**Acadian Lines** 6040 Almon St, Halifax, Nova Scotia (☎902/454-9321).

**Arctic Frontier Carriers** PO Box 1860, Yellowknife NWT (☎403/873-4892).

**Autobus Auger** 147 Rue Principale, Chateauguay, Québec (☎514/691-1654).

**Canada Coach Lines**, 330 Wentworth St North, Hamilton, Ontario (☎416/527-2100).

**Cha-Co Trails** 100 Currie St, PO Box 248, Chatham, Ontario (☎519/681-2861).

**Go Transit** 1120 Finch Ave West, Downsview, Ontario (☎416/665-0022).

**Gray Coach Lines**, 180 Dundas St West, Suite 1100, Toronto, Ontario (☎416/393-7911).

**Greyhound Lines of Canada** 877 Greyhound Way SW, Calgary, Alberta (☎403/265-9111).

**Grey Goose** 301 Burnell St, Winnipeg, Manitoba (☎204/786-8891).

**Mackenzie Bus Lines**, PO Box 249, 210 York St, Bridgewater, Nova Scotia (☎902/543-2491).

**Norline Coaches (Yukon) Ltd** Box 5237, Yukon Y1A 4Z1 (☎403/928-3995).

**Ontario Northland** 555 Oak St East, North Bay, Ontario (☎705/472-4500).

**Orleans Express** 533 rue Ontario Est, Bureau 350, Montréal, Québec (☎514/847-4000).

**Penetang – Midland Coach** 475 Bay St, Midland, Ontario (☎475/526-0161).

**Saskatchewan Transportation Company** 2041 Hamilton St, Regina, Saskatchewan (☎306/787-3357).

**SMT (Eastern) Ltd** 98 St George St, PO Box 310, Moncton, New Brunswick (☎506/859-5100).

**Terra Transport CN Roadcruiser** Water St West, PO Box 310, St John's, Newfoundland (☎709/737-7882).

**Vancouver Island Coach Lines** 700 Douglas St, Victoria, British Columbia (☎604/388-5248).

**Voyageur Colonial** 265 Catherine St, Ottawa, Ontario (☎613/238-5900).

**Voyageur Inc** 505 boulevard Maisonneuve, Montréal, Québec (☎514/843-4231).

*Canada* lines (Toronto–Vancouver on the Trans-Canada; throughout Alberta and mainland British Columbia; New York–Montréal; New York–Toronto) and *Voyageur Colonial* services (Québec, parts of Ontario and destinations east). Prices are as follows, with high-season (mid-June to mid-Sept & mid-Nov to Dec) prices in brackets: seven days £80 (£105); fifteen days £120 (£155); thirty days £175 all year.

The **All Canada Pass** covers the same routes plus the services of *Orleans Express* in Québec, *Acadian Lines* in Nova Scotia and *SMT Lines* in New Brunswick for fifteen days (£158/£185) and thirty days (£210/£225). Extensions can be bought at the rate of £10 a day when you buy the pass.

In the UK the passes are available from *London Student Travel*, 52 Grosvenor Gardens SW1W 0AG (☎071/730 3402), through any branch of *Thomas Cook* or from *Greyhound's* office at Sussex House, London Rd, East Grinstead, W Sussex RH19 1LD (☎0342/317317).

If you are exploring just **Ontario and Québec** it could be worth investing in a **Tour Pass**. Available from May to mid-October from major bus terminals in the two provinces, it costs $115 for ten consecutive days and is valid on nearly all the bus lines. Up to seven additional days can be purchased for $12 per day.

If you are coming in from the US, note that *Greyhound's* **Ameripass** is not valid for travel in Canada except for the **Seattle to Vancouver** route.

## BY TRAIN

The railway may have created modern Canada but passenger trains are now few and far between – at the beginning of 1990 over half of **VIA rail** services were eliminated at a stroke and remaining fares were increased dramatically. Services are notoriously slow and delays common as passenger trains give way to freight, though the city links between Montréal and Toronto are still speedy and efficient. However, rail travel can still be a very rewarding experience, especially on trains with special "dome cars" that allow an uninterrupted roof-top view of the countryside.

One of the saddest losses of the *VIA* cutbacks was the legendary **Canadian** train that followed the *Canadian Pacific* lines daily from Montréal to Vancouver. Today's *Canadian* departs three times a week from Toronto and uses the more northerly *Canadian National* lines, through the monotonous muskeg of northern Ontario before hitting Jasper – the scenery between there and Kamloops, the last big station before Vancouver, provides some of the Rockies' best . The trip is scheduled to take four nights but usually runs late; it costs a minimum of $404 per person one way.

The other major *VIA* trains still running are the **Western Canada** services from Winnipeg to Churchill, Jasper to Prince Rupert and Victoria to Courtenay; the **Windsor/Québec City** services between Toronto, Ottawa, Niagara Falls, Montréal and Québec City; and the **Eastern Canada** network between Montréal, Halifax and the Gaspé.

## FARES

One-way fares from Toronto to Winnipeg give an idea of the cost of rail travel. **Coach** class, the Canadian equivalent of second class, with reclining seats, costs $200; **section** class, with large seats that become curtained bunks at night, costs from $168–227, or $336 for two; **roomettes** are private single rooms with a toilet and a bed that folds out from the wall, and cost $309; finally, **bedrooms** are spacious cabins with two armchairs, large windows, a table, toilet, wardrobe and bunk bed, costing $618 for two.

Ten percent reductions are available for the over-60s, and two- to eleven- year-olds are half fare. **Off-peak fares**, for "Coach" travel only, are forty percent cheaper on the Windsor/Québec City corridor every day except Friday, Sunday and holidays, but seats are limited and five-day advance purchase is obligatory. Between the Maritimes and Ontario or Québec the "Coach" discount applies all year except from mid-June to early September and from mid-December to early January, with the requirement of seven days' advance purchase. In western Canada, a 33 percent reduction applies from November to mid-December and early January to late April; again a week's advance purchase is necessary.

## PASSES

Non-North American visitors can cut fares greatly by buying a **Canrailpass**, which allows unlimited "Coach" class travel for thirty consecutive days and discounted car rental from *Hertz*. There are two types of pass: the **System** ($299/$439 late April to Oct), allows travel on the entire network; the **Eastern** pass ($179/$269) is only valid on the

Québec City to Windsor corridor and destinations east of Montréal. The passes are cheaper for under-24s and students – System $249/$399, Eastern $159/$219. In the UK the passes can be obtained from *Long-Haul Leisurail*, PO Box 113, Peterborough PE1 1LE (☎0733/51780); *Compass Travel*, 3rd floor, Priest Gate House, 527 Priest Gate, Peterborough PE1 1LE (☎0733/53809); or *Thistle Air Ltd*, 22 Bank St, Kilmarnock, Scotland KA1 1HA (☎0563/71159). They can also be purchased from any *VIA rail* station, but are about $40 more expensive if you don't buy seven days in advance.

*Canadian Airlines* offer a **SkyRail** pass which has to be bought 21 days before departure on a round-trip to Canada. It consists of three air and rail coupons which can be exchanged for "Coach" class rail journeys or domestic flights between eighteen major destinations, though you must use at least one rail and one air coupon. If you cross the Atlantic with *Canadian* the pass costs $579 from mid-June to mid-September and from mid-December to mid-January and $469 during the rest of the year; up to eight additional coupons can be purchased for $70 each. For transatlantic passengers not using a *Canadian Airlines* flight, rates are around $180 more expensive.

---

**VIA TOLL-FREE INFORMATION**

☎1-800-561-3926 in Newfoundland.

☎1-800-561-3952 in Prince Edward Island, Nova Scotia and New Brunswick.

☎1-800-361-5390 in Québec.

☎1-800-361-1235 in Ontario.

☎1-800-561-8630 from northwest Ontario, Manitoba, Saskatchewan, Alberta, British Columbia, Yukon and NWT.

---

**PRIVATE LINES**

Other than *VIA*, various private companies operate passenger trains which pass through otherwise inaccessible wilderness. Most spectacular is the **Rocky Mountaineer** from Vancouver to Banff and then on to Calgary, or to Jasper, which is best experienced through a package from *Rocky Mountaineer Railtours* (☎1-800-665-7245). These tours, which are swiftly booked out, run from June to September and cost $390 one way for two to Jasper and Banff ($695 return), plus

$35 per person for one-way travel between Banff and Calgary. Rates do not include tax but do include light meals, and a night's hotel accommodation in Kamloops. In Ontario shorter trips can be made on the **Polar Bear Express** from Cochrane to Moosonee (see p.307) and the **Algoma Central Railway** from Sault Ste Marie to Hearst (see p.316).

---

### BY PLANE

The complexity of Canada's internal flight network is immense, and throughout this guide we have given indications of which services are most useful. Having merged with *Wardair*, *Canadian Airlines* offers the most prolific intercountry service, with planes serving over 125 destinations, but both *Air Canada* and *Canadian Airlines* link up with numerous minor lines to reach the farthest-flung recesses of Canada – for example *Labrador Airways* in Labrador. Nobody could pretend that flying round Canada is a low-budget option, but bargains do appear in the travel sections of local newspapers, especially on Sundays, and VUSA passes can bring hefty discounts. If you're set on exploring the deep north, there is no alternative to air transport, as these are zones which no rail line or road can penetrate.

**PASSES**

A multitude of **VUSA** (Visiting US and Canada) tickets provide internal air travel at special rates. The passes have to be bought before taking a transatlantic flight, and are available in the UK from *Air Canada*, *Canadian Airlines* and *British Airways*, usually with the proviso that you fly to Canada with that carrier.

All VUSA air-pass deals are broadly similar, involving the purchase of at least two coupons for around £180, with a maximum purchase of eight, extra coupons costing around £60. Each coupon is valid for a flight of any duration within the continent. *Canadian Airlines*, with the strongest domestic connections, has a good variety of passes: study the possibilities carefully before committing yourself. The main **unlimited** pass within Canada is the *Air BC* **Western Canada AirPass** purchasable from UK travel agents before departure; it costs £169 for fourteen days, £245 for thirty days and allows unlimited travel between Winnipeg and a range of destinations to the west.

## MAJOR AIRLINE NUMBERS IN CANADA

| **Air Canada** | **Canadian Airlines** |
| --- | --- |
| Montréal ☎1-800-361-8200 | Montréal ☎1-800-363-0372 |
| Toronto ☎1-800-268-7240 | Toronto ☎1-800-263-6133 |
| Vancouver ☎1-800-663-3721 | Vancouver ☎1-800-663-3502 |

## BY CAR

Travelling by car is the best way to see Canada, even though a vehicle can be a bit of a liability in towns, with their stringent parking areas, efficient traffic wardens and rush-hour gridlocks. Any US and UK national over 21 with a full driving licence is allowed to drive in Canada, though rental companies may refuse to rent to a driver who has held a full licence for less than one year, and under-25s will probably get lumbered with a higher insurance premium. Car rental companies will also expect you to have a credit card; if you don't have one they may let you leave a hefty deposit (at least $300) but don't count on it.

Most of Canada's vehicles run on unleaded petrol, which is sold by the litre; prices vary, but are generally around 70–80¢ per litre. It is also worth bearing in mind that gas is nearly half the price in the US, so if you are near the border it's worth crossing over to fill up the tank — Canadians who live near border crossings do this regularly.

### CAR RENTAL

Often the cheapest way to **rent a car** is either to take a fly-drive package (see p.5) or book in advance with a major agent like *Avis*, *Budget*, *Hertz*, *Thrifty* or *Tilden*. *Budget* and *Thrifty* tend to offer the best bargains, charging from around £80 a week for their cheapest vehicles. If you take a transatlantic flight, check to see if your airline offers discounted car hire for its passengers.

In Canada, expect to pay from around $200 a week for a two-door economy saloon in low season to $400 for a four-door medium car in high season, though throughout the year special promotions are offered by the major companies, which can get rates down to as low as $80 per week. Provincial **taxes** and GST (see p.14) are also not included in the rates, but the biggest **hidden surcharge** is often the **drop-off charge**, levied when you intend to leave your car in a different place from where you picked it up.

This is usually equivalent to a full week's or more rental, and can go as high as $500. Also be sure to check if **unlimited mileage** is offered, an important consideration in a country where towns are so widely dispersed: the usual free quota is 150–200km per day, after which an extra charge of 20¢ per kilometre is standard. Some companies, like *Rent-a-Wreck*, rent out used cars which are cheaper if you just want to spin around a city for a day, but as free mileage is not included, they work out far more costly for long-distance travel.

The **Loss Damage Waiver** (LDW) is a form of insurance which often isn't included in the initial rental charge but which you should think about taking out. At around $12 a day, it can add substantially to the total cost, but without it you're liable for every scratch to the car — even if it wasn't your fault. For breakdown problems, there'll be an emergency number attached to the dashboard.

### DRIVEAWAYS

A variation on car rental is a **driveaway**, whereby you drive a car from one place to another on behalf of the owner. The same rules as for renting apply, but you should look the car over before taking it as you'll be lumbered with any repair costs and a large fuel bill if the vehicle's a big drinker.

Most driveaway companies will want you to give a personal reference as well as a deposit in the $200–400 region. The most common routes are along the Trans-Canada and between Toronto or Montréal and Florida in the autumn and winter, although there's a fair chance you'll find something that needs shifting more or less to where you want to go. You needn't drive flat out, although not a lot of leeway is given — around eight days is the allocation for driving from Toronto to Vancouver. We have put some driveaway companies in our city listings, but check under "Automobile Driveaways" in the telephone directory.

## MAJOR CAR RENTAL COMPANIES

### IN THE UK

**Avis** ☎081/848- 8733.
**Budget** ☎0800/181181.
**Hertz** ☎081/679-1799.

**Thrifty** ☎0494/442110.
**Tilden** ☎081/950-5050.

### IN THE US

**Avis** ☎1-800-331-1212.
**Budget** ☎1-800-527-0700.
**Dollar** ☎1-800-421-6868.
**Hertz** ☎1-800-654-3131.

**National** ☎1-800-227-7368.
**Rent-a-Wreck** ☎1-800-535-1391.
**Thrifty** ☎1-800-367-2277.
**Tilden** ☎1-800-227-7368.

### IN CANADA

**American International Rent-a-Car** ☎1-800-527-0202.
**Avis** ☎1-800-387-7600 from Ontario and Québec; ☎1-800-268-2310 from elsewhere.
**Budget** ☎1-800-268-8970 from Québec; ☎1-800-268-8900 from elsewhere.
**Dollar** ☎1-800-421-6868.

**Hertz** ☎1-800-620-9620 from Toronto; ☎1-800-263-0600 from elsewhere.
**Rent-a-Wreck** ☎416/961-7500 (Toronto); ☎514/521-5771 (Québec); ☎902/543-4100 (Halifax).
**Sears** ☎1-800-527-0770.
**Thrifty** ☎1-800-367-2277.
**Tilden** ☎1-800-361-5334.

## RENTING AN RV

**Recreational vehicles** (RVs) can be rented through most travel agents who specialise in Canadian trips. It's best to arrange rental before getting to Canada, as RV rental outlets are not too common there, and agents will often give cheap rates if you book a flight through them as well. You can rent a huge variety of RVs right up to giant mobile homes with two bedrooms, showers and fully fitted kitchens. A price of around $700 for a five-berth van for one week is fairly typical, and on top of that you have to take into account mileage charges, the cost of petrol (some RVs do less than fifteen miles to the gallon), drop-off charges, and the cost of spending the night at designated trailer parks, which is what you're expected to do. Canada also has strict regulations on the size of vehicle allowed; in Ontario, for example, the maximum length for a trailer is 48 feet, 75 feet for trailer plus car — so if you are coming in from the US check that your RV isn't over the limit. The best UK-based rental company is *Caravan Abroad Ltd*, 56 Middle St, Brockham, Surrey RH3 7HW (☎0737/842 735), with various packages and pick-up points throughout Canada.

## ROADS, RULES AND REGULATIONS

The best **roads** for covering long distances quickly are the straight and fast multi-lane highways which radiate for some distance from major population centres. These are a maximum of six lanes divided by an intersection and are marked on maps as yellow lines with red borders and red shields that contain the highway number. Out of populated areas highways (marked by a red line on maps) go down to one lane each way and, though generally paved, are bordered by gravel — if you hit the gravel you will go into a spin, a potentially lethal experience. Up in the north, highways may be entirely of gravel — broken windscreens are an occupational hazard of the Alaska Highway, for example. The Trans-Canada highway from coast to coast is marked by a maple leaf sign at regular intervals along its length. Lesser roads go by a variety of names — county roads, provincial routes, rural roads or forest roads; out in the wilds many of these are not paved.

Canadians drive on the **right-hand** side of the road. In most **urban areas** streets are arranged on a grid system, often with octagonal "Stop" signs ("Arrêt" in Québec) at all four corners of junctions: **priority** is given to the first car to arrive, and to the car on the right if two or more cars arrive at the same time. Except in Québec, you can turn right on a red light if there is no traffic approaching from the left. Traffic in both directions must stop if a yellow schoolbus is stationary with its lights on, as this means children are getting on or off.

**Out of town**, exits on multi-lane highways are numbered by the kilometre distance from the beginning of the highway, as opposed to sequentially – thus exit 55 is 10km after exit 45. Rural road **hazards** include bears, moose and other large animals lumbering into the road – particularly in the summer, when the beasts crash through the undergrowth onto the highway to escape the flies, and in spring, when they are attracted to the salt on the roads.

Driving laws are made at provincial level, but the uniform **maximum speed limit** is 100kph on major highways, 80kph on rural highways and 50 kph in built-up areas. Canadians have a justifiable paranoia about speed traps and the traffic-control planes that hover over major highways to catch offenders – if you see one, slow down. On-the-spot fines are standard for speeding violations, for failing to carry your **licence** with you, and for having anyone on board who isn't wearing a **seat belt**. Canadian law also requires that any alcohol be carried unopened in the boot of the car, and it can't be stressed enough that **drunk driving** is a very serious offence. Bars in some provinces now have **designated driver schemes** whereby the driver of a group gives the keys to the head barperson and is then given free soft drinks all night; if the driver is spotted taking a sip of alcohol, he or she must pay for all the soft drinks consumed and leave their keys in the bar until the following morning. On the road, spot-checks are frequently carried out, and the police do not need an excuse to stop you. If you are over the limit your keys and licence will be taken away, and you may end up in jail for a few days.

In cities **parking meters** are commonplace, charging 25¢–$1 per hour. Car parks charge up to $20 a day. If you park in the wrong place (such as within five metres of a fire hydrant) your car will be towed away – if this happens, the police will tell you where your car is impounded and then charge you upwards of $150 to hand it back. A minor parking offence will set you back around $20; clamps are also used in major cities, with a fine of $120.

If you're a member of the *AA* or *RAC* in the UK or of the *AAA* in the States, a reciprocal agreement entitles you to free **breakdown service** from the *Canadian Automobile Association* (emergency number: ☎1-800-336HELP). Otherwise you should sit tight and wait for the police, who patrol regularly on major highways.

## HITCHING

Where it's legal **hitch-hiking** is the cheapest way to get around, but it may take some time to get a lift in less frequented areas – though in out-of-the-way areas many people customarily get around by thumb and visitors will often get picked up even when they are not attempting to hitch. Hitching on highways is illegal, but the sliproads on summer weekends are very busy, and you'll be up against a lot of competition on the Trans-Canada – count on a good week to get from Montréal to Vancouver. Drivers on multi-lane highways like the Ottawa to Montréal link treat the road like a Grand Prix circuit, so if you're trying to hitch between neighbouring cities stick to the lesser highways, which are usually parallel to a faster route.

An institutionalised system of ride-sharing is available in Québec and Ontario with *Allo-Stop*, which costs $8 to join and then fixes needy passengers with drivers who want company, all for just the share of petrol costs – a trip from Montréal to Toronto will set you back around $30, less if you are with other people. *Allo-Stop* numbers are given in the guide wherever appropriate.

## CYCLING

**Cyclists** are very well cared for in environment-friendly Canada: most cities have cycling lanes and produce special maps for cyclists, and long-distance buses and trains will allow you to transport your bike, perhaps for a small fee. The *Canadian Cycling Association (CCA)*, 1600 James Naismith Drive, Gloucester, Ontario K1B 5N4 (☎613/748-5829), can offer information on cycling throughout the country and publish several books, including the invaluable *Complete Guide to Cycling in Canada* ($15 excluding postage and packing). Standard bike rental costs are around $10 per day, plus a sizeable cash sum or a credit card as deposit; outlets are listed in the guide.

# ACCOMMODATION

Accommodation isn't too expensive in Canada, but is still likely to take a good portion of your budget. You can reduce outlay by camping, which costs from as little as $5, or by using hostels, where prices start at around $10. Campgrounds and hostels in cities, however, are heavily used, and you may have to resort to hotels or motels, were you can usually find rooms from about $30, or even less in rural areas away from the big sights. Most places will set up a third single bed in a double room for $5–15 extra. But travellers on their own will have a hard time: single rooms, especially in motels, are usually doubles let out at only a slightly reduced rate.

If you're heading into remote parts of the country, always check the availability of accommodation before setting off. Places which look large on the map often have no facilities at all, and US visitors will find motels far scarcer than in similar regions back home. Wherever you intend to stay, it's best to try to book a room well before you arrive, especially in summer – and if you're arriving late, stress the fact, as reservations are generally held only until 6pm, or even 4pm in major resorts. It can also be worth confirming check-in/check-out times, particularly in busy areas, where your room may not be available until late-afternoon. Also be prepared to pay in advance, and be ready for a few dollars' surcharge to a room's advertised price, usually the result of provincial taxes.

Local tourist information offices can help out if you get stuck: most offer free advice and will book a place free of charge, but few are willing to commit themselves to specific recommendations. Many large resorts, like Banff and Jasper in the Rockies, have a privately run central reservations agency which will find rooms for a small fee. Before going to Canada it's worth picking up the full accommodation and camping listings put out by the provinces (see p.12 for office addresses); they all give details of prices, size and facilities.

## HOTELS AND MOTELS

Canada's **hotels** tend to fall into one of two categories: high-class five-star establishments in big cities and resorts; or grim downtown places, often above a bar. Middle-ground spots are thin on the ground, their role being filled by motels, which are basically out-of-town hotels by another name.

**Top-of-the-range** hotels can be very grand indeed, particularly those run by *Canadian Pacific* in big resorts like Banff and Lake Louise. Most cater unashamedly for Japanese and US tourists, or to business travellers in the big cities, charging anywhere between $150 and $500 in high season; $250 would get you a double in most cities, though rates can fall to around $100 off-season.

**Mid-price** hotels are often part of a chain such as *Holiday Inn*, *Sandman* or *Best Western*, and usually offer a touch more comfort than middling motels. You should be able to find a high-season double in such places from around $80.

**Bottom-bracket** hotels – those costing around $20–35 – are mostly hangovers from the days when liquor laws made it difficult to run a bar without an adjoining restaurant or hotel. Found in most medium- and small-sized towns, they have the advantage of being extremely central, but the disadvantage that the money-generating bars come first, with the rooms usually an afterthought. Many have strip joints or live music likely to pound until the small hours, and few pay much attention to their guests, many of whom are long-stay clients as seedy as the hotel itself. Rooms are mostly battered but clean, but probably won't have much in the way of facilities beyond a wash basin and broken TV. Basic meals are often on hand in the bar. Such places still fill up, though, and it pays to call ahead to check for space if you're forced to use them.

**Motels** may be called inns, lodges, resorts or motor hotels, but they all amount to much the same thing; reasonably priced and reliable places on the main highways just outside town. The simplest rooms start at around $25, with the **average** price nearer $50 – though in resorts and more remote areas it's not unusual to find $100 being charged. As a rule of thumb, prices drop in the larger centres the further you move from downtown. Many offer **off-season rates**, usually between October and April, some have triple or quadruple berth rooms, and most are fairly relaxed about introducing an extra bed into "doubles" for a nominal charge. Many also offer a **Family Plan**, whereby youngsters sharing their parents' room stay free.

In all but the most basic motels you can expect a good-sized double bed, a private bathroom, TV and phone, and in smarter places there may be frills like free coffee and the use of saunas, sun-beds and swimming pools. Some have rooms with **kitchenettes**, or basic cooking facilities. More ritzy spots may also have a small restaurant, but generally you can expect nothing in the way of **food and drink** except for a soft drinks machine.

## BED AND BREAKFAST

**Bed and breakfast** is an accommodation option that's rapidly colonising most Canadian towns, and is already well established in cities such as Toronto, Montréal, Vancouver and Québec. Standards in B&B homes or **guesthouses** are generally very high, and prices are around $50 and upwards per couple – no real saving over cheaper hotels and motels, but you may wind up with a wonderful room in a heritage building in a great location, with the chance to meet Canadians on closer terms. B&B establishments have a quite rapid turnover, so to find one it's often best to visit tourist offices, many of which have bulging cata-logues and photographs of what's available, or contact one of the many private agencies who can line you up with something suitable.

## HOSTELS AND STUDENT ACCOMMODATION

Canada has about 60 **Canadian Hostelling Association** (*CHA*) hostels affiliated to the *IYHF*, and many more non-affiliated **mini-hostels** (or Homes) which also figure in *CHA* literature. Hostels are graded in four categories (basic, simple, standard and superior), and accommoda-tion is usually in single-sex dorms which cost about $8–16 for members, depending on category and location. In theory you're supposed to be an *IYHF* member to use hostels; in practice you can join the *IYHF* on the spot, or rely on most hostels making a higher charge for non-members (about $12–25) – though hostels will generally give pref-erence to members. Most offer communal recrea-tion and cooking areas, plus pillows and blankets, though you're expected to provide your own sleeping bag and towels. And of course you may have to help with chores.

Things are changing in the *CHA*: increasingly efficient advance bookings schemes are being set up; hostels are open longer and later; cafeterias are being introduced; and you can often book into smaller hostels, notably in the Rockies, through the bigger city hostels. Some major hostels now accept credit card bookings, but a more common way of securing a bed is still to send a deposit for the first night's stay or an *IYHF Advance Booking Voucher*, available from any *IYHF* office or specialist travel agents – though check that the hostel you're after accepts them.

**Mini-hostels** tend to be private homes or tiny commercial hotels with small breakfast included. Prices are about $10–20, with a surcharge for non-members, and you must have your own sleeping bag. A full current list is avail-able from most larger youth hostels.

## YOUTH HOSTEL INFORMATION

**Canada**

*Canadian Hostelling Association* (*CHA*), National Office, 333 River Rd, Tower A-3, Vanier City, Ottawa, Ontario K1L 8H9 (☎613/748-5638).

**United Kingdom**

*Youth Hostel Association* (*YHA*), Trevelyan House, 8 St Stephen's Hill, St Albans, Herts AL1 2DY (☎0727/55215).

**US**

*American Youth Hostels* (*AYH*), PO Box 37613, Washington DC 20013 (☎202/783-6161).

Both the **YMCA** and **YWCA** have establishments in most Canadian cities. In many cases the quality of accommodation matches that of the better hotels, and invariably exceeds that of most other hostel-type lodgings. Often the premises have cheap **cafeterias** open to all, and sports facilities, gymnasium and swimming pools for the use of guests. **Prices**, however, reflect the comforts, and though you can usually find bunks in shared dorms from about $15, the trend is increasingly to single, double and family units, ranging between $30 and $60. The old demarcation of the sexes is also breaking down, though many YWCAs will only accept men if they're in a mixed-sex couple. Some YWCAs accept women with children, others only in emergencies.

In Canada's university cities it's possible to stay in **student accommodation** during vacations. Anyone can use the facilities, though priority is usually given to other students. Often the accommodation is good if soulless, and you'll have access to the campus's sports facilities; on the downside most places are a good distance from city centres. Prices for single and double rooms start from about $30. Most campuses have a special office to handle such accommodation, and it's a good idea to call well ahead to be sure of a room.

## FARM VACATIONS

**Farm vacations**, on which you spend time as a paying guest on a working farm, give you the chance to eat well, sleep cheaply – and even work (if you want) – with your hosts, often with a wide range of outdoor activities on tap. Most places offer daily and weekly accommodation, either on rough campsites from as little as $5 per day, bed and breakfast from $20, or room and full board from $35 daily. Most provinces now have farm vacation associations to prepare lists of farms and inspect facilities. For further details consult tourist offices, provincial accommodation guides or contact the *Canadian Country Vacations Association*, PO Box 2580, Winnipeg, Manitoba R3B 4C3 (☎204/475-6624).

## CAMPING

Few countries offer as much scope for **camping** as Canada. Most urban areas have a campground; all national parks and the large proportion of provincial parks have outstanding government-run sites, and in most wilderness areas and in the vast domain of Canada's federally owned Crown Lands you can camp rough more or less where you please, though you should ask permission where possible. If you're travelling with a tent, check a campground's small print for the number of **unserviced** (tent) sites, as many places cater chiefly for **recreational vehicles** (RVs), providing them with **full or partial hookups** for water and electricity (or "serviced sites"). Anywhere described as an "RV Park" ought to be avoided completely.

During July and August campgrounds can become as busy as all other types of accommodation in cities, and particularly near mountain, lake or river resorts. Either aim to arrive early in the morning or book ahead – we've given phone numbers wherever this is possible). And check that the site is open – many campgrounds only open seasonally, usually from May to October.

### CAMPGROUND TYPES

At the bottom of the pile are **municipal campgrounds**, usually basic affairs with few facilities, which are either free or cost only a few dollars – typically $5 per tent, $10 per RV, though these usually are tent places only. **Private campgrounds** run the gamut: some are as basic as their municipal cousins, others are like huge outdoor pleasure domes with shops, restaurants, laundries, swimming pools, tennis courts, even saunas and jacuzzis. As for **price**, private campgrounds have several ways of charging. Some charge by the vehicle; others per couple; comparatively few on a tent or per person basis. Two people sharing a tent might pay anything between $2.50 and $15 each, though an average price would be nearer $5–7. You can book places in private campgrounds but there's often no need as most are obliged to keep a certain number of pitches available to passing custom.

Campgrounds in **national and provincial parks** are run by *Parks Canada* and individual provincial governments respectively. All are immaculately turned out and the bulk are **open** in theory only between May and September, but in practice most are available year-round, and in the bigger national parks, particularly in the Rockies, you'll find at least one site serviced for **winter camping**. **Prices** vary from about $5 to $15 per tent depending on location, services and the time of year – prices may be higher during July and August.

Sites in the major national parks, especially close to towns, usually offer a full range of amenities for both tents and RVs, and often have separate sites for each. As a rule, though, provincial sites and more remote national park campgrounds tend to favour tents and offer only water, stores of firewood and pit toilets. Hot showers, in particular, are rare. But both national park and provincial sites, of course, invariably score highly on their scenic locations. Both types of park campground fill the bulk of their pitches on a **first come first served** basis, but in a few parks there is a growing trend to set up a reservation service.

### PRIMITIVE CAMPING

Camping rough – or **primitive camping**, as it's known in Canada – has certain rules that must be followed. Check that fires are permitted before you start one – in large parts of Canada they aren't allowed in summer because of the risk of **forest fire.** If they are permitted, use a fire pit if provided, or use a stove in preference to local materials. In wilderness areas, try to camp on previously used sites. Be especially aware of the precautions needed when in bear country (see p.442). Where there are no toilets, bury human waste at least four inches into the ground and a hundred feet from the nearest water supply and campsite. Canadian parks ask for all rubbish to be carried away; elsewhere burn rubbish, and what you can't burn, carry away. **Never drink** from rivers and streams, however clear and inviting they may look. Before you drink it, **water** that isn't from taps should be boiled for at least five minutes, or cleansed with an iodine-based purifier (such as *Potable Aqua*) or a *Giardia*-rated filter, available from camping or sports shops.

## EATING AND DRINKING

Canada's sheer number of restaurants, bars, cafés and fast-food joints is staggering, but for the most part there's little to distinguish Canada's mainstream urban cuisine from that of any American metropolis: the shopping malls, main streets and highways are lined with pan-American food chains, trying to out-do each other with their bargains and special offers. However, this overall uniformity is leavened in the big cities by a plethora of ethnic and speciality restaurants, and even out in the country – the domain of often grim family-run diners – you'll find the odd ethnic restaurant to save the day. For specifically Canadian meals non-vegetarians should be all right with the provincial specialities, mostly based on local game and fish.

### BREAKFAST

**Breakfast** is taken very seriously all over Canada, and with prices averaging between $3 and $5 it's often the best-value and most filling meal of the day. Whether you go to a café, coffeeshop or hotel snack bar, the breakfast menu, on offer until around 11am, is a fairly standard fry. **Eggs** are the staple ingredient: "sunny side up" is fried on one side leaving a runny yolk; "over" is slipped over in the pan to stiffen the yolk; and "over easy" is flipped for a few seconds to give a hint of solidity. Scrambled, poached eggs and omelettes are popular too. The usual meat is **ham or bacon**, streaky and fried to a crisp, or skinless and bland **sausages** – except for Nova Scotia's famous Lunenburg sausage, a hot spicy version pioneered by settlers from Germany. Whatever you order, you nearly always seem to receive a dollop of fried potatoes, called **hash browns** or sometimes **home fries**. Other favourite breakfast options include **English muffins** or, in posher places, **bran muffins**, a glutinous fruitcake made with bran and sugar, and **waffles or pancakes**, swamped in butter with lashings of maple syrup. Also, because the breakfast/lunch division is never hard and fast, mountainous meaty **sandwiches** are common too.

Whatever you eat, you can wash it down with as much **coffee** as you can stomach: for the price of the first cup, the waiters will keep providing free refills until you beg them to stop. The coffee is either **regular** or **decaf** and is nearly always freshly ground, though lots of the cheaper places dilute it until it tastes like dish water. As a matter of course, coffee comes with cream or **half-and-half** (half cream, half milk) — if you ask for skimmed milk, you're often met with looks of disbelief. **Tea**, with either lemon or milk, is also drunk at breakfast, and the swisher places emphasise on the English connection by using imported brands — or at least brands which sound English.

## LUNCH AND SNACKS

Between 11.30am and 2.30pm many big-city restaurants offer special **set-menus** that are generally excellent value. In Chinese and Vietnamese establishments, for example, you'll frequently find rice and noodles, or dim sum feasts for $4 to $6, and many **Japanese** restaurants give you a chance to eat sushi for under $10, far cheaper than usual. **Pizza** is also widely available, from larger chains like *Pizza Hut* to family-owned restaurants and pavement stalls. Favourites with white-collar workers are **café-restaurants** featuring whole- and vegetarian foods, though few are nutritionally dogmatic, serving traditional meat dishes and sandwiches too; most have an excellent selection of daily lunch specials for around $7.

For quick **snacks** many **delis** do ready-cooked meals from $3, as well as a range of sandwiches and filled bagels. Alternatively, shopping malls sometimes have **ethnic fast-food stalls**, a healthier option than the inevitable **burger chains**, whose homogenised products have colonised every main street in the land. Regional snacks include **fish and chips**, especially in Newfoundland; Québec's traditional thick pea soup and *poutines* (fries doused in mozzarella cheese or cheese curds and gravy); and the Maritimes' ubiquitous **clam chowder**, a creamy shellfish and potato soup.

Some city **bars** are used as much by diners as drinkers, who turn up in droves to gorge themselves on the free **hors d'oeuvres** laid out between 5pm and 7pm from Monday to Friday in an attempt to grab commuters. For the price of a drink you can stuff yourself with pasta and chilli. **Brunch** is another deal worth looking out for, a cross between breakfast and lunch served up in bars at the weekend from around 11am to 2pm. For a set price ($8 and up) you get a light meal and a variety of complimentary cocktails or wine.

## MAIN MEALS

Often swamped by the more fashionable regional and ethnic cuisines, traditional **Canadian cooking** largely relies on local game and fish, with little in the way of vegetables and salads. In terms of price, meals for two without wine cost from $15 to $30 on average.

**Newfoundland's** staple food is the cod, usually prepared as fish and chips, supplemented by salmon, halibut and hake and more bizarre seafood dishes like cod tongues, dulse (dried seaweed) and seal flipper pie. The island's restaurants are not usually permitted to sell moose or seal meat, but many islanders join in the annual licensed shoot and, if you befriend a hunter, you may end up across the table from a hunk of either animal.

In the **Maritimes**, lobster is popular everywhere, whether it's boiled or broiled, chopped up or whole, as are oysters, scallops and herrings either on their own or in a fish stew or clam chowder. Fish are also **Ontario**'s most distinctive offering — though the pollution of the Great Lakes has badly affected the catch. Try the whitefish, lake trout, pike and smelt, but bear in mind that these are easier to come by in the north of the province rather than the south. Pork forms a major part of the **Québec** diet, both as a spicy spread known as *creton* and in *tourtière*, a minced pork pie. There are also splendid thick pea and cabbage soups, beef pies (*cipâte*), and all sorts of ways to soak up maple syrup — *trempette* is bread drenched with it and topped with fresh cream.

Northern **Saskatchewan and Manitoba** are the places to try fish like the goldeye, pickerel and arctic char. The **Arctic** regions feature caribou steak, and Alberta is also noted for its steaks. Finally, **British Columbia** cuisine features Pacific fish and shellfish of many different types, from cod, haddock and salmon to king crab, oysters and shrimp. Here and there, there's also the odd native peoples' restaurant, most conspicuously at the **Wanuskewin Heritage Site** in Saskatoon, Saskatchewan, where the restaurant serves venison, buffalo and black-husked wild rice.

Although there are exceptions, like the Ukrainian establishments spread across central Manitoba, the bulk of Canada's **ethnic restaurants** are confined to the cities. Here, amongst dozens of others, Japanese restaurants are fashionable and fairly expensive; Italian food is popular and generally cheap providing you stick to pizzas and basic pasta dishes; there's the occasional Indian restaurant, mostly catering for the inexpensive end of the market; East European food is a good, filling stand-by, especially in central Canada; cheap Chinese restaurants are common throughout the country; and French food is available too, though it's nearly always the cuisine of the expense account.

### TIPPING

Almost everywhere you eat or drink, the service will be fast and friendly – thanks to the institution of tipping. Waiters and bartenders depend on tips for the bulk of their earnings and, unless the service is dreadful, you should top up your bill by at least fifteen percent. A refusal to tip is considered rude and mean in equal measure. If you're paying by credit card, there's a space on the payment slip where you can add the appropriate tip.

### DRINKING

Canadian bars, like their American equivalents, are mostly long and dimly lit counters with a few punters perched on stools gawping at the bartender, and the rest of the clientele occupying the surrounding tables and booths. Yet, despite the similarity of layout, bars vary enormously, from the male-dominated, rough-edged drinking holes concentrated in the blue-collar parts of the cities and the resource towns of the north, to the far more fashionable city establishments which provide food, live entertainment and an inspiring range of cocktails. Indeed, it's often impossible to separate restaurants from bars – drinking and eating are no longer the separate activities they mostly were up until the 1960s.

The legal drinking age is eighteen in Alberta, Manitoba and Québec and nineteen in the rest of the country, though it's rare for anyone to have to show ID, except at the government-run liquor stalls, which exercise a virtual monopoly on the sale of alcoholic beverages of all kinds direct to the public: the main exception is Québec, where beer and wine are sold at retail grocery stores.

### BEER

For the most part, Canadian beer is as unremarkable as that of the States: freezing cold, fizzy and tasteless, designed to quench your thirst rather than to satisfy your palate. There are just two major Canadian brewers, **Molson** and **Labatts**, who market a remarkably similar product under all sorts of names – Molson Canadian, Molson Export, Labatts Blue – that inspire, for reasons that elude most foreigners, intense loyalty. The tastier **Great Western Beer** is made by the country's third largest brewer, a workers' cooperative based in Saskatoon, Saskatchewan, and there's also a niche market for foreign beers, although **Heineken**, the most popular, is made under licence in Canada. American beers like Budweiser and Coors are commonly available too. Some of the large cities have the odd brewpub, where ales are brewed on the premises, and the occasional independent brewer producing small quantities of natural (real) beer.

For bottled beers, expect to pay anything from $1.75 to $3.50. For draught beer, a cheaper way to drink, a 170ml glass can cost as little as 85¢; if there's a group of you, a pitcher containing about six glasses averages $5.

### WINE AND SPIRITS

Often akin to paint stripper, most Canadian **wines** come from Ontario's Niagara-on-the-Lake region. As imported wines are widely available and not too pricey, you probably won't want to experiment, but if you do, look out for Hillebrand Estates and Inniskillen wine. But as for **spirits**, this is where Canada, copying its giant neighbour, really excels. Even in run-of-the-mill bars there are startling arrays of gins and vodkas, and usually a good selection of rums. In the more traditional places, the most popular liquor is **whiskey** – either Scottish and Irish imports or the domestically made Canadian Club and VO rye whiskey. In the smarter places, you can experiment with all sorts of cocktails, costing anywhere between $3 and $10, whose basic ingredients are ice, topped with one or more shots of spirit and some type of fruit juice or sweet liquid like grenadine. Some bars feature their own concoctions, but by and large it's best to stick to the standards like those opposite.

## COCKTAILS

**Black Russian** vodka with coffee liqueur, brown cacao and cola.

**Bloody Mary** vodka, tomato juice, lemon or lime juice, salt and pepper, Worcestershire sauce and, if they know what they're doing, a celery stick.

**Brandy Alexander** brandy, brown cacao and cream.

**Harvey Wallbanger** vodka, orange juice and Galliano.

**Highball** any spirit plus a soda water or ginger ale.

**Manhattan** vermouth, whiskey, lemon juice and soda.

**Margarita** tequila, triple sec and lime or lemon juice.

**Piña Colada** dark rum, light rum, coconut cream and pineapple juice.

**Screwdriver** vodka and orange juice.

**Singapore Sling** sloe gin, dry gin, apricot brandy, cherry brandy, lime juice, sugar, seltzer water.

**Tequila Sunrise** tequila, orange juice and grenadine.

**Tom Collins** gin, lemon juice, soda and sugar.

**Vodka Collins** vodka, lemon juice, soda and sugar.

**Whisky Sour** bourbon, lemon juice and sugar.

## COMMUNICATIONS

General **post office** opening hours are Mon–Fri 8.30am–5.30pm, though a few places open on Saturdays between 9am and noon. Offices are sometimes found inside larger stores, so look out for *Canada Post* signs. **Stamps** can also be bought from automatic vending machines, the lobbies of larger hotels, airports, train stations, bus terminals and many retail outlets and newsstands. First-class **rates** for a letter or card are currently 37¢ within Canada; 43¢ to the US and 74¢ to the UK. There is no separate airmail rate.

Letters can be sent **poste restante** to any Canadian post office by addressing them c/o General Delivery at the main post office. Mark a pick-up date if known, or write "Hold for 15 Days", the maximum period mail will usually be held. Take some ID when collecting. Letters will also be held by hotels – mark such mail "Guest Mail, Hold for Arrival". If you're holding an *American Express* card or travellers' cheques you can have mail marked "Client Mail Service" sent to *Amex* offices throughout Canada. Others can pick up mail from *Amex* for a small fee.

### TELEPHONES AND TELEGRAMS

**Coin-operated telephones** are available in most public places. Whenever you are dialling a number outside the telephone region of the call box you are using, you have to prefix the number with 1-; this puts you through to the operator, who will tell you how much money you need to get connected. The operator asks for an amount (about $1.25) to cover the initial time period, which even within a province is fairly brief. Thereafter you'll be asked to shovel money in at regular intervals, so unless you're making a return charge (or "collect") call you need a stack of coins – usually quarters (25¢). Some connections within a single telephone code area are charged at the long-distance rate, and thus need the 1- prefix: a recorded message will tell you if this is necessary as soon as you dial the number. Local calls cost 25¢ from a public phone and are dialled direct; private subscribers pay nothing for these, so you'll find that shops often don't mind you using their phone for local calls.

Needless to say, using pocketloads of quarters is an inconvenient way of making international calls. Pay phones taking major credit cards, however, are increasingly common, especially in transport and major tourist centres. In some cities there are *Bell* offices that enable you to make your call and pay afterwards. Also growing in popularity are **affinity cards**, combined credit and phone cards, available in the US and Canada.

More upmarket hotels and motels have **direct dial** phones where the call is automatically charged to your bill. Elsewhere the hotel switchboard operator will place a call for you, or you'll be linked to an operator who will ask for the room number to which to charge the call – but be warned that virtually all hotels will levy a service charge in the region of 65–85 percent.

Many hotels, tourist offices and transport companies have **toll-free numbers** (prefixed by ☎1-800). Many can only be called from phones in the same province; others from anywhere within Canada; a few from anywhere in North America – as a rough guideline, the plusher the organisation, the wider its toll-free net.

To send a **telegram** either within Canada or abroad ask at your hotel or tourist office for the nearest *CN/CP Public Message Centre*. You can also phone in **Telepost** messages, a guaranteed next-day or sooner service in Canada and the US. **Intelpost** is an international fax service available at main post offices.

---

### OPERATOR NUMBERS AND TELEPHONE CODES

#### DIRECTORY ENQUIRIES

Canada's nationwide number for telephone information is ☎555-1212. If you need a number in another province, dial the area code (see below) + 555-1212. In most cities you can also dial ☎411 for local info. Operator number ☎0.

#### PROVINCE CODES

| | | |
|---|---|---|
| Alberta ☎403. | Nova Scotia ☎902. | Prince Edward Island ☎902. |
| British Columbia ☎604. | Newfoundland & Labrador ☎709. | Québec ☎514 (Montréal region) |
| Manitoba ☎204. | Ontario ☎416 (Toronto region)/ | / 819 (north)/ 418 (east). |
| New Brunswick ☎506. | 705 (central and n.east) / 519 | Saskatchewan ☎306. |
| Northwest Territories ☎403 / | (s.west peninsula)/ 613 (Ottawa | Yukon ☎403. |
| 819. | region) / 807 (n.west). | |

Calling Canada from the UK, dial 0101 + province code + subscriber number.
Calling Canada from the US, dial province code + subscriber number.

#### INTERNATIONAL CALLS

For direct **international calls**, dial the country code, the area code minus its first 0, and then the subscriber's number.

UK: ☎011 44      IRELAND: ☎011 353      AUSTRALIA: ☎011 61      NEW ZEALAND: ☎011 64

# OPENING HOURS, TIME ZONES AND HOLIDAYS

Most **shops and supermarkets** open from about 9am to 5.30pm Monday to Saturday, though in bigger towns and cities supermarkets and **malls** may open as early as 7.30am and close around 9pm. Enforced Sunday closing of shops, bars and restaurants operates over much of the country, but the law varies slightly in each province; as a balance many retail shops open late on Thursday and Friday evenings. In cities you'll usually find a **pharmacist** open 24 hours, and you can usually find a **convenience store** like *Mac's* or *7-11* that's open round the clock.

Time of year makes a big difference to the opening times of **information centres**, **museums** and other attractions, many of which, particularly in remote areas, have shorter winter hours or close altogether from late September to mid-May. In cities, more upmarket **restaurants** usually open from around noon to 11pm, longer at weekends; many diner-type places, however, close around 8pm, and small-town restaurants tend to close early too. Opening regulations for **bars** – often part of a hotel or restaurant – vary tremendously from province to province: most open daily from 10am–1am, but in certain provinces, notably Alberta, all bars except a few hotel lounges are shut on Sundays.

## TIME ZONES

Canada has six **time zones**, but because the two most easterly zones – Newfoundland Standard Time (NST) and Atlantic Standard Time (AST) – are only half an hour apart, the time difference between east and west coasts is 4hr 30min. Newfoundland on NST is 3hr 30min behind Greenwich Mean Time (GMT) in the UK, and British Columbia and the Yukon on the west coast (Pacific Standard Time) are 8hr behind GMT.

Train, bus and plane **timetables** are always given in local time, something it's worth bearing in mind if you're making long journeys across several zones. Most timetables use the 24-hour clock; those that do not, notably *Greyhound* bus schedules, use light type for am, bold for pm.

**Daylight saving time** takes effect in Canada in all regions except Saskatchewan and the northeast corner of British Columbia. Clocks go forward one hour on the first Sunday of April, and back one hour on the last Saturday in October.

## HOLIDAYS

Banks, schools and government buildings are closed all over the country on Canada's **national holidays**, and are closed within the relevant region on the **provincial holidays** that fall on certain – often moveable – days throughout the year; many shops, restaurants, museums and sights remain open, however. Hotels, campgrounds and smaller information centres often use Victoria Day and Labour Day or Thanksgiving as markers for their open and closed seasons.

### NATIONAL HOLIDAYS
New Year's Day.
Good Friday.
Easter Monday.
Victoria Day (Monday before May 25).
Canada Day (July 1).
Labour Day (first Monday in September).
Thanksgiving (second Monday in October).
Remembrance Day (November 11).
Christmas Day.
Boxing Day (December 26).

### PROVINCIAL HOLIDAYS
**Alberta**: Alberta Heritage Day (first week in August).
**British Columbia**: British Columbia Day (first week in August).
**New Brunswick**: New Brunswick Day (first week in August).
**Newfoundland and Labrador**: St Patrick's Day (March 17); St George's Day (around April 21); Discovery Day (penultimate Monday in June); Memorial Day (first week in July); Orangeman's Day (third week in July).
**Novia Scotia**: Sir John A MacDonald's Birthday (January 11).
**Manitoba**, **NWT**, **Ontario** and **Saskatchewan**: Civic Holiday (first Monday in August).
**Québec** Epiphany (January 6); Ash Wednesday; Ascension (forty days after Easter); Saint-Jean Baptiste Day (June 24); All Saints' Day (November 1); Immaculate Conception (December 8).
**Yukon** Discovery Day (August 19).

## OUTDOOR PURSUITS

Canada's mountains, lakes, rivers and forests offer the opportunity to indulge in a vast range of **outdoor pursuits**. We've concentrated on hiking, skiing, canoeing and fishing – the most popular activities – and on the national parks, which have been established to preserve and make accessible the best of the Canadian landscape. Whatever activity interests you, you should send off to the provincial tourist offices for information before you go, and once in Canada you can rely on finding outfitters, equipment rental, charters, tours and guides to help you in most areas. Also make a point of visiting Canadian bookshops – most have a separate outdoor pursuits section with a wide variety of specialist guides.

### THE NATIONAL PARKS

Canada's thirty or so **national parks** are administered by *Parks Canada*, a federal body, and are supervised locally by **park information centres** (the terminology may vary from park to park). Visit these to pick up **permits** if you intend to fish or camp in the backcountry, and for information and audio-visual displays on flora, fauna and outdoor activities. Many offer talks and nature walks presented by park naturalists, as well as reports on snow, weather and recent bear sightings. **Regulations** common to all parks include a total ban on firearms, hunting, snowmobiles or off-road vehicles, the feeding of wildlife, and the removal or damaging of any natural objects or features.

Note that most national park regulations relating to the care of the environment and campground behaviour are usually applicable to **provincial parks**. Entry to these parks is free but you'll have to pay for fishing and hunting permits – though the specifics vary from province to province.

### PERMITS

At most national parks all motor vehicles, including bikes, must buy a **park permit** before entering, usually from a roadside booth at the point where the road crosses the park boundary. People entering on foot, bicycle, boat or horseback are exempt, and there are exemptions for vehicles passing straight through certain parks without stopping overnight. An annual permit, valid until March of the following year, costs $26.75 per vehicle; a four-day permit costs $9.50; and a day permit $4.25, valid until noon the following day. Permits bought for one park are valid for all other national parks.

Permits are also required to **fish** in national parks (over and above any provincial permits; see "Fishing", overleaf). These are available from park centres, wardens or park administration buildings, and cost $10.75 (annual); $5.25 (weekly); $3.25 daily. There may well be quotas on the types and numbers of fish which can be taken, which you can find out when you buy a permit; in all parks there's a $10.75 surcharge to fish for salmon.

### CAMPING IN THE PARKS

Most parks have large, well-run campgrounds close to the park's main town, some for tents or RVs only, others mixed. **Fees** depend on facilities, and currently run from $6.50 per tent or per vehicle for **semi-primitive sites** (with wood, water and pit toilets) up to $16 for those with electricity, sewage, water and showers. Park permits do not cover campground fees.

Most parks also have **primitive campgrounds**, which are basic backcountry sites providing, as a rule, just fire pits and firewood. Regulations for **rough camping** vary enormously. Some parks, like Jasper in the Rockies, allow backcountry camping only in tightly defined sites; others, like Banff, have a special **primitive wildland** zone where you can pitch a tent within a designated distance of the nearest road or trail-head. Whether you want to use a primitive camp-ground or camp rough you must obtain an **overnight permit** from the park centre (either free or $1–2); this enables the authorities to keep a check on people's whereabouts and to regulate the numbers in the backcountry.

## HIKING

Canada boasts some of North America's finest **hiking**, and whatever your abilities or ambitions you'll find a walk to suit you almost anywhere in the country. All the national and provincial parks have well-marked and maintained trails, and a visit to any park centre or local tourist office will furnish you with adequate **maps** of local paths. Park trails are usually sufficiently well marked not to need more detailed maps for short walks and day hikes. If you're venturing into backcountry, though, try to obtain the appropriate 1:50,000 (or 1:250,000) sheet from the *Canadian Topographical Series*. For key hiking areas we've given a brief summary of the best trails in the appropriate parts of the guide, though with over 1500km of paths in Banff National Park alone, recommendations can only touch the surface of what's on offer. Park staff can advise on other good walks, and **trail guides** are widely available for most of the country's prime walking regions.

It's essential, of course, to be **properly equipped** if you're walking in high or rough country: good boots, waterproof jacket and spare warm clothing. Be prepared for sudden changes of weather and the sort of health problems asso-ciated with the Canadian backcountry (see "Health and Insurance"). Outdoor clothing can be bought easily in most towns, and in walking areas there's a good chance of being able to **hire** tents and specialised cold-weather gear.

### MAIN HIKING AREAS

In picking out the country's prime **walking areas** we've chosen the parks which are accessi-ble by road, where maps are available and the trail system developed, and where you can turn up without too much planning or special wilder-ness training.

Best-known and most developed of these are the **Rockies national parks** of Alberta and British Columbia. Thousands of kilometres of well-kept and well-tramped paths criss-cross the "big four parks"– Banff, Jasper, Yoho and Kootenay – as well as the smaller enclaves of Glacier, Revelstoke, Kananaskis and Waterton lakes. Scope for hiking of all descriptions is almost limitless.

More modest areas dotted all over British Columbia boast walking possibilities out of all proportion to their size: all the following provin-cial parks offer a variety of day hikes, short strolls and longer trails that could keep you happy for a week or more: **Wells Gray**, north of Kamloops; **Kokanee Glacier**, near Nelson: **Manning**, east of Vancouver; **Garibaldi**, north of Vancouver; and **Strathcona**, on Vancouver Island.

In Manitoba, the **Riding Mountain National Park** offers about thirty hiking trails, but though there's plenty of upland walking to be had in the so-called prairie provinces, you have to move east to Québec's **Mauricie**, **Forillon** and **Gatineau** parks for a taste of mountains compar-able to the western provinces. In Ontario, **Lake Superior Provincial Park** and the **Algonquin** park are the most challenging terrains. New Brunswick's **Fundy National Park** offers coastal walks, while Newfoundland's hiking centres on its two national parks: **Terra Nova** on the east coast, and the high plateau and fjords of the the west coast's **Gros Morne**. For the truly bold, however, nothing can match the arctic extremes of **Baffin Island**, whose principal trail lies over an ice-cap that never melts.

### LONG-DISTANCE FOOTPATHS

In areas with highly developed trail networks, seasoned backpackers can blaze their own **long-distance footpaths** by stringing together several longer trails. Recognised long-haul paths, however, are relatively rare, though more are being designated yearly. One of the best is the **Chilkoot Trail** from Dyea in Alaska to Bennett in British Columbia, a 53-kilometre hike that closely follows the path of prospectors en route to the Yukon during the 1898 gold rush. The most popu-lar is probably Vancouver Island's demanding **West Coast Trail**, which runs for 80km along the edge of the Pacific Rim National Park.

More far-reaching walks include the **Rideau Trail** which follows paths and minor roads for 386km from Kingston to Ottawa, the 690-kilometre **Bruce Trail** from Queenston on the Niagara River to Tobermory on the Bruce Peninsula, and the soon-to-be-completed **Voyageur Trail** along the north shores of lakes Superior and Huron, which will be the longest and most rugged route in the province.

The **Alpine Club of Canada**, Box 519, Indian Flats Road, Canmore, Alberta T0L 0M0 (☎403/678-5855), is an invaluable source of information and organises hiking and skiing trips around the country.

## SKIING

Wherever there's hiking in Canada, there's also usually **skiing**. The increasingly popular resorts of the Rockies and British Columbia are the main areas, followed by Québec, but there's also skiing in Newfoundland and the Maritimes, and even a few runs in Manitoba and Saskatchewan. Most **cities** are close to excellent downhill and cross-country runs: Vancouver is ninety minutes' drive from Whistler, one of the world's top three resorts; Calgary is the same distance from the Rockies' six big centres; Ottawa lies just half an hour from Camp Fortune and Mont Cascade; and Montréal is around an hour from 300 runs in the Laurentians and 100-plus slopes in L'Estrie (the Eastern Townships).

Canadian **ski packages** are available from most UK and US travel agents, but it's perfectly feasible to organise your own trips, as long as you book well ahead if you're hoping to stay in some of the better-known resorts. **Costs** for food, accommodation and **ski passes** are still fairly modest by US and European standards – a day's pass in one of the Rockies' resorts, for example, costs around $30. Tourist offices in skiing areas are open in winter to help with practicalities, and all nearby towns have ski shops to buy or rent equipment. Companies and hotels in some cities even organise their own mini-packages to nearby resorts. Skiing provinces publish regional ski and winter sports directories, all available in the UK and US from state or provincial tourist offices.

## FISHING

Canada is a fishing nirvana. While each region has its specialities, from the arctic char of the Northwest Territories to the Pacific salmon of British Columbia, excellent fishing can be found in most of the country's super-abundant lakes, rivers and coastal waters. Most towns have a fishing shop for equipment, and any spot with fishing possibilities is likely to have companies running boats and charters. As with every other major type of outdoor activity, most provinces publish detailed booklets on everything that swims within the area of their jurisdiction.

Fishing is governed by a range of **regulations** which vary from province to province. These are baffling at first glance, but usually boil down to the need for a **non-resident permit** for freshwater fishing, and another for salt-water fishing. These are obtainable from most local fishing or sports shops for about $30 and are valid for a year. Short-term (one- or six-day) licences are also available in some provinces. In a few places you may have to pay for extra licences to go after particular fish, and in national parks you need a special additional permit (see p.32). There may also be quotas or a closed season on certain fish. Shops and tourist offices always have the most current regulations.

## CANOEING

Opportunities for **canoeing** are limited only by problems of access and expertise – some of the rapids and portages on the country's more challenging routes are for real pros only. The most straightforward regions to canoe are in **Ontario**, with its estimated 250,000 lakes and 35,000 kilometres of waterways, some 25,000 kilometres of which have been documented as practical canoe routes. The key areas are the Algonquin, Killarney and Quetico provincial parks, though the single most popular run is the 190-kilometre **Rideau Canal**, a tame run from Kingston to Ottawa.

The rivers of **British Columbia** offer generally more demanding whitewater routes, though the lake canoeing – in the Wells Gray Provincial Park, for example – is among the country's most beautiful. One of the province's other recognised classics is the 120-kilometre trip near Barkerville on the Cariboo River and the lakes of the Bowron Lakes Provincial Park. More challenging still are the immense backcountry lakes and rivers of the **Mackenzie** system and the barren lands of the Northwest Territories, where you can find one of the continent's ultimate river challenges – the 300-kilometre stretch of the **South Nahanni River** near Fort Simpson. Growing in popularity, partly because of improved road access, are trips on and around the **Yukon river system**, particularly the South Macmillan River east of Pelly Crossing. Other areas that will test the resources of any canoeist are to be found in Manitoba and Labrador – all detailed in the guide.

Once you've decided on an area, provincial tourist offices can send you full lists of outfitters and rental agencies whose brochures provide a good idea of what you can expect in their various regions. When you arrive, **outfitters** are available in most centres to rent equipment, organise boat and plane drop-offs, and arrange provisions for longer trips. Typical **costs** are in the region of $80 for weekly canoe rental, $25 daily for a wet suit. Most also supply **maps**, but for longer trips you should obtain maps from the *Canada Map Office*, 615 Booth St, Ottawa, Ontario K1A 0E9 (☎613/952-7000). Specialist canoe **guides** are also widely available in Canadian bookshops, many giving extremely detailed accounts of particular river systems or regions.

## SPECTATOR SPORTS

Canadians are sports-mad – ice-hockey, baseball and Canadian football matches are a riot of over-excitement both on and off the field of play. Just as exciting as the professional games, and usually much less expensive, are the inter-collegiate competitions, the intensity of whose rivalries can be gauged from the fact that Ottawa actually banned their college games.

### ICE HOCKEY

Technically lacrosse is the "national" sport in all of Canada except Québec, but unofficially, it is **ice-hockey** that ignites the passions of all Canadians. With players hurtling around at nearly 50 kilometres per hour and the puck clocking speeds of over 160, this would be a high-adrenalin sport even without its relaxed attitude to combat on the rink – as an old Canadian adage has it, "I went to see a fight and an ice-hockey game broke out" indicates. Players, especially in the minor leagues, are as adept at a right hook as they are at skating and a few years ago the national team waged such a battle against the Soviet Union that the fight only stopped when officials turned all the lights off.

The North American **National Hockey League (NHL)** consists of 21 teams, of which seven are from Canada: the Montréal Canadiens, Québec Nordiques, Toronto Maple Leafs, Vancouver Canucks, Winnipeg Jets, Calgary Flames, and the Edmonton Oilers. There are two conferences – **Wales** and **Campbell** – both divided into two divisions. The Montréal Canadiens and the Québec Nordiques meet teams from Buffalo, Boston and Hartford in the Adams division of the Wales conference and the Toronto Maple Leafs face Chicago, Detroit, St Louis and Minnesota in the Norris division of the Campbell conference. The other Canadian teams play in the Smythe division of the Campbell conference, where they come face to face with the Los Angeles Kings – whose line-up includes Edmonton's own **Wayne Gretsky**, known throughout North America as the "Great One".

**Teams** have six players and perpetual substitutions are allowed during the game – players rarely spend more than a minute on the ice at one time. There are three twenty-minute periods in a match but the clock is frequently stopped for a variety of reasons so play usually goes on for three hours. Each team plays over ninety games a **season**, which lasts from October to May, and on alternate weeks will play two and then three games. At the end of the season the top three teams in each league go on into the play-offs for the **Stanley Cup**, ice-hockey's most prestigious title. The Montréal Canadiens are the Liverpool of Canada, having won the Stanley Cup 23 times, whilst the Toronto Maple Leafs are Canada's Manchester United with 11 victories; the Québec Nordiques are generally considered something of a joke. A season **schedule** is available from the National Hockey League, 960 Sun Life Building, 1155 Metcalfe, Montréal H3B 2W2 (☎514/817-9220).

**Ticket** prices range from around $10 to hundreds of dollars for a Stanley Cup final – you can forget about getting into this event unless you have contacts like Mulroney or Gretsky. For nearly all matches you will buy a ticket in advance.

Other than the NHL there are also numerous **minor league** clubs composed of **farm teams**, so-called because they supply the top clubs with talent. Ontario and Québec both have their own minor leagues; the rest of the country plays in the Western League, all with play-offs for a variety of awards. For **college hockey** the University of Toronto and York in Toronto, Concordia in Montréal, St Mary's in Halifax and the University of Alberta in Edmonton all have good teams.

## NHL TEAMS AND VENUES

### WALES CONFERENCE

**Montréal Canadiens** Forum, 2313 St-Catherine Ouest, Montréal (☎514/932-6131).

**Québec Nordiques** Colisée de Québec, 2205 du Colisée, Parc de l'Exposition, Québec City (☎418/529-8441).

### CAMPBELL CONFERENCE

**Calgary Flames** Calgary Olympic Saddledome, Stampede Park, Calgary (☎403/261-0455).

**Edmonton Oilers** Northlands Coliseum, 7424 118th Ave, Edmonton (☎403/474-8561).

**Toronto Maple Leafs** Maple Leaf Gardens, 60 Carlton St, Toronto (☎416/977-1641).

**Vancouver Canucks** Pacific Coliseum, Exhibition Park, Vancouver (☎604/254-5141).

**Winnipeg Jets** Winnipeg Arena, 1430 Muronnes Rd; Winnipeg (☎204/786-5448).

## CANADIAN FOOTBALL

Professional **Canadian football**, played under the aegis of the **Canadian Football League (CFL)**, is largely overshadowed by the National Football League in the US, chiefly because the best home-grown talent moves south in search of better money while NFL cast-offs move north to fill the ranks. However, the two continents football games vary only slightly, and what differences do exist tend to make the Canadian version more exciting. In Canada the playing field is larger and there are twelve rather than eleven players on each **team**. There is also one fewer **down** in a game – ie after kickoff the attacking team has three, rather than four, chances to move the ball forward ten yards and score a first down en route to a **touchdown**. Different rules about the movement of players and the limited time allowed between plays results in a faster-paced and higher-scoring sport in which ties are often decided in overtime or in a dramatic final-minute surge.

Despite the sport's potential, the CFL has suffered a blight of media and fan indifference which has caused immense financial problems, epitomised by the plight of the Toronto Argonauts, who began 1991 in serious trouble, largely as a result of their move to the oversized SkyDome. However, recent events at the Argos might signal a new lease of life for the CFL. A partnership of Los Angeles Kings owner Bruce McNall and Wayne Gretsky stepped in to rescue the club, offering the richest contract in pro football – $18 million for four years – to **Raghib (Rocket) Ismail**, probably the fastest man on a football field. His inspirational play rocketed the

## CFL TEAMS

### WESTERN CONFERENCE

**British Columbia Lions** BC Place Stadium, 777 Pacific Blvd South, Vancouver (☎604/669-2300).

**Calgary Stampeders** McMahon Stadium, 1817 Crowchild Trail NW, Calgary (☎403/289-0258).

**Edmonton Eskimos** Commonwealth Stadium, 9021 111th Ave, Edmonton (☎403/429-2881).

**Saskatchewan Roughriders** Taylor Field, 2940 10th Ave, Regina (☎303/569-2323).

### EASTERN CONFERENCE

**Hamilton Tiger-Cats** Ivorwynne Stadium, 14 Hughson St South, Hamilton (☎416/527-1508).

**Ottawa Rough Riders** Lansdowne Park, 1015 Bank, Ottawa (☎613/563-1212).

**Toronto Argonauts** Skydome, 277 Front St West, Toronto (☎416/595-1131).

**Winnipeg Blue Bombers** Winnipeg Stadium, Broadway and Balmoral, Winnipeg (☎204/775-9751).

Argos to a decisive victory in the **Grey Cup**, the culmination of the play-offs at the end of the 72-match **season** played by the two divisions of eight teams. On a wider scale, the Argos' dashing success has provided impetus for the transfer of the Ottawa and Calgary teams to more stable ownerships, and focused attention back on the CFL.

The season lasts from August to November, each team playing a match a week; tickets are fairly easy to come by, except for important games, and vary in cost from $10 to a Grey Cup final price of over $100.

## BASEBALL

**Baseball**, with its relaxed summertime pace and byzantine rules, is generally considered an exclusively American sport, but the **Toronto Blue Jays** and the **Montréal Expos** perform in two of the US's four leagues. Though neither has yet managed to lift the somewhat misnamed **World Series** title from the States, the Blue Jays in 1985, 1989 and 1991 won the American League East division despite tough rivals like the Boston Red Sox and the New York Yankees. Led by **Cito Gaston**, only the fourth black manager in baseball history, their most inspirational players are second baseman Roberto Alomar and outfielders Devon White and Joe Carter. The Expos are a lowlier bunch, though they became the first non-

US team to play in a US league in 1968, eight years before the Blue Jays. Their one asset is the Nicaraguan-born Dennis Martinez, who is arguably the best pitcher in the National League.

Even if you don't understand what's going on, a game can be a pleasant day out, drinking beer and eating burgers and popcorn in the sun, with friendly family-oriented crowds. Moreover, the home ground of each team is a vast, wondrous modern stadiums – the Skydome in Toronto and the Olympic Stadium in Montréal. With six teams in each division, there are eighty-one home games each season, played from April to late September, with play-offs continuing through October; there is no set match day and games are either played in the afternoon or evening. Lasting for two to three hours baseball games never end in a tie; if the scores are level after nine innings, extra innings are played until one side wins.

**Tickets** for the Blue Jays, priced from $4 to $900 for a hotel room that overlooks the pitch, are hard to come by – in 1991 more than two-thirds of their games sold out and they entered the record books with a seasonal attendance that topped the four million mark. In Montréal, with less glamour and tickets costing from $1 to $14, it is easier to get in. Nothing can match the glitz of the big two, but minor league **farm teams** include the Edmonton Trappers, Calgary Cannons and Vancouver Canadians.

---

### BASEBALL TEAMS

**Calgary Cannons** Foothills Baseball Stadium, PO Box 3690, Station B, Calgary (☎403/284-1111).

**Edmonton Trappers** John Ducey Park, 10233 96th Ave, Edmonton (☎403/429-2934).

**Toronto Blue Jays** Skydome, 277 Front St West, Toronto (☎416/595-0077).

**Montréal Expos** Olympic Stadium, 4141 Pierre-de-Coubertin Ave, Montréal (☎514/253-3434).

**Vancouver Canadians** Nat Bailey Stadium, 4601 Ontario St, Vancouver (☎604/872-5232).

---

## DISABLED TRAVELLERS

Canada is one of the best places in the world to travel if you have mobility problems or other physical disabilities. All public buildings are required to be wheelchair accessible and provide suitable toilet facilities, almost all street corners have dropped kerbs, and public telephones are specially equipped for hearing-aid users. Though wheelchair users will probably encounter prob-

lems when travelling on city public transport, main population centres are gradually introducing suitable buses.

The *Canadian Paraplegic Association* can provide a wealth of **information** on travelling in specific provinces, and most of its regional offices produce a free guide on the most easily accessed sights. The *Canadian Rehabilitation*

*Council for the Disabled* produces a useful publication called *Handi-Travel* ($12.95 plus $3 postage), and provincial tourist offices in London and Canada (see p.12) are also excellent sources of information on accessible hotels, motels and sights. Some also supply special free guides, like *Montréal – Useful Information for the Handicapped*, available from Québec House. You may also want to get in touch with *Kéroul* in Montréal, an organisation which specialises in travel for mobility-impaired people, and publishes the bilingual guides *Accèss Montréal* (free) and *Accèss Tourisme* ($10).

Most **airlines**, both transatlantic and internal, will do whatever they can to ease your journey, and will usually let attendants of more seriously disabled people accompany them at no extra charge – *Air Canada* is the best-equipped carrier.

The larger **car rental** companies, like *Hertz* and *Avis*, can provide cars with hand-controls at no extra charge, though these are only available on their most expensive models; book one as far in advance as you can – *Hertz* insists on the request being made five days before the car is needed. A wheelchair-accessible **coach** with hydraulic lift and on-board accessible toilet can be rented from *National Motor Coach Systems*, Box 3220, Station B, Calgary, Alberta T2M 4L7 (☎403/240-1992). In order to obtain a **parking privilege permit**, disabled drivers must

complete the appropriate form as supplied by the *Canadian Paraplegic Association* and produce a letter from their doctor stating their disability; a fee of around $6 is charged.

All *VIA rail* **trains** can accommodate wheelchairs that are no larger than 81cm by 182cm and weigh no more than 114kg, though 24 hours' notice is required for the Québec-Windsor corridor and 48 hours' on other routes. They offer an excellent service, including served meals, roomettes at no extra charge for blind people travelling with a guide dog, as well as help with boarding and disembarking. Those who need attendants can apply for a two-for-one fare certificate under the **"Helping Hand"** scheme; it's available from the *Canadian Rehabilitation Council for the Disabled*, if you submit a medical certificate and an application signed by a doctor.

Although **buses** are obliged to carry disabled passengers if their wheelchairs fit in the luggage apartment, access is often difficult. However, nearly all bus companies accept the two-for-one "Helping Hand" certificates, and drivers are usually extremely helpful.

Larger **hotels** like *Holiday Inn* have specially designed suites for disabled guests, and major motel chains like *Best Western* and *Journey's End* have full access – but it is always worth checking with the tourism offices to confirm facilities.

---

## USEFUL ADDRESSES

**Canadian Paraplegic Association**, 520 Sutherland Drive, Toronto M4G 3V9 (☎416/422-5640).

**Canadian Rehabilitation Council for the Disabled** 1 Yonge St, Suite 2110, Toronto, Ontario M5E 1E5 (☎416/862-0340).

**Kéroul** 4545 Pierre-de-Courbetin, CP 1000, Montréal (☎514/252-3104).

**VIA rail information** and reservations for the speech and/or hearing impaired are available on ☎416/368-6406 from Toronto, ☎1-800-268-9503 from elsewhere.

---

# POLICE, TROUBLE AND SETBACKS

There's little reason why you should ever come into contact with either the **Royal Canadian Mounted Police** (RCMP), who patrol most of Canada, or the provincial forces of Ontario and Québec. In contrast to the US, there's very little street crime and even in Toronto and Montreal you shouldn't have any problems in terms of

**personal safety**, though it's obviously advisable to be cautious late at night. However, blue collar Canada is not renowned for its gentleness and, if you're drinking in one of the country's many rough and ready bars, don't be too surprised if there's a fight, though the males (very rarely females) involved will almost always be too busy thumping people they know to bother with a stranger – and hitting a woman (in this context) is almost unheard of. **Theft** is also uncommon, though it's obviously advisable to be on your guard against petty thieves: secure your things in a locker when staying in hostel accommodation and avoid leaving valuables on a beach or in a tent or car.

Canadian officials are notorious for coming down hard if you're found with **drugs** – especially on non-Canadians. Stiff penalties are imposed even when only traces of any drug are found: so don't even think about it.

If you are unlucky enough to be attacked or have something stolen, phone the police on ☎**911**. If you're going to make an **insurance claim** or **travellers' cheque refund application**, ensure the crime is recorded by the police and make a note of their crime reference number.

Should you lose your **passport** go to the nearest consulate (see box below) and get them to issue a **temporary passport**, which is basically a sheet of paper saying you've reported the loss. This will get you home, but if you were planning to travel on from Canada, you'll need a new passport – a time-consuming and expensive process.

Another possible problem is **lost** airline tickets. On scheduled and most charter flights, the airline company will honour their commitment on the lost ticket, but for some bargain-basement tickets they will make you pay again unless you can produce the lost ticket's number. Similarly if you lose your travel insurance policy document, you won't be able to make a claim unless you quote its number. To avert both calamities, keep a copy of the numbers at home. For **lost travellers' cheques**, if you've followed the issuer's suggestion and kept a record of the cheque numbers separate from the actual cheques, all you have to do is ring the issuing company on their given toll-free number to report the loss. They'll ask you for the cheque numbers, the place you bought them, when and how you lost them and whether it's been reported to the police. All being well, the missing cheques should be reissued within a couple of days – and you may get an emergency advance to tide you over.

---

## CONSULATES AND EMBASSIES

### UNITED STATES

**Calgary**, 615 MacLeod Trail SE (☎403/266-8962).

**Halifax**, Cogswell Tower, Scotia Square (☎902/429-2480).

**Montréal**, 1155 rue St-Alexandre (☎514/398-9695).

**Ottawa**, 100 Wellington St (☎613/238-5335).

**Québec City**, 2 Terrace Dufferin (☎418/692-2095).

**Toronto**, 360 University Ave (☎416/595-1700).

**Vancouver**, 1095 West Pender St (☎604/685-4311).

### UNITED KINGDOM

**Edmonton**, Suite 1404, 10025 Jasper Ave (☎403/428-0375).

**Halifax**, Suite 1505, Purdy's Wharf Building, 1955 Upper Water St (☎902/429-4230).

**Montréal**, 1155 Université (☎514/866-5823).

**Ottawa**, 80 Elgin St (☎613/237-1530).

**St John's**, 34 Glencoe Drive (☎709/364-1200).

**Toronto**, Suite 1910, College Park, 777 Bay St (☎416/593-1290).

**Vancouver**, Suite 800, 1111 Melville St (☎604/683-4421).

**Winnipeg**, 111 Aldershot Building (☎204/896-1380).

## DIRECTORY

**ELECTRIC CURRENT** Electricity in Canada is supplied at an alternating current of 110 volts and at a frequency of 60Hz, the same as in the US. Visitors from the UK will require transformers for electrical appliances like shavers and hair dryers, and a plug converter for Canada's two-pin sockets.

**MEASUREMENTS** Canada officially uses the metric system, though many people still use the Imperial system. Distances are in kilometres, temperatures in degrees Celsius, and food, petrol and drink are sold in grams, kilograms or litres.

**NEWSPAPERS** Canada has no truly national newspaper: the closest thing is the *Globe and Mail*, an Ontario broadsheet also published in a western edition and available more or less throughout the country. Most cities have a quality paper, like the *Toronto Star*, *Calgary Herald* or *Vancouver Sun*, also often available throughout their provinces – though in rural areas you're more likely to find small-town tabloids on newsstands. The weekly *Maclean's* is the most widely read news magazine.

**PUBLIC TOILETS** Rare even in cities, but bars, fast-food chains, museums and other public buildings invariably have excellent facilities.

# PART TWO

# THE

# GUIDE

# CHAPTER ONE

# THE MARITIME PROVINCES

The **MARITIME PROVINCES** – Nova Scotia, New Brunswick and Prince Edward Island – are Canada's three smallest provinces, and their combined population of around one and a half million has been largely confined to the coasts and river valleys by the thin soils of their forested interiors. The undulating fields of PEI and the lowlands around New Brunswick's Grand Falls might produce massive crops of potatoes, and Nova Scotia's Annapolis Valley might be a major fruit-producing area, but the bulk of the region remains intractable – 84 percent of New Brunswick, for example, is covered by pine, maple and birch forests.

Most visitors to the Maritimes come for the coastal scenery and the slow pace of the "unspoilt" fishing villages, but the Maritimes were not always as sleepy as they appear today. When the three provinces joined the Dominion in the middle of the nineteenth century, their economies were prospering from the export of its fish and timber and the success of its shipyards. As opponents of the union had argued, the Maritimers were unable to prevent the passage of protectionist measures favouring Ontario and Québec. This discrimination, combined with the collapse of the shipbuilding industry as steel steamers replaced wooden ships, precipitated a savage and long-lasting recession that, within the space of thirty years, transformed the Maritimes from a prosperous, semi-industrialised region to a pastoral backwater dependent on the sale of its raw materials – chiefly wood and fish.

Despite this decline, the Maritimes offer more variety than their image suggests. In **Nova Scotia**, the southwest coast does indeed have a clutch of quaint fishing ports, but it also harbours the busy provincial capital of **Halifax**, whilst at **Port Royal** it boasts a fine reconstruction of the fort Samuel de Champlain built here in 1605. Further east, **Cape Breton Island**, separated from the mainland by the narrow Strait of Canso, is divided into two by **Bras d'Or Lake**: the hilly plateaux around industrial Sydney are unremarkable, but in the west the elegaic wooded hills and lakes around the resort of **Baddeck** lead into the mountainous splendour of **Cape Breton Highland National Park**. Moving on, **New Brunswick** has few urban pleasures, but provides the compensating delights of **Fundy National Park** and the culture of the Acadian settlers, while on **PEI** sedate **Charlottetown** is within a short hop of the magnificent sandy beaches of the **Prince Edward Island National Park**.

---

**TOLL-FREE INFORMATION NUMBERS**

Nova Scotia Department of Tourism ☎1-800-565-0000 from within Canada; ☎1-800-341-6096 from within the rest of mainland North America.

Tourism New Brunswick ☎1-800-442-4442 from within the province; ☎1-800-561-0123 from elsewhere in North America.

PEI Department of Tourism ☎1-800-565-7421 from within the Maritimes; ☎1-800-565-0267 from elsewhere in North America.

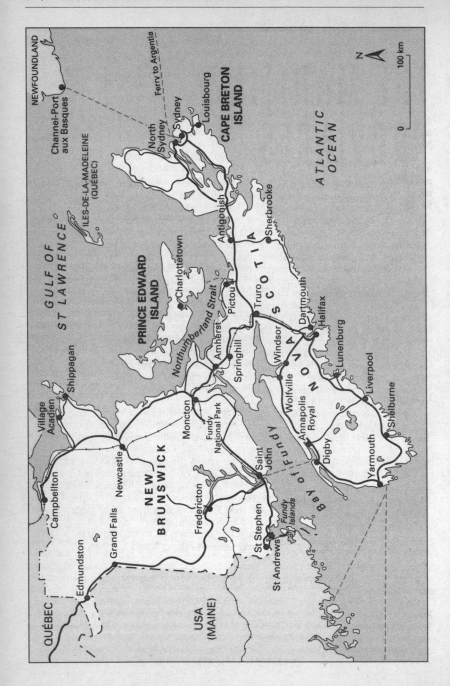

# NOVA SCOTIA

The character of **Nova Scotia** has been conditioned largely by the whims of the north Atlantic weather, a climate so harsh that the Nova Scotian colonists of the eighteenth century earned the soubriquet *Bluenoses* for their ability to stand the cold. The descendants of these privateers and hardened sailors do not typify the whole province, however: the farmers of the Annapolis Valley and their Acadian neighbours are quite distinct from the mariners of the Atlantic seaboard, and are different again from the mixed bag of emigrants who came to work the coal mines and steel mills of central Nova Scotia and Cape Breton Island from the 1880s.

To get the full sense of Nova Scotia you have to do a tour, and the logical place to start is the capital, **Halifax**, which sits on a splendid harbour on the south coast. The place itself is not all that attractive but it can fill a couple of days, after which it's best to take in the beguiling fishing villages of the southwest shore, turning inland at Liverpool for the sumptuous forests and lakes of **Kejimkujik National Park**, then on to **Annapolis Royal**, the old capital of Acadia, and Champlain's *habitation* at **Port Royal**. Heading east along the Annapolis Valley, it's a further 100km to the pleasant town **Wolfville** and another 90km back to Halifax.

Nova Scotia's other outstanding circular tourist route is the **Cabot Trail**. Named after the explorer John Cabot, who is supposed to have landed here in 1497, it encircles the northern promontory of **Cape Breton Island**, where the mountainous landscapes of **Cape Breton Highlands National Park** constitute some of eastern Canada's most stunning scenery. Cape Breton Island and the strip of Nova Scotia coast bordering the Northumberland Strait attracted thousands of Scottish highlanders at the end of the eighteenth century, mostly tenant farmers who had been evicted by Scotland's landowners when they found sheep raising more profitable than renting farmland. Many of the region's settlements celebrate their Scots ancestry and Gaelic traditions in one way or another – museums, highland games and bagpipe-playing competitions – and in **South Gut St Ann's**, on the Cabot Trail, there's even a Gaelic college. The final attraction of Cape Breton is the reconstructed eighteenth-century French fortress of **Louisbourg**, stuck in splendid isolation on the southeast tip.

Southwest Nova Scotia is well served by **bus**, with daily connections running between Halifax and Yarmouth via both the south shore and the Annapolis Valley, but to see anything of the wilder sections of the Cabot Trail you need a car.

---

The Nova Scotia **telephone code** is ☎902.

---

## A brief history of Nova Scotia

The original inhabitants of the Maritime Provinces were the **Micmacs** and **Malecites**, Algonquian-speaking peoples who lived a semi-nomadic life based on crop cultivation, fishing and hunting. Never numerous, both groups were ravaged by the diseases they contracted from their initial contacts with Basque and Breton fishermen in the late fifteenth century. Consequently, they were too weak to contest European colonisation, although the Micmacs were later employed by the French to terrorise the colonists of northern Maine.

Founded by the French in 1605, **Port Royal**, on the south shore of the Bay of Fundy, was Nova Scotia's first European settlement, but it was abandoned in 1614. Seven years later, James I granted **"Nova Scotia"**, as New Scotland was termed in the inaugural charter, to William Alexander, whose colony beside Port Royal lasted just three years. The French returned in the mid-1630s to re-establish Port Royal on the site of today's Annapolis Royal, this time designating the region as the French colony of

**Acadie**. These competing claims were partly resolved by the **Treaty of Utrecht** in 1713 – when Britain took control of all the Maritimes except Cape Breton Island and today's PEI – and finally determined after the fall of New France in 1759, a British victory tarnished by the cruel expulsion of the Acadians from their farms along the Bay of Fundy.

With France defeated and the British keen to encourage immigration, there was a rapid influx of settlers from New England, Ireland, England and Scotland. This increase in the population precipitated an administrative reorganisation, with the creation of Prince Edward Island in 1769 and New Brunswick in 1784. The new, streamlined Nova Scotia prospered from the development of its agriculture and the expansion of its fishing fleet. Further profits were reaped from shipbuilding, British-sanctioned privateering, and the growth of Halifax as the Royal Navy's principal north Atlantic base. In 1867 Nova Scotia became part of the Dominion of Canada confident of its economic future. However, the province was too reliant on shipbuilding and, when this industry collapsed, Nova Scotia experienced a dreadful recession, whose effects were only partly mitigated by the mining of the province's coal fields and the industrialisation of Cape Breton's **Sydney**, which became a major steel producer. The pits and steel mills were closed in the 1950s, and the province is now dependent on farming, fishing and tourism.

# Halifax

**HALIFAX**, set on a steep and spatulate promontory beside one of the world's finest harbours, has become the focal point of the Maritimes, the region's financial, educational and transportation centre, whose metropolitan population of over 300,000 makes it three times the size of its nearest rival, New Brunswick's Saint John. This preeminence has been achieved since World War II, but long before then Halifax was a naval town par excellence, its harbour defining the character and economy of a city which rarely seemed to look inland.

The British were the first to develop Halifax, founding a base here in 1749 to counter the French fortress of Louisbourg on Cape Breton Island. When New France was captured shortly afterwards, the town became a heavily fortified guarantor of the Royal Navy's domination of the north Atlantic, a role reinforced when the British lost control of New England. The needs of the garrison called the tune throughout the nineteenth century: the waterfront was lined with brothels; martial law was in force till the 1850s; and most Haligonians, as the local citizenry are known, were at least partly employed in a service capacity.

In this century Halifax acted as a key supply and convoy harbour in both world wars, but since then its military importance has declined, even though the ships of the Canadian navy still dock here. Disfiguring office blocks reflect the city's new commercial successes, interrupting the sweep of the town as it tumbles down to the harbour from the **Citadel**, the old British fortress which is the town's only significant sight. Nevertheless, Halifax retains a compact, quite leafy centre whose relaxing air is a far cry from the tense industriousness of many a metropolis.

## Arrival, information and transport

**Halifax International Airport** is located 32km northwest of the city centre. From here, *Airport Transfer* runs a bus **shuttle** service to the classier downtown hotels (daily 8am to midnight every 30min; 50min; $11). Ask the driver to let you off at the *Delta Barrington Hotel*, which is on Barrington Street right in the centre. The **taxi** fare for the same journey is around $40. The long-distance **bus station** is in the *Acadian Lines*

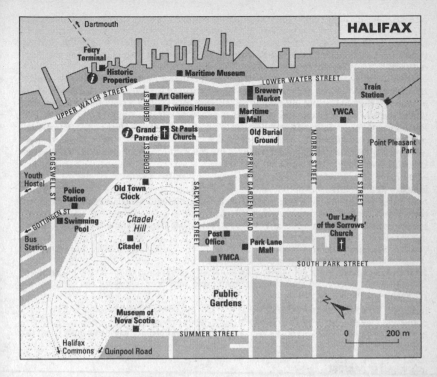

terminal, 6040 Almon St, about 4km northwest of the centre: transit buses #7 or #80 connect with downtown. The *Via rail* station, Terminal Rd, handles just six **trains** in and out per week, connecting Halifax with Truro, New Brunswick, and Montréal. From the train station it's a fifteen-minute walk into the centre down Barrington Street, or else catch the #9 bus.

## Information

Halifax's two **tourist offices**, one covering the city and the other the province, are both centrally situated. The *City Visitors Information Centre* (June–Aug daily 9am–6pm; Sept–May Mon–Fri 9am–6pm; ☎421-8736) is in city hall on the corner of Duke and Barrington streets. They will gladly fix up accommodation, advise on tours and provide you with armfuls of maps, brochures and leaflets. Five minutes' walk away, just off the waterfront in the area known as the Historic Properties, is the *Nova Scotia Tourist Information Centre* (mid-June to mid-Sept daily 9am–9pm; mid-Sept to mid-June Mon–Fri 8.30am–4.30pm; ☎424-4247), a mine of information about all aspects of the province, from history to bird-watching. The centre operates a room reservation service.

## Getting around

The best way to see downtown Halifax is on foot, but for outlying attractions and accommodation, **Metro Transit** bus services are reliable and efficient, though they are sharply curtailed in the evenings and on weekends. There's a flat fare of $1.10 for the inner city, or $1.50 to Dartmouth and the outer zones – exact fare only. If you need to change buses on the same journey, ask for a free transfer ticket at the outset.

# Accommodation

Finding a **place to stay** in Halifax is rarely a problem and the Visitors Information Centre is especially helpful in emergencies. Most downtown **hotels** are in the expense-account bracket, but there are a couple of small, inexpensive family-run places within a stone's throw of the train station – a far better alternative than the city's **motels**, which are inconveniently concentrated about 10km northwest of town along the Bedford Highway (Hwy 2), beside the Bedford Basin bay. Halifax has lots of **bed and breakfasts**, small, comfortable and sometimes seasonal places where reservations are strongly advised, either direct or through the **Halifax Bed and Breakfast Organisation** (☎429-7685). The main budget alternatives are the **college rooms** offered by four of Halifax's universities between mid-May and mid-August, and the **youth hostel**. There is no city campground.

## Hotels and motels

**Delta Barrington**, 1875 Barrington St (☎429-7410). Bang in the middle of downtown; scrubbed and polished luxury; from $80.

**Gerrard Hotel**, 1234 Barrington St (☎423-8614). One block from the train station; a delightful small hotel in a registered historical property; $45.

**Halifax Sheraton**, 1919 Upper Water St (☎421-1700). The city's grandest hotel, overlooking the waterfront; saunas, swimming pool and whirlpool; $120–175.

**Halliburton House Inn**, 5184 Morris St (☎420-0658). Central location, off Barrington St; splendidly restored series of old town houses; garden, patio and library; breakfast and afternoon tea included in room rates, $95–105.

**Prince's Lodge Motel**, 554 Bedford Hwy (☎443-0348). Small and pleasant; $40; June–Sept.

**Sea King Motel**, 560 Bedford Hwy (☎443-0303). Straightforward motel rooms; $60.

**Twin Elms Hotel**, 5492 Inglis St (☎423-8974). Medium-sized hotel in Victorian premises near the train station. $40.

## Bed and breakfast

**Fountain View Guest House**, 2138 Robie St (☎422-4169). Located 1km west of downtown, this has seven basic rooms; $24–30.

**Harvey House Inn**, 5220 Harvey St (☎423-8614). One block from the train station; ten rooms; laundry facilities; $45.

**Heritage House**, 1253 Barrington St (☎423-4435). Comfortable place near the train station; $49.

**Illusions Tourist Home**, 1520 Robie St (☎425-6733). Situated 1500m west of downtown; three simple rooms; $35; April–Oct.

**Upper House B&B**, 6253 Allan St (☎423-3214). Nice rooms; 1km west of downtown; $44.

**Waken 'n Eggs**, 2114 Windsor at Allan St (☎425-1146). Located 2km west of downtown; bus #14 or #20; a cosy little place; $40.

## Hostels and college rooms

**Dalhousie University**, west end of University Ave (☎494-8840, or ☎494-2108 after 5pm). Situated 2km southwest of the centre, bus #1; all campus facilities open to guests, including swimming pool and sports halls; singles $27; doubles $40.

**Halifax International Youth Hostel**, 2445 Brunswick St (☎422-3863). Located about 2km north of the centre in a spacious old wooden building; 50 dormitory beds at $11.45.

**Mount Saint Vincent University**, 166 Bedford Hwy (☎443-4450). Attractively wooded campus about 10km northwest of the centre; bus #80 or #82; singles $23; doubles $34.

**St Mary's University**, 923 Robie St (☎420-5486 or ☎420-5591 after 5pm). About 2km south of the centre, on the way to Point Pleasant Park; bus #10; singles $22; doubles $34.

**Technical University of Nova Scotia**, O'Brien Hall, Bishop St. Situated off Barrington St, ten minutes' walk south of the centre. The residence office is centrally located at 5217 Morris St (☎420-7780); singles $22; doubles $36.

**YWCA**, 1239 Barrington St (☎423-6162). On the way to the train station; women only; swimming pool and gym; $38.
**YMCA**, 1565 South Park St (☎422-6437). Opposite the Public Gardens, downtown just south of Citadel Hill; swimming pool; men and women; $38.

## The City

The commercial and social heart of modern Halifax lies amongst the malls and tower blocks of the **Scotia Square** and in the waterfront **Historic Properties**, both on the north side of the city centre. This is the least prepossessing part of central Halifax, and you're better off starting a visit at the **Citadel**, the Vaubanesque fortress at the top of the hill overlooking the downtown core. From here, it's the easiest of walks down George Street through the incidental attractions of the centre to the splendid **Maritime Museum**, and a stiffer walk southwest to the pleasant **Public Gardens**. On a sunny day it's a pleasant diversion to visit a couple of the **outer fortifications** built to defend Halifax harbour.

### The Citadel

The distinctively bright Georgian **Clock Tower**, the landmark sitting at the top of George Street beside the path up to the Citadel, looks somewhat confused, its dainty balustraded tower set on top of the dreariest of rectangular shacks. Completed in 1803, the tower is a tribute to the architectural tastes of its sponsor, Edward, Duke of Kent, the father of Queen Victoria, who was sent here as military commandant in 1794. The Duke insisted the tower had a clock on each of its four faces so none of the garrison had an excuse for being late, a preoccupation typical of this unforgiving martinet.

Up above the Clock Tower, the present fortifications of the **Citadel National Historic Park** (daily 9am–5pm; mid-June to Aug $2, otherwise free) were completed in 1856, the fourth in a series dating back to Edward Cornwallis's stockade of 1749. The star-shaped fortress, constructed flush with the crest of the hill to protect it from artillery fire, seems insignificant until you reach the massive double stone and earth walls flanking the deep encircling ditch, a forbidding approach to one of Britain's most important imperial strongholds. Spanning the ditch, a slender footbridge leads into the fort, where the **Cavalier Building** (same times) beside the gate has been restored to its 1869 appearance, complete with barrack rooms and library. Across the parade ground, the majority of the south end of the fort has also been returned to the mid-nineteenth century and offers insights into military life both in an hour-long film entitled *The Tides of History* and through its summertime "inhabitants" who re-enact drills and parades. If militarism leaves you cold, enjoy the view out over the city and harbour instead.

### Downtown

If you retrace your steps past the Clock Tower and head east down George Street, you'll hit the tree-lined, elongated square known as the **Grand Parade**, the social centre of the nineteenth-century town. For the officer corps, this was the place to be seen walking on a Sunday, when, as one obsequious observer wrote, "their society generally [was] sought, frequently courted, and themselves esteemed" – a judgement rather different from that of the radical journalist Joseph Howe, who hated their "habits of idleness, dissipation and expense". The southern edge of the parade borders the tiny **St Paul's Church** (Mon–Fri 9am–5pm), whose graceful cupolas and simple timber frame date from 1750, making it both the oldest building in town and the first Protestant church in Canada. The church bears a mark of the 1917 Halifax explosion (see p.51): look for the piece of metal embedded in the plaster above the entrance doors.

Charles Dickens, visiting in 1842, described the graceful sandstone **Province House**, five minutes' walk from Grand Parade down George Street (mid-June to mid-Sept Mon–Fri 9am–6pm, Sat & Sun 9am–5pm; mid-Sept to mid-June Mon–Fri 8.30am–4.30pm; free), as "a gem of Georgian architecture" whose proceedings were "like looking at Westminster through the wrong end of a telescope". If you want to see how things have developed in the seat of Nova Scotia's Legislature, you can watch a debate from the gallery or take one of the frequent guided tours.

Across the road from the Province House, the **Art Gallery of Nova Scotia**, 1741 Hollis St (Tues & Thurs 10am–9pm, Wed, Fri & Sat 10am–5.30pm, Sun noon–5.30pm; $2, free on Tues) occupies an imposing Victorian building which previously served as a courthouse, police headquarters and post office. The bulk of the collection is a long series of uninspired local artists, but the small displays of Japanese prints and Inuit art are mildly diverting, and the temporary exhibitions are sometimes excellent. The basement tends to have more experimental work and also features an interesting section on the development of artistic expression in children.

### The waterfront

Near the foot of George Street stands the **Maritime Museum of the Atlantic**, 1675 Lower Water St (mid-May to mid-Oct Mon–Fri 9.30am–5.30pm, open till 8pm Tues, Sun 1–5.30pm; mid-Oct to mid-May Tues–Sat 9.30am–8pm & Sun 1–5pm; free), is a fascinating exhibition covering all aspects of Nova Scotian seafaring from colonial times to the present day. By the entrance, the highlight is a reconstruction of a nineteenth-century chandlery, stocked with everything from chains, ropes, couplings and barrels of tar through to ships' biscuits and bully beef. Other displays include a collection of small boats and cutaway scale models illustrating the changing technology of shipbuilding, a shipwreck section and a number of gaudy ships' figureheads: look out for the turbanned Turk once attached to the British barque *Saladin*. In 1844 the *Saladin*'s crew mutinied in mid-Atlantic, killed the captain and ran the boat aground near Halifax, where they were subsequently tried and hanged. There's also a feature on the Halifax Explosion, entitled *One Moment in Time*, and don't miss the short video on the first submarine exploration of the wreck of the *Titanic*.

The much-vaunted **Historic Properties** comprise an area of refurbished wharves, warehouses and merchants' quarters situated below Upper Water Street, 400 metres north of the Maritime Museum. The ensemble has a certain urbane charm – all bars, boutiques and bistros – and the narrow lanes and alleys still maintain the shape of the waterfront during the days of sail, but there's not much to stare at until you reach the star attraction, the schooner **Bluenose II**, which is moored here when it's not on courtesy voyages. The present vessel is an exact copy of Canada's most celebrated ship, the *Bluenose*, whose picture is on the 10¢ coin because of its fame as the fastest vessel of its kind in the 1920s. Although the original boat ended her days ingloriously as a freighter, foundering off Haiti in 1946, the replica has been adopted by the province as a floating standard-bearer, representing Nova Scotia at events such as the Montréal Expo. In July and August *Bluenose II* undertakes harbour tours that are pleasant and expensive in about equal measure (Tues–Sun 3 daily; $15).

### The Old Burying Ground and the Nova Scotia Museum

Mysterious and spooky, especially in low light, the **Old Burying Ground**, ten minutes' walk south of Grand Parade along Barrington Street (June–Sept daily 9am–5pm; free), looks something like the opening shot of David Lean's *Great Expectations*. "A dozen neat things to do in the Old Burying Ground", a leaflet available from the Maritime Museum, tracks through the more interesting graves, beginning with the oldest, that of a certain John Connor, who ran the first ferry service over to Dartmouth before passing over himself in 1754.

## THE HALIFAX EXPLOSION

Nothing in the history of the Maritimes stands out like the **Halifax Explosion** of 1917, the greatest human-caused cataclysm of the pre-atomic age. It occurred when Halifax was the departure point for convoys transporting troops and armaments to Europe. Shortly after dawn on December 6, a Belgian relief ship called the *Imo* and a French munitions carrier called the *Mont Blanc* were manoeuvring in Halifax harbour. The Belgian ship was steaming for the open sea, while the *Mont Blanc*, a small, barely seaworthy vessel, was heading for the harbour stuffed with explosives and ammunition, including half a million pounds of TNT – though it flew no flags to indicate the hazardous nature of the cargo. As the ships approached each other the *Imo* was forced to steer into the wrong channel by a poorly positioned tugboat. With neither ship clear about the other's intentions and each attempting to take evasive action, they collided, and the resulting sparks caused the ignition of the drums of flammable liquid stored on the *Mont Blanc's* deck. A fire took hold, and the crew abandoned their vessel, which drifted under the force of the impact towards the Halifax shore.

A large crowd had gathered on the waterfront to witness the spectacle when the TNT exploded. The blast killed 2000 people instantly and flattened over 300 acres of north Halifax, with fire engulfing much of the rest. Windows were broken in Truro over 80km away and the shock-wave was felt in Cape Breton. Nothing remained of the *Mont Blanc*, and part of its anchor, a piece of metal weighing over half a ton, was later found more than 4km away. To make matters worse, a blizzard deposited sixteen inches of snow on Halifax during the day, hampering rescue attempts. The bodies of many victims were not recovered until the spring.

It's hard to appreciate today the vision of Armageddon which haunted Halifax after the explosion, but haunt them it did, as the poignant newspaper cuttings in the Maritime Museum show.

Walking west up Spring Garden Road from the Burying Ground, it's about 800 metres to the edge of the city's **Public Gardens**, off South Park Street (May–Oct 9am–sunset; free), whose sixteen acres were first planted in the 1870s. Meticulously maintained, the exotic shrubs and trees make a pleasant stroll en route to the **Nova Scotia Museum**, situated below the citadel at 1747 Summer St (mid-May to Oct Mon–Sat 9.30am–5.30pm, open till 8pm Wed, Sun 1–5.30pm; Nov to mid-May Tues–Sat 9.30am–5pm, open till 8pm Wed, Sun 1–5pm; free). At the museum, a comprehensive range of exhibits covers the human and natural history of Nova Scotia, at their strongest in their depiction of the region's marine and land-based wildlife. Other galleries concentrate on ceramics, domestic interiors and the **Micmacs**, the native people of the region. Unfortunately the portrayal of Micmac culture is stuck in the pre-colonial age – while there's no doubting the skill shown in fashioning items from materials such as birch-bark and porcupine quills, something on the effects of European colonisation would not have gone amiss.

### The outer fortifications

In the eighteenth century the British navy protected the seven-kilometre-long sea passage into **Halifax harbour** with coastal batteries strung along the shore between the city and the Atlantic. Two of these are worth a visit, though more for their commanding views than the rag-bag of military remains. There's one at **Point Pleasant**, at the tip of the Halifax peninsula about 3km south of the city; the other is on **McNab's Island**, sitting in the middle of the main seaway, 4km south of the city.

**Point Pleasant Park** (bus #9 from Barrington St) incorporates the remains of four gun batteries overlooked by the squat **Prince of Wales Martello Tower** (mid-June to early Sept daily 10am–6pm), which was built at the end of the eighteenth century to cover and supply the guns. The surrounding park, 200 acres of wooded hills and shoreline, boasts thousands of butterflies and birds, and is one of the few places in North America where heather grows, supposedly originating from seeds shaken from the bedding of Scots regiments stationed here.

**McNab's Island**, 5km long and 2km wide, contains the remnants of five different fortifications, dating from the middle of the eighteenth century to the establishment of Fort McNab in 1880. The island, half of which is parkland, is criss-crossed with hiking trails and dotted with picnic spots, making a pleasant retreat from the city. However, in 1991 plans were announced to build a large waste-disposal plant on the island, an idea that's provoked bitter opposition from conservationist groups. To reach McNab's Island take a **ferry** from the downtown jetty on Cable Wharf at the bottom of George Street (frequent sailings mid-June to mid-Sept; 20min; $7).

## Eating, drinking and entertainment

It's easy to **eat** well and cheaply in Halifax. At the **downtown** snack bars and restaurants listed below – all within ten minutes' walk of Grand Parade – a substantial meal will set you back about $15 excluding booze, snacks around $8. **Lobsters** are a local speciality, and in the tourist season quite a few places serve the crusty crustacea on a fixed-price, all-you-can-eat basis for $15 and up: watch for the ads, or try the couple of more permanent eateries below. They say Halifax has more **bars** per head than anywhere in Canada, except St John's Newfoundland, and though many of them are eminently forgettable, those we've listed rise well above the general standard and offer a reasonable menu as well. If you want to go out and rave, Halifax has plenty of **clubs** and **discos**, but it's a constantly changing scene and, unless you've a contact, you're likely to miss the best because the city lacks a good entertainment guide. The clubs below are at least well established, though they take few musical risks.

### Snacks and restaurants

**Athens**, 1558 Barrington at Blowers St. Greek-run place serving great specials. Perfect breakfasts for $4.

**Czech Inn**, 5163 South St. East European delicacies; try the goulash.

**Food Centre**, beneath the Maritime Mall, corner of Barrington and Salter St. Adventurous and high-quality fast food. About a dozen outlets, featuring bagels, chicken, pizza, Chinese food, sandwiches etc. Crammed with office workers between noon and 2pm.

**Halifax Lobster Feast**, next to the ferry terminal by the Historic Properties. All-you-can-eat lobster aboard an old ferry boat.

**Hungry Hungarian**, 5215 Blowers St. Borsch and all manner of East European delights from $8.

**King Spring Roll**, 1284 Barrington St. Cheap and simple Vietnamese place.

**Mexicali Rosa's**, 5680 Spring Garden Rd. Good Mexican food from $6.

**Misty Moon**, corner of Sackville and Barrington St. This café, beneath a nightclub, does spicy Jamaican food in uninspiring surroundings.

**Mrs Murphy's Kitchen**, 5670 Spring Garden Rd. Good for wholesome homestyle vegetarian breakfasts. Near the Public Gardens. Closed Sat & Sun.

**Original Lobster Feast**, 1577 Barrington St. All-you-can-eat lobster from $15.

**Satisfaction Feast**, 1581 Grafton St. Vegetarian restaurant, with vegan options available. Open from early morning until mid-evening daily.

### Bars

**Double-Dance Roundhouse Tavern**, 1560 Hollis St. Good for C&W, live bands at the weekend.

**Flamingo Lounge**, basement of Maritime Mall. Fairly sophisticated watering hole, with a mixed bag of live sounds, two or three times weekly.

**The Graduate**, 1565 Argyle St. Sports videos on several screens, which compete with live music and a generally hectic atmosphere.

**Granite Brewery**, 1222 Barrington St. Advertises itself as a genuine English pub. Of course it's not, but it's still charmingly intimate and they brew most of the ale on the premises. Try their *Peculiar*, a fair approximation of the oily grandeur of the legendary British *Theakston's*.

**Lawrence of Oregano**, 1726 Argyle St. Cavernous and chaotic pick-up spot. Good cheap beer and a modestly priced Italian menu.

**Split Cow**, 1855 Granville St at Duke St. Another supposedly English pub. Very central, sometimes featuring live maritime fiddle music.

## Clubs and discos

**Bogarts**, 1575 Argyle St. Brash and noisy.

**Jaguars**, 5184 Sackville St. Good sound systems and obligatory flashing lights.

**Misty Moon**, 1595 Barrington St. Big and popular, sometimes with interesting live music – the only place in town to take reggae seriously.

## Folk and jazz

**The Grad-House**, on the Dalhousie campus. High-quality folk acts on the first Saturday of every month; cheap admission, food and drinks.

**Earl of Dalhousie** pub, also on the Dalhousie campus. Each Wednesday there's a coffee-house night where anyone can turn up and play folk. Nominal admission, cheap snacks and drinks.

**Lower Deck Bar**, in the Privateers Warehouse, one of the Historic Properties. Traditional maritime folk music.

**Pepe's**, 5680 Spring Garden Rd. Frequent trad and modern jazz.

## Cinemas

**Canadian National Film Board Theatre**, 1571 Argyle St. Egghead films free of charge each Friday at 8pm.

**Famous Players**, 5657 Spring Garden Rd. In the Park Lane Mall complex; mainstream.

**Hyland Theatre**, 7211 Quinpool Rd. Mainstream.

**Oxford Theatre**, 6408 Quinpool Rd. Mainstream.

**Wormwood's Dog and Monkey**, 2015 Gottingen St at Cogswell. The city's art-house cinema; named after a vaudeville show which brought the first moving pictures to Halifax.

## Theatre and classical music

**Neptune Theatre**, 5216 Sackville St (☎429-7070). The doyen of Halifax's live theatres, offering a wide range of mainstream dramatic productions, but closed for three months during the summer.

**Scotia Festival of Music**, Sir James Dunn Theatre, Dalhousie University (☎429-9469). A fortnight of classical music, usually in late May or early June, featuring chamber works and master-classes.

**Symphony Nova Scotia**, 1646 Barrington St (☎421-7311). Concert season runs from October to May.

# Listings

**Airlines** *Air Canada*, Scotia Square, facing Duke St (☎429-7111); *Canadian Airlines*, Suite 518, Cogswell Tower, Scotia Square (☎427-5500); *KLM*, 1701 Hollis St (☎455-8282).

**Banks** *Canada Trust Bank*, 1718 Argyle St (Mon–Fri 8am–8pm, Sat 9am–5pm).

**Bike rental** The *Trail Shop*, 6260 Quinpool Rd (☎423-8736).

**Books** Bookshops abound on the central part of Granville St, both new and secondhand. The *Book-Room* at no. 1664 originated in 1839 (Canada's oldest) and makes for compulsive browsing. *Red Herring Co-op Books* at no. 1555 is left of centre, with well-stocked ecological, women's and gay sections.

**Car rental** *Rent-a-Wreck*, 5516 Kaye St (☎454-6401); *McFrugal Rent-a-Car*, on the corner of Kempt Rd and Staits St (☎453-7368).

**Consulate** *USA*, Cogswell Tower (☎429-2480).

**Hospital** *Halifax Infirmary*, 1335 Queen St (☎428-2781).
**Laundry** *The Lint Trap*, 5576 Fenwick St, a combined launderette and bar (daily 10am–11pm).
**Police** Main station is on the corner of Cogswell and Gottingen streets (☎4105).
**Post office** Central office at 1526 Dresden Row.
**Weather** ☎426-9090.

# Dartmouth

Gritty **DARTMOUTH**, across the harbour from Halifax, is often neglected by visitors as it lacks the more obvious appeal of its neighbour. Nevertheless, it is the province's second largest town, with 90,000 inhabitants, and although it's primarily an industrial centre there are enough sights here to justify at least one sortie over the water: don't be put off by the horrible waterfront – it's the tiny, old residential area behind that attracts.

## The town

Dartmouth ferry terminal abuts Wyse Road and Alderney Drive, the latter home to the **Shubenacadie Canal Interpretive Centre**, at no. 140 (June to early Sept Mon–Fri 10am–6pm, Sat & Sun 1–5pm), which commemorates the ill-fated ninety-kilometre canal which linked the Bay of Fundy to Dartmouth. Begun in 1826, this monumental feat of engineering, linking a dozen existing lakes with new water courses and locks, was completed in 1860, but the canal only made a profit for ten years before it was superseded by the railways – and left to rot.

After the American War of Independence, several Quaker whaling families emigrated from Nantucket Island, off Cape Cod, to Dartmouth. One of their dwellings has survived, the charming **Quaker House** at 57 Ochterloney St (June–Aug daily 10am–6pm; free), a small, grey clapboard residence sitting three blocks north of the ferry dock. The interior has been painstakingly restored to its late eighteenth-century appearance, its spartan fittings reflecting Quaker values. Among the exhibits are a 200-year old pair of shoes found under the floorboards during renovations in 1991, and the eye of a Greenland whale preserved in formalin – though the staff won't show you this if they think you're squeamish. Don't miss the herb-garden behind the house and, when you've finished, pop across the road to crook your little finger at the *Temptations English Tea Room*.

**Dartmouth Heritage Museum**, 100 Wyse Rd (June–Aug Mon–Fri 9am–7pm, Sat noon–5pm, Sun 2–7pm; Sept–May Mon–Sat 1–5pm, Wed 1–9pm, Sun 2–5pm; free), a fifteen-minute walk northwest of the ferry terminal, has a mundane art gallery beneath a museum whose exhibits dutifully track the history of the town from its establishment in 1750 by a party of soldiers from Halifax. However, amongst the dross, look out for the sections on the Micmacs, the Nantucket whalers and the 1917 explosion.

## Practicalities

The Dartmouth **ferry** leaves the Halifax waterfront near the Historic Properties (every 15min June–Sept daily 6.30am–11.30pm; Oct–May Mon–Sat only; 15min; 50¢). The twin cities are also connected by two road bridges, the MacDonald, running just to the northwest of both city centres, and the Mackay, part of the outer ring road. **Metro Transit** buses #1 and #10 use the MacDonald. The Dartmouth **tourist office** is in the same building as the Dartmouth museum and keeps similar hours. If you want to **stay** here, try the *Prince Albert Hotel*, 313 Prince Albert Rd (☎469-5850; doubles from $40), about 2km north of the centre by Lake Banook. For **food**, head for the restaurants and snack bars dotted along central Portland Street, especially *Healthy Habit*, at no. 86, which caters for vegetarians, or the *Harbour House Dining Room*, 23 Alderney Drive, which specialises in seafood.

# Southwest Nova Scotia

The jagged coastline running southwest of Halifax to **Yarmouth**, a distance of 300km, boasts dozens of tiny fishing villages and a trio of quite elegant towns – **Lunenburg**, **Liverpool** and **Shelburne** – whose prosperity largely derived from the now defunct shipbuilding business and from privateering. Today, it's a subdued region whose wild shoreline is explored by the **Lighthouse Route**, a tourist trail that fetishises anything of any possible interest: you're better off sticking to the main road, Highway 103, and dropping down to the coast for the highlights. After Shelburne there's not much to detain you and it's a good idea to retrace your steps to Liverpool, where route 8 cuts across the peninsula direct to Annapolis Royal, past the wilderness splendours of the **Kejimujik National Park**.

*Mackenzie Bus*, based in the Halifax bus station, operate a daily service between Halifax and Yarmouth along the southern shore, and *Acadian Bus Lines* connect the two via the Annapolis Valley, Digby and the French shore twice daily. Local bed and breakfasts are the most economical places to stay and you can live cheaply for days on the ubiquitous fish chowder soup with salad, the favourite local dish.

## Peggy's Cove

Tiny **PEGGY'S COVE**, 45km southwest of Halifax along route 333, is a cliché of old maritime Canada that hauls in the tourists to snap away at the ramshackle cluster of fishing shacks and wooden jetties on their wiggly stilts. The harbour is picturesque and the boats appealingly sturdy, but the large granite boulders littering the landscape refuse to accommodate the scenic cosiness, while the solitary lighthouse looks positively forbidding. If you're keen to visit, come at sunrise or sunset, when there are no coach parties.

## Mahone Bay and Lunenburg

In 1813, the wide waters of **Mahone Bay** witnessed the destruction of the splendidly named American privateer the *Young Teaser*, which had been hounded into the bay by a British frigate. On board was a British deserter who knew what to expect if he was captured, so he blew his own ship up instead – a tribute to the floggers of the Royal Navy. Legend has it that the ghost of the blazing vessel reappears each year.

Comely **LUNENBURG**, 6km south of Mahone Bay town, perches on a narrow bumpy peninsula, its older central streets sloping steeply down to the waterfront, decorated by brightly painted wooden houses. The town was founded in 1753 by German and Swiss Protestants who mixed farming, fishing and shipbuilding to create a prosperous community that now possesses its own fleet of trawlers and scallop-draggers. Lunenburg makes a pleasant place to break your journey; while you're here you might visit the **Fisheries Museum of the Atlantic** (daily mid-May to June & Sept–Oct 9.30am–5.30pm; July & Aug 9.30am–7pm; free), at the western end of the quayside, which has aquaria, live demonstrations of fish-filleting and processing, and displays on fishing and boat-building techniques.

Lunenburg **tourist office** (May–Oct daily 9am–9pm) is in an imitation lighthouse on Blockhouse Hill Road, above the village and next to the municipal **campground** (mid-May to mid-Oct; ☎634-8100). There's cheap **accommodation** at the *Margaret Murray B&B*, 20 Lorne St (☎634-3974; doubles $40), but pay a little more and you can enjoy the splendour of the *Compass Rose Inn*, 15 King St (☎634-8509; doubles $60), a sea captain's house of 1825. There are a couple of motels out of town heading southwest towards Mason's Beach; try the *Ranch-O Motel* (☎634-8220; $42).

**Eating** places abound in the centre. The *Magnolia Grill*, 128 Montague St, is a small café with a good atmosphere and delicious snacks, while *Big Red Family Restaurant*, on the harbour front, is an inexpensive pan-American style diner. If you're crying out for a lobster supper there's no better place than here – but it's expensive: the *Rum-Runners Inn*, 56 Montague St, or else the downstairs part of the *Dolphin Beverage Room*, 90 Pelham St, serve them for around $20. The other culinary delight is the **Lunenburg sausage**, made of lean pork and beef, flavoured with coriander and allspice; traditionally, it's served at breakfast.

## Liverpool

Like its British namesake, **LIVERPOOL**, 140km from Halifax along Highway 103, skirts the mouth of a River Mersey and has a strong seafaring tradition, but there the similarities end. Nova Scotia's Liverpool was founded by emigrants from Cape Cod in 1759, who established a fearsome reputation for privateering during both the American Revolution and the War of 1812, when their most famous ship, the *Liverpool Packet*, claimed 100 American prizes. These piratical endeavours are cheekily celebrated by a memorial in the park at the end of Main Street, inscribed "they upheld the best tradition of the British Navy". Nowadays, Liverpool is a minor fish-processing and papermaking town, whose past successes are affirmed by the fine old houses dotted round the leafy centre, one of which, the **Perkins House** on Main Street (mid-May to mid-Oct Mon–Sat 9.30am–5.30pm, Sun 1–5.30pm; free), has been returned to its general appearance at the end of the eighteenth century.

Liverpool has one fine **bed and breakfast**, the *Hopkins House*, 120 Main St (☎354-5484; doubles $40), a beautiful Loyalist home dating from the early nineteenth century. The primitive **youth hostel** (Aug only; ☎345-3533; $5) is in the Trinity Church Parish Hall on Main Street, near the bus station. For simple sustaining **meals** and bargain lunch specials try the *Lunch Kettle*, 179 Main St.

## Kejimkujik National Park

There's no better way to experience the solitude and scenery of the southwest Nova Scotian hinterland than to head north 70km from Liverpool along route 8 to MAITLAND BRIDGE, the entrance to the **Kejimkujik National Park**. This magnificent tract of wilderness has a richly varied terrain of thick forests and grassy meadows punctuated by rivers and brooks linking about a dozen lakes. The park is a riot of wildflowers in the spring and autumn and provides the habitat for an abundance of porcupines, white-tailed deer and beavers, as well as the endangered Blandingo Turtle.

Call in at the **information centre** (mid-May to Sept daily 9am–5pm; ☎682-2772), beside the entrance, for trail maps, canoe and mountain-bike rental details and to register for backcountry **camping** – a better bet than the large campground at Jeremy's Bay, 5km inside the park from the entrance. The nearest beds are at the tiny *Whitman Inn* (☎682-2226; doubles $50), just south of Maitland Bridge on route 8.

An alternative is to press on a further 30km to SOUTH MILFORD, where a right turn leads to the **Sandy Bottom Lake Youth Hostel** (☎532-2497; $4), whose primitive conditions – it's no more than a rough wood cabin with communal sleeping space for nine – are redeemed by the splendid isolation of its forested lakeside setting and the range of wildlife: beavers, otters, mink, snakes and toads especially. The area has lots of lovely walks, but it's best toured by canoe and these can be hired from the warden, though advance bookings are advised. At the hostel, you're responsible for providing your own wood for the stove, which provides the only heat or means of cooking; the nearest shops are in Annapolis Royal, 30km away.

## Lockeport

Well off the beaten track, 65km west of Liverpool, lies **LOCKEPORT**, a sleepy backwater tucked away on a narrow peninsula and separated from the ocean by the mile-long swathe of **Crescent Beach**. The surf is good, the white sand is never crowded and the village features a row of five grandly contrasting houses built by the merchant Samuel

Locke for his children in the middle of the nineteenth century. The **tourist office** (summer daily 9am–7pm), on the causeway into town, has the details of a handful of **B&Bs** at about $40 per double. The **campground** at Rood's Head is wonderfully situated with Crescent Beach on one side and views over to the Gull Rock Lighthouse on the other.

## Shelburne
**SHELBURNE**, 70km west of Liverpool, has a faintly complacent air, its well-kept shingle and clapboard houses strung along leafy and level Water Street. This, the main drag, runs parallel to the third largest harbour in the world, after Halifax and Sydney – easily big enough, so the plan went, to accommodate the British fleet if Hitler managed to launch a successful invasion. The British would have been welcome: Shelburne has been intensely anglophile ever since thousands of Loyalists fled here in the 1780s – including two hundred free blacks, ancestors of the town's present black community.

Shelburne is home to the **Nova Scotia Museum Complex**, centred on Dock Street, which has three distinct elements. The **Shelburne County Museum** (mid-May to mid-Oct daily 7.30am–5.30pm; mid-Oct to mid-May Tues–Sat 2–5pm; free) provides a broad overview of the town's history and its maritime heritage; the adjacent **Ross-Thomson House** (mid-May to mid-Oct daily 9.30am–5.30pm; free) is a Loyalist merchant's store and home, restored to its appearance circa 1800; and the nearby **Dory Shop** (mid-June to Sept Mon–Sat 9.30am–5.30pm, Sun 1.30–5.30pm; free) comprises a boat-factory-cum-museum stuck beside the waterfront. Rarely more than five metres long and built to ride the heaviest of swells, the flat-bottomed dory was an integral part of the fishing fleet during the days of sail. Each schooner carried about six of them: manned by a crew of two, they were launched from the deck when the fishing began, fanning out to maximise the catch. The Dory Shop produces three a year, but they are obsolete – the dories you see today, used in the offshore fishery, are steel-hulled.

Shelburne **tourist office** (summer daily 9am–7pm) is set in a small booth on Dock Street. There are plenty of small **motels** and **bed and breakfasts**: try the *Cape Cod Colony Motel*, 234 Water St (☎875-3411; doubles $50), or the *Toddle In B&B* (☎875-3229; doubles $50), at Water and King, which is pleasant and central. Wooded, lakeside **camping** is available 5km west round the bay at the *Islands Provincial Park* (mid-May to mid-Oct). There's inexpensive and unpretentious Canadian **food** at *Gloria's Diner*, 149 Water St; at the other end of the scale, the *Cooper's Inn*, 36 Dock St, is one of the province's best restaurants, with meals from around $40. At the far end of Dock Street, *McGowan's Seafood Restaurant*, with *Bruce's Wharf Tavern* downstairs, is a good place for a **drink**, particularly at weekends.

## Barrington
Occupying a spectacular bayside setting some 25km west of Shelburne, minuscule **BARRINGTON** makes a scenic stop on the way to Yarmouth. After you've done with the views, at their best from the top of the **Lighthouse Museum** (mid-June to Sept Mon–Sat 9.30am-5.30pm, Sun 1.30–5.30pm; free), have a look at the mid-eighteenth century **Old Meeting House** (same hours), the oldest non-conformist place of worship in Canada, and the **Barrington Wooden Mill** (same hours), an example of early water-turbine technology, complete with the original carding, spinning and weaving machines. The *Lighthouse Walk B&B* (☎637-3409; doubles $40) is the only place to stay – and very good it is too.

## Yarmouth
Arriving by ferry from Maine, many American visitors get their first taste of Canada in **YARMOUTH**, and most of them leave quickly. It is grim, but the town's **tourist office**, beside the terminal (May–June & Sept–Oct daily 9am–5pm; July & Aug daily 8.30am–

8.30pm) has buckets of free tourist information. If you're stuck here for the night, there's a comfortable **B&B** right opposite the ferry port entrance, the *Murray Manor Guest House*, 17 Forest St (☎742-9625; doubles from $35). Alternatively, the *Mid-Town Motel*, 13 Parade St (☎742-5333; units about $50), offers rooms right in the centre of town. For **food**, try the *Five Corners Restaurant*, 626 Main St, a decent Italian place.

## THE ACADIANS

**Acadia** – *Acadie* in French – has at different times included all or part of Maine, New Brunswick and Nova Scotia. The etymology of the name is as vague as the geographical definition, derived from either the local Micmac word "akade", meaning abundance, or a corruption of "Arcadia", an area of Greece that was a byword for rural simplicity when transient French fishermen arrived here in the early 1500s.

Whatever the truth, the origins of Acadian settlement date to 1604, when a French expedition led by Pierre Sieur de Monts and Samuel de Champlain built a stockade on the islet of **Saint-Croix**, on the west side of the Bay of Fundy. It was a disaster: with the onset of winter, the churning ice floes separated the colonists from the fresh food and water of the mainland, and most died of malnutrition. The following spring the survivors straggled over to the sheltered southern shore of the bay, where they founded **Port Royal**, considered Canada's first successful European settlement.

However, Champlain and Sieur de Monts soon despaired of Port Royal's fur-trading potential and moved to the banks of the St Lawrence, leaving Acadia cut off from the main flow of French colonisation. Port Royal was **abandoned** in 1614, and although it was refounded on the site of present-day Annapolis Royal in 1635, there were few immigrants. Indeed, the bulk of today's Acadians are descendants of just forty French peasant families who arrived in the 1630s. Slowly spreading along the **Annapolis Valley**, the Acadians lived a semi-autonomous existence in which their trade with their English-speaking neighbours was more important than grand notions of loyalty to the French Empire. When the British secured control of Port Royal under the Treaty of Utrecht in 1713, the Acadians made no protest.

But then, in the 1750s, the tense stand-off between the colonial powers highlighted the issue of Acadian loyalty. In **1755**, at the start of the Seven Years' War, government officials attempted to make the Acadians swear **an oath of allegiance** to the Crown. They refused, so Governor Lawrence decided – without consultation with London – to **deport** them en masse to other colonies. The process of uprooting and removing a community of around 13,000 was achieved with remarkable ruthlessness. As Lawrence wrote to a subordinate: "You must proceed with the most vigorous measures possible not only in compelling them to embark, but in depriving those who should escape of all means of shelter or support, by burning their houses and destroying everything that may afford them the means of subsistence in the country."

By the end of the year over half the Acadians had arrived on the American east coast, where they faced a cold reception – the Virginians even re-routed their allocation to England. Most of the rest spread out along the north Atlantic seaboard, establishing communities along New Brunswick's Miramichi Valley, on Prince Edward Island and in St-Pierre et Miquelon. Many subsequently returned to the Bay of Fundy in the 1770s and 1780s, but their farms had been given to British and New England colonists and they were forced to settle the less hospitable lands of the **French Shore**, further west. For other deportees the expulsion was the start of wider wanderings. Some went to Louisiana, where they were joined in 1785 by over 1500 former Acadian refugees who had ended up in France – these were the ancestors of the **Cajuns**, whose name is a corruption of Acadian.

The Acadian communities of the Maritime Provinces continued to face discrimination from the English-speaking majority and today they remain firmly planted at the bottom of the economic pile. Nevertheless, the Acadians have resisted the pressures of assimilation and have recently begun to assert their cultural independence, most notably in New Brunswick, where Moncton University has become their academic and cultural centre.

# The Annapolis Valley

The **Annapolis Valley**, stretching 133km northeast from **Annapolis Royal** to Windsor, is sheltered by ranges of gently undulating hills from the winds and fog which afflict much of the central part of the province. This factor, combined with the fertility of the soil, makes the valley ideal for fruit growing, and the brief weeks of apple-blossom time, from late May to early June, are the subject of much sentimental and commercial exploitation – as well as the communal knees-ups of the **Apple-Blossom Festival**. The valley's string of modest towns were settled by Loyalists from New England after the expulsion of the Acadians, but the only one worth a second look, apart from Annapolis Royal and the historic site of Fort Royal, is **Wolfville**, which is also near the **Grand Pré National Historic Site** and the harsh scenery of **Cape Blomidon**.

In the opposite direction, the road skirts the lagoon called the Annapolis Basin before reaching the small fishing port of **Digby**, which is notable for three things: the swirling effect of the Fundy tides through the narrow channel known as the Digby Gut; the delicately smoked herrings known as "Digby chicks"; and the **ferry** service over to Saint John, New Brunswick, which leaves from the port about 8km along Shore Road (1–3 daily; 2hr 30min). From Digby it's 110km to Yarmouth across the **French Shore**, whose villages house the largest concentration of Acadians in the province which nevertheless fail to make this zone of Nova Scotia anything other than extremely boring.

## Annapolis Royal

With a population of just 700, the township of **ANNAPOLIS ROYAL**, 114km north of Liverpool, spreads across a podgy promontory tucked between the Annapolis River and the Allain River, its tributary. The long main drag, St George Street, part of route 8, sweeps through the southern outskirts to reach the end of the promontory, where it turns right to run parallel to the Allain and onto the town wharf. This is the heart of Annapolis Royal: the broad square beside the dock is home to a vibrant **Farmers' Market** (May–Oct Sat morning & Wed afternoon), while the neighbouring streets are lined with self-important late eighteenth- and early nineteenth-century villas. Take a peek at the **Farmer's Hotel**, on the junction of St George and Church streets, a ruddy timber structure from 1730 that was the site of Canada's first Masonic Lodge.

Retracing your steps back along St George Street, it's about ten minutes' walk to **Fort Anne** (mid-May to mid-Oct daily 9am–6pm; mid-Oct to mid-May Mon–Fri 9am–5pm; free), whose earthen ramparts, stone powder magazine and storehouse date from the last years of French control. The largest remaining building, the officers' quarters in the middle of the compound, were completed by the British during the Napoleonic Wars; surmounted by three outsize chimney-stacks, it houses the town's tourist office and a small **museum**, comprising tedious military memorabilia, a reconstruction of an Acadian domestic interior and an outline of the fort's development.

Across the road from the fort lie the ten-acre **Historic Gardens** (mid-May to mid-Oct daily 8am–dusk; $3.50), which feature five "theme gardens", from Acadian allotments to the fussy formalism of the Victorian flower border. The whole site slopes gently down towards the Allain River, with its salt marshes and duck sanctuary.

### Practicalities

Two **buses** a day in each direction stop in the centre of town on the *Acadian Lines* route between Halifax and Yarmouth. The **tourist information bureau** at Fort Anne (late May to mid-Oct daily 9am–6pm) can arrange accommodation. Best are the **bed and breakfasts**, several of which are in immaculately maintained heritage properties: try the *Turret*, 372 St George' St (☎532-5770; doubles $40), or the *Bread and Roses Inn*,

82 Victoria St (☎532-5727; doubles $60). For cheaper accommodation, *Helen's Cabins* (☎532-5207), near the beginning of route 201 going northeast, has doubles from $30. The *Dunromin* **campground** (mid-April to Oct; ☎532-2808), just across the Annapolis River on route 8 at Granville Ferry, occupies a wooded position by the water.

**Eating** well and in style is easy here, but prices are high and several restaurants expect a formal standard of dress – it's that kind of town. The *Garrison House*, 350 St George St, has excellent meals at around $20; the *Fort Anne Café*, opposite the site, is good for breakfasts and snacks; and *Tom's Pizza*, next to *Helen's Cabins*, does what it does acceptably and inexpensively. The fine *Ye Olde Towne* at 9 Church St serves good draught **beer** and daily food specials from about $7.

## Port Royal

**Port Royal National Historic Park** (mid-May to mid-Oct daily 9am–6pm; free), 10km west of Annapolis Royal on the opposite side of the river, was where Samuel de Champlain and Pierre Sieur de Monts first set up camp in 1605 after their dreadful winter on the Île Saint-Croix. Their scurvy-ridden men, scared of English attack, hastily constructed a *habitation* similar in design to the fortified farms of France, where a square of rough-hewn, black-painted timber buildings presented a stern, partly stockaded face to any enemy. The stronghold dominated the river from a small bluff, as does today's replica, a painstaking reconstruction relying solely on the building techniques of the early seventeenth century.

Up the hill overlooking the *habitation* is the site of the **Scotch Fort**, which was established in 1629, fifteen years after the French had abandoned their original settlement. The fort was the idea of Sir William Alexander who, supported by King James I, wished to found a New Scotland – in the Latin of the deeds, "Nova Scotia" – at Port Royal. After three years of hardship and starvation, the Scots settlers were forced to return, and nothing remains to mark the fort except a cairn and plaque.

For both French and Scot settlers alike, the problem of survival was compounded by acute boredom during the months of winter isolation. To pass the time Champlain constituted the **Order of Good Cheer**, whose "entertainments programme" starred the poet Marc Lescarbot – though the role hardly filled him with colonial zeal to judge from a poem he wrote for a gang of departing buddies:

"We among the savages are lost
And dwell bewildered on this clammy coast
Deprived of due content and pleasures bright
Which you at once enjoy when France you sight."

There are no bus services from Annapolis Royal to the *habitation*, but there is **accommodation** next door to the site at the *Auberge Sieur de Monts* (May–Sept; ☎532-7883; doubles $40).

## Wolfville and around

The well-heeled university town of **WOLFVILLE**, 108km northeast from Annapolis Royal, was originally called Mud Creek until the daughter of a local dignitary, Justice DeWolf, expressed her embarrassment at the hick-sounding name. He modestly had it renamed after himself, but the mud-flats around the tiny harbour, off Main Street, remain the town's most distinctive feature. They are the creation of the **Fundy tides**, which rush up the River Cornwallis from the Minas Basin to dump the expanse of silt that's become home to hundreds of herons and waders. From the wharf, there's a pleasant walk along the causeway which encircles some of the wetland and its enclosing dikes, giving a panoramic view of Wolfville – the skyline dominated by the classical lines of **Acadia University**, whose 3000 students double the resident population.

Wolfville's other curiosity is the **Robie Tufts Nature Centre**, down Elm Avenue from Main Street, which is best visited an hour before sunset on a summer's evening, when there's an amazing performance by an enormous flock of **chimney swifts**. After a long day of hunting for insects, the birds fly in ever-decreasing circles above the centre, which is built round an old chimney, then suddenly swoop en masse into the chimney to roost for the night.

## Practicalities

Wolfville is on the *Acadian Lines* **bus** route connecting Halifax and Yarmouth. The centrally sited **tourist office**, at Willow Ave and Main St (daily May–June & Sept–Oct 9am–5pm; July & Aug 8am–8pm), has information on the whole of the Annapolis Valley as well as local accommodation lists. The cheapest **rooms** are those rented out in the summer by Acadia University, University Ave (☎542-2201) – $32 for a single, $47 a double, including breakfast, and there's a fifty percent discount with a student ID. Alternatively, the *Harmony House B&B*, 285 Main St (☎542-7100; doubles from $30), is central, small and agreeable, and the *Blomidon Inn*, 127 Main St (☎542- 2291), is an elegant Victorian country inn with doubles from $50.

For **food**, there are fine snacks, cakes and coffee at *The Coffee Merchant*, Elm Ave at Main; stylish burgers and steaks at the *Garage Road-House*, 203 Main St, and pizzas at *Elmer's*, just across the road. If you're flush, try one of Canada's most celebrated restaurants: the *Chez la Vigne*, 17 Front St, with its exquisite French regional cuisine. The *Wolfshead Tavern*, on Gaspereau Avenue near the harbour, is the best **bar** in town.

## Grand Pré

In 1847, Henry Wadsworth Longfellow chose **GRAND PRÉ**, 4km east of Wolfville beside the Minas Basin, as the setting for his epic poem *Evangeline – a Tale of Acadie*, which dramatised the deportations through the star-crossed love of Evangeline for her Gabriel. Horribly sentimental and extremely popular, the poem turned the destruction of this particular community into a symbol of Acadian suffering and British callousness. Strangely, the **Grand Pré National Historic Site** (daily 9am–6pm; free) celebrates Longfellow's poetry rather than the Acadians, though the small chapel standing on the site of the original church does have a modest Acadian display. Overlooking the site is the **Grand Pré Estate Vineyard** (Mon–Sat 9am–6pm), probably the most prestigious winery in eastern Canada and the source of some excellent white wines (tours & tastings 10.30am, 1.30pm & 3.30pm).

## Cape Blomidon

Angling out into the sea 25km north of Wolfville, the lumpy **Cape Blomidon Peninsula** takes its name from the sailors' phrase "Blow me down", or at least that's what they say. To get there from Wolfville, take route 358 through CANNING, all overhanging elms and Loyalist homes, before climbing steeply to the highest point of the peninsula, the **Blomidon Look-off**, where the view over the Annapolis Valley and the Minas Basin is truly spectacular. Behind the café here, the *Look-off* **campground** (mid-May to Sept; ☎582-3373) is one of the best sited in the province.

From the look-off, it's 16km to the end of the road, where five hiking trails, all roughly 12km one way, lead to the tip of **Cape Split**; the Wolfville tourist office has maps. The trails pass sheer towering cliffs, heavily eroded rock formations and precipitous waterfalls, before ending up on a small beach of eccentrically shaped boulders – keep an eye out for amethysts and agates.

# Central Nova Scotia

Most visitors hurry through **central Nova Scotia**, the chunk of land north and east of Halifax, on their way to Cape Breton Island, PEI or New Brunswick. By and large they're right, but there is the odd pleasant diversion en route, and a couple of places make for a convenient overnight stay. One place it's difficult to avoid is glum-faced **Truro**, the region's largest town, from where the Trans-Canada Highway heads west to New Brunswick, via the old mining town of **Springhill**. In the opposite direction, the Trans-Canada travels the **northeast shore**, whose gently rolling countryside was a centre of Scottish settlement from the end of the eighteenth century. The Scots first landed in **Pictou**, near New Glasgow, and this is the pick of the fishing and agricultural communities round here – especially as it's conveniently close to the PEI ferry terminal.

An alternative route between Halifax and Cape Breton is along the **southeast shore**, a remote region of skinny bays and the tiniest of fishing villages connected by a tortuous 320-kilometre road. The coastal scenery is magnificent, but the villages don't deserve their redolent names – Spanish Ship Bay, Ecum Secum, Mushaboom – and the only place worthy of attention is **Sherbrooke**, whose attractively restored nineteenth-century houses lie some 200km east of the capital.

## Springhill

**SPRINGHILL**, a town of 5000 people 190km from Halifax and 30km from New Brunswick, has had more than its share of tragedies, mostly associated with the coal mine which was sunk here in 1872 – 125 miners perished in a subterranean disaster in 1891; 39 died in a gas explosion in 1956; and a tunnel collapse in 1958 accounted for 76 more. In addition, two fires in 1957 and 1975 wiped out the town's commercial district. The collieries are closed now, but the mining tradition is kept alive at the **Springhill Miners' Museum**, on the western edge of town along the Black River Road (daily June & Sept to mid-Oct 10am–5pm; July & Aug 9am–8pm; $3). There you can see the wash-house and lamp-room, looking exactly as they did in the 1950s, but the real highlight is the trip down to a coal-face in the company of retired pitmen. However, central Nova Scotia's most popular attraction is the **Anne Murray Centre**, 22–32 Main St (May–Oct daily 10am–7pm; $5), an exercise in organised sycophancy to the Springhill-born balladeer.

The only **place to stay** in Springhill is the *Rollways Motel*, 9 Church St (☎597-3713; doubles $40). As for **food**, inexpensive breakfast and lunch specials are available at the *Candy Kitchen*, 18 Main St; the *Jade Palace*, 2 Fir St, is a recommended Chinese restaurant; and there's the *Imperial Pizza*, 40 Main St. The latter doubles as the **bus stop** for *Acadian Lines*: Springhill is on the Halifax-to-Fredericton route (2 daily).

## Pictou

Signs proclaim **PICTOU**, 170km from Halifax, as the "Birth-Place of New Scotland" on the basis of the arrival in 1773 of the ship *Hector*, loaded with settlers from Rosshire, the advance guard of the subsequent Scots migrations. To maintain the connection, the town has its own Scottish Cultural Centre, teaching Gaelic, traditional dancing and the playing of the bagpipes, and researching clan genealogies. Pictou is also having a replica of the *Hector* built in the harbour, an expensive and time-consuming project because they're sticking to the original shipbuilding techniques. The attractive town centre has a number of stone buildings from the early nineteenth century, and the old railway station is home to the **Northumberland Fisheries Museum** (June–Aug Mon–Sat 9.30am–5pm & Sun 1.30–5.30pm; free), which concentrates on the local lobstering.

Pictou's **tourist office** (daily mid-May to June & Sept to mid-Oct 9am–5pm; July & Aug 8am–10pm) lies on the Trans-Canada to the west of town. For a **place to stay**, the *Walker Inn*, 34 Colermaine St (☎485-1433; doubles $50), is a charmingly renovated Victorian mansion right in the centre. Less expensive are two **B&Bs** on the High Street: *Fraser's* at no. 12 (☎485 4294) and *Munro's* at no. 66 (☎485 8382), where doubles cost about $35. The *Storehouse Café*, 12 Water St, is a cut above most of the **restaurants** in town, but for a really posh meal head for the *Braeside Inn*, east of the centre at 80 Front St.

Pictou is 8km south of **CARIBOU**, where there are hourly car ferries to Prince Edward Island most of the year (late April to mid-Dec; 75min; $8 return; $25 for cars; schedules ☎1-800-565-0201).

## Sherbrooke

Developed as a timber town in the early nineteenth century, **SHERBROOKE** boomed when gold was found near here in 1861, the start of a gold rush that fizzled out just twenty years later. About half of the village has been restored to its appearance at that time, comprising a thirty-building **museum** (mid-May to mid-Oct daily 9.30am–5.30pm; $2), each staffed by a guide dressed in immaculate period clothes and going about an appropriate business. There's a post office, smithy, print works and furniture shop and, just outside the main site, an impressive water-powered sawmill. More buildings are incorporated into the site each year, and it takes a good two and a half hours to do it justice.

The most convenient of the three places to **stay** in Sherbrooke is the *St Mary's River Lodge* (☎522-2177; doubles $40), next to the rear entrance of the restored village. There's not much choice about where to eat, but fortunately the *Bright House*, in the centre of the modern village, is an excellent restaurant – be sure to try the seafood casserole.

# Cape Breton Island

"I have travelled the globe. I have seen the Canadian and American Rockies, the Andes and the Alps and the Highlands of Scotland: but for simple beauty Cape Breton outrivals them all." With these words Alexander Graham Bell summed up a part of Nova Scotia whose scenery continues to attract its share of hyperbole. From the lakes and hills of the southwest to the wild and inhospitable promontory of the northeast, **Cape Breton Island** offers the most exquisite of landscapes, reaching its melodramatic conclusion along the stark coast of the **Cape Breton Highlands National Park**. Encircling the park and some of the western shore is the **Cabot Trail**, a 300-kilometre loop that's reckoned to be one of the most extraordinary drives on the continent.

Cape Breton Island is effectively divided in two by the **Bras d'Or Lake**, and its east portion was once a busy coal-mining and steel-milling region, centred on the town of **Sydney**. Both industries have collapsed, but the de-industrialised sprawl remains, only enlivened by the splendid reconstruction of the French fortress town of **Louisbourg**, stranded out on the coast. However, Sydney is still the area's largest settlement and all of the island's **bus** services end here: there are regular connections from Halifax, Fredericton and Moncton, whilst the main ferries to Newfoundland leave from the nearby port of **North Sydney**. Unfortunately, there are no buses to Louisbourg, but the southern part of the Cabot Trail, along Highway 105, is on the main Halifax–Sydney bus route, which crosses the **Strait of Canso** by the causeway that's the only road route onto Cape Breton. There's a toll charge of $1.50 per vehicle on the way in, though not on the way out.

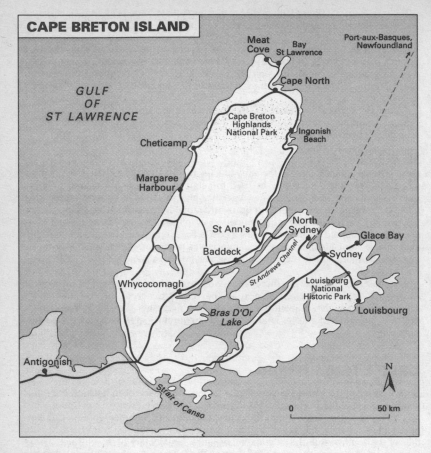

## The Cabot Trail

Sitting beside the Canso causeway, the **Port Hastings Tourist Information Centre** (mid-May to mid-Oct daily 9am–5pm; July–Aug 9am–9pm; ☎625-1717) will help you get your bearings and makes advance room reservations on Cape Breton Island. From here it's 50km along Hwy 105 to the tiny resort village of **WHYCOCOMAGH**, nestling by a small inlet at the western end of the Bras d'Or Lake, a lovely introduction to the splendours beyond. If you decide to stay, the *Fair Isle Motel*, on Hwy 105 (☎756-2291), has quality rooms for $40, and you can eat well and cheaply at the nearby *Norma's Diner*. From Whycocomagh, route 395 crosses the spartan interior of the peninsula – past the Twin Rock Valley turning for the *Glenmore Youth Hostel* (☎258-3622; $8), set in a wooded wilderness 4km from the road – to the remote MARGAREES, a total distance of 50km.

### Chéticamp
The fishing village of **CHÉTICAMP**, 40km north of Margaree Harbour, is the home of an Acadian community founded by returning deportees in the 1780s. Celebrating their

traditions, the interesting **Acadian Museum** on Main Street (mid-May to June & Sept to late Oct daily 9am–6pm; July & Aug daily 8am–9pm; free) features a selection of the crudely patterned hooked rugs which are a characteristic craft of the area. Nearby, the towering church of **St-Pierre** has a splendid interior decorated with ornately gilded mouldings and expansive frescoes. To stay the night, the *Albert's Motel* (☎224-2077) and the *Chéticamp Motel* (☎224-2711), both on Main Street, charge $35 per double. The *Acadian Restaurant*, upstairs from the museum, is good and cheap –the *poulet fricot* (chicken stew) is mouth-watering. A highly reputable **whale-watching** company, *Whale Cruises Ltd* (☎224-3376), operates excursions once or twice daily during the summer from opposite St-Pierre's; the trips cost $25 and last four hours.

## Cape Breton Highlands National Park

The 958 square kilometres of **Cape Breton Highlands National Park**, immediately north of Chéticamp, offer some of the most gorgeous scenery anywhere in the country – a mix of mountain passes, steep hairpin descents, undulating forestland, long-range valley and mountain views, and rocky coastal headlands. Although visitors get a sniff of the park travelling by car – 110km of highway trimming all but its southern edge – the essence of the place is only revealed on foot: thirty **hiking trails** are signposted from the road, some of them the easiest of woodland strolls, others striking deep into the interior to the small lakes and wetlands of the central plateau. Most of the wildlife inhabits these inner reaches – garter snakes, red-backed salamanders, snowshoe hares and moose are common; bald eagles, black bear and lynx are rare. The only artificial sight is the **Lone Sheiling**, a replica of a Highland crofter's cottage, set near the road on the northern perimeter of the park.

The park has two **Reception Centres**, one at Chéticamp on the west coast (mid-May to late June & Sept to late Oct daily 9am–5pm; late June to Aug daily 8am–9pm; late Oct to mid-May Mon–Fri 8am–4.30pm; ☎224-2306), the other at Ingonish Beach on the east (same hours; ☎285-2691). Both have 1:50,000 scale maps, guides to local flora and fauna, and exhaustive details of the hiking trails. They also levy an entry fee of $4.25 for one day per vehicle, or $9.50 for four days, and issue backcountry camping permits. The park has six serviced **campgrounds**, all within easy reach of the road, and a variety of **wilderness campsites** along the more arduous trails. At the Chéticamp centre, mountain bikes are available for $15 per day.

## Cape North

Beyond the northern perimeter of the National Park is **Cape North**, a jagged slab of land jutting out into the sea where the Gulf of St Lawrence meets the Atlantic Ocean. The cape's tiny villages begin with **CAPE NORTH** itself, which provides the area's only **accommodation**, the *Oakwood Manor B&B* (May–Oct; ☎383-2317; doubles $30), just under 2km north of the village, and the inferior *Macdonald's Motel* (☎383-2054; $45), at the main intersection near the excellent *Morrisson Pioneer Restaurant*. The hamlet of **BAY ST LAWRENCE**, 17km further, is far more beautiful, its small, white church set against the most photogenic of harbours. From Bay St Lawrence three-hour **whale-watching** cruises depart in the summer (3 daily; $25; ☎383-2981) and a gravel road leads northwest to CAPSTICK – famous for its dramatic cliff-top sunsets – and MEAT COVE, where a small makeshift campsite is full of the roar of the ocean.

## The Gaelic Coast

Leaving the National Park at Ingonish Beach, the Cabot Trail slips down the 90-kilometre **Gaelic Coast**, passing through SOUTH GUT ST ANN'S, the location of the **Nova Scotia Gaelic College of Arts and Culture**. Standing on its own landscaped campus in the hills, the college looks like a small university, and it offers courses in Gaelic language and all manner of highland activities – bagpiping, tartan-weaving, dancing and Scots folklore. The main focus of a visit here is the **Great Hall of the Clans** (mid-May to mid-Oct daily 8.30am–4.30pm, open till 8pm July & Aug), which provides a graphic depiction of the nineteenth-century Nova Scotian migrations. The seven-day **Gaelic Mod**, one of the province's principal Scottish festivals, takes place here during the first full week in August, with all traditional sports, crafts and contests featured. The *St Ann's Motel* (☎295-2876) has doubles for $45, and the place to eat is the *Harbour House*, overlooking the bay.

## Baddeck

The resort and yachting town of **BADDECK**, 20km southwest of St Ann's, enjoys a beautiful lakeside setting on the St Patrick's Channel, an inlet of the Bras d'Or Lake, and is home to the fascinating **Alexander Graham Bell Museum** (daily Oct–June 9am–5pm; July–Sept 9am–9pm; free), which overlooks the lake from a tiny park. Bell (1847–1922) spent his last thirty-seven years in Baddeck, working away at **Beinn Bhreagh**, across the bay from the museum, which does full justice to the fertility of his mind. Most famous for the invention of the telephone, Bell also made extraordinary advances in techniques for teaching hearing-impaired children, in animal husbandry and in the development of aircraft and boats – his nautical adventures culminated in 1919 with the launch of the world's first hydrofoil, the HD-4, which reached a speed of 70mph on the lake right in front of the town.

Baddeck is on the main *Acadian Lines* **bus** route between Sydney and Halifax, with three buses daily in each direction stopping at the *Ultramar* service station at the eastern end of town. **Accommodation** here tends to be expensive because of Baddeck's popularity as a holiday spot, but there are two cheap tourist homes by the lake, ten minutes' walk west of the tiny centre on Shore Road: the *Restawyle* (☎295-3428) and the *Sealladh Aluinn* (☎295-2807), both open from May to October with doubles from $30. Of the motels, the *Telegraph House*, Chebucto St (☎295-9988; doubles from $65), is the most central, while the nearest **campground** is the *Bras d'Or* (☎295-2329), about 6km west on Hwy 105.

There are a couple of good-value **cafés** in the centre: try the *Highwheeler* for wholefood snacks and salads – it's opposite the post office and close to the *Switchboard*, which does a good daily special and first-class ice cream. For a full **seafood** menu, try the *Bell Buoy*, on Lower Chebucto Street.

## Sydney and around

Poor old **SYDNEY**, 430km from Halifax on the east bank of the Sydney River, was once the industrial dynamo of eastern Canada. From the late nineteenth century to the 1950s its steel mills processed Newfoundland iron ore with Nova Scotian coke, but as gas and oil came on stream, this arrangement became uneconomic and the subsequent decline has been severe and long lasting: the city regularly records an unemployment rate twice the national average. If you're marooned here, head for *Pauls Hotel* (☎562-5747), dead central on the corner of Pitt Street and the Esplanade: it's comfortable, intimate and has doubles for $35; the *Royal Hotel*, 345 Esplanade (☎539-2148), is similarly priced. For **food**, *Soupy's*, 191 and 350 Charlotte St, has substantial breakfasts and lunches from $3.50, while the *Cactus Café*, 100 Townsend St, has Mexican dishes from $7. *Smooth Hermans*, at Esplanade and Falmouth, is a good place for a **drink**.

The *Acadian Lines* **bus station**, on Terminal Road off Prince Street, roughly six blocks east of the Esplanade, has regular services to Baddeck and Halifax. Also based at the bus station, *Overland Transit* operate a thrice-weekly route to Chéticamp during the summer. Alternatively, *Briands Cabs* (☎564-6161) organise limo tours of the Cabot Trail for about $40 per person, and *Rent-a-Wreck*, 180 Kings Rd (☎564-8366), is the cheapest of the car rental firms.

Although long-distance buses run to meet the sailing times of the **ferries to Newfoundland** from **NORTH SYDNEY**, 28km west, consider breaking your journey at Sydney if the crossing promises to be rough. Local bus #5 connects Sydney with the ferry port, where the *Kawaja Lodge B&B*, 88 Queen St, about 2km west of the jetty, is the only place to stay (☎794-4876; doubles for $30). Sydney is also the obvious base for a visit to Glace Bay, where there's no accommodation – take bus #1 for the one-hour trip from the corner of Dartmouth and George streets.

## Glace Bay

In its heyday following World War II, **GLACE BAY**, shoved against the coast 23km east of Sydney, was a busy coal town with over 30,000 inhabitants. With the mines closed, the population is now falling fast – it's too remote to easily attract other industries and too ugly to pull in the tourists. That said, the town has one modest sight, the **Quarry Point Miner's Museum** (June–Aug daily 10am–6pm; Sept–May Mon–Fri 9am–4pm; $2.75), on Birkley Street – a twenty-minute walk from Main Street. The museum has standard-issue displays on the formation of coal and early mining techniques, but its films are more original, tracing the struggles of the miners against the pit companies. The worst dispute began in the early 1920s when the owners, British Empire Steel Corporation (*BESCO*), decided to cut the men's wages by a third. The miners struck and the dispute escalated until *BESCO* persuaded prime minister King to send in the militia. The miners were defeated, but the death of one of them, William Davis – shot by company police on June 11, 1925 – is still celebrated as **Miner's Memorial Day**.

After the films, there are guided tours of the rest of the museum complex, which includes a trip down the **Ocean Deeps Mine** ($2.25 extra), sloping out under the Atlantic, and of the **Miners' Village**, comprising four restored houses and a company store. A snack at the *Miners' Village Restaurant* rounds off the trip nicely.

## Louisbourg

The French constructed the coastal fortress of **LOUISBOURG**, 34km south of Sydney, to guard the Atlantic approaches to New France and salvage their imperial honour after the humiliation of the Treaty of Utrecht. The result was a staggeringly ostentatious stronghold covering a hundred acres and encircled by ten-metre-high stone walls: it took so long to build and was so expensive that Louis XV said he was expecting its towers to rise over the Paris horizon. However, Louisbourg was wildly ill-conceived: the humid weather stopped the mortar from drying, the fort was overlooked by a score of hillocks, and developments in gunnery had already made high stone walls an ineffective means of defence. As Charles Lawrence, the British governor, confirmed, "the general design of the fortifications is exceedingly bad and the workmanship worse executed and so disadvantageously situated that . . . it will never answer the charge or trouble". And so it proved: Louisbourg was only attacked twice, but it was captured on both occasions – Wolfe, on his way to Québec, destroyed the fortress in 1758.

The modern fishing village of Louisbourg has a **tourist office** in the central railway museum (June & Sept Mon–Fri 9am–5pm; July–Aug daily 9am–7pm) and several **B&Bs**, like the *Ashley Manor*, on Main St (☎733-3268; doubles $35), and the *Greta Cross*, 81 Pepperell St (March–Nov; ☎733-2833; doubles $30). The *Louisbourg Motel*, 1225 Main St (☎783-2844), is a little more expensive, with doubles at $49. Of the several **eating** places, the *Grubstake*, 1274 Main St, is recommended for its fish platters and home-baked pastries.

A visit to the **Louisbourg National Historic Park** (May, June & Sept daily 9.30am–5pm; July–Aug daily 9am–6pm; $6.50) begins at the Reception Centre, 2km from the village, where there's a good account of the fort's history and its reconstruction in the 1960s. From here, a free shuttle bus runs to the fort, whose massive walls rise from the sea to enclose over four dozen restored buildings, a mid-eighteenth century fortress-town including a luxurious governor's mansion, guardhouses, warehouses, barracks and the spartan abodes of the soldiers. From June to September a couple of hundred costumed guides provide extra atmosphere. Authentic refreshments are available at the fort's taverns and eating houses, but cheaper and most sustaining of all is the soldiers' bread (wheat and rye wholemeal) sold at the military bakery – eat it with a ration of cheese from the Destouches House on the waterfront.

# NEW BRUNSWICK

The province of **NEW BRUNSWICK**, roughly 320km long and 240km wide, has a population of just 725,000, of whom about one third are French speakers, the descendants of those Acadians who settled here after the deportations of 1755. To avoid further persecution, these refugees clustered in the remote northern parts of the province, some settling the rolling **Acadian Peninsula** of the northeast, others moving to the hilly region around **Edmundston** in the northwest. Since the 1960s the Acadians have become more assertive – following the example set by their Québecois cousins – and have made **Moncton**, in southeast New Brunswick, the effective capital of modern Acadia, with a French-speaking university as their cultural centre. However, Moncton itself is a somewhat charmless place, so if you're after a flavour of Acadian life, head for the fishing village of **Caraquet** on the Acadian Peninsula, and visit the nearby **Village Historique Acadien**.

Easily the most attractive town hereabouts is the provincial capital **Fredericton**, which besides offering the bonus of the Beaverbrook Art Gallery is also a useful starting point for exploring the scenic delights of **Passamaquoddy Bay** to the south. From Fredericton, the Saint John River flows southeast to reach the Bay of Fundy at the busy port of **Saint John**. Along with most of the settlements of southern New Brunswick, Saint John was founded by New England Loyalists, whose descendants, mingled with those of British colonists, account for almost all the remaining two-thirds of the province's population. Despite its fine setting and quality restaurants, Saint John is of little interest, and is chiefly appealing for its proximity to the splendidly rugged **Fundy National Park**.

There are frequent **bus** connections along the Saint John River Valley and regular **bus and boat** services from Fredericton, Saint John and Moncton over to Charlottetown on PEI, via the Cape Tormentine ferry.

> The New Brunswick telephone code is ☎506.

## A brief history of New Brunswick

Administered as part of the British colony of Nova Scotia until 1784, **New Brunswick** was created to cope with the sudden arrival of thousands of Loyalists in the early 1780s. The New Englanders were concentrated in Saint John, which they expected to be the new provincial capital. However, they were out-manoeuvred by the governor's aristocratic claque who managed to get Fredericton chosen as the seat of government. This unpopular decision led to an unusual separation of functions, with Fredericton developing as the province's political and administrative capital, whereas Saint John became the commercial centre. Throughout the nineteenth century conservative Fredericton stagnated whilst liberal Saint John boomed as a shipbuilding centre, its massive shipyards, dependent on the vast forests of the New Brunswick interior, becoming some of the most productive in the world. By 1890 the province was Canada's most prosperous region, but within the space of twenty years its economy had collapsed as wooden ships were replaced by steel steamers. Never developing a diversified industrial economy, New Brunswick has spluttered along on the profits from its raw materials, principally timber, fish and potatoes, plus zinc, lead and copper from the northeast around Bathurst. Like its neighbours, New Brunswick exercises no control over the prices it receives for its raw materials, and unemployment and poverty dog the province.

# Fredericton

Situated 100km inland from the Bay of Fundy on the banks of the Saint John River, **FREDERICTON**, the capital of New Brunswick, has a well-padded air, the streets of its tiny centre graced by well-established elms and genteel villas. There's scarcely any industry here and the population of 45,000 mostly work for the government or the university, at least partly fulfilling the aims of one of the town's aristocratic sponsors, who announced in 1784 "it shall be the most gentlemanlike place on earth". Fredericton has few specific sights, just the odd building left from the **Military Compound** that once housed the garrison, and the **Beaverbrook Art Gallery**, the gift of that crusty old reactionary Lord Beaverbrook.

## Arrival and information

The *SMT* **bus** terminal is at 101 Regent Street, about five minutes' walk from the river. There are no **trains** to Fredericton: the nearest service is to Fredericton Junction, about 35km south, which handles three trains a week in either direction between Saint John and Montréal. The connecting coach arrives at the central *Beaverbrook Hotel*, next to the art gallery.

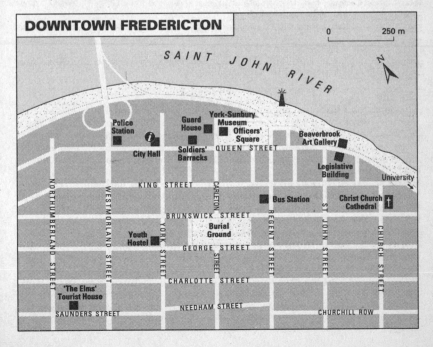

Fredericton has a downtown **Visitors Information Centre** in City Hall on the corner of Queen and York Streets (mid-May to early Sept daily 8am–8pm; early Sept to mid-May Mon–Fri 8.15am–4.30pm), and another out on the Trans-Canada, next to exit 289 (daily June & Sept 9am–5pm; July & Aug 8am–8pm). Both will ring ahead for accommodation.

## Accommodation

Finding a place to stay in Fredericton is rarely a problem, though there are surprisingly few choices: the downtown area has just one hotel, a handful of bed and breakfasts and a high-season youth hostel. Try to avoid the dreary motels on the outskirts and stick to the centre or, if you're strapped for cash, the university's campus rooms.

### HOTELS AND BED & BREAKFAST

**Back Porch B&B**, 266 Northumberland St (☎454-6875). Pleasant downtown place with doubles for $40.

**Elms Tourist Home**, 263 Saunders St (☎453-3410). A large yellow house in a dignified downtown residential area. Singles $27, doubles $40.

**Happy Apple Acres**, Hwy 105 (☎472-1819). A B&B north of the river about 7km from town. Lovely little place, enormous breakfasts; doubles $55.

**Kinheim B&B**, 270 Church St (☎455-6848). Downtown; doubles $45.

**Lord Beaverbrook Hotel**, 659 Queen St (☎455-3371). The city's grandest hotel; doubles from $96.

**Fredericton Inn**, 1315 Regent St (☎455-1430). About 1km south of the river. Expense account doubles from $70 to $130.

### HOSTEL, COLLEGE ROOMS AND CAMPING

**Hartt Island Campground**, on the Trans-Canada near Silverwood (☎450-6057). The nearest camping to town, 6km west of the city; sites $12.

**UNB Tourist Hotel**, University of New Brunswick, off Beaverbrook St (☎453-4891). Between June and September the university has over a thousand rooms for rent in or near the Macleod Building, about 2km south of the river; singles $28, doubles $35.

**Youth Hostel**, 193 York St (☎454-1233). July and August only, set in a Victorian schoolhouse bang in the middle of town; meals available; dormitory bunks $9.

## The city

The **Saint John River**, running from northern Maine to the Bay of Fundy, was for long the fastest way to reach Fredericton, whose early streets, bounded by Brunswick Street to the west and York Street to the north, were laid out close to a curve of the west bank. Here the provincial administration set up shop and the garrison, stationed to counter the threat of American attack, paraded on the **Officers' Square**, at the foot of Regent Street. Partly turned into an ornamental garden, the square still has space for the Changing of the Guard, a re-enactment of British drill that takes place during the summer (Tues–Sun 11am & 7pm). Close by, the **Lighthouse** (July & Aug daily 10am–9pm; June & Sept Mon–Fri 9am–4pm, Sat & Sun noon–4pm; May & Oct Mon–Fri 9am–4pm; $2) has pleasant views over the city and is the spot where the *Pioneer Princess*, a Mississippi-style riverboat, departs for ninety-minute **cruises** from June to August ($12).

The square forms the eastern perimeter of the **Military Compound**, which once stretched over to York Street between Queen and the river. The elegant officers' quarters, on the square's west side, now house the **York-Sunbury Historical Museum** (May to early Sept daily 10am–6pm, open till 9pm Tues & Thurs; early Sept to April Mon, Wed & Fri 11am–3pm; $1), whose military and domestic hardware are only partly redeemed by a reconstruction of a World War I trench and the alleged remains of the twenty-kilo "Coleman Frog", the pet of a local innkeeper. Nearby, at the bottom of

Carleton Street, the **Guard House** (June–Aug daily 9am–6pm; free) contains a restored orderly room, guardroom and detention cells that create a fearsome picture of military life in the middle of the nineteenth century – the guardroom is not too different from the airless cells where villains were locked up waiting to be flogged, branded or transported. A couple of minutes' walk away, with its back to Queen Street, is the **Soldiers Barracks** (same times) an unlovely three-storey block which at one time accommodated over 2000 squaddies. Most of the building now houses offices, but one room has been restored to its appearance in 1860, when it housed nineteen soldiers.

Lord Beaverbrook, the newspaper tycoon and champion of the British Empire, was raised in New Brunswick's Newcastle, and although he moved to England in 1910 at the age of 31 – becoming a close friend of Churchill and a key member of his war cabinet – he sustained a sentimental attachment to his homeland. In Fredericton his largesse was extended to the university, the Playhouse Theatre and the **Beaverbrook Art Gallery**, by the river at the foot of St John Street (July–Aug Sun & Mon noon–8pm, Tues & Wed 10am–8pm, Thurs–Sat 10am–5pm; Sept–June Sun & Mon noon–5pm, Tues–Sat 10am–5pm, $3), whose half-dozen rooms display an eclectic collection of mostly British and Canadian art. However, the entrance is dominated by three Salvador Dali canvases, including the monumental *Santiago el Grande* depicting St James being borne up towards a vaulted firmament on a white charger. After Dali's blitzkreig, it takes time to adjust to the subtler works beyond, where the Brits are represented by Hogarth, Reynolds, Gainsborough, Constable, Turner, Landseer, Augustus John, and Lowry. The fulsome Canadian collection features Paul Kane, the Group of Seven, Emily Carr and several pastoral scenes by Cornelius Krieghoff, who made a packet churning out souvenir pictures of Indians for British soldiers and tourists in the late 1840s, but also painted finely detailed, carefully composed anecdotal scenes of French Canadian life – two of the best, *Merrymaking* and *Coming Storm at the Portage*, are here.

The **Legislative Building** (guided tours June–Aug daily 9am–9pm; Sept–May Mon–Fri 9am–4.30pm), the home of New Brunswick's Parliament, stands behind the art gallery, its robust and imposing exterior topped by a small white cupola. The highlight of the free tour is the sumptuously decorated Legislative Chamber, adorned with portraits of George III and Queen Charlotte by Joshua Reynolds. The pictures were rescued from the previous parliament building, which burned down in 1880. The Legislature occupies the poshest building in Fredericton, but the nearby **Christ Church Cathedral**, Queen St (Mon–Sat 8.45am–5pm), comes a close second. A mid-Victorian copy of the fifteenth-century parish church of Snettisham, in Norfolk, it's distinguished by the elegance of its tapering spire and the intricate grace of its hammer-beam ceiling.

## Eating and drinking

Fredericton offers a good mix of **eating** places in and around the centre. For breakfast the choice has to be *Grandma T's Bakery*, 459 King St, which has quality wholesome food and great rye bread; it's good for lunch too, with a variety of soups and chowders from around $7. *Gerry's Restaurant and Muffin Ship*, a small family-run place at 88 Regent St, features filling lunch specials for around $5; *McGinnis' Landing*, 339 King St, offers a reliable wide-ranging menu; and the *Lunar Rogue* pub, 625 King St, dishes out good bar food from around $7. More expensive, *La Vie en Rose*, in a small alley off 570 Queen St opposite Officers' Square, serves great food.

Most of Fredericton's **clubs** stay open until 2am. *Cosmo's*, 458 King St, is a well-established dance spot with a "meat-rack" reputation, though it does showcase some good local bands. There's serious drinking at the *Hilltop Pub* on Prospect Street – cheap beer and large steaks – and the *Chestnut*, 440 York St, has live music every night and a games room.

# Passamaquoddy Bay

In the southwest corner of New Brunswick, abutting the state of Maine, lies **Passamaquoddy Bay**, a deeply indented inlet of the Bay of Fundy. The prettiest of the region's coastal villages is **St Andrews**, a Loyalist settlement perched on a headland 135km south of Fredericton. However, most visitors head for the **Fundy Islands** archipelago at the mouth of the inlet, whose two most accessible islands – **Deer Island** and **Campobello** – lie close to the frontier.

## St Andrews

ST ANDREWS, its grid of well-maintained wooden homes sloping up from Water Street, was once a busy fishing port, but is now a leafy, elegant resort that makes a restful place to spend a night. For a diversion walk to the west end of the main street, where the **West Point Blockhouse** (summer daily 10am–6pm), a squat little wooden fort of 1813, was built to protect the area from the Americans.

Accessible by bus from Saint John (1 daily; 1hr 30min), St Andrews has a **tourist office** on the waterfront near the fishing pier (mid-May to early Sept daily 9am–5pm). They will happily help you with accommodation – though advance bookings are a good idea in the season — and give information on the various boat tours around the bay. Most illustrious of all the **hotels** is the *Algonquin* (☎529-8823), whose turrets and gables dominate the northwest of town: in low season $50 will sneak you into the cheapest single room, but expect to pay three times that much for a double. More economically, the village has a number of **bed and breakfasts**: try the *Puff Inn*, 38 Earnest St (☎529-4191; doubles $40), or *Shady Maples*, 132 Sophia St (☎529-4426; doubles $50). Seafood dominates the **restaurant** menus. The *Sea Breeze*, 180 Water St, offers reliably priced fish platters while *Cappy's Deli* next door is good for coffee, snacks and lunch. For a special meal in a splendid location try the *Smuggler's Wharf*, 223 Water St, with a beautiful dining lounge looking out over the bay.

## Deer Island

Measuring just 10km from end to end, **Deer Island**, reached by ferry from LETETE on the southeast shore of Passamaquoddy Bay (free; every 30min), is dotted with the tiniest of fishing villages, strung along a road that provides enchanting views over to the mainland as it crosses from the ferry wharf in the east to FAIRHAVEN in the west, the site of the world's largest lobster pound and the island's only **motel** and **restaurant**, the *45th Parallel* (☎747-2231; doubles $45). **Deer Island Point**, at the southwest tip, overlooks a narrow sound where it's possible to see and sometimes hear the whirlpool known as the *Old Sow*, caused by the Fundy tides as they sweep round the island, at its peak three hours before high tide. There's a **campground** on the point (mid-May to Aug; ☎747-2423). The best bathing **beaches** are on the north shore, near two **B&Bs**: *Mitchell's* (☎747-2275) at LORD'S COVE, and *Darby Hill* (☎747-2069) at LAMBERTVILLE, both charging $35 for a double.

## Campobello Island

Franklin D Roosevelt loved **Campobello Island** for its quiet wooded coves, rocky headlands and excellent fishing, but today the island swarms with visitors who come here by **ferry** from the southwest tip of Deer Island (late June to early Sept 7 daily; car & driver $10; foot passengers $2) or over the bridge from Lubec in Maine. The **Roosevelt Cottage** is surrounded by woods and gardens about 4km south of the landing stage (late May to early Oct daily 9am–5pm; free), though "cottage" is an understatement – it's a thirty-five room mansion built in a Dutch colonial style and packed with memorabilia. The site forms the key feature of the **Roosevelt-Campobello International Park**, whose scenic drives and footpaths occupy the southern portion of the island.

The Roosevelt connection bumps up the price of Campobello **accommodation**. Nevertheless, if you head for the village of WILSON'S BEACH, at the northern tip of the island about 12km from the park, you'll escape most of the crowds and find a couple of reasonably priced **B&Bs** – the *Ship's Wheel* (☎752-2496; doubles $40) and the *Fleets' Retreat* (☎752-2126; doubles $45).

# Saint John

At first sight **SAINT JOHN** seems a confusing hotchpotch of industrial and residential zones spread over the bluffs, valleys and plateaux where the Saint John River empties into Fundy Bay, 100km southeast of Fredericton. In fact, the cramped and modern downtown is squeezed onto a chubby peninsula immediately east of the harbour and south of the short main drag, King Street, to form a surprisingly compact centre for a city of 120,000 people. In 1877 a fire wiped out most of the town, but Saint John was sufficiently wealthy, as a major shipbuilding centre, to withstand the costs of immediate reconstruction, so almost all the city's older buildings – at their most conspicuous on the east side of the peninsula – are late Victorian. Most of the shipyards have now gone and the place survives as a modest seaport and manufacturing town, with a bustling nightlife and an excellent range of restaurants. Saint John's attractions are largely confined to the outskirts, where the **Reversing Falls Rapids** are yet another place to see the effects of the Fundy tides.

### The city centre

The tiny rectangular harbour at the foot of King Street, known as the **Market Slip**, witnessed one of the more dramatic Loyalist migrations, when 3000 refugees disembarked here in 1783. They were not overly impressed by their new country; one recorded that it was "the roughest land I ever saw . . . such a feeling of loneliness came over me that I sat down on the damp moss with my baby in my lap and cried". The Slip no longer functions as a port, but it's still at the heart of Saint John, and is close to its most entertaining shop, **Barbour's General Store** (mid-May to mid-Oct 9am–6pm), a refurbished place specialising in Victorian paraphernalia from formidable-looking sweets to parasols. The opposite side of the Slip has been gentrified, the old wooden wharf-stores converted into wine-bars, restaurants and boutiques that contrast with the brash Market and Brunswick Square shopping malls behind.

Nearby, the white wooden **Loyalist House**, one block north of King at 120 Union St (July–Aug Mon–Sat 9am–5pm, Sun 1-5pm; Sept–June Mon–Fri 10am–5pm; $2), was erected in 1810 for merchant David Merritt, whose family lived here for five generations. Inside, the early nineteenth-century furnishings and fittings include a fine, sweeping staircase and intricate plaster mouldings. Returning to King Street, it's an easy stroll to Union Jack flowerbeds of **King Square** and the lively **City Market** (Mon–Sat 8.30am–5.30pm), heaped with the characteristic foods of New Brunswick – fiddleheads, a succulent fern-tip akin in flavour to asparagus, and dulse, a seaweed which enlivens the chowders hereabouts.

### The outskirts

Like just about every other place in the vicinity of the Bay of Fundy, Saint John is proud of its tidal bore. What you have here is the **Reversing Falls Rapids**, created by a sharp bend in the Saint John River about 3km west of the centre (bus #4). At low tide the river flows quite normally, but the incoming tide puts it into reverse, causing a brief period of equilibrium when the surface of the water is totally calm, then a surge upstream that is particularly noticeable here. You need to stick around for a couple of hours to see the complete process, but it's a particularly windy spot and the noxious

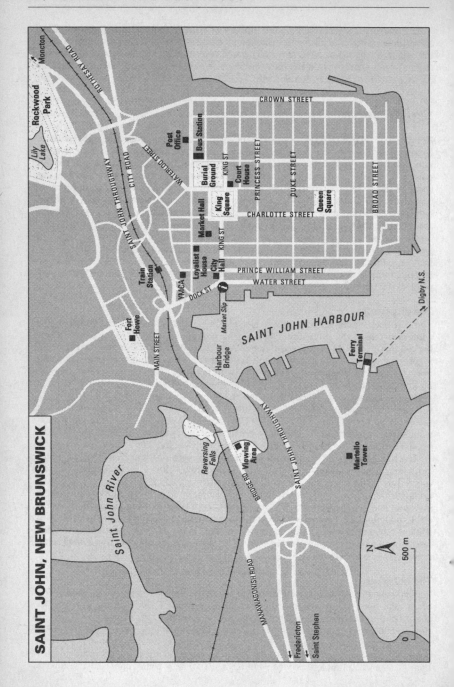

fumes from the neighbouring pulp mill could well erode your patience. There are viewing stations on each side of the river, connected by a bridge, and an **information centre** on the south side (summer daily 10am–6pm; $1), which shows a film telescoping a day's tidal flow into fifteen minutes.

When you've finished with the river, it's a twenty-minute trek east, or another ride on the #4 bus, to the **Carleton Martello Tower** on Fundy Drive (mid-May to mid-Oct daily 9am–5pm; free). The tower was raised as part of a projected series to protect the Fundy coast from American attack, but the scheme was abandoned in 1815. Visit for the splendid views over town and bay.

From here, it's a further twenty-minute walk east to the Saint John–Digby ferry terminal and the wharf for organised excursions to **Partridge Island** (June to early Sept 1–2 daily; 2-hr round trip; $20), the first quarantine station in North America, which sits in the bay beyond the harbour entrance. Less than a kilometre long, the island bristles with ruins and cemeteries, where 2000 unfortunate would-be immigrants are buried. It's uninhabited now, except for a coastguard station, and the whole island is being turned into a museum to commemorate its former function.

## Practicalities

Both Saint John **bus station**, 300 Union St, and the **rail station**, on City Rd, are ten minutes' walk from Market Slip – the first to the east, the other to the north. The **ferry terminal** for services from Digby is 3km west of the centre, served by the "East-West" bus. The main **tourist office** is on the eleventh floor of city hall, near the foot of King St (Mon–Fri 9am–4.30pm), close to the seasonal office beside Market Slip (mid-May to mid-Oct daily 9am–6pm). Most buses start and finish at King Square.

### ACCOMMODATION

Most of Saint John's cheap accommodation is on the outskirts of town, with a cluster of **motels** a couple of kilometres northeast of the centre along Rothesay Avenue (bus #8). These include the *Bonanza*, no. 594 (☎633-1710; doubles $30); the *Glen Falls*, no. 650 (☎633-0113; doubles $35); and the *Park Plaza*, no. 607 (☎633-4100; doubles $50). For downtown alternatives consider the *YMCA*, two blocks from Market Slip at 19–25 Hazen Ave (☎634-7720; $22 single, $17 with IYHA card), where you get the use of the swimming pool, sauna and gym facilities. Also central are two **B&Bs**: the pleasant *Earl of Leinster Inn*, 96 Leinster St (☎693-3462; doubles $40); and *Cranberry's Bed and Breakfast*, 168 King St East (☎657-5173; doubles $40). The *Rockwood Park* **campground** (June–Sept; ☎652-4050; $10), is located near the southern entrance of Rockwood Park, about 2km north of the centre off route 1.

### EATING, DRINKING AND NIGHTLIFE

Saint John is a boisterous, lively place to **eat and drink**. *Reggie's*, at 26 Germain St near the city market, has a dozen breakfast specials from $5; down on Prince William Street, the *Historic Café* at no. 181 and the *Heritage* at no. 112 are equally dependable. For lunch, head for the city market, where *Jeremiah's Deli* and *Slocum and Ferris* serve great sandwiches and salads, while *Lords* specialises in lobster rolls and clams. In the evening, *Diana's Restaurant*, King St at King's Square, has great spaghetti; *Mexicali Rosa's*, 88 Prince William St, serves excellent Tex-Mex food, with the emphasis on the Tex; and the *Café Creole*, Charlotte St at King Square, specialises in spicy Cajun food. Best of all, at around $25 per head, *Incredible Edibles*, 42 Princess St, has a wide-ranging menu, simply prepared and thoughtfully presented.

After dark, the rollicking *Gene's Country Palace*, 148 Union St, has draught **beer** and live country **music** most nights; the *Loyalist Pub*, Charlotte at Union St, is a no-frills, serious drinking bar; *O'Leary's* is an Irish place at 46 Princess St; and *Club 74*, 74 Prince William, is a cosy and intimate club.

# Moncton and around

**MONCTON**, 180km east of Fredericton, named after colonel Robert Monckton (sic), was originally known by the Acadian name **Le Coude** ("the elbow"), which at least hinted at its setting on a sharp bend of the Petitcodiac River. Indeed, the river provides Moncton with its only attraction, the tidal bore, which sweeps up from the Bay of Fundy, 25km downstream. A humdrum industrial town, Moncton hosts the province's only French-speaking university, boasts of its bilingualism – the result of Acadian ex-deportees settling here in the 1790s – and lies conveniently near the coastal delights of the **Fundy National Park** and Cape Tormentine, where **ferries** leave for PEI.

Moncton is proud of its **tidal bore**, a wave that varies from a few centimetres to a metre in height, depending on weather conditions and the phase of the moon. At low tide you'll be in no doubt as to why the locals call the Petitcodiac the "chocolate river" – but the bore is followed by a rise in the river level of up to eight metres. **Bore Park**, downtown at Main and King streets, has information plaques on the tide times and a small grandstand so you can watch the phenomenon in comfort.

The city is commonly regarded as the capital of modern Acadia, and Moncton University, its cultural bastion, is the home of the **Acadian Museum** (June–Sept Mon–Fri 10am–5pm, Sat & Sun 1–5pm; Oct–May Tues–Fri 1–4.30pm, Sat & Sun 1–4pm; free), in the campus's Clément Cormier Building, 3km from the centre off Archibald Road (bus #5). The star exhibit is a huge, plaintive canvas entitled *Les Dispersions des Acadiens* by Henri Beau, but there are also thematic displays on every-day Acadian life, with sections on furniture, folk art, textiles, fishing and architecture.

## Practicalities

The town's **bus** and **train** stations are quite close together on either side of Main Street, about ten minutes' walk southwest of the centre. From the bus station, a twice-daily service takes four hours to reach Charlottetown, PEI, via the Cape Tormentine **ferry** (12–18 daily; 45min; $6 return). Moncton has two **tourist information** offices, one in city hall, 774 Main St (Mon–Fri 9am–4pm), the other at 575 Main St (June–Aug daily 9am–7pm). They'll book accommodation at no charge and give information on forthcoming events as listed in *Dimensions*, their free fortnightly magazine. For budget **accommodation**, try the *Sunset Hotel*, 162 Queen St (☎382-1163; doubles $35), a clean and well-kept place right in the centre, two blocks from the prominent NBTel tower, or the gracious *Park View B&B*, 254 Cameron St (☎382-4504; doubles $45). During the summer student rooms are available at Moncton University (☎858-4008), singles for $20, doubles $30, though rates are cheaper with a student ID.

For **food**, start the day at *Len's*, 540 Main St, where a substantial breakfast special costs around $4. *Jean's Diner*, 369 St George St, is worth a look at lunchtime or evening, especially for the clams. The *Fancy Pocket*, 589 Main St, serves kebabs and Middle Eastern dishes; if you're flush, go to *Gaston's*, 644 Main St (in the Blue Cross Mall), where there are French meals to savour. For **nightlife**, *Ziggy's Bar*, 730 Main St, is a brash, noisy place open till 2am, while the *Urban Corral*, 333 St George St, show-cases C&W acts nightly.

## Fundy National Park

Heading south from Moncton on route 114, there are delightful views of the widening Petitcodiac River and its tidal basin. At the mouth, where it flows into Shepody Bay 40km from town, is Cape Hopewell, the site of the **Hopewell Rocks**, which at high tide resemble stark little islands covered in fir trees, but at low tide look like enormous termite hills. The rocks were pushed away from the cliff face by glacial pressure during the ice age, and the Bay of Fundy tides have defined their present, eccentric shape.

**Fundy National Park**, 40km west of the Hopewell Rocks on route 114, encompasses a short stretch of the Bay of Fundy shoreline, whose jagged cliffs and tidal mudflats edge the forested hills and gorges of the central plateau. This varied scenery is crossed by over 120km of hiking trails, described in booklets available at either of the two **information centres** beside the highway across the park – one at the east entrance near the village of ALMA (mid-June to early Sept daily 8am–10pm), the other to the west at WOLFE LAKE (mid-May to mid-Oct daily 10am–6pm). The park is geared up for **camping**, with several serviced grounds and dozens of backcountry sites. Alternatively, the *Fundy Park Chalets* (☎887-2808; $58 per cabin) is in the park near Alma, which itself has several places to stay, including the *Burns Central Motel*, Edgewater Drive (☎887-2909; doubles $32), and the *Captain's Inn*, Main St (☎887-2017; $60). In 1992/93 a park **youth hostel** will be opened at the *Devil's Half-Acre* campground, overlooking Fundy Bay.

# The Saint John River Valley

The **Saint John River Valley** between Fredericton and Edmundston, 275km away, is not consistently beautiful but does have its moments, when it threads through maple and pine forests or, to the north, where its low-lying hills and agricultural land are finally replaced by more mountainous, heavily forested terrain. The valley towns, threaded along the Trans-Canada, are not especially memorable, but the restored pioneer village of **King's Landing** is worth a couple of hours, as is the waterfall at **Grand Falls**.

### King's Landing

Some 30km west of Fredericton on the Trans-Canada lies the **Mactaquac Dam**, part of a hydro-electric project whose reservoir stretches 75km up the valley. Close to the generating station, the **Fish Culture Station** attempts to rectify one of the worst consequences of the scheme, the interruption of the spawning cycle of the Atlantic salmon. The **King's Landing Settlement** (daily June & Sept to mid-Oct 10am–5pm; July & Aug 10am–6pm; $6), 10km west of the dam, also exists because of the Mactaquac project. Making a virtue of necessity, several dozen nineteenth-century buildings were carefully relocated to form a fictitious agricultural community as of 1850. Like similar reconstructions, King's Landing aims to provide a total experience to its visitors, with its "inhabitants" engaged in bread-making, horse-shoeing, logging, milling, weaving, cattle-driving and so on. Even if it all seems a bit daft, the setting amidst the waterside woods and fields is splendid.

### Hartland and Grand Falls

Surrounded by forest, **HARTLAND**, some 60km from King's Landing, advertises itself exclusively on the size of its wooden covered **bridge**, which at 390 metres is by far the longest in the world. There's nothing graceful or aesthetically satisfying about the thing, however – it's just long.

North of Hartland, the scenery changes as the maples give way to the beginning of a great undulating belt of potato fields. This is really dreary, but a surprise lies in store at **GRAND FALLS**, 105km from Hartland. Here, right in the centre of an otherwise nondescript town, a spectacular weight of water crashes past hydro-electric barriers and down a twenty-six-metre pitch. Even if the diversion of water through nearby turbines has deprived the falls of their earlier vigour, they're still impressive, as is the two-kilometre gorge they've carved downstream, a steep-sided ravine encircling half the town. There are two short walks from the bridge over the gorge: one leads to near the base of the falls themselves, the other to the bottom of the gorge, where, amid the pounding of the water and the sheer faces of the rock, it's hard to believe you're still in the middle of town.

There's nothing else to see in Grand Falls, and the **visitors' centre** on the bridge (May to early Oct daily 9am–9pm) is concerned only with the falls and explaining hydro-electric technology. In emergencies, there's **accommodation** north of town on the Trans-Canada: try the *Scenic Motel* (☎473-2211; doubles $44) or the *Auberge Héritage Tourist Home* (☎473-4806; doubles $30).

### Edmundston

Lying at the confluence of the Saint John and Madawaska rivers, wood-pulping **EDMUNDSTON** is the largest town in the north of New Brunswick, with a population of nearly 12,000. It's a brash, modern place, a profusion of flashing neon signs and ranks of old-style American cars proclaiming the proximity of the USA, just over the bridge. The town is mainly French-speaking and, curiously, regards itself as the capital of the enclave known as the **Republic of Madawaska**, the snout-shaped tract of Canadian territory jutting out into the state of Maine. While the idea of an independent state here is preposterous, the "Republic" is more than a publicity stunt: it signifies the frustration of a people over whom the British and Americans haggled for thirty years until 1842, and who still feel ignored by Fredericton. Yet the town packages the Republic frivolously, with Ruritanian touches such as a coat of arms, a flag, honorary knights and a president, otherwise the Mayor of Edmundston.

The **tourist information office** is in the Parc Centennaire, downtown by the Boucher Bridge (summer daily 9am–6pm), a short walk from the **bus depot** at 169 Victoria St. Close by, at 127 Victoria St, is the admirably cheap and snazzy *Hotel Praga* (☎735-5567), where a comfortable double averages $29. For a standard-issue Canadian cooked breakfast in the centre of town, try *Restaurant Bélanger* opposite the international bridge; small and friendly, it also offers weekday lunch specials at about $3.50.

# The Acadian Peninsula

The **Acadian Peninsula**, which protrudes some 130km into the Gulf of St Lawrence in the northeast corner of New Brunswick, is promoted as a part of the province where the twentieth century has yet to gain a foothold. For the Acadians who fled here to avoid the deportations, the isolation was a life-saver, and more than anywhere else in the Maritimes this is where they have maintained their traditional way of life, based on fishing and marshland farming. The port of **Caraquet**, on the north shore near the replica **Village Historique Acadien**, serves as the peninsula's cultural focus, but it is 300km of dreary road from Fredericton, the nearest major town of any charm.

### Caraquet

Heading east from the mining town of BATHURST, route 340 sticks religiously to the Acadian Peninsula's northern shore, trimming the edge of the rolling countryside and slicing through a string of villages where fresh fish is sold from roadside booths and signs advertise homemade bread, smoked herrings and hand-churned butter. Forty kilometres along the road lies unassuming **CARAQUET**, founded by Acadian fugitives in 1758. The **Acadian Museum**, near the harbour at 15 blvd St-Pierre (June–Aug 9am–6pm; $1), chronicles the hardships of those early settlers, while a few minutes' walk to the west, a thick grove of pine trees secretes the **Shrine of Ste Anne de Bocage**, a quaint white chapel built at the end of the eighteenth century. Caraquet is the setting for the region's most important **Acadian Festival**, a week-long programme of music and theatre held during the second week of August, which begins with the blessing of the fishing fleet by the Bishop of Bathurst.

The **Village Historique Acadien** (June–Sept 10am–6pm; $6), 6km west of Caraquet, consists of seventeen old Acadian buildings relocated from other parts of New Brunswick – only the church was purpose-built. Costumed "inhabitants" emphasise the struggles of the settlers and demonstrate traditional agricultural techniques as well as old methods of spinning, cooking and so on.

Getting to Caraquet by **bus** is a pain: the twice-daily bus from Moncton takes three and a half hours, while the daily bus from Fredericton involves a one-day wait in Bathurst for the onward connection. The village does have two cheap and simple **hotels** though: the *Hotel Paulin* at 143 blvd St-Pierre (☎727-9981; doubles $28) and the *Hotel Dominion* at no. 145 (☎727-2876; doubles $23). The *Hotel Paulin* offers genuine Acadian on request. The *Auberge de la Baie*, 139 blvd St-Pierre (☎727-3485), is a more expensive alternative, with doubles from $55.

# PRINCE EDWARD ISLAND

The freckly face and pert pigtails of Anne of Green Gables are emblazoned on most of **Prince Edward Island**'s publicity material, and her creator, local-born novelist Lucy Maud Montgomery, was the island's most gushing propagandist, depicting the place floating "on the waves of the blue gulf, a green seclusion and haunt of ancient peace ... invested with a kind of fairy grace and charm". William Cobbett was not so dewy-eyed, and saw instead "a rascally heap of sand, rock and swamp . . . a lump of worthlessness [that] bears nothing but potatoes". Each had a point. The economy may not be quite as uniform as Cobbett suggested, but PEI does remain thoroughly agricultural – Million-Acre Farm, as it's sometimes called. On the other hand, the country's smallest province – a crescent-shaped slice of land separated from Nova Scotia and New Brunswick by the Northumberland Strait – can be beguiling. The 220-kilometre shoreline is serrated by dozens of bays and estuaries, where the ruddy soils and grassy tones of the rolling countryside are set beautifully against the blue of the sea.

**Charlottetown**, the capital and only significant settlement, sits on the south coast beside one of these inlets, the tree-lined streets of the older part of town occupying a chunky headland that juts out into a wide and sheltered harbour. With its graceful air, wide range of accommodation and good restaurants, this is easily the best base for exploring the island, especially as almost all of PEI's villages are formless affairs whose houses are strung along the road. One exception is **Victoria**, a compact fishing village southwest of Charlottetown, that makes a peaceful overnight stay. Otherwise, **Orwell Corner Historic Village**, just to the east of the capital, is an agreeable attempt to re-create an island village as of 1890; **Cavendish**, on the north coast, boasts the house that Montgomery used as the setting for her books; and, close by, **Prince Edward Island National Park** has miles of sandy beach. Further east, the rough-and-ready township of **Souris** is also worth a peek, located just down the coast from the delightful fishery museum at **Basin Head**. In the west, the chief interest is social: descendants of PEI's **Acadian** settlers – once the majority of the population – today constitute some fifteen percent of its people, many of them living on the wedge of land that runs down from the village of Wellington to Cap-Egmont.

In recent years, PEI has become a major holiday spot, so there's plenty of **accommodation** to choose from, though it's a good idea to make advance reservations during July and August – and note that there's hardly any **public transport** once you're on the island. On a culinary note, the island has a reputation for the excellence of its **lobsters**, which are trapped along the north shore from June to July, and along

The Prince Edward Island telephone code is ☎902.

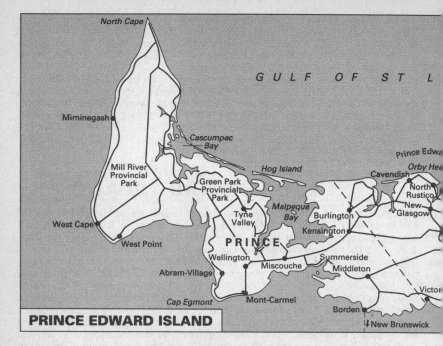

PRINCE EDWARD ISLAND

the south coast between August and September. A number of restaurants specialise in lobster dishes, but keep a look out for local posters advertising lobster suppers, cheap and delicious buffet meals served in some church and community halls during the summer.

## Getting to the island

There are regular domestic **flights** to Charlottetown airport from most cities in eastern Canada, but the main budget options are the three **ferry** routes. The *Northumberland Ferries* boat makes the frequent 45-minute crossing between **Cape Tormentine**, New Brunswick, and **Borden**, 56km west of Charlottetown ($6 return; $16 for cars; schedules on ☎855-2030). The Borden ferry is used by the twice-daily *SMT* **bus** service connecting Fredericton, New Brunswick, with Charlottetown via Saint John, Moncton and Amherst.

The second ferry, run by *Marine Atlantic*, takes 75 minutes to cross from **Caribou**, Nova Scotia, to **Wood Islands**, 61km east of Charlottetown, at least hourly for most of the year ($8 return; $25 for cars; schedules on ☎1-800-565-0201 from within the Maritimes, ☎566-3838 from elsewhere). The *Island Transit* once-daily summer bus service uses this ferry to connect New Glasgow, Nova Scotia, with Charlottetown. Neither of these ferries accepts reservations.

Except in February and March, a third ferry does the five-hour hop between **Cap-aux-Meules** on the Îles-de-la-Madeleine and **Souris**, 81km northeast of Charlottetown, every day except Tuesday ($26 single, $49.50 per car; mid-June to Aug 2 daily, but none on Tues; schedules ☎902/687-2181, reservations ☎418/986-3278). From Souris, *Island Transit* provides a Monday to Saturday once-daily bus service to Charlottetown, but the times of the boat and bus do not coincide.

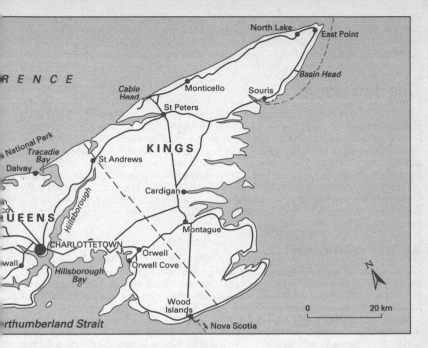

## A brief history of Prince Edward Island

Jacques Cartier claimed Prince Edward Island for France on the first of his voyages across the Atlantic, naming it the **Île-St-Jean** in 1534. However, the French and the Acadian farmers they brought with them from the Bay of Fundy only began to clear the land some two hundred years later, when they founded their tiny capital at **Port La Joye**, near the site of present-day Charlottetown. In 1754, there were about 3000 settlers, but their numbers doubled the following year with the arrival of refugees from the deportations (see p.58), a sudden influx with which the island was unable to cope. After the capture of Louisbourg in 1758, the British army turned its attention to Île-St-Jean and its starving, dispirited population. **Lord Rollo** rounded up and shipped out all but 300 of the Acadians and the colony was subsequently renamed the Island of St John in 1763, **Prince Edward Island** in 1799.

As the island's population climbed from around 7000 to 80,000 in the first half of the nineteenth century, the majority were tenant farmers or squatters, victims of an absentee landowning system that was patently unjust and inefficient. Although most of these immigrants were drawn from the poor of the Scottish Highlands and Ireland, the new citizens had come here in the hope of owning land. Their ceaseless petitioning eventually resulted in the compulsory **Land Purchase Act** of 1875, and within a decade PEI became a land of freeholders.

With the agricultural, fishing and logging industries buoyant, the late 1870s marked the high point of the island's fortunes, but this prosperity was short lived. The Canadian government's protectionist **National Policy** discriminated in favour of the manufactured goods of Ontario and Québec and the result was a long-lasting recession that helped precipitate a large-scale emigration which left PEI a forgotten backwater, derisively nicknamed **Spud Island**. Depopulation remains a problem, which many argue can only be solved by exploiting the island's tourist potential. The plan to build a bridge between PEI and the mainland will, its proponents argue, provide a desperately needed economic boost. Others argue that the island will simply be swamped by outsiders, its farms bought up as second homes and its closely knit communities overwhelmed.

# Charlottetown

Tiny **CHARLOTTETOWN**, the administrative and business centre of PEI, is the most civilised spot on the island, its comfortable main streets – Grafton and Kent – hemmed in by leafy avenues of clapboard villas, the most opulent of which spread southwest of the centre towards **Victoria Park**. But although these well-disposed streets give the place a prosperous and sedate appearance, this is not the whole truth: Charlottetown has a high rate of unemployment and a level of poverty that is evident by the abject stuff on show in its cheaper department stores and the grimness of some of its snack bars. That said, Charlottetown is a pleasant place to spend a couple of days and it also has, in small-island terms, a reasonable **nightlife**, with a handful of excellent restaurants and a couple of good bars.

## Arrival and information

Connected with all of Canada's major cities, Charlottetown **airport** is located 8km north of the town centre. There's no public transport from here to town, but the **taxi** fare costs just $6. What few **buses** there are all arrive centrally: the *SMT* depot is at 330 University Avenue and *Island Transit* is at 308 Queen Street and Euston.

Inside the airport there's a **tourist information** free phone (mid-June to mid–Sept daily 8am–8pm), which provides accommodation advice and a room reservation service. In the town centre, Charlottetown's **tourist office**, located in city hall at Queen Street and Kent (mid-June to Aug daily 8am–4pm; Sept to late Oct Mon–Fri 8.30am–5pm; ☎566-5548), also offers accommodation assistance and has all the basic information about the town and the island. PEI's main **Visitor Information Centre** is about 1km north of the town centre, along University Ave (mid-May to early June & mid-Sept to Oct daily 8.30am–6pm; early June to mid-Sept daily 8am–8pm; Nov to mid-May Mon–Fri 8.30am–5pm; ☎368-4444); its free literature includes a comprehensive *Visitors' Guide* and leaflets on the island's B&Bs and farm vacation spots.

## Accommodation

Charlottetown has no shortage of **places to stay** and only in the height of the season is there any difficulty in finding somewhere reasonably convenient. However, most of the downtown **hotels** and **motels** are expensive and undistinguished, so you're better off staying in one of the handful of **inns** located in some of the town's oldest properties, or in one of the dozens of small guesthouses, listed as either bed and breakfasts or tourist homes. Cheaper still, there's a **youth hostel**, a **campground** and university **rooms** in the summer. As well as the tourist offices, PEI has a free **room reservation service** (☎1-800-565-7421 from the Maritimes, ☎368-5555 from elsewhere).

### Hotels, motels, inns and guesthouses

**Aloha Tourist Home**, 234 Sydney St (☎892-9944). Simple and quite comfortable; doubles $32. Open mid-May to mid-Dec.

**Anchor's Aweigh**, 45 Queen Elizabeth Drive (☎892-4319). A few minutes' walk west of the centre just north of Victoria Park; pleasant rooms; doubles $36.

**Best Western MacLauchlan's Motor Inn**, 238 Grafton St (☎892-2461). Good facilities but characterless rooms; doubles $80–120.

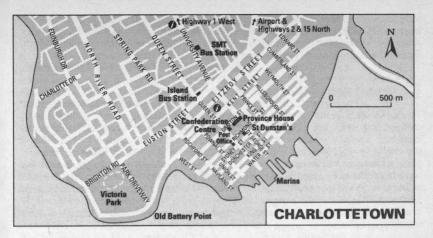

**Birchview B&B**, 139 Rochford St (☎368-1704). Attractive rooms in "heritage home"; doubles $50. Open mid-June to mid-Sept.

**The Charlottetown**, Kent at Pownal (☎894-7371). A grand 1930s hotel with a colonnaded portico; doubles $100–130.

**Duchess of Kent Inn**, 218 Kent St (☎566-5826). The cheapest of the town's inns, simple rooms with shared bathroom facilities located in a nineteenth-century home; doubles $55. Open May–Nov.

**Dundee Arms Inn and Motel**, 200 Pownal St (☎892-2496). Delightful rooms and location; doubles $80.

**Great George Inn**, 68 Great George St (☎566-3137). Charming house with four lovely rooms; doubles $85–125.

**Inn on the Hill**, corner of University and Euston (☎894-8572). Agreeable rooms, but overpriced; doubles from $90.

**Prince Edward Hotel**, 18 Queen St (☎566-2222). Charlottetown's premier hotel, overlooking the harbour; standard-issue luxury; doubles $120–150.

### Hostel, college rooms and camping

**The Charlottetown Youth Hostel**, 153 Mount Edward Rd (☎894-9696). Inconveniently situated 4km from the town centre, behind the university campus; there's no bus. $10 per night; bike rental and kitchen facilities. Open June–Aug.

**Marion Hall**, Prince Edward Island University, University Ave (☎566-0439). Rooms from July to the third week in August; singles $21, doubles $42.

**Southpark Trailer Park**, 20 Stratford Rd (☎569-2287). Charlottetown's most central campground, at the far end of the bridge across the Hillsborough River about 4km east of town – signposted off Hwy 1. From $10; open May–Oct.

## The Town

The island's most famous historical attraction, the **Province House** (Oct–May Mon–Fri 9am–5pm; June & Sept daily 9am–5pm; July & Aug daily 9am–8pm; free) is right in the heart of Charlottetown, at University and Grafton. This squat brownstone structure, dominated by its over-large portico, hosted the first meeting of the **Fathers of Confederation** in 1864, when representatives of Nova Scotia, New Brunswick, Ontario, Québec and PEI met to discuss a union of the British colonies in North America. Today it's used by the island's legislature, but most of its rooms are open to visitors. On the ground floor, a fifteen-minute film provides a melodramatic account of that original meeting and, close by, the Colonial Secretary's Office has been pleasantly restored to its mid-nineteenth-century appearance. On the first floor, the Confederation Chamber remains pretty much unchanged, but frankly it's not much to look at – just a huge table and some heavy-duty chairs.

Next door, the **Confederation Centre of the Arts** (July–Aug daily 9am–8pm; Sept–June Mon–Sat 9am–6pm & Sun 2–5pm; free) is housed in a glass and concrete monstrosity built in 1964 to commemorate the centenary of the epochal meeting. Each of Canada's provinces paid 15¢ per resident to cover its construction and they continue to contribute towards its upkeep. The centre contains the island's main library, a couple of theatres and a combined art gallery and museum, whose changing exhibitions are usually drawn from its permanent collection of Canadian paintings. Most of the work on display is tedious, but look out for the portraits of Robert Harris, who painted most of PEI's business elite in the 1880s, and the manuscripts, papers and scrapbooks of Lucy Maud Montgomery. Close by, beside the gift shop, are displayed *The Lord Nelson Tiles*, a self-explanatory series of ceramics created by the Florida artist Katherine Pancoast in the 1960s.

A couple of minutes' walk away, fringed by the pretty terraced houses of Great George Street, the spires and neo-Gothic facade of the extravagant **St Dunstan's Basilica** mark the centre of the oldest part of Charlottetown. Many of this district's buildings date from the middle of the nineteenth century, with rows of simple wood and brick buildings concentrated along **King Street** and **Water Street**.

Below Water Street, the sequence of jetties that make up the **harbourfront** have been refurbished to hook the upmarket tourists with a couple of expensive restaurants, a yacht club, the lavish *Prince Edward Hotel* and the twee souvenir shops of Peake's Wharf. From the harbourfront, it's a pleasant ten-minute stroll west to **Victoria Park**, which incorporates the scant remains of the gun battery built here in 1805. Looking out over the harbour, it adjoins the grandiose lieutenant-governor's residence.

## Eating, drinking and nightlife

Charlottetown's government workers are catered for by a couple of excellent **snack bar-cum-restaurants**: the *Perfect Cup*, 42 University, where there's a range of vegetarian dishes from about $6; and the rather more expensive *Strawberry Patch*, 104 Water St at Great George. Less polished alternatives in the same category include the *Lunch Bar*, 34 University, which serves Lebanese specialities, and, in emergencies, the cheap and basic fare of the *Island Food Centre*, 117 Queen at Richmond.

PEI is justifiably famous for its **lobsters** and, although they're cheaper and possibly even tastier out of town, *Samuels'*, the **restaurant** of the *Inn on the Hill*, serves excellent lobster dinners for around $11 per pound. Other options include the delightful *Off-Broadway Café*, 125 Sydney, which specialises in exotic crêpes; seafood and Yugoslav dishes at the *Stagecoach Steak House*, 75 Queen; and good quality pasta and steaks at *Pat's Rose and Grey Room*, 132 Richmond. The *Claddagh Room Restaurant*, 131 Sydney, has a good selection of reasonably priced seafood and beef dishes and is also attached to the busy *Olde Dublin Pub*, where there's often live **folk music**. A few minutes' walk away, *Pat and Willy's Bar and Grill*, 119 Kent, has **rock and pop** till late at night, and the *Tradewind*, down the road at no. 189, is the town's busiest **club**. For a quiet drink, try *Doc's Corner* at Kent and Prince.

The programme of events at the **Confederation Centre of the Arts** (☎566-2464) encompasses a wide range of acts, from rock and jazz through to comedians, magicians, theatre, opera and ballet. The centre is also the home of the main show of the annual **Charlottetown Festival**, which – surprise, surprise – is a musical adaptation of *Anne of Green Gables*. Alternatively, the *Off-Stage Theatre Company*, 64 King (☎628-2216), offers often adventurous modern Canadian plays.

## Listings

**Airlines** *Air Canada* (☎892-1007) and *Canadian Airlines* (☎566-4035) are both at the airport.

**Bike rental** *MacQueen's*, 430 Queen St, and the youth hostel.

**Bus companies** *Island Transit* (☎892-6167); *Beach Shuttle* (☎566-3243).

**Car rental** *Avis*, at the airport and at the corner of University and Euston (both ☎892-3706); *Budget*, at the airport and 215 University Ave (both ☎566-5525); *Thrifty*, at the airport (☎566-1696); *Rent-a-Wreck*, at the *PetroCanada* station, 114 St Peter's Rd (☎894-7039).

**Ferry companies** *Northumberland Ferries*, 94 Water St (☎566-3838); *Marine Atlantic*, 119 Kent St (☎566-7059).

**Hospital** Queen Elizabeth Hospital, Riverside Drive (☎566-6111).

**Laundry** *Uptown Laundromat and Café*, 288 University Ave at Bishop (daily till 10pm).

**Pharmacy** *Shoppers Drug Mart*, 128 Kent (Mon–Wed 9am–6pm; Thurs–Fri 9am–9pm; Sat 9am–5pm).

**Police** 450 University Ave (☎368-2677).

**Post office** 97 Queen St at Richmond.

# The Island

Prince Edward Island is divided into three counties: in the middle, **Queens County** incorporates the province's most popular tourist attractions and has some of its prettiest scenery and best beaches; to the east, **Kings County** covers two broad geographical areas, the tree-dotted farmland and estuary townships of the south giving way to wilder scenery further north; and to the west, **Prince County** makes up the flattest part of PEI, its broad-brimmed, sparsely populated landscapes curving round a handful of deep bays. The provincial government has worked out three **scenic drives** covering each of the counties: *Lady Slipper Drive* (287km) to the west, *Blue Heron Drive* (191km) in the centre, and the *Kings Byway Drive* (367km) to the east. However, although these drives visit everything of interest, they are frequently dreary, so unless you really love driving, it's better to be more selective.

PEI's **public transport** system is rudimentary, but *Island Transit* operate a limited bus service from the capital to Summerside, Miscouche and Tignish (5 weekly), and another service to Souris (May–Oct Mon–Sat 1 daily). From late June to August, there's also a **Beach Shuttle** between the visitor information centres in Charlottetown and Cavendish, which runs four times daily. Alternatively, three Charlottetown companies operate **sightseeing tours**: *Abegweit*, 157 Nassau St (☎894-9966); *Prince Edward Tours*, 18 Queen St (☎566-5466); and *Ed's Taxi*, 73 University (☎892-6561).

## Queens County

Bisected by Hwy 2, Queens County divides easily into north and south districts, the latter in turn split into east and west by the deep inlet of Charlottetown harbour. If time is pressing, head north.

### North Queens

The main attraction in Queen's County is the north-shore **Prince Edward Island National Park**, just half an hour's drive from Charlottetown. Some forty kilometres long, it's mostly no more than one or two hundred metres wide, a sliver of sandy beach, low red cliff and marram-covered sand dune that together create a superb place to sun- and sea-bathe. A narrow road runs behind almost all of the shoreline and it's easy enough to drive along here until you find a place to your liking, though the chain of tourist facilities bordering the road is often dire.

The drive from Charlottetown to Cavendish, at the west end of the park, is a delight. **Route 224** passes dozens of prettily painted, high-gabled timber homesteads before threading through the tiny settlement of **NEW GLASGOW**, whose matching pair of black and white clapboard churches sit on opposite sides of an arm of Rustico Bay. In the centre of the village, the *Prince Edward Island Preserve Company* is a great place to buy local jams, mustards and maple syrups, while the attached coffee bar has superb breakfasts for about $5 and evening meals for about $10 – try the Atlantic salmon. Just to the west, **Saint Ann's Church**, in the hamlet of the same name, organises regular lobster suppers from late June to late September (Mon–Sat; reservations ☎964-2385).

North of New Glasgow, off route 13 en route to Cavendish, **NORTH RUSTICO** is the home of the *Fisherman's Wharf Restaurant*, an excellent place to sample the island's lobsters. A short distance southeast of here on route 6, the hamlet of **SOUTH RUSTICO** has excellent accommodation at the *Barachois Inn* (May–Oct; ☎963-2194; doubles from $45), a lovely Victorian house with views over Rustico Bay.

The straggling hamlet of **CAVENDISH**, clumped around the junction of routes 6 and 13, has a **visitor information centre** that supplies detailed maps and brochures on the national park (daily early June to mid-June & mid-Aug to early Oct 10am–6pm; mid-June to mid-Aug 9am–9pm). There's nothing to the village itself, but it does boast a particularly fine strip of beach, a couple of walking trails and the **Green Gables House** (daily May to mid-June & Sept 9am–5pm; mid-June to Aug 9am–8pm; free), situated in a little dell just 500m from the crossroads. The two-storey wooden farmhouse was once occupied by the cousins of Lucy Maud Montgomery, one of Canada's best-selling authors. In 1876, when she was just two years old, her mother died and her father emigrated to Saskatchewan, leaving her in the care of her grandparents in Cavendish. Here she developed a deep love for her native island and its people, and although she spent the last half of her life in Ontario, PEI remained the main inspiration of her work. Completed in 1905 and published three years later, *Anne of Green Gables* was her most popular book, a tear-jerking tale of a red-haired, pig-tailed orphan girl that Mark Twain dubbed "the sweetest creation of child life ever written". The mildly diverting period bedrooms and living rooms – supposedly the setting for *Anne* – attract scores of Japanese tourists every day as the book has a cult following in Japan. If you decide to stay in Cavendish, go for the *Kindred Spirits Country Inn and Cottages*, on Hwy 6 near Green Gables House (mid-May to mid-Oct; ☎963-2434; doubles from $50).

West of Cavendish, route 6 passes through the most commercialised part of the island on its way to NEW LONDON, where route 20 branches north to provide some delightful views across the bay and over to the national park before it approaches SPRINGBROOK. From here, route 234 heads west towards Burlington and the area's most bizarre sight, the large-scale reproductions of famous British buildings that make up **Woodleigh** (daily June & Sept to mid-Oct 9am–5pm; July–Aug 9am–8pm; $5.50). Built by a certain Colonel Johnston, who developed an obsessional interest in his ancestral home in Scotland, it features models of such edifices as the Tower of London, York Minster and Anne Hathaway's cottage. Some of the structures are even big enough to enter and their interiors have also been painstakingly re-created, right down to the Crown Jewels in the Tower.

## South Queens

In the southwest corner Queens County, apart from paltry remains of the British fort at **Fort Amherst National Historic Park**, the only spot worth a call is the tiny village of **VICTORIA**, overlooking the Northumberland Strait. There's nothing remarkable among its unpretentious gridiron streets and nineteenth-century timber houses, but it's a relaxing place to break a journey between Charlottetown and the Borden ferry, and it has two old **hotels**: the *Orient* (☎658-2503; doubles $45–65) and the *Victoria Village Inn* (☎658-2288; doubles $40–75).

It's half an hour's drive east of Charlottetown, along the Trans-Canada Highway, to the delightful **Orwell Corner Historic Village** (mid-May to mid-June & Sept to mid-Oct Mon–Fri 10am–3pm; mid-June to Aug daily 9am–5pm; $3), which was settled by Scottish and Irish pioneers in the early nineteenth century, taking its name from Sir Francis Orwell, an English minister of plantations. At first, the village prospered as an agricultural centre, but by the 1890s it was undermined by the expansion of Charlottetown and mass emigrations to the mainland. Orwell was finally abandoned in the 1950s, but a handful of buildings remained, principally the main farmhouse-cum-post-office-cum-general-store and the church. In recent years, these have been restored and supplemented by replicas of some of the early buildings, like the blacksmith's shop, the shingle mill and the school.

## Kings County

Near Orwell Historic Village, **route 210** turns off the Trans-Canada to snake its way east across the rich farmland bordering the Montague River before reaching **Highway 4**, the county's principal north–south road. This leads to the northeast corner of the province, where **SOURIS**, curving round the shore of Colville Bay, has a busy fishing port and harbour with a regular ferry service to the Magdalens. The docks are a few hundred metres from the town centre, and the stretch of shoreline between the two is the most elegant part of Souris, a sequence of Victorian mansions that includes the excellent *Matthew House Inn*, on Breakwater St (mid-June to Sept; ☎687-3461; doubles from $50). Nearby, Souris's main drag is a grim and grimy affair edged by cheap and tatty snack bars, its ugliness only partly redeemed by the graceful lines of several older buildings tucked away down the side streets.

The **Basin Head Fisheries Museum** (mid-June to Aug daily 9am–5pm; Sept Mon–Fri 9am–5pm; $2.50), a few minutes' drive up the coast from Souris, has a gorgeous setting, lodged on a headland overlooking sand dunes and a fine sandy beach that's trapped between the sea and a narrow, gurgling stream which runs out from an elongated lagoon. Too isolated and barren for any settlement, Basin Head was never more than a fishermen's outpost, and the museum details the lives of these men with displays of equipment, photographs of boats, and miniature dioramas showing the fishing techniques they employed.

From here, it's possible to drive right round the northeast corner of PEI along route 16 but, with the possible exception of the mid-nineteenth-century lighthouse at **East Point**, there's nothing much to see.

## Prince County

Forty kilometres west of Charlottetown Hwy 2 crosses the **Prince County** boundary, from where it's another 30km to **SUMMERSIDE**, PEI's second largest settlement, a sprawling and boring bayside town of 8000 people that was once the island's main port. If you're in town, pop into the **International Fox Hall of Fame and Museum**, 286 Fitzroy St (May–Oct Mon–Sat 9am–7pm; free), which traces the strange history of the island's fox-farming industry from its beginnings in 1894 to its heyday in the 1920s, when fox fur collars reached the height of their popularity in the cities of Europe and the States. At this time, fox pelts became PEI's leading export and a breeding pair of silver foxes sold for as much as $35,000.

Heading west from Summerside, it's a few minutes' drive to **MISCOUCHE**, where the **Acadian Museum** (mid-June to Aug Mon–Sat 9.30am–5pm & Sun 1–5pm; Sept to mid-June Mon–Fri 9am–5pm; $2) is devoted to the island's French-speaking community. It contains a series of modest displays which outline the group's historical development, from pioneer days and deportation through to modern attempts to balance the pressures of assimilation with the Acadians' desire to maintain their own culture. Though the Acadians remain at the bottom of the social ladder, they have maintained a strong sense of identity, and the museum also includes an Acadian Research Centre, complete with a library and extensive archives.

Continuing west, the headland south of the village of WELLINGTON is a centre of Acadian settlement, but it doesn't look any different from the surrounding districts until you reach **MONT-CARMEL**. This tiny coastal village is dominated by the hulking red brick mass and mighty spires of the Église Notre-Dame, whose fantastically ugly appearance is made bizarre by a series of peculiarly sentimental statues and statuettes dotted around the entrance.

After the church, there's nothing else of any real interest anywhere around here, and it's a long drive north before you leave the flattened farmland of this part of Prince County for the slightly hillier scenery along the west shore of **Malpeque Bay**. If you make the trip, head for the village of **TYNE VALLEY**, a cosy little place with a good bed and breakfast, the *Tyne Valley Inn*, on route 12 (☎831-2042; doubles from $50). From here, it's 7km further north to the **Green Park Shipbuilding Museum** (mid-June to Aug daily 9am–5pm; $2.50), inside the park of the same name, which features a restored mid-nineteenth-century shipyard, an industrial museum, and the grand mansion of the one-time shipbuilding magnate, James Yeo.

About 70km away on the other side of the island, west of Hwy 2 along route 142/14, the remote and windswept **West Point Lighthouse** (mid-May to mid-Oct daily 8.30am–6pm; $1.65), contains a small collection of photographs and memorabilia portraying the lives of the lighthouse keepers. Next door, the *West Point Lighthouse Inn* (mid-May to mid-Oct; ☎859-3605; doubles $30–65) makes the most of a great seaside location, overlooking a long sandy beach. The lighthouse and inn are surrounded by the **Cedar Dunes Provincial Park**, which has a **campground** about 500km down the coast (July–Aug; ☎859-2711; from $10).

## travel details

### Trains

**From Halifax** to Truro (6 weekly; 1hr 30min); Moncton (6 weekly; 4hr 45min); Saint John (3 weekly; 7hr); Montréal (6 weekly; 19hr 30min).

**From Moncton** to Saint John (3 weekly; 2hr); Halifax (6 weekly; 4hr 45min); Montréal (6 weekly; 14hr 30min).

**From Saint John** to Moncton (3 weekly; 2hr); Halifax (3 weekly; 7hr); Montréal (3 weekly; 12hr).

**From Campbellton** to Moncton (3 weekly; 4hr); Halifax (3 weekly; 9hr 30min); Matapédia, Québec (3 weekly; 1hr); Montréal (3 weekly; 9hr 45min).

### Buses

**From Halifax** to Sydney (4 daily; 6–8hr); Yarmouth (4 daily; 6hr); Truro (7 daily; 1hr 30min); Moncton (2 daily; 4hr 30min); Fredericton (1 daily; 7hr 30min); Charlottetown (2 daily; 8hr 30min); Liverpool (2 daily; 3hr); Annapolis Royal (2 daily; 3hr 30min); Montréal (1 daily; 19hr).

**From Sydney** to Halifax (4 daily; 6–8hr); Cheticamp (3 weekly; 2hr 30min); Moncton (1 daily; 9hr); Charlottetown (1 daily; 7hr 30min).

**From Yarmouth** to Halifax (3 daily; 6hr); Annapolis Royal (2 daily; 2hr 30min); Liverpool (1 daily; 3hr); Shelburne (1 daily; 2hr).

**From Fredericton** to Saint John (2 daily; 1hr 45min); Moncton (2 daily; 3hr 15min); Edmundston (3 daily; 4hr); Bathurst (1 daily; 4hr 30min); Montréal (1 daily; 12hr).

**From Saint John** to Moncton (4 daily; 2hr); Fredericton (2 daily; 1hr 45min); St Stephen (1 daily; 2hr); Halifax (2 daily; 7hr 30min); St Andrews (1 daily; 1hr 30min).

**From Moncton** to Fredericton (3 daily; 3hr 30min); Saint John (3 daily; 2hr 15min); Charlottetown (2 daily; 4hr); Newcastle (1 daily; 2hr 45min); Caraquet (2 daily; 3hr 30min).

**From Campbelltown** to Fredericton (1 daily; 6hr); Saint John (1 daily; 8hr 30min); Moncton (1 daily; 5hr 45min); Gaspé, Québec (2 daily; 5hr).

**From Edmundston** to Fredericton (3 daily; 4hr); Halifax (1 daily; 12hr 30min); Rivière du Loup, Québec (3 daily; 2hr); Québec (2 daily; 5hr).

**From Charlottetown** to Borden (2 daily; 1hr 25min); Moncton (2 daily; 4hr 45min); St John (2 daily; 7hr 40min); Fredericton (2 daily; 9hr 30min); Halifax (1daily; 8hr 20min); Sydney (1 daily; 13hr).

### Ferries

**From Saint John**, New Brunswick, to Digby, Nova Scotia (1–3 daily; 2hr 30min).

**From Cape Tormentine** to Borden, PEI (12–18 daily; 45min–1hr).

**From Sydney**, Nova Scotia, to Argentia, Newfoundland (June–Oct 2 weekly; 14hr).

**From Caribou**, Nova Scotia, to Wood Islands, PEI (late April to mid-Dec 9–20 daily; 1hr 15min).

### Flights

**From Halifax** to Charlottetown (8 daily; 35min); Deer Lake (7 daily; 1hr 30min); Fredricton (5 daily; 1hr 20min); Montréal (3 daily; 2hr); Toronto (7 daily; 2hr 25min).

# CHAPTER TWO

# NEWFOUNDLAND AND LABRADOR

n 1840 an American clergyman named Robert Lowell described **Newfoundland** as "a monstrous mass of rock and gravel, almost without soil, like a strange thing from the bottom of the deep, lifted up, suddenly, into sunshine and storm", an apt evocation of this fearsome island. Its distant position between the Atlantic and the Gulf of St Lawrence has fostered a distinctive, inward-looking culture that's caricatured by many Canadians in the stereotype of the dim "Newfie" – a term coined by servicemen based here in World War II. This ridicule can be traced to the poverty of the islanders, the impenetrability of their dialect – an eclectic and versatile mix of Irish and English – and even to their traditional **food**. Fish and chips, the favourite dish, is reasonable enough in the eyes of most people, but many stomachs churn at stand-bys such as cods' tongues, fried bread dough with molasses ("toutons"), and seal flipper pie.

Isolated from the rest of the country, Newfoundland is also a place of great isolation within its own boundaries. Only in recent years have many of the **outports** – the ancient **fishing settlements** that were home to the first Europeans – been linked by road to the solitary highway, the Trans-Canada, which sweeps 900km from the southwest corner of the island to the **Avalon Peninsula**, where **St John's**, the capital, sits on the northeast shore. Ferries from Nova Scotia touch the southwest and the Avalon, but most visitors fly straight to St John's, the island's only significant town and the obvious place to start a visit, for its museums, its flourishing **folk music** scene and its easy access to the **Witless Bay** seabird reserve. Yet there are more delightful spots than this: tiny **Trinity**, near the Avalon isthmus, is easily the most beguiling of the outports; the French-owned archipelago of **St-Pierre et Miquelon** is noted for its restaurants; **Gros Morne National Park**, in the west, features wondrous mountains and glacier-gouged lakes; and at the far end of the **Northern Peninsula** you'll find the scant but evocative remains of an eleventh-century Norse colony at **L'Anse aux Meadows**, the only such site in North America.

The definition and control of **Labrador** is the subject of a seemingly interminable dispute between Québec and Labrador, a row so intense that a Newfoundland senator, Alexander Baird, was once roused to declare: "We Newfoundland-Canadians don't want to fight, but by jingo if we have to, then I say we have the ships, the money and the men"; to which Québécois senator Maurice Bourget added sneeringly – "and the fish". The major point of contention was the establishment of the massive **Churchill Falls** hydroelectric project, whose completion was a boost to the Newfoundland-Labrador economy, yet despite the last few years of industrial development and the construction of a few incongruous planned towns, Labrador remains a scarcely explored wilderness, boasting some of Canada's highest mountains, wonderful fjords, crashing rivers, a spectacular shoreline with minuscule coastal settlements, and a forested hinterland teeming with wildlife. A trip to Labrador is not something to be undertaken lightly, but its intimidating landscapes are the nearest thing eastern Canada can offer to the challenge of the deep north.

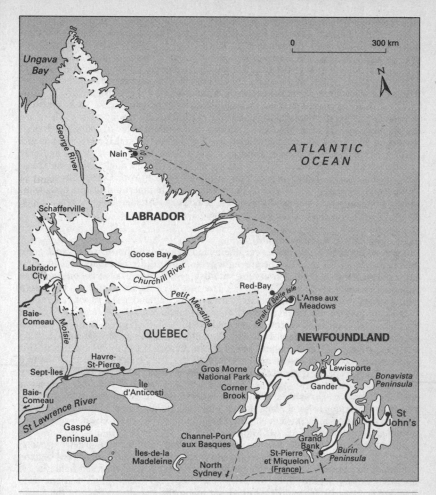

# THE ISLAND OF NEWFOUNDLAND

The inhospitable interior and the fertile ocean kept the first European settlers on the **Island of Newfoundland** – most of English and Irish extraction – glued to the coast when they founded the outports during the sixteenth and seventeenth centuries. Though they hunted **seals** on the winter pack ice for meat, oil and fur, they were chiefly dependent on the cod fish of the **Grand Banks**, whose shallow waters, concentrated to the south and east of the island, constitute the richest fishing grounds in the world. It was a singularly harsh life, prey to vicious storms, dense fogs and the whims of the barter system operated by the island's merchants, who exercised total control of the trade price of fish until the 1940s in some areas.

To combat the consequent **emigration**, various populist premiers have attempted to widen the island's economic base, sometimes with laughable ineptitude – as in the case of a proposed rubber factory, sited ludicrously far from the source of its raw materials. Furthermore, efforts to conserve the fisheries, primarily by extending Canada's territorial waters to 200 nautical miles in 1977, have failed to reverse the downward spiral, and the over-fished Grand Banks are unable to provide a livelihood for all the reliant Newfoundlanders. Ottawa will spend $39 million bailing out the Atlantic fishery in 1992 alone, but there is one bright spot – the discovery of oil and gas just offshore in the **Hibernia** field will transform the economy if the profits are shrewdly spent.

The mixture of coastal deprivation and intermittent industrialisation makes most of Newfoundland's settlements unprepossessing places that are readily missed. There are exceptions – chiefly **St John's** and **Trinity** – but really it's the 10,000 kilometres of **coastline** which appeals, and to get anything like the best from this terrain you need a car, for Newfoundland's **public transport** is appalling. There are no trains and only one daily long-distance **bus**, the *CN Roadcruiser*, which travels the length of the Trans-Canada. Elsewhere, *Viking Express* run a limited service from Corner Brook to St Anthony, at the end of the Northern Peninsula, and a number of **minibus** companies connect St John's with various destinations, principally Argentia, Bonavista for Trinity, and Fortune for the boat to St-Pierre et Miquelon.

## A brief history of Newfoundland

Numerous Europeans may have seen the island before him, but it was **John Cabot**, sailing for Henry VII in 1497, who stirred a general interest in Newfoundland when he reported back that "the sea is swarming with fish, which can be taken not only with the net, but in baskets let down with a stone". This was the effective start of the **migratory ship fishery**, with boats sailing out from France and England in the spring and returning in the autumn, an industry that was soon dominated by the merchants of the English West Country, who grew fat on the profits.

In the early 1700s the English fishery began to change its *modus operandi*, moving towards an offshore **bank fishery** based in the harbours of the eastern coast. This encouraged greater permanent settlement, with the Brits concentrated in **St John's** and the French around **Placentia**, their main fishing station since the 1660s. Mirroring the wars of Europe, these rival nationalities fought a series of desultory campaigns until the **Treaty of Utrecht** in 1713, when France gave up her claims to the island in return for the right to catch, land and dry fish on the northwest coast, the so-called **French Shore** – an arrangement that lasted until 1904. In 1763 the French also swapped Labrador for St-Pierre et Miquelon.

Meanwhile, in 1729 the British government had introduced a bizarre system, whereby the commanders of the naval convoy accompanying the fishing fleet became the temporary **governors** of Newfoundland, even though they returned home in the autumn. Largely left to their own devices, the English and Irish settlers, who numbered about 30,000 by 1790, spread out along the coasts, massacring the native **Beothucks** on the way – they died out in 1829. A permanent governor was eventually appointed in 1817; the island was recognised as a colony in 1824; and representative, ultimately **responsible government** followed shortly after.

Struggling through a period of sectarian violence, Protestant English against Irish Catholic, Newfoundlanders decided not to join newly formed Canada in the 1860s, opting instead for self-governing **dominion** status. However, by the 1910s class conflict had replaced religious tension as the dominant theme of island life, reflecting the centralisation of the economy in the hands of the bourgeoisie of St John's – a process which impoverished the outports and fuelled the growth of the trade unions. The

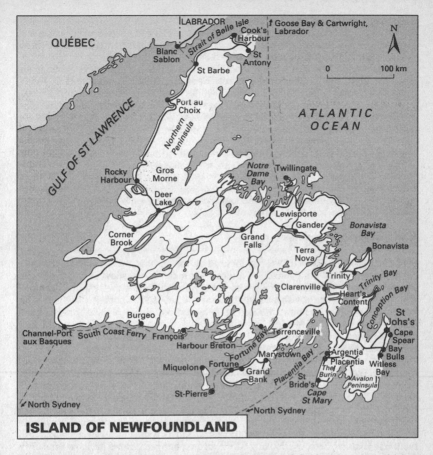

**ISLAND OF NEWFOUNDLAND**

biggest of these, the **Fishermen's Protective Union**, launched a string of hard-fought campaigns that greatly improved the working conditions of the deep-sea fishermen and sealers. Newfoundland's export-orientated economy collapsed during the Great Depression of the 1930s, and the bankrupt dominion turned to Great Britain for help. The legislative chamber was suspended and replaced by a London-appointed commission. However, almost before they could start work, the economy was revived by the boom created by World War II, which also saw Newfoundland garrisoned by 16,000 American and Canadian servicemen.

Though a narrow majority voted for **confederation** in the referendum of 1949, many islanders remain at least suspicious of the rest of Canada, blaming Ottawa for the decline of the fishing industry and the high levels of unemployment. Many more regard Québec's claims to distinct status with a mix of contempt and incredulity – after all, they argue, no one's as distinctive as themselves and anyway it's their fellow fishermen on St-Pierre et Miquelon who should be respected as proper "Parisian French", not the charlatan Québécois. These sentiments underlie the assertive stance taken by the present premier, **Clyde Wells**, in the constitutional wranglings that have become a constant feature of Canadian politics.

## Getting to Newfoundland island

There are regular domestic **flights** to St John's from all of Canada's major cities and frequent services onward across the island to several smaller settlements, most usefully Deer Lake, for Gros Morne National Park.

*Marine Atlantic* operates two **ferries** from North Sydney, on the Nova Scotia mainland. The first goes to **Channel-Port aux Basques**, 900km southwest of St John's (June–Oct 1 daily; 5–6hr; $16 per person, $46 for cars; reservations ☎902/794-5700), from where the **CN Roadcruiser** bus leaves for St John's (1 daily; 25hr; $76). The second serves **Argentia** (June–Oct 2 weekly; 14hr; $41 per person one way; $99 for cars; same number), 131km southwest of St John's, where **Newhook's** minibuses connect with the capital, a two-hour drive away, for $15. A third *Marine Atlantic* ferry connects Goose Bay, Labrador, with **Lewisporte** (mid-June to early Sept 2 weekly; $69 per person, $110 for cars; 34hr; reservations ☎709/896 5698).

---

The Newfoundland and Labrador telephone code is ☎709.

---

# St John's and around

For centuries life in **ST JOHN'S** has focused on the harbour, which in its heyday was crammed with ships from a score of nations but today is a shadow of its former self, with just the odd oil tanker or trawler creeping through the 200-metre-wide channel of The Narrows into the jaw-shaped inlet. Once a rumbustious port, it's become a far more subdued place, the rough houses of the waterfront mostly replaced by shops and offices, its economy dominated by white-collar workers who are concentrated in a string of downtown tower blocks and in Confederation Building, the huge government complex on the western outskirts.

Yet although the town's centre of gravity has begun to move west, the waterfront remains the social centre, home of lively bars that feature the pick of Newfoundland **folk music** – the best single reason for visiting. Almost all of the older buildings were destroyed by fire in the nineteenth century, so although St John's looks splendid from the sea, with tier upon tier of pastel-painted houses rising from the harbour, there are precious few sights to see, with the notable exception of two museums which provide an excellent introduction to the history of the island and its people. Elsewhere, **Signal Hill National Historic Site**, overlooking The Narrows, has great views back over the town and out across the Atlantic, while the drive out to the rugged shoreline of **Cape Spear**, the continent's most easterly point, makes for a pleasant excursion, as does the trip to the **Witless Bay Ecological Reserve**.

## Arrival and information

St John's **airport** is about 6km northwest of the city centre and there's a seasonal **tourist information desk** inside (early June–mid to Sept daily 8am–6pm; ☎772-0011). There's no public transport from the airport to the centre, but *Gulliver's Taxis* operate a shared **limo** service for only $5.50 per person; should there not be a limo in sight when you arrive, use *Gulliver's* direct free phone in the concourse. **Taxis** charge $11 for the same journey. The **bus station** is on the western edge of the centre, in the defunct railway station beside the junction of Water and New Gower streets. It's a good fifteen minutes' walk from here to downtown, straight down Water Street, or you can catch a city bus from the **Metrobus** stop on the far side of Water Street, opposite the station. Buses have a standard single fare of $1.10, with tickets available from the drivers –

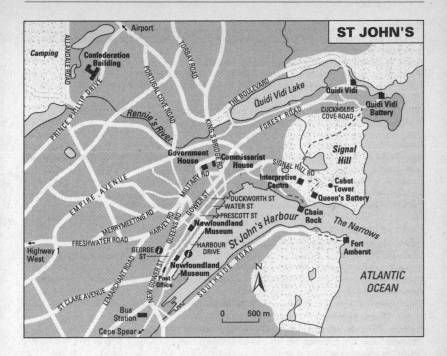

exact fare only. If you're not quite sure where you're going, head for the *Hotel Newfoundland*, the city's most prominent and convenient landmark.

St John's has two downtown **tourist offices**, one in city hall, at New Gower and Adelaide streets (Mon–Fri 9am–4.30pm; ☎576-8106), the other in the old railcar next to the waterfront, halfway along Harbour Drive at the foot of Bairds' Hill Cove (June to mid-Sept daily 9am–7pm; ☎576-8514). Both outlets have bucketfuls of free literature, most usefully a *St John's Tourist Information Guide*, which lists everything from accommodation and events through to church services and radio station frequencies. They also have free city and provincial maps, the tourism department's comprehensive *Newfoundland and Labrador Travel Guide* and a variety of specialist leaflets detailing local sights, guesthouses and bed and breakfasts.

## Accommodation

St John's has a handful of convenient downtown **hotels**, but their charges are high and, with the possible exception of the *Hotel Newfoundland*, they're of precious little distinction. The town's **motels** also tend to the mundane and most of them are inconveniently located on the main roads into town, with charges that start at about $50 per double. On the other hand, several of the city's **bed and breakfasts – hospitality homes –** are outstanding, the best located in some of the fine nineteenth-century houses and villas that are spread across the centre: reckon on $60 per double including breakfast. Far cheaper, the **university** offers rooms throughout the summer and, although Newfoundland's weather is too wet and windy for most campers, there is a city campground.

## Hotels

**Holiday Inn Government Centre**, 180 Portugal Cove Rd (☎722-0506). Standard-issue modern luxury hotel on the northwest edge of the city centre; $115.

**Hotel Newfoundland**, Cavendish Square (☎726-4980). Convenient location at the northern end of Water Street. Grand and a rather pompous place, but many of the rooms have great views over the harbour; swimming pool, sauna and whirlpool; $150; weekend and off-season discounts of up to 20 percent.

**Radisson Plaza Hotel**, 120 New Gower St (☎739-6404). Luxurious tower block with swimming pool, saunas and gym; $125.

## Motels

**Best Western Travellers Inn**, Kenmount Rd (☎722-5540 or ☎1-800-528-1234). About 5km southwest of the centre, along the Trans-Canada Highway. Comfortable rooms for $75.

**Centre City Motel**, 389 Elizabeth Ave (☎726-0092). Roughly 3km west of the centre. Basic and a bit tatty; $50.

**Parkview Inn**, 118 Military Rd (☎753-2671). Central location; basic rooms for $45.

## Bed and breakfast

**Bonne Esperance**, 20 Gower St (☎726-3835). Pleasant and central; $56.

**Compton House**, 26 Waterford Bridge Rd (☎739-5789). Delightful old home, about 2km south of the centre, straight along Water Street; $70–95; breakfast extra.

**Fort William**, 5 Gower St (☎726-3161). Lovely house and rooms just across from the *Hotel Newfoundland*; $62.

**The Gables**, 115 Gower St (☎754-2318). Mundane, but cheap and central; $52.

**Gower House**, 180 Gower St (☎754-0047). Basic; $54.

**Kincora**, 36 King's Bridge Rd (☎576-7415). Central location in fine old house; $65.

**Prescott Inn**, 17–19 Military Rd (☎753-6036). Lovely rooms complete with period furniture; a bargain at $62.

**The Roses**, 9 Military Rd (☎753-6036). Another pleasant and convenient old house; $65; breakfast extra.

**Sea Flow Tourist Home**, 53 William St (☎753-2425). A few minutes' walk west of the centre, along Prescott Street and Monkstown Road. Basic and cheap; $30; breakfast extra.

**Victoria Station Inn**, 290 Duckworth St (☎722-1290). Splendid old house next door to the cathedral. More like a hotel than a B&B; $65–85; breakfast extra.

## Hostel and college rooms

**Catherine Booth House Travellers' Hostel**, 18 Springdale St (☎738-2804). On the southern edge of downtown, near the bus terminal; a Salvation Army hostel, next door to a drug rehabilitation centre; spartan rooms; $35.

**Memorial University of Newfoundland** (MUN), off Elizabeth Ave (☎737-7590). Reasonably pleasant rooms available from mid-May to mid-August, 3km west of the centre; $32 non-students; $24 students; reservations essential.

## Campground

**CA Pippy Park Campground**, in Pippy Park (May–Sept; ☎737-3655). About 4km west of the town centre, turn off Elizabeth Avenue at Allandale Road and subsequently Nagles Place; unserviced sites $5; serviced $14.

# The City

Running the length of the town centre, **Water Street** has long been the commercial hub of St John's, though the higgledy-piggledy storefronts of the chandlers and tanners, ship suppliers and fish merchants have mostly been replaced by a series of ill-considered redevelopments. In the architectural gloom, look out for the odd elegant stone and brick facade or take a peek at the old **courthouse**, a monumental Romanesque Revival building of 1904 that overlooks the harbour from Water Street at Baird's Cove.

## The Newfoundland Museum at the Murray Premises

The best place to start a visit to St John's is the **Newfoundland Museum at the Murray Premises** (Mon–Fri 9am–4.30pm; Sat–Sun 10am–5.30pm; free), located in a refurbished fish merchant's property on Beck's Cove, off Water Street a couple of minutes' walk south of the courthouse. Don't bother with the first two floors, but head straight up to the third, where a series of small, well-designed display areas deal with all things maritime, from the development of navigational aids and the evolution of ship design and construction, through to the history of the fishing industry and the domination of the island by a merchant oligarchy.

There's also a display on the Basque whalers who worked Red Bay during the sixteenth century and another on **shipwrecks**. The island's waters are notoriously dangerous and it's estimated that they've accounted for about 10,000 vessels in the last 500 years. Indeed, when Edward Wix, the archdeacon of the island's Anglican church, made a tour of the southern coast in 1835, his host remarked, "I have had so much to do with dead bodies, that I think no more of handling them, than I do of handling so many codfish". A further section deals with the **seal fishery**, or more accurately the seal hunt, which has been a vital source of income for many Newfoundlanders since the early nineteenth century. An old photograph album provides some extraordinary pictures of an early twentieth-century sealer, the crew pushed up against the gunwales waiting for the signal to deploy over the ice, and later the boats awash with blood and guts. The long wooden gaffs were used to bash the seals' heads in and, held horizontally, stopped the men from falling through ice holes.

## The Newfoundland Museum

It's the briefest of walks up the hill from the courthouse to the other part of the **Newfoundland Museum** (Mon–Fri 9am–4.30pm, plus Thurs till 8.30pm, Sat & Sun 10am–5.30pm; free), housed in a sturdy stone edifice on Duckworth Street at Cathedral. Here, one floor is devoted to the prehistoric peoples of Newfoundland and Labrador, beginning with the few bits and bobs that are the sole traces of the Maritime Archaic Indians and their successors, the Dorset Eskimos. This is pretty dull stuff, but the series of displays on the **Beothucks** are more diverting. These Algonquian-speaking people reached Newfoundland in about 200 AD and were seminomadic, spending the summer on the coast catching fish, seals and sea birds, moving inland during the winter to hunt caribou, beaver and otter. They were also the first North American natives to be contacted by British explorers, who came to describe them as **Red Indians** – from their habit of covering themselves with red ochre, perhaps as some sort of fertility ritual. The initial contacts between the two cultures were quite cordial, but the whites soon began to encroach on the ancient hunting grounds, pushing the natives inland with tactics summarised by Joseph Banks, a contemporary observer – "the English fire at the Indians whenever they meet them, and if they happen to find their houses or wigwams, they plunder them immediately". The last of the tribe, a young woman by the name of **Shanadithit**, died in 1829. Shanadithit had spent the last years of her life in the protective custody of the attorney general in St John's and it was here that she made ten simple drawings of her people and their customs. Copies of these are on display, a modest memorial to a much-abused people.

Upstairs on the third floor are displayed various Newfoundland furnishings and fittings, ranging from the comfortable rooms of the bourgeoisie down to the impoverished fishermens' dwellings. Many of the outports remained beyond the cash economy right up until the 1940s and consequently much of their furniture was made from packing cases and driftwood. The kitchen stuff was painted in bright, primary colours, but much of the rest was stained dark brown, a decorative graining which gradually assumed the styles and patterns exemplified by the charming Trinity Bay **chest of drawers** of around 1900. In the outports, it was one thing to have living room furniture, but quite another to have anything to put in or on it: most of the drawers are false.

## Military Road

**Military Road** and adjacent **Kings Bridge Road** boast St John's finest old buildings, a handful of elegant structures beginning near the *Hotel Newfoundland* with the clapboard and elongated chimneys of the **Commissariat House** on Kings Bridge Road (June–Aug daily 9am–5pm; free), whose interior has been restored to its appearance circa 1830. Costumed staff provide entertaining guided tours of the building and the attached coach house. Close by, the trim black and white painted clapboard of the Anglican **Church of St Thomas** completes the ensemble.

Continuing along Military Road, it's a couple of minutes' walk to the imperial pomposities of **Government House**, the governor's residence until 1949. Next door, the impressively stylish **Colonial Building** once housed the provincial assembly and now contains the island's historical archives. From here, it's a further five minutes along Military Road to the grandest of the town's churches, the mid-nineteenth-century Catholic **Basilica of St John the Baptist**, whose twin-towered limestone and granite mass overlooks the harbour from the crest of a hill. The basilica is fronted by a magnifi-

### SEALING

The Newfoundland seal hunt has always been dependent on the **harp seal**, a gregarious animal that spends the summer feeding around the shores of Greenland, Baffin Island and northern Hudson Bay. In the autumn, they gather in a gigantic herd which surges south ahead of the arctic ice pack, passing the coast of eastern Labrador before dividing into two – one group pushing down the Strait of Belle Isle into the Gulf of St Lawrence to form the **Gulf herd**, the other continuing south as far as Newfoundland's northeast coast where they congregate as the **Front herd**. From the end of February to early March, the seals of the Front herd start to breed, littering the ice with thousands of helpless baby seals or **whitecoats**, as they're known. It's just two or three weeks before the pups begin to moult and their coats turn a shabby white and grey.

From early days, the Front herd provided the people of northeast Newfoundland with fresh meat during the winter, but it was the value of the whitecoats' fur that spawned a clutch of hunting centres – such as Bonavista, Trinity and Twillingate – and thousands of jobs: in 1853, the seal fleet consisted of 4000 ships manned by 15,000 sailors, who combined to kill no fewer than 685,000 harps. However, in the 1860s **steamers** made the old sailing ships obsolete and provoked a drastic restructuring of the industry. The new vessels were too expensive for the shipowners of the smaller ports and control of the fleet fell into the hands of the wealthy traders of St John's. By 1870, the bulk of the fleet was based in the capital and hundreds of Newfoundlanders were obliged to travel here for work every winter.

For those "lucky" enough to get a berth, conditions on board were appalling: as a government report noted, a captain could "take as many men as he could squeeze onto his ship. . . . When the seal pelts began to come aboard, the crew had to make way until, by the end of a successful voyage, the men would be sleeping all over the deck, or amongst the skins piled on the deck, even in the most savage weather conditions". All this hardship was endured on a basic diet of "hardtack", hard bread or ship's biscuit, and "switchel", black unsweetened tea, enlivened by the odd plate of "duff", a boiled-up mixture of old flour and water. "Small wonder", as one of the sealers – or **swilers** –

cently unsuccessful entry arch, but otherwise it's a reasonable attempt to mimic the Romanesque churches of Italy. It's at its best inside, where the crudely coloured stained glass illuminates a delightfully ornate maroon and deep green ceiling.

From the basilica it takes about ten minutes to walk back down the hill to Water Street, passing through the oldest residential part of town, rows of simple pastel-painted clapboard (or vinyl imitation) houses festooned by a quaint cobweb of power and telephone cables: there's nothing special here, but it's a beguiling district that maintains the flavour of old St John's.

## Signal Hill

Soaring high above The Narrows, **Signal Hill National Historic Site** (daily mid-June to Aug 9am–8pm; Sept to mid-June 8.30am–4.30pm; free) is a massive, grass-covered chunk of rock with views that are dramatic enough to warrant the strenuous half-hour walk up from the northern end of Water Street. Known originally as the Lookout, Signal Hill took its present name in the middle of the eighteenth century when it became common practice for flags to be hoisted here to notify the merchants of the arrival of a vessel – giving them a couple of hours to prepare docking facilities and supplies. The hill was also an obvious line of defence for the garrison of St John's, and the simple fortifications that were first established during the Napoleonic Wars were restructured every time there was a military emergency right up until World War II. Since then, it's become the easiest and most comfortable place for lots of young Newfoundlanders to try a bit of alfresco fraternisation – a popular 1970's folk song suggested most of the town's babies should be re-christened in its honour.

recalled, that "most of us learned to eat raw seal meat. The heart, when it was cut out and still warm, was as good as steak to we fellows". There were two compensations: money and status – as it left for the Front the seal fleet was cheered on its way and the men of the first ship back, the **highliner**, dispensed seal flippers, an island delicacy, and got free drinks all round.

In the early 1900s, the wooden walled steamships were, in their turn, replaced by **steel steamers**. Once again, the traders of St John's invested heavily, but the shrinking seal population reduced their profit margins. Increasingly, they began to cut corners which threatened the safety of the swilers. The inevitable result was a string of disasters that culminated in the loss of the **Southern Cross** with all 173 hands in 1914. Shortly afterwards, a further 78 men from the **Newfoundland** died on the ice as a consequence of the reckless greed of one of the captains. These twin catastrophes destroyed the hunt's communal popularity, and a decade later the economics of the industry collapsed during the Great Depression. By 1935 most of the sealing firms of St John's had gone broke.

After World War II sealing was dominated by the ships of Norway and Nova Scotia, with the Newfoundlanders largely confining their activities to an inshore cull of between twenty and forty thousand whitecoats per year, enough work for about 4000 people. Thus, sealing remained an important part of the island's bedraggled economy up until the 1960s when various conservationist groups, spearheaded by **Greenpeace**, started a campaign to have it stopped. Slowly but surely, the pressure built up on the Canadian government until it banned all the larger sealing ships and closely restricted the number of seals the islanders were allowed to kill. This remains the position today.

The **conservationists** have always objected to the cruelty of the cull and it's certainly true that the killing of a hapless whitecoat is a brutal act. Yet the furore has much to do with the doleful eyes and cuddly body of the baby seal, an anthropomorphism that doesn't wash with an island people whose way of life has been built on the killing of animals, and who are convinced that the increasing number of seals has damaged the fisheries. Nothing angers many Newfoundlanders more than the very mention of "Greenpeace", whose supporters are caricatured as well-heeled, urban outsiders who have no right to meddle in their traditional hunting practices.

Signal Hill is bare and treeless, but there's the odd diversion as you clamber up the approach road. The first is the **Visitors' Centre** (daily June 15 to Aug 9am–6pm; rest of year 8.30am–4.30pm), which explores the history of the town and the island. Close by, the antiquated guns of the **Queen's Battery** peer over the entrance to the harbour directly above Chain Rock, which was used to anchor the chain that was dragged across the channel in times of danger. Right on the top of Signal Hill, the squat and ugly **Cabot Tower** was built between 1898 and 1900 to commemorate both John Cabot's landing of 1497 and Queen Victoria's Diamond Jubilee. The tower is closed until 1993, when it will be reopened as part of the "Lookout Project" detailing Signal Hill's past. There's also a plaque in honour of Guglielmo Marconi who confirmed the reception of the first transatlantic radio signal here in December 1901. From the top you can walk down to the rocky headland below, a wild and windswept route on all but the balmiest of days.

## Quidi Vidi

**Quidi Vidi** is one of the province's most photographed scenes, a couple of fishing shacks and drying racks flanked by sharp-edged cliffs about 3km from the town centre – take Kings Bridge Road and turn right down Forest Road. The cliffs stick out from the deep blue waters of a tiny inlet that's connected to the sea by the sweetest of narrow channels; although the village itself is a bore, the scenery's great and you can walk round the coast to the nearby **Quidi Vidi gun battery** (June–Aug daily 9am–5pm; free).

# Eating, drinking and entertainment

St John's has a small but flourishing "counterculture", whose denizens congregate in a handful of vaguely alternative **restaurants** on Duckworth Street, where the food is generally good and reasonably priced. Slightly cheaper, there are a number of central **café-cum-restaurants** catering for the town's office workers, whilst many of the downtown pubs also sell reasonably appetising **bar food** at lunchtime and sometimes at night. The town's high rate of unemployment means there are lots of inexpensive – and often nasty – **snack bars**, usually fish and chip shops, the best of which serve hearty meals for as little as $5. For **drinking**, St John's has dozens of **bars**, though many of them get both rowdy and obnoxiously sexist late at night: as a general rule, stick to the pubs where there's **folk music**, which you shouldn't miss in any case.

There are some half dozen pubs and bars dotted around the centre which regularly showcase island musicians, who vary enormously in quality and the type of music they play, ranging from what sounds like country and western with an eccentric nautical twist, through to traditional unaccompanied ballads. If you're content to take pot luck, follow the crowds, but otherwise ask for advice at **O'Brien's Music Store**, 278 Water St, where you can also get a comprehensive list of up-and-coming gigs. Another good contact is the **St John's Folk Arts Council** (☎576-8508), who organise a folk club at Bridget's (see opposite) on Wednesday nights and a monthly folk dance at various locations where you can learn the dances and join in a "real Newfoundland time". Finally, the best of the island's dozen folk festivals, the **Newfoundland and Labrador Folk Festival**, is held in St John's on the first weekend in August.

## Snacks, cafés and restaurants

**Cavendish Café**, 73 Cavendish Square. Good-quality sandwiches and fancy, expensive cakes.

**Ches's**, 9 Freshwater Rd at Lemarchant (☎726-3434). Situated fifteen minutes' walk from the *Hotel Newfoundland*, along Military and then Harvey Road, *Ches's* is one of the best fish and chip shops in town.

**The Coffee House**, 246 Duckworth St at Prescott. A students' favourite with a good range of cheap snacks.

**Duckworth Lunch**, 192 Duckworth St. Health-food snacks and light meals; closes around 5pm.

## NEWFOUNDLAND FOLK MUSIC

The musical culture of Newfoundland was defined by the early settlers from England and Ireland, whose evenings would typically begin with step dances and square sets performed to the accompaniment of the **fiddle** and the **button accordion**, followed by the unaccompanied **singing** of "old country" songs. The music was never written down, so as it passed from one generation to another a distinctive **Newfoundland style** evolved, whose rhymes and rhythms varied from village to village – though its Irish and English roots always remained pronounced.

Newfoundland's musical fabric began to unravel in the 1930s and 1940s with the arrival of thousands of American soldiers during World War II and the advent of radio and television. A multitude of influences became interwoven with the indigenous forms, none more pronounced than country and western, whose introduction has produced a hybrid in which an old story or ballad is given a C&W melody and rhythm, the accordion supported by lead and bass guitar and drum. The unadulterated style of folk music is becoming increasingly hard to find, especially after the recent death of the island's most famous fiddler, **Rufus Guinchard**, and despite the efforts of **Emile Benoit**, an unaccompanied singer from the Port au Port Peninsula. Nevertheless, marginally modified versions of Newfoundland's traditional songs are regularly performed by younger generations of **revivalists**: singer-songwriters such as Jim Payne and Ron Hynes, musician-producers such as Jim Kelly, and groups such as **Figgy Duff** have all played important roles in this process. Other musicians to look out for include **Dermot O'Reilly**, **Phyllis Morrissey** and the **Irish Descendants**, the most popular group on the island today.

More than 350 recordings of the island's music are available at two principal St John's outlets: **O'Brien's Music Store**, 278 Water St, and **Fred's**, 198 Duckworth. The **Pigeon Inlet Productions** label is the one to look out for; the company is run by Jim Kelly and you can get a comprehensive brochure or the recordings themselves direct from him at Pigeon Inlet Productions, PO Box 1202 Station C, St John's (☎754-7324).

**The Fishing Admiral**, 203 Water St. Spruce and touristy place with good seafood crêpes and grilled chicken.

**The Flake House**, Quidi Vidi village. Popular with tourists and locals alike; good range of seafood; dinners from $12.

**Heritage Deli**, 325 Duckworth St. Great atmosphere, big juicy sandwiches. Closes 5.30pm.

**Leo's**, 27 Freshwater Rd. Superb fish and chips; try the cods' tongues and, in season, flipper pie.

**Stella's**, 183 Duckworth. Imaginative and well-conceived menu with a health-food slant; excellent lunches for around $7, main evening courses from $9. Closed Mon & Tues evening.

**Stone House**, 8 Kenna's Hill (☎753-2380). Located near the west end of Quidi Vidi Lake, this expensive place serves traditional Newfoundland game and seafood dinners; reservations advised.

**Victoria Inn**, 288 Duckworth at Cathedral. Cosy and fairly expensive restaurant with well-prepared dishes from a wide-ranging menu – though their portions are rather mean; lunchtime specials for just $7; dinners from $15.

**Woolco restaurant**, Water St and Queen. Emergency rations; full meals for $5.

## Music bars, pubs and clubs

**Bar None**, McMurdo's Lane at 208 Water St. A bit of a dive; all sorts of music, especially jazz, but the quality is very inconsistent.

**Blarney Stone Irish Pub**, George St at Adelaide. Good live folk acts; boisterous atmosphere after about 10pm.

**Bridgett's Pub**, 29 Cookstown Rd. Access from Freshwater Road, fifteen minutes' walk from Water St. Generally considered the town's best traditional pub; good-quality folk musicians especially on Wednesdays.

**The Cage**, Water St near Baird's Cove. Scheduled to open in the summer of 1992; intended to be St John's trendiest nightspot.

**Cruisers**, George St. A busy bar featuring all sorts of live music ranging from the dire to the excellent.

**Erin's Pub**, 186 Water St. Popular bar; good live folk acts.

**Nautical Nellie's**, 203 Water St. Over-elaborate decor, but consistently good and frequent folk acts.

## Listings

**Airlines** International and domestic flights: *Air Canada, Hotel Newfoundland*, Cavendish Square and Scotia Centre, Water St (both ☎726-7888); *Canadian Airlines, Hotel Newfoundland*, Cavendish Square (☎576-0274). Local flights: *Atlantic Airways*, St John's airport (☎576-1800); *Provincial Airlines*, St John's airport (☎576-1666).

**Bookshops** *Dicks*, in the Scotia Centre, Water St, specialises in books about Newfoundland; *After Words*, 166 Water St, has a good selection of new and secondhand texts.

**Bus services** There are several **minibus** companies connecting St John's with the outports, but the biggest and most reliable is **Newhooks**, at Prince and George (☎726-4876), with frequent services to Argentia ($15 each way) and Bonavista village ($19). *CN Roadcruiser* details, ☎737-5912.

**Car hire** *Budget*, at St John's airport and behind the *Hotel Newfoundland* (both ☎747-1234 or ☎1-800-268-8900); *Rent-a-Wreck*, 43 Pippy Place (☎753-2277); *Thrifty*, St John's airport (☎576-4351 or ☎1-800-367-2277).

**Gay and lesbian information line** 11 Johnson Crescent (☎754-3926).

**Hospital** *Grace Hospital*, 241 Le Marchant Rd (☎778-6222).

**Laundry** *Mighty White's*, 152 Duckworth, near the *Newfoundland Hotel*.

**Pharmacy** *Lawtons Drugs*, 186 Duckworth at King's Rd (Mon–Sat 9am–10pm & Sun 1–10pm).

**Police** ☎772-5400.

**Post office** The main central post office is at Water and Queen (Mon–Fri 8am–5pm).

**Sightseeing tours** The best land-based sightseeing tours of St John's and its environs are by *McCarthy's Party*, Topsail, Conception Bay (May to early Sept daily; ☎781-2244). They charge $15 for a two-and-a-half hour trip that includes all the main sights, but it's the historical gossip that makes it worth the money. There's also one particularly good boat trip, on the *Scademia*, a refurbished two-masted schooner which sails to Cape Spear and offers a chance to do some "cod-jigging" (handline fishing); it leaves from Harbour Drive, just near the rail car, for two-hour excursions up to four times daily (May–Sept; ☎754-1672; $30). Similar and slightly cheaper sea trips are organised by *Harbour Charters*, on the waterfront at Pier 7, opposite the Murray Premises (☎754-1672).

**Taxis** *Bugden's*, 266 Blackmarsh Rd (☎726-4400); *Gulliver's*, 5 Adelaide St (☎722-0003); ranks outside the *Newfoundland Hotel*.

**Weather** ☎772-5534.

**Women's contacts** *Womens' Centre*, 83 Military Rd (☎753-0220).

## Around St John's: Cape Spear and Bay Bulls

It's a twenty-minute drive along route 11 from St John's to the rocky headland that makes up **Cape Spear National Historic Park**, often visited because it's nearer Europe than any other part of mainland North America. To cater for the tourists, the Cape is encirled by a winding walkway, an intrusive affair which connects all of the park's incidental attractions – the remains of a World War II gun emplacement and a couple of lighthouses.

Far more interesting is the trip to the straggling village of **Bay Bulls**, 30km southwest of St John's along route 10, sitting at the head of a deep and pointed bay that witnessed the surrender of one of the last active German U-boats in 1945 – much to the amazement of the local inhabitants, who watched from the shoreline. There's nothing to the place itself, but it's the base for two excellent **boat tour** operators, *Bird Island Charters*, beside the waterfront on Southside Road (☎753-4850), and *Gatheralls*, on Northside Road (☎334-2887). Between April and October, both companies run sea trips to the **Witless Bay Ecological Reserve**, three sea bird-covered islets just south of Bay Bulls. These trips depart eight times daily, last for two and a half hours and cost $25; reservations are recommended and *Bird Island Charters* will also provide transport from St John's for around $15. The best time to visit is between mid-June and mid-July when over five million birds gather here – the reserve has the largest puffin colony in eastern Canada and there are also thousands of storm-petrels, kittiwakes, razorbills, guillemots, cormorants and herring gulls. Humpback, fin and minke whales are often spotted in the area between June and August.

If you decide to **stay** in Bay Bulls, *Gatherall's Bed and Breakfast*, Northside Rd (May to mid-Oct; ☎334-2887), has three double rooms for $48. Nearby, the *First Choice Restaurant* has gooey cods' tongues and enormous plates of fish and chips for only $5.

# Around the Avalon Peninsula

St John's lies on the eastern shore of the **Avalon Peninsula**, a jagged, roughly rectangular slab of land that's connected to the rest of Newfoundland by a narrow isthmus. Concentrated around Conception Bay, whose eastern shoreline lies 15km west of the capital, the Avalon's settlements stick resolutely to the coast, hiding from a bare and rocky interior that received its ludicrous name when **George Calvert**, later Lord Baltimore, received a royal charter to colonise the region in 1623. Calvert subsequently became the victim of a confidence trick: the settlers he dispatched sent him such wonderful reports that he decided to move there himself. He only lasted one winter, writing to a friend – "I have sent [my family] home after much sufferance in this wofull country, where with one intolerable wynter were we almost undone. It is not to be expressed with my pen what wee have endured".

## Harbour Grace

Conception Bay's bonniest settlement is **HARBOUR GRACE** on its western shore, tucked in against route 70, 100km from the capital. This elongated village stretches out along another Water Street, which is at its prettiest near the northern end, where a handful of elegant clapboard houses and a handsome silver and green-spired church are set against a slender, rock-encrusted inlet. The old red-brick Customs House has been turned into a mildly entertaining **museum** (June–Aug daily 9am–5pm; free), featuring photos of the village and its Victorian inhabitants, and an outdoor plaque commemorating **Peter Easton**, the so-called "Pirate Admiral" who was based here at the start of the seventeenth century. Easton's phenomenally successful fleet was run by 5000 islanders, who made their leader rich enough to retire to a life of luxury in the south of France. Next door, the tiny park has a further plaque in honour of the early aviators who flew across the Atlantic from the Harbour Grace area, including **Amelia Earhart**, the first woman to complete the journey solo.

There's no reason to spend more than a couple of hours here, but if you decide to **stay** there's just one place, *Hunt's Hotel*, Water St (☎596-5156; doubles $60).

## Heart's Content

In the middle of the nineteenth century, **HEART'S CONTENT**, 30km northwest of Harbour Grace on the eastern shore of Trinity Bay, was packed with engineers attempting to connect North America with Britain by **telegraph cable**, a project that had begun when the *USS Niagara* hauled the first transatlantic line ashore here in 1858. However, after Queen Victoria and the American president James Buchanan had swapped inaugural jokes, the cable broke and it was eight years before an improved version, running from Valentia in Ireland, could be installed. Heart's Content became an important relay station to New York, a role it performed until technological changes made it obsolete in the 1960s. Squatting by the waterfront, in the centre of the village, the old **Cable Station** (June–Aug daily 9am–5pm; free) houses a series of displays on the history of telecommunications, including a replica of the original cable office and details of the problems encountered during the laying of the first telegraph lines.

Heart's Content is approached from Harbour Grace along route 74 or from the Trans-Canada Highway, 60km to the south, via route 80. The village is about 2km from the junction of routes 74 and 80, where the two double rooms of *Legge's Hospitality Home* (☎588-2577) cost $35, and the attached restaurant has reasonable fish and chips.

### Castle Hill National Historic Park and Cape St Mary's

The thumb-shaped promontory filling out the southwest corner of the Avalon Peninsula is a windswept wilderness trimmed by St Mary's and Placentia Bay. Its northern section is crossed by **route 100**, branching off the Trans-Canada Highway at WHITBOURNE, 80km from St John's, and as this is the main road to the ferry terminal at ARGENTIA, most people drive straight past the turning for the tiny **Castle Hill Park**, just 5km short of the port (mid-June to Aug daily 8.30am–8pm; Sept to mid-June daily 8.30am–5pm; free). This is a pity, because the park occupies a magnificent site overlooking a watery web of harbour, channel and estuary that combine to connect the fjord-like inlets of the South East Arm and North East Rivers with Placentia Bay.

The topography makes **Placentia Harbour** one of Newfoundland's finest anchorages, and its sheltered waters attracted the French, who in 1662 established PLAISANCE, their regional headquarters, here. Castle Hill was the area's key defensive position and so, as the fortunes of war see-sawed, it was successively occupied and refortified by the British and the French. Today, little remains of these works, just a few stone walls and ditches, but make the trip for the views and drop into the trim **Visitor Information Centre** (same times) for a useful account of the district's history.

Seen from the top of Castle Hill, the village of **PLACENTIA**, at the start of the road leading to Cape St Mary's, looks pretty enough, a ribbon of buildings sandwiched between the green of the hills and the blue of the bay. However, on closer inspection, the village is the most miserable of places and you're better off quickly continuing south for the fifty-kilometre drive to the tiny community of ST BRIDE'S. From here, it's a further 5km to the start of the fifteen-kilometre gravel track down to the lighthouse and information centre of the **Cape St Mary's Ecological Reserve**. The reserve is best visited between the middle of June and early August when hundreds of thousands of sea birds, principally gannets, kittiwakes, murres and razorbills, congregate on the rocky cliffs and stumpy sea-stacks along the shore. The main vantage point is about half an hour's walk from the lighthouse. St Bride's is the nearest village to Cape St Mary's and has one **place to stay**, the *Bird Island Motel* (☎337-2450; doubles $50).

# The Burin Peninsula

The 250-kilometre-long, bony **Burin Peninsula** juts south into the Atlantic between Fortune and Placentia Bay from the west side of the isthmus connecting the Avalon Peninsula with the rest of Newfoundland. It's crossed by route 210, a turning off the Trans-Canada about 160km from St John's, a road that starts promisingly with the melodramatic scenery of the **Piper's Hole River** estuary. After that, the journey becomes tedious, a long and dismal trip across an interior plateau of intimidating harshness. On the way, a side road leads down to the port of **Terrenceville**, where there's a fairly regular boat service along the south coast to Channel-Port aux Basques (see p.114), but the main reason for travelling the Burin is to catch the ferry to St-Pierre et Miquelon from **Fortune**, near its southern tip. From St John's, *Shirran's* (☎722-8032) run an irregular minibus service to Terrenceville ($35); for services to Fortune, see opposite.

## Grand Bank

Spreading out beside the sea 200km from the Trans-Canada, the older streets of **GRAND BANK** incorporate a charming assortment of late nineteenth-century timber houses, a few of which are equipped with the so-called "widow's walks", rooftop galleries where the women watched for their returning menfolk. Some of these houses are splendid, reflecting a time when the village's proximity to the Grand Banks fishing grounds brought tremendous profits to the shipowners, if not to the actual fishermen. Nowadays the fishery is in an acute state of decline, much to the frustration of local people, who apportion blame amongst a number of old enemies – foreigners who overfish, big marketing corporations who are indifferent to their interests, and a government that imposes unrealistic quotas. With many of its fishermen out of work, the future of Grand Bank looks grim, especially as many feel an inflexible affinity to the fishing that it's hard for outsiders to understand: as one of their representatives recently declared, "Without fish there is no soul, no pride, no nothing".

To see something of this tradition, visit the **Southern Newfoundland Seamen's Museum** (Mon–Fri 9am–4.45pm, Sat & Sun 10am–1pm & 2–5pm; free), situated in a modern building on the edge of the village – it has all sorts of models, paintings and photographs of different types of fishing boats, and a relief model of Newfoundland and the surrounding ocean that shows where the illustrious "Banks" actually are.

Grand Bank has one hotel, the *Thorndyke*, a fine old house at 33 Water Street (mid-June to Aug; ☎832-0820; doubles $35 with breakfast), but it may well be closing down. For **food**, the *Ocean Breeze Restaurant*, in between the centre and the museum, sells a substantial plate of fish and chips for $7.

## Fortune

**FORTUNE**, perched on the seashore a couple of kilometres from Grand Bank, is a slightly smaller village whose 2500 inhabitants are mostly employed in the fish processing plant and the inshore fishery. A modest and sleepy little place, it has one delightful **bed and breakfast**, the *Eldon House*, just up from the harbour at 56 Eldon Street (mid-June to Sept; ☎832-0442; doubles $40), and one reasonable **motel**, the *Fair Isle*, just back down the main road towards Grand Bank (☎832-1010; doubles $60). The *Fair Isle* also serves up superb **seafood**, at about $10 for a main course. For **campers** there's the *Horse Brook Trailer Park* (May–Sept; ☎832-1800) on the outskirts of the village, with unserviced sites for $4. The only public transport to the ferry from St John's is provided by *Richard Foote's* (☎364-1377), who operate a daily route to Grand Bank and Fortune ($27); and *SPM Tours Ltd* (☎722-3892), whose services coincide with the departure times of the *MV Arethusa*, one of two ferries running to St-Pierre (see below).

# St-Pierre et Miquelon

The tiny archipelago of **St-Pierre et Miquelon** became a fully fledged *département* of mainland France in 1976, giving a legalistic legitimacy to the billing of the islands as "a little bit of France at your doorstep" – a phrase that attracts several thousand visitors each year and manages to gloss over the lack of actual attractions and the wetness of the climate. Yet the islands are still worth a day or two for the francophone atmosphere of the main settlement, **ST-PIERRE**, whose fine restaurants and simple guesthouses have a genuinely European flavour. All but 700 of the 6500 islanders live in town, with the remainder marooned on Miquelon to the north – the third and middle island, **Langdale**, is uninhabited.

> The Saint-Pierre et Miquelon telephone code is ☎508.

## A brief history

The uninhabited islands of St-Pierre et Miquelon were claimed for the French king by **Jacques Cartier** in 1536. Subsequently settled by French fishermen, they were alternately occupied by Britain and France until the French finally lost their North American colonies in 1763, whereupon they were allowed to keep the islands as a commercial sop. St-Pierre et Miquelon soon became a vital supply base and safe harbour for the French fishing fleet, and provided France with a yearly harvest of salted cod.

After World War I, the French colonial authorities wanted to expand the local fishing industry, but their efforts became irrelevant with **Prohibition** in 1920. Quite suddenly, St-Pierre was transformed from a maritime backwater into a giant transit centre for booze smuggling – even the main fish-processing plant was stacked high with thousands of cases of whisky. It was an immensely lucrative business, but when Prohibition ended thirteen years later, the St-Pierre economy dropped through the floor. These were desperate days, but more misery followed during World War II, when the islands' governor remained controversially loyal to the **Vichy** regime. Both the Canadians and the Americans considered invading, but it was a **Free French** naval squadron that got here first, crossing over from their base in Halifax and occupying the islands without a shot being fired in late 1941.

There was further trouble in 1965 when a **stevedore's strike** forced the administration to resign. De Gaulle promptly dispatched the navy, who occupied the islands for no less than nine years. Perhaps surprisingly, the St-Pierrais remained largely loyal to France, and they certainly needed the support of Paris when the Canadians extended the limit of their territorial waters to 200 nautical miles in 1977. The ensuing wrangle between Canada and France over the islands' claim to a similar exclusion zone remains unresolved, although the tightening of controls on foreign vessels has largely ended St-Pierre's role as a supply centre.

## Arrival, information and getting around

The cheapest **flights** into the islands are from St John's on *Provincial Airlines* (three weekly; $230 return; ☎709/576-1666) and from Sydney, Nova Scotia, with *St-Pierre Airlines* (2–5 weekly; $160; ☎902/562-3140), but there are also regular connections with Halifax and Montréal. St-Pierre **airport** is located just south of town, and is connected by taxi to the centre (☎41.38.39).

Flights here are often delayed by fog and the **ferries** plying between Fortune and the town of St-Pierre are more dependable and far cheaper, though the crossing can get mighty rough. There are two ferries: *St Eugene* (mid-June to early Sept 4–7 weekly; 1hr; $29 single; ☎709/832-2006); and *MV Arethusa* (April to early Oct 2–7 weekly; 1hr 45min; $29 single; ☎709/738-1357). If you come by ferry, it usually means you have to stay the night, but about eight times each summer the *St Eugene* makes the return trip on the same day; the excursion fare is $43 per adult.

To clear St-Pierre et Miquelon's **customs control**, Canadians and citizens of the United States need only present an identity document such as a driver's licence or social security card; EC visitors need a passport. The islands' currency is the French franc, but Canadian dollars are widely accepted.

The **Office du Tourisme de St-Pierre et Miquelon**, on the waterfront at 1 quai de la République (May–Sept daily 9am–5pm; ☎41.22.22), has the timetables of the **ferries** which run from the town of St-Pierre to the village of Miquelon (July & Aug Tues, Fri & Sun 2 daily; 2hr; F120 return), and details of the excellent **boat and bus day-trips** that start in St-Pierre and then head north to cross between the islands of Langdale and Miquelon along the Dune of Langdale; reckon on about F230 per person for the entire excursion.

## The islands

The tidy, narrow streets of the town of **ST-PIERRE** edge back from the harbour fronted by a string of tall, stone buildings of quintessentially French demeanour. However, although the central area makes for an enjoyable stroll, there's nothing particular to aim for, with the possible exception of the **cathedral**, which does at least attempt to look imposing, and the tiny **museum**, on rue Dr-Henri-Dunan (daily 2–5pm), which provides a general historical background to the islands. Otherwise, it's easy to walk out into the surrounding countryside, passing bare hillocks and marshy ponds to reach the rugged cliffs of the northern shore, just 8km away.

At the north end of the archipelago, the dumpy-looking island of **Miquelon** is mostly peat bog and marsh, sloping west from its only village, which bears the same name. The island's pride and joy is the **Dune of Langdale**, a sweeping ten-kilometre sandy isthmus that connects with the middle island, **Langdale**. The Dune began to appear above the ocean two hundred years ago and it has continued to grow to its current width of up to 2500 metres. In heavy seas, parts of the Dune can be engulfed by sea water, so stick to the guided tours (see opposite), which stop at the **Grand Barachois**, a large saltwater pool at the northern end of the isthmus that's a favourite haunt of breeding seals.

## Practicalities

**St-Pierre** has a good selection of hotels and pensions, though reservations are strongly recommended from July to early September. The town's deluxe **hotels** include the *Hôtel Île de France*, 6 rue Maître Georges-Lefèvre (☎41.28.36; doubles F440), and the *Hôtel Robert*, quai de la République (☎41.24.19; F395). For **pensions**, which charge a fixed rate of F210 per double including breakfast, try the comfortable *Chez Marcel Hélène*, 15 rue Beaussant (☎41.31.08); *Chez Roland Vigneau*, 12 rue des Basques (☎41.38.67); or *L'Arc-en-Ciel*, 26 rue Jacques Cartier (☎41.25.69). The village of **Miquelon** has just one hotel and one pension: the *Hôtel l'Escale*, 24 rue Victor Briand (☎41.62.04; doubles F240); and *Chez Paulette*, 8 rue Victor Briand (☎41.62.15; doubles F225).

St-Pierre's **restaurants** are splendid, combining the best of French cuisine with local delicacies such as *tiaude*, a highly seasoned cod stew. Prices are quite high – reckon on about F70 for a main dish – but it really is worth splashing out at *La Ciboulette*, rue Marcel-Bonin, for nouvelle cuisine at its fanciest; at *Chez Dutin*, 20 rue Amiral-Muselier, for the salmon; or at *Chez Eric*, rue Boursaint, the place to try local specialities. If you're on a tight budget, stick to the **snack bars** or drop into *Le Maringouin'fre*, 22 rue Général-Leclerc, with its quality crêpes.

# The Bonavista Peninsula

The stumpy **Bonavista Peninsula**, crossed by route 230 – which leaves the Trans-Canada 190km west of St John's at Clarenville – is trimmed by lots of little outports which were first settled by the English in the seventeenth century.

**TRINITY**, 70km along the peninsula off the main road on route 239, is the most enchanting of these, a gem of a place whose narrow lanes are lined by delightfully restored pastel-coloured clapboard houses that reflect its importance as a supply centre during the 1800s. Sandwiched between a ring of hills and the sea, it also boasts the island's finest wooden church, **St Paul's Anglican Church**, whose graceful and dignified interior has a ceiling built to resemble an upturned boat. There's also a modest **Community Museum** (June–Aug daily 10am–4pm; free), in the saltbox house opposite St Paul's, with an eccentric collection of bygones, such as an old shoemaker's kit and an early cooperage. Nearby, the orange and green **Hiscock House** (same times) has been returned to its appearance circa 1910 when it served as a merchant's house; as ever, costumed guides give the background.

Trinity's early twentieth-century *Village Inn* (☎464-3269; doubles $50) is a great **place to stay**, its grand double beds and clapboard-lined rooms enough to make you forget the antiquated plumbing. The inn also has a good **restaurant** (mid-June to Sept only), where substantial, filling meals average out at about $14; after, you can stroll over to *Rocky's Place* for a drink. It's impossible to reach Trinity by **bus**, but the *CN Roadcruiser* drops passengers at the *Holiday Inn*, on the edge of Clarenville, and the waiting taxis charge $25 for the trip on to Trinity. Alternatively, *Newhook's Transportation*, in St John's, runs a twice daily minibus service to Bonavista village, which comes within 5km of Trinity at LOCKSTON, beside the junction of routes 230 and 239 – you'll have to walk or hitch from here.

## Whale-watching

Based at the *Village Inn* in Trinity, *Ocean Contact* (same number) run an extensive programme of **whale-watching** excursions, or rather, as they insist, whale "contact" trips designed to encourage close encounters between whales and humans. They can't guarantee contact, of course, but there is an excellent chance of sighting minke, fin and humpbacks, particularly between mid-June and early August. Expertly run, these excursions take place every day during the peak whale season, and prices begin at $40 for a half-day trip. If the sea is too rough for a boat trip, *Ocean Contact* provide escorted whale-watching walks along the nearby cliffs at half the price.

## Cape Bonavista

Some 55km north of Trinity, the red-and-white striped lighthouse on **Cape Bonavista** looks out over a violent coastline of dark gray rock and pounding sea. This beautifully desolate headland is supposed to be the spot where the British-sponsored Genoese explorer **John Cabot** first clapped eyes on the Americas in 1497. The tourist literature claims he exclaimed "Buono vista!" – "O, happy sight"; whatever the truth of the matter, a statue has been built here in his honour. The cape is 5km from the ugly and drab fishing village of Bonavista, a place to avoid.

# Terra Nova Park to Deer Lake

The **Trans-Canada Highway** is the only major road running along Newfoundland's central northern shore, slicing through Terra Nova National Park before connecting the towns of the interior – Gander, Grand Falls and Deer Lake – a distance of about 450km. Heading north from Clarenville along the Trans-Canada, it's about 40km to the southern entrance of the **Terra Nova National Park**, whose coniferous forests, ponds and marshes border the deeply indented coastline of southwest Bonavista Bay. It's a further 20km to the main **Visitor Information Centre** (daily mid-May to mid-Oct 10am–8pm; ☎533-2801), which sits by the highway 2km up the hill from the west end of the **Newman Sound** fjord. This spot serves as the park's principal tourist area with the full range of seasonal amenities, including a **campground**, grocery store, gas station and restaurant. Frankly, the tourist village is rather crass, but it does give ready access to several excellent **walking trails**, most notably the strenuous hike round the Sound to the rugged cliffs of **Mount Stamford**.

## Gander

The Trans-Canada leaves Terra Nova Park to sprint 70km to **GANDER**, an inconsequential town built around an airport, whose site was chosen by the British in the 1930s – they considered it ideal because it was far enough inland to escape Newfoundland's coastal fogs and near enough to Europe to facilitate the introduction of regular transatlantic flights. During World War II, the airport was a major staging point for American planes on their way to England and, since then, it has become the air traffic control centre for much of the northwest Atlantic. The airport is also a major stopover destination for incoming flights from Europe and, in the last few years, hundreds of refugees have decamped here to ask for political asylum. There's no reason to stop, but in emergencies the *Cape Cod Inn*, 66 Bennett Drive (☎651-2269), situated not far from the tourist chalet on the Trans-Canada, has pleasant double rooms for $55.

## Twillingate's icebergs

The myriad headlands and inlets around the northern outport of **TWILLINGATE**, 100km north of Gander along routes 330/331, ensnare dozens of **icebergs** as they drift down from the Arctic between June and mid-September. Tinted by reflections from the sea and sun, they can be wonderously beautiful and, if you're particularly lucky, you might witness the moment when one of them rolls over and breaks apart, accompanied by a tremendous grating, wheezing explosion. **Twillingate Island Boat Tours**, South Side, Twillingate (☎884-2242), run excellent two-hour iceberg-watching tours three times daily during the summer for $25 per person.

Again, there's no reason to stay here, but the best of the **accommodation** is the *Hillside Bed and Breakfast*, 5 Youngs Lane (June–Sept; ☎884-5761; doubles $40); for **food**, try the simple *R&J Restaurant*.

## Lewisporte

Ugly **LEWISPORTE**, just 11km from the Trans-Canada along route 340, is the terminal for the twice-weekly **ferry** to Goose Bay, in Labrador. The *CN Roadcruiser* bus from St John's drops you either at the *Irving Restaurant*, on the Trans-Canada 16km from the dock, or at the *Brittany Inn*, on the southern edge of Lewisporte, 3km from the dock. In either case, *Cyril's Taxis* (☎535-8100) will come and collect you, but the times of the buses don't usually tally with those of the boats, which mostly leave at mid-morning. Between September and the middle of November there's also a weekly **freighter/foot passenger ferry** from Lewisporte to St Anthony on the Northern Peninsula. In heavy weather this is a tumultuous journey, but it's a bargain at $70 for passage and a further $70 for a cabin (reservations essential, ☎535-6876). For overnight accommodation in Lewisporte, stick to the *Northgate Bed and Breakfast*, close to the ferry at 92 Main Street (☎535-2258; doubles $45).

## Grand Falls and Windsor

**GRAND FALLS**, 90km west of Gander, sits in the middle of some of the island's best stands of timber, an expanse of forest that has been intensively exploited ever since Alfred Harmsworth, later Lord Northcliffe, had a paper mill built here in 1905. Harmsworth, the founder of the *Daily Mirror* and the *Daily Mail*, funded the project to secure a reliable supply of newsprint well away from Europe, which he believed was heading towards war. It was an immensely profitable venture, which also established the first Newfoundland community sited, as one contemporary put it, "out of sight and sound of the sea". For many of the employees, recruited from the outports, it was the first time they had ever received a cash wage, though this particular pleasure was countered by some bitter management-union disputes. The worst was in 1959, when the Mounties broke a well-supported strike with appalling barbarity, at the behest of island premier, Joey Smallwood.

Grand Falls remains a company town, a singularly unprepossessing place built up around the hulking mass of the paper mill that towers over the Exploits River. Nevertheless, there is one surprise, the **Mary March Museum** on St Catherine Street (Mon–Fri 9am–4.45pm, Sat–Sun 10am–5.45pm; free), just to the south of the Trans-Canada where it separates Grand Falls and the adjacent township of **WINDSOR**. The museum has a good section on the history of the town and an intriguing series of displays on the Beothucks, including an explanation of the tragic story of Mary March, or Demasduit, who was captured near here in March 1819.

The **CN Roadcruiser Terminal**, on Main Street, Windsor, is about 2km north of the museum. The nearest accommodation to the station is the *Poplar Inn Bed and Breakfast*, 22 Poplar Rd (☎489-2546; doubles $40), 3km away to the southeast – walk straight down Catherine from the museum, then along Birch and it's on the left.

## Deer Lake and Corner Brook

**DEER LAKE**, 200km west of Grand Falls, lies at the start of route 430, the only road up to L'Anse aux Meadows, and has the nearest airport to Gros Morne National Park (see below), so if you fly in and hire a car at the airport, you miss the long trek across the island. There are regular reasonably priced flights in from St John's (from $134 return) and a clutch of **car hire** offices inside the terminal building: try *Budget* (☎635-3211); *Tilden* (☎635-3282); or *Avis* (☎635-3252).

At **CORNER BROOK**, 50km south of Deer Lake, the *CN Roadcruiser* stops at the bus station near the Trans-Canada, about 2km from the centre. From here, *City Cabs* (☎634-6565) or *Star Taxi* (☎634-4343) will take you down into town, where the Millbrook Shopping Mall stands near the stop for the *Viking Express* (☎634-4710) **bus**, the only service up the Northern Peninsula. The bus calls at Rocky Harbour (Mon–Fri 1 daily; $12) and St Anthony, for L'Anse aux Meadows (3 weekly; $41), but be warned that *Viking* do not have a reputation for punctuality and reliability, so always ring ahead to confirm schedules. If you get stuck, there's cheap and fairly central **accommodation** at *Power's Tourist Home*, 33 Main St (☎634-2048; doubles $30); the *Delightful Guest Home*, 1 Elswick Rd (☎634-2165; doubles $35); or, just down the road at no. 22, the *Stoneway Hospitality Home* (June–Sept; ☎634-2730; doubles $38).

# The Northern Peninsula

Stretching between Deer Lake and the township of St Anthony, a distance of about 450km, the **Northern Peninsula** is a rugged and sparsely populated finger of land whose interior is dominated by the spectacular **Long Range Mountains**, a chain of flat-topped peaks punctuated by the starkest of glacier-gouged gorges above the bluest of lakes – or "ponds" as the locals incongruously call them. Most of the region remains inaccessible to all except the most experienced of mountaineers, but **route 430** – whose bus services are so poor that it's hard to manage without a car – trails along the length of the peninsula, connecting the insignificant fishing villages of the narrow coastal plain with the remains of the Norse colony at **L'Anse aux Meadows**.

## Gros Morne National Park

The southern section of the Long Range Mountains, beginning about 35km from Deer Lake and bordering the Gulf of St Lawrence, has been set aside as the **Gros Morne National Park**, some 1800 square kilometres of the peninsula's finest and most approachable scenery. The bays, scrawny beaches, straggling villages and sea-stacks of the littoral are set against bare-topped, fjord-cut mountains, whose forested lower slopes are home to moose, woodland caribou and snowshoe hare. The best place to start a tour is the **Visitor Information Centre** (daily July & Aug 9am–10pm; Sept–June 9am–5.30pm; ☎458-2066), situated beside route 430 as it approaches Rocky Harbour just 70km from Deer Lake. The centre has a series of excellent displays on the geology, botany, biology and human history of the park, issues free maps, brochures on Gros Morne's key hiking trails and boat excursions, and runs a programme of guided walks. If you intend to use one of the park's free primitive **campsites**, which are dotted along the longer trails, then you have to register here first.

## Rocky Harbour

It's a couple of minutes' drive from the visitor centre to **ROCKY HARBOUR**, the park's largest and most felicitous village, which curves around a long and sweeping bay with the mountains lurking in the background. Although there's nothing special to do or see here, the long walk round to the **Lobster Head Cove Lighthouse** is a pleasant way to spend an afternoon. Rocky Harbour is also near several of Gros Morne's **hiking trails**, notably the lung-bursting 16km of the *James Callaghan Trail*, curiously named after the British ex-prime minister. The trail begins beside route 430, just 7km east of the village, and climbs to the top of Gros Morne Mountain where, at 806m above sea level, the views are stupendous. If you decide to stay on the mountain overnight, there's a primitive **campsite** on the way down from the summit.

Rocky Harbour is the best place to stay in the park, not least because it's relatively compact and has a reasonable range of tourist facilities. **Accommodation** includes the comfortable *Ocean View Motel*, beside the waterfront (☎458-2730; doubles $54); *Bottom Brook Cottages*, Main St (☎458-2236; doubles $58); and *Parson's Harbour View Cabins and Hospitality Home*, near the waterfront (☎458-2544; doubles $40). In all cases, advance bookings are recommended in July and August. The nearest **campground** is at **Berry Hill**, 3km north of Rocky Harbour along route 430. For **food**, the restaurant of the *Ocean View Motel* serves excellent seafood dishes for around $12; the nearby *Fisherman's Landing Restaurant* is a mundane second best.

## Bonne Bay, Woody Point and the Tablelands

**BONNE BAY**, just along the coast from Rocky Harbour, sits at the mouth of a great gash that slices inland from the Gulf of St Lawrence framed by the severest of mountains. Most of the park's villages lie on the shore of the fjord and it's possible to drive right round, but you're better off heading for **NORRIS POINT**, 9km from Rocky Harbour, where a **ferry** (June to early Sept every 2hr 8am–6pm; $3 per person, $11 per car and driver) crosses the neck of the bay to minuscule **WOODY POINT**, which has a pleasant guesthouse, the *Victorian Manor Hospitality Home* (☎453-248; doubles $45). Close by, there's also the grim *Stornoway Lodge* (☎453-2282), with motel-style doubles for $52, and the small and basic *Woody Point Youth Hostel* (June–Sept; ☎453-2442; $10).

Heading west from Woody Point along route 431, it's 4km to the start of the **Tablelands Hiking Trail**, a four-kilometre circular track that cuts across a forbidding area of bare and barren rock, and another 8km to the **Green Gardens Trail**, which twists its way to some secluded coves, caves and sea-stacks – a nine-kilometre loop equipped with three primitive campgrounds. Continuing down the road, it's a further 4km to **Trout River Pond**, sandwiched by the yellowed bareness of the Tablelands and the massive cliffs bordering the Gregory Plateau. The views here are splendid and the best way to see the lake is on the **Tablelands Boat Tour** (early June to early Sept 3 daily; $23; ☎451-2101).

## Western Brook Pond

**Western Brook Pond**, reached by just one access point, 25km north of Rocky Harbour beside route 430, is one of eastern Canada's finest landscapes, 16km of deep, dark-blue water framed by mighty mountains and huge waterfalls. From the access point it's a forty-minute walk to the edge of the lake's gorge along the **Western Brook Pond Trail**, which crosses the narrow coastal plain. When you get to the end don't skimp on the **boat trip** – weather permitting, they run three or four times daily in July and August, once or twice daily in the shoulder season ($25; ☎458-2730). Western Brook Pond also boasts a couple of extremely difficult hiking trails, the 27-kilometre **Snug Harbour-North Rim** route, which branches off from the main path between the road and the pond; and the 35-kilometre **Long Range Mountains** trail at the eastern end of the pond. Both these tracks have primitive campsites – advice and permits from the information centre. If you're without a car, *Pittman's Taxis* in Norris Point (☎458-2486) will take you from Rocky Harbour to the access point for $25.

# Port au Choix

The tiny fishing village of **PORT AU CHOIX**, 160km from Rocky Harbour, sits on a bleak headland beside the **Port au Choix National Historic Park** (mid-June to Aug daily 9am–6pm; free), established where a mass of prehistoric bones, tools and weapons were accidentally discovered in the 1960s. The ensuing archaeological dig unearthed three ancient cemeteries, confirming the area as a centre of settlement for the Maritime Archaic People, hunters and gatherers who lived here around 2000 BC. The nearby **Visitor Information Centre** (same times), opposite the fish-processing plant, provides the background, but it's all pretty speculative stuff and the scant remains of this and the later Dorset Eskimo culture are hardly awe-inspiring. Port au Choix area has a handful of **accommodation**: try the *Jean-Marie Guest House* (☎861-3023; doubles $45), or the *Sea Echo Motel* (☎861-3777; doubles $54).

# St Anthony – and the Norse village

Pressing on from Port au Choix, it's about 80km to the hamlet of ST BARBE, where there's a twice-daily summer **ferry** service across the Strait of Belle Isle to BLANC-SABLON, on the Québec-Labrador boundary (☎722-4000; see p.212). From St Barbe, route 430 slips through a handful of fishing villages before cutting east across the peninsula for the fishing and supply centre of **ST ANTHONY**. With a population of 3500, this is the region's largest settlement, but it's not much more than a dreary port stretched out around the wide sweep of its harbour, the only recompense being the remains of the Norse village at L'Anse aux Meadows, 42km away (see below). In town, the one meagre attraction is the **Grenfell House Museum** (June–Aug daily 9am–5pm; $1), the restored home of the pioneering missionary doctor, Sir Wilfred Grenfell, who first came here on behalf of the Royal National Mission to the Deep Sea Fishers in 1892. He never moved back home and, during his forty-year stay, he established the region's first proper hospitals, nursing stations, schools and cooperative stores.

### Practicalities

There are daily **flights** to St Anthony from most of Newfoundland's larger settlements and from several of eastern Canada's main cities. The **airport** is near Hare Bay, a few kilometres to the south of town, and onward transportation to the centre is by taxi only – reckon on $20. Otherwise, *Viking Express* runs a **bus** service (see p.110), and there's a weekly **ferry** from Lewisporte (see p.109). For central **accommodation** there's *Howell's Tourist Home*, 76B East St (☎454-3402; doubles $35); the *St Anthony Motel*, 14 Goose Cove Rd (☎454-3200; doubles $65); and the *Vinland Motel*, West St (☎454-8843; doubles $60–90).

Unfortunately, there are no public transport connections between St Anthony and L'Anse aux Meadows, and the return taxi fare will cost you about $60. Alternatively, *Tilden*, next door to the *St Anthony Motel* (☎454-8522), has reasonably priced, short-term car rental deals.

### L'Anse aux Meadows

**L'Anse aux Meadows National Historic Park** (daily dawn–dusk), comprising the scant remains of the earliest verified European settlement in the Americas, is a tribute to the obsessive drive of **Helge Instad**, the Norwegian who hunted high and low to find Norse settlements on the North Atlantic seaboard from 1960. His efforts were inspired by two medieval Icelandic sagas, which detailed the establishment of the colony of **Vinland** somewhere along this coast in about 1000 AD.

At L'Anse aux Meadows, Instad was led by a local to a group of grassed-over bumps and ridges beside Epaves Bay. This unremarkable area, next to a water-logged peat bog, contained the remnants of the only **Norse village** ever to have been discovered in America – the foundations of eight turf and timber buildings and a rag-bag of archaeological finds, including a cloak pin, a stone anvil, nails, pieces of bog-iron, an oil lamp, and a small spindle whorl.

The site was thoroughly excavated between 1961 and 1968 and there followed an acrimonious academic debate about whether it was actually "Vinland". The geographical clues provided in the sagas are extremely vague, so the argument is essentially linguistic, hinging on the various possible interpretations of the old Icelandic word "Vinland", with one side insisting that it means "Wine-land" and therefore cannot refer to anywhere in Newfoundland, the other suggesting the word means "fertile land" and therefore it could be.

Whatever the truth of the matter, hundreds of tourists come here every summer and begin their tour at the **Visitor Reception Centre** (mid-June to Aug daily 9am–8pm), where the Norse artefacts and changing exhibitions on Viking life and culture are beefed up by an excellent if somewhat melodramatic film entitled *The Vinland Mystery*. From here it's a few minutes' walk to the cluster of gentle mounds that make up what's left of the original village and another short stroll to a group of full-scale replicas of a long house, a forge and an animal shed.

Most people use St Anthony as a base for visiting L'Anse aux Meadows, but if you're travelling by car it's also worth considering a stay at the **Tickle Inn** (June–Sept; reservations essential on ☎452-4321; doubles $45), an attractive late nineteenth-century house located at remote **Cape Onion**. The Cape is approached along route 437, a rough gravel track about 25km long that branches off from route 436, the main road between St Anthony and L'Anse aux Meadows.

## VINLAND AND THE VIKINGS

The first **Viking** voyages, in the eighth century, had no wider purpose than the plunder of their Scandinavian neighbours, but by the start of the ninth century overpopulation at home had pushed them towards migration and colonisation. By 870 they had settled on the shores of Iceland and by the start of the eleventh century there were about 3000 Norse colonists established in Greenland. As good farmland became scarce, so it was inevitable that there would be another push west.

The two **Vinland sagas** – the *Graenlendinga* and *Eirik's Saga* – give us the only extant account of these further explorations, recounting the exploits of Leif Eriksson the Lucky and Thorfinn Karlsefni, his brother-in-law, who founded a colony they called **Vinland** in North America around 1000 AD. Although eventually forced to abandon Vinland by relentless threats from the local peoples – whom they called *skraelings*, literally "wretches" – the Norse settlers continued to secure resources from the region for the next few decades, and it seems likely that the site discovered at **L'Anse aux Meadows** is the result of one of these foragings.

The Norse carried on collecting timber from Labrador up until the fourteenth century when a dramatic deterioration in the climate made the trip from Greenland too dangerous. Attacks from the Inuit and the difficulties of maintaining trading links with Scandinavia then took their toll on the main Greenland colonies. All contact between Greenland and the outside world was lost around 1410 and the last of the half-starved, disease-ridden survivors died out towards the end of the fifteenth century – when Christopher Columbus was eyeing up his "New World".

# Channel-Port aux Basques and the south

**CHANNEL-PORT AUX BASQUES** sits by the ocean right in the southwest corner of Newfoundland, serving as the region's fishing and transportation centre, with regular ferry connections to North Sydney in Nova Scotia, and a daily bus service to St John's, twenty-five hours' drive away. The town divides into two distinct sections, an older part stuck on a bare and bumpy headland behind the ferry terminal, and a newer section spread out around Grand Bay Road, about 2km to the west.

Apart from the ferries, there's no possible reason to come here, but in emergencies it's useful to know that the place has a clutch of reasonably priced **accommodation**. Walking out of the ferry port, turn left towards the old part of town, along Caribou Street, where you'll find the *Heritage Home Bed and Breakfast*, 11 Caribou Rd (May–Oct; ☎695-3240; doubles $40), and *Walker's Motel*, just off Caribou on Marine Drive (☎695-7355; doubles $65). Alternatively, in the newer part of town, there's the *Caribou Bed and Breakfast*, 30 Grand Bay Rd (May–Oct; ☎695-3408; doubles $45), which is near the *Hotel Port aux Basques* (☎695-2171; doubles $64) and the *Grand Bay Motel* (☎695-2105; doubles $55). Driving out of town along the Trans-Canada, the **tourist information chalet** (mid-May to Aug daily 6am–10pm & Sept–Oct daily 7am–9pm; ☎695-2262) has a range of literature about the whole of Newfoundland.

## The south coast

The submerged rocks and jutting headlands of Newfoundland's **south coast** have witnessed the shipwreck of hundreds of vessels as they attempted to steer round the island into the Gulf of St Lawrence, some running aground in a fog bank, others driven ashore by tremendous gales. Such was the frequency of these disasters that many outports came to rely on washed-up timber for firewood and building materials, a bonus for communities all too dependent on the trade price of fish. The flotsam and jetsam days are long gone, but the south coast remains one of the poorer parts of Newfoundland, an isolated region where most of the tiny villages remain accessible only by sea. If you're after seeing a slice of traditional outport life, then this is the nearest you'll come, though it's difficult to select one place over another. Most have simple **guesthouses**, which provide all your meals and a bed for around $30 per day; there are usually lists of them at the Channel-Port aux Basques tourist information chalet, but if they're out of stock, ring the *Penguin Area Development Association* in Burgeo (☎886-2867); advance reservations are strongly advised.

The **CN Coastal Boat Service** (May to mid-June & mid-Sept to Nov 2 weekly; mid-June to mid-Sept & Dec–April 3 weekly; ☎695-7081), leaving from the dock next to the Nova Scotia ferry terminal in Channel-Port aux Basques, runs along the south coast to Terrenceville, 260 nautical miles away, calling at whichever outports require a call. Passengers are charged 16¢ per nautical mile. In the summer, the trip is by a **motor launch** that nips along at about 18 knots, but in the winter the traditional **boat** is far slower. There are too many imponderables to be precise about times, but in the summer reckon on about 18 hours for the entire one-way trip between Channel-Port aux Basques and Terrenceville, though the boat often overnights at BURGEO or HERMITAGE. None of the outports have other onward transportation.

One of the prettier outports is **RAMEA**, perched on a tiny island stuck out in the ocean near Burgeo, 83 nautical miles from Channel-Port aux Basques. There's guesthouse accommodation here with *John Fudge* (☎842-3191); *Harvey Baggs* (☎842-3226); and *Gladys Marsden* (☎842-3486). A second attractive spot is FRANCOIS, 40 nautical miles further east, an ancient settlement sitting precariously under the steep slopes of the Frior Mountain – you can lodge here with *Russel Hatcher* (☎625-2719) or *Clyde Pink* (☎625-2708).

# LABRADOR

**LABRADOR**, 292,220 square kilometres of sub-arctic wilderness on the northeastern edge of the Canadian Shield, is a place so desolate that it provoked Jacques Cartier to remark "I am rather inclined to believe that this is the land God gave to Cain". **Goose Bay**, located on the westernmost tip of the huge Hamilton Inlet, has an average maximum temperature of -16°C/3°F in January and an annual snowfall of 445cm, much of which remains on the ground for half the year. Further inland and up north the climate is even worse. Just 29,000 people live here, concentrated in coastal villages that are linked by weekly ferry, and inland mining areas that have only received road access in the last five years – the road from Labrador City to Goose Bay was completed in 1991.

This desolate terrain has long been a bone of contention between Québec and Newfoundland, whose current **common border** was set in the 1920s by the Privy Council when it ordained that Newfoundland had jurisdiction not just over the undisputed northern shore – the traditional domain of Newfoundland fishermen – but also

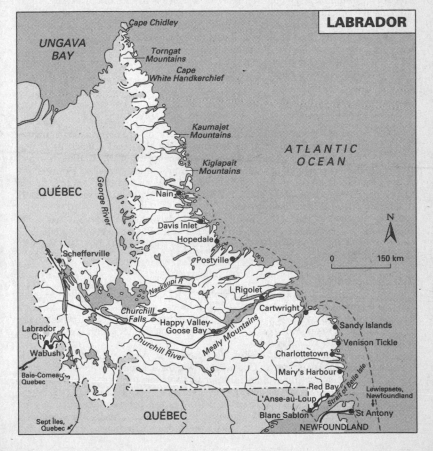

over the central Labrador plateau, from which the north shore's rivers drained. Newfoundland's territory was expanded by some 292,219 square kilometres, twice the size of the island itself, whilst Québec was left ranting about anglophone imperialism. The border again became a problem in 1961, when it was decided to develop the hydro-electric potential of Labrador's Churchill Falls, a project which required Québec's participation, as Québec would have to buy some of the electricity if it were to be a viable scheme, and the power lines would encroach on its land as well. Eventually a compromise was reached whereby Newfoundland could receive Labrador's power via a toll-free route through Québec, in return for which Québec could tap the headwaters of five rivers in southern Labrador. However, the Québécois remain indignant about their loss of territory and the issue is likely to be debated again as they move towards separation.

The original owners of this land, the Naskapi and Inuit, who collectively number around 4000, were more or less left alone until the last few decades, when the economic potential of Labrador was realised. Dams and mines have disrupted the local ecology – the Labrador Trough in western Labrador has the highest concentration of iron ore in North America – but even more destructive is the use of the area by Dutch, British and German air forces to practise wartime drills and bombing raids. Inuits have been imprisoned for staging sit-ins and chaining themselves to the gates of the Goose Bay air base, which is built on their land, and do not intend to halt the protests until the low-level sorties (up to 10,000 a year) and bombings are halted. With the demise of the Cold War this may well happen soon, and Canada's minister of defence recently hinted that it may be shut down in 1995.

# Practicalities

Labrador is one of Canada's most forbidding areas, so any trip needs a fair amount of organisation, and a great deal if you are heading for the hinterland – it is perhaps best to opt for one of the various tours available (see box opposite) which, though expensive, make the exploration of Labrador's wilds as trouble-free as possible. However you go it's important to take the strongest fly ointment you can find (workers in Labrador carry emergency syringes of the stuff) and heavy winter clothing, as even in the height of summer savage snowstorms can occur.

Maps, timetables and other **information** is available in advance from *The Department of Development Tourism Branch*, PO Box 8730, St John's, Newfoundland (☎576-2830) or the *Department of Development and Tourism*, PO Box 490, Wabush, Labrador (☎282-5600).

### Getting to Labrador

Labrador has **airports** at Goose Bay, Wabush and Churchill Falls, with scheduled services by *Inter-Canadian* (☎1-800-361-0200) from various points in Québec and regular flights by *Canadian Airlines* from Newfoundland (☎1-800-565-1800). Expect to pay around $500 for a return Montréal to Wabush flight, half that for a flight from St John's and Deer Lake in Newfoundland.

Less expensive are the **ferries from Newfoundland**. A ninety-minute ride from St Barbe Bay, 96km north of Port au Choix, takes you the 31km across the Strait of Belle Isle to Blanc-Sablon, on the southern border of Labrador; the ferry runs twice a day from May to December, and is operated by *Puddister Trading Company* (☎722-4000; adult $15.70 return, car $31.50). To get into the heart of Labrador, there's a 34-hour ferry trip on the *Sir Robert Bond* from Lewisporte to Goose Bay, run by *Marine Atlantic* of North Sydney, Nova Scotia; it runs twice a week from early June to mid-September

(☎1-800-563-7701 from Newfoundland, ☎1-800-565-9411 from Ontario and Québec; adults $68.75 one way, cars $110.25; single cabins $34 per night, doubles $68). *Marine Atlantic* also runs two foot-passenger steamships from Lewisporte: the *Northern Ranger* and the *MV Taverner*, which visit numerous coastal settlements in Labrador from June to November, usually travelling as far north as Nain. Sailing at weekly intervals on average, they take two weeks to complete a return journey from Lewisporte to Nain, and it is possible to travel just a segment of the journey; rates are 18¢ per nautical mile plus the cost of a cabin, which is $65 per night for a double.

The 416-kilometre **rail** line that links Sept-Îles in Québec to Labrador City and Schefferville is primarily an industrial link, but there is limited space for passengers and the journey is an exhilarating ride over high bridges, through dense forest and stunted tundra, past seventy-metre waterfalls, deep gorges and rocky mountains – a special dome car allows passengers to appreciate this awesome land. Trains for Labrador City leave Sept-Îles every Monday and Thursday and take around eight hours ($82.55 return); a fourteen-hour train leaves for Schefferville every Thursday ($113.15 return). Contact the *Québec North Shore and Labrador Railway* (☎944-8205 or ☎514/871-1331) for reservations.

It is possible to **drive** to Labrador from Québec via the new 600-kilometre route 389 from Baie Comeau to Labrador City and Wabush. As yet there are no services on this stretch of road, so you will need petrol and food for the journey. There are rumours of a planned bus service – contact the station in Baie Comeau for the latest (☎418/296-2593).

## SPECIALIST TOUR COMPANIES

**Drover's Labrador Adventures**, PO Box 121, Labrador City, Labrador A2V 2K3 (☎944-6947). Outfitters for hiking and canoe expeditions in Labrador (April–Dec) and snowmobile tours (Dec–April), from $250 per day.

**Eastern Edge Outfitters**, Box 13981, Station A, St John's, Newfoundland A2B 4G8 (☎368-9720). Day long, weekend and ten-day sea kayak expeditions to the wilds of northern Labrador. Around $200 a day including all equipment and food as well as hotel accommodation for first and last days of tours.

**Inuilak Labrador**, North West River, Labrador A0P 1M0 (☎497-8326).

Wilderness tours lasting up to two weeks and costing from around $150 a day. May–Oct & March–April.

**Labrador Adventure**, PO Box 86, Churchill Falls, Labrador A0R 1A0 (☎925-3235). Four- and six-day tours in various areas of Labrador from $200 a day, with all accommodation, food and transportation included.

**Sobek Expeditions**, 159c Main St, Unionville, Ontario L3R 2GB (☎416/479-2600). Sea kayak expeditions in the more northerly regions of Labrador. Around $2000 for a two-week trip, including all necessary equipment, food and accommodation.

## Getting around Labrador

With the exception of the rail line that terminates at Schefferville, there is no land-based public transport in Labrador, and the new unpaved road linking Goose Bay to Labrador City via Churchill Falls can be used just in summer. The only other road is the 81-kilometre route 510 which runs north from Blanc-Sablon to Red Bay. For non-drivers, or for those who want to reach the far-off outposts, there are **internal flights** run by *Labrador Airways* in Goose Bay (☎896-3387), the return trip from Goose Bay to Nain costing around $260. Alternatively, but more expensive, are the coastal services of the *Northern Ranger* or *MV Taverner* steamships (see above).

# Blanc-Sablon to Red Bay

The car ferry from St Barbe in Newfoundland across the Strait of Belle Isle to Blanc-Sablon makes it possible to explore the coastal settlements along route 510 to Red Bay, then return to Newfoundland on the second boat of the day – a possibility which more tourists exploit every year. The trip over is an experience in itself, with the vessel dwarfed by icebergs floating down the Strait from Greenland, and minke and humpback whales a constant sight.

This coast has been inhabited for over 9000 years, first by caribou-hunters, then Vikings and Basque whalers, but permanent settlements did not evolve until the turn of the eighteenth century when fishermen from Newfoundland began summer migrations to these well-stocked waters. Those that chose to live here all year were known in Newfoundland as "livyers" and led terribly harsh lives under the control of the English merchants' corrupt truck system and the supplies of alcohol that kept them in a constant state of debt. Their standard of living was greatly improved by Wilfred Grenfall, the superintendent of the Mission to Deep Sea Fishermen in 1890, who established hospitals, orphanages and nursing stations all along the coast, and succeeded in bringing the truck system to an end. The livyers, incidentally, were the first to train **Labrador retrievers**, which were trained catch any fish that fell off the hook.

Villages such as L'ANSE-AU-LOUP, CAPSTAN ISLAND and WEST ST MODESTE are the descendants of the fishing camps that huddled against eastern Labrador's cliffs. Though the only sight that might detain you is the **Labrador Straits Museum** (May–Dec daily 8am–6pm; $1) between Forteau and L'Anse-au-Loup, the only places to stay on the east coast are along this strip south of Red Bay – *Beachside Hospitality Home* (☎931-2662; doubles $38) and the *Northern Lights Inn*, (☎931-2332; doubles $58–68), both in L'Anse-au-Clair, only 8km from the ferry terminal; *Seaview Housekeeping Units* (☎931-2840; doubles $58), in Forteau, the next settlement northeast; and *Barney's Hospitality Home* (☎927-5634; doubles $33) in L'Anse-au-Loup.

## Red Bay

**RED BAY**, terminus of route 510, was the largest **whaling port** in the world in the late sixteenth century and is the most worthwhile visit on the east coast. At its peak over a thousand men lived here during the whaling season, producing half a million gallons of whale oil to be shipped back on a month-long voyage to Europe. Whale oil was used for light, lubrication and as an additive to drugs, soap and pitch, and one 55-gallon barrel could fetch a price equal to $10,000 today – so for the **Basques** the discovery of Labrador's right whale stocks was equivalent to striking oil. However, as well as the treacherous journey from Spain to what they knew as Terranova, the Basques withstood terrible hardships to claim their rich booty. Once in Labrador, they rowed fragile wooden craft called *chalupas* into these rough seas and then attached drogues to the whales to slow them down. It was then a matter of following their prey for hours until the whale surfaced and could be lanced to death. Three factors brought the whale boom to an end: first, the Basques were so successful that within thirty years they had killed off more than 15,000 whales; second, the industry became more hazardous with early freeze-ups in the 1570s; and finally, the Basque ships and men were absorbed into the ill-fated Spanish Armada of 1588.

Serious study of this fascinating area began in 1977 when marine archaeologists discovered the remains of three Basque galleons and several *chalupas*. Most notable of these vessels was the *San Juan* galleon, which was split in half by an iceberg in 1565, with the loss of one black rat – its bones were found in a wicker basket with a scattering of codfish bones which showed that the heading and splitting techniques were identical to those used by the Labrador fishermen today. On land, excavations uncovered tryworks (where the whale blubber was boiled down into oil), personal artefacts and, in 1982, a cemetery on Saddle Island where the remains of 160 young men were found. Many were lying in groups, indicating that they died as crew members when chasing the whales, but some had not been buried – which may show that the community had died of starvation when an early freeze dashed their chances of getting home.

New objects are constantly being discovered and a new **visitors' centre** (mid-June to Sept Mon–Sat 8am–8pm, Sun noon–8pm; free) allows you to explore the archaeological sites, including a boat trip to Saddle Island (Mon–Sat 3 daily). An excellent hour-long documentary film at the centre shows footage of the discovery that revealed so much about Canada's early history.

# Northern Labrador

So far, the north is the most untouched area of Labrador, a region where the nomadic Inuit and Naskapi have managed to escape the clutches of modern Canadian society – though the production of souvenirs such as the soapstone carvings available all over Canada is now an intrinsic part of their economy. Few visitors venture this far: once you've reached **GOOSE BAY** from Lewisporte on the *Sir Robert Bond* or the slower steamships, it takes a further three and a half days for the latter to reach their northerly limit of Nain ($85 per person one way, plus $65 for a double cabin per night) – and a sudden storm can leave you stranded for days in one of the tiny settlements. If you have to wait for the ships in Goose Bay, **accommodation** is available at the *Aurora Hotel*, 132 Hamilton River Rd (☎896-3398; doubles $97); the *Royal Inn*, 5 Royal Ave (☎896-2456; doubles $65); and the *Labrador Inn*, Station C (☎896-3351; doubles $68–86).

Most of the coastal villages beyond Goose Bay began as fur-trading posts in the nineteenth century, though some date back to the eighteenth-century establishment of missions by the Moravian Brethren, a small German missionary sect. Their old mission still stands at HOPEDALE (150km south of Nain) and at **NAIN** the mission has been converted into a museum called **Piulimatsivik** – Inuit for "place where we keep the old things" (year-round by appointment ☎922-2810). From Nain you can travel onwards to the flat-topped **Torngat Mountains**, the highest range east of the Rockies; contact *Nunatsuak Limited* at the *Atsankik Lodge* (☎922-2910; doubles $68), who charter boats for up to five people at $600 a day. They will take you wherever you want to go and pick you up when you have finished exploring but you need all your own equipment. An astounding trip is to the **Nachvak Fjord**, near Labrador's northernmost extremity, where the Razorback Mountains soar out of the sea at an angle of nearly eighty degrees to a height of 915 metres. En route you're likely to spot grey seals, whales, peregrine falcons and golden eagles.

# Labrador City, Wabush and Schefferville

From Goose Bay it is also possible in the summer months to drive across to Labrador City via Churchill Falls on the Trans-Labrador Highway – one of the least frequented stretches of road in eastern Canada, so take all necessary supplies, including petrol, with you.

Rising from a spring high on the Labrador plateau, the **Churchill River** plunges through the Beaudoin Canyon and in a space of 32 kilometres drops 300 metres – 75 metres of which are accounted for by the **Churchill Falls**, about 240km west of Goose

Bay. In order to exploit the massive power of this tumult, an area three and a half times the size of Lake Ontario was dammed for the incredible Churchill Falls hydro-electric development, a project conceived by Joey Smallwood in 1952 as part of a drive to save Newfoundland's economy, whose only industrial plant at that time was a small copper mine on the northeast coast. Wrangling with possible US backers and then with the Québec government delayed its commencement until 1967, when a workforce of 30,000 finally began the largest civil engineering project in North America. The town of **CHURCHILL FALLS** is simply an outgrowth of the power plant; if you want to stay here for a long look at the falls – which are half as high again as Niagara – **accommodation** and **food** are available at the *Churchill Falls Inn* (☎925-3211; doubles $79).

A further 200km west it's a shock to come across **LABRADOR CITY** and neighbouring WABUSH, two planned mining communities of wide streets and a couple of malls in the middle of nowhere. Labrador City, as a terminus of the **rail line** from Sept-Îles, is a convenient gateway into Labrador's hinterland, but little else will bring you here. If you want to stay, **accommodation** is available at the *Carol Inn*, 215 Drake Ave (☎944-7736; doubles $85), and the *Two Seasons Inn* on Avalon Drive (☎944-2661; doubles $82).

When the *IOC* mining operation opened the first Labrador iron-ore mine in the 1950s at **SCHEFFERVILLE** – the other rail terminus, 190km beyond Labrador City – they recruited a band of migratory Naskapi as cheap labour, so beginning a particularly woeful episode in the history of Canada's native peoples. In 1978 the natives signed an agreement giving them compensation for their lost land and exclusive hunting and fishing rights, but by that time the majority were so debilitated by alcohol that a return to their former existence was impossible. When the mine closed in the late 1980s, the Naskapi were left to fend for themselves while the white workers moved on to employment in other mines. Schefferville is now a run-down, blackfly-ridden reserve where houses can be bought for less than $10. Lying just over the border in Québec, the town is essentially a dead-end spot and only worth visiting for the spectacular rail journey from Sept-Îles, and the only **accommodation** is the *Hôtel-Motel Royal*, 182 rue Montagnais (☎585-2605; doubles $66–103).

## travel details

### Trains
**From Labrador City** to Sept-Îles (2 weekly; 8hr).
**From Schefferville** to Sept-Îles (1 weekly; 14hr).

### Buses
**From St John's** to Clarenville/Lewisporte/Grand Falls/ Corner Brook/ Channel-Port aux Basques (1–2 daily; 2hr 30min/ 5hr 30min/ 6hr 15min/ 9hr 50min/ 13hr 50min).

### Ferries
**From Lewisporte** to Goose Bay (mid-June to early Sept 2 weekly; 34hr); Nain, via Labrador north shore ports (mid-June to mid-Nov weekly; 7 days).

**From Channel-Port aux Basques** to Terrenceville (May to mid-June & mid-Sept to Nov 2 weekly; mid-June to mid-Sept & Dec–April 3 weekly; 18hr); North Sydney, Nova Scotia (Sept to mid-April 1 daily; mid-April to May 3 daily; June–Aug 6 daily; 5hr–7hr 30min).
**From Argentia** to North Sydney, Nova Scotia (June–Oct 2 weekly; 14hr).
**From St Barbe** to Blanc-Sablon (May–Dec 2 daily; 2hr).

### Flights
**From Goose Bay** to St John's (5 weekly; 2hr); Deer Lake/St John's (1 daily; 1hr 20min/2hr 20min); Deer Lake/Halifax/Charlottetown (daily;

1hr 20min/3hr 10min/3hr 45min); Churchill Falls/ Wabush/Québec/Montréal (1 weekly; 45min/1hr 15min/3hr 25min/4hr).

**From Wabush** to Sept-Îles/Québec/Montréal (6 weekly; 50min/2hr 20min/3hr 10min); Sept-Îles/ Québec/Montréal/Ottawa (6 weekly; 50min/2hr 20min/3hr 10min/3hr 45min); Québec/Montréal (1 daily; 2hr 10min/2hr 55min); Churchill Falls/ Deer Lake/St John's (2 weekly; 40min/2hr 15min/ 3hr 15min); Deer Lake/St John's (3 weekly; 1hr 55min/2hr 55min); Churchill Falls/Goose Bay/St John's (1 weekly; 40min/1hr 15min/3hr 15min).

# CHAPTER THREE

# QUÉBEC

As the only French-speaking enclave in North America, **QUÉBEC** is totally distinct from the rest of the continent – so distinct, in fact, that it seems to be moving inexorably towards independence. This political separation of Québec from its English-speaking neighbours is the culmination of a process that began over two hundred years ago, with France's ceding of the colony to Britain in 1760. At first this transfer saw little change in the life of most Québécois. Permitted to retain their language and religion, they stayed under the control of the Catholic Church, whose domination of rural society – evident in the huge churches of Québec's tiny villages – resulted in an economically and educationally deprived sub-class, but a sub-class whose huge families were eventually to bring about the so-called "revenge of the cradle".

The creation of Lower and Upper Canada in 1791 served to emphasise the inequalities between anglos and francos, with the French-speaking majority in Lower Canada ruled by the so-called **Château Clique**, an assembly of francophone priests and seigneurs who had to answer to a British governor and council appointed in London. Rebellions by French *patriotes* in 1837 against this anglo hierarchy led to an investigation by Lord Durham, who concluded that French-Canadians had "peculiar language and manners" and should be immersed in the English culture of North America. The establishment of the Province of Canada in 1840 was thus a deliberate attempt to marginalise francophone opinion within an English-speaking state.

French-Canadians remained insulated from the economic mainstream until twentieth-century **industrialisation**, financed and run by the better-educated anglos, led to a mass francophone migration to the cities, where a French-speaking middle class soon began to articulate the grievances of the workforce and to criticise the suffocating effect the Church was having on francophone opportunity. The shake-up of Québec society came with the so-called **Quiet Revolution** of the 1960s, when the provincial government, led by the newly elected Liberals, took over the control of welfare, health and education from the Church, as well as instigating the creation of state-owned industries to reverse the financial domination of the anglophones.

In order to implement such legislation, Québec needed a disproportionate share of the nation's taxes, and the Liberals, despite being staunchly federalist, were constantly at loggerheads with Ottawa. Nationalist feeling intensified as Québec became increasingly isolated from the rest of the country, reaching a violent peak in 1970 with the terrorist actions of the largely unpopular **Front de Libération du Québec** (FLQ) in Montréal. Six years later a massive reaction against the ruling Liberals brought the separatist **Parti Québécois** to power in Montréal. Led by René Lévesque, the Parti Québécois accelerated the process of social change with the Charte de la langue française, better known as **Bill 101**, which established French as the official language of the province. With French now dominant in the workplace and the classroom, the Québécois thought they had got as close as possible to cultural and social independence. Still reeling from the terrorist activities of the FLQ and scared that Lévesque's ultimate objective of separatism would leave Québec economically adrift, the 6.5 million population voted 60:40 against sovereignty in a 1980 referendum.

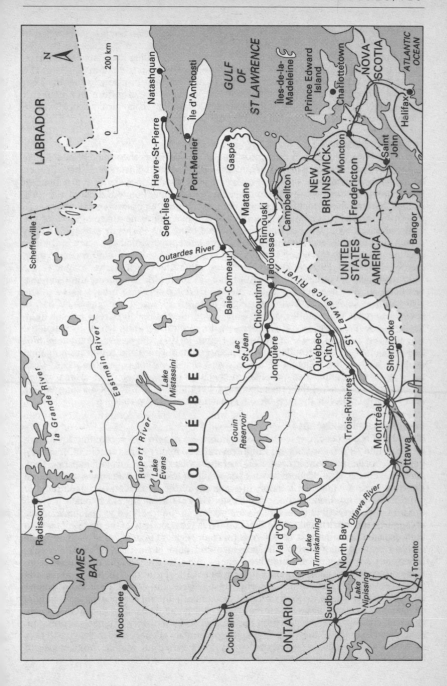

However, the collapse of the 1990 **Meech Lake** talks, when the provinces failed to find a way to accede to Québec's demand to be regarded as a "distinct society" – to be able to opt out of any federal legislation it didn't like, including the Canadian Charter, the equivalent of the Bill of Rights – left Ottawa no choice but to confront Québec. The provincial government were told in effect to either find their own way to stay in or get out, and a **deadline** of October 1992 was set for a new **referendum** in Québec. It seems likely that the outcome will favour separation, an economically more feasible proposition than a decade ago – at least for the Québécois.

## The native peoples

Independence won't be plain sailing for Québec, however. Franco-anglo relations may be the principal concern of most Québécois – eighty percent of Québécois have French as their mother tongue – but the province's population also includes ten nations of **native peoples**, the majority of whom live on reservations "granted" them by the early French settlers. Resentment and racism are as rife here as elsewhere in Canada – as shown by the fact that it was only a decade ago that the name above a portal of the National Assembly in Québec City was changed from "Les Portes de sauvage" to "Les portes de la Famille Amerindienne". Native grievances are particularly acute in Québec because most of the province's tribes are English-oriented, and until recently most learned English if they spoke any language other than their native tongue – the **Mohawks** near Montréal even fought on the side of the British during the conquest. Relations are bad between the authorities and French-speaking groups as well. The **Hurons** near Québec City battled for eight years, all the way to the Supreme Court of Canada, to retain their hunting rights, while around James Bay the **Crees** are still fighting to block the expansion of Québec's hydro-electric network, which if completed would cover an area the size of Germany. Begun in 1971, the project is only one-third finished but has already resulted in the displacement of Crees and **Inuits** from flooded lands as well as the pollution of those rivers that have not been channelled. Until recently native groups used peaceful methods to register their land claims, which amount to 85 percent of the province's area, but the violent Mohawk uprising at Oka near Montréal indicates the possible onset of a more militant phase.

## The cities and landscapes

Should Québec secede, Canada will lose its **largest province** – accounting for a sixth of the country's territory; its 1.5 million square kilometres are capable of enclosing Portugal, Spain, Germany, France, Belgium and Switzerland. Of this vast expanse, sixty percent is **forest land** peppered with over a million **lakes** and waterways, and though some mining towns dot the interior, the majority of the population is concentrated in the rich **arable lands** along the southern stretches of the mighty St Lawrence.

The Gallic ancestry of most Québécois is clear in their attitude to hedonistic pleasures – they eat and drink in a style that combines the simplicity of the first settlers with the rich tastes of the French. Nowhere is this more evident than in the island metropolis of **Montréal**, premier port of the province and home to a third of all Québécois. Montréal's skyscrapers and nightlife bear witness to the economic resurgence of French-speaking Canada, whereas in **Québec City** the attraction lies more in the ancient streets and architecture. Beyond these centres, the **Gaspé Peninsula**, poking into the eastern side of the Gulf of the St Lawrence, is the most appealing area with its old-fashioned fishing villages, some of them still home to Acadian people, a French-speaking community separated from the Québécois by a history of terrible repression. Furthermore, much of the Gaspé's inspiring mountain scenery and rocky coastline is protected as parkland, providing sanctuary for a variety of wildlife, from moose to herons.

The opposite shore of the St Lawrence, north of Montréal, is a sparsely populated and often bleak region, but its villages – principally **Tadoussac** – offer magnificent opportunities to go **whale-watching**, while the contrasting landscapes of **Saguenay fjord** and the northerly **Mingan Archipelago** are among Québec's most dramatic sights. Beyond the regions covered in this guide, Québec's inhospitable and largely roadless tundra is inhabited only by pockets of Inuits and other native peoples; it's a destination only for those travellers who can afford an expensive bush-plane and the equipment needed for survival in the wilderness.

**Train** services within the province serve Montréal, Gaspé, Québec City and the north, and there are also services to Ontario, New Brunswick, Newfoundland and the States – with Montréal very much the pivot. **Buses** are your best bet for getting around, with the major places connected by *Voyageur* services, supplemented by a network of smaller local lines. However, distances between communities in the outlying areas can be immense, and in order to reach remoter parks and settlements on secondary roads a **car** is useful, though hitching is often a viable and safe alternative. Around Montréal and Québec City the shores of the St Lawrence are linked by bridges, and towards the north a network of **ferries** links the Gaspé with the Côte Nord. In the far north the supply ship *Nordik Express* serves the Île d'Anticosti and the roadless lower north shore as far as the Labrador border – the ultimate journey within Québec.

---

### TOLL-FREE INFORMATION NUMBER

Tourisme Québec ☎1-800-363-7777.

---

# MONTRÉAL

**MONTRÉAL**, Canada's second largest city, is geographically as close to the European coast as to Vancouver, and in look and feel it combines some of the finest aspects of the two continents. Its North American skyline of glass and concrete rises above churches and monuments in a medley of European styles, a medley as complex as Montréal's social mix. This is the second largest French-speaking metropolis outside France, but only two-thirds of the city's two million population are of French extraction, the other third being a cosmopolitan mish-mash of *les autres* – including Eastern Europeans, Chinese, Italians, Greeks, Jews, South Americans and West Indians. The result is a truly multi-dimensional city, with a global variety of eateries, bars and clubs, matched by a calendar of festivals that makes this the most vibrant place in Canada.

Montréal has long been the dynamo behind Québécois **separatism**, the tension between the two main language groups culminating in the terrorist campaign that the **Front de Libération du Québec** focused on the city in the 1960s. The consequent political changes affected Montréal more than anywhere else in the province: in the wake of the "francisation" of Québec, English-Canadians hit Highway 401 in droves, tipping the nation's economic supremacy from Montréal to Toronto. However, though written off by Canada's English-speaking majority, the city did not sink into oblivion – rather it has reached its 350th year on a peak of resurgence.

Everywhere you look there are the signs of civic pride and prosperity. In the historic quarter of **Vieux-Montréal**, on the banks of the St Lawrence, the streets and gracious squares are flanked by well-tended buildings, from the mammoth **Basilique de Notre-Dame** and steepled **Chapelle de Notre-Dame-de-Bonsecours**, to the sleek and stately commercial and public buildings. Old houses have been converted into lively restaurants and shops, abandoned warehouses into condos and the disused

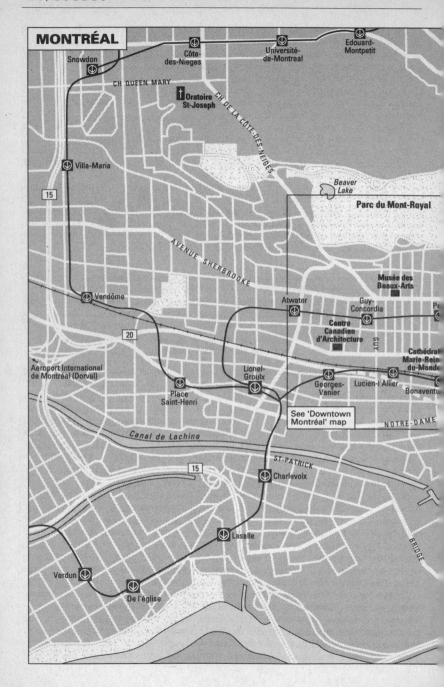

**MONTRÉAL**

Snowdon

Côte-
des-Nieges

Université-
de-Montreal

Edouard-
Montpetit

CH QUEEN MARY

✝ Oratoire
St-Joseph

CH DE LA CÔTE-DES-NEIGES

Villa-Maria

15

Beaver
Lake

**Parc du Mont-Royal**

AVENUE SHERBROOKE

Vendôme

**Musée des
Beaux-Arts**

Atwater

Guy-
Concordia

Pe

20

**Centre
Canadien
d'Architecture**

GUY

**Cathédral
Marie-Rein
du-Monde**

Aéroport International
de Montréal (Dorval)

Lionel-
Groulx

Georges-
Vanier

Lucien-l'Allier

Bonaventu

Place
Saint-Henri

See 'Downtown
Montréal' map

NOTRE-DAME

Canal de Lachine

ST-PATRICK

15

Charlevoix

BRIDGE

Lasalle

Verdun

De l'église

Laurier

BOULEVARD ST-JOSEPH

AVENUE DE LAURIMIER

AVE DU MONT-ROYAL

Mont-Royal

Jardin Botanique &
Olympic Stadium

RACHEL

AV DU PARC

RUE DULUTH

Préfontaine

ST-DENIS

AVENUE SHERBROOKE

Sherbrooke

Youth
Hostel

Frontenac

AYLMER

Bus
Station

1cGill

Place-
des-Arts

Saint-
Laurent

Berri-
Uqam

Beaudry

Papineau

niversité

BOULEVARD RENÉ-LÉVESQUE

AUTOROUTE VILLE-MARIE

NOTRE-DAME

Square-
Victoria

Place-
d'Armes

Champ-
de-Mars

*i*

La Ronde

DE LA COMMUNE

See 'Vieux-
Montréal' map

Île
Sainte-Hélène

PONT DE LA
CONCORDE

AVENUE PIERRE-DUPUY

ST LAWRENCE RIVER

Île
Notre-Dame

20

N

0                    1 km

Vieux-Port into a summer playground with state-of-the-art exhibitions in the old hangars. Beneath the forested rise of **Mont Royal**, the grid of downtown boulevards and leafy squares is alive from the morning rush hour right through to the early hours, when revellers return from Montréal's clubland – centred on Ste-Catherine and the bohemian **Latin Quarter**. Below ground, the walkways of the Underground City and the outstanding **Métro** system link the nodal points of the city, while towards the eastern outskirts, the **Olympic Stadium** has finally been completed by the addition of a leaning tower that overshadows the vast **Jardin Botanique**, second in international status only to London's Kew Gardens.

To mark the 350th anniversary Montréal's **museums** are also being transformed – the recently opened **Centre Canadien d'Architecture**, one of the continent's most impressive specialist collections, has already been matched by the splendid new wing of the **Musée des Beaux Arts**, and there are many more projects imminent: the re-opening of the **Musée McCord d'Histoire Canadienne** after a multi-million-dollar expansion, a modern art gallery in the **Place des Arts** cultural centre, an ambitious **Biodôme** in the Parc Olympique and a brand new **Centre Archéologique** in Vieux-Montréal.

Beyond the city limits, Montréalers are blessed with superb vacation regions, most within an hour or two of the metropolis. To the north, the fertile banks of the St Lawrence and the lake-sprinkled mountains of the **Laurentians** offer a reprieve from muggy summer temperatures, while in winter the mountain ski resorts are among the busiest in the country. To the east the charm of **L'Estrie** lies in the acres of farmlands, orchards, maple woods and lakeshore hamlets. En route to Québec City, the **Mauricie** valley, the province's smallest national park, is a glorious summer haven, with a web of waterways and lakes amidst a landscape of mountainous forest.

## A brief history of Montréal

The island of Montréal was first occupied by the St Lawrence **Iroquois**, whose small village of Hochelaga (Place of the Beaver) was sited at the base of Mont Royal. European presence began in October 1535 when Jacques-Cartier was led here while searching for a northwest route to Asia. However, even after the arrival of Samuel de Champlain the French settlement was little more than a small garrison, and it wasn't until 1642 that the colony of Ville-Marie was founded by the soldiers of **Paul de Chomedey**, Sieur de Maisonneuve. They were on orders from Paris to "bring about the Glory of God and the salvation of the Indians", a mission which predictably enough found little response from the natives. Bloody conflict with the Iroquois, fanned by the European fur trade alliances with the Algonquins and Hurons, was constant until a treaty signed in 1701 prompted the growth of Ville-Marie into the main embarkation point for the fur and lumber trade.

When Québec City fell to the British in 1759 Montréal briefly served as the capital of New France, until the Marquis de Vaudreuil was forced to surrender to General Amherst. The ensuing **British occupation** suffered a seven-month interruption in 1775, when the Americans took over, but after this hiatus a flood of Irish and Scottish immigrants soon made Montréal North America's second largest city. It was not an harmonious expansion, however, and in 1837 there was an uprising of the French against the British ruling class, an insurgency followed by hangings and exiles.

With the creation of the **Dominion of Canada** in 1867, Montréal emerged as the new nation's premier port, railroad nexus, banking centre and industrial producer. Its population reached half a million in 1911 and doubled in the next two decades with an influx of emigrés from Europe. It was also during this period that Montréal acquired its reputation as Canada's "sin city". During Prohibition in the US, Québec province became the main alcohol supplier to the entire continent: the Molsons and their ilk made their fortunes here, while prostitution and gambling thrived under the protection of the authorities. Only in the wake of World War II and the subsequent economic boom did a major anti-corruption operation begin, a campaign that was followed by rapid architectural growth, starting in 1962 with the beginnings of the Underground City complex. The most glamorous episode in the city's facelift came in 1967, when land reclaimed from the St Lawrence was used as the site of the **World Expo**, a jamboree that attracted fifty million visitors to Montréal in the course of the year. However, it was Montréal's anglophones who were benefiting from the prosperity, and beneath the smooth surface francophone frustrations were reaching dangerous levels.

The crisis peaked in October 1970, when the radical **Front de Libération du Québec** (FLQ) kidnapped the British trade commissioner, James Cross, and then a Québec cabinet minister, Pierre Laporte. As ransom the FLQ demanded the transportation to Cuba of 25 FLQ prisoners awaiting trial for acts of violence, the publication of the FLQ manifesto and $500,000 in gold bullion. Prime Minister Pierre Trudeau responded with the War Measures Act, suspending civil liberties and putting troops on the streets of Montréal. The following day Laporte's body was found in the boot of a car. By December the so-called **October Crisis** was over, as Cross was released and his captors and Laporte's murderers were arrested, but the reverberations shook the nation.

At last recognising the need to redress the country's social imbalances, the federal government poured money into countrywide schemes to promote French-Canadian culture. Francophone discontent was further alleviated by the provincial election of **René Lévesque** and his Parti Québécois in 1976, the year the Olympic Games were held in Montréal. The consequent language laws made French a compulsory part of the school curriculum and banned English signs on business premises in Québec unless the company employed fewer than fifty people, in which case bilingual signs were permitted, provided that the French was printed twice as big as the English. For many anglophones these measures were pettily vindictive, and nearly 100,000 English speakers left Montréal – twenty percent of the city's population. They took with them over a hundred companies and a massive amount of capital, provoking a steep decline in house prices, a halt on construction work and the withdrawal of investment. For a while it seemed that Montréal's heyday was over, but soon the gaps left by the departing anglos were filled by young francophones who at last felt in charge of their own culture and economy. Today Montréal's francophone entrepreneurs control sixty percent of the province's workforce and account for seventeen percent of Canada's exports.

# Arrival, information and city transport

Montréal has two international **airports**. **Aéroport de Mirabel**, 55km northwest of the city, is the arrival point for flights from Europe, Africa, South America and Asia. *Aéro Plus* runs a bus service to the downtown *Queen Elizabeth* hotel and Terminus Voyageur at least hourly; the trip takes about 45 minutes and costs $11. A taxi will set you back around $45. Flights from North and Central America touch down at **Aéroport de Dorval**, 22km southwest of Montréal. From Dorval to the same locations downtown takes around half an hour by *Aérocar/Murray Hill* buses (every 20–30min until midnight; $8.50–11). A cheaper but more complicated way to reach downtown from Dorval is to take local bus #204 to Dorval train station ($1.50), then a train to Windsor station ($3), where you can transfer to the Métro system. Ask for a transfer (*une correspondance*) from the ticket seller on the train, which allows you to complete your journey by bus or Métro for no extra cost. Several local buses also connect Dorval train station to downtown but they take ages. The same journey by taxi costs $19.

Montréal's main **train** station, Gare Centrale, is below the *Queen Elizabeth* hotel on the corner of René-Lévesque and Mansfield. The station is the major terminus for

Canada's *Via Rail* trains from Halifax, Toronto, Ottawa, Québec and the Gaspé as well as US *Amtrak* trains from Washington and New York. The Bonaventure Métro station links it with the rest of the city.

Long-distance **buses** arrive and depart from Terminus Voyageur on Boulevard de Maisonneuve Est. The Berri-UQAM Métro is right in the station.

## Orientation

Though Montréal island is a massive 51km by 16km, the heart of the city is very manageable, and is divided into **Vieux-Montréal** – along the St Lawrence River – and a **downtown** high-rise business core, on the south side of the hill of **Mont Royal**. Sherbrooke, de Maisonneuve, Ste-Catherine and René-Lévesque are the main east-west pedestrian arteries, divided into east (*est*) and west (*ouest*) sections by the north-south boulevard St-Laurent, known locally as "The Main". Street numbers begin from St-Laurent and increase the further east or west you travel: thus 200 Sherbrooke Ouest is about three blocks west of the Main and 1000 René-Lévesque Est is about ten blocks east of the Main. North-south street numbers increase north from the St Lawrence River.

> The Montréal area telephone code is ☎514.

## Information

Montréal's main **information** centre, *Infotouriste* (daily April to mid-May & Sept to mid-Oct 9am–7pm; mid-May to Aug 8am–7pm; mid-Oct to March 9am–6pm; ☎873-2015), is on the corner of Metcalfe and Square-Dorchester at 1001 Square-Dorchester. The nearest Métro is Peel, from where painted footprints lead you to the information centre. In addition to masses of useful free information – including the *Montréal* booklet and an excellent guide to walks in Vieux-Montréal – it offers an accommodation service which will make any amount of free calls to suss out vacancies for you. Other than the small information offices at Montréal's **airports** (Mirabel daily noon–2.30pm & 3–8pm; Dorval daily 1–8pm), there is also a branch in **Vieux-Montréal** on the corner of Place Jacques-Cartier, at 174 Notre-Dame Est (daily early June to Aug 9am–7pm; Sept to early June 9am–1pm & 2–5pm).

## Transport

The **public transport** system is one of the city's greatest assets, linking the 65-station Métro to 118 bus routes. The clean, speedy, convenient, reliable and cheap **Métro** system has four colour-coded lines, the major interconnecting stations being Berri-UQAM (which links the orange, green and yellow lines), Lionel Groulx (green and orange), and Snowdon and Jean-Talon (blue and orange). Coloured signs indicate the direction of each line by showing the name of the terminus; maps of the system can be picked up at stations and information centres. One-way fares are a flat $1.50, or 75¢ for under-18s, students and over-65s; a strip of six – a *carnet de tickets* – costs $6.50 or $2.50. A *correspondance*, available from machines at the Métro stations, is valid for an hour and allows you to complete your journey by bus at no extra cost. The transfer system also works in reverse from buses to Métro – ask the driver for one as you board. Most **buses** stop running at 12.30am, shortly before the Métro, though some run all through the night; they have the same fare system as the Métro, but only exact change is accepted.

It is rarely necessary to take a **taxi**, though they are not too expensive if you're in a group; they cost $2 plus $1 per kilometre, and a 10–15 percent tip is normal. Taxis can be boarded at ranks outside hotels and transport terminals, although if you flag madly they usually stop.

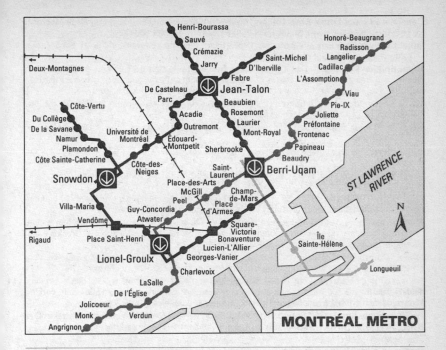

MONTRÉAL MÉTRO

# Accommodation

Montréal has no shortage of places to stay, though the majority of accommodation is geared towards expense-account travellers in the downtown hotels. However, hotel rooms in the range of $25–60 per person are conveniently concentrated around the Voyageur bus terminal or the livelier St-Denis area, and a growing number of bed and breakfast places offer budget accommodation in Vieux-Montréal. Rock-bottom prices are charged in the city's hostels and the university residences left vacant in the summer. For campers the outlook is not so good, as the campgrounds are at least twenty minutes' drive out of town, with no public transport. The peak season is from May to the end of October, with July and August especially busy.

## Hotels

**Château Versailles**, 1659 Sherbrooke Ouest (☎933-3611 or ☎1-800-361-7199). A unique and beautifully furnished hotel that occupies four stone buildings in downtown. Book well in advance, as the Château is one of the city's most popular hotels. Singles $80–129, doubles $86–139; family discounts and cheap winter weekend rates also available.

**Hôtel l'Appartement in Montréal**, 455 Sherbrooke Ouest (☎284-3634 or ☎1-800-363-3010). Apartments fitted with kitchenettes, bathrooms, air-conditioning, telephones and TVs. There's free use of an outdoor pool and sauna though parking costs extra. Apartments from $84–139 per night; 25 percent discount per week, 45 percent per month.

**Hôtel Bon Accueil**, 1601 St-Hubert (☎527-9655). Central red-brick hotel near the bus station. All rooms with private bathrooms; singles and doubles $55.

**Hôtel Le Breton**, 1609 St-Hubert (☎524-7273). Within spitting distance of the bus station. Clean air-conditioned rooms with TVs, and friendly reception. Singles $25–60, doubles $40–59. Some rooms sleep up to four people with $7.50 charged for each extra person.

**Hôtel Castel Saint-Denis**, 2099 St-Denis (☎842-9719). One of the best budget hotels in Montréal. Right in the trendy St-Denis area, but quiet. Singles $30–45, doubles $30–50.

**Hôtel Château Napoléon**, 1030 Mackay (☎861-1500). Pleasant, renovated old hotel. Singles from $45, doubles from $58; $6 per extra person.

**Hôtel de l'Institut**, 3535 St-Denis (☎282-5120). Run by the Institut de Tourisme et d'Hôtelerie in Québec as a training hotel for students of tourism. Consequently the staff bend over backwards to look after you, though the dull look of the place is not very inspiring. Doubles from $98.

**Hôtel Louisbourg**, 1649 St-Hubert (☎598-8544). Budget hotel with sparse facilities in the bus station area. Singles from $35, doubles from $40.

**Hôtel du Manoir Saint-Denis**, 2006 St-Denis (☎843-3670). In the heart of the action. Singles $46–60, doubles $52–60.

**Hôtel Pierre**, 169 Sherbrooke Est (☎288-8519). Nine-bedroom hotel with free parking. Singles and doubles $25–80.

**Hôtel Viger Centre-Ville**, 1001–1005 St-Hubert (☎845-6058). On the corner of Avenue Viger, close to bus station. Singles from $35, doubles from $40.

**Lord Berri**, 1199 Berri (☎845-9236 or ☎1-800-363-0363). Modern hotel in a renovated old building next to the Université de Québec-Montréal. Air-conditioned doubles from $86.

**Manoir des Alpes**, 1245 St-André (☎845-9803 or ☎1-800-465-2929). Right next to the bus station, this Victorian house has been renovated into a hotel with tacky Swiss overtones. Breakfast and parking included in the price. Singles $50–78, doubles $55–78.

**Manoir Ambrose**, 3422 Stanley (☎288-6922). A couple of blocks from the heart of downtown. Very cheap rooms, some with air-conditioning and bathrooms. Singles $25–70, doubles $45–75.

**Nouvel Hôtel Montréal**, 1740 René-Lévesque Ouest (☎931-8841 or ☎1-800-363-6063). Studios, condos, apartments and hotel rooms in one huge complex. Swimming pool, health club, parking and continental breakfast included in the price. Singles and doubles from $120.

**Le Roussillon Royal**, 1600 St-Hubert (☎849-3214 or ☎1-800-363-6223). Four-star, central, rather sterile hotel adjacent to bus station. Singles and doubles from $72. Free parking.

## Bed and breakfast agencies

**Bed and Breakfast à Montréal**, 4912 Victoria (☎738-9410). The longest established B&B service in the city. Over fifty homes available. Singles $30–45, doubles $45–70.

**Chambre et Petit Déjeuner Bienvenue**, 3950 Laval (☎844-5897). Offers rooms in Victorian homes. Singles $30–55, doubles $40–65.

**Downtown Bed and Breakfast Network**, 3458 Laval (☎289-9749). Numerous homes in the downtown area and Vieux-Montréal. There is nearly always a vacancy. Singles $25–40, doubles $35–55, triples $55–75.

**Montréal Oasis B&B Network**, 3000 de Breslay (☎935-2312). Downtown and Vieux-Montréal B&Bs. Singles $45–60, doubles $50–85, triples $75–110.

## Hostels and student accommodation

**Auberge de jeunesse internationale de Montréal**, 3541 Aylmer (☎843-3317). Friendly and fun official youth hostel, despite the cramped conditions – 104 beds in 19 mixed dorms. During the winter some double rooms are available. Curfew 2am. Kitchen and laundry facilities. Members $13, non-members $16.

**Collège Francais**, 5155 de Gaspé (☎495-2581). Often used by school groups so can be booked out. Open July & Aug, with a few rooms available in Sept. Curfew 2am. Dormitory accommodation $8.50, singles and doubles $29, rooms with four beds $12.50 per person.

**Concordia University Residences**, 7141 Sherbrooke Ouest (☎848-4756). Summer only. Special rates for students with ID (singles $17, doubles $34); otherwise singles are $23, doubles $36.

**McGill University Residences**, 3935-Université (☎398-6367). Popular residence for visiting anglophones and consequently often full. $23 for students, $32 for others.

**Université de Montréal**, 2350 Édouard-Montpetit (☎343-6531). West of downtown. $19.95 with a student card, $30 for those without.

**YMCA**, 1450 Stanley (☎849-8393). Expensive, mixed YMCA with a floor for women only. Single ($33) and double rooms ($48), swimming pool and cafeteria.

**YWCA**, 1355 René-Lévesque Ouest (☎866-9941). Women only, near the station. Laundry facilities as well as swimming pool and cafeteria. From $33 for singles, $45 for doubles.

## Camping

**Camping Parc Mont Laval**, 675 bd St-Martin Ouest, Ste-Dorothée. 25km northwest of downtown on neighbouring Laval island; take exit 60 off Hwy 40 to Hwy 13, then exit 12. Sites $13–20.

**Camping Pointe-des-Cascades**, 2 Chemin du Canal, Pointe-des-Cascades. 40km west of downtown; take Hwy 20 to Dorion, then it's a further 6km on Hwy 338 – follow signs to the theatre. Sites $11–15.

**Koa Montréal Sud**, 130 bd Monette, St-Philippe-de-la Prairie. About 20km west of downtown; take exit 38 off Hwy 15, turn left, and it's 3km on. Sites $15–22.50.

# The City

Most visitors to Montréal sample first the old world charm of **Vieux-Montréal**. The narrow cobblestoned streets, alleys and squares are perfect for strolling, at every corner revealing an architectural gem, from monumental public edifices to the city's first steep-roofed homes. Close by, in contrast, are the futuristic exhibitions in the hangars of the **Vieux-Port** – also the departure point for thrilling jet boat trips down the Lachine Rapids. To the north, in the compact **downtown** area, the glass frontages of the office blocks reflect Victorian row-houses and the spires of numerous churches, clustered within the shadow of the city's landmark, **Mont Royal**. To the east of the hill the eateries and bars of the **Main** make this the spot where the city's pulse beats fastest, while on the city's outskirts the magnificent **Olympic Stadium** complex and the vast green of the **Botanical Gardens** are the main pull. Beneath street level the passages of the **Underground City** link hotels, shopping centres and offices with the Métro.

## Vieux-Montréal

Severed from downtown by the Autoroute Ville-Marie, the gracious district of Vieux-Montréal was left to decay until fairly recently, when the developers stepped in with generally tasteful renovations that brought colour and vitality back to the area. The continent's greatest concentration of seventeenth-, eighteenth- and nineteenth-century buildings has its fair share of tourists, but it's just as popular with Montréalers too – formerly as a symbolic place to air francophone grievances, more recently as a spot to while away the hours in a café or restaurant.

### Place d'Armes and around

The focal point of Vieux-Montréal is the **Place d'Armes**, its centre occupied by a century-old statue of Maisonneuve, whose missionary zeal raised the wrath of the displaced Iroquois. The mutt among the luminaries represents the animal who warned the French of an impending attack in 1644; legend has it that the ensuing battle ended when the unarmed Maisonneuve killed the Iroquois chief on this very spot.

Despite the addition of an ugly skyscraper on its west side, the square is still dominated by the twin-towered, neo-Gothic **Basilique Notre-Dame** (daily July–Sept 7am–8pm; Oct–June 7am–6pm), the cathedral of the Catholic faithful since 1829. Its architect, the Protestant Irish-American James O'Donnell, was so inspired by his creation that he converted to Catholicism. The western of the two towers, named Temperance and Perseverance, holds the ten-ton Jean-Baptiste bell, whose booming can be heard 25km away. The breathtaking gilt and sky blue interior, flooded with light from three rose windows in the ceiling, was designed by Montréal architect Victor Bourgeau and some talented craftsmen. Most notable of the detailed furnishings are Louis-Philippe Hébert's fine wooden carvings of the prophets on the pulpit and the awe-inspiring main altar by French sculptor Bouriché. Imported from Limoges in France, the stained glass windows depict the founding of Ville-Marie. Behind the main altar is the Chapelle Sacré-Coeur, destroyed by an arsonist in 1978 but rebuilt with an impressive bronze reredos by Charles Daudelin. Next to the chapel is a small **museum** (Sat & Sun 9.30am–4pm; $1) dealing with the history of the basilica and of Catholicism in Québec. The collection includes paintings and sculptures, church vestments, ornaments and a silver Madonna presented by Louis XV.

Behind the fieldstone walls and wrought iron gates to the right of Notre-Dame is the low-lying, mock-medieval **Séminaire de Saint-Sulpice**, saved from blandness by a portal that's topped by North America's oldest public timepiece, which began chiming in 1710. Generally considered Montréal's oldest building, the seminary was founded in 1685 by the Paris-based Sulpicians, who instigated the establishment of Montréal by Maisonneuve as a religious enterprise. They liked the place so much that they bought the whole island, and until 1854 were in charge of religious and legal affairs in the colony. The seminary is still the Canadian headquarters of the Sulpicians, but their duties are now limited to maintaining the basilica.

The domed shrine of Montréal's financial rulers, the **Banque de Montréal**, stands opposite. This grand, classical-revival building still houses the headquarters of Canada's oldest bank, which rose from its foundation by a few Scottish immigrants to serve the entire nation until the creation of the Bank of Canada in the 1930s. Inside, the original marble counters, black pillars and gleaming brass and bronze fittings ooze wealth and luxury, while a small **museum** (Mon–Fri 10am–4pm; free) displays early account books, banknotes, coins and pictures of the bank.

British names once controlled the finances of the continent from the stately limestone, griffin-capped institutions along **Rue St-Jacques**, once the Wall Street of Canada. French businesses now rule the roost: the Art Deco Aldred Building has been renamed the Prévoyance Building, and the city's first skyscraper – on the corner of côte de la Place d'Armes and St-Jacques – is dwarfed by a soaring block occupied by thriving francophones. Transformations have also occurred alongside the basilica, in the area around **Rue St-Sulpice**, where the warehouses constructed in the Victorian era to cope with the growing trade of Montréal harbour have been converted into luxurious flats and offices. Many of the continent's first explorers once lived here – such as Pierre Gaulthier de Varennes, who charted South Dakota, the Rockies and Wyoming, and Daniel Greysolon du Luth, who roamed over Minnesota.

## Along Rue Notre-Dame

Ville-Marie's first street, **Rue Notre-Dame**, was laid out in 1672 and runs east–west from one end of Vieux-Montréal to the other. Other than the financial buildings of Rue St-Jacques there is little of interest to the west of Place d'Armes; it's more rewarding to head east along Notre-Dame from the top of rue St-Sulpice, past the 1811 **Maison de la Sauvegarde** at no. 160. It stands opposite the imposing **Old Courthouse**, erected by the British to impress upon the French population the importance of abiding by their laws, but now usurped by the shiny black glass of the **Palais de Justice** on the corner of St-Laurent. Beside the Old Courthouse, **Place Vauquelin**, with its pretty fountain and statue of the naval commander Jean Vauquelin, gives views of the Champ de Mars to the north; once a military parade ground, now a car park, and soon to be a venue for outdoor performances.

East of the square is the ornate **Hôtel de Ville**, built in the 1870s and a typical example of the area's civic buildings of the time when French-speaking architects looked to the mother country for inspiration. On a visit to the Montréal Expo, General de Gaulle chose its second-floor balcony to make the "Vive le Québec Libre" that left the anglos reeling at the thought that Québec was on its way to independent status and infusing the francophones with a fervour that culminated in the October Crisis.

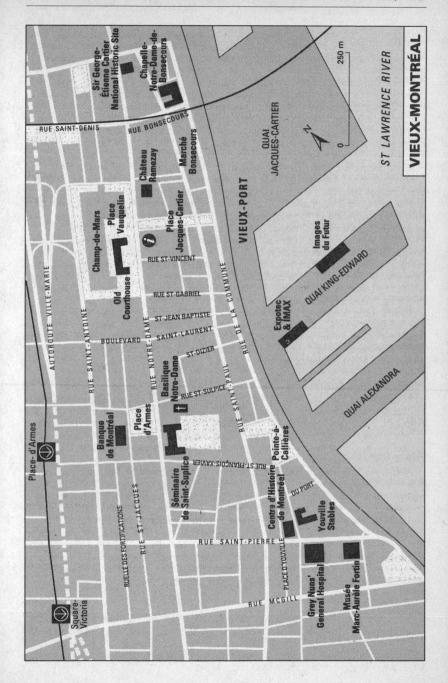

**VIEUX-MONTRÉAL**

ST LAWRENCE RIVER

0    250 m

QUAI JACQUES-CARTIER

VIEUX-PORT

Images du Futur

QUAI KING-EDWARD

Expotec & IMAX

QUAI ALEXANDRA

Sir George-Étienne Cartier National Historic Site

Chapelle-Notre-Dame-de-Bonsecours

RUE SAINT-DENIS

RUE BONSECOURS

Château Ramezay

Marché Bonsecours

Champ-de-Mars

Place Vauquelin

Place Jacques-Cartier

RUE ST-VINCENT

Old Courthouse

RUE ST-GABRIEL

ST-JEAN BAPTISTE

AUTOROUTE VILLE-MARIE

RUE SAINT-ANTOINE

RUE NOTRE-DAME

BOULEVARD SAINT-LAURENT

RUE DE LA COMMUNE

ST-DIZIER

Basilique Notre-Dame

RUE ST-PAUL

RUE ST-SULPICE

Place d'Armes

Banque de Montréal

Place-d'Armes

Séminaire de Saint-Sulpice

RUE ST-FRANÇOIS-XAVIER

Pointe-à-Callières

RUELLE DES FORTIFICATIONS

RUE ST-JACQUES

Centre d'Histoire de Montréal

DU PORT

Youville Stables

RUE SAINT-PIERRE

PLACE D'YOUVILLE

Square-Victoria

RUE MCGILL

Grey Nuns' General Hospital

Musée Marc-Aurèle Fortin

Opposite is the long, low fieldstone manor house of the **Château Ramezay** (mid-June to Sept daily 10am–4.30pm; Oct to mid-June Tues–Sun 10am–4.30pm; $2), looking much as it did in 1705, the only addition being an incongruous tower which hoisted the building into "château" status in the 1800s. One of the oldest buildings in North America, Château Ramezay was built as the residence for the French governors, then passed into the hands of the British. During the fleeting American invasion Benjamin Franklin stayed here in an attempt to persuade Montréalers to join the States, but he lost public and church support by not promising the supremacy of the French language in what would have been the fourteenth state. Nowadays, after a variety of other uses, it's an historical **museum**, displaying oil paintings, domestic artefacts, tools, costumes and furniture from the eighteenth and nineteenth centuries. The most impressive room is a reconstruction of the Grande Salle of the Compagnie des Indes, the fur-trading company that had a monopoly on beaver pelts until the coming of the British. Though the company used the château as their headquarters, the ornately carved wood panelling is an import from Nantes in France, donated to Montréal during the Expo. Other rooms are furnished in the bourgeois style of New France, while in the deep stone vaults the life of the native peoples before European settlement is the subject.

At the intersection of Notre-Dame and Berri the **Sir George-Étienne Cartier National Historic Site** (mid-May to Aug daily 9am–5pm; Sept to mid-May Wed–Sun 10am–5pm; free) comprises two adjoining houses which were inhabited by the Cartier family from 1848 to 1871. The cocky Sir George-Étienne Cartier was one of the fathers of Confederation, persuading the French-Canadians to join the Dominion of Canada by declaring "We are of different races, not for strife but to work together for the common welfare". Today leaders of French-Canadian nationalism decry Cartier as a collaborator, and the displays in the east house diplomatically skirt over the issue of whether he was right or wrong and emphasise instead his role in the construction of Canada's railways. The rooms in the west house have been furnished with over a thousand original artefacts to evoke the period when Sir George lived here.

## Place Jacques-Cartier

Sloping down to the river from Place Vaquelin, the cobbled **Place Jacques-Cartier** is one of Montréal's favourite hang-outs, its buzz generated at the restaurants and cafés that spill out of the square's historic buildings and by the buskers and horse-drawn calèches that serve the tourist crowds. Just off the square, the narrow rue St-Amable is choked with struggling artists who produce pastel sketches of Madonna and oils of Burt Reynolds for the same audience.

At the top of the square itself the controversial **Monument to Nelson** stands above the flower stalls that are the only reminders that this was once Montréal's main market-place. The monument, only a third of the size of its more famous London counterpart but a few years older, was funded by anglophone Montréalers delighted with Nelson's defeat of the French at Trafalgar in 1805. Québec separatists adopted it as a rallying point in the 1970s – and ironically the anglos don't like it much either, because it faces away from the water. The most notable buildings on the square are Maison Vandelac, Maison del Vecchio and the Maison Cartier, showing the architectural features typical of Montréal architecture in the 1800s with pitched roofs to shed heavy snowfalls and small dormer windows as a defence against the cold.

## Rue St-Paul

Running parallel to rue Notre-Dame along the southern end of Place Jacques-Cartier, **Rue St-Paul** is one of Montréal's most attractive thoroughfares, lined with nineteenth-century commercial buildings and Victorian lampposts. Though the buildings differ little from when Charles Dickens stayed here, they now house restaurants and specialist shops selling everything from Inuit crafts to kites.

A block from Place Jacques-Cartier, the silver-domed **Marché Bonsecours**, with its long facade of columns, is to be opened to the public as the nerve centre of the city's anniversary celebrations, after years of use as municipal offices. Hopefully the building's exhibition space will do justice to the grandiose exterior.

Mark Twain noted that in Montréal "you couldn't throw a brick without hitting a church", and just past Marché Bonsecours is Montréal's favourite, the delicate and profusely steepled **Chapelle de Notre-Dame-de-Bonsecours** (daily May–Oct 9am–5pm; Nov–April 10am–5pm), or the Sailors' Church. The outstretched arms of the Virgin on the tower became a landmark for ships on the St Lawrence, and once safely landed the mariners would endow the chapel with wooden votive lamps in the shape of ships, many of which are still here. The chapel dates back to the earliest days of the colony, when Maisonneuve helped cut the wood for what was Ville-Marie's first church, under the instigation of Marguerite Bourgeoys, who had been summoned to Ville-Marie to teach the settlement's children. The devout Bourgeoys also founded the nation's first religious order and was in charge of the *filles du Roi* – orphaned French girls sent to marry bachelor settlers and multiply the colony's population. She was canonised in 1982, becoming Canada's first saint. Today's chapel, post-dating Bourgeoys by some seventy years, contains a small **museum** devoted to her life (May–Oct Tues–Sun 9am–4.30pm; Nov–April Tues–Sun 10.30am–4.30pm; $2). Be sure to climb the narrow stairs leading to the summit of the tower above the apse, known as **Le Monument**, for excellent views.

Opposite the chapel is the three-storeyed, high-chimneyed **Maison du Calvet**, built in 1725 and one of Montréal's best examples of French domestic architecture. Photographed, painted and admired more than any other house in the district, it was the home of a Huguenot draper called Pierre Calvet, a notorious turncoat who changed his allegiances from the French to the British and then to the Americans. When the British returned to power after the American invasion they threw their former Justice of the Peace into prison. On his release three years later he discovered that the Americans had no intention of paying for the services he had rendered, then drowned at sea before his claims for compensation reached court. The house is now a gourmet food shop.

**Rue Bonsecours**, which links rue St-Paul to Notre-Dame, is another typical Vieux-Montréal street. The **Maison Papineau** at no. 440 was home to four generations of the Papineau family, including Louis-Joseph who, as Speaker of the Assembly, championed the *habitants* of the St Lawrence farmland against the senior Catholic clergy, the British government and the Montréal business class. Calling for democratic election of the executive officers of church and government, he fuelled the rage of the *Patriotes* – the leaders of Lower Canada reform – but deserted the scene as the 1837 rebellion reached a bloody climax.

## Vieux-Port

At the southern end of Bonsecours lies the **Vieux-Port** of Montréal, once the import and export conduit of the continent. When the main shipyards shifted east in the 1970s they left a vacant lot which has been renovated for public use, with biking and jogging paths and excellent exhibitions in the quayside hangars.

The fences and disused railway tracks are best crossed opposite Porte St-Laurent, five blocks west of Bonsecours, to reach the King Edward quay. In hangar 7, an interpretation centre has a small exhibition on the changing face of the quays, but the real attraction lies next door in the mammoth **Expotec** hangar (June–Aug daily 10am–11pm; Sept Wed–Sun 10am–11pm; $10.50). Its enthralling sound and light exhibitions cover wide-ranging themes, declared in great banners across the front of the hangar, but are usually family-oriented high-tech displays combining entertainment and education. Films at Expotec's **IMAX** cinema take full advantage of the seven-storey screen, the camera scanning vast panoramas and launching into occasionally sickening plunges.

At the end of the quay **Images du Futur** (daily June to mid-Aug 10am–11pm; mid-Aug to mid-Sept noon–10pm; $9.50) is a showcase for futuristic artistic creations using lasers, holograms, neon, computer-generated images and digital music. International artists, scientists and industrial designers create bizarre exhibits that often encourage the viewer's interaction. Small screens show equally off-the-wall films, and in the larger cinema the summer-long International Computer Animation Competition features non-stop screening of the best of the genre. In the lower half of the Images du Futur hangar, the **Jacques-Cartier Flea Market** sells everything from chipped crockery to local art (May & Sept–Oct Fri–Mon 11am–8pm; June Wed–Sun 11am–10pm; July–Aug Mon 11am–8pm & Wed–Sun 11am–10pm).

The Vieux-Port is also the departure point for various **boat trips** and tours. The best by far is the **Jet Boat** from the Victoria quay at Bonsecours (May–Sept; $40). Scooting through the Lachine Rapids, the trip is wet, exhilarating and terrifying. Another unmissable trip is by **amphibus** from the Jacques-Cartier quay (May–Oct; $15). In true James Bond style the amphibus sails the water and drives along the streets of Vieux-Montréal.

## Place Royale to Place d'Youville

Once the site of duels, whippings and public hangings amidst the pedlars and hawkers who sold wares from the incoming ships, **Place Royale** is dominated by the neat classical facade of the **Old Customs House**, fronted by the Founder's Obelisk, a monument to the founders of the city. After a nine-day journey from Québec City Maisonneuve and his posse moored their boats at nearby **Pointe-à-Callières**, now landlocked after the changes in the Vieux-Port. At the extremity of the point stands a monument to **John Young**, who was responsible for enlarging Montréal's port in the seventeenth century, an act that enabled the city to expand as a trading centre. In 1992 a major **archaeological centre** is scheduled to open here, which, judging by the amount of money being spent, promises to be one of the most impressive museums in the city.

Rue de la Commune – in the nineteenth century a morass of taverns and brothels – continues past the **Old Docks** to rue d'Youville. From here, turn right into rue St-Pierre for the **Musée Marc-Aurèle Fortin** at no. 118 (Tues–Sun 11am–5pm; $3), a small gallery dedicated to a Québec painter whom the proprietors seem to believe was the greatest artist since the Impressionists. Unfortunately Fortin's directionless experiments with various styles do nothing to justify the praise. His twee oils of pastoral Laurentian scenes convey no real depth of feeling and though his paintings were bought by French-Canadians they were hung in Montréal homes as decoration, not as great statements. Fortin became increasingly frustrated with what he took to be the misunderstandings of the public and his later works – completed just before he went blind – are both sombre and frantic.

Continuing north takes you past the renovated wing of the **Grey Nuns' General Hospital**, where the sick, old and orphaned of Ville-Marie were first cared for. In the centre of the adjacent square, **Place d'Youville**, the red-brick fire station has been converted into the **Centre d'histoire de Montréal** (mid-May to mid-Sept daily 9am–5pm; mid-Sept to mid-May Tues–Sun 11am–4.30pm; $3), with dioramas of the city's history from its days as an Iroquois settlement to its present expansions under and above ground. Nothing goes into great depth but it is fine for a sketchy overview; an English booklet is available free from reception for translations of the displays. Usually more stimulating are the temporary exhibitions upstairs, highlighting unusual aspects of the city from its back alleys to prominent citizens. The future of this museum is in doubt as the impending opening of the archaeological centre on Pointe-à-Callières threatens to overshadow it.

On the south side of the square the **Youville Stables**, with its shady courtyard, gardens, restaurants and offices, was one of the first of the area's old buildings to be yuppified. The complex was in fact a warehouse – the stables were located next door. Dating from 1825, the courtyard layout is a throwback to a design used by the earliest Montréal inhabitants as a protection against the hostilities of the Iroquois.

# Downtown Montréal

Even if you're not staying in one of the area's hotels, you'll spend at least some time in **downtown** Montréal, as it's here that you'll probably arrive – either at the train stations or the *Voyageur* bus station. Though the main sights are the high-rises and shopping complexes, the area is dotted with old churches and museums, and Montréal is also one of the cities that has a downtown business area as alive at night as during the day.

### Dorchester Square and around

People tend to gravitate towards **Dorchester Square**, originally a Catholic cemetery and now a leafy spot right in the centre of downtown. In the summer the office blocks around the square empty their personnel onto the park benches for a snack and a chat while tourists mill around the Art Deco-inspired **Infotouriste** building – starting point for various guided tours in summer. The oldest building here is the Victorian **St George's Anglican Church**, with an impressive tapestry from Westminster Abbey.

The adjacent **Place du Canada** was bought in 1840 by Thomas Phillips, who insisted that the buildings around the square should be the most beautiful in Montréal. Most of the resulting edifices still stand. Dwarfed by its high-rise neighbours, the **Cathédrale Marie-Reine-du-Monde** (May–Sept daily 7am–7pm; Oct–April Sat 8am–7.30pm & Sun 9.30am–7.30pm), is a quarter-size replica of St Peter's in Rome. It was commissioned in 1870 by Bishop Ignace Bourgeau as a reminder that Catholicism still dominated the largest city in the new Dominion of Canada. Inside it's not as opulent as one would expect, though the high altar of marble, onyx and ivory is surmounted by a gilded copper reproduction of Bernini's baldachin over the altar in St Peter's. To your right on entering is the **Chapelle des Souvenirs**, which contains various relics including the wax-encased remains of the immensely obscure Saint Zoticus.

Opposite the cathedral is the grey granite **Sun Life Building**, built in 1914 and for a quarter of a century the largest building in the British Commonwealth.

### Ste-Catherine and around

Continuing north up Metcalfe brings you to **Rue Ste-Catherine**, the city's main commercial throughfare since the early 1900s, with the main shopping centres – *Eaton*, *La Baie* and *Ogilvy* – interspersed with exclusive boutiques, souvenir shops and fast-food outlets. For all its consumerist gloss the road was until recently pretty seedy, but the peep shows and strip clubs have been driven further east.

Montréal's Anglican **Christ Church Cathedral** (daily 8am–6pm), built in 1859, is to be found four blocks east of Metcalfe, at 1444 Union Avenue. By 1927 its slender stone spire was threatening to crash through the wooden roof and was replaced with the peculiar aluminium replica. Inside, the soaring Gothic arches are decorated with heads of saints, gargoyles and angels, but the most arresting feature is the *Coventry Cross*, made from nails salvaged from the bombed Coventry Cathedral. With the decline in its congregation, the cathedral is desperate for money. Some income is generated by the concerts held here throughout the year, and the authorities have sold off all the land around and beneath the church to accommodate new buildings and the Promenade de la Cathédrale in the Underground City. There is now a possibility that it may be developed as a college for one of the city's universities.

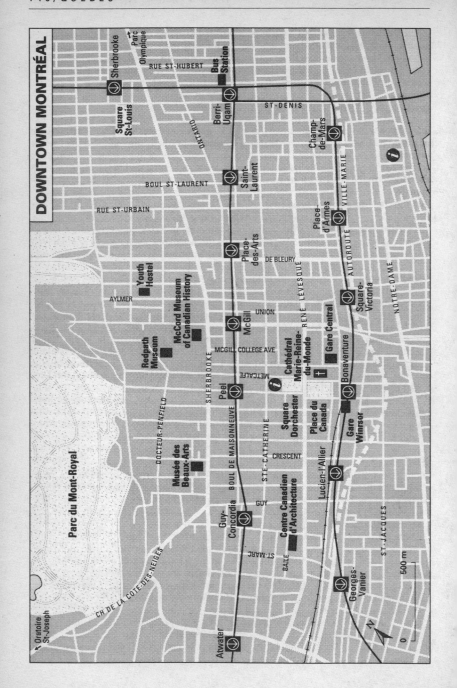

The most prestigious of the universities can be reached by backtracking one block to **McGill College Avenue**, which has been recently redeveloped as a principal boulevard – the wide pavements are adorned with sculptures, most notably Raymond Mason's *Illuminated Crowd*, portraying a mass of larger-than-life Montréalers. Continuing up McGill College Avenue brings you to the leafy campus of **McGill University**. Founded in 1813 from the bequest of James McGill, a Glaswegian immigrant fur trader, the university is now world famous for its medical and engineering schools, and has more than 20,000 students. The campus of ornate limestone buildings and their modern extensions is perfect for relaxing or for a walk above the street level of downtown. A boulder on the campus near Sherbrooke marks the spot where the original Iroquois village of Hochelaga stood before European penetration.

The university boasts a couple of fine museums. At 859 Sherbrooke Ouest there's the **Redpath Museum** (Sept–June Mon–Fri 9am–5pm; July–Aug Mon–Thurs 9am–5pm; free), the first custom-built Canadian museum. Its eclectic anthropological collection includes a rare fossil collection, dinosaur bones and two Eygptian mummies. The better-known **McCord Museum of Canadian History** in the McGill Union building, 690 Sherbrooke Ouest, is in the throes of a $20-million expansion programme, due to be completed in 1992. When it re-opens the McCord will be Canada's best history museum, displaying much of its vast collection of costumes, textiles and paintings, and its famed photographic archives.

Another major overhaul is being carried out on Place des Arts, to the east of the campus, where the **Musée d'art Contemporain de Montréal** – the city's foremost showcase for work by living Québécois artists – is being installed inside the Place des Arts complex.

## Rue Sherbrooke and around

**Rue Sherbrooke** crosses half of Montréal island, but other than the Olympic Stadium far out east its most interesting part is the few blocks from the university to Rue Crescent, an elite stretch of private galleries, exclusive hotels and outlets for the likes of Saint Laurent, Ralph Lauren and Armani.

At the corner of Drummond is the **Ritz Carlton Hotel**, Montréal's most ornate hotel – Elizabeth Taylor married Richard Burton here. The hotel remains a symbol of what was once known as the Golden Square Mile, the area between Sherbrooke, Mont Royale, côte de Neiges and avenue de Parc. From the late nineteenth century to World War II it is estimated that seventy percent of Canada's wealth was owned by a few hundred people who lived here. Known as the Caesars of the Wilderness, the majority were Scottish immigrants who made their fortunes in brewing, fur trading and banking, and who financed the railways and steamships that contributed to Montréal's industrial growth.

Almost opposite the Ritz stands Montréal's **Musée des Beaux Arts** (Tues–Sun 10am–7pm; $4), Canada's oldest museum. Recently extended for a second time, the building can at last do justice to its permanent collection, much of which used to be displaced whenever one of the museum's prestige temporary exhibitions was on. The Canadian art collection is one of the country's most impressive, covering the spectrum from the devotional works from the days of New France, through paintings of the local landscape by, among others, James Wilson Morrice, Maurice Cullen and Clarence Gagnon, to the more radical canvases by the Automatistes – Paul Emile Borduas and Jean-Paul Riopelle – who transformed Montréal's art scene in the 1940s. Predictably enough, the Group of Seven get a showing too, but the most accomplished paintings are in the European section, where many of the canvases – by such masters as El Greco, Rembrandt and Memlinc – were donated by the merchants of Montréal's heyday. Their contributions are supplemented by equally high-class later acquisitions by Rodin, Picasso, Henry Moore and other twentieth-century luminaries.

To the left of the museum is another reminder of the Scottish roots of this neighbourhood, the **Church of St Andrew and St Paul**, the regimental church of the Black Watch, the Highland Regiment of Canada. Though the Gothic Revival building is not particularly impressive, Tiffany's stained glass windows are worth a quick peek.

### The Centre Canadien d'Architecture

Continue west on Sherbrooke to St-Marc then walk down to Baile, and you'll come face to face with the gigantic **Centre Canadien d'Architecture** (Wed & Fri 11am–6pm, Thurs 11am–8pm, Sat & Sun 11am–6pm; $3). A wonderfully sleek building with a curiously windowless facade and vast glass doors that open smoothly with the least amount of effort, the centre was heaped with accolades when it opened in 1989. The Peter Rose design incorporates the beautifully restored Shaughnessy mansion and its Art Nouveau Devencore conservatory, while the light-filled galleries display the museum's vast collection of prints, drawings and books in exhibitions which range from individual masters to whole movements from all cultures and periods.

Behind the museum on boulevard Rene Lévesque, on an area known as the Dorchester Plateau, are the **CCA Sculpture Gardens** (free). This whole area, once full of rambling villas like the Shaughnessy mansion, was ripped apart in 1969 for the construction of the Autoroute Ville-Marie, and the gardens have restored pride in what was until recently a derelict area. Designed by prominent Montréal artist and architect Melvin Charney, the sculptures are a wacky mishmash of architectural references, arranged in a way reminiscent of ancient stone circles.

### Underground City

From the CCA it's about a ten-block walk east back to Dorchester Square and nearby **Place Ville-Marie**, the beginning of Montréal's famous **Underground City**, planned as a refuge from weather that is outrageously cold in the winter and humid in the summer. The underground network began with the cruciform Place Ville-Marie in the 1960s. Montréalers flooded into the first climate-controlled shopping arcade, and the Underground City duly spread. Today its 22km of passages provide access to the Métro, major hotels, shopping malls, transport termini, thousands of offices, flats and restaurants and a good smattering of cinemas and theatres. Everything underground is well signposted, but you're still likely to get lost on your first visit, unless you pick up a map of the ever-expanding system from a tourist office.

## The Main – and East Montréal

Boulevard St-Laurent – the **Main** – leads all the way up from Vieux-Montréal to the northern extremities of the city. North of Sherbrooke is the most absorbing episode along the way, a district where Montréal's cosmopolitan diversity is evident in distinct enclaves of immigrant neighbourhoods. Crossed by **Rue St-Denis**, the heart of the upbeat studenty Latin Quarter, this zone is where the most fun can be had in Montréal, with a huge array of ethnic food outlets and bars spilling out onto the streets. If the party atmosphere is too much, you can head for the landscaped expanse of **Mont Royal** or the overwhelming **Olympic Stadium** and the vast **Botanical Gardens** further east.

### Boulevard St-Laurent and Mont Royal Plateau

Traditionally **Boulevard St-Laurent** divided the British in the west from the French in the east of the city. Montréal's immigrants, first Russian Jews then Greeks, Portuguese, Italians, East Europeans and more recently South Americans, settled in the middle and though many prospered enough to move on, the area around the Main is still a cultural mix where neither of the two official languages dominates. Delis, bars, nightclubs, hardware stores, bookshops and an increasing number of trendy boutiques provide the perfect background to a wonderful jumble of sights, sounds and smells.

Wandering north from downtown will bring you one of Montréal's few pedestrianised streets, **Prince Arthur**, thronged with buskers and caricaturists in the summer. Turning right leads to the beautiful **Square St-Louis**, the city's finest. Designed in 1876, the square was originally the domain of rich corporate Montréalers, but the magnificent houses are now occupied by artists, poets and writers – including Leonard Cohen. During the winter the square's pathways are converted into skating rinks.

The east side of the square divides the lower and upper areas of **St-Denis**, a relaxed, bohemian district of balconied red-brick houses and a wealth of cafés, bars and clubs. The part of St-Denis back towards downtown has long had a rather grubby reputation, but though this is still a favourite haunt of drug pushers it is becoming increasingly colonised by terrace cafés crammed with students well into the early hours. Further north lies the stamping ground of the francophone intellectual set, where a different yet equally heady atmosphere pervades the sidewalks.

## Mont Royal

Little more than a hill to most tourists but a mountain to Montréalers, **Mont Royal** reaches a less than lofty height of 225 metres but its 190 hectares of greenery are visible from anywhere in the city. Mont Royal holds a special place in the history of the city – it was here that the Iroquois established their settlement and that Maisonneuve declared the island to be French – but for centuries the mountain was privately owned. Then, during an especially bitter winter, one of the inhabitants cut down his trees for extra firewood. Montréalers were outraged at the desecration and in 1875 the land was bought by the city for the impressive sum of $1,000,000. Frederick Law Olmsted, designer of New York's Central Park and San Francisco's Golden Gate Park, was hired to landscape the hill, which now boasts 56km of jogging paths and 20km of skiing paths to keep the city's inhabitants happy all year round.

The city has steadfastly refused any commercial developments on this lucrative site, the only construction being **Beaver Lake**, built in the 1930s as a work creation scheme for the unemployed. In the 1950s protection of the mountain reached a puritanical extreme when a local journalist revealed that young couples were using the area for amatory pursuits and, even worse, that people were openly drinking alcohol. Consequently all the underbush was uprooted, which only succeeded in killing off much of the ash, birch, maple, oak and pine trees. Within five years Mont Royal was dubbed Bald Mountain and a replanting campaign had to be instigated.

From avenue Mont Royal you can turn left onto avenue du Parc to the **George-Étienne Cartier monument** where every Sunday buskers and people of all ages congregate until the sun goes down. Paths lead up to the summit via an illuminated cross marking the spot where Maisonneuve placed his cross in 1642. Olmsted road, which leads up to the summit from downtown, has various look-out points for views of the city.

## Oratoire St-Joseph

On the west side of the mountain the awesome **Oratoire St-Joseph** (daily 6.30am–9.30pm) rises from its green surroundings on Montréal's highest point. If you don't want to walk across the summit, the nearest Métro is Côte des Neiges, from where the oratory is signposted.

In 1904 a certain Brother André built a small chapel here to honour Saint Joseph, Canada's patron saint. Before long André's ability to heal people had earned him the soubriquet "The Miracle Man of Montréal", and huge numbers of delighted patients donated so much money that in 1924 he could afford to begin work on this immense granite edifice. It was completed in 1967, thirty years after Brother André's death, and is topped by a dome that is second in size only to St Peter's in Rome. The interior of St Jo's – as it's known locally – does not live up to the splendour of the Italianate exterior, though the chapel in the apse is richly decorated with green marble columns and a gold leaf ceiling. The roof terrace, above the portico, has excellent views of the city and the St Lawrence beyond. A small **museum** in the basement displays items relating to Brother André's life, including the room in which he died, which was shifted here from a local hospice. Even stranger is Brother André's heart enclosed in a glass case; the devout believe it quivers occasionally.

Outside the **Way of the Cross** has some particularly beautiful sculptures in smooth white Carrara marble and Indiana buff stone by Montréal artist Louis Parent – a tranquil site used as the setting for Canada's most famous film, *Jesus of Montreal*. On the other side of the oratory the original chapel and Brother André's tiny room can be visited.

## The Parc Olympique and around

It's best to take the Métro to Pie IX to view Montréal's most infamous architectural construction, the **Parc Olympique**. The main attraction, the **Olympic Stadium**, is known by Montréalers as The Big O for two reasons: its circular shape and the fact that the city owes so much money for its construction. The main facilities for the 1976 Olympics were designed by Roger Taillibert, who was told that money was no object – the complex ended up costing $1.2 billion, and was not even completed in time for the event. It's now the most heavily used stadium in the world, in a desperate attempt to pay the debts; the ceaseless schedule features everything from Pink Floyd concerts to regular baseball games played by the Expos. Daily **guided tours** are also available (June & Aug 9am–5pm; Sept–May 12.40–3.40pm; $5.50).

The stadium's 168-metre **tower** is a major engineering feat: the highest inclining tower in the world, its main function is to hold the 65-tonne roof when it is retracted, a process that takes 45 minutes. The latest attraction here is a **shuttle ride** up the tower to an observation deck, with 80-kilometre views and displays on the history of the complex (daily Oct–April 10am–6pm; May–Sept 10am–11pm; $5.50).

Also in the Parc Olympique is the globe-shaped **Vélodrome**, used for the biking events during the Olympics and currently being redeveloped as the **Biodôme**. Due to open in June 1992, this unique environment museum will re-create four North American ecosystems – it will be possible to see polar bears, reptiles and whales all living under one roof in replicas of their natural habitats.

Near the stadium and linked by a free shuttle bus from mid-May to mid-September are the **Jardin Botanique de Montréal**, 4101 Sherbrooke Est (daily 8am–sunset; $6 from mid-May to mid-Oct, free the rest of the year). Covering 73 hectares, they comprise some thirty different types of gardens from medicinal herbs to orchids. Highlights include a Japanese garden designed by the landscape architect Ken Nakajima, its ponds of water lilies bordered by greenish sculpted stone and crossed by delicate bridges. In 1991 the Japanese garden was joined by the Chinese garden, the largest of its kind outside China – over 1500 tonnes of materials from China were used to reproduce a replica of the Ming Gardens of fifteenth-century Shanghai. Other attractions in the gardens include the **Insectarium** (daily 9am–6pm; $4), a bug-shaped building containing insects of every shape and size. The museum is mainly geared towards children but adults will learn a fascinating thing or two – like the fact that the house fly has more than five thousand muscles.

Near the southwest corner of the gardens, on the junction of Pie IX and Sherbrooke, is the stately mansion of the **Château Dufresne** (Wed–Sun 11am–5pm; $3), built in the 1910s for the Dufresne brothers – one an engineer, the other an industrialist – who were both instrumental in Montréal's expansion. Its impressive Edwardian interior houses post-1935 *objets d'art*, plus occasional special decorative arts exhibitions.

# Montréal's other attractions

The islands of Montréal, Île Ste-Hélène and Île Notre-Dame and their environs offer various slightly out-of-the-way sights, all well served by public transport but mostly worth the trip only if you have time to kill. Lying just south of Montréal, the combined 263 hectares of the **smaller islands** were the main venue for Expo '67 and have been developed as playgrounds for the city's inhabitants, with **La Ronde** amusement park the main draw. The **Maison St-Gabriel** is included in this section as it is a bit of a hike from central Montréal. The fur-trading centre of **Lachine** is located on the western shore of Montréal island, about the same distance from downtown as the art museum in the suburb of **St-Laurent**, while the **Canadian Railway Museum** is located off the island on the south shore of the St Lawrence.

**La Ronde**, Île Ste-Hélène (late May to Aug Fri & Sat 11am–1am, rest of week 11am–midnight; adults $17.25, children $8, families $38.50). Ticket gives unlimited access to every ride in the amusement park and admission to the nearby Aqua Parc, a waterslide park. La Ronde is also the location for various celebrations through the year, including the annual Fireworks Competition. Île Ste-Hélène Métro.

**David M Stewart Museum**, Old Fort, Île Ste-Hélène (10am–5pm; closed Tues; $2). Located in the fortified arsenal commissioned by the Duke of Wellington, the museum contains a collection of weapons and assorted domestic and scientific artefacts. In addition the fort is the summer venue for the re-enactment of seventeenth- and eighteenth-century military manoeuvres by the Fraser Highlanders and Compagnie Franche de la Marine.

**Palais de la Civilisation**, Île Notre-Dame (mid-May to Sept daily 10am–8pm; admission varies). Originally the French pavilion for the Expo, this now holds exhibitions on subjects from clothing to archaeology. Bus #167 from Île Ste-Hélène Métro.

**Maison St-Gabriel**, 2146 Place Dublin (guided tours mid-April to mid-Dec Tues–Sat 1.30–3pm, Sun 1.30–3.30pm; donation). Dating from 1668, this stone house was the home of Marguerite Bourgeoys (see p.137); antique furniture and the restored kitchen are the main attractions. Bus #61 from Square Victoria Métro.

**National Historic Site – The Fur Trade in Lachine**, 1255 St Joseph Boulevard, Lachine (mid-Feb to mid-May Wed–Sun 10am–noon & 1–5pm; mid-May to Aug Mon 1–6pm, Tues–Sun 10am–12.30pm & 1–6pm; Sept to mid-Oct daily 10am–noon & 1–5pm; mid-Oct to Nov Wed–Sun 10am–noon & 1–5pm; free). Right on the shore of Lac St-Louis, the old Lachine warehouse houses an exhibition on the fur trade, and the staff wear the costumes of the natives, *coureurs des bois* and the Scottish merchants who worked here in the eighteenth and early nineteenth centuries. Bus #191 from Lionel-Groux Métro.

**Musée de Lachine**, 110 chemin LaSalle, Lachine (Wed–Sun 11.30am–4.30pm; closed Jan & Feb; free). This seventeenth-century fur-trading post contains a humdrum collection of contemporary artefacts and a display on the history of the Lachine canal. Bus #110 from Angrignon Métro.

**Musée d'Art de St-Laurent**, 615 Ste Croix Boulevard, Ville St-Laurent (Tues–Fri & Sun noon–5pm; free). A small museum in the former neo-Gothic chapel of St-Laurent college, featuring early arts and crafts from Québec. Du Collège Métro.

**Musée ferroviaire Canadien**, 122A St-Pierre, St-Constant (May to Aug daily 9am–5pm; Sept to late Oct Sat & Sun 9am–5pm; $2.25). Special buses connect Longueuil and Angrignon métros to Canada's largest collection of railway, tramway and steam locomotives.

# Eating

Montréalers conduct much of their business and their social lives in the city's eating places, and Montréal food is as varied as its population, ranging from the rich meat dishes of typical Québécois cuisine to bagels bursting with cream cheese. Masses of restaurants line the area around **Ste-Catherine** in downtown, though American fast-food chains seem to be taking over, while **Vieux-Montréal** has an ever-expanding number, though here most are touristy and slightly overpriced. The most upbeat atmosphere is around the **Latin Quarter** and further east in the more French area of the metropolis. Though Montréal has its own **Chinatown** just north of Vieux-Montréal, a **Little Italy** around Jean-Talon Métro and a **Greek** community concentrated along Prince Arthur, most prominent of the ethnic eateries are the **Eastern European** establishments dotted around the city. Opened by immigrants who came to work in the garment factories, their speciality is **smoked meat**, which has become a Montréal obsession – coming in various degrees of fattiness, from lean to positively dripping, it's served between huge chunks of rye with pickles on the side. Montréal comes a close second to New York as the **bagel** capital of the world, and they are sold everywhere from grimy outlets to stylish cafés.

For those on a **tight budget** the delis, diners and cafés are perfect – $5–10 will see you well fed. "Apporter son vin" establishments, of which there are many on Prince Arthur and Duluth, are the cheaper restaurant alternatives. Remember when checking the menu that the present federal and provincial **taxes** will add just under 16 percent to the meal, and tips are a further 15 percent.

## Snacks and cafés

**Bagel Etc.**, 4320 St-Laurent. Trendy New York-type diner. Excellent bagels from the simple cream cheese to caviar. Open until 6am Sat & Sun, until 3.30am Tues–Fri.

**Beauty's**, 93 Mont-Royal Ouest. The best bargain eatery in this area and a brunch favourite with Montréalers. Wonderful 1950s decor and typical diner fare on the menu.

**Ben's Delicatessen**, 1475 Metcalfe. Lithuanian Ben Kravitz opened his deli in 1908 and his sons and grandsons still run the place. Ben's has become much more than a family business and is now a Montréal institution. Around 3am the gaudy 1930s interior is packed with customers from truckers to jewellery-adorned theatre-goers. The wall of fame is constantly being added to, as anyone who is anyone drops by. The speciality Big Ben Sandwich ($7.40) is an inch thick and the equally famous Strawberry Cheese Cake ($4.50) is exceptional. Open Sun–Thurs 7am–4am, Fri & Sat 7am–5am.

**La Binerie Mont-Royal**, 367 Mont-Royal. Only four tables and a chrome counter for the hundreds of people who drop into this Montréal institution every day. Basically the menu is beans, beans and more beans served with ketchup, vinegar or maple syrup. On the side the choices are pork, beef, tourtière or the Binerie's famous stew.

**Briskets**, 4006 Ste-Catherine Ouest, 1073 Beaver Hall & 2055 Bishop. Plain decor with wooden tables, popular with students. Smoked meat to eat in or take away. Closed Sun.

**Café Ciné-Lumière**, 5163 St-Laurent. Antique Parisian decor, inexpensive French food and continuous movies.

**Café El Dorado**, 5226 St-Laurent. Coffees from all over the world, and fine desserts.

**Café Santropol**, 3990 St-Urbain. Vegetarian café on the corner of Duluth. Popular with health-conscious anglophones having mid-life crises – known locally as "granolas" because they always munch health-food snacks. Enormous sandwiches, quiches and salads as well as a wide range of herbal teas and coffees.

**Café Toman**, 1421 Mackay. A quiet Czech coffeeshop in downtown. The cakes are great but soups and salads are also available. Popular with students from nearby Concordia. Closed Sun & Mon.

**La Chartreuse**, 3439 St-Denis. Upmarket café with delicious cakes. Closed Mon.

**Le Daphnée**, 3808 St-Denis. Hyper-civilised and expensive *salon de thé*.

**La Desserte**, 5258 St-Laurent. The most unbelievable cakes, particularly the cheesecake, but they are all divine. Expensive but worth every cent. Serves discounted specials for cinema-goers on some nights – keep your tickets. Open until 1am at weekends.

**Dunn's**, 892 Ste-Catherine Ouest. Open 24 hours a day. An excellent deli with great jars of pickles in the window and a wealth of smoked meats. Frantic atmosphere and friendly service. A favourite with local business types, and thus packed at lunchtimes.

**Fairmount Bagel Bakery**, 74 Fairmount Ouest. Possibly the best bagel outlet in the Western hemisphere. There is nowhere to sit, but arm yourself with a bag of bagels, a pot of cream cheese and some smoked salmon (lox), sit on the nearest kerb and you'll soon be in bagel heaven. A huge variety of bagels is on offer 24 hours a day, 7 days a week.

**Faubourg Ste-Catherine**, 1616 Ste-Catherine Ouest. A gigantic restored building on the corner of Guy. Downstairs is a wealth of food stalls from cookies to fresh veg; upstairs a fast-food mall to surpass all others – everything from fresh salmon to crêpes and cookies.

**Le Petit Peu**, 318 Ontario Est. Very cheap vegetarian and health-food café. Closed Sat.

**Schwartz's Montréal Hebrew Delicatessen**, 3895 St-Laurent. Small, narrow deli. Schwartz tends to stay at the top of the word-of-mouth "Who does the best smoked meat?" competition more often than its competitors. The sandwiches are colossal.

**Wilensky's Light Lunch**, 5167 Clark. Used for countless film sets because the decor hasn't changed since 1932 and that includes the till, the grill and the drinks machine. The Wilensky Special includes four types of salami and costs around $4. Closed weekends.

# Restaurants

**Arachova**, 256 St-Viateur. Plain Greek restaurant with excellent prices. Bring your own alcohol. Open until 4am.

**Azuma**, 901 Sherbrooke Est (☎525-5262). Not too expensive (about $20 a head) considering this is a Japanese restaurant. Reserve if possible.

**Bar-B-Barn**, 1201 Guy. Just off Ste-Catherine. Brilliant spare ribs served in Western "Yeee-Ha" decor; a favourite with the local "cowboy" business world – hundreds of cards are stuck in the log rafters.

**Basha**, 2140 Guy and 930 Ste-Catherine Ouest. Cheap central Lebanese, open late at weekends.

**Le Bistro Bagatelle**, 4806 du Parc (☎273-4088). Pricey, French seafood restaurant. Wood-panelled rooms and engraved mirrors imported from Belgium. Reservations a good idea.

**Le Bistro Méditerranéen**, 3857 St-Denis. Very cheap North African restaurant.

**Le Bonaparte**, 443 St-François-Xavier. Moderately priced, well-situated French restaurant in Vieux-Montréal. The fish is good and there are tables on the balconies.

**La Casa Greque**, 200 Prince Arthur. Another cheap Greek place. There are numerous other Greek restaurants in this area, all much the same standard.

**Le Caveau**, 2063 Victoria. Three-floored restaurant in a twee downtown house. Inside you might be in France – red-and-white tablecloths and dripping candles as well as great French food. Very pricey but worth the splurge.

**Chez Delmo**, 211 Notre-Dame Ouest. Popular with anglophones and workers from the nearby stock exchange in Vieux-Montréal. Eat in the first room with its two long oyster bars. Fish and seafood dishes are the speciality, and the chowder is excellent. Closed Sun.

**Citrus**, 5282-St-Laurent (☎276-2353). Tiny restaurant with three-course menu for $35, six-course for $55. The French/American food is of the highest quality.

**Le Commensal**, 680 Ste-Catherine Ouest & 2115 St-Denis. Conveniently located cheap vegetarian with hot or cold buffet. Not licensed. The St-Denis location has a better atmosphere. Open every day until late.

**Eduardo**, 404 Duluth Est. Crowded cheap Italian with huge portions. Bring your own alcohol and expect a queue.

**L'Express**, 3927 St-Denis (☎845-5333). Fashionable Parisian-style bistro, with hectic service. Pretty expensive, and reservations essential.

**Fiesta Tapas**, 479 St-Alexis. Another of Vieux-Montréal's restaurants that conjures up another world – this time a Madrid tapas bar. Not too expensive. Closed Mon.

**Les Filles du Roy**, 415 Bonsecours (☎849-3535). Québécois restaurant that caters for the Vieux-Montréal tourists. Seventeenth-century decor of stone walls and heavy wooden furniture, with waitresses wearing the costume of the orphaned "daughters of the king". Food's good though.

**Il était une fois**, 600 Place d'Youville. Old train station converted into hamburger restaurant. One of the best deals in Vieux-Montréal.

**Katsura**, 2170 de la Montagne. Large and popular downtown Japanese restaurant. Fairly reasonable.

**Laloux**, 250 des Pins Est. On the east side of the city, this chic Parisian-style bistro serves expensive nouvelle cuisine.

**Laurier BBQ**, 381 Laurier Ouest. Great hunks of Québec-style barbequed chicken and huge salads; a Montréal favourite for half a century.

**Maison Kam Fung**, 1008 Clark. Montréal's vast temple to dim sum in the heart of Chinatown. Well-priced menu but not dirt cheap. Dim sum is *élan du coeur* in Québécois.

**La Marée**, 404 Place Jacques-Cartier (☎861-9794). Very refined and expensive fish restaurant with an excellent reputation and perfect Vieux-Montréal location.

**Mazurka's**, 63 Prince Arthur. You'll hear more Polish spoken here than either French or English. Cheap, with a midday special.

**Le Mer Rouge**, 256 Roy Est. Cheap Ethiopian restaurant with African paintings and sculptures. Seating is on the floor and you eat the spicy food with your hands.

**Modigliani**, 1251 Gilford. Lots of plants and a pianist. Reasonable prices for great Italian food.

**Moishe's**, 3961 St-Laurent (☎845-3509). Excellent steaks, but very expensive with notoriously bad-tempered service. Favourite haunt of Montréal's business community. Reservations recommended.

**Le Palmarium**, 4128 St-Denis. Very cheap Tunisian food.

**La Paryse**, 302 Ontario Est. Delicious homemade hamburgers and chips in a 1950s-style diner. Highly recommended.

**Pattaya**, 1235 Guy. Small Thai restaurant. Closed Mon.

**Le Petit Extra**, 1690 Ontario Est. Large, lively and inexpensive bistro.

**Le Pique Assiette**, 2051 Ste-Catherine Ouest. Cheap Indian buffet.

**La Pizzaïolle**, 5100 Hutchison. Thick-crusted pizzas straight out of a brick oven. Pricey but worth it.

**Pizzédélic**, 3509 St-Laurent. Modern decor and experimental pizzas.

**Pizzeria Napoletana**, 189 Dante. Very cheap place in Little Italy. Take your own alcohol. Expect a queue at the weekend.

**Prego**, 5142 St-Laurent. Stylish Italian restaurant with loaded clientele. Expensive but delicious.

**La Selva**, 862 Marie-Anne Est (☎525-1798). Tiny, plain restaurant with unbeatable prices for fish and Peruvian food. Bring your own wine – there are six off-licences (*dépanneurs*) in the area. Reservations are recommended purely because of the size of the place. Closed Sun & Mon.

**Shed Café**, 3515 St-Laurent and 1333 Ste-Catherine Est. Hamburger, salad and sandwich joint where trendy Montréalers come to see and be seen. Avant-garde, wacky interior. Open until 5am Fri & Sat.

**Le St-Honoré**, 1616 Ste-Catherine Ouest (☎932-5550). One of Montréal's top restaurants, situated behind Faubourg Ste-Catherine in a former part of the Grey Nuns' mother-house. The food is magnificent but expect to pay around $50 without wine. Reservations a must.

**Le Witloof**, 3619 St-Denis (☎281-0100). Upmarket bistro serving Belgian and French food. Around $50 for two before wine.

# Bars and nightlife

Montréal's **nightlife** keeps going to the small hours of the morning, and its bars and clubs cater for everyone – from the students of the Latin Quarter and the punks who hang out on the corner of Ste-Catherine and St-Denis, to the anglophone yuppies of Crescent Street. The places listed here are the best of the bunch and are open until 3am unless stated otherwise. Always tip the bar staff – the perks constitute the main whack of their wages. Many of the bars have regular music nights, with jazz being especially popular. Other than the bars there are numerous venues in the city, with top-name touring bands playing at the Forum and the Olympic Stadium .

For up-to-date **information**, the *Mirror* is a free English weekly newspaper with an excellent listings section. The English-language daily *The Montréal Gazette* also carries comprehensive listings – the Friday weekend guide is particularly good. *Montréal Scope*, available in tourist information offices and the better hotels, is primarily for mainstream tourists.

## Bars

**Bar Salon St-Laurent**, 3874 St-Laurent. Popular student bar with loud South American and West Indian music on the first floor.

**Les Beaux Esprits**, 2073 St-Denis. Local blues and jazz artists can be seen here for free.

**La Bibliothèque**, 1647 St-Denis. Quiet bar with outside terrace. Done up like a library. Two drinks for one on Friday and Saturday nights.

**Café Campus**, 3315 Queen Mary. A long way out (take the Métro to Côte des Neiges) but worth it for the great atmosphere, free popcorn and French singers on Sundays. Popular with students.

**Le Central**, 4479 St-Denis. Unpretentious, old jazz bar. Another student hang-out as the drinks are cheap and admission is free.

**Le Cheval Blanc**, 809 Ontario Est. Old Montréal pub that does not seem to have been redecorated since the 1940s. Strange beers, including chocolate flavour. Closes at midnight; closed Sun.

**L'Escapade**, Château Champlain, 1 Place du Canada. On the top floor of the cheese grater skyscraper of Château Champlain. The "holes" reveal excellent views of the whole city.

**Le Grand Café**, 1720 St-Denis. Loud bar that spills out into trendy St-Denis in the summer. Live jazz and blues from Wednesday through Saturday. Free entry.

**Le Pub...de Londres à Berlin**, 4557 St-Denis. Excellent atmosphere with the trendiest of Montréal's young bohemian crowd – particularly up-and-coming actors, comedians and artists. Big sacks of free popcorn, numerous draught beers and pool tables. Closes at 2am Sat & Sun.

**Le St-Sulpice**, 1682 St-Denis. A three-floored beautifully decorated fashionable bar in the heart of Montréal's Latin quarter. Terrace at the back and front, perfect for people-watching.

**Lux**, 5220 St-Laurent. Magnet for Montréal's night owls, hitting its stride at around 3.30am. Cheap draft beer. Avoid the burgers.

**Pub le Vieux-Dublin**, 1219A Université. Irish pub with Celtic music and a massive choice of draught beers. Popular with everyone.

**Pub Sir Winston Churchill**, 1459 Crescent. Known locally as Winny's, this English-style pub attracts local and visiting anglophone professionals. Pool tables and a small dance floor.

**Thursday's**, 1449 Crescent. Another mainstay of Montréal's dwindling English population. Very popular with anglos but a pretty horrendous cattle market. Closes at 12.45am so everyone can get to bed early!

**Les Zéclopés**, 500 Rachel Est. Unpretentious, laid-back and friendly bar with a mainly young clientele. Cheap drinks.

## Venues, clubs and discos

**L'Air du Temps**, 194 St-Paul Ouest (☎842-2003). The most famous of Montréal's jazz spots. In the heart of Vieux-Montréal with ornate antique interior. Live acts from 10pm Thurs–Sun, closed Mon–Wed. Entrance $7, arrive early to get a decent seat.

**Aux Deux Pierrots**, 104 St-Paul Ouest. Québécois folksingers are the mainstay of this club. There's usually a good crowded atmosphere but don't expect to understand a word unless your French is excellent. Outside terrace in the summer. Admission from $3.

**Le Balattou**, 4372 St-Laurent. Montréal's only African nightclub. Dark, smoky, crowded, hot, loud and friendly. Live acts every night; entrance $5 on weekdays, $8 at weekends (which includes one drink).

**Le Belmont**, 4483 St-Laurent. Yuppie disco dance bar. Closed Mon–Wed. Entrance Thurs $3, Fri & Sat $4, Sun free.

**Blue Dog**, 3556 St-Laurent. Popular, free, trendy, student dance bar.

**Le Club Soda**, 5240 du Parc. One of Montréal's most popular venues. Attracts good acts, especially during the comedy and jazz festivals. Admission charge depending on act.

**Les Foufounes Électriques**, 87 Ste-Catherine Est. A bizarre name (The Electric Buttocks) for a bizarre and wonderful bar/club/venue. The best place in Québec for alternative bands, attracting all of Montréal's young crowd from punks through to medical students. Wacky interior of graffittied walls and strange sculptures. Has a huge outside terrace perfect for summer evenings. Tickets for bands from $10, otherwise admission is free and pitchers of beer are cheap.

**Le Lézard**, 4177 St-Denis. Dingy, avant-garde club with frequently changing decor – on Wednesdays and Thursdays pots of paint are available to the clientele who then redecorate the place with weird and often disastrous murals. On Sunday things get even stranger when the punters paint each other's bodies. Entrance Fri & Sat $2. Closed Mon.

**Le Lolas Paradise**, 3604 St-Laurent. Chic, expensive disco. The extortionately priced drinks include imaginative cocktails. Open until 5am.

**Le Métropolis**, 59 Ste-Catherine. A huge converted theatre that's now Montréal's premier discothèque. No jeans. Admission Thurs & Fri $5, Saturday $8. Closed Mon–Wed & Sun.

**Le Passeport**, 4156 St-Denis. Small dance-music club with long queues at weekends. Frequented by Quebec's rich and famous; drinks are overpriced. Thurs–Sat entry is $3.50, free the rest of the week.

**Spectrum**, 318 Ste-Catherine Ouest. Huge jazz club, acts from 9pm. Loud, smoky atmosphere. Admission from $10.

**Le Vieux Munich**, 1170 St-Denis. This huge Bavarian-style building attracts all ages for nights of beer-stomping. Great atmosphere. Entrance $3 on Fridays and Saturdays. Closes 2am.

# The performing arts and cinema

Montréal's most prestigious centre for the performing arts is the *Place des Arts*, 1501 Jeanne Mance (information ☎285-4200; tickets ☎842-2112), a four-hall complex with a comprehensive year-round programme of dance, music and theatre. The *Théâtre de Verdure* in Lafontaine Park is an outdoor theatre with a summer-long programme of free plays, ballets and concerts. Another eclectic venue is the *Théâtre St-Denis*, 1594 St-Denis (☎849-4211), which presents blockbuster musicals and other shows. The *Saidye Bronfman Centre*, 5170 chemin de la Côte Ste-Catherine (☎739-2301), contains an exhibition centre and a 300-seater venue for music, dance, film and theatre.

The city's foremost French-language **theatre** is the *Theatre du Rideau Vert*, 4664 St-Denis (☎845-0267), which gives prominence to Québec playwrights, while the *Theatre du Nouveau Monde*, 84 Ste-Catherine Est (☎861-0563), presents a mix of contemporary and classic plays in French. Montréal's main English-language theatre is the *Centaur Theatre*, housed in the former stock exchange at 453 St-François-Xavier (☎288-3161).

Montréal has more than ten excellent **dance** troupes from the internationally acclaimed *Les Grandes Ballets Canadiens* and *Ballets Classiques de Montréal* to the avant-garde *LaLaLa Human Steps* and *Tangente*, who perform at various times at the *Place des Arts*, *Théâtre de Verdue* and during the festivals. The continent's premier contemporary dance festival is the **Festival International de Nouvelle Danse**, held at various city locations every two years from late September to early October.

Montréal has two well-known **orchestras**, the *Montréal Symphony Orchestra* (☎842-3402) and the *McGill Chamber Orchestra* (☎487-5190), each of whom holds regular concerts at *Place des Arts* and the Basilique Notre-Dame. The city also has a programme of free summer concerts in various city parks (information ☎842-3402). *L'Opera de Montréal* produces five bilingually subtitled productions a year at *Place des Arts*.

**Films** in English, usually the latest releases from the States, can be caught at nearly all the city's cinemas, as they are shown for about a fortnight before the dubbed versions are available – central ones include *Eaton*, 705 Ste-Catherine Ouest; *Centre Ville*, 2001 Université; and *Palace*, 698 Ste-Catherine Ouest. The city's only English rep cinema is the *Rialto Cinema*, 5723 du Parc; French rep cinemas include the *Ouimetoscope*, 1204 Ste-Catherine Est, and *Cinéma de Paris*, 896 Ste-Catherine Ouest. For Québécois filmmakers, check out *Cinématique Québécoise*, 335 de Maisonneuve Est.

# Festivals and other events

The **Montréal International Jazz Festival** is North America's largest jazz festival, with 90 indoor and 240 outdoor shows, many of them free. From late June to early July more than 2000 international musicians descend on the city, including the likes of Cab Calloway, Dave Brubeck, Ben E King and Branford Marsalis. Continuing the superlatives, there's the mid-July **Juste Pour Rire** (Just For Laughs), the world's largest comedy festival; the 1991 programme included the Glaswegian Gerry Sadowitz, who got punched for joking that all the French should be sent home.

Noisiest of the city shindigs is the **International Fireworks Competition**, whose participants are competing to get contracts for the July 4 celebrations in the States. Held from late May to early June, the music-coordinated pyrotechnics are a breathtaking sight. The action takes place at La Ronde and tickets are around $20, but across the water and on the Jacques-Cartier Bridge the spectacle is free, and the music for the displays is broadcast live on local radio.

Montréal has **film festivals** practically every month, some thematic, some devoted to individuals. The most notable is the **Montréal World Film Festival** in late August, the city's answer to Cannes, Berlin and Venice.

Finally, the **Cirque du Soleil** (information ☎522-2324) is a fantastic circus company that travels all over the world but every year has a big-top season in its home city. Refusing to exploit animals, the circus's acrobats, trapeze artists, clowns, jugglers and contortionists present an incredible show, with original music scores, extravagant costumes and mind-blowing stunts.

# Gay Montréal

Montréal has an excellent gay scene, with the action concentrated in the area known as the **Village** – it's located between St-Denis and Papineau, along Ste-Catherine and the cross streets. There are two **information lines** for up-to-date info on the latest events in the city: *Gai-Info* (☎768-0199), which is bilingual, and *The Gay Line* (☎931-8668), in English only. For contacts *L'Androygyne*, 3636 St-Laurent, is a gay and lesbian bookstore and *Priape*, 1311 Ste-Catherine Est, is Canada's largest gay department store. In late June a massive Gay Pride and Lesbian Parade is held along Ste-Catherine, ending with shows in Campbell Park.

## Cafés and restaurants

**L'Anecdote**, 801 Rachel Est and 3751 St-Urbain. Small, cosy hamburger joint.

**Callipyge**, 1493 Amherst. Good-value Sunday brunch and classic French *table d'hôte*. Closed Mon.

**Chez Better**, 1310 de Maisonneuve. Friendly place in the heart of the Village. Imported beers and excellent music.

**El Sombrero**, 1451 Ste-Catherine Ouest. Well-priced Mexican specialities. Open until 1am on Fridays.

**L'Exception**, 1200 St-Hubert. Chilli, salads and burgers. Young gay crowd.

## Bars, clubs and discos

**La Boîte en Haut**, 1320 Alexandre-de-Sève. Male disco.

**Caberet l'Entre Peau**, 1115 Ste-Catherine Est. Drag shows, mixed fun-loving clientele.

**La California**, 1412 Ste-Elizabeth. Popular and relaxed mixed hang-out, with pool tables.

**Club Date**, 1218 Ste-Catherine Est. Piano bar in the Village. Good singers. Mainly older, male punters.

**L'Exit**, 4282 St-Denis. Patio bar with a packed happy hour. Mostly women, though men are welcome.

**Le Joy**, 1450 Montcalm. Young mixed multi-level disco with roof terrace.

**Le Kiev**, 812 Rachel Est. Pool tables and chart music disco, popular with gay women. Closed Mon.

**Max**, 1166 Ste-Catherine Est. Relaxed men's hang-out.

**La Track**, 1584 Ste-Catherine Est. Gay bar and disco. Cruisy male leather crowd.

**Station C**, 1450 Ste-Catherine Est. Four-bar gay complex: *K.O.X*, Montréal's most well-established gay disco; *Katacombes*, a cruisy male-only leather bar; *K2*, a lesbian hang-out; and *Kaché*, a mixed Key-West-style lounge.

**Vogue**, 1950 de Maisonneuve Est. Live female vocalists. Mainly '50s and '60s music. Older women-only crowd.

**Zorro**, 4123 St-Denis. Intimate bar that resembles a grotto. Avant-garde art exhibits. Good place to meet people. Men in the majority.

# Listings

**Airlines** *British Airways*, 1021 de Maisonneuve (☎287-9133); *Air Canada, Air Alliance, Air Nova & Air Ontario*, 2020 Université (Canada & USA ☎393-3333); other destinations ☎393-3111); *Air France*, 2000 Mansfield (☎284-2825); *Canadian Airlines*, 999 de Maisonneuve (☎847-2211); *Swiss Air*, 1253 McGill College (☎879-1367).

**Airport enquiries** Mirabel ☎476-3010; Dorval ☎633-3105.

**Baseball** The Montréal Expo's home ground is the Olympic Stadium, 4545 Pierre-de-Coubertin (Métro: Pie IX). Tickets cost $1–13.50 (information ☎253-3434; tickets ☎522-1245).

**Bike rental** *Accès Cible*, Vieux-Port just south of Place Jacques-Cartier (mid-May to Aug Mon noon–8.30pm, Tues–Sun 11am-8pm; ☎525-8888).

**Books** English books can be bought from most major bookstores, specifically *Coles*, 1171 Ste-Catherine Ouest and *W H Smith*, 625 Ste-Catherine Ouest and Gare Central. *Double Hook*, 1235A Greene, specialises in English-Canadian authors. An excellent selection of travel books in English and French are available from *Ulysses Travel Bookshop*, 4176 St-Denis, 560 President-Kennedy, and downstairs at *Ogilvy* on the corner of Ste-Catherine and de la Montagne.

**Bus enquiries** Local services ☎288-6287; long-distance ☎842-2281.

**Car rental** *Avis*, 1225 Metcalfe (☎866-7906); *Budget*, Gare Central (☎866-7675); *Hertz*, 1475 Alymer (☎842-8537); *Mini-Prix 2000*, 2000 Ste-Catherine Est (☎524-3009); *Thrifty*, 1600 Berri, Suite 9 (☎845-5954); *Tilden*, 1200 Stanley (☎878-2771); *Via Route*, 1255 Mackay (☎871-1166).

**Consulates** *Great Britain*, 1155 Université (☎866-5863); *Netherlands*, 1245 Sherbrooke Ouest (☎849-4247); *USA*, Complexe Desjardins, South Tower (☎281-1468).

**Dental emergencies** 24-hour dental clinic, 3546 Van Horne Street (☎342-4444).

**Drive-away** *Auto Drive-Away*, 1117 Ste-Catherine Ouest (☎844-1033); *Montréal Drive-Away*, 4036 Ste-Catherine Ouest (☎937-2816). Expect to pay $200–400 deposit plus petrol.

**Exchange** *Bank of America Canada*, 1240 Peel (Mon–Fri 8.30am–5.30pm; Sat 9am–5pm; Sun 10am–4pm); *Deak International*, 625 René-Lévesque Ouest (daily 9am–5pm) & 1155 Sherbrooke Ouest (Mon–Fri 9am–5pm).

**Hospitals** Montréal General Hospital, 1650 Cedar (☎937-6011).

**Ice-hockey** Canada's most successful ice-hockey team, the Montréal Canadiens, play at the Montréal Forum, 2313 Ste-Catherine Ouest (Métro: Atwater). Tickets and information ☎932-2582.

**Laundry** *Le Nettoyeur*, 1001 Université, 1447 Drummond & 4090 Ste-Catherine (Mon–Fri 8am–6pm; Sat 8am–noon).

**Left luggage** There are $1 lockers at the Gare Central and Terminus Voyageur.

**Métro information** General information ☎280-5666; timetable information ☎288-6287; lost and found ☎280-4637.

**Pharmacy** *Pharmaprix Drug Store*, 5122 Côe-des-Neiges, is open 24 hours.

**Post office** The main post offices are Station B, 1250 Université (Mon–Fri 8am-5.45pm, Sat 8am–noon) and Station C, 1250 Ste-Catherine Est (Mon–Fri 8am–5.45pm). The city's poste restante is located at Station A, 285 St-Antoine Ouest (Mon–Fri 8am–5.45pm, Sat 8am–noon).

**Ride-sharing** *Allo-Stop*, 4317 St-Denis (Mon–Wed 9am–5pm, Thurs & Fri 9am–7pm, Sat 10am–5pm, Sun 10am–7pm). Membership costs $7 plus the share of petrol. Typical prices are: Ottawa $14, Toronto $26, Québec $25, New York $50.

**Sexual Assault Centre** Bilingual, 24-hour crisis line ☎934-4504.

**Taxis** *Co-op* ☎725-9885; *Diamond* ☎273-6331; *Lasalle* ☎272-2552. $2 minimum fare, then 75c per kilometre.

**Telephones** *Bell-Canada*, Bureau Public, 700 de la Gauchetière Ouest on the corner of Université (Mon–Fri 9am–5pm).

**Train information** *Via Rail* ☎871-1331; *Amtrak* ☎1-800-426-8725.

**Travel agencies** *La Billeterie*, 800 Place Victoria (☎282-1022), offers good prices on air tickets as well as selling bus and train tickets. *Tourbec*, 535 Ontario Est (☎288-4455) is excellent for budget travellers.

**Weather information** Montréal ☎636-3026; outside Montréal ☎636-3284.

**Whitewater rafting** The Rivière Rouge offers the best whitewater rafting in the Montréal vicinity. *Adventures en Eau Vive*, R. R. 2 chemin Rivière Rouge, Calumet (☎242-6084 or ☎1-800-567-6881) runs rafting trips for $67 at the weekend, $63 during the week for groups over eight people; a smaller group costs more.

# Around Montréal

The lake-dotted countryside around Montréal offers a range of recuperative pleasures for the city-dwellers, from the peaks of the **Laurentian Mountains** north of the metropolis to the lush farmland of **L'Estrie**, east towards the US border. Where the Lower Laurentians meet the St Lawrence's north shore, historic argricultural and religious settlements give an insight into the early days of New France. Further north, the more dramatic Upper Laurentians have sprouted ski resorts by the dozen, but brief hikes from the main centres – all linked by bus to Montréal – will soon get you into a seemingly never-ending forest, patched with deserted lakes and waterways. The developers are also moving in on L'Estrie, but lakeside hamlets, tranquil farms and apple orchards still present an enticing rural escape. Finally, if you are heading for Québec City, consider breaking your journey in the small town of Trois-Rivières – an excellent jumping-off point for the beautiful interior of the Mauricie valley.

## The Laurentians (Les Laurentides)

Don't expect dramatic, jagged peaks when exploring the Laurentians – 500 million years of erosion have moulded one of the world's oldest ranges into a rippling landscape of undulating hills and valleys. The mountains extend all the way along the north side of the St Lawrence from the Ottawa River to the Saguenay, with the zone closest to Montréal the most accessible. Immediately north of Montréal, the Lower Laurentians are dotted with whitewashed farm cottages and manor houses, but settlement in Upper Laurentians did not begin until the 1830s, when the construction of the P'tit Train du Nord let in the mining and lumber industries. When the decline in both industries left the area in a depression, salvation came in the form of the recreational demands of the growing populace of Montréal. The region is now one of North America's largest ski areas, with the number of resorts multiplying annually.

### The Lower Laurentians (Les Basse Laurentides)

Once the domain of various native groups, the **Lower Laurentians** were granted by Ville-Marie's governors to the colony's first seigneurs who, using a modified version of the feudal land system of the motherland, oversaw the development of the land by their tenants, or *habitants*. As the St Lawrence was the lifeline of the colony, these tenant farms were laid out perpendicular to the river in long, narrow rectangular seigneuries. Typical of these is the **Seigneurie de Terrebonne** on the Ile des Moulins, a twenty-minute drive via highways 25 and 440. This was a seigneurie from 1673 to 1883, and the restored nineteenth-century buildings – including the manor house of the area's last seigneur and Canada's first francophone millionaire, Joseph Masson – powerfully evoke life under the long regime.

A forty-minute drive northwest of Montréal via Hwy 13 or 15 then Hwy 640 lies the town of **ST-EUSTACHE**, also served by the slow Montréal to Ottawa *Voyageur* bus. It was here that the frustrations of the *habitants* with the British occupancy met a tragic end in the 1837 Rebellion. In the early 1800s the British immigrants to Lower Canada were offered townships (*cantons*) while the francophones were not allowed to expand their holdings, exacerbating the resentment caused by the favouritism extended to the English-speaking businesses in Montréal. The situation was worsened by high taxes on British imports and a savage economic depression in 1837. Wearing garments of *étoffe du pays* as a protest against British imports, the leaders of Lower Canada reform – known as the *Patriotes* – rallied francophones to rebel in Montréal. As Louis-Joseph Papineau, the seigneur whose speeches in the Assembly had encouraged the rebellions, fled the city, fearful that his presence would incite more rioting, the government sent out military detachments to the countryside, the hotbed of the *Patriotes*. Two hundred *Patriotes* took refuge in St-Eustache's church, where eighty of them were killed by British troops, who went on to raze much of the town.

Today, over thirty of the period buildings that survived the battle are still intact – the **church**, at 123 St-Louis, still bares the scars. Rue St-Eustache has the main concentration of sights, with the wedding-cake **Manoir Globensky** at no. 235 (May–Nov Mon–Fri 8.30am–4pm) and the eighteenth-century **Moulin Légaré** at no. 232 (late April to mid-Nov Mon–Fri 9am–noon & 1–4.30pm), the oldest water-powered flourmill in Canada. If you have time, you could drop by at **La Maison Jean-Hotte**, 405 Grand Côte (April–Nov daily 9am–9pm; $4), a hotchpotch collection of old cars, trains and antique toys.

## OKA

Southwest of here, on Hwy 344, lies the small lakeside town of **OKA**, which can also be reached by taking the commuter train from Montréal's Gare Windsor to Hudson on the opposite shore, then catching the free ferry to Oka. Until recently a quiet resort, Oka achieved national prominence in the summer of 1990 when it became the stage for a confrontation between **Mohawk** warriors and the federal government. The crisis began when Oka's town council decided to expand its golf course onto a sacred burial ground, a provocation to which the Mohawks responded by arming themselves and barricading Kanesataka, a small reserve near Oka. Although the Native Affairs Minister for Québec was close to reaching an agreement with the Mohawks, the mayor of Oka sent in the provincial police to storm the barricades. In the ensuing fracas a policeman was killed – no one knows by whom, but the autopsy established it was not by a police bullet. Hostilities now reached a new pitch and the two sides became ever more polarised: as the Mohawks set up barricades across the Mercier Bridge, one of Montréal's main commuter arteries, groups of white Québécois attacked them with stones, while sympathetic groups of native people sprang up all over Canada and the USA. The federal government then offered to buy the land for the natives on the condition that they surrender, but the stand-off continued as negotiators failed to agree on terms. In the end the crisis lasted 78 days, until the core of fifty Mohawks was encircled by 350 soldiers and forced to give up. The fate of the disputed land, along with hundreds of other similar claims, is still being negotiated. However, many believe that the natives went too far at Oka, and the existing distrust between the first peoples and other Canadians seems to have deepened. As George Erasmus, national chief of the Assembly of First Nations, said – "Our demands are ignored when we kick up a fuss – but they are also ignored if we do not".

In complete contrast, one of North America's oldest monasteries, the **Abbaye Cistercienne d'Oka**, 1600 chemin d'Oka (Mon–Fri 9.30–11.30am & 1–5pm, Sat 9am–5pm), commands a spectacular site just outside town, its century-old bell tower rising amidst enveloping hills. The Trappists arrived here from France in 1880, their life in Canada beginning in a miller's house that's now totally overshadowed by the rest of the complex and the landscaped gardens of the abbey. The monastery shop sells a wealth of organic Trappist products, from maple syrup and chocolates to variations on the famed Oka cheese. The nearby **Calvaire d'Oka** with its mid-eighteenth-century chapels is best visited on September 14, when native pilgrims hold the Feast of the Holy Cross along the banks of the Lac des Deux Montagnes. The surrounding area has several cottage resorts but the only **place to stay** in Oka itself is the *Auberge Le Faitout*, 28 de l'Annonciation (☎514/479-6908), which charges from $35 for singles, from $60 for doubles.

## The Upper Laurentians (Les Hautes Laurentides)

The slopes of the **Upper Laurentians**, a vast sweep of coniferous forests dotted with hundreds of tranquil lakes and scored with rivers, was once Montréal's "wilderness backyard". Nowadays the huge silence is shattered in the winter as Québécois take to the slopes at over twenty-five ski resorts, yet some of the land has been left relatively untouched – like in the Parc du Mont Tremblant – and the area is a must when the colours of autumn take over.

The Upper Laurentians really cater for families on a week's sporty vacation, and much **accommodation** is pricey, as it includes gyms, tennis courts, golf courses and the like. However, a smattering of B&Bs and numerous motels offer an alternative to those on a tight budget, as does the youth hostel in Val David. You could also check out travel agents in Montréal – weekend packages can be a bargain. There's a free telephone accommodation service for the region too (☎1-800-363-5606).

Two **roads** lead from Montréal to this area of the Laurentians: the Autoroute des Laurentides (Hwy 15) and the slower Hwy 117. *Limocar Laurentides* from the Voyageur **bus** station offer regular services to most of the towns. In winter the slightly more expensive *Aerocar* offers a ski bus from Dorval and Mirabel airports to various resorts. Express ski-bus services are also run by *Limocar, Murray Hill*, and *Tour Autocar* from various downtown hotels and the Voyageur bus station.

Rates for **skipasses** are around $25 a day in the decent areas, a few dollars more at weekends. **Information** on the resorts is available from the main tourist office in Montréal and offices in the majority of Laurentian towns – pick up the useful *Laurentides* booklet. During the ski season *SkiLine* (☎514/875-7558) reports ski conditions as does "The Snow Report" column printed in *The Montréal Gazette*.

### ST-SAUVEUR-DES-MONTS

The ski resorts start at **ST-SAUVEUR-DES-MONTS**, 60km from Montréal. Boasting a total of 42 pistes in the immediate vicinity and an ever-increasing number of condominium complexes, its resident population is just 4000, compared to a peak-season weekend population of 30,000. The main drag, Principale, is packed with every type of restaurant, separated by designer boutiques and craft shops competing for the charge cards. Nighttime sees numerous flash clubs and discos boogying till the early hours.

For those with money, this is *the* place to be seen, and hotel prices reflect the fact – the excellent *Auberge St–Denis*, 61 St-Denis (☎514/227-4766), leads the way for class, with luxurious rooms from $230. Budget travellers will be pretty well limited to the **food** at *Dunns*, a branch of Montréal's famous smoked meat deli, located on chemin Lac Milette. **Information** on shopping and skiing is available from the *Bureau Touristique de la Vallée de Ste Sauveur*, 220E chemin du Lac Millette (daily 9am–5pm).

## VAL-DAVID

Further north, **VAL-DAVID** is the bohemian resort of the Laurentians, chosen by artists and craftspeople as a haven from the yuppie developments elsewhere in this beautiful region: the main street, Rue d'l'Église, has various galleries and craft shops run by the artisans themselves. Val-David's excellent **youth hostel**, *Chalet Beaumont*, 1451 Beaumont (☎819/322-1972; dorm beds $10.50, private rooms with bathrooms $18), is the only one in the region, a massive log chalet with roaring fires in the winter, and great views all year. Located a twenty-minute walk from the bus station, the hostel offers a pick-up service. Other **accommodation** in Val-David is fairly expensive: *Parker's Lodge*, 1340 Lac Pacquin (☎819/322-2026), is in the shadow of the ski slopes of Vallée Bleue and charges $55–90 for rooms, which is about as cheap as they come. The swishest ski lodge is *La Sapinière*, by Mont Alta at 190 Val-David (☎819/322-2020), with rooms from $172 and some of the most highly regarded cuisine in the area. There are two **campgrounds** along Hwy 117, *Camping La Belle Etoile* and *Camping Laurentien*, both with pitches from $15. Rue d'l'Église has a selection of decent, well-priced **restaurants**.

## STE-AGATHE-DES-MONTS

Nearby, on the shores of Lac des Sables, is **STE-AGATHE-DES-MONTS**, a luxurious resort since the 1850s and now the largest town in the Laurentians. Located 97km from Montréal and not entirely quashed by tourism, it is a good base for exploring the less developed towns and the wildlife reserves further north. The cheapest **accommodation** is above a rowdy bar at the *Auberge du Coin*, 55 Préfontaine Est (☎819/326-4901; singles $15, doubles $30), a couple of blocks from the main drag. A quieter but pricier stay can be had at the *Auberge des Neiges*, 173 chemin du Tour du Lac (☎819/326-1276; singles $60, doubles $75) – one of the town's most beautiful historic homes with its pointed roof and wraparound veranda – or the duller *Motel Clair de Lune*, 30 Morin (☎819/326 3626; singles and doubles $55–65). **B&B** is only available at *La Bergerie du Mouton Noir*, 2107 chemin Brunet (singles $30, doubles $45; ☎819/326-6037), a sheep farm about 4km from the town centre – ring for a lift. The nearest **campground** is *Camping Ste Agathe* (from $15), 15km from town, accessible via exit 53 of Hwy 15. **Restaurants and bars** are concentrated on the lakefront, the most attractive area of town. The **bus** arrives at the shopping mall on Hwy 117; the **information** centre is across the road.

## ST-JOVITE–MONT-TREMBLANT

Situated some 130km north of Montréal, **ST-JOVITE–MONT-TREMBLANT** is the Laurentians' oldest and most renowned ski area, focused on the range's highest peak, **Mont Tremblant** (960m), so-called because the native population believed it was the home of spirits that were capable of moving the mountain. There are 34 slopes on the mountain for all levels, with a maximum vertical drop that is over 640-metres – the longest ski run in Québec.

St-Jovite is the commercial centre of the area, while Mont-Tremblant (10km north) is a tiny village with only the most basic services. In and around the two are a variety of lodges including the most glamorous in the Laurentians: *Le Tremblant Club*, by Lac Tremblant at the base of the mountain (☎1-800-567-8341), and *Auberge Gray Rocks*, near St-Jovite (☎1-800-567-6767), upwards of $200 per night. **Information** is available from *Bureau Touristique St-Jovite–Mont-Tremblant*, 305 chemin Brébeuf in St-Jovite (daily June–Sept 9am–7pm; Oct–May 9am–5pm).

The **Parc du Mont Tremblant**, a wilderness area of over 1000 square kilometres spreading northwards from the villages, is a favourite with Québécois. Skiing, snowmobiling and snowshoeing are the sports in winter; in summer the park attracts campers, canoeists, hunters and hikers – in the more remote areas you may see bears, deer and moose. The park's three lakeside **campsites** need to be reserved in advance (☎819/688-2336). There's no public transport, but hitching is possible.

## L'Estrie (The Eastern Townships)

Situated about 80km southeast of Montréal and extending to the US border, **L'ESTRIE** was once Québec's best-kept secret, but its nineteenth-century villages are fast becoming no more than shopping arcades fringed with condominium complexes for Montréal commuters. A growing ski industry – concentrated around Mont Sutton, just north of the Vermont border – is making its mark on the land too. However, the region's agricultural roots are still evident, especially in spring, when the maple trees are tapped for syrup. At this time of year remote *cabanes a sucre* offer sleigh rides and Québec fare such as "Taffy" – strips of syrup frozen in the snow.

The land, once the domain of scattered groups of natives, was first cultivated by United Empire Loyalists hounded out of the States after the American Revolution. Their loyalty to the crown resulted in land grants from the British, and townships with very English names like Sherbrooke and Granby were founded at this time. In the mid-nineteenth century the townships opened up to industry which attracted an influx of French-Canadians seeking work: today, 95 percent of the 400,000 population are francophone. The term Eastern Townships was abandoned only recently for the more French name of L'Estrie, a combination of "est" for east and "patrie" for homeland.

L'Estrie can be reached from Montréal by the Autoroute de L'Estrie (Hwy 10) or the more picturesque Hwy 112. Most of the villages and towns are served regularly by *Voyageur* **buses** from Montréal, and *VIA rail* runs a Montréal-to-Sherbrooke **train**.

### Granby

Coming from Montréal, L'Estrie begins at the pleasant but mundane town of **GRANBY**, renowned for the **Jardin Zoologique de Granby** (May–Oct daily 10am–5pm; adults $12, children $6) – Québec's best known zoo and an absolute nightmare. The animals are kept in terrible conditions without a blade of grass in sight and most look suicidal. The town redeems itself during October with a month-long Québécois **food festival**. Granby's **information centre** at 650 Principale (May–Sept daily 8am–6pm; Nov–April Mon–Fri 9am–noon & 1–4.30pm) can supply a copy of the *L'Estrie* booklet, which has up-to-date listings of the region's accommodation and activities. There are numerous **motels** along Principale, should you get stuck here.

### Around Lac Memphremagog

The summer resort town of **MAGOG**, less than 60km further east, gets its name from a corruption of a native word meaning "great expanse of water". The expanse of water in question is one of L'Estrie's largest lakes, **Lac Memphremagog**, which is right in the town but unremarkable unless you're impressed by the fact that Sylvester Stallone and Donald Sutherland have homes on its shore.

The **bus** stops on Sherbrooke; turn right and right again to reach the main drag, Principale, where the **information centre** is located at no. 1032 (June–Aug daily 9am–9pm; Sept–May 9am–5pm). The cheapest **accommodation** is the *Hotel Union*, 259 Principale (☎819/843-3363), which charges around $25 for adequate rooms. Several **bars and restaurants** can be found along Principale, while at 27 des Pins, just off Principale, is the *Pâtisserie Gaby*, one of the best cake shops in the area.

About 25km south of Magog, just off the road to Austin, is the **Abbaye St-Benoit-du-Lac**, its presence signalled by its white granite turrets. Occupied by about sixty Benedictine monks (many of them under a vow of silence) and a small number of nuns, it's renowned as a refuge for flustered politicians and prominent figures who need a time of contemplation, but the abbey's doors are open to anyone who wants to stay in accordance with the order's tradition of hospitality. Food and **accommodation** are free, though a donation is expected. There is no public transport to the abbey; hitching is a reliable alternative, or a taxi costs about $25 from Magog.

On the opposite shore lies **GEORGEVILLE**, accessible via Hwy 247 from Magog. A totally unspoilt hamlet, its clapboard buildings, which include an antique general store, are set around a village green on the lake border.

## Sherbrooke and around

The 100,000-strong university town of **SHERBROOKE**, 147km east of Montréal, revels in the title "Queen of the Eastern Townships", a strange accolade for the town with the lowest average wage in Canada. To be fair, it doesn't feel overly impoverished, but it's no great shakes, with just one mild attraction in the shape of the **Musée des Beaux Arts de Sherbrooke**, 174 Palais (Tues–Sun 1–5pm; free), a display of local work that includes a fairly impressive collection of Naïve painters.

The **bus** station with connections to and from Montréal, Québec City and various local towns is at 20 King Ouest. The **information** centre is located in the **train** station at 48 Dépôt (mid-June to Sept daily 9am–8pm; Oct to mid-June 9am–5pm). The cheapest **accommodation** in summer is the student residence at 2500 boulevard Université Sherbrooke (☎819/821-7000; $20 per person). Otherwise there are numerous modern motels along King Street Ouest: the cheapest are *L'Ermitage* at no. 1888 (☎819/569-5551) and *Motel La Réserve* at no. 4235 (☎819/566-6464), both with singles around $40, doubles around $50. **Restaurants, bars** and **cafés** are also concentrated along King Street Ouest and the cross streets of Wellington, just by the bus station, and Belvédère, four blocks further west. Try the well-priced bistro *Bla-Bla Café*, 2 Wellington or *Da Toni*, 15 Belvédère, for a sound Italian meal.

The region south of Sherbrooke holds its Loyalist connections dear, and this is one of the few areas in Québec where you'll encounter a hangover of the snobbish anglophone attitudes that once pervaded the whole province. **NORTH HATLEY**, a ten-minute drive from Sherbrooke, is a veritable anglophone bastion, with boutiques selling Lipton teas, Liberty products, tweeds and Aran jumpers – and a population that steadfastly refuses to have their home's name changed to Hatley Nord. Situated right on the shore of Lake Massawippi, with clapboard houses painted in pastel shades, the hamlet is primarily a resort for rich Canadians and Americans, who first adopted the area for vacations during Prohibition. The village boasts two of Québec's classiest inns, the romantic turn-of-the-century *Manoir Hovey* (☎819/842-2421) and *Auberge Hatley* (☎819/842-2451), both of which charge around $150 for a double. If you can afford to stay, book rooms early. The cuisine in the inns is also renowned but those on a tight budget will be limited to *Le Pilsen*, an English-style **pub** with locally brewed draught and basic meals.

# Montréal to Québec City

There are two **autoroutes** between Montréal and Québec City: the boring Highway 20 along the south shore, and Highway 40 along the north shore, which is flanked by the farms of the seigneurial regime. The slower Highway 138 meanders along the north shore, giving a closer look at rural Québec. *VIA rail* **trains** and *Voyageur* **buses** connect the two cities with regular services, the slower buses stopping at various towns en route.

## Trois-Rivières

The major town between the two cities is **TROIS-RIVIÈRES**, straddling the three channels of the St Maurice River midway between Montréal and Québec. European settlement dates from 1634 ,when the town established itself as an embarkation point for the French explorers of the continent and as an iron ore centre. Lumber followed, and today Trois-Rivières is one of the world's largest producers of paper, the delta chock-full with logs to be pulped. It's often dismissed as an industrial city and little else, but its shady streets of historic buildings – neither as twee as Québec City, nor as monumental as Vieux Montréal – are well worth a wander, and the town is a good starting point for exploring the Maurice Valley.

Trois-Rivières compact downtown core is centred on the small square of Parc du Champlain. Rue Bonaventure runs from near the bus station to the square and the neo-Gothic **Cathédrale de Trois-Rivières** (daily 7–11.30am & 2–5.30pm; free), with its Florentine stained glass windows. One of the town's oldest buildings, now the information centre, is just past the opposite corner of the square – the **Manoir Boucher-de-Niverville**, a pretty white manor that dates from 1730, when it was the home of the local seigneur. Further down Bonaventure, a left turn leads into the narrow and ancient Rue des Ursulines, where at no. 864 the three-storey **Manoir de-Tonnancour** (Tues–Sun 2–5pm, Thurs & Fri 7–9.30pm; free) holds temporary exhibitions on various themes from stamps to sculpture. Local art is on display at **Maison Hertel-de-la-Fresnière** at no. 802, which also serves as a Maison des Vins. Dominating the street is the slender silver dome of the **Monastère-des-Ursulines**, established by a small group of Ursuline nuns who arrived from Québec City in 1697. The chapel, though badly damaged by fire in 1897, has attractive frescoes and gilt sculptures, whilst the nunnery's treasures are displayed in a little museum in the old hospital quarters (May–Aug Tues–Fri 9am–5pm, Sat & Sun 1.30–5pm; Oct–April Wed–Sun 1.30–5pm, closed Sept; donation).

On the nearby renovated and characterless waterfront, the **Centre d'Exposition sur l'Industrie des Pâtes et Papiers**, 800 Parc Populaire (mid-June to Aug daily noon–9.30pm; Sept to mid-June Sat & Sun noon–6pm; $1) has an informative if unthrilling exhibition on the industry that's the backbone of the community. Finally, the ruined buildings of the **St-Maurice forges**, which put the town on the map as a supplier to the farmers and arsenals of Québec and Europe, is now a national historic park, linked to downtown by bus #4 (Feb–March Sat & Sun 1–4pm; mid-May to Aug daily 9.30am–5.30pm; Sept to mid-Nov Thurs & Fri 9.30am–5.30pm, Sat & Sun 9.30am–4pm; free).

The *Bureau de tourisme* at 168 Bonaventure (May–Sept Mon–Fri 9am–8pm, Sat & Sun noon–8pm; Oct–April Mon–Fri 9am–5pm) has **information** on all the town's activities and sights. For **accommodation** the cheapest option is the clean and comfortable **youth hostel**, *Auberge La Flottille*, in the heart of downtown at 497 Radisson (☎819/378-8010; $11.50). Centrally located **hotels** include the *Delta*, 1620 Notre Dame (☎819/376-1991) and the *Des Gouverneurs*, 975 Hart (☎819/379-4550), both charging upwards of $100 a night for a double. If these are too expensive, there's the *Motel Democrate*, northwest of the town centre at 2070 Bellefeuille (☎819/378-2881), charging $60 for a double. For **food**, *Le Bolvert*, 1556 Royale, does sandwiches and salads.

## The Mauricie

North of Trois-Rivières lies the mountainous area of the St-Maurice valley – the **Mauricie** – where the best of the landscape is demarcated by the **Parc National de la Mauricie** (May–Nov) over 500 square kilometres of soft-contoured hills, lakeland, rivers, waterfalls, sheer rock faces and breathtaking views. There is no public transport to the park, but a *Voyageur* bus leaves Trois-Rivières for Grand-Mère (45km) at 12.15pm, returning at 6.35pm. Hitching the 20km from Grand-Mère to the park's southeast entrance should not take too long, so this allows for an afternoon in the park. Information centres at the park's entrances have excellent maps and booklets about the park's well-maintained hiking trails, canoe routes and bike paths, and also provide canoe rental. **Camping** places are allocated at the centres on a first come, first served basis, though the hundreds of places are rarely filled.

# QUÉBEC CITY

Spread over Cap Diamant and the banks of the St Lawrence, **QUÉBEC CITY** is Canada's most beautifully located and most historic city. The Vieux-Québec quarter of the Haute-Ville, surrounded by solid fortifications, is the only walled city in North America, a fact which prompted UNESCO to classify it as a World Heritage Treasure in 1985. In both parts of the centre – Haute and Basse – the winding cobbled streets are flanked by seventeenth- and eighteenth-century stone houses and churches, graceful parks and squares, and countless monuments. Although some districts have been overly renovated to give the tourists as seductive an introduction to Québec as possible, this is an authentically and profoundly French city – 95 percent of its 500,000 population are French-speaking, and it is often difficult to remember which continent you are in as you tuck into a croissant and a steaming bowl of coffee in a café full of the aromas and sounds of Paris. Moreover, despite the fact that the city's symbol is a hotel, the **Château Frontenac**, the government remains the main employee, not tourism, and some of the most impressive buildings remain government-run and off-limits.

Arriving from Montréal you're immediately struck by the differences between the province's two main cities. Whilst Montréal is international, dynamic and forward-thinking, Québec City is more than a shade provincial, often seeming too bound up with its religious and military past – a residue of the days when the city was the bastion of the Catholic Church in Canada. On the other hand, the Church can claim much of the credit for the creation and preservation of the finest buildings, from the Basse-Ville's quaint Église **Notre-Dame-des-Victoires** to Haute-Ville's decadently opulent **Basilique de-Notre-Dame** and the vast **Seminary**. In contrast, the austere defensive structures, dominated by the massive **Citadelle**, reveal the military pedigree of a city dubbed by Churchill the "Gibraltar of North America", while the battlefield of the **Plains of Abraham** are now a national historic park. Of the city's rash of museums, two are essential visits – the modern **Musée de la Civilisation**, expertly presenting all aspects of French-Canadian society, and the recently expanded **Musée du Québec**, the finest art collection in the province.

Outside the city limits, the neighbouring towns of **Lévis** and **Wendake** – a Huron reservation – make worthwhile excursions, whilst the farmlands, manors, churches and cottages of the **Côte de Beaupré** and the **Île d'Orléans** hark back to the days of the seigneurs and *habitants*. The gigantic **Basilique de-Sainte-Anne-de-Beaupré**, attracting millions of pilgrims annually, is one of the most impressive sights in Québec, and for equally absorbing natural sights there are the spectacular waterfalls at **Montmorency** and **Sept-Chutes**, and the wildlife reserve in the **Laurentians**.

## A brief history of Québec City

For centuries the clifftop site of what is now Québec City was occupied by the **Iroquois** village of **Stadacona**, and though Cartier visited in the sixteenth century, permanent European settlement did not begin until 1608, when Samuel de Champlain established a fur-trading post here. To protect what was rapidly developing into a major inland trade gateway, the settlement shifted to Haute-Ville in 1620 when Fort St-Louis was built on the present-day site of the Château Frontenac. Québec's steady expansion was noted in London and in 1629 Champlain was starved out of the fort by the British, an occupation that lasted just three years.

Missionaries began arriving in 1615, and by the time Bishop Laval arrived in 1659 Québec City and the surrounding province were in the grip of Catholicism. In the city's earliest days, however, power rested with the merchants of the fur trade, who frequently came into conflict with the priests, who wanted a share in the profits in order to spread their message amongst the native peoples. The wrangles were resolved by **Louis XIV**, who assumed power in France in 1661 and was advised to take more interest in his kingdom's mercantile projects. By 1663 New France had become a royal province, administered by a council appointed directly by the crown and answerable to the king's council in France. Three figures dominated the proceedings: the governor, responsible for defence and external relations; the intendent, administering justice and overseeing the economy; and, inevitably, the bishop.

Before the century was out, the long-brewing European struggles between England and France spilled over into the colony with French attacks on the English in New York and New England in 1689 and a foiled naval attack on the city by Sir William Phipps, governor of Massachusetts, in the following year. It was at this time that the **Comte de Frontenac**, known as the "fighting governor", replaced Champlain's Fort St-Louis with the sturdier Château St-Louis, and began work on the famous fortifications.

In September 1759, during the Seven Years' War, the most significant battle in Canada's history took place here, between the British general **James Wolfe** and Louis Joseph, **Marquis de Montcalm**. The city had already been under siege from the opposite shore for three months and Montcalm had carefully protected the city from any approach by water. Wolfe and his 4000 troops took the only unguarded route, scaling the cliff of Cap Diamant and creeping up on the sleeping French regiment from behind. The twenty-minute battle on the Plains of Abraham left both leaders mortally wounded and the city of Québec in the hands of the English, a state of affairs confirmed by Treaty of Paris in 1763. Madame de Pompadour commented: "It makes little difference; Canada is useful only to provide me with furs".

In 1775 – the year after the Québec Act of 1774 allowed French-Canadians to retain their Catholic religion, their language and their culture – the town was attacked again, this time by the Americans, who had already captured Montréal. The battle was won by the British and for the next century the city quietly earned its livelihood as the centre of a **timber trade** and **shipbuilding** industry. By the time it was declared the provincial capital of Lower Canada in 1840, though, the accessible supplies of timber had run out. The final blow came with the appearance of steamships which could travel as far as Montréal, while sailing ships found it difficult to proceed beyond Québec City. Ceasing to be a busy seaport, the city declined into a centre of small industry and local government, its way of life still largely determined by the Catholic Church.

With the Quiet Revolution in the 1960s and the rise of Québec nationalism, Québec City became a symbol of the glory of the French heritage – for example, the motto *Je me souviens* (I remember) above the doors of its Parliament buildings was transferred to the licence plates of Québec cars, to sweep the message across Canada. Though the city played little active part in the changes, it has grown with the upsurge in the francophone economy, developing a suburbia of shopping malls and convention centres as slick as any in the country.

> The Québec area telephone code is ☎418.

# Arrival, information and city transport

Québec City's **airport**, 20km east of the city, is served only by *Air Canada* domestic flights – all international flights arrive at Montréal. An hourly bus run by *Maple Leaf Tours* runs into Vieux-Québec and costs $8; the twenty-minute trip by taxi will set you back about $25.

**Trains** from Montréal arrive at Gare du Palais in Basse-Ville, whereas services from the Atlantic provinces arrive at Lévis, across the St Lawrence, from where there's a regular ferry. The terminal for long-distance **buses** is some way outside the city walls at 225 Charest Est. Turn right outside the station and then right again onto Dorchester;

from here *CTCUQ* bus #3 takes about ten minutes to reach Vieux-Québec for $1.40. A taxi costs around $5. It is best to leave your **car** outside the centre, off Grande Allée.

## Information

For **information** about Québec City's sights and events, the central *Maison du tourisme de Québec* is on the other side of Place d'Armes from Château Frontenac at 12 Ste-Anne (early June to Aug daily 8.30am–7.30pm; Sept to early June 9am–6pm; ☎643-2280 or ☎1-800-443-7000). The other main information centre is near Porte St-Louis at 60 d'Auteuil (July–Aug daily 8.30am–8pm; Sept to mid-Oct daily 8.30am–5.30pm; mid-Oct to mid-April Mon–Fri 9am–5pm; mid-April to June Mon–Fri 8.30am–5.30pm; ☎692-2471). Both centres provide an adequate free map and a booklet, *Greater Québec Area*, which lists the latest opening hours and entrance fees. They also run a free accommodation booking service, and will do all your phoning for you, though the queues can be long.

## Transport

Québec City's sights and hotels are packed into a small area, so walking is the best way of getting around. For sights further out, like the Musée du Québec, *CTCUQ* local buses are efficient and run from around 6am to 1am. Fares are a standard $1.40 per journey; if you need more than one bus to complete your journey pick up a transfer (*une correspondance*) from the driver which enables you to take the second bus for no extra charge. The main bus stop in Vieux-Québec is on the west side at Place d'Youville, near Porte St-Jean. The terminus for all *CTCUQ* buses is at Place Jacques-Cartier, reachable by buses #3, #5, #7, #8 and #30 from Place d'Youville.

# Accommodation

The accommodation in Québec City is perfect for budget travellers. In the Haute-Ville there are two youth hostels, and the budget hotels are as well located as those at the top end. However, the city is one of North America's most frequented tourist cities, so try to reserve in advance, particularly during the summer months and the Carnaval in February. Even at those times, though, you're not likely to find the city completely full, as the suburbs have masses of motels, all of them just a local bus ride away. All of Québec City's campgrounds are around 20km outside town, which means they are only convenient for those with their own transport; the ones recommended here are the closest.

The hotels in Québec City are usually renovated town houses with the rooms fitted to provide a variety of accommodation. For cheaper rooms, in the $30 region, head for the area around St-Louis and Ste-Ursule, which are lined with budget hotels; the posher places are around the Jardin des Gouverneurs in the shadow of the prestigious Château Frontenac and in the Latin Quarter. In Basse-Ville hotel accommodation is surprisingly more expensive and options are limited to a couple of places and motels.

## Hotels

**Auberge La Chouette**, 71 d'Auteuil (☎694-0232). In the road running parallel to Ste-Ursule, in the shadow of the city walls. All rooms with bathrooms, $70–85.

**Auberge St-Louis**, 48 St-Louis (☎692-2424). The cheapest two-star inn in the St-Louis area. Recently renovated. Rooms $37–82.

**Auberge du Quartier**, 170 Grande Allée Ouest (☎525-9726). 1852 house near the Plains of Abraham, a twenty-minute walk into the city. Free parking. Singles $59, doubles $69.

**Hôtel Belley**, 249 St-Paul (☎692-1694). Eight-bedroom, slickly designed hotel near the Gare du Palais. Three-star rooms $50–90, cheaper off season.

**Hôtel Cap-Diamant**, 39 Ste-Geneviève (☎694-0313). Two star, nine-bedroom guesthouse with Victorian furnishings near Jardin des Gouverneurs. Rooms all have bathrooms. $65–95.

**Hôtel Château Bellevue**, 16 Laporte (☎692-2573). Modern hotel in an old building. Views of the Jardin and the Château Frontenac. Free parking. Singles $59–89, doubles $64–89.

**Hôtel au Château Fleur de Lys**, 15 Ste-Geneviève (☎694-1884). Just off the Jardin, on the corner of Laporte. Air-conditioned rooms $73–105.

**Château Frontenac**, 1 des Carrières (☎692-3861 or ☎1-800-268-9420). This opulent 535-roomed castle has accommodated such dignitaries as Churchill, Roosevelt, Madame Chiang Kai-shek and Queen Elizabeth II. Naturally it's the most expensive place in town; rooms are in the $200–300 range.

**Hôtel Château de Léry**, 8 Laporte (☎692-2692). One of the less pricey hotels right on the Jardin des Gouverneurs and recently renovated. Two-star rooms $58–85.

**Hôtel Le Château de Pierre**, 17 Ste-Geneviève (☎694-0429). 1853 mansion with plush rooms also on the Jardin. $90–110.

**Hôtel Château de la Terrasse**, 6 Terrasse Dufferrin (☎694-9472). The better rooms have the best views in town, overlooking the St Lawrence. Rooms $64–85.

**Hôtel Clarendon**, 57 Ste-Anne (☎692-2480 or ☎1-800-361-6162). Québec City's oldest hotel, dating from 1870. Renovated in the 1930s, it has a classic Art Deco reception area. Rooms $99–125.

**Hôtel Le Clos St-Louis**, 71 St-Louis (☎694-1311 or ☎1-800-461-1311). Another two-star with simple, clean rooms with TVs from $50–85.

**Hôtel L'Ermitage**, 60 Ste-Ursule (☎694-0968). The cheapest three-star in the area. Ten bedrooms all with bathrooms and air-conditioning. Rooms $75–80, $10 for an extra person. Free parking.

**Hôtel au Jardin du Gouverneur**, 16 Mont-Carmel (☎692-1704). On the corner of Mont Carmel and Laporte, next to the Château Frontenac. Seventeen rooms all with adjoining bathrooms. $81–100.

**Hôtel La Lucarne**, 69 St-Louis (☎694-1311). A variety of rooms, from the plain and simple to the luxurious (with whirlpool etc). Rooms $47–85.

**Hôtel Maison Acadienne**, 43 Ste-Ursule (☎694-0280). Little rooms with sinks and shared bathrooms. Singles $38–65, doubles $43–75.

**Hôtel La Maison Demers**, 68 Ste-Ursule (☎692-2487). Parking and breakfast included in the price; the more expensive rooms have ensuite bathrooms. Singles $30–40, doubles $45–60.

**Hôtel La Maison Doyon**, 109 Ste-Anne (☎694-1720). Helpful landlord and well situated near the Latin Quarter. Rooms from $45–75.

**Maison du Fort**, 21 Ste-Geneviève (☎692-4375). Another small guesthouse near Jardin des Gouverneurs with air-conditioned rooms. Rooms $55–100.

**Hôtel Maison du Général**, 72 St-Louis (☎694-1905). One of the best budget hotels in the area with a friendly French-speaking landlady. Singles from $28, doubles from $33.

**Hôtel Maison Ste-Ursule**, 40 Ste-Ursule (☎694-9794). Built in 1780 – the doors are tiny. Rooms with TVs and bathrooms. Singles $44, doubles $54.

**Hôtel Le Manoir d'Auteuil**, 49 d'Auteuil (☎694-1173). Lavish 1835 town house by the city walls. Three-star rooms from $75–120.

**Hôtel Manoir des Remparts**, 3.5 des Remparts (☎692-2056). At the north end of Vieux-Québec on the ramparts, near the Latin Quarter. Views of the St Lawrence. Singles from $45, doubles from $50, breakfast included.

**Hôtel Manoir la Salle**, 18 Ste-Ursule (☎647-9361). Well located, clean budget hotel. Rooms from $25–40.

**Hôtel Manoir Ste-Geneviève**, 13 Ste-Geneviève (☎694-1666). Charming four-star hotel dating from 1880, in the shadow of the Château Frontenac. Beautiful Victorian rooms. Singles $75–100, doubles $87–120.

**Hôtel Manoir sur le Cap**, 9 Ste-Geneviève (☎694-1987). Cheapest hotel overlooking the Jardin des Gouverneurs. Some rooms have air conditioning and all have TVs. Singles $35–75, doubles $40–75.

**Manoir Victoria**, 44 du Palais (☎692-1030 or ☎1-800-463-6283). Just off trendy St-Jean. Four-star hotel with rooms from $99 to $225.

**Au Petit Hôtel**, 3 ruelle des Ursulines (☎694-0965). Located in a peaceful cul-de-sac just off Ste-Ursule, parallel to St-Louis. Rooms $60–80.

**Hôtel de la Place d'Armes**, 24 Ste-Anne (☎694-9485). Perfectly located opposite the Anglican Cathedral, on the pedestrianised part of Ste-Anne. Two-star rooms $60–100.

**L'Hôtel du Vieux-Québec**, 8 Collins (☎692-1850). Popular modernised hotel in the Latin Quarter. Singles for $110, doubles for $121. Rooms are around $20, cheaper off season.

## Motels

**Motel Delisle**, 7979 Wilfred Hamel (☎872-7476). Open in summer only. Cheap rooms but around 10km from other motels in this strip. Rates are $24–30 per person.

**Motel Doyon**, 1215 Ste-Foy (☎527-4408). The cheapest motel around, basic but clean, with free parking. Ten-minute bus ride to Vieux-Québec. Singles from $20, doubles from $24.

## Hostels and student accommodation

**Auberge de la Paix**, 31 Couillard (☎694-0735). Situated in the Latin Quarter, this is by far the best hostel in Québec City. Bike rental is available, and the $13 rate includes breakfast. Curfew is 2am.

**Centre International de Sejour de Québec**, 19 Ste-Ursule (☎694-0755). The official youth hostel, located in a former boarding school, is often full and is very impersonal, though it does offer laundry facilities, bike rental, luggage lockers and tourist information. Curfew is 11pm. In the summer rooms and dormitories for members are $12 and $9 respectively; in winter $13 and $10.

**Services des Residences de l'Université Laval**, Pavillion Parent, local 1643, Université Laval, Ste-Foy (☎656-2921). From early May to late August rooms are available in the student residences, a ten-minute bus ride from Haute-Ville. $25 for a single, $30 for a double.

**YWCA**, 855 Holland (☎683-2155). Chiefly for women only, though couples are allowed in the summer. Located just off Chemin St-Louis, about a twenty-minute bus ride into Haute-Ville. Singles $30, doubles $50.

## Campgrounds

**Camping Aéroport**, de l'Eglise Sud, Ste-Foy. Take exit 10 off Hwy 440 onto Route de l'Aeroport – the campsite is around 20km north of the airport itself. From $12.

**Camping Base de Plein Air Ste-Foy**, off Hwy 440 in Ste-Foy (☎654-4641). Exit 10 or 11 leads to this park-set campsite. Reservations recommended. $10.50.

**Camping municipal de Beauport**, Serenité, Beauport. Off Boulevard Rouchette. Take exit 322 off Hwy 40. From $12.

# The City

Québec City spreads from its historical heart into bland surburbia but the interesting area lies beside the St Lawrence, the main sights evenly distributed between the upper and lower towns. Haute-Ville is divided by the city walls which encircle Vieux-Québec; beyond the walls the furthest you need to wander is to the Musée du Québec, set in the vast parkland of the Plains of Abraham. This itinerary begins at Haute-Ville's Place d'Armes and then explores this upper district within and outside the walls as far west as the gallery. However, the equally historic area of Basse-Ville to the east can also be reached directly from Place d'Armes, so there is a choice of itinerary from this central hub.

## Place d'Armes and around

The ten square kilometres of Haute-Ville encircled by the city walls is the Québec City of the tourist brochures, and its centre of gravity is the main square, the **Place d'Armes**, whose central fountain serves in the summer as a resting place for weary sightseers. It was here that Champlain established his first fort, on the site now occupied by the gigantic **Château Frontenac**, probably Canada's most photographed building. Commissioned by the *Canadian Pacific Railway* in 1893, New York architect Bruce Price drew upon the French-Canadian style of the surroundings to produce a pseudo-medieval red-brick pile crowned with a copper roof – an over-the-top design to make the most of the stupendous location atop Cap Diamant.

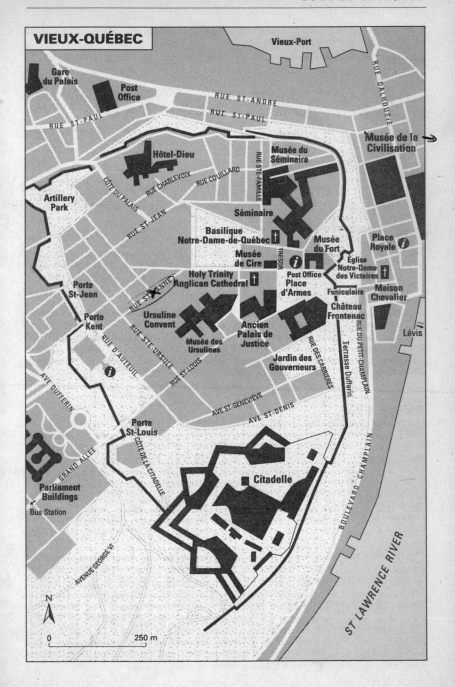

The cape's clifftop is fringed by the wide boardwalk of the **Terrace Dufferin**, which runs alongside the Château to the fortifications of the Citadelle overlooking the narrowing of the river that was known to the natives as the *kebec* – the source of the province's name. At the beginning of the walkway – which gives breathtaking panorama takes of the Île d'Orléans and the Laurentian mountains – stands a romantic statue of Champlain and beside it a modern sculpture symbolising Québec's status as a UNESCO site. From here the steep Frontenac steps and a funicular descend to Basse-Ville (see p.173).

Beside the Château Frontenac on the corner of St-Louis is the **Maison Maillou**, which houses the Québec chamber of commerce. Dating from 1736, this grey limestone house, with blue shutters for insulation and a steeply slanting roof, displays the chief elements of the climate-adapted architecture brought over by the Norman settlers. On the west side of the square, on the spot where the Récollet missionaries built their first church and convent, stands the largely ignored **Ancien Palais de Justice**, a Renaissance style courthouse designed in 1887 by Eugène-Étienne Taché, architect of the city's Parliament Buildings.

On the northeast corner of Place d'Armes, where Ste-Anne intersects rue du Fort, is the **Musée du Fort** (summer daily 10am–6pm; spring & autumn Mon–Sat 10am–5pm, Sun 1–5pm; winter Mon–Fri 11am–5pm, Sat 10am–5pm, Sun 1–5pm; closed Dec; $4.25), whose sole exhibit is a 400-square-foot model of Québec City circa 1750. Amid the streets of plastic the city's six major battles, including the battle of the Plains of Abraham and the American invasion of 1775, are re-enacted in an entertaining thirty-minute sound and light show.

Parallel to rue du Fort is the narrow alley of **Rue du Trésor** where French settlers paid their taxes to the Royal Treasury; nowadays it is a touristy artists' market. Visitors who want to take home a portrait rather than a saccharine cityscape should shuffle into the pedestrianised section of Ste-Anne to the west of Trésor, which is full of portraitists and their subjects. At no. 22, in the impressive 1732 Maison Vallée, the **Musée de Cire** (June–Sept daily 9am–11pm; Oct–May 10am–5pm; $3) is populated by unrealistic figures of Québécois luminaries from Champlain to Lévesque.

## The Latin Quarter

Québec City's small **Latin Quarter**, in the northeast section of Vieux-Québec, is dominated by the seventeenth-century seminary in whose grounds stands the **Basilique Notre-Dame de Québec** (daily 6.30am–8pm; free). The oldest parish north of Mexico, the church was burnt to the ground in 1922 – one of many fires it has suffered – and was rebuilt to the original plans of 1647. Absolute silence within the cathedral heightens the impressiveness of the rococo-inspired interior, culminating in a ceiling of blue sky and billowy clouds. The silver chancel lamp, beside the main altar, was a gift from Louis XIV and is one of the few treasures to survive the fire. In the crypt over nine hundred bodies, including three governors and most of Québec's bishops, are interned. Champlain is also rumoured to be buried here, though archaeologists are still trying to work out which body is his.

Next door to the cathedral, in the Maison du Coin, the seminary's **information centre** (Tues–Sun 10.30am–5.30pm; $2) is the departure point for guided tours of the seminary during the summer. The vast **Seminary**, currently undergoing a $30-million renovation, was founded by the aggressive and autocratic **Monseigneur Francois-Xavier de Laval-Montmorency** in 1663. In the three decades of his incumbency Laval secured more power than the governor and intendent put together and any officer dispatched from France found himself on the next boat home if Laval did not care for him. Laval retired early due to ill health, brought on by a religious fervour that denied him blankets and proper food. Death finally came after freezing his feet on the stone floor of the chapel during his early-morning prayer session.

At its construction the seminary was the finest collection of buildings the city had seen, leaving Governor Frontenac muttering that the bishop was now housed better than him. Primarily a college for priests, the seminary was also open to young men who wanted to follow other professions, and in 1852 it became Laval University, the country's first francophone university.

The wrought iron gates between the basilica and the Maison du Coin lead into a vast courtyard flanked by austere white buildings with handsome mansard roofs. Adjoining the Roman-style chapel to the left as you enter is a funeral chapel housing Laval's ornate marble tomb. Across the courtyard the **Musée du Séminaire** (Tues–Sun June– Sept 10am–5.30pm; Oct–May 10.30am–5pm; $2) displays changing exhibitions based on the eclectic items gathered by Québec's bishops and academics at Laval: stuffed animals from the biologists, an Eygptian mummy from the historians, a fine collection of European and Canadian paintings from the art historians, as well as a wealth of silverware and some of Laval's personal belongings.

To the east, between the upper and lower parts of the city, lies **Parc Montmorency**, its monuments recalling the historic figures of the area. This land was granted by Champlain to Canada's first agricultural settler and seigneur, Louis Hébert, and was later the meeting place of Québec's first legislature in 1694. The park gives wonderful views of Québec's port and its massive grain elevators, as does the flanking Rue des Remparts, where the cannons that once protected Haute-Ville still point across to Lévis.

## Hôtel-Dieu and Artillery Park

Rue des Remparts leads to the seventeenth-century **Hôtel-Dieu du Précieux Sang**, the first hospital in North America. The stone buildings, with barred windows as protection from Iroquois attack, are still occupied by the Augustinian order of nuns who founded the hospital in 1639. Turning left up Côte du Palais leads to the **Musée des Augustines de l'Hôtel-Dieu de Québec**, 32 Charlevoix (Tues–Sat 9.30–11.30am & 1.30–5pm, Sun 1.30–5pm; free), where the artworks include some of Québec's oldest paintings – including the earliest known portrayal of the city in the background of the portraits of the Duchess of Auguillon and her uncle Cardinal Richelieu, who together funded the hospital. Another notable painting is the *Martyrdom of the Jesuits*, a gruesome tableau showing the torture of Jesuit missionaries in southern Ontario by the Iroquois in 1649. Each section shows a different missionary undergoing trial and punishment by baptism with boiling water, wearing a collar of red-hot hatchets and other forms of excruciating pain. Grateful patients also donated a fine collection of antique furniture, copperware and ornaments. Many of the items are French as the first settlers usually found themselves interned in the hospital to recover from the diseases rife on the ocean crossing. Ancient medical instruments of the early settlement are also displayed. On request the Augustines offer free guided tours of the chapel where Catherine de St Augustin, their first Mother Superior, is buried, and the cellars where the nuns sheltered from the British in 1759.

Backtracking to Rue des Ramparts leads to the northwest corner of Vieux-Québec and **Artillery Park**, whose immense defensive structures were raised in the early 1700s by the French, in expectation of a British attack from the St Charles river. After the fall of Québec the British added to the site, which was used primarily as a barracks for the Royal Artillery Regiment. Under the Canadians a foundry and cartridge factory provided the army with ammunition in both world wars, but was finally closed in 1964. The massive Dauphine Redoubt, named after Louis XIV's son, typifies the changes of fortune here: used by the French as the barracks for their garrison, it became the officers' mess under the British and then the residence of the superintendent of the Canadian Arsenal. A reception and **interpretation centre** (April–Oct Mon 1–5pm, Tues–Sun 10am–5pm; Nov–March Mon–Fri 10am–noon & 1–5pm) in the former foundry has displays on the military pedigree of the city, including a vivid model of Québec City in 1808. The

Officers' Quarters where the British officers lived until 1871 is now a military museum for children with costumed guides providing a prettified version of events.

The steep rue d'Auteuil running alongside the park rises to Porte Kent, close to the **Chapelle des Jésuites**, 20 rue Dauphine (Mon–Sat 8am–1pm & 2.30–5pm, Sun 7.15–9.30am; free). The church's delicately carved altar and ecclesiastical sculptures are by Pierre-Noel Levasseur, who was one of the most illustrious artists to work on the early Québec parish churches.

## Around the Jardins de l'Hôtel de Ville

Rue Dauphin continues to rue Cook which leads to the **Jardins de l'Hôtel-de-Ville**, scene of numerous live shows in the summer. The park is overlooked by the Hôtel-de-Ville, which dates from 1883, and the far more impressive Art Deco buildings of the **Hôtel Clarendon** and the **Édifice Price** (the city's first skyscraper), at nos. 57 and 65 Ste-Anne respectively.

On the corner of Ste-Anne and Rue des Jardins stands the first Anglican cathedral built outside the British Isles, the **Holy Trinity Anglican Cathedral** (May–June Mon–Sat 9am–5pm, Sun noon–5pm; July–Aug Mon–Sat 9am–9pm, Sun noon–9pm; Sept–Nov Mon–Fri 10am–3pm; Dec–April Tues–Sat 1–3pm; free guided tours). The site was given by the King of France to the Récollet Fathers but their church burned down in the late eighteenth century. Its replacement was constructed in 1800–04 on orders from King George III, following the lines of London's church of St Martin in the Fields. The simple interior houses the 1845 bishops' throne, reputedly made from the wood of the elm tree under whose branches Samuel de Champlain used to confer with the Iroquois. Many of the church's features came from London, including the silverware from George III and the wood for the pews from Windsor's royal forest. The golden bars on the balcony denote the seats for the exclusive use of British sovereigns. In the courtyard is the *L'Atelier Plein Air*, a small crafts and clothes market which avoids selling tourist tack.

## The Chapelle des Ursulines and around

Heading back south along rue des Jardins brings you to the narrow rue Donnacona and the **Chapelle des Ursulines**, built by a tiny group of Ursuline nuns who arrived in Québec in 1639 calling themselves "the Amazons of God in Canada". Their task was to bring religion to the natives and later to the daughters of the settlers, a mission carried out in the classrooms of North America's first girls' school – the buildings still house a private school. They also cared for the *filles du roi*, marriageable orphans and peasant girls imported from France to swell the population. These girls were kept in separate rooms in the convent for surveillance by the local bachelors who were urged to select a wife within fifteen days of the ship's arrival – a fine of three hundred livres was levied on any man who failed to take his pick within the period. Fat girls were the most desirable, as it was believed they were more inclined to stay at home and be better able to resist the winter cold.

The Ursuline's first Mother Superior, Marie de l'Incarnation, was widowed at the age of nineteen and left a son behind in France. Her letters to him give some sharp insights into the early days of the city: "It would be hard to live here an hour without having the hands protected and without being well covered. Although the beds are covered well with quilts or blankets, scarcely can one keep warm when lying on them". Her likeness can be seen in a replica of a posthumous portrait by Pommier in the interesting little **museum** (Tues–Sat 9.30am–noon & 1.30–4.45pm, Sun 12.30pm–5.15pm; closed Dec; $2), housed in the former home of one of the first nuns. Documents, paintings and household items testify to the harshness of life in the colony, but lace work and embroidery are the highlights, particularly the splendid ornamental gowns produced by the Ursulines in 1739. As a grisly counterpoint, Montcalm's skull and one of his bones are also on display.

Montcalm himself is buried in the **chapel** (May–Oct Tues–Sat 9.30am–noon & 1.30–4.45pm, Sun 12.30–5.15pm; free), rebuilt in 1902 but retaining the sumptuous eighteenth-century interior by sculptor Pierre-Noel Levasseur. A painting by Frère Luc, though executed in France, pictures a Canadian version of the Holy Family: Joseph is shown presenting a Huron girl to Mary, while through the window one can glimpse Cap Diamant and the St Lawrence flowing past wigwams and campfires. Next to the museum is the **Centre Marie-de-l'Incarnation** (Tues–Sat 10–11.30am & 2–4.30pm, Sun 2–4.30pm; free) which sells religious and historical books, and has a few of Marie's personal effects on show.

On the corner of rue des Jardins and rue St-Louis – the main restaurant strip in Vieux-Québec – stands **Maison Jacquet**, occupied by the restaurant *Aux Anciens Canadiens*. The name comes from Québec's first novel, whose author, Philippe Aubert de Gaspé, lived here for a while in the middle of the last century. Dating from 1677, the house is another good example of seventeenth-century New France architecture, as is the blue and white **Maison Kent** at no. 25 on St-Louis, which was built in 1649. Once home of Queen Victoria's father, the Duke of Kent, it's best known as the place where the capitulation of Québec was signed in 1759.

## Jardin des Gouverneurs and around

Rue Haldimand, beside Maison Kent, leads to the beautiful **Jardin des Gouverneurs**, whose wonderful prospect of the St Lawrence was once the exclusive privilege of the colonial governors who inhabited Château St-Louis. The garden's Wolfe-Montcalm obelisk monument, erected in 1828, is rare in paying tribute to the victor and the vanquished. Converted manor houses border this grandiose area, and the nearby streets are some of the most impressive in Vieux-Québec – check out Rue Laporte and the parallel Rue des Grisons on the park's west side, which boasts some fine eighteenth-century homes, the outstanding example being the **Maison Allaire-Langan** at no. 12.

From the Jardin des Gouverneurs, avenue Ste-Geneviève runs west to Porte St-Louis. En route turn right onto rue Ste-Ursule for the **Chalmers-Wesley United Church** at no. 78, which was built in 1852 and is one of the most beautiful in the city. Its slender, Gothic revivalist spires are a conspicuous element of the skyline, and inside the stained glass windows are worth a look. Opposite, the 1910 **Sanctuaire Notre-Dame-du-Sacré-Coeur** (daily 7am–8pm; free) also has impressive stained glass windows.

A left turn on rue St-Louis leads to the Porte St-Louis, one of the four gates in the city wall. It's surrounded by **Parc de l'Esplanade**, the main site for the Carnaval de Québec, and departure point for the city's smart horse-drawn calèches. The park's **Poudrière de l'Esplanade**, 10 St-Louis (mid-May to June Mon–Fri 10am–5pm; July–Aug daily 10am–5pm; Sept–Oct daily 1–5pm; free), a powderhouse constructed in 1810, has a dull exhibition on the fortifications of Vieux-Québec. It is sometimes possible to take a 4.6-kilometre walk along the city wall, but restoration work occasionally blocks the path.

## The Citadelle

Dominating the southern section of Vieux-Québec, the massive star-shaped **Citadelle** is the tour de force of Québec City's fortifications. Occupying the highest point of Cap Diamant, 320 feet above the St Lawrence, the site was first built on by the French, but the majority of buildings were constructed by the British under orders from the Duke of Wellington, who was paranoid about American attack after the war of 1812.

The complex of twenty-five buildings covers forty acres and is the largest North American fort still occupied by troops – it's home to the Royal 22nd Regiment, Canada's only French-speaking regiment. Within the courtyard are ranged various monuments to the campaigns of the celebrated "Van-Doos", encircled by the summer residence of Canada's governor general and two buildings dating back to the French period – the

1750 powder magazine, now a mundane museum of military artefacts, and the Cap Diamant Redoubt, built in 1693 and thus one of the oldest parts of the Citadelle.

In addition to entertaining hour-long guided tours around the Citadelle (March–April & Oct Mon–Fri 9am–4pm; May to mid-June & Sept daily 9am–5pm; mid-June to Aug daily 9am–7pm; Nov Mon–Fri 9am-noon; $3), other activities include the colourful Changing of the Guard (mid-June to Aug daily 10am), the Beating of the Retreat tatoo (July–Aug Tues, Thurs, Sat & Sun 7pm) and the firing of the cannons every day at noon and 9.30pm.

## The Parliament Buildings

Sweeping out from Porte St-Louis and flanked by grand Victorian mansions, the tree-lined boulevard of **Grande-Allée** is proclaimed the city's equivalent of the Champs Élysées, with its upper-bracket restaurants and bars. Near its eastern end stand the stately **Parliament Buildings** (free tours late June to Aug daily 9am–4.30pm; Sept to late June Mon–Fri 9am–4.30pm), designed by Étienne Taché in 1877 in imitation of the Louvre. The ornate facade includes niches for twelve bronze statues by Québec sculptor Louis-Philippe Hébert of Canada's and Québec's major statesmen, while finely chiseled and gilded walnut panels in the entrance hall depict important moments in Québec history, coats of arms and other heraldic features. From here the corridor of the President's Gallery, lined with portraits of all the Legislative Assembly's speakers and presidents, leads to the Chamber of the National Assembly, where the 122 provincial representatives meet for debate (early March to May & early Oct to Nov Tues & Thurs 2–10pm, Wed 10am–6pm; early June & early Dec Mon–Fri 10am–6pm).

## National Battlefields Park

Westward of the Citadelle are the rolling grasslands of the **National Battlefields Park**, a vast area that encompasses the historic Plains of Abraham. Named after Abraham Martin, the first pilot of the St Lawrence River in 1620, the Plains were to become the site on which Canada's history was rewritten. In June 1759 a large British force led by **General Wolfe** sailed up the St Lawrence to besiege **General Montcalm** in Québec City. From the end of July until early September the British forces shuttled up and down the south side of the river, razing much of the city with cannon fire. Montcalm and the governor, Vaudreuil, became convinced that Wolfe planned an assault on the citadel from Anse de Foulon, the only feasible approach to the Plains of Abraham, an opinion confirmed when lookouts observed a British detachment surveying Cap Diamant from across the river in Lévis. Montcalm thus strengthened the defences above Anse de Foulon, but made the mistake of withdrawing the regiment stationed on the Plains themselves. The following night the British performed the extraordinary feat, which even Wolfe had considered "a desperate plan", of scaling the cliff below the Plains, and on the morning of September 16 Montcalm awoke to find the British drawn up a mile from the city's gate. The hastily assembled French battalions, flanked by native warriors, were badly organised and rushed headlong at the British, whose volleys of gunfire mortally wounded Montcalm. On his deathbed Montcalm wrote a chivalrous note of congratulations to Wolfe, not knowing that he too was dead. Québec City surrendered four days later.

The dead of 1759 are commemorated by a statue of Joan of Arc in a sunken garden just off Laurier by the Ministry of Justice. More conspicuous, standing out amid the wooded parklands, scenic drives, jogging paths and landscaped gardens, are two Martello towers, built between 1805 and 1812 to protect against the Americans. **Martello Tower 2**, on the corner of Laurier and Taché, has a slide show on Québec's battles and exhibits on the history of Battlefields Park (early June to early Sept Mon noon–5.30pm, Tues–Sun 9.30am–5.30pm; free); **Martello Tower 1** (same hours), further south in the park, has superb views of the St Lawrence from its rooftop lookout.

## The Musée du Québec

Canadian art had its quiet beginnings in Québec City three hundred years ago, and the full panoply of subsequent Québécois art is displayed in the **Musée du Québec**, 1 Wolfe-Montcalm (May–Sept daily 10am–5.45pm, open till 9.45pm Wed; Oct–April closed Mon; $5, free on Wed). If you don't fancy walking, bus #11 connects Vieux-Québec to Avenue Wolfe-Montcalm along Grande Allée Est.

The Church was the first patron of the arts in Canada, and the work produced under the sponsorship of Bishop Laval was enriched by the 1670 arrival of the Récollets, who included in their number the painter **Frère Luc**, a former assistant to Poussin. His influential output is represented here by the *Guardian Angel*, depicting the story of Tobias and the archangel Raphael. Secular art began with the fashion for portraiture among Québec City's upper classes: **Francois Malepart de Beaucourt's** portraits of the affluent Eustache-Ignace Trottier and his wife (1793) are the earliest examples of this genre, and his approach is far from servile – bonneted Madame is shown as the perfect hostess, but her husband is shown frittering away the family's fortune at the gaming table. One of Québec's most prolific artists was the travelling portraitist **Jean-Baptiste Roy-Audy**, whose primitive style, heavily influenced by his artisan background as the son of a woodworker, is best seen in his *Monsigneur Rémi Gaulin* (1838) with its ivory-like surface. Roy-Audy's modest roots are reflected in the inconspicuous placement of his signature on the spine of the meticulously painted books in the background.

The most favoured portrait painter of the bourgeoisie was **Antoine Plamondon** who had trained in Paris under Charles X's court painter Guérin, himself a pupil of the classicist David – a lineage evident in Plamondon's poised *Madame Tourangeau* (1842). Plamondon was a very quarrelsome man, described as being unable to find "excellence but in himself", and having railed against anyone who threatened to establish themselves in Québec he finally sulked out of the scene altogether to manage a farm. **Théophile Hamel**, a pupil of Plamondon's, combined what he learnt from his tour around Europe in the 1840s – the palette of Rubens and the draughtsmanship of the Flemish masters – in his *Self-portrait in the Studio*, painted soon after his return. A successful career painting Canada's leading citizens lay ahead of him, and he was to influence a whole generation of post-Confederation painters.

The first artist to depict Canadian scenes for their own sake was the Québec-born **Joseph Légaré**, whose sympathy with radical French-Canadians led to his imprisonment after the 1837 Rebellion. His *Fire in the Saint-Jean Quarter* – depicting the 1845 conflagration that made 10,000 homeless – is one of his many paintings recording local scenes and events. His counterpart in Montréal was the Irish immigrant **James Duncan** who worked mainly in watercolour but is represented here by the only oil painting he signed, *Montréal from the Mountain* (1845), a classical view of the city with its spires lit by the rays of the sun. Another contemporary, **Cornelius Kricghoff**, emigrated to America in 1836 from Amsterdam, and worked as a sign painter in Montréal before moving to Québec City in 1853, the year of his *Québec Seen from Pointe-Lévis*. His romanticised works were a major hit and he became one of the country's best-known artists.

Of the **sculptures** dotted around these galleries – all of them taken from Québec's churches – the most notable are by just two dynasties. Brothers Pierre-Noel and Francois-Noel Levasseur dominated the beginning of the eighteenth century, then three generations of Baillairgés took over in the second half.

The collections of **modern art** on the first floor begin with the works of artists disparagingly termed the "fossil school" – for reasons made plain by the lifeless children in **Napoléon Bourassa's** *The Little Fishermen* (1870). The more emotive work of **Horatio Walker** is typified by his painting of mighty oxen ploughing. Walker was born in Ontario but moved to Québec in the 1880s and became completely engrossed in the lives of the French-Canadian *habitants*. Though his work recalls Millet in its subject matter he lacks the sociological dimension: Millet's peasants are bent by labour; Walker's *habitants* simply love every minute of it.

Canada's art scene was rejuvenated by the impact of Impressionism and Post-Impressionism, first seen in the work of Newfoundlander **Maurice Cullen** – the rich orange and green hues of his *L'Anse-des-mères* (1904) shows the touch of Gauguin. Cullen's compatriot, the rich anglophone **James Wilson Morrice**, hobnobbed with the likes of Whistler in Paris and London, an acquaintance that shows in his *The Citadelle of Québec* (1897), showing the fortification covered in snow, a theme that was to occur over and over again in the coming decades. A more colourful winter scene appears in **Clarence Gagnon's** *Laurentian Village* (1915) – he used to grind his own colours to achieve greater intensity.

The works of the Group of Seven are more usually associated with the remote wilds of Ontario, but **Arthur Lismer**, one of the founders of the Group, visited Charlevoix many times, producing pieces such as *Québec Village, Ste-Hilarion* (1925). Urban life at the time is admirably recorded by **Adrien Hébert**, son of sculptor Louis-Philippe Hébert: his *Port of Montréal* (1924) is one of many canvases dominated by grain elevators, steamers and harbour installations, symbolically dwarfing the men in the foreground. The contemporaneous **Marc-Aurèle Fortin's** best works were his impressionistic renditions of trees, as seen in *Elm at Pont-Viau* (1935) where one gigantic tree of numerous intense greens dominates the entire riverscape.

The modernism of Matisse and Picasso was introduced to Canada by **Alfred Pellan**, who returned from Paris in 1940 to teach at Montréal's École des Beaux Arts. Pellan's comparative radicalism – represented here by his *Young Woman with a White Collar* (1932) – caused confrontations with his bosses, the clash reaching its peak with a semi-riot at the 1945 degree show, precipitated by the conservative director's removal of controversial items by Pellan's students.

**Sculpture** underwent a similar process of European-led development, beginning with the production of religious votary objects. Secular art flourished in the nineteenth century, when of the most prolific sculptors was **Louis-Philippe Hébert**, whose classical works grace most of Québec's buildings and parks. He is represented here most strikingly by *The Halt in the Forest*, a copy of which graces the Parliament Buildings as a tribute to the province's native peoples. By the 1920s and 1930s the influence of Rodin had become overwhelming, as evident in **Suzor-Côte's** *Women of Chaughnawaga* and **Aldred Laliberté's** *The Spirit of Marble*, in which a smooth nude emerges from a block of hewn marble.

**Contemporary art** on the second floor is dominated by the work of Montréal's Automatistes, who held their first exhibition in 1947 and were greatly influenced by the Abstract Expressionists in New York. This is clear in the splashy work of **Paul Émile Borduas**, whose 1948 manifesto *Refus Global* was adopted as a general manifesto for disgruntled young French-Canadians. Other strands of abstraction appear in **Ferdinand Leduc's** *L'Alphiniste* (1957), a work indebted to Mondrian, and the monochrome grey canvas of **Yves Gaucher's** *R-M-III N/69* (1969). Extremely simplified forms spilled over into the sculpture of the period, as is evident in Louis Archambault's scarcely detailed *Head* (1948) and Vaillancourt's massive *Tree on Rue Durocher*. On the same floor there's a gallery showcasing avant-garde paintings and sculptures from Québec.

The red brick of the adjoining former jail has been spruced up to create a warm interior far removed from the sombre exterior. Montréal sculptor David Moore has created a unique two-storey sculpture in the prison's tower with huge torsos and legs of wood scaling the walls and a central figure diving from the summit. As well as a variety of prestigious temporary exhibitions, this part of the museum houses the impressive drawing and print collection.

## Basse-Ville

The birthplace of Québec City, **Basse-Ville**, can be reached from Terrasse Dufferin by either the steep **Escalier Casse-Cou** (Breakneck Stairs) or by the **funicular** alongside (daily 7am–midnight; 65¢). The Basse-Ville station of the funicular is the 1663 **Maison Louis-Jolliet**, 16 Petit-Champlain, built for the retired discoverer of the Mississippi, Louis Jolliet, the first Québécois to make history. It now houses a second-rate souvenir shop, a ghastly introduction to this interesting area.

Dating back to 1685, the narrow cobbled **Rue du Petit-Champlain** is the city's oldest street, and the surrounding area – known as **Quartier Petit-Champlain** – is the oldest shopping area in North America. The boutiques and art shops in the quaint seven-teenth- and eighteenth-century houses are not too overpriced and offer an array of excel-lent crafts, from weird and wonderful ceramics to Inuit carvings. Older artefacts can be seen closer to the harbour, on the corner of boulevard Champlain and rue du Marché Champlain, where three merchant houses – **Maison Chanaye-de-la-Garonne**, **Maison Fréot** and the **Maison Chevalier** – are now used by the Musée de la Civilisation for changing exhibits of period furniture, costumes, toys, folk art and domes-tic objects (daily 10am–5pm; free).

### PLACE-ROYALE

From here it's a short walk along rue Notre-Dame to **Place-Royale**, where Champlain built New France's first permanent settlement in 1608, to begin the trade of fur with the native peoples. The square – known as Place du Marché until the bust of Louis XIV was erected here in 1686 – remained the focal point of Canadian commerce until 1759, and after the fall of Québec the British continued using the area as a lumber market, vital for shipbuilding during the Napoleonic wars. After 1860 Place-Royale was left to fall into disrepair, a situation reversed as recently as the 1970s, when the scruffy area was renovated. Its pristine stone houses, most of which date from around 1685, are undeni-ably photogenic with their steep metal roofs, numerous chimneys and pastel-coloured shutters, but it's a Legoland townscape, devoid of the scars of history. Fortunately the atmosphere is enlivened in summer by entertainment from classical orchestras to juggling clowns – a nearby information centre, 215 Marché Finlay (late June–Aug daily 10am–6pm) has listings of upcoming activities.

**Interpretation centres** at 3A Place-Royale and 25 St-Pierre (mid-May to Sept daily 10am–6pm; free) outline the stormy past of Place-Royale, the former concentrating on the mercantile aspects and the latter on the changes in the look of the square from the days when it was inhabited by the Iroquois to its renovation.

The **Église Notre-Dame-des-Victoires** (May to mid-Oct Mon–Sat 9am–4.30pm, Sun 7.30am–4.30pm; mid-Oct to April Tues–Sat 9am–noon, Sun 7.30am–1pm), on the south side of the square, was instigated by Laval in 1688 but has been completely restored twice – after being destroyed by shell fire in 1759 and after a fire in 1969. Inside, the fortress-shaped altar alludes to the two French victories over the British navy that gave the church its name: the destruction of Admiral Phipp's fleet by Frontenac in 1690 and the sinking of Sir Hovenden Walker's fleet in 1711. Above the altar, paintings depicting these events hang by copies of religious paintings by Van Dyck, Van Loo and Boyermans, gifts from early settlers to give thanks for a safe passage. The model ship suspended in the nave has a similar origin.

Opposite the church, the **Maison des Vins**, designed by the architect of Notre Dame, is now a touristy wine outlet – though it does offer free samples to visitors.

### THE MUSÉE DE LA CIVILISATION AND VIEUX-PORT AREA

Rue de la Place leads to **Place de Paris**, where a modern sculpture called *Dialogue with History* marks the disembarkation place of the first settlers from France. The **ferry to Lévis** leaves from one block south, while a walk north along Rue Dalhousie brings you to Québec City's most impressive and dynamic museum, the **Musée de la Civilisation**, 85 rue Dalhousie (mid-June to early Sept daily 10am–7pm; early Sept to mid-June Tues–Sun 10am–5pm, Wed 10am–9pm; $5, free on Tues). Designed by Canada's top-rank modern architect, Moshie Safdie, the building reflects the steeply pitched roofs of Québec's earliest architecture and has won numerous awards for the way it blends with the historic surroundings. It actually incorporates three historic structures, including the two-storey merchant's house called the Maison Estèbe, whose arched cellars now contain an excellent gift shop.

Concentrating primarily on Canada but also diversifying into a wider perspective, the museum presents various changing exhibitions under the broad themes of "The Body", "Matter", "Society", "Language" and "Thought". The only permanent show – except the foyer sculpture, Astri Reusch's *La Débâcle*, symbolising the break-up of the ice in the spring thaw – is "Memories", which expertly displays life in Québec from the early days of the settlers to the present. Until 1993 an exhibition called "Food for Thought" will be installed, a surprisingly fascinating exploration of every aspect of the subject, from dietary comparisons with other cultures to the history of the humble baked bean.

To the east, on the confluence of the St Charles and the St Lawrence, lies the seventeenth-century **Vieux-Port de Québec**, the busiest harbour in the province until its eclipse by Montréal. Much of the harbour has been renovated as a recreational area, with theatres, yuppie flats, sheltered walkways, restaurants and a marina packed with pleasure boats and yachts. A throwback to how the port used to be is the **Marché du Vieux-Port** at the north end of the port (March–Nov daily 8am–8pm), a market selling organic produce from the local area. A remodeled cement plant bordering the Louise Basin at 100 Ste-Anne now houses an **interpretation centre** for the Vieux-Port (March–April & Sept–Nov Tues–Fri 10am–noon & 1–4pm, Sat & Sun 11am–5pm; mid-May to June Mon 1–4pm, Tues–Fri 9am–4pm, Sat & Sun 10am–5pm; July–Aug Mon 1–5pm, Tues–Sun 10am–5pm), housing a display on the lumber trade and shipbuilding in the nineteenth century.

A block south of the Louise Basin lies rue St-Paul, heart of Québec's **antiques district**. Numerous cluttered antique shops, art galleries, cafés and restaurants now occupy warehouses and offices abandoned after the demise of the port. From Rue St-Paul the steep Côte Dambourges leads to Rue des Remparts on the northern borders of the Latin Quarter.

# Eating

It is when you start **eating** in Québec City that the French ancestry of the Québécois hits all the senses: the eateries of the city present an array of culinary delights adopted from the mother country, from beautifully presented gourmet dishes to humble baguettes. In the finer **restaurants** high-quality French cuisine is easy to come by, and although prices tend to be rather high, even the poshest restaurants have cheaper lunchtime and *table d'hôte* menus. For a change of taste, the dishes of other countries are also represented, including Italian, Greek, Swiss, Thai – and the good old hamburger. Strangely though, typical French-Canadian cooking – game with sweet sauces followed by simple desserts with lashings of maple syrup – is available at very few places in town.

Whether you are on a tight budget or not, the lively **cafés** are probably where you will want to spend your time, washing down bowls of soups and croutons (toasted baguettes dripping with cheese) with plenty of coffee. Decked out in a variety of decors, from the traditional to the stylish, they are always buzzing with activity, as students and workers drop in throughout the day. Haute and Basse-Ville have their fair share of restaurants and cafés, but the best area for atmosphere and selection is along the stretch of St-Jean outside the city walls.

## Snacks and cafés

**Bouche Bée**, 383 St-Paul. Cheap café in Vieux-Québec. Sandwiches, quiches, soups, etc.

**Le Café Canadien**, Château Frontenac. Considering the location, looking across the St Lawrence, this place is not too badly priced.

**L'Esplanade**, 1084 St-Jean. Plain and simple but cheap. Sandwiches and the like.

**Café Krieghoff**, 1089 Cartier. Trendy café, with a patio area and cheap and delicious food. Fifteen types of coffee. Fairly far out, but worth the trip.

**Café Loft**, 49 Dalhousie. Sleek yuppie café in a converted warehouse. Good bagels.

**Restaurant Liban**, 23 d'Auteuil. Cheap Lebanese fast food just inside the city walls – kebabs and felafels for $3.95.

**Café du Monde**, 57 Dalhousie. Fairly pricey and chic bistro.

**Café Retro**, 1129 St-Jean. Well priced but fairly touristy. A variety of food from sandwiches to T-Bone steaks.

**Café Sainte-Julie**, 865 des Zouaves. One of the cheapest places to eat in Québec City. Tiny, greasy spoon café popular with young people. Just off St-Jean.

**Café Taste-Vin**, 32 St-Louis. Centrally located café. Set meals around $20.

**Chez Temporal**, 25 Couillard. Bowls of steaming café au lait, croissants and chocolatines make this a perfect place for breakfast. Soups and sandwiches also available throughout the day and night. In the Latin Quarter, a few doors from the Peace Hostel.

**Croissant Plus**, 50 Garneau. One of a chain of fast-food croissant places. Cheap but not particularly tasty.

**La Luncheonette**, 50 Côte de la Fabrique. Chrome tables and great ice creams in the heart of Vieux-Québec.

## Restaurants

**À la Table de Serge Bruyère**, 1200 St-Jean (☎694-0618). Probably the best restaurant in Canada. Fresh produce, beautifully prepared and presented. Dinner for two $150. Reservations a must. Closed Sun & Mon.

**L'Apsara**, 71 d'Auteuil. Cambodian, Vietnamese and Thai food in Vieux-Québec near Porte St-Louis. Three-course lunch around $10, dinners in $30 region.

**L'Astral**, 1225 Place Montcalm. Rotating restaurant on the top floor of the *Hôtel Loews le Concorde*. The food is generally expensive but the views can't be beaten. On Sundays the all-you-can-eat brunch costs $20, which competes with some of the budget places around town.

**Aux Anciens Canadiens**, 34 St-Louis (☎692-1627). Located in one of the oldest homes in Québec City. Expensive (around $50 a head) and touristy, but serves such typical Québécois food as duck glazed with maple, turkey in hazelnut sauce and lamb in blueberry wine sauce. As a side dish such delicacies as baked beans are given a whole new meaning, and to finish off there's a slab of blueberry tart or maple syrup pie.

**Buffet de l'Antiquaire**, 95 St-Paul. Cheap and cheerful Canadian fast food.

**Café de la Paix**, 44 des Jardins (☎692-1430). The desserts displayed in the front window taste every bit as good as they look – and the rest of the menu is equally delicious. Approximately $40 per person. Closed Sunday.

**La Cagouille**, 17 Stanislas. Antique restaurant with a good reputation. Fairly expensive but worth it.

**Casse-Crêpe Breton**, 1136 St-Jean. Delicious crêpes made right in front of your eyes for around $5. One of the best budget restaurants. Open until 2.30am at the weekends.

**Chalet Suisse**, 32 Ste-Anne. Touristy fondue place. Perfect for people-watching as the restaurant spills out onto the pedestrian-only part of Ste-Anne in the heart of Vieux-Québec.

**Le Cochon Dingue**, 46 Champlain and 46 St-Cyrille Ouest. Fun and reasonably priced pasta- and burger bistros – the first in Basse-Ville, the second way out west. Great strawberry tart.

**Le Graffiti**, 1191 Cartier. French food in a Parisian-style bistro, complete with dripping candles and chequered tablecloths.

**Grambrinus**, 15 du Fort (☎692-5144). Excellent Italian and French food in the shadow of Château Frontenac. Menu of the day around $35.

**Le Hobbit**, 700 St-Jean. One of the best bargains around: great vegetarian food, good studenty atmosphere.

**Le Marie Clarisse**, 12 Petit-Champlain (☎692-0857). Fine fish restaurant in Basse-Ville. Four-course meal around $40.

**Le Mykonos**, 1066 St-Jean. Well-priced Greek restaurant. A full meal will set you back around $15.

**Le Onze Bourg**, 469 St-Jean. Great submarines for around $5 and the poutine is good too. Open until 4am on Fridays and Saturdays.

**Le Paris Brest**, 590 Grande Allée (☎529-2243). One of Québec City's best restaurants. Traditional French food, very expensive.

**Restaurant au Parmesan**, 38 St-Louis. Bland Italian and French food, but popular with tourists because of its central Haute-Ville location and reasonable prices.

**Le Petit Coin Latin**, 8 Ste-Ursule. Delicious but fairly expensive baguettes and quiches. Open until 2.30am at weekends, 1am weekdays.

**Pizzeria d'Youville**, 1014 St-Jean. Variety of brick-oven pizzas in the heart of the Latin Quarter.

**Piazzetta**, 707 St-Jean & 1191 Cartier. There's always a queue outside these trendy pizzerias – the pizzas come close to perfection and are dead cheap.

**Le Saint-Amour**, 48 Ste-Ursule (☎694-0667). Romantic French restaurant. Excellent food at around $100 for two.

# Bars and nightlife

Nightlife in Québec City is far more relaxed than in Montréal: an evening in an intimate bar or a jazz or blues soirée are more popular than big gigs or discos – and few major bands tour here, except during the Festival d'Éte, when everyone lets their hair down. As with restaurants, Québec City's main bar and nightclub strip is around St-Jean, outside the city walls. For up-to-date **information** on the goings-on check out the listings section in the French daily newspapers *Le Soleil* and *Journal de Québec*. The quarterly bilingual magazine for tourists *Voilà Québec* also carries information, as does the English *Québec Chronical-Telegraph*, published every Wednesday.

### Bars and live music

**Ainsi Soit-il**, 1135 Cartier. Local rock and blues bands. Free admission.

**Le d'Auteuil**, 35 d'Auteuil. Cheap blues, folk and jazz bands, above the *Fourmi Atomix*.

**Bar Chez Son Pére**, 24 St-Stanislas. Just off St-Jean in Haute-Ville, above street level. Québécois folk singers create a great thigh-slapping atmosphere. Free admission.

**Bull Dog**, 624 Grande Allée Est. Two-floored sports bar with big screens.

**L'Acropole**, 219 St-Paul. Video bar with billiard tables.

**L'Amour Sorcier**, 789 Ste-Geneviève. Intimate mixed gay bar with cheap beers and soft music. Popular with everyone.

**Le Chantauteuil**, 1001 St-Jean. Relaxed French-style bar.

**L'Emprise**, Hôtel Clarendon, 57 Ste-Anne. Art deco decor attracts a sophisticated touristy crowd to evenings of jazz and blues.

**Le Fou Bar**, 519 St-Jean. Trendy, packed student bar.

**Fourmi Atomix**, 33 d'Auteuil. The trendiest bar in Haute-Ville. Cheap beers, snacks, pool tables and loud music.

**Le Pape Georges**, 8 Cul-de-sac. Near Place Royale. Small wine bar with traditional folk singing.

**Le Pub Saint Alexandre**, 1987 St-Jean. Over 190 beers in this yuppie English-style pub.

**Taverne Le Drague**, 804 St Augustin. A gay bar, café and nightclub. Cheap imported beers. Popular with Québec's small transvestite population.

### Clubs and discos

**Le Ballon Rouge**, 811 St-Jean. Gay male disco. Loud, good music. Free entry.

**Chez Dagobert**, 600 Grande Allée Est. A huge club in a renovated warehouse. Dance floor on the first floor, and a stage for mainly rock bands downstairs. Free unless a band is playing.

**Merlin**, 1175 Cartier. Young Québécois disco hang-out.
**Le Tube Hi-fi**, 139 St-Pierre. Massive glitzy disco on the corner of St-Paul, with Greek columns and lashings of '70s disco tack. Like a visit into a John Travolta movie, except everyone is dressed in black.
**Studio 157**, 157 Ste-Foy. Locally known as the *Venus*. Disco/bar for gay women.
**Le Vogue**, 1170 d'Artigny. Trendy dance-music club, on the top of the hip-list.

# Entertainment and festivals

Québec City is not especially renowned for its high culture, but from May to September there are dance, theatre and music events at various outdoor venues, and throughout the year performances can be caught at the city's theatres. The liveliest periods are in February and July, when the entire city is animated by its two principal festivals: the excellent Carnaval and the equally frenzied Festival d'Été. Tickets for most events can be purchased through the *Billetech* agency which has outlets at the *Grand Théâtre de Québec*, *Provigo* supermarkets and *La Baie* shopping centre in Place Laurier.

## Theatre

Québec City has a fair smattering of **theatres**, all producing plays in French only. The city's main theatre for the performing arts is the *Grand Théâtre de Québec*, 269 St-Cyrille Est (☎643-8131), which has a sound programme of drama, as well as dance shows and classical music concerts. Other main theatres include *Palais Montcalm*, 995 Place d'Youville (☎670-9011), and *Salle Albert Rousseau*, 2410 Ste-Foy (☎659-6710). For small-scale dramatic productions check out the *Théâtre de la Bordée*, 1143 St-Jean (☎694-9631), and *Théâtre du Petit-Champlain*, 68 du Petit-Champlain (☎692-0100).

Open-air **summer theatres** are particularly popular in Québec. The largest is the *Agora*, in the Vieux-Port at 160 Dalhousie (☎692-0100), a huge amphitheatre used for a range of productions from comedies to classical music. *Théâtre du Bois du Coulonge* (☎692-3064), set near the Musée du Québec in Battlefields Park, is a perfect venue for a summer theatre. A summer-long programme of activities is also enacted on open stages in the Jardin de l'Hôtel-de-Ville, the *Pigeonnier* on Parliament Hill and in the Place d'Youville.

## Music

Canada's oldest symphony orchestra, *L'Orchestre Symphonique de Québec*, performs at the *Grand Théâtre*. Other classical concerts can be caught at the *Bibliothèque Gabrielle-Roy*, 350 St-Joseph (☎529-0924). In Place d'Youville and Place Royale there are various free classical music concerts in the summer, and the *Agora* is used for summer concerts too.

## Cinema

The city has a large number of cinemas. Popular ones include *Cinéma Ste-Foy*, 2500 Laurier; *Cinéma de Paris*, Place d'Youville; and *Place Québec*, 5 Place Québec, all of which feature undubbed English films when they first come out, as well as Québécois and French movies. *Cinéma Le Clap*, 2360 Ste-Foy (bus #7), is the city's rep cinema.

## Festivals

Québec City is renowned for its two large annual **festivals**, the first of which is the **Carnaval de Québec** in freezing February, when large quantities of the lethal but warming caribou are consumed amid parades and ice-sculpture competitions, all presided over by the mascot snowman called Bonhomme Carnaval. In early July, the **Festival d'Été** is an equally cheery affair, especially as the provincial law prohibiting drink on the streets is temporarily revoked. The largest festival of francophone culture in North America attracts hundreds of artists, and everyone is roped into the celebration, with restaurants offering discounts and all of Québec's major performers pitching up to dance, make music and lead the party from massive open-air stages.

It is also worth being in the city on **St-Jean Baptiste Day** on June 24, the provincial holiday when an outpouring of Québécois pride spills onto the streets in a massive parade with the entire city decked with thousands of fleur-de-lis flags.

# Listings

**Airlines** *Air Alliance*, Aeroport de Québec (☎872-7622); *Air France*, 610 Place Québec (☎692-0733); *Air Canada* and *Intair*, 2700 Laurier (☎692-1031) and 1200 Germain des Pres, Ste-Foy (☎692-0770); *Canadian Airlines*, Aeroport de Québec (☎692-0912).

**Bicycle hire** *Location Petit-Champlain*, 92 du Petit-Champlain, and the youth hostel *Auberge de la Paix*.

**Books** English books can be purchased at *Librairie Garneau*, 47–49 Buade; *La Maison Anglaise*, 33 St-Cyrille Ouest; *Classic Bookshop*, Place Laurier.

**Bus enquiries** Long distance: *Terminus Voyageur*, 255 Charest Est (☎524-4692). Local: *CTCUQ*, Place Jacques-Cartier, 325 du Roi (☎627-2511).

**Car hire** *Agency Rent-a-Car*, 103–3914 Wilfred Hamel (☎871-9191); *Avis*, Hôtel Hilton (☎523-1075); *Budget*, 380 Wilfred Hamel (☎687-4220); *Discount*, 2360 Ste-Foy (☎652-7289); *Hertz*, 44 du Palais (☎694-1224) and 580 Grande Allée Est (☎647-4949); *Thrifty*, 2605 Wilfred Hamel (☎683-1542).

**Car parks** Hôtel-de-Ville, Chauveau (near Hôtel-de-Ville), Haldimand (near Jardin des Gouverneurs), Complex "H" (off St-Louis), Complex "G" (St-Cyrille), Youville (St-Jean off Dufferin).

**Consulates** *US*, 2 Terrasse Dufferin (☎692-2095).

**Exchange** *Banque d'Amerique*, 24 de la Fabrique (summer daily 9am–7pm; winter Mon–Fri 9am–5pm, Sat & Sun 10am–4pm); *Deak International*, 615 Grande Allée Est (May–Sept daily 10am–9pm; Oct–April 9am–5pm).

**Hospitals** *Hôtel-Dieu Hospital*, 11 du Paris (☎694-5042); *Jeffrey Hale Hospital*, 1250 Ste-Foy (☎683-4471).

**Ice hockey** The *Québec Nordiques* play at the Colisée de Québec, 2205 du Colisée, Parc de l'Exposition (information ☎529-8441; tickets ☎523-3333).

**Laundry** *Lavoir la Lavandiére*, 625 St-Jean and 17 Ste-Ursule (Mon–Sat 9am–9pm).

**Left luggage** Both the train and bus stations have $1 luggage lockers.

**Medical emergencies** 24-hr medical service (☎687-9915).

**Pharmacy** 24-hr service: *Jean Coutu*, 1455 Ste-Foy.

**Post office** 300 St-Paul (Mon–Fri 8am–5.45pm).

**Ride sharing** *Allo-Stop*, 467 St-Jean (☎522-0056).

**Taxis** *Taxi Coop* (☎525-5191); *Taxi Québec* (☎522-2001); *Taxi Québec-Metro* (☎529-0003).

**Train enquiries** *Via Rail* (☎692-3940 or ☎1-800-361-5390); *Gare du Palais*, 450 de la Gare du Palais (☎524-6452); *Gare de Lévis*, 5995 St Laurent, Lévis (☎833-8056).

**Travel agencies** *American Express Inter-Voyage*, 1155 Claire Fontaine (☎524-1414).

**Weather information** ☎648-7293.

# Around Québec City

If you're staying in Québec City for a while, there are various options for a swift or protracted trip out from the city. **Lévis**, on the opposite shore of the St Lawrence, is less inundated by visitors than Québec City and the views of its more illustrious neighbour should not be missed. In nearby **Wendake**, the past and present crafts of Canada's only surviving Huron community can be seen, while to the east the fertile

**Côte-de-Beaupré** and the offshore **Île d'Orléans** still recall the lives of the province's first argricultural settlers. The Côte also offers the attractions of the spectacular water-falls of **Montmorency** and **Sept-Chutes**, but for something wilder, the wilderness of the **Réserve Faunique des Laurentides** is within easy reach too.

**Buses** run to Chute Montmorency, Wendake and Ste-Anne-de-Beaupré, while a quick **ferry** trip lands you in Lévis. The only places for which your own transport is essential are the Île d'Orléans and Sept-Chutes.

## Lévis

It's hard to think of any commuters who have as pleasant a morning trip as those who cross the St Lawrence from **LÉVIS** to Québec City each day. Lévis itself is an attractive Victorian town, but it's really the views of Québec that make the visit a treat. The regular ferry leaves day and night from opposite Place Royale, and costs $1.05 for the fifteen-minute crossing – and no extra for the return if you stay on the boat.

Most tourists stay on the ferry for the free return trip but those dauntless enough to scale the staircase to the Terrasse on the heights of Lévis are rewarded with an even greater panorama. The Terrasse runs through a landscaped park whose centrepiece is a statue of Father Joseph David Déziel, founder of Lévis. The main street of Lévis, Carré Déziel, is a couple of blocks east of the Terrasse, and the streets running off it are as narrow and steep as those in Québec City - and on Notre Dame, Wolfe and Guinette streets there are examples of elaborate brickwork and ornate roof lines as fine as those across the water. The massive **Notre-Dame-de-Lévis** (1851), which dominates the town's skyline, was commissioned by Déziel and has some noteworthy wooden furnishings by the Baillargé family, and stained glass windows depicting scenes from the life of the Madonna.

## Wendake

Just to the north of Québec City lies the only **Huron reserve** in Canada, L'Ancienne-Lorette or **WENDAKE**, a word derived from the Hurons' own name for their people – Wendat, meaning "people of the peninsula". French Jesuit missionaries led three hundred Huron from Ontario's Georgian Bay to the Île d'Orléans in 1650, as their numbers were being depleted by wars, epidemics and famines. After the Iroquois attacked them again, their French allies gave them this land close to the city's protection in 1697. Now with a population of 2000, the central village core of the reserve retains typical Québécois wooden houses with sloping and gabled roofs, but the main reason tourists visit is to shop for Huron crafts – moccasins, mittens, beaded belts, jewellery and embroidered duffle coats.

The #71 and #73 *CTCUQ* buses run every half-hour from Place Jacques-Cartier to the reserve; the trip takes about forty minutes and costs the standard $1.40. The red-roofed chapel where the bus arrives, **Notre-Dame-de-Lorette** (May–Oct Mon–Fri 9am–9pm, Sat & Sun 9am–6pm; Nov–April Mon–Wed, Sat & Sun 10am–6pm, Thurs–Fri 10am–9pm), was built 250 years ago and is now a small museum containing old manuscripts and religious objects. Opposite the chapel, one of the original wooden houses contains the **Musée Arouanne** (May–Sept Mon–Sat 9.30am–5pm, Sun noon–4pm; $1), whose impressive collection of native cultural objects includes ceremonial attire beaded with pearls and porcupine quills, drums of moose hide and feathered head-dresses used for festive occasions.

Every summer a Huron village of tepees is reconstructed on Maurice Bastien for the benefit of the tourists; August is the best time to visit, for the local powwow celebrations. Of the village's numerous artisan shops, *Le Huron* and *Petit Huron Moc* on Maurice Bastien and *Rolland P. Sioui* on Grand Rue are recommended.

# The Réserve Faunique des Laurentides

The zone of the Laurentians to the north of Québec City is considerably more wild than the mountains north of Montréal, thanks to the creation of the 14,600-square-kilometre **Réserve Faunique des Laurentides**. The vast wooded terrain, reaching summits over 1000m towards the east, was once a hunting ground of the Montagnais, until the Hurons, supplied with arms by the French, drove the small population further north. The area became a park in 1895 to protect the caribou herds, an intervention that was not a great success – very few exist today. However, though it allows controlled moose-hunting, the park's main function is still to preserve native animals such as the beaver, moose, lynx, black bear and deer, all of which you may see in the remoter areas.

The best way to see the park is to drive through it via Hwy 175 to Chicoutimi (see p.204); halfway through the park the highway branches, with Hwy 169 leading to Alma on Lac St-Jean (see p.205). *Autocars Fournier*, 2200 Lavoisier, Ste-Foy (☎688-1222), run a bus service through the park from Québec City to Alma, stopping at Camp Mercier, Mare du Sault and L'Étape. There are two campgrounds along the highway and several cottage resorts ($50–100; reservations ☎622-9781).

# The Côte-de-Beaupré

Dubbed the "coast of fine meadows" by Jacques Carter, the **Côte-de-Beaupré** stretches along the St Lawrence to the basilica of Ste-Anne-de-Beaupré, 40km from Québec City. There are two roads along the coast: the speedy Dufferin-Montmorency autoroute (Hwy 440) and the winding Avenue Royale (Hwy 360), which is served by local buses. The latter gives a far better introduction to the province's rural life, with ancient farmhouses and churches lining the way.

### Chute Montmorency

Nine kilometres northeast of Québec City the waters of the Montmorency river cascade from the Laurentians 83 metres into the St Lawrence, which makes the **Chute Montmorency** one and a half times the height of Niagara, though the volume of water is considerably less. Named by Champlain in honour of the governor of New France, the falls were the site of Wolfe's first attempt on the colony, but they were driven off by Montcalm's superior forces. In those days – before a hydro-electric dam cut off much of the flow – the falls were a far more spectacular sight, but it remains an awesome spectacle, especially in winter, when the water and spray become a gigantic cone of ice, known locally as the sugar loaf. Local *CTCUQ* bus #53 stops at the bottom of the falls, #50 at the top; both buses leave from Place Jacques-Cartier and take around fifty minutes, costing $1.40.

### Ste-Anne-de-Beaupré

Québec's equivalent of Lourdes, the **Basilique de Ste-Anne-de-Beaupré**, 39km from Québec City (1hr by *CTCUQ* bus #50 from Place Jacques-Cartier; $1.50), stands more or less isolated in acres of countryside, totally engulfing the tiny village. The legend of its foundation has it that some Breton sailors were caught in a storm on the St Lawrence in 1650 and vowed to build a chapel to Saint Anne if she saved them. The sailors did survive and building began in 1658 on the spot where they came ashore. The first miracle occurred when a crippled peasant was cured so that he could help build the chapel, and from then on everyone caught in the St Lawrence's frequent storms prayed to Saint Anne and donated ex votos to the shrine. In the early days the devout came to this site on their knees from the beach or walked shoeless from

Québec City; now one and a half million pilgrims flock to the site every year in comfortable coachloads.

The neo-Romanesque granite cathedral with lofty symmetrical spires is the fourth church to stand here, fires and floods having destroyed the first three. It has a capacity of 10,000, and most of its decoration – countless stained glass windows and massive murals – depict the miraculous powers of Saint Anne, though the wooden pews bear delightful animal carvings. Behind the ornate golden statue of Saint Anne, depicted holding her daughter Mary, is a chapel containing a portion of Anne's forearm, donated by the pope in 1960. Those who have been cured by her intervention have left a vast collection of crutches and wooden limbs hanging on the basilica's back pillars. The information office in front of the basilica (early May to mid-Sept daily 8.30am–5pm) runs pious, free, guided tours daily at 1pm.

Numerous little chapels cringe in the basilica's shadow. The simple **Chapelle Souvenir** (early May to mid-Sept daily 6am–8pm), across the street, was built in the nineteenth century using the stones of the first chapel; some of its paintings date from the shrine's earliest days. The fountain in front is the apparent agency through which Anne performs her healing. Nearby, the small white chapel of the **Scala Santa** (early May to mid-Sept daily 6am–8pm) is the container for a set of holy stairs that replicate those climbed by Christ on his meeting with Pontius Pilate. Lumps of earth from various holy places are contained in glass boxes embedded in each stair, and the devout accomplish the ascent on their knees. Another obligatory part of the penitential route is the nearby **Way of the Cross**, which curves steeply up the hillside; on summer evenings torchlit processions wend their way through each station. Less athletic visitors can pay their respects to the basilica's collection of ex votos and treasures in the **Historial** (mid-June to Sept daily 9am–7.30pm, Oct to mid-June 9.30am–5pm; $2), which also contains a missable wax museum depicting scenes from the life of Saint Anne.

## Sept-Chutes

Just off Hwy 138 some 10km further east from Ste-Anne-de-Beaupré, the falls at **Sept-Chutes** (daily mid-May to Aug 9am–7pm; Sept 10am–5pm; $3.50) can only be reached by car, which takes about thirty minutes from Québec City. The tourist bumph describes the gorge created by the 73-metre falls as a Grand Canyon, which is pushing the hyperbole a little far, but the area is spectacular – with the water tumbling through a chasm fringed with woodlands that are criss-crossed by short nature trails. Over the falls a precarious rope bridge allows for splendid and terrifying views, whilst other, sturdier look-out points cling to crevices on the side of the gorge.

# Île d'Orléans

From just north of Québec City to a short distance beyond Ste-Anne-de-Beaupré, St Lawrence is bottlenecked by the **ÎLE D'ORLÉANS**, an area which retains the atmosphere of eighteenth-century French Canada in a purer form than most places on the mainland. This island of old stone churches, little cottages and seigneural manors has remained in a pristine state because it was cut off from the mainland until the construction in 1932 of the suspension bridge from Hwy 440, about 10km out of the city, to the west end of the island.

To its first inhabitants, the **Algonquins**, the island was known as Minigo, which means "enchanting place". Jacques Cartier christened it Île de Bacchus because the vines he saw here were "such as we had seen nowhere else in the world". (He was soon to change the name to Île d'Orléans in honour of the son of the king.) Agriculture is still the mainstay for the 7000 population: roadside stalls heave under the weight of fresh fruit and vegetables, jams, dairy products, homemade bread and maple syrup, and the island's restaurants and B&Bs are some of the best in the province, thanks to the supplies from local farms.

Encircling the island, the chemin Royal (route 368) dips and climbs over gentle slopes and terraces past acres of neat farmland and orchards, passing through the six villages on the island's periphery. The island's **information** office is situated on the right just after the bridge at 490 côte de Pont. Nearly all the information is in French, except the free *Île d'Orléans* booklet, which has an adequate map and accommodation listings.

From here it's best to head west to the area known locally as the "end of the island", a district still characterised by the grand homes of the merchants who made their fortunes trading farm produce with Québec City. In the eighteenth century rich anglophones spent their leisure time in **STE-PÉTRONILLE**, the island's oldest and most beautifully situated settlement, with the noble rise of Québec City dominating the skyline – Wolfe used this spot to observe the city before his bombardment. The white **Maison Gourdeau-de-Beaulieu** at no. 137 Royal was the island's first permanent dwelling, built in 1648 and still home to the Beaulieu family. Some of the best views can be had from Rue Horatio Walker, where the home of landscape painter **Horatio Walker** stands at no. 13. Known unofficially as the grand seigneur of Ste-Pétronille, Walker lived here from 1904 until his death in 1938. He despised his English heritage, continually emphasising a French branch in his ancestry and refusing to speak English. His subject matter was almost entirely based on the Île d'Orléans, which he viewed as a "sacred temple of the muses and a gift of the gods". Though most of his paintings now grace Canada's larger galleries, some of his lesser-known works and sketches can be viewed in his studio (late May to Oct; reservations only, ☎828-2275).

Budget **accommodation** in the village is limited to two often booked-out **B&Bs**: *La Vielle École*, 25 Royal (☎828-2737), and the *Gîte le "91"*, 91 du bout de l'Île (☎828-2678), both with singles for $30, doubles for $45. A pricier stay can be had at *La Goéliche*, 22 du Quai (☎828-2248; doubles from $75), an inn with delicious French/Québécois cuisine and great views.

The south shore of the island was once the domain of sailors and navigators, most of them living in **ST-JEAN**, where the cemetery of the hull-shaped local church contains the gravestones of numerous mariners. St-Jean has a museum of antique furniture and domestic objects housed in the stately **Manoir Mauvide-Genest**, 1451 Royal (late May to Oct daily 10am–5pm; $2.50), the one-time home of Louis XV's surgeon; its metre-thick walls withstood the impact from Wolfe's bombardment. Nearby, at no. 1457, *La Sucerie de la Ferme Louis-Hébert* has a filling table d'hôte for around $10. Nearby **ST-LAURENT** was the island's supplier of *chaloupes*, the long rowing boats that were the islanders' only means of getting to mainland before the bridge was built.

From St-Jean, the road continues to the island's southwest tip and the village of **ST-FRANCOIS**, where a precarious observation tower is the only attraction since a suicidal driver wrecked the 1734 church. Unless you intend to pitch camp at *Camping Orléans*, 357 chemin Royal ($16), take Route du Milan across the interior to **STE-FAMILLE**. Among its wealth of French-regime stone buildings, the **Maison Canac-Marquis**, 4466 chemin Royal, is a particularly fine example, and the richly decorated **church**, built in 1743, includes a painting of the Holy Family by Québec's foremost early painter, Frére Luc. The local boulangerie, *G.H.Boulin*, is one of the island's oldest and best, with mouth-watering bread and local fare. Another of the village's Normandy manors is now the highly recommended Québécois **restaurant** *L'Atre*, 4403 chemin Royal.

The remaining village, **ST-PIERRE**, to the west of Ste-Famille, is notable for its **church**; constructed in 1718, it has pews with special hot-brick holders for keeping bums warm on seats.

# THE GASPÉ PENINSULA AND ÎLES-DE-LA-MADELEINE

The **Gaspé Peninsula** has always been sparsely inhabited and poor, its remote communities eking out an existence from the turbulent seas and the rocky soil. In recent years it's become a major summer holiday spot, yet the new service industry jobs have failed to dent the high rate of unemployment. The people of the peninsula are predominantly and proudly Québécois, though there are pockets of long-established English-speaking settlement, particularly in and around Gaspé town, while Carleton and Bonaventure are centres of Acadian culture, established in 1755 in the wake of the British deportation of some 10,000 Acadians from the Bay of Fundy in Nova Scotia. Neither of these communities has created visually distinctive villages or towns, however, and the Gaspé looks as French as the heartlands of rural Québec.

Bounded by the Gulf of St Lawrence to the north and west and by the Baie des Chaleurs to the south and east, the peninsula is roughly 550km long, with a chain of mountains and rolling highlands dominating the interior and the northern shore – providing some wonderful scenery of forested hills, deep ravines and craggy mountains tumbling to a jagged coastline. This landscape makes the coastal drive along Highway 132 a delight, though the principal towns strung along this shore – **Rimouski**, **Matane** and **Gaspé** – are in themselves less appealing than smaller villages like **Sainte-Anne-des-Monts**, **Marsoui** and **Mont-Saint-Pierre**. If you're travelling in summer, be sure to book your accommodation before you arrive. The Gaspé also has two outstanding parks: the extravagantly mountainous **Parc de la Gaspésie**, inland from Sainte-Anne-des-Monts; and the **Parc National de Forillon**, at the tip of the peninsula, with its mountain and coastal hikes and wonderfully rich wildlife. Just to the south of the Forillon park, the village of **Percé** is famous for the offshore **Rocher Percé**, an extraordinary limestone monolith that has been a magnet for travellers for over one hundred years. East of here, stuck out in the middle of the Gulf of St Lawrence, the **Îles-de-la-Madeleine** are most easily reached by ferry from Prince Edward Island; the windswept archipelago is not the most enthralling part of the province, but cyclists and walkers might find it a good place to unwind.

The **south coast** of the Gaspé is, for the most part, flatter and duller than the north, and public transport is problematic, as buses and trains from Montréal, Québec City and Halifax favour the northern coast route. However, the seaside resort of **Bonaventure** is a pleasant little place to bathe and relax, while at **Carleton**, further to the west, the mountains return to tower over the coast, offering yet more fine scenery and strenuous hikes.

> The Gaspé and Îles-de-la-Madeleine telephone code is ☎418.

# Rivière-du-Loup

Whether you're coming up from the heartlands of Québec or crossing over from New Brunswick on the Trans-Canada Highway, **RIVIÈRE-DU-LOUP** is to all intents and purposes the beginning of the Gaspé Peninsula. The town is a prosperous-looking place whose centre comes complete with broad, tree-lined streets and handsome Victorian villas, and owes its development to the timber industry and the coming of the railroad in 1859, which established Rivière-du-Loup as a crossroads for traffic between

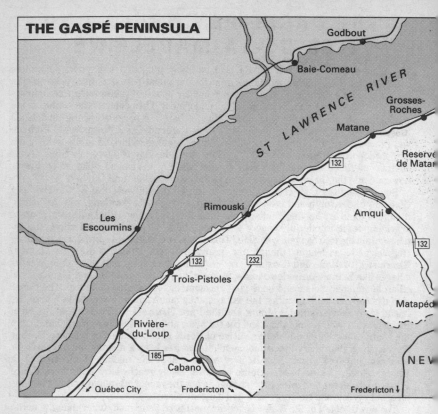

**THE GASPÉ PENINSULA**

Godbout

Baie-Comeau

ST LAWRENCE RIVER

Grosses-Roches

Matane

Reserve
de Matar

132

Rimouski

Amqui

Les
Escoumins

132

132

232

Trois-Pistoles

Mataped

Rivière-
du-Loup

185

Cabano

N E V

Québec City    Fredericton    Fredericton ↓

the Maritimes, the peninsula and the rest of the province. Its significance as an administrative and commercial centre has grown accordingly and today it has a population of around 16,000.

The river which gives the town its name crashes down a thirty-metre drop close to the centre, at the top of rue Frontenac. However, although the **waterfall** generates a lot of noise and spray, even the specially built platform fails to make the view enthralling. Similarly modest, the town has two museums: the central **Musée du Bas-Saint-Laurent**, 300 rue St Pierre (June–Sept Mon–Fri 10am–5pm & Sat–Sun 1–5pm; Sept–June Tues–Fri 10am–1pm & 2–5pm & Sat–Sun 1–5pm; $3), which combines ethnological displays of the region with historical exhibits and works of modern art by local artists; and the **Musée des Carillons**, on the eastern edge of town at 393 rue Témiscouata (June–Oct daily 9am–9pm; $2.50), which has bells of all types and sizes.

If you're interested in the architectural heritage of the place, you could pick up the interpretive booklet from the tourist office and take a stroll round the centre: there's nothing special, but it's a pleasant way to while away an hour. For less sedate pleasures, the amusement park of **Château de Rêve**, 65 rue de l'Ancrage (daily June 9am–5pm, July–Sept 9am–9pm), has bumper cars, miniature golf, bumper boats and roller coasters. It's situated on the tongue of land which protrudes north of the harbour.

Rivière-du-Loup is a good place for **boat trips** on the St Lawrence River. Beginning at around $25 per person per trip, these excursions are not cheap, but they are well

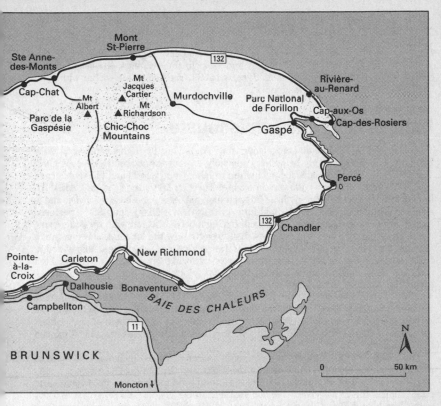

organised and there's a good chance of seeing beluga, minke and finback whales throughout the summer. The *Société Linnéene*, 200 rue Hayward (☎862-9454), specialises in whale-watching trips; alternatively, the *Duvetnor Society*, at the same address (☎867-1660), has cruises to various midstream sanctuaries for sea birds and mammals, with overnight stops a possibility.

## Practicalities

The main coastal road, Highway 132, runs right through the centre of Rivière-du-Loup. The town's **bus station** is on boulevard Cartier, about ten minutes' walk northeast of the centre, where the **tourist office**, at 65 rue Hôtel de Ville (Mon–Fri 8.30am–5pm; ☎862-1981), will help you get your bearings and provide accommodation listings. The **youth hostel** (June–Aug; ☎862-7566), on the same street at no. 46, occupies a fine wooden building with ornate banisters and balustrades, and has beds at $11. A similarly inexpensive and equally convenient option is the **Cégep**, 335 rue St Pierre (☎867-2733), a college hall of residence where hundreds of spartan rooms are on offer throughout the summer at $20 per person per night. There are two decent **motels** with doubles from $40: the **Auberge de l'Anse** (☎867-3463), a couple of kilometres east of town on Hwy 132; and the **Motel Dubé**, 182 Rue Fraser (☎862-6354), which also offers **camping** facilities. The municipal **campground**, rue Hayward (mid-May to Sept; ☎862-4281), is near the Château de Rêve, off Hwy 132.

Pricey high-class **restaurants** abound in the centre of town, but a walk down rue Lafontaine, near the river, reveals some less expensive alternatives. Best value is *La Gourmande*, no. 168, where salads and vegetarian meals average out at about $9; *Mike's Pizza*, at no. 370, is in the same range. Down on boulevard Cartier, around the bus station, is the spot for fast food, steaks and ribs. In the evenings, the bright young things of Rivière-du-Loup gather at *La Terrasse*, at 392 rue Lafontaine – a **bar** with beer, cocktails, flashing lights and loud music.

# Cabano and Lake Témiscouata

The area east of Rivière-du-Loup, along the Trans-Canada Highway towards New Brunswick, is outstandingly beautiful, especially around the graceful sweep of **Lake Témiscouata**, where a magical combination of lake, river, woods and hills is adorned by a dazzling display of wildflowers in spring. The tiny lakeside village of **CABANO**, linked with Rivière-du-Loup by three buses a day, makes a good base for a visit and is also the location of **Fort Ingall** (mid-June to Aug daily 9.30am–6pm; $5), a restored British fortification dating from 1839. Built during a border dispute with the Americans, the fort was part of a series of schemes that strengthened the land link between the St Lawrence and the Bay of Fundy, protecting the area's timber resources. Abandoned in 1842, having seen no action, Ingall has been painstakingly reconstructed, its high stockade surrounding a squat wooden barracks, block house and officers' quarters. Inside the last there are displays on the background to the fort's construction, contemporaneous army life and local archaeological finds. There's also a section on Archie Belaney, aka **Grey Owl**, the British conservationist turned Indian who settled in the area in the 1920s (see p.305). From Fort Ingall, Hwy 232 tracks some of the prettiest stretches of Lake Témiscouata before snaking back to the St Lawrence at Rimouski (see opposite).

There are several **campgrounds** in and around Cabano, including the *Cabano* municipal site on Hwy 185 (June–Aug; ☎854-3358), and the *Témilac*, 33 rue de la Plage, near the junction of Highways 232 and 185 (mid-May to mid-Oct; ☎854-7660). The latter adjoins the *Hébergement Témilac* (same number), where doubles cost $75 per night. The **Motel Royal**, 19 rue Saint-Louis (☎854-2307), is a decent and inexpensive place to stay, with doubles from $35.

# Trois-Pistoles

Heading northeast from Rivière-du-Loup along the St Lawrence, with the far bank clearly visible, the coastal highway passes through a succession of farming communities and fishing villages on its way to **TROIS-PISTOLES**, named after a silver goblet worth three *pistoles* (gold coins) which a French sailor once lost here. The town is dominated by the enormous church of **Notre-Dame-des-Neiges-de-Trois-Pistoles** (mid-May to mid-Sept daily 9am–6pm), built in 1887. From a distance it looks like something out of Disneyland, as the roof, surmounted by four pinnacles, is clad in reflective metal. Inside, the vaulted Italianate ceiling is supported by massive marble columns with ornate gilded capitals, while the walls are dotted with old devotional paintings.

A **ferry** service crosses from here to Les Escoumins (June–Oct 6 daily; 1hr 15min; $10), and excursions are also available to the **Île aux Basques**, a couple of kilometres offshore. As early as the sixteenth century, the island was used as a whaling station by Basque sailors who built huge stone furnaces to render the blubber into whale oil; the remains of these can still be seen.

Should you be breaking your journey in Trois-Pistoles, try the **Hôtel Le Marmiton**, 70 rue Notre-Dame (☎851-3202; doubles from $35), or the **bed and breakfast** *Gîte Coucher de Soleil* at 175 rang 2 est (☎851-3622; from $25 per person). For **snacks**, coffee and cakes, the *Quaides Brumes*, on the corner opposite the church door, is the place to go, while *Le Michalie*, nearby at 53 rue Notre-Dame, has good lunch and dinner specials and excellent mussel dishes from around $9.

# Bic and Rimouski

North from Trois-Pistoles the main road crosses a district of fertile agricultural land, giving views of rocky wooded hummocks along the shoreline, interrupted by spectacular sea vistas and a handful of tiny little villages – most notably **BIC**, a beautifully situated settlement just inland from the St Lawrence. Bic is on the edge of the forests of the **Parc du Bic**, a naturalist's paradise that's pushed up tight against the river, from where it's possible to see herds of grey seals. The park has a series of hiking trails, a beach and a **campground**, *Camping Bic* (early June to early Sept; ☎736-4711), with pitches from $11. Back in the village, there's one **motel**, the *Au Petit Lac*, 2356 route 132 est (☎736-5063; doubles $35).

Some 20km northeast of Bic lies **RIMOUSKI**, the administrative capital of eastern Québec. It's an unremarkable town of 30,000 souls, best visited during the **Jazz Festival** at the end of August or the **Film Festival** in late September. There's not much else to see here, but you could pop into the **Galerie Basque** (June–Aug Mon–Sat 10am–12pm & 1–5pm; Sept–May Tues–Sun 1–5pm & Thurs–Fri 7–9pm; free), on the western edge of town at 1402 boulevard St-Germain Ouest. This is an eclectic commercial art gallery of some renown, featuring work by modern French-Canadian painters. A couple of kilometres northeast of town, beside the St Lawrence, the **Musée de la Mer** (mid-June to early Sept daily 9am–5pm; $3) has an interesting series of displays on the *Empress of Ireland*, a luxury liner which sank just offshore with the loss of over 1000 lives in 1914. The staff here will also unlock the door of the adjoining **Pointe-au-Père Lighthouse**, which marks the point at which the St Lawrence River becomes the Gulf of St Lawrence.

Rimouski's **tourist office**, 50 rue St-Germain Ouest (Oct–May Mon–Fri 8.30am–4.30pm; June–Sept daily 8am–8pm; ☎723-2322) is right in the centre of town, on the waterfront. They have **accommodation** listings that include college rooms available during the summer vacation at the **Cégep**, 320 rue Potvin (☎723-4636), for around $20 per person per night. The town's cheapest **motel** is the *Motel-Chalets Belle Vue*, 1038 rue St-Germain Ouest (☎723-0034; doubles from $38), or you could try the *Motel Colonial*, at no. 438 (☎723-8960; doubles $45). Rimouski has a couple of outstanding **restaurants**: the *Riverain*, 42 rue St Germain, and *La Renaissance*, 130 rue Belzile, which emphasise regional dishes such as lobster.

# Rimouski to Matane

Between Rimouski to Matane the only place to stop is the village of **SAINTE-FLAVIE**, where the **Gaspésie Regional Tourist Office** (mid-June to Aug daily 8am–8pm; Sept to mid-June Mon–Fri 8.30am–5pm) has armfuls of literature on the whole of the peninsula and operates a free room reservation service.

At first sight, **MATANE** looks as if it's dominated by oil refineries and cement works, but in fact fishing and forestry have been the mainstays of the local economy. The town is bisected by the Matane River and right in the centre there's a barrage and fish ladder, built to help the salmon head upstream to spawn. In the same vein, the

**Festival de la Crevette**, held during the last ten days in June, takes its name from the prawn harvest but in fact celebrates the entire range of local seafood – all the town's restaurants and bars participate.

Matane's **tourist office** is in the lighthouse at 968 avenue du Phare (June–Aug daily 9am–6pm; ☎562-1065). Simple institutional **accommodation** can be rented at the *Cégep*, 616 avenue St-Redempteur (☎562-1240; doubles $30), and there's a comfortable **bed and breakfast** called *La Seigneurie*, near the centre on the west side of the river, at 621 avenue St-Jérôme (☎562-0021; doubles $50). Most of Matane's **hotels** and **motels** are pricey, but check out *Motel les Mouettes*, 298 rue McKinnon (☎562-3345; doubles $45). There's a basic **campground** west of the centre of town on boulevard Dion (mid-June to Aug; ☎562-3414). Good for **coffee and cakes** is the tiny un-named café in place Centre Ville. The best bet for serious **eating** is *Le Moussaillon*, 50 rue d'Amours, where they feature seafood, but also have delicious pizzas baked in a wood oven for around $10.

From Matane, a **ferry** runs to Godbout and Baie-Comeau on the north side of the St Lawrence (1–2 daily; 2hr 30min; information ☎562-2500).

### Around Matane: the wildlife reserve

About an hour's drive from the town along Hwy 195 lies the **Réserve Faunique de Matane**, a chunk of wooded hills and mountains interspersed with lakes and rivers that are noted for salmon fishing. Beside the road, the park's **Reception Centre** has the details of various hiking routes and there's a well-established **campground** close by, *Camping John* (early June–Aug; ☎224-3345; from $11.50).

# Sainte-Anne and the Gaspésie park

East of Matane the highway hugs the shoreline through a rugged scenery of forested hillsides punctured by harsh rocky outcrops. A string of pretty little fishing villages breaks up this empty landscape – places like GROSSES-ROCHES, with its boulder-strewn beach, and CAP-CHAT, where a seaside rock formation appears to represent a crouching cat. Near here, the **Éolienne de Cap-Chat** (June–Aug daily 8.30am–5pm; $5) dominates the skyline for miles around – at 100 metres in height, it's the tallest and most powerful vertical axis wind-tower in the world.

Just 16km from Cap-Chat, tiny **SAINTE-ANNE-DES-MONTS** is a good place to break your journey before heading on to the cape or inland to the parc de la Gaspésie. There are some attractive old houses in the town and a fine beach, but it's the relaxed atmosphere and setting that appeal rather than any particular sight. For **accommodation**, try the *Motel Manoir sur Mer*, 475 1ère avenue Ouest (☎763-7844; doubles from $40), where the rooms back onto the beach, or the **bed and breakfast** *Chez Lepage*, on the same road at no. 268 (☎763-2692; doubles from $30). Decent fast-food platters of shellfish and fries are to be had at *Dixie Lee*, on the main strip by the bus stop.

### The Parc de la Gaspésie

As you travel south from Sainte-Anne-des-Monts on Hwy 299, the snow-peaked **Chic-Choc Mountains** – which make up most of the **Parc de la Gaspésie** – can be spotted in the distance, a stark and forbidding backdrop to the coastal plain. The Chic-Chocs are the most northerly protrusions of the Appalachian Ridge which extends deep into the USA, and the serpentine road reveals the full splendour of their alpine interior. The sequence of valleys framed by thickly wooded slopes culminates in the staggering ravine which lies at the foot of the towering **Mont Albert**. In this ravine, the park's **Reception and Interpretation Centre** (June–Aug daily 8am–8pm; ☎763-3301) has details and maps of half a dozen well-signposted **hiking trails**, each of about a day's duration; prospective hikers should come fully equipped and log their intended route at the centre. These mountain trails ascend to the summits of the area's three highest mountains – Mont Jacques-Cartier, Mont Richardson and Mont Albert – and are remarkable in that they climb through three distinctive habitats. Herds of **Virginia deer** thrive in the rich vegetation of the lowest zone, whereas **moose** live in the boreal forest and **caribou** in the tundra at the peaks. This is the only place in Québec where the three species exist in close proximity.

There are good **campgrounds** at the start of all the trails. Alternatively, the **Auberge Gîte Mont Albert** (☎763-2288) offers the only fixed lodgings in the park. It's a well-established traditional hostelry set a few hundred metres from the Reception Centre and, although rooms are not cheap, particularly during the summer and skiing seasons when doubles cost between $70 and $120, there are off-season discounts of up to thirty percent – and it's well worth the expense, as the views from here are simply superb. The *auberge* also controls a number of **chalets** around the park, offering simple but reliable facilities; reckon on $65 for two per night.

# Sainte-Anne to the Forillon park

Heading east from Sainte-Anne-des-Monts towards the tip of the Gaspé Peninsula, the road often squeezes between the ocean and the sheer rock faces of the mountains, its twists and turns passing tumbling scree and spectacular waterfalls. Aim to be hungry by the time you reach **MARSOUI**, a tiny fishing village with a remarkable **restaurant**, *La Couquerie* – dead cheap and one hundred percent French-Canadian. It started life in 1937 as the refectory of the defunct local lumber mill, and the interior remains functional, with simple hard benches beside six long tables. However, the daily specials here are glorious – try the salmon or the meat and vegetable stew (*cipaille*), real bargains at around $10. If you feel like sticking around, the *Hôtel Marsoui* (☎288-5677), just a couple of doors down, has a handful of simple doubles for $30, and the village has a sheltered sandy beach.

The view as you approach **MONT-SAINT-PIERRE** is majestic, the curving seashore and the jagged mountains together framing this little community set at the mouth of a wide valley. Mont-Saint-Pierre is a quiet place, dedicated to bathing and sea-fishing, except during the **hang-gliding festival** at the end of July. The *Auberge les Vagues* youth hostel, on the waterfront at 84 rue Prudent Clontier (☎797-2851), is the cheapest place to stay, with beds at $10. There are several other **motels** along the same street: try the *Mont-Saint-Pierre* at no. 60 (☎797-2202; doubles about $50) or the *Flots Bleus* at no. 18 (☎797-2860; doubles $40). For **camping**, the *Du Pont* on Hwy 132 (June–Sept; ☎797-2951) has places at $15.

## The Parc National de Forillon

Lying at the very tip of the peninsula, the **Parc National de Forillon** is also the scenic culmination of the Gaspé, encompassing some 250 square kilometres of thick forest and mountain, crossed by hiking trails and fringed by stark cliffs along a deeply indented coastline. The splendour of the landscape is complemented by the **wildlife**: black bears, moose, beavers, porcupines and foxes are all common, and over 200 species of birds have been seen, ranging from sea birds like gannets, cormorants and guillemots to songbirds such as the skylark and chaffinch. From the coastal paths, particularly around Cap Gaspé itself, **whales and porpoises** can also be spotted between May and October. As Thomas Anburey, a British soldier, observed in the 1770s – "They cause most beautiful fire works in the water: for being in such abundance, and darting with amazing velocity, a continued stream of light glides through the water, and as they cross each other, the appearance is so picturesque that no description can reach it".

Roughly triangular in shape, the park is sandwiched between the Gulf of St Lawrence and the Baie de Gaspé and encircled by Highways 197 and 132, the former passing through the handful of tiny, nondescript settlements that cling precariously to the shore-line: RIVIÈRE-AU-RENARD, L'ANSE-AU-GRIFFON and CAP-DES-ROSIERS to the north and CAP-AUX-OS on the south side. There are **visitor centres** (both ☎892-5873) at the two road entrance points – one on the southern shore, the other on the northern, both on Hwy 132 – but the main **interpretation centre** (June–Aug daily 8am–7pm; ☎368-5505), close to the lighthouse near Cap-des-Rosiers, is the best place to start a visit. Here, the natural and human history of the area is imaginatively presented, with a wealth of suggestions as to how to spend your time. Perhaps the best **hike** is to the tip of **Cap Gaspé**. This ninety-minute round trip starts a few kilometres to the south of the interpretation centre from the end of the paved road near GRANDE-GRAVE, a pleasant reconstruction of a small fishing village founded by immigrants from Jersey. The path follows the southern coast of the cape, rising and falling until it makes the final steep ascent to the **lighthouse** at the end, set on a 150-metre cliff with the ocean on three sides. On a clear day, you can see the rock at Percé, 40km to the south.

On the south side of the park, along the road west of Cap-aux-Os, lie the remains of **Fort Péninsule**, the bay's World War II coastal gun battery, located in an under-ground bunker whose history is detailed by a series of explanatory plaques. The fort was built to protect Gaspé town and harbour from German U-boats, who ventured as far as Matane in search of victims. It was a particularly important defence as Gaspé town, along with Shelburne in Nova Scotia, was scheduled to be the base for the Royal Navy in the event of a successful German invasion of Great Britain. Nearby, a small tongue of land called **Penouille** pokes out into the bay, its woods and sand dunes making it ideal for swimming, sunbathing and picnicking.

*PARK PRACTICALITIES*

There are half a dozen **campgrounds** in the park and all of them are pleasantly situ-ated and well maintained: *Camping Cap Bon-Ami* (early June–Sept ☎892-5100) has a particularly delightful setting just south of Cap-des-Rosiers. The visitor centres and interpretation centre have details of all sites, and can arrange accommodation in **chalets** around the park – doubles are around $65 per night, though it's cheaper by the week. At L'Anse-au-Griffon on the north shore there's a **B&B** called *Le Gîte Forillon* (☎892-5335), and on the south coast at Cap-aux-Os there's another called *Le Gîte du Parc* (☎892-5864); both have doubles for $45 per night. Cap-aux-Os also has a **youth hostel**, at 2095 boulevard Grande-Grève (open all year; ☎892-5153; $11 per person). The hostel has laundry facilities and rents out mountain bikes.

# Gaspé

The resort of **GASPÉ**, situated on a hillside above the estuary of the York River, is a disappointment after the scenic drama of the surrounding area, a humdrum settlement of about 17,000 people whose popularity is hard to understand. This is the spot where the French navigator and explorer **Jacques Cartier** landed in July 1534, on the first of his three trips up the St Lawrence. He stayed here for just eleven days, time enough to erect a wooden cross engraved with the escutcheon of Francis I, staking out the king's – and Christianity's – claim to this new territory. Cartier's first aim was to find a sea route to the Orient, but he also had more extensive ambitions – to acquire land for himself and his men, exploit the Indians as fur gatherers and discover precious metals to rival the loot the Spaniards had taken from the Aztecs. Naturally, Cartier had to disguise his real intentions on the first trip and his initial contacts with the Iroquois were cordial. Then in the spring of 1536, on his second visit, he betrayed their trust by kidnapping a local chief and nine of his men, and taking them back to Francis I. None of the captives ever returned, and when Cartier made his third trip in 1541 the Iroquois were so suspicious that he was unable to establish the colony he had been instructed to found. Desperate to salvage his reputation, Cartier sailed back to France with what he thought was a cargo of gold and diamonds. They turned out to be iron pyrites and quartz crystals.

Just to the east of the town centre, at 80 boulevard Gaspé, the **Jacques Cartier Monument** looks out over the bay from the grounds of the town museum. It consists of six bronze dolmens carved in relief with a record of Cartier's visit supplemented by some anodyne homilies on the nature and unity of humankind. The **museum** itself (late June–Aug daily 8.30am–9.30pm; Sept–May Mon–Fri 9.30am–noon & 1–5pm, Sat–Sun 2–5pm; $2.50) illuminates the social issues which have confronted the inhabitants of the peninsula to the present – isolation from the centres of power, depopulation and, more recently, unemployment. There are also interesting displays on the history of steam shipping and on local fishing techniques.

A good ten minutes' walk away, near the top of rue Jacques Cartier, stands the controversial **Gaspé Cathedral**. Built in 1934 to commemorate the fourth centennial of Cartier's landing, it's the only cathedral in North America to be built of wood, and from the outside it has an extraordinarily dour and industrial appearance. The interior is completely different: the nave – all straight lines and symmetrical simplicity – is bathed in warm, softly coloured light that pours in through an enormous stained glass window in the style of Mondrian. Directly in front of the cathedral stands a massive granite **cross**, also erected in 1934.

### Practicalities

Gaspé **bus station** is right in the centre on the main street, rue Jacques-Cartier. The **tourist office** (mid-June to Aug daily 8am–8pm) is to the west of the centre on Hwy 132: it has accommodation listings and sketch maps of the town. **College rooms** are available during the summer at the *Cégep de la Gaspésie* at 94 rue Jacques-Cartier (☎368-2749; doubles from $35). *La Normande*, 19 rue Davis (☎368-5468; doubles $45), is the only registered **B&B**. Cheapest of **motels** and **hotels** is the *Maison Bérubé*, 239 montée Sandy Beach (☎368-3644), about 3km down the road towards Percé, which offers doubles from $25. Others worth a try are the *Motel Plante*, 137 rue Jacques-Cartier (summer only; ☎368-2254; doubles from $46); *Motel Fort Ramsay*, 254 boulevard Gaspé (summer only; ☎368-5094; doubles $30); and the *Motel la Grande Hermine*, 21 boulevard Gaspé (☎368-3553; doubles $55).

For **food**, *Le Bourlingueur*, next to the Jacques-Cartier Mall opposite the main bridge, is recommended for breakfast at about $4, though the evening menu is rather pricey, with main courses at around $13. Otherwise, *Maestro Pizzeria*, at the bottom of rue Jacques-Cartier, has competent Italian food for about $9, and there's also a decent café-bar in the bus depot. If you're feeling flush, check out *La Belle Hélène*, 135a rue de la Reine – it's one of the best restaurants on the peninsula.

# Percé

Once a humble fishing community, **PERCÉ** is a prime holiday spot, thanks to the tourist potential of the gargantuan limestone rock which rears up from the sea here. One of Canada's most celebrated natural phenomena, the **Rocher Percé** is nearly 500 metres long and 100 metres high, and is an almost surreal sight at dawn, when it appears bathed in an eerie golden irridescence. The town is now replete with facilities for the sightseers, with gift shops, private art galleries, restaurants and bars, but off season, when much of the resort closes down, Percé maintains a pleasantly relaxed and sleepy feel which makes it worth an overnight stay.

At low tide it's possible, if you hurry, to walk almost round the rock, an excursion that will be accompanied by the overpowering screams of the sea birds that nest in the cliffs. One of the most spectacular longer-range views of the monolith is from the top of **Mont Sainte-Anne**, which rises directly behind Percé town; the path is signposted from behind the church and the walk takes about an hour.

Apart from the rock, there's precious little else to see in Percé, though the **Centre d'Interprétation faunique** (mid-June to Aug daily 9am–6pm; free), some 2km to the south of the centre on route d'Irlande, does have some pleasant displays on the area's flora and fauna. Otherwise, Percé makes a useful base for visiting several natural attractions, notably the **Great Crevasse**, a volcanically formed split in a rocky outcrop that's just a few millimetres wide but several hundred metres deep. The clearly marked path takes about an hour to walk and begins behind the *Auberge de Gargantua*, a first-class restaurant on route des Failles, a couple of kilometres west of town.

From the wharf in the centre of Percé, there are frequent boat trips round the Île **Bonaventure** bird reserve, whose precipitous cliffs are favoured by gannets, kittiwakes, razorbills, guillemots, gulls, cormorants and puffins. You can also arrange to disembark at the island's tiny jetty, where an hour-long walking trail leads to the cliff tops above the bird colonies, but be sure to book your return in advance. The round trip costs $12.

### Practicalities

Highway 132 bisects Percé and passes just to the north of the main wharf, where the **Tourist Office** (mid-June to Aug daily 8am–8pm) has a comprehensive list of accommodation and boat timetables. Some of the cheapest **rooms** in town are at the *Maison Avenue House* guesthouse, 38 avenue de l'Église (☎782-2954), with doubles at about $35. Alternatively, there are a couple of similarly priced **B&Bs**: the *Chez Georges and Rita*, 16 rue Ste-Anne (☎782-2980) and the *Gîte l'Extra*, to the south of the centre at no. 222 on Highway 132 (☎782-5347). There are lots of **motels** dotted along Highway 132 and, although there's little to distinguish them, advance bookings are advised in July and August. Some of the options include the *Bleu Blanc Rouge*, no. 103 (☎782-2142; doubles $40–70); *Motel Bellevue*, no. 183 (summer only; ☎782-2182; doubles $45–70); *Auberge la Table à Rolland*, no. 190 (summer only; ☎782-2606; doubles $50); *Le Macareux*, no. 262 (summer only; ☎782-2414; doubles $40); and *Le Mirage du Rocher*, at no. 288 (summer only; ☎782-5151; doubles $48). The south end of town is where you'll find the **campgrounds**: try *Camping de la Côte Surprise* on Hwy 132 (☎782-5443; sites from $9), where there are great views of the rock.

For **food**, *La Maison du Pêcheur*, just up from the wharf, has fine seafood dishes; the *Restaurant Biard*, on the main street at no. 99, has a reasonably cheap and enjoyable set-price buffet for $12. Substantial snacks, coffees and vegetarian dishes are best in the faintly bohemian atmosphere of *Les Fous de Bassan*, also on the main street, just two hundred metres south of the centre.

# The Baie des Chaleurs

Along the coastal road to the southwest of Percé, the dramatic mountains that dominate the north and east of the peninsula are replaced by a gently undulating landscape of wooded hills and farmland. **CHANDLER**, the first town of any size on this route, is an ugly lumber port notable solely for the wreck of the Peruvian freighter *Unisol* in the mouth of the harbour. It ran aground in a gale in 1983, allegedly because its captain, unable to negotiate entry into the port for his cement-laden vessel, got drunk and allowed the vessel to run onto the sandbank where it remains today. Beyond Chandler lies the **Baie des Chaleurs**, the long wedge of ocean that separates the heart of the Gaspé from New Brunswick. As its name implies, this sheltered inlet has relatively warm waters, and the bay is dotted with seaside resorts-cum-fishing-villages and farming communities, all connected by the coastal highway.

## Bonaventure

The most easterly resort on the bay is **BONAVENTURE**, attractively situated at the end of a lagoon and cut off from the sea by a narrow spit of land. The town is, uniquely, a centre for the production of fish-leather products, such as purses and wallets, but it's usually visited for its salmon fishing and sandy beach. Bonaventure is also a stronghold of **Acadian culture**, whose traditions and heritage are celebrated at the **Musée acadien du Québec**, 97 avenue Port-Royal (mid-June to Aug daily 9am–7pm; Sept to mid-June Mon–Sat 9am–noon & 1–5pm & Sun 1–4.30pm; $2.50), set in an imposing blue and white wooden building in the town centre. Highlights of the collection include some delightful handmade furniture dating from the eighteenth century and a whole range of intriguing photographs that encapsulate something of the hardship of Acadian rural life.

Across the road, Bonaventure's **tourist office**, 91 avenue Port-Royal (mid-June to Aug daily 9am–6pm), has background information on the town and **accommodation** lists. The latter includes the *Motel aux Bocages*, 173 av Port-Royal (☎534-3430; doubles $30–$45), *Motel de la Place*, 136 av Port-Royal (☎534-2934; doubles $50), and the *Chez Arsenault*, a B&B at 188 Rang Thivierge (☎534-2697; doubles around $30). *Camping Beaubassin*, 154 rue Beaubassin (early June to Aug) is a municipal **campground** right by the waters of the lagoon. Nearby, with its name emblazoned in whitewash on the roof, the excellent *Café Acadien* has imaginative French-Canadian **food** – try the home-baked bread and the fiddlehead soup, made from fern shoots.

## New Richmond

**NEW RICHMOND**, 30km from Bonaventure, has only one attraction, the **British Heritage Centre of the Gaspésie**, located towards the west end of town at 351 boulevard Perron Ouest (early June to Aug daily 9am–6pm; $2.50). Set in wooded parkland around the old lighthouse at Duthie's Point, near the mouth of the Cascapédia river, it's a kind of Loyalist theme park, made up of a collection of wooden buildings assembled from the surrounding region, all restored to their early twentieth-century appearance. None of the buildings is outstanding, but the historical displays on the three most influential groups amongst the region's English-speaking colonists – the Irish, the Scots and the Loyalist Americans – are diverting, and the Centre is spacious enough for a pleasant stroll along the shore. It even has its own tiny beach.

If you're staying in New Richmond, the **Seashore Lodge Motel**, 185 boulevard Perron (☎392-9701), has doubles from $25, but frankly there's nothing to keep you here.

## Carleton and around

Just to the west of New Richmond, Highway 299 runs north along the banks of the Cascapédia towards the Parc de la Gaspésie (see p.188), while the coastal Highway 132 continues on to the popular bayside resort of **CARLETON**, where the mountains of the interior return to dominate the landscape. Founded in 1756 by Acadian refugees, Carleton is a pretty little place that stands back from the sea behind two broad lagoons, linked to the narrow coastal strip by a couple of long causeways. The town has a bird sanctuary – a favourite haunt of wading species like the sandpiper and plover – and several good bathing beaches, but what makes it special is the contrast between the coastal flatlands and the backdrop of wooded hills which rise up behind the town. At 594 metres, **Mont Saint-Joseph** is the highest of these, ascended by a maze of steep footpaths that slip past streams and waterfalls before they reach the summit, where there are splendid panoramic views over the bay and across to New Brunswick.

Carleton is a good place for an overnight stay and, while you're here, the **Miguasha Peninsula**, some 20km to the west off Hwy 132, makes a pleasant excursion. Famous for its fossils, this tiny peninsula is home to the **Parc de Miguasha**, where the cream of the fossil crop is displayed at the combined research centre and **museum** (June to late Sept daily 9am–5pm; free). Frequent and free guided tours include the museum, the research area and a walk along the beach and cliffs. Also on the peninsula, about 500 metres from the park, is the port for the little **ferry** (hourly 7.30am–7.30pm; 20min) which crosses over to Dalhousie in New Brunswick, a shortcut that avoids the tip of the Baie des Chaleurs.

Carleton's ten **motels** are dotted along the main street, boulevard Perron. Cheaper choices include: *De La Mer*, no. 326 (summer only; ☎364-7672; doubles around $50); *L'Abri*, no. 360 (☎364-7001; doubles $50); *Belle Plage*, no. 474 (☎364-3388; doubles $40–95); *Auberge des Caps*, no. 1435 (☎364-7091; doubles around $45); and the *Shick-Shock*, no. 1746 (summer only; ☎364-3288; doubles around $35). The town has one reasonable **campground**, the *Carleton*, on banc de Larocque (mid-June–Aug; from $11).

For **food**, there's *Café Ciné*, serving delicious waffles in the centre of town at 681 boulevard Perron, while more substantial seafood dinners are available just down the road to the west at *Restaurant Heron*.

## Pointe-à-la-Croix and around

Some 50km to the west of Carleton, **Pointe-à-la-Croix** is the site of the inter-provincial bridge over to Campbellton, New Brunswick. During the summer, a **tourist booth** (daily 9am–6pm) offers a full range of information on the Gaspé Peninsula from the tiny wooden house right by the main crossroads on the Québec side of the bay. Within sight of the bridge, the little waterside community of **SAINTE-ANNE-DE-RESTIGOUCHE** lies at the heart of a Micmac Indian reservation which, oddly enough, functions on New Brunswick time because all the children go to school in Campbellton. The village is home to the **Interpretive Centre for Micmac Culture**, 4 rue Riverside Ouest (daily June–Sept 9am–7pm; Oct–May 9am–4pm), which provides a modest exhibition of the history and traditions of the Micmacs, an Algonquian-speaking people who spread across the Atlantic seaboard from Nova Scotia through to the Gaspé and east Newfoundland. Their story is the familiarly sad one: trading furs for European knives, hatchets and pots, the Micmacs quarrelled with other native groups over hunting grounds until there was a state of perpetual warfare. In later years, the Micmacs proved loyal allies to the French military cause, but, like all the other native groups, their numbers were decimated by European diseases and they have remained a neglected minority until the last few years.

A couple of kilometres west of the bridge, the **Parc historique national de La Bataille-de-la-Ristigouche** chronicles the crucial naval engagement of 1760 which effectively extinguished French hopes of relieving their stronghold in Montréal, the year after the fall of Québec City. The French fleet, which had already taken casualties in evading the blockade of Bordeaux, was forced to take refuge in the mouth of the Restigouche river and then, despite assistance from local Micmacs and Acadians, was overpowered by superior British forces. The site's **Interpretive Centre** (mid-June toAug daily 9am–5pm) contains relics of the French fleet, especially the frigate *Le Machault*, which has been partly reconstructed. There's also an audio-visual display providing a graphic account of the battle and of its strategic significance.

For reasonably priced **accommodation** in the area, try the *Motel Clipper*, near the bridge at 94 rue Riverside Est, Pointe-à-la-Croix (☎788-2950;, doubles from $40), or the nearby **B&B** *Chez Savoie* (☎788-2084; doubles around $30). There's also a **youth hostel**, the *Auberge du Château* (☎788-2048; $12), in Pointe-à-la-Garde, some 6km east of the bridge along Hwy 132. It's located in an eccentrically Renaissance-style wooden castle built by the owner, who adds new wings and turrets each year.

## Matapédia

Located at the western tip of the Baie, beside the confluence of the Ristigouche and Matapédia rivers, the tiny village of **MATAPÉDIA** is surrounded by rolling green hills and lies at the centre of an excellent salmon-fishing region. Not a lot else happens here, but there is an excellent and reasonably priced **restaurant**, *Café l'Entracte*, at 50 boulevard Perron Ouest, which serves fine seafood dishes for around $12. The café also has a handful of rooms, with doubles at $50 per night (☎865-2734). From Matapédia, Highway 132 cuts north across the interior of the peninsula through AMQUI, a dreary little town that serves as a ski resort in the winter.

# The Îles-de-la-Madeleine

The archipelago of the **Îles-de-la-Madeleine** (Magdalen Islands), scattered in the middle of the Gulf of St Lawrence some 200km southeast of the Gaspé Peninsula and 100km north of Prince Edward Island, consists of twelve main islands of which seven are inhabited and six are connected by narrow sand spits, crossed by paved and gravel roads. Together these dozen islands form a crescent-shaped series of dunes, lagoons and low rocky outcrops that's 65km from end to end, with the main village and ferry port roughly in the middle at **Cap-aux-Meules**. The islands lie in the Gulf Stream, which makes the winters warmer than those of mainland Québec, but they are subject to almost constant winds which have eroded the red sandstone cliffs along parts of the shoreline into an extraordinary array of arches, caves and tunnels. These **rock formations**, the archipelago's most distinctive attraction, are at their best on the central **Île du Cap-aux-Meules** and the adjacent **Île du Havre-aux-Maisons**.

In 1534, **Jacques Cartier** stumbled across the Îles-de-la-Madeleine on his way west to the St Lawrence River. Cartier, always keen to impress his sponsors with the value of his discoveries, wrote with characteristic exaggeration, "The islands are full of beautiful trees, prairies, fields of wild wheat, and flowering pea plants as beautiful as I've ever seen in Brittany". Despite Cartier's eulogy, the islands attracted hardly any settlers until the Deportations of 1755, when a few Acadian families escaped here to establish a mixed farming and fishing community. Remote and isolated, the **Madelinots**, as the islanders came to be known, were unable to control their own economic fortunes, selling their fish at absurdly low prices to a series of powerful merchants who, in turn, sold them tackle and equipment at exorbitant rates. One of the most notorious of these men was a certain **Isaac Coffin**, who developed a classically colonial form of oppression in the 1790s when he forced many of the islanders to sell their lands to his company. Only in 1895 did a provincial statute allow the Madelinots to buy them back. Today the 15,000 inhabitants are largely dependent on fishing in general, and the lobster catch in particular.

Although the archipelago's tiny villages are rather drab and desultory, it has become a relatively popular tourist destination, mostly visited for its wide open landscapes and sense of isolation. Bear in mind, though, that throughout the islands, powerful currents and changeable weather conditions make sea-bathing dangerous.

Every month except February and March there's a daily car **ferry** to Cap-aux-Meules from Souris, on Prince Edward Island (☎902/687-2181); a one-way ticket costs $26 per person, $49 per vehicle, and it's a five-hour trip. There's also a cargo and passenger ship, the *CTMA Voyageur*, that leaves Montréal for the islands once weekly (☎986-6600). By **plane**, there are regular, scheduled flights to the islands on *Intair* and *Air Atlantic* from Montréal, Québec City, Ottawa, Toronto and Halifax. *Air Alliance* also offer daily flights from Gaspé town.

# The islands

In the middle of the archipelago, Île du Cap-aux-Meules boasts the islands' largest community, CAP-AUX-MEULES, a useful base for exploring the other islands. Just a couple of kilometres west of the village, there are fine views of the entire island chain from the Butte du Vent, the area's highest hill. Further west, on the other side of the island near the fishing port of L'ÉTANG-DU-NORD, you'll find some particularly extravagant coastal rock formations. In the opposite direction, the main road skirts the southern tip of the islands' longest lagoon before heading on across the Île du Havre-aux-Maisons, whose smooth green landscapes contrast with the red cliffs of its southern shore. Criss-crossed by narrow country roads and littered with tiny straggling villages, this island is arguably the most appealing of the group, and the weird shapes of the coastal rocks around Dune-du-Sud are well worth a visit.

North of here, along Highway 199, the hamlet of Pointe-aux-Loups is edged by two long and deserted beaches. Beyond, at the far end of the archipelago, the twin islets of Grosse-Île and Île de la Grande-Entrée border the wildlife reserve of the Pointe-de-l'Est, whose entrance is beside the main road. It's possible to stroll across part of the reserve, but it's better to join one of the guided walks that are arranged throughout the season; inquire at the tourist office in Cap-aux-Meules for details. On its south side, the reserve is edged by the enormous sandy expanse of the Plage de la Grande Échouerie, whose southern end is framed by yet more splendid rock formations at Harry's Point.

To the south of the Île du Cap-aux-Meules, Île du Havre-Aubert has one significant community, HAVRE-AUBERT, a pretty little place that's edged by round sloping hills. The village is home to the Musée de la Mer (daily 10am–6pm; $2), which has a series of displays on local fishing techniques and the history of the islands – especially their many shipwrecks. To the southeast, tiny Île d'Entrée is the only inhabited island that's not linked by land to the rest of the archipelago. This hilly and bare outcrop is encircled by footpaths and makes a pleasant day out, providing the sea is calm on the ferry trip from Cap-aux-Meules (Mon–Sat 2 daily; information ☎985-2148).

## Practicalities

The islands' **airport** is inconveniently situated at the north end of Île du Havre-aux-Maisons, some 20km from Cap-aux-Meules. Some of the flights have connecting buses to Cap-aux-Meules, but otherwise you'll have to take a *Lafrance* **taxi** (about $35), **or hire a car** from the *Tilden* or *Budget* desks at the airport. The **ferry terminal** at Cap-aux-Meules is near the **tourist office**, 128 chemin du Débarcadère (late June to Aug daily 7am–9pm; Sept to late June Mon–Fri 9am–noon & 1–5pm; ☎986-2245). They have masses of free leaflets and operate a free room reservation service with a special emphasis on **B&B**.

There are just fifteen **inns**, **motels** and **hotels** on the Magdalens, so it's a good idea to book a bed before you fly or sail here. More reasonably priced options in Cap-aux-Meules include the *Motel Boudreau*, 280 rue Principale (☎986-2391; doubles around $70); the *Motel Bellevue*, 40 rue Principale (☎986-4477; doubles from $60); the *Auberge du Village*, 205 rue Principale (☎986-3312; doubles around $45); and the basic *L'Étang-du-Nord*, Chemin de Gros-Cap (☎986-2875; doubles around $35). On Île du Havre-aux-Maisons, the *Motel Thériault*, Dune-du-Sud (☎969-2955), has doubles at $70 and the *Motel des Îles*, route 199 (summer only; ☎969-2931), has doubles for around $50.

The tourist office also has details of the islands' many **bed and breakfast** addresses (reckon on $35 per double), and a substantial number of **cottage** and **apartment** rentals, beginning at roughly $250 per week. There are two **campgrounds** on Île de Cap-aux-Meules: *Le Barachois*, chemin du Rivage, Fatima (mid-May to mid-Sept; ☎986-6065; from $9), and *Camping Gros Cap*, chemin du Laboratoire (June to mid-Sept; ☎986-4515; from $10).

For **food**, you should try the lobster at the *Restaurant Alexandre*, Cap-aux-Meules, or the *Au Vieux Couvent*, route 199, Havre-aux-Maisons. Cheaper options include Chinese dishes and burgers at the *Bellevue* and sandwiches and submarines at *Café Le Bistrot*, both in Cap-aux-Meules.

The best way to tour the principal islands is by **bike**, available for rent at *Le Pédalier*, 365 chemin Principal, Cap-aux-Meules. **Boat** and **fishing trips** leave from near the ferry terminal throughout the summer (information ☎986-2304); the cliff and cave excursions are best, at about $25 per person.

# NORTH QUÉBEC

Québec's true north is a mighty, inhospitable tundra inhabited only by mining communities, groups of Inuits, and the hardy characters who staff the hydro-electric installations with which so many of the rivers are stoppered. This section deals with the only readily accessible region, along the north shore of the St Lawrence and its main tributary, the Saguenay, covering an area that changes from trim farmland to a seemingly never-ending forest bordering the barren seashore of the St Lawrence.

Immediately northeast of Québec City is the beautiful **Charlevoix** region of peaceful villages and towns that bear the marks of Québec's rural beginnings – both in the architecture of the seigneurial regime and in the layout of the land. Often the winding highways and backroads pass through a virtually continuous village, where the only interruptions in the chain of low-slung houses are the tin-roofed churches. The sublime hills and valleys give way to dramatic ravaged rock near the Charlevoix borders, where the **Saguenay River** crashes into the immense fjord that opens into the St Lawrence at the resort of **Tadoussac**. Inland, **Lac Saint-Jean** – source of the Saguenay – is an oasis of fertile land in a predominantly rocky region, and its peripheral villages offer glimpses of native as well as Québécois life. The adventurous can head beyond Tadoussac to **Havre-Saint-Pierre** through a desolate, sparsely populated region where the original livelihood of fishing and lumber have largely given way to ambitious mining and hydro-electric projects. The remoteness of northern islands such as the **Île d'Anticosti** and the sculptured terrain of the **Mingan archipelago** – as a national park, well served by boats from Havre-Saint-Pierre – is matched by the isolation of the unmodernised fishing communities along the **Lower North Shore**, where no roads penetrate and visits are possible only by supply ship.

> The telephone code for North Québec is ☎418.

# Charlevoix

Stretching along the north shore of the St Lawrence east of Québec City, from the Beaupré coast to the Saguenay River, the area of **CHARLEVOIX** is the world's only inhabited UNESCO World Biosphere Reserve. Species like the arctic caribou and great wolf, not usually associated with such southerly latitudes, can be seen in the more remote areas, and because the ice age that shaped the rest of eastern Canada missed this breathtaking region, numerous preglacial plants still thrive here. The 6000-square-kilometre region consists of gently sloping hills, sheer cliffs and vast valleys veined with rivers, brooks and waterfalls: a landscape that Québec's better known artists – Clarence Gagnon, Marc-Aurèle Fortin and Jean-Paul Lemieux – chose for inspiration. Though Charlevoix has been a tourist resort for centuries, the land has been carefully preserved, and the quaint villages and tin-roofed churches still nestle in an unspoiled countryside.

Highway 138, the main route through Charlevoix, travels 225km from Québec City to Baie-Ste-Catherine on the Saguenay. The main towns along this highway are served by *Intercar* buses from Québec City, but many of the quintessential Charlevoix villages – in particular those along the coastal Hwy 362 – are not served by public transport. Be prepared to hitch (which is relatively simple) or hire a car or bike – the expense is well worth it.

# Baie-Saint-Paul

One of Charlevoix's earliest settlements and long-time gathering place for Québec's landscape painters, the picture-perfect **BAIE-SAINT-PAUL** is tucked into the Gouffré valley at the foot of the highest range of the Laurentian mountains. Dominated by the twin spires of the church, the streets wind from the centre of town flanked by houses that are over two hundred years old – and just wandering around Baie-Saint-Paul is the main attraction.

From the bus station take Rue St-Jean-Baptiste to reach the church. Along the way you will pass numerous quaint cottages characteristic of Québec's earliest houses, with curving roofs and wide verandahs, many converted into commercial galleries. At no. 152, the **Centre d'histoire naturelle de Charlevoix** (June–Oct daily 10am–6pm; $2.25) has displays on the flora, fauna, geology and inhabitants of Charlevoix. The centre also runs excellent guided tours of the environs: their two-hour excursion by bus (late June to Aug; $15) is a good taster, but the best trip is the one-day hike around the incredible canyons of the Hautes-Gorges de la Rivière Malbaie (mid-May to late June & late Aug to late Oct every Sat & Sun; $12; reservations essential ☎435-6275). The centre also rents out canoes and bikes.

At no. 58, **Maison René Richard** (late June to late Aug 10am–6pm; $4) offers an insight into the works of René Richard, an associate of the Group of Seven. The 1842 house has been left exactly the same since Richard died; bilingual guided tours take you around his studio and living quarters. An overview of the works of art produced in Charlevoix is exhibited in the centrally located **Centre d'Art de la Baie-Saint-Paul**, 4 Fafard (daily 9am–5pm; free), which has excellent exhibitions of paintings and sculptures inspired by the surrounding countryside. The centre's boutique also sells local crafts, and every August a symposium is held here, when the public can watch young Canadian and European artists at work.

Baie-Saint-Paul's nearest park is the **Parc des Grands-Jardins** (late May to late Oct), 42km away on Hwy 381 but with no public transport. Within the park, the 900-metre Mont du Lac des Cygnes gives the best of all Charlevoix panoramas; it's a four-hour climb there and back from the park's activity centre on Hwy 381. Hwy 381 continues to La Baie on the Saguenay river (see p.202).

## Practicalities

The **information centre** for Baie-Saint-Paul and the whole Charlevoix area is in the Centre d'Art, 4 Fafard (Mon–Fri 8.30am–noon & 1–4.30pm; ☎435-5795 or 665-4454); there is also a seasonal office on Hwy 138 (mid-June to Sept daily 9am–9pm).

For a town its size, Baie-Saint-Paul has an excellent variety of **accommodation**, from luxurious historic hotels to an outstanding youth hostel. The four-star **hotels** are the 1840 *Auberge Maison Otis*, 23 St-Jean-Baptiste (☎435-2255), and the *Auberge La Pignoronde*, 750 Mgr-de-Laval (☎435-5505 or 1-800-463-5250), both with doubles upwards of $120. Next door to each other on the waterfront are the *Auberge Belle-Plage et Motels*, 192 Ste-Anne (☎435-3321), and the *Auberge Le Cormoran* at no. 196 (☎435-6030) have comfortable doubles for $65. **Bed and breakfasts** are located along the winding lane of St-Jean-Baptiste: the best is *La Muse* at no. 39 (☎435-6839; singles $40, doubles $50–55). Cheaper B&B is available at the *Residence Belley*, 183 St-Jean-Baptiste (☎435-

2289; single $25, doubles $36). The town's best bargain is the **hostel/campsite** *Le Balcon Vert*, Hwy 362 (mid-May to mid-Oct; ☎435-5587), about 3km out on the road to Malbaie; four-berth cabins are $12.50 per person, camping is around $7, and there's a restaurant and bar on site. Camping is also available during the summer at the riverside *Camping du Gouffré*, 439 St-Laurent ($12–14) or the larger *Camping Le Genévrier*, 1175 Mgr-de-Laval ($16).

The cheapest **food** is at *L'Oasis*, 1 Fafard, a trendy café with great sandwiches and smoked meat; alternatively there is an excellent sandwich and vegetarian café opposite the Centre d'Art. For a more expensive nosh the award-winning *Le Mouton Noir*, 43 Ste-Anne, serves mouth-watering dishes. The restaurant of the *Belle-Plage* also has an excellent reputation, and the adjoining *Bleu Nuit* **disco** is good. For a great atmosphere check out *Le Bistro de la Maison Otis*, a Québécois singing club in the poshest hotel in town.

## Highway 362

From Baie-Saint-Paul the main route onwards is Hwy 138, but if you have your own transport you should opt for the coast-hugging detour of **Highway 362**, which twists and turns its way through a succession of clifftop villages.

The first settlement out of Baie-Saint-Paul is **LES ÉBOULEMENTS**, which means "landslide" – after the massive earthquake of 1663, one of many that shaped this region. The main road, Principale, has a couple of buildings worth a look. At nos. 157–159 is the eighteenth-century **Manoir de Sales-Laterrière** (daily 9–11am & 2–4pm; free), whose farmhouse and mill are among the few intact structures left from the seigneurial regime of New France. Further down the road at no. 194, the **Galerie de la Vieille Forge** (May–Oct daily 10am–5pm; $1.50), dating from 1891, still operates as a forge.

The road dips and climbs on to **SAINT-IRÉNÉE**, 34km from Baie-Saint-Paul, where there are stunning views all year round. However, the best time to visit is during the **Festival International**, a two-month musical event which starts at the end of June.

From Les Éboulements a steep secondary road that has been paved only in recent years leads to the tiny village of **SAINT-JOSEPH-DE-LA-RIVE**, a once-important shipyard whose maritime connections are reduced now to the hourly free ferry to Île aux Coudres. Pop into the local church (June–Oct 9am–8pm) on Chemin de l'Église, where the altar is propped up by anchors and the font is a huge seashell from Florida.

### Île aux Coudres

The ferry takes fifteen minutes to reach the sixteen-kilometre-long island of **ÎLE AUX COUDRES**, which is said to have been formed when an earthquake shook it from the escarpment at Les Éboulements. Cartier celebrated Canada's first mass here in 1535 and named the island after its numerous hazelnut trees. Missionaries were the first permanent settlers, arriving in 1748, and the growing population came to depend on shipbuilding and beluga whale hunting for their livelihoods. Ship- and canoe-building still takes place here, but the main industry of its 1600 inhabitants is harvesting peat moss from the bogs in the centre of the island.

The island's stone manors and cottages nowadays attract huge numbers of visitors, who drive and cycle around the peripheral road that connects the three villages of **ST-BERNARD, LA BALEINE** and **ST-LOUIS**. There is an **information centre** (May–Sept daily 8am–noon & 1–5pm) near the ferry dock in St-Bernard, with maps of the island. Bikes can be rented from *Velo-Coudres*, 743 des Coudriers in La Baleine, 15km from the dock. Most hotels are located in La Baleine – the best deals are the *Motel La Baleine*, 128 Principale (☎438-2453; doubles $45), and *Motel Écumé*, at no. 808 (☎438-2733; doubles $40). There's also an ever-expanding number of B&Bs, but the island's best bargain is the splendidly located *Motel l'Islet*, 10 l'Islet (☎438-2423; doubles $38) in an isolated spot near St-Louis, on the west tip of the island. The island's **campgrounds** are *Camping La Baleine*, 165 La Baleine ($12), and *Camping Slyvie*, 191 Royale, St-Bernard ($9–14), with some chalets available.

For **food**, *T-Coq* is a burger place near the ferry wharf in St-Bernard, while *La Quenouille*, the restaurant of the *Motel l'Islet* in St-Louis, has good local food, as does the nearby *La Mer Veille*, 160 des Coudriers. The island's posh hotel, the *Cap-aux-Pierres* at 230 Principale in La Baleine, serves reasonably priced lunchtime buffets.

# From La Malbaie to Saint-Simeon

Highways 362 and 138 converge about 50km from Baie-Saint-Paul, at **LA MALBAIE** – Bad Bay, so called because Champlain ran aground here in 1608. Situated at the mouth of the Malbaie River, the town has little to keep you but is an excellent springboard for trips into the Charlevoix interior. The main sight is the **Pelican**, a tallship moored on the east bank of the Malbaie River; it's a replica of the vessel which destroyed three British warships in Hudson Bay in 1697, only to be sunk by a surprise storm. The *Office du Tourism* is located at 166 de Comporté (mid-June to Sept daily 9am–9pm; Oct to mid-June Mon–Fri 8.30am–noon); the bus arrives on the same road. *Motel Murray*, 40 Laure Cohen (☎665-2441; singles $35, doubles $60) is a good accommodation option, as is the plusher *Auberge sur la Côte*, 205 Chemin des Falaises (☎665-3972; singles $90, doubles $140). If you have the equipment head for Charlevoix's oldest and most beautifully situated campsite, *Camping Chutes Fraser*, 500 de la Vallée (mid-May to mid-Oct; sites $13–16), located by the falls of the same name about 3km north from Malbaie.

### The Hautes-Gorges

One sight that must not be missed in the Charlevoix region is the **Parc régional des Hautes-Gorges de la rivière Malbaie** (June to mid-Oct daily 9am–6pm), a network of valleys that slice through a maze of lofty peaks 45km west of La Malbaie. To get there take Hwy 138 to ST-AIMÉ-DES-LACS, from where a stunning thirty-kilometre unpaved forest road leads to the park's **information centre**, Chalet l'Ecluse, beside the Malbaie river. On all sides the cliff faces rise over 700 metres, constituting Canada's deepest canyon east of the Rockies, formed by a slip in the earth's crust 800 million years ago. The uniqueness of the park lies not just in this astounding geology but also in the fact that all Québec's forest species grow in this one comparatively small area. From the Chalet l'Ecluse a tiring but rewarding five-kilometre hike leads to the canyon's highest point, passing through a Laurentian maple grove on the way to the arctic–alpine tundra of the 800-metre summit – it's a good idea to take food, water and a jacket as protection against the mountain breezes. Other shorter trails offer less strenuous alternatives, and from the l'Ecluse dam, beside the information centre, leisurely river cruises depart regularly in summer ($18). As well as free maps, the centre has canoes to rent ($8 an hour, $18 a day) for the six-kilometre paddle along the calm "Eaux Mortes" of the river.

### Pointe-au-Pic, Cap-à-l'Aigle and Port-au-Persil

If you've got the cash you could head for the magnificent grey stone castle of the $200-a-night *Manoir Richelieu* (☎665-3703) that dominates the clifftop village of nearby **POINTE-AU-PIC** on Hwy 362, a magnet for rich Americans and the bourgeoisie of Québec. The town also boasts the best of Charlevoix art galleries, the **Musée de Charlevoix**, 1 du Hâvre (late June to Aug daily 10am–8pm; Sept to late June Mon–Fri 10am–5pm; $3.50).

Enroute to Saint-Siméon you'll pass by a couple of peaceful Québécois villages worth a stop for their vistas of the St Lawrence: **CAP-À-L'AIGLE**, 2km from La Malbaie, an agricultural village with a hideous modern church; and the harbour community of

**PORT-AU-PERSIL**, 25km further. The former has an excellent B&B, 215 St-Raphael (☎665-2288; singles $25, doubles $40), a thatched grange that is one of the best examples of Québécois rural architecture.

## Saint-Siméon

The hillside village of **SAINT-SIMÉON** marks the junction of Hwy 138 to the Côte Nord and Hwy 170 to the awesome Parc du Saguenay and Lac Saint-Jean (see p.205) – public transport serves only the former. Saint-Siméon also has a ferry service across to Rivière du Loup (2–5 daily; see p.183). Missing the last boat is about the only eventuality that will make you want to stay; should it arise, the *Motel-Restaurant Les Flots Bleus*, by the ferry wharf at 101 du Festival (☎638-2967), has singles for $30, doubles for $60. *La Détente*, 800 Port-au-Persil (☎638-2666), is the cheapest B&B, with rooms under $25.

# The Parc du Saguenay

A stupendous expanse of rocky outcrops, sheer cliffs and thick vegetation, the **Parc du Saguenay** perches above one of the world's longest fjords, which cuts through the Canadian Shield from Tadoussac to Lac Saint-Jean. Coming from the south, the best approach is to drive along the wriggling Hwy 170 from Saint-Siméon, a road that strikes the fjord about 50km from Saint-Siméon, close to **L'ANSE-ST-JEAN**. The only village on the Saguenay when it was founded in 1838, L'Anse-Saint-Jean is famous now for its Pont du Faubourg, the covered bridge featured on the back of the Canadian $1000 note. From here it is possible to hike through the Parc du Saguenay, 35km west to Rivière-Éternité or 8km east to Petit Saguenay, though it is best to enter the park at Rivière-Éternité. Horse riding can be arranged at the *Centre Équestre A dos de Cheval*, 31 St-Thomas Nord (☎272-3321). For **accommodation** *Auberge Perron*, 370 St-Jean-Baptiste (☎272-2626; singles $25, doubles $25) has superb views of the St-Jean river. There are two B&Bs as well. *Ferme des Trois Cours d'Eau*, 34 St-Thomas Nord (☎272-2944; singles $22–25, doubles $35–40) is 1km beyond the far side of the covered bridge – the owners will pick you up if you have no transport. The *Maison du Capitaine*, just on the right past the church (☎272-3491), is slightly more pricey but still a bargain with singles for $30, doubles $40. For **eating** there's a mouth-watering patisserie at 328 St-Jean-Baptiste, and there are restaurants by the marina.

**RIVIÈRE-ÉTERNITÉ**, 83km from Saint-Siméon and 59km east of Chicoutimi (see p.204), is the main gateway to the Parc du Saguenay (mid-May to mid-Oct daily 8am–7pm; free, but parking $5.50). The park's **information centre** (mid-May to mid-Oct daily 9am–5pm), 8km from the village, has free maps of hiking trails, exhibitions on the flora and fauna, and expert naturalists on hand. A smaller information post is 1.5km from the village, on the park's border. A word of warning about the park's only unpleasant feature – arm yourself with anti-bug cream and long-sleeved tops and trousers, as the blackflies love this place.

From the main information centre two short hikes and a long one are laid out through the park. Of the short hikes, the **statue hike** is a four-hour round trip up the massive bluff of Cap Trinité, which – with the equally intimidating Cap Éternité – flanks the deep blue water of the Baie Éternité. The summit is topped by a huge statue known as Our Lady of the Saguenay, erected in 1881 by Charles-Napoléon Robitaille after he was saved from drowning in the river. The easier **interpretation hike** (1.6km in total) winds along the banks of the Éternité river; various panels along the way explicate the wildlife and geographical phenomena of the area. The park's long-distance hike (35km) follows the bay of the Éternité river back to L'Anse-St-Jean via massive plateaus, ravines, waterfalls and stunning views. The hike takes about three days and there are campsites and a couple of refuges along the way; reservations are a must (☎272-3008).

If you don't want to hike, one-hour **cruises** of the Baie Éternité leave from near the information centre ($13). Alternatively, and perfect if you are heading for Chicoutimi, are the longer cruises (late June to Aug; $28) to VILLE DE LA BAIE on the Baie des Ha! Ha!, which is linked by *CITS* buses #50 and #51 to Chicoutimi.

# Tadoussac to Lac Saint-Jean

The "gateway to the Kingdom of the Saguenay", Tadoussac lies some 40km north of Saint-Siméon, at the confluence of the St Lawrence and the Saguenay, whose source – the vast Lac Saint-Jean – lies 200km inland. Traffic along Hwy 138 crosses the neck of the Saguenay fjord by a free **car ferry** to Tadoussac, which runs 24 hours a day. The area around Tadoussac and along the fjord is protected by park status, to the benefit of the migratory whale population, which can be observed here at their southern limit. Closer to the lake a glut of aluminium and paper plants using the river as a power source has resulted in the growth of characterless industrial towns, the largest of which is Chicoutimi. Further west, the lake's farmland periphery is still relatively untouched and offers the opportunity to stay on the Montagnais reserve at Pointe Bleue, a unique zoo at Saint-Félicien and the strange sight of Val-Jalbert, Québec's most accessible ghost town.

## Tadoussac

One of Canada's oldest villages, **TADOUSSAC** is beautifully situated beneath the rounded hills that gave the place its name – it comes from the Algonquian word *tatou-shak*, meaning "breasts". Basque whalers were the first Europeans to live here and by the time Samuel de Champlain arrived in 1603 Tadoussac was a thriving trading post. The mid-nineteenth century saw Tadoussac evolve into a popular summer resort for the anglophone bourgeoisie: the first hotel opened in 1846 and by the 1860s steamer-loads of rich anglos were arriving every summer to escape the heat of the city.

The waterfront Bord de l'Eau is dominated by the red roof and green lawns of the *Hôtel Tadoussac*, a landmark in Tadoussac since 1864 and the focus of the historic quarter. Next door is the tiny **Chapelle des Indiens** (late June to Aug daily 9am–9pm; $1), built by the Jesuits in 1747 and the oldest wooden church in Canada; inside there are displays of clothing and icons. Tucked on the other side of the hotel, the steep-roofed wooden **Maison Chauvin** (June–Sept daily 10am–10pm; $2) exactly replicates – right down to the handmade nails – the first trading post on the north shore of the St Lawrence as described in Champlain's 1603 diary; it houses a small museum of beaver pelts and bits and pieces pertaining to the fur trade.

Following the waterfront towards the harbour brings you to the new **Centre d'interprétation du milieu marin**, 108 de la Cale-Sèche (mid-June to mid-Oct daily 10am–6pm; $3.50), which is a must if you intend to go whale-watching, as its excellent documentary films and bilingual displays explain the life cycles of the whales in the St Lawrence and the efforts being made to save their ever-diminishing numbers.

The Tadoussac sector of the **Saguenay National Park** offers some easy **hikes** around the village: an **information office** (mid-June to Sept daily 9am–5pm) in the car park just after the ferry terminal supplies free maps of the trails. To the northeast of Tadoussac are the long terraced **sand dunes** on the Baie du Moulin-à-Baude, known locally as *le désert*. To reach the dunes follow Chemin du Moulin-à-Baude 5km northeast to the **interpretation centre**, the Maison des Dunes (mid-June to Sept daily 9am–5pm; free). The 112-metre-high dunes are popular with sand-skiers, and skis can be rented from the youth hostel (see opposite).

## The Saguenay Marine Park

The **Saguenay Marine Park**, in Tadoussac's immediate vicinity, contains six different ecosystems supporting hundreds of marine species. This region is part of the hydrographic basin of the St Lawrence and the Great Lakes, and the toxic waste tipped into the St Lawrence once made this the most polluted waterway in Canada. Since the creation of the park, the federal government has promised to reduce ninety percent of the pollutants from fifty industrial plants in the immediate vicinity by 1993. The damage has already been done, though – the numbers of the **St Lawrence beluga whale** are down from 5000 to 500, placing them on Canada's list of endangered species. That said, the area continues to attract the whales because the mingling of the cold Labrador sea waters with the highly oxygenated fresh water of the Saguenay produces a uniquely rich crop of krill and other plankton. The white St Lawrence beluga lives in the area all year round and from May to October it is joined by six species of migratory whales including the minke, finback and the blue whale, the largest mammal on earth.

Several companies offer **whale-watching trips** from Tadoussac from mid-May to mid-October, charging around $30 for a trip of up to three hours with qualified bilingual naturalists on board. The inflatable Zodiac dinghies can get really close to the whales and only carry a small number of people – contact *La Companie de la Baie de Tadoussac*, 145 Bord de L'Eau (☎235-4548). A more sedate excursion is the one on the *Hôtel Tadoussac's* 1922 schooner *Marie Clarisse*. Less thrilling trips are offered on the fibreglass boats of *Les Crosières du Grand Fleuve*, 100 Bord de l'Eau (☎235-4585 or 1-800-463-6761) and *Croisière Express*, 119 Bord de l'Eau (☎235-4770). If you can't afford a boat trip take the short hike around the Pointe de l'Islet from the marina, which has lookout points for whale-watching.

## Practicalities

The **bus** terminus is on des Pionniers, outside the *Auberge du Lac*. Close by, on the corner of des Jésuites and des Pionniers, the small **information office** (mid-June to Sept daily 8am–8pm) has free maps of Tadoussac and leaflets on the town's activities and accommodation. Pick of Tadoussac's wealth of **accommodation** is the *Hôtel Tadoussac*, 165 Bord de L'Eau (☎235-4421 or ☎1-800-463-5250), with singles from $129, doubles from $188. A cheaper historic hotel is the *Hôtel-Motel Georges*, 135 du Bateau Passeur (☎235-4393; singles $35–80, doubles $40–80). *Auberge du Lac*, 187 des Pionniers (☎235-4326; singles $40, doubles $50), is convenient, and the similarly priced *Le Pionnier*, 251 de l'Hôtel de Ville (☎235-4666), is a clean if characterless motel. **Bed and breakfasts** are situated along des Pionniers. *Maison Clauphi* at no. 188 (☎235-4303; singles $32–55, doubles $48–80) is a B&B/motel place opposite the bus terminus. *Maison Hovington*, no. 285 (June–Oct; ☎235-4466; singles $40–50, doubles $50–60), is a century-old B&B with four beautifully decorated rooms – and the bilingual owners will pick you up from the bus station. Finally, at no. 176, Madeleine Fortier (☎235-4215; singles $25–35, doubles $35–45) runs an extremely hospitable and good value B&B.

The **youth hostel** *Maison Majorique*, 158 Bateau Passeur (☎235-4372), is one of the best youth hostels in Québec. Bikes, skis for sand-skiing, canoes, skidoos, snowshoes and cars are available for rent, and various activities such as guided hikes and dog-sleigh trips are organised in their relative seasons. Rates are $10 for members, $3 for camping with the option of $6 suppers and $3 all-you-can-eat breakfasts. The quieter and more comfortable new *Maison Alexis*, 285 des Pionniers, is run by the same people at the same rates; the hostel's huskies are kept here and volunteers are always needed to take them walking through the woods. Family style **camping** away from the hostels is available in summer at *Camping Tadoussac*, 428 des Pionniers ($11–16), 2km from the ferry terminal on Hwy 138.

For eating the *Hôtel Tadoussac* has a fairly reasonable set menu, while *La Bolée*, 164 Morin, has crêpes and salads and a take-out deli underneath. For **drinking**, the *Bar Fjord* is the young people's hang-out near the youth hostel; the music is good and the atmosphere is kicking throughout the summer. For a quieter drink check out the small *Bar le Gibard*, 137 Bord de L'Eau, which is open until 3am.

## Ste-Rose-du-Nord

The daily *Intercar* bus from Tadoussac to Chicoutimi follows Hwy 172 parallel to the fjord, a route that gives occasional panoramas over the water. About 30km along the way is the turn-off for **STE-ROSE-DU-NORD**, a tiny village of white houses crammed beneath the precipitous walls of the fjord, 3km from the main road. The **Musée de la Nature**, 197 de la Montagne (daily 8.30am–9pm; $2.50), is a small but surprisingly informative museum housing an eclectic range of exhibits from stuffed animals to knotty roots, all found in the local region. The church of **Ste-Rose-de-Lima**, with its interior of wood, bark, branches and roots, is also worth a peek. If you intend to visit Lac Saint-Jean, you could continue your journey by a two-hour **cruise** to Chicoutimi ($16), along the most stunning stretch of the fjord. Should you want to **stay** over, the award-winning *Auberge Le Presbytère*, 136 du Quai (☎675-2503; singles $75, doubles $120), also has an excellent restaurant, with full local menus at around $40. Rooms are also available above the *Musée de la Nature* (☎675-2348; singles $30, doubles $45), while *Camping La Descente des Femmes* has sites from $10.

## Chicoutimi

Since its founding by a Scottish immigrant in 1842 the regional capital of **CHICOUTIMI** has grown from a small sawmill centre into one of the province's largest towns. Though it's crossed by the Saguenay, Chicoutimi and Moulin rivers, it's not a particularly enticing place, but you will probably end up here as the **train** from Montréal terminates at Jonquière (10km west), **buses** from Montréal, Québec City, Lac Saint-Jean, Tadoussac and Charlevoix all connect here, and highways 172 and 170 converge on the town.

Chicoutimi's main attraction is the **Vieille Pulperie** at 300 Dubuc (mid-June to mid-Sept daily 9am–5pm; ☎543-2729; $3) five austere brick buildings raised on the rapids by the Chicoutimi Pulp Company, which was founded in 1896 and quickly became Canada's largest producer of paper pulp. Left to rot in 1930, these gigantic ghosts of Chicoutimi's industrial past are gradually being restored to prime condition; guided tours are given every thirty minutes, but need to be reserved for English-speakers.

Not far from the *pulperie* is the strange **Maison-Musée du peintre Arthur Villeneuve**, 669 Taché Ouest (mid-May to mid-Oct Mon–Fri 1.30–4pm; reservations only ☎549-6841; $2). Home of naive painter Arthur Villeneuve, the house is in effect one big painting, with murals of Canadian scenes covering inside and out. Despite the unadventurous subject matter, Villeneuve has built himself quite a reputation in the Canadian art scene, and will probably be on hand to talk about his work. In the **Musée du Saguenay–Lac Saint-Jean**, 534 Jacques-Cartier (late June to Aug Mon–Fri 8.30am–5pm, Sat & Sun 1–5pm; Sept to late June Mon–Fri 8.30am–noon & 1.30–5pm, Sat & Sun 1–5pm; $3), the usual mock-ups of Victorian rooms are counterbalanced by good displays on the Montagnais and Inuit native peoples, and the museum's temporary exhibits on local artists, influential people, ecology and history can be interesting.

### Practicalities

Chicoutimi's **bus station** is on the corner of Tessier and Racine, right in the centre; the *CITS* local bus link with Jonquière's **train station** runs at least hourly from 7.15am to 9.45pm. The most central **information centre** is the one in the town hall, 320 de l'Hôtel de Ville (mid-June to Sept daily 8am–8pm); the all-year office at 198 Racine Est (Mon–Fri 9am–noon & 1.30–4.30pm) has information on the whole Saguenay–Lac Saint-Jean region. *Allo-Stop* is located at 236 Morin (☎543-3992).

**Accommodation** is readily available in Chicoutimi, as the town hosts a variety of business conferences all year round. The **youth hostel** *Auberge Saguenay*, 27 Bossé (☎543-5103; $11), is fairly seedy but well located. *Auberge Centre-Ville*, 104 Jacques Cartier (☎543-0253; singles $22–38, doubles $28–48), is a small, central **hotel** with cheap rates. On the main drag, *Hotel Chicoutimi*, 460 Racine (☎549-7111 or 1-800-463-9656; singles $36–160, doubles $42–160), has air-conditioned rooms with all mod cons in a range of prices.

There are numerous **fast-food** places and little restaurants on Racine. Recommended are *Le Troquet* at no. 387 which has French food in the $10–20 range and great cakes. *Le Fleur de Jasmin* is a cheap unlicensed Vietnamese restaurant at no. 331, while *Chez Georges* is an excellent and very cheap greasy spoon at no. 433. For a better class of meal, *La Bourgresse*, 260 Riverin (☎543-3178), serves French cuisine for $20–40. Most **bars** are also located on Racine – *Downtown Rock* at no. 198 and *Pile ou Face* at no. 375 are both young, lively spots. The main **disco/club** is *Le Cent Limites* at no. 362.

*Crosières La Marjolaine* offer once-daily summer **cruises** on the Saguenay as far as Ste-Rose-du-Nord (see opposite). Finally, the town is host to one of the best of Québec's **festivals**. For the ten-day **Carnival Souvenir** in February what seems like the entire population dresses in costumes from circa 1890; lumber camps, can-can clubs and operetta shows and heavy drinking augment the pioneer atmosphere.

## Lac Saint-Jean

To the west of Chicoutimi, around **Lac Saint-Jean**, stretches a relatively untouched area whose tranquil lakeshore villages are linked by the circular route of Hwy 169. Named after Father Jean Duquen, the first European to visit the region in 1647, the huge glacial lake is fed by most of the rivers of northeastern Québec and – unusually for an area of the rocky Canadian Shield – is bordered by sandy beaches and a lush, green terrain that has been farmed for over a century. The local cuisine, especially the delicious coarse meat pie called a *tourtière* and the thick blueberry pie, are renowned throughout the province. Further bonuses for budget travellers are the lake's two excellent youth hostels and its **public transport**: there's a daily bus service between Chicoutimi and both Alma and Dolbeau, the latter running round the south side of the lake; during the winter and spring a bus runs on Fridays and Sundays from Dolbeau to Alma via the villages on the north shore, and on Fridays only there's a service in the opposite direction.

### Val-Jalbert

From Chicoutimi Hwy 170 runs west to Hwy 169, which continues to one of the main tourist attractions of the region, **VAL-JALBERT** (late May to mid-June daily 9am–5pm; mid-June to Aug daily 9am–7pm; $4). The seventy-metre Ouiatchouan waterfall, which dominates the town, led to the establishment of a pulp mill here at the turn of the century, and by 1926 the village had around 950 inhabitants, with a convent serving the educational needs of the community. In the following year, though, the introduction of chemical-based pulping made the mill redundant, and the village was closed down. Val-Jalbert was left to rot until 1985, when the government decided to renovate it as a tourist attraction.

From the site entrance a bus (with on-board French commentary) runs around the main sights of the village, ending at the mill at the base of the falls. You can then wander around whatever caught your eye along the way – the abandoned wooden houses, the nunnery (now a museum) or the general store (now a souvenir shop).

From the mill – itself converted into an excellent crafts market and cafeteria – a cable car ($3) leads to the top of the falls, from which there are stunning views of the village and Lac Saint-Jean beyond. It is possible to stay in Val-Jalbert's renovated **hotel** (☎275-3132; singles $52, doubles $60), in apartments in the converted houses on St-George Street ($75 a day for four people), or in the **campground** just outside the village.

## Mashteuiatsh

Ten kilometres west, at ROBERVAL, a turn-off leads to the Montagnais reserve of **MASHTEUIATSH**, also known as Pointe-Bleue. Before European contact the Montagnais were a migratory people who split into small family groups for summer hunting, often directed to new grounds by a shaman who would locate the animals by "reading" the cracks on burnt animal bones. When the Europeans arrived they found the Montagnais in bitter conflict with the Iroquois, an enmity which Champlain intensified by allying himself with the Montagnais for trade. By the late seventeenth century their population had been greatly weakened by warfare, European diseases, depletion of game and displacement from their lands. This reserve was created in 1856, and today around 1500 of eastern Québec's 10,000 Montagnais live here. Like many Canadian reserves, Mashteuiatsh is dry in an attempt to reduce alcoholism and its attendant problems, yet the Montagnais suffer a great deal of prejudice from the surrounding white communities – so much so that there's no bus service, because Québécois bus drivers refuse to go there.

The village is situated right on the lake, and has an **information centre** on the main street at 151 Ouiatchouan (mid-June to Sept daily 8am–8pm). Up the hill from the information office, at 407 Amishk, is the only **Montagnais museum** in Canada (June–Sept Mon–Sat 9am–6pm, Sun noon–5pm, Tues & Thurs 7–9pm; Oct–May Mon–Fri 9am–noon & 1.30–4pm; $2). Exhibits include the band council's beautifully carved meeting table and chairs, their hunting implements and their clothing, which includes snowshoes patterned exclusively for each hunting group – any poachers could be identified by the distinctive mark of their snowshoes in the snow. On request you'll be shown a fascinating short film on the craft of birchbark biting, a technique for producing intricate patterns merely by making teeth marks in sheets of bark. At the end of July a **powwow** is held on the waterfront by the four concrete tepee sculptures that represent the seasons.

The only place to stay is the loghouse **youth hostel**, the *Auberge Kukum*, 241 Ouiatchouan (☎275-0697; from $15). The *Kukum* is no mere hostel – it is an introduction to the life of the native peoples of Canada, with nightly discussions of Montagnais issues over a communal supper of local dishes. Traditional music fills the *auberge* and documentary films are shown regularly. The *Kukum* also organises **adventure trips** into the bush: three-day canoe trips with a Montagnais guide cost $150 with all meals and equipment supplied, or you can live with the Montagnais in the bush for five days for $40 a day all-in. Using birchbark canoes, snowshoes and toboggans, you are completely submerged in the traditional way of life, relying on the resources of the surrounding woodlands and rivers to build shelters, make fires and prepare food.

## Saint-Félicien, Dolbeau and Mistassini

Situated on the western extremity of the lake on the Ashuapushuan river, **SAINT-FÉLICIEN** is the site of Québec's best zoo, the **Jardin Zoologique de St-Félicien** (daily 9am–5pm, open till 7pm in July; $12.50), located on Chamouchouane Island. The 130 mainly Canadian species roam free all over the site – the humans are the ones in cages, hauled around on the back of a mini-train. The zoo also has an historical angle, with mock-ups of an Indian village, trading post, loggers' camp and settlers' farm. Closer to town there's a vintage-car museum, **Musée de l'Auto**, 2203 boulevard du

Jardin (May–Sept daily 8am–10pm; $2). The **information office** is located at 976 Sacré-Coeur (mid-June to Sept daily 8am–8pm). For **accommodation** check out the cheap *Hôtel Bellevue*, 1055 Sacré-Coeur (☎679-0162; singles $22, doubles $27), or the B&B *Au Grand Jardin Fleuri*, near the bus station at 1179 Notre-Dame (☎679-0287; singles $30, doubles $40).

Continuing clockwise around the lake from Saint-Félicien brings you to **DOLBEAU**, 39km further. It's at its best during mid-July's ten-day **Western Festival**, with rodeos and people wandering around in stetsons and spurs. If you get stranded, the cheapest **accommodation** option is the *Hôtel Maison Blanche*, 218 7e Avenue (☎276-0797; doubles from $25). Nearby **MISTASSINI**, the region's blueberry capital, hosts a better fest in early August, the **Festival du bleuet** – one big blowout on blueberries dipped in chocolate, blueberry pie, blueberry cheesecake and an extremely potent blueberry wine. Over the Mistassini River the **Monastère des Pères Trappistes** sells its own organic produce – a large quantity of the berries are on offer in season.

### Sainte-Monique and Alma

Another 42km round the shore is the village of **SAINTE-MONIQUE**, on whose outskirts you'll find an island-based **youth hostel** and **campground**: the *Auberge Île du Repos de Péribonka* (June–Sept; ☎347-5649; chalets $10, camping from $9). Bikes can be rented for $25 a day, useful for an excursion to **Pointe-Taillon park** (late June to early Sept). Occupying a finger of land that juts into Lac Saint-Jean, the park is bordered by long and often deserted beaches.

From Sainte-Monique it's 29km to the dull aluminium-producing city of ALMA, useful only for its **buses** to Chicoutimi and Québec City.

# The Côte Nord

The **St Lawrence River** was the lifeline of the wilderness beyond Tadoussac until Hwy 138 was constructed along the **Côte Nord** to Havre-St-Pierre, 625km distant. The road sweeps from high vistas down to the rugged shoreline through the vast regions of Manicouagan and Duplessis, the few distractions offered in the villages and towns enroute being supplemented by panoramas of spruce-covered mountains, the vast sky and the mighty river. **Bears** and **moose** often lumber out of the stunted forest onto the highway, and in the summer the shiny backs of **whales** are frequently spotted arching out of the water.

Basque whalers were the first Europeans to penetrate this chilly shore in the sixteenth century, but when they began to trade fur with the native Montagnais, Naskapi and Inuit they were ousted by French merchants in the next century. After the British conquest the fur trade continued but fishing remained the main industry until this century, when mining, lumber and hydro-electric projects led to the growth of a few settlements into fair-sized towns. Despite this, the region has a population density of just five people per square mile, and the distances between communities becomes longer and longer the further you travel, overwhelming the visitor with the sense of Canada's vastness.

The Québec City to Tadoussac *Intercar* **bus** serves the north shore as far as Baie-Comeau, from where *Autobus du Littoral* travels to Sept-Îles and onwards to Havre-St-Pierre. At Havre-St-Pierre the highway gives out altogether and the only onward transport is by supply **ship** from Sept-Îles and Havre-St-Pierre, which serves the wildlife haven of Île d'Anticosti and undertakes a breathtaking journey along the inlets of the windswept coastline of the Lower North Shore. Other ferries link various points to the south shore and the Gaspé, which means you can plot a varied return trip.

# Tadoussac to Port-Cartier

The craggy terrain is the chief attraction of the 200km of highway from Tadoussac to Baie-Comeau, though within the first half of the route the communities of GRANDES-BERGERONNES, LES ESCOUMINS and SAULT-AU-MOUTON (22km, 31km & 56km from Tadoussac) have regular **whale-watching** trips (June–Oct 1–2 daily; $25). Grandes-Bergeronne's **Centre d'Interprétation de la Nature**, 424 rue de la Mer (mid-June to mid-Sept 9am–8pm; mid-Sept to mid-Oct 9am–5pm; $3), built around the Cap Bon Désir lighthouse, has displays on the whale life and lookout post by a popular whale feeding ground – but you may well have a fruitless wait. From Les Escoumins there's a ferry across the St Lawrence to Trois-Pistoles (see p.186).

## Baie-Comeau

The road to **BAIE-COMEAU** passes a monstrous newsprint mill plant that churns out poisonous emissions 24 hours a day. Established in 1936 by Colonel Robert R McCormick, the publisher of the *Chicago Tribune*, Baie-Comeau has done nothing but boom ever since – with a population of 26,000, it dwarfs the communities around it. There's no real reason to hang around here, but if you have time to kill while waiting for a northward bus or a ferry to the south shore you might stroll through the **quartier Sainte-Amélie** in the eastern Marquette sector, where the streets are lined by grand American houses dating from the 1930s. The **Sainte-Amélie Church**, 37 avenue Marquette, is worth a quick peek for its stained glass windows, designed by Italian artist Guido Nincheri.

The *Maison régionale du tourisme*, 871 rue de Puyjalon (Mon–Fri 9am–noon & 1–5pm), has **information** on the entire region. **Buses** terminate at 330 boulevard Lasalle; the departure point for the **car ferry** to Matane is at the western end of boulevard Lasalle (1–2 daily; journey time 2hr 20min; $8.25 single, cars $20).

**Accommodation** is available at the rambling brick hotel *Le Manoir*, 8 Cabot (☎296-3391), which overlooks the St Lawrence and has singles and doubles from $65–170. Less expensive is the modern *Hôtel-Motel La Caravelle*, 202 boulevard Lasalle (☎296-4986; singles $40, doubles $50). Other similarly priced motels are located along this street. The cheapest place is *Hôtel Baie-Comeau*, 49 place Lasalle (☎296-4977), with singles from $34, doubles from $39. For **camping** *Camping Manic 2* on Hwy 389 has places from $10. *La Manoir Hôtel* is pricey for **eating** but has an excellent reputation, and there are various fast-food places, including the major chains, on Lasalle and Laflèche boulevards.

## The Manic Dams

One of the few roads to penetrate the bleak terrain north of the St Lawrence is the partly paved Hwy 389 (Manic Road), which runs 215km into the forest from the east end of Baie-Comeau. The road was built as a supply route for the hydro-electric company who built the colossal **dam system** on the Manicouagan river, the only artificial site to rival the landscape in these parts. The *Hydro-Québec* **information** kiosk at 135 boulevard Comeau (mid-June to Sept daily 8am–3pm), where Hwy 389 branches off from Hwy 318, offers a cheap **bus** service to the two massive dams along the Manic Road on request.

The first dam in the system, **Manic 2**, is a half-hour drive from Baie-Comeau, a journey that takes in great views of the rocky Canadian Shield. A free guided tour of the dam takes you inside the massive wall (mid-June to Sept daily 9am, 11am, 1pm & 3pm), but an even more stupendous structure awaits two and a half hours' drive further north – the awesome **Manic 5** or Daniel Johnson dam. Constructed in 1968, it is named after the premier of Québec who died here on the morning of the opening ceremony. With a length of 1314 metres and a central arch of 214 metres, the dam is the world's largest multiple arch structure. Free guided tours take visitors to the foot of the dam (mid-June to Sept daily 9am, 11am, 1.30pm & 3.30pm) and across the top, giving panoramic views of the Manicouagan Valley and the 2000-square-kilometre reservoir. There is **accommodation** right by the Manic 5 at the *Motel de L'Énergie* (☎584-2301; doubles $80).

## Godbout and onwards

The attractive fishing village of **GODBOUT**, situated on a crescent-shaped bay 45km from Baie-Comeau, is not just the most pleasant place hereabouts – it also has an excellent **Musée Amérindien et Inuit**, 134 chemin Pascal-Comeau (June–Sept daily 9am–10pm; $1.50). The museum was founded by Claude Grenier, who spent ten years in the frozen north in the 1970s on a government scheme to boost the Inuit economy by promoting native culture. Consequent commercialism has diluted the output since then, but the private collection of the Greniers features nothing but genuine pieces, from the characteristic soapstone carvings to domestic artefacts. The village is linked to Matane on the south shore by a daily **ferry** ($8.25 single, $20 for cars). For **accommodation**, the *Motel Chantal*, 111 Hwy 138 (☎568-7511), has singles for $40 and doubles for $50, while *Aux Berges*, 180 Pascal Comeau (☎568-7748), offers **B&B** with singles for $30, doubles for $40. There's **camping** at *Camping L'Estuaire* on the highway, with pitches from $10.

Situated where the St Lawrence River merges into the Gulf of St Lawrence, **POINTE-DES-MONTS**, 24km from Godbout, has not changed since the nineteenth century. Mind you, there's not a lot to change – all that stands on this rocky outcrop is a red and white **lighthouse** dating from 1830 – the oldest in Canada – and a small missionary **chapel** built in 1898. The lighthouse, listed as an historical monument, now contains a **museum** (late June to mid-Sept daily 9am–7pm; $1.50), a fairly expensive seafood **restaurant** and a **B&B** (June–Aug; ☎939-2332; singles $32, doubles $40). From late June to mid-September there are also **whale-watching** excursions from the lighthouse (2/4 hr; $15/30); the boats are small and need to be reserved in advance at the B&B.

From here it's an uneventful journey over the 113km to Sept-Îles, passing through POINTE-AUX-ANGLAIS and, 63km further, the lumber and iron ore centre of **PORT-CARTIER**. The town's only attraction is as the entrance to the **Réserve faunique de Sept-Îles–Port-Cartier**, a wilderness park popular with hunters, anglers and experienced canoeists, who ride the rapids on the Rochers River. There are basic **camping** facilities here at *Camping Lac Walker*.

# Sept-Îles

The largest ore-exporting port in eastern Canada, **SEPT-ÎLES** is a good base for trips further north, owing to its rail links with Labrador. With its alphabetically named streets of dull prefab houses, the town itself has as much character as a pile of iron ore, but it's pleasantly located on the St Lawrence shore and you could spend an enjoyable day here – especially in August, when one of Québec's foremost native music festivals is held nearby.

An interesting overview of local history is offered by the **Vieux Poste** located on the shores of the Rivière du Poste at the town's Uashat reserve (June–Sept 9am–6pm; $2.50). Prior to the British conquest when the Hudson Bay Company took over the trade here, Sept-Îles was leased by the French crown to merchant traders. Settlements like these opened up Québec for the Europeans but practically destroyed the lives of the native Montagnais. Converted to Christianity and overwhelmed by European goods – particularly firearms which aided them in their battles against the feared Iroquois – the Montagnais were forced by market pressure to hunt more and more fur-bearing animals. The resulting depletion of game was worsened so much by the later lumber and mining industries that the Montagnais were obliged to live on official reserves in order to become eligible for state hand-outs. The reconstructed Vieux Poste, with its small chapel, store and postmaster's house, presents an absorbing portrayal of the Montagnais culture and is staffed by local Montagnais who produce crafts and food which are sold at a decently priced handicrafts store.

The name of the town comes from the archipelago just offshore, whose largest island, **Grande Basque**, is served by a ferry from Urban Park off Arnaud (7 daily; $8). There's a campsite on the island, and a cruise boat tours the islands from the same departure point daily at 1pm ($14). Whales and sea birds are the main attraction.

## The Innu Nikamu Festival

One of the more offbeat Canadian chart successes of recent years has been the local native group Kashtin, the only nationally known band to perform in a native tongue. Their appearance is now a highlight of the excellent **Innu Nikamu Festival** of song and music, held every August 14km east of Sept-Îles in the Montagnais reserve of Maliotenam. Inspired by Kashtin's success, numerous other groups travel to the festival to produce some of the best of Canada's contemporary and traditional native music. As well as the music, the festival includes native food and craft stalls – despite the reserve's alcohol ban, there is always a good buzz. There is no public transport to the reserve: by car take Hwy 138 towards Havre-St-Pierre and turn left at the Moisie intersection for the Maliotenam entrance. Tickets cost around $5 and are available from the tourist information kiosk.

## Practicalities

The **information** office is on Hwy 138 on the western outskirts of town (late June to late Aug daily 9am–5pm). The *Le Tangon* **youth hostel**, 555 Cartier (mid-June to mid-Sept; ☎962-8180), is grotty and characterless but cheap at $10 for members, $8 for campers; curfew is midnight. *Hôtel Carmelo*, 386 Gamache (☎962-3841), has singles for the rock bottom price of $10; *Hôtel Royal*, 232 Evangéline (☎968-4909), has doubles at $30–40; and the luxurious *Auberge des Gouverneurs*, 666 Laure (☎962-7071), has doubles for $100. The *Camping Uashat* **campsite** is at 1149 Dequen ($15). For the dauntless traveller, *Aventure Nomade* (☎962-1123) organise dog-sleigh, kayak and hiking trips using traditional Inuit equipment and methods.

The **bus** station, 126 Blanche (☎962-2126), has buses north to Havre-St-Pierre; the **train** station, with weekly trains to Wabush, Labrador City and Schafferville, is to the north of town (☎968-7805). There is also an **Allo-Stop** office here (☎962-5035). The *Nordik Express* supply **ship** (☎1-800-463-0680) leaves Sept-Îles on Wednesday morning every month except February and March, arriving at Port-Menier on the Île d'Anticosti ($45) that evening and Havre-St-Pierre ($81) early the next morning, before continuing along the lower north shore to almost as far as Labrador. On Monday afternoons it shuttles over to Rimouski ($67) on the Gaspé, arriving early Tuesday morning.

# Havre-St-Pierre and offshore

There is little of interest along the blackfly-ridden stretch of shore known as the Mingan coast until you reach **HAVRE-ST-PIERRE**, where the stunning islands of the Mingan archipelago offer a unique environment of sculpted rock formations and profuse wildlife. The community of Havre-St-Pierre would have remained a tiny fishing village if it hadn't been for the discovery in the 1940s of a huge deposit of ilmenite, the chief source of titanium. The quarries are 45km north of the town itself, where fishing and tourism provide employment for the non-miners, the latter industry having received a major boost when the forty islands of the **Mingan archipelago** were made into a national park in 1983. Before setting off to the park check out the **Centre** d'Accueil et d'Interprétation, Réserve du Parc National de l'Archipel de Mingan, 975 de l'Escale (mid-June to Sept 8am–8pm; free), with photographic displays and info on the flora, fauna and geology of the islands.

Havre-St-Pierre's **information centre** is at 957 de la Berge (June–Aug daily 9am–5pm). The *Auberge de la Minganie* **youth hostel** is inconveniently located 25km west of town, but the bus from the south will let you off early – and hitching is easy. An old fishing camp with minimum renovations and lots of bugs, the hostel charges $10 for members and serves $3 breakfasts. In town, the *Hôtel-Motel du Hâvre*, 970 de l'Escale (☎538-2800), has doubles from $45, but the cheapest accommodation is in the **B&B** *Le Gîte Chez Louis*, 1045–1047 Boréal (May–Aug; ☎538-2799; singles $30, doubles $45). The *Centre Culturel et d'Interprétation de Havre St Pierre*, 957 de la Berge (☎538-2512), runs a network of **private homes** that offer cheap rooms to visitors. *Camping Municipal* is on Hwy 138 ($6–12). The **bus station** is near *Hôtel-Motel du Havre*. The wharf is the departure point for the *Nordik Express* (see overleaf).

## The Mingan Archipelago

Just 3.5km offshore from Havre-St-Pierre, the **Mingan National Park Reserve** offers some of the weirdest and most beautiful landscapes in Québec. Standing on the islands' white sand shorelines are innumerable eight-metre-high rocks like ancient totem poles, with bright orange lichen colouring their mottled surfaces and bonsai-sized trees clinging to their crevices. These formations originated as underwater sediment near the equator, which were thrust above sea level over 250 million years ago and then covered in an ice cap several kilometres thick. As the drifting ice melted the islands emerged again, 7000 years ago, at their present location. The sea and wind gave the final touch by chipping away at the soft limestone to create the majestic monoliths of today.

Bizarre geology isn't the archipelago's only remarkable feature. The flora constitutes a unique insular garden of 452 arctic and rare alpine species, which survive here at their most southern limit due to the limestone soil, long harsh winters and cold Gulf of Labrador current. As for wildlife, other than the Gulf's whale populations the permanent inhabitants of the national park include puffins who build nests in the scant soil of three of the islands from early May to late August.

Various **boat tours** round the island are available from Havre-St-Pierre, but need to be booked in advance: *La Relève II* operates from 1167 des Anciens (3 daily; $20; ☎538-2865); the *Perroquet de Mer* (3 daily; $20) and *Rocher Percé II* (2 daily; $20) are run by *La Tournée des Îles Inc*, 1155 de la Digue (☎538-2547). Free camping is allowed on six of the islands but the only transport is the more expensive water taxis, available from *Taxi des Îles*, 879 Acara (☎538-3161). Permits must be obtained from the interpretation centre.

## Île d'Anticosti

Situated in the Gulf of St Lawrence between the Jacques Cartier and Honguedo Straits, the remote **ÎLE D'ANTICOSTI** was once known as the "Graveyard of the Gulf", as over 400 ships were wrecked on its shores, including Admiral Phipp's fleet, retreating from Québec City in 1690. Its 7770-square-kilometre expanse is made up of windswept beaches and forests of twisted pine, criss-crossed by turbulent rivers and sheer ravines.

Known as Notiskuan – "the land where we hunt bears" – by the natives, and a walrus- and whale-fishing ground for the Basques, Île d'Anticosti became the private domain of Henri Menier, a French chocolate millionaire, in 1873. He imported white-tailed Virginia deer, red fox, silver fox, beaver and moose to his domain in order to gun them down at his leisure. Nowadays a less exclusive horde of hunters and fishers come here to blast the deer from the back of their four-wheel-drives and to hoist the salmon from the rivers, which now fall under the jurisdiction of the province. For other travellers it presents an opportunity to explore an area that's untamed and still practically deserted, with a population of just 340.

Menier established the tiny village of Baie Ste-Claire on the western tip in 1873; less than thirty years later the settlers moved to **PORT-MENIER** on the south side of this tip, and Baie-Ste-Claire's homes were left to the ravages of the salt air. The human population is now concentrated in the blue-roofed houses of Port-Menier, where the weekly *Nordik Express* from Havre-St-Pierre or Sept-Îles comes in. A small museum in Port-Menier, the **Ecomusée d'Anticosti** (daily 8am–noon & 1–5pm; free), has small displays on the history and ecology of the island, while moccasins, gloves and other objects made of Virginia deer leather are readily available in the handicraft stores of the village.

The twisting, pot-holed road that crosses the island, jokingly called the "Trans-Anticostian", provides access to the **Réserve Faunique de l'Île d'Anticosti** located in the centre and on the eastern tip. Driving or hitching is the only way of getting there – you can hire a car in Port-Menier at *Location Georges Lelièvre Anticosti*. The island can boast Québec's largest cave, the glacial **Caverne de la Rivière à la Patate** on the island's north side, where a modest opening leads into a cathedral-like chamber and a warren of 500-metre-long passages. With attractions such as this and the plethora of wildlife, the reserve is endeavouring to encourage adventure tourism during the summer months. Their ecologically sound packages are pricey (around $500 a week) but include transport, meals, accommodation and four-wheel-drive vehicles (information ☎1-800-463-0863).

The *Nordik Express* from Havre-St-Pierre or Sept-Îles costs $45 return per person; the round trip from Sept-Îles to Port-Menier and back to Havre-St-Pierre costs $81 per person. Apart from the municipal **campsites** at Baie-Ste-Claire and Port-Menier, the only other organised **accommodation** is in Port-Menier at *Chalets Touristiques Anticosti* (☎535-0346; doubles $20–25) and *Auberge de Port-Menier* (☎535-0122; doubles $60).

## The Lower North Shore

With Highway 138 terminating at Havre-St-Pierre, the dozen or so villages along the rugged **Lower North Shore** have been cut off from the rest of Québec for centuries – to such an extent that most of the inhabitants speak only English. The original inhabitants of the area were Montagnais, Naskapi and Inuits, who were invaded by Vikings in the year 1000. Cartier saw the coast in 1534 but did not register it as a discovery because it was already seasonally occupied by Basque, Spanish and Portuguese fishermen, and fishing is still the only industry on this desolate coast. The current 6500 inhabitants are descendants of fishermen from the Channel Islands and Newfoundland.

The trip by *Nordik Express* from Havre-St-Pierre affords stunning views of a rocky, subarctic landscape that is so cold that icebergs float past the ship even in the height of summer. During the day whales, dolphins and a wealth of sea birds are a common sight and at night the northern lights present an unforgettable display. At each stop the village inhabitants surround the boat as its weekly arrival is about all that happens here. Chief stops include the village of KEGASKA, whose roads are covered with white seashells and pavements are made of wood, and VIEUX-FORT, where you can always see seals sunning themselves on the rocks surrounding the bay.

To visit the Lower North Shore the **Nordik Express** leaves Havre-St-Pierre on Thursday morning and arrives in BLANC-SABLON, Québec's most easterly village, in the very early morning of the following Saturday. The boat then returns, arriving back in Havre-St-Pierre late Sunday night. The price is pretty hefty but includes meals and a cabin berth: Havre-St-Pierre to Blanc-Sablon is $393 return. **Accommodation** in Blanc-Sablon is available at *Auberge Bremen* (☎461-2920; singles $43, doubles $49).

From Blanc-Sablon it is possible to get a ferry across to Newfoundland (May–Dec 2 daily; 1hr 30min) or drive along the coast into Labrador (see p.112).

# travel details

## Trains

**From Montréal** to Québec City (2 daily; 3hr); Lévis (12 weekly; 3hr 30min); Sherbrooke/St John/Moncton/Halifax (3 weekly; 2hr 30min/ 13hr/15hr/20hr); Lévis/Rivière-du-Loup/Trois-Pistoles/Rimouski/Moncton/Halifax (3 weekly; 3hr 30min/5hr 45min/7hr 15min/8hr/17hr/21hr 30min); Lévis/Rivière-du-Loup/Trois-Pistoles/ Rimouski/Carleton/New Richmond/Bonaventure/ Percé/Gaspé (3 weekly; 3hr 30min/5hr 45min/7hr 15min/8hr/12hr/12hr 40min/13hr 15min/15hr 45min/17hr); Jonquière (3 weekly; 9hr); Ottawa (2–3 daily; 2hr); Grand-Mère (4 weekly; 2hr 45min); Kingston/Toronto (2–3 daily; 2hr 20min/ 4hr 50min); Cornwall/Brockville/Kingston/ Belleville/Oshawa/Toronto (2 daily; 1hr 10min/ 2hr/2hr 30min/3hr 30min/4hr 40min/5hr 30min); Moncton/Halifax (6 weekly; 15hr–16hr 50min/ 20hr–21hr 55min).

Note: All train services from Québec City are routed via Montréal.

## Buses

**From Montréal** to Québec City (18 daily; 3hr 5min); Lévis (5–6 daily; 2hr 40min); St-Eustache (2 daily; 45min); St-Jovite (4–9 daily; 2hr); St-Sauveur (7 weekly; 1hr 30min); St-Jovite (1–2 daily; 2hr); Val-David/Ste-Agathe (3–4 daily; 1 hr 50min; 2hr); Ste-Agathe/St-Jovite (1–2 daily; 1hr 45min/2hr 15min); Val-David/Ste-Agathe/St-Jovite (1–3 daily; 1hr 45min/1hr 55min/2hr 20min); Val-David/Ste-Agathe/St-Jovite/Mont-Tremblant (1–2 daily; 1hr 45min/1hr 55min/2hr 30min/3hr); St-Sauveur/Val-David/Ste-Agathe/ St-Jovite (4 weekly; 1hr 25min/2hr/2hr 10min/2hr 40min); Granby (9 daily; 1hr 15min); Granby/ Magog/Sherbrooke (6 daily; 1hr 40min/2hr 45min/3hr 20min); Magog/Sherbrooke (11 daily; 1hr 20min/2hr); Trois-Rivières (1 daily; 2hr 30min); Lévis/Rivière-du-Loup/Rimouski (1 daily; 2hr 40min/5hr 20min/6hr 40min); Lévis/Rivière-du-Loup (1 daily; 2hr 40min/5hr 30min); Rivière-du-Loup/Rimouski (1 daily; 4hr 30min/6hr 45min); Toronto (10 daily; 6hr 10min); Cornwall/Kingston/ Toronto (5 daily; 1hr 35min/3hr 25min/6hr 35min); Ottawa (18 daily; 2hr 10min).

**From Sherbrooke** to Trois-Rivières (1–2 daily; 2hr 30min); Québec City (2–4 daily; 4hr).

**From Trois Rivières** to Grand-Mère (2 daily; 1hr).

**From Québec City** to Rimouski (6 daily; 3hr 40min–5hr 20min); Lévis/Rivière-du-Loup/Trois-Pistoles/Bic/Rimouski (1 daily; 35min/3hr 40min/ 4hr 30min/5hr/5hr 20min); Lévis/Rivière-du-Loup (2 daily; 35min/3hr 40min); Rivière-du-Loup/Trois-Pistoles/Bic/Rimouski (1 daily; 2hr 15min/3hr/3hr 40min/4hr); Lévis/Rivière-du-Loup/Bic/Rimouski (1 daily; 30min/3hr 45min/5hr 30min/6hr); Lévis/ Rivière-du-Loup/Trois-Pistoles/Rimouski (1 daily; 2hr 15min/2hr 50min/3hr 40min); Lévis/Rivière-du-Loup/Rimouski (1 daily; 35min/2hr 50min/4hr 10min); Rivière-du-Loup/Rimouski (1 daily; 4hr 30min/6hr 45min); Chicoutimi (5–9 daily; 2hr 40min); Parc des Laurentides/Alma/Val-Jalbert/ Roberval/St-Félicien/Dolbeau (2 daily; 1hr/2hr 40min/3hr 30min/3hr 45min/4hr 10min/5hr); Parc des Laurentides/Alma (1 daily; 1hr/2hr 40min); La Malbaie/Forestville/Baie-Comeau (1 weekly; 2hr 50min/5hr/6hr 20min); Baie-St-Paul/La Malbaie (1 weekly; 1hr 45min/2hr 40min); Baie-St-Paul/La Malbaie/Pointe-au-Pic (1–4 daily; 1hr 50min/2hr 35min/2hr 40min); Baie-St-Paul/La Malbaie/St-Siméon / Tadoussac / Grandes-Bergeronnes / Les Escoumins/Forestville/Betsiamites/ Baie-Comeau (2 daily; 1hr 15min/2hr 10min/3hr 20min/4hr 15min/4hr 45min/5hr 5min/5hr 50min/6hr 45min/ 7hr 45min).

**From Rimouski** to Matane (3 daily; 1hr 10min– 1hr 35min); Carleton/New Richmond/ Bonaventure/Percé/Gaspé (1 daily; 3hr 45min/ 4hr/4hr 30min/6hr 45min/7hr 45min); Pointe-au-Père/St-Flavie/Matane/Cap-Chat/Ste-Anne-des-Monts/Gaspé (2 daily; 10min/30min/1hr 30min/ 1hr 30min/2hr 55min/6hr 45min); Pointe-au-Père/ St-Flavie/Val-Brillant/Amqui/Matapedia/Carleton (1 daily; 10min/20min/1hr 30min/1hr 40min/2hr 45min/4hr); Pointe-au-Père/St-Flavie/Matane (1 daily; 10min/30min/1hr 35min); Val-Brillant/ Amqui (1 daily; 1hr 30min/1hr 40min); Val-Brillant/ Amqui / Matapedia / Carleton / New Richmond/Bonaventure/Percé/Gaspé (1 daily; 1hr 30min/1hr 40min/2hr 45min/4hr 10min/5hr 10min/5hr 40min/8hr/9hr).

**From Chicoutimi** to Jonquière/Val-Jalbert/ Roberval/St-Félicien/Dolbeau (1–2 daily; 30min/ 1hr 50min/2hr/2hr 20min/3hr 30min); Jonquière/ Alma (1–3 daily; 25min/1hr). .

**From Dolbeau** to Péribonka/Ste-Monique/Alma (late August to late April, 2 weekly; 30min/40min/ 1hr 15min).

**From Baie Comeau** to Godbout/Baie-Trinité/ Pointe-aux-Anglais/Port-Cartier/Sept-Îles (1–2 daily; 40min/1hr 15min/2hr/2hr 45min/3hr 30min).

**From Sept-Îles** to Havre-St-Pierre (5 weekly; 3hr 10min).

### Ferries

**From Québec City** to Lévis (1–3 hourly; 15min).

**From Rivière-du-Loup** to St-Siméon (April–Dec 3-8 daily; 1hr 15min).

**From Trois-Pistoles** to Les Escoumins (June–Oct 1–6 daily; 1hr 15min).

**From Matane** to Baie-Comeau (2 daily to 5 weekly; 2hr 30min); Godbout (2 daily to 5 weekly; 2hr 15min).

**From St-Joseph-de-la-Rive** to St-Bernard (hourly to 11 daily; 15min).

**From Baie-Ste-Catherine** to Tadoussac (1–4 hourly; 10min).

**From Rimouski** to Sept-Îles/Port Menier/Havre-St-Pierre/Blanc Sablon (1 weekly; 11hr/18hr/23hr/68hr).

**From Blanc-Sablon** to St Barbe, Newfoundland (2 daily; 1hr 30min).

### Flights

**From Montréal** (Dorval) to Québec City (10–14 daily; 45min); Québec City/Mont-Joli (Rimouski)/ Gaspé/Îles-de-la-Madeleine (2 daily; 45min/1hr 35min/2hr 25min/3hr 40min); Québec City/ Gaspé/Îles-de-la-Madeleine (1 daily; 45min/2hr 5min/2hr 55min); Québec City/Sept-Îles/Wabush (1 daily; 45min/2hr/2hr 50min); Québec City/ Mont-Joli (Rimouski)/Baie Comeau (6 weekly; 45min/1hr 45min/2hr 5min); Bagotville (Chicoutimi) (1–4 daily; 1hr 5min); Ottawa (7–10 daily; 40min); Toronto (36–40 daily; 1hr 15min); Halifax (4–5 daily; 1hr 20min); Moncton (3–5 daily; 1hr 20min); Calgary (1–2 daily; 4hr 20min); St John's (1 daily; 2hr 20min); Winnipeg (1 daily; 2hr 50min); Fredericton/St John's/Halifax (1 daily; 1hr 5min/1hr 35min/2hr 20min); Bathurst (6 weekly; 1hr 40min).

**From Québec City** to Toronto (2–3 daily; 1hr 30min); Ottawa (5 weekly; 1hr 5min); St John's/ Halifax (1 daily; 1hr 10min/1hr 50min).

**From Sept-Îles** to Québec City/Montréal/ Ottawa (2–3 daily; 1hr 30min/2hr 20min/3hr).

# CHAPTER FOUR

# ONTARIO

he one million square kilometres of **ONTARIO**, Canada's second largest province, stretch all the way from the St Lawrence River and the Great Lakes to the frozen shores of Hudson Bay. Some two-thirds of this territory – all of the north and most of the centre – is occupied by the forests and rocky outcrops of the Canadian Shield, whose characteristically flat, lake-studded landscapes the Iroquois called Ontario, literally "glittering waters". **Algonquian** and **Iroquoian** natives were the first to cultivate the more hospitable parts of southern Ontario, a fertile flatland in which the vast majority of the province's ten million people are now concentrated.

The first **Europeans** to make regular contact with these peoples were the **French explorers** of the seventeenth and eighteenth centuries, most famously the intrepid Brulé and Champlain, but these early visitors were preoccupied with the fur trade, and it wasn't until the end of the American War of Independence and the immigration of the **United Empire Loyalists** that mass settlement began. Between 1820 and 1850 a further wave of migrants, mostly English, Irish and Scots, made Upper Canada, as Ontario was known until Confederation, the most populous and prosperous Canadian region. This pre-eminence was reinforced towards the end of the nineteenth century by the industrialisation of its larger towns, a process underpinnned by the discovery of some of the world's richest mineral deposits – in the space of a few years nickel was found near Sudbury, silver at Cobalt, gold in Red Lake and iron ore at Wawa.

Nowadays, a highly mechanised timber industry, massive hydro-electric schemes and thousands of factories – making more than half the country's manufactured goods – keep Ontario at the top of the economic ladder. However, this industrial success has created massive **environmental problems**, most noticeable in the wounded landscapes around Sudbury and the heavily polluted waters of the Great Lakes. Furthermore, despite the diversity of its economy and its tremendous natural resources, Ontario in the 1980s experienced a slump that contributed to the electoral success of the New Democratic Party in 1990, an upset in a province that had always chosen to vote Conservative or Liberal before.

With over three million inhabitants, **Toronto** is Canada's biggest city, a financial and industrial centre that might lack grace and elegance but compensates in terms of museums, restaurants and nightlife. To the south of the metropolis, **Lake Ontario** is ringed by nondescript suburbs and ugly industrial townships that culminate in the polluted steel city of Hamilton, a few kilometres from Canada's premier tourist spot, **Niagara Falls** – best visited on a day-trip from Toronto or from colonial **Niagara-on-the-Lake**. Most of the southernmost region, sandwiched between lakes Huron and Erie, is farming terrain that's as flat as a Dutch polder. Nevertheless, the car-producing town of **Windsor** is a lively place to spend a night, and **Goderich** is a pretty little place tucked against the bluffs along the Lake Huron shoreline. For landscape, the most attractive regions of southern Ontario are the **Bruce Peninsula** and the islands of the adjacent **Georgian Bay**, unspoiled oases in an area much favoured by Ontarian vacationers.

Much of **central Ontario**, approximately the triangle formed by Toronto, Ottawa and Sudbury, is cottage country, where the province's city folk escape to isolated lakesides to fish, boat and swim. Yet even this largely domesticated idyll has its wilderness, in the shape of **Algonquin Park**, where beavers and black bears roam a land that

Pickle Crow

*Albany River*

Winnipeg

Kenora

Dryden

Sioux Lookout

*Lake of the Woods*

*Lake Nipigon*

Aroland

Geraldton

**ONTARIO**

Hearst

Kapuskasir

Fort Frances

*Quetico Provincial Park*

Nipigon

White River

Thunder Bay

Pukaskwa National Park

*Missinai Lake*

Wawa

*Lake Superior*

Lake Superior Provincial Park

Sault Ste Marie

*MICHIGAN*

Manito Islan

*Lake*

Minneapolis

**WISCONSIN**

*Lake Michigan*

Sarni

Detroit

Windsor

Chicago

N

**OHI**

0        200 km

**UNITED STATE**

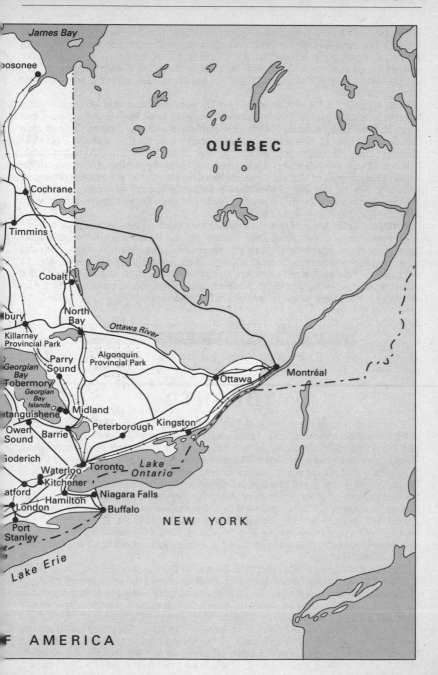

James Bay

oosonee

QUÉBEC

Cochrane

Timmins

Cobalt

bury
North
Bay

Killarney
Provincial Park
*Ottawa River*

Parry
Sound
Algonquin
Provincial Park

*Georgian
Bay*
Tobermory
*Georgian
Bay
Islands*
Ottawa
Montréal

tanguishene
Midland

Owen
Sound
Barrie
Peterborough
Kingston

Goderich

Waterloo
Toronto
*Lake
Ontario*

Kitchener

atford
Hamilton
Niagara Falls

London
Buffalo

Port
Stanley
NEW YORK

*Lake Erie*

F AMERICA

inspired Canada's most prestigious art movement, the Group of Seven. To the east of the park lies the Loyalist heartland, centred on the militaristic and handsome city of **Kingston**, strategically situated on the shores of the St Lawrence. From here, the **Rideau Canal** runs north to **Ottawa**, the nation's capital but a surprisingly small city of impeccable streets and parks, high-class museums and galleries, and incessant bureaucratic bustle.

From Ottawa the **Trans-Canada** (Hwy 17) wends its way west through endless forest to Manitoba, passing by the shore of the mighty **Lake Superior** – a journey that takes in revitalised **Sudbury**, **Sault Ste Marie** – where the **Agawa Canyon** train affords a glimpse of the otherwise inpenetrable hinterland – and the sprawl of **Thunder Bay**, the major port on the greatest of the Great Lakes. Further north, Highway 11 cuts through a region whose mining towns are moribund testimony to the extraordinary impact of Canada's mineral-based boom and the subsequent ravages of recession. Beyond this line of habitation lies a brutal country where hunters are the only regular visitors, though the passing tourist can get a taste of the terrain on board the Polar Bear Express from **Cochrane**.

Toronto is at the heart of Ontario's **public transport** system, with regular bus and rail services along the shore of Lake Ontario and the St Lawrence between Niagara Falls and Ottawa, from where there are frequent links to Montréal. Away from this core, though, the picture is far more sketchy. There are fairly regular bus services on the London–Windsor–Detroit route and along the Trans-Canada and Highway 11, but connections between the province's smaller towns are few and far between – reckon on about one per day even for prominent places like Goderich.

---

### TOLL-FREE INFORMATION NUMBER

Ontario Ministry of Tourism ☎1-800-ONTARIO.

---

# TORONTO

The economic and cultural focus of English-speaking Canada, **TORONTO** sprawls along the northern shore of Lake Ontario in a jangle of satellite townships and industrial zones that cover a hundred square kilometres. The country's largest metropolis, Toronto was for decades saddled with unflattering soubriquets – "Toronto the Good", "Hogtown" – that reflected a reputation for complacent mediocrity and greed. Spurred by the bad press into years of image-building, the city's postwar administrations have lavished millions on glitzy architecture and slick museums, on a careful mix of residential and business projects, on sponsorship of the arts, on an excellent public transport system, and on the reclamation and development of the lakefront. The result might be too clean and safe for some tastes, like "New York run by the Swiss" as Peter Ustinov commented, but with some pride its people maintain a modest motto – Toronto is, they say, "a city that works".

Huge new shopping malls reflect the economic successes of the last two or three decades, a boom that has attracted immigrants from all over the world, transforming an overwhelmingly anglophone city into a cosmopolitan one, with some sixty significant minorities. Its multi-culturalism goes far deeper than an extravagant diversity of restaurants and a slightly self-conscious ethnicity of street signs ("Chinatown", "Little Italy" etc): the city schools, for instance, have extensive "Heritage Language" programmes, positively encouraging the maintenance of the immigrants' first cultures. Getting the feel of Toronto's diversity is one of the great pleasures of a stay, but the city is replete with attention-grabbing sights as well, of which the most celebrated is perhaps the **CN**

**Tower**, the world's tallest free-standing structure. Other attractions include the wide-ranging collection of the **Royal Ontario Museum**, a good selection of European and Canadian painting at the **Art Gallery of Ontario**, the mock-Gothic extravagances of **Casa Loma**, a lavish **Science Centre**, and a replica of the colonial settlement where Toronto began, **Fort York**. And at the day's end, in addition to the excellent restaurants, the city offers one of Canada's most energetic rock and performing arts scenes.

## A brief history of Toronto

Situated on the approximate triangle of land separating Lake Ontario and Georgian Bay, **Toronto** was on one of the three early portage routes to the northwest, its name taken from the Huron for "place of meeting". The first European to visit the district was the French explorer Etienne Brulé in 1615, but it wasn't until the middle of the eighteenth century that the French made a serious effort to control the area with the development of a simple settlement and stockade, **Fort Rouillé**. The British pushed the French from the northern shore of Lake Ontario in 1759, but then chose to ignore the site for almost forty years until the arrival of hundreds of Loyalist settlers in the aftermath of the American Revolution. In 1791 the British divided their remaining American territories into two, Upper and Lower Canada, each with its own legislative councils. The first capital of Upper Canada was Niagara-on-the-Lake, but this was too near the American border and the province's new lieutenant governor, **John Graves Simcoe**, moved his administration to the relative safety of Toronto in 1793, calling the new settlement **York**. Simcoe had grand classical visions of colonial settlement, but even he was exasperated by the conditions of frontier life – "the city's site was better calculated for a frog pond . . . than for the residence of human beings". Soon nicknamed "Muddy York", the capital was little more than a village when, in 1812, the Americans attacked and burnt the main buildings.

In the early nineteenth century, effective economic and political power lay in the hands of an anglophilic oligarchy christened the **Family Compact** by the radical polemicists of the day. Their most vociferous opponent was a radical Scot, **William Lyon Mackenzie**, who promulgated his views both in his newspaper, the *Colonial Advocate*, and as a member of the Legislative Assembly. Mackenzie became the first mayor of **Toronto**, as the town was renamed in 1834, but the radicals were defeated in the elections two years later and a frustrated Mackenzie drifted towards the idea of armed revolt. In 1837, he staged the **Upper Canadian insurrection**, a badly organised uprising of a few hundred farmers, who marched down Yonge Street, fought a couple of half-hearted skirmishes and then melted away. Mackenzie fled across the border and two of the other ringleaders were executed, but the British parliament, mindful of their earlier experiences in New England, moved to liberalise Upper Canada's administration instead of taking reprisals. In 1841, they granted Canada responsible government, reuniting the two provinces in a loose confederation, prefiguring the final union of 1867 when Upper Canada was redesignated Ontario. Even Mackenzie was pardoned and allowed to return.

By the end of the nineteenth century Toronto had become a major manufacturing centre dominated by a conservative mercantile elite who were exceedingly loyal to British interests and maintained a strong Protestant tradition. Well into this century Sunday was preserved as a "day of rest" – *Eaton's* store even drew its curtains to prevent Sabbath window-shopping. For all its capital status, until the 1950s the city was strikingly provincial by comparison with Montréal, but the opening of the St Lawrence Seaway in 1959 gave the place a kick, and the complexion of Toronto changed completely with the arrival of immigrant communities. More recently, Toronto was an indirect beneficiary of the assertion of francophone identity in Québec, as many of Montréal's anglophone-dominated financial institutions and big businesses transferred their operations to the Ontario capital.

> The Toronto area telephone code is ☎416.

# Arrival, information and city transport

Toronto's main **airport**, Lester Pearson International, is about 25km northwest of the city centre. The volunteer-run **Travellers' Aid** desk (daily 9am–10pm; ☎676-2868) will telephone to book accommodation at no charge, and can often get hotel discounts of up to fifteen percent. From outside the terminal building, an express **bus** service takes about forty minutes to reach downtown (every 20min 6–1am, hourly 1–5am), dropping passengers at all the major hotels. Most of the drivers are also prepared to stop near less obvious destinations – just ask. Tickets can be purchased at the kiosk by the bus stop or from the driver. A one-way fare costs $10, a return $17.25, and there's no expiry date. There's also a **limo** service to the centre leaving from beside the bus platform, a shared taxi system that costs about $25 per person; limos only leave when they're full. **Taxis** charge about $35.

*City Express Airline* flights from Montréal, Ottawa and London, Ontario, land at the smaller **Toronto Island Airport**, which is by the lakeshore close to downtown. From here, there's a minibus service to Union Railway Station.

Well connected to most of the major towns of eastern Canada, Toronto's **bus station** is conveniently situated downtown on Elizabeth Street, near the junction of Bay and Dundas. The nearest subway station is five minutes' walk east at Yonge and Dundas. The **Union Railway Station** is also in the downtown core, at the junction of York Street and Front Street West, with regular services from the larger cities of Ontario and Québec, supplemented by more occasional trains from the Maritime Provinces, the Prairies and Vancouver. Union Station is at the heart of Metropolitan Toronto's public transport system.

## Information

The Metropolitan Toronto Convention and Visitors Association (MTCVA) operate a number of **information kiosks** across the city, with a main desk just outside the Eaton shopping centre (daily 9.30am–5.30pm), at the corner of Dundas and Yonge. The other all-year kiosk is at the Skyplace in the Skydome (event days 9.30am–7.30pm, non-event days 9.30am–6.30pm), off Front Street West at John, and there are seasonal kiosks at the Royal Ontario Museum and Toronto City Hall (late June to Labour Day daily 9am–7pm). The **MTCVA office** is by the lakeshore, on the fifth floor of the Queen's Quay complex, 207 Queen's Quay West, near the southern end of York Street (Mon–Fri 8.30am–5pm; ☎416-368-9821 or ☎1-800-363-1990). All these outlets provide a comprehensive range of free information, including city maps, a *Ride Guide* to the transport system, accommodation listings in the *Annual Visitor's Guide*, and entertainment details in the monthly magazine *Where*. Theatre and concert tickets are also available at the Eaton kiosk. In addition, the **Ontario Travel Centre** (Mon–Fri 10am–9pm, Sat 9.30am–6pm & Sun noon–5pm), inside the Eaton shopping centre, has an excellent range of information on all the province's major attractions and provides free road maps and an accommodation book listing nearly all of Ontario's hotels.

## Orientation and transport

Toronto's downtown core is sandwiched between Front Street to the south, Bloor to the north, Spadina to the west and Jarvis to the east. **Yonge Street** is the main north–south artery: principal street numbers start and names change from "West" to "East" from here. To appreciate the transition between the different neighbourhoods, it's best

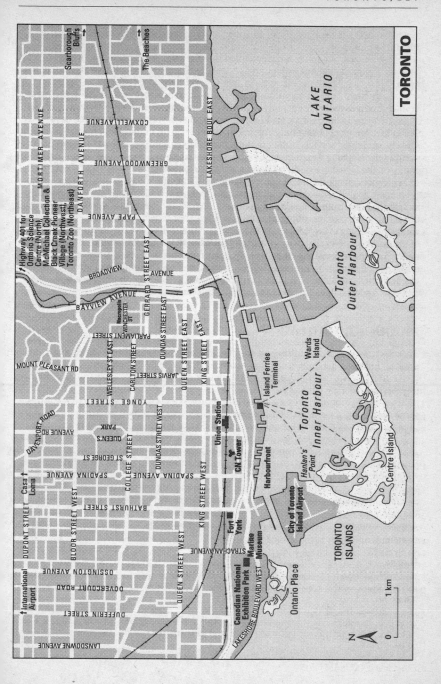

TORONTO

LAKE ONTARIO

Scarborough Bluffs
The Beaches

COXWELL AVENUE
GREENWOOD AVENUE
LAKESHORE BOUL EAST

↑ Highway 401 for
Ontario Science
Centre (North),
McMichael Collection &
Black Creek Pioneer
Village (Northwest),
Toronto Zoo (Northeast)

DANFORTH AVENUE
MORTIMER AVENUE

PAPE AVENUE

BROADVIEW AVENUE

BAYVIEW AVENUE

GERRARD STREET EAST

Necropolis
WINCHESTER ST

PARLIAMENT STREET

DUNDAS STREET EAST

QUEEN STREET EAST

KING STREET EAST

Toronto Outer Harbour

Wards Island

Island Ferries Terminal

Toronto Inner Harbour

MOUNT PLEASANT RD

WELLESLEY ST EAST

CARLTON STREET

JARVIS STREET

YONGE STREET

QUEEN'S PARK

ST GEORGE ST

COLLEGE STREET

DUNDAS STREET WEST

Union Station

CN Tower

Harbourfront

Hanlan's Point

Centre Island

DAVENPORT ROAD

AVENUE ROAD

SPADINA AVENUE

SPADINA AVENUE

KING STREET WEST

City of Toronto Island Airport

Casa Loma

DUPONT STREET

BATHURST STREET

BLOOR STREET WEST

KING STREET WEST

Fort York

Marine Museum

STRACHAN AVENUE

TORONTO ISLANDS

↑ International Airport

OSSINGTON AVENUE

DOVERCOURT ROAD

QUEEN STREET WEST

Canadian National Exhibition Park

Ontario Place

DUFFERIN STREET

LANSDOWNE AVENUE

LAKESHORE BOULEVARD WEST

N

0          1 km

to **walk** round the centre – Front to Bloor is about 2km; Spadina to Jarvis 1km. In an attempt to protect shoppers from Ontario's climate, there's also an enormous sequence of pedestrianised shopping arcades called the **Toronto Underground**, which begins beneath Union Station and twists up as far as the Eaton centre – the MTCVA has free maps.

Fast, frequent and efficient, the city's **public transport** is run by the Toronto Transit Commission (TTC) and is pivoted on a simple **subway** system. One line crosses from east to west along Bloor and the other forms a loop heading north from Union Station, along University Avenue and Yonge. The immediate area around each subway station is serviced by complementary **buses** and **streetcars**. There's also a small **Light Railway Transit** (LRT) which heads south and west from Union Station to points on the lakeshore as far as the southern end of Spadina.

Main services operate from 6am to midnight (9am on Sundays), with a limited night-time operation. You can buy single **tickets** from bus and trolley drivers and single metallic **tokens** from subway stations for $1.20. More economically, a batch of eight tickets or tokens can be bought for $8. Each ticket or token entitles passengers to one complete journey of any length on the TTC system. If this involves more than one sort of transport, it's necessary to get a paper **transfer** at the point of entry; there are automatic machines providing transfers at subway stations. A **day pass** costs $5 and provides one adult with unlimited TTC travel all day on Saturdays and after 9.30am on weekdays. On Sundays, the same pass covers two adults. For the physically disabled, TTC has a special door-to-door service, **Wheel-Trans** (☎393-4111).

# Accommodation

Toronto has no shortage of **places to stay**, and only during major festivals and exhibitions is there any difficulty in finding somewhere reasonably convenient. In addition to the tourist information offices, help in finding a hotel place can be obtained from the free *Accommodation Toronto* service (☎369-9200).

Most of Toronto's **hotels** are characterless skyscrapers with standardised furnishings and a range of charges that scrupulously reflects floor space. Prices are high, but there's considerable seasonal variation and some hotels will offer discounts if you stay for a few days and are prepared to haggle. Compared to other North American cities of comparable size, Toronto has surprisingly few **motels**. However, there are a cluster on the west side of town along Lake Shore Boulevard West, near Humber Bay Park, which benefit from cool lake breezes in summer. The best of these are listed below. If you're strapped for cash, it's best to use one of the **Bed and Breakfast** agencies we've listed, or try a guesthouse, hostel or – from mid-May to August – one of the university colleges. There are no **campgrounds** near downtown Toronto and without your own transport the five sites on the outskirts are virtually impossible to reach.

## Hotels

**Bond Place Hotel**, 65 Dundas St East (☎362-6061). Popular with package-tour operators and ideally located, just a couple of minutes' walk from the Eaton Centre. From $80; weekend reductions.

**Delta Chelsea Inn**, 33 Gerrard St West (☎595-1975). Close to the Eaton centre, this is the biggest hotel in town with excellent leisure facilities, including a swimming pool, gymnasium, sauna and child-care programme. The sumptuous rooms are a comparative bargain at $160. Substantial weekend discounts.

**Executive Inn**, 621 King St West (☎362-7441). Cheap and rather like a motel; near Bathurst and King; doubles from $65.

**Journey's End Hotel**, 111 Lombard St (☎367-5555). Part of a drearily uniform chain; doubles from $80.

**The Royal York Hotel**, 100 Front St (☎368-2511). Finished in 1927, the *Royal York* was, at the time, the largest hotel in the British Empire and retains much of its original grandeur. Rooms aren't as expensive as you'd expect, with singles from $140, doubles from $160.

**Selby**, 592 Sherbourne St (☎921-3142). One of the few hotels with some character, the 67-room *Selby* prides itself on its Victorian ambience, and is popular with gay men; from $50.

**Strathcona Hotel**, 60 York St (☎363-3321). A couple of minutes' walk from Union Station; reasonable rooms from $65; weekend discounts.

**Victoria**, 56 Yonge St (☎363-1666). Sandwiched between the tower blocks at the southern end of Yonge, this small hotel has rooms from $95.

**The Westin Harbour Castle**, 1 Harbour Square (☎869-1600). A tower block right on the edge of Lake Ontario, opposite the Toronto Islands. Facilities include an indoor pool, saunas and a jogging track, whilst a revolving rooftop restaurant provides fine views over the city and lake. Rooms from $130; substantial weekend discounts.

**The Whitehouse Hotel**, 76 Church St (☎362-7491). A small hotel near the southern end of Church Street, with rooms from only $55.

## Guesthouses

**Amsterdam**, 209 Carlton St (☎921-9797). Near Ontario Street, with doubles from $60 including breakfast.

**Casa Loma Inn**, 21 Walmer Rd (☎924-4540). Singles from $38, doubles from $50; non-smokers only.

**Grayona Tourist Home**, 1546 King St West (☎535-5443). An agreeable place overlooking Lake Ontario, 3km west of the centre near Roncesvalles; singles from $35, doubles from $45.

**Karabanow Tourist Home**, 9 Spadina Rd (☎923-4004). Near the Spadina subway, with simple rooms from $30.

## Motels

**Beach Motel**, 2183 Lake Shore Blvd West (☎259-3296). Doubles from $60.

**Hillcrest Motel**, 2143 Lake Shore Blvd West (☎255-7711). Doubles from $55.

**Inn on the Lake**, 1926 Lake Shore Blvd West (☎766-4392). Doubles from $60.

**North American Motel**, 2147 Lake Shore Blvd West (☎255-1127). Doubles from $60.

## Bed and breakfast agencies

**At Home-in-the Beach Guest Homes**, 237 Lee Ave (☎690-9688). Small agency that specialises in providing rooms in the Beaches area, with doubles from $50.

**Beaches Bed and Breakfast**, 174 Waverley Rd (☎699-0818). Singles in the Beaches area from $40, doubles around $60.

**Bed and Breakfast Homes of Toronto**, College Park Post Office, 444 Yonge St (☎363-6362). Singles from $35, doubles from $45.

**Downtown Association of Bed and Breakfast Guest Houses**, PO Box 190, Station B, Toronto (☎977-6841 or ☎598-4562; try to ring between 9.30am & noon). Rooms in renovated Victorian homes. Singles $45–$60; doubles $55–$75; non-smokers only.

**Metropolitan Bed and Breakfast Registry**, Suite 269, 615 Mt Pleasant Rd (☎964-2566). Premises all over the city; singles from $35, doubles from $45.

**Toronto Bed and Breakfast Inc**, Box 269, 253 College St (☎588-8800). At the top end of the market; doubles from $55 to $85.

## Hostels and college rooms

**Admiral House**, 32–34 Admiral Rd (☎923-9233). Near St George subway station; rents out a handful of dormitory rooms; $40–50.

**The Neill Wycik College Hotel**, 96 Gerrard St East (☎977-2320). The 250 rooms here are small, but the location is excellent. Singles $38, doubles $41–49.

**Toronto International Youth Hostel**, 223 Church St (☎368-0207). Located in the heart of the city at Dundas and Church, three blocks east of the main entrance to the Eaton centre on Yonge. There are some 200 beds here, divided into rooms of between 4 and 10, with a coin laundry and a kitchen. Reservations are advised in the summer, and required for groups of more than 6 all year. Members $15; $19 for non-members.

**University of Toronto Residence Services**, Room 240, Simcoe Hall, 27 Kings College Circle (☎978-8735). Total of 800 rooms at various sites. Doubles from $40.

**Victoria University**, 140 Charles St (☎585-4524). One block south of Bloor, with singles at $40–48 and doubles at $58–64, including breakfast.

**YWCA**, 80 Woodlawn Ave East (☎923-8454). Located off Yonge St, near Summerhill subway. There are 115 rooms with singles at $35 and doubles at $50; women only.

## Campgrounds

**Glen Rouge Campground**, on Hwy 2 to the east of Port Union Rd (☎392-2541). On the edge of the township of Scarborough. From $12; open May–Oct.

**Indian Line Tourist Campground**, Indian Line Rd (☎678-1223). Closest campground to the centre, in the Clairville Conservation Area, near the junction of Steeles Avenue West and Hwy 427. From $12; open mid-May to mid-Oct.

### TORONTO'S NEIGHBOURHOODS

One of Toronto's most striking features is its division into distinct **neighbourhoods**, many of them based on ethnic origin, others defined by sexual preference or income. Bilingual street signs identify some of these neighbourhoods, but architecturally they are often indistinguishable from their surroundings. The following run-down will help you get the most from the city's demographic mosaic, whether you want to shop, eat or just take in the atmosphere.

**The Beaches**, lying along and south of Queen St East between Woodbine and Victoria, is a prosperous suburb with chic boutiques and a sandy beach trimmed by a popular boardwalk.

**Cabbagetown**, just to the east of Yonge St, roughly bounded by Gerard St East on its south side, Wellesley to the north and Sumach to the east, is renowned for its Victorian housing, now occupied by a mixture of haut bourgeois and urban poor. It's supposed to take its name from the district's nineteenth-century immigrants who filled their tiny front gardens with cabbages.

**Chinatown** is concentrated along Dundas between Bay and Spadina, and along Spadina to King. One of the most distinctive of Toronto's neighbourhoods, it has a multitude of crowded restaurants and stores, selling anything from porcelain and jade to traditional herbs and pickled seaweed.

**The Gay and Lesbian Village** is around Church and Wellesley.

**Greektown**, along Danforth Avenue, between Pape and Woodbine.

**Kensington Market**, just north of Dundas between Spadina and Augusta, is the most ethnically diverse part of town, based on a combination of Portuguese, West Indian and Jewish Canadians, who pack the streets with a plethora of tiny shops and open-air stalls.

**Little India** is along Gerrard St East, one block west of Coxwell.

**Little Italy** runs along St Clair Avenue West between Bathurst and Lansdowne.

**Queen St West**, between University and Spadina, is a strip of old warehouses, factories and shops that is now the haunt of students and punks. This is a good area for cheap bars and restaurants, secondhand clothes and books.

**Yorkville**, situated just above Bloor between Yonge and Avenue Rd, was vaguely "alternative" in the 1960s, with regular appearances by the figureheads of the counter culture, notably Gordon Lightfoot and Joni Mitchell. Today, it's the home of some of Toronto's most expensive clothes shops and art galleries.

# Downtown Toronto

Toronto evolved from a lakeside settlement, but its growth was sporadic and often unplanned, resulting in a cityscape that can strike the visitor as a random mix of the run-down and the new. This apparent disarray, combined with the city's muggy summers, means that most newcomers to Toronto spend their time hopping from sight to sight on the public transport system, rather than walking the streets, and there's no doubt that if you've only got a day or two to spare, that's the way to get a grip on the city. However, if you've the time to get below the surface, the best thing to do is stroll

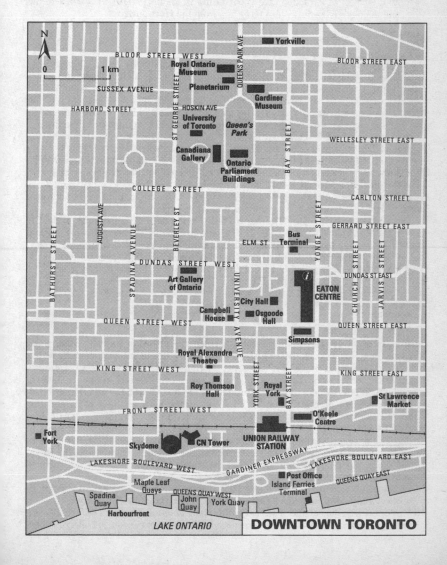

through downtown Toronto, and the logical place to start is the **CN Tower**, from where you can take the lie of the land for miles around. Nearby **Union Station**, hub of the city's public transport system, lies on the edge of the **business** district, whose tower blocks march up Yonge as far as Queen Street, where they give way to the main **shopping** area, revolving around the enormous Eaton Centre. To the west of this commercial zone there's **Chinatown** and the **Art Gallery of Ontario**; to the northwest, along University Avenue, there's the most obviously English-influenced area of town around **Queen's Park**, incorporating the Ontario Parliament building, the University of Toronto and the city's major museum, the **Royal Ontario**. On the periphery of central Toronto the principal attractions are **Casa Loma** in the north, **Old Fort York** to the west, and the city's **islands**, a short ferry hop from the **Harbourfront**.

## The CN Tower and around

The obligatory start to a Toronto visit is to take your place in the queue at the foot of the minaret-thin **CN Tower** (July–Aug Mon–Sat 9am–midnight, Sun to 10pm; Sept–June daily 10am–10pm; $10), which tapers to a point 553.33 metres above the waterfront. Tourists are whisked up its outside in leg-liquefying glass-fronted elevators to the *Sky Pod* viewing platform at 340 metres, from where it's another 100 metres to the *Space Deck* (an extra $2) and views as far as Niagara Falls and Buffalo. Timorous souls can join the schoolkids in the *Tour of the Universe* show ($13) at the base of the tower.

Next door to the CN Tower is the home of the Blue Jays baseball team and the Argonauts football squad – the magnificent **Skydome** complex, which despite housing a colossal *McDonalds* and hosting major concerts, has been a financial disaster in its first two years of operation. Skydome **tours** (daily 9am–6pm; $7) give you a chance to marvel at the retractable roof – taking twenty minutes to cover no less than eight acres of turf and terrace – and the world's largest video replay screen, but there's not much point going in if you're not getting some action for your money.

The same goes for the **Roy Thomson Hall** (3 tours daily; $3), just north of the CN Tower at 60 Simcoe Street. Home of the Toronto Symphony Orchestra, it was finished in 1982 to a design by Arthur Erickson that looks like an upturned soup bowl by day, but at night is transformed as the glass-panelled walls cast light over the sidewalks. This is not the most engrossing area of downtown Toronto, but for a good selection of contemporary art, visit **Art at 80** (Tues–Sat 11am–6pm), a few minutes' walk west of the Roy Thomson Hall at 80 Spadina Avenue, where no fewer than fifteen galleries are squeezed under one roof.

## The banking district

To the east of the CN Tower, the Beaux Arts splendour of **Union Railway Station** and the matching **Royal York** Hotel mark the boundary of the banking district, whose bizarre juxtapositions of old buildings and high-rises are due to one of Toronto's stranger city ordinances. Toronto's buildings have been decreed to have a notional maximum altitude; owners of historic properties are not allowed to extend their buildings, but they are permitted to sell the empty space between their roofs and this notional maximum to the builders of new structures, who may add this volume of air to that maximum, thereby creating the skyscrapers that the ordinance would seem to forbid. The arrangement brings the best in neither the old nor the new, but some of the high-rises are undeniably impressive, such as the colossal twin towers of the **Royal Bank Plaza**, at Bay and Front Street, and the reflective black blocks of the **Toronto Dominion Centre**, along Wellington Street West.

On the south side of Wellington, the **IBM Tower**, fringed by Joe Fafard's sculpture of seven grazing cows, contains a **Gallery of Inuit Art** (Mon–Fri 8am–6pm & Sat–Sun 10am–4pm; free), one of the most exquisite collections of its sort. The exhibits are owned by the Dominion Bank, who commissioned a panel of experts to collect the best of postwar Inuit art in 1965. Their haul features some simple and forceful stone carvings by Johnny Inukpuk, whose impressionistic style contrasts with the precision of the *Wonderful Migration* by Joe Talirumili, in which the rowers crane forward in eagerness and anxiety. Even more detailed is the incised caribou antler from Cape Dorset, on which natural dyes pick out a cartoon strip of Inuit life.

## City Hall, the Eaton Centre and around

One of the most distinctive of Toronto's landmarks lies across Queen Street, to the north of the banking zone – **Nathan Phillips Square**. Laid out by the Finnish architect Viljo Revell, the square is overlooked by his **City Hall**, whose curved glass and concrete towers bracket a sort of central mushroom, in turn fronted by *The Archer*, a Henry Moore sculpture that resembles a giant kidney. Revell won all sorts of awards for this project, which seemed the last word in thrusting dynamism but has faded into a desolate symbol of 1960s urban planning. On a positive note, it is at least associated with political change – its sponsor, Nathan Phillips was Toronto's first Jewish mayor. Had Phillips' grand scheme been carried out fully, the city would have lost the **Old City Hall**, on the east side of the square, a flamboyant pseudo-Romanesque building, whose front is dominated by a sequence of thick stone arches beneath a copper-green roof.

### THE EATON CENTRE AND THE THOMSON GALLERY

At the back of the Old City Hall, the **Eaton Centre** stretches south from its main entrance at Dundas and Yonge all the way to Queen Street, its four-storey assortment of shops and restaurants spread out underneath a glass and steel arched roof. Timothy Eaton, an Ulster immigrant, opened his first store here in 1869, and his cash-only, fixed-price, money-back-guarantee trading revolutionised the Canadian market. Soon a Canadian institution, Eaton kept a grip on the pioneer settlements in the west through his mail-order catalogue, known as the "homesteader's bible" – or the "wish book" amongst the native people. The company runs a mail-order business and has department stores in all of Canada's big cities, but recently it's tried to keep ahead of the competition by investing heavily in shopping complexes like this one.

At the southern end of the Eaton Centre, a first-floor walkway crosses Queen Street into *Simpsons* store, where, on the eighth floor, you'll find the **Thomson Gallery** (Mon–Sat 11am–4pm; $2), an excellent, manageable introduction to many of Canada's finest artists, especially the Group of Seven (see p.230). Highlights include an impressive selection of paintings by Lawren Harris, like his almost surrealistic *Lake Superior*, and a small selection of paintings by JEH MacDonald, whose *Rowan Berries* of 1922 stands out. Tom Thomson, the main inspiration of the Seven, is represented by the vivid *Autumn's Garland*, a blotchy contrast with AY Jackson's smooth-flowing *Yellowknife Country*, in which a mass of trees swirls above a heaving, purplish earth. A contemporary of the Group of Seven, Emily Carr was famous for her paintings of west coast Indian villages and the totemic figures she developed as a symbol of native culture. *Thunderbird Camp River BC* and *Thunderbird* are good examples of her later style, a marked progression from the fastidiousness of the early *Gitwangak, Queen Charlotte Islands*.

The gallery's assortment of early and mid-nineteenth century Canadian and Canada-based artists is often distinctly second rate, but there are exceptions, such as the curiously unflattering *Portrait of Joseph Brant* by William Berczy. Interesting in a different way is the series by the artist-explorer **Paul Kane**, whose paintings show a conflict of subject and style that highlights the achievement of the Group of Seven in finding an indigenous manner – his *Landscape in the Foothills with Buffalo Resting*, for example, looks more like a placid German valley than the prairies. Born in Ireland in 1810, Kane first emigrated to Toronto in the early 1820s, but returned to Europe at the age of

## GLENN GOULD

In the 1970s, anyone passing the Eaton department store around 9pm on any day of the year might have seen the door unlocked for a distracted-looking figure swaddled in over-coat, scarves, gloves and hat. This character, making his way to a recording studio set up for his exclusive use inside the shop, was perhaps the most famous citizen of Toronto and the most charismatic pianist in the world – **Glenn Gould**.

Not the least remarkable thing about Gould was that very few people outside the CBS recording crew would ever hear him play live. In 1964, aged just 32, he had retired from the concert platform, partly out of a distaste for the accidental qualities of any live perfor-mance, partly out of hatred for the cult of the virtuoso. Yet no pianist ever provided more material for the mythologisers. He possessed a memory so prodigious that none of his acquaintances was ever able to find a piece of music he could not instantly play perfectly, but he loathed much of the standard piano repertoire, dismissing romantic composers such as Chopin, Liszt and Rachmaninoff as little more than showmen. Dauntingly cere-bral in his tastes and playing style, he was nonetheless an ardent fan of Barbra Streisand – an esteem that was fully reciprocated – and once wrote an essay titled "In Search of Petula Clark". He lived at night and kept in touch by phoning his friends in the small hours of the morning, talking for so long that his monthly phone bill ran into thousands of dollars. Detesting all bloodsports (a category in which he placed concert perfor-mances), he would terrorise anglers on Lake Simcoe by buzzing them in his motorboat. He travelled everywhere with bags full of medicines and would never allow anyone to shake his hand, yet soaked his arms in almost scalding water before playing in order to get his circulation going. At the keyboard he sang loudly to himself, swaying back and forth on a creaky little chair made for him by his father – all other pianists sat too high, he insisted. And even in a heatwave, he was always dressed as if a blizzard were immi-nent. To many of his colleagues Gould's eccentricities were maddening, but what mattered was that nobody could play like Glenn Gould. As one exasperated conductor put it, "the nut's a genius".

Gould's first recording, Bach's *Goldberg Variations*, was released in 1956, became the bestselling classical record of that year, and has remained available ever since. Soon after, he became the first western musician to play in the Soviet Union, where his reputa-tion spread so quickly that for his final recital over a thousand people were allowed to stand in the aisles of the Leningrad hall. On his debut in Berlin, the leading German critic described him as "a young man in a strange sort of trance", whose "technical ability borders on the fabulous". The technique always dazzled, but Gould's fiercely wayward intelligence made his interpretations controversial, as can be gauged from the fact that Leonard Bernstein, conducting Gould on one occasion, felt obliged to inform the audi-ence that what they were about to hear was the pianist's responsibility, not his. Most notoriously of all, he had a very low opinion of Mozart's abilities – and went so far as to record the Mozart sonatas in order to demonstrate that Wolfgang Amadeus died too late rather than too soon.

Gould's legacy of recordings is not confined to music. He made a trilogy of radio documentaries on the theme of solitude – *The Quiet in the Land*, about Canada's Mennonites, *The Latecomers*, about the inhabitants of Newfoundland, and *The Idea of North*, for which he taped interviews with people who, like himself, spent much of their time amid Canada's harshest landscapes. Just as Gould's Beethoven, Bach and Mozart sounded like nobody else's, these were documentaries like no others, each a complex weave of voices spliced and overlaid in compositions that are overtly musical in construction. However, Gould's eighty-odd piano recordings are the basis of his enduring popularity, and nearly all of them have been reissued on CD, spanning western keyboard music from Orlando Gibbons to Arnold Schoenberg. One of the most poignant is his second version of the *Goldberg*, the last record to be issued before his sudden death in 1982 at the age of 50 – the age at which he had said he would give up playing the piano entirely.

thirty, where, ironically enough, he was so impressed by an exhibition of paintings on the American Indian that he promptly decided to move back to Canada. In 1846, he finally wangled himself a place on a westward-bound fur-trading expedition and started an epic journey – travelling from Thunder Bay to Edmonton by canoe, crossing the Rockies by horse, and finally returning to Toronto two years after setting out. During his time away Kane made some 700 sketches which he then proceeded to paint onto canvas, paper and cardboard, and in 1859 published *Wanderings of an Artist among the Indian Tribes of North America*, the story of his journey. It includes this account of Christmas dinner at Fort Edmonton: "At the head, before Mr Harriett, was a large dish of boiled buffalo hump; at the foot smoked a boiled buffalo calf . . . one of the most esteemed dishes among the epicures of the interior. My pleasing duty was to help a dish of mouffle, or dried moose nose (while) the worthy priest helped the buffalo tongue and Mr Randall cut up the beaver's tails. The centre of the table was graced with piles of potatoes, turnips and bread conveniently placed, so that each could help himself without interrupting the labours of his companions. Such was our jolly Christmas dinner at Edmonton".

## WEST OF CITY HALL

Just to the west of Nathan Phillips square, along Queen Street, stands **Osgoode Hall**, a Neoclassical pile built for the Law Society of Upper Canada early in the nineteenth century. Looking like a cross between a Greek temple and an English country house, it's protected by a wrought iron fence and gates, designed to keep cows and horses off the lawn. The elegant Georgian mansion on the opposite side of University Avenue is **Campbell House** (June–Sept Mon–Fri 9.30am–4.30pm & Sat–Sun noon–4.30pm; Oct–May Mon–Fri 9.30–11.30am & 2.30–4.30pm; $2), built on Adelaide Street for Sir William Campbell, Chief Justice and Speaker of the Legislative Assembly – it was transported here in 1972. Guides in contemporary costume lead hourly tours of the period interior and provide a well-researched overview of early nineteenth-century Toronto, illustrated by a detailed model of the town in 1825.

## The Art Gallery of Ontario

Just west of University Avenue, hemmed in by the bustle of **Chinatown**, looms the lumpen concrete home of the **Art Gallery of Ontario** – or AGO (Tues–Sun 11am–5.30pm, plus Mon 11am–5.30pm June–Sept; $4.50, Wed free 5.30pm–9pm) – a place renowned both for its excellent temporary exhibitions and for its comprehensive collection of international art.

Straight ahead of the information desk, on the left side of Walker Court, are two rooms of **nineteenth- and early twentieth-century** paintings, including a brace of Picassos, Degas' archetypal *Woman Drying Herself after a Bath*, Renoir's screaming pink *Concert* of 1918, and Monet's wonderful *Vetheuil in Summer*, with its hundreds of tiny jabs of colour. To the rear and to the right of Walker Court, the assembly of **Old Masters** contains Pieter Bruegel the Younger's incident-packed *Peasants' Wedding* and his unusual *Proverbs*, featuring such strange subjects as "He pisses against the moon". Close by, there's an extraordinary fifteenth-century *Expulsion of the Money Changers* by the Master of the Kress Epiphany, the belligerent Christ dispelling the uglies with a length of knotted rope. An *Adam and Eve* by Lucas Cranach creates a disconcerting set of colour contrasts, a strong green background set against the crystalline white of the two figures and the silver-white of the forbidden fruit.

On the first floor, the strong suit of the **Canadian Collection** in the west wing is the cross-section of work from the **Group of Seven** (see box on next page) and their contemporaries, where the key paintings are accompanied by a wealth of background information. One of the most distinctive artists of the Group of Seven was **Lawren**

**Harris**, whose *Above Lake Superior* of 1922 is a pivotal work – nothing he had done before had the same clarity of conception, with its bare birch stumps framing a dark mountain beneath Art Deco clouds. Nearby, his large and brilliant *Leyton Mountains* has a mass of frosty ice spitting into the sky above deep green mountains and a silvery green lake, an ejaculatory image if ever there were one.

**Fred Varley**, another founder member, preferred softer images and subtler colours, exemplified by the sticky-looking brushstrokes of *Moonlight after Rain*, whereas his friend **JEH MacDonald** was fond of dark and rich effects, his panoramic *Falls, Montréal River* setting turbulent rapids beside hot-coloured hillsides. A sample of **AY Jackson**'s work includes the characteristically carpet-like surface of *Algoma Rocks, Autumn, 1923*, while **AJ Casson**'s intimate watercolour *Hillside Village* offers a break from the monumentalism of the rest of the Seven. **Emily Carr**, represented by several works here, was a great admirer of the Seven, but she was never accepted as a member despite her obvious abilities. Perhaps the most famous of all Canadian paintings is here too – *The West Wind* by the greatly influential **Tom Thomson**, who was the first to approach wilderness landscapes with the determination of an explorer. It accompanies less familiar but no less powerful works, including a Cubist-influenced panel, *Autumn Foliage 1915*.

The AGO'S **modern art** collection hangs in an adjoining corridor, a cramped space that's due to be relieved by a new wing in 1993. In the meantime, watch out for Marc Chagall's tilted Orthodox church in *Over Vitebsk*, Augustus John's sensual *Marchesa Casati*, Picasso's classically cubist *Seated Woman*, and an alarming *Portrait of Doctor Hendrik Stadelmann* by Otto Dix. The corridor continues past the **Henry Moore Sculpture Centre**, the world's largest assembly of pieces by HM, which displays a

---

## THE GROUP OF SEVEN

In the fall of 1912, a commercial artist by the name of **Tom Thomson** returned from an extended trip to the Mississauga country, north of Georgian Bay, with a bag full of sketches that were to add a new momentum to Canadian art. His friends, many of them fellow employees of the art firm of *Grip Ltd* in Toronto, saw Thomson's naturalistic approach to native subject matter as a pointer away from the influence of Europe, declaring the "northland" as the true Canadian "painter's country". World War I and the death of Thomson – who drowned in 1917 – delayed until 1920 the formation of the **Group of Seven**: Franklin H Carmichael, Lawren Harris, AY Jackson, Arthur Lismer, JEH MacDonald, FH Varley and Frank Johnston (later joined by AJ Casson, LL Fitzgerald and Edwin Holgate). Working under the unofficial leadership of Harris, they explored the wilds of Algoma in the 1920s, travelling around in a converted freight car, and later foraged even further afield, from Newfoundland to BC.

They were immediately successful, staging forty shows in eleven years, a triumph due in large part to Harris's many influential contacts. However, there was also a genuine popular response to the intrepid frontiersman element of their aesthetics. Art was a matter of "taking to the road" and "risking all for the glory of a great adventure", as they wrote in 1922, whilst "nature was the measure of a man's stature" according to Lismer. Symbolic of struggle against the elements, the Group's favourite symbol was the lone pine set against the sky, an image whose authenticity was confirmed by reference to the "manly" poetry of Walt Whitman.

The legacy of the Group of Seven is double-edged. On the one hand, they rediscovered the Canadian wilderness and established the autonomy of Canadian art. On the other, their contribution was soon institutionalised, and well into the 1950s it was difficult for Canadian painters to establish an identity that didn't conform to the Group's precepts. Among many practising artists the Group is unpopular, but the Ontario artist Graham Coughtry is generous: "They're the closest we've ever come to having some kind of romantic heroes in Canadian painting".

changing exhibition drawn from some 300 examples of his output, from woodcuts and etchings to bronze and plaster sculptures. The show is dominated by Moore's bombastic abstractions.

On the west side of the AGO, approached along Beverley Street, **The Grange** (Tues & Thurs–Sun noon–4pm, Wed 6–9pm, plus Mon noon–4pm June–Sept) is a Georgian house that's just about worth a peek for its pleasantly restored early nineteenth-century interior; costumed staff, as ever, provide guided tours.

## The Parliament and university

University Avenue cuts north from Dundas to College lined by gleaming tower blocks and overlooked by the pink sandstone mass of the **Ontario Parliament Building** (Mon–Fri 8.30am–5pm, plus Sat & Sun in summer; also frequent guided tours – ring ☎965-4028). Accusations of political corruption have always been ten-a-penny in Ontario, but even so the choice of architect was a surprise, for Richard Waite, the chairman of the appropriate committee, selected himself.

Behind the Parliament Building, modest **Queen's Park** is bordered by the various faculties of the **University of Toronto**, opened in 1843 and the province's most prestigious academic institution. Its older buildings, with their quadrangles, ivy-covered walls and Gothic interiors, deliberately evoke Oxbridge: **Hart House**, on the west side of the park, directly opposite Wellesley Street, is the best example, attached to the **Soldier's Tower**, a memorial to those students who died in both world wars.

## The Royal Ontario Museum

The various buildings of the **Royal Ontario Museum (ROM)**, to the north of Queen's Park, house one of the country's most ambitious collections of fine and applied art, albeit a collection whose intended scope sometimes over-stretches its physical resources. It's basically a jumble of disparate private collections, but there's more than enough first-rank stuff here to fill an afternoon. A combined ticket for the principal collection and the Gardiner Museum costs $6 and entitles visitors to a same-day discount at the **McLaughlin Planetarium**, next to the main block.

The main part of the ROM, at Queen's Park Avenue and Bloor (June–Aug daily 10am–6pm, Tues & Thurs to 8pm; Sept–May closed Mon), starts with two colossal **totem poles** from British Columbia, bolted into the stairwells just beyond the domed entrance hall. Amazing, elemental objects, they're decorated with stylised carvings representing the supernatural animals and birds that were associated with their owners and their particular clan. The best known of native art forms, totem poles were a by-product of European trade – imported metal tools enabled the Indians to increase the size of their carvings, while the fur trade brought both economic prosperity and intense rivalry, from which the totem pole emerged as a symbol of clan status. Production peaked on the Pacific coast in the 1860s, but, mirroring the collapse of the local economy, the art had virtually disappeared by the turn of the century.

On the **first level** of the ROM, you have to plough past a dreary display on the behind-the-scenes work of the museum to get to the exhibits from the **Far East**, including fine Hindu and Buddhist sculptures and a sample of Imperial Chinese applied art, notably a collection of ceramic head cushions and an extraordinary number of snuff bottles made from quartz, bronze, silver, glass – even tangerine skin. However, the highlight here is the monumental Ming Tomb, the only complete example on display in the West. Thought to date from the seventeenth century, the tomb and its archways are guarded by beautifully carved animals and servants. The **second level** deals with the life sciences, featuring several sections on evolution, innumerable stuffed animals, an "interactive" mock-up of a bat cave, and a magnificent set of dinosaur skeletons recovered from the Alberta badlands. The **third level** concentrates on the ancient Mediterranean, though it has a pretty feeble section on European decorative arts.

Across the road, the **Gardiner Museum** (same hours) is the purpose-built home of the stunning ceramics collection of George Gardiner, local businessman turned aesthete. In the Delftware section, look out for the delightful series of seventeenth-century serving plates decorated with portraits of English kings.

Five minutes' walk to the south, immediately west of the Parliament, the **Canadiana Gallery** (Tues–Sun 10am–5pm; free), the ROM's second annexe, has some good examples of early Canadian pottery and an interesting sample of homemade wooden toys, but is noted for the intimate wood-panelled Belanger room, carved in the 1820s and transported here from St-Jean-Port-Joli in Québec.

## Casa Loma and Spadina

A couple of minutes' walk north of Dupont subway station, along Spadina to Davenport Road, a flight of steps leads to Toronto's most bizarre attraction, **Casa Loma** (daily 10am–4pm; $7), an enormous towered and turreted mansion built to the instructions of Sir Henry Pellatt between 1911 and 1914. Every inch the self-made man, Pellatt made a fortune by pioneering the use of hydro-electricity, harnessing the power of Niagara Falls to light Ontario's expanding cities. Determined to construct a house no-one could ignore, Sir Henry gathered furnishings from all over the world and even imported Scottish stonemasons to build the wall around his six-acre property. He spent over three million dollars fulfilling his dream, but business misfortunes and the rising cost of servants forced him to move out in 1923, earning him the nickname of "Pellatt the Plunger". His legacy is a strange mixture of medieval fantasy and early twentieth-century technology: secret passageways and an elevator; claustrophobic wood-panelled rooms confused by gargantuan pipes and plumbing.

Free diagrams of the layout of the house are available at reception – taped commentaries along the suggested route elucidate such mysteries as why Sir Henry took to dressing up in a costume that combined a British colonel's uniform with the attire of a Mohawk chief. The main entrance is on the first floor, near Sir Henry's favourite room, the study, with secret passageways leading to the wine cellar and his wife's suite. Nearby, the Great Hall is a pseudo-Gothic extravagance with a sixty-foot-high, cross-beamed ceiling and enough floor space to accommodate several hundred guests. In a touch worthy of Errol Flynn, the hall is overlooked by a balcony at the end of Pellatt's second-floor bedroom; in a typically odd contrast, the bathroom behind the bedroom is 1910s white marble high-tech, featuring an elaborate multi-nozzled shower.

Next-door **Spadina** (tours Mon–Sat 9.30am–5pm & Sun noon–5pm; $4) is an elegant Victorian property whose modesty is in striking contrast to the pretensions of its neighbour. Until 1980, it was the residence of the Austin family, the descendants of the Irish founder of the Toronto Dominion Bank, and as a result nearly all the contents are genuine antiques. Particular highlights include an inventive and delicate Art Nouveau decorative frieze in the billiard room, an assortment of period chairs designed to accommodate the largest of bustles, and a trap door in the conservatory that allowed the gardeners to come and go unseen by their employers. The open transoms above the doors were inspired by Florence Nightingale, whose much-publicised experiences of sickness in the Crimea had convinced her of the need for a good flow of air.

## The Harbourfront and the islands

In recent years, an ambitious and massively expensive redevelopment programme has transformed **the Harbourfront**, the zone at the southern end of Yonge, into one of the more fashionable parts of the city. It's best reached from Union Station by the LRT, from whose first stop – at **Queen's Quay** and Bay – a pleasant lakeside walkway extends west as far as Spadina, passing chic shops, restaurants, lakeside condominiums, arts centres, office suites and marinas. From beside the walkway, at the foot of York and Yonge, a number of operators run hour-long harbour **boat trips** for about

$10 from May to October. From the bottom of Bay Street, there are also trips on the *PS Trillium*, a 1910 steam paddle-boat (July to mid-Sept, Wed–Sun, 2 daily; $5).

If you're on a tight budget, you can get just as good a view more cheaply from the **Toronto Islands**, the low-lying, crescent-shaped sand banks that protect the city's natural harbour. From the late nineteenth century, the islands were popular with day-tripping Torontonians, who rowed across to enjoy the cool lake breezes and sample some rather odd attractions – including JW Gorman's "diving horses", who would jump into the lake from a high-diving board. Today, the marinas, beaches and amusement areas are run by the Toronto Parks Department, who keep the islands spotless and car-free. There are three main sections, connected by bridges: to the east is **Ward's Island**, a quiet residential area; in the middle, **Centre Island** is the busiest and the most developed; and to the west, **Hanlan's Point**, edging Toronto's tiny Island's Airport, has the best sandy beach – though Lake Ontario is too polluted for swimming.

**Ferries** to the islands leave from the foot of Yonge Street, taking ten minutes to make the crossing and costing $2.25 return. (Ward's Island daily June–Sept 6.35am–11.15pm, at least hourly; Oct–May 6.35am–11pm, at least every 2hr. Hanlan's Point June–Sept daily 8am–9.30pm, at least hourly; Oct–May Mon–Fri, 4 daily. Centre Island June–Sept hourly 9am–10.30pm.)

## West of the Harbourfront: Fort York and Exhibition Park

Modern Toronto improbably traces its origins to the ill-starred **Fort York** (daily 9.30am–5pm; $4.25), built to reinforce British control of Lake Ontario in 1793. It was never properly fortified, partly through lack of funds and partly because it was too remote to command much attention, and within ten years the stockade was in a state of disrepair, even though the township of York had become the capital of Upper Canada. In 1811 the deterioration in Anglo-American relations prompted a refortification, but its main military achievement was entirely accidental. Forced to evacuate the fort in 1812, the British blew up the gunpowder magazine, but underestimated the force of the explosion. They killed 10 of their own number and 250 of the advancing enemy, including the splendidly named American general, Zebulon Pike. After the war, Fort York was refurbished and its garrison – the largest local consumer of supplies – made a considerable contribution to the development of Toronto, as York was renamed in 1834.

Situated a twenty-minute walk west from Union Station, Fort York was opened as a museum in 1934, and is now staffed by guides who provide informative, free tours that take about an hour. The meticulously restored ramparts enclose eight log, stone and brick buildings, notably the elegant **Officers' Quarters** and a **powder magazine**, built with two-metre-thick walls and sparkproof copper and brass fixtures. The **Blue Barracks**, or junior officers' quarters, has a small exhibition of Canadian military artefacts from 1792 to 1967.

From the front entrance of Fort York, it's a five-minute walk to Princes Gate, the grandiose gateway to the grounds of the **Canadian National Exhibition** at Lake Shore Boulevard and Strachan, close to the terminus of the Bathurst streetcar, #511. Used for trade fairs and sports events, the area also has three modest **museums**. The **Hockey Hall of Fame** (daily June–Aug 10am–7pm; Sept–May 10am–4.30pm; $3), a five-minute walk west of Princes Gate, has displays on the history of the game, is the home of the Stanley Cup, and has a special section dedicated to superhero Wayne Gretsky. In the same building, **Canada's Sports Hall of Fame** (same times) has more general exhibits from cycling to rowing. The **Marine Museum of Upper Canada** (Mon–Sat 9.30am–5pm; Sun noon–5pm; $2.50), located in an old barracks close to Princes Gate, concentrates on the development of local shipping.

From beside the Marine Museum, a footbridge crosses Lake Shore Boulevard to **Ontario Place**, a grossly unattractive Disney-style entertainment complex built on three artificial islands.

# Metropolitan Toronto

The satellite suburbs and industrial areas that make up most of **Metropolitan Toronto** are of little appeal, a string of formless settlements sprawling over a largely flat and dreary landscape that extends from Scarborough in the east to Mississauga in the west and north as far as the districts around Steeles Avenue. In all this area, there's only one really distinctive geographic feature, the cliffs that make up the **Scarborough Bluffs**. Yet the metropolitan area and its immediate surrounds are home to several impressive attractions, notably the **Ontario Science Centre**, which comes complete with dozens of interactive science displays, the **McMichael Collection** of the Group of Seven's paintings, and the garish extravagance of Disney's **Wonderland**.

## The Scarborough Bluffs

The **Scarborough Bluffs**, which begin about 5km from the city centre, on the eastern edge of the Beaches, are a sixteen-kilometre line of jagged cliffs that run along the lakeshore, a mixture of ancient sands and clay that have provided geologists with a wealth of information about the last ice age. There are especially good views of the cliffs from **Scarborough Bluffs Park**, at the foot of Midland Avenue, off Kingston Road: take bus #20 east from Main Street subway station, get off at the junction of Midland Avenue and Kingston Road, and it's a two-kilometre walk down to the park.

## Ontario Science Centre

Opened in 1969, the **Ontario Science Centre**, 11km from downtown at 770 Don Mills Road (daily 10am–6pm; $5.50), bills itself as a "vast playground of science" and draws more than one million visitors a year. The centre traces the development of technology through some 700 exhibits, many of which invite participation – staring at strangely coloured Canadian flags until you go dotty, piloting a spacecraft, having your hair raised by a Van der Graaf generator. You could spend a day here on your own, though it's a lot more enjoyable with kids. To get there, take the Bloor Street subway east to Pape, transfer to the Don Mills bus and get off on the Don Mills Road at St Dennis Drive.

## Canada's Wonderland

Located at Vaughan, 30km from downtown and immediately east of Hwy 400 at the Rutherford Road exit, **Canada's Wonderland** (June–Aug daily 10am–10pm; late May & Sept Sat & Sun 10am–8pm; one-day pass $23.95) is Toronto's Disneyworld, a theme park featuring three dozen different rides spread across several different themes such as "Hanna Barbera Land" and the "Medieval Faire". Wonderland's roller-coaster rides are enough to make the strongest stomachs churn, if the kitsch doesn't do it first. By public transport, catch the Wonderland Express GO bus from Yorkdale or York Mills subway station; buses leave every half hour and take forty minutes ($2.50 each way).

## Toronto Zoo

**Toronto Zoo** (daily, summer 9.30am–7pm; winter 9.30am–4.30pm; $7), 40km from downtown near Hwy 401 at Meadowdale Road in Scarborough, covers no less than 710 acres and has over 4000 animals exhibited in simulations of their natural habitats – which in the case of the African species means an enormous wood and glass pavilion. The North American animals are kept in the Rouge River Valley surrounding the main part of the zoo, and they can be visited by monorail ($2 extra).

For access from the city, take the Bloor subway to Kennedy and transfer to bus 86A.

## The McMichael Art Collection

The **McMichael Art Collection** (May–Oct daily 10am–5pm; Nov–April Tues–Sun 11am–4.30pm; $3; free guided tours Wed afternoon) is situated in the commuter township of Kleinburg, roughly 40km northwest of downtown, off Hwy 400. The collection, housed in a series of handsome log and stone buildings in the wooded Humber River valley, was put together by Robert and Signe McMichael, devoted followers of the Group of Seven, and given to the province in 1965. Of particular interest is the Tom Thomson Gallery, featuring many of the small panels the artist painted on location in preparation for the full-sized canvases he worked on back in his studio. Gallery 5, *The Spirit of the Land*, is of similar interest as it concentrates on the early work of the Group as they explored their country from coast to coast. Three other exhibition areas are devoted to Canada's native peoples, including contemporary Indian art and Inuit soapstone carvings and lithographs.

From Toronto, it's only possible to make a day-trip to the McMichael on public transport by taking the subway to Islington, then taking bus #37 to Steeles and Islington (45min), and then catching the 11.40am bus #3 or #3a to Kleinburg (15min), five minutes' walk from the gallery entrance. The only return bus leaves at 5.30pm, so pack a picnic and take a hike in the woods.

# Eating and drinking

Toronto prides itself on the quality and diversity of its cuisine, with over 4000 establishments offering a spectacular range of foods from all over the world. To get the best from the city's kitchens, head for any one of the city's **ethnic neighbourhoods**, where there's an abundance of good **restaurants**, or go to one of the many downtown **restaurant/bars** that have carefully nurtured a good reputation. Toronto's shopping malls are dominated by chain restaurants, most of which offer bland and basic fare, and a similar criticism also applies to most of the city's hotels, whose snack bar/restaurants serve mundane food at prices that roughly parallel the hotel's tariff. The city does have a couple of places with Canadian menus, where the emphasis is on fish and wild animal meat, but there's no real distinctive local cuisine – if there is a Toronto dish, it's hamburger, fries and salad.

Prices range from the deluxe, where a meal will set you back upwards of $50, to the cheap fast-food chains, where a decent-sized snack or sandwich works out at about $5. The majority of Toronto's restaurants fall somewhere in between – a $15 bill per person for a two-course meal, excluding drinks, is a reasonable average. Most of the city's popular restaurants feature bargain daily specials from about $7 upwards and serve food till about 10pm, drinks till 1am.

For **drinking**, many of Toronto's neighbourhood bars are rough-and-ready places that look and feel like beer halls. Dominated by men – until fairly recently, it was common for them to have one entrance for men accompanied by women, the other for men only – the beer halls remain popular with many of the city's blue-collar workers, but are being replaced by the combined **restaurant/bar**, whose development has made the traditional distinction between eating and drinking houses redundant.

## Cafés and snacks

**Amsterdam Brasserie and Brewpub**, 133 John St, south of Queen. Warehouse decor, excellent draft beer and bar meals from $7.

**Arcadian Court**, 8th floor of Simpson's store, 176 Yonge St at Queen. Spectacular dining room – crystal chandeliers and Greco-Roman decor; dishes from $8. It's overlooked by the equally appealing *Gallery Restaurant*, where prices are similar. (Mon–Sat 11.30am–3pm plus Thurs–Fri 4.30–7.30pm.)

**The Artful Dodger**, 12 Isabella St, just off Yonge south of Bloor. English-style pub with darts and British beer. Reasonable steak-and-kidney and shepherd's pies from $6.

**Bellair Café**, 100 Cumberland St, in Yorkville. Good pasta and salads; pleasant, relaxed setting; snacks from about $12.

**Ciao Café** at 551 Bloor St West, east of Bathurst, & 534 Church St, south of Wellesley. Good pasta dishes and daily specials from $7.

**Lick's**, 285 Yonge at Dundas & in the south food court of the Eaton Centre. Hamburger and ice cream bars. Arguably the best of the cheaper burger chains.

**The Pickle Barrel Restaurant/Deli**, 151 Front St West & 595-Bay St at Dundas. Chicken from $7 and deli meat plate from $12. Huge portions.

**Queen Mother Café**, 206 Queen St West. Popular spot with a good range of basic, well-prepared dishes. Snacks from about $7.

**Renaissance Café**, 509 Bloor St West, two blocks east of Bathurst. Vegetarian; good soups and salads.

**Rotterdam Brewing Company**, 600 King St West. Good draft beers and bar food (Mon–Sat), from $7.

**Shopsy's Delicatessen/Restaurant**, 33 Yonge St at Front. One of the city's oldest delis, popular with visitors to the O'Keefe Centre across the road. Large portions at cheap prices; corned-beef hash from $6; meat platters from $9.

**Simpson's Food Hall**, in the basement of Simpson's store, Yonge at Queen. A series of food counters specialising in different sorts of cuisine – Japanese, Mexican, Italian to name just three. A shoppers' favourite and, despite the plastic cutlery, nice and tasty. A filling meal will set you back about $7.

**Toby's Goodeats**, the Eaton Centre, 542 Church St, 725 Yonge St, 93 & 386 Bloor St West. One of the more upmarket burger chains; good salads; meals from $9.

**Wheatsheaf Tavern**, 667 King St West. Good beer and hot wings from $8.

# Restaurants

**Astoria**, 390 Danforth Ave, near Chester subway. In Greektown; excellent shish kebabs and souvlakis; moderate prices.

**Avocado Club**, at John and Queen. Middle-range restaurant with the emphasis on seafood; dishes from $10.

**Biagio Ristorante**, 155 King St East. Expensive and excellent Italian restaurant located in the nineteenth-century elegance of St Lawrence Hall.

**Centro**, 2472 Yonge St at Eglinton. Excellent Italian food at one of the most expensive places in town.

**Continental Restaurant**, 521 Bloor St West, west of Spadina. Hungarian dishes with huge schnitzels and goulash from $7. Established in the 1940s, this is a pleasant place with the standard red and white chequered table cloths. No license; no credit cards; closes at 10pm.

**Il Fornello**, 486 Bloor St West & 214 King St West. Clay-oven pizzas from $12.

**Fred's Not Here** & **The Red Tomato**, 321 King St West. Two restaurants in one. Good basic menus, fish specialities.

**King's Noodle House**, 296 Spadina at Dundas. Chinese food; very cheap and rather grubby.

**Lee Garden**, 358 Spadina. Cantonese restaurant with exceptionally varied menu; the seafood is a treat.

**The Madras Durbar**, 1435 Gerrard St East at Coxwell. Tamil vegetarian dishes from $6.

**Masa**, 205 Richmond St West (☎977 9519). Japanese food, with part of the restaurant equipped with mats and partitions. Reservations advised at weekends.

**Metropolis**, 838 Yonge. Canadian menu includes east-coast seafood, and cheeses and sausages from Ontario.

**Moghal Restaurant**, 563 Bloor St West. Standard but tasty Indian menu; meals from $20.

**Old Fish Market**, 12 Market St, next to St Lawrence Market. Fantastic selection of fish, but twee setting. Full meals from $15.

**Le Papillon**, 106 Front St East at Jarvis. French food and delicious crêpes from $10.

**Pappas Grill**, 440 Danforth Ave, near Chester subway. Good Greek food; reasonable prices.

**The Parrot**, 325 Queen St West. Exotic dishes and rapidly changing menu from $14. Popular and busy.

**Peter Pan**, 373 Queen St West. Good basic menu at affordable prices.

**P.J. Mellons**, 489 Church St. Superb food in the heart of the Gay Village. Fine pasta selection; excellent daily specials from $9. Very busy.

**Sai Woo**, 130 Dundas St West, one block from Yonge. Reasonably priced Chinese restaurant specialising in Cantonese cuisine. Open daily till 2.30am.

**Santa Fe Bar & Grill**, 129 Peter St, off Richmond. Well-prepared southern California specialities at affordable prices.

**Scaramouche Restaurant**, 1 Benvenuto Place, at Edmund Ave & Avenue Rd (☎961-8011). One of Toronto's premier restaurants; magnificent French cuisine at arm-and-a-leg prices. Dinner only; closed Sun. Reservations recommended.

**Le Select Bistro**, 328 Queen St West. Standard French-style menu; slick decor; jazz and classical background music. Meals from $15.

**Strathcona Hotel**, 60 York St. Good, cheap breakfasts and lunches (Mon–Fri) served in the hotel's ground-floor restaurant in the centre of the business district. Packed at lunch times.

**Swiss Chalet**, 234 & 570 Bloor St West;,151 Front St West, 261 Spadina Ave, 362-Yonge St. One of the few Canadian-owned restaurant chains; the decor may be grim, but the chicken is cheap and tasty.

**The Vegetarian Restaurant**, 4 Dundonald St, east of Yonge & one block north of Wellesley. One of the few specifically vegetarian establishments in the city, the food here is cheap and tasty. No smoking.

**Whistling Oyster**, 11 Duncan St, just west of Queen and University. Great shellfish; meals from $15.

# Nightlife and entertainment

Toronto thinks of itself as the cultural centre of English-speaking Canada and has gone to great expense to maintain a wide-ranging programme of highbrow performance, from **theatre** and **opera** to **ballet** and Brahms. Prices vary from $8 to around $30, but *Five Star Tickets* (Mon–Sat noon–7.30pm & Sun 11am–3pm), in a booth outside the Dundas and Yonge entrance of the Eaton Centre, sell spare dance and theatre tickets at half price for that day's performances. The city of the Cowboy Junkies obviously has some life in its **music** scene, and though most local bands who hit the big time move to the States, the city does have its fair share of venues, especially for **jazz**. Several bars and clubs sponsor a range of modern and traditional jazz, and there are free open-air jazz concerts at various downtown locations throughout the summer. Four local **bands** to look out for are the Skydiggers (acoustic rock), the Phantoms (blues rock), the Leslie Spit Treeo (folk rock) and the Shadowy Men (indie). Toronto's mainstream **cinemas** show Hollywood releases long before they reach the UK, and as you'd expect from a university city, it has good outlets for art-house stuff.

For **listings and reviews** check out either of the city's main free newspapers, *Metropolis* and *Now*. The MTCVA office outside the Eaton Centre has two other free publications, an *Annual Visitors' Guide* and *Where*, which also have listings sections, but their reviews are bland and uncritical. For happenings in the Gay Village, see *Xtra*, the city's third free newspaper.

### Venues, music bars and clubs

**Apocalypse**, 750 College St. Local new wave bands, and left-of-centre benefit concerts.

**The Black Bull**, 298 Queen St West. Local rock groups.

**The Cameron**, 408 Queen St West. Showcase for local bands of varying abilities and styles.

**C'est What**, 67 Front St East. Avant-garde jazz.

**El Mocambo**, 464 Spadina Ave, just south of College. Has seen the likes of Elvis Costello and the Rolling Stones, and still has appearances by big names.

**The Gasworks**, 585 Yonge St. Toronto's premier heavy metal club.

**Horseshoe**, 370 Queen St West. For good-quality and better-known bands.

**Grossman's**, 379 Spadina Ave. R&B venue.

**Meyers Deli**, 69 Yorkville Ave, Yorkville. Well-established trad and modern jazz place.

**The Pilot**, 22 Cumberland St. High-quality modern jazz.

## Discos

**Bamboo**, 312 Queen St West. Has live acts, but is best for its ska, reggae and salsa discos.

**The Copa**, 21 Scollard St, just north of Bay and Bloor. A reliable disco with a good, wide mixture of music.

**Diamond**, 410 Sherbourne St, south of Wellesley. Lively, if somewhat rough and ready.

## Performing arts

**O'Keefe Centre**, 1 Front St East at Yonge (☎393-SHOW). Home of the *Canadian Opera Company* and the *National Ballet of Canada*.

**Pantages Theatre**, 263 Yonge (☎872-2222). Splendidly restored Victorian auditorium, featuring mainstream plays and musicals.

**Poor Alex Theatre**, 296 Brunswick Ave (☎927-8998). One of the city's best venues for inventive and engaging modern drama.

**Royal Alexandra Theatre**, 260 King St West (☎872-3333). Refurbished nineteenth-century theatre, concentrating on top-drawer transfers from London and Broadway.

**Roy Thomson Hall**, 60 Simcoe St at King St West (☎872-HALL). Base of the Toronto Symphony Orchestra.

**St Lawrence Centre for the Performing Arts**, 27 Front St East (☎366-7723). Home to the *Canadian Stage Company*, which produces modern Canadian plays and is responsible for a classical music programme, and *Theatre Plus*, the city's only resident acting ensemble, whose contemporary international and Canadian season runs from April to September.

**Tarragon Theatre**, 30 Bridgman Ave (☎531-1827). Specialises in new Canadian plays.

## Cinema

**Bloor Cinema**, 506 Bloor St West. A student favourite, with an excellent programme of international and art-house films; three different shows daily.

**Carlton Cinema**, 20 Carlton St at College subway. Best mainstream cinema; eight screens, four shows daily.

**The Revue**, 400 Roncesvalles. Two different films daily.

**The Roxy**, 1215 Danforth Ave. Noted for its pop, rock and cult films as well as its noisy late-night shows.

## Festivals

One of the biggest and best of Toronto's many festivals is the **Caravan**, a nine-day multi-ethnic celebration at the end of June, with some forty pavilions dotted across the city representing Toronto's different communities. In July bluegrass and Indian music performances dominate the **Mariposa**, followed by the **Carabana** in early August, a West Indian carnival with a fantasic parade plus music and dance. The **Molson Canadian Hispanic Fiesta** is a Latin music shindig at the Harbourfront in late August/early September. Also in early September the city hosts the **Festival of Festivals**, a ten-day showing of new films from around the world. The most sedate annual event is perhaps the **International Festival of Authors**, held at the Harbourfront in early October.

# Listings

**Airlines** *Air Canada* (☎925-2311); *Canadian Airlines* (☎675-2211); *Wardair* (☎620-9800). *City Express* (☎360-4444) has regular, bargain deals from Toronto Island Airport to London, Montréal and Ottawa. For more obscure destinations within Ontario try *Air Ontario* (☎925-2311); for flights to the States try *American Airlines* (☎283-2243) and *USAir* (☎361-1560).

**Airport enquiries** Pearson International (☎676-3506); Toronto Island (☎868-6942).

**Bike rental** *High Park Cycle*, 1168 Bloor St West, west of Dufferin; *Brown's Sports and Cycle*, 2447 Bloor St West, near Jane.

**Bookshops** Best of the general bookshops is *The World's Biggest Bookshop*, 20 Edward St, near Yonge and Dundas. *Lichtman's* is good for bestsellers and newspapers, with outlets at Yonge and Bloor and Yonge and Richmond. For travel books, try *Open Air Books and Maps*, downtown at 25 Toronto St, or *Ulysses Travel Bookshop*, 101 Yorkville.

**Bus information** *Greyhound* (☎367-8747); *Gray Coach* (☎393-7911); Toronto Transit Commission (☎393-INFO).

**Camping equipment** *Trail Head*, 40 Wellington St East; *Mountain Equipment Co-op*, 35 Front St East.

**Car rental** *Avis*, in the *Bay Department Store* at Yonge and Bloor (☎964-2051); *Budget*, 141 Bay St (☎364-7104); *Discount Car Rental*, 700 Bay St (☎597-2222); *Hertz*, 39 Richmond St West (☎363-9022); *Thrifty Car Rental* at the *Sheraton Centre Hotel*, 123 Queen St West (☎868-0350); *Tilden*, beside Union Station (☎364-4191).

**Embassies** *Australia*, 175 Bloor St East (☎323-3919); *Ireland*, 160 Bloor St East (☎929-7394); *Netherlands*, 1 Dundas St West, suite 2106 (☎598-2520); *UK*, 777 Bay St (☎593-1267).

**Emergencies** *Assaulted Women's Helpline* ☎863-0511; *Rape Crisis* ☎597-8808.

**Hospital** 311 Sherbourne (☎969-4264).

**Laundry** *Bloor Laundromat and Dry Cleaners*, 598 Bloor St West at Bathurst; *Crystal Coin*, 768 Queen St West; *Reynoldo's*, 816 Dundas St West.

**Lost property** *TTC*, Bay subway (☎393-4100); *GO* transit (☎665-0022); *VIA* (☎366-8411).

**Pharmacies** 24-hour services at *Owl Drug*, 68 Wellesley St East at Church, and *Shoppers Drug Mart*, 700 Bay St at Gerard.

**Post offices** The main post office is at 20 Bay St.

**Sports** The *Toronto Maple Leafs*, of the National Hockey League, play home fixtures in Maple Leaf Gardens at Carlton and Church, College subway (☎977-1641). The *Argonauts*, of the Canadian Football League, play in the Skydome (☎595-1131); the *Blue Jays*, of the American Baseball League, also play there (☎341-1000).

**Weather** ☎676-3066.

**Winter sports** Ring *Metro Parks* (☎392-8184) for information on outdoor rinks and cross-country ski routes. Ski hire available at *Rudy's Sport Centre Ltd*, 1055 Eglinton Ave West (☎781-9196).

# SOUTHERN ONTARIO

The chain of towns to the east and west of Toronto, stretching 100km along the edge of Lake Ontario from Oshawa to Hamilton, is often called the **Golden Horseshoe**, a misleadingly evocative name that refers solely to their geographic shape and economic success. This is Ontario's manufacturing heartland, and the only place of any real interest here is the steel-making city of **Hamilton**, the home of the Royal Botanical Gardens and the delightful mansion of Dundurn Castle. Further round the lake, the melodramatic **Niagara Falls** adjoin the seedy town of the same name – it's best to use the charmingly twee, colonial village of Niagara-on-the-Lake as a base for a visit. At neighbouring Queenston the **Niagara Escarpment** begins its journey across the region to the Bruce Peninsula, the major interruption in a generally tedious terrain. Most of southern Ontario's remaining attractions are on the coast, most notably the **Point**

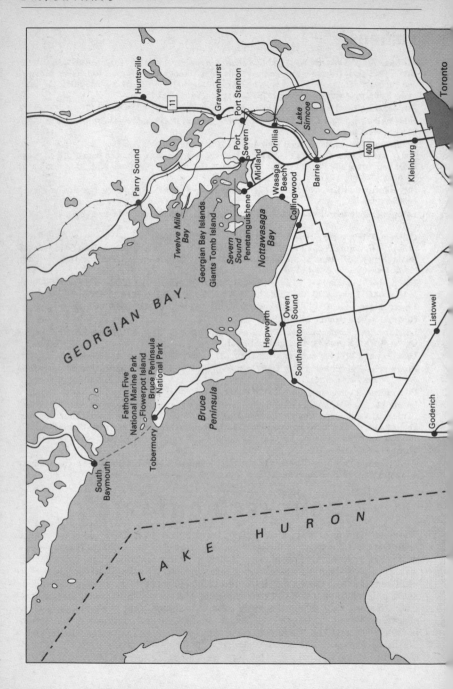

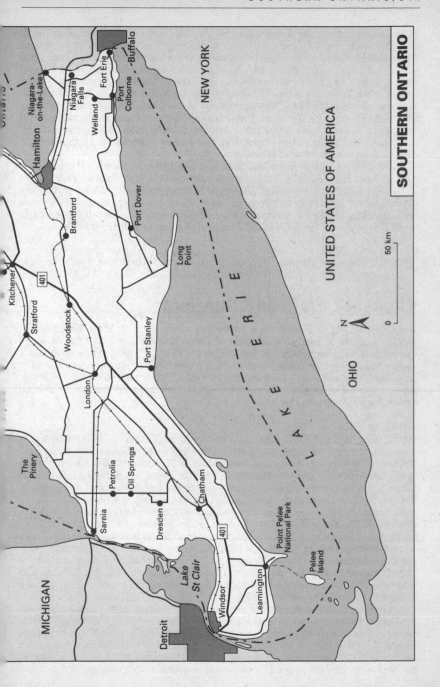

Pelee National Park; the vigorous town of **Windsor**, and the small-town pleasures of little **Goderich**. Further north, the dramatic scenery along the edge of the **Bruce Peninsula** incorporates two outstanding **national parks**, which make for some great walking, climbing and scuba-diving. Nearby, along the southern shore of **Severn Sound**, there's a string of moribund ports, the cosiest of which is **Penetanguishene**, located a few kilometres from the sturdy palisades of the Jesuit mission of **Sainte-Marie among the Hurons**. The eastern shore of the Sound boasts the lion's share of the stunningly beautiful **Georgian Bay Islands National Park**, an elegaic land and waterscape of rocky, pine-dotted islets and crystal blue lake. The islands are best approached by boat from the tourist resort of **Honey Harbour** or on the summer island cruises from the town of **Midland**.

There are fast and frequent **buses** and **trains** between Toronto, Hamilton and Niagara Falls, and a similarly efficient service between the region's other major settlements, like Windsor, London and Kitchener. Most of the smaller towns, particularly Penetanguishene, Midland and Goderich, have the odd bus connection, but there are no buses along the Bruce Peninsula, where Tobermory has a **ferry boat** service to South Baymouth on Manitoulin Island – a useful shortcut to northern Ontario.

---

Unless stated otherwise, the telephone code for southern Ontario is ☎519.

---

# Kitchener, Elora and Stratford

The industrial city of **Kitchener** is southern Ontario at its drabbest, but amid the prevailing gloom it does have a couple of sights that are worth an hour or so. In marked contrast, **Elora**, 30km north of Kitchener, is a pretty little village of old stone houses and mills on the **Elora Gorge**, a narrow limestone ravine that's a popular spot for a day's walk and picnic. Fifty kilometres west of Kitchener, **Stratford** is different again, a modest country town that hosts one of Canada's most prestigious cultural events, the **Shakespeare Festival**.

### Kitchener

Strung along Hwy 401 about 80km west of downtown Toronto, **KITCHENER** lies at the centre of an industrial belt whose economy is based on rubber, textiles, leather and furniture. The town was founded as **Sand Hills** in 1799 by groups of **Mennonites**, a tightly knit Protestant sect who came here from the States, where their pacifist beliefs had incurred the wrath of their neighbours during the Revolution. Soon after, German farmers began to arrive in the area, establishing a generally good-humoured trading relationship with the Mennonites. The new settlers had Sand Hills renamed **Berlin** in 1826, but during World War I it was thought prudent to change the name yet again, to prove their patriotism: they chose **Kitchener** after the British field marshal. Today around sixty percent of Kitchener's inhabitants are descendants of German immigrants, a heritage celebrated every year during **Oktoberfest**, nine days of alcoholic stupefaction when even the most reticent men can be seen wandering the streets in lederhosen. The Mennonites have drifted out of Kitchener itself, and are concentrated in the villages north and west of Waterloo, Kitchener's glum neighbour.

Kitchener's centre is marked by the **Farmers' Market**, open on Saturdays and Wednesdays from mid-May to mid-October – be sure to sample the delicious German sausages. The Mennonite traders are unmistakeable, for unlike their Manitoba cousins (see p.348), the men wear traditional black suits and broad-brimmed hats, the women ankle-length black dresses and matching bonnets. Members of the traditional wing of the Mennonite movement, sometimes called **Ammanites**, they own property communally and shun all modern machinery, travelling to the market and around the back lanes on spindly horse-drawn buggies.

The only conventional tourist sight in Kitchener is **Woodside**, boyhood home of prime minister William Lyon Mackenzie King, about 1km northeast of the centre at 528 Wellington St North (daily 10am–5pm; free; bus #6 from King St). Set in a pretty little park, the house has been restored to its late-Victorian appearance and has an interesting display in the basement on King's life and times, though it doesn't give much away about his eccentricities – a dog lover and spiritualist, he amalgamated the two obsessions by believing his pets were mediums.

*PRACTICALITIES*

Kitchener's **bus station** is on Charles Street, five minutes' walk from the town centre. The **train station** is a ten-minute walk north of downtown, at Victoria and Weber. The **tourist office** at 67 King Street and Frederick (Mon–Fri 9am–5pm) has **accommodation** listings, including a couple of bed and breakfasts with doubles from about $35; many families offer similarly priced rooms just during Oktoberfest. Cheaper still, the University of Waterloo, 200 University Ave West (☎884-5400), and Wilfrid Laurier University, 75 University Ave West (☎884-1970), have doubles at around $25 from May to mid-August. There's also a clutch of **motels** north of the centre along Victoria Street, including the *Barons Motor Inn* at no. 901 (☎744-2215); the *Mayflower*, no. 1189 (☎745-9493); and the *Kitchener*, no. 1485 (☎745-1177). Doubles at all these start at about $40. For **food**, try the German specialities of the *Rathskeller*, 151 Frederick St, the Italian dishes at *Angelo's Place*, 255 King St West, or the standard Canadian menu of *MacArthur's*, 103 King St West.

## Elora

Pushed up against the craggy banks of the Grand River, **ELORA** was founded in the 1830s by settlers who harnessed its waterfall to run their mills. Nearly all of their limestone cottages have survived, but most visitors come here to walk along the riverside and gaze at the falls, even though they're only a few metres high.

A ten-minute walk from end to end, Elora is approached from the south across a narrow bridge that leads into the main street, Metcalfe – which runs into tiny Mill Street, adjoining the falls. The **tourist office**, 136 Metcalfe (June–Aug Mon–Fri 9am–5pm), has the details of a handful of **B&Bs**, including the attractive *Gingerbread House* (☎846-0521), just by the bridge, with doubles from $60. Elora has two **hotels**, the tacky and expensive *Elora Mill Inn*, on Mill St (☎846-5356; doubles from $90); and the grim-looking *Dalby House*, 143 Metcalfe (☎846-9811; from $40). For cheap **food**, head for *Tiffany's Fish and Chiperie*, 146 Metcalfe, or the *Dalby House* across the street.

Some 2km southwest of Elora, signposted from the bridge, the **Elora Gorge Conservation Area** (daily Jan–March 10am–5pm; May to mid-Oct 10am–dusk; $2.50) spreads out on the flanks of the most dramatic part of the Grand River, the twenty-metre-deep limestone **Elora Gorge**. The park has over 10km of trails and tracks, plus camping spaces.

## Stratford

Surrounded by flat farmland that stretches west as far as Lake Huron, **STRATFORD** is an inconsequential town of 27,000 people, saved from complete architectural indifference by a grandiose city hall, a brown-brick fiesta of cupolas, towers and limestone trimmings. More importantly, the town is also the home of the **Shakespeare Festival**, which started in 1953 and is now one of the most prestigious theatrical occasions in North America, attracting no fewer than half a million visitors from May to October. Although the core performances are still Shakespearean, the festival has broadened its appeal to include other drama, from Racine to Beckett.

The **Festival Box Office** at the Festival Theatre (March–Aug Mon–Sat 9am–8pm & Sun 9am–5pm; Sept–Oct Mon–Sat 9am–5pm; ☎273-1600) accepts applications in person or by letter (PO Box 520) or phone. Tickets cost between $20 and $40, and from $9 for students. Many plays are sold out months in advance, but the box office does set aside a limited number of **rush tickets** for two of the three theatres at about $17. These are for sale from 9am on the day of the performance, but the seats are the worst in the house. The box office also organises a number of discount packages with savings upwards of ten percent for various categories of performance, plus **accommodation** ranging from **hotels** at $65 for a double, down to **guesthomes** at $29.

Stratford **bus** and **train stations** are on Shakespeare Street, a fifteen-minute stroll from the town centre. There are two **tourist offices**: a main Visitor Information Booth (April–Sept Mon–Sat 9am–8pm & Sun 9am–6pm; Sept–Thanksgiving Mon–Fri 9.30am–3.30pm & Sat–Sun 9am–6pm; Thanksgiving to April Mon–Fri 10.30am–4.30pm, Sat 9am–5pm & Sun 9am–3.30pm; ☎273-3352), on the riverbank at Erie and York, immediately northwest of Downie at Ontario; and Tourism Stratford, 88 Wellington St (Mon–Fri 8.30am–4.30pm), which is on the west side of the Market Place.

Stratford has over 250 guesthouses and a dozen or so hotels and motels, but **accommodation** can be hard to find during the Festival's busiest weekends in July and August. The walls of the Information Booth are plastered with pictures and descriptions of many of the town's **guesthouses** and **B&Bs**, with prices from $35 for a double. There are a few **hotels** near the centre, including the *Stone Maiden Inn*, 123 Church St (☎271-7129), the *Jester Arms Inn*, 107 Ontario St (☎271-1121) and the *Queen's Inn*, 161 Ontario St (☎271-1400), all with doubles from $85. The *Albert Place, Twenty Three*, 23 Albert St (☎273-5800), has doubles from $65. For **food**, most of the posher places on Ontario Street sell average food at inflated prices. Better alternatives include the excellent *Let Them Eat Cake*, by the Market Place at 90 Wellington St, and cheap pizzas at *Domino's Pizza*, 127 Erie St.

# Hamilton and around

Some 70km from Toronto, **HAMILTON** lies at the extreme western end of Lake Ontario, focus of a district first surveyed by George Hamilton, a Niagaran storekeeper-turned-landowner who moved here in 1812 to escape the war between America and Britain. Strategically located, the town was soon established as a trading centre, but its real growth began with the development of the farm-implements industry in the 1850s. By the turn of the century, Hamilton had become a major steel producer and today its mills churn out sixty percent of the country's output.

For a city of half a million people, Hamilton has very limited attractions. The finest building in the centre is **Whitehern** (tours daily June–Aug 11am–4pm; Sept–May 1–4pm; $1.75), a couple of minutes' walk south of the city hall at 41 Jackson St West. A good example of early Victorian architecture, it has an overhauled interior with an eccentric mix of styles ranging from a splendid mid-nineteenth-century circular stairway to a dingy wood-panelled 1930s basement.

About twenty minutes' walk west of the town centre, straight down York Boulevard from James, you come to **Dundurn Castle** (daily tours mid-June–Sept 11am–4pm; Oct to mid-June 1–4pm; $3.25), a Regency villa built in the 1830s for Sir Allan Napier MacNab, a soldier, lawyer and land speculator who became one of the leading conservative politicians of the day. He was knighted for his loyalty to the Crown during the Upper Canada Rebellion of 1837, when he employed bands of armed Indians to round up supposed rebels and loot their property. Carefully renovated, Dundurn is an impressive Italianate building with an interior that easily divides into "upstairs" and "downstairs": the former filled with fine contemporaneous furnishings, the latter a warren of poorly ventilated rooms for the dozens of servants. Nearby, the gatekeeper's cottage has been turned into a small **military museum** (same times; free admission with castle), detailing local involvement in the War of 1812 and in the Fenian (Irish-American) cross-border raids of the 1860s.

From Dundurn Castle, York Boulevard crosses the four-kilometre-long isthmus that spans the west end of Hamilton harbour before heading into the neighbouring city of Burlington. The **Royal Botanical Gardens** (daily dawn to dusk; free) cover some 3000 acres around the northern end of the isthmus, spread over 15km of shoreline. There are no public transport connections from either Hamilton or Burlington, so it's difficult to get round without a car. The displays are gorgeous, though – especially the arboretum (best in late May and early June) and Hendrie Park with its scented, medicinal and rose gardens (best June–Oct).

## Practicalities

Hamilton **bus station** is on Rebecca Street at John, five minutes' walk from the junction of Main Street and James. Less conveniently, the **train station** is about 2km north of the city centre at James Street North and Murray. The **Tourist Information Office** (daily 9am–6pm), 127 King St East at Catherine, has brochures on the city and its surroundings, plus restaurant and hotel lists. There's very little cheap downtown **accommodation** except the *YMCA*, 79 James St South (☎416/529-7102; $23), the *YWCA*, 75 MacNab St South (☎416/522-9922; from $25), and the *Town Manor Motor Hotel*, 175 Main St West at Caroline (☎416/528-0611; doubles from $40).

For cheap downtown **food**, *Christopher's Restaurant and Tavern,* 60 James St at Rebecca, sells basic snacks and sandwiches, *The Black Forest Inn*, 255 King St East at Ferguson, specialises in inexpensive German and Austrian cuisine, and *Bronzie's Place*, 201 James St South, has Italian dishes from $8.

### Brantford and the Bell Homestead

The modest manufacturing town of **BRANTFORD**, to the west of Hamilton near the Grand River, takes its name from **Joseph Brant**, who led a large group of Loyalist Iroquois here after the American War of Independence, then worked to form a confederation of Iroquois to keep the United States out of Ohio. His dream was undermined by jealousies amongst the Indian nations, whereupon he withdrew to Burlington, where he lived the life of an English gentleman. The town was later the birthplace of hockey's greatest player, **Wayne Gretzky**, but no-one's built a museum yet.

The only thing to see in the town itself is the **Brant County Museum**, 57 Charlotte St (May–Aug Tues–Fri 9am–5pm & Sat–Sun 1–4pm; Sept–April closed Sun & Mon; $1), where there's a reasonable collection of Iroquois artefacts. However, 6km southwest of Brantford, in the low wooded hills overlooking the river, stands the **Bell Homestead**, 94 Tutela Heights Rd (mid-June to Aug daily 10am–5pm; Sept to mid-June Tues–Sun 10am–5.30pm; free). **Alexander Graham Bell** left Edinburgh for Ontario in 1870 at the age of twenty-three, a reluctant immigrant who came only because of fears for his health after the death of two close relatives from tuberculosis. Soon afterwards he took a job as a teacher of the deaf, motivated by his mother's loss of hearing and, in his efforts to discover a way to reproduce sounds visibly, he stumbled across the potential of transmitting sound along an electrified wire. The consequence was the first long-distance call, made in 1876 from Brantford to the neighbouring village of Paris. The site consists of two simple, clapboard buildings. The first, moved here from Brantford in 1969, housed Canada's original *Bell* company office and features a series of modest displays on the history of the telephone. The second, the cosy family home, fronts a second small exhibition area devoted to Bell's life and research. There's no public transport from Brantford to the Homestead.

# Niagara Falls and the Niagara River

In 1860 thousands watched as Charles Blondin walked a tightrope across **Niagara Falls** for the third time; at the midway point he cooked an omelette on a portable grill and then had a marksman shoot a hole through his hat from the *Maid of the Mist* tug boat, fifty metres below. As attested by Blondin's subsequent career, by the antics of innumerable lunatics and publicity seekers, and by several million waterlogged tourist photos, the Falls can't be beaten as a theatrical setting. Yet the stupendous first impression of the Niagara doesn't last long on jaded modern palates, and to prevent each year's twelve million visitors becoming bored by the sight of a load of water crashing over a 54m cliff, the Niagarans have ensured that the Falls can be seen from every angle imaginable – from boats, viewing towers, helicopters, cable-cars and even tunnels in the rock face behind the cascade. The **tunnels** and the **boats** are the most exciting, with the entrance to the first right next to the Falls and the second leaving from the bottom of the cliff at the end of Clifton Hill, 1500m downriver. Both give a real sense of the extraordinary force of the waterfall, a perpetual white-crested thundering pile-up that had Mahler bawling "At last, fortissimo" over the din.

**Trains** and **buses** from Toronto and most of southern Ontario's larger towns serve the revolting town of **NIAGARA FALLS**, 3km to the north of the action; the horribleness of the town and the availability of discount excursion fares make a day-trip the best way to see the Falls. If you're travelling under your own steam, the best place to stay is 26km downstream at quaint **Niagara-on-the-Lake**, beside Lake Ontario.

## Niagara practicalities

Niagara Falls' **bus terminal**, 420 Bridge St at Erie, is situated directly opposite the **train station**. Five minutes' walk away is the **Visitor and Convention Bureau** (June–Sept daily 9am–8pm; Oct–May Mon–Fri 9am–5pm), 4673 Ontario Ave at Queen; there are also a number of seasonal **tourist kiosks** near the Falls themselves. For motorists, the **Ontario Welcome Centre** (daily April to mid-May & Sept 8am–6pm; mid-May to Aug 8am–8pm; Oct–March 8.30am–4.30pm), beside Hwy 420 at Stanley Ave, is well stocked with literature on the whole of the province.

Next door to the bus station, the **Niagara Transit** depot is the starting point for town and suburban services, including the **Falls Shuttle** (mid-May to Sept daily 8.30am–11.30pm), which runs to the Falls every twenty minutes. A second shuttle route runs along Lundy's Lane, the main motel strip, and across to the Falls every thirty minutes. Both connect with the Niagara Parks' **People Mover System** (daily mid-May to early June & Sept to early Oct 10am–7pm; mid-June to Aug 9am–midnight), whose buses travel along the riverbank between the Spanish Aero Car, north of the Falls, and the Rapids' View parking lot to the south. An all-day **pass** for both services costs $4.75.

**Sightseeing tours** run by *Double Decker* leave from beside the ticket office at the bottom of Clifton Hill three times daily from mid-May to October, travelling north as far as Queenston Heights and south to the rapids. Passengers can get on and off the bus when they wish; the $30 ticket is valid for two days and includes admission to the river's major tourist attractions. The same company runs buses from Clifton Hill and the town bus station to Niagara-on-the-Lake (mid-May to Oct 3 daily; $15 one way), but the future of this service is uncertain.

### Accommodation and eating

Niagara Falls is billed as the "Honeymoon Capital of the World", which means that many of its motels and hotels have an odd mix of cheap, basic rooms and gaudy suites with heart-shaped bathtubs, waterbeds and the like. Out of season it's a buyer's market, so it's well worth trying to haggle – but if you want the easy option, assistance

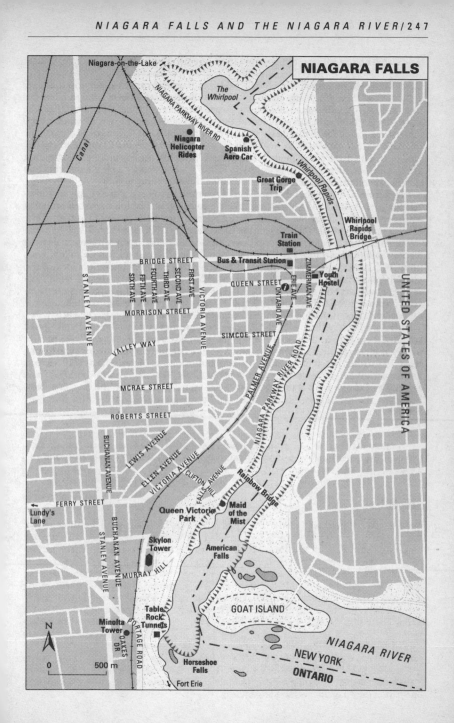

# NIAGARA FALLS

Niagara-on-the-Lake
The Whirlpool
NIAGARA PARKWAY RIVER RD
Canal
Niagara Helicopter Rides
Spanish Aero Car
Whirlpool Rapids
Great Gorge Trip
Whirlpool Rapids Bridge
Train Station
Bus & Transit Station
BRIDGE STREET
SECOND AVE
THIRD AVE
FIRST AVE
FOURTH AVE
FIFTH AVE
SIXTH AVE
Queen Street
ZIMMERMAN AVE
ERIE AVE
ONTARIO AVE
Youth Hostel
STANLEY AVENUE
VICTORIA AVENUE
MORRISON STREET
SIMCOE STREET
VALLEY WAY
MCRAE STREET
ROBERTS STREET
PALMER AVENUE
NIAGARA PARKWAY RIVER ROAD
LEWIS AVENUE
ELLEN AVENUE
VICTORIA AVENUE
CLIFTON HILL
FALLS AVENUE
BUCHANAN AVENUE
Rainbow Bridge
FERRY STREET
Lundy's Lane
Queen Victoria Park
Maid of the Mist
BUCHANAN AVENUE
STANLEY AVENUE
Skylon Tower
American Falls
MURRAY HILL
Table Rock Tunnels
GOAT ISLAND
N
Minolta Tower
PORTAGE ROAD
OAKES DR
NIAGARA RIVER
NEW YORK
0        500 m
Horseshoe Falls
ONTARIO
Fort Erie
UNITED STATES OF AMERICA

is available on the **Visitor Infoline** (☎416/356-6061). The pick of the premier **hotels** are the *Sheraton*, 6755 Oakes Drive (☎416/374-1077; doubles from $230), and the *Oakes Inn*, 6546 Buchanan Ave (☎416/356-4514; doubles from $90), both on the bank to the west of the Falls. Many of the town's **motels** are dotted along Lundy's Lane, the long westward continuation of Victoria Avenue and Ferry Street. Averaging out at about $90 per double in the summer, cheaper alternatives include the *Bonanza* at no. 6267 (☎416/356-5135), *Falls Manor* at no. 7104 (☎416/358-3211), *Parkwood* at no. 8054 (☎416/354-3162), *Seneca* at no. 8405 (☎416/356-2942), and *Willow* at no. 8646 (☎416/374-2664). The more convenient motels along Clifton Hill are far more expensive, but the *Quality Inn Fallsway*, no. 4946 (☎416/358-3601), has comfortable rooms from $50 at the beginning and end of the season – at other times reckon on $120.

Niagara Falls has a handful of **bed and breakfast** addresses and a couple of **guesthouses** from around $55 per double. Ask for details at any of the tourist information offices or try along River Road at the *Butterfly Manor*, no. 4917 (☎416/357-1124), *White Knight*, no. 4939 (☎416/374-8767), or the *Glen Manor*, no. 5381 (☎416/354-2600).

The **youth hostel**, 4699 Zimmerman Ave (☎416/357-0770), is a five-minute walk from the bus station, down towards the river along Bridge Street, and has dormitory beds from $10. There are several **campgrounds** on Lundy's Lane, including *Orchard Grove*, no. 8123 (☎416/358-9883; from $15), *Niagara Falls KOA*, no. 8625 (☎416/356-6472; from $17) and the *Campark Resort*, no. 9387 (☎416/358-3873; from $14). *The Niagara Glen-View Tent and Trailer Park* (☎416/358-8689), occupying a more agreeable location at the corner of Victoria Avenue and the Niagara Parkway, has 200 sites starting at $18.

There are literally dozens of cheap chain **restaurants** and fast-food bars along and around Clifton Hill. Most of them are pretty grim, though the *Fallsway Restaurant*, in the *Quality Inn* at 4946 Clifton Hill, has a good basic menu with main courses from around $7. Other possibilities include pizzas and snacks at *Mama Mia's*, 5719 Victoria Ave, and Chinese meals at the *Jade Gardens*, 5306 Victoria. There's authentic and expensive Japanese food at the *Yukiguni*, a few minutes' walk from the Skylon at 5980 Buchanan Ave and Ferry; nearby there are Polynesian dishes in the *Mia Kai*, 5402 Ferry St.

---

A **combined ticket** for all four riverside attractions – the Table Rock scenic tunnels, the Maid of the Mist, the Great Gorge Adventure and the Spanish Aero Car – is available at each of them and costs $11.

---

## The Falls

Though you can hear the growl of the **Falls** miles away, nothing quite prepares you for the spectacle, the fearsome white arc shrouded in clouds of dense spray, with the tiny river boats struggling below, mere specks against the surging cauldron. There are two cataracts, the accelerating water being sliced into two channels by tiny Goat Island: on the far side, across the frontier, the river slips over the precipice of the **American Falls**, 300m wide but still only one third of the width of the **Horseshoe Falls** on the Canadian side. If anything, it's an even more amazing scene in winter, with snow-covered trees edging a jagged armoury of frozen mist and heaped ice-blocks. It looks like a scene of untrammelled nature, but it isn't. Since the 1950s, successive hydro-electric schemes have greatly reduced the water flow, and all sorts of tinkering has spread what's left of the Niagara more evenly over the crestline. As a result, the process of erosion, which has moved the Falls some 11km upstream in 12,000 years, has slowed down from 1m per year to 3cm. This obviously has advantages for the tourist industry, but the environmental consequences of training this deluge for decades on one part of the Niagara riverbed are unclear.

Beside the Horseshoe Falls, **Table Rock House** has a small, free observation platform and elevators which travel to the base of the cliff, where **tunnels** ($5) lead to points behind the waterfall. A couple of minutes' walk from the river, the **Minolta Tower**, 6732 Oakes Drive (daily June–Sept 9am–midnight; Oct–May 9am–11pm; $4.95), has three observation platforms looking out over the Falls, but the views are a little bit better from the neighbouring **Skylon** tower, 5200 Robinson at Murray Hill (daily 9am–11pm; $5.40).

From Table Rock House, a wide and crowded path leads north along the cliffs beside the river, with the manicured lawns of Queen Victoria Park to the left and views over to the American Falls to the right. A few minutes further on, at the foot of Clifton Hill – the main drag of Niagara Falls town – **Maid of the Mist boats** edge out into the river and push up towards the Falls, an exhilarating and extremely damp trip (May to late June & mid-Sept to Oct Mon–Fri 10am–5pm & Sat–Sun 10am–6pm; late June to mid-Aug daily 9am–8pm; mid-Aug to early Sept daily 9am–7.30pm; at least every 30min; $7). **Clifton Hill** itself is a tawdry collection of fast-food joints and bizarre attractions, from the innocuous "House of Frankenstein" to the grotesque voyeurism of the "Guinness World of Records Museum" and the absurdity of the "That's Incredible Museum", where you can talk to a live genie trapped inside a crystal bottle.

Continuing north, it's a further 4km to the **Great Gorge Adventure** ($4), a grubby boardwalk beside the Whirlpool Rapids, and another ten minutes' walk downstream to the brightly painted **Spanish Aero Car** ($4), a cable-car ride across the gorge that's as near as you'll come to emulating Blondin's antics.

## Downstream from the Falls

From the Falls, the **Niagara Parkway** road follows the river parallel to the **Niagara Parks Recreation Trail**, a combined cycle and walking track. The road and trail loop round the treacherous waters of the whirlpool (see above), before cutting along to the **Niagara Glen Nature Reserve**, whose paths lead down from the clifftop to the bottom of the gorge, a hot and sticky trek in the height of the summer.

About 3km further on, **Queenston Heights Park** (mid-May to Aug daily 10am–6pm; free) marks the original location of the Falls, before the force of the water eroded the riverbed 11km upstream, adjusting the 120-metre differential between the water levels of lakes Erie and Ontario. Soaring above the park, there's a grandiloquent monument to Sir Isaac Brock, the Guernsey-born general who was killed here in the War of 1812, leading a head-on charge against the Americans. From beside the park, the road begins a curving descent down to the pretty little village of **QUEENSTON**, whose importance as a transit centre disappeared when the Welland Canal was completed in 1829, creating a placid waterway between lakes Erie and Ontario. On the main street, the **Laura Secord Homestead** (June–Aug daily 10am–6pm; $1) is a reconstruction of the house of Massachusets-born Laura Ingersoll Secord, whose dedication to the imperial interest was such that she ran 30km through the woods to warn the British army of a surprise attack planned by the Americans in the War of 1812–14.

### Niagara-on-the-Lake

A day-trippers' favourite, **NIAGARA-ON-THE-LAKE** is rather special, a finely preserved early nineteenth-century town with lines of elegant clapboard houses surrounded by well-kept gardens, all spread along tree-lined streets. The town, then named Newark, became the first capital of Upper Canada in 1792, but four years later lost this distinction in favour of York (Toronto) because of its proximity to the frontier – a wise decision, for the Americans crossed the river and destroyed the place in 1813. Given the name by which it's known today, it was rebuilt immediately afterwards, and has barely changed since.

The charm of the town lies in the whole rather than in any particular sight, but **Queen Street**, which cuts right across the town centre to the lake, is the setting for the **Apothecary** (June–Aug daily noon–6pm), worth a look for its beautifully carved wooden cabinets and porcelain jars, while the **Niagara Historical Society Museum**, 43 Castlereagh St (Jan–Feb Sat & Sun 1–5pm; March–April & Nov–Dec daily 1–5pm; May–Oct daily 10am–5pm; $2), has a mildly interesting collection of local artefacts.

There were so many desertions from the British military post of **Fort George** (June daily 9am–5pm; July–Aug daily 10am–6pm; Sept–Oct 10am–5pm; $2), 1km south of Niagara-on-the-Lake, that it eventually had to be garrisoned by the Royal Canadian Rifle Regiment, a force consisting mostly of married men approaching retirement who were unlikely to forfeit their pensions by high-tailing it down south. If they did try and were caught, they were branded on the chest with the letter "D" and then either lashed or transported to a penal colony – except in war time, when they were shot. The fort, part of a line of stockades slung across the waterways of the Great Lakes, was destroyed during the War of 1812 and today's site is a splendid reconstruction. Its **compound** harbours ten buildings, among them three pine blockhouses and the powder magazine, its inside finished in wood and copper to reduce the chances of an accidental explosion – and the soldiers who worked here wore shoes with no metal fastenings.

*PRACTICALITIES*
The only **public transport** to Niagara-on-the-Lake are the *Double Decker* buses from Niagara Falls, and the *Gray Coach* day-trips from the Bay Street terminal in Toronto between June and the middle of October (2–6 weekly; $31 return). Both services stop at Queen Street and King, a couple of minutes' walk from the **tourist office**, 153 King St at Prideaux (May–Aug Mon–Fri 9am–7pm, Sat 11am–7pm & Sun 10am–6pm; Sept–Oct Mon–Fri 9am–5pm & Sat 10am–6pm; Nov–April Mon–Fri 9am–5pm; ☎468-4263), which has free town maps and a **room reservation service** – useful during the Shaw Festival (late April to mid-Oct), when theatre-goers book out most of the rooms.

Some of the province's most elegant **hotels and inns** are within easy walking distance of the centre, all with doubles from around $110. These include the *Prince of Wales*, 6 Picton St (☎416/468-3246), the *Moffat Inn*, 60 Picton St (☎416/468-4116), the *Oban Inn*, 160 Front St (☎416/468-2165), and the *Angel Inn*, 224 Regent St (☎468-3411). More reasonably priced alternatives, from about $90 for a double, include the *Royal Anchorage Hotel*, 186 Ricardo St (☎416/468-2141) and the *Kiely House Heritage Inn*, 209 Queen St (☎416/468-4588). The tourist office also has details of some 100 **bed and breakfasts** with prices between $55 and $95 per double.

For **eating**, the *Buttery Theatre Restaurant*, 19 Queen St, has wonderful homemade pies on its outstanding and reasonably priced menu; *The Angel Inn*, 224 Regent St, just off Queen, sells good snacks and sandwiches, as does the *Colonel Butler Inn*, 278 Mary St. *The Harbour Inn*, 35 Melville St, specialises in seafood.

## Upstream from the Falls: Fort Erie

The 32 kilometres of the **Niagara Parkway** south of the Falls are less appealing than the stretch to the north, even though the road sticks close to the riverbank and gives some pleasant views over to the States. Beyond dreary CHIPPAWA the river is wide and quiet, divided into two channels by Grand Island, just downstream of **Fort Erie**, a small industrial town that sits opposite the American city of Buffalo. Roughly 2km south of the town, **Old Fort Erie** (May to mid-Oct 9.30am–6pm; $2.50) overlooks the lake from the mouth of the Niagara River. A reconstruction of the third fort the British built on the site, which was razed by the Americans in 1814, the fort is entered across a wooden drawbridge which leads to a central compound, where there's the usual array of army buildings and a tiny museum of military equipment.

# London

The citizens of **LONDON** are proud of their clean streets, efficient transit system and neat suburbs, but to the outsider there's nothing to justify a detour, apart from the city's two **music festivals** in July – the Big Band Festival and the three-day Home County Folk Music Festival. London owes its existence to the governor of Upper Canada, **John Graves Simcoe**, who arrived in 1792 determined to develop the wilderness north of Lake Ontario. Because of its river connections to the west and south, he chose the site of London as his new colonial capital and promptly renamed its river the Thames. Unluckily, Simcoe's headlong approach to his new job irritated his superior, Governor Dorchester, who vetoed his choice with the wry comment that access to London would have to be by hot-air balloon. When York, present-day Toronto, was chosen as capital instead, Simcoe's chosen site lay empty until 1826, yet by the 1880s London was firmly established as the economic and administrative centre of a prosperous agricultural area. With a population of 340,000, it remains so today.

## The city

London's **downtown core** is laid out as a gridiron on either side of its main east–west axis, Dundas Street. At the west end of Dundas, close to the river, the **Art Gallery**, 421 Ridout St North (Tues–Fri noon–5pm, Sat 10am–6pm & Sun noon–6pm; free) was designed by Raymond Moriyama, of Toronto, a once fashionable architect whose ugly concrete buildings are characterised by a preference for contorted curves and circles rather than straight lines. The gallery's permanent collection isn't much better, mostly an indeterminate mix of obscure eighteenth- and nineteenth-century Canadian paintings, but look out for the temporary modern art exhibitions – some of them come here straight from Toronto and are excellent.

London's oldest residence, **Eldon House** (daily June–Sept noon–5pm; Oct–Dec & March–May 2–5pm; $3) is a couple of minutes' walk north from the gallery at 481 Ridout St North. Built by John Harris, a retired Royal Navy captain, in the 1830s, the house is a graceful clapboard dwelling, whose interior has been returned to its mid-nineteenth-century appearance.

The only other sights of any interest are the two rival Victorian cathedrals. **St Paul's Anglican Cathedral** – take Fullarton from the Eldon House as far as Richmond – is a simple red-brick structure built in the English Gothic Revival style in 1846. In marked contrast, **St Peter's Catholic Cathedral**, just to the north at Dufferin and Richmond, is a flamboyant, high-towered, pink stone edifice, in the French Gothic style so popular amongst Ontario's Catholics in the late nineteenth century.

About 8km northwest of downtown London, the **Lawson Prehistoric Indian Village** (April–Nov daily 10am–5pm; Dec–March Wed–Sun 1–4pm; $3), 1600 Attawandaron Rd, is a careful but dreary reconstruction of a Neutral Indian village that stood here 500 years ago – cedar palisades and elm longhouses, but not much else. Next door, the **Museum of Indian Archaeology** (same hours) traces the history of these local Iroquois-speaking bands through audio-visual displays and a ragbag of archaeological finds. To get to the site, take bus #9 from Wharncliffe at Kensington, near the western end of Dundas; get off on Wonderland Road and just follow the signs.

## Practicalities

London's **train station** is centrally situated at York and Richmond, a couple of minutes' walk east of the **bus depot** at York and Talbot. The most central **tourist office** is in the city hall at Dufferin and Wellington (Mon–Fri 8.30am–4.30pm). As far as **accommodation** is concerned, several of the downtown hotels are just flophouses, but there are two reasonably priced, central **places**, the *Travellers Motor Inn*, 636 York

(☎433-8161; doubles from $50), and the *Journey's End Hotel*, 374 Dundas (☎661-0233; doubles from $65). Doubles at around $40 are available at a cluster of **motels** east of the centre along Dundas Street: *Motor Court*, no. 1883 (☎451-2610); *White Village*, no. 1739 (☎451-5840); and *Maple Glen*, no. 1609 (☎451-8300). Even cheaper are the **bed and breakfast** places listed at the tourist office or available direct from *London B&B Association*, 720 Headley Drive (☎471-6228).

London has a good range of convenient and reasonably priced **restaurants** and **snack bars**. *Captain John and Suzy Wong's*, by the bus station at 304 Talbot St, is the most popular place in town, with excellent fixed-price, all-you-can-eat meals for around $10. Others to try are the *London Chinese Cafe*, 200 Dundas, for cheap and filling snacks and lunches; *Riccardi's*, 380 Dundas, for bargain Italian dishes; and *Anthony's Bistro*, 434 Richmond, for a superb and expensive selection of fresh fish.

# Windsor and around

"I'm going to Detroit, Michigan, to work the Cadillac line" moans the old blues number, but if he'd crossed the river he would have been equally at home amongst the car plants of **WINDSOR**. The factories are American subsidiaries built as part of a complex trading agreement which, monitored by the forceful Canadian United Automobile Workers Union, has created thousands of well-paid jobs. Living opposite Detroit makes the "Windsors" feel good in another way too: they read about Detroit's murders and mayhem, the crime and the crack, and shake their heads in disbelief and self-congratulation. A robustly working-class place, it has a handful of good restaurants and cafés, a lively rock scene, and is also a good base for **Leamington** and **Point Pelee Park**.

Windsor itself has few specific sights, but **Dieppe Gardens**, stretching along the waterfront from the junction of Ouellette and Riverside, is a good place to view the stark Detroit skyline, and is just five minutes' walk west of the **Art Gallery of Windsor**, at 445 Riverside West (Tues, Wed & Sat 11am–5pm, Thurs & Fri 11am–9pm, Sun 1–5pm; free). Well over half the space here is given over to temporary and often excellent exhibitions, while the well-displayed permanent collection, on the second and third floors, includes some good examples of the work of the Group of Seven – including Lawren Harris's skeletal *Trees and Snow* and the dramatic perspectives of Arthur Lismer's *Incoming Tide, Cape Breton Island*. Also on the third floor, a highlight of the first-rate Inuit art collection is *Hunters and Polar Bear*, a dark and elemental soapstone carving by Juanasialuk.

A couple of minutes' walk south of the gallery, the **Hiram Walker Historical Museum**, 254 Pitt St West (Tues–Sat 10am–5pm & Sun 2–5pm; free), is devoted to items of local historical interest, from displays of chairs and china to doorknobs and documents. It occupies the Georgian mansion built by Francois Baby (pronounced Baw-bee), scion of a powerful French-Canadian clan who proved consistently loyal to the British interest after the fall of New France, an example of the money going with the power. The museum takes its name from its sponsor, *Hiram Walker Vintners*, who made a fortune smuggling whiskey into the US during Prohibition.

## Practicalities

Well connected to Detroit, London, Toronto and Niagara Falls, Windsor's **bus station** is right in the centre of town on Chatham, just east of the main street, Ouellette. The **train station** is some 3km east of the city centre, near the waterfront at Walker and Wyandotte; taxi ($6) is the only public transport into town. Windsor's **Convention and Visitors' Bureau** (Mon–Fri 8.30am–4.30pm), across the road from the bus station at 80 Chatham, has details of a handful of **bed and breakfasts** from $40 per double, but most of their addresses are far from the centre. Indeed, central accommodation is limited and expensive, with the cheaper **hotel** rooms averaging out at around $75 for a double. Pick of this category are the *Best Western Rose City Inn*, 430 Ouellette (☎25-7281); *Relax Plaza Hotel*, 33 Riverside East (☎258-7774); and the *Royal Windsor Hotel*, 675 Goyeau (☎258-8411). Alternatively, there are a number of cheaper **motels** along Hwy 3B, which connects Hwy 401 with the city centre via Dougal and subsequently Ouellette. Averaging around $45 per double, this group includes the *Star Economy*, 3260 Dougal (☎969-8200); *ABC*, 3048 Dougal (☎969-5090); *Cadillac*, 2498 Dougal (☎969-9340); *Madrid Motor Hotel*, 2530 Ouellette (☎966-1860); and the *Bavarian Inn*, 1280 Ouellette (☎254-5123).

For **food**, the art gallery has a reasonably priced, third-floor restaurant with fine views over to Detroit. Other downtown restaurants include the *Traiteur's Bistro*, 656 Pitt St West, with excellent seafood and satays; *Casa Bianca*, 345 Victoria, which specialises in Italian dishes; *The Old Fish Market*, 156 Chatham St West, featuring a fine selection of seafoods; and the *Orient Express*, 188 Pitt St West, for quality Chinese cuisine.

The *Park Press*, available at the tourist office and in downtown record stores, is a free bimonthly news-sheet with comprehensive **listings** of gigs and clubs. In the city centre, there's **jazz** at *Cyrano's*, 327 Ouellette, **folk** at *Changez by Night*, 961 Wyandotte, and the *Second Cup*, 300 Ouellette, and all sorts of local bands at *Stanley's*, 340 Pitt St East, and *Key West*, 170 Wyandotte.

# Leamington and Point Pelee

About 500km long, the largely flat and often tedious northern shoreline of **Lake Erie** is broken up by a string of provincial parks and a handful of modest port-cum-resorts, such as Port Stanley, whose popularity declined when the more beautiful landscapes around Georgian Bay became accessible. The elongated peninsula of **Point Pelee National Park**, the southernmost tip of Canada's mainland, is the north shore's most distinctive attraction, most easily reached from **LEAMINGTON**, 50km southeast of Windsor, the largest agricultural centre in this highly productive region. The main drag is Erie Street, which runs up from the harbour to the town centre at Talbot, where the **Tourist Office** (May–Aug daily 9am–5pm & Sept–Oct daily 10am–4pm) is sited in a large plastic tomato, a reminder that Leamington is billed as the "tomato capital of Canada" – there's a massive *Heinz* factory here as well. The **bus station** at Erie and Mill streets, one block south of Talbot, has regular services from Windsor, London and Toronto, though there are no connections on to Point Pelee Park, which begins 8km to the south. Leamington has a handful of **motels**, with doubles from about $40, including a cluster along Talbot Street East – *Wigle's Colonial Motel* at no. 133 (☎326-3265), *Manery's Motel* at no. 161 (☎326-4436), and the *Town and Country Motor Inn*, no. 200 (☎326-4425). Another good alternative is the *Sun Parlor Motel*, 135 Talbot St West (☎326-9002).

## Point Pelee National Park

Occupying the same latitude as northern California, **Point Pelee National Park** (daily 6am–10pm; cars $5; no camping) – filling the southern half of a twenty-kilometre sandspit – can boast a variety of habitats unequalled in Canada. The park incorporates marshlands and open fields, but most remarkably it is one of the few places where the ancient **deciduous forest** of eastern North America has survived: one third of its area is covered by jungle-like forest, packed with a staggering variety of trees, from hackberry, red cedar, black walnut and blue ash to vine-covered sassafras. The park's mild climate and its mix of vegetation attract thousands of **birds** on their spring and fall migrations, and in the latter season the sandspit also funnels thousands of southward-moving **monarch butterflies** across the park, their orange and black wings a splash of colour against the greens and the browns of the undergrowth.

From the **park entrance**, it's a three-kilometre drive down behind the beach to the start of the **Marsh Boardwalk** nature trail; there's a restaurant plus bike and canoe rental facilities here. It's a further 4km to the **Visitors' Centre** (April–Sept daily 10am–6pm), where Tilden's Wood Trail and the Woodland Trail head off into the forest. Propane-powered "trains" provide a shuttle service from here to the tip of the Pelee peninsula, about 2km away, where the boardwalk is the best place to spot the monarch butterflies. From there, you can walk back along the beach.

# Sarnia and around

The land south and east of **SARNIA**, a border town 100km from London, was one of the last parts of southern Ontario to be cleared and settled, as its heavy clay soil was difficult to plough and became almost impassable in rain. Established as a lumber port in 1863, Sarnia is a negligible place in itself, but offers the nearest accommodation to a couple of southern Ontario's minor sights.

With connecting services to London, Toronto, Port Huron in Michigan, and Chicago, Sarnia's **train station** is on the southern edge of town, at the end of Russell Street, a $6 taxi ride from the centre. Far more convenient, the **bus station** is right in the centre on Christina near Cromwell, fifteen minutes' walk from the **tourist office** at 224 Vidal St North (Mon–Fri 9am–5pm). There's a cluster of **motels** with $35 doubles on London Road, the main route into Sarnia from exit 6 on Hwy 402: *Barbara Motel*, no. 1625 (☎542-5523); *Bluewater*, no. 1626 (☎542-5535); *East Court*, no. 1612 (☎542-7747); and *Faulds*, no. 1675 (☎542-5566). Downtown accommodation is limited – try the *Drawbridge Inn*, 283 Christina St North (☎337-7571; doubles from $65) or ask the tourist office for information on the handful of **bed and breakfasts**, from $30 per double.

## Petrolia and Oil Springs

About 30km southeast of Sarnia, the village of **PETROLIA** strings out along its one main drag, an agreeable little place whose street lamps are cast in the shape of oil derricks. There are several fanciful Victorian mansions here, notably **Fairbank House** (private), at Petrolia and Oil, a turreted extravagance of 1890, and **Nemo Hall**, at 419 King, an impressive brick building with splendid wrought iron trimmings that's home to an antique business (Thurs–Sun 10am–6pm).

Some 10km to the south, the hamlet of **OIL SPRINGS** was once known as the "oil capital of Canada", a rough-and-ready frontier settlement packed with hundreds of eager fortune-seekers and their hangers-on. The first prospectors were attracted to the area by patches of black and sticky oil which had seeped to the surface through narrow fissures in the rock. These **gum beds** had long been used by local native peoples for medicinal and ritual purposes, but it was not until Charles and Henry Tripp of Woodstock incorporated their oil company in 1854 that serious exploitation began. Four years later, James Miller Williams dug North America's first commercial oil well, and in 1862 a certain Hugh Shaw drilled deeper than anyone else and, at 160 feet, struck the first gusher. The shock of seeing the oil fly up into the trees prompted Shaw, a religious man, to use the words of his Bible – "And the rock poured me out rivers of oil" (Job 29:6). Shaw became rich, but his luck ran out just one year later when he was suffocated by the gas and sulphur fumes of his own well. At the height of the boom, the oil fields produced about 30,000 barrels of crude a day, most of it destined for Sarnia, transported by stage coach and wagon along 40km of specially built plank road.

On the southern edge of Oil Springs, signposted off Hwy 21, the **Oil Museum of Canada** (May–Oct daily 10am–5pm; Nov–April Mon–Fri 10am–5pm; $2.50) has been built next to the site of James Williams' original well. Highlights of the open-air display area include a nineteenth-century blacksmith's shop, with some fascinating old sepia photos taken during the oil boom, and an area of gum bed. The inside of the museum has a motley collection of oil industry artefacts and background geological information. Oil is still produced in the fields around the museum, drawn to the surface and pushed on into an underground system of pipes by some 700 low-lying pump-jacks.

## Uncle Tom's Cabin

Just 2km to the southwest of tiny DRESDEN – 25km south of Oil Springs – lies **Uncle Tom's Cabin Historic Site** (mid-May to mid-Oct daily 9am–4pm), whose clapboard house was once the home of the **Reverend Josiah Henson**, a slave who fled from Maryland to Canada in 1830 by means of the Underground Railroad (see box). Eleven years later, he and a group of abolitionist sympathisers bought 200 acres of farmland round Dresden and founded a vocational school for runaway slaves known as the "British American Institute". In 1849, Henson narrated his life experiences to **Harriet Beecher Stowe**, who went on to write the most influential abolitionist text of the day, *Uncle Tom's Cabin*, basing her main character on Henson's tales. Most of the Dresden refugees returned to the States after the Civil War, but Henson stayed till he died in 1883. The site consists of a tiny church, a cemetery and the house, containing a slave-trade museum displaying whips, handcuffs and posters advertising slave sales.

---

### THE UNDERGROUND RAILROAD

The **Underground Railroad** – the UGRR – started in the 1820s as a loose and secretive association of abolitionists dedicated to smuggling slaves from the southern states of America to Canada. By the 1840s, the UGRR had become a well-organised network of routes and safe houses, but its real importance lay not so much in the number of slaves rescued – the total was small – but rather in the psychological effect it had on those involved in the smuggling. The movement of a single runaway might involve hundreds of people, if only in the knowledge that a neighbour was breaking the law. To the extent that white Americans could be persuaded to accept even the most minor role in the Railroad, the inclination to compromise with institutional slavery was undermined, though the psychology of racism remained intact: like Uncle Tom, the freed negroes were supposed to be humble and grateful, simulating child-like responses to please their white parent-protectors.

---

# Goderich

A popular summer resort area, the southern section of the **Lake Huron shoreline** has some fine sandy beaches and the water is less polluted than Lake Ontario, but most of the coastal settlements have little to recommend them. There are two exceptions, however. The most southerly is the village of **Bayfield**, a wealthy and good-looking resort on the tree-lined bluffs overlooking the lake about 80km north of London. The other is **GODERICH**, at the mouth of the Maitland River, a delightful country town of 8000 inhabitants that's saved from postcard prettiness by its working harbour.

Goderich really began life in 1825, when the British-owned Canada Company bought two and a half million acres of southern Ontario – the **Huron Tract** – from the government at the ridiculously low rate of twelve cents an acre, amid rumours of bribery and corruption. Eager to profit on their investment, the company pushed the **Huron Road** through from Cambridge in the east to Goderich in the west, an extraordinary effort that was witnessed by a certain Mr Moffat – "The trees were so tall, the forest was eternally dark and with the constant rains it was endlessly damp . . . Clearing the centuries of undergrowth and tangled vines was only the beginning, the huge rotted deadfalls of hardwood had to be hauled deeper into the bush, already piled high with broken pine . . . Since each man was responsible for cooking his own food after a hard day's work, the men sometimes ate the fattest pork practically raw . . .To make up for such fare, a barrel of whiskey with a cup attached always stood at the roadside." Completed in 1828, the road attracted the settlers the company needed. Indeed, within thirty years, the Huron Tract had two flourishing towns, Stratford and Goderich, and was producing large surpluses of grain for export, as it continues to do today.

## The town
The wide tree-lined avenues of the geometrically planned centre radiate from a grand octagonal circus dominated by the whitestone courthouse. From here, the four main streets follow the points of the compass.

A couple of minutes' walk up North Street, the compendious **Huron County Museum** (May–Aug Mon–Sat 10am–4.30pm & Sun 1–4.30pm; Sept–April Mon–Fri 10am–4.30pm, Sun 1–4.30pm; $2) concentrates on the district's pioneers. Highlights include a fantasic array of farm implements, from simple hand tools to gigantic, clumsy machines like the steam-driven thresher. There's also a beautifully restored Canadian Pacific steam engine and intriguing displays on the history of Huron County and the Canada Company, as well as exhibition areas featuring furniture, transportation, military memorabilia and reconstructed rooms.

A ten-minute walk up to the far end of North Street and right along Gloucester brings you to the **Huron Historic Jail** at 181 Victoria Street (June–Aug daily 9am–4.30pm; Sept–Nov Mon–Fri 10am–4pm & Sat–Sun noon–4pm; $1.75), which was constructed as a combined courthouse and gaol between 1839 and 1842. The tour begins on the third floor of the main block, whose claustrophobic courtroom and council chamber were originally situated next to a couple of holding cells. The design was most unpopular with local judges, who felt threatened by the proximity of those they were sentencing. The other problem was the smell: several judges refused to conduct proceedings because of the terrible odour coming from the privies in the exercise yard below. In 1856, the administration gave way and built a new courthouse in the town centre. On the second and first floors, there's the original jailer's apartment and a string of well-preserved prison cells, reflecting various changes in design between 1841 and 1972, when the prison was finally closed. The worst is the leg-iron cell for "troublesome" prisoners, where unfortunates were chained to the wall with neither bed nor blanket. The final part of the tour is through the Governor's House, with its pleasantly restored late Victorian interior.

Back in the centre, **West Street** leads through a cutting in the bluffs to the Lake Huron shoreline, just south of the town's harbour and salt workings. The adjoining beach is pretty awful, but Goderich's sunsets are spectacular, particularly on cloudy autumnal evenings.

## Practicalities
Goderich **bus terminal** is at Victoria and East streets, a couple of minutes' walk from the town centre; there's a daily **bus** service from London to Owen Sound, via Bayfield, Goderich and Southampton, and another daily service from London to Goderich. Five minutes from the terminal, the **Visitor Centre** (mid-May to Aug daily 9am–9pm; Sept to early Oct Mon–Fri 10am–5pm) is at Victoria and Elgin; for out-of-season enquiries, head for the **City Hall**, 57G West St (Mon–Fri 9am–5pm).

Goderich has one outstanding and reasonably priced **hotel**, the *Hotel Bedford*, right in the centre at 92 The Square (☎524-7337), with doubles from $50. Built in 1896, the

*Bedford* has an enormous open stairwell fitted with a grandiose wooden staircase just like a saloon in a John Ford movie – though the modernised rooms are a bit of a disappointment. Alternatively, there are a number of slightly cheaper **motels** dotted along Hwy 21 on the outskirts of town; the *Maple Leaf Motel* (☎524-2302) is more centrally situated at 54 Victoria Street. The visitor centre and city hall have the details of a number of **bed and breakfasts**, starting at $30 per double. Most of their addresses are near the town centre and some are located in fine Victorian houses, with charges rising to $45 per double. Goderich **youth hostel**, RR#2 (☎524-8428; $8.50), is a lakeside log cabin, 7km from town (no buses). There's **camping** in the *Maitland Falls Conservation Area* (☎524-6429), around 8km east of town, to the north of the hamlet of Benmiller.

For **eating**, the *Goderich Steak House and Tavern*, 42 West, serves up excellent, standard dishes at reasonable prices, and the *Park House*, 168 West, is popular with the town's teenagers and has good salads. *Bailey's Restaurant*, 120 The Square, has a more imaginative menu, but it's far more expensive. If you're on a tight budget, try *Woolworth's Snack Bar*, South St.

# The Bruce Peninsula

Dividing the main body of Lake Huron from Georgian Bay, the **Bruce Peninsula** boasts two of Ontario's most impressive national parks: the Bruce Peninsula Park, whose magnificent cliff-line walks cross the best part of the east shore, and the Fathom Five Marine Park, whose extraordinary rock formations, plentiful shipwrecks and pellucid waters provide wonderful sport for divers. You'll need a car to visit, though – the peninsula has no bus services.

## Owen Sound
Just under 200km northwest from Toronto, **OWEN SOUND** lies in the steep ravine around the mouth of the Sydenham River, at the base of the peninsula. In its heyday, Owen Sound was a rough and violent town packed with brothels and bars, prompting the Americans to establish a consulate whose main function was to bail out drunk and disorderly sailors. For the majority it was an unpleasant place to live, and the violence spawned the Women's Christian Temperance Organisation, whose success was such that an alcohol ban was imposed in 1906 and only lifted in 1972. The town was in decline long before the return of the bars, its port facilities undercut by the railways from the 1920s. It's now a desultory sort of place, with only three sights of any interest: the **Marine-Rail Museum**, overlooking the harbour in the old railway station at 1165 1st Ave West (June–Sept Tues–Sat 10am–noon & 1–4pm; Sun 1–4pm; donations), with photos of old sailing ships and their captains; the **Tom Thomson Memorial Art Gallery**, 840 1st Ave West (June–Aug Mon–Sat 10am–5pm & Sun 1–5pm; Sept–May Tues–Sat 10am–5pm; donations), which has temporary exhibitions by Canadian artists and a clutch of Thomson's less familiar paintings; and the **Billy Bishop Museum** on 3rd Ave West (Sat & Sun 1–4pm; donations), concentrating on the military exploits of Canada's VC-winning air ace.

Owen Sound **bus station** is at 10th Street East and 3rd Ave East, five minutes' walk from the **tourist office**, at 832 2nd Ave East (Mon–Fri 9am–5pm; ☎371 9833). Reasonably priced downtown **accommodation** is limited; try the *Company Motor Inn*, 840 3rd Ave East (☎371-2266), with doubles from $50. There's also a handful of **motels** east of the town centre along 9th Ave East, Hwy 6/10 – best bet is the *Diamond*, no. 713 (☎371-2011), with doubles from $50. Alternatively, the tourist office has the details of half a dozen **bed and breakfasts**, with doubles from $35 per night. For downtown

**food**, stick to *Green's Deli*, 261 9th St East, which serves excellent, cheap snacks and meals that include homemade *latke*, a potato pancake, and *beef knish*.

## The Bruce Peninsula National Park

Most of the peninsula's villages are inconclusive affairs, little more than a few shops and restaurants surrounded by second homes, and the first place worth stopping along Hwy 6 is just 10km south of Tobermory, at the sign marked **Cyprus Lake**. From here, it's 5km down to the campgrounds and walking trails of the **Bruce Peninsula National Park** (all year; ☎596-2233), a magnificent mixture of limestone cliff, rocky beach, wetland and forest that's best visited in June when the wildflowers are in bloom and it's not too crowded. The park has four walking tracks which start at the northern edge of Cyprus Lake; three of them connect with the **Bruce Trail**, the 700-kilometre hiking trail from Queenston to Tobermory.

## Tobermory

Sitting on the northern tip of the peninsula, **TOBERMORY** is an unpretentious fishing village fanning out from a sheltered double harbour – known as Big Tub and Little Tub. Many motorists pass straight through, making use of the **car ferry** to South Baymouth on Manitoulin Island (June–Aug 6 daily; late April to May & Sept–Oct 2–3 daily; 2hr; $9 single, $20 cars), but quite a few hang around to explore the Fathom Five Park, calling in first at the **National Park Visitor Centre** right on the Little Tub waterfront (July–Aug daily 9am–9pm; June & Sept Mon–Fri 9am–4.30pm).

There are a dozen or so **hotels** and **motels** in and around the village, with the cheaper establishments charging around $60 per double, though there are considerable seasonal variations. Convenient choices include the *Blue Bay Motel* (☎596-2392), *Bruce Anchor* (☎596-2555), *Harbourside* (☎596-2422), and the *Tobermory Lodge* (☎596-2224) – the last also owns some **cottages** and **chalets** overlooking Little Tub, charging $50 daily for one or two people. The village has a couple of **restaurants** specialising in seafood – try the whitefish and ocean perch at the *Lighthouse*, just up from the ferry.

Prospective divers need to book in at the **Registration Centre** (mid-May to Oct daily 8am–4.30pm), beside the Little Tub, and **diving gear** can be hired round the corner at *G&S Watersports*. **Boat rental** is available along the waterfront, working out at about $40 per day. For less immediate exploration of the waters and shipwrecks of the Fathom Five, a multitude of **boat trips** begin at Little Tub; the longer, more worthwhile excursions stop at Flowerpot Island (see below) and average out at about $9.

### FATHOM FIVE MARINE NATIONAL PARK

Tobermory's main attraction is the **Fathom Five Marine National Park**, whose nineteen uninhabited islands are enclosed within a boundary drawn round the waters off the end of the peninsula. To protect the natural habitat, only **Flowerpot Island**, 4km from the mainland, has any amenities, with six tiny campgrounds and five marked walking trails of roughly two hours each. A delightful spot, Flowerpot takes its name from two pink and grey rock pillars that have been eroded away from its eastern shore – best seen from the Flowerpot Loop Trail.

Surprisingly, there are usually vacancies at the **campgrounds** – places can be booked at the Park Visitor Centre in Tobermory, which also provides a good guide to the island's fauna and flora. Flowerpot is accessible from Tobermory by **water taxi**, with a going rate of around $15 for the round trip. Make sure you arrange a collection time with the pilot and pack your own food and drink.

The telephone code for all the following towns in southern Ontario is ☎705.

# Lake Simcoe: Barrie and Orillia

Highway 400 north from Toronto, the obvious route to the southern shore of Georgian Bay and to Algonquin Park, runs through **BARRIE**, a mundane industrial and commuter town beside a western arm of Lake Simcoe. The town centre has been recently spruced up with pinkish pavement bricks and ornate lampposts, and there really isn't anything else to say, except that Barrie has good bus connections to the south and north. Half an hour's drive from Barrie, **ORILLIA** makes a more pleasant stop on Hwy 11, the road to Algonquin. The town lies close to the narrow channel that connects the northern tip of Lake Simcoe with Lake Couchiching, a waterway that was once a centre of Huron settlement. When **Samuel de Champlain** arrived here in 1615, he promptly handed out muskets to his Huron allies, encouraging them to attack their Iroquois rivals in order to establish French control of the fur trade – an intervention that was to lead to the destruction of the Jesuit outpost at Sainte Marie in 1649 (see below). Two hundred years later, a second wave of Europeans cleared the district's forests, and today Orillia is a trim town of 24,000 citizens, part lakeside resort, part farming centre – and the hometown of the poet and musician Gordon Lightfoot.

Orillia **town centre** spreads out on either side of the main drag, Mississaga Street, which runs west from Lake Couchiching. At the foot of Mississaga, **Centennial Park** incorporates a brand new marina and has a boardwalk running north to **Couchiching Beach Park**, complete with an Edwardian bandstand and a bronze statue of Champlain. Centennial Park is the embarkation point for sightseeing **cruises** of lakes Simcoe and Couchiching on board the *Island Princess*, a replica of a paddle-boat steamer. The main non-aquatic attraction is 3km east along Hwy 12 – the **Stephen Leacock House** (daily mid-June to Aug 10am–5pm; mid-April to mid-June & Sept to mid-Dec 10am–2pm; $2). Built in 1928 in the colonial style, with symmetrical pitched roofs and an ornate verandah, this was the summer home of the humorist and academic Stephen Leacock until his death in 1944. His most famous book, *Sunshine Sketches of a Little Town*, gently mocks the hypocrisies and vanities of the people of Mariposa, an imaginary town so clearly based on Orillia that it caused great local offence. There's not much to look at in the house, just a few cartoons based on his novels and some incidental memorabilia, but the gift shop sells almost all of his works.

The ODCVA, Orillia's combined **bus terminal**, **train station** and **Convention and Visitors' Association** (Mon–Fri 9am–5pm; ☎326-8687), is a ten-minute walk south of Mississaga Street, straight along Front Street. There are several cheap **motels** on Laclie, the northern extension of Front Street, with doubles at around $40: the *Northcourt* at no. 320 (☎325-2751), *Orillia* at no. 370 (☎325-2354), and the *Holiday* at no. 436 (☎325-1316). More pleasant than these, though, is the *Lakeside Inn*, 86 Creighton St (☎325-2514; doubles $65), overlooking Lake Simcoe, about 5km east of town – drive across the narrows and take the signposted turning off Hwy 12. The ODCVA also has the details of a handful of **bed and breakfasts**, from $35 per double. The town's **youth hostel** (mid-July to Sept; ☎325-0970; $11), accessible by bus from the station, is located on Lake Couchiching at 198 Borland Street East.

For **food**, *Belamy's*, 16 Front St North, has a good range of burgers and sandwiches, and the *Blue Anchor Brewpub*, 47 West St South at Mississaga, serves tasty lunches.

# Nottawasaga Bay and Severn Sound

East of Owen Sound the southern curve of Georgian Bay forms **Nottawasaga Bay**, whose largest town is the busy and unremarkable port of COLLINGWOOD. Though it's a few minutes' drive from two much-visited outcrops of the Niagara Escarpment – the **Blue Mountain**, now a major winter sports centre, and the **Devil's Glen**, preferred by

# GEORGIAN BAY & SEVERN SOUND

Algonquin

Parry Sound

Five Mile Bay

Otter Lake

Huntsville

Lake Joseph

Lake Rosseau

Georgian Bay Islands

Twelve Mile Bay

Moon River

GEORGIAN BAY

Go Home R.

Lake Muskoka

Bracebridge

Georgian Bay Islands

Giants Tomb I

Beausoleil Island

Awenda Provincial Park

Gravenhurst

Honey Harbour

Big Chute

Severn River

SEVERN SOUND

Penetanguishene

Port Severn

Port Stanton

Midland

North River

Sainte Marie among the Hurons

Orillia

Collingwood

Wasaga Beach

Owen Sound

Nottawasaga River

LAKE SIMCOE

Coates River

Barrie

Angus

Mad River

Cookstown

N

0        20 km

↓ Toronto

walkers – this is not a place to linger. Just about the only attractive spot in this over-crowded holiday zone is the **Wasaga Beach Provincial Park** (April–Sept & mid-Dec to March), several kilometres of protected sand close to **WASAGA BEACH**, Ontario's busiest resort. The resort's **travel information centre** is behind Beach Area 3, roughly 3km west of Nancy Island at 35 Dunkerron Street (June–Aug daily 9am–5pm; May & Sept Mon–Fri 9am–5pm; ☎429-2247). This has extensive **accommodation** listings, anything from trailer rental to hotels and cottages. There's also a number of reasonably priced **motels** along Mosley Street, which runs the length of the resort, a few minutes' walk from the beach. Try the *Lucky Strike* at no. 148 (☎429-2622), *Mayfair* at no. 790 (☎429-2004), or the *Mermaid* at no. 1600 (☎429-3643), all at between $25 and $35 per double.

In contrast to the tawdriness of Nottawasaga, **Severn Sound**, the southeastern inlet of Georgian Bay, is one of the most beautiful parts of Ontario, its sheltered southern shore lined with tiny ports and its deep blue waters studded by the outcrops of the **Georgian Bay Islands National Park**.

## Penetanguishene

The most westerly town on Severn Sound, homely **PENETANGUISHENE** – "place of the rolling white sands" – was the site of one of Ontario's first European settlements, a Jesuit mission founded in 1634, then abandoned in 1649 following the burning of Sainte Marie. Europeans returned some 150 years later to establish a trading station where local Ojibwa exchanged pelts for food and metal tools. However, the settlement remained insignificant until just after the War of 1812, when the British built a naval dockyard that attracted shopkeepers and suppliers from both French and British communities. Today Penetanguishene is one of the few places in southern Ontario which maintains a bilingual tradition.

As is so often the case, it's the atmosphere and setting that please rather than any individual sight, though the long main drag, **Main Street**, is a pleasant enough place for a stroll, its bars and shops installed behind sturdy red-brick facades. While you're here, take a peek also at the **Centennial Museum**, 13 Burke St (June–Aug daily 10am–5pm), a couple of minutes east of Main Street along Nelson. The museum is sited in a reconstruction of a general store, and features a good collection of old photos and postcards illustrating the town's early history. From the north end of Main Street, there are also three-hour **cruises** of the southern stretches of Georgian Bay and the Thirty Thousand Islands (June to early Sept, 1 daily; $10). Finally, some 7km east of the town centre – follow the signs – is the **Historic Naval and Military Establishments** (June–Aug 10am–5pm; $5), a replica of the British base that was founded here in 1817, staffed by replica military personnel.

Well connected to Midland and Toronto, Penetanguishene **bus station** is just off Main Street, a ten-minute walk south of the harbour, where the **tourist office** (July–Aug daily 9am–7pm; May–June & Sept–Oct Mon–Fri 9am–5pm) has details of **bed and breakfasts** at $35 per double, the town's best bet. There are also two downtown **hotels**, *The Brule*, 118 Main St (☎549-8983; doubles from $50), and the rough-and-ready *Commodore*, 59 Main St (☎549-4464; doubles from $40). As for **eating**, *Memories Roadhouse*, 32 Main St, has an excellent cheap menu, and *The Watergate*, 7 Nelson St, specialises in steaks.

### AWENDA PROVINCIAL PARK

**Awenda Provincial Park** (mid-May to mid-Sept & mid-Dec to mid-March; ☎549-2231), just 11km northwest of Penetanguishene, is one of Ontario's larger parks, its delightful mainland portion dominated by a dense deciduous forest that spreads south from the Nipissing Bluff on the edge of Georgian Bay. The other section lies offshore, around Giants Tomb Island, but you'll need to bring your own boat to get there.

Awenda has a few small rock-and-pebble beaches, four good campgrounds (no hook-ups), and five hiking trails starting near the park office, which has trail guides and maps. A recommended route is to take the Brule Trail through the forest to connect with the Dune Trail, which leads to a vantage point above the bay – 5km in all.

## Midland

MIDLAND has suffered badly from recurrent recession, losing its engineering plants in the 1930s, its shipyards in 1957 and much of its flour mill capacity in 1967. Despite provincial and governmental attempts to entice new companies here, the town remains a comparatively poor community whose main street – King Street – is a parade of cheap fast-food joints, pool halls and traditional barbers' shops. Recent efforts to cash in on the tourist industry have included the construction of a marina and the re-development of the harbourfront, where cruises of the Thirty Thousand Islands leave from mid-May to early September (1–4 daily; $11).

Sooner or later, every schoolkid in Midland gets taken to the Huronia Museum and Huron Indian Village (mid-May to mid-Oct Mon–Sat 9am–5pm & Sun 10am–5pm; April to mid-May & mid-Oct to mid-Dec closed Sun; $4), a twenty-minute walk south of the harbour along King Street. Highlights of the museum include a large number of Huron artefacts and a series of photos tracing the pioneer settlement of Midland. The adjacent Indian Village is a replica of a sixteenth-century Huron settlement, its high pali-sade encircling storage pits, drying racks, a sweat bath, a medicine man's lodge and two longhouses. These characteristic Huron constructions, with their bark-covered walls of cedar poles bent to form a protective arch, contain tiers of rough wooden bunks draped with furs, whilst herbs, fish, skins and tobacco hang from the roof to dry.

Midland bus station is close to the waterfront, a couple of minutes' walk east of the Tourist Information Centre, at the foot of King Street (June–Aug Mon–Fri 8.30am–5pm & Sat–Sun 10am–6pm; Sept–May Mon–Fri 8.30am–5pm). The centre has details of a wide range of accommodation, including a handful of central bed and break-fasts, from $40 per double, as well as a dozen cheap bed and breakfasts in the small communities along the bay shoreline. In Midland itself there are several reasonably priced motels on Yonge Street, which cuts across King about 1km south of the harbourfront, including the *Park Villa* at no. 751 (☎526-2219; doubles from $50), and the *Shamrock* at no. 955 (☎526-7851; doubles from $60).

For food, try the *La Mar Steak and Seafood Restaurant*, 238 Midland Ave at Dominion, one block east of King, or the cheaper *Pizza Delight*, 301 King. The *Midland Boatworks*, by the town dock, is a popular, boisterous bar, but the meals are dreadful.

## Sainte-Marie among the Hurons

One of Ontario's most arresting historical attractions is Sainte-Marie among the Hurons (late May to mid-Oct daily 10am–5pm; $5), the carefully researched and beau-tifully maintained site of a crucial episode in Canadian history. It's 5km east of Midland beside Hwy 12 – there are no buses, but the taxi fare from Midland is only $5.

In 1608, Samuel de Champlain returned to Canada convinced that the only way to make the fur trade profitable was by developing alliances with the native hunters. The Huron were the obvious choice, as they already acted as go-betweens in the exchange of corn, tobacco and hemp from the bands to the south and west of their territory, for the pelts collected to the north. In 1611, having participated in Huron attacks on the Iroquois, Champlain cemented the alliance by a formal exchange of presents. His deci-sion to champion one tribe against another was to entirely disrupt the native societies of the St Lawrence and Great Lakes area.

Social cohesion within the Huron community was undermined after 1639, when the Jesuits established their centre of operations at Sainte Marie, where they succeeded in converting a substantial minority of the native people, by then enfeebled by three

## THE HURONS

From around the thirteenth to the middle of the seventeenth century, three main **Iroquoian-speaking confederacies** occupied the lands around lakes Huron and Ontario. The Five Nations Iroquois lived in the forests of what is today upper New York State; the Neutrals, or Atiwandaronks, were settled in southern Ontario, between the Niagara Peninsula and the Detroit River; and the third, the **Hurons**, ancient enemies of the Five Nations, were found to the south of Georgian Bay.

In the fourth century BC, the Maya of Central America had learnt how to cultivate corn, beans, squash and sunflowers, four main crops which formed the basis of a relatively balanced diet. It took several hundred years for these skills to be passed north to the peoples of the Great Lakes, but once they were learnt, the Iroquois quickly developed an agrarian economy. The area around Georgian Bay is dotted with the remains of **Huron villages**, which grew so rapidly with the advance of agriculture that some were home to as many as 5000 people by the time the French arrived. Each was built within a defensive palisade which protected a series of fields, work areas and communal longhouses, yet they were not permanent settlements – they were abandoned when the local timber supply was exhausted and the soil became less productive, and were often left empty when there were full-scale hunting, fishing or trading expeditions.

The Hurons had a sophisticated **social structure**. Leadership was shared by various short-term chiefs, each with his own area of responsibility, from organising war parties to settling internal disputes. There was no rigid caste system, but Huron society did allow for the personal accumulation of wealth, on the understanding that the better-off would give generously to the community and sponsor lavish feasts. Another check to the development of a prosperous elite was the Hurons' ambivalent attitude to "theft". They treated it as a contest of skills between the individuals concerned, and there was no formal system of punishment or reparation.

Like the Iroquois peoples, the Hurons were **animists**, investing all that surrounded them with *oki*, or spirits, which had the capacity for both good and evil. Containment of these spirits was the office of the powerful **shaman**, a priestly medicine man who bridged the gap between the seen and the unseen. Huron dead were placed on wooden platforms just outside the village, but every ten years or so, during the **Feast of the Dead**, the bodies were collected, cleaned of their flesh and dropped in a communal bone pit. During the Feast, no special reverence was paid to dead warriors, but **warfare** was an important part of their culture, whether to avenge a wrong, displace an enemy or merely to prove the valour of their young men. However, major engagements were rare and the Hurons preferred to ambush small groups of hostiles, killing them on the spot or offering to incorporate them in their clan. For reasons which remain obscure, though it may partly be connected with fertility rites, some captives were savagely tortured and occasionally eaten.

It was chiefly the interference of the Europeans that enabled the Five Nations Iroquois to overwhelm the Hurons in the war of 1649. The few who survived fled to Québec, and their lands were left empty until the Algonquian-speaking Ojibwa spread down from the north in the next century.

European sicknesses: measles, smallpox and influenza. In 1648 the Dutch on the Hudson River began to sell firearms to the Iroquois, who launched a full-scale invasion in March 1649, slaughtering their enemies as they moved in on Sainte Marie. Fearing for their lives, the Jesuits of Sainte Marie burnt their settlement and fled. Eight thousand Hurons went with them; most starved to death on Christian Island, but a few made it to Québec. During the campaign two Jesuit priests, fathers Brébeuf and Lalemant, were captured at the outpost of Saint-Louis, near Victoria Harbour, where they were bound to the stake and tortured: the image of Catholic bravery and Indian cruelty lingered in the minds of French-Canadians long after the sufferings of the Hurons had been forgotten.

By the entrance through Sainte-Marie's palisade the site **museum** features a variety of audio-visual displays on the culture of the Hurons, the history of the mission and its reconstruction. Behind the museum, the large **mission** has been painstakingly restored, its 22 wooden buildings divided into two sections: the Jesuit area with its watchtowers, chapel, forge and stables, and a native area including a bark-covered longhouse, a hospital and simple tepees. It takes some imagination to see the place as it appeared to Father Lalemant, who saw " a miniature picture of hell . . . on every side naked bodies, black and half-roasted, mingled pell-mell with the dogs . . . you will not reach the end of the cabin before you are completely befouled with soot, filth and dirt". Summer guides act out the parts of Huron and European with great gusto, though they show a certain reluctance to eat the staple food of the region, *sagamité*, a porridge of cornmeal seasoned with rotten fish.

Overlooking Sainte-Marie, the twin-spired church of the **Martyrs' Shrine** (daily 9am–7pm) was built in 1926 to commemorate the eight Jesuits who were killed in Huronia between 1642 and 1649. Blessed by Pope John Paul II in 1984 – when he bafflingly remarked that it was "a symbol of unity of faith in a diversity of cultures" – the church is popular with pilgrims, who've left a stack of discarded crutches in the transept.

## Port Severn and Honey Harbour

Perched on the northern shore of Severn Sound, beside Hwy 69, straggling **PORT SEVERN** is the gateway to the **Trent-Severn Waterway** (open June–Sept), a 400-kilometre canalised route which connects Georgian Bay with Lake Ontario. With a minimum depth of only two metres, it's of little commercial importance today, but until the late nineteenth century it was one of southern Ontario's principal cargo routes. From Lock #45 in Port Severn, two-hour **cruises** (May–Sept 1 daily; $10) travel as far as the **Big Chute Marine Railway**, where boats are lifted over the 18-metre drop between the upper and lower levels of the river.

It's 10km northwest from here across the mouth of the Severn to **HONEY HARBOUR**, the nearest port to the Georgian Bay Islands National Park. Little more than a couple of shops and a few self-contained hotel-resorts, the village is very much a family place today, but was a wild spot in the 1970s, when the bar of the *Delawana Inn* was the site of violent confrontations between Toronto's Hell's Angels and local Ojibwa families. The feud ended with the Angels walking home after their bikes had been dynamited.

The *Gray Coach* **bus** service from Toronto to Sudbury passes through Port Severn, but there are no connections on to Honey Harbour. The area's cheapest hotel is the *Port Severn Inn* (☎538-2675), off Hwy 69, with doubles from $40; at the other end of the scale are the attractively sited cabins of the *Delawana Inn* (mid-May to Sept; ☎756-2424) – full board and lodging here starts at $200 per cabin in the season, with substantial discounts on various sorts of package deals. Honey Harbour also has two **bed and breakfasts**: in the home of Gail Barrie, just across from the *Delawana* (☎756-2404; doubles $60); and the *Elk's Hideaway* (☎756-2706; doubles $45), right in the centre of the village opposite the national park office. **Restaurants** are few and far between – your best bet is to eat where you sleep.

### THE GEORGIAN BAY ISLANDS NATIONAL PARK

A beautiful area to cruise, the **Georgian Bay Islands National Park** consists of a scatter of about sixty islands spread between Twelve Mile Bay and Honey Harbour, a distance of about 50km. The park's two distinct landscapes – the glacier-scraped rock of the Canadian Shield and the hardwood forests and thicker soils of the south – meet at the northern end of the largest island, **Beausoleil**, a forty-minute boat ride west of

Honey Harbour. The most visited and scenically diverse part of the park, Beausoleil has eight **hiking trails**, including two which start at the **Cedar Spring landing stage**, on the southeastern shore – the Treasure Trail, which heads north behind the marshes along the edge of the island, and the Christian Trail, which cuts through beech and maple stands to the balsam and hemlock groves overlooking the rocky beaches of the western shoreline. At the northern end of Beausoleil, within comfortable walking distance of the **Little Dog** and **Chimney jetties**, the Cambrian and Fairy trails are two delightful routes through the harsher Canadian Shield scenery, while just to the west, the Dossyonshing Trail tracks through a mixed area of wetland, forest and bare granite that covers the transitional zone between the two main landscapes.

A visit to the **national park** office in Honey Harbour (daily 8am–4.30pm; ☎756-2415) is essential, not only because it provides a full range of information on walking trails, flora and fauna, but also because you should let the warders know where you're going and when you expect to return. The park is open all year and, in the winter, the wardens also advise on where it's safe to ski across to the islands. The park has fifteen **campgrounds**, thirteen on Beausoleil and one each on Island 95B and Centennial Island – all charge $7 a night and operate on a first-come, first-served basis. In July and August they can be fully occupied, so ask about availability at the office before you set out. Next door to the national park office is the **water taxi** service to Centennial Island ($20 one way), Island 95B ($20), and Beausoleil ($20); there are no set times, but in summer boats leave for Beausoleil every hour or so. Fares to the park's other islands are negotiable, but make sure there's an agreed pick-up time wherever you go. If you want to head southwest, a one-way water taxi-trip to Midland costs around $60.

# CENTRAL ONTARIO

Lying between Lake Ontario's north shore and the Ottawa Valley border with Québec, **central Ontario** is a region that now relies on the lumber industry and tourism, but until the late eighteenth century this was the hunting ground of the Ojibwa, Cree and Ottawa tribes. This native population was squeezed out by the arrival of United Empire Loyalists escaping from the newly independent States, a group who initially settled along the St Lawrence Valley then spread north in parallel with the construction of the **Rideau Canal** from Kingston to Ottawa. Once the economic potential of the vast interior had been realised, rail lines were laid down and the **Trent-Severn** waterway was opened up from Trenton to Georgian Bay, to serve the farmers, merchants and timber barons who rushed to populate the wilderness.

With Ontario's industries using road transport, most of the traffic on the Rideau Canal and Trent-Severn are now recreational boats, and the lakelands of the **Muskokas** and **Kawarthas** also attract vanloads of anglers and canoeists. However, the wondrous expanse of **Algonquin Park** is the best reason for visiting central Ontario, giving a glimpse of the state of this region before the white invaders got at it. Apart from the road into Algonquin, there are three other broad routes through this region: from Toronto to Ottawa, either directly via **Peterborough** and Highway 7 or the longer route via the Loyalist towns of Lake Ontario's north shore, past historic **Kingston** and along a broad sweep of the St Lawrence; and from Port Severn along Highway 69 towards Sudbury, following the beautiful east coast of the vast **Georgian Bay**.

The Parry Sound, Muskoka, Peterborough and Algonquin telephone code is ☎705.

# Parry Sound and around

**PARRY SOUND**, 225km north of Toronto, is the principal resort on the shore of Georgian Bay. Named after the Arctic explorer Sir William Edward Parry, it earned the nickname of "Parry Hoot" because the log-drivers on the river chose this as the place to get drunk in. These days the town has become a popular stopover for boats roaming the Thirty Thousand Islands, of which you can get a taster by taking a **cruise** from the Government Wharf at the end of Bay Street. Canada's largest sightseeing cruise ship – the *Island Queen* – just manages to squeeze through the Thirty Thousand Islands in a spectacular and hair-raising trip (June to early Sept 1–2 daily; $12). Should you want to **stay**, the best idea is to contact the *Parry Sound and District Bed and Breakfast Association* (☎746-8372), who can fix you up with a place to suit your needs and budget; their average doubles are $40. Parry Sound's eateries are nothing to get excited about, but most are along James Street in the south end of town.

### Killbear Provincial Park

The wild Georgian Bay shoreline, formed by glaciers which scoured the rock and dumped mighty boulders onto its long beaches, is seen at its finest in **Killbear Provincial Park** (mid-May to early Oct), reached by driving 18km north from Parry Sound on Hwy 69 then 20km southwest on Hwy 559. Along the shore, windswept, crooked cedars and black spruce cling precariously to the Canadian Shield's southern rocky outcrops, whilst the interior of this peninsular park is a forest of maple, beech and yellow birch. The three-and-a-half-kilometre loop of the **Lookout Point Trail**, which starts about 1.5km east of the park office and heads to a lookout across Parry Sound, is the best of the park's three short hiking trails. **Campgrounds**, some by the water and others in the forest, need to be pre-registered at one of the two campground offices, situated on the park's only road (☎342-5226). For **canoe rental** the nearest outlet is *Killbear Park Mall Ltd* (☎342-5747) in NOBEL, about 5km south of the Hwy 559 turnoff.

# The Muskokas

Served by *Gray Coach* buses and *VIA* trains as far as Huntsville, the route to Algonquin from Toronto passes through the **Muskokas**, a region of more than one and a half thousand lakes and hundreds of urbanite cottage retreats. Named after an Ojibwa chief, Mesqua-Ukee, who settled here with his people after aiding the British in their defence of Little York during the war of 1812, the area was opened to tourism in 1860, when two hikers made the two-day trek from Toronto to a small Ojibwa settlement where Gravenhurst now stands. By the 1890s this had become the in-place to holiday for the wealthy families of southern Ontario, and it's still primarily the preserve of city folks with lots of loot.

### Gravenhurst

The gateway to Muskoka is **GRAVENHURST**, sited at the southern end of Lake Muskoka 163km north of Toronto. A favourite with painters ever since the Group of Seven painted here, Gravenhurst is also host to the **Muskoka Festival** (late June to early Sept), a springboard for young Canadian performers. Outside of festival time, the main attraction is the **Bethune Memorial House**, 235 John St (daily June to early Sept 9am–6pm; early Sept to May 10am–5pm; free), the birthplace of Norman Bethune, a doctor who introduced Western medicine to the Chinese in the 1930s. His fame even spread to Chairman Mao, who dedicated an essay to him after the revolution. Restored to its appearance in 1890, the house has displays on Bethune's accomplishments – detailed in English, French and Chinese for the benefit of the Chinese leaders who make frequent pilgrimages to the house. Having surveyed the good doctor's career, you could hop aboard *RMS Segwun*, a 105-year-old steamship, which cruises up Lake Muskoka (June to early Oct 5–7 weekly; $15) giving a fine view of the hills and the summer mansions of Ontario's plutocrats.

The **information centre** at 150 Second St (Mon–Fri 9am–5pm) offers an **accommodation** service; for **bed and breakfast** you could also contact the *Muskoka Bed and Breakfast Association* (☎687-4395), whose average rate is $50 per double. *KOA* have a campground with full facilities on Hwy 3 just outside town. For very posh food head for *Ascona Place*, 1 Bethune Drive (☎687-5906), possibly the best **restaurant** in the Muskokas – stick to an average bottle and the bill should not exceed $50 each; a good alternative is *Sloanes*, 155 Muskoka St, which has been here as long as Gravenhurst.

## Bracebridge

Situated 25km north of Gravenhurst, **BRACEBRIDGE** prides itself on being "Halfway to the North Pole" – the powers that be have decided this is the summer home of Santa Claus, decorating the town with all-year banners of the jolly soul and building a horrendous **Santa's Village** just west of town (mid-June to early Sept daily 10am–6pm; $12, under-5s free). Admission price includes unlimited use of rides like Rudolf's Roller Coaster Sleigh Ride, Elves' Island and the Christmas Ball Ferris Wheel, as well as a meeting with Santa Claus so the kids can get their orders in nice and early.

The town's **information centre** at 63 Kimberley Avenue (Mon–Fri 9am–5pm) has details on **accommodation** in the area.

## Huntsville

The main attraction of **HUNTSVILLE** – 35km beyond Bracebridge – is that it's as near as the buses and trains get to Algonquin Park, though it does have the pleasant **Muskoka Pioneer Village** on Brunel Road (daily late June to early Sept 10am–5pm; early Sept to Oct 10am–4pm; $4), where costumed staff demonstrate mid-nineteenth-century cooking and the like. If you need a place to stay before heading into Algonquin, cheap **motels** are located along King William Street – check out *Towne House Motel* at no. 23 (☎789-9661; doubles $42); *Sunrise Motel* at no. 33 (☎789-9673; doubles $40); or the *Rainbow Motel* at no. 32 (☎789-5514; doubles $45).

# Algonquin Park

Created in 1893, **Algonquin Park** is Ontario's oldest provincial park and for many people is the quintessential Canadian landscape. Located on the southern edge of the Canadian Shield, the park straddles a transitional zone, with the hilly two-thirds to the west covered in a hardwood forest of sugar maple, beech and yellow birch, whilst in the drier eastern part jack pines, white pines and red pines dominate. Throughout the park, the lakes and rocky rounded hills are interspersed with black spruce bogs, a type of vegetation typical of areas far further north.

Wildlife is as varied as the flora – any trip to Algonquin is characterised by the echo of birdsong, from the loons' ghostly call to the screech of ravens. Beavers, moose, black bears and racoons are all resident, as are white-tailed deer, whose population thrives on the young shoots that replace the trees felled by the park's loggers. Public "howling parties" set off into the wilderness during August in a search of **timber wolves** – each expedition takes a park ranger who knows exactly where to head, as the movements of the packs are charted with radio transmitters. If you don't have your own transport enquire at the information centres in case there's a spare seat.

Access to the park is via either the **West Gate**, 45km from Huntsville on Hwy 60, or the less convenient **East Gate**, 56km away through the park's southern end. There's an **information centre** at each gate (late April to mid-Oct daily 8am–6pm, open till 8pm Fri). Because Algonquin is the most popular of Ontario's parks, the park operates a **permit system** which allows a limited number of cars through each entrance every day; to avoid being turned away, either arrive early or book your $5 day permit by credit card (☎633-5538). Away from Hwy 60 – or the Parkway Corridor as it's known within the park boundary – walking and canoeing are the only means of transport; before striking off into the interior, it's worth investing in *Backpacking Trails of Algonquin Provincial Park* ($1.50) and *Canoe Routes of Algonquin Provincial Park* ($2.75), available at the information centres.

### The Parkway Corridor

Accommodation along the **Parkway Corridor** is provided by eight lakeside **campgrounds**, whose location is indicated by distances from the West Gate. The less popular sites are those which prohibit motorboats – namely Canisbay Lake (km 23), Coon Lake (km 40) and Kearney Lake (km 37). Camping from October to March is only available at Mew Lake (km 30), and the only sites that can be **reserved** (☎633-5538 or ☎633-5725; $4 fee) are Pog, Two Rivers, Mew Lake and Canisbay. Though meagre **food** supplies are available near Canoe Lake (km 14), Two Rivers (km 31) and Opeongo Lake (about 6km north of km 45), you are best advised to bring your own.

Of the ten **day-treks** from Hwy 60, the two-kilometre **Beaver Pond Trail** (km 45) is a rugged but easy trail which takes you past huge beaver dams, while the equally short but steeper **Lookout Trail** (km 39) gives a remarkable view of the park. For a longer trail with greater chances of spotting wildlife, the eleven-kilometre **Mizzy Lake Trail** (km 15) is recommended. Other points of interest in the Parkway Corridor include two small **museums**: the Park Museum at km 20 (mid-May to mid-June Sat & Sun 9am–5pm; mid-June to early Oct daily 9am–5pm) and a Pioneer Logging Exhibit at the East Gate. A totem pole at Canoe Lake marks the spot where Tom Thomson, the artist who inspired the Group of Seven, died by drowning – the mystery of whether the expert canoeist died accidentally or by murder has never been solved.

### The Park Interior

The depths of the **Park Interior** are best explored by **canoe**, and there are several outfitters in the small towns around the park's periphery, and in the Parkway Corridor itself from May to mid-October – the *Portage Store* at Canoe Lake and the *Opeongo Store* at Opeongo Lake. The latter also runs a useful water taxi service and shuttle into the Park Interior. Because of Algonquin's popularity, two weeks' advance reservation for canoe rental is recommended (☎635-2243).

If you don't want to embark on the 1500km of canoe routes you can experience the Park Interior via two long-distance hiking trails from Hwy 60. The **Western Uplands Hiking Trail** (km 2.5) is composed of a series of loops which allow you to construct a hike of up to 71km, while the equally challenging **Highland Hiking Trail** (km 29) has loops of up to 35km. **Campgrounds** in the interior are limited to nine people at a time; permits ($3 per person per night) must be obtained from the information offices.

# Peterborough and around

Though it has one of Ontario's major universities, for most people **PETERBOROUGH** is worth a call only for its access to the Kawartha Lakes and a couple of Ontario's more diverting ancient sites. It does, however, have one strange sight – the largest hydraulic **lift lock** in the world. The star turn on the Trent-Severn Waterway, the lock operates by counterbalancing two watertight boxes, each large enough to hold a vessel – an ingenious piece of engineering explained in the neighbouring interpretive centre on Hunter Street, where it's possible to watch the lock in action from May to September daily. If you want to experience being lifted and lowered twenty metres in a boat, a lift lock **cruise** sets off from the centre (mid-May to mid-Oct 1–4 daily; $12–20).

The rest of Peterborough has very little of any interest. Once you've done the dull **Centennial Museum and Archives**, near the lift lock on Hunter Street East (Victoria Day to Thanksgiving daily 10am–5pm; rest of year Mon–Fri 10am-5pm, Sat & Sun noon–5pm; $1.25), there's just the **Hutchinson House** at 270 Brock Street (May–Oct Tues–Sun 1–5pm; Dec Wed, Sat & Sun; $1.50), celebrating local physician Dr John Hutchinson, an Irish immigrant who died in 1847 after contracting typhus from one of his patients. The house and gardens include a museum with exhibits pertaining to Hutchinson's second cousin Sandford Fleming, the originator of Standard Time, adopted across the continent in 1883 and responsible for the design of Canada's first postage stamp.

Peterborough's *Voyageur Bus Terminal* is in the middle of town at 202 King Street. For **tourist information**, the *Peterborough Kawartha Tourism and Convention Bureau*, 135 George St (mid-May to mid-Sept daily 8am–8pm; mid-Sept to mid-May Mon–Fri 9am–5pm) is beside the now defunct train station. Cheap **rooms** are best sought via the *Bed and Breakfast Registry of Peterborough and Area* (☎652-6290), with doubles from $38. For **restaurants** the best deal is at *The India Food House*, 217 Hunter St West, which offers superb Indian food at incredibly low prices. For high quality but relatively expensive dining try *Fleming's*, 267 George St. George Street is good stamping ground for a number of cheap coffeeshops, including the *George Street Café* at no. 241 with a good selection of muffins and the like; *Papa's Coffee Shop* at no. 407 has good cheap lunches and a billiard table.

## The Kawartha Lakes

Stretching northwards to the Canadian Shield, the drumlin terrain of the **Kawartha Lakes** are prime fishing country, most of whose visitors arrive laden with maggots and rods. Of the area's villages, one of the most attractive is **LAKEFIELD**, off Hwy 28 on the shores of Lake Katchewanooka, famous as the home of sister pioneer authors Catherine Parr Traill and Susanna Moodie. Moodie emigrated to Canada in 1832 with her new husband, a half-pay officer, and, as she explained in her most famous book *Roughing It in the Bush*, regarded emigration "as a severe duty performed at the expense of enjoyment". Needless to say she detested her life in the New World, living in constant fear of the remoteness and wildlife and finding it impossible to sustain any level of gentility in the pioneer environment. Her sister, however, was fascinated by life in Upper Canada – her *Backwoods of Canada* relishes the flora and fauna like a trained botanist, and envisages the full potential of the emergent nation.

Further north on Hwy 50, **BUCKHORN** hosts the **Wildlife Art Festival** on the third weekend in August, when painters, sculptors and woodcarvers from all over North America bring their works to sell. At other times of the year the **Gallery on the Lake** exhibits works by over twenty artists, including potters, in a hexagonal building built of knotty pine. If you want to explore the Kawarthas by canoe, Buckhorn is a good base – *Club Whitesands* (☎657-8432) rents canoes and supplies partial outfitting. If you're planning to stay there's a concentration of reasonably priced ($40–60) lakeside cottage resorts by the supermarket on Hwy 507 – the approach from Peterborough.

## Serpent Mounds Provincial Park

From 100 to 300 AD the peoples of the so-called Point Peninsula culture conducted their ceremonial burials at the site now given over to the **Serpent Mounds Provincial Park** (late April to late October), 20km southeast of Peterborough (Hwy 7 east for 9km to the turn-off for Keene, then south for 11km). The largest of the burial mounds – sixty metres in length and up to two metres high – would be a compound grave: high status individuals were interred in pits beneath the mound, while the remains of others were scattered throughout the mound fill. The rituals of burial and the development of pottery distinguish this culture from its contemporaries, and they evidently had also established extensive trade networks: this site has yielded copper from Lake Superior, silver from northern Ontario, and a conch shell from the Gulf of Mexico. An activity centre located near the mounds has displays on the exploration of the site; opening times vary but a free video presentation on the outside of the building explains the origins of the mounds. You can camp in the park from mid-May to early September (☎519/422-1952).

## Petroglyphs Provincial Park

To the Ojibwa the sacred land of the **Petroglyphs Provincial Park** (mid-May to mid-Oct), 55km northeast of Peterborough, is known as Kinomagewapkong, meaning "the rocks that teach". Etched into the white crystalline limestone surface between 900 and 1400, this is Canada's largest array of petroglyphs, including over 900 figures of spirits, people, animals, boats, weapons and other objects recounting the aboriginal story of life. Whenever a male Ojibwa entered adolescence, the elders would lead him to this site by a secret route marked by rocks that only they could decipher. The boy was then left alone in the forest, refraining from food, drink or sleep until a vision of his guardian spirit appeared, when he would be told of the particular powers he was to receive later in life – in hunting, in warfare or in shamanism.

The Ojibwa carvings teach that humans must coexist with nature, a lesson squandered on later settlers – a specially designed building now protects the carvings from acid rain. However, despite being beset by the socio-economic problems that many of Canada's native peoples suffer, the Ojibwa are determined that their culture will survive. Though the traditional initiation is no longer observed, many Ojibwa make the pilgrimage to the site, where they are forced to stand with tourists to look at the petroglyphs from behind barriers. An excellent film at the site fills in the cultural background.

---

The telephone code for all the following places in central Ontario is ☎613.

---

# Prince Edward County

East from Toronto Hwy 401 zips straight along the north shore of Lake Ontario to Québec, paralleled by the slower Hwy 2, which cuts right through the heart of most of the communities in this mainly agricultural locale. From Oshawa, the roads pass the pretty towns of PORT HOPE and COBOURG to TRENTON, which has been all but ruined by motels and fast-food chains catering for the crews of pleasure boats on the Trent-Severn Waterway. Here and at humdrum BELLEVILLE there's a road link to **Prince Edward County**, essentially a backwater of winding lanes and isolated farms, despite the popularity of its long sandy beaches.

Referred to by its residents as Quinte's Isle – after the Mohawk settlement of Kente, once situated on the site now occupied by Belleville – the island has been occupied since 1000 BC, but it wasn't until the exodus of United Empire Loyalists in the late eighteenth century that any towns grew up. After the war of 1812, when the US government slapped a tax on whiskey and Americans switched to drinking beer, Prince Edward County became Ontario's major barley producer to the breweries of the US, but nowadays the farmers concentrate their efforts on fresh fruit and veg, of which they are among Ontario's largest producers.

## Picton

Birthplace of Canada's first prime minister, Sir John A Macdonald, **PICTON** is the main hub of the island and the terminus for long-distance buses, but it's no more than a peaceful, laid-back village – with a wacky diversion in the shape of **Birdhouse City** to the south of the centre, a collection of 92 birdhouse replicas of local public buildings and landmarks. The **information** centre is located next to the war monument at 116 Main Street (Mon–Fri 9am–5pm) and has details on the whole island. Their lists of **farm vacations** are excellent value and give a chance to sample real Ontarian cooking.

The two **motels** in Picton itself – *Picton Bay Family Motel*, 33 Bridge St (☎476 2186), and *Tip of the Bay Motel*, 35 Bridge St (☎476 2156) – are fairly pricey, charging around $70 for doubles. Alternatively, cheap **bed and breakfasts** can be obtained anywhere on the island through the *Bed and Breakfast Independents of Prince Edward County* (☎399-3085; doubles from $50) or *Bed and Breakfast Prince Edward County* (☎969-9925; doubles from $38).

One of the best places to **eat** is the *Inn on the Bay*, 73 Bridge St, but the island's best is *The Waring House Restaurant*, 1.5km west of Picton on the intersection of County Road 1 and Hwy 33 (☎476-7367; closed Sun & Mon and from mid-Jan to mid-Feb). Moving on from Picton to the mainland, Hwy 33 is connected by the Glenora free ferry to Aldophustown (2–4 hourly; Nov to mid-May at least every 30min), where the bulk of the first Loyalists landed in this part of Ontario in 1794.

## Lake on the Mountain Provincial Park

On an eastern finger of the island, 9km from Picton, **Lake On The Mountain Provincial Park** (early May to early Oct) preserves an extraordinary sight – a lake on top of a mountain above the Bay of Quinte. The Mohawks believed this was inhabited by powerful spirits, and European settlers were mystified by the lake's lack of apparent source – despite recent scientific studies geologists can only guess that the sixty-metre-deep basin is replenished by groundwater from neighbouring marshy grounds. An outlet flows to the Bay of Quinte, but no one has been able to explain how the lake's fluctuations exactly replicate those of Lake Erie, 200km away.

## Sandbanks Provincial Park

The **Sandbanks Provincial Park** (early May to early Oct), about 20km southwest of Picton, is the location of the island's most spectacular sand bars and dunes – the West Lake formation is the largest freshwater sand dune system in the world (8km long, 2km wide), and the smaller East Lake side is almost as impressive. The once straight West Lake Road is now a meandering route, evidence of the distance the dunes have moved. When barley became the staple crop of Prince Edward County the cattle that had formerly occupied the fields were moved to the dunes, where they ate the stabilising grasses and shrubs; it wasn't until government assistance in the 1950s and 1960s that the drift was halted. Today the sand is all but swamped by people on summer days, with an atmosphere reminiscent of Australian beach life without the surf. Reserved **campgrounds** are available in the last fortnight of May and from late June to early September (☎969-8368); for a touch more luxury stay at *Burrowood Jersey Farm* near the park, 2km south of Cherry Valley, a tiny hamlet about 10km south of Picton (☎476-2069; doubles $45), a century-old dairy farm, where breakfast milk comes straight from the udder.

## North Beach Provincial Park

Located 35km west of Picton on the south side of the island, **North Beach Provincial Park** (late June to early Sept) boasts a three-kilometre sandy beach that becomes absolutely packed in summer. The North Bay side of the sand bar is usually less crowded because the beach is steep there and visitors are advised to keep children on the Lake Ontario side.

# Kingston

Located on the Cataraqui River where Lake Ontario begins to narrow into the St Lawrence, the self-proclaimed Limestone City of **KINGSTON** is the finest looking and largest of the communities along this stretch of coast. The city's roots go back to Champlain's initiation of the fur trade with the Iroquois of Cataraqui village. By 1673 the French, under the governorship of Comte de Frontenac, had built a fortified trading post here, but its beginnings were disastrous. During Frontenac's absences the acting governor, Denonville, pursued a policy of trading the Iroquois rather than fur, inviting natives to attend conferences at the fort then shipping them back to France as slaves. Denonville was eventually forced to abandon the fort, but when it reopened in 1696 it was caught in the midst of hostilities between the Huron and Iroquois, whose long enmities were intensified by the European traders.

In 1758 the fort fell to a force of British-Americans and Iroquois, a victory soon followed by an influx of United Empire Loyalists who equipped the scrubby wooden town of Kingston with Ontario's first grist mill. By the war of 1812 Kingston had become a shipbuilding centre and the construction of the mighty *St Lawrence* ensured that no enemy ship ventured near the place. With the completion of the Rideau Canal, Kingston's population was swelled by the now unemployed navvies, whose ranks included a fair number of Scottish masons. The limestone houses these masons built for themselves, following the model of the homes they had left behind, transformed the city and are still its greatest aesthetic asset.

Short-lived capital of Canada from 1841 to 1844, Kingston retains a wealth of links with the nineteenth century, and the scenic Thousand Islands, nearby, further enhance its appeal. Yet Kingston's main importance lies not in its tourist potential but in its military and educational institutions: Queens University is one of the best-known in the country, and the city is also home to Canada's equivalent of Sandhurst and West Point.

## Arrival, information and accommodation

Kingston's small **airport**, in the southeast outskirts, is served by *Canadian Partners* (☎384-7072) and *Voyageur Airways* (☎1-800-461-1636), with regular flights to and from Toronto. **Trains** from Toronto, Ottawa and Montréal terminate at the *Via Rail* station on Hwy 2, northeast of the city at the junction of Princess and Counter streets; bus #1 goes into downtown. The terminus for *Voyageur* long-distance **buses** is on the corner of Division and Counter streets in the north of the city; bus #2 goes into downtown. Maps and **information** can be picked up at the *Kingston Area Visitor and Convention Bureau*, 209 Ontario St (Mon–Fri 9am–5pm), located in the former Kingston-Pembroke Railway Station opposite the city hall.

Though prices are usually steep, much of Kingston's **accommodation** is in attractive historic buildings, all of which need advance booking in summer. For B&Bs contact *Kingston and Area Bed and Breakfast*, 10 Westview Rd (Mon–Sat 7.30am–10pm, Sun 12.30–10pm; ☎542-0214), who can book B&Bs with doubles around $50.

### Hotels, motels and B&B

**Alexander Bed and Breakfast**, Marine Museum, 55 Ontario St (☎542-2261). A moored icebreaker provides a unique B&B right downtown. Singles $30, doubles $50. Closed from early September to May.

**Hotel Belvedere**, 141 King St East (☎548-1565). Beautifully decorated rooms, and rates include delicious continental breakfast. Rooms from $79 to $129.

**Gardiner House**, 9 Kennedy St (☎544-0933). A Georgian house with singles $45, doubles $65.

**Journey's End**, 1454 Princess St (☎549-5550). Three-star accommodation in Canada's budget motel chain. Singles $50, doubles $52.

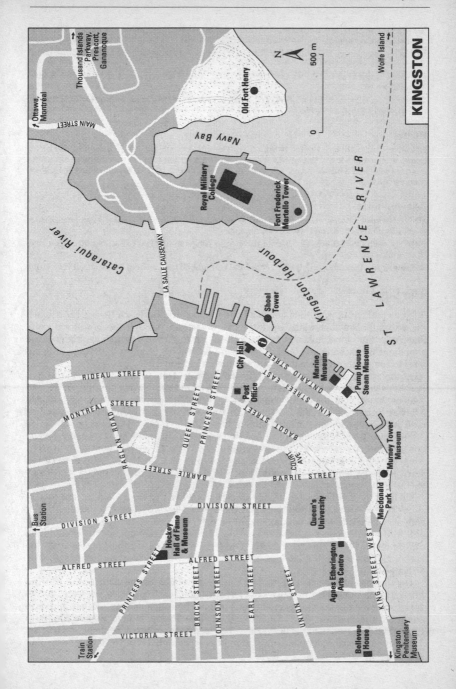

KINGSTON

N

500 m

Wolfe Island

Thousand Islands
Parkway,
Prescott,
Gananoque

Ottawa,
Montréal

MAIN STREET

Old Fort Henry

Navy Bay

Cataraqui River

Royal Military
College

Fort Frederick
Martello Tower

LA SALLE CAUSEWAY

Kingston Harbour

ST LAWRENCE RIVER

Shoal
Tower

City Hall

RIDEAU STREET

MONTREAL STREET

QUEEN STREET

PRINCESS STREET

Post
Office

KING STREET EAST

ONTARIO STREET

Marine
Museum

Pump House
Steam Museum

RAGLAN ROAD

BAGOT STREET

BARRIE STREET

COURT
AVE

Murney Tower
Museum

Macdonald
Park

Bus
Station

DIVISION STREET

DIVISION STREET

BARRIE STREET

Queen's
University

Hockey
Hall of Fame
& Museum

PRINCESS STREET

ALFRED STREET

ALFRED STREET

BROCK STREET

JOHNSON STREET

EARL STREET

UNION STREET

Agnes Etherington
Arts Centre

KING STREET WEST

Train
Station

VICTORIA STREET

Bellevue
House

Kingston
Penitentiary
Museum

**Kelly's House Bed and Breakfast**, 35 Wellington St (☎548-4796). An old oak home within walking distance of downtown. Singles $35, doubles $45.

**Prince George Hotel**, 200 Ontario St (☎549-5440). An expensive but beautiful 1809 heritage home. Singles $75, doubles $130.

**Princess Motor Hotel**, 720 Princess St (☎542-7395). Air-conditioned rooms and cable TV. Singles $50, doubles $60.

**Queen's Inn**, 125 Brock St (☎546-0429). Four-star accommodation in an old hotel with seventeen rooms. Singles $45, doubles $95.

## Hostel

**Kingston International Hostel** (☎546-7203). The CNA-recognised hostel is looking for a new home. It is possible it will stay at 323 William Street during the summer months, whereas winter quarters will be in a private home. All year the hostel is closed 10am–4pm and curfew is 11.30pm. Members $10.

## Campgrounds

**Hi-Lo Hickory Campground**, Hogan Rd, Wolfe Island (☎385-2430). Twelve kilometres east of *Wolfe Island's* ferry berth off Hwy 96. Beach location.

**KOA**, Hwy 38 (☎546-6140). Five-minute drive from Kingston off Hwy 401 at exit 611. Open mid-May to mid-Oct.

**Rideau Acres Campground**, Hwy 15 (☎546-2711). Eight kilometres from Kingston, off Hwy 401.

# The City

To get a real feel of what Kingston is all about wander down **Brock Street**, the original main throughfare that winds up from the waterfront through the downtown core, flanked by limestone buildings that have been left to grow old gracefully. Many of the shops remain unchanged – *Cooke's Old World Shop* at no. 61 is worth popping into, not least to sample the coffee and the outrageously good smells.

At the end of Brock Street stands the domed **City Hall**, intended as the Parliament Buildings but completed too late to fulfill that function. Having housed shops and saloons, it now contains municipal offices. Canada's first farmers' market, next door in **Market Square**, still specialises in fresh fruit and veg, but there are also excellent craft stalls and an antiques market on Sundays.

For many years Kingston's main function was a shipbuilding port responsible for the construction of war vessels; the first ship of the Great Lakes was built here in 1678. Kingston is still an aquatic-orientated city and opposite the city hall, **Confederation Park** runs the length of the waterfront with a modern marina crammed with fancy yachts in the summer.

**Cruises** of the Thousand Islands depart from the Crawford Dock at the foot of Brock Street – take your pick between the *Island Queen Showboat*, a paddle-wheeler with live vaudeville acts (mid-May to mid-June & Sept 1 daily; mid-June to Aug 2 daily; 3hr; $13) or the modern catamaran *Sea Fox II* (mid-May to mid-June 2 daily; mid-June to Aug 3 daily; Sept 2 daily; 2hr; $9). The ferry to Wolfe Island just across from the harbour offers a free but far less scenic and very brief view of the islands (hourly 6.15am–2am).

On the site of the old shipyard in the western area of the park is the **Marine Museum**, 55 Ontario St (April–Oct daily 10am–5pm; Nov to mid-Dec Tues–Sun 10am–4pm; $4), which has a nineteenth-century engine house containing the machinery to pump out the drydock. At 23 Ontario Street, **The Pump House Steam Museum** (Tues–Sun 10am–5pm; $2) is best visited between June and early September when the Victorian municipal water-pumping station is in action; otherwise you'll have to content yourself with model trains.

## West Kingston: Queen's University and around

West from downtown along Union Street lies **Queen's University**, whose small art gallery, the **Agnes Etherington Art Centre** on the corner of University Avenue and Queen's Crescent (Tues–Fri 10am–5pm; Sat & Sun 1–5pm; Thurs 5–9pm, closed July & Aug; $2) has an excellent reputation both for its changing exhibitions and its permanent collection of Canadian art. Major pieces include Tom Thomson's painterly *Autumn, Algonquin Park*, and Inuit prints by Kenojuak, Pitseolak and Lucy – some of the best known Inuit artists of modern times. Other interesting items are the heritage quilts from eastern Ontario which date back to 1820, a comprehensive collection of West African sculptures, Canadian costume from the 1790s to the 1960s, and some seventeenth-century Dutch and Flemish paintings.

Sir John A Macdonald, Kingston's most famous past resident, lived as a child at 110 Rideau Street and later at **Bellevue House**, 35 Centre St, on the western borders of the campus (daily June to early Sept 9am–6pm; early Sept to May 10am–5pm; free). Macdonald rented this bizarrely asymmetrical, pagoda-type house in the 1840s in the hope that the country air would improve the ill-health of his wife, whose headaches were made worse by the treatment – opium. Both the house and gardens have been restored to the period of the late 1840s.

In nearby Macdonald Park, on the corner of Barrie and King Street East, the **Murney Tower** (May–Aug daily 10am–5pm; $1) is the most impressive of four such towers built during the Oregon Crisis of 1846–47 to defend the city's dockyards against the anticipated US attack. Displays inside elucidate the military principles, spiced with social artefacts from nineteenth-century Kingston.

On Christmas Day 1885, members of the Royal Canadian Rifles regiment took their field hockey sticks and a lacrosse ball onto the frozen lake at Kingston, thereby inventing a sport that has become a national passion. In the **International Hockey Hall of Fame and Museum**, on the corner of York and Albert streets (mid-June to mid-Sept daily 10am–5pm; mid-Sept to mid-June Sat & Sun 2–5pm; $2), the history of the game is illustrated by a mass of memorabilia, from the square puck used in an 1896 match between Queen's and the Royal Military College, through to the number 9 sweater and gloves of Gordie Howe, who was the oldest player in the history of the professional game when he retired at the age of 52. An old NHA contract values Alf Smith of Ottawa at $500 a year; a facsimile of the million-dollar cheque awarded to prolific goal-scorer Bobby Holst in the early 1970s shows how the popularity of the game has rocketed in the last century.

Nowadays Kingston's prisons are among the most civilised in North America, enabling people to spend weekends with their jailed spouses for what are known as "trailer weekends". Things have come a long way since 1850, when members of the public paid to watch the torture of prisoners, and warden Henry Smith allowed his son to chase inmates around the yard with a bow and arrow – Smith was finally taken to court, where he was represented by none other than John A Macdonald. The **Kingston Penitentiary Museum** opposite the men's prison at 555 King Street West (Mon–Fri 8am–4pm; free) dwells on the prison's darker days with a collection of torture instruments, inmate art and primitive escape devices.

## East Kingston: Old Fort Henry and around

Over the La Salle Bridge on a finger of land just east of the Cataraqui River stands **Old Fort Henry** (daily May–June 10am–5pm; July & Aug 10am–6pm; Sept 10am–4.30pm; Oct–April 10am–4pm; $5), built to repel American invaders during the war of 1812. Though it never saw a shot fired in anger, the fort was used as a British garrison up to 1870 and as a Canadian garrison for the next twenty years until, as a mark of respect to those across the border, it was allowed to fall into disrepair.

Inside the stout restored walls, the vast parade ground comes to life in summer when students from the Royal Military College fill the fort with the smoke of muskets and cannons and the racket of drums, bugles and fifes (July & Aug 2pm daily, plus Mon, Wed & Sat 7.30pm). In the quieter hours guided tours explore the ramparts, with their vistas of Lake Ontario and the Thousand Islands, as well as the magazines, kitchen and officers' quarters, and the fort's collections of firearms, medals and military equipment.

On the opposite side of Navy Bay stands the **Royal Military College**, training academy for officers of all three services. Within the beautiful grounds, the **Fort Frederick Martello Tower** houses a museum outlining the history of the college, the exploits of its graduates, and an arms collection that once belonged to General Porfirio Diaz, president of Mexico at the turn of the century.

## Eating, drinking and nightlife

For a city its size, Kingston has a large number of excellent places to eat: for those on a tight budget there are several **cafés** worth checking out, and many of the **restaurants** are reasonably priced as well. Kingston also has several decent English-style pubs and bars that often feature live music sessions. **Nightlife** outside of the bar scene is limited to a few disco-clubs populated in the main by Queen's students and a couple of small theatres. For **listings**, see the monthly *Key to Kingston* available from major hotels, restaurants and the tourist office, or the upfront *Between the Lines*, a free biweekly available from pubs, clubs and restaurants.

### Cafés and snacks

**Canoe Club**, Prince George Hotel, 200 Ontario St. Seafood bar with a half-price happy hour 4.30–6pm.

**The Chinese Laundry Café**, 291 Princess St. Trendy café with homemade bagels and bread. Outdoor patio in the summer.

**Delightfully Different Café**, 118 Sydenham St. Homemade muffins and cakes, as well as salads, soups and sandwiches. Open Mon–Fri 7am–4pm.

**Tea and Company**, 237 Brock St. Basic homemade foods, like steak-and-vegetable pie and Cornish pasties. Open Tues–Sat 7am–4pm.

### Restaurants

**Chez Piggy**, 68 Princess St (☎549-7673). Kingston's best-known restaurant is housed in a restored stable that dates back to 1810. The patio is always packed in summer and the interior is just as pleasant, with handcrafted pine and limestone walls. Unfortunately the food does not really live up to the excellent atmosphere. Lunchtime specials $7. Closed Mon.

**Cultures**, 335 King St. Popular student hang-out with great salads.

**The Curry Village**, 169A Princess St (☎542-5010). Popular, reasonably priced Indian restaurant. Reservations recommended.

**The Sunflower**, 20 Montreal St. Cheap vegetarian restaurant producing such delights as Szechwan Stir-Fry and Mediterranean Crêpes. Pasta, lunch and dinner specials daily. Closed Sun & Mon.

### Bars, pubs and clubs

**Duke of Kingston**, 331 King St East. The best of Kingston's English pubs, with darts and pool tables. Live bands on Thursdays and Sundays.

**Kingston Brewing Company**, 34 Clarence St. A brew pub serving natural ales and lagers brewed on the premises. The brewery is open to the public and there is also a beer garden.

**The Sports**, 125 Brock St. Excellent sports bars with big screens and free popcorn. It is rumoured that the Ontario Hockey Association was formed here.

**Stages**, 390 Princess St. Popular nightclub on three levels with laser shows and live entertainment. Open until 3am on Fridays and Saturdays. $2 admission.

**Stetson's**, Shamrock Hotel, 671 Princess St. Country-and-western bar with cowboy movie-murals. Live bands every Thursday and Saturday.

**The Toucan**, 76 Princess St. Student pub with excellent live music from blues to traditional Irish. Thursdays is underground night, which can produce some surprises.

## Kingston to Ottawa: the Rideau Canal

The **Rideau Canal**, which cuts through 200 kilometres of coniferous and deciduous forest, bogs, limestone plains and granite ridges, was completed in 1832 after a mere six years' work, but at the cost of the lives of scores of workers, many of whom had immigrated from Scotland and Ireland to dig the canal. Though intended to provide continental transport with a safer route than the St Lawrence, which after the war of 1812 was considered vulnerable to American attack, the canal never became anything more than an artery for regional commerce – albeit one that lead to the development of Canada's capital and attracted more settlers to eastern Ontario. The introduction of the railways in the 1850s further diminished its significance, and by the end of the last century pleasure boats were already plying the route regularly. Today the holiday traffic is thicker than ever; if you want to weave your way through the bow-to-stern pleasure craft, *Adventures Unlimited* in Kingston (May–Oct; ☎547-4263) provides a shuttle service to the canal, camping equipment and canoes. The route can also be walked on the waymarked **Rideau Hiking Trail** – information from the *Rideau Trail Association* in Kingston (☎545-0823). There are campgrounds near all 24 lockstations.

# The upper St Lawrence

Heading east from Kingston along the shore of the St Lawrence, the first sixty or so kilometres are dominated by the **Thousand Islands** – the meandering Highway 2 is known as the Thousand Islands Parkway, and the towns along it have little interest other than as jumping-off points for island cruises. Beyond the islands, the river was an eighty-kilometre sequence of rapids until, in the 1950s, the US and Canadian governments created the **St Lawrence Seaway** – the world's longest artificial shipping lane. The project made the waters navigable by the massive ocean-going freighters and created power-plants to harness the river's hydro-electric potential, most notably at Cornwall, Ontario's easternmost town and site of the biggest dam in the northern hemisphere. On a negative note, the seaway necessitated the destruction of many riverside towns, a process at which one local newspaper scribe bewailed – "once again another patch of Ontario is sicklied o'er with the pale cast of progress". One threatened patch has survived by transplantation to the **Upper Canada Village**, near Morrisburg, the region's most popular and worthwhile sight.

### The Thousand Islands

The **Thousand Islands** – the 1768 chunks of Canadian land that have inspired a salad dressing – were called Manitouana (Garden of the Great Spirit) by the native population, who believed they were created when petals of heavenly flowers were scattered on the mighty river. Part of the Frontenac axis, a ridge of billion-year-old rock that stretches down into New York State, the islands are mostly pink granite covered in pine, birch and poplar trees, and in spring they become a wonderful show of white when the provincial flower, the trillium, blooms.

The populated islands range from **Wellesley Island**, with its *Millionaire's Row*, right down to **Just Room Enough Island**, with its single tiny home. Along with Irving Berlin and Jack Dempsey the most famous resident of the islands was George Boldt, owner of New York's *Waldorf Astoria*, who in 1899 bought one of the islands and reshaped it into a heart as a tribute to his wife – hence the name **Heart Island**. He spent two million dollars building the huge turreted **Boldt Castle** (mid-May to early Oct daily 10am–6pm; $3.50) with material from around the world, then abandoned it when his wife died, taking his new salad dressing recipe back to New York. The Thousand Islands Bridge Authority purchased the castle for $1 in 1978, and it can be explored on a trip from Gananoque (see below) – take your passport, as it's in American waters. Other sights you might pick out from the boat are the island of **St Helena**, which has a house built in the shape of Napoleon's hat, and Canada's shortest international bridge between the two Zavikon Islands.

## Gananoque

**GANANOQUE**, 29km beyond Kingston, offers the best trips to the Thousand Islands from this side of the border, of which the most rewarding is the cruise to Boldt Castle (May to mid-June & Sept 4 daily; mid-June to Aug 9 daily; early Oct 2 daily; $12). There are masses of **motels** around Gananoque – most convenient for the cruises is the *Blinkbonnie Motor Lodge*, 50 Main St (☎382-7272; doubles from $40), one block from the dock. The **information centre** at 2 King St East (Mon–Fri 9am–5pm; ☎382-3250) has details of other vacancies.

## Brockville

The industrial city of **BROCKVILLE**, 80km from Kingston, is a nice-looking but rather dull community, founded in 1785 by the Loyalist William Buell, and once claiming more millionaires per capita than anywhere else in Canada. You get some idea of the level of excitement in modern Brockville from the fact that its chief sight is the oldest **railway tunnel** in the country, dank, damp and disused since 1954. Tunnel Bay, opposite this bore, is the departure point of Thousand Island **cruises** on a replica of a St Lawrence steamboat (mid-May to mid-Oct 2 daily; $7–11), passing St Helena, Heart and Wellesley islands. From Tunnel Bay a walk through the Armagh S Price Park brings you to the one of the town's oldest homes, **Brockville Museum,** 5 Henry St (daily Jan to mid-March 1–4pm; mid-March to Dec 10am–4pm; donation), which illustrates the history of the town. Nearby, William Buell's village green, at the end of Broad Street, is dominated by the 1842 county courthouse and jail, and the four churches which mark each corner.

    **Information** is available from the city hall, 1 King St West (Mon–Fri 8.30am–4.30pm). If you are forced to stay over, the pricey *Manitouana Hotel*, 5 King St East (☎345-5655; doubles $80), is the only central **hotel**, so you are best to stick to **bed and breakfast** – *Brockville Bed and Breakfast*, 331 King St West (☎345-4600), and *Jasmine House*, 59 Wall St (☎345-1831), both have doubles around $35. Alternatively head north along Stewart Boulevard for reasonably priced **motels** – try the *Queen's Grant Motor Hotel* at no. 325 (☎345-1437; doubles $45).

## Prescott

The deepwater port of **PRESCOTT** – rather eclipsed since the opening of the St Lawrence Seaway – was founded in 1810 by General Prescott with land granted to him in thanks for his efforts during the American Revolution. Though now tied to the US by the bridge to Ogdensburg, NY, the people of Prescott raucously celebrate their Loyalist origins in the third week of July, when the ten-day Loyalist Days Festival includes the largest military pageant in Canada.

    The pageant takes place at **Fort Wellington National Historic Site** on Hwy 2 east (mid-May to early Sept daily 10am–6pm; free), which was built, like Kingston's Fort Henry, to protect the vulnerable St Lawrence frontier during the war of 1812. It was completed in 1814 and was never attacked, though its garrison captured two American fortifications in Ogdensburg. After the completion of the Rideau Canal the fort fell into disrepair and it wasn't until 1837 that the British rebuilt it as a guard against the Canadian rebels and their American sympathisers. The subsequent bloody four-day engagement known as the Battle of the Windmill was the last action seen by the troops of Fort Wellington apart from the short-lived Irish-American Fenian raids of 1865. The four original 1813 structures are surrounded by artillery-resistant earthworks, while the 1838 stone blockhouse contains a guard room, armoury, powder magazine and barracks, all refurnished as of the mid-nineteenth century.

## Upper Canada Village

During the construction of the St Lawrence Seaway the villages of IROQUOIS and **MORRISBURG** were relocated to escape the river's rising waters, and are now situated 18km and 31km respectively from Prescott. The finest of the endangered buildings were painstakingly reconstructed 11km east of Morrisburg to form the **Upper Canada Village** (daily late June to early Sept 9.30am–6pm; mid-May to late June & early Sept to mid-Oct 9.30am–5pm; $6), situated off Hwy 401 in Crysler Farm Battlefield Park. This is an entirely self-sufficient settlement, whose inhabitants are skilled at producing cheeses, quilts, brooms, bread and cloth in exactly the same way as their ancestors – not one nail is machine-made. The site is easily accessible by public transport, as the *Colonial* Montréal–Toronto and Ottawa–Cornwall buses both serve the village.

# OTTAWA

**OTTAWA** has three major claims to fame: it's the capital of the second biggest country on the planet; it's the Western world's coldest capital; and popular opinion holds that it is one of the world's dullest. The Canadian government, all too aware of the third, have spent lashings of dollars to turn Ottawa into "a city of urban grace in which all Canadians can take pride". The grid-planned streets virtually sparkle. Buggies guzzle up the litter even in pouring rain, snow is whisked off the pavements as soon as it hits the deck, and because Ottawa's main industry is chin-wagging, pollution is almost non-existent. Ottawa has been painstakingly groomed to impress visitors and stimulate its population of just over 750,000 with parks and gardens, bicycle and jogging paths, six national museums, cultural facilities like the National Arts Centre and a downtown farm – just in case the four-kilometre-wide greenbelt isn't close enough.

This investment is resented by many Canadians, an attitude that has been almost constant since Queen Victoria, inspired by some watercolours of the **Gatineau Hills**, declared Ottawa the capital, leaving Montréal and Toronto smarting at their rebuff. Once Victoria had made her momentous decision things started to happen in Ottawa – it changed from a brawling, boozy lumbering town to a place where Canada's future would be decided. As nineteenth-century pundit Goldwin Smith curtly pointed out, Ottawa was "a sub-arctic lumber village converted by royal mandate into a political cockpit".

Yet despite the promotion in status, the capital has a small-town atmosphere and an easily manageable size. It is divided by the Rideau Canal into Upper and Lower Town: to the west, on the steep banks of the Ottawa River, the Gothic-inspired **Parliament Buildings** are the high point of Upper Town, whilst in Lower Town the focal point is the boulevard of Sussex Drive, which curves along the river to the posh locale of Rockcliffe in the northeast, passing the glasshouse of the **National Gallery** and several other smaller museums on the way. To the south, beyond the Lower Town, the **National Museum of Science and Technology** is the main draw.

As Parliament Hill resounds to politicians debating the complexities of Québec nationalism, exemplary Canadian diplomacy has ensured that the national capital is not an anglophone bastion. The Québécois town of **Hull**, just across the Ottawa River in a region known as the Outaouais, is linked to Ottawa by four bridges and is fast becoming an integrated part of the city, though Hull is still very proud of its French heritage – after the introduction of Québec's language laws one local shopkeeper was fined $1000 for displaying an English "Merry Christmas" poster. Federal investment has created in Hull the wonderful **Musée Canadiens des Civilisations**, and the marriage of the two settlements is confirmed by the five-kilometre tourist route called **Confederation Boulevard**, which links the main attractions on both sides of the river.

Various immigrant communities – including Italians, Lebanese and Chinese – have enriched the atmosphere of Ottawa in recent years, bringing international **restaurants** and numerous festivals to the scene. Renovations of historic districts such as the **Byward Market** in Lower Town have paved the way for the development of trendy boutiques, eateries and open-air markets – finding a ready market among the students from Carleton University and the University of Ottawa. A city dubbed too perfect for excitement is at last reforming its reputation.

## A brief history of Ottawa

Ottawa's earliest history is much like that of every other logging town in Ontario. The Outaouais, a tribe of Algonquian Indians, hunted in this area for thousands of years. Then in 1613 Samuel de Champlain pitched up, paused to watch his Indian guides make sacrifices of tobacco to the misty falls which he christened **Chaudière** (French for "cauldron") and took off in search of more appealing pastures. Later, when Champlain established Canada's fur trade with Europe, the **Ottawa River** became a major transportation route but the area where Ottawa now stands remained just a camping stop for the voyageurs, Jesuit missionaries and European explorers who trickled slowly into this newly discovered wilderness.

Permanent settlement began in 1800 on the north side of the river, when **Philemon Wright** snowshoed up the frozen Ottawa River from Massachussetts. Wright called the small settlement Wrightstown, a name he later changed to **Hull** in honour of his parents' birthplace in England. At this time Britain was embroiled in the Napoleonic Wars and desperate for shipbuilding wood, and it didn't take long for Wright to realise the economic potential of the pine that grew all around him. He had soon worked out a way of shifting the tall trees by squaring them off, tying them together and floating them as rafts down the river to Montréal.

It wasn't until the construction of the **Rideau Canal** in 1826 that development shifted from the north to the south side of the river. The area was then settled by a mixed workforce of Irish, Scottish and French workers, army engineers and British veterans from the Napoleonic and American wars, all of them under the command of **Lieutenant-Colonel John By** and the Royal Engineers. **Bytown**, as the new town was called, became the centre for not only the canal workers and military personnel, but also a rush of immigrants from Ireland escaping the potato famine, and a seasonal population of raftsmen from winter logging camps. The loggers drank most of their earnings in the taverns of Bytown, while the English, Irish, Scottish and French did not leave their political differences in Europe – the result was that nights in Bytown were characterised by drunken brawls and broken bones.

Despite these raucous goings-on, a group of American lumber barons were attracted to the area: the workers were already there, the Ottawa River and Rideau Canal provided perfect access, and wood was plentiful. By the mid-1830s, Wrightsville and Bytown were the centre of the Ottawa River Valley's squared timber trade.

In 1855 Bytown became **Ottawa** in a bid to become the capital of the Province of Canada, hoping that a change of name would relieve the town of its sordid reputation. In order to secure the title the community stressed its attractive location conveniently between Upper and Lower Canada, its remoteness from America, and its industrial prosperity. Queen Victoria's decision in 1857 upset the other contenders, but an

American newspaper noted that it was an easily defended capital as any "invaders would inevitably be lost in the woods trying to find it". America may have been able to see the wisdom in the Queen's choice but the politicians sent to work in the capital did not – Sir Wilfred Laurier, prime minister from 1896, found it "hard to say anything good" about the place. Nonetheless, this did not stop him and his successor Mackenzie King from endeavouring to convert Ottawa from the "Westminster in the wilderness" to the "Washington of the North".

For all their efforts it remained a rough-and-ready town until the late 1940s, when the Paris city planner, Jacques Greber, was commissioned to beautify the city with a profusion of parks, wide avenues and tree-lined pathways. A decade later the railway and its associated noise and dirt were removed from the city centre, and the huge green belt was established to prevent urban sprawl. For many years there was a law against building structures higher than the Parliament Buildings Peace Tower, which is 89.5m high. Later changes in the regulations paved the way for the construction of high-rise office buildings and apartments, transforming but not engulfing a capital that is now a showpiece for the nation.

---

The Ottawa telephone code is ☎613. The Hull telephone code is ☎819.

---

# Arrival, information and transport

The **Ottawa International Airport** is a twenty-minute drive south of the city. An airport bus run by *Carleton Bus Lines* links the airport to various downtown hotels and leaves every half-hour at a cost of $6. The cheaper local bus #96 from outside the airport travels to Billings Bridge at the south end of the city, where you can pick up a transfer and change to the #1 for Elgin in downtown (for fares, see "City transport", below). A taxi from or to downtown will set you back about $15.

Ottawa's spanking new **train station** is on the southeastern outskirts at 200 Tremblay Road, about 5km from Parliament Hill. There are direct *VIA Rail* trains to and from Belleville, Brockville, Kingston, Montréal and Toronto, but they are frequently late, especially in the winter, and massive cuts in the services occur every year. Local bus #95 goes downtown; taxi fare to the centre is approximately $10.

Long-distance **buses** arrive at and depart from the *Voyageur* bus station at 265 Catherine Street on the corner of Kent just off the Queensway. Take local bus #4 to get further downtown.

## Information

The *Ottawa and Hull Tourism Inc. Visitor Information Centre*, in the National Arts Centre at 65 Elgin St (May–Aug daily 9am–9pm; Sept–April Mon–Fri 9am–5pm, Sun 10am–4pm; ☎237-5158), is usually understaffed but will provide any amount of free bumph on the immediate area and Ontario; it also offers a free summertime booking service for hotels, motels and B&Bs. *Canada's Capital Visitor Information Centre*, 14 Metcalfe St just opposite the Parliament Buildings, has more detailed information on Ottawa and Hull only (mid-May to August daily 8.30am–9pm; Sept to mid-May Mon–Sat 9am–5pm, Sun 10am–4pm; ☎239-5000), as does its equivalent in Hull – the *Association touristique de l'Outaouais*, 25 Laurier St (mid-June to Aug Mon–Fri 8.30am–8.30pm, Sat & Sun 9am–5pm; Sept to mid-June Mon–Fri 9am–5pm; ☎778-2222). During the summer months there is also an Infotent on Parliament Hill and an information booth at Sparks St Mall.

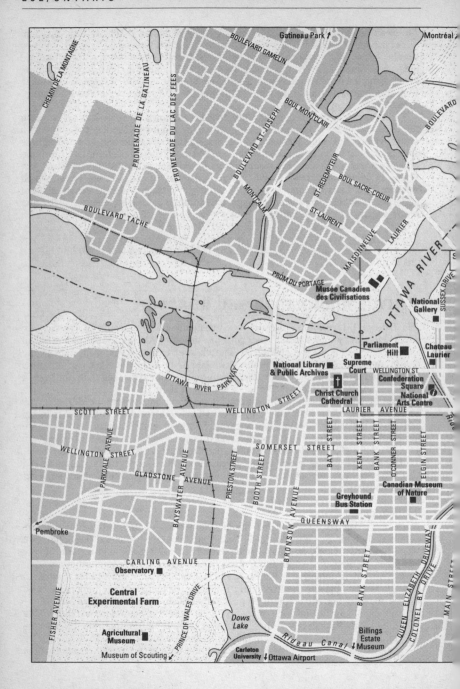

Montréal

BOULEVARD GAMELIN

Gatineau Park

CHEMIN DE LA MONTAGNE

PROMENADE DE LA GATINEAU

PROMENADE DU LAC DES FEES

BOULEVARD ST-JOSEPH

BOUL MONTCLAIR

MONTCALM

ST-REDEMPTEUR

BOUL SACRE-COEUR

ST-LAURENT

BOULEVARD TACHE

BOULEVARD

MAISONNEUVE

LAURIER

OTTAWA RIVER

SUSSEX DRIVE

PROM DU PORTAGE

Musée Canadien
des Civilisations

National
Gallery

OTTAWA RIVER PARKWAY

Parliament
Hill

Chateau
Laurier

National Library
& Public Archives

Supreme
Court

WELLINGTON ST

Confederation
Square

Christ Church
Cathedral

National
Arts Centre

WELLINGTON STREET

LAURIER AVENUE

SCOTT STREET

Rideau

WELLINGTON STREET

SOMERSET STREET

BAY STREET

KENT STREET

BANK STREET

O'CONNOR STREET

ELGIN STREET

PARKDALE AVENUE

GLADSTONE AVENUE

PRESTON STREET

BOOTH STREET

BAYSWATER AVENUE

BRONSON AVENUE

Canadian Museum
of Nature

Greyhound
Bus Station

Pembroke

QUEENSWAY

CARLING AVENUE

Observatory

Central
Experimental Farm

FISHER AVENUE

PRINCE OF WALES DRIVE

Dows
Lake

BANK STREET

QUEEN ELIZABETH DRIVEWAY

COLONEL BY DRIVE

MAIN STREET

Agricultural
Museum

Museum of Scouting

Carleton
University

Ottawa Airport

Rideau Canal

Billings
Estate
Museum

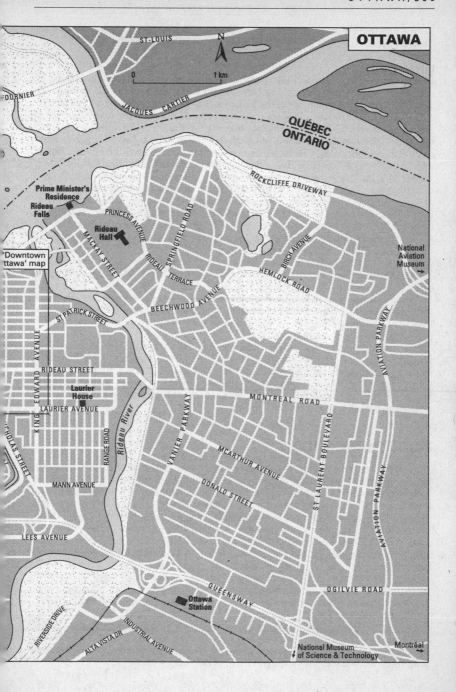

**OTTAWA**

ST-LOUIS

N

0      1 km

JACQUES CARTIER

QUÉBEC
ONTARIO

ROCKCLIFFE DRIVEWAY

FOURNIER

Prime Minister's
Residence
Rideau
Falls

PRINCESS AVENUE

SPRINGFIELD ROAD

BIRCH AVENUE

National
Aviation
Museum

Rideau
Hall

MACKAY STREET

RIDEAU TERRACE

HEMLOCK ROAD

'Downtown
ttawa' map

ST PATRICK STREET

BEECHWOOD AVENUE

AVIATION PARKWAY

KING EDWARD AVENUE

RIDEAU STREET

Rideau River

MONTREAL ROAD

Laurier
House

LAURIER AVENUE

VANIER PARKWAY

ST-LAURENT BOULEVARD

NICHOLAS STREET

RANGE ROAD

MCARTHUR AVENUE

MANN AVENUE

DONALD STREET

AVIATION PARKWAY

LEES AVENUE

QUEENSWAY

OGILVIE ROAD

RIVERSIDE DRIVE

Ottawa
Station

ALTA VISTA DR

INDUSTRIAL AVENUE

National Museum
of Science & Technology

Montréal

Free information on the capital can be obtained by phoning ☎1-800-267-7285 from eastern Canada or ☎1-800-267-0450 from other parts of Canada and the US.

## City transport

Downtown Ottawa, incorporating parts of both Upper and Lower towns, is an extremely compact area and can be crossed by foot in a little over half an hour. To make the most of the entire capital the best idea is to hire a **bicycle** and take advantage of Ottawa's 150km of safe and scenic pathways (see "Listings"), but if you'd prefer to roam without effort, there's the efficient **bus** service run by *OCTranspo* on the south side and *CTCRO* on the north side of the river. The buses from both companies interconnect along Rideau and Wellington streets in Ottawa and around the Portage Bridge area and at Place d'Accueil in Hull. All routes in downtown Ottawa meet at the Rideau Transit Mall on Rideau between Nicolas and Sussex and the Mackenzie King Bridge. Buses run from 6am to around midnight and the whole system works on a two-tier **fare** system. From Monday to Friday during peak hours (6–8.30am and 3–5.30pm) fares are the most expensive in Canada at $1.80; at all other times tickets cost 90¢. Tickets can be bought at corner stores, or on the bus itself if you have the correct change. If you need to change buses to complete your journey, ask for a transfer (at no extra cost) – they are valid for both systems for up to an hour.

From June to September a shuttle bus service, **Visibus**, links all the major tourist attractions along Confederation Boulevard and runs from 9am to 6pm daily. A **Visipass** costs $3 per person ($7 per family) and is valid all day on both the Visibus and *OCTranspo* buses. The pass is available from the *OCTranspo* office at 294 Albert, or from major hotels, museums and information centres. A **Minipass** ($2), also available from the *OCTranspo* office, allows you unlimited travel for one day after 9am, but from 3 to 5.30pm a 70¢ top-up fare is charged.

It is only really necessary to take a **taxi** after midnight, when most of the buses have finished. All are metered and start with $1.70 on the clock, charging $1 per kilometre, with a tip of ten percent average. Taxis can only be boarded at ranks, which are located outside major hotels and nightspots: central ones include *Chateau Laurier* and *The Novotel* on Nicolas, and during the small hours fleets of taxis wait outside Promenade de Portage in Hull to return revellers to Ottawa.

# Accommodation

With all the business conferences in Ottawa, there is no shortage of rooms in the city, but average **hotel** prices tend to be quite high. On the other hand, even the poshest hotels knock a good chunk off their price tags in the summer, when Parliament is in recess, and special weekend rates are also widely available – make sure you ask about these, as some places might neglect to mention them. The best bet for a low-cost room in downtown Ottawa, though, is **bed and breakfast**; the number of these increases every year and they offer one of the few ways to stay in a heritage building – and most have free parking. Should the places we've listed be booked out, try one of Ottawa's three referral services, all of whom have B&Bs in and around the capital that charge around $40 for singles and $50 for doubles: *Capital Bed and Breakfast*, 2071 Riverside Drive (☎737-4129); *Ottawa Area Bed and Breakfast Association*, 488 Cooper (☎563-0161); or *Ottawa Centretown Bed and Breakfast Association*, 253 McLeod (☎234-7577).

Of course the other way drivers can avoid Ottawa's mob of traffic wardens is to stay in a **motel**; the majority are located to the east and west of town, but there are a couple downtown too. The cheapest beds in town are at the official CHA **hostel**, which is open all year round and is right downtown. There are also **campgrounds** close to the heart of the city, with a single reservation service (☎456-3016).

## Hotels

**Aristocrat Suite Hotel**, 131 Cooper (☎236-7500). Suites for up to four people with fully equipped kitchens for $80; prices drop in the summer and at weekends.

**Auberge de la Salle Inn**, 245 Dalhousie (☎233-0201). Friendly and cheap, with sixteen air-conditioned rooms; singles $49, doubles $54. Weekend rates available.

**Beacon Arms Hotel**, 88 Albert (☎235-1413). A few blocks from Parliament Hill, this 158-year-old hotel has been around almost as long as Ottawa and has recently been completely renovated. Singles $75, doubles $85.

**Chateau Laurier**, 1 Rideau (☎232-6411 or ☎1-800-268-9420). It is not easy to miss this place, slap bang next to the Parliament Buildings and reminiscent of a stocky Disney castle. A favourite drinking hole of politicians – dress up to check in or risk being thrown out. There are 500 rooms, with rates from $105, reduced in summer to $79 (single or double occupancy).

**Doral Inn**, 486 Albert (☎230-8055). Five minutes from the Parliament Buildings, next to the Bay Mall. A restored 1879 inn, this is one of the few relatively cheap Ottawa hotels with a touch of character. Both doubles and singles start from $59 and there are special weekend rates. It has a coffeeshop, pool and Spanish restaurant.

**Lord Elgin Hotel**, 100 Elgin (☎235-3333 or ☎1-800-267-4298). This Ottawa landmark has all the pomp of a classy hotel but the prices are not too bad. Singles $77–83, doubles $85–90; special weekend and summer rates, free parking.

**Hotel Roxborough**, 123 Metcalfe (☎237-5171 or ☎1-800-263-8967). A European-style hotel with prices reflecting the level of service – continental breakfast, newspaper and shoeshine are included. Singles from $94, doubles from $104. Rates drop to $68 for a double from June to September.

**Somerset House Hotel**, 352 Somerset West (☎233-7762). Downtown's cheapest hotel has recently been bestowed a couple of stars. Singles from $25, doubles from $35.

## Motels

**Britannia Motor Inn**, 2980 Carling (☎829-9411). West Ottawa three-star without the charge – singles/doubles for $46.95/$49.95.

**Motel Concorde**, 333 Montreal (☎745-2112). The cheapest motel in East Ottawa, with a swimming pool and all mod cons. Rates are $42 for single, $53 for doubles.

**Journey's End Motel**, 1252 Michael (☎744-2900 or ☎1-800-668-4200). The better located of Ottawa's two *Journey's End* motels, in East Ottawa. $47.88 single, $54.88 double.

**Parkway Motor Hotel**, 475 Rideau (☎232-3781). A good downtown location but rather characterless. Three-star bonuses of a cheap coffeeshop, free parking, air-conditioning and TVs in every room. Singles $54–60, doubles $58–66, $5 for an extra person.

**Richmond Plaza Motel**, 238 Richmond (☎722-6591). A small West Ottawa motel and very cheap with singles for $34.95 and doubles for $41.95.

**Town House Motor Hotel**, 319 Rideau (☎236-0151). A three-star, dull motor hotel, but with an excellent location. Singles and doubles start at $58.95.

**WelcomINN**, 1220 Michael (☎748-7800 or ☎1-800-387-4381). In East Ottawa. One of a chain across Canada; very modern. Rates from $59.77, with continental breakfast.

**West Park Motor Inn**, 1655 Carling (☎728-1861). Cheap West Ottawa motel with singles at $44 and doubles $48.

## Bed and breakfasts

**Albert House**, 478 Albert (☎236-4479 or 1-800-267-1982). Seventeen-bedroomed heritage mansion which has been well restored to include bathrooms en suite. $55 single, $62 double, $10 for each additional person.

**Appletreewick Guest House**, 58 Marlborough (☎237-2753). A good place for homesick anglophones; Beth and John Bycroft from Yorkshire stayed in this 80-year-old building in 1981 and liked it so much that they bought the place. Singles from $30, doubles from $40.

**Auberge du Marche**, 87 Guiges (☎235-7697). Often full as it is very popular and has only four bedrooms. Singles $38, doubles $48.

**Auberge McGee's Inn**, 185 Daly (☎237-6089). A restored Victorian mansion with 14 bedrooms, some with jacuzzis. Doubles $68–108.

**Australis Guest House**, 35 Marlborough (☎235-8461). Air-conditioned rooms with fireplaces in this tiny, three-bedroomed heritage home, a twenty-minute walk from Parliament Hill. Single $32, double $40 including continental breakfast.

**Beatrice Lyon Guest House**, 479 Slater (☎236-3904). Another three-bedroomed place right downtown, just off Bank Street. Singles start at $30, doubles from $35, including full breakfast.

**Constance House**, 62 Sweetland (☎235-8888). Built in 1895 in what is now a secluded area of downtown. Excellent breakfasts. Singles from $48, doubles from $54; $10 for an extra person.

**Le Gîte Park Avenue Bed and Breakfast**, 54 Park (☎230-9131). A non-smoking B&B; singles $30–35, doubles $45.

**Haydon House**, 18 The Driveway (☎230-2697). Victorian home with antiques and Canadian art. Singles $40, doubles $50, extra person $10.

**Laurier Guest House**, 329 Laurier East (☎238-5525). Well located, very cheap, but with only three rooms. Singles from $25, doubles $35. Weekend and family rates.

**O'Connor House**, 172 O'Connor (☎236-4221). Claims to be the most centrally located B&B in Ottawa. Rates include all-you-can-eat breakfast, free bicycles and skates. Parking is free but limited. Single $49, double $55.

**Robert's Bed and Breakfast**, 488 Cooper (☎563-0161). A heritage home with three rooms; from $34 single, $44 double.

## Hostels and student accommodation

**Carleton University Residence**, 223 Commons Building, 1233 Colonel By (☎788-5609). South of the central core, but with bonuses of air-conditioning, Olympic-sized swimming pool, saunas and a whirlpool. Singles $25, doubles $38 – reductions with student card. Open May to Aug.

**Nicholas Gaol International Hostel**, 75 Nicholas (☎235-2595). Ottawa's nineteenth-century jail was converted in 1973 into a hostel, but conversions were kept to a minimum and accommodation is in cells complete with bars on the windows and doors. The solitary confinement area is now a laundry but Death Row remains unchanged –the 3ft-by-6ft cells and the gallows are still there. "Dormitories" are $10 for members, $15 for non-members. Reservations can only be made for family rooms, for others check-in is before 10am or after 5pm. Between those hours the hostel is closed, though it is possible to dump luggage; curfew is 1am. From the bus station take bus #4 to the corner of Rideau and Nicolas; from the train station take bus #95 and get off at Rideau Shopping Mall.

**Ottawa YMCA-YWCA**, 180 Argyle (☎237-1320). Slightly less convenient than the hostel, but it's a better standard of accommodation and there is a pool, gym and cafeteria. Singles $30.98, doubles $38.33.

**University of Ottawa**, 85 University (☎564-5400). From May to August, student dormitory accommodation is available at the Stanton residence just off Nicolas Street; the reception is at 100 Hastey on the west side of the university buildings. The rates for students are $12.50 single, $25 double – for non-students $28.35/$37.80 double.

## Campgrounds

**Camp Le Breton**, corner of Fleet St and Booth. Just west of Parliament Hill right in the heart of downtown; 200 sites; $6 per person.

**Lac La Peche Canoe-Camping**, Gatineau Park. A small campground beside Lac La Peche off Hwy 366; $11 a site.

**Lac Philippe Family Campground**, Gatineau Park. Right in the centre of the park, a massive campground on the banks of Lac Philippe; on-site store, showers, toilets and canoe rental. $13 a site.

# The City

The National Capital Region officially spans thousands of square kilometres along the Ottawa Valley encompassing several separate communities. The major sights, however, lie within a small area around the Ottawa River in the downtown centres of Ottawa and its French neighbour Hull: once on Parliament Hill, the symbolic and topographical apex of the city, a short walk brings you to all the major sights.

## DOWNTOWN OTTAWA

N

0    250 m

Musée Canadien
des Civilisations

OTTAWA RIVER

ALEXANDRA BRIDGE

Nepean
Point

Royal Mint

War Museum

National
Gallery

Caricature
Museum

Notre Dame
Basilica

Major's Hill
Park

Ski Museum

Parliament
Buildings

Bytown
Museum

Chateau
Laurier

Byward
Market

WELLINGTON STREET

Confederation
Square

Post Office

SPARKS STREET MALL

National Arts
Centre

Rideau Centre

RIDEAU STREET

Nicholas Goal
International
Hostel

National Postal
Museum

LAURIER AVENUE

LAURIER AVENUE

DOTELER STREET

PARENT AVENUE

DALHOUSE ST

CUMBERLAND

ST PATRICK STREET

MURRAY STREET

CLARENCE ST

YORK ST

GEORGE ST

KING EDWARD AVENUE

STREET

SUSSEX DRIVE

MACKENZIE AVENUE

BANK STREET

O'CONNER STREET

METCALFE STREET

ELGIN STREET

NICHOLAS ST

## Parliament Hill

Ottawa's *raison d'être*, the **Parliament Buildings**, are dramatically situated on the limestone bluff of **Parliament Hill** overlooking the Ottawa River, the geographic high-point originally used by the British military as barracks during the building of the Rideau Canal. In summer the Governor General's Foot Guards and Grenadier Guards march onto the Hill for the 10am **Changing of the Guard**; Ottawa's winters are too cold for stationary guards.

The entrance to the Hill through the south gate from Wellington Street leads past the **Centennial flame**, lit in 1967 to commemorate a century of Confederation. In front stand the three Parliament Buildings – begun in 1860 – which like Britain's Houses of Parliament are built on mock-Gothic lines, but unlike the London version it's the acreage of green copper roofing that catches the eye, rather than fiddly stonework. (Reputedly the workmen urinated on the roof to speed up the oxidisation.) In 1916 a fire destroyed the **Centre Block** (free tours late May to Aug Mon–Fri 9am–8.30pm, Sat & Sun 9am–6pm; Sept to late May daily 9am–4.30pm) and the present building, which contains the Senate and the House of Commons, dates from 1920 when it was built along the original plans but increased to one and a half times the size. From the

centre of the facade rises the **Peace Tower** (late May to Aug Mon–Fri 9am–9pm, Sat
& Sun 9am–6pm; Sept to late May daily 9am–5pm), which was added in 1927 as a
memorial to Canadians who served in World War I – the floor is paved with stone
brought from the battlefields of Europe. From the top, nearly ninety metres above the
river, you can see forty miles in all directions.

Entrance to the Centre Block itself is through the Peace Tower entrance, which
leads to **Confederation Hall** and the **House of Commons**, where the Speaker's chair
is made of English oak from Westminster Hall and from Nelson's ship *Victory*. The red-
carpeted **Senate** is far more impressive, though, with its murals of scenes from World
War I surmounted by a beautiful gilded ceiling. Adjoining the Centre Block is the
**Library**, the only part of the building to survive the fire of 1916; the circular design and
the richly carved wooden galleries make this the most handsome of the buildings.

The **West Block** is closed to the public but the **East Block** (late June to late Aug
daily 9am–5pm) has four rooms open to the public – the original Governor General's
office, the offices of Sir John A Macdonald and Sir George Étienne Cartier, and the
Privy Council Chamber. More a museum than an insight into Ottawan politics today,
the interiors have been restored to look as they did in the 1870s.

More entertaining than the buildings themselves are the **debates** in the House of
Commons (Mon, Tues, Thurs 11am–1pm & 2–6.30pm, Wed 2–6pm, Fri 11–1pm & 2–
5pm) and the Senate (Tues 8pm, Wed & Thurs 2pm), both of which are open to the
public – a white light at the top of the Peace Tower indicates when Parliament is in
session. For **Question Period** in the House of Commons you'll certainly have to
queue (Mon–Thurs 2.15–3pm, Fri 11.15am–noon), but watching the right honourable
ladies and gentlemen rant and rave can be the best show in town.

Of the buildings' lawny surroundings the most interesting part lies on the Ottawa
River side of the Hill where there are excellent views from a paved pavillion. The
grounds themselves are formally laid out with various statues of Canada's greater
statesmen, with one of Queen Victoria thrown in for good measure. The National
Capital Commission (NCC) has spent $2.5 million bringing more attention to what is
considered Canada's symbol of freedom and democracy with a free summer **sound
and light show** illustrating Canada's history.

## Wellington Street and around

Practically next door to the Parliament Buildings stands the **Supreme Court of
Canada**, a rather austere Art Deco building, beyond which you'll find the **National
Archives and the National Library of Canada**; both feature regular free exhibitions.
The western area of Wellington leads to Ottawa's business district, with tall, modern
office blocks and streets crowded with the bureaucrats that Ottawa is infamous for.

**Sparks Street Mall**, parallel to Wellington Street, was once the site of a pioneer
farm and is now an expensive open-air shopping zone. In the thick of the boutiques, at
245 Sparks, the **Currency Museum** (May–Aug Mon–Sat 10.30am–5pm; Sept–April
Tues–Sat 10.30am–5pm, Sun 1–5pm; free) is housed in the old HQ of the Bank of
Canada – when they expanded their premises they encased the original 1937 stone
building in two green glass towers with an indoor jungle garden court. Within the
garden, in front of the museum, is a huge Yap stone, a symbol of wealth in the South
Pacific; such stones usually remain at the bottom of the sea, their possession simply
changing hands among the islanders by agreement. Inside the museum the stress is
on Canadian currencies, from the small beads and shells known as wampum through
to playing cards, beaver pelts and modern banknotes.

## Confederation Square and the Rideau Canal

The eastern end of Sparks Street Mall meets the triangular **Confederation Square**,
site of the **National Arts Centre** (tours May–Aug daily noon, 1.30pm, 3pm; Sept–April

Tues, Thurs & Sat noon, 1.30pm, 3pm), a complex of low hexagonal buildings housing an opera hall, theatres and the main information centre. The free tours are very popular with tourist groups and last a bit too long – far better to visit as part of an audience and to appreciate the excellent design and acoustics of the place.

The National Arts Centre hugs the side of the **Rideau Canal**, which in winter becomes the world's longest skating rink, with hot chocolate and muffin stands providing sustenance for the skaters, many of whom use the route to get to work. The canal joins the river at the foot of Parliament Hill, where a flight of locks lowers pleasure boats into the river. Beside the locks you'll find the **Bytown Museum** (mid-May to Sept Mon & Wed–Sat 10am–4pm, Sun 2–5pm; April to mid-May & Oct–Nov Mon–Fri 10am–4pm; $2), Ottawa's oldest building, where military supplies were stored during the construction of the canal. The history of the waterway is shown in a short video display, while the rest of the museum contains assorted Ottawan memorabilia, including some of Colonel By's belongings.

## Sussex Drive and Major's Hill Park

Crossing the canal beside the locks takes you past Ottawa's most ostentatious hotel, the *Chateau Laurier*, to **Sussex Drive**, whose southern section is one of Ottawa's oldest streets: the buildings between George and St Patrick might seem brand new, but they date from Ottawa's pioneer days. The general stores that once lined the city's busiest throughfare have been gutted and their fronts restored to house expensive shops and galleries. The most excessive renovation has been carried out on the east side of the street – in **Tin House Court**, for example, the entire facade of a tinsmith's house has been hung on the side of a stone building. On the opposite side of the road, **Major's Hill Park** is the area chosen by Colonel By as the site of his home so he could overlook the progress of the canal; the park has a beautiful setting, its peace disturbed only by the **Noon Day Gun** – except Sundays, so as not to disturb church-goers – a tradition introduced in 1869 to regulate the postal service. Major's Hill Park merges with **Nepean Point**, an area of land that juts out into the Ottawa River, with excellent views of the Chaudière Falls, Hull and the Laurentian Mountains.

## The National Gallery

In the area between Nepean Point and Sussex Drive rises the magnificent **National Gallery** (May–Aug daily 10am–6pm, open till 8pm Wed–Fri; Sept–April Tues–Sun 10am–5pm, open till 8pm Thurs; $4, free on Thurs), designed by Moshe Safdie to reflect the circular design of the Parliament Library. The collection was founded in 1880 by the Marquis of Lorne, the Governor General of the time, who persuaded members the Royal Canadian Academy to donate a work to the government. Over the next century artworks were gathered from all over the world, resulting in a collection that now contains over 25,000 pieces.

### THE CANADIAN GALLERIES

Predictably, the **Canadian Galleries**, laid out in roughly chronological succession on level one, are the finest in the building, following the history of Canadian painting from the mid-eighteenth century to the mid-twentieth. They begin with religious art from Québec and the gilded high altar by Paul Jourdain from Longueuil, followed by a room showing the emergence of secular art in the early nineteenth century, with paintings by immigrant artists trained in Europe. The most notable of these was Joseph Légaré, who was not only a painter but also a politician and nationalist – his *Cholera Plague, Québec*, is a fine example of his work. For popularity, though, none could match Cornelius Krieghoff, who could turn his hand to anything requested by his patrons from the emerging middle classes – as illustrated by his *Winter Landscape* and *White Horse Inn by Moonlight*.

Next comes the gallery's most intriguing exhibit, the Rideau Street Convent Chapel, rebuilt piece by intricate piece after it was threatened by demolition in 1972. Designed in 1887 by the architect-priest Canon Georges Bouillon for a convent school in Ottawa, it has slender cast-iron columns supporting a fan-vaulted ceiling – one of the few examples of its kind in North America. Contained in the chapel is a collection of silver and wooden church sculptures from Québec.

The growth of the Maritimes and Upper Canada during the nineteenth century are depicted in the following rooms. John Poad Drake's *The Port of Halifax* and John O'Brien's dramatic depictions of storm-tossed frigates illustrate the importance of the Atlantic provinces in this period, while the effects of colonisation in Upper Canada on the native population are shown in the forceful portraits by Paul Kane, Canada's first artist-explorer. At the centre of the Kane gallery is the unique Croscup room from Nova Scotia. Once the living room of a shipping family, it is covered in murals that juxtapose images from nineteenth-century North America and Europe – portraits of Micmac Indians next to Queen Victoria and family.

The construction of the railroads enabled artists to explore the wilder zones of Canada, a development encapsulated in Lucius O'Brien's *Sunrise on Saguenay*. However, painters of this period were still in thrall to European masters – the Royal Canadian Academy of Arts sent its students to Paris to complete their training – and the influence of Europe remained unshakeable right into this century, as shown by the impressionistic work of Cullen and Suzor-Côte, and the sombre rural scenes of Morris, Williamson, Watson and Walker, inspired by the Dutch and Barbizon school.

However, with the **Group of Seven** a purely Canadian style emerged. The first room dedicated to their works concentrates on their apprenticeship under Tom Thomson, whose startling *The Jack Pine* could be taken as the Group's clarion call – trees, often windswept or dead, are a constant symbol in the Group's paintings of Canada's *terre sauvage*. Using rapid, brash, often brutal brushstrokes, their works are faithful less to the landscape itself than to the emotions it evoked – Lawren Harris's *North Shore, Lake Superior* and JEH Macdonald's *The Solemn Land* are good awestruck examples.

Following Macdonald's death in 1932 the Group of Seven formed the Canadian Group of Painters, embracing all Canadian artists of the time whatever their style. Initially landscape remained the predominant genre but the effects of the Depression forced socio-political subjects to the fore – *Ontario Farm House* by Carl Schaefer turns a landscape into a social statement, while Jack Humphrey, Miller Brittain and Sam Borenstein depict the harsh reality of urban environments.

Emily Carr's mystical, monumental paintings dominate the room given over to pictures of BC's landscape, a section followed by works produced in 1940s Montréal, the most cosmopolitan arts centre in the country. Abstraction was first explored by the Montréal Automatistes, whose emphasis on the expressive qualities of colour was rejected by the Platiciens, with whom geometrical and analytical forms were a preoccupation. Both groups are represented here, as are postwar artists from Vancouver and Toronto – like William Ronald, known for aggressive images such as *The Hero*. The last rooms contain temporary exhibitions of works from the 1950s.

## THE CONTEMPORARY ART COLLECTION

The **Contemporary Art Collection**, on the lower level, spans the years between 1960 and 1980, and again shows Canadian artists looking for a lead outside their country. The shadow of New York's Abstract Expressionists falls over Charles Gagnon's *Cassation/ Open/Ouvert*, while the genealogy of mixed-media pieces like Jeff Wall's *The Destroyed Rooms* becomes clearer when you get to the collection of American contemporary art. Highlights here include Andy Warhol's *Brillo* sculpture, George Segal's lifesize assemblage *The Gas Station* and Carl Andre's minimalist *Lever* – a line of firebricks.

## THE EUROPEAN AND AMERICAN GALLERIES

The **European and American Galleries** begin with pieces from the workshops of Duccio in Siena and Giotto in Florence, accompanied by Filippino Lippi's *Triumph of Mordecai* and *Ester at the Palace Gate*, painted for chests that contained a bride's dowry. Northern European art in the fifteenth and sixteenth centuries is also represented primarily by religious art – note Quentin Matys's *Crucifixion*, with Jerusalem looking decidedly like a Flemish town circled by ramparts.

The collection of works from seventeenth-century Europe is particularly impressive: apart from Bernini's sculpture of his patron Pope Urban VIII, there's Claude Lorrain's *Landscape with a Temple of Bacchus*, an *Entombment* by Rubens, Rembrandt's sumptuous *Heroine from the Old Testament* and Van Dyck's *Suffer the Little Children to Come Unto Me*, an early work that includes portraits thought to be of Rubens and his family. From Britain in the eighteenth century there are portraits by Reynolds and Gainsborough, and Romney's *Joseph Brant (Thayendanegea)*, a portrait of a Mohawk chief on a visit to London to discuss the native involvement in the American Revolution with George III. Also here is *The Death of General Wolfe* by Benjamin West, an American who became George III's official painter.

The nineteenth-century selection is basically a show of minor paintings by great artists: Delacroix's romantic *Othello and Desdemona*, Corot's orderly *The Bridge at Narni*, Constable's *Salisbury Cathedral from the Bishop's Grounds* and Turner's *Mercury and Argus*, with a sunset that anticipates his future masterpieces. In stark contrast, the realist strain of the nineteenth century is represented by Courbet's *The Cliffs at Etretat* and Millet's *The Pig Slaughter*, though tranquillity is soon restored by Monet's *Waterloo Bridge: The Sun through the Fog*, beautifying London's notorious pea-soupers, and two canvases by Pissarro. Van Gogh's *Iris* and Cézanne's *Forest* are the only worthy Post-Impressionist works.

American art takes over in the following room, residence of Barnett Newman's *Voice of Fire*, the very mention of which causes some Canadians to break out in a cold sweat – not because of its artistic significance but because it cost $1.76 million. The artist intended the 18-foot-high piece to give the viewer a "feeling of his own totality, of his own separateness, of his own individuality, and at the same time of his connection to others, who are also separate"; unfortunately the purchase of the painting caused a furore, with one Manitoba Tory MP ranting that it could have been "done in ten minutes with two cans of paint and two rollers".

The final galleries have works from twentieth-century Europe, a diverse and high-class assembly that includes the disturbing *Hope I* by Gustav Klimt, Matisse's *Nude on a Yellow Sofa*, Francis Bacon's macabre *Study for Portrait No.1*, and pieces by Picasso, Leger, Epstein, Mondrian, Dali and Duchamp.

## INUIT AND PHOTOGRAPH GALLERIES

On the same level are the Asian art, Inuit art, prints, drawings and photograph galleries. The **Inuit art** section includes *The Enchanting Owl* by Kenojuak, whose flamboyant depictions of fantasy birds are the most famous of Inuit works. The **Photograph Gallery** displays a changing selection from the gallery's 17,000 photographs, covering the entire history of photography from its invention in 1838 to today.

## The war museum, Notre-Dame and around

Next door to the Gallery, surrounded by tanks and cannons, is the **Canadian War Museum** (daily 9.30am–5pm; $2; free on Thurs), the largest military collection in the country. One of the main exhibits is "Hitler's car" – the museum acquired it as Goering's car but the vehicle was renamed in the hope that it would encourage more visitors. The windscreen has bullet holes in it, added by the previous owner to fool people into thinking the Nazis had driven the Merc into battle. Other exhibits include a mock-up of a World War I trench, a gallery of medals and insignias, an intricate frigate constructed out of matchsticks by a bored sailor and an arsenal of weapons from Indian clubs to machine guns.

Opposite the National Gallery is the capital's Catholic cathedral, the plain-looking **Notre Dame Basilica**. Completed in 1890, it took fifty years to build and is Ottawa's oldest church. Inside, the altar is surrounded by over one hundred wooden sculptures – some with a kitschy marble finish – many of which were created by the sculptors who worked on the Parliament Buildings.

Behind the cathedral on St Patrick is the small **Canadian Centre for Caricature** (Sat–Tues 10am–6pm, Wed–Fri 10am–8pm; free), showing a rotating display of satirical cartoons from the eighteenth century to the present day. Back on Sussex, at no. 457a, is the **Canadian Ski Museum** (May–Sept Tues–Sat 11am–4pm; Oct–April noon–4pm; $1), one of the few museums in Ottawa that has failed to squeeze any money out of the NCC. Amid the haphazard collection of skis, photos, and paraphernalia, check out the 5000-year-old cave drawing of men on skis.

## Byward Market and the Laurier House

Since the 1840s the **Byward Market**, just east of Sussex and north of Rideau Street, has been a centre for the sale of farm produce, but in the last few years it has become Ottawa's hippest district. The 1927 Byward Market building has been renovated to house the **Ottawa Arts Exchange**, whose arts and crafts merchandise spills out onto the streets to merge with market stalls selling a variety of wares from ethnic gear to fresh fruit and veg. Most of Ottawa's best restaurants and bars are located here and during the day the area is busy with shoppers and buskers; at night it's buzzing until 1am, when everyone makes an exodus to Hull.

Northeast of here, closer to the Rideau River in the upmarket area of Sandy Hill, is the **Laurier House**, 335 Laurier Ave East (April–Sept Tues–Sat 9am–5pm & Sun 2–5pm; Oct–March Tues–Sat 10am–5pm & Sun 2–5pm; free), former home of prime ministers Sir Wilfred Laurier and William Lyon Mackenzie King. Laurier, Canada's first French-speaking prime minister, served from 1896 to 1911; Mackenzie King, his self-proclaimed "spiritual son", was Canada's longest-serving (1921–30 & 1935–48). Notoriously pragmatic, he enveloped his listeners in a fog of words through which his political intentions were barely discernible, as exemplified by his most famous line, "Not necessarily conscription, but conscription if necessary" – supposedly a clarification of his plans at the onset of World War II, which most Québécois viewed as a European imperialist conflict. Even more famous than his obfuscating rhetoric was his personal eccentricity. His fear that future generations would view him as the heir of his grandfather William Lyon Mackenzie – who in the 1830s led rebellions in Upper Canada – eventually led him into spiritualism: he held regular seances to tap the advice of great dead Canadians, including Laurier, who allegedly communicated to him through the agency of his pet dog.

The house is dominated by King's possessions, including his crystal ball and a portrait of his obsessively adored mother, in front of which he placed a red rose every day. Other mementoes include the programme Abraham Lincoln held the night of his assassination and a guest book signed by Churchill, Roosevelt, De Gaulle, Nehru, the Dionne quintuplets and Shirley Temple. The house also contains a reconstruction of a study belonging to prime minister Lester B Pearson, who was awarded the Nobel Peace Prize for his role in the 1956 Arab-Israeli dispute.

Laurier Avenue East eventually meets the **Rideau River**, which is escorted by walkways and bicycle paths to the **Rideau Falls**, whose twin cataracts are separated by Green Island – the site of the Ottawa City Hall, an unattractive building built in the 1950s. The Falls themselves were once enveloped in an industrial complex which has now been cleared away to allow excellent views across the river to Hull.

## Rockcliffe

North of the Falls lies **Rockcliffe**, Ottawa's Beverly Hills, a tranquil haven colonised by parliamentary bigwigs and diplomats – and in the evening by local lovers, who canoodle in the pavilions on the river shore, looking across to the Gatineau Hills. The prime minister resides in a stately mansion barely visible through the trees at 24 Sussex, while the stately **Rideau Hall**, at no. 1, has been the home of Canada's governors-general since Confederation. The Hall's gardens of maples and fountains are open to the riff-raff for guided tours (every half-hour mid-June to mid-Aug daily 10.15am–6.15pm; on the hour Oct to mid-May Sat & Sun 10am–3pm; mid-May to mid-June daily 10am–4pm; mid-Aug to Sept Wed–Sun 10am–3pm; free).

At the east end of Rockcliffe, 4km from downtown, is the huge hangar of the **National Aviation Museum** (May–Aug Wed–Fri 9am–8pm, Sat–Tues 9am–6pm; Sept–April Tues–Sun 9am–5pm, Thurs 9am–8pm; $4, free on Thurs) – served by bus #198. Highlights include a replica of the *Silver Dart*, which made the first powered flight in Canada in 1909; it flew for a full nine minutes, a major achievement for a contraption that seems to be made out of spare parts and old sheets. There are also bombers from both world wars and some excellent videos, including a programme to simulate a helicopter flight.

## South Ottawa

Of south Ottawa's straggle of attractions, the most central is the **Canadian Museum of Nature**, installed in a fortress-like building on the corner of McLeod and Metcalfe, just one block south of Gladstone (June–Sept daily 9.30am–5pm, open till 8pm Sun, Mon & Thurs; Sept–April daily 10am–5pm, open till 8pm Thurs; $2, free on Thurs). Covering the evolution of the natural world from the beginning of life on the planet, the museum contains a couple of million zoological specimens, including a good collection of dinosaur skeletons. The dioramas of present-day Canadian wildlife are the most interesting – everything you ever wanted to know about the moose and grizzly.

Following the canal south along Queen Elizabeth Driveway brings you to Dows Lake, which before the building of the canal was known as Dow's Great Swamp. Surrounding the lake is the arboretum of the **Central Experimental Farm** (daily 8.15am–dusk; free; bus #3), among whose 2000 tree species are many non-native to Canada. The farm itself, covering 500 hectares on the other side of Prince of Wales Driveway, began in 1886 as an attempt by the government to improve existing farm practices and help pioneers get the most from the wilderness. Now one of five such farms, it is still primarily concerned with agricultural experimentation and the study of how flora survive in Canada's harsh climate. Beside the information building at the junction of Maple Drive and the Driveway, the **Agricultural Museum** (daily 9.30am–5pm; free) has a collection of turn-of-the-century farming equipment and special shows on such riveting subjects as "Haying in Canada" and "A Barn in the 1920s". Although the farm has various livestock herds, the Clydesdale horses are the only animals put to work, pulling wagonloads of visitors along the lanes from outside the museum. Other than animals the farm also has a varied collection of plants – the Tropical Plant Greenhouse has over 500 tropical plants including orchids and banana trees. At the intersection of Carling Avenue and Maple Drive, still within the bounds of the farm, the now redundant **Observatory** (Mon–Fri 8.30am–4pm) houses a collection of instruments used to measure earthquakes and the like.

East of the farm lies the **Billings Estate Museum** at 2100 Cabot Street (mid-May to Oct 10am–5pm; closed Fri & Sat; free; bus #96), home of Bradish Billings and his wife – the first white settlers to take up land on the south side of the Rideau River. The grounds have great views, and the house contains exhibits on Ottawa's growth from wilderness to capital.

About three kilometres further east, a lighthouse from Cape North in Nova Scotia marks the site of the **National Museum of Science and Technology,** 1867 St Laurent Blvd (May–Aug Wed–Fri 10am–8pm, Sat–Tues 9am–5pm; Sept–April Tues–Sun 9am–5pm, open till 8pm Thurs; $4, free on Thurs; buses #114 and #111). Surrounding the museum is the so-called Technology Park, whose steam locomotive and other vehicles indicate the museum's main thrust. For although the museum has a fair showing of hands-on exhibits on scientific topics from agriculture to astronomy – you can make your own paper, see chicks hatch in an incubator and queue for a peek through Canada's largest refracting telescope – the main draws are the hardware of land, sea and space transportation. The cars section has vintage vehicles as well as the popemobile used on John Paul II's 1984 tour of Canada; old cruisers and models of ships fill out the story of marine transport; and the pristine Apollo 7 space capsule sits beside the burnt-out chunk of a Soviet satellite that landed in northern Canada in 1978.

## Hull

**Hull,** though recognised as part of Canada's capital region in 1969, remains distinctly separate and predominantly francophone. For years it was a paper milling town, an industrial, working-class area removed from the rat-race atmosphere on the south side of the river. However, pressure on the government has led to the building of a number of high-rise administration buildings and the capital's newest national museum, the Musée Canadien des Civilisations, which now dominates the waterfront. At the moment, though, Hull is still best known as Ottawa's nightlife spot and receives its heaviest tourist influx after dark.

### THE MUSÉE CANADIEN DES CIVILISATIONS

The **Musée Canadien des Civilisations,** right by the foot of the Alexander Bridge, is the one museum in the capital region that must not be missed (May–Aug daily 9am–5pm, open till 9pm Thurs; Sept–April closed Mon; adults $4, children free; combination ticket including Cineplus adults $9, children $4). The building itself is an amazing sight – undulating over 24 acres, it was designed by Douglas Cardinal, an Indian architect, to represent the landscape created by the meeting of the rocky Canadian Shield and the snow and ice of the deep north. Inside, the museum is a state-of-the-art presentation of the human history of Canada, from the native populations, through European domination to today's immigrants.

In the **Grand Hall** the world's largest collection of totem poles serves as a backdrop to displays on native ceremonies and excellent videos which present a balanced account of the plight of the Indians today. The **History Hall** – still being completed – will eventually illustrate Canada's history from 1000 AD to the present day, its exhibits taking the form of life-size reconstructions of historical environments. Beginning with Norsemen embarking on Newfoundland's shores, the early history concentrates on the Basques who crossed the Atlantic to trawl the fertile Gulf of St Lawrence and Labrador Sea. Permanent settlement by the French on the Atlantic coast is recreated with an Acadian settlement, focusing on the dike-making techniques that enabled them to turn salt marshes into arable land. The farming communities of New France, which by the eighteenth century were strung along the St Lawrence, are represented by farmhouses, a cooperage, a pub and a hospital. A separate section deals with the fur trade that opened up Canada – a fur trading post and Métis camp are followed by the wagons of the new immigrants from America. A mock-up of a British officers' quarters, based on a painting by Cornelius Krieghoff, illustrates the military's expansion of Canada's transport and communication lines in the nineteenth century, while a full-scale section of a schooner gives a sharp insight into the maritime life at the time. The liveliest part of the show is the Ontarian main street of the turn of the century, populated by the resident theatre company. Future exhibits will include sections on the Prairies, the west coast and the arctic, with special emphasis on the effects of modern development on the Inuit. In the meantime, elsewhere in the museum you'll find changing exhibitions of Indian and Inuit art, and a **Children's Museum** whose interactive displays include a "world tour" bus that takes children on an imaginary journey through eight different countries.

In addition to all this, there's the **Cineplus** (adults $6, children $4), a space-age cinema with two huge screens – the Imax and the Omnimax – which together virtually engulf the audience. Canadian-made films on natural wonders and human skills like acrobatics and rock-climbing take full advantage of the immense size of the screens – indeed the effects are so overwhelming that before performances a guide advises the audience to close their eyes should they feel any motion sickness. Films are shown at regular intervals during the day.

### GATINEAU PARK

Ottawa's playground in the wilderness, the 88,000-acre **Gatineau Park** was founded in 1934 when the government purchased the land to stop the destruction brought on by the need for cheap firewood during the Depression. It's located on Hull's western borders, about a fifteen-minute drive from Parliament Hill, and there is no public transport except during the Fall Festival, when a bus operates from outside the Musée Canadien des Civilisations. Alternatively, there's a bicycle path from opposite the National Gallery – a lengthy but pleasant ride.

Other than the standard hiking and cross-country ski trails – where you may be lucky enough to spot a few beavers – the main attraction is **Kingsmere** (mid-May to Aug daily; Sept Wed–Sun 11am–6pm; free), the Mackenzie King estate in the southern sector of the park. King retreated here to escape the rigours of public life and in a characteristically eccentric manner strewed the grounds with various architectural fragments – chunks of the old Parliament Buildings, Corinthian columns and blocks of the British House of Commons retrieved after the Blitz. The summer-house tea room is open in summer and serves a decent cup.

# Eating, drinking and nightlife

**Eating out** is not an aspect of the average Ottawan day, and despite the relatively recent explosion in the numbers of **restaurants** – ethnic eateries in particular – the capital is not on the list of the world's best cities to eat in. Moreover, keeping track of the best places is tricky, as restaurants come and go in Ottawa faster than in anywhere else in Canada – eighty percent of establishments change hands in the first five years, due largely to the Ottawan habit of eating in and going to bed early. The trendiest joints are in the Byward Market area, but there are also a number of good places along Elgin and Bank, and a small Chinatown on Somerset West and Bronson. Considering the majority of eateries are located in the centre of a capital city, the price tags are extremely reasonable – a decent meal with drink can be had for less than $20.

**Snack and fast-food** outlets seem to have most staying power, probably because they don't take up too much of the workaholics' time and get a lot of their custom from the more relaxed blue-collar workers. Chip vans have become an Ottawan institution – be sure to try their mouth-watering *poutine* – fries covered in gravy and chunks of mozzarella. Other excellent places for cheap food are the numerous Lebanese establishments, where kebabs and vegetarian felafels are both reasonable and delicious.

Most **bars and pubs** depend on a student crowd to fill the tills, and during the week most places are pretty dead. Beer does not come cheap either – tax is heavy and the policy of tipping the bartender soon empties your wallet. It is illegal to sell drink in Ottawa without providing food, so all the pubs and bars sell finger foods – the current fads are Mexican snacks and spicy chicken wings. Ottawa's **nightlife** is in Hull and everybody knows it: at 1am the Ontario bars shut while the Québec bars stay hot until the 3am close-down. Hull's Happy Hours and Ladies Nights can get a bit childish ("Ladies without bras" nights, etc), but there's always something worth the trip across the river – take bus #8 or a taxi, costing $5 from downtown Ottawa. Because of the later licensing hours, Hull's bars are quite clubby, with dance floors and loud music, though few charge an entrance fee. On both sides of the river the clubs and **discos** tend to be your average Top 40 boppy music and good old-fashioned rock and roll – though Hull's bars are a bit more experimental.

As for **live music**, Ottawa has a good selection of venues, but decent bands are few and far between. Live **jazz**, however, is extremely popular and there is a *Jazzline* (☎232-7755) with the latest info on gigs.

For **listings** on events of all sorts, there's the free bilingual *WHERE Ottawa-Hull*, a monthly promotional magazine designed for tourists. On Fridays the *Ottawa Citizen* prints a list of current entertainment, but for gig details as well as other more objective listings and information the monthly *Metro-Eye* magazine is the capital's trendiest and most comprehensive source.

## Snacks and cafés

**Bagel Bagel**, 92 Clarence. Nine different types of bagel with an assortment of fillings for 40¢. Open 24 hours at the weekend.

**Boko Bakery**, 87 George. Mini-pizza, croissants and *pain de chocolat*, pricey but worth every penny. Open 7am–6pm.

**Café Bohemian**, 89 Clarence. A well-established market eatery. Simple decor and imaginative food from cognac paté to strawberry pancakes.

**Café Deluxe**, 279 Dalhousie. Fashionable café with black furnishings and black-clad people. There is also a patio area in the summer. Fairly expensive.

**Hooker's All Canadian Beavertails**, Sparks St Mall and on the corner of York and William (Byward Market). Specialises in the Ottawan snack that is half pizza, half doughnut, covered either in garlic butter and cheese or homemade jam.

**Marrous**, 380 Elgin. Lebanese take-out with great kebabs; open daily till 2am.

**Nate's**, 316 Rideau. At $1.50 the cheapest full breakfast in the capital's most popular deli.

**Rideau Mall**, Rideau St. The food market has a choice of fast-food outlets from Canadian to Chinese.

**Royal Smoke Shop**, 1 Nicholas. Lebanese deli and supermarket. A variety of salads and kebabs to take away.

**Toni's**, corner of Dalhousie and George. A greasy spoon with free coffee refills and the advantage of being open 24 hours daily.

**Yogen Fruz**, 42 Byward Market. Fresh fruit blended with frozen yogurt – refreshing, delicious and healthy, from $1.65. Open daily, weekends until 1am.

## Restaurants

**Crystal Dragon**, 704 Somerset West. Ottawa's best and most reasonable Chinese restaurant, usually packed with Chinese taking advantage of the lengthy Cantonese menu. Open daily.

**Festival Japan**, 149 Kent. Authentic sushi and excellent service; an average meal will set you back $20.

**Guadala Harry's**, 18 York. Cheap, multi-storied, Mexican-village style restaurant with a good atmosphere and a Spanish crooner at the weekends. Open daily.

**Haveli**, Market Mall, George St. Elegant Indian restaurant. The all-you-can-eat lunch buffet is one of the best buys in Ottawa.

**Hurley's Roadhouse**, 73 York. With a seating capacity of 300 and chicken wings and burgers as the staple fare.

**Khyber Pass**, 271 Dalhousie. Generous servings of Afghan dishes; good for vegetarians.

**Mama Teresa**, 300 Somerset West. Homemade pasta, fresh parmesan, filtered water, fresh olives and real Italian coffee; most pasta dishes under $10. Very popular. Closed Sun.

**Newfoundland Pub and Restaurant**, on the corner of Hochelage and Montreal Rd. Far out of downtown but if you are not going out east, a chance to try such Newfie delicacies as cod cheeks and tongues. Bus #2.

**Old Fish Market Restaurant**, 54 York. Great-value fresh fish with different specials every day. Closed Sun lunchtimes.

**Passage to India**, 544 Rideau. The most reasonable and highly recommended Indian restaurant in the area. Closed Sat lunchtime.

**Pho Quynh Café**, 881 Somerset. Vietnamese food including beef barbequed in front of you for $6.50 with all the trimmings.

**The Ritz**, 15 Clarence, 274 Elgin, 375 Queen Elizabeth Driveway, 1665 Bank and 226 Nepean. Ottawa's biggest success story and the best place for a bit of a splurge. There are five *Ritzes*, all varying slightly. The one on Clarence is an old brick house with brick-oven pizzas and homemade bread; the original and the best *Ritz* is the one on Elgin; the Canal Ritz has the best location of any restaurant in Ottawa. Closed Sun lunchtimes.

**The Sitar**, 417A Rideau. More expensive than the *Passage*, but with excellent curries and reputedly the best nan in Ottawa. Closed Sun lunchtime.

**Yan's**, 224 Besserer. Malaysian and Chinese food. During the week, huge buffets cost $5.95 at lunchtime, $8.95 for dinner.

**Zak's Diner**, 16 Byward Market. A '50s style time-warp with chrome decor, rock 'n' roll blaring from the jukebox and good all-American food. Open daily until midnight.

# Bars and pubs

**Chateau Lafayette**, 42 York. A dark and dingy dive that has been here as long as Ottawa. Take a glimpse of Ottawan life beneath the comfy veneer, as the old timers add salt to their beer. Try and avoid the inevitable fights – and make sure you tip if you want to leave in one piece.

**Club 166**, 166B Laurier West. Good male gay bar.

**The Mayflower**, 247 Elgin and 201 Queen. Twinned English pubs – the one on Queen has a better buzz.

**On Tap**, 160 Rideau. Ottawa's trendiest bar, with pitchers of beer for under $5 and big screens for the sport.

**Royal Oak**, 360 Bank. An English-style pub good with tasty, cheap homemade soups and a generous combo plate.

**Tramps**, 53 William. The best bar in the Market, with excellent finger foods – try the deep-fried zucchini. Chicken wings are 10¢ at the weekends. The sports bar upstairs has the mandatory screens as well as table ice-hockey and basketball.

# Music bars and venues

**Bank Café**, 294 Bank. A licensed old-style folk bar dating back to the 1930s. Local singers perform Thurs–Sat 9pm–1am.

**Barrymores**, 323 Bank. Commercial, mainstream and local bands live every night except Sun. Both U2 and Tina Turner have played in this huge seven-level venue. Cover can be as high as $25 depending on the band.

**Downstairs Club**, 307 Rideau. Small, smoky venue with excellent free blues on Tues, live bands with a cover charge of $4–5 at the weekend.

**Grand Central**, 141 George. Cover bands playing mainstream rock Thurs through Sat, big-screen movie nights earlier in the week. $1 cover at weekends.

**The New Live Penguin**, 292 Elgin. Bursting at the seams on the weekend; a variety of live bands and no cover charge.

The Rainbow Bistro, 76 Murray. The best R&B club, highly regarded on the blues circuit. Cover charge varies from $2 to $8.

Vineyard's Wine Bar Bistro, 54 York. Free live jazz every Wed night.

Zaphod Beeblebrox, 413 Rideau. Upstairs for indie and alternative – often European – bands, downstairs for upbeat country and western.

Zoes, Chateau Laurier Hotel. Ottawan jazz trios Wed nights in this very elegant bar.

## Dance bars, discos and clubs

Le Bistro, 115 Promenade de Portage, Hull. The best bar in Hull but from Thurs through to Su it's the watering hole of Ottawa's bar staff – unless you are in with the in crowd it's impossible to get in. Mon and Tues are promotion nights with a beer and a shot for $2.50.

Le Bop, 180 Promenade de Portage, Hull. A loud, heaving dance bar. Promotions on Mon and Tues (rock 'n' roll night), when all beers are $2.

Chez Henri, 179 Promenade de Portage, Hull. Hull's hottest nightspot, with laser shows and numerous dance floors. $2 Thurs, $4 Fri and Sat, with half price drinks on Fri and Sun before 11pm; no jeans or trainers on Thurs, Fri and Sat.

Club Zinc, 191 Promenade de Portage, Hull. Another Hull disco with a cover of $5.

Gigi's, 53 York. White-faced, black-clad Goths and alternative music.

Stoney Mondays, 62 York. Open-air disco which attracts a young studenty crowd.

Zap, 75 Promenade de Portage, Hull. Nightclub with impressive laser show.

### Gay venues

Central Park & Zipper Club, 340 Somerset West. Popular male gay venue – during the day for its belowstairs café, at night for its dance bar.

Le Club, 77 Wellington, Hull. Ottawa's longest-established gay nightclub.

Shadows, 433 Cooper. Ottawa's only women-only club.

## Performing arts and cinema

Ottawa's focus of culture, the *National Arts Centre*, 53 Elgin (☎755-1111), presents **plays** by the resident company and touring groups, **concerts** by the resident orchestra, **operas** with simultaneous French and English subtitles and **dance** from, among others, the National Ballet of Canada and the Royal Winnipeg Ballet. As a further attraction, the Canadian Film Institute also presents **films** here. Tickets begin at $10 and wherever you sit the acoustics are outstanding.

Quality **theatre** is also presented by *The Great Canadian Theatre Company*, 910 Gladstone (☎236-5196), which presents avant garde Canadian plays with strong social or political overtones; *Ottawa Little Theatre*, 400 King Edward (☎233-8948), an amateur group who perform a variety of popular plays, usually comedies; and Hull's *Théâtre l'Île*, 1 Wellington (☎595-7455), on an island in the Ottawa River. Hull also has its own **opera house** at *Le Theatre Lyrique*, 109 Wright (☎770-8031).

Free **concerts** are held during the summer at *Astrolabe*, a 1500-seat open-air amphitheatre in Nepean Point Park behind the *Chateau Laurier Hotel*, while the *Nepean Symphony Orchestra* sometimes gives free concerts at parks in and around the capital.

Ottawa has a good selection of **cinemas**, with Thursday as cheap night at most venues. The *Bytowne Cinema*, 325 Rideau, is the capital's most popular repertory cinema. The *Canadian Film Institute*, 395 Wellington, shows arty programmes arranged by theme. *Rideau Centre Cinemas*, 50 Rideau, has the latest releases, as does the *Mayfair Theatre*, 1074 Bank.

For **comedy**, *Yuk Yuks*, 88 Albert, features stand-up comedians from Canada, the States and Europe; Wednesday is "New Talent Night".

# Festivals

The NCC uses every excuse in the book to put on **festivals**, and its munificence is evident at every jamboree. Public holidays like Canada Day are celebrated here with the sort of spectacle that other cities muster, but with extra dollars to boost the show, while seasonal festivals like the Winterlude and the Canadian Tulip Festival are as lavish as any in the country. Other than these large bashes, ethnic festivals embracing Canada's diverse population are smaller but equally entertaining and fun affairs – with the Franco-Ontarien fest becoming more popular every year. The list below is arranged chronologically.

**Winterlude.** A ten-day snow-and-ice extravaganza, usually scheduled at the beginning of February. Concentrated around the frozen Rideau Canal, it includes ice sculptures at Confederation Park – renamed the Crystal Garden for the duration – and snow sculptures around Dows Lake. Other events include speed-skating, bed-races and dog-sled races.

**Odawa Powwow.** Held in May at Nepean Tent and Trailer Park. Ottawa's powwow is less spectacular than others in the country but there are competitions in dancing, drumming and singing as well as stalls selling crafts and food.

**Canadian Tulip Festival.** Held in mid-May, this is the oldest of Ottawa's festivals – it began in 1945 when the Dutch sent 100,000 tulip bulbs to the capital to thank the Canadian soldiers who helped liberate the Netherlands. More bulbs arrived the following year from Queen Juliana, who had taken refuge in Ottawa when the Netherlands were occupied. The transformation of the city didn't meet with universal approval at first – Mackenzie King thought the planting of tulips around the Parliament Buildings was "undignified", but his staff planted thousands in secret anyway. Nowadays the bulbs are planted around Parliament, along the canal and around Dows Lake, an outbreak of colour that's accompanied by concerts, parades, fireworks and a huge craft show. The major events take place in Major's Hill Park and Dows Lake – but few are free, and the festival has a reputation for being rather upmarket and touristy.

**Ottawa-Hull Children's Festival.** June. Children-oriented performances in mime, dance, music and theatre.

**Ital-Canada Festival.** June. A celebration of the Italian contribution to Canadian life, with Italian films, outdoor concerts and expensive gala performances.

**Franco-Ontarien Festival.** Mid-June. This festival has built up a reputation as being the party that brings a bit of wildness to conservative Ottawa. Dalhousie St is closed off to traffic for up to ten days, so the bands and street dancers can take over.

**Canada Dance Festival.** End of June. Dance troupes from around the country rock and roll, tap and generally swing their pants in various locations across the capital, including a barge on the canal.

**Donnie Gilchrist Festival.** July. Traditional fiddling and step-dancing competitions.

**Cultures Canada.** Held from early July to early September, this programme of the performing arts attracts entertainers from all over the country to celebrate the "diverse ethnic and regional character of Canada". The performances take place at locations along Confederation Boulevard in Ottawa and Hull. Many of the performances are free and those that do require ticket purchase are rarely more than $4.

**Ottawa International Jazz Festival.** Mid-July. This is one of the most popular festivals in the capital with performances by over 400 musicians. The main stage is in Confederation Park with concerts at noon, 6.30pm and 8.30pm ($5); however, you'll find local bands swinging all around Byward Market and Sparks St Mall.

**Festival of the Arts.** Mid-September. Includes video and film presentation, visual art exhibits, crafts and concerts.

**Fall Rhapsody.** End of September to early October. An attempt to promote environmental awareness through a range of events at Gatineau Park; at the weekends there is a free shuttle bus from 14 Metcalfe St in Ottawa and the Musée Canadien des Civilisations in Hull.

**Oktoberfest.** End of September to early October. Plenty of beer, stomping and traditional Germanic entertainment at the Ottawa Civic Centre, 1015 Bank St.

**Japan Fest**. October. Hosted by the Japanese Embassy, with art exhibitions, theatre, dance and martial arts demonstrations.

**Lebanese Festival**. November. Parades and special guests from the Lebanon.

# Listings

**Airlines** *Air Canada, Air Alliance, Air Nova* and *Air Ontario*, 275 Slatter (☎237-5000); *Canadian Airlines International*, 50 O'Connor (☎237-1380 or 1-800-361-7413); *First Air*, 100 Thad Johnson (☎839-3340 or 1-800-267-1247).

**Airport enquiries** ☎998-3151.

**Babysitters** *Quickcare* ☎233-8280.

**Bike rental** *Rent-a-Bike*, Mackenzie Ave, behind *Chateau Laurier* (April to Thanksgiving daily 9am–6pm; ☎233-0268).

**Books** *Books Canada*, 71 Sparks St, has a fine selection of Canadian literature and non-fiction. *The Book Market* on the corner of Dalhousie and Rideau buys and sells secondhand books. *The Nicolas Goal Hostel* and the *Canadian Hostelling Association*, 18 Byward Market, sell travel books.

**Bus information** Local services: *OC Transpo* (Ottawa ☎741-4390); *CTCRO* (Hull ☎770–3242). Long-distance: *Voyageur Colonial* (☎238-6668).

**Camping equipment** *The Expedition Shoppe*, 43 York; *Blacks Camping International*, 901 Bank; *Trailhead*, 126 York.

**Car parks** The most central car parks are by the National Gallery on Sussex Drive and beside the National Arts Centre in Confederation Square.

**Canadian football** Ottawa's league team, the Rough Riders, play at Lansdowne Park, 1015 Bank (☎563-1212). Tickets cost around $10; take bus #7 or #1 to Lansdowne Park.

**Car rental** *Budget*, 443 Somerset West (☎230-6666); *Hertz*, 881 St Laurent (☎746-9969); *Myers*, 1200 Baseline (☎225-8006); *Tilden*, 418 Somerset West (☎232-3536).

**Dental emergencies** Ottawa ☎523-4185; Hull ☎568-3368.

**Embassies** *Australia*, 50 O'Connor (☎236-0841); *Great Britain*, 80 Elgin (☎237-1303); *Ireland*, 170 Metcalfe (☎233-6281); *Netherlands*, 275 Slater, 3rd Floor (☎237-5030); *USA*, 100 Wellington (☎238-5335).

**Gay Ottawa** *Gays of Ottawa,* 318 Liskeard St, operate an excellent information service (Mon–Fri 7.30–10.30pm, Sat & Sun 6–9pm; ☎238-1717) and publish *GO Info*, which is free from most bars. For books and magazines, check out *Mags and Fags* at 286 Elgin.

**Hospitals** *Ottawa General*, 501 Smythe Rd (☎737-7777; bus #85); *St Anne's Medical Centre*, 500 St Patrick (☎238-1552), is the most central.

**Ice hockey** The Ottawa area has two Junior A teams. The Ottawa 67s play at the Civic Centre, 1015 Bank (bus #7 or #1); the Hull Olympiques play at the Robert Guertin Arena, 125 Carillon Blvd in Hull. Wayne Gretsky's team, the Los Angeles Kings, occasionally train at the Guertin Arena.

**Laundry** *Rideau Coinwash*, 436 Rideau; and several along Bank.

**Left luggage** There are lockers at the train and bus stations; downtown, the Nicolas Gaol Hostel charges a nominal fee for left luggage.

**Pharmacy** *Rideau Pharmacy*, 390 Rideau (daily 9am–9pm).

**Post office** 59 Sparks St Mall.

**Ride-sharing** *Allo-Stop* (☎778-8877).

**Soccer** Ottawa Intrepid play at Lansdowne Park, 1015 Bank (bus #7 or #1) or the Terry Fox Stadium, Riverside Drive (bus #96). Tickets cost around $10.

**Taxis** *Blue Line* (☎238-1111); *A-1* (☎746-1616); *Blondeau* (☎749-5838).

**Train information** ☎238-8289.

**Travel agencies** *Voyageur Travel*, 300-161 Laurier West (☎237-2700); *Ottawa Travel*, 197 Sparks (☎563-0744); *Club Adventure*, 115 Parent Ave, Byward Market (☎236-5006).

**Weather information** ☎998-3439.

**Women's Ottawa** The *Ottawa Women's Bookstore*, 380 Elgin, is the best place to go for contacts (Mon–Sat 10am–6pm; Thurs–Fri 10am–9pm). Useful in emergencies are the *Ottawa Distress Centre* (☎238-3311) and *Sexual Assault Support Centre* (☎234-2266).

# NORTHERN ONTARIO

Stretching from the north shores of lakes Huron and Superior to the frozen reaches of Hudson Bay, **northern Ontario** is a land of sparse population and colossal distances, summed up thus by Canadian humorist Stephen Leacock – "The best that anyone could say of the place was that it was a 'sportsman's paradise', which only means a good place to drink whiskey in". Attracted by the exploitable skills of the nomadic Ojibwa, Cree and Algonquian natives and by the strategic waterways, European fur traders were the first people to establish permanent settlements here, though sizeable communities began to develop only at the end of the last century, with the rise of the lumber industry. Later mineral strikes brought prospectors flooding in, but now that most of the mines have closed or dwindled and the timber industry is declining through ill-planned replanting and the switch to recycling, towns are having to rely on the passing trade of lorry drivers, freight trains and tourists. Most of the visitors who linger here tend be equipped with rod or gun, for despite the poisons from local pulp industries, the wildlife is abundant and the thousands of lakes and rivers well stocked. However, an increasing number of non-hunting clientele are attracted by Lake Superior Provincial Park and by the **tour trains** from Sault Ste Marie and Cochrane – convenient ways of reaching the wilderness.

Northern Ontario's two main thoroughfares – highways 11 and 17 – diverge on North Bay, 345km north of Toronto. The older Highway 11, which runs 1896km from Toronto to Rainy River on the Ontario–Minnesota border, heads north through the mining towns that made Ontario's fortune, passing through Cochrane, from where a lone rail line strikes north to Moosonee on the shores of James Bay. The more scenic Highway 17 heads west via **Sudbury**, historic **Sault Ste Marie** and along the shore of the magnificent Lake Superior to the inland port of **Thunder Bay**. Most towns on both highways are served by regular buses (passenger train connections diminish every year), but all the provincial parks require private transportation.

---

Unless stated otherwise, the North Ontario telephone code is ☎705.

---

# North Bay and Highway 11

At **North Bay**, the transport nexus of northern Ontario, **Highway 11** begins a thousand-kilometre loop to Nipigon, passing though a region which, far from the moderating effects of Lake Superior, has a climate as savage as any in the world. The long winters are so cold that inhabitants who die in the winter cannot be buried until the spring. Though the highway's infrequent towns are served by *Greyhound, Grey Goose* and *Ontario Northland* buses, this is definitely a region where a car is needed – you don't want to be hanging around too long for a connection. Note also that food and drink are more expensive in this region than elsewhere in Ontario; your best bet is to eat where you sleep.

## North Bay

Despite being a city since 1935, **NORTH BAY** is not much more than a small dull town, handy as a springboard for points north or west. *Ontario Northland* **trains** from Cochrane and Toronto and all long-distance **buses** terminate at the Intermodal station at 100 Station Road, to the east of town (☎495-4200). To get to Main Street walk through the shopping mall opposite, and take a bus from the front of the mall to the local bus terminal on Oak Street, one block from Main Street – the fare is $1.

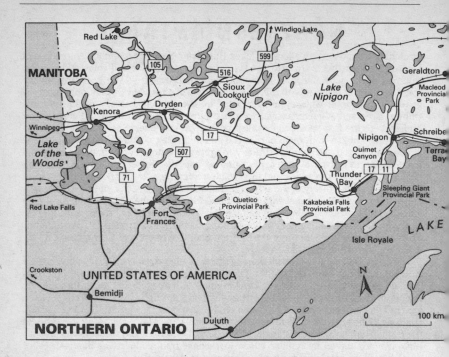

NORTHERN ONTARIO

The #4 bus goes to North Bay's only interesting museum, the **Dionne Homestead Museum**, on the corner of Franklin and Seymour where Hwy 11 hits the south side of town (June–Sept daily 9am–9pm; $2). The museum is housed in the small log cabin from Corbeil, just west of North Bay, where the Dionne quintuplets were born on May 28, 1934. Kept alive with drops of whiskey, the quints were considered miracle children by the economically depressed nation, and at the age of three the government took custody of them, removing them from their parents and five brothers and sisters. Until they were nine years old the quints were put on display in a glassed-in playground, to the delight of up to 6000 sightseers who turned up each day to watch them – and to pay for souvenirs such as "birth-promoting" stones picked up from the North Bay area. The girls were educated in a synthetic "normal school atmosphere" provided by ten class-mates, five of whom were English to help the quints with their second language. This bizarre childhood eventually caused a highly publicised estrangement between the quints and their parents, and doubtless contributed to the unhappiness of their later lives – a story dominated by illness, depression and failed marriages. The three surviv-ing quints – Yvonne, Annette and Cecile – now live in Québec. The small museum contains dresses, toys, photographs, advertising hoardings and souvenirs of the quints' childhood, including the bed they were born in.

## Practicalities

The **information centre** is by the Dionne Homestead Museum at 1375 Seymour Street (Mon–Fri 9am–5pm). North Bay's glut of **accommodation** is concentrated along Lake Nipissing on Lakeshore Drive, served regularly by the Marshall and Lakeshore buses. Cheap **motel** rooms are available at the *Rock Haven Motel* at no. 812 (☎472-6470; doubles $30), *Bayshore* at no. 566 (☎472-5350; doubles $35), *Lancelot Inn*

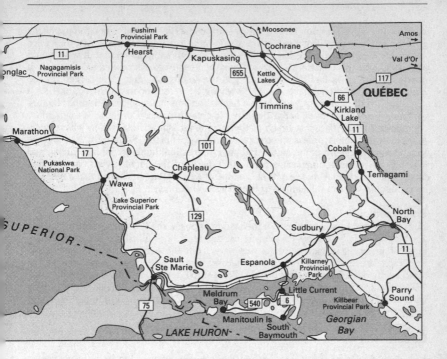

at no. 295 (☎476-0200; doubles $39) and the *Manitou Motel* at no. 710 (☎472-1900; doubles $40). If you prefer **bed and breakfast**, *B&B* at no. 653 (☎472-4734; doubles $35) nccds to be booked in advance. Family-style **campgrounds** are *Del Rio Motel Tent and Trailer Park*, at no. 676, and *Franklin Motel Tent and Trailer Park* at no. 444.

For **eating, drinking** and **nightlife** head for the area around Main Street. The *Windmill Café*, 168 Main St is a decent, family-run greasy spoon with all the usuals on offer. For soup and sandwiches *The Magic Kettle*, 407 Ferguson St, is cheap and delicious. *Mike's Seafoods*, 406 Lakeshore Drive, serves reasonably priced fish dishes while *Traditions*, 246 First Ave West (☎476-4600), is the best and most expensive restaurant. Students keep the bars along Main Street alive; check out the popular dance **bars** – *Madams* at no. 200 and *Waves* at no. 134. *The Lions Heart*, 147 Worthington East, is a British-style pub with good brews. Finally, Yuk Yuk's **comedians** perform on Wednesday nights in the *Empire Motor Hotel*, just off Main Street at 425 Fraser.

## Temagami

The resort village of **TEMAGAMI**, 97km past North Bay, started as a rest stop on the long portage from Snake Lake into Lake Temagami. With its hundreds of bays and islands, Lake Temagami has been attracting tourists since the turn of the century, when it built the region's first grand hotel and introduced a steamship company and rail line to transport the holidaymakers. It's a tranquil place, but has recently become the focus of intense controversy. Temagami's old-growth **red and white pines** are complicated ecosystems that support thousands of species of plant and animal life, but since the 1920s ninety percent of the forest has been cut down, leaving fifty-metre-wide buffer zones around the rivers, lakes and roads to mask the extent of the destruction.

Local people were compromised by the need to conserve jobs, but when the provincial government began an illegal extension of a logging road deep in the forest they were galvanised into campaigning for the preservation of this unique habitat. It wasn't until May 1989 that the Ontario Ministry of Natural Resources acknowledged that only a quarter of the trees had been replanted in the 1980s and that forty percent of the replanted forests "do not have enough surviving trees to support future logging". As a consequence the mill was closed but no legislation was made to prevent other lumber companies clear-cutting or harvesting the old-growth pines. The issue is made more complicated by the fact that much of the land is an Ojibwa reservation whose occupants have been more or less ignored during the whole battle. Both the natives and the locals favour multi-use of the land, combining recreation, hunting, fishing, mining and logging, whilst environmentalists from other parts of the country want the area left totally untouched. Stalemate exists at the time of writing, but it is hoped that a renewed investment in tourism will jump-start the village's economy.

## Practicalities

Both **trains** and **buses** terminate at the station opposite the **Welcome Centre** on Hwy 11 (May to early Sept Mon–Fri 9am–5pm); the centre has details on accommodation, most of which is in tourist camps that vary from the luxurious to the very basic. Preferable are the **B&Bs** from the *Temagami Bed and Breakfast Association* (☎569-3309), with rates from $45 per double. For complete **canoe outfitting** *Smoothwater Wilderness Outfitters* (☎569-3539) can provide everything from first-aid kits to frying pans; the *Temagami Wilderness Centre* (☎569-3733), 22km south on the highway, also organises canoe trips at reasonable rates.

# Cobalt

Less than a century ago it was neither Toronto nor Ottawa that brought visitors to Ontario – it was **COBALT**, the town that silver built and silver destroyed. Local legend contends that it all started when a blacksmith named Fred LaRose threw a hammer at a fox and hit a rock instead, uncovering the silver vein. In fact the first strike was by two lumberjacks called McKinley and Darraugh, but in the summer of 1903 both the McKinley-Darraugh mine and the LaRose mine began operating, changing the landscape of the area almost overnight.

New mine shafts were dropped every few weeks and by 1911 the haphazard collection of tents, log cabins and huts had become a community of 7000. As output burgeoned, Cobalt merged with nearby Haileybury and New Liskeard to form the "tritowns", the miners living in Cobalt, the managers living on the Lake Temiskaming waterfront in Haileybury, and the mine owners and investors keeping their distance in New Liskeard. Life in Cobalt was perilous: typhoid, smallpox and flu were common and many of the homes were built from wooden dynamite boxes, and so were regularly wrecked by fires. Yet Cobalt survived the slumps caused by enlistment in World War I and by the Depression, only to be killed off by the recent world reduction in silver prices. The last mine closed in 1990, and every year the blue population signs at the entrance to the town are repainted. At one time 12,000 people lived here; now the number is down to 1000, all living in the hope that Cobalt's boom will come again.

## The town and the mines

On Cobalt's main street, Silver Street, only one shop – a pet shop – remains. Just up the road, an old headframe protrudes from the roof of what was once the grocery store (the store used the disused shaft as a refrigerator); opposite, a small park has a large painted sign listing the 104 mines operating in 1908. At no. 38 Canada's oldest **Mining Museum** (daily June & Sept 1–5pm; July & Aug 9am–5pm; donation) is housed in a converted

## GREY OWL

Temagami was once the domain of one of Canada's most colourful characters – Wah-Sha-Quon-Asin or **Grey Owl**, as he was more commonly known. One of the world's first conservationists, he travelled Canada, Britain and the US spreading the Indian message of respect for the flora and fauna of the wilderness, publishing articles in such magazines as *Country Life,* and turning out books that became bestsellers. In 1938, at the age of 50, Grey Owl died. It was only then that it became known just how extraordinary his life had been.

Grey Owl was in fact **Archie Belaney**, an Englishman from Hastings who had emigrated at the age of seventeen to escape his authoritarian aunt. Arriving in Canada, Archie made his way to the silver strike in Cobalt but on a sudden whim got off the train at Temagami. There he worked as a guide in the tourist camps and became fascinated with the Ojibwa population of the reserve on Lake Temagami's Bear Island. He learned the native stories and customs, and eventually married a young Ojibwa named **Angele**, with whom he produced a daughter. Prone to drinking and causing trouble, Archie was finally run out of town after a brawl that ended in bloodshed.

Archie moved to Biscotasing and became a forest ranger, but soon his arrest warrant caught up with him and he had to leave town again – though not before impregnating another Indian woman, **Marie Girard**. She died of consumption shortly after giving birth to their child. During World War I, Archie temporarily abandoned his Indian ways to fight with the army in Flanders, where he was wounded by shrapnel. During his convalescence in England he met and married his nurse, thereby adding bigamy to his many accomplishments. The call of the Canadian wilderness proved this marriage's undoing, and Archie returned to Biscotasing, stopping en route to see **Angele** for four days, and inevitably conceiving another child.

Since his departure Biscotasing had been taken over by the whites, who were busy cutting down the trees and scaring away the wildlife that Archie had grown to love. His determination to renounce his European roots now became even stronger, and his anarchic attitude made his persona as a "drunken Injun" the more convincing to the locals. In 1925 Archie – by this time almost exclusively known as Grey Owl – returned to Temagami to live with Angele and their two children and resume work as a guide. It was there that he met **Anahereo**, a nineteen-year-old Iroquois. Angele was duly dumped as Anahereo and Grey Owl eloped to a hut in northern Québec, where their only companions were two beavers, McGinnis and McGinty. It was these two animals and Jelly Roll, a later addition, that inspired much of Grey Owl's writing and prompted him to start a beaver colony to prevent the extinction of Canada's national animal. To raise money for the project Grey Owl began writing and lecturing about his life as a Canadian native, a publicity campaign that also secured him the post of warden of Riding Mountain National Park and later Prince Albert National Park.

Grey Owl's long absences and the days spent writing led to the break-up of his relationship with Anahereo, but it didn't take long for him to marry someone else, this time a French-Canadian who adopted the Indian name of Silver Moon. Grey Owl made a final lecture tour of Britain and America in 1938, which included an audience with King George and the princesses Elizabeth and Margaret. The tour left Grey Owl suffering such exhaustion that he died later that same year. Only then did his wives, friends and family find out about his charade.

newspaper office, with a vast collection of ores from the mines, including a collection of luminous stones. A block away stands Cobalt's grandest building, the former train station; renovated in 1990, it contains the **Bunker Military Museum** (June–Aug daily 9am–5pm; $2), one man's immense collection of military artefacts and uniforms.

In the surrounding area, where abandoned headframes have become the homes of red squirrels, skunks and birds, huge holes appear regularly as shafts give way. A fire in 1977 destroyed all records of the shafts' locations, so the Geological Society constantly combs the wilderness marking the areas that are about to collapse. It's unwise to go out into this region unaccompanied, so the Ontario Ministry of Northern Development and Mines have laid out a six-kilometre **Silver Heritage Trail**. It begins at the foundations of the McKinley-Darraugh mill, which burned down in 1928 – probably an insurance scam, as it was destined for closure. To take the tour your own vehicle is preferable but if you are without a car enquire at the Mining Museum, as it may be possible to join a tour – provided on demand to groups with their own transport – which actually goes down the old mine shafts, left unchanged since the early days.

## Practicalities

The only **accommodation** in Cobalt is the *Buffalo Mill House Bed and Breakfast*, 102 Galena (☎679-8360; doubles $25). In New Liskeard – connected by the *Tritown Trolley*, a regular bus service costing 90¢ – the cheapest rooms are in *Wheel Inn Motel*, 208 Armstrong St (☎647-6116; doubles $38). In Haileybury, also served by the bus, the *Haileybury Motel* on Farr Avenue (☎672-3354; doubles $45) has views of the lake. For **camping**, there's *Sharpe Lake Park* just outside Cobalt and *Bucke Park* near Devil's Rock on Hwy 567, off Hwy 11B. The liveliest time to be in Cobalt is for the five days around the August Civic Holiday weekend, when the **Cobalt's Miners' Festival** features mining contests, a flea market and a large amount of drinking.

---

### KIRKLAND LAKE AND SIR HARRY OAKES

About 100km north of Cobalt on Hwy 66 lies the mining community of **Kirkland Lake**, producer of one fifth of Canada's gold. The main street, Government Road, is actually paved with gold – the construction crew used the wrong pile of rocks to construct the road, resulting in a main street made from gold ore instead of waste rock. There's no real reason to head off this way, but the town featured prominently in one of the most sensational stories of Canada's recent past – the story that Nic Roeg made into the film *Eureka*.

In the summer of 1911 **Sir Harry Oakes** arrived in Swastika, close to Kirkland Lake, with $2.65 in his pocket. He left in 1934 with $20 million, the largest fortune ever gained through mining in Canada. Oakes began his quest for gold in 1898, his search taking him to Alaska, where his vessel was blown into the Bering Strait and then captured by Cossacks. He escaped under rifle fire and continued his explorations in the relatively safer regions of Australia, West Africa, Mexico and California until, on the run from a revolution in South America, he joined the budding gold rush in northern Canada. In 1912 he founded a mine in what was to become known as Kirkland Lake, where the narrow vein produced $100,000-worth of gold a month, and in 1928 opened up the Lake Shore mine, the most lucrative one ever discovered in Canada. Oakes, obsessed with keeping his wealth from the revenue services, then emigrated to the tax-free Bahamas.

Around midnight on July 8, 1943, Oakes was murdered in his bed in Nassau, a crime that knocked the war off the front pages of the newspapers. Detectives immediately arrested Alfred de Marigny, a handsome playboy who had eloped with Oakes' daughter, Nancy, two years previously. The case against him was thin, resting on the presence of a single fingerprint in Oakes' bedroom and the motive of money – with Oakes dead his daughter would inherit a fortune. During the trial it became obvious that the detectives had planted the fingerprint and de Marigny was acquitted. The case was never reopened, but the murder of Sir Harry Oakes has prompted a variety of theories. Alfred de Marigny implicated Oakes' debt-ridden friend Harold Christie, who had defrauded Oakes in a property deal that was about to be exposed by the auditors. Rumours of voodoo and Mafia involvement were rife at the time, but more intriguing is a possible cover-up involving Oakes' confidant the Duke of Windsor. It has come to light that the Duke and Oakes were involved in a money-laundering operation with a Swedish industrialist and alleged Nazi agent; the suggestion is that the Duke, terrified that the scam would come to light in the course of a prolonged police investigation, might have wanted de Marigny's quick arrest in order to throw people off the scent.

If you're running short of things to read, call in at the **Highway Bookshop** (daily 9am–10pm), 8km south of the town on Hwy 11. This huge warehouse in the middle of nowhere has 10,000 secondhand and new books piled from floor to ceiling on incredibly rickety shelves.

## Timmins

Fourteen kilometres north of the Hwy 11 and Hwy 66 junction, about 105km from Cobalt, Hwy 11 passes through the **Arctic Watershed**, or Height of Land, an elevation in the Canadian Shield which divides the flow of water in the province. North of this area all water flows to James and Hudson bays, and south of here it flows to the Great Lakes and the St Lawrence. Just north of the watershed, 61km west along Hwy 101, lies **TIMMINS**, home to the richest silver-zinc mine in the world and once one of the largest gold-mining camps in North America – with the highest number of bars per capita on the continent. The numerous small mining communities of this region have now been subsumed into the city, making Timmins the largest municipality in Canada, with an area in excess of 3100 square kilometres and a population of just 50,000. Boom time came just after World War I – in 1914 the population was 935, by 1929 it was 13,000 – and to see a genuine relic from this era you should take a walk around **Hollinger Housing**, a few blocks north of the main route through town, where row after row of identical tiny wooden shacks are covered in red and green tar-paper. Their occupants included immigrants from all over Europe, in particular Croats, Finns, Italians, Poles, Scots and Ukrainians, whose contribution to the city is traced in the **Ukranian Museum** at 78 Mountjoy (June to early Sept daily 10am–5pm; early Sept to May Sat & Sun 1–5pm).

Of the various mines open to the public in Timmins, the most interesting are the **Dome Mines** in South Porcupine (tours July & Aug Thurs 1pm; $2), the oldest and largest gold mine in this area. It was discovered in 1909 when a man named Harry Preston, flapping his hands to get rid of flies, slipped down a rock and landed on one of the richest gold veins in the world. Buses leave from the Chamber of Commerce, 76 McIntyre Rd on Hwy 101 east of Timmins in the suburb of Schumacher. **Kidds Creeks Mines**, 26km east of the city on Hwy 101 (tours July–Aug Tues, Wed & Fri 1pm; $3), is the world's richest zinc plant, with the added attraction of a herd of buffalo who regularly graze near the complex. Timmins **accommodation** consists of a series of motels concentrated along Algonquin Boulevard – try *Bon Air* at no. 355 (☎264-1275), *Journey's End* at no. 939 (☎264-9474) or *Parkview* at no. 536 (☎254-4334), all with doubles in the $50 region.

### Kettle Lakes Provincial Park

**Kettle Lakes Provincial Park** technically lies within the boundaries of Timmins, but is actually 40km east of the centre on Hwy 101 and can only be reached by car. The park's twenty small glacial lakes – known to geologists as "kettles" because they have no inlets or outlets – are surrounded by jack pine and aspen, the species that recovered best from a forest fire that devastated this area in 1911. The two campgrounds in the park are located by the park entrance and by Island Lake in the south of the park. Of the park's hiking trails the best goes via Mud Lake, a popular spot for moose who submerge themselves to escape the flies.

## Cochrane

**COCHRANE**, 50km from the junction of Hwy 101 and Hwy 11, grew up as a repair and turntable station for the railroad companies serving the north. Most of the workshops have closed down but this is still the departure point for the *Ontario Northland* railway's *Polar Bear Express* to James Bay and into the land of the Cree. That's really the only attraction of this workaday town, but if you have time to spare check out the railcars and native crafts in the **Railway Museum** on 13th Avenue beside Union Station (mid-June to mid-Sept daily 9.30am–10pm). The **information centre** (mid-June to early Sept daily 9am–5pm) is by "Chimo", the huge white polar bear at the entrance to Cochrane. The *King George Hotel*, 101 Railway St (☎272-9883; doubles $30), is your best bet if you're catching the express – or there's a mass of motels on the highway west of town.

### The Polar Bear Express

The supply-train journey from Cochrane to Moosonee, known as the **Polar Bear Express** (late June to early Sept daily except Fri; departs Cochrane 8.30am, arrives Moosonee 12.50pm; departs Moosonee 5.15pm, arrives Cochrane 9.20pm; $38 return), traverses a region where there are in fact no polar bears, but the train goes as far north as anyone can easily go in Ontario and is increasingly popular as a tourist excursion. The tourist bumph promises that on arrival at Moosonee the traditional Cree greeting "Watchi" will resound around the station and you'll have a unique view of Crees and non-natives living and working together in harmony. The reality is different: the government administrators live in pleasant homes in Moosonee, while the 2000 Cree are confined to shacks on the reserve on Moose Factory Island just offshore in the Moose River. Nonetheless, it's a remarkable 300-kilometre trip across the tundra line, the train occasionally stopping along the way to pick up trappers, fishers, hunters and Crees, whose ancestors first arrived here 10,000 years ago. Europeans arrived somewhat later – in 1673 the first English-speaking settlement in Ontario was established at Moose Factory by the Hudson's Bay Company, and Moosonee itself was founded in 1903 by Revillon Frères, a French fur-trading company. In those days the journey from Cochrane took ten days of hard graft on snowshoes or canoe but since 1932 the two towns have been connected by rail, which remains the only way – bar flying – of reaching the settlement.

*MOOSONEE*

A couple of museums in **MOOSONEE** outline its history: the **Revillon Frères Museum**, in one of the original company buildings, explores the bloody conflicts between the British and French over the area's fur trade, while the **Railway Car Museum** concentrates on the cultural and natural history of James Bay. More worthwhile, though, is to hop into a Cree canoe to Moose Factory Island, or – if you plan to stay – take the *Polar Princess* cruise boat (daily late June to early Sept; 6hr 30min; $35.50 including lunch), which goes via James Bay, the Island Bird Sanctuary and Tidewater Provincial Park to Moose Factory for a bus tour. At the reserve itself the **Hudson's Bay Staff House**, built in 1820, still stands, as do the blacksmith's shop and gunpowder magazine, located near another small museum. St Thomas **Anglican Church**, built in 1860, has an altarcloth of moose hide, prayer books written in Cree and floor plugs that can be removed to prevent the church floating away in floods. No driving licence is required on the island and the trucks are pretty reckless – so take care or end up in the Moose Factory General Hospital, which dominates the south end of the island.

If you want to stay longer than the time allowed by the return train (4hr 30min), make sure you reserve your **accommodation** in advance, either at the *Moosonee Lodge* (☎336-2351; doubles $69) or at *Polar Bear Lodge* (☎336-2345; doubles $69). **Camping** is available at Tidewater Provincial Park on Charles Island.

## Kapuskasing and beyond

Kapuskasing marks the halfway point between North Bay and Thunder Bay, beyond which the highway continues west through a stark land of stunted spruce and balsam.

The towns have very little of interest and the provincial parks, though often deserted compared to their more southern counterparts, are not really worth the detour.

## Kapuskasing

Once known as the model town of the north, **KAPUSKASING**, locally known as the Kap, began as MacPherson Siding in 1913 on the newly completed National Transcontinental Railway, but it was when the community turned to forestry in the 1920s, utilising the hydro-electric potential of the falls on the Kapuskasing River, that Kap really developed. The Ontario government financed the building of a planned town, with Tudor-style buildings and a layout like a cartwheel whose hub is now marked by a monstrous metal K, the ugly symbol of a town that's hit the skids – uneconomical forestry management by the town's main employer, Spruce Falls Power and Paper Company, has driven Kap's young people to seek better opportunities in the south.

For **accommodation**, the rail hotel of *Kapuskasing Inn*, 80 Riverside Drive (☎335-2261; doubles $49), is as old as Kap itself and makes a nice change from modern motels. **Campgrounds** are located at Rene Brunelle Provincial Park just off Government Road and at Remi Lake, 13km to the north. For **eating** *John's Grill*, 15 O'Brien, has been producing the finest hamburgers for the last thirty years, while *Dante's Tavern*, 9 Lang Ave has an $11.95 special of garlic bread, pasta, meat dish, a nine-inch pizza and vegetables.

## Hearst and Fushimi

Linked by the *Algoma Central Railway* to Sault Ste Marie, **HEARST** has a large sign outside town proclaiming it the moose capital of the world, which really means "Welcome to huntsville". Yet this largely French-speaking lumber centre is also a university town, with comparatively chic boutiques and restaurants reflecting a self-confidence that many northern towns are sadly lacking. The helpful **information** centre (Mon–Fri 9am–5pm), on the highway east of town, has information on the whole of northern Ontario, while *Hearst & Area Bed and Breakfast Association* (☎362-4442) can fix up cheap **accommodation** in local **B&Bs**.

If you want to see moose, head for **Fushimi Provincial Park** (mid-May to mid-Oct), 35km from Hearst and 13km north of Hwy 11, or **Nagagamisis Provincial Park** (same months), on Hwy 631 about 100km southwest of Hearst. The former, named after Prince Fushimi of Japan who visited the area in 1907, is a favourite breeding ground of the blood-sucking blackfly, so stock up on repellent if you're heading for one of its half-dozen campgrounds. The latter is an ancient Algonquian hunting ground, where many thousand-year-old relics have been found – it is possible to canoe to two ancient burial sites from the campground.

## Longlac and Geraldton

**LONGLAC**, 213km from Hearst, is a lumber and sawmill town that's home to the largest Ojibwa reserve in northern Ontario. It's also the only town in the area that has not banned buck nights, the Canadian equivalent of a stag night. Ontarian buck nights involve trailing the bridegroom around the streets to be subjected to indignities such as pelting with eggs – the missiles are sold to passers-by in aid of charity.

The first thing anyone notices when arriving in **GERALDTON**, 35km away, are the wide streets, a reminder of Geraldton's glory days during the mining boom. *The Geraldton Hotel*, 100 First Ave (☎807/854-0660; doubles from $25), is another local landmark which still looks like you should park your horse outside. The **Macleod Provincial Park** (June to mid-Sept), 6km south of Geraldton, is your best bet if you are under canvas. It's a further 160km to Nipigon.

# Sudbury

**SUDBURY**, the economic centre of northeastern Ontario, is parked on the edge of the Sudbury Basin, a pit created either by a volcano or, the preferred theory, by a giant meteor. Whatever did the damage, the effect was to throw one of the world's richest deposits of nickel and copper towards the surface. It was the nickel – used to temper steel – that made Sudbury's fortune, but its by-products caused devastation. Most of the damage was done by a smelting method known as heap roasting, used until the 1920s, which spread clouds of sulphurous fumes over forests already ravaged by lumber firms and mineral prospectors, who often started fires to reveal the traces of metal in the bare rocks. Likened to Hell or Hiroshima, the bleak landscape had only one advantage: in 1968 it enabled Buzz Aldrin and Neil Armstrong to practise their great leap for mankind in a ready-made lunar environment.

Having continued to produce sulphur-laden smoke from the stacks of their nickel smelters, the mining companies were finally forced to take action when a whole community of workers from Happy Valley, just northeast of Sudbury, were evacuated in the 1970s because of the number of sulphur-induced illnesses, particularly lung cancer. Pollutants in the immediate environs of the city have been reduced, albeit by means such as building the world's tallest superstack, which now belches poisons out half a kilometre above the city, where they drift off to contaminate areas way to the north. Thousands of acres have spluttered back to life, and the thirty lakes in the vicinity, including one in the middle of town, are no longer stagnant pools of vinegar. Sudbury's multi-national population of 80,000 – over half of them French-speaking – are fiercely proud of a city that has received nothing but lousy publicity for decades. Though it can seem that the main effect of the recent redevelopment has been an efflorescence of shopping malls, the city can boast two of north Ontario's most impressive tourist sights, Science North and Big Nickel Mine. And it gets warmer than any other of Ontario's other industrial cities – the pollution-blackened rocks retain the heat of the sun.

## Arrival and accommodation

Sudbury's new **train** station, the terminus of trains from the east, is about 20km northeast of town, near the airport in Falconbridge; local buses from outside go to the downtown terminus on the junctions of Elm and Cedar – the flat fare, payable on board, is $1. The *Greyhound* **bus** depot is at 200 Falconbridge Road, east of town; local bus #303 goes into Sudbury. For **information**, the Sudbury Welcome Centre (daily 9am–5pm) is to the south of town on Hwy 69, but unless you just want to ask about the main attractions – Science North or the Big Nickel – they haven't got a clue.

The official youth **hostel**, the *Auberge Sudbury Hostel*, 302 Cedar St (☎674-0104; $10), has just twenty-five beds, reduced to eight from September to May. During the summer student rooms are also available at Laurentian University, Ramsey Lake Road (☎675-1151 ext 300; doubles $30). For **bed and breakfast** there's the *David Street Guest House*, 142 David St (☎673-7977; doubles $45), or the *Red Geranium Guest House*, on the corner of Paris and Van Horne (☎675-8000) with similar rates. The two central budget **hotels** in town are grotty and usually full with transient workers; most have a policy of only renting out for the week. The *Hotel Coulson* (☎675-6436; $25–35) on the corner of Durham and Larch is worth checking out; for posher accommodation *The President Hotel*, 117 Elm St West (☎674-7517; doubles $66), is a three-star place right in the middle of town. The proliferation of **motels** west of town on Lorne Street are all pretty characterless; it's best to head for Pioneer Road south of town – *The Brockdan Motor Hotel* at no. 1222 (☎522-5270; doubles $45) is cheap with air-conditioned rooms.

For **camping** *Carol's Campground* (☎522-5570) and *Mine Mill Campground* (☎673-3661) are 8km south on Hwy 69 in a pretty wilderness area; you need to reserve at both.

## The City

Sudbury is a sprawling city with a small central core that offers very little except the opportunity to browse through the **Farmer's Market** (May–Oct Sat & Sun 7am–5pm) on Shaughnessy Street, a limp imitation of Ottawa's Byward Market, or check out the arts and crafts shows at **Laurentian Museum and Arts Centre** on John Street, just off Paris (Tues–Sun noon–5pm; $2).

The main attractions of Sudbury are located to the south of the central core. In trying to change it from a black hole into a resort, the powers that be have made the most out of the city's unusual geology, and most of the exhibits in **Science North** (daily May–June & Sept 9am–5pm; July–Aug 9am–7pm; Oct–April 10am–4pm; $5.95; bus #500 or #181), a huge snowflake-shaped structure on Ramsey Lake Road, are installed in a cavern blasted into the rock of the Canadian Shield. The hands-on displays permit you to simulate a miniature hurricane, gauge your fitness, lie on a bed of nails, prospect for gold, float weightlessly in space and learn to lip read, all under the guidance of students from Laurentian University. The museum also has a collection of insects and animals including a porcupine called Ralf, a tarantula called Charlotte and Fergie the snake. An excellent 3-D film allows you to make a fool of yourself ducking from flying geese and multi-coloured fish.

The town's symbol, a nine-metre-high steel replica of a five-cent piece imaginatively known as the Big Nickel, stands with four other large coins in Big Nickel Numismatic Park, by the Trans-Canada on the western approach to town. The nickel marks the entrance to the **Big Nickel Mine** (daily May–June & Sept 9am–5pm; July–Aug 9am–7pm; $4.95; bus #940), where there's an underground mailbox so you can let the folks back home know that you've travelled twenty metres below the earth's surface and seen an experimental subterranean kitchen garden. Samples of lettuce are given away if the crop has been good.

To discover more about mining and to escape the heat of Sudbury's summer days it's worth taking the **Path of Discovery** (May–Aug 3 daily, 2hr 30min; $9.95), a guided tour in an air-conditioned coach from Science North and the Big Nickel Mine. The tour visits the place where nickel was first discovered, the Inco surface plant – one of the world's largest open-cast mines – and the base of the superstack. Various **combination tickets** save money on these attractions: the *Gold passport* ($18.95) is for Science North, Big Nickel and the Path of Discovery; the *Nickel passport* ($9.95) is for Science North and the Nickel; and the *Copper passport* ($12.95) is for the Nickel and the Path.

One of the most spectacular sights in the province is **slag-pouring**, which you can watch from **Copper Cliff**, the workers' estate beneath Inco's ever-growing slag heaps in the west end beyond the Big Nickel. At the end of the smelting process the red-hot slag is poured into hopper cars which are pulled by an electric train to the top of huge slag piles, from where it's poured like volcanic lava down the hill. The best view is from the Lasalle Boulevard bypass, reached by bus #940 (information on times ☎682-6666).

Bus #940 continues to a hilltop west of Copper Cliff, site of **Little Italy**, a quarter built by Italian miners at the turn of the century to re-create the hillside villages of their home country. Italian is still more commonly spoken than English here, and it's one of the more atmospheric parts of the city.

## Eating, drinking and nightlife

To **eat** cheaply, *Grandma Lees*, 65 Elm St, is good for homebaked goodies and soups, and is open on Sundays. *Frank's Delicatessen*, 112 Durham, is also good for light meals, and upstairs at the City Centre Mall there is an adequate food court with the usual selection of bargain fast-food outlets. Fresh pickerel from the lakes in the vicinity can be sampled at *The Red Lobster*, 1600 Lasalle, or the more expensive *Teklenburg's* at no. 1893.

Italian food is cheap at *Mingle's*, 762 Notre Dame, a studenty pizza and pasta restaurant, whilst *Marconi's*, 1620 Regent St South, is Sudbury's best restaurant, with homemade pasta and a varied antipasto bar. For Indian, *Taste of India*, 1873 Kingsway, is reasonable. The reliable chains also have branches here – *Beef and Brand* in the City Centre Mall; *Swiss Chalet*, 1349 Lasalle, for chicken; and *Casey's* for Mexican and Canadian fare.

The best **bars** are the *Coulson* on the corner of Larch and Durham, the popular *Trevi Tavern*, 1837 Lasalle, and *The Pub* at Laurentian University. The busiest **night-clubs** are *Citylights* on Elgin Street North and *Studio 4* in Brady Street.

# Killarney Provincial Park

Located on the north shore of Georgian Bay, 100km southwest of Sudbury, is the so-called crown jewel of Ontario's provincial parks, **Killarney Provincial Park**. Dominated by the white quartzite ridges of the La Cloche Mountains, this was a popular haunt of the Group of Seven – Franklin Carmichael even had a cottage here and was reported to find the park "the most challenging and gratifying landscape in the province".

Driving south from Copper Cliff, you will pass the park entrance 10km before the tiny village of **KILLARNEY**, close to the southern tip of the park. The village is the closest community to the park, and has **accommodation** at the *Sportsman's Inn* (☎287-2411; doubles $60) and the *Rock House Inn* (☎287-2331; doubles $45), both on Channel Street. *Killarney Outfitters*, 3 Commissioner St (May–Oct; ☎287-2828) located on Hwy 637, 5km east of Killarney, offers complete outfitting for canoe trips.

Places in the campgrounds around **George Lake** (mid-May to early Oct; $4), close to the park gate, must be reserved at the nearby park office (☎287-2368); canoeists and hikers heading into the interior must obtain permits from the office and also register a route plan that does not allow for any detours. The three short **hiking trails** from the George Lake campground can often be crowded with day-trippers, but the interior hiking is unsurpassable. **La Cloche Silhouette Trail** across the north ridges of the La Cloches requires a week to ten days of hiking and is not for the unfit – the camp-grounds along the way are primitive and you need to be self-sufficient for the whole trip. The highlight of the trail is **Silver Peak**, 543m above sea level, where views over Georgian Bay are awe-inspiring. Off-trail hiking is also permitted but needs to be well organised and is strictly for experienced hikers.

The **canoe routes** have well-marked portages and are generally suitable for begin-ners as well as experienced canoeists. The waters are sparkling and beautiful, but don't drink them – acid rain coupled with the natural acidity of the quarzite has all but wiped out the fish population. It is also possible to canoe into Georgian Bay, but this is not advised for beginners as the weather on the coast is unpredictable.

# Manitoulin Island

The Ojibwa believe that when Gitchi Manitou (the Great Spirit) created the world he reserved the best bits for himself and created Manitoulin (God's Island) – the world's largest freshwater island – as his own home. A continuation of the limestone Niagara Escarpment, Manitoulin is beautifully different from the harsh grey rocks of the Canadian Shield, with its white cliffs skirting lakes and woodland that's home to a substantial population of white-tailed deer. For the time being, despite the popularity of the ferry link with Tobermory on the Bruce Peninsula as a route between the south and north of the province, this is a place of solitary villages and quiet lanes that wind past hundreds of lakes and acres of farmland neatly divided by low tree-stump fences. This may soon change, however – the farms, unable to keep up with the levels of production in more southern regions, are changing into cottage resorts and campgrounds for the rapidly expanding tourist industry, and Manitoulin may not much longer present a contrast with the overloaded rural retreats on the other side of Georgian Bay.

Over a quarter of the island's 11,000 population are native peoples, descendants of groups who arrived over 10,000 years ago, leaving some of the oldest human traces on the continent. An Iroquois invasion in 1652 – two years after Champlain arrived here – forced the island's natives to flee, and it wasn't until the early nineteenth century that the Ojibwa, Odawa and Pottawatomi people were brought back by missionaries. In 1838 the government sponsored an establishment at Manitowaning, legendary home of the Great Spirit, to "instruct the Indians in the ways of civilisation", a lamentable experiment that collapsed in 1861, when the natives were persuaded to cede their land to white settlers instead. It was only the Ojibwa band living on the eastern tip of the island at Wikwemikong who refused the treaty, and today the majority of Manitoulin's Indians still live on this unceded reserve, which is officially not a part of Canada. During the August Civic long weekend Wiky – as it's always known – holds the largest **pow-wow** in the country.

## Practicalities

Manitoulin has a tiny **airstrip** at Gore Bay, used by daily *Manitoulin Air Service* (☎1-800-461-3504) flights to and from Toronto. Most people arrive on the island via the *MS Chi-Cheemaun* or *MS Nindamaya*, the two **car ferries** that travel between Tobermory on the Bruce Peninsula and South Baymouth on the south side of the island (late April to late Oct 2–6 daily; 1hr 45min; ☎1-800-265-3163; $9 single, $20 cars). From northern Ontario Hwy 6 connects Espanola on Hwy 17 with the north shore of Manitoulin – if you're in your own car it is worth taking a detour to the tiny village of Willisville for stunning views of the whole island and the La Cloche mountains. Arriving by *Greyline* or *Greyhound* long-distance **buses** from northern Ontario involves changing at Espanola to buses run by *AJ Bus Lines* (☎368-2540), which run along Hwy 6 to South Baymouth via Little Current, Wiky and Manitouwaning.

Getting around by **public transport** on the island is limited to *AJ Bus Lines* school buses from Little Current west to Gore Bay and south to South Baymouth. There are no services west of South Baymouth or into the central core of the island, but **hitchhiking** is easy in any season. Alternatively, from Monday to Saturday during July and August a tour bus run by *Manitoulin Sightseeing Tours* (☎282-2848) operates between South Baymouth and Gore Bay.

There are **information centres** in Gore Bay, Manitowaning and South Baymouth and Little Current. The centre at 16 Manitowaning Road in Little Current is the only one open all year; the others are closed from early September to May. For information on B&Bs contact *Manitoulin Bed & Breakfast Association* in Little Current (☎368-3021).

## East Manitoulin: South Baymouth to Little Current

First sight of Manitoulin for most visitors is **SOUTH BAYMOUTH**, a pleasantly situated if nondescript village that grew on its fish-salting factories. Your best advice is to keep moving once you're off the ferry. If you're heading north along Hwy 6 to the mainland, your route runs through **MANITOWANING** on the southwestern shore of Manitowaning Bay, where the **Assignack Museum** (daily June–Aug 9am–6pm; Sept 11am–4pm; $1.75) details the history of the Manitowaning Experiment. **Accommodation** in Manitowaning is limited to two dull **motels** right on the highway or a modern **B&B** on Wellington Street (☎859-3136).

## WIKWEMIKONG

At Manitowaning a branch road runs east to the reserve of **WIKWEMIKONG**, 14km from Hwy 6 on the western shore of Smith Bay. Home to 2500 people of the Three Fire Tribes – Odawa, Ojibwa and Pottawatomi – this is the only unceded reserve in North America, but it looks much like every other run-down reserve in Canada with its gravel track flanked by wooden yellow shacks, and like so many of them it's generally a sad place of massive unemployment and alcoholism. Every August Civic Weekend, though, Wiky is transformed by the country's largest **powwow**, which brings in the best of the continent's performers and is packed with stalls selling native foods and crafts. Amongst the programme of traditional dances and ceremonies, the local theatre group *De-Be-Jeh-Mu-Jig* retell native legends and perform contemporary plays by native playwrights; during the rest of the summer they perform at the disused Pontiac School in Wiky.

Only in July is it possible to stay on the reserve, when *Kino.Mud.Win* of Parry Sound (☎746-2622) run one-week **workshops** led by elders. Participants sleep in tepees, live on native foods, learn crafts such as basket-making to beading, and perform harder chores like skinning game. Though a 24-hour fast is part of the week, and the workshop costs $450 per person, places are booked fast.

## Sheguiandah and Little Current

A few kilometres beyond the amazing **Ten Mile Point Lookout,** which overlooks the waters of Lake Huron as they funnel into the North Channel, you come to **SHEGUIANDAH** and the **Little Current-Howland Museum** (daily May–June noon–5pm; July–Sept 9am–5pm; $1.50). It was in this woodland setting that archaeologists found pieces of local quartzite that had been fashioned into tools 30,000 years ago, the oldest evidence of human habitation in North America. Yet the museum makes little reference to the prehistoric discoveries, instead housing the normal run-of-the-mill tools and furnishings of early Victorian settlers.

Though it's the largest community on Manitoulin and the only all-year gateway to the island, **LITTLE CURRENT** is a drowsy place that can make a pleasant stopover: *Little Current Motel*, 18 Campbell St (☎368-2882; doubles $35), is the most central **accommodation**. *The Olde English Pantry* opposite the waterfront has some of the best cream teas you'll find anywhere in Canada, while *Farquhar's Dairy*, Manitouwaning Rd, turns out a mean ice cream.

## North Manitoulin: Little Current to Meldrum Bay

Highway 540 stretches the length of Manitoulin along the shore of the North Channel, one of Ontario's foremost areas for folks with boats and the route with the remotest villages and the most interesting of Manitoulin's **hiking trails**. The six-kilometre **Cup and Saucer** is the best-known trail, located 18km west of Little Current at the junction of Hwy 540 and Bidwell Road, just east of West Bay; the trail reaches the highest point of the island (460m) and involves climbing ladders through natural rock chimneys. Several short hikes lead from behind *Abby's Dining Lounge* at the Ojibwa reserve at **WEST BAY**, 30km southwest of Little Current – the eight-kilometre **M'Chigeeng** trail is accompanied by signs retelling local folklore and legends.

Another 30km west brings you to **GORE BAY**, an attractive village right on the shore, worth visiting if only to stay in the beautifully situated *Hill House*, 6 Borron St (☎282-2072; doubles $40) – the best **bed and breakfast** on the island.

Highway 540 continues west through hamlets that you'll miss if you blink, passing backroads that lead to bays deserted enough for skinny-dipping. The road peters out at the most westerly point of the island marked by **MELDRUM BAY** a tiny settlement of white wooden buildings. There are two **bed and breakfasts** here – *The Four Seasons* (☎283-3256; doubles $40) and the *Meldrum Bay Inn* (☎283-3190; doubles $45).

## Southern Manitoulin

Though south Manitoulin is less impressive than the north, its proximity to the Bruce Peninsula has led to more tourist development. The most worthwhile part is **Providence Bay**, about 40km west of South Baymouth, which boasts the island's longest sand beach plus the unique attraction of the "burning boat", a glowing apparition that appears on the horizon around 3am on nights with a full moon. **Camping** on the beach is available at *Providence Bay Camping Park* (May–Oct; ☎377-4650).

# Sault Ste Marie

Strategically situated on the rapids of St Mary's River, the link between lakes Superior and Huron, **SAULT STE MARIE** – more popularly called the Soo – sits opposite an American town of the same name and sees constant two-way traffic: tourists flow over the International Bridge to experience Canada's wilderness, while a stream of Canadians heads across to the States for cheaper groceries and petrol. The river is bordered by an American and a Canadian **canal**, each constructed in the nineteenth century when the relationship between the halves of the continent was not the reciprocal one of today. These waterways enabled the Soo to graduate from a major pulp-and-paper producer to the province's second largest producer of steel, but since the Canadian locks experienced engineering difficulties a couple of years ago the freighters have travelled exclusively via the four American locks on what is one of the busiest sections of the Great Lakes.

Northern Ontario's oldest community, the Soo was originally settled by fishing parties of the Ojibwa called Saulteux – "people of the falls" – by the French. In 1667 Jesuit missionaries renamed the town, a prelude to its development as a fur-trading post; it was here that Sieur de St Lusson proclaimed France's lawful claim to the whole of America in 1671. The following centuries present a steady tale of economic growth, and the only significant event of recent years was the Soo's declaration of English as its official language, a symbolic protest which duly caused a furore in Québec. Despite the Soo's industrial make-up it is a cosy, well-tended town with handsome red sandstone buildings and the added unmissable attraction of the **Algoma Central Railway**.

## Arrival and accommodation

The Soo's **bus** station is on the town's main street at 33 Queen Street East. Because the Soo receives so many American tourists, the **Ontario Travel Information Centre**, 120 Huron St (daily mid-May to early Sept 8am–8pm; early Sept to early Oct 8.30am–7pm), a five-minute walk from the bus station, is an excellent source of information on the whole province.

As ever the cheapest **accommodation** is in the **youth hostel**, 8 Queen St East (☎946-4804; $11; closed 10am–5pm; curfew 11pm), located in the back of the old *Royal Hotel*, which still has a rusty sign on its roof – the entrance is actually on Gore Street just off Queen Street. Be warned that the hostel is small and often full.

The cheapest **bed and breakfasts** are at 99 Retta St (☎253-8641; doubles $25) and 345 Elizabeth St (☎253-2349; doubles $26). For slightly more luxurious B&B try *Snuggleden Bed and Breakfast*, 1245 Old Garden River Rd (☎942-7627; doubles $35), ten minutes' walk from downtown, with a creek in the garden. Others worth considering are *Top o'the Hill*, 40 Broos Rd (☎253-9041; doubles $45), and *Hillsview Bed and Breakfast*, 406 Old Garden River Rd (☎759-8819; doubles $40), the latter for non-smokers only.

Centrally, the budget **hotel** is the *Algonquin*, 864 Queen St East (☎253-2311; doubles $22), a scruffy building that has been a hotel since 1888. More expensive, *The Stel*

*Hotel*, 320 Bay St (☎759-8200; doubles $75), is right opposite the *ACR* train station, with all mod cons and a good brew pub; rates are $10 cheaper out of season. Of the profusion of motels, the *Algoma Cabins and Motels*, 1713 Queen St East (☎254-4371; singles $39, doubles $59), is the most centrally located.

**Camping** is available in various locations just out of town – *KOA* have a campground with hook-ups at 501 Fifth Line, 8km north of the Soo off Hwy 17, and *Blueberry Hill Tent and Trailer Park* is 2km further north on Hwy 17.

## The City

The Soo's agreeable downtown area is centred on Queen's Road, parallel to the waterfront, which contains all of the Soo's sights in a pleasant renovated area. Of the designated historic sites the most impressive is the **Marie Ermantinger Old Stone House**, 831 Queen St East (April–May Mon–Fri 10am–5pm; June–Sept daily 10am–5pm; Oct–Nov Mon–Fri 1–5pm; donation), built in 1814 and originally home to the fur trader Charles Ermantinger, his Ojibwa princess wife Manonowe – who was unceremoniously renamed Charlotte – and their thirteen children. Since then the house has served as a hotel, the sheriff's house, a meeting hall for the YWCA and a social club. Restoration has returned it to the look of 1814–30, and the period-costumed staff bake delicious cakes in the summer. Across the road in the old post office, the **Sault Ste Marie Museum** (Mon–Sat 9am–4.30pm, Sun 1–4.30pm; donation) has various exhibits on the Soo's history, from a birchbark Ojibwa house to a recreation of Queen Street in 1910.

Soo's waterfront, just a block south of the museum, is a good area to wander for a couple of hours, and its recent rebuilding includes the better-than-average **Art Gallery of Algoma**, 10 East St (Mon–Sat 10am–5pm, Thurs open till 9pm, Sun 1.30–4.30pm; donation), whose exhibitions of Canadian art often feature local artists inspired by the Algoma countryside. Further west is the restored **Museum Ship Norgoma**, Foster Drive Water Front (daily June & Sept 10am–6pm; July & Aug 9am–8pm; $3.75), the last passenger ship built on the Great Lakes. The *Norgoma* just missed becoming the youth hostel and is now an overpriced museum with a unimpressive collection of marine memorabilia. From the *Norgoma* there are two-hour **cruises** through the **Soo lock** system (mid-May to mid-Oct 3–8 daily; $12.50), which handles more tonnage than the Suez and Panama put together. Unless you are crazy about cruises it is far better to view the locks and the traffic from the boardwalk of the **National Historic Park**, which leads through a wooded area to the edge of the St Mary's Rapids from the south end of Huron Street.

## The Algoma Central Railway

The main attraction of the Soo is as the departure point for the **Algoma Central Railway** (ACR), a 500-kilometre rail line constructed in 1901 to link the factories to the vital timber resources further north. It was first used for recreational purposes by the Group of Seven, who shunted up and down the track in a converted boxcar which they used as a base to canoe into Canada's wilds. The ACR now offers everyone an opportunity to journey into the Algoma fastnesses, where the train snakes through a vista of deep ravines and countless secluded lakes, hugging the hillsides and crossing gorges on skeletal trestle bridges. To see everything sit on the left-hand side – otherwise your window will look out onto a wall of rock.

Three tours now depart from the Algoma Central Railway Terminal, 129 Bay St. The **Agawa Canyon Train Tour** takes the whole day (June to mid-Oct departs 8am, returns 4.30pm; $37.50; ☎254-4331), and its popularity with the Americans means that it is always necessary to book, often two days in advance. A two-hour stop within the canyon's 180-metre walls allows for a lunch break and a wander around the well-marked nature trails, which include a look-out post from where the rail line is a thin silver thread far below. Unless you are properly equipped don't miss the train back – the canyon gets very cold at night even during the summer and the flies are merciless.

During the winter when the lakes are frozen and the country is laden with snow, the **Snow Train** (late Dec to mid-March Sat & Sun, departs 8.30am, returns 4.30pm; $41.50; ☎946-7300) travels right through the canyon to the dramatic exit, where the walls are only fifteen metres apart, before returning to the Soo.

The third and longest trip is the **Tour of the Line** (mid-May to mid-Oct Tues–Sun; mid-Oct to mid-May Fri–Sun; departs 9.30am, arrives 7.15pm; $88 return, accommodation extra; ☎254-4331), a round trip that takes two days with one overnight stay in Hearst, at the end of the line (see p.309). North of the canyon the scenery of low coniferous forest can be flat and dreary – though you'll probably spot a few moose – and Hearst is no great shakes, but if you are heading west anyway and are sick of travelling by *Greyhound*, the journey is worth considering.

In addition to these tourist-oriented expeditions, every day from mid-May to mid-October you can jump on board the ACR's so-called "moose meat special", which picks up the hunters and trappers at various points along the track, allowing you to simply step out into the great unknown alone. The cost is 21¢ per mile, which makes it more expensive than the tour train (to get to the canyon from the Soo costs $23.60 one way), and because it stops all the time it takes longer, but camping in this kind of country is as far away from civilisation as you can get, with the security of knowing that you can always flag down the next train if you get completely sick of the flies. There are several lodges en route, most of which are located beside clear, silent lakes; information about them is available at the terminal in the Soo.

## Eating and drinking

Sault Ste Marie has an excellent variety of eateries to suit all budgets and taste. The proliferation of American-style **diners** with chrome bars and low bar stools provide huge amounts of grub for low prices, though most close early. *Ernie's Coffee Shop*, 13 Queen St East (Tues–Sat 7am–7pm), is the best and most popular of these with lengthy queues for its non-stop coffee, breakfast specials for $2.95, and juke-boxes on each table. Operating since 1932, *Mike's Quick Lunch*, 518 Queen St East (closed Sun), is equally popular, while nearby *Mary's Lunch*, 663 Queen St East, has breakfast specials all day.

The best of the budget **restaurants** is *Life Supports Natural Foods Service*, 21 King St (closed Sat & Sun), a rare vegan restaurant and food store; the smoothies – cashew milk blended with fresh strawberries and blueberries – have to be tasted to be believed, and the delicious, all-you-can-eat buffet costs just $4.95. The Soo's proximity to vast expanses of water has yielded a good set of fish restaurants: *Pisces Restaurant*, 151 Trunk Rd, is a take-out place specialising in English style fish 'n' chips; *Gino's*, 1076 Great Northern Rd, has local lake trout for $6; and pricier *Aurora's*, 384 McNabb, has a reputation for great lobster. For a splurge *Zak's*, 708 Queen St East (☎759-1793), is good for such exotic creations as sherried crab. Top of the tree, though, is *A Thymely Manner*, 531 Albert St (closed Mon; ☎759-3262), which despite the hideous name is one of Canada's top restaurants, famed for its lamb from nearby St Joseph's Island and its great Caesar salad; it'll cost you around $30 per head, and reservations are a must.

**Nightlife** is pretty thin on the ground and you're limited to the bars of the hotels – the *Algonquin* has the town's cheapest beer.

## Listings

**Airlines** *Air Ontario*, at the airport (☎1-800-268-7240).
**Bike rental** *Vernes's Hardware*, 51 Great Northern Rd (☎254-4901).
**Bus information** Local: ☎759-5438. Long distance: *Greyhound*, ☎949-4711.
**Canoe rental** *Oskar's Heyden Crafts Company*, RR 2 (☎777-2426).
**Car rental** *Tilden*, 440 Pim St (☎949-5121); *Avis*, 95 Second Line East (☎254-4349); *Budget*, 100 Queen St East (☎942-1144); *Thrifty*, 680 Great Northern Rd (☎759-0120).
**Ice hockey** The Soo Greyhounds of the Ontario Hockey League play at the 3500-seater rink, Memorial Gardens, 269 Queen St East (☎759-5251; $8).
**Hiking** Over 400km of Ontario's longest hiking trail, the *Voyageur Trail,* has been completed – it now reaches the Soo from Manitoulin, passing through the La Cloche Mountains via the rocky shore of Lake Superior. For more information and a detailed guidebook contact the *Voyageur Trail Association*, Box 66, Sault Ste Marie, ON P5A 5L2 (☎759-2480).
**Laundry** *Station Mall Laundromat*, 293 Bay (daily 8am–9pm).
**Post office** 451 Queen St East.
**Weather information** ☎779-2240.

# The north shore of Lake Superior

With a surface area of 82,000 square kilometres, **Lake Superior** is the largest freshwater lake in the world, and one of the wildest. The north shore, stretching for nearly 700 kilometres from Sault Ste Marie to Thunder Bay, is a windswept, forested, rugged region formed by volcanoes, earthquakes and glaciers, its steep forested valleys often overhung by a steely canopy of grey sky. In 1872 Reverend George Grant wrote of Superior – "It breeds storms and rain and fog, like a sea. It is cold . . .wild, masterful and dreaded". The native Ojibwa also lived in fear of the storms that would suddenly break on the lake they knew as Gitche Gumee, the Big-Sea-Water, and propitiated their gods to placate it. With icy waters that cause its many victims to sink like stones, Lake Superior is hauntingly known as the lake that never gives up its dead.

The highlights of this region are the vast parks of **Lake Superior** and **Pukaskwa**, whose innumerable waterways and treks are a challenging route into some of Ontario's most dramatic wilderness, and the **Sleeping Giant** provincial park, between Nipigon and Thunder Bay – which is also close to the wonderful canyon of Ouimet. With few exceptions, the small towns are humdrum places based on railroading, mining, lumber and the endless stream of truckers and tourists who motor through on the Trans-Canada. Though passenger trains only serve White River, nearly all the other communities are regularly served by *Greyhound* buses.

## Lake Superior Provincial Park

Stretching on either side of the Trans-Canada, its southern border 124km from Sault Ste Marie, the **Lake Superior Provincial Park** (May to late Oct) is an awesome yet easily accessible portion of Superior's granite shoreline and its hinterland. Fall is perhaps the best times to visit, when the blackflies have abated and the forests of sugar maples and yellow birch are an orgy of colour, but the scenery and wildlife are enthralling throughout the year. Moose, chipmunks and beavers are the commonest mammals, sharing their habitat with more elusive species including white-tailed deer, woodland caribou, coyote, timber wolves and black bears, as well as myriad migratory and resident birds. The **Park Office** (May to early Oct daily 9am–6pm; ☎856-2284), beside the highway about 194km from the Soo, provides maps of the park's outstanding **hikes** and canoe routes, and information on vacancies at the park's three major **campgrounds** – located at **Crescent Lake** on the southern boundary, **Agawa Bay**, 8km further north, and at **Rabbit Blanket Lake** just north of the Park Office. A camping permit must be purchased from the office or the campgrounds if you plan to stay overnight. You must also register at the office or at the trail entrances before embarking on any of the long-distance hikes; the staff will warn you if weather conditions look perilous, but always expect the worst – the park receives more rain and snow than any other area in Ontario.

### Agawa Rock

For thousands of years the Ojibwa used the park area for hunting, a single hunter's territory sometimes extending for as much as 1300 square kilometres. Their sacred rock carvings, created at inaccessible sites in order to heighten their mystery, are best seen on **Agawa Rock**, where the pictures represent a crossing of the lake by Chief Myeegn and his men, during which they were protected by Misshepexhieu, the horned lynx demi-god of Lake Superior. To reach Agawa Rock take the short access road west of Hwy 17 about 16km from the southern border of the park; from here a four-kilometre trail leads to a rock ledge from where the pictographs can be viewed.

### The Coastal Trail

The finest of the park's trails – the **Coastal Trail** – begins some 140km from Sault Ste Marie at Katherine Cove and runs north to Indian Harbour, a challenging route of high cliffs, sand and cobbled beaches, sheltered coves and exposed granite ledges. The only organised campground is at Gargantua Harbour, 8km south of Indian Harbour, though the burnt-out fires on the beaches indicate where most people choose to pitch. The entire trek takes about four to five days but access points from Katherine Cove, Orphan Lake Trail (an 11-km loop from the highway, starting 12km from Katherine Cove) and Gargantua Harbour enable you to do shorter sections of the trail.

## Wawa to Nipigon

Past the park's northern border, the mixed deciduous-coniferous forest gives way to boreal forest of balsam fir, white birch, trembling aspen, white and black spruce. From Wawa to Marathon the highway travels inland, losing sight of Lake Superior behind a continuous screen of conifers before resuming the panoramic stint along the lake, whose white fringe of beaches looks like a frigid Caribbean. There is little to stop for other than to take a few snaps, but if you are after a rest stop, Rossport is your best bet.

### Wawa

The inconsequential iron-mining town of **WAWA**, just north of the park, was named by the natives after the cry of the Canadian geese and was developed as a Mormon camp at the end of the nineteenth century, when gangs of Seventh Day Adventists were hired to work on the CPR. However, the present population stems from the workers brought here during the Depression when deposits of low-grade iron ore were developed. There is nothing to keep you here, but as it is less than 10km from Lake Superior provincial park's northernmost point it's a good embarkation point or recovery station.

The **tourist information centre** (June to early Sept 8.30am–5.30pm), situated on Pinewood Drive just off the highway, is marked by a daft massive statue of a goose. Next door *U-Paddle-It* rents out canoes if you want to canoe to the park, and a useful drop-off and pick-up service is also available. Several **motels** in Wawa offer a comfortable bed for the night including the *Wawa Motor Inn*, 100 Mission Rd (☎856-2278; doubles $70), and the older *Lakeview Hotel*, 28 Broadway Ave (☎856-2625; doubles from $30), opposite the lake in town. The *Wawa Motor Inn* is also the best place for food, with Lake Superior trout and wall-eye for dinner, and excellent muffins and home-made soups for snacks.

> The telephone code for all the following towns in northern Ontario is ☎807.

## White River

The next settlement of any size is **WHITE RIVER**, 90km north of Wawa, which has billed itself as the coldest spot in Canada since the winter of 1935 when temperatures dropped to -72°F. Another odd claim to fame is that this was the original home to Winnie the Pooh, a small bear cub named Winnipeg who was exported to Regents Park Zoo in London in 1914. In 1992, White River won the rights off Disney to erect a statue of the tubby honey-lover – it should appear soon on the highway near the huge thermometer that symbolises the big freeze. White River is linked to Sudbury by **train**; the station is on Winnipeg Road, about four blocks from the Trans-Canada. If you need to stay here the *Continental Motel* (☎822-2500) and the *White River Motel* (☎822-2333), both with doubles in the $35–45 region, are located on the Trans-Canada near the junction with Hwy 631. Just to the west of town, the waste disposal site is a good place to see bears at dusk.

## Pukaskwa National Park and Marathon

**Pukaskwa National Park**, 1878 square kilometres of hilly boreal forest and stunning coastline, can only be reached by car via the well-marked Hwy 627, a turnoff from the Trans-Canada 85km west of White River. Campgrounds, parking facilities, a visitor information centre and a park office (early June to Sept 8.30am–6.30pm; ☎229-0801) are located at Hattie Cove in the northwest corner of the park, from where the **Coastal Hiking Trail** travels 60km south over the ridges and cliffs of the Canadian Shield. Open throughout the year but best visited from early June to September, it is not an easy trail and should only be embarked upon after gaining permission at the park office.

**MARATHON**, 7km beyond the junction with Hwy 627,would be a perfect jumping-off point for Pukaskwa National Park if it weren't for the fact that a newly opened mine has filled every motel with migratory workers. Marathon has long had a reputation for being the Trans-Canada's most inhospitable spot – one believable tale tells of a hitch-hiker who was thumbing for so long that he ended up marrying a local girl. Now that rooms are non-existent, Marathon is best avoided altogether.

## Rossport

**ROSSPORT** is one of the most picture-perfect and friendly little towns along the Trans-Canada. The natural harbour made Rossport the perfect spot for bringing in fish, but the industry has declined rapidly and the town now relies on its natural assets to earn tourist money from camping, sailing and fishing. The best place to **stay** is the six-roomed *Rossport Inn* on Bowman Street (☎824-3213; doubles from $45), a nineteenth-century inn with a well-priced restaurant. *Rossport campground* is just west of town on the shore of Lake Superior (June–Aug), a beautiful site.

## Nipigon

**NIPIGON**, where the northern Hwy 11 meets the Trans-Canada, is a typical northern pulpwood town and fishing centre. Located at the mouth of the Nipigon River, the site was occupied by Ojibwa for hundreds of years until the fur trade ousted the natives and made Nipigon the first white community on the north shore of Lake Superior. Essentially a centre for anglers, Nipigon has **accommodation** at the *Chalet Lodge* on Hwy 11 (☎887-3030; doubles $42) and several other resorts and motels, but unless you can't face another inch of tarmac press on to Thunder Bay, just over 100km west.

---

### TERRY FOX

West of Nipigon, highways 17 and 11 merge to become the **Terry Fox Courage Highway**, named after Terrance Stanley Fox, one of modern Canada's most remarkable figures. At the age of eighteen Terry developed cancer and had to have his right leg amputated. Determined to advance the search for a cure, he planned a money-raising run from coast to coast and on April 12, 1980, set out from St John's in Newfoundland. For 143 days he ran 26 painful miles a day, covering five provinces by June and raising $34 million. In September, at mile 3339, just outside Thunder Bay, Terry was forced by lung cancer to abandon his run; he returned home to Port Coqitlam in British Columbia, where he died the following summer. More than $85 million has now been raised for cancer research in his name.

On the eastern outskirts of Thunder Bay, the end of the Terry Fox Courage Highway is marked by the **Terry Fox Monument**, erected in June 1982 at the Scenic Lookout. Great views of the Sleeping Giant and Lake Superior ensure a constant crowd of people with cameras.

---

## Ouimet Canyon Provincial Park – and the amethyst mines

Some 45km west of Nipigon and 11km north of the Trans-Canada is one of Ontario's most spectacular and curiously ignored sights – the **Ouimet Canyon Provincial Park**. The canyon was formed during the last ice age, when a sheet of ice two-kilometres thick crept southward, bulldozing a fissure 3km long, 150m wide and 150m deep. Nearly always deserted, the canyon has two look-out points which hang over the terrifyingly sheer sides looking down to the permanently dark base – an anomalous frozen habitat whose perpetual snow supports some very rare arctic plants. The vistas are particularly awe-inspiring in autumn, when the forests become bunches of red, orange and yellow. Unfortunately there is no public transport to the canyon, but Bayway Tours, 308 Memorial in Thunder Bay (☎345-3678), runs the odd bus tour to Ouimet during the summer.

### The mines
The stretch of the Trans-Canada beyond Ouimet gives access to several **amethyst mines**, source of Ontario's official mineral, a purple-coloured variety of quartz first discovered in this area in the 1800s. The best are the family-run **Diamond Willow** and **Pearl Lake**, reached by taking the road from the tiny hamlet of PEARL – you just walk in, pick up a bucket, gather as many lumps of rock as you want, and pay for your booty on the way out. More tourist-oriented is the **Thunder Bay Amethyst Mine Panorama**, 65km west of Nipigon off Hwy 11/17 on East Loon Lake Road north.

## The Sleeping Giant Provincial Park

Leaving the Trans-Canada 69km west of Nipigon, Hwy 587 runs the 42-kilometre length of **Sibley Peninsula**, whose entire area is given over to the dramatically scenic **Sleeping Giant Provincial Park**, so named because of the recumbent form of the four mesas that constitute its backbone. Established in 1944 to protect what the logging companies had left of the red and white pines, the park covers 243 square kilometres of high, barren rocks and lowland bogs, criss-crossed with 100km of trials. Acting as a sort of catchnet for animals, the peninsula is inhabited by a beavers, foxes, porcupines, white-tailed deer and moose, though the moose are becoming scarce. There are also wolves in the more remote areas – on a still night you can hear their howls.

## THE LEGEND OF THE SLEEPING GIANT

Ojibwa explain the unique formation of the four mesas of the peninsula with a legend that illuminates the ancient resentment between Canada's native peoples and the whites. It is said that the giant was once Nanabijou, the son of the west wind and protector of the Ojibwa, who lived on Mount MacKay. When Nanabijou discovered silver here, he made the Ojibwa bury the metal on an islet off the southern tip of the peninsula, warning them that if they told the whites of its whereabouts they would lose their land and he would turn to stone. The secret was kept until a vain Ojibwa made himself weapons of silver and was killed in a battle with the Sioux. When the whites, led by the Sioux, arrived from Lake Superior to seek out the source, Nanabijou created a storm to drown them all. The next morning he had turned to stone and still lies in the lake to protect the lode.

Hwy 587 enters the park about 6km south of the village of PASS LAKE, and driving into the park will set you back $5. The park office (May–Sept Mon–Fri 8am–4.30pm; ☎933-4332) is situated at the south end of Lake Marie Louise, about 20km from the park entrance; it's advisable in summer to pay the $4 fee to book a place at the nearby **campgrounds**; if you intend to camp in the park interior, a permit from the office costs $3. The gatehouse beside the office (May–Sept daily 10am–10pm) provides maps and leaflets on the hiking trails.

Of the park's hikes, the forty-kilometre **Kaybeyun Trail** is the most spectacular and the hardest. Beginning at the southern end of Hwy 587, it runs around the tip of the peninsula via the rock formation known as the Sealion to the **Chimney**, at the Sleeping Giant's knees, then on to **Nanabijou Lookout** at the chest of the Giant, and finally to the Thunder Bay Lookout. You have to be fit – the walk to the Chimney takes about nine hours' of hard graft up rugged pathways where the boulders are the size of cars, and in one kilometre you go up 800 feet.

For those who can't take the pace there are two far easier trails – the **Talus** and the **Sawyer** – which leave the Kabeyun at Sawyer Bay on the southwest side of the peninsula. Easier still are the **Joe Creek Trail** and the **Pinewood Hill Trail**, both of which are situated in the northern end of the park near Hwy 587; the latter leads to a fine viewpoint over Joeboy Lake – a favourite spot for moose escaping the flies. The brief **Sibley Creek Trail**, which passes a number of beaver dams, begins near Lake Louise, and so you're likely to share the wilderness with a number of other walkers.

At the most southern end of Hwy 587, the unusual sight of **Silver Islet** is worth a visit, particularly in the cooler months when it is less crowded. A century ago this was one of Canada's greatest silver towns but now all that remains are fifty houses, a customs house, a log jail, a weathered general store with rusted *Pepsi* signs and a population of two. The settlement was begun in 1872 by mining magnate Alexander Sibley and engineer William Frue, who built a wall to keep Lake Superior's tempestuous waters from a silver deposit by the tiny islet that's visible just offshore. Over the years the town exhausted the local firewood supply and had to rely on coal for fuel. One winter, the coal boat was caught in frozen waters – the last straw for the miners, who had already seen many lives lost when the damp shafts collapsed.

# Thunder Bay

The inland port of **THUNDER BAY**, known locally as T-Bay, is much closer to Winnipeg than to any of the other large urban centres of Ontario, and the population of just over 112,000 refer to themselves as Westerners. Economics as well as geography define this self-image, for this was until recently Canada's largest grain-handling port, and the grain, of course, is harvested in the Prairies. Established as a fur-trading depot,

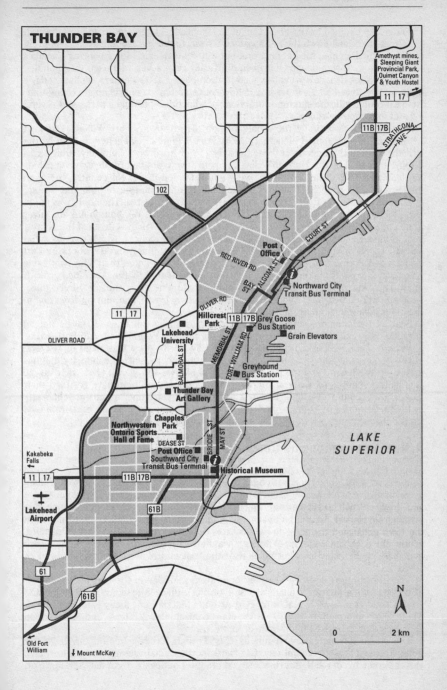

**THUNDER BAY**

Amethyst mines,
Sleeping Giant
Provincial Park,
Ouimet Canyon
& Youth Hostel

11 | 17

11B | 17B

STRATHCONA AVE.

102

COURT ST.

Post
Office

RED RIVER RD.

ALGOMA ST.

BAY ST.

Northward City
Transit Bus Terminal

OLIVER RD.

Hillcrest
Park

11B | 17B Grey Goose
Bus Station

Grain Elevators

Lakehead
University

MEMORIAL ST.

FORT WILLIAM RD.

BALMORAL ST.

OLIVER ROAD

11 | 17

Greyhound
Bus Station

Thunder Bay
Art Gallery

Chapples
Park

Northwestern
Ontario Sports
Hall of Fame

BRODIE ST.

MAY ST.

DEASE ST.

Kakabeka
Falls

Post Office
Southward City
Transit Bus Terminal

11 | 17

11B | 17B

Historical Museum

*LAKE
SUPERIOR*

Lakehead
Airport

61B

61

61B

N

Old Fort
William

Mount McKay

0          2 km

Thunder Bay boomed as the great Canadian lakehead, shipping grain and ore through the Great Lakes and down the St Lawrence Seaway to the sea 3200km away. The grain elevators still dominate the habourfront, but with federal legislation favouring Canada's Pacific ports their significance has been drastically cut – seven years ago they handled sixty percent of Canada's wheat exports and employed 1700 workers, against today's figure of less than 400. Thunder Bay is now concentrating its efforts on attracting tourists year-round with the summer attractions of wilderness provincial parks and several ski areas for winter visitors.

Thunder Bay is actually the amalgamation of two towns, Fort William and Port Arthur, which were united in January 1970. **Fort William**, established in 1789 by the British, became the upcountry headquarters of the Northwest Company, which was displaced in 1816 by the Hudson's Bay Company, five years before the two companies amalgamated. When the beaver hat went out of fashion in the old country, the main industry of the fort declined, but in the mid-nineteenth century a rumour that a huge silver lode lay close to **Port Arthur** drew prospectors to the area. The boom was not to last, and the Port Arthur, Duluth and Western railway (PD & W), built to link the silver mines, was nicknamed "the Poverty, Distress and Welfare" as the effects of the depression in the silver market set in. The Canadian Northern Railway, which took over the abandoned PD &W lines, did much to rescue the local economy but did not bring Fort William and Port Arthur closer together. Rudyard Kipling noted that "The twin cities hate each other with the pure, passionate, poisonous hatred that makes cities grow. If Providence wiped out one of them, the other would pine away and die." Even today residents will immediately inform you which area they live in, and moving from one to the other is viewed as an act of betrayal.

Scarred by industrial complexes and criss-crossed by rail lines, T-Bay is not an attractive city, and the five-kilometre waterfront between Fort William and Port Arthur – officially Thunder Bay South and Thunder Bay North – is a wasteland of fast-food chains, motels and garages. But it has a unique atmosphere, since the industry that has carved up the town has attracted workers from all over the world. Over forty ethnic groups have chosen to settle in Thunder Bay, and many of them have retained their language and culture. Thunder Bay is thus the nearest you'll find to a cosmopolitan city in hicksville northern Ontario, and can make a pleasant stopover on the *Greyhound* trans-Canada journey – it is, after all, a long way to Winnipeg.

## Arrival, information and transport

Thunder Bay's **Lakehead Airport** is a fifteen-minute drive from town in the western suburbs; an airport bus runs from here to the now defunct train station in Fort William every twenty minutes for $3, while local bus #4 departs at least every forty minutes for the Brodie Street **bus terminal** in Fort William. There are two long-distance **bus** stations: *Greyhound*, 815 Fort William Rd, is the terminal for buses arriving from Sault Ste Marie, Hearst, Winnipeg (via Kenora) and Duluth; *Grey Goose*, 395 Fort William Rd, is the depot for buses from Winnipeg via Fort Frances. The local bus #1, which connects the Brodie Street terminal with the east end of Port Arthur, serves both stations.

The **information centres** are only open from mid-May to the end of September. The main one is in Fort William at Paterson Park (daily 8am–8pm; ☎623-7577), and there's another in the CN Station in Port Arthur's Marina Park (daily 8am–8pm; ☎345-6812). For information in other months contact the Visitors and Convention Department, 520 Leith St (daily 9am–5pm; ☎625-2149).

The public transport service run by **City Transit** has two bus depots useful for getting around this spread-out city: the Northward terminal, serving Port Arthur, is in Water Street by the CN information centre; the Southward terminal, serving Fort

William, is at Brodie Street South, opposite the Paterson Park information centre. The flat fare is $1.10; ask for a transfer if you need more than one bus to complete your journey. Most buses run from 6am to midnight during the week and have a habit of not running at weekends.

# Accommodation

Campers with a vehicle are well catered for in Thunder Bay, but otherwise budget accommodation is a problem, as the CHA-approved **hostel** is a long way out of town and there is only one bed and breakfast in the area – which leaves a profusion of characterless but well-priced motels. If you are under canvas there are several campgrounds but most are situated some distance from Thunder Bay proper without any public transport links.

## Hotels and B&B

**Landmark Inn**, 1010 Dawson Rd (☎767-1681). Thunder Bay's top hotel, with four stars and rates to match. Singles $70.95, doubles $77.95.

**Park Place**, 221 Brodie North (☎622-9335). A B&B opposite the Tourist Office with only two rooms. Singles $30, doubles $35; homebaked muffins for breakfast.

**Ramada Inn/Prince Arthur**, 17 Cumberland North (☎345-5411). 121 bedrooms, all mod cons and a swimming pool. Central but quite expensive, with doubles $89, singles $77.

**Venture Inn**, 450 Memorial (☎345-2343). Over 90 Canadian-style rooms with air-conditioning and an indoor pool. Singles $60, doubles $70 – including breakfast.

## Motels

**Circle Inn**, 686 Memorial Ave (☎344-5744). Singles $44, doubles $48.

**Crest Motor Hotel**, 875 Red River Rd (☎767-1627). In the Red River-Dawson Road area. Singles $34, doubles $38.

**Inntowner Motel**, 301 Brodie St South (☎623-1565). Singles $32, doubles $37.

**Lakeview Motel**, 391 Cumberland North (☎345-1711). Small motel with singles or doubles for $32.

**Old Country Motel**, 500 Cumberland North (☎344-2511). Cheapest motel in Thunder Bay – singles $28, doubles $30.

**Ritz Motel**, 2600 Arthur East (☎623-8189). Three-star accommodation with reasonable rates – singles $45, doubles $47.

**Shoreline Motor Hotel**, 61 Cumberland North (☎344-9661). Within walking distance of the harbour with doubles for $40, singles $35. Has dubious live entertainment seven nights a week from local rock bands and cabaret singers.

**Sleeping Giant Motor Hotel**, 439 Memorial (☎345-7316). Smack between Port Arthur and Fort William. Air-conditioned rooms and indoor swimming pool. Singles $38, doubles $43, with breakfast.

**Strathcona Motel**, 573 Hodder Ave (☎683-8136). A six-bedroomed cheap motel near the lakefront. Singles $30, doubles $35.

## Hostels and student accommodation

**Longhouse Village Hostel**, 1594 Lakeshore Drive (☎983-2042). Run by husband and wife team Lloyd and Willa Jones, who were once missionaries in Borneo and continue their Christian work with refugees. The first home of many immigrants, the hostel has a commune-like atmosphere, a beautiful setting and no curfew. The only disadvantage is that it is 22km east of Thunder Bay and not served by city buses. It is easy to hitch to, though, and the eastbound *Greyhound* bus will drop you off at the end of Mackenzie Station Road on Hwy 11/17, which is a twenty-minute walk from the hostel. The hostel is never full, and beds cost $10 for members; camping outside is available for a small fee.

**Lakehead University**, 953 Oliver Rd (☎343-8612). Dormitory beds or single rooms available in summer in the $20–30 region. Buses #2A and #2B run from the Water Street terminal to the university.

## Camping

**Chippewa Park Tourist Camp**, City Rd (☎623-3912). On junction Hwy 61 and Hwy 61B, 8km south of Thunder Bay. From $11; also has 18 log cabins for up to 6 persons, from $24.

**KOA Kampground**, Hwy 11/17 at Spruce River Rd turn-off (☎683-6221). The largest campground, just 2.5km east of the Terry Fox Lookout on the Trans-Canada. There is also a restaurant and grocery store. Open mid-May to mid-October. From $12.75.

**Trowbridge Falls Campground**, Copenhagen Rd (☎683-6661). Close to the junction of Hwy 11/17 and Hodder Avenue, within walking distance of Centennial Park. Open mid-May to mid-September. From $11.

# Fort William

The tourist industry is concentrating its attentions on **Fort William**, the more depressed area of the city, but frankly most of its "sights" might well make you a depressed area. The **Historical Museum**, 219 May St (mid-June to mid-Sept daily 11am–5pm; mid-Sept to mid-June Tues–Sun 1–5pm; free), has the usual collection of local antiquities and mock-ups of Victorian businesses, but the Indian beadwork is worth a look as are the displays about local oddities White Otter Castle and Silver Islet. Two blocks north the **Amethyst Factory**, 400 East Victoria Ave (Mon–Fri 8.30am–6pm; free), has tours showing the production of various tacky souvenirs.

A ten-minute walk northeast brings you to the **Northwestern Ontario Sports Hall of Fame**, 435 Balmoral St (Mon–Fri 10am–4.30pm, Sun 1–4pm; free), whose heroes are predominantly of the ice hockey variety. Further north across Chapples Park, on Confederation College campus off Balmoral, is the **Thunder Bay Art Gallery** (Tues–Thurs noon–8pm, Fri & Sun noon–5pm; free), whose collection includes works by local-born Norval Morisseau, one of Canada's most famous native artists, who came to public attention in the 1960s. Known as the originator of the Cree-Ojibwa art style usually referred to as "Woodlands art", he initially came into conflict with his elders by using Ojibwa legends as his subject matter – in Ojibwa tradition it is taboo for anyone other than a shaman to depict legendary figures. The Woodlands art movement is now one of the main vehicles of native identity amongst the Cree and Ojibwa. The gallery also has a knack of getting native art exhibits on loan from major national and international museums and galleries.

**Mount McKay**, southwest of the Kaministikwia River on City Road, is the tallest mountain in the Northwestern chain, rising 488 metres above sea level and 305 metres above the city. This massive mesa is the reservation of the Mission Indians who charge a fee of $5 for car parking; it is possible to see the whole of Thunder Bay from the top, but you'll get more scenic views free of charge from Hillcrest Park in Port Arthur (see opposite).

## Old Fort William

Thunder Bay's *tour de force* is the reconstructed fur-trading post of **Old Fort William** (mid-May to mid-June & mid-Aug to mid-Sept Mon–Fri 10am–4pm; mid-June to mid-Aug daily 10am–6pm; mid-Sept to mid-May daily 10am–4pm; $4.50), about 15km west of Fort William centre. The forty-two buildings and Ojibwa camp are staffed by students dressed as merchants, workers, servants and natives, giving demonstrations of barrel-making in the cooperage, canoe-building and nineteenth-century bush-cooking – the canteen food is delicious and very reasonable. Old Fort William is especially enjoyable in July when free food is dished out at the **Great Rendezvous** – a re-enactment of the annual shindig when Nor'Westers from the inland forts would meet their Montréal partners to conduct the company's business, barter furs with the natives and generally party. In the winter the fort is more or less deserted except for the occasional sleigh ride and skating parties on the river.

To get to the fort, local bus #10 goes from Fort William every twenty minutes. A pleasant alternative is the ninety-minute cruise on the Kaministikwia River from the Port Arthur marina to the fort on the *Cruiseship Welcome*; a bus returns to the marina later in the day (mid-May to early Oct; $12).

## Port Arthur

Thunder Bay North, still obdurately called **Port Arthur**, is the more upbeat side of town, and its most attractive enclave is the Finnish district of **Little Suomi**, stretching from Oliver Road to Pearl Street and from Hillcrest Park to the waterfront. Arriving in Thunder Bay in 1872, the Finns created here the world's largest Finnish community outside the homeland, and as you wander the streets you will still hear more Finnish spoken than English – even the signs are bilingual. The most pleasant area is the intersection of Bay and Algoma, which is dotted with good restaurants and older buildings.

Port Arthur has some good city parks. On the High Street **Hillcrest Park** has panoramic views of the harbour and the Sleeping Giant. **Waverley Park**, on the corner of Waverley and Red River Road, holds free open-air concerts in the summer – from Sinatra-type crooners to rap artists from Toronto. Finally, along the shores of Current River 9km out of town, the more natural-looking **Centennial Park** features a 1910 bush camp, a small logging history museum and a farm for the city kids, with rabbits, sheep and pigs.

## Eating, drinking and nightlife

The best place to **eat** is in Little Suomi, at the junction of Bay and Algoma, where you can sample tasty Finnish food in healthy portions. The majority of the area's eateries close early, and for late eating there's little on offer except the standard burgers and pizzas. **Nightlife** is restricted to a few decent bars and nightclubs – most bars serve finger foods and have a dance floor and the occasional live band, usually churning out the re-hashed Top 40 numbers.

### Snacks and restaurants

**Boston Pizza**, 217 Arthur St and 505 Memorial Ave. Average pizzas, ribs and pasta with the advantage of being open until 3am on Fri and Sat.

**Calabria Restaurant**, 287 Bay St (☎344-9376). Southern Italian food. Spaghetti with dandelion roots and anchovies for $6.95. Advisable to book at the weekends.

**Cultures Fresh Food Restaurant**, 11 Cumberland South. Deli-type restaurant; good for vegetarians.

**Hoito Restaurant**, 314 Bay St. Established in 1918, Thunder Bay's best-known Finnish restaurant is always full and the specials on the board should not be missed. Open daily until 8pm.

**Kangas Sauna**, 379 Oliver Rd. This used to just be a small counter service for the sauna users but is now a larger restaurant with great homemade soups and delicious omelettes, as well as sweet berry pies. Closed Sun & Mon.

**Ozzie's Family Restaurant**, corner of Dawson and Government Rd. English fish and chips and Canadian food, open 24 hours daily.

**The Prospector Restaurant**, 27 Cumberland South (☎345-5833). Excellent steaks from a local ranch served with homemade bread; the hamburgers are good too. Advisable to book.

**Scandinavian Homemade**, 147 Algoma South. A friendly, cosy café with full breakfasts for $3.75 and delicious Finnish pancakes. Open Mon–Sat 7am–4pm.

**Thunder Bay Restaurant**, 188 Bay St. Billed as "the working man's place to eat" this greasy spoon has generous helpings and a fine collection of the baseball caps that are the uniform of this area. Non-stop coffee and full breakfast for $2.99. Open daily until 7pm.

**Trifon's Pizza and Pasta**, 131 May North and 428 Cumberland North. Buy one pizza and get one free. Closed Sun.

## Bars, clubs and live music

**The Blue Line**, 920 Tungsten St. The best sports bar.

**Brasserie**, 901 Red River Rd. A trendy American-type brew pub which is packed at weekends. Expensive beer.

**The Brown Street Station**, 1408 Brown St. An old fire station converted into a bar.

**Casey's**, Venture Inn, 450 Memorial Ave. A small dance bar, patronised mainly by thirtysomething singles.

**Horseshoe Tavern**, 246 Cumberland St. A variety of bands from country to rock.

**Inntowner**, corner of Arthur and Brodie. Leather jackets and hard rock. Admission charge if there is a live band.

**The Office**, 215 Red River Rd. Features live blues bands.

**Pacific Club**, 201 Syndicate Ave. High-tech lights and Thunder Bay's largest dance floor.

**The Wayland**, 1019 Gore St West. A popular bar, with free pizza for groups of six or more.

## Listings

**Airlines** *Air Canada*, airport (☎623-3313); *Canadian Air*, airport (☎577-6461).

**Bus information** Local: *City Transit* (☎344-9666). Long-distance: *Greyhound* (☎345-2194); *Grey Goose* (☎345-8231).

**Camping equipment** *Wildwaters Wilderness Shop & Expeditions*, 119 Cumberland North (☎345-0111). *Gear Up For Outdoors*, 894 Alloy Place (☎345-0001).

**Car rental** *Avis*, 330 Memorial (☎345-9929) and 1475 Walsh West (☎577-5766); *Tilden*, 556 Arthur West (☎577-5783); *Budget*, 899 Copper Crescent (☎345-2425); *Thrifty*, 899 Tungsten (☎345-7111).

**Hospital** Port Arthur General, 460 Court North (☎343-6621).

**Laundry** *Algoma Home Style Laundry*, 213 Algoma South (daily 8am–11pm); *Honey's Washeteria*, 230 Leland South (Mon–Sat 8.30am–10pm, Sun 10am–10pm).

**Post office** 321 Archibald North and 33 Court South.

**Ski information** *Ski Thunder*, 79 North Court St (☎345-7312).

**Taxi** *Amber Cab/Central Taxi* (☎475-4050).

**Weather information** ☎475-4224.

# West of Thunder Bay

Heading west from Thunder Bay, the nearest attraction that might make you stop is Kakabeka Falls Provincial Park, a pleasant spot if not quite the most enthralling aquatic spectacle in the country. Some 39km further the Trans-Canada splits into Hwy 11 and Hwy 17 – the latter the more frequented and faster route to Winnipeg via the attractive lakeshore-based Kenora, the former running past the border-crossing at Fort Frances, where the relatively secluded Hwy 71 turns north to rejoin Hwy 17 via the east shore of the beautiful and vast Lake of the Woods. All three highways are served by regular long-distance buses.

## Kakabeka Falls Provincial Park

Thirty kilometres west of Thunder Bay, close to Hwy 11/17, the Kaministikwia River plunges nearly forty metres into a gorge, creating the **Kakabeka Falls** – taking its name from the Ojibwa word for "thundering waters". Local legend has it that Greenmantle, the daughter of an Ojibwa chief, promised to guide the fearsome Sioux to the Ojibwa camp in return for her own life, and then steered the Sioux to their deaths in the cataract. It is said she sometimes appears in the mist of the falls, but these days she doesn't have too many opportunities, as a hydro-electric dam now controls the flow to such an extent that locals jokingly refer to the "Only on a Sunday

Falls". In summer there's usually just a yellow trickle here, but during the spring and autumn the river flows at full force if the dam allows it – which is usually at the weekends. Now with provincial park status, the area has been adapted for family outings with picnic tables, viewing posts and a spanking new information centre.

## Quetico Provincial Park – and on to Kenora

**Quetico Provincial Park** (April to early Oct, and day use Dec to early March), 161km west of Thunder Bay on Hwy 11, is a wild but well-organised park located between the highway and the border with Minnesota. A perfect destination for canoeists, it presents a landscape typical of the region, with its rocky cliffs and forests of black spruce and jack pine laced with countless waterways. As well as an impressive array of animal and bird life – including wolves, black bears, bald eagles and ospreys – the park has the additional attraction of the thirty or so cliff faces decorated with miniature pictographs whose origins and age still remain uncertain.

The service town for the park is ATIKOKAN, 48km west of the park gate, which is the nearest you can get to the park by bus. If you need to stay here, your best bet is the *Radisson Motel*, located on the main street into town at 310 Mackenzie Avenue (☎597-2766; doubles $50). There are several outfitters in Atikokan, but none is as convenient as the *Quetico Trading Post* (☎929-2177), 5km west of the park entrance, which rents out canoes for $35 a day – it is best to reserve in advance. Right by the entrance the **Quetico Information Pavilion** provides maps of the park's extensive canoe routes and details of the pictograph sites, which are visible only from the water; camping ($10–14) and vehicle permits ($5) are also issued here. Camping can be reserved by phone from February to the end of August, for a $4 fee (Mon–Fri 8am–4.30pm; ☎597-2735).

## Lake of the Woods

Some 400km west of Thunder Bay, segmented by the provincial and international borders, lies the **Lake of the Woods**, whose 14,000 islands gave rise to the Ojibwa name "Min-es-tic" (Lake of the Islands) – which the French settlers misinterpreted as "Mis-tic", the native word for woods. Today's Ojibwa live on scruffy reserves, some located on the lake's remoter islands. Fierce prejudice, which seems to stem from the fact that their native status allows them to catch as many fish as they like, prevents their employment in the region's main town of Kenora. Their situation has worsened since 1974, when the Ojibwa, sick of the slow pace of land-claims negotiations, staged an armed but bloodless protest that prompted a local backlash whose effects can still be felt.

For the visitor, this is principally an area for boating and fishing, but even for land-lubbers the lake is impressive, its myriad islands a refreshing change from the usual unbroken expanses of water. The echoing sound of the loons is all that breaks the stillness of the area, while fantastic sunsets change the water into a kaleidoscope of colour.

### Kenora

The Lake of the Woods' reputation as an angler's paradise is indicated by "Husky the Muskie", a forty-foot statue of a fish at **KENORA**, a town that used to be known as Rat Portage until a flour company refused to build a mill here, arguing that the word "rat" on sacks of their product would not do much for sales. Nowadays the permanent population of 9000 quadruples in the summer, when droves of Americans hit the lake – a fortunate boost to the town's economy as the main employer, the newsprint paper mill, is threatened with closure as the continent switches to recycled paper. Renting a boat costs over $1000 for a week, so unless you are loaded you will be probably be land-based, but it's an enjoyable spot – especially in summer when there's a really laid-back feel to this beautifully located town.

The impressive **Lake of the Woods Museum**, 300 Main St (summer Mon–Sat 10am–5pm, Sun noon–5pm; winter Tues–Sat 10am–5pm; $2), relates the history of the area with a fine selection of native ceremonial pipes and clothing, including a sacred jingle dress which is thought to have healing properties – its design came as a vision to a chief whose sick daughter was cured when she wore it.

At the foot of Main Street the *MS Kenora* **cruises** the Lake of the Woods' islands and channels for two hours (mid-May to Sept 1–3 daily; $9.50), offering an opportunity to see **Devil Gap's Rock** at the entrance to Kenora harbour. In 1884 the rock's resemblance to a human face was emphasised with paint and it has been repainted ever since, but this is not a gimmicky attraction – it's an Ojibwa spirit rock, to which food and tobacco sacrifices were made in order to propitiate the supernatural giant known as Windigo – the personification of winter. His powers could only be controlled by powerful shamen, and when hunters disappeared in the bush they were thought to have been eaten by Windigo. When winter food shortages drove starving Ojibwas to develop a craving for human flesh they would request execution rather than be taken over by Windigo. Passing vacationers still throw the odd cigarette at the rock.

Kenora's **bus** terminus is the *Greyhound Bus Depot*, 630 Lakeview Drive – the arrival point for buses from Fort Frances, Thunder Bay and Winnipeg. A five-minute walk from the station is the *Lake of the Woods Tourism Centre*, located on Hwy 17 east of town (summer daily 9am–5pm; winter Mon–Fri 9am–5pm). First choice for **accommodation** is the *Kenrica Hotel*, 155 Main St (☎468-6461; doubles $65), which has been around as long as Kenora. There's the usual string of **motels** stretching along the highway just outside town, all of which require reservations in the summer – *Lake-Vu Motel*, 740 Lakeview Drive (☎468-5501; doubles $60), is a moderately priced three-star place. **Camping** is available downtown at the shoreside *Anicinabe Park* (☎468-8233). For **eating**, the renowned steaks in the Kenrica Hotel dining room cost $11.95, while the *Plaza Restaurant*, 135 Main St, is a friendly Greek place with sandwiches as well as full meals.

## travel details

### Trains

**From Toronto** to Kingston (2–3 daily; 2hr 20min); Kingston/Montréal (4–5 daily; 2hr 30min/5hr 25min); Ottawa (3 daily; 4hr 40min); Montréal (5–6 daily; 5hr); Parry Sound (3 weekly; 4hr); Barrie/Orillia/Gravenhurst/Huntsville/North Bay/Temagami/Cobalt/Cochrane/Kapuskasing/Hearst (6 weekly; 1hr 15min/1hr 40min/2hr 15min/3hr/4hr 50min/6hr 40min/7hr 20min/10hr 10min/11hr 25min/12hr 45min); Parry Sound/Sudbury Jct/Winnipeg (3 weekly; 5hr/8hr/33hr 30min).

**From Ottawa** to Kingston/Toronto (2–3 daily; 1hr 50min/4hr); Montréal (3–4 daily; 2hr).

**From Cochrane** to Moosonee (6 weekly in summer; 4hr 20min).

**From Sault Ste Marie** to Hearst (1–2 daily; 9hr).

**From Sudbury** to White River (6 weekly; 8hr 20min).

### Buses

**From Toronto** to Ottawa (10 daily; 4hr 30min–8hr); Peterborough/Ottawa (4 daily; 2hr 40min/8hr); Port Hope/Cobourg/Trenton/Kingston (3 daily; 2hr 10min; 2hr 30min/3hr 25min/5hr 25min); Kingston/Cornwall/Montréal (7 daily; 3hr/5hr 15min/7hr); Montréal (12 daily; 6hr 30min–7hr); Peterborough (12 daily; 2hr–2hr 40min); Gravenhurst/Parry Sound/Sudbury (1 daily; 3hr/4hr 15min/5hr 40min); Parry Sound/Sudbury (5 daily; 2hr–4hr 15min; 5hr 15min–5hr 40min); Gravenhurst/Hunstsville/North Bay (3 daily; 3hr/4hr 15min/8hr); Gravenhurst/North Bay (1 daily; 2hr 30min/4hr 45min); Gravenhurst/Huntsville (1 daily; 3hr/3hr 50min); Sudbury/Espanola/Sault Ste Marie/Wawa/White River/Nipigon/Thunder Bay/Kenora/Winnipeg (4 daily; 5hr/6hr/10hr 50min/13hr 50min/17hr/18hr 15min/21hr 30min/29hr/30hr 30min).

**From Kingston** to Ottawa (10 daily; 3hr 30min–3hr 45min).

**From Ottawa** to North Bay (9 daily; 4hr 35min–7hr); Montréal (18 daily; 2hr); North Bay/Sudbury (4 daily; 6–7hr/9–9hr 45min); North Bay/Sudbury/Espanola/Sault Ste Marie (1 daily; 3hr/6hr/9hr/10hr).

**From North Bay** to Sudbury (1 daily; 1hr 35min); Timmins/Cochrane/Hearst/Longlac/Geraldton (1 daily; 8hr/11hr/14hr 15min/18hr/19hr).

**From Sudbury** to Timmins (1 daily; 4hr 15min).

**From Espanola** to South Baymouth (3 daily; 1hr).

**From Little Current** to Gore Bay (1 daily; 1hr).

**From Sault Ste Marie** to Wawa/Timmins (1 daily; 3hr/7hr 35min).

**From Thunder Bay** to Fort Frances/Winnipeg (2 daily; 4hr 10min/11hr).

**From Fort Frances** to Kenora (1 daily; 3hr).

**From Longlac** to Nipigon/Thunder Bay (1 daily; 1hr 30min/4hr 30min).

**From Hearst** to Nipigon/Thunder Bay/Fort Frances/Winnipeg (1 daily; 5hr/7hr 30min/11hr/16hr 30min).

**Planes**

**From Toronto** to Calgary/Banff (5–7 daily; 4hr 15min); Edmonton (5–7 daily 1hr 40min); Fredericton (5–6 daily; 1hr 45min); Halifax/Dartmouth (7–9 daily; 2hr); Moncton (5 daily; 2hr); Montréal (15–26 daily; 1hr 15min); Ottawa (11–22 daily; 1hr); Québec City (8–19 daily; 1hr 45min); Saint John (4–5 daily; 1hr 45min); Saskatoon (2–3 daily; 3hr 30min); St John's (6–7 daily; 3hr); Thunder Bay (2–5 daily; 1hr 30min); Vancouver (6–7 daily; 5hr); Winnipeg (5 daily; 2hr 45min).

**From Ottawa** to Calgary/Banff (5–9 daily; 3hr 40min); Halifax/Dartmouth (3–6 daily; 2hr); Montréal (7–16 daily; 30min); Vancouver (8 daily; 5hr 20min); Winnipeg (6–7 daily; 2hr 20min); Québec City (6–18 daily; 1hr).

# CHAPTER FIVE

# CENTRAL CANADA

The provinces of **Manitoba** and **Saskatchewan**, a vast tract bounded by the Ontario border and the Rockies, together comprise a region commonly called "the Prairies". In fact, flat treeless plains are confined to the southern part of **central Canada** and even then they are broken up by the occasional river valley and range of low-lying hills, which gradually raise the elevation from sea level at Hudson Bay to nearly 1200m near the Rockies. Furthermore, the plains themselves are divided into two broad geographical areas: the semi-arid short **grasslands** which border the States in Alberta and Saskatchewan; and the **wheat-growing** belt, a crescent-shaped expanse to the north of the grasslands. In turn, this wheat belt borders the low hills, mixed farms and sporadic forests of the **aspen parkland**, a transitional zone between the plains and the **boreal forest**, whose trees, rocky outcrops, rivers and myriad lakes cover well over half of the entire central region, stretching to the Northwest Territories in Saskatchewan and Alberta and as far as the treeless **tundra** beside Hudson Bay in Manitoba.

If you're here in the winter, when the temperature falls to minus 30°c or 40°c and the wind rips down from the North Pole, it's hard to imagine how the European pioneers managed to survive, huddled together in remote log cabins or even sod huts. Yet survive they did, and between about 1895 and 1914 the great swathe of land that makes up the wheat belt and the aspen parkland had been turned into one of the most productive wheat-producing areas in the world. By any standards, the development of this farmland was a remarkable achievement, but the price was high: the nomadic culture of the **Plains Indians** was almost entirely destroyed and the disease-ravaged, half-starved survivors were dumped in a string of meagre reservations. Similarly, the **Metis**, descendants of white fur traders and native women who for more than two centuries had acted as intermediaries between the two cultures, found themselves overwhelmed, their desperate attempts to maintain their independence leading to a brace of futile rebellions under the leadership of Louis Riel in 1870 and 1885.

With the Metis and the Indians out of the way, thousands of European immigrants concentrated on their wheat yields, but they were the victims of a one-crop economy, their prosperity dependent on the market price of grain and the freight charges imposed by the railroad. Throughout this century, the region's farmers have experienced alarming changes in their fortunes as bust has alternated with boom, a situation which continues to dominate the economies of Saskatchewan and eastern Alberta today. As the *Globe and Mail* newspaper lamented in 1991 – "A bumper crop sits in the grain bins without a market and, by January, it's expected 20,000 more disillusioned souls will join the 24,000 who left Saskatchewan last year for a future elsewhere."

Central Canada is not a popular tourist destination, its main cities caricatured as dull and dreary, its scenery considered flat and monotonous. To some extent, these prejudices stem from the route of the **Trans-Canada Highway**, which contrives to avoid nearly everything of interest on its way from Winnipeg to Calgary, a generally boring and long drive that many Canadians prefer to do at night when, they say, the views are better. However, on the Trans-Canada itself, the busy city of **Winnipeg** – easily the largest town in Central Canada – is well worth a visit for its museums, restaurants and nightlife, whilst, just to the south of the highway on the Saskatchewan-Alberta border, there are the delightful wooded ridges of the **Cypress Hills Inter-Provincial Park**, which incorporates the restored Mountie outpost of **Fort Walsh**. It has to be said, though, that the **Yellowhead Route** from Winnipeg – Highway 16 – makes a far more agreeable journey, with pleasant stops at **Saskatoon** and the **Battlefords**. This road is also within easy reach of central Canada's two outstanding parks, **Riding Mountain National Park** in Manitoba and **Prince Albert National Park** in Saskatchewan, both renowned for their wild lakes, forest-hiking and canoeing routes.

Most of central Canada's boreal forest is inaccessible except by private float plane, but all the major cities and the region's tourist offices have lists of tour operators and suppliers who run or equip a whole variety of trips into the outback – from whitewater rafting and canoeing, through to hunting, fishing and bird watching. It's also possible to fly or travel by train to **Churchill**, a remote and desolate settlement on the southern shore of Hudson Bay that's one of the world's best places to see polar bears. One word of warning: the boreal forests swarm with voracious insects such as blackflies and mosquitoes, so don't forget your insect repellent.

---

### TOLL-FREE INFORMATION NUMBERS

Travel Manitoba ☎1-800-665-0040.
Tourism Saskatchewan ☎1-800-667-7538 from within Saskatchewan,
☎1-800-667-7191 from elsewhere in Canada and the US.

---

# WINNIPEG

With 600,000 inhabitants, **WINNIPEG** accounts for roughly two-thirds of the population of Manitoba, and lies at the geographic centre of the country, sandwiched between the American frontier to the south and the infertile Canadian Shield to the north and east. The city has been the gateway to the plains since 1873, and became the transit point for much of the country's transcontinental traffic when the railroad arrived just twelve years later. From the very beginning, Winnipeg was described as the city where "the West began", and its polyglot population, drawn from every country in Europe, was attracted by the promise of the fertile soils to the west. But this was no classless pioneer town: as early as the 1880s the city had developed a clear pattern of residential segregation, with leafy prosperous suburbs to the south, along the Assiniboine River, while to the north lay "Shanty Town". The long-term effects of this division have proved hard to erase, and today the dispossessed still gather round the flophouses just to the north of the business district, a sad rather than dangerous corner near the main intersection at Portage and Main. Winnipeg's skid row is a tiny part of the downtown area, but its reputation has hampered recent attempts to reinvigorate the city centre as a whole: successive administrations in the last twenty years have refurbished warehouses and built walkways along the river, but the new downtown apartment blocks remain hard to sell, and most people stick resolutely to the suburbs.

That apart, Winnipeg makes for an enjoyable brief stopover, and all of the main attractions are within easy walking distance of each other. The **Manitoba Museum of Man and Nature** has excellent displays on the history of the province and its various geographic areas; the **Exchange District** features some good examples of Canada's early twentieth-century architecture; the **Art Gallery** has the country's best collection of Inuit art; and, just across the Red River, the suburb of **St Boniface** has a delightful museum situated in the house and chapel of the Grey Nuns, who arrived here by canoe from Montréal in 1846. Winnipeg is also noted for the excellence and diversity of its **restaurants**, whilst its flourishing performing arts scene features anything from ballet and classical music through to country and western and jazz.

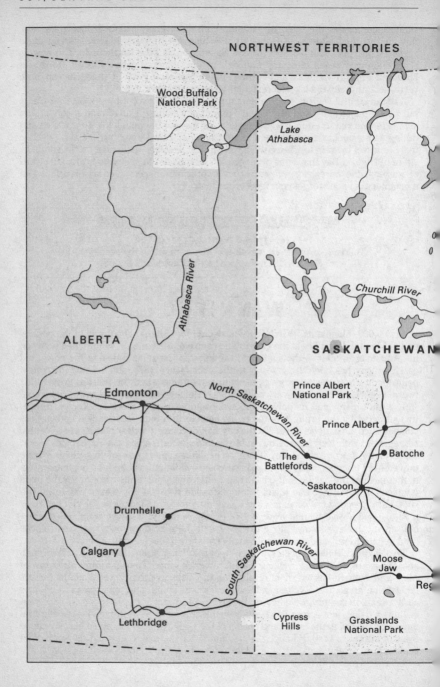

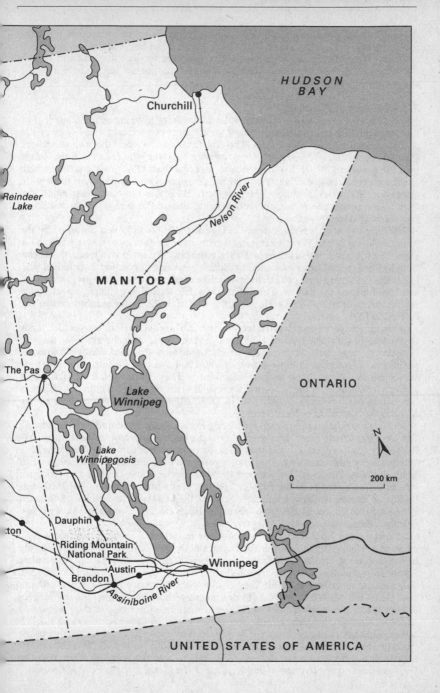

Finally, the city makes a useful base for exploring the area's attractions, the most popular of which – chiefly **Lower Fort Garry** – are on the banks of the Red River as it twists its way north to Lake Winnipeg, 60km away. On the lake itself, **Grand Beach Park** has the province's finest stretches of sandy beach, just two hours' drive from the city centre.

## A brief history of Winnipeg

Named after the Cree word for murky water ("win-nipuy"), Winnipeg owes much of its history to the Red and Assiniboine rivers, which meet just south of today's city centre at the confluence called **The Forks**. The first European to reach the area was Pierre Gaultier, Sieur de la Vérendrye, an enterprising explorer who founded **Fort Rouge** near the Forks in 1737. This settlement was part of a chain of fur-trading posts he built to extend French influence into the west and, prospering from good connections north along the Red River to Lake Winnipeg and Hudson's Bay and west along the Assiniboine across the plains, the fort became one of the region's most important outposts within twenty years.

After the defeat of New France in 1763, local trading activity was absorbed by the Montréal-based **North West Company**, which came to dominate the fur trade at the expense of its rival, the **Hudson's Bay Company**. The latter continued to operate from fortified coastal factories staffed by British personnel, expecting their Indian trading partners to bring their pelts to them – unlike their rivals, who were prepared to live and travel among the natives. This inflexible policy looked like ruining the company until it was rescued by Thomas Douglas, the Earl of Selkirk, who bought a controlling interest in 1809.

In the three years **Lord Selkirk** took to turn the business round, he resettled many of his own impoverished Scottish crofters around The Forks, buying from his own company a huge tract of farmland which he named the **Red River Colony** or Assiniboia. The arrival of these colonists infuriated the Nor'Westers, who saw their settlement as a direct threat to their trade routes. They encouraged their Metis allies and employees to harry the Scots and for several years there was continuous skirmishing, which reached tragic proportions in 1816, when 21 settlers were killed by the Metis in the **Seven Oaks Massacre**.

Just five years later the two rival fur-trading firms amalgamated under the "Hudson's Bay Company" trade name, bringing peace and a degree of prosperity to the area. Yet the colony remained a rough-and-ready place, as a chaplain called John West lamented: "Almost every inhabitant we passed bore a gun upon his shoulder and all appeared in a wild and hunter-like state." For the next thirty years, the colony sustained an economic structure that suited both the farmers and the Metis hunters, but in the 1860s this balance of interests collapsed with the decline of the buffalo herds, and the Metis faced extreme hardship just at the time when the Hudson's Bay Company had itself lost effective administrative control of its territories.

At this time of internal crisis, the politicians of eastern Canada agreed the federal union of 1867, opening the way for the transfer of the Red River Colony from British to Canadian control. The Metis majority – roughly 6000 as compared to some 1000 whites – were fearful of the consequences and their resistance took shape round **Louis Riel**, under whose dextrous leadership they captured the Hudson's Bay Company's Upper Fort Garry and created a provisional government without challenging the sovereignty of the crown. A delegation went to Ottawa to negotiate the terms of their admission into the Dominion, but their efforts were handicapped by the execution of an English settler, **Thomas Scott**, back on the Red River. The subsequent furore pushed prime minister John Macdonald into dispatching a military force to restore "law and order"; nevertheless, the **Manitoba Act** of 1870, which brought the Red River into the Dominion, did accede to many of the demands of the Metis, at the price of Riel's exile.

The eclipse of the Metis and the security of Winnipeg – as it became in 1870 – were both assured when the **Canadian Pacific Railway** routed their transcontinental line through The Forks in 1885. With the town's commodity markets handling the expanding grain trade and its industries supplying the vast rural hinterland, its population was swelled by thousands of immigrants: in 1872 Winnipeg had a population of 1,500; by 1901 it had risen to 42,000; and by 1921 it had reached 192,000. More recently, the development of other prairie cities, like Regina and Saskatoon, has undermined something of Winnipeg's pre-eminence, but the city is still the economic focus of central Canada.

> The Manitoba telephone code is ☎204.

# Arrival, information and transport

Winnipeg **airport** is some 7km west of the city centre. There's a **tourist information desk** inside the airport concourse (daily 8.30am–10pm), which has a good range of leaflets on the city and its principal attractions, along with accommodation listings. Close by, a display board advertising the city's grander hotels is attached to a free phone for on-the-spot hotel reservations. From outside the terminal building, a *Winnipeg Transit* **bus** service (every 20–30min, 6am–midnight; $1.15) runs downtown, dropping passengers at or near most of the larger hotels; the trip takes about twenty minutes, and tickets are bought from the driver. **Taxis** charge around $12 for the same journey, but cut the price down to $5 per person if you're prepared to share; **limos** cost $25 per person, $9 shared.

The **bus station** is on the west side of the downtown area at Portage Avenue and Memorial Boulevard. The city's **train station** is on Main Street, just south of Portage, with connecting trains to Churchill, Toronto and Saskatoon for Vancouver.

### Information

*Winnipeg Tourism* has an **information office** on the first floor of the city's Convention Centre at York and Carlton (mid-May to Aug daily 9am–5pm; Sept to mid-May Mon–Fri 9am–5pm; ☎943-1970), but the Manitoba **tourist desk**, inside the foyer of the Legislative Building at Broadway and Memorial (mid-May to Aug daily 8am–9pm; Sept to early Oct Mon–Fri 8.30am–4.30pm; ☎942-2535), has a far more comprehensive range of leaflets on both the city and the province. Both outlets provide free city maps, a *Winnipeg Transit* bus plan, accommodation listings and the free *Where* magazine.

If you're heading off to one of the provincial parks, you should visit the **Manitoba Natural Resources Department**, 258 Portage at Garry (Mon–Fri 9am–4.30pm; ☎945-4374). They have a comprehensive range of maps and will provide specialist advice on anything from weather conditions to details of suitable outfitters and guides. The **Canadian Parks Information Office**, 457 Main St (same hours; ☎983-2290), offer a similar service for the region's national parks.

### Orientation and city transport

Winnipeg's main north–south artery is **Main Street**, which runs roughly parallel to the adjacent Red River. The principal east–west drag is **Portage Avenue**, which begins at its junction with Main. The downtown core falls on either side of Portage, beginning at Main and ending at Memorial; it's bounded by Broadway to the south and Logan to the north. A twenty-minute stroll takes you from end to end, whilst the suburbs and the more outlying attractions are easy to reach by **bus**. **Winnipeg Transit** has an excellent range of city-wide services that includes two free downtown shuttle routes: *99 Dash* (Mon–Fri 11am–3pm), connecting the Forks with Broadway, Memorial, Graham and then Main at King; and *96 The Forks* (Mon–Fri 11am–6pm; Fri–Sat 9am–6pm), which runs east from Portage at Spence to Pioneer Boulevard and on down to The Forks. On other routes, there's a flat fare of $1.15 per journey, with tickets and transfers for trips involving more than one bus available from the driver – exact fare only. The **Transit Service Centre**, in the underground concourse at Portage and Main, sells a book of ten tickets for $10. Free route maps are available here, as well as at the tourist offices, and details of services are printed at the back of the Winnipeg telephone directory. Winnipeg also has a 24-hour transit **information service** (☎986-5700) and a **Handi-Transit** door-to-door minibus facility for disabled visitors (information on ☎986-5722 Mon–Sat 8am–midnight & Sun 9am–10pm).

# Accommodation

Most of Winnipeg's hotels are within walking distance of the bus and train stations, and there's rarely any difficulty in finding somewhere to stay. The modern **hotels** are standard-issue skyscrapers that concentrate on the business clientele; charges are between $100 and $150 for a double, but some of them offer weekend discounts and up to twenty percent reductions if you stay for three or four nights. The smaller and older downtown hotels start at around $35 for a double, but at this price the rooms are basic and often grimy – a more comfortable place averages out at about $50. (Avoid the flophouses calling themselves "hotels" on Main Street, just north of Portage.) Breakfasts are extra almost everywhere.

The major approach roads are dotted with **motels**, with doubles starting at around $40 per night, and drifting up towards $80. The largest concentrations are along the Pembina Highway, which runs south from the city centre as route #42, and along Portage, which runs west forming part of the Trans-Canada.

*Winnipeg Tourism* has the details of some thirty **bed and breakfast** addresses with doubles mostly around the $40 mark, with breakfasts that vary from frugal continental to a complete meal. Most of these are affiliated to *Bed and Breakfast of Manitoba*, 93 Healy Crescent (☎256-6151), an agency that makes reservations upon payment of a deposit equivalent to one night's stay. Unfortunately, most of their places are far from the centre, but a handful of the more convenient locations are given below. The **youth hostel**, within easy walking distance of the bus station, is supplemented in summer by less convenient rooms at the city university.

The tourist offices will help arrange hotel and B&B accommodation and there's also a free phone number for reservations (☎1-800-665-0040).

## Hotels

**Aberdeen Hotel**, 230 Carlton (☎942-7481). Convenient location, just by the Convention Centre. Old and charmless place with partial air-conditioning; doubles $34.

**Carlton Inn**, 220 Carlton (☎942-0881). Motel-style rooms; convenient location; one of the more agreeable cheap hotels; doubles $57.

**Charterhouse**, 330 York at Hargrave (☎942-0101). Central location; all rooms with balcony. doubles $55.

**The Delta Winnipeg**, 288 Portage at Smith (☎956-0410). The city's largest hotel, with a gymnasium, swimming pool, babysitting services and fine views from the top floors; doubles $135.

**Gordon Downtowner**, 330 Kennedy at Ellice (☎943-5581). Probably Winnipeg's most comfortable cheap hotel; doubles $50.

**Holiday Inn Crown Plaza**, 350 St Mary at Hargrave (☎942-0551). Adjoins the city's Convention Centre. Tasteful, opulent doubles for $132.

**Hotel Fort Garry**, 222 Broadway (☎942-8251). Near the train station. Built in neo-Gothic style in 1913; lavishly refurbished, with an elegant, balconied foyer leading to 600 rooms; doubles $109.

**The Marlborough Inn**, 331 Smith (☎942-6411). Unremarkable rooms from $60.
**Osborne Village Motor Inn**, 160 Osborne (☎452-9824). Basic, but right at the heart of Osborne Village; doubles $34.

## Motels
**Assiniboine Gordon Inn on the Park**, 1975 Portage Ave (☎888-4806). $50.
**Birchwood Inn**, 2520 Portage Ave (☎885-4478). $80.
**Capri Motel**, 1819 Pembina Hwy (☎269-6990). $47.
**Downs Motor Inn**, 3740 Portage Ave (☎837-5831). $40.
**Journey's End Motel**, 3109 Pembina Hwy (☎269-7390). $50.
**Norlander Inn**, 1792 Pembina Hwy (☎269-6955). $50.
**Ramada Inn**, 1824 Pembina Hwy (☎269-7700). $80.
**Travelodge Hotel Astoria**, 2935 Pembina Hwy (☎275-7711). $56.
**St Norbert**, 3540 Pembina Hwy (☎269-1290). $36.
**Viscount Gort**, 1670 Portage Ave (☎775-0451). $64.

## Bed and breakfast
**Ollie Hillman**, 701 Sherburn (☎775-5820). $45.
**Fred & Daisy Paulley**, 141 Furby St (☎772-8828). $40.
**Geoff & Nancy Tidmarsh**, 330 Waverley St (☎488-0084). In the River Heights area, a 10-minute bus ride from The Forks; $42.

## Hostel and college rooms
**Ivey House International Youth Hostel**, 210 Maryland at Broadway (☎772-3022). Rooms for between two and four people at a cost of $10 per member. There are also laundry and kitchen facilities and bicycle rental. In summer it's often full. Closed 10am–5pm.
**University of Manitoba**, Fort Garry campus (☎474-9942). Rooms from mid-May to mid-August, 10km south of the city centre. Doubles around $36, dormitory beds from $15.

## Campground
**KOA Winnipeg**, Murdoch Rd (May–Sept; ☎253-8168). The nearest campground, some 14km southeast of the centre, just off the Trans-Canada. From $11.

# The City

The traditional centre of Winnipeg is the **Portage and Main Street intersection**, close to the Red River at the start of what was once the main Metis cart track across the prairies. Despite its historic associations, the city council accepted a real-estate deal in 1979 which closed most of the junction to pedestrians in return for the construction of an underground shopping concourse. Recently the councillors have had second thoughts and negotiations are underway to have the junction reopened by 1993. While you're here, have a look at the grand neoclassical **Bank of Montréal** on the southeast side of the intersection, its fussily carved capitals in stark contrast to the sharp, clean lines of its skyscraper neighbours.

### The Centennial Centre
A couple of minutes' walk to the north, at 190 Rupert Avenue, the province's **Centennial Centre** incorporates the **Manitoba Museum of Man and Nature** (mid-June to Aug daily 10am–8pm; Sept to mid-June Tues–Fri 10am–5pm & Sat–Sun noon–6pm; $3.50), an excellent introduction to the province's geographical regions and the history of its peoples. Highlights of the natural history galleries include an imposing polar bear diorama, a well-illustrated explanation of the Northern Lights, and an off-

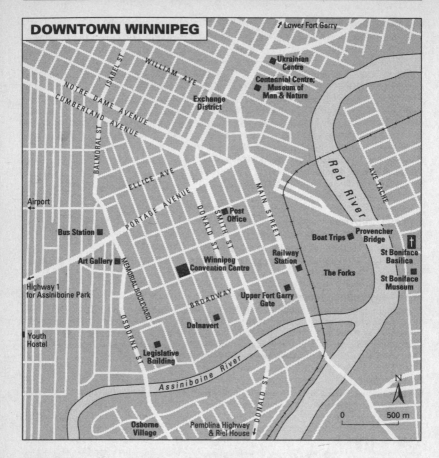

**DOWNTOWN WINNIPEG**

Lower Fort Garry

Ukrainian Centre

Centennial Centre; Museum of Man & Nature

Exchange District

WILLIAM AVE

ISABEL ST

NOTRE DAME AVENUE

CUMBERLAND AVENUE

BALMORAL ST

ELLICE AVE

Red River

AVE TACHE

Airport

PORTAGE AVENUE

MAIN STREET

Bus Station

Post Office

SMITH ST

DONALD ST

Boat Trips

Provencher Bridge

St Boniface Basilica

Art Gallery

Winnipeg Convention Centre

MEMORIAL BOULEVARD

Railway Station

The Forks

St Boniface Museum

Highway 1 for Assiniboine Park

BROADWAY

Upper Fort Garry Gate

Youth Hostel

OSBORNE ST

Dalnavert

Legislative Building

Assiniboine River

DONALD ST

N

0    500 m

Osborne Village

Pembina Highway & Riel House

putting section devoted to the more malicious insects of Manitoba – starring the "no-see-um", a deer fly that specialises in burrowing into the nostrils of caribou. The museum's most popular exhibit, moored in a massive display area of its own, is a full working replica of the **Nonsuch**, the ship whose fur-collecting voyage to James Bay in 1668 led to the creation of the Hudson's Bay Company.

The museum's *Grasslands* gallery has a small display of Assiniboine Indian artefacts, along with a reconstruction of a tepee and a copy of a pioneer log cabin. There's also an example of the sod houses that the pioneers were forced to build in many parts of the treeless southern plains, and a replica of a Red River cart, the Metis' favourite form of land transportation. The final part of the museum is the *Urban* gallery, which re-creates the Winnipeg of the early 1920s, a street complete with drugstore, dentist, boardwalk and cinema showing period films.

Also in the Centennial Centre are the **planetarium** (shows mid-June to Sept daily; Sept to mid-June closed Mon; $4) and the *Touch the Universe* **science gallery** (mid-June to Aug daily 10am–8pm; Sept to mid-June Tues–Thurs 10am–5pm, Fri 10am–7pm, Sat noon–7pm & Sun noon–6pm; $3), where the exhibits focus on the way the universe is perceived by the five senses. A combined ticket for all three attractions cost $7.50.

## The Ukrainian Centre

Just north of here, the **Ukrainian Cultural and Educational Centre**, 184 Alexander Ave East at Main (Tues–Sat 10am–4pm & Sun 2–5pm; free), occupies a 1930s office block on the edge of the Exchange District. The second largest ethnic group in Manitoba, the Ukrainians arrived here around the turn of the twentieth century, a peasant people united by language and custom, but divided by religion and politics – Orthodox against Catholic, nationalist against socialist. By 1940, the various factions managed to amalgamate to create the Ukrainian Canadian Committee, a loose coalition committed to the country's British institutions and the promotion of Ukrainian interests. Their collection of folk arts in the fifth-floor **museum** of the complex is an excellent introduction to their strongly maintained traditions, with delightful examples of embroidery, weaving, wood carving and the exquisite designs of *pysanky*, Easter egg painting.

## The Exchange District

Just to the north of Portage at Main, the **Exchange District** is a rough rectangle of old warehouses and commercial buildings whose effective centre is the **Market Square** at King, Bannantyne and Albert, with its weekend flea markets and buskers. This part of town was built during Winnipeg's boom, a period of frenzied real-estate speculation and construction that peaked in 1882, but lasted until the outbreak of World War I. The standard architectural design, used for most of the office blocks and nearly all the warehouses, was simple and symmetrical, the plain brick walls topped off by a decorative stone cornice, and there are dozens of examples of this basic model in the Exchange District. One or two companies financed extravagant variations, notably the **Electric Railway Chambers Building** at 213 Notre Dame Ave, an imaginative blend of Italian Renaissance and early twentieth-century motifs, its terracotta facade lined with a magnificent dazzle of 6000 electric lights.

## The Forks

South of Portage along Main Street rises the ponderous dome of **Union Station**, opposite the stone gate that's the sole remnant of **Upper Fort Garry**, a Hudson's Bay Company fort from 1837 to 1870 and thereafter the residence of Manitoba's lieutenant governors until 1883. The pointed dormers and turrets behind belong to the **Hotel Fort Garry**, a chateau-like structure built for the Grand Trunk Railroad in 1913.

Behind the station, the chunk of land bordering the Red River as it curves round to **The Forks** was, until recently, one of the country's largest railway yards. In the last couple of years it's been redeveloped as a leisure centre, incorporating a riverside walkway, a quay for boat trips, an outdoor amphitheatre, shops and restaurants in The Forks Market and a tidy parcel of riverbank set aside as the **The Forks National Historic Site**, with plaques celebrating the role of the fur traders and pioneers who first settled here.

## Portage Avenue and the Art Gallery

Lined by department stores and office blocks, downtown **Portage Avenue** is the city's main shopping street, equipped with a brand new mall called Portage Place. The web of enclosed walkways from the main entrance at Kennedy provide welcome relief from the summer heat and winter cold, but the architectural honours go to the splendid piered facade and delicate cornice of the **Paris Building** at 259 Portage, and the cream and bronze terracotta decoration of the **Boyd Building** at no. 388.

The uncompromisingly modern **Winnipeg Art Gallery**, 300 Memorial Blvd at Portage (mid-June to Aug Mon & Tues, Fri–Sun 10am–5pm; Wed & Thurs 10am–9pm; Sept to mid-June opens 11am, closed Mon; $3), owns the most comprehensive collection of Inuit art in the world and a reasonable assortment of modern European art, including work by Mirò, Chagall and Henry Moore. The problem is that little of either of these collections is on display at any one time – much of the available space is taken up by offices whilst the main display area, on the third floor, is given over to temporary and often dire exhibitions of modern Canadian art. The tiny mezzanine level is devoted to the Inuits, each temporary display developing a particular theme – from the symbolic significance of different animals to the role of women sculptors in the isolated communities.

## The Legislative Building, Osborne Village and Dalnavert

A few minutes' walk south of the Art Gallery, surrounded by trim lawns and flower borders, is the **Manitoba Legislative Building**, whose central pediment is decorated with splendidly pompous sculptures representing the ideals of Canadian nationhood. A half-kneeling figure, symbolising progress, beckons his lazy neighbour to come to the land of promise, whilst a muscular male figure, with a team of powerful horses, ideal-ises the pioneer spirit. High above, a central tower rises to a copper-green dome that's topped by the **Golden Boy**, a four-metre-high figure that's supposed to embody the spirit of enterprise and eternal youth. Inside (tours every 30min Mon–Fri 9am–7pm & Sat–Sun 9am–4pm; free), the marble columns and balconies of the foyer house two magnificent life-size buffalo bronzes by the French artist Charles Gardet, framing a staircase of brown-veined Carrara marble. Upstairs, the legislative chamber follows the inevitable model of Westminster's House of Commons.

Just behind the Legislative Building, across the Assiniboine, lies **Osborne Village**, the "bohemian" part of town, whose cheap bars, restaurants and music joints – strung along Osborne Street – are favourites with the city's students.

A couple of blocks east of the Legislative Building, **Dalnavert**, at 61 Carlton (guided tours June–Aug Tues–Thurs & Sat–Sun 10am–6pm; Sept–Dec & March–May same days noon–5pm; Jan & Feb Sat & Sun noon–5pm; $3), was the home of Hugh Macdonald, the son of Canada's first prime minister and, briefly, premier of Manitoba. Built in 1895, the house has been painstakingly restored, its simple red-brick exterior engulfed by a fanciful wooden verandah, the interior all heavy, dark-stained woods and strong deep colours. Macdonald's conservatism, reflected in the decor, was mellowed by a philanthropic disposition – he even reserved part of his basement for some of the city's destitute.

## St Boniface

The suburb of **St Boniface**, a ten-minute walk east of the downtown area just across the Red River, was a centre of early French-Canadian and Metis settlement. Founded by Catholic priests in 1818, it retains something of its distinctive character and even today, twenty years after its incorporation into the city of Winnipeg, roughly 25 percent of its population speaks French as a first language.

St Boniface's principal historic sites are situated beside the river, along Taché Avenue. Walking south from the Provencher Bridge, the massive white stone facade on the left is all that remains of **St Boniface Cathedral**, a huge neo-Romanesque structure that was largely destroyed by fire in 1968. Its replacement, just behind, was designed with an interior in the style of a giant tepee. In front, the cemetery contains the grave of **Louis Riel**, whose modest tombstone gives little indication of the furore surrounding his execution in Regina on November 16, 1885. Only after three weeks had passed did the authorities feel safe enough to move the body, which was then sent secretly by rail to St Boniface. The casket lay overnight in Riel's family home just south of town before its transfer to the cathedral, where a requiem mass was attended by most of the Metis population. That same evening, across the river, Riel's enemies burnt his effigy on a street corner, a symptom of a bitter divide that was to last well into this century.

Housed in an attractive whitewashed and green-shuttered building across from the cathedral, the **St Boniface Museum** (June–Aug Mon–Fri 9am–9pm, Sat 10am–5pm & Sun 10am–9pm; Sept–May daily 10am–5pm; donation), was built in 1846 as a convent for the Grey Nuns, a missionary order whose four-woman advance party had arrived by canoe from Montréal two years before. Subsequently, the building was adapted for use as a hospital, a school and an orphanage. Inside, a series of cosy rooms are devoted to the Red River Colony, notably an intriguing collection of Metis memorabilia that includes photographs of a fierce-looking Gabriel Dumont – Riel's commander in the battle of Batoche (see p.386) – and examples of the colourful sashes that were the most distinctive feature of Metis dress. There's also a lovely little chapel, whose papier-mâché Virgin was made from an old newspaper which one of the original Grey Nuns found outside Fort Garry when she walked across the frozen river to buy food.

## South of the centre: the Riel House

The **Riel House National Historic Site** (mid-May to Aug daily 10am–6pm; Sept Sat & Sun 10am–6pm; free) is at 330 River Road in the suburb of St Vital, about 10km south of the city centre, and is just about worth the trip – it can be reached by bus #16 from the Portage Place Mall. The main feature of the site is a tiny clapboard house that was built by the Riels in 1880 and stayed in their possession until 1968. Louis Riel never actually lived here, but this was where his body was brought after his execution and the house has been restored to its appearance at that time, complete with black-bordered photographs and a few artefacts left by his wife, Marguerite. Other period furnishings and fittings give a good idea of the life of a prosperous Metis family in the 1880s. The railroad had reached St Boniface in 1877 and this was a time when the simple products of the Red River could be supplemented by manufactured goods from the east with relative ease – the iron stove, the most obvious import, improved the quality of the Riels' life immeasurably. Costumed guides provide an enjoyable twenty-minute tour of the house and the garden, the sole remnant of the once sizeable Riel land holdings.

## West of the centre: Assiniboine Park and the Living Prairie Museum

Some 8km west of the city centre, to the south of Portage Avenue, a great chunk of land has been set aside as the **Assiniboine Park** (daily 9am–sunset; free; bus #66 from Broadway at Smith), whose wooded lawns attract hundreds of visitors every summer weekend. Its **zoo** (daily 10am–sunset; free) has over 1000 animals and a giant tropical conservatory, whilst the most developed part of the park has a full range of amenities from a miniature train to a formal garden and restaurants. Adjoining the park, the 700-acre nature reserve of **Assiniboine Forest** is home to deer, ruffled grouse and waterfowl.

A couple of kilometres further west, the **Living Prairie Museum** at 2795 Ness Avenue (May, June & Sept Sat & Sun noon–5pm; July & Aug daily 10am–6pm; free; bus #24 along Portage) is worth a brief visit, its twelve hectares of land forming the largest area of unploughed tall grass prairie in Manitoba. A small visitors' centre provides a wealth of background information on the indigenous plants, whose deep-root systems enable them to withstand both the extreme climate and prairie fires. There's a daily programme of half-hour guided walks, or you can pick up a brochure and stroll alone.

# Eating and drinking

Winnipeg boasts literally dozens of good and cheap places to **eat**, though many of them are long on quantity and short on finesse. The wide variety of ethnic restaurants are the exception, ranging from deluxe establishments serving exquisite French and Italian delicacies, through to Ukrainian and French-Canadian restaurant-bars that cater mainly for their own communities. In the more expensive places it's possible to pay upwards of $40 per person for a full dinner, but $10 per head is a reasonable average elsewhere. Many of Winnipeg's more staid **restaurants** and **restaurant-bars** are concentrated in and around the downtown shopping malls, but there's a cluster of more interesting places in **Osborne Village**, and several other good restaurants dotted around the edges of the centre. For **drinking**, most of the city's bars are grim and cheerless places and it's best to stick to the restaurant-bars.

## Restaurants and restaurant-bars

**Alycia's**, 559 Cathedral and McGregor. Situated about 4km north of the city centre, this long-established Ukrainian restaurant also serves as an informal social centre. The food is cheap and filling – reckon on about $12 for a three-course meal.

**Basil's**, 117 Osborne. One of Winnipeg's trendiest restaurants, complete with open-air dining area. Meals from about $13; superb cheesecake.

**Le Beaujolais**, 131 Provencher Blvd, St Boniface (☎237-6306). Winnipeg's premier French restaurant, with prices to match; reservations recommended.

**Bradbury's**, 121 Osborne. Lively restaurant-bar with good quality, varied menu; steaks from $13.

**Carlos & Murphy's**, 129 Osborne. Filling Mexican food, and a raucous and dingy bar.

**Centre Culturel Franco-Manitobain**, 340 Provencher at rue des Meurons, St Boniface. Has an attractive open-air restaurant featuring traditional French-Canadian food – try the meat pies (*tourtière*) and the bread pudding. Open lunch times only, with a complete meal costing around $15.

**Dimitri's**, 121 Osborne. Good Greek food at reasonable prices.

**Edohei**, 355 Ellice. Good Japanese meals from $14.

**Forks Market**, The Forks. A converted railway shed that incorporates a number of cheap and pleasant snack bars, including *Yudyta's* for Ukrainian and *Tavola Calda* for Italian food. Upstairs, the *Sandpiper* is an excellent and expensive French restaurant.

**Grand Garden**, 224 King. Cantonese specialities.

**Impressions Café**, 102 Sherbrooke and Westminster. A charming, off-beat neighbourhood bar 2km west of the centre, where you can settle down to read the paper, listen to good music and eat East European and Jewish specialities from as little as $5.

**India Curry House**, 595 Broadway. Excellent meat and vegetarian curries from $7.

**Kelekis**, 110 Main St between Aberdeen and Redwood. Popular Jewish deli-restaurant; quality sandwiches and soups from $7.

**The Marigold**, 245 King. Fine Chinese cuisine within the medium price range.

**Mr Greenjeans**, opposite the Holiday Inn at Donald and St Mary. A fashionable restaurant-bar with mammoth portions and an imaginative menu; meals from $7.

**Pasquale's**, 204 Osborne. Delightful, busy little place with well-prepared Italian dishes from $6.

**Salisbury House**, 212 Notre Dame. One of a chain specialising in simple inexpensive food.

# Nightlife and entertainment

Winnipeg tries hard to be the cultural centre of the Prairies, and generous sponsorship arrangements support a good range of **theatre**, **ballet**, **opera** and **orchestral music**. The city also has some lively **night spots**, featuring the best of local and Canadian **rock** and **jazz** talent. These venues are supplemented by an ambitious summer programme of open-air concerts, notably the week-long **International Jazz Festival** towards the end of June, and the **Winnipeg Folk Festival**, a four-day extravaganza held in the third week of July at Bird's Hill Provincial Park, roughly 40km north of town. For **listings** consult the weekend editions of the *Winnipeg Free Press* newspaper or the free newssheet *Interchange*, available throughout Osborne Village. The tourist office's free magazine *Where* also has listings, but their reports are never critical.

## Music venues and clubs

**Centre Culturel Franco-Manitobain**, 340 Provencher Blvd. Hosts weekly concerts by French-Canadian musicians.

**Jazz on the Rooftop**, Winnipeg Art Gallery, 300 Memorial Blvd. Frequent performances by some of Canada's better known jazz musicians.

**The Rorie Street Marble Club**, 65 Rorie St. One of the city's slicker nightclubs, with occasional live bands.

**Spectrum**, 176 Fort. Spotlights some of Canada's best, up-and-coming bands, like the Leslie Spit Treeo.

**Times Change**, 234 Main. Rough-and-ready jazz and blues place.

**Toad in the Hole**, 112 Osborne. Blues acts twice a week.

**The Tom Tom Club**, second floor, 108 Osborne. Showcases good local rock bands.

**The West End Cultural Centre**, 586 Ellice. Everything from jazz and folk through to reggae and salsa.

## Classical music, opera and ballet

Major performances by the **Winnipeg Symphony Orchestra** and the **Manitoba Opera Association** take place at the Centennial Concert Hall, 555 Main (☎949-3950); tickets for both start at $10. The **Royal Winnipeg Ballet**, 380 Graham at Edmonton (☎956-2792), has an international reputation and an extensive programme of traditional and contemporary ballets; tickets from $12, student discounts up to twenty percent.

## Cinema and theatre

Winnipeg's largest mainstream **cinema** is the *Cineplex-Odeon*, 234 Donald, while *Cinema 3*, 585 Ellice at Sherbrook, shows foreign and second-run films, and *Cinematheque*, 304-100 Arthur, concentrates on Canadian releases.

The city has a couple of professional **theatre** groups, principally the *Popular Theatre Alliance of Manitoba*, whose modern and imaginative plays are performed at the *Gas Station*, Osborne and River (☎284-2757). The *Warehouse Theatre*, 140 Rupert Ave (☎943-3222), also features local talent, though Winnipeg's main theatrical events are performed by international touring companies in the Centennial Concert Hall.

# Listings

**Airlines** *Air Canada*, Richardson Building concourse, 355 Portage (☎943-9361); *Canadian Airlines*, Scotia Bank concourse, 200 Portage (☎632-1250); *Air Manitoba*, Winnipeg airport (☎783-2333).

**Bike rental** At the youth hostel.

**Books** *Mary Scorer*, 389 Graham at Edmonton, is the city's best bookshop, with an excellent range of titles on the Canadian West. *The Global Village*, 736 Osborne, is a map and travel store with a comprehensive selection of specialised maps.

**Bus enquiries** *Greyhound* (☎783-8840); *Gray Line* (☎942-4500).

**Car rental** The following firms will collect customers at no extra charge: *Discount*, at the airport (☎775-2282); *Airways* (☎783-0031); and *Budget*, at the airport (☎783-2512) and downtown at Ellice and Sherbrook (☎786-5866).

**Festivals** Apart from the city's music festivals (see above), the biggest event is *Folklorama*, held during the middle two weeks of August. This celebrates Winnipeg's multi-ethnic population with over 40 pavilions spread out over town, each devoted to a particular ethnic group. St Boniface's French-Canadian heritage is honoured annually in the *Festival du Voyageur*, ten days of February fun, whose events lead up to a torchlit procession and the Governor's Ball, where everyone dresses up in period costume.

**Gay Winnipeg** *Gay and Lesbian Resource Centre*, 1-222 Osborne (☎284-5208).

**Hospital** The *Grace General Hospital*, 300 Booth; out-patient emergencies on ☎837-0157.

**Laundry** *Clean All*, 187 Isabel at Portage; *Zip Kleen*, 110 Sherbrook at Westminster.

**Left luggage** 24-hour coin-operated lockers at the rail and bus stations.

**Lost property** *VIA* baggage information on ☎949-7481; *Winnipeg Transit*, at the Portage and Main office (☎986-5054).

**Pharmacies** *Shoppers' Drug Market* at 297 Portage and Smith, and at 471 River Ave and Osborne, are open until 10pm.

**Outfitters** The *United Army and Navy Store*, 460 Portage Ave at Colony, sells a wide range of camping and wilderness equipment.

**Post office** The main office is at Smith and Graham.

**Sexual Assault Crisis Line** ☎786-8631.

**Taxis** *Unicity*, 340 Hargrave Place (☎947-6611); *Duffy's*, 871 Notre Dame (☎775-0101).

**Train enquiries** *VIA* ☎949-1830.

**Weather** ☎983-2050.

**Women's contacts** *Women's Resource Centre*, 100-290 Vaughan (☎943-0381).

# Around Winnipeg

As Winnipeg's dull and ugly suburbs fade into the seamless prairie landscape, the only major interruption is provided by the course of the **Red River** to the north. The sixty-kilometre stretch from the city to Lake Winnipeg – the Red River Corridor – was once a tiny part of the supply route which connected the Red River Colony to Hudson Bay, and nowadays it harbours the region's most absorbing tourist attractions, notably a couple of elegant nineteenth-century houses and the refurbished **Lower Fort Garry**. Ornithologists might want to make the trip to the **Oak Hammock Marsh Wildlife Area**, 40km north of Winnipeg, home to thousands of migrating birds, particularly snow and Canada geese between April and September. In the opposite direction, about 60km southeast of the city, the **Mennonite Heritage Village** is worth a peek for its pleasant reconstruction of a nineteenth-century pioneer settlement.

## The Red River Corridor

The trip along the Red River Corridor is easily the best day out from Winnipeg, a pleasing diversion along the gentle hills that frame the wide and sluggish river. Driving out from the city on Main Street, it's about 10km to the turning for the **River Road Heritage Parkway**, a rough twisting gravel track that leads to some of the Corridor's lesser attractions, or you can keep on the main road for **Selkirk** and **Lower Fort Garry**. The *Beaver* **bus** company run a regular service from Winnipeg to Lower Fort Garry and Selkirk, but there's no public transport along the Parkway and it's too rough a road to cycle. Alternatively, *Gray Line* organise summer **cruises** to the Fort, which leave from the dock near the Provencher Bridge on the edge of The Forks (June–Aug 5 weekly; $15.90); the boat takes about three hours to make what is frankly an extremely dull trip.

### The Heritage Parkway

Turning off the main road, down the **River Road Heritage Parkway**, it's a few minutes' drive to **Twin Oaks**, which was built in the 1850s as part of a girls' school, before curving round to **St Andrew's Rectory** (mid-May to Aug daily 10am–6pm; Sept Sat & Sun only; free), containing exhibits about the building and its early occupants, stern-looking Victorians determined to save the Metis from themselves. Just opposite, the tidy mid-Victorian **St Andrew's Church** has a number of benches still partly covered by buffalo hide, and stained glass windows brought here from England packed in barrels of molasses. A couple of minutes' drive further north, the pretty **Kennedy**

**House** (same times; free) was once the home of Captain William Kennedy, an English-speaking Metis who resigned his Hudson's Bay Company commission because of its increasing involvement with the debilitating liquor trade. The house's three main-floor rooms are furnished in the style of the 1870s, the gardens are a delight, and there's a twee little glassed-in tea room.

## Lower Fort Garry

A few minutes' drive further north, on Hwy 9 just 32km from Winnipeg, stands **Lower Fort Garry** (mid-May to Aug daily 10am–6pm; Sept Sat & Sun only; $3.25), built as the new headquarters of the Hudson's Bay Company in the 1830s. It was the brainchild of **George Simpson**, governor of the company's northern department, an area that was bounded by the Arctic and Pacific oceans, Hudson Bay and the Missouri Valley. Nicknamed the "Little Emperor" for his autocratic style, Simpson selected the site because it was downriver from the treacherous waters of the St Andrew's Rapids and was not prone to flooding, as Upper Fort Garry had been. However, the settlers round The Forks were reluctant to cart their produce down to the new camp and when the governors of Assiniboia refused to move here, his scheme collapsed. The new settlement became a minor provisioning depot and boat-building yard, until it was sold to the Mounties in 1871.

Sandwiched between Hwy 9 and the Red River, the **Lower Fort Garry Historic Site** begins at the Visitor Reception Centre, where there's a comprehensive account of the development of the fort and its role in the fur trade. A couple of minutes' walk away, the low limestone walls of the fort protect reconstructions of several company buildings, including the retail store, where a small museum is devoted to Inuit and Indian crafts. Several of the exhibits here are exquisite, particularly the decorated skin pouches and an extraordinary necklace fringed by thin strips of metal cut from a sardine can. Next door, the combined sales shop and clerk's quarters has a fur loft packed with pelts, whilst the middle of the compound is dominated by the Big House, built for Governor Simpson in 1832.

## Selkirk and Netley Creek Marsh

About 8km north of the fort, along Hwy 9, the township of **SELKIRK** was originally chosen as the point where the proposed transcontinental railroad was to cross the Red River. Realising the importance of the railway, the business leaders of Winnipeg – Selkirk's great trade rival – launched a campaign to have the route changed. Their efforts were successful, not least because one of the leading lights of the CPR syndicate, Donald Smith, was a key shareholder in the Hudson's Bay Company, which owned 500 acres of land around The Forks. Bypassed by the trains, Selkirk slipped into relative obscurity, though it did achieve a degree of prosperity through its shipyards.

Selkirk's only real attraction is the **Marine Museum of Manitoba** (mid-May to June daily 10am–4pm; July–Oct 10am–6pm; $3), situated on the edge of Selkirk Park at Eveline and Queen Street. The museum consists of five passenger and freight ships, dragged out of the water and parked on a lawn, plus a mildly interesting video on the history of Lake Winnipeg's shipping and fishing industries.

From the Marine Museum, County Road 320 continues north some 16km to the edge of **Netley Marsh**, a huge swampy delta formed by the Red River as it seeps into Lake Winnipeg. At the end of the road, there's a small **Recreation Park** with a snack bar, an observation tower and a series of plaques that detail the way of life of the area's native peoples. The marsh is an impenetrable maze for the inexperienced, but you can hire a boat and guide at the park for about $80 a day. On the lake side of the delta, the **Bird Refuge** is one of Canada's largest waterfowl nesting areas and there are lots of good fishing spots: the pickerel, or wall-eye, are delicious.

## Oak Hammock Marsh

The **Oak Hammock Marsh Wildlife Area** (daylight hours all year; no camping; free) is all that remains of the wetlands that once stretched from St Andrews, near the Red River, up to the village of Teulon, to the west of Netley Creek. Most of this wetland was drained and farmed around the turn of the century, but in the 1960s some of the area was restored to its original state and protected by a series of retaining dikes. In addition, a number of islands were built to provide marshland birds a safe place to nest.

To get there from Winnipeg take Hwy 7 north, turn east along Hwy 67, and follow the signs to the Main Mound Area, where there's an **information centre**, a picnic site and a couple of observation decks, all connected by a system of dikes. The best time to come is in spring or fall, when the grebes, coots and other residents are joined by thousands of migrating birds, from falcons through to Canada geese. Another part of the Wildlife Area has been returned to tall grass prairie, carpeted with the blooms of wildflowers like the purple Blazing Star and the speckled red Prairie Lily from mid-June to August.

## The Mennonite Heritage Village

A spruce reconstruction of a pioneer settlement of the late 1800s is to be found just 2km north of the township of STEINBACH, which is an hour's drive from Winnipeg along highways 1 and 12 (2 buses daily). In and around the main street of the **Mennonite Heritage Village** (June–Aug Mon–Sat 9am–7pm & Sun noon–7pm; May & Sept Mon–Sat 10am–5pm & Sun noon–5pm; $3) there's a church, a windmill and a couple of stores and farmhouses, but it's the general flavour of the place that appeals rather than any particular structure. The Mennonites, a Protestant sect, were founded in the Netherlands under the leadership of Menno Symons in the early sixteenth century. Subsequently the movement divided into two broad factions, with one group refusing to have anything to do with the secular state and sustaining a hostile attitude to private property, and the more "liberal" clans being inclined to compromise. Many of the former – the **Ammanites** – moved to the States and then Ontario, settling in and around Kitchener-Waterloo, while the more liberal **Untere** migrated to Russia and then Manitoba in the 1870s. Few of these Manitoba Mennonites, who congregated in and around Steinbach, wear the traditional black and white clothes or live on communal farms, but like all Mennonite communities they maintain a strong pacifist tradition. Costumed guides at the heritage village provide an intriguing account of their history, augmented by the displays in the tiny museum.

# AROUND MANITOBA

Most of Manitoba's significant attractions are concentrated in and around Winnipeg, and few of the province's smaller villages and towns are really worth a visit. The notable exception is remote **Churchill**, a weird and wild outpost on the shores of Hudson Bay that's a great place for seeing beluga whales and polar bears. Elsewhere, **Neepawa** and **Dauphin** are two of the more agreeable prairie towns, but almost all the other settlements are virtually indistinguishable, even though the European immigrants who cleared and settled Manitoba in the late nineteenth century came from a wide range of backgrounds. Most of them were rapidly and almost entirely assimilated, but the villages around **Dauphin** are still dominated by the onion domes of the Ukrainians' Orthodox churches, and **Gimli**, on the west side of Lake Winnipeg, has a pleasant museum tracing the history of its Icelandic settlement.

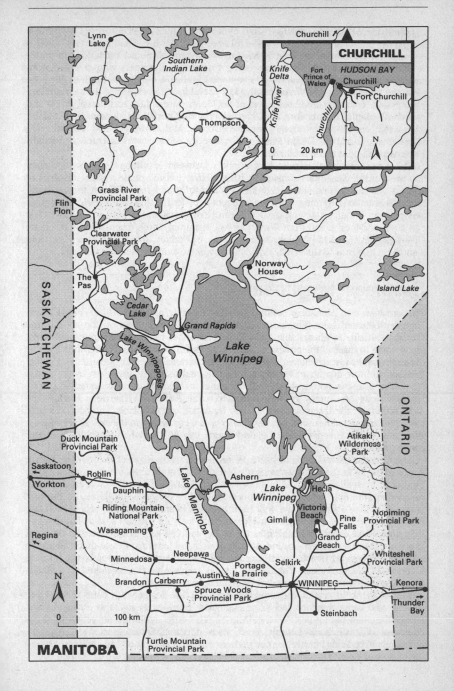

Lynn Lake

*Southern Indian Lake*

Thompson

Grass River Provincial Park

Flin Flon

Clearwater Provincial Park

The Pas

*Cedar Lake*

Grand Rapids

*Lake Winnipegosis*

*Lake Winnipeg*

Norway House

*Island Lake*

SASKATCHEWAN

ONTARIO

Duck Mountain Provincial Park

Atikaki Wilderness Park

Saskatoon

Yorkton

Roblin

Dauphin

Ashern

*Lake Manitoba*

*Lake Winnipeg*

Hecla

Riding Mountain National Park

Nopiming Provincial Park

Regina

Wasagaming

Gimli

Victoria Beach

Pine Falls

Minnedosa

Neepawa

Grand Beach

Whiteshell Provincial Park

Brandon

Carberry

Austin

Portage la Prairie

Selkirk

WINNIPEG

Kenora

Spruce Woods Provincial Park

Steinbach

Thunder Bay

N

0        100 km

**MANITOBA**

Turtle Mountain Provincial Park

**CHURCHILL**

Churchill

*HUDSON BAY*

Knife Delta

*Knife River*

Fort Prince of Wales

Churchill

Fort Churchill

*Churchill*

0        20 km

N

Otherwise, Manitoba is distinguished by its **parks**, thousands of acres of wilderness lake, river and forest that boast wonderful scenery, great hikes and hundreds of miles of canoe routes. One of the best is **Riding Mountain National Park**, 250km north-west of Winnipeg, which derives its name from the fur trappers who changed from canoe to horseback to travel across its wooded highlands. On the southern edge of the park, the tourist village of **Wasagaming** is a useful base for exploring the surrounding countryside, which incorporates areas of deciduous forest, lake and boreal forest and grassland. Manitoba's **provincial parks** include the dramatic landscapes and difficult whitewater canoe routes of the remote **Atikaki Wilderness Park**, the lakeside marshes and forests of **Hecla Park**, and yet more canoe routes in **Duck Mountain Park**, which is also noted for its fishing.

There are reasonably regular **bus** services between Manitoba's main settlements, and most of the village bus stops are within relatively comfortable walking distance of at least one hotel. However, nearly all of Manitoba's parks are difficult to reach and impossible to tour by bus, with the exception of Riding Mountain Park where the service from Winnipeg stops right in the centre of Wasagaming. *VIA rail* operates just two **train** services to and from Winnipeg, each running three times weekly: the main east–west line connects Winnipeg with Toronto, Saskatoon, Jasper and Vancouver, and a northern line runs to Churchill, via The Pas, well beyond the reach of the road.

# Southeast Manitoba

The great slice of Manitoban wilderness that extends north from the Trans-Canada Highway between Lake Winnipeg and the Ontario border is set on the rock of the Canadian Shield, an inhospitable and sparsely inhabited region of lake, river and forest that's home to three of the province's largest **parks**. To the south, **Whiteshell Park** is the oldest and most developed, with a relatively extensive road system, fifteen camp-grounds and one quarter of Manitoba's holiday and fishing lodges. Just to the north, **Nopiming Park** is more isolated, with a handful of lakeside campgrounds that can be reached along two bumpy gravel roads, whilst the **Atikaki Wilderness Park** is the most remote of the three, accessible only by canoe or float plane. The Atikaki's mile upon mile of rugged forest and granite outcrop are connected to the east shore of Lake Winnipeg by the Bloodvein and Leyond rivers, two of Manitoba's wildest whitewater canoe routes.

The Canadian Shield ends at **Lake Winnipeg**, a giant finger of water some 350km long that connects the Red River with the Nelson River and subsequently Hudson Bay to the north. It's a shallow lake, subject to violent squalls, and, apart from the odd Indian reservation, the only settlement has been around its southern rim. Here, on the east shore, Winnipeg's wealthy have built their cottages in and around **Victoria Beach** and **Hillside Beach**, but **Grand Beach Provincial Park** has the lake's finest bathing and long lines of sand dune stretching as far as the eye can see. The beaches of the west shore are poor by comparison, and the old fishing and farming villages that trail up the coast from Winnipeg Beach to Riverton are dull and dreary. Immediately to the north of Riverton, **Hecla Provincial Park** is slightly more agreeable, the developed resort facili-ties of *Gull Harbour* supplemented by unspoilt marsh and forest.

Known as the **Interlake**, the marginal farmland that lies between Lake Winnipeg to the east and lakes Manitoba and Winnipegosis to the west, is as flat as a pancake and one of the most boring parts of the Prairies. The only significant attraction is at the **Narcisse Wildlife Management Area**, 90km north of Winnipeg on Hwy 17, where thousands of red-sided garter snakes gather to mate in April and May, writhing around the bottom of a series of shallow pits in slithering heaps. It's not for the sqeamish.

From Winnipeg, there's a once-daily **bus** service to Rennie and West Hawk Lake in the Whiteshell; one or two buses daily to Lac du Bonnet, the nearest point to Nopiming Park; a once-daily service to *Doris's Grocery Store*, 2km from Grand Beach; and one bus daily to Gimli and Gull Harbour, on Hecla Island.

## Whiteshell Provincial Park

**Whiteshell Provincial Park** takes its name from the small, white seashell, the *megis*, that was sacred to the Ojibwa, who believed the Creator blew through the shell to breathe life into the first human being. These shells, left by the prehistoric lake that covered the entire region, were concentrated along the park's two main rivers, the **Whiteshell** to the south and the **Winnipeg** to the north, the latter an important part of the canoe route followed by the voyageurs of the North West Company on their way from Montréal to the Red River.

Most of the park's visitors head for **FALCON LAKE** and **WEST HAWK LAKE**, two well-developed tourist townships situated on either side of the Trans-Canada Highway, near the Ontario border. Crowded throughout the summer, neither site has much to recommend it, though both have a full range of facilities from serviced campgrounds, gas stations and grocery stores through to boat and water sports equipment rental. For day-trippers, there's a $3 entrance fee. On the south side of West Hawk Lake, the sixteen-kilometre loop of the **Hunt Lake Hiking Trail** passes through cedar and white pine forests, across sticky aromatic bogs and over rocky outcrops all in the space of about eight hours. There's a primitive campground on the trail at Little Indian Bay, but be sure to register at the West Hawk Lake park office if you're planning to stay overnight.

From West Hawk Lake, route 44 cuts north towards **CADDY LAKE**, where there are grocery stores, a couple of campgrounds and a sprinkling of holiday lodges. The lake is also the starting point for one of the area's most beautiful **canoe routes**, the 160-kilometre journey along the Whiteshell River to Lone Island Lake, in the centre of the park. Experienced walkers could tackle the 60-kilometre loop of the **Mantario Hiking Trail** just to the east of Caddy Lake, along Provincial Road 312; for beginners there are the **Bear Lake** (8km) and **McGillivray** (4km) **trails**, clearly signposted walks from Hwy 44 to the west of Caddy Lake; they reveal a good sample of the topography of the park – dry ridges dominated by jack pine, bogs crammed with black spruce, and two shallow lakes brown from algae and humic acid. Opposite the start of the Bear Lake Trail, the **Frances Lake** canoe route makes for a pleasant overnight excursion, a twenty-kilometre trip south to the Frances Lake campground with three portages past the rapids, and twelve hauls round beaver dams. It's the most popular canoe route in the park.

Further west, 32km from West Hawk, the village of **RENNIE** is home to the **park headquarters** (Mon–Fri 8.30am–4.30pm & July–Aug Sat–Sun 9am–4.30pm; ☎369-5232), which has a comprehensive range of information on local trails and canoe

---

### WILDERNESS TRIPS

The **Manitoba Naturalists' Society** run an excellent programme of Whiteshell Wilderness Adventures during July and August. Their trips last for five days, cost $200, and are based at a cabin on secluded Lake Mantario. They provide all the equipment and the services of fully experienced guides, who organise classes in canoeing and survival skills. Reservations are essential: write or ring the *Mantario Summer Programme*, 302-128 James Ave, Winnipeg (☎943-9029).

routes. The nearby **Alfred Hole Goose Sanctuary** is best visited in spring or fall when the Canada geese pass through on their migration. From Rennie, the eighty-kilometre stretch of route 307 passes most of the park's other campgrounds, lodges, trails and canoe routes. It's hard to distinguish between them, but the **Nutimik Lake** campground (May–Sept) has all the usual facilities and gives access to a section of the **Winnipeg River** canoe route, whose 820km connect Winnipeg with Kenora in Ontario.

## Nopiming Park

Separated from the Whiteshell by the Winnipeg River, **Nopiming Provincial Park** is a remote rocky area whose shoreline cliffs spread out above spruce bogs and tiny sandy beaches. The park's handful of campgrounds lie close to its two gravel roads: route 314, which meanders across the 80km of its western edge, and the far shorter route 315, a thirty-kilometre track that cuts east below Bird Lake to the Ontario border. Nopiming Park is crossed by the **Oiseau** and **Manigotagan** waterways, whose creeks and rivers trickle or rush from lake to lake, forming no less than 1200km of possible canoe route. Towards the south of the park, **BIRD LAKE** makes for a useful base, with a main settlement on the south shore that's equipped with a campground, a grocery store, the cabins of the *Nopiming Lodge* (☎884-2281), and motor-boat, canoe and guide hire.

## Atikaki Wilderness Park

Accessible by float plane from Winnipeg and Lac du Bonnet, the **Atikaki Wilderness Park** has half a dozen holiday and fishing lodges dotted across some of the finest Canadian Shield scenery in the province. There are no campgrounds or roads through the park, but the rough gravel track that makes up most of route 304 does reach Wallace Lake, at its southern tip, via the east shore of Lake Winnipeg or Nopiming Park's route 314. The Atikaki is criss-crossed by canoe routes that give glimpses of the region's ancient pictograph sites, but they all include difficult whitewater stretches that should only be attempted by experienced canoeists.

The park's more popular canoe routes include the dramatic journey down the **Bloodvein River** to Lake Winnipeg, its rapids, falls and wild twisting sections balanced by peaceful flows past quiet lakes and wild rice marshes, and the **Kautunigan Route**, a 500-kilometre excursion which starts at Wallace Lake and threads its way to the mouth of the Berens River on Lake Winnipeg, well to the north of the park. Both routes pass stands of white birch, black spruce, jack pine, elm, oak and maple, and you may catch sight of moose, timber wolves, coyotes and black bears.

Maps are available from the Manitoba Department of Natural Resources, 1007 Century St, Winnipeg, and trip plans should be filed with the Lac du Bonnet Natural Resource Office, Box 850, Lac du Bonnet (☎345-2231). As an alternative, several of the outfitters in Winnipeg and Lac du Bonnet organise guided excursions; for details enquire at the Manitoba Natural Resources Office, 258 Portage Ave, Winnipeg (☎945-4374).

## Lake Winnipeg

Approached along Hwy 59, the southeast shore of **Lake Winnipeg** has one major attraction, **Grand Beach Provincial Park**, whose long stretch of powdery white sand and grass-crowned dunes make it the region's most popular day-trip. The beach is divided into two distinct parts, separated by a narrow channel that drains out of a knobbly lagoon, set just behind the lake shore. The channel is spanned by a tiny footbridge, but the two parts of the beach are very different: to the west there are privately owned cottages, sports facilities, motor- and rowboat hire, grocery stores and a restaurant; the eastern section is less developed, although it does have a large **campground** (May–Sept; ☎754-2212) tucked away amongst the dunes. By the campground office, the **Ancient Beach Trail** follows the line of the prehistoric lake that dominated southern Manitoba in the last ice age; allow about an hour for the walk.

Roughly 20km north of Grand Beach, the twin townships of **HILLSIDE BEACH** and prettier **VICTORIA BEACH** have good sandy beaches, but their well-heeled inhabitants avoid catering for outsiders. There are no campgrounds and the only **motel**, the *Birchwood* (☎754-2596), is a crummy affair on the highway, 6km south of Victoria Beach.

## Gimli and Hecla Provincial Park

In 1875, some 2000 Icelanders moved to the southwestern shore of Lake Winnipeg, where they had secured exclusive rights to a block of land that stretched from today's Winnipeg Beach to Hecla Island. The next year the colonists were struck by a smallpox epidemic, yet they managed to survive and found the **Republic of New Iceland**, a large self-governing settlement with its own Icelandic-language school, churches and newspaper, supported by an economy that was based on farming and fishing. Their independence lasted just twenty years, for in 1897 they acquiesced in the federal government's decision to open their new homeland to other ethnic groups. An identifiable Icelandic community had ceased to exist by the 1920s, but their descendants still organise the *Islendingadagurinn* (Icelanders' Day) festival, a rather tacky affair of plastic Viking helmets and beauty competitions held in Gimli on the August long weekend.

There's precious little to attract visitors to this part of the lake, and the largest township, **GIMLI** (literally "paradise"), is only worth a brief visit for its **Historical Museum** (mid-May to June Wed–Sun 11am–5pm; July–Aug daily 11am–6pm; $1.50), which chronicles the history of New Iceland.

Roughly 100km to the north, **Hecla Provincial Park** consists of several islands that jut out into Lake Winnipeg, almost reaching the eastern shore. The park is approached along Hwy 8, which runs across a narrow causeway to the largest of the islands, **Hecla**, where the tourist township of **GULL HARBOUR** has a comprehensive range of facilities. Nearby, on the east side of the island, the original **Hecla Village** has a number of old houses dating from the early years of Icelandic settlement; a short heritage trail tours the highlights, or you can strike out on one of the island's hiking trails through forest and marsh.

For **accommodation**, the *Gull Harbour Resort* (☎475-2354) has doubles from $70 and there's a medium-size **campground** (May–Sept; ☎378-2945) on the neck of land between Gull Harbour and the lake.

# Southwest Manitoba

West of Winnipeg, the Trans-Canada Highway slices across the Prairies on its way to Regina, 600km away in Saskatchewan. Dotted with campgrounds and fast-food joints, the Trans-Canada follows the route of the original transcontinental railroad, passing a series of charmless towns that are at the heart of the province's most fertile farming region. **Brandon**, the province's second largest town, has a handful of Victorian mansions, and lies not too far from the **Spruce Woods Provincial Park**, a mixed area of forest and desert. Before you get to Brandon, however, immediately to the east of Portage la Prairie, the **Yellowhead Highway** cuts northwest from the Trans-Canada to form a more attractive route across the Prairies, passing through the pretty little village of **Neepawa** before running to the south of **Riding Mountain National Park**.

# The Trans-Canada and points south

The first major settlement west of Winnipeg, **PORTAGE LA PRAIRIE** is a food-processing centre with only one mildly interesting attraction, the **Fort la Reine Museum and Pioneer Village** (May to mid-Sept Mon–Fri 8am–6pm, Sat–Sun 10am–6pm; $1), located on the outskirts of town at the junction of highways 1A and 26. The original fort served as the headquarters of Pierre Gaultier de la Vérendrye during his explorations in the 1740s; the present complex depicts life in the nineteenth century, and includes a trading post, a log homestead, a trapper's cabin, a schoolhouse and a railway caboose.

Further west near AUSTIN, 3km south of the Trans-Canada on Hwy 34, the **Manitoba Agricultural Museum** (May to mid-Oct daily 10am–6pm; $2.50) has an exhaustive collection of early twentieth-century farm machinery, from gigantic steam tractors through to threshing machines and balers. The site also includes a **homesteaders' village**, which simulates village life of the early 1900s and has the province's largest collection of pioneer household articles. The immensely popular **Manitoba Threshermen's Reunion and Stampede** is held here every year, featuring all things "western" – four days of rodeo riding, threshing displays, plowing competitions, square dancing, jigging and a Fiddlers' Festival.

## Spruce Woods Provincial Park

In between Austin and Brandon, about 15km south of the Trans-Canada along Highway 5, **Spruce Woods Provincial Park** falls on either side of the Assiniboine River, whose confused loops twist slowly south and west. The park has a number of walking trails that begin beside or near the road. To the north, the **Epinette Creek Trails** run through woodland and marsh, the longest being the 25-kilometre Newfoundland Trail. There are a number of unserviced campgrounds along the various paths.

Roughly 5km south of the Epinette Creek Trails, the **Spirit Sands Trails** cross an area of mixed grass prairie before entering the shifting sand dunes and pots of quicksand that constitute Manitoba's only desert. These "Spirit Sands" were of great religious significance to the Ojibwa who, according to one of the earliest fur traders, Alexander Henry, told "of the strange noises heard in its bowels, and its nightly apparitions". If it's too hot to walk, try one of the horse-drawn wagon tours which leave from the start of the trail throughout the summer (mid-May to June Sat & Sun 1 daily; July & Aug 2–3 daily; $6; ☎827-2800).

A kilometre or so south of the start of the Spirit Sands, there's a full range of tourist facilities at **Kiche Manitou Lake**, including a large campground (May–Sept; ☎827-2458), a caravan park, grocery stores, restaurants, a beach, canoe and paddle-boat hire and a summer Visitor Services Centre.

## Brandon

In 1881, when the CPR decided to route the transcontinental railroad through Winnipeg, it was clear that they would need a refuelling depot in the western part of the province. The ideal location was on the east bank of the Assiniboine River, opposite today's **BRANDON**, 160km from Winnipeg, but a certain Dugald McVicar was already established here. The sudden arrival of all sorts of speculators encouraged McVicar to overreach himself, and he attempted to sell his farm and sod hut to the CPR for around $60,000 dollars, prompting a railway negotiator to exclaim "I'll be damned if a town of any kind is built here." It wasn't, and Brandon was founded 4km to the west. Nowadays, the town is a major agricultural centre, home to several research institutions, Manitoba's largest livestock show, and the professional rodeo competitions of the *Provincial Ex*, held in mid-June.

The Brandon tourist office on the Trans-Canada has a glossy brochure detailing an **Architectural Walking Tour** of the town, but the only buildings worth a second look are on the south side of Rosser Avenue between 9th and 10th streets. Here, an attractive terrace in the Romanesque Revival style includes the former *Mutter Grocery Store*, whose interior has been removed to the **Daly House Museum**, 122–18th St (daily 10am–noon & 1–4.30pm; $2), the restored home of Brandon's first mayor.

### Turtle Mountain Provincial Park

Situated some 90km south of Brandon along Hwy 10, **Turtle Mountain Park** is a mixed area of marsh and deciduous forest, whose 400 shallow lakes form an ideal habitat for the western painted turtle, after which the park takes its name. There's also a substantial moose population, most visible in late September. Turtle Mountain's main facilities are beside the main road at **Adam Lake**, where there's a large campground, a beach, a store, a park office (☎534-7204) and a number of walking trails. Nearby, the landscaped shrub and formal flower garden of the **International Peace Gardens** span the American border at the southeast corner of the park.

Alternatively, there's a smaller, prettier campground at **Max Lake** (May–Sept) on Provincial Road 446. This campground gives easy access to the **Oskar Lake Canoe Route**, a 19-kilometre paddle and portage excursion across ten of the park's lakes. Best in the spring or fall, the route should be tackled in an anti-clockwise direction to eliminate the need to climb steep hills, and can be completed in one or two days. There's an overnight cabin at James Lake – register at the Adam Lake park office if you intend to use it. There are no canoe-hire facilities in the park.

## The Yellowhead Highway and points north

Highway 16, one of central Canada's most appealing long-distance drives, is better known as the **Yellowhead Route** – taking its name from a light-haired Iroquois explorer and guide who was called *Tête Jaune* by the voyageurs. About 90km along the road from Portage la Prairie lies one of Manitoba's more agreeable townships, tiny **NEEPAWA**. The town's oldest buildings are spread along and around the tree-lined principal drag, Mountain Avenue – notably the cosy neo-Gothic **Knox Presbyterian Church** at Mill and First Avenue, and the tidy late Victorian **County Court House**, close to Mountain and Hamilton. Also in the centre, in the old CN station at the west end of Hamilton, the **Beautiful Plains Museum** (June–Sept daily 10am–4.30pm; $1) has fairly diverting displays on the life of the district's pioneers.

The Yellowhead Highway doubles as Neepawa's Main Street, marking the southern perimeter of the town centre. The **tourist office** (June–Aug daily 11am–7pm) is 1km east of Main at Mountain, with the **bus station** immediately to the west. For **accommodation**, there's a central riverside **campground** on Hamilton Street, the *Lions Riverbend Park* (May–Oct; from $7; ☎476-2317), and two convenient **hotels**, the down-at-heel *Hamilton* at Mountain and Mill (☎476-2368) and the rudimentary *Vivian Hotel*, 236 Hamilton at First (☎476-5089), both with doubles from around $35. Neepawa's **restaurants** are far from outstanding – try the *Bamboo Gardens* at 442 Mountain, where a full Chinese meal will set you back about $15.

### Riding Mountain National Park

Bisected by Hwy 10 on its way from Brandon to Dauphin, **Riding Mountain National Park** is a vast expanse of wilderness roughly 50km wide and 100km long that provides some of Manitoba's finest hiking trails and most beautiful scenery. Its eastern perimeter is formed by a 400-metre-high ridge studded with a dense evergreen forest of spruce, pine, balsam fir and tamarack. This soon gives way to a highland plateau whose mixed forests and lakes form the central, and most scenic, part of the park, bordered to the west by an area of aspen woodland, meadow and open grassland – the habitat of moose, elk and a carefully tended herd of buffalo.

The only settlement of any significance is the tacky tourist centre of **WASAGAMING**, beside the main highway on the southern edge of the park, adjoining Clear Lake. The village has campgrounds, hotels and restaurants, grocery stores, gas stations, and boat and canoe hire, but the narrow and scrawny beach is desperately overcrowded in July and August, whilst the lake is infested with a parasitic flatworm that can cause the painful skin irritation called "Swimmer's Itch".

Beside the beach, the park's **Visitor Information Centre** (mid-May to June daily 9am–6pm; July–Aug 9am–8pm; Sept to mid-Oct 9am–5pm; ☎848-2811) incorporates a collection of stuffed animals and environmental displays, and has a comprehensive range of maps and pamphlets, including the *Bugle*, a free broadsheet guide to the park's amenities. The staff here organise a programme of summer events that features frequent and free day-long **walks** and **hikes**; reservations are necessary for the more infrequent overnight excursions that take place from July to early September. The centre also issues **fishing permits** and free **backcountry permits**, which are compulsory for overnight stays in the bush. In the winter, when the centre is closed, the adjacent **Administration Office** (Mon–Fri 9am–5pm) provides a similar service.

Wasagaming lies at the centre of Riding Mountain's paved road and gravel track system, which gives ready access to its network of 32 **walking and hiking trails**, ranging from a half-hour walk through the woods to a strenuous 73-kilometre cross-country hike. Most of the trails that begin in or near Wasagaming are short and easy, the most testing one being the 18-kilometre **Grey Owl Trail** to Beaver Lodge Lake, where Grey Owl (see p.305) lived for six months in 1931. This trail connects with the nearest of the overnight routes, the **Cowan Lake Trail**, which branches off to pass through a region of dense forest, small lakes and meadows. All the overnight trails have primitive **campgrounds**.

### WASAGAMING PRACTICALITIES

Served by daily buses from Winnipeg, Brandon and Dauphin, Wasagaming's main **bus stop** is opposite the **tourist office** (June–Sept daily 9am–5pm), which provides a comprehensive list of **accommodation**. *The Mooswa*, Mooswa Drive (☎848-2533), has delightfully designed, modern chalets and motel rooms from $64, with bungalows from $57; basic bungalows and log cabins at *Johnson Cabins*, Ta-Wa-Pit Drive (☎848-2524), are just a bit cheaper. *Clear Lake Lodge*, at Ta-Wa-Pit Drive and Columbine (☎848-2345; doubles from $70), is a comfortable hotel, but if you want to save money, head for the *Manigaming Motel*, 137 Ta-Wa-Pit Drive (☎848-2459; doubles from $40). There's only one **campground** in the village, *Wasagaming Campground* (mid-May to mid-Sept; from $9.50).

Wasagaming's **restaurants** are poor, with the notable exception of the *Mooswa*, where a delicious fresh fish meal will set you back about $20. The best of the cheaper establishments is the mundane *Cinnamon Bun*, at the corner of Wasagaming and Buffalo Drive. The Petro Canada station opposite rents out **mountain bikes**, whilst **canoe** and **power-boat** rentals are available from the jetty on Clear Lake.

## Dauphin

Relatively pleasant **DAUPHIN**, founded as a fur-trading post by the French in 1739, is now a town of 9000 people that straggles across the flat prairie landscape just to the east of the Vermilion River. Its elongated **Main Street** features some good examples of early twentieth-century Canadian architecture, but there's only one real attraction, **The Fort Dauphin Museum** (May to mid-Sept daily 9am–5pm). This is a tidy wooden replica of a North West Company trading outpost, located by the river at the end of 4th Avenue SW, fifteen minutes' walk from Main Street. Inside the stockade, there are reconstructions of several sorts of pioneer building, including a trapper's cabin, a house, a school, a store and a church.

The fertile river valley that runs west of Dauphin towards Roblin was a centre of **Ukrainian** settlement between 1896 and 1925, and its village skylines are still dominated by the onion-domed spires of their Orthodox and Catholic churches. There's a modest collection of Ukrainian pioneer artefacts and traditional handicrafts in Dauphin at the **Selo Ukraina Office**, 119 Main St South (Mon–Fri 9am–5pm), but their main task is to organise the **National Ukrainian Festival**, which takes place on the first weekend of August at a purpose-built complex 12km south of Dauphin, just off Hwy 10 on the edge of Riding Mountain Park. The complex has a heritage village dedicated to the early Ukrainian settlers and a splendid amphitheatre, ideal for the festival's music and dance performances.

*PRACTICALITIES*

Dauphin's **bus station** is at Fourth Avenue NE and Main Street, a couple of minutes' walk from the town centre at Main and First Avenue NE, where the **Chamber of Commerce**, 107 Main St North (Mon–Fri 9am–noon), provides tourist information. There's also a **tourist bureau** (mid-May to Aug daily 8am–8pm) 2km away on the southern edge of town beside Hwy 10. For **accommodation**, the *Boulevard*, 22 Memorial Blvd (☎638-4410), the *Dauphin Inn*, 35 Memorial Blvd (☎638-4430), and the *Dauphin Community Inn*, 104 Main St N (☎638-4311), are seedy downtown **hotels** with doubles for around $30. The *Rodeway Inn* (☎638-5102), roughly 4km south of town near the junction of highways 5 and 10, has a pool, a sauna and more appealing doubles from $55. The **Vermilion Park Campground** (mid-May to mid-Sept; from $8; ☎638-3740) is ten minutes' walk north of Main Street at 21-2nd Ave NW. For **food**, try *Irving's Pizza*, 302 Main St South, or the *Grey Goose Restaurant*, 404 Main St North, though neither would win any gourmet prizes.

## Duck Mountain Provincial Park

**Duck Mountain Provincial Park**, some 100km northwest of Dauphin, is a large slice of the Manitoba Escarpment comprising several thousand acres of thickly wooded rolling hills, punctuated by meadows, bogs, streams and hundreds of tiny lakes. Most of the park is boreal forest, a mixture of white spruce, jack pine, balsam fir, aspen and birch, but many of its eastern slopes are covered by maple, bur oak and elm, which are usually found further south. The park is noted for its fishing, with pickerel, pike and trout in most of its lakes, and the delicious arctic char to the north.

Access to Duck Mountain Park is along two partly paved roads: **route 367**, which cuts across the middle from east to west, connecting Hwy 10 with Hwy 83, a distance of 80km; and **route 366**, which crosses from south to north, connecting the town of GRANDVIEW, on Hwy 5 just 45km west of Dauphin, with the village of MINITONAS, 130km away. Approached along route 366, the best part of the park is its southeast corner, where **Baldy Mountain** is the highest point in Manitoba, complete with an observation tower which provides good views over the forest. A few kilometres to the north, the twin **West** and **East Blue Lakes** are among the park's finest lakes, narrow curving strips of clear water fed by underground springs. Situated beside the road between the lakes is the **Blue Lakes Campground** (May–Oct; ☎542-3482), close to both the Blue Lakes Trail, a six-kilometre cross-country hike, and the Shining Stone Trail, a short path along the peninsula that juts out into West Blue Lake. The campground has a beach, a dock, a grocery store and a gas station; the camp office will advise on boat rental and fishing.

# Northern Manitoba

Running east from the northern end of Lake Winnipegosis and across through Grand Rapids, the 53rd parallel was Manitoba's boundary until 1912 when it was moved up to the 60th parallel on Hudson Bay. This tripled the size of the province and provided its inhabitants with new resources of timber, minerals and hydro-elecricity as well as a direct sea route to the Atlantic Ocean. Today's **northern Manitoba** is a vast and sparsely populated tract mostly set on the Canadian Shield, whose shallow soils support a gigantic coniferous forest broken up by a complex pattern of lakes and rivers. It's a hostile environment, the deep cold winter alternating with a brief, bright summer, when the first few inches of topsoil thaw out above the permafrost to create millions of stagnant pools of water, ideal conditions for mosquitoes and blackflies. There are compensations: out in the bush or along the shores of Hudson Bay, there is a sense of isolation, of desolate wilderness that's hard to find elsewhere, and a native wildlife that includes caribou, polar bear and all sorts of migratory birds.

Most of the region is inaccessible and its limited **highway** system was built to service the resource towns just to the north of lakes Winnipeg and Winnipegosis. One of these, the paper-and-pulp complex at **The Pas**, is served by buses from Dauphin and Winnipeg and provides a convenient base for the region's two main parks, **Clearwater Lake** and **Grass River**. Northern Manitoba's key tourist centre, however, is **Churchill**, a remote and windswept township on the southern shore of Hudson Bay where the main attractions are the **polar bears** that congregate along the Bay shore from July to early November. Churchill is well beyond the reach of Manitoba's highways, but it is connected to Winnipeg and The Pas by **train** along one of the longest railway lines in the world. The trip from Winnipeg takes 36 hours, but if you haven't the time, there are regular, reasonably priced excursion flights from Winnipeg.

## The Pas and around

Situated 400km north of Dauphin on Hwy 10, on the southern bank of the Saskatchewan River, **THE PAS** is a town with no specific sights, but it does host the **Northern Trappers' Festival** every February, four days of revelling that features competitions in a number of traditional pioneer skills, like tree felling, trap setting, ice fishing and muskrat skinning. The highlight is the World Championship Sled Dog Race, which features three daily races of 50km.

The town's **bus** and **train stations** are right in the centre, a few minutes' walk from the **Municipal Offices** (Mon–Fri 9am–5pm; ☎623-7256), at 1st St West and Fischer, which will provide basic tourist information. There's also a **tourist booth** (June–Aug daily 9am–5pm) about 1km south of town on Hwy 10, beside the tiny *Devon Park and Kinsmen Campground* (May–Sept; ☎623-2233) and close to three **motels**: the *Golden Arrow*, 1313 Gordon Ave (☎623-5451; doubles from $45); the *New Laverendrye*, 1326 Gordon Ave (☎623-3431; doubles from $50); and the *M&M*, on Hwy 10 (☎623-6447; doubles $45). Back in the centre, near the train station, the *Wescana Inn* at 439 Fischer Avenue (☎623-5446) has doubles from $50 and is a good place to **eat**. If you're after a wilderness excursion, **Clearwater Canoe Outfitters**, Box 3939 (☎624-5467), hire out a full range of equipment and organise canoe trips between here and Churchill.

### Clearwater Lake Provincial Park

Just 19km north of The Pas, the square-shaped lake and adjoining strip of coniferous forest that constitute **Clearwater Lake Park** are a favourite haunt of the region's anglers, who come here to catch northern pike, whitefish and highly prized lake trout. The park's amenities are concentrated along **route 287**, a turning off Hwy 10, which runs along the lake's southern shore past The Pas airport. Beside the road there are two summer **campgrounds** and a couple of **hunting lodges** that can be booked at the tourist office in The Pas.

## Grass River

A further thirty-minute drive north up Hwy 10 brings you to the channels and lakes of the **Grass River** water system, which were first charted in the 1770s by **Samuel Hearne**, an intrepid employee of the Hudson's Bay Company who became the first European to reach the Arctic Ocean by land. Hearne witnessed both the development of the Grass River's fur trade and the cataclysmic effects of the smallpox epidemic that followed. He estimated that about ninety percent of the local Chipewyan population was wiped out in the space of a decade, an indication of the scale of a tragedy whose results were compounded by other European diseases, particularly whooping cough and measles. On this and other matters, Hearne was an acute observer of Indian culture and customs. His *Journey to the Northern Ocean* records, for example, the comments of his Chipewyan guide concerning the importance of women:

"'Women,' added he, 'were made for labour; one of them can carry, or haul, as much as two men can do. They also pitch our tents, make and mend our clothing, keep us warm at night; and, in fact, there is no such thing as travelling any considerable distance in this country without their assistance. Women' he said again, 'though they do everything, are maintained at trifling expense; for as they always stand to cook, the very licking of their fingers, in scarce times, is sufficient for their subsistence.'"

### GRASS RIVER PROVINCIAL PARK

**Grass River Provincial Park** is made up of several thousand acres of evergreen forest, lake and river interspersed by the granite outcrops of the Canadian Shield. It's noted for its **canoe routes**, the most popular of which runs 180km from the Cranberry Lakes, on the park's western perimeter, to its eastern boundary, where the southern tip of Tramping Lake is located near Hwy 39. It's an excursion of about ten days – all of the route's portages are short and fairly easy and there are lots of basic campgrounds on the way.

At the start of the canoe route, the first of the three Cranberry Lakes is situated close to **CRANBERRY PORTAGE**, a straggling township on Hwy 10, which runs along the western edge of the park. The settlement has its own park **information kiosk**, a small **campground** (mid-May to Sept; ☎472-3219), a simple **hotel**, the *Northern Inn* on Portage Road (☎472-3231; doubles from $20), and a handful of holiday **lodges** along its lakeshore – like the *Viking Lodge* (☎472-3337) and the *Caribou Lodge* (☎472-3351). Most of the lodges have boat and canoe rentals, and can arrange guided wilderness trips.

There are other access points to Grass River Park along **Highway 39**, which runs along its southern boundary. This 100-kilometre stretch of road passes three small summer **campgrounds** – *Gyles* (24km east of Hwy 10), *Iskwasum* (40km) and *Reed Lake* (56km) – where park entry points lead to circular canoe trips that can be accomplished within one day.

## Flin Flon

At the northern end of Hwy 10, about 60km from Cranberry Portage, the mining township of **FLIN FLON** gouges copper, gold, lead and zinc from a massive seam that was discovered in 1914. An ugly blotch on a barren rocky landscape, the town takes its name from the hero of an obscure novel entitled *The Sunless City*, which one of the first prospectors was reading at the time of the discovery – in the book, Josiah Flintabbatey Flonatin builds a submarine and enters the bowels of the earth, where he discovers everything is made of gold. The nearest you'll come to his trip is on the free guided tours of the town's **Hudson Bay Mining and Smelting Plant** (June–Aug Mon, Wed & Fri 8.30am; reservations ☎687-2385). There's also a **Miner's Museum** (May to mid-Sept daily 10am–6pm; $1), with a collection of picks and shovels, an old ore car and a dilapidated tractor.

The town's **bus station** is right in the centre at 63 3rd Avenue. About 1km to the east, along Hwy 10A, the **tourist office** (May–Aug daily 9am–5pm; ☎687-4560) adjoins the main **campground** (May–Sept; ☎687-4518). There are five **hotels**, including two cheap and central places on Main Street: the *Royal*, at no. 93 (☎687-3437; doubles at $45), and the *Flin Flon*, at no. 140 (☎687-7534; doubles at $50). For simple, basic **food**, try *Mary's Place*, 111 Main St.

# Churchill

Sitting on the east bank of the Churchill River where it empties into Hudson Bay, **CHURCHILL** has the neglected appearance of nearly all the settlements of the far north, its ill-kempt open spaces littered with the houses of its mixed Inuit, Cree and white population. These grim buildings are heavily fortified against the biting cold of winter and the insects of the summer – ample justification for a local T-shirt featuring a giant mosquito above the inscription "I gave blood in Churchill". That said, the town has long attracted a rough-edged assortment of people with a taste for the wilderness, and nowadays tourists flock here for the wildlife – a lifeline now that Churchill's grain-handling facilities are under-used.

In 1682, the Hudson's Bay Company established a fur-trading post at **York Factory**, a marshy peninsula some 200km southeast of today's Churchill. The move was dictated by the fact that the direct sea route here from England was roughly 1500km shorter than the old route via the St Lawrence, while the Hayes and Nelson rivers gave access to the region's greatest waterways. Within a few years, a regular cycle of trade had been established, with the company's Cree and Assiniboine go-betweens heading south in the autumn to hunt and trade for skins, and returning in the spring laden with pelts they could exchange for the company's manufactured goods. Throughout the eighteenth century, before the English assumed control of all facets of the trade and laid off their native intermediaries, both sides seem to have benefitted economically, and the reports of the company's traders are sprinkled with bursts of irritation at the bargains forced on them by the natives. The company was always keen to increase its trade and it soon expanded its operations to **Churchill**, building the first of a series of forts here in 1717.

In the nineteenth century the development of faster trade routes through Minneapolis brought decline, and by the 1870s both York Factory and Churchill had become remote and unimportant. Then the development of agriculture on the Prairies brought a reprieve. Many of the politicians and grain farmers of this new west were determined to break the trading monopoly of Sault Ste Marie and campaigned for the construction of a new port facility on Hudson Bay, connected by rail to the south through Winnipeg. In the 1920s the Canadian National Railway agreed to build the line, finally reaching Churchill in April 1929. Unfortunately, despite all the effort of the railway workers in the teeth of the ferocious climate, the port has never been very successful, largely because the Bay is ice-free for only about three months a year.

## The town

On the northern side of town, the unprepossessing Bayport Plaza is a good place to start a visit as it incorporates the **Canada Parks Visitor Centre** (June–Aug daily noon–4pm & 5–9pm; Sept to mid-Nov daily 8am–noon & 5–9pm; mid-Nov to May Mon–Fri 8am–noon & 1–5pm; free), where displays on the history of the fur trade and the Hudson's Bay Company are jazzed up by films dealing with arctic wildlife, Fort Prince of Wales and the construction of the railway. Opposite the plaza, the purpose-built **Town Centre Complex** offers a good view over Hudson Bay and an assortment of recreational facilities, including a curling rink, a bowling alley and a cinema.

Just down the road, the **Eskimo Museum** (June–Aug Mon 1–5pm, Tues–Sat 9am– noon & 1–5pm; Sept–May Mon & Sat 1–5pm, Tues–Fri 10.30am–noon & 1–5pm; free) houses the Inuit collection of the Oblate Fathers of Mary Immaculate, whose mission- ary work began around here at the turn of the century. The museum's one large room is dominated by two animal-hide canoes and several stuffed arctic animals, with Inuit art arranged in cases round the walls. It's a fine range of material, from caribou antler pictographs and highly stylised soapstone figurines through to walrus tooth scrim- shaws and detailed ivory and stone carvings. The sculptures fall into two distinct periods. Up until the 1940s, the artistic work of the local Inuit was essentially limited to the carving of figurines in walrus ivory, modelled on traditional designs. However, in 1949 a Canadian painter by the name of James Houston travelled the east coast of the Bay, encouraging the Inuit to vary their designs and experiment with different materi- als – which led, in particular, to the development of larger and more naturalistic sculp- tures carved in soapstone.

One corner of the museum functions as a **gift shop**. A five-minute walk away, *Northern Images*, on Kelsey Blvd, sells similar work at higher prices – but its profits go back to the producers.

### CAPE MERRY AND FORT PRINCE OF WALES

A couple of minutes' walk from the town centre, Churchill's grain elevators and silos stand at the base of a narrow peninsula that sticks out into the mouth of the Churchill River. At the tip, approached along a gravel track, **Cape Merry National Historic Site** (free tours June–Aug daily 8am–noon & 5–9pm) has the remains of an eighteenth- century gun emplacement and a cairn commemorating the Danish explorer Jens Munck, who led an expedition that was forced to winter here in 1619; most of the crew died from cold and hunger.

On the other side of the estuary, **Fort Prince of Wales National Historic Site** (July–Aug free tours daily, times dependent on tides – ask at the visitor centre) is a partly restored eighteenth-century stone fortress that was built to protect the trading interests of the Hudson's Bay Company from the French. Finished in 1771, this massive structure took forty years to complete, but even then it proved far from impregnable. When a squadron of the French fleet appeared in the bay in 1782 the fort's governor, Samuel Hearne, was forced to surrender without firing a shot because he didn't have enough men to form a garrison. The French spiked the cannon and undermined the walls, and after this fiasco the company never bothered to repair the damage. The fort is only accessible as part of a guided tour of the Churchill River or by water taxi. *Churchill Wilderness Encounter* (☎675-2248) organises both, with excursions costing $20, taxis around $10.

### EAST OF THE CENTRE: THE BAY SHORE ROAD

**East of town**, a rough road runs behind the shoreline past a series of rather eccentric attractions. Near the airport, the **polar bear "prison"** is a large hangar-like compound where dangerous bears are kept until they can be released safely. The problem is that some of the beasts wander into town in search of food and, although most can be scared off quite easily, a handful return. These more persistent specimens are shot with tranquillizers and transported to the compound. It's a necessary precaution, as polar bears can run and swim faster than humans and there are occasional horror

## CHURCHILL WILDLIFE AND SPECIALIST AGENCIES

Churchill occupies a transitional zone where the stunted trees of the taiga (sub-arctic coniferous forests) meet the mosses of the tundra. Blanketed with snow in the winter and covered by thousands of bogs and lakes in the summer, this terrain is completely flat until it reaches the sloping banks of the Churchill River and the ridge around Hudson Bay, whose grey boulders have been rubbed smooth by the action of the ice, wind and water. This environment has splendid **wildlife**, including Churchill's premier attraction, the **polar bears** who come ashore when the ice melts on the bay in late June and congregate near town waiting for the freeze. In the middle of June, as the ice breaks on the Churchill River, the spreading patch of open water also attracts schools of **beluga whales**, who stay till the end of August, joining the **seals**, who arrive in late March. The area around town is also on one of the major migration routes for **birds** heading north or nesting here from late April to June and returning south in August or early September. A couple of hundred species are involved, including gulls, terns, loons, Lapland Longspurs, ducks and geese. Available throughout town and at the Eskimo Museum, the *Birders' Guide to Churchill* by Bonnie Chartier lists them all for $7. Finally, Churchill is a great place to see the **Aurora Borealis**, whose swirling curtains of blue, green and white are common between September and April, best from January to March.

Several local companies organise **wildlife tours**, the cheapest run by *Churchill Wilderness Encounter* (☎675-2729 in summer; otherwise ☎604/336-8414), whose blue and white bus meets the train. Their programme includes four-hour **tundra tours** in June and July for $35 per person, which concentrate on local flora and fauna; **beluga whale and Fort Prince of Wales** boat trips during the same months for $15; afternoon **nature tours** from July to September that comprise a drive through the taiga and a walk in the Akudlik Marsh for $35; **polar bear** tours from mid-October to early November for $40; and **bird-watching** trips from May to mid-July, $35. Based in the Bayport Plaza, *North Star Tours* (☎675-2629) operate a similar package of excursions along with **iceberg trips** in the middle of June and **Churchill River nature tours** in July and August, both for $38. They also have various **Tundra Buggy Trips** from June to September, from a half-day excursion for $60 to an overnight trip including meals and lodge accommodation for $244. The cumbersome vehicles protect tourists from wandering bears and are designed to avoid damaging the delicate tundra. *Sea North Tours*, 39 Franklin St (☎675-2195), specialise in sea trips, including iceberg tours in June, whale trips in July and August and deep-sea diving throughout the summer. *Dymond Lake Air Services* (☎675-2583) run expensive air tours out across the Bay from May to November.

stories. In the last one, the owner of a fire-damaged house returned to empty his freezer, whereupon a bear trapped and killed him.

A few kilometres further east, clearly visible from the shoreline, there's the wreck of the **Ithaca**, a coal-fired steamer that came aground in 1961. The shipwreck was the subject of considerable speculation as the crew were never found and the vessel was supposed to be worth a fraction of its insurance value. Nearby, the **Rocket Range** finally closed in 1987 after thirty odd years of quasi-military research that included firing barium missiles into the Northern Lights to track their movements.

### Practicalities

Churchill can only be reached by **plane** or **train**, with *VIA rail* running a service three times weekly from Winnipeg (from $300 return), and *Canadian Airlines* operating a weekday service ($666 return – half-price with two weeks' advance booking). The town's **airport** is 7km from the centre, and each flight attracts the minibuses of the main tour operators, who will provide onward transportation for about $5. Alternatively, there's one **taxi** firm, *J&S*, at 7 Selkirk St (☎675-2345), who charge about $10 for the same service. The **train station** is right in the town centre, a few yards from the Visitor Information Bureau (June–Aug daily 9am–5pm; ☎675-2022) and a five-minute walk from the Bayport Plaza, where there's a Canada Parks **Visitor Centre** (April–May & mid-Nov to March Mon–Fri 8am–noon & 1–5pm; June–Aug daily noon–4pm & 5–9pm; Sept to mid-Nov daily 8am–noon & 5–9pm). Both these offices provide the full range of tourist information, including town plans and accommodation listings.

There are no campgrounds or hostels in Churchill, so visitors are dependent on the town's **hotels**, which are so uniformly drab it's hard to see why they vary in price. All are within easy walking distance of the train station, and all should be booked in advance no matter what the time of year. The full list is as follows: *Arctic Inn*, Kelsey Blvd (☎675-8204; $70); *Kelsey Lodge*, Kelsey Blvd (☎675-8801; $60); *Beluga Motel*, The Flats (☎675-2150; $60); *Polar Motel*, Franklin St (☎675-8878; $70); the overpriced *Tundra Inn*, Franklin St (675-8831; $80); and the ugly new *Seaport Hotel*, Munck St (☎675-8807; $70).

Churchill's handful of **restaurants** leave a lot to be desired, with the exception of the expensive *Trader's Table*, on Kelsey Blvd, where you can try the local speciality, arctic char, for $20. The best alternative is the snack bar in the *Town Centre Complex*, with burgers from $5.

## York Factory

The remote **York Factory National Historic Site** (roughly June to mid-Sept Mon–Fri 8am–noon & 1–5pm, depending on river conditions), lies some 200km southeast of Churchill, at the mouth of the Hayes and Nelson rivers. This was the central store-house of the northwestern fur trade throughout the eighteenth century, its wooden palisades the temporary home of soldiers and explorers, travellers and traders, and settlers bound for the Red River Colony. With the amalgamation of the North West and Hudson's Bay companies in 1821, it was here that the new governor, **George Simpson**, set about the delicate task of reconciling the feuds stirred by a generation of inter-company rivalry. In October he arranged his first formal joint banquet, seventy three traders facing each other across two long and narrow tables. It was, according to a contemporary, "dollars to doughnuts [whether it would be] a feed or fight", but Simpson's diplomatic skills triumphed, leading to a successful reorganisation of trading operations. In its heyday, there were some fifty buildings within the stockade, including a guesthouse, fur stores, trading rooms, living quarters and shops, but they were all destroyed in the 1930s, with the exception of the **main warehouse**, a sturdy wooden building that serves as a reminder of the fort's earlier importance.

This remote spot can only be reached by **charter flight** from the town of GILLAM, a hydro-electric centre on the rail line between Winnipeg and Churchill, or by **canoe** along the Hayes River from NORWAY HOUSE – an extremely difficult journey of 600km, which should not be undertaken without advice from the Manitoba Parks Department, 258 Portage Ave, Winnipeg (☎945-4374).

## The Seal River

The wild rivers that drain into Hudson Bay constitute some of the most challenging **canoe routes** in Canada, their long stretches of whitewater demanding considerable planning, experience and skill. One of the more popular is the **Seal River**, whose principal canoe route begins at the tiny Chipewyan village of TADOULE, and then passes through regions of boreal forest and tundra before emptying into Hudson Bay, just 45km west of Churchill. There's float plane transportation to the start of the canoe route and from the mouth of the river at the end, which can take between two and four weeks to reach. For details, contact *Dymond Lake Outfitters*, 23 Selkirk, Churchill (☎675-2583).

# SASKATCHEWAN

"You'd marry anyone to get out of Moose Jaw, Saskatchewan", Susan Sarandon tells Burt Lancaster in Louis Malle's film *Atlantic City*, and the whole province is regarded with similar disdain by many Canadians. It's certainly not one of the country's glamour regions, remaining as dependent on agriculture as it was when the province was established in 1905. It produces 42 percent of Canada's wheat, 39 percent of its canola, 35 percent of its rye and 20 percent of its barley, but even so, its one million people still live in one of Canada's poorest provinces, with an unemployment rate stuck in the region of twenty percent. Saskatchewan's farmers often struggle to make ends meet when international prices fall, and consequently they have formed various **Wheat Pools**, which attempt to control freight charges and sell the grain at the best possible time. The political spin-off has been the evolution of a strong socialist tradition, built on the farmers' mistrust of the market. For many years Saskatchewan was a stronghold of the **Cooperative Commonwealth Federation**, the forerunner of the NDP, and in 1944 the CCF formed the country's first leftist provincial government, pushing through bills to set up state-run medical and social security schemes.

However underprivileged Saskatchewan might be, its image as a featureless zone is grossly unfair. Even the dreariest part of the province, to the south of the Yellowhead Highway, has some splendid diversions, notably **Regina**'s intriguing Royal Canadian Mounted Police Museum, and the coulees and buttes of the **Grasslands National Park**. On the Yellowhead itself, **Saskatoon**, Saskatchewan's largest city, has an attractive riverside setting and boasts good restaurants, plus a brand-new complex devoted to the culture of the Northern Plains Indians. Further west, **Battleford** has a splendidly restored Mountie stockade, while to the north **Batoche National Historic Park**, occupying a fine location beside the South Saskatchewan River, commemorates the Metis rebellion of 1885. Not far away from Batoche, **Prince Albert National Park** marks the geographical centre of the province, where the aspen parkland of the south meets the boreal forests and lakes of the north. There are some wonderful walks and canoe routes here, even though the park's tourist village, **Waskesiu Lake**, is rather tacky. North of Prince Albert Park, the desolate wilderness of the Canadian Shield is mostly inaccessible except by float plane; the main exception is the town of **La Ronge**, which is on the edge of the canoe routes and good fishing waters of **Lac La Ronge Provincial Park** and the **Churchill River**. By comparison, the area bordering eastern Alberta has little to offer, though the desultory prairie landscape that makes up its south and centre does incorporate some of the hills, forests and ravines of the **Cypress Hills Inter-Provincial Park**.

The region's **public transport** system is limited, but there are regular scheduled **bus** services between most of the major towns and a useful, once-daily summertime bus from the town of Prince Albert to Waskesiu Lake, in Prince Albert Park, and La Ronge.

---

The Saskatchewan telephone code is ☎306.

---

# Regina

The capital city of Saskatchewan, **REGINA**, is the commercial and administrative centre of one of the more densely populated parts of central Canada, its services anchoring a vast network of agricultural villages and towns. Yet despite its capital status, brash shopping malls and population of 180,000, Regina acts and feels like a small prairie town. It's a comfortable if unremarkable place to spend a couple of days, with the offbeat attraction of the Royal Canadian Mounted Police museum, and the opportunity to explore some of southern Saskatchewan's less familiar destinations – like the Big Muddy Badlands and the Grasslands National Park.

### A brief history of Regina

In 1881, the Indian commissioner **Edward Dewdney** became lieutenant governor of the North-West Territories, a vast tract of land that spread west from Ontario as far as the Arctic and Pacific oceans. Almost immediately, he decided to move his capital south from the established community of Battleford to **Pile O'Bones**, an inconsequential dot on the map that took its name from the heaps of bleached buffalo bones left along its creek by generations of native hunters. The reason for Dewdney's decision was the routing of the Canadian Pacific transcontinental railroad across the southern plains: he renamed the capital **Regina** after Queen Victoria, and petitioned for it to be expanded on land to the north of the creek, a plot coincidentally owned by Dewdney. The site was terrible: the sluggish creek provided a poor water supply, the clay soil was muddy in wet weather and intolerably dusty in the summer, and there was no timber for building. Accordingly the railway board refused to oblige, and the end result was farcical: Government House and the Mounted Police barracks were built where Dewdney wanted them, but the train station was a three-kilometre trek to the south.

In 1905 Regina became the capital of the newly created province of **Saskatchewan**, and settlers flocked here from the States and central Europe. At the heart of an expanding wheat-growing district, the city tripled its population in the 1910s. It also overcame its natural disadvantages by an ambitious programme of tree-planting, which provided shade and controlled the dust, and by damming the creek to provide a better source of water. However, the city's success was based on the fragile prosperity of a one-crop economy, and throughout this century, boom has alternated with bust.

## Arrival, information and transport

Regina **airport** is about 5km west of the centre; there's a **limo** service into town for around $5 per person and the taxi trip costs roughly $10. A ten-minute walk east of the airport, *Regina Transit*'s **bus** #4 leaves for the city centre from the junction of Regina Avenue and Pasqua Street every half-hour from Monday to Saturday between 6am and midnight; it runs hourly on Sunday from 2 to 8pm. The **bus station** is downtown at 2041 Hamilton Street, just south of Victoria Avenue; the train station is defunct.

The **Saskatchewan Tourist Office** (Mon–Fri 8am–7pm & Sat 10am–4pm; ☎787-2300), in the *Ramada Renaissance* hotel downtown at 1919 Saskatchewan Drive and Hamilton, has a comprehensive range of leaflets and booklets on Regina and the province as a whole. In addition, *Tourism Regina* operates a **tourist bureau** east of town on Hwy 1 (May–Aug daily 8am–7pm; Sept–April Mon–Fri 8.30am–4.30pm; ☎789-5099).

The best way to see the centre is on **foot**, though the area around McIntyre and Saskatchewan Drive and sections of Osler Street are run-down neighbourhoods that are best avoided. Similarly accessible is the **Wascana Centre**, a large multi-purpose park and recreational area, whose northern boundary is a few minutes' stroll south of the centre. For longer journeys within the city, **Regina Transit** runs bus services with a standard single fare of $1.25 (exact fare payable to driver), or $10 for a book of ten (available at the tourist office).

## Accommodation

Central Regina has a reasonable range of moderately priced and convenient **hotels**, as well as an excellent **youth hostel**. There's rarely any difficulty in finding a room, but most of the very cheapest places listed by the tourist office are effectively flophouses,

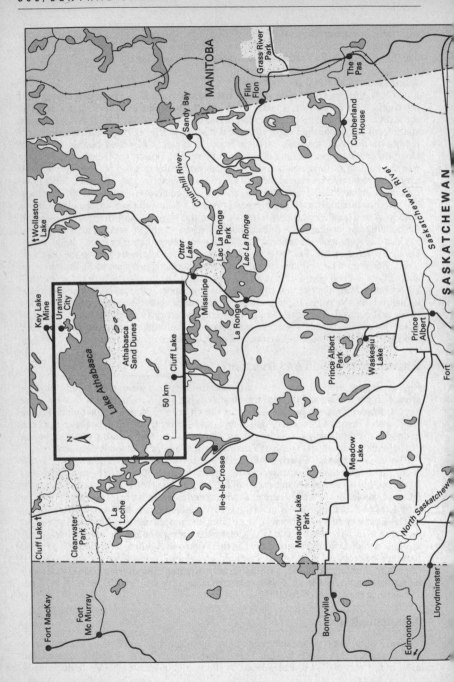

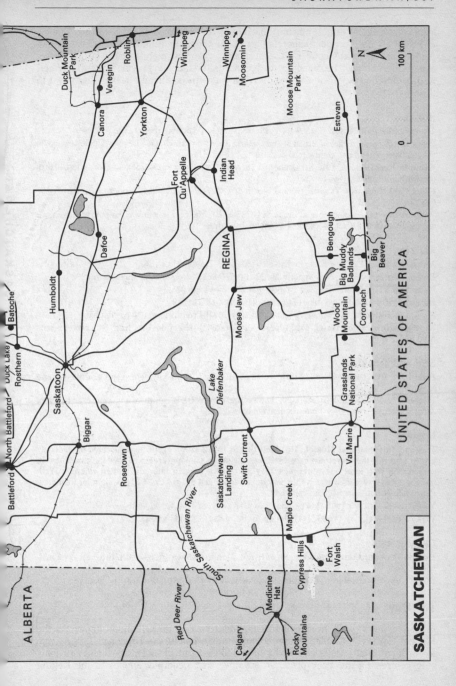

SASKATCHEWAN

grim and cheerless establishments inhabited by the town's poor and desperate. There's a cluster of cheap, standard **motels** east of the town centre along Highway 1, which doubles as Victoria Avenue East, and another group of motels south of the centre, along Albert Street. The remaining budget accommodation is provided by two tiny **bed and breakfast** places and the two main **campgrounds** situated beside Highway 1 to the east of the city centre.

## Hotels

**Chelton Inn**, 1907 11th Ave (☎569-4600). Pleasant and large double rooms from $60.

**Delta Inn Regina**, corner of Broad St and Victoria Ave (☎569-1666). Good, basic doubles from $75; substantial weekend and commercial discounts.

**Ramada Renaissance**, 1919 Saskatchewan Drive at Hamilton (☎525-5255). Regina's most luxurious, with doubles from $65 to $200.

**Hotel Saskatchewan**, Victoria Ave and Scarth St (☎522-7691). Standard modern rooms from $55 to $100.

**Victoria Inn**, 1717 Victoria Ave at Broad St (☎757-0663). The best downtown bargain, with comfortable doubles from $40 and occasional weekend discounts.

## Motels

**Journey's End**, 3221 East Eastgate Drive (☎789-5522). Doubles from $42.

**Regina Super 8 Motel**, 2730 Victoria Ave East (☎789-8833). Comfortable doubles from $39.

**Relax Inn**, 1110 Victoria Ave East (☎565-0455). Doubles from $35.

**Imperial 400 Motel**, 4255 Albert St (☎584-8800). Doubles at $49.

**Regina Travelodge**, 4177 Albert St South (☎586-3443). 164 rooms from $50 per double.

**Sandman Inn Motor Hotel**, 4025 Albert St (☎586-2663). Hotel doubles from $45, motel rooms from $35.

## Bed and breakfast

**B and J's**, 2066 Ottawa St (☎522-4575). Situated just north of the city centre and near the general hospital; doubles $25.

**Eileen's**, 2943 Grant Rd (☎586-1408). The second-choice B&B, south of the centre and east of Albert Street, near the Hwy 1 intersection; doubles $25.

## Hostels

**Turgeon International Hostel**, 2310 McIntyre St (☎522-4200). IYHF hostel located immediately to the south of the downtown core. Facilities include a cooking area and washing machines. In conjunction with local bus companies, they also run a bargain bus fare system whereby IYHF members can travel anywhere within Saskatchewan for just $11 return. $10 per night for members. Reservations 7am–10am & 5pm–midnight.

**YMCA**, 2400 13th Ave (☎757-9622). Rooms for $17 a day, $72 per week.

**YWCA**, 1940 McIntyre (☎525-2141). Rooms for $27 a day, $105 per week.

## Campgrounds

**Buffalo Lookout Campground**, south of Hwy 1, 5km from town (☎789-4110). From $8; open mid-May to Sept.

**Kings' Acre Campground**, 1km east of town on Hwy 1 (☎522-1619). From $9; open all year.

# The City

Fifteen minutes' walk from end to end, Regina's downtown core is known as the **Market Square**, a simple gridiron bounded by Saskatchewan Drive and 13th Avenue to north and south, Osler and Albert streets to east and west. This business and shopping centre is a mundane place, an adjective that generally applies to the **Regina**

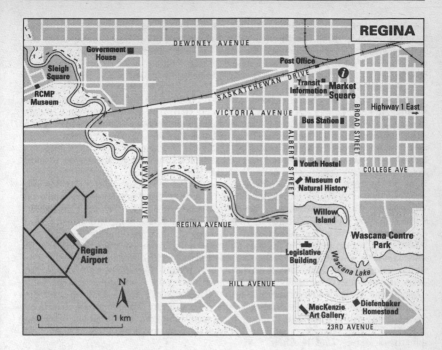

**REGINA**

DEWDNEY AVENUE

Government House

Post Office

Sleigh Square

Transit Information

Market Square

RCMP Museum

SASKATCHEWAN DRIVE

VICTORIA AVENUE

Highway 1 East

Bus Station

BROAD STREET

LEWVAN DRIVE

ALBERT STREET

Youth Hostel

COLLEGE AVE

Museum of Natural History

Willow Island

REGINA AVENUE

Wascana Centre Park

Regina Airport

Legislative Building

Wascana Lake

N

HILL AVENUE

MacKenzie Art Gallery

Diefenbaker Homestead

0        1 km

23RD AVENUE

**Plains Museum** (May–Oct Mon–Fri 11.30am–5pm & Sat–Sun 1–5pm; Nov–April Wed–Fri 11.30am–5pm & Sat–Sun 1–5pm; $2), on the fourth floor of the mall at 1801 Scarth and 11th Avenue – its modest displays on the city's history are less diverting than the stories of the elderly volunteers who staff the museum.

## Wascana Centre Park
Roughly eight times the size of the Market Square, Regina's most distinctive feature is **Wascana Centre Park**, which begins three blocks south of 13th Avenue and extends southeast to the city limits, following the curves of **Wascana Lake**, which was created as part of a work project for the unemployed in the 1930s. The city's main recreation area, the park is equipped with a bandstand, barbecue pits, snack bars, boating facilities, and waterfowl ponds, but for the most part it's a dreary combination of murky water and bare lawn.

In the northwest corner of the park, near College and Albert Street, the **Museum of Natural History** (daily May–Aug 9am–8.30pm; Sept–April 9am–4.30pm; free) is devoted to the province's geology and wildlife, starring a giant animated dinosaur called *Megamunch*. Most of the wildlife dioramas were recently destroyed by fire, and restoration work will last until 1993. A couple of minutes' walk to the east, the swimming pool (June–Aug daily noon–8pm) has bikes for rent, and close by there's a ferry boat to **Willow Island** (mid-May to Aug Mon, Thurs & Fri noon–4pm), a favourite picnic spot.

On the other side of the lake, accessible from Albert Street, is the grand **Legislative Building** (free tours every half-hour, May–Sept 8am–9pm & Sept–May 8am–5pm), a self-confident structure of Manitoba limestone with an impressive domed tower at its centre. Guided tours take in the oak-and-marble panelled Legislative Chamber and six small art galleries, the best of which houses Edmund Morris's portraits of local Indian leaders, presented to the province in 1911. A neighbouring corridor is occupied by the paintings of the **Native Heritage Foundation**, some thirty canvases featuring the work of contemporary Metis and native artists, notably Allen Sapp from North Battleford, who has won some international acclaim for his softly coloured studies of life on Saskatchewan's Indian reserves as he remembers them from the 1930s.

A few minutes' walk south of the Legislative Building, just off Albert Street at 23rd Avenue, the **Mackenzie Art Gallery** (daily 11am–6pm, Wed & Thurs till 10pm; free) is devoted to temporary exhibitions by modern Canadian artists. It's also the stage for the city's principal theatrical event, **The Trial of Louis Riel** (Aug Thurs, Fri & Sat 7.30pm; $9), whose text is based on the transcripts of the trial in Regina in September, 1885. No other single event in Canada's past has aroused such controversy: at the time, most of English-speaking Canada was determined he should hang as a rebel, whereas his French-Canadian defenders saw him as a patriot and champion of a just cause. Though Riel was subject to visions and delusions, the court rejected the defence of insanity on the grounds that he knew what he was doing. As he exclaimed – "No one can say that the North West was not suffering last year . . . but what I have done, and risked, rested certainly on the conviction [that I was] called upon to do something for my country." The jury found him guilty, but the execution was delayed while prime minister John A Macdonald weighed the consequences; in the end, he decided against clemency.

The **Diefenbaker Homestead** (mid-May to Aug daily 10am–7pm; free), about 1km east of the gallery but still within the park, was the boyhood home of John Diefenbaker, Conservative prime minister of Canada from 1957 to 1963. Moved from the township of Borden, Saskatchewan, in 1967, the tiny wooden house has been decked out with original and contemporary furnishings and memorabilia reflecting both Diefenbaker's homespun philosophies and the immense self-confidence that earnt him the nickname "Dief the Chief".

## The Royal Canadian Mounted Police Barracks

All Mounties do their basic training at the **Royal Canadian Mounted Police Barracks**, some 4km west of the city centre, accessible by bus #6 from 11th Avenue at Cornwall Street. Beside the main parade ground, Sleigh Square – site of the closely choreographed Sergeant Major's parade (Mon–Fri 1pm) and Sunset Retreat Ceremony (July to mid-Aug Tues 6.45pm) – the RCMP **Museum** (daily June to mid-Sept 8am–8.45pm; mid-Sept to June 8am–4.45pm; free) traces the history of the force from early contacts with the Plains Indians and Metis, through to its present role as an intelligence-gathering organisation.

Near the entrance hangs one of the prime exhibits, the splendid painted buffalo skin of the Blood Indian **Crop-eared Wolf**, its starkly simple hieroglyphics representing the achievements of its warrior owner. For once, the caption provides a thorough explanation, describing the importance of "coup counting" in Plains Indian culture, whereby an act of "bravery" such as slashing an enemy's tent or hitting him with a stick was as important as drawing blood. Nearby, a series of contemporary quotations illustrate the **Long March** that first brought the Mounties to the west from Ontario in 1874. Their destination was Fort Whoop-up, near today's Lethbridge, Alberta, where they intended to expel the American whiskey traders. However, by the time they arrived they were in a state of complete exhaustion, and it was fortunate that the Americans had already decamped. Another small section deals with **Sitting Bull**, who crossed into Canada after his victory at the Battle of the Little Big Horn in 1876. Fearing reprisals from the furious American army, Sitting Bull spent four years in and around the Cypress Hills, where he developed a friendship with Police Inspector James Walsh. A picture of the chief and his braves, taken at Fort Walsh in 1877, shows an audience of curious Mounties in their pith helmets.

## THE MOUNTIES

The heroes of a hundred adventure stories, from *Boys' Own* yarns to more eccentric epics like the movie *Canadian Mounties versus the Atomic Invaders*, the **Mounties** have been the continent's most charismatic good guys ever since Inspector James Morrow Walsh rode into Chief Sitting Bull's Canadian encampment to lay down the law. Coming straight after the Sioux's victory at the battle of the Little Big Horn in 1876, this was an act of extraordinary daring, and it secured the future of the Mounties. The **North West Mounted Police**, as the Mounties were originally called, had been created in Ottawa during the autumn of 1873, simply in order to restore law and order to the "Whoop-up Country" of southern Saskatchewan and Alberta in the aftermath of the Cypress Hills Massacre. There was no long-term strategy: the force's areas of responsibility were undecided, and even their uniforms had been slung together from a surplus supply of British army tunics that happened to be handy. However, they did a brilliant job of controlling the whiskey traders who had created pandemonium through the unscrupulous sale of liquor to the Plains Indians, and it was soon clear – after Walsh's dealings with Sitting Bull – that they were to become a permanent institution.

The Mounties came to perform a vital role in administering the west on behalf of the federal government, acting both as law enforcement officers and as justices of the peace. From the 1880s their patrols diligently criss-crossed the territory, their influence reinforced by a knowledge of local conditions that was accumulated in the exercise of a great range of duties – from delivering the mail to providing crop reports. Despite this level of autonomy, the Mounties saw themselves as an integral, if remote, part of the British Empire, their actions and decisions sanctioned by the weight of its authority. In this sense, they despised the individualism of the American sheriff and marshall, for the Mounties expected obedience because of the dignity of their office, not because their speed with a firearm.

The officer corps, most of whom were recruited from the social elite of the eastern provinces, became respected for an even-handedness that extended, remarkably for the period, to their dealings with the Plains Indians. **Crowfoot**, the Blackfoot leader, was even moved to remark, "If the police had not come to the country, where would we all be now? They have protected us as the feathers of a bird protect it from the frosts of winter." Yet the officers' class prejudices had a less positive influence on their approach to law and order – socially disruptive crimes of violence were their main priority, whereas prostitution and drunkenness were regarded as predictable and inevitable nuisances that were confined to the "lower orders". They had a cohesive view of the society they wanted to create, a Waspish patriarchy where everyone knew their place.

After 1920, when the force lost its exclusively western mandate to become the **Royal Canadian Mounted Police**, this conservative undertow became more problematic. Time and again the RCMP supported reactionary politicians who used them to break strikes – like prime minister Bennett in Saskatchewan in 1933 and 1934, and Joey Smallwood in Newfoundland during 1959 – and they have often been accused of bias in their dealings with the Québécois. That said, although the Mounties are seen by some as a bastion of reaction at odds with multi-cultural definitions of Canada, for the most part they remain a potent symbol of nationality. And for Labatts' brewery, the endorsement of Malcolm the Mountie is a sure-fire way to sell beer.

## Government House

**Government House**, a couple of kilometres west of the city centre at 4607 Dewdney and Lewvan (guided tours every half-hour Tues–Fri 1–4pm & Sun 1–5pm, plus July & Aug Sat 1–4pm; free; bus #1), was the residence of the lieutenant governors of the North-West Territories and subsequently Saskatchewan from 1891 to 1945. A stolid yellow-brick building, it has been delightfully restored to its appearance at the end of the last century, with a chain of offices and reception areas downstairs and a splendid, balconied staircase leading up to the first-floor bedrooms. The men's smoke room comes decorated with an enormous bison head and a lemon-water stand, where the governor and his cronies would dip their fingers to hide the smell of the cigars. There are also a couple of mementoes of one of the more eccentric governors, Amédée Forget, whose specially designed "salesman's chair", beside the entrance, was meant to be uncomfortable, with protruding gargoyles sticking into the visitor's spine, legs shorter at the front than the back and a flesh-pinching crack cut across the middle of the seat. The rocking horse in the office was for Forget's pet monkey. High tea, complete with finger sandwiches and fragile china cups, is served in the ballroom at the weekend.

## Eating and drinking

Regina has a clutch of good downtown **restaurants**, lively places whose prices are usually very reasonable – reckon on about $12 for a full meal. However, many of them close early and don't open at all on Sundays; in emergencies try the big hotels whose standard-issue snack bars are nearly always open daily till 9.30pm. The city's **nightlife** is hardly inspiring, but the university students provide a little stimulation for the couple of downtown clubs, whilst local roustabouts and government workers alike tend to stick to country and western. As a general rule, avoid the downtown **bars**, which are really not very pleasant.

### Restaurants

**Alfredo's**, 1801 Scarth St at 11th Ave. Specialises in homemade pasta dishes; a tasty and imaginative menu from $9.

**Bartleby's**, 1920 Broad St at 12th. Wide-ranging menu with steaks, burgers and seafood from around $8; karaoke from 9pm.

**The Copper Kettle**, 1953 Scarth St at 11th Ave. Basic pizzas and Greek dishes from $7.

**The Keg**, Hamilton and 8th Ave. Good chicken and seafood dishes from $10.

**Lang's**, 1745 Broad St. Filling, very cheap Vietnamese food; noodle dishes from $5.

**Mieka's**, 1810 Smith St. Nouvelle cuisine, pasta and seafood from $15 – but it's a 2-km walk north of the centre.

**The Sergeant Major's**, 1764 Broad St between 11th and Saskatchewan Drive. Buffalo steaks from $10 in an interior littered with Mounties' bric-a-brac.

**Trifon's**, Victoria and Broad. Standard salads and good vegetarian pizzas from $7.

### Discos and venues

**The Manhattan**, 2300 Dewdney Ave. Disco with a chaotic mixture of music.

**The Original California Club**, in the mall attached to the Regina Inn at 1975 Broad St at Victoria. Student favourite, with mostly New-Wave music.

**The Pump**, 641 Victoria Ave East. Country and western venue.

## Listings

**Airlines** *Canadian*, 2002 Victoria Ave (☎569-2307); *Air Canada*, 2015 12th Ave (☎525-4711).

**Airport** Enquiries ☎565-0081.

**Bike rental** *Youth Unlimited*, beside the Wascana Park pool (June–Aug daily noon–6pm; ☎525-8494); *Western Cycle*, 1745 Hamilton St (☎522-5678).

**Books** Both *Canada Book* and *Sutherland Books*, at 1861 and 1821 Scarth St, off 11th Ave, have a good range of titles. The *Book Cellar*, 1km north of the centre in the shopping mall at 1230 Broad St and 7th, has a superb collection of antiquarian Canadian texts, with a special emphasis on the early explorers of the Prairies.

**Buses** *Regina transit*, at 2124 11th Ave (☎777-RIDE). The city bus station, 2041 Hamilton St, just south of Victoria, has *Greyhound* (☎787-3340) for long-distance services, and two provincial carriers, *Moose Mountain Lines* (☎721-6707) and the *Saskatchewan Transportation Company* (☎787-3340).

**Car rental** *Avis*, 2010 Victoria Ave (☎757-1653); *Dollar Rent-a-Car*, 1975 Broad St (☎525-1377); *National*, 3476 Saskatchewan Drive (☎522-3696).

**Festivals** *Buffalo Days* is a week-long festival held at the end of July and the start of August; it begins with the "Pile O' Bones" picnic in Wascana Park on a Sunday, followed by several days of craft and livestock exhibitions and music shows that culminate in a firework display. The *Big Valley Jamboree*, held in Craven, a 20-minute drive north of town, is a four-day country and western shindig in the middle of July.

**Hospital** Regina general hospital, 1400 14th Ave (☎359-4444).

**Laundry** *Cathedral Laundromat*, 2911 13th Ave (☎525-2665); *Coin Laundry*, Broad St at 14th (☎352-3908).

**Left luggage** Coin-operated lockers at the bus station.

**Post office** Main office at 2200 Saskatchewan Drive, opposite the Cornwall shopping centre.

**Taxis** *Capital Cab*, 2730 Dewdney Ave (☎522-6621); *Regina Cabs*, 3405 Saskatchewan Drive (☎543-3333).

**Womens' contacts** Regina Women's Community and Counselling Centre, 306-2505 11th Ave (☎522-2777).

# Northeast of Regina

The slow-moving **Qu'Appelle River** flows 350km from Lake Diefenbaker – 160km west of Regina – to the border with Manitoba, its lush, deep and wide valley a welcome break from the Prairies. Punctuated by a series of narrow lakes and home to half a dozen modest provincial parks, this is one of the province's more popular holiday areas.

## Fort Qu'Appelle

The river's most pleasant township is **FORT QU'APPELLE**, which sits beside Hwy 10 an hour's drive northeast of Regina, its centre sandwiched between the road and the grooved escarpments of the neighbouring lakes. Roughly ten minutes' walk from end to end, its leafy gridiron streets fall on either side of Broadway, the main drag, whose attractively restored red-brick **Hudson's Bay Company store** dates from 1897. Nearby, at the top end of Bay Avenue, the **museum** (mid-May to Aug daily 10am–noon & 1–5pm; $2) has a small display on the area's European pioneers and is joined to the Hudson's Bay Company trading post of 1864. Three blocks to the south, the stone **obelisk** at Fifth Street and Company commemorates the signing of Treaty Number 4 between the Ojibwa, Cree and Assiniboine of the southern prairies and Lieutenant-Governor Morris in 1874. It was a fractious process. The Ojibwa insisted that the Hudson's Bay Company had stolen "the earth, trees, grass, stones, all that we see with our eyes", hectoring Morris to the point where he finally snapped. He confined the more militant Indian leaders to their tents, an authoritarian manoeuvre that undermined the unity of the Indians, who then signed the treaty in return for various land grants, pensions and equipment.

Near Fort Qu'Appelle, the river bulges into a chain of little lakes known collectively as the **Fishing Lakes**. It's possible to drive alongside all of them, but the pick of the bunch is the nearest, **Echo Lake**, which affords pleasant views over the river valley.

An early-morning bus makes the seventy-kilometre journey each day from Regina to Fort Qu'Appelle, where there are three **motels**. The most central is the modern *Country Squire Motel* (☎332-5603), beside Hwy 10 at the bottom end of Bay, where doubles start at $35. On the north side of town, beside the lake and near the golf course, the *Valley Park* **campground** (☎332-4614) has an unimaginative setting and sites from $8. There are several **restaurants** on Broadway, including Chinese meals at the *Jade Palace*.

## Yorkton

Beyond Fort Qu'Appelle, the only town of any note on Hwy 10 before you hit Dauphin (see p.356) is **YORKTON**, which was founded as an agricultural community in the 1880s. The silver-painted dome of **St Mary's Ukrainian Catholic Church** is the town's most distinctive feature, and the Ukrainian community features strongly in Yorkton's branch of the **Western Development Museum** (mid-May to mid-Sept daily 9am–6pm; $3.50), devoted to the various ethnic groups who have settled in the region. It's unlikely you'll want to stay here, but there are several reasonably priced, central **hotels**, including the *Holiday Inn*, 100 Broadway East (☎783-9781; doubles from $45); the *Imperial 400 Motel*, 207 Broadway East (☎783-6581; doubles from $40); and the basic *Yorkton City Limits Inn*, off Broadway at 8 Betts Ave (☎782-2435; doubles from $22).

## Veregin

An hour's drive northeast of Yorkton, the tiny town of **VEREGIN** is named after Peter Verigin, the leader of the pacifist Doukhobor sect whose 7000 members migrated to Saskatchewan at the end of the last century. The town is home to the **National Doukhobor Heritage Village** (mid-May to mid-Sept daily 10am–6pm; mid-Sept to mid-May Mon–Fri 9am–5pm; $2), where a modest museum traces the history of the sect and a refurbished two-storey prayer home contains the living quarters of their leader, complete with many original furnishings. Most of the other buildings have been moved here from Doukhobor colonies in other parts of the province, including a blacksmith's shop, a granary, a bakery and a bathhouse, equipped with dried oak leaves that were used to cleanse the skin. Another, smaller prayer home features a Russian library and a display on Tolstoy, whose financial support helped them to migrate.

### THE DOUKHOBORS

The first **Doukhobors** developed their dissenting beliefs within the Russian Orthodox Church during the eighteenth century, rejecting both the concept of a mediatory priesthood and the church's formal hierarchy. Later they established an independent sect, but their pacifist and proto-communist views made them unpopular with the tsars, who subjected them to periodic persecution. In the 1890s they fled Russia for Saskatchewan under the leadership of **Peter Verigin**, a keen advocate of communal labour and the collective ownership of property, Verigin maintained his authority until 1907, when the Canadian government insisted that all Doukhobor homesteads be registered as private property. The colonists were divided, with over one-third accepting the government's proposals despite the bitter opposition of the collectivists, who showed their contempt for worldly possessions by destroying their belongings; some even burnt their clothes and organised Canada's first nude demonstrations. Irretrievably divided, Verigin and his supporters left for British Columbia, but the rest stayed behind to create a prosperous, pacifist and Russian-speaking community, which remained separate and distinct until the 1940s.

# Southern Saskatchewan

The 600-kilometre drive across southern Saskatchewan on the **Trans-Canada Highway** is crushingly boring, and apart from Regina the only town worth a look is **Moose Jaw**, once a prohibition hang-out of American gangsters. Otherwise the rest of southern Saskatchewan is mostly undulating farmland, broken up by a handful of lakes and rivers, stretches of arid semi-desert and the odd range of wooded hills. In the southeast corner of the province, the lakes, hillocks and aspen, birch and poplar forests of **Moose Mountain Provincial Park** come complete with campgrounds, nature trails and a resort village. Further west, just south of Regina and near the US border, it's possible to drive across the **Big Muddy Badlands**, but these weathered buttes and conical hills are best explored on the tours that leave the tiny town of **Coronach** throughout the summer. Directly west of here, the **Grasslands National Park** is still being developed and extended, two separate slices of prairie punctuated by coulees and buttes that add a rare touch of drama to the landscape. Some 200km further, straddling the Alberta border, **Cypress Hills Inter-Provincial Park** is also well worth a visit, its heavily forested hills and ridges harbouring a restored Mountie outpost, **Fort Walsh**. Apart from the daily bus services along the Trans-Canada, the region's **public transport** system is abysmal; to see the parks, you'll need a car.

## Moose Mountain Provincial Park

**Moose Mountain Provincial Park**, just 60km south of the Trans-Canada on route 9, 230km from Regina, is a rough rectangle of wooded hill and lake whose main resort, **KENOSEE LAKE**, is packed with holidaymakers throughout the season. There's a full range of amenities here, including restaurants, bars, sports facilities and canoe rental, but it's still easy enough to escape the crowds and wander off into the surrounding woods. For **accommodation**, the *Kenosee Gardens* (☎577-2211), on the lakefront, has motel rooms and cabins from $40 per double, and there are also a number of **campgrounds** spread out around the lake. The *Fish Creek* and *Lynwood* campgrounds have the advantage of being right on the western edge of the developed area, a good 2km from the busiest part of the park.

A short-lived experiment in transplanting English social customs to the Prairies is the subject of the **Cannington Manor Provincial Historic Park** (mid-May to Aug daily 10am–6pm; free), a partly rebuilt Victorian village about 30km east of Kenosee Lake. Founded in 1882 by Edward Pierce, the would-be squire, the village attracted a number of British middle-class families who were determined to live as "gentlemen farmers", running small agricultural businesses, organising tea and croquet evenings and even importing a pack of hounds to stage their own hunts. Their efforts failed when the branch rail line was routed well to the south of Cannington Manor, and by 1900 the settlement was abandoned. By the entrance, an information centre provides the background.

## Moose Jaw

**MOOSE JAW**, 70km west of Regina, was founded as a railway depot in 1882 and is now Saskatchewan's third largest town, with 35,000 inhabitants. It achieved some notoriety during Prohibition, when liquor was smuggled south by souped-up car or by train along the *Soo Line*, which ran from Moose Jaw to Chicago. For most locals this period of boot-leggers, gangsters, gamblers and "boozoriums" – liquor warehouses – was not a happy one, and various schemes to attract tourists by developing the "Roaring Twenties" theme have met with considerable opposition from the substantial portion of the population that actually experienced them. As for the town's weird name, it may have come from an Indian word for "warm breezes", or the jaw-like turn the river takes just outside town, or even the repairs made to a cartwheel by an early pioneer with the assistance of a moose's jawbone.

The downtown area is bisected by Main Street, running from north to south, and Manitoba Street, the east–west axis, which is adjacent to the railway line and the river. The central area is for the most part dispiriting, though a string of **murals** of early pioneer days, concentrated along 1st Avenue NW between Manitoba and Hochelaga, do their best to cheer things up. That apart, some of the streets look like they haven't changed much since the 1920s, the wide treeless avenues framed by solemn brick warehouses and hotels. One block north of Manitoba, the best example is **River Street**, whose rough-and-ready *Royal* and *New Brunswick* hotels were once favourite haunts of the gangsters. There's a network of tunnels running underneath River Street from their basements, but efforts to have them opened up have been resisted and their extent and purpose remain obscure – most likely they were built both for extra storage space and as possible escape routes.

The chief sight is the huge **Western Development Museum** (April to mid-May & mid-Sept to mid-Oct daily except Sat 10am–6pm; late May to early Sept same times; $3.50), about 4km from the centre, beside the Trans-Canada as it loops around the northern edge of town. Divided into sections covering air, land, water and rail transport, its exhibits include a replica of a steamship, several Canadian Pacific railway coaches, a number of fragile old planes, and a 1934 Buick car converted carrying the chief superintendent up and down the rail line.

### Practicalities

Moose Jaw's **bus station**, 63 High St East, is a couple of minutes' walk from Main Street and two blocks north of Manitoba; there are no trains. The **tourist bureau** (mid-May to Sept daily 10am–8pm) is next to a giant concrete moose near the Western Development Museum. There's also **Tourism Moose Jaw** (Mon–Fri 9am–5pm) beside Main Street at 15 Hochelaga Street West, roughly ten minutes' walk north of the bus station. The town has several reasonably priced, central **hotels** and **motels**, including the *Best Western Motor Lodge*, 45 Athabasca St East (☎693-7919; doubles $40–65); the grim *City Centre Motel*, at the corner of Main and Manitoba (☎692-6422; rooms from $40); the primitive *Dreamland Motel*, 1035 Athabasca St East at 10th (☎692-1878; doubles from $25); and the recently refurbished *Harwood Moose Jaw Inn*, 24 Fairford St East (☎692-2366; doubles $50–80). The **River Park Campground** (mid-May to Sept; ☎694-4447) is 2km southeast of the centre, with sites from $10 per night.

For **food**, *Houston Pizza*, 117 Main St, has Italian dishes from $8; the *Arbor Room*, 20 Main St, has a daily smorgasbord from $10; and the *Hopkins Dining Parlour*, 65 Athabasca St West, located in a pleasant Victorian house, is a more formal affair with a wide-ranging menu and main courses from $14.

## The Big Muddy Badlands

At the end of the last ice age, torrents of meltwater produced a massive gash in the landscape to the south of the site of Moose Jaw, near the US frontier. Edged by rounded hills and flat-topped buttes that rise up to 200 metres above the valley floor, the **Big Muddy Valley** can only be explored with organized tours, the best of which are the five-hour minibus trips from dreary **CORONACH** about 200km from Regina (mid-May to Sept 2 weekly; $15; ☎267-3312). The tours include visits to Indian burial cairns and a couple of outlaw caves, the refuge of American rustlers and robbers like Butch Cassidy and Dutch Henry. Cassidy and his gang, the Wild Bunch, established an outlaw trail that connected the Big Muddy with Mexico via a series of safe houses; their antics were curtailed by the arrival of a detachment of Mounties in 1904 led by a certain Corporal Bird, known ruefully as the "man who never sleeps". There's **accommodation** in Coronach at the *Country Boy Motel* on Hwy 18(☎267-3267; doubles $35–50), the *South Country Inn* on Main Street (☎267-2063; from $30), and *Coronach Campground* on the south side of town (May–Sept; ☎267-2318), with sites from $8.

# Grasslands National Park

Directly west of the Big Muddy, accessible along Hwy 18, the **Grasslands National Park** is predominantly mixed grass prairie, a flat, bare landscape broken up by splendid coulees, buttes and river valleys – notably the wide ravine edging the Frenchman River in the western block. Far from the moderating influence of the oceans, the area has a savage climate, with an average low in January of -22°C and temperatures that soar to 40°C in summer. This terrain is inhabited by many species that are adapted to cope with the shortage of water, from flora such as prairie grasses, greasewood, rabbitbrush, sagebrush and different types of cacti, to fauna like the pronghorn antelope, the rattlesnake and Canada's only colonies of black-tailed prairie dog.

At the moment the park consists of east and west sections separated by private ranches and farms, which the federal government eventually intends to buy, creating a single park stretching from Hwy 4 in the west to Hwy 2/18 in the east. The **west** is both more scenic and accessible, its limited system of gravel tracks and roads cutting off from highways 18 and 4, south and east of **VAL MARIE**. This tiny township houses the **Grasslands Information Centre** (Mon–Fri 8am–4.30pm; ☎298-2257), whose rangers provide advice on weather and road conditions, hand out maps, issue camping permits and give tips on animal-spotting and hiking. There are no **campgrounds** within the park, but camping is allowed within 1km of its roads – take a good supply of water, a stout pair of walking shoes, and a stick to sweep in front of you in tall grass or brush as a warning to rattlesnakes. Animal activity is at its height at dawn and dusk and during spring and fall; whatever the season, you'll need a pair of binoculars.

Val Marie also has one **hotel**, the *Val Marie* (☎298-9080), where a double room costs $30, and a centrally located, all-year **campground** (☎298-2022).

# Maple Creek

Driving west from Moose Jaw along the Trans-Canada Highway, it's about 180km to SWIFT CURRENT, an industrial town and farm research centre, and another 130km to **MAPLE CREEK**, situated just 8km to the south of the highway on the way to the Cypress Hills. Nicknamed "old cow town", Maple Creek lies at the heart of ranching country, its main streets all pick-up trucks, cowboy boots and stetsons. Some of the late nineteenth-century brick storefronts have survived, and the trim and tidy **Old Timers' Museum** at 218 Jasper Street (June–Aug daily 9am–5pm; Sept–May Mon–Fri 1–4pm;

---

### THE HUTTERITES

The **Hutterites**, the only prairie community to have maintained a utopian communal ideal, are members of an Anabaptist sect that takes its name from their first real leader, Jacob Hutter. Originating in the Tyrol and Moravia in the sixteenth century, they gradually moved east across central Europe, ending up in Russia, which they abandoned for South Dakota in the 1870s. It was fifty years before they felt obliged to move again, their pacifism recoiling from the bellicosity that gripped their American neighbours during World War I. They moved north between 1918 and 1922, established a series of colonies where they were allowed to educate their own children, speak their own language and have no truck with military service. In these largely self-sufficient communities tasks are still divided according to ability and skill, property is owned communally, and social life is organised around a common dining room and dormitories. Economically prosperous, they continue to multiply, a new branch community being founded whenever the old one reaches a secure population of between 100 and 200. Apart from the occasional skirmish with the outside world when they buy new land, the Hutterites have been left in peace and have resisted the pressures of assimilation more staunchly than their kindred spirits the Mennonites and the Doukhobors.

$2) has pleasant displays on pioneer life and the Mounties. The town is also a supply centre for a number of **Hutterite colonies**, agricultural communities of mid-European descent; the men are indistinguishable from the other locals, but the women stand out with their floral dresses and headscarves (see box).

Maple Creek has a couple of cheap **cafés**, including the *Star*, on Pacific Avenue near Jasper Street, and a handful of **hotels** and **motels**. The grim *Commercial Hotel*, Pacific Ave (☎662-2673), has doubles from $20, and the marginally more agreeable *Cypress Hills Motor Inn* (☎662-2639) has doubles from $25, but it's better to move on.

# The Cypress Hills

South of the Trans-Canada Highway, between Maple Creek and Irvine, in Alberta, the wooded ridges of the **Cypress Hills** rise above the plains in a 130-kilometre-long plateau that in places reaches a height of 1500m – the highest point in Canada between Labrador and the Rockies. Due to their elevation, the Cypress Hills have a wetter and milder climate than the plains, creating a rich variety of woodland, wetland and grassland. In turn, this comparatively lush vegetation supports a wealth of wildlife, from the relatively rare elk, lynx, bobcat and coyote through to the more common gopher and racoon, plus about 200 species of bird, over half of whom breed in the hills. One surprise, considering the name, is the absence of cypress trees: the early French voyageurs seem to have confused the area's predominant lodgepole pines with the jack pines of Québec, a species they called *cyprès*. Literal-minded translation did the rest.

## Cypress Hills Provincial Park

In amongst the cattle ranches two separate sections of the Hills have been set aside to form the **Cypress Hills Provincial Park**; Saskatchewan's **Centre Block** lies to the south of Maple Creek along Hwy 21, and the larger **West Block** spans the Saskatchewan-Alberta border, accessible from Maple Creek along Hwy 271 in the east and via Alberta's Hwy 41, off the Trans-Canada, in the west. The Saskatchewan part of the West Block is also attached to **Fort Walsh National Historic Park**, incorporating a partly refurbished Mountie station and a replica of one of the Battle Creek trading posts. The three north–south access highways present no problems, but it's difficult to drive across the park from east to west as the paved road is interrupted by two long stretches of gravel and clay track, which are positively dangerous in wet weather.

### *SASKATCHEWAN'S CENTRE BLOCK*

Just 30km south of Maple Creek on Hwy 21, a paved side road heads into the park's **Centre Block**, a rough rectangle of hilly land dominated by lodgepole forest. At the centre, a pleasant tourist resort surrounds tiny **Loch Leven**, complete with canoe and bike rental, stores, a gas station and a café. There's also a modest nature centre adjoining the park's **administration office** (daily 8am–6pm, plus Fri–Sun 8pm–10pm in season), which has useful maps and trail brochures and a good deal of local information. The resort is a popular holiday destination, but it's easy to escape the crowds along the half-dozen hiking trails.

For **accommodation**, there's one **hotel**, the modern *Cypress Four Seasons Resort* (☎662-4477; doubles from $60, cabins from $50). Close by there are several summer **campgrounds**, which have to be booked at the campground office on Pine Avenue to the west of the centre (mid-May to Aug daily 8.30am–10pm; ☎662-4459).

### *SASKATCHEWAN'S WEST BLOCK AND FORT WALSH*

The eastern side of the park's **West Block** has alternating areas of thick forest and open grassland broken up by steep hills and deep, sheltered ravines. Highway 271 enters this section from the east and becomes increasingly bumpy as it twists south

## THE CYPRESS HILLS MASSACRE

From the middle of the eighteenth century, the Cypress Hills lay in a sort of neutral zone between the **Blackfoot** and the **Cree**, whose intermittent skirmishing was small scale until the 1860s, when the failure of the Crees' traditional hunting grounds forced them to move west. Some 3000 Crees reached the Cypress Hills in 1865 and the violence began just four years later with the murder of the Cree peacemaker, Maskepetoon. The ensuing war was overshadowed by the Red River rising of 1869–70, but casualties were high and its effects were compounded by two smallpox epidemics. In 1871 the Crees sued for peace, but both sides were exhausted, their morale, health and social structures further undermined by the whiskey traders who had moved into the region.

These **whiskey traders**, who were mostly American, brought their liquor north in the autumn, returning south in late spring laden with furs and buffalo robes. Though it was illegal to supply the Indians with booze, the traders spread out across the southern plains, aptly nicknamed **Whoop-up Country**, establishing dozens of trading posts whose occupants were protected from their disorderly customers by log stockades. (They needed to be, as the stuff they sold was adulterated with such substances as red ink, gunpowder and strychnine.) In the spring of 1873, there were two such outposts beside **Battle Creek**, deep in the Cypress Hills, owned by a certain Abel Farwell and his rival Moses Solomon. For reasons that remain obscure, though the prevailing drunkenness played a part, this was the scene of a violent confrontation between a group of white wolf-hunters and a band of Assiniboine. Equipped with the latest fast-action rifles, the hunters riddled an Assiniboine camp with bullets, killing twenty-one and raping a further five before returning to the trading posts to celebrate. News of the incident, known as the **Cypress Hills Massacre**, filtered back to Ottawa, where John A Macdonald acted quickly. He speeded the recruitment of the newly formed **North West Mounted Police**, and posted the first detachment west in the autumn. The police reached Fort Whoop-up, near today's Lethbridge, Alberta, in early 1874, where they set about suppressing the whiskey trade and establishing law and order.

To consolidate their control of the area, the Mounties built **Fort Walsh**, near Battle Creek, the following year. An unpopular posting, the fort was considered "unhealthy, isolated and indefensible", but it could not be abandoned until 1883 when the last of the restless Indian bands were moved to reservations further north. It was during this period that the fort's first inspector, **James Morrow Walsh**, was faced with an extremely delicate situation. In 1876, **Chief Sitting Bull's** Sioux had exterminated General Custer's army at the battle of the Little Big Horn. Fearing reprisals, 5000 Sioux moved north, establishing their camp at Wood Mountain, 350km east of Fort Walsh. Aware of the danger, Walsh rode into the Sioux encampment with just four other constables to insist that they obey Canadian law. This act of bravery established a rough rapport between the two leaders and by his tactful dealings with the Sioux, Walsh enhanced the reputation of the Mounties, whose efficiency ensured there were no more massacres in the Canadian west.

towards **Fort Walsh National Historic Park** and **Visitor Information Centre** (mid-May to Sept 9am–5.30pm), which has excellent displays on the Plains Indians, the history of the fort and the development of the RCMP.

A five-minute walk behind the information centre, **Fort Walsh** (mid-May to Sept 9am–5.30pm; free) sits in a wide, low-lying valley, its trim stockade framed by pine forests. Built in 1875, the fort was abandoned in favour of Maple Creek just eight years later; in 1942 the RCMP acquired the land, and most of the present buildings date from that decade. Costumed guides enliven a dreary tour of whitewashed log buildings, but there are plans to return the whole site to its 1880s appearance, down to the toilets, which were segregated by rank – even out here, British class distinctions remained precise. Every half-hour a minibus makes the trip from the information centre over the hills to Battle Creek, where Abel Farwell's **trading post** has been reconstructed and staffed with costumed guides to act out the parts of Farwell and his entourage.

The only **accommodation** in this part of the park is the *West Block Campground* (May to mid-Nov; free), 5km north of Fort Walsh. It's in an isolated spot, so take your own food and water.

### ALBERTA'S WEST BLOCK

The lodgepole forests and deep coulees of the Alberta section of the park are centred on the tourist resort of **ELKWATER**, 34km south of the Trans-Canada on Hwy 41. Curving round the southern shore of Elkwater Lake, the village has a comprehensive range of facilities, from boat and bike rental through to a sandy beach and sauna baths. There's also a **park office** (Mon–Fri 9am–5pm; ☎893-3777) and a **visitor centre** (mid-May–Sept daily; ☎893-3833), which has maps and hiking brochures and runs guided walks throughout the summer. For **accommodation**, the *Green Tree Motel* (April–Dec; ☎893-3811) has doubles from $65, while the *Elkwater Campground* is relatively luxurious, with both simple and hooked-up sites.

Southwest of Elkwater, a paved road leads to Horseshoe Canyon and **Head of the Mountain**, where there are striking views over the hills towards Montana; other roads lead east to Reesor Lake and Spruce Coulee Reservoir. Beside the roads there are twelve other **campgrounds**, bookable through the visitor centre.

# Saskatoon

Set on the wide South Saskatchewan River at the heart of a vast wheat-growing area, **SASKATOON** is a commercial, manufacturing and distribution centre with a population of around 200,000 – making it Saskatchewan's largest town and, in the opinion of many of its inhabitants, a better claimant to the title of provincial capital than Regina. Ontario Methodists founded the town as a temperance colony in 1883, but in spite of their enthusiasm the new settlement made an extremely slow start, partly because the semi-arid farming conditions were unfamiliar to them and partly because the Northwest Rebellion of 1885 raised fears of Indian hostility. Although the railroad reached Saskatoon in 1890, there were still only 113 inhabitants at the turn of the century. In the next decade, however, there was a sudden influx of European and American settlers and as the agricultural economy of the Prairies expanded, so the city came to be dominated by a group of entrepreneurs nicknamed **boomers**, under whose management Saskatoon became the economic focus of the region. This success was underpinned by the development of a particularly sharp form of municipal loyalty – people who dared criticise any aspect of the city, from the poor quality of the water to tyrannical labour practices, were dubbed **knockers**, and their opinions were rubbished by the press. The boomers established a city where community solidarity overwhelmed differences in income and occupation, a set of attitudes that palpably still prevails, making this a pleasant, well-groomed place, albeit one with just a trio of tourist attractions – the **Mendel Art Gallery**, a branch of the **Western Development Museum**, and, on the outskirts, **Wanuskewin**, a complex dedicated to the Plains Indians.

## Arrival, information and transport

Some 7km north of the city centre, Saskatoon **airport** is connected to downtown by taxi at a cost of roughly $10. The nearest bus service is line #21, which leaves from the junction of Airport Drive and 45th Street, a good fifteen-minute walk from the terminal building. The **train station** is 7km west of the town centre, on Chappell Drive, a five-minute walk from the route of bus #3 on Dieppe Street; once again, a taxi to the downtown core costs about $10. Far more convenient, the city's **bus station** is in the centre at 23rd Street East and Pacific Avenue.

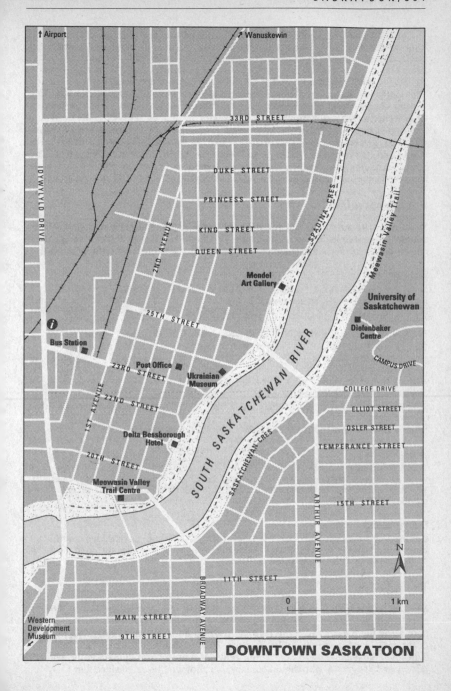

↑ Airport

↗ Wanuskewin

33RD STREET

DUKE STREET

PRINCESS STREET

KING STREET

QUEEN STREET

IDYWYLYD DRIVE

2ND AVENUE

SPADINA CRES

Meewasin Valley Trail

Mendel
Art Gallery ■

University of
Saskatchewan

■ Diefenbaker
Centre

CAMPUS DRIVE

25TH STREET

ℹ

Bus Station ■

23RD STREET

Post Office ■

Ukrainian
Museum ■

1ST AVENUE

22ND STREET

SOUTH SASKATCHEWAN RIVER

COLLEGE DRIVE

ELLIOT STREET

OSLER STREET

TEMPERANCE STREET

Delta Bessborough
Hotel ■

SASKATCHEWAN CRES

20TH STREET

Meewasin Valley
Trail Centre ■

ARTHUR AVENUE

15TH STREET

N

11TH STREET

BROADWAY AVENUE

0          1 km

Western
Development
Museum ↙

MAIN STREET

9TH STREET

**DOWNTOWN SASKATOON**

The main office of **Tourism Saskatoon** (Mon–Fri 8.30am–5pm & June–July Sat 9am–4.30pm; ☎242-1206) is centrally sited at no. 102, 310 Idylwyld Drive North and 24th St East. In addition to maps and brochures, it has copies of *The Broadway Theatre*, a free bimonthly newssheet that carries details of cultural events. The local newspaper, *The Star Phoenix*, has bland reviews and nightlife listings at the weekend.

Saskatoon's compact city centre is best explored on **foot**, though it takes a little time to work out the street plan. Edged to the south and east by the river and the adjacent strip of city park, the **downtown core** is bounded by 25th Street East to the north and 1st Avenue to the west. Numbered sequentially, these central **streets** are all "East", with their western extensions starting at either 1st Avenue or Idylwyld Drive. On the other hand, the **avenues** change from "south" to "north" right in the centre at 22nd Street East. For the suburbs, **Saskatoon Transit** operates an efficient and fairly comprehensive bus transport system, with a standard adult fare of $1 (pay on board).

## Accommodation

Saskatoon has a good choice of downtown **hotels** with prices starting at around $35 per double, through to luxury accommodation for about $130. Cheap and convenient alternatives include a YWCA and summer **youth hostel** for women, and a **campground**.

### Hotels

**Delta Bessborough Hotel**, Spadina Crescent and 21st St East (☎244-5521 or ☎1-800-268-1133). Built for the CNR in 1931, the *Bessborough* is an enormous turreted and gabled affair in a "French chateau" style that makes it the city's most striking building. Tastefully refurbished, it has doubles from $80.

**Holiday Inn**, 90 22nd St East (☎244-2311). Reasonably priced doubles start at $60 per night.

**King George Hotel**, 157 2nd Ave North (☎244-6133). A bargain, with doubles at $40.

**Parktown Motor Hotel**, Spadina Crescent and 25th St East (☎244-5564). Peasant place with doubles for $50.

**Patricia Hotel**, 345 2nd Ave North at 25th St East (☎242-8861). Easily the best of the low budget hotels; clean, basic doubles from $25 to $35.

**Ramada Renaissance**, 405 20th St East (☎665-3322). Tower block with luxurious doubles from $120 per night.

**Senator Hotel**, 3rd Ave and 21st St East (☎244-6141). Primitive doubles from $36.

### Hostel

**YWCA Residence**, 510 25th St East, at 5th Ave North (☎244-0944). Accommodation for single women; long- and short-term stays possible; $30 per day, $150 for 2 weeks. At the same address, the YWCA Summer Youth Hostel offers dormitory beds from June to August for women only; hostel members $6.25.

### Campground

**Gordon Howe Campground**, Avenue P South (☎975-3328). Most comfortable and central of the three campgrounds in the city, which is located near the South Saskatchewan River about 4km south of the centre. From $6. Open mid-April to Sept.

## The City

Most of Saskatoon's principal sights are on or near the **Meewasin Valley Trail**, a circular, fifteen-kilometre walking and cycle route which follows the narrow strip of park along the river between the Idylwyld Drive and Circle Drive bridges. At the start of the trail, the **Meewasin Valley Centre**, 3rd Ave South at 19th St East (Mon–Fri 9am–5pm; Sat–Sun 10.30am–5pm; free), provides a useful introduction to the region's history and geography with the aid of maps, old photographs and a video film.

A few minutes' walk from the Valley Centre, along the west bank, the **Ukrainian Museum of Canada**, 910 Spadina Crescent East at 24th St East (mid-June to Aug Mon–Sat 10am–4.30pm & Sun noon–5pm; Sept to mid-June Mon–Fri & Sun 1–4.30pm; $2), is the more interesting of the city's two Ukrainian museums, representing the Orthodox as distinct from the Catholic tradition. Displays cover the history of Ukrainian migration, traditional textile design, festivals and Easter egg painting, the most appealing Ukrainian folk art.

The **Mendel Art Gallery** (daily 10am–10pm; free), overlooking the river from Spadina Crescent, just north of 25th Street East, features temporary shows of modern Canadian art and a rotating exhibition drawn from the possessions of local magnate Fred Mendel. His collection includes many of the country's best artists – Emily Carr, Lawren Harris and David Milne – and a good selection of Inuit sculpture, a small sample of which is always on display. Other parts of the building contain a snack bar, a delightful conservatory and an excellent gift shop.

Across the river from the Mendel Art Gallery, over University Bridge, the campus of the **University of Saskatchewan** occupies a prime riverbank site just to the north of College Drive. Departmental collections include a dull **Museum of Natural Sciences** (daily 12.30–5pm; free) and a similar **Museum of Antiquities**, in the main library (Mon–Thurs 9am–4pm & Fri 9am–noon; closed Aug, Dec & Jan; free). Neither of them draws as many visitors as the **Diefenbaker Centre** at the west end of the campus, beside the river (Mon–Fri 9.30am–4.30pm & Sat–Sun 12.30–5pm; free). Prime minister from 1957 to 1963, Diefenbaker was a caricaturist's dream with his large flat face, protruding teeth and wavy hair, and the museum's high point is its assortment of newspaper cartoons. He was buried just outside the centre in 1979.

On the south side of the river, 8km from the centre, is the Saskatoon branch of the **Western Development Museum**, 2610 Lorne Ave South (opening times under review; ring ☎931-1910; $3.50), a few minutes' walk from the route of bus #1. The principal exhibit here is **Boomtown**, an ambitious reconstruction of a typical Saskatchewan Main Street circa 1910. More like a film set than a museum, its mixture of replica and original buildings includes a school, a general store, a church, a theatre, a train station and a combined pool hall and barbershop.

Opening in the summer of 1992, **Wanuskewin Heritage Park**, 405 Third Ave South, ten minutes' drive north of the city centre along Warman Road, is designed to be Saskatoon's principal tourist attraction, a lavish tribute to the culture of the northern Plains Indians. Bordering the South Saskatchewan River, the park embraces a string of marshy creeks and wooded ridges that have been used by native peoples for at least 5000 years. Its nineteen sites will be connected by trail and walkway to a visitors' centre which will feature reconstructions of tepees, a buffalo pound and a buffalo jump as well as displays on traditional skills as diverse as tool-making and story-telling. The attached restaurant will specialise in indigenous foodstuffs such as buffalo meat and pemmican, a mixture of fat, berries and dried meat that's supposed to last for years. Wanuskewin has been developed with the cooperation of local native peoples, who will, it is hoped, provide most of the interpretative staff.

## Eating, drinking and entertainment

Saskatoon has a useful assortment of **restaurants** clustered in and around the downtown core and along the first couple of blocks of **Broadway Avenue**, which lies just across the river via the bridge at 4th Avenue South and 19th Street East. Broadway is the nearest thing the city has to a "cultural centre", the home of the Broadway Theatre and a handful of vaguely "alternative" shops and cafés. While you're in town, try a bottle of **Great Western Beer**, the product of a local factory whose future was recently threatened by the merger of two of Canada's giant brewing companies, Molson and

Carling O'Keefe. The workers bought the factory themselves and can barely keep up with demand.

## Snack bars and restaurants

**Adonis**, 3rd Ave North at 22nd St East. Soups, salads and sandwiches from around $4.

**Broadway Café**, 806 Broadway Ave. Wholesome meals from $7.

**Calories**, 721 Broadway Ave. Pleasant little café where snacks start at $5.

**Earls**, 610 2nd Ave North and Queen. Trendy place with an imaginative menu; vegetarian and other dishes between $5 and $15.

**Johnny's Cooky and Serious Sandwich Bar**, 101 3rd Ave North at 22nd St East. Good for sandwiches and hamburgers from about $5.

**The Keg**, 301 Ontario Ave. Standard steak and seafood dishes from $10.

**The Mid-town Shopping Plaza**, 1st Ave South and 21st St East. Houses a number of fast-food joints and snack bars, like the *A&W* hamburger stall and the restaurant in Eaton's department store, where simple, main courses cost around $5.

**Nino's**, 801 Broadway Ave. Homely place with filling pizzas and Greek dishes from as little as $7.

**Pinocchio's**, 123 2nd Ave South. Classic Italian cuisine; expensive.

**St Tropez Café**, 243 3rd Ave South. Quiches and crêpes from about $8.

## Bars and clubs

**Bar-K Ranch House**, 2415 22nd St West. Quality country music.

**The Bassment**, 245 Third Ave South. Jazz sets.

**Buds**, 817 Broadway. Rough-and-ready bar with R&B acts.

**Patricia Hotel**, 345 2nd Ave North and 25th St East. Most of Saskatoon's central bars are grim places, but the tap room of this hotel is okay.

**Texas "T"**, 3331 8th St East. Country and western venue.

## Film, theatre and classical music

The *Broadway Theatre*, 719 Broadway Ave, has the best of foreign and domestic films, while the *Midtown Plaza Cinema*, 1st Ave South and 21st St East, has mainstream releases. For **theatre**, the *Persephone*, 2802 Rusholme Rd (☎384-7727), is the best known of the city's professional companies, with performances featuring mostly modern plays; their season runs from October to May. The *25th Street Theatre Centre*, 420 Duchess St (☎664-2239), perform more occasionally and concentrate on local work. Visiting ballet, theatre and opera stars appear at the *Saskatoon Centennial Auditorium*, 35 22nd St East (☎938-7800).

## Festivals

Saskatoon's biggest and best shindig is the **Du Maurier Ltd Saskatchewan Jazz Festival** in the last week in June; over 200 musicians perform across the town, often for free. The *25th Street Theatre Company* organises **The Fringe on Broadway Theatre Festival**, a week of alternative performances held at the end of July and the beginning of August, featuring some fifty theatre groups from all over the world, performing on stages dotted along Broadway; tickets are all under $8.

# Listings

**Airlines** *Air Canada*, 123 2nd Ave South (☎652-4181); *Canadian Airlines*, at the airport (☎665-7688).

**Bike rental** *Joe's Cycle and Sports*, 220 20th St West; *Bike 'n Blade*, 205 Idylwyld Drive South.

**Buses** *Greyhound* and *The Saskatchewan Transportation Company* are both on ☎933-8000.

**Car rental** *Avis*, 3-2130 Airport Drive (☎652-3434); *Budget*, 234 1st Ave South (☎244-7925); *Tilden*, 321 21st St East (☎652-3355).
**Hospital** *St Paul's*, 1702 20th St East (☎382-3220).
**Laundry** *The Idylwyld*, 24-1715 Idylwyld Drive North (daily 8am–10pm).
**Left luggage** Coin-operated machines at the bus station.
**Police** 130 4th Ave North (☎975-8200).
**Post office** Main post office at 4th Ave North and 23rd St East.
**Taxis** *United Cab* (☎652-2222).
**Train enquiries** ☎384-5665.
**Weather** ☎975-4266.

# Central Saskatchewan

North of Saskatoon you have a choice of two routes. Following the Yellowhead north-west towards Edmonton, you'll come to the **Battlefords**, consisting of grimy and impoverished **North Battleford** and, on the opposite bank of the North Saskatchewan River, the trim riverside streets and refurbished Mountie stockade of **Battleford**. Due north of Saskatoon, the road shadows the South Saskatchewan River on its way to the town of Prince Albert, a distance of 140km, passing the **Batoche National Park**, where the Metis rebellion of 1885 reached its disastrous climax (see box overpage). Further north still, the lakes and wooded hills of **Prince Albert National Park** are among the region's finest, with innumerable wilderness canoe and hiking routes. Central Saskatchewan's **public transport** is poor, but there are reasonably regular **buses** between the major towns and a once-daily summertime service to Waskesiu Lake.

## Saskatoon to Prince Albert Park

From Saskatoon, Hwy 11 cuts across the narrow slice of prairie that separates the final stretches of the North and South Saskatchewan Rivers, before they flow together further to the northeast. There's nothing to see on the road itself, but, on the way, the briefest of detours will take you to one of the province's more interesting attractions, Batoche National Park.

### Batoche National Historic Park

The site of the Metis' last stand, **Batoche National Historic Park** (mid-May to June & Sept to mid-Oct daily 9am–5pm; July–Aug daily 10am–6pm; free) occupies a splendid site beside the east bank of the South Saskatchewan River, 90km from Saskatoon just off Provincial Highway 225. At the entrance to the park, a Visitor Reception Centre has displays on the culture of the Metis and provides a detailed account of the rebellion, supplemented by a glossy brochure and a 45-minute film.

Behind the centre, the main footpath leads to a refurbished Catholic church and adjacent rectory, all that's left of the original village. A few minutes' walk away, in the cemetery, memorials inscribed with the hoary commendation "a credit to his race" contrast with the rough chunk of rock that commemorates Riel's commander-in-chief **Gabriel Dumont**. A stern and ferocious man, Dumont insisted that he be buried standing up, with a good view of the river.

The church and cemetery are at the centre of the park's **walking trails**, which extend along the riverbank in both directions. Roughly 1km to the south, there's a military graveyard, a Metis farmhouse and the remains of some rifle pits; about the same distance to the north, there's the site of the old ferry crossing, more rifle pits and the foundations of several Metis buildings. With a knowledge of the history, the park becomes an extremely evocative spot.

## THE NORTHWEST REBELLION

The 1870 Red River rebellion led by Louis Riel won significant concessions from the Canadian government, but failed to protect the Metis way of life against the effects of increasing white settlement. Many **Metis** moved west to farm the banks of the **South Saskatchewan**, where the men worked as freighters, traders, horse breeders and translators, acting as intermediaries between the Indians and the Europeans. In itself, the development of these homesteads was a recognition by the Metis that the day of the itinerant buffalo hunter was over. However, when the government surveyors arrived here in 1878, the Metis realised, as they had on the Red River twenty years before, that their claim to the land they farmed was far from secure.

Beginning with the Metis, a general sense of instability spread across the region in the early 1880s, fuelled by Big Bear's and Poundmaker's increasingly restless and hungry **Cree** and by the discontent of the white settlers at the high freight charges levied on their produce. The leaders of the Metis decided to act in June 1884, when they sent a delegation to Montana, where **Louis Riel** was in exile. Convinced that the Metis were God's chosen instrument to purify the human race, and he their Messiah, Riel was easily persuaded to return to Canada, where he spent the winter unsuccessfully petitioning the Ottawa government for confirmation of Metis rights.

In March 1885 Riel and his supporters declared a provisional government at Batoche and demanded the surrender of the nearest Mountie outpost, **Fort Carlton**, just 35km to their west. The Police Superintendent refused, and the force he dispatched to re-establish order was badly mauled at **Duck Lake**. When news of the uprising reached Big Bear's Cree, some 300km away, they attacked the local Hudson's Bay Company store and killed its nine occupants in the so-called **Frog Lake Massacre**. Within a couple of weeks, no fewer than three columns of militia were converging on Big Bear's Cree and the meagre Metis forces at Batoche. The total number of casualties – about fifty altogether – does not indicate the full significance of the engagement, which for the Metis marked the end of their independence and influence. Riel's execution in Regina on November 16, 1885, was bitterly denounced in Québec and remains a potent symbol of the deep divide between English- and French-speaking Canada. In Ontario there was a mood of unrepentant triumphalism, the military success – however paltry – stirring a deep patriotic fervour that excluded Metis and Indian alike.

## Duck Lake and Fort Carlton

Back on Hwy 11, on the west side of the river, the tiny farming community of **DUCK LAKE** is home to a **Regional Interpretive Centre** (mid-May to mid–Sept daily 9am–6pm; $2), whose displays are devoted to Indian, Metis and pioneer society from 1870 to 1905. Prize exhibits include some elaborate Cree costumes, an outfit that belonged to the Sioux chief Little Fox, an adviser to Sitting Bull, and Gabriel Dumont's gold watch, presented to him in New York where he was appearing in Buffalo Bill's Wild West Show.

Continue 26km west along Hwy 212 and you'll reach **Fort Carlton Provincial Historic Park** (mid-May to Aug daily 10am–6pm), a reconstruction of a Hudson's Bay Company trading post circa 1860. Founded in 1810, the riverbank station was fortified in successive decades and became an important centre of the fur and pemmican trade, until the demise of the buffalo brought an end to its success. Reduced to a warehouse facility in the early 1880s, the fort was garrisoned by the Mounties during the Northwest Rebellion, but it was finally burnt down and abandoned in 1885.

The visitor centre provides an historical introduction to the fort, whose stockade shelters replicas of a sail and harness shop, a fur and provision store, the clerk's quarters and a trading shop, where the merchandise included gunpowder – which meant the clerks were forbidden to light a stove here, no matter what the temperature.

## Prince Albert

Founded as a Presbyterian mission in 1866, **PRINCE ALBERT** has a thriving timber industry and is a major transportation centre, but it's a dull spot, its long main drag, **Central Avenue** (Hwy 2), lined with fast-food joints, gas stations and shopping malls. The only conceivable attraction is the **Historical Museum** at River Street and Central Avenue (mid-May to Aug Mon–Sat 10am–6pm & Sun 10am–9pm; $1.50), given over chiefly to the area's first farmers and loggers.

The appeal of the place is that it has the only **bus** to Prince Albert National Park and La Ronge, the service leaving from the **station** at 20 14th Street East and Central Avenue. A couple of minutes' walk away, the **tourist information office** (Mon–Fri 8am–5pm), on the third floor of City Hall at 1084 Central Avenue and 11th Street East, provides free town maps and brochures. There's no real reason to stay here, but the town has several cheap and central **hotels**, including the *Avenue Hotel*, 1015 Central Ave (☎763-6411), where grim and basic doubles start at $25, and the *Marlboro Inn*, 67 13th St East (☎763-2643), with better doubles from $45. For **campers**, the *Mary Nesbit Campground* (mid-May to mid-Sept; ☎763-3883) is situated about 2km north of town, on the other side of the river, beside Hwy 2.

## Prince Albert National Park

Some 230km north of Saskatoon, **Prince Albert National Park** is a great tract of wilderness where the aspen parkland of the south meets the boreal forest of the north, a transitional landscape that incorporates a host of rivers and creeks, dozens of deep lakes, pockets of pasture and areas of spruce bog. The shift in vegetation is mirrored by the wildlife, with prairie species such as coyote and wild bison giving way to black bear, moose, wolf, caribou, osprey and eagle further north. Tourists are principally drawn here by the marvellous canoe and hiking **trails**, a series of splendid routes that range from the simple and short to longer excursions suitable only for experienced canoeists and backpackers.

The tacky tourist village of **WASKESIU**, approached from the south by Hwy 263 and from the east by highways 2 and 264, is the only settlement in the park. Spread out along the southern shore of Lake Waskesiu, it has accommodation, sports facilities, gas stations, grocery stores and a narrow sandy beach that gets ridiculously overcrowded in summer. The resort is also home to the park's **nature centre**, on Lakeview Drive (late June–Aug daily 10am–5pm), which has a modest display on the region's habitats. In the centre of Waskesiu, at the junction of Lakeview Drive and Waskesiu Drive, the park's main **information office** (mid-May to Aug daily 8am–10pm; Sept 8am–4.30pm; ☎663-5322) gives advice on wildlife and the condition of the hiking trails, along with weather forecasts – particularly important if you intend to use one of the canoe routes. The information office also runs a programme of **guided walks** in July and August and issues free camping permits, which allow visitors to use the primitive, seasonal **campgrounds** dotted along most of the more substantial trails. Whatever you do, remember to take insect repellent.

Several of the park's easier **hiking trails** begin in or near Waskesiu, most notably the thirteen-kilometre Kingfisher Trail, which loops through the forest just to the west of the resort. However, the best trails and **canoe routes** begin roughly 15km further north at the bottom end of Lake Kingsmere, which is accessible by boat or car from Waskesiu. They include a delightful week-long canoe trip that skirts the west shore of Lake Kingsmere before heading through a series of remote lakes amidst dense boreal forest. There's also a twenty-kilometre hike or canoe paddle to **Grey Owl's Cabin** (May–Sept), situated beside tiny Lake Ajawaan, near the northern shore of Lake Kingsmere. Grey Owl (see p.305) lived in this cabin from 1931 until 1937, the year before his death, and it was here that he wrote one of his better books, *Pilgrims of the Wild*.

*PRACTICALITIES*

Connected by bus to La Ronge to the north and the town of Prince Albert to the south, Waskesiu's **bus stop** is right in the centre, beside a seasonal **tourist kiosk**, which provides free maps of the town and accommodation listings. Waskesiu's main street, **Waskesiu Drive**, runs roughly parallel to and just south of the lake, its western section curving round behind **Lakeview Drive**. Almost all the **hotels** and **motels** are dotted on or near these two streets. Convenient options include the *Lakeview Hotel*, Lakeview Drive (☎663-5311; doubles \$55); *Northland Motel*, Waskesiu Drive (☎663-5377; doubles \$30–50); *Skyline Motel & Cedar Village*, Waskesiu Drive (☎663-5461; cabins and doubles \$30–80); and the *Waskesiu Lake Lodge*, Lakeview Drive (☎663-5975; plush doubles from \$90).

**Bungalow** and **cabin** accommodation tends to be block-booked throughout the summer, but you could try the *Armstrong Hillcrest Cabins*, Waskesiu Drive (☎663-5481; \$40), or *Baker's Bungalows*, Waskesiu Drive (☎663-5211; \$30–65). If you're keen to escape the seediness of central Waskesiu, there's the *Kapasiwin Bungalows* (☎663-5225; from \$50), 2km round the lake to the east of the resort, whose cabins form a quiet mini-resort with their own private beach.

There's also a **youth hostel**, the *Waskesiu International Hostel*, up from the bus stop along Montréal Drive (mid-May to Aug; ☎663-5450; \$10), which has family, twin and single rooms. Waskesiu has two park's department **campgrounds**, the centrally situated *Waskesiu Trailer Park* (mid-May to mid-Sept; \$13), and *Beaver Glen* (late June to early Sept; \$9.50), just to the east of the centre; for reservations ring the park office.

There are several cheap **restaurants** and **snack bars** in the centre, including the *Park Centre Café* opposite the information office, the neighbouring *Mike's Place* and *Pizza Pete's*, on Lakeview Drive. For more expensive dining, try the restaurant of the *Hawood Inn*, Lakeview Drive, where main courses start at around \$15.

Waskesiu's stores sell a full range of outback **equipment**, but no one hires out camping gear. **Boat rentals** are available at the jetty, a couple of minutes' walk from the information office, while **mountain bikes** are available from *Pizza Pete's* and the *Park Centre Café*.

# The Battlefords and westward

Roughly 150km west of Saskatoon, the twin townships of **NORTH BATTLEFORD** and **BATTLEFORD** face each other across the wide valley of the North Saskatchewan River, the former a rough-and-ready industrial settlement, the latter a more sedate little place. From the middle of the eighteenth century, this stretch of the North Saskatchewan River near today's Battlefords formed a natural boundary between the **Blackfeet** to the south and the **Cree** to the north. These two groups were temporary trading partners, the Cree and their Ojibwa allies controlling the flow of European goods, the Blackfeet providing the horses. However, with the arrival of white traders at the start of the nineteenth century, the Blackfeet developed a flourishing trade direct with the Europeans, and by 1870 the Cree and Blackfeet were waging war across the entire length of their frontier, from the Missouri to Fort Edmonton.

In the 1870s, apprehensive after the Cypress Hills Massacre and the arrival of Sitting Bull and his warriors, the government speeded its policy of containment and control, determined to push the Plains Indians into reservations and thereby open the area for European settlers. Their chosen instrument was the North West Mounted Police, who in 1876 established a post at **Battleford**, which then became the regional capital.

With the virtual extinction of the buffalo herds in the late 1870s, the Plains Indians began to starve and Lieutenant-Governor Dewdney used his control of emergency rations to force recalcitrant Indians onto the reservations. Several bands of Cree resisted the process, fighting a series of skirmishes at the same time as the Metis rebe-

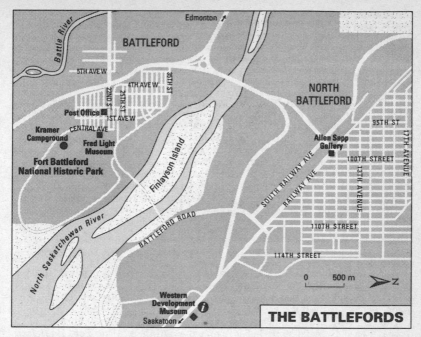

THE BATTLEFORDS

lion in Batoche, but by the mid-1880s their independence was over. Meanwhile, Battleford had lost its pre-eminence when the Canadian Pacific Railway routed their transcontinental line through Regina, which became the new capital in 1883. Twenty years later, its prospects were further damaged by the Canadian Northern Railway, who laid their tracks on the other side of the river, creating the rival town of **North Battleford**. Since then, Battleford has stagnated and shrunk, whilst its rival has become a moderately successful industrial and distribution centre, with a population of around 14,000.

## Arrival, information and accommodation

Situated on the east side of the river valley, **North Battleford**'s downtown core is arranged into streets running north–south and avenues running west–east, forming a central gridiron that intersects with Railway Avenue, which runs southeast to northwest. Across the river, some 5km away, **Battleford** sprawls next to Hwy 4, its streets running from west to east and avenues from north to south.

All long-distance and local bus services use **North Battleford bus station**, located on the edge of the town centre at 75 East Railway Avenue. The **Tourist Information Centre** (June–Aug daily 8am–8pm; ☎445-6226) is on the outskirts 2km away, at the junction of highways 16 and 40 East. There are no buses to Battleford, but North Battleford does have one **taxi** firm, *Crown Cab* (☎445-8155), who charge about $10 for the trip from the bus station to Fort Battleford.

Most of **North Battleford's** central **hotels** are grim and dreary, the haunt of the drunk and the dispossessed. Better alternatives include the *Capri Motor Hotel*, 992 101st St at Railway Ave (☎445-9425), where reasonably comfortable doubles start at $40, and the *Tropical Inn*, on Hwy 16 (☎446-4700), about 1km east along the Yellowhead from the bus station, where pleasant doubles start at $50.

**Battleford** has just one **motel**, the *Five Star*, 322 22nd St West (☎937-2651), where simple, clean doubles start at $30. It also has a splendid **campground** – *Kramer Campground* (mid-May to Aug; ☎937-3366; from $7) – overlooking the river valley from beside Fort Battleford.

## North Battleford

The old municipal library in the centre of North Battleford, at 1091 100th St at 11th Ave, now houses the **Allen Sapp Art Gallery** (June–Sept daily 1–5pm, plus 6–9pm Tues–Thurs; Oct–May closed Mon; free), showcase for the work of Allen Sapp, a local Cree who is often in attendance dressed in flamboyant cowboy boots, a wide-brimmed stetson and long braids. Perhaps the best known of Canada's contemporary native artists, Sapp trawls his childhood recollections of life on the Red Pheasant reserve in the 1930s for most of his material. His simply drawn figures are characteristically cast in the wide spaces of the Prairies, whose delicately blended colours hint at a nostalgic regard for a time when his people had a greater sense of community.

About 5km southeast of the gallery, beside the tourist information centre on Hwy 16, the North Battleford **Western Development Museum** (late May to Sept daily 8.30am–6pm; $3.50) is dedicated to the region's farmers and settlers, the prime exhibit a reconstruction of a prairie village circa 1920.

## Battleford

From North Battleford there are two roads over the North Saskatchewan River: a modern flyover that's part of Hwy 16, and the shorter old route 16A, carried on a pair of rickety wooden bridges that span the narrow channels on either side of Finlayson Island. Across the river, the **Fred Light Museum**, at Central Ave and 20th St (mid-May to Aug daily 9am–7pm; $2), has a substantial collection of early firearms and a replica of an old general store, but is thoroughly upstaged by the **Fort Battleford National Historic Park** (May–Aug daily 9am–6pm; free), overlooking the river valley from the top of a steep bluff just down the road. At the entrance to the park, the visitor information centre provides a general introduction to the fort and, next door, the restored barracks contains a display explaining its history, assisted by well-informed, costumed guides.

Within the replica stockade stand four original buildings, including the **Sick Horse Stable**, where the delicate constitutions of the Mounties' horses – most of which came from Ontario – were coaxed into accepting the unfamiliar prairie grasses. Centrepiece of the park is the **Commanding Officer's Residence**, which has been returned to its appearance in the 1880s. Broadly Gothic Revival in style, the hewn-log house contains an enormous carved bedhead and a couple of magnificent black and chrome oven ranges, which must have been a nightmare to transport this far west. However, the house was not as comfortable as it seems today, principally because the high ceilings made the rooms almost impossible to heat. As the first commanding officer, James Walker, moaned in 1879, "This morning with the thermometer 37 degrees below, water was frozen on the top of the stove in my bedroom."

## Restaurants

North Battleford is short on good **restaurants**, but there are several cheap and central places with filling menus. Try the *Dragon Palace*, 1292 101st St at 13th Ave, where simple Chinese dishes start at $6, or the *Kresge* department store, 101st St at 12th Ave, which has burgers and sandwiches from $4. Alternatively, *Smitty's Family Restaurant*, just outside the town centre in the *Tropical Inn*, has good, basic dishes from $8. Best of all, *Pennydale Junction*, over the river in Battleford at 92 22nd St and 1st Ave West, has great seafood, pizzas and steaks from $9.

## On from the Battlefords: Lloydminster

Some 140km west of the Battlefords you hit the Alberta-Saskatchewan border, and the dreary town of **LLOYDMINSTER**, which was founded in 1903 by a group of 2000 British pioneers known as the Barr colonists. The only attraction is the **Barr Colony Heritage Cultural Centre**, located beside the Yellowhead at 44th Street and 45th Avenue (June–Aug daily 10am–8pm; Sept–May Wed–Fri 1–6pm & Sat–Sun 1–5pm; $2.50), and even this is scarcely pulse-racing – a small display on the founders together with a couple of art galleries and a wildlife exhibition.

Yet Lloydminster is a popular town for a break in the journey, and has lots of **hotels** and **motels** along its two main streets, 44th Street (the Yellowhead) and 50th Avenue (Hwy 17). The pick of these are the *Capri Motor Inn*, 4615 50th Ave (☎875-7000; doubles from $25); *Cedar Inn Motel*, 4526 44th St (☎825-6155; doubles $30), *Imperial 400 Motel*, 4320 44th St (☎825-4400; doubles from $54); and the *Esquire Motor Inn*, 5620 44th St (☎875-6113; doubles from $45). For **camping**, *Weaver Park Campground* (mid-April to Oct; ☎825-3726), next door to the heritage centre, has sites from $8. The Chamber of Commerce has a **tourist office** at 4905 50th Ave (Mon–Fri 9am–5pm; ☎825-4390) and both *Tourism Saskatchewan* and *Alberta Tourism* run seasonal **visitor reception centres** on either side of the border.

# Northern Saskatchewan

Stretching from Prince Albert National Park to the border with the Northwest Territories on the 60th parallel, the inhospitable and largely uninhabited expanse of **northern Saskatchewan** accounts for almost half the province. The region divides into two slightly different areas, the marginally richer flora and fauna of the **Interior Plains** lying south of the more spartan landscapes of the **Canadian Shield**, whose naked rock stretches north of a rough curve drawn between La Loche, La Ronge and Flin Flon, on the Manitoba boundary.

Northern Saskatchewan's shallow soils are unable to support any form of agriculture and its native peoples, the **Woodland Cree**, have traditionally survived by hunting, trapping and fishing. In recent times, this precarious and nomadic existence has been

---

### WILDERNESS CANOEING

Northern Saskatchewan has an abundance of **canoe routes** sprinkled across its thousands of lakes. However, it's important that prospective canoeists come fully prepared both in terms of equipment and knowledge of the proposed route. For independent and experienced wilderness travellers, the **Saskatchewan Parks Department** issue a comprehensive range of free material that includes route descriptions, lists of outfitters, details of campgrounds and information on climate, wildlife and potential hazards. They also sell detailed local maps and will help you book lodge or cabin accommodation – reckon on $20 per person per night, though costs vary according to the size of the group and the type of lodge. The department has **offices** in a number of towns, but their **headquarters** are at 3211 Albert Street, Regina (Mon–Fri 8am–5pm; ☎787-2700). This office also operates a **toll-free advice line** in summer on ☎1-800-66 PARKS.

Saskatchewan has a host of **tour operators** running hunting, fishing and canoe excursions into the north of the province from the middle of May to September. A full list of these is provided in the *Saskatchewan Outdoor Adventure* booklet, available at most tourist offices and travel agents. Alternatively, the parks department coordinates *Parkspirit Adventure and Leisure Packages*, 3211 Albert St, Regina (☎787-7828), whose programme of activities includes hiking in Clearwater Park for $300 per week and canoe trips in and around Lac La Ronge Park from about $400 for five days.

replaced by a more settled and restricted life on the reservations which are concentrated around **Lake Athabasca**. Nearly all the other settlements in the north are **mining towns**, the result of the discovery of uranium in the 1950s. The main exception is the tourist-resort-cum-mining centre of **La Ronge**, situated on the edge of the lakes and forests of **Lac La Ronge Provincial Park**. La Ronge is also near a section of the **Churchill River**, whose remote waters boast some of the north's best canoe routes. Finally, **Clearwater River Provincial Park**, near the Alberta border, provides some of the region's most challenging whitewater canoeing.

Although northern Saskatchewan attracts hundreds of hunters, anglers and canoeists throughout the summer, it has an extremely poor public transport system. There's just one really useful **bus**, a seasonal weekday service connecting Saskatoon, Prince Albert, Waskesiu and La Ronge.

## La Ronge and around

About 240km north of Prince Albert, readily accessible along Hwy 2/102, the scrawny, straggling resort of **LA RONGE** is sandwiched between the road and the western edge of Lac La Ronge. An unremarkable place, it was home to an isolated Cree community until the road reached here in 1948. Since then, gold mines have been opened just to the north of town and the area's lakes and rivers have proved popular with visiting canoeists and anglers.

Falling either side of Boardman Street, the town is fronted by La Ronge Avenue, which runs parallel to the waterfront, the location of the **bus depot**. A few minutes' walk away, in Mistasinihk Place, there's the office of the **Saskatchewan Parks Department** (Mon–Fri 8am–5pm; ☎425-4234) and an interpretive centre with exhibits on northern lifestyles, crafts and history. The nearest **visitor reception centre** (mid-May to mid-Sept Mon–Thurs 10am–9pm & Fri–Sun 10am–10pm; ☎425-2777) is 2km south of town beside Hwy 2.

A good base for exploring the region, La Ronge has several reasonably priced and central **hotels** and **motels**. These include the *Drifters Motel*, at the entrance to town, beside Hwy 2 (☎425-2224; doubles $50); *Kikinahk Hostel*, at Boardman St and Bedford (☎425-2051; doubles $30, dormitory beds $15); *La Ronge Motor Hotel*, 1120 La Ronge Ave (☎425-2190; doubles from $45); and the *Northland Motor Hotel*, La Ronge Ave at Hastings St (☎425-2323; doubles $40–60). There's a series of **campgrounds** strung along Hwy 102 north of town, the nearest of which is *Nut Point* (mid-May to Aug; ☎425-4234), 1km north via La Ronge Avenue.

### LAC LA RONGE PROVINCIAL PARK

La Ronge is on the western edge of **Lac La Ronge Provincial Park**, which incorporates all 1300 square kilometres of Lac La Ronge and extends north to encompass a number of smaller lakes and a tiny section of the **Churchill River**, once the main route into the northwest for the voyageurs. The Churchill swerves across the width of the province, from west to east, before heading on into Manitoba, its waterways providing some of the region's longest canoe routes. The parks department provide a detailed description of the river and its history in their booklet entitled *Voyageur Highway*. Less strenuously, these waters are also good for fishing – the wall-eye, pike and lake trout are delicious.

A number of La Ronge **tour operators** and **outfitters** run and equip fishing and canoeing trips into the park, most of them using its web of lakeside holiday **lodges** and **cabins**; the parks department office has the details. There are also several **campgrounds** along Hwy 102 including the *Missinipe* (mid-May to Aug; ☎425-4234) on Otter Lake, where the highway crosses the Churchill River.

North of La Ronge, Hwy 102 deteriorates long before it reaches **MISSINIPE**, 80km away, the home of *Horizons Unlimited* (☎635-4420), one of the best wilderness holiday companies. Beyond here, the road joins **route 905**, a bumpy 300-kilometre track that leads to the uranium mines around Wollaston Lake.

## Clearwater River Provincial Park

Apart from Highway 2/102, the only other paved road running into the heart of northern Saskatchewan is **Highway 155**, which extends as far as the tiny town of **LA LOCHE**, near the Alberta border. From here, a rough, gravel track, **route 955**, passes through **Clearwater River Wilderness Park** before continuing on to the uranium mines of Cluff Lake. The park's main feature is the rugged **Clearwater River Valley**, whose turbulent waters are recommended only to the experienced whitewater canoeist. There's a small and simple free **campground** (May to mid-Nov; ☎822-2033) where the river meets the road, but otherwise the nearest accommodation is back in La Loche, 60km to the south. The town has one **motel**, the *Northern Lights* (☎822-2222; doubles $50), located beside the highway, and a parks department office (Mon–Fri 9am–4.30pm; ☎822-2030).

## Lake Athabasca

A particular favourite of the hook-and-bullet brigade, wild and remote **Lake Athabasca**, close to the 60th parallel, can be reached only by private **float plane**. This is the region's largest lake, and much of its southern shore is protected as the **Athabasca Sand Dunes Parkland Reserve**, the most northerly sand dunes in the world. Several companies organise excursions to the area that include flights, food, accommodation and boat rental; if you can afford $3000 for a six-day trip, try *Athabasca Camps*, Box 7800, Saskatoon (☎306/653-5490), or *Tourama Tours*, 2606 Lindsay St, Regina (☎306/352-8313).

## travel details

### Trains

**From Winnipeg** to Sioux Lookout/Sudbury/Toronto (3 weekly; 8hr/26hr/34hr); Saskatoon/Edmonton/Vancouver (3 weekly; 9hr 35min; 18hr; 44hr); Dauphin/The Pas/Churchill (3 weekly; 4hr/12hr/36hr); Flin Flon (2 daily; 12hr 40min).

### Buses

**From Winnipeg** to Thunder Bay/Sault Ste Marie/Sudbury/Toronto (3 daily; 14hr/18hr/23hr/26hr); Brandon/Regina/Moose Jaw/Calgary/Vancouver (3 daily; 3hr/7hr/8hr/17hr/32hr); Portage la Prairie/Neepawa/Dauphin/Flin Flon/The Pas (1–3 daily; 1hr/2hr 30min/6hr 30min/11hr 30min/14hr 30min); Saskatoon/North Battleford/Vancouver (3 daily; 19hr/20hr/30hr); Rennie/West Hawk Lake (1 daily; 2hr/2hr 30min); Kenora (4 daily; 2hr 30min); Gimli (1 daily; 1hr 30min); Lac Du Bonnet (3 daily; 2hr); Grand Beach Provincial Park (1 daily; 1hr 40min).

**From Saskatoon** to Prince Albert (3–5 daily; 1hr 40min); North Battleford (4 daily; 1hr 35min).

**From Regina** to Saskatoon (4 daily; 3hr); Coronach (1 daily; 4hr 15min); Prince Albert (2 daily; 6hr 30min).

**From Prince Albert** to La Ronge (1 daily; 3hr 50min); Waskesiu Lake (early May–mid-Sept Mon–Sat 1 daily; 1hr 40min).

### Flights

**From Winnipeg** to Churchill, Manitoba (Mon–Fri 2 daily; 3hr 40min); The Pas (1 daily; 1hr 30min); Regina (5 daily; 1hr 10min); Saskatoon (6 daily; 1hr 20min); Calgary (7 daily; 2hr 20min); Toronto (12 daily; 2hr 20min); Vancouver (10 daily; 4hr).

**From Regina** to Saskatoon (9 daily; 40min); Calgary (6 daily; 1hr 20min); Toronto (8 daily; 3hr); Vancouver (8 daily; 2hr 30min).

**From Saskatoon** to Regina (8 daily; 40min); Calgary (5 daily; 1hr); Toronto (6 daily; 4hr); Vancouver (8 daily; 2hr 10min).

# CHAPTER SIX

# ALBERTA AND THE ROCKIES

**A**lberta is Canada at its best, and for many people the legendary beauty of the **Canadian Rockies**, which rise with awesome majesty from the rippling prairies, is the main reason for coming to the country. Most visitors confine themselves to the four contiguous national parks – **Banff**, **Jasper**, **Yoho** and **Kootenay** – that straddle the southern portion of the range, a vast area whose fairly arbitrary boundaries spill over into British Columbia. Two smaller parks, **Glacier** and **Mount Revelstoke**, lie firmly in BC and not, technically speaking, in the Rockies, but scenically and logistically it makes sense to group them with the others. Managed with remarkable efficiency and integrity, all the parks are easily accessible terrains of recreation carved out of a much wider wilderness of peaks and forests that extend from the Canada–US border northwards before merging into the huge ranges of the Yukon and Alaska.

If you're approaching the Rockies from the east, you'll have no choice but to spend time in either Edmonton or Calgary, the province's only two cities of any size, and the transport hubs for northern and southern Alberta respectively. Poles apart in feel and appearance, the two cities are locked in an intense rivalry, and one in which **Calgary** comes out top in almost every respect. Situated on the **Trans-Canada Highway** – which takes you to the heart of Banff National Park in less than ninety minutes – it's closer to the main towns of the Rockies and offers a more logical itinerary if you want to take in Yoho, Kootenay, Glacier or Revelstoke, and is undisputedly more convenient for pushing on to southern British Columbia and the west coast. As a city to spend time in, it's also got far more going for it: the weather is kinder (there's more sunshine here than anywhere else in the country), the Calgary Stampede offers one of the country's rowdiest festivals, and the vast revenues from the oil and natural gas that make Alberta one of Canada's richest provinces have been spent to good effect on its downtown skyscrapers and civic infrastructure.

**Edmonton** is a bleaker city, resting on the edge of an immense wilderness of boreal forest and low hills that stretches to the border of the Northwest Territories and beyond. Ignored by the Canadian Pacific Railway which brought an early boom to Calgary, its main importance to travellers is as a gateway to the Alaska Highway and the arctic extremities of the Yukon, and to the more popular landscapes of northern British Columbia – the **Yellowhead Highway** and Canada's last transcontinental **railway** link Edmonton to the town of Jasper and its national park in about four hours.

---

## TOLL-FREE INFORMATION NUMBERS

Alberta Tourism ☎1-800-222-6501 within Alberta,
☎1-800-661-8888 from elsewhere in Canada and the US.
Tourism British Columbia ☎1-800-663-6000.

# EDMONTON AND NORTHERN ALBERTA

Unless your choice of transport and approach specifically consigns you to **Edmonton**, there's no substantial reason, apart from the Folk Music Festival, to make a trip to the more downbeat of Alberta's pair of pivotal cities. Onward movement means either heading west into the Rockies and Jasper National Park or traversing the unimaginable distances of the far northern interior. Northern Alberta contains the only all-weather road link to Yellowknife, capital of the Northwest Territories, but other than **Wood Buffalo National Park** – the largest protected area in Canada – and a surfeit of fishing possibilities, the region has nothing to waylay most visitors.

> The **telephone code** for Alberta is ☎403.

# Edmonton

Alberta's provincial capital, **EDMONTON** is the most northerly city in North America, and at times – particularly in the teeth of its bitter winters – it can seem a little too far north, as if it had developed reluctantly where a city was needed but not really wanted. Much of the downtown area still has the unfinished feel of a frontier town; windfall oil revenues have been put to less spectacular architectural effect here than they have been in Calgary. Against this background, perhaps it's appropriate that the premier attraction for seventy percent of visitors is a shopping centre. Once you've done **West Edmonton Mall**, however, there's little cause to delay your departure, unless you're around during one of its occasionally outstanding **festivals**.

Fort Edmonton was founded in 1795 by William Tomison for the Hudson's Bay Company and quickly built to compete with nearby Fort Augustus, which was opened earlier that year by the rival North West Company. Though it soon became a major trading post, **settlers** arrived in force only after 1870, when the company sold its governing right to the Dominion of Canada, and even then the city only became firmly established during the Yukon gold rush of 1897, through a scam of tragic duplicity. Prompted by the city's outfitters – virtually the only breed to make any money from the rush – newspapers lured prospectors with the promise of an "All Canadian Route" to the goldfields that avoided Alaska and the dreaded Chilkoot Trail (see p.582). In the event this turned out to be a largely phantom trail across 1900 miles of intense wilderness, and hundreds of men perished as they pushed north; many of those who survived, or who never set off, ended up settling in Edmonton. World War II saw the city's role reinforced by its strategic position relative to Alaska and the new Alaska Highway, and its postwar growth was guaranteed by the Leduc oil strike in 1947. If Edmonton has achieved any fame since, it has been in the field of **sports**, as the seat of the 1978 Commonwealth Games and the home of Wayne Gretzky, the greatest player in ice-hockey history – though he has now defected from the Edmonton Oilers to a more lucrative future in Los Angeles.

## Arrival, accommodation and transport

Edmonton is one of the easiest places to reach in western Canada. Road and rail links are second to none, and the airport receives its share of long-haul flights from Europe and the United States. After the closure of the famous Rockies railway via Calgary, Edmonton is also where you'll arrive if you take Canada's last remaining transcontinental passenger train.

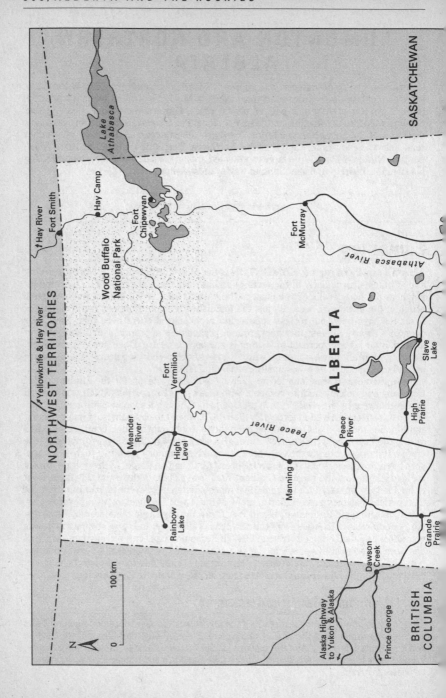

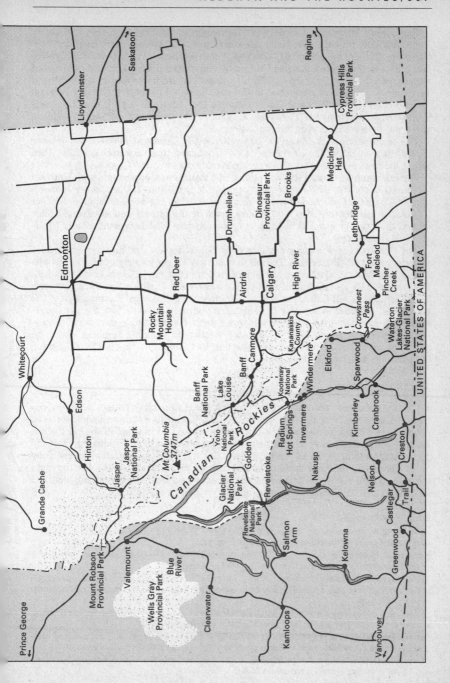

Edmonton's international **airport** is 29km south of downtown off Hwy 2 (Calgary Trail). A shuttle **bus**, the *Grey Goose Airporter*, runs to downtown every half-hour from 5.15am to 12.15am for around $11 one way – cheaper than a taxi (about $35) if you're on your own. Edmonton is served by many American, British and other European airlines, and the majority of internal flights – especially from the Yukon and Northwest Territories – fly here in preference to Calgary; numerous shuttle flights ply between the two cities. Some short-hop flights may use the municipal airport, north of downtown off 97th Street near 118th Avenue. City buses connect it to downtown and there's also a shuttle service between the two airports.

The **train station** is downtown beneath the CN Tower at 10004–104th Avenue Equally convenient for the city centre is the *Greyhound* **bus terminal** at 10324–103rd Street, the centre of a network that extends over most of western Canada.

For **information** contact the well-equipped **Edmonton Convention and Tourism Authority** at no. 104, 9797-Jasper Ave (summer daily 8.30am–4.30pm; winter Mon–Fri only; ☎422-5505). If necessary they'll also help with finding accommodation. Smaller information centres are also located downtown at the airport and at several points around the city. For material on the rest of the province visit **Travel Alberta** at 10015-102nd St (☎427-4321).

The downtown area is easily negotiated on foot. Without a car, however, you'll have to get to grips with **Edmonton Transit** to make any longer journeys. Maps of the integrated bus/light-rail system are available throughout the city. Tickets cost $1.25–1.50, day passes $3.50, and during off-peak periods travel is free within the downtown area. **Taxis** are cheap, but difficult to hail on the street: see "Listings" for numbers of cab companies. **Addresses** are easy to decipher if you remember that avenues run east–west, with numbers increasing as you travel further north, while streets run north–south, the numbers increasing as you move westwards. Building numbers tend to be tacked on to the end of street numbers, so that 10021-104th Avenue is 21 100th Street, at the intersection with 104th Avenue.

## Accommodation

Edmonton sees far fewer tourists than Calgary, leaving the city's budget **accommodation** less burdened but also less salubrious than that of its southern neighbour. You should have few problems finding a reasonably priced bed in some of the big middle-ranking hotels, many of which cut their prices out of season. If you're driving, there are plenty of **motels** in the bleak outskirts of the city, the main concentrations being along Stony Plain Road (north of downtown) and on the Calgary Trail (south). For the more intimate though not necessarily cheaper option of **bed and breakfast** lodgings, call the *Alberta Bed and Breakfast Association*, 4327-86th St (☎462-8885).

### Hotels and motels

**Best Western Ambassador Motor Inn**, 10041-106th St (☎423-1925 or ☎1-800-528-1234). Mid-sized central motel with covered parking; rooms from $49.

**Edmonton Centre Travelodge**, 10209-100th Ave (☎428-6442). Reliable downtown motel with covered parking, TV, phones; singles from $50, doubles from $65.

**Grand Hotel**, 10266-103rd Street (☎422-6365). Anything but grand – clean but knocked about, it's used mainly by long-stay residents – but its location almost alongside the bus terminal is handy; rooms $20 and up.

**Hotel Cecil**, 10406-Jasper Ave (☎428-7001). Extremely central and convenient for the bus terminal, but you're probably taking your life in your hands here; rooms from $20.

**Inn on 7th**, 10001-107th St (☎429-2861 or ☎1-800-661-7327). Modern, quiet and civilised, and probably the best of the middle-range hotels; singles from $59, doubles from $69; extra beds $10.

**Mayfair Hotel** 10815-Jasper Ave (☎423-1650). Elegant and recently reurbished rooms; singles from $50, $6 per additional person (breakfast included).

**Renford Inn at 5th**, 10425-100th Ave (☎423-5611). Full range of facilities, including jacuzzis; all rooms $65, $6 for each additional bed.

**Royal Park Apartment Hotel**, 9835-106th St (☎420-0809). Downbeat, slightly off-centre spot with suites from $35–65.

## Hostels and student rooms

**Edmonton Youth Hostel**, 10422-91st St off Jasper Ave (IYHF; ☎429-0140). A friendly place within walking distance of both the station and bus terminal with views south over the city; however, women alone should take care if walking here at night. The common room is a good spot to pick up travel information, particularly if you're heading north. Closed daily 10am–5pm, with a rigidly observed midnight curfew. Members $10, non-members $15.

**St Joseph's College**, 114th St & 89th Ave (☎492-7681). Small, cheap and popular student rooms; reservations required in summer. Well out of the centre but served by several buses including the #43. Singles $20; doubles $28; breakfast $5.50.

**University of Alberta**, 97th Ave between 112th & 114th St (☎492-4281). Basic institutional student rooms available in summer from $25.

**YMCA**, 10030-102nd Ave (☎421-9622). Men and women welcome in clean, sprightly and largely refurbished building. Singles from $20, doubles from $35; three-bunk dorms $10 per person (2 nights maximum).

**YWCA**, 10305-100th Ave (☎429-8707). Quiet and pleasant women-only accommodation with free use of swimming pool and cheap cafeteria (open to all). Dorm bunks from $10; singles from $25.

## Campgrounds

**Androssan Campground**. Located 18km east of downtown on Hwy 16; 24 free pitches, but no water or facilities other than fire pits.

**Bretona Campground**. On Hwy 14 about 18km southeast of Edmonton; free but no facilities.

**Half Moon Lake Resort**, Sherwood Park (☎922-3045). A private site with extensive facilities, 29km east of town on Hwy 14 and then 4km down a signposted side road.

**Klondike Valley Tent and Trailer Park**, Hwy 2 (south), Ellerslie Rd (☎988-5067). May–Sept only.

**Shakers Acres Tent and Trailer Park**, 21530-103rd Ave (☎447-3564). On the northwest edge of the city.

# The City

Edmonton comes across as a strangely dispersed place, even in the **downtown** area around Sir Winston Churchill Square and along the main east–west drag known as Jasper Avenue (101st Avenue). Bounded on the south by the North Saskatchewan River, this roughly six-block grid contains the train and bus stations and a few odd points of interest. Cosmopolitan Edmonton, such as it is, resides south of the river in **Old Strathcona** (see "Eating and drinking"). Trips further afield entail long bus journeys to outer suburbs, though you might want to pay homage to the past at the **Provincial Museum of Alberta** or **Fort Edmonton Park**, or worship at one of the great temples of contemporary consumer culture, **West Edmonton Mall**.

## Downtown

Downtown Edmonton only really comes alive as a place to wander on sunny days when office workers pour out for lunch; it's not much of a place to linger, but the following low-key sights would keep you occupied if you had some time to kill.

Vista 33 (daily 10am–5pm; 50¢) is a viewpoint on the thirty-third floor of the Alberta Telephone Tower, 10020-100th St – the panorama doesn't reach the mountains, but it does open your eyes to the vast prairie domain of Edmonton's hinterland. The **Edmonton Art Gallery** (daily 10am–5pm; $2, free Wed 5–9pm), part of the Civic Centre on the north edge of Sir Winston Churchill Square, deals mainly in modern Canadian artists, though it also hosts many visiting exhibitions. More satisfyingly

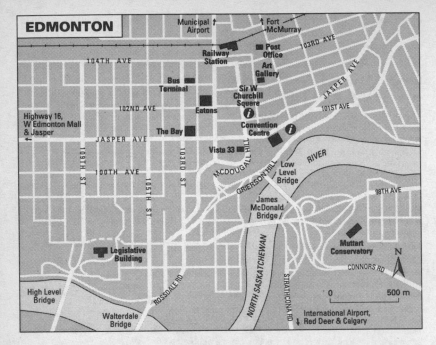

offbeat is the **Police Museum**, on the third floor of the central police station at 9620-103A Ave (Tues–Sat 10am–3pm; free), which traces the long arm of Albertan law enforcement from the RCMP's formation in 1873 to the flatfoots of the city's current force. Marvel at handcuffs, old jail cells, and a stuffed rat that served time as an early RCMP mascot.

For a little leg-stretch, you could head out to the distinctive glass pyramids of the **Muttart Conservatory** (daily 11am–9pm; $5), located just south of downtown and reached by walking across the Low Level Bridge or taking the #51 bus. Three high-tech greenhouses duplicate tropical, temperate and arid climates, together with the trees, plants and tangy aromas that go with them; a fourth houses a potpourri of experimental botanical projects.

Finally, you might stop by for a guided tour of the **Alberta Legislative Building**, located south of Jasper Avenue on 108th Street (every 30min Mon–Fri). Set in the manner of a medieval cathedral over an ancient shrine, the domed sandstone pile of Alberta's provincial legislature was built in 1912 on the original site of Fort Edmonton.

### The Provincial Museum of Alberta

Edmonton badly needs a new museum that lives up to its role as provincial capital. Housed in a drab building well out in the western suburbs at 12845-102nd Avenue, the **Provincial Museum of Alberta** (daily 9am–8pm; free) is loaded with dated, utilitarian displays. Nonetheless, it makes a reasonable introduction to western Canada if Edmonton is your first stop in the region, and if you haven't already seen the much better museums of Calgary, Victoria and Vancouver. To reach it by bus, take the #1, #2, #115, #116 or #120 from Jasper Avenue dowtown.

The **natural history** exhibits feature numerous painted dioramas and stuffed animals, taxidermy being the didactic stock in trade of virtually all western Canada's museums; by far the best section concerns the region's bison herds and their virtual extinction. Other displays include a pretty humdrum collection of "Artefacts of Domestic Utility" (pots and pans, in plain language), one or two beautiful chrome stoves and vintage juke-boxes, and a rundown of the **native peoples** of the province. The latter collection is merely workaday, though the "Self Torture" section contains some harrowing exhibits, the nipple-stretching implements being particularly eye-watering.

## Fort Edmonton Park

Located southwest of the city on a deep-cut bend of the North Saskatchewan River, **Fort Edmonton Park** (daily 10am–6pm; $5) undertakes to re-create the history of white settlement in Edmonton during the nineteenth century. Everything has been built from scratch, and while you can't fault the attention to detail, the pristine woodwork of the supposedly old buildings hardly evokes period authenticity. Buses #32 and #123 go directly from downtown to the site, which is off the Whitemud Freeway near the Quesnell Bridge.

The heart of the complex is a facsimile of **Fort Edmonton**, a fur-trading post dominated by the Big House, home of the Chief Factor, John Rowland, head of the then ill-defined Saskatchewan District from 1828 to 1854. Arranged around it are the quarters of the 130 or so people who called the fort home, their place today taken by appropriately dressed guides pretending to be blacksmiths, clerks, shopkeepers, schoolteachers and so forth. Edmonton's later, pre-railway era is represented by a rendition of Jasper Avenue as it appeared in 1885, complete with shops, RCMP station and Alberta's first Protestant church. Two other streets, simulating 1905 and 1920, offer rides on steam engines and tram cars to bolster the period effect.

## West Edmonton Mall

"Your Adventure Awaits" announces the brochure to **West Edmonton Mall**, preparing you for the sort of hoopla you'd expect from a place that gets eleven mentions in the *Guinness Book of Records*, including its main claim to fame as "largest shopping mall in the world". Built at a total cost of $1.1 billion, the complex extends over the equivalent of 115 American football fields and boasts over 800 shops, 11 department stores, the world's largest indoor lake, a vast swimming complex, and the world's largest indoor amusement arcade. The mall's effect on Edmonton has been double-edged: it has captured thirty percent of the city's retail business, thus decimating the downtown shopping area, but it has also succeeded, to everyone's surprise, in attracting an estimated nine million tourists a year.

The sheer size of the place could keep you browsing all day in horror and amazement, and it's hard not to get sucked in by the whole extravaganza. The **Indoor Lake**, for instance, contains a full-sized replica of Columbus's galleon, the *Santa Maria*, and four working submarines – more than are owned by the Canadian navy. The **amusement arcade** features such attractions as the "Drop of Doom", a thirteen-storey "free-fall experience", and the fourteen-storey "Mindbender" roller-coaster. The **World Waterpark**, by contrast, is a superb collection of swimming pools, immense water slides and wave pools; you can hire a towel and swimming togs for a dip in what'll probably be the biggest swimming pool you've ever seen (day pass $18.95; after 5pm $12.95). You could round off the day in one of the mall's many **cinemas**, and if you want to go the whole hog spend the night in the **Fantasyland Hotel**, which offers rooms "themed in six different fantasies": Roman, Hollywood, Arabian, Victorian Coach, Canadian Rail and, most intriguing of all, Truck.

The #10 **bus** goes straight to the mall, heading west out of town along Jasper Avenue west of 101st Street. Maps of the mall are available throughout the main building.

# Eating and drinking

Few places stand out amongst Edmonton's 2000-odd **restaurants**, but if you want a bit of nocturnal zip to go with your meal you'd do best to head out to Old Strathcona, a vibrant district of café culture, nightlife and alternative arts located along 82nd (Whyte) Avenue between 102nd and 105th streets – any bus marked "University Transit Centre" from 100th Street will get you there. Ethnic options – notably restaurants serving Edmonton's large Ukrainian and Eastern European populations – complement the standard steak-and-salmon offerings. Otherwise, the stalls in the *Eaton's* mall and downtown streetfront eateries are lively at lunchtime, and all the usual fast-food, snack and cheap breakfast options are available, the best of which are the *YWCA* and *YMCA* cafés. If you're a beer drinker, be sure to try the local real ale, *Big Rock*.

## Cafés, snacks and bars

**Café le Gare**, 10308a-81st Ave. Small tea-and-coffee joint in Old Strathcona, the sort of place where you can read a book or paper for hours; poetry readings Mon nights.

**Grabbajabba**, 82nd Ave & 104th St. Great music and coffee at this very popular non-smoking café in the heart of Old Strathcona.

**Hot Pastrami**, 1044-108th St. Office-worker favourite for its deli-style food (from 6.30am) and home of the $2.50 breakfast.

**9th Street Café**, 8615-109th St. Relaxed and cosy student hang-out – generous helpings, imaginative soups and renowned desserts.

**Old Strathcona Coffee Factory**, 8224-104th St. Amongst the most lively and popular coffee, food and beer places in Old Strathcona. You'll have to queue most nights and it's especially busy during the Fringe.

**Old Strathcona Diner Beer and Wine Garden**, 8223-104th St. Near the above, similarly friendly and casual, and with live jazz some nights. Good menu, including some innovative salads.

## Restaurants

**Bistro Praha**, 10168-100A St. One of the best places to sample Eastern European cuisine, Edmonton style, but highbrow and awfully expensive – better for lunch or late at night.

**Café Select**, 10018-106th St (☎423-0419). An excellent, intimate place, trendy without being intimidating. Serving fine simple food, it's downtown's best choice for a late-night splurge.

**Mongolian Food Experience**, 10160-100A St. A downtown Edmonton institution, hugely popular for lunchtime barbecue; a wide range of Chinese and Mongolian specialities also available.

**Oriental Noodle House**, 10718-101th St. A much-patronised spot for Vietnamese and Southeast Asian food at rock-bottom prices.

**Rose Bowl**, 10111-117th St. A frenetic and smoky den, probably the most popular of the city's countless pizzerias.

**Sceppa's Restaurant and Lounge**, 10921-101th St. Coffee bar, pool table, and Edmonton's best Italian restaurant alongside.

**Silk Hat**, 10251 Jasper Ave (☎428-1551). First choice amongst Edmonton's eateries – and also a fine place to knock back a *Molson* (the brewery's up the road) – this is a city institution whose dim, diner interior hasn't altered in 40 years. It's best known for the Fifties juke-boxes at each booth, but the cheap, basic food's as good as the ambience.

**Strathcona Gasthaus**, 10105-82nd Ave. Long-established Eastern European eatery renowned for its huge, stolid helpings and bargain-basement prices.

**Veggies**, 10221-82nd Ave. Good, full-blown vegetarian/non-smoking restaurant with extensive main course menu plus herbal iced teas and fruit and yogurt milkshakes.

**Vi's**, 112th St & 100th Ave (☎482-6402). Housed in an old residence with great views, an excellent place for a special occasion.

# Nightlife and entertainment

Edmonton's enthusiastic self-promotion as the "Festival City" may have something to do with its shortage of indigenous **nightlife**. But while clubs capable of attracting big names are thin on the ground, there are any number of small-time spots with live music, and the summer festivals certainly do liven things up. Most of the best clubs and live-music venues are in Old Strathcona. Big-name acts – as well as theatre, ballet and opera companies – tend to play at the University of Alberta's *Jubilee Auditorium*, 87th Avenue and 114th Street, and the *Coliseum*, 118th Avenue and 74th Street.

The best **listings** source is the free monthly, *Something Entertaining*, which gives a clear idea of what's on in the live music field and a more cursory survey of theatre, opera and cinema. Otherwise check out the alternative *Edmonton Bullet*, another free monthly, or the entertainment sections of the city's two main newspapers, the *Journal* and the *Sun*. For **tickets** to most events, visit one of the several *BASS* ticket outlets around the city (☎451-8000) – they'll also sell you tickets for Edmonton Oilers **ice-hockey** games, which are played in the *Northlands Coliseum*, 118th Avenue and 74th Street.

## Clubs, discos and live music

**Blues on Whyte** at the *Commercial Hotel*, 10329-82nd Ave. Widely acknowledged as one of the city's best live music clubs.

**Club Malibu** 10310-85th St. Top-40 disco in a converted armoury.

**Cook Country Saloon**, 8010-103rd St. Old Strathcona-based country-and-western venue that's much praised by locals.

**Esmeralda's at the Edmonton Inn**, 11830-Kingsway Ave. Another highly rated country-and-western hoedown.

**Goose Loonies**, 6250-99th St. Outlying but highly popular live music club.

**Sidetrack Café**, 10323-112th St. Despite its disconcertingly bombed-out surroundings, this is the best of the city's live music venues and where you're most likely to see international acts of some standing.

**The 6th Street Bar**, 10041-106th St. Downtown blues club with shows at 9.30pm and special 2pm Saturday jam session.

**Yardbird Suite**, 10203-86th Ave. Live groups nightly in the city's top jazz venue.

**Yuk Yuk's**, 7103-78th Ave. Assorted comedy acts every night, featuring well-known US and Canadian names.

## Festivals

Hardly any area of entertainment goes uncelebrated by a festival at some time of the year in Edmonton. Few merit a special pilgrimage to the city, a notable exception being the **Edmonton Folk Music Festival**, rated the best in North America by *Rolling Stone* – it's held at Gallagher Park (near the Muttart Conservatory) at the end of the first week in August. Also well regarded are the **International Street Performers Festival** in early July; the **International Jazz City Festival** at the end of June; and the August **Fringe Festival**, a nine-day theatrical jamboree that's the largest event of its kind in North America.

The more contrived and commercial **Klondike Days** is less compelling, a blowout that claims to be the continent's largest "outdoor entertainment" but has rather too obviously been cobbled together to steal some of Calgary's Stampede thunder. Held for ten days during July, it revolves around a re-creation of the 1890s gold-rush era, a dubious premise for a festival given the scam that brought many men to the city and then sent them to their deaths along a bogus trail. Nonetheless, it's a popular outing, with plenty for kids, and events along the lines of the Fun Tub Race and the Hairiest Chest Competition.

## Listings

**Airlines** *Air Canada* (☎423-1222 or ☎1-800-222-6596); *Canadian Airlines* (☎421-1414); *American* (☎1-800-433-7300); *Delta* (☎426-5990 or ☎1-800-221-1212).

**Bike rental** *River Valley Cycle and Sports*, 9701-100A St (☎421-9125); *Campus Outdoor Centre*, University of Alberta, 116th St & 87th Ave (☎492-2767).

**Books** *Greenwood's*, on 82nd Ave between 103rd & 104th, is one of the city's best; *Athabasca Books*, on 105th St north of 82nd Ave, is a quality secondhand outlet.

**Bus enquiries** *Greyhound* (☎421-4242); bus terminal (☎421-4211).

**Car rental** *Rent-A-Wreck*, 10140-109th St (☎423-1755); *Thrifty*, 10036-102nd St (☎428-855); *Hertz* (☎423-3431); *Budget* (☎448-2000).

**Consulates** *Great Britain*, 1404-0025 Jasper Ave (☎428-0375).

**Hospital** Edmonton General Hospital, 1111 Jasper Ave (☎268-9111).

**Police** ☎423-4567.

**Post office** 9808-103A Ave.

**Taxis** *Alberta Co-op* (☎425-8310); *Checker Cabs* (☎455-2211); *Prestige* (☎462-4444); *Yellow Cabs* (☎462-3456).

**Train information** *VIA rail* (☎422-6032).

**Weather information** ☎468-4940.

# Northern Alberta

North of Edmonton stretches an all but uninhabited landscape of rippling hills, rivers, lakes, lonely farms, open prairie and the unending mantle of the northern forests. Compared to the spectacular mountain scenery off to the west, however, northern Alberta is more akin to the pristine monotony of the central plains of Saskatchewan and Manitoba. Unless you're fishing or boating, or just into sheer untrammelled wilderness, little here is worth detouring for, with the possible exception of **Wood Buffalo National Park** on Alberta's northernmost border with the Northwest Territories.

Two great north-flowing waterways, the **Peace River** and **Athabasca River**, were the area's traditional arteries, but today they have been superseded by three basic roads, each of vital importance if you're heading north or west. The most travelled is **Highway 16** (the Yellowhead Highway) which runs due west from Edmonton to Jasper and onwards through the Rockies to Prince George and Prince Rupert (BC). The second is **Highway 43–Highway 2** to Grande Prairie and Dawson Creek (BC) – Mile Zero of the Alaska Highway. The third route is **Highway 43–Highway 35** (the Mackenzie Highway), which bisects northern Alberta and provides its only road link to the Northwest Territories.

Direct long-haul *Greyhound* **buses** run on all these routes from Edmonton, supplemented by the *VIA* **rail** service from Edmonton to Jasper (with connections on to Vancouver or Prince Rupert). In all cases you'll be able to sit tight on the bus without a break until your destination and shouldn't need to worry about overnight stops in any of the backwoods settlements en route. The distances in the area, coupled with the relatively monotonous scenery, however, means that few roads are worth travelling for their own sake, and on the trips to Wood Buffalo National Park or Hay River (NWT) in particular it's well worth thinking about **flying** as a time-saving option.

## Highway 16 to Jasper

**Highway 16**, or the Yellowhead Highway, is, as Edmonton's Chamber of Commerce likes to call it, "the other Trans-Canada Highway"; the second and less-travelled transcontinental route and – by comparison to the Calgary–Banff route – a duller way of making for the Rocky Mountain national parks. Jasper lies 357km west of Edmonton on the highway, an easy journey by car, **bus** (4 daily; $35), or on the **train** whose tracks run parallel to the highway for its duration (Tues, Fri & Sun; $67).

Numerous **campgrounds** and **motels** service the road at regular intervals, the main concentrations being at EDSON and HINTON. Edson, which lies at about the halfway mark to Jasper, makes the more obvious spot to break a journey. Its fourteen motels are all much of a muchness, the cheapest being the *Cedars*, 5720-4th Ave (☎723-4436), with doubles from $29. Two sites provide for campers: the *Lions Club Campground*, on the east side of town, and the *Willmore Recreation Park*, 6km south on the McLeod River.

## Highway 43–Highway 2 to Dawson Creek (BC)

**Highway 43** out of Edmonton to Grande Prairie, and **Highway 2** thereafter, ambles through terminally unexceptional towns, hills and prairie scenery on its way west to Dawson Creek (p.577). It's a mind-numbing day's journey however you tackle it, whether by car or **bus** (2 daily; $55); additional bus connections run as far as Grande Prairie, 463km from Edmonton, which is the town you're likely to wash up in if you're forced to break your journey.

Failing to live up to its evocative name, **GRANDE PRAIRIE**'s unfocused sprawl is, as with many similar-sited towns, a legacy of having the luxury of unlimited space in which to build. The **infocentre** is by Bear Creek Reservoir, off the main highway, which bypasses the main part of town to the west. Most of Grande Prairie's many **motels** are on the strip known as Richmond Avenue (100th Avenue), which links the southern part of the highway bypass to downtown. All are vast affairs with bargain prices – the top-of-the-line *Golden Inn Hotel*, 11201-100th Ave (☎539-6000), charges just $50 for rooms, and the cheapest, the *Econo-Lodge Motor Inn*, 10909-100th Ave (☎539-4700), $30 for doubles.

If you want perhaps Canada's ultimate cowboy **bar**, make for *Kelly's Bar* in the Sutherland Inn at CLAIRMONT, immediately north of Grande Prairie. Owned by a Calgary Stampede chuck wagon champion, it's the sort of place that has saddles for barstools and serves up shooters in bull-semen collection tubes.

## Highway 35 and Peace River Country

Alberta's northern reaches are accessible only from **Highway 35**, still a route for the adventurous and one which, according to Albertans, shows the real side of the province: a world of redneck homesteads, buffalo burgers, and the sort of genuine country-and-western bars where strangers on a Friday night meet silent stares but wind up being invited to the hoedown anyway. You'll find such spots more or less everywhere along the route, but very little in the way of motels, garages or campgrounds, so come prepared. The road itself is well kept and straight, allowing you to make healthier progress than on the more serpentine Alaska Highway to the west. If you're sticking to **buses**, *Greyhound* runs two services daily from Edmonton to Peace River and one all the way to Hay River (NWT).

If you're travelling under your own steam you'll probably have to overnight in **PEACE RIVER**, 486km from Edmonton and the starting point of Hwy 35. The largest town in the region, it has a couple of **motels**, the largest being the *Crescent* (☎624-2586), with rooms starting at $60; there's also a **campground** at Lion's Club Park ($12). **MANNING**, 50km north of Peace River, is the last sizeable community for another 200km, making its trio of **motels** vital and often surprisingly busy watering holes. The *Aurora* (☎836-3381) has doubles from $35, though only half the rooms have bathrooms; the *Hillcrest Motel* (☎836-3381) has more facilities for the same price; while the *Manning Motor Inn* (☎836-2801) has more expensive doubles ($45) but, unlike its competitors, admits additional beds to double rooms for just $3. For the municipal **campground** on the Notikewin River, turn east at the summer-only infocentre on the highway.

Only a couple of basic campgrounds and the odd windblown store disturb the peace **north of Manning**, though if you're **camping** it's as well to know you can expect the unwelcome nocturnal attention of bears in these parts. Official tenting spots are *Notikewin River*, a short way off the road at the junction with Hwy 692, 22km from the town; and *Twin Lakes Campground* another 15km up the road. The latter is close to the *Twin Lakes* **motel** (☎554-1348; $40), whose eight rooms are the only ones available between Manning and High Level.

As with all the larger settlements hereabouts, you're only going to stop in **HIGH LEVEL**, 199km north of Manning, as a place to bed down. Rates begin to creep up the further north you go, and you'll be paying around $50 for rooms in all four of the town's **motels**, the ritziest of which is *Our Place Apartment Hotel* (☎926-2556), followed by the *Lanner Motor Inn* (☎926-3736) and the *Sunset* (☎926-2272). Campers can overnight free at the drab municipal **campground** east of town on Hwy 58, but are better off splashing out for the private facilities of *Aspen Ridge Campground* (☎926-4540; $8), 3km south of the centre on the main road.

Between High Level and Hay River (NWT), a string of campgrounds provide the only accommodation, and three native hamlets – MEANDER RIVER STEEN RIVER and INDIAN CABINS – offer only food and petrol.

# Wood Buffalo National Park

Straddling the border between Alberta and the Northwest Territories, **Wood Buffalo National Park** covers an area larger than Switzerland, making it Canada's largest national park and the world's second largest protected environment. Primarily famous as home on the range for one of the world's only remaining free-roaming buffalo herds, it's also the last refuge of the critically endangered whooping crane – first discovered in a remote part of the park as late as 1954 – and the world's only river rookery of rare white pelicans, a species which elsewhere in its domain nests only on lakes. In addition to some 46 species of mammals found in the park, including bear and lynx, the Peace-Athabasca river delta in the southeast corner boasts an enormous concentration of wildfowl – 227 species – and no fewer than four major migration routes overfly the area, bringing millions of transient birds during seasonal movements. If its wildlife is spectacular, however, the park's topography, though wild and vast in its extent, is limited to low hills, grasslands, boreal forest and marsh.

The refuge was created initially in 1922 to protect an estimated 1500 **wood buffalo** (*Bison bison athabascae*), a longer-legged, darker and more robust relative of the plains buffalo (*Bison bison bison*). Six years later the federal government moved some 6000 plains buffalo to the park from the now nonexistent Buffalo National Park near Wainright, Alberta, when their grazing lands were appropriated for a firing range. Most of the present herd, now down to some 3000 members, is probably a hybrid strain, and has understandably become the subject of considerable controversy over plans to wipe it out (see box). At present, however, you'll still see plenty at the roadsides, more often than not wallowing in dust to escape the region's ferocious mosquitoes.

## Access and getting around

**Getting to** the park by road can be a slow business, and is possible only along a 280-kilometre stretch of Hwy 5 from Hay River (NWT) to Fort Smith. *North of 60 Bus Lines* runs **buses** from Hay River to Fort Smith (weekdays only; $35 one way; ☎874-6411 for information), with services timed to connect with the daily *Greyhound* from Edmonton. You can also easily **fly** to Fort Smith on scheduled flights from Edmonton (daily except Sun on *Canadian*), Hay River, Yellowknife and Vancouver, as well as on any number of wing-and-a-prayer charter planes that link the communities of the Northwest Territories and northern Alberta.

Highway 5, the only all-weather road in the park, makes a 150-kilometre run through the northeastern quadrant, and unless you're prepared to backpack or fly into the interior this is the only reliable **access** to the park proper. Branching off Hwy 5, 8km south of Fort Smith, is a 298-kilometre summer-only loop through the southeast corner, but some stretches are impassable after heavy rain, and you should check conditions with the park centre in Fort Smith (see below). The west leg of the loop leads to three of the only developed **trails** in the park – Salt River (after 15km), Rainbow Lakes (after 20km) and Pine Lake (after 65km), the latter with a nearby **campground**. Backwoods camping is allowed anywhere as long as it's at least 1500m from Pine Lake or any road or trail. **Canoeing** is wide open: the Athabasca and Peace River system was once the main route for trade from the south, and still offers limitless paddling options.

## Fort Smith

Though it's actually in the Northwest Territories, **FORT SMITH** is the only conceivable base for exploring Wood Buffalo National Park. Virtually the last settlement for several hundred kilometres east and north, the town started life as a Hudson's Bay

### THE BUFFALO KILL

Clean-living Canada rarely causes environmental outrage on an international scale, but since 1990 the federal government has been at the heart of a row with conservationists following proposals to wipe out Wood Buffalo's entire herd of buffalo. The herd has been found to be infected with **tuberculosis** and **brucellosis**, and government scientists claim the only way to keep these highly contagious diseases from spreading to Alberta's valuable beef herds is to **kill off** one of the only remaining populations of wood buffalo, a unique subspecies of the plains buffalo. Scientists opposed to the government plan point out that the herd has been infected for years, and as well as keeping the disease to itself, has survived by internal regulation and natural balance. Locals, who are largely opposed to the cull, point out that killing every animal would be a daunting task, given the immensity of the animals' range, and that it would presumably be fruitless if even a few were missed, as disease would erupt afresh when the herd regenerated.

The **restocking** issue has opened another can of worms, for there are just eighteen pure-bred, disease-free wood buffalo in captivity, and it is from these that the government intends to restart the herd. However, most experts argue that this would create a weak, inbred group which would compare badly with the large and long-evolved gene pool of the present herd. Other scientists take a completely different, laissez-faire line, maintaining that wood buffalo aren't genetically different from their plains cousins and therefore it wouldn't matter if they were wiped out as they could easily be replaced.

The dispute has quickly become extremely messy, reflecting fundamental changes in Canadian attitudes towards the rival claims of business and the environment in a tough financial climate. Beneath the whole question, many people see the hand of Canada's powerful **beef lobby** guiding the government's actions. Others see it as part of a move to relax the powerful injunctions protecting Canada's national parks and open the way for **economic growth** in what are, almost by definition, regions of depression and high unemployment. This has already started, with Alberta's government taking plains buffalo off the protected list and putting it onto restaurant menus by promoting buffalo farming as a means to boost its northern economy.

In the saga's most ironic twist, however, tuberculosis and brucellosis have turned up in **farmed game animals** (mainly elk), and a huge recent increase in game farming has led to an explosion in the very diseases that farmers are seeking to eradicate by culling the wild herds; animals bred in captivity are more susceptible to such diseases, and as farmed elk escape they are spreading them to areas far beyond the range of Wood Buffalo's supposed culprits. At the time of writing, the federal government had appointed a committee of interested parties to review the affair; the park's buffalo, for their part, are still nibbling contentedly as the debate continues.

trading post, and despite being only 1km from the Alberta border, was the NWT administrative centre until 1967, when the Ottawa government moved it to Yellowknife.

Call ahead to reserve rooms in one of Fort Smith's two **hotels**: the *Pelican Rapids Inn* (☎872-2789), with kitchenettes in every room, or the smaller *Pinecrest Hotel* (☎872-2320). For half the price of the hotels, however, you could try one of a dozen or so **bed and breakfasts** – the best contact is *Subarctic Wilderness Adventures* (☎872-2467), who'll ring around for a bed or put you up themselves in their lodge with singles at $40 with breakfast, $60 for full board. They also organise tours and **hire camping equipment**. There's a public **campground** alongside the Slave River on the northern edge of town, though Fort Smith's other stores and its two restaurants are clustered in a tiny two-block area of downtown. Make a point of dropping into the **Northern Life Museum**, 110 King St, which packs one of the best collections of the far north's traditional artefacts, crafts and archive photographs.

For more details on Wood Buffalo National Park, the park superintendent can be contacted at Fort Smith's summer-only **infocentre** (June–Sept 9am–9pm; ☎872-2349).

# CALGARY AND SOUTHERN ALBERTA

**Calgary** is the obvious focus of southern Alberta, but with some of the continent's most awesome mountains practically on its doorstep, it takes some self-restraint to give the city the couple of days it deserves. Perfectly placed where the prairies buckle suddenly into the Rockies, the city is by far the best point from which to strike west into the mountains or spend a couple of days gathering your wits if you've journeyed in from the east. Within day-tripping distance lie two unexpected gems: the dinosaur exhibits of the **Royal Tyrrell Museum**, near Drumheller in the strange badlands country east of Calgary; and the **Head-Smashed-In Buffalo Jump**, a Native American site in the heart of Alberta's beef and cowboy country to the south. However, the latter is most easily visited if you're following Hwy 3, the extreme southerly route across the province, as is **Waterton Lakes National Park**, which is isolated well to the south of the other Canadian Rockies parks.

# Calgary

Cities in North America don't come any more glittering than **CALGARY**, a likeable place whose impressive downtown skyscrapers rose almost overnight on the back of an oil boom in the Seventies to turn it into Canada's very own Dallas. The tight high-rise core is good for wandering, and contains Calgary's most prestigious sight, the **Glenbow Museum**, while the simple wooden houses of the far-flung suburbs show a different, homelier side to the city, recalling its pioneering frontier origins. These are further celebrated in the annual **Calgary Stampede**, a hugely popular cowboy carnival in which the whole town – and hordes of tourists – revel in a boots-and-stetson image that's still very much a way of life in the surrounding cattle country.

**Blackfoot** natives ranged over the site of present-day Calgary for several thousand years, and traces of old campsites, buffalo kills and pictographs litter the area – though tribal lands are now locally confined to a few reserves such as the one visible alongside the Trans-Canada Highway west of the city. Whites began to hover around the confluence of the Bow and Elbow rivers from about the turn of the nineteenth century, but it wasn't until the 1870s that a North West Mounted Police fort was established here to curb the lawlessness of the whiskey traders. Christened **Fort Calgary** after the

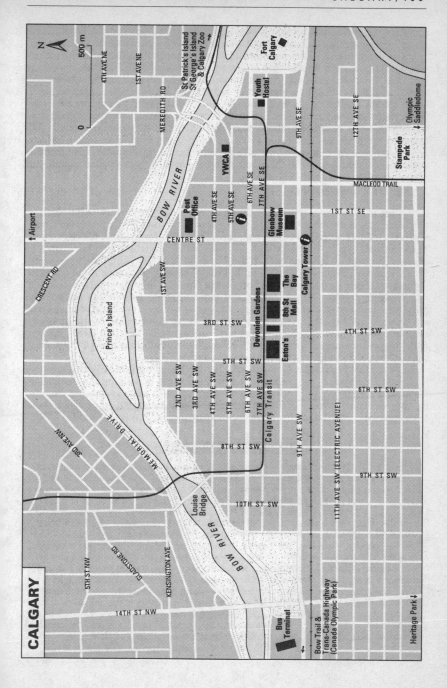

Scottish birthplace of its assistant commissioner, the new town quickly attracted ranchers and British gentlemen farmers to its low, hilly bluffs – which are indeed strongly reminiscent of Scottish moors and lowlands – and cemented an Anglo-Saxon cultural bias still far more apparent in latter-day Calgary than in other Albertan towns.

**Cattle** and the coming of the Canadian Pacific Railway generated exceptional growth and prosperity in the early part of this century; and when the Dingman No. 1 **oil** well blew, in 1914, it started a boom that set the stage for Calgary, by the early Seventies, to take on the mantle of a world energy and financial centre. Although falling commodity prices subsequently punctured the city's ballooning economy, it still managed to attract the 1988 **Winter Olympics**, two weeks of glory which Calgary seems loath to relinquish and which, like the legacy of its oil and cattle riches, continues to make the city seem a brash, self-confident and apparently prospering boomtown.

## Arrival and information

One of the best ways to approach Calgary is **by air**, if only for the view of the Rockies stretching across the western horizon as you come in to land. The city's international **airport**, a modern, often half-deserted strip, is about 10km northeast of the city centre. Taxis to downtown are expensive ($25), and the widely advertised free hotel coaches elusive. The most reliable ride in is on the **Airporter Bus** ($6), with departures every twenty minutes (5.30am–11.30pm) from in front of Level 1, the lowest of the airport's concourses. There's a small **information centre** (7am–11pm) in Level 2 (arrivals).

Arriving by **bus** at Calgary's brand-new terminal is comfortable but not terribly convenient. Located west of downtown at 8th Avenue SW and 16th Street, it leaves you a somewhat seedy thirty-minute walk to the city centre. Free transit buses, however, are available during the day to the C-Train at 7th Avenue SW and 10th Street, the key to the city's central transit system (see "City transport", opposite). **Taxis** for this short run cost around $5 and are plentiful outside the terminal.

Be aware that **hitching** is illegal within the city limits, following a series of gruesome assaults on and by hitch-hikers. However, buses run to downtown from outlying points, and often people will make a point of dropping you in a convenient spot. Outside the city you should have few problems picking up lifts. Take bus #51 either east or west to escape downtown, and ask the driver for connections onto the Trans-Canada.

---

### CHINOOKS

Winters in Calgary are occasionally moderated by **chinooks**, sudden warming winds that periodically sweep down the eastern flanks of the Rockies. Often heralded by a steely cloud band spreading from the mountains over the city, a chinook can raise the temperature by as much as 50°F in a couple of hours and evaporate a foot of snow in a day. Chinooks are the result of a phenomenon that occurs on leeward slopes of mountains all over the world, but nowhere more dramatically than in the plains of southwestern Alberta. The effect has to do with the way prevailing westerly winds are forced to rise over the Rockies, expanding and cooling on the way up and compressing and warming up again on the way back down. On the way up the cooling air, laden with Pacific moisture, becomes saturated – in other words, clouds form – and drops much of its rain and snow on the windward (western) side of the mountains. All this condensation releases latent heat, causing the rising air to cool more slowly than usual; but on the leeward descent the air, now relieved of much of its moisture, warms up at the normal rate. By the time it reaches Calgary it's both drier and warmer than it was to start with.

The name comes from the tribe that traditionally inhabited the area around the mouth of the Columbia River in Washington and Oregon, from where the winds seem to originate; the Chinook tribe also gives us the name of the largest species of Pacific salmon.

The main city **Tourist and Convention Bureau** is in the Burns Building at 237-8th Avenue SE (daily 8.30am–4.30pm; ☎ 263-8510); in July and August a more modest information booth at the same address is open from 8.30am to 7pm. Both dole out huge amounts of information and also provide a free accommodation-finding service. Other minor offices operate on the Trans-Canada Highway and on Macleod Trail (Hwy 2) heading south. For information on Alberta as a whole, head for **Travel Alberta** in the MacDougall Centre at 455-6th Street SW (Mon–Fri 8.15am–4.30pm; ☎297-8510).

For all its rapid expansion, Calgary is a well-planned and straightforward city engineered around an inevitable grid. The metropolitan area is divided into **quadrants** (NW, NE, SE and SW) with the Bow River dividing north from south, Centre Street–Macleod Trail east from west. **Downtown**, and virtually everything there is to see and do, is in a small area in or close to the SW quadrant. Streets run north–south, avenues east–west, with numbers increasing as you move out from the centre. As with Edmonton, the last digits of the first number refer to the house number – thus 237-8th Avenue SE is on 2nd Street at no. 37, close to the intersection with 8th Avenue.

## City transport

Almost everything in Calgary, barring Stampede locations and a few minor diversions, is a comfortable walk away – except in winter, when temperatures can make any excursion an ordeal. The city's much-vaunted **Plus 15 Walking System** is designed to beat the freeze. The network of enclosed walkways fifteen feet above ground is invaluable in winter, when you can walk through downtown without setting foot outside, but it's so confusing – the system's signs (blue and white circles) and tunnels directing you through a maze of malls – that you might as well ignore it if the weather's fine. Desperately complicated maps, if you can find them, are located at strategic points to guide you through the labyrinth.

**Public transport** is cheap, clean and efficient, comprising an integrated network of buses and the **C-Train**, the latter a cross between a bus and a train which is **free** for its downtown stretch along the length of 7th Avenue SW between 10th Street and City Hall. An on-board announcement tells you when the free ride is over.

**Tickets**, valid for both buses and C-Train, are available from machines on C-Train stations, from shops with a Calgary Transit sticker, and from the main **Information and Downtown Sales Centre**, 206-7th Ave SW (Mon–Fri 8.30am–5pm). The single adult fare is $1.35 (free for under-6s; 75¢ for 6–14); books of ten tickets cost $10, day passes $3.50. Note that you can board a bus without a ticket as long as you have the exact change to shovel into the box alongside the driver.

The sales centre also provides timetables and an invaluable **information line** (☎276-7801 Mon–Fri 6am–11pm, Sat & Sun 8am–9.30pm): tell them where you are and where you want to go, and they'll give you the necessary details. In winter they'll also save a wait in the cold by telling you when the next bus is due.

## Accommodation

Cheap **accommodation** in Calgary is not plentiful, but what little exists is rarely at a premium except during Stampede (mid-July) when prepaid reservations, in central locations at least, are essential. In addition to the recommendations given below, motels abound and make good stand-bys if you have a car – most are well away from the centre, along Macleod Trail heading south and on the Trans-Canada heading west. If you run into difficulties, try the main tourist office, which is primed to hunt out rooms at short notice, or consult the Alberta Hotel Association's ubiquitous *Accommodation Guide*.

## Hotels and motels

**The Cecil**, corner of 4th Ave & 3rd St SE (☎266-2982). Cheap and, by budget standards, clean, but on a busy junction (the airport road) and with a downstairs bar with a rough reputation. No phones, TV or private baths; doubles from $45.

**Glenbow Inn**, 708-8th Ave SW (☎263-7600 or ☎1-800-661-8683). A large, comfortable hotel with doubles from $80 (weekend discounts); $10 for a third person sharing.

**Hotel Regis**, 124-7th Ave SE (☎262-4641). One of the cheaper, and by definition dingier, central hotels, but only two blocks from the Calgary Tower. Bathroom facilities are all shared and rooms only have sinks; beware the bar. Doubles from $60.

**Lord Nelson Inn**, 1020-8th Ave SW (☎269-8262). A new ten-storey block, each room with TV and fridge – a bit more salubrious than the bottom-of-the-barrel jobs. Doubles from $55.

**Prince Royal Inn**, 618-5th Ave SW (☎263-0520 or ☎1-800-661-1592). A mixture of 300 studio, one- and two-room suites with full facilities and free continental breakfast. Doubles from $75, $10 for third person sharing.

**Relax Inns**, 2750 Sunridge Blvd NE (☎291-5581) and 9206 Macleod Trail (☎253-7070). Cheapest of the out-of-town motels, with doubles at around $60.

**Sandman Hotel**, 888-7th Ave SW (☎237-8626 or ☎1-800-663-6900). More expensive than the York and Nelson but, with 300 rooms, a good chance of finding space. Doubles from $80, $10 for third bed.

**St Louis Hotel**, 430-8th Ave SE (☎262-6341). Seedy location, extremely cheap and extremely basic; the management is friendly, the long-term residents less so. Doubles from $35.

**York Hotel**, 636 Centre St SE (☎262-5581). Central, with good-sized rooms, TV, baths, laundry service; doubles from $65 (student and weekend discounts).

**Westward Inn**, 119-12th Ave SW (☎266-4611). Amenity-loaded hotel with rooms priced at $80–90; $7 for a third person sharing a room.

## Hostels and student accommodation

**Calgary International Youth Hostel**, 520-7th Ave SE (☎269-8239). A convenient position close to downtown, buses and C-Train. Laundry and cooking facilities, snack bar. Closed 10am–5pm; midnight curfew. Members $10.

**Calgary YWCA**, 320-5th Ave SE (☎263-1550). Hotel comfort for women only in a quiet and safe area; book in summer. Singles from $27.50; dorm beds $17.50. Sleeping bag space is provided in summer.

**University of Calgary**, 3330-24th Ave NW (☎220-3203). Way out in the suburbs, but a cheap last resort with a huge number of student rooms in the peak summer period. Take the C-Train or bus #9. The room rental office (call first) is in the Kananaskis Building on campus (24hr). Student ID card secures a 33 percent discount. Singles $25, shared rooms $35.

## Campgrounds

**Bow Bend**, 5227-13th Ave NW (☎288-2161). Alongside parkland and the Bow River – leave the Trans-Canada at Home Rd and follow 13th Ave. Showers and laundry facilities; open year-round.

**Whispering Spruce**, fifteen minutes' beyond the city limits on Hwy 2 north (☎226-0097). All facilities. Open mid-May to mid-Oct.

# The City

**Downtown Calgary** lies in a self-evident cluster of mirrored glass and polished granite facades bounded by the Bow River to the north, 9th Avenue to the south, Centre Street to the east and 8th Street to the west. A monument to oil money, the area is about as sleek as an urban centre can be; much of the modern architecture is easy on the eye, and virtually everything is brand new – in marked contrast to a decade ago, when the building boom turned Calgary into an inferno of continual construction.

Any city tour should start with a trip to the **Glenbow Museum**, a fine introduction to both the city and Alberta's cultural heritage, and can be followed up by a jaunt up the **Calgary Tower**, immediately across the street, for a literal overview of the Calgarian hinterland. Thereafter a good deal of the city lends itself to wandering on foot, whether around the mall-laden main streets or to **Prince's Island**, the nearest of many parks, and **Kensington**, the heart of Calgary's small alternative scene. The appeal of attractions further afield – **Fort Calgary**, **Heritage Park** and the **Calgary Zoo** – will depend on your historical and natural history inclinations.

## The Glenbow Museum

The excellent and eclectic collection of the **Glenbow Museum** is, aside from the Stampede, the only sight for which you'd make a special journey to Calgary. It's located across the street from the Calgary Tower at 130-9th Ave SE, but the entrance is a hidden door alongside the Skyline Plaza complex (Tues–Sun 10am–6pm; $3; free Sat & holidays). Built in 1966 as a state-of-the-art museum, the no-expense-spared presentation is a testament to sound civic priorities and the cultural benefits of booming oil revenues. If you're coming from eastern Canada, the three floors of displays make a fine introduction to the heritage of the Canadian West – as well as preparing you for the pattern of pioneer exhibits you'll see time and again in the small-town museums of British Columbia.

The permanent collection embraces the something-for-everyone approach, starting with a section devoted to ritual and **sacred art** from around the world and an **art gallery** tracing the development of western Canadian indigenous art. Better still is the **Images of the Indian** section, a detached and fascinating look at the art that flowed back to Europe after white contact with native peoples. Two outlooks prevail – the romantic nineteenth-century image of the Indian as "noble savage" and the more forward-looking analysis of artists such as Paul Kane, a painter determined to make accurate representations of a people and culture before their assimilation by white expansion.

The place to spend most time is the second floor, which runs the gamut of western Canadian history and heritage, including an outstanding exhibit on **Native Canadian peoples** – underscoring the interest contemporary Canadians in this part of the country take in native culture, which is in many ways the most meaningful long-term history they have. Make a point of searching out the **treaties** section, hidden in a corner almost as if in shame, where the museum text skates over the injustices with a glossary of simple facts. The original treaties are on display, and provide eye-opening examples of incomprehensible jargon and legal gobbledegook. All facets of native **crafts** are explored, with stunning displays of carving, costumes and jewellery, and whilst their emphasis ·is on the original inhabitants of Alberta, the collection also forays into the Inuit and the Metis – the latter being the offspring of native women and white fur traders, and the most marginalised group of all. Following a historical chronology, the floor moves on to exhibits associated with the fur trade, North West Rebellion, the Canadian Pacific, pioneer life, ranching, cowboys, oil and wheat – each era illustrated by interesting and appropriate artefacts of the time – adding up to a glut of period paraphernalia that includes a terrifying exhibit of frontier dentistry, an absurdly comprehensive display of washing machines, and a solitary 1938 bra.

The top floor is the most eccentric of all, kicking off with a pointless display of Calgary Stampede merchandising and then moving on to one of the largest collections of **military paraphernalia** in the world and a dazzling display of **gems and minerals**, said to be amongst the world's best. These exhibits are mainly for genre enthusiasts, though the gems are worth a look if only to see some of the extraordinary and beautiful things that come out of the drab mines that fuel so much of western Canada's economy.

## Other downtown sights

The **Calgary Tower** (daily 7.30am–11pm; $4), the city's favourite folly and symbol, is a good deal shorter and less imposing than the tourist material would have you believe. An obligatory tourist traipse, the 190-metre saltcellar stands in a relatively dingy area at 101-9th Ave SW, somewhat overshadowed by downtown's more recent sprouting. Nevertheless, as a long-term landmark it makes a good starting point for any conscientious tour of the city, offering outstanding **views**, especially on clear days when the snow-capped Rockies fill the western horizon; whether it's worth the price of admission is another matter. Up on the observation platform you'll find a snack bar (reasonable), cocktail bar and revolving restaurant (expensive).

Hidden behind the soaring high-rises are any number of shopping malls, most notably Toronto Dominion Square (8th Ave SW between 2nd & 3rd), the city's main shopping focus and the unlikely site of **Devonian Gardens** (9am–9pm; free). Like something out of an idyllic urban future, the three-acre indoor garden supports a lush sanctuary of streams, waterfalls and full-sized trees (some 138 species of plants and 20,000 individual specimens), no mean feat given that it's located on the fourth floor of a glass and concrete glitter palace. Benches beside the garden's 1km of paths are perfect for picnicking on food bought in the takeaways below. Chances are you'll catch an impromptu concert on one of the small stages dotted around, and quite probably become an unwitting observer of fresh conjugal bliss, this being the favourite spot for Calgary's newlyweds to pose for their wedding pictures.

Calgary inevitably pays homage to its oil industry, notably in the small but oddly interesting **Energeum** plonked in the main lobby of the Energy Resources Building, 640-5th Ave SW (Mon–Fri 10.30am–4.30pm, plus Sun in June, July & Aug; free). The gamut of audio-visual and presentational tricks takes you through the formation, discovery and drilling for coal and oil. Alberta's peculiar and problematic oil sands are explained, and there's dollops of the stuff on hand for some infantile slopping around. The tiny **Natural Gas Museum**, at the corner of 11th Avenue and 8th Street SW, fills in any gaps left in your fossil-fuel education. Science buffs, and anyone who's never been to a planetarium, might take in the **Alberta Science Centre** and **Centennial Planetarium** at 11th Street and 7th Avenue SW (daily July & Aug 1–9pm; closed Mon & Tues Sept–June; $5); also on hand is a small observatory, open nightly (weather permitting), with telescopes trained on moon, planets and stars.

### Prince's Island, the Bow River and Kensington

Five minutes' walk north of downtown via a footbridge, **Prince's Island** is a popular but peaceful retreat offering plenty of trees, flowers, a snack bar, kids' playground and, most importantly, enough space to escape the incessant stream of joggers pounding the walkways.

Swimmers might be tempted by the broad, fast-flowing **Bow River**, but it's for passive recreation only – the water is just two hours from its icy source in the Rockies, and its dangers are underlined by lurid signs on the banks. The river is the focus for Calgary's civilised and excellent system of **recreational walkways**, asphalt paths (also available to cyclists) which generally parallel the main waterways – the Bow and Elbow rivers, Nose and Fish creeks, Confederation Park and Glenmore Reservoir. The network totals some 200km, plus an additional 100km of signed on-street bikeways.

A twenty-minute jaunt along the walkway system from Prince's Island, **Kensington** is a revitalised nightlife centre of bars and restaurants centred on 10th Street NW and Kensington Road. As alternative as Calgary gets, it's slightly self-conscious in the nature of such places – this is the city's self-proclaimed "People's Place" – and the whiff of patchouli and counterculture hang in the air despite a tide of encroaching gentrification. Shops here are the type that sell healing crystals and advertise yoga and personal-growth seminars, though the older and more appealing cafés, bookshops and wholefood stores are beginning to give way to trinket shops. The C-Train station at Sunnyside is handy for the area if you don't want to walk out here.

### Fort Calgary

**Fort Calgary**, the city's historical nexus, stands at 750-9th Avenue SE, a manageable eight-block walk east of downtown; you could also take bus #1 from 7th Avenue to Forest Lawn, or the C-Train free to City Hall and walk the remaining five blocks. Built by the North West Mounted Police in 1875, the fort was the germ of the present city, and remained operative as a police post until 1914, when it was sold – inevitably – to the Canadian Pacific Railway. Today only a few stumps of the original building remain, much having been torn down by the developers, and what survives is its site, now a pleasant forty-acre park contained in the angled crook of the Bow and Elbow rivers.

An **interpretive centre** makes sense of the history, tracing Calgary's century-odd development with the aid of artefacts, audio-visual displays and a series of "interpretive walks" along the river (daily 9am–5pm; closed Mon & Tues early Oct to early May). Amongst the sillier things on offer – and you may never get the chance again – is the opportunity to dress up as a Mountie. Across the river to the east is the newly renovated **Deane House**, built in 1906 by Mountie supremo Richard Deane (free tours daily 9am–5pm). Its neighbour, **Hunt House**, built by the Hudson's Bay Company, is Calgary's oldest building.

## St George's Island

**St George's Island** is home to **Calgary Zoo, Botanical Gardens and Prehistoric Park** (daily 9am–dusk; $6, free Tues), and can be reached from downtown and Fort Calgary by riverside path, by C-Train (to Calgary Zoo station), or by car (take Memorial Drive East). Whether or not you enjoy the **zoo**, whose 1400 animals and 400 species make it Canada's biggest, will depend on your attitude to captive wild animals. Sensitive to criticism, the Calgary Zoological Society regales you constantly with its "Zoo Philosophy"; self-justifying or not, there are no actual cages, and animals are left as far as possible in their "natural" habitats. Lavish amounts of money have obviously been spent, and the displays are innovative and exciting: underwater viewing areas for polar bears and sea creatures, darkened rooms for nocturnal animals, greenhouses for myriad tropical birds, and any number of pens for the big draws like gorillas, tigers and giraffes. Check out the extended North American section for a taste of Rocky Mountain fauna.

The **Botanical Gardens** are dotted throughout the zoo, some of them indoors and intended as aids to understanding the interrelationship between plants, birds and butterflies. The **Prehistoric Park** is an annex of the zoo linked by suspension bridge across the Bow River (daily mid-May to mid-Nov). Reputedly unique, it boasts life-sized – but not too convincing – dinosaur models in somewhat incongruous settings. This is a poor substitute, however, for the superb site and museum at Drumheller (see p.419), and only the collection of fossils in two adjoining buildings are of more than fleeting interest.

Natural history enthusiasts might also visit the **Inglewood Bird Sanctuary** on the Bow River's forested flats at 9th Avenue and 20A Street SE, 3km downstream of the zoo. Some 230 species are present year-round – more during migratory cycles.

## Heritage Park

A sixty-acre theme park centred on a reconstructed frontier village 16km southwest of downtown, **Heritage Park** replicates life in the Canadian West before 1914 and panders relentlessly to the myth of the "Wild West" (May–Sept daily; $4). Full of gushing presentations and original costumes, it's a family affair which nonetheless offers a thorough run-through of the period: see this "heritage" offering – the largest of its type in Canada – and you won't feel you have to see any more.

The aim has been to produce a living, working museum comprising more than 100 **restored buildings**, all of them originals transported from other small-town locations. Each has been assigned to one of several communities – fur post, native village, homestead, farm and turn-of-the-century town – and most fulfill their original function. Thus you can see a working blacksmith, buy fresh bread, buy a local paper, go to church, even get married. Transport, too, is appropriate to the period – steam trains, streetcars, horse-drawn bus, stagecoaches, and the highlight, the restored paddle-steamer **SS Moyie**, which runs trips across the local reservoir.

## THE CALGARY STAMPEDE

The annual **Calgary Stampede** is an orgy of all things cowboy and cowgirl, and a gift to Calgary's tourist industry, bringing hordes of spectators and participants into the city for the middle two weeks of July. In return the city obliges visitors by losing its collective head, and all and sundry turn out in obligatory white stetsons, bolo ties, blue jeans and hand-tooled boots, and everyone appears to address one another in a bastardised cowboy slang that's normally only heard in poor country-and-western songs. It's all largely good, friendly fun, and almost certainly unlike anything you'll have seen before.

For all its heavily worked tourist appeal, however, the competition end of things is taken very seriously. Most of the cowboys are for real, as are the injuries – the rodeo is said to be North America's roughest – and the combined prize money is a very serious $500,000. Even the first show in 1912, masterminded by entrepreneur Guy Weadick, put up $100,000 and attracted 14,000 people to the opening parade, a line-up which included 2000 Indians in full ceremonial rig and Pancho Villa's bandits in a show erroneously billed as a swan song for the cowboy of the American West. Nowadays the ten days of **events** still start after a huge, heavily attended parade, and encompass bronco riding, bull riding, native buffalo riding, branding, calf roping, steer wrestling, cow tackling, wild cow milking, and – the recognised highlight – the ludicrously dangerous chuck wagon races. The events run for three hours daily, with the wagon races (the "World Championship") held over until each evening.

**Nightlife** is a world unto its own, with Stampede locations giving way to music, dancing and mega-cabarets which involve casts of literally thousands. There's also lots of drinking, a multitude of gambling opportunities, and fireworks and general party time way into the small hours. Barbeques are the norm, and even breakfast is roped into the free-for-all – outdoor bacon, pancake and flapjack feasts being the traditional way to start the day. "White hatter stew" and baked beans – inevitably – are other much-gobbled staples.

Most events take place at **Stampede Park**, southeast of downtown and best reached by C-Train to Stampede Station, which contains an amusement park, concert and show venues, bars and restaurants. Some action reverts to the Olympic Saddledome close by, and there's a panoply of extra on-street entertainments throughout the city.

**Accommodation** during Stampede is greatly stretched, and prices for most things are hiked for the duration. **Tickets** for the key events go quickly, and cost anything between $5 and $50. Even without tickets, however, you'll still get most of the flavour of the thing just by being there. For ticket order forms, advance sales and **general information** write to Calgary Exhibition and Stampede, Box 1860, Station M, Calgary T2P 2L8 (☎261-0101, elsewhere in Alberta ☎1-800-661-1260) or call in person at Stampede Headquarters, 1410 Olympic Way SE, or the central tourist office.

To get there by **car**, take either Elbow Drive or Macleod Trail south and turn right on Heritage Drive (the turn-off is marked by a huge, maroon steam engine); **bus** #53 makes the journey from downtown.

## Eating, drinking and nightlife

When not international – Italian, Greek, French or Chinese – Calgary's cuisine is meat-orientated; Alberta claims, with some justification, to have some of the best **steaks** in the world. With its particular immigration history, however, the city lacks the Ukrainian influences that grace cooking to the north, and prefers instead to rehash so-called "Californian cuisine", western Canada's latest culinary trend.

The Toronto Dominion Square and Stephen Avenue malls, on 8th Avenue SW between 1st and 3rd, are riddled with cheap ethnic **takeaways** and café-style eateries – hugely popular and perfect for lunch or snacks on the hoof. The nicest thing to do is buy food and eat it – with half of Calgary – amidst the greenery of Devonian Gardens.

Elsewhere in the city you'll stumble across an impressive range of middle- to upper-bracket **restaurants** spawned by the expense accounts of the city's boom years. Prices are low by most standards, even in the upmarket places, though wine is overpriced.

Calgary is no party town, except during Stampede and a brief fling in summer when the weather allows barbecues and nighttime streetlife. Nonetheless, its bars and clubs are all you'd expect of a city of this size, the vast majority of them found in four distinct areas: **Kensington**, with its varied cafés, restaurants and clubs, and the best summer evening wandering possibilities; **"Electric Avenue"**, as 11th Avenue SW between 5th and 6th streets is called, all identikit pubs and bars, bright, brash and very popular; **17th Avenue SW**, a quieter and more varied collection of pubs, bars, speciality shops and ethnic eating; and **downtown**, fine during the day but fairly desolate in the evening.

Many a café boasts solo singers, and in the specialist clubs the quality of live music is good – especially in jazz, blues and the genre dear to cowtown Calgary, country-and-western. If you share the enthusiasm, call the **Country Music Association** for details of local gigs (☎233-8809). For details of the annual **Jazz Festival** (third week in June) and for daily information on who's playing where, call the **Jazz Line** (☎265-1321). Prince's Island is the venue for a **folk festival** at the end of July.

**Tickets** for virtually all events are available through *BASS*, a central booking agency (☎270-6700), and through several *Marlin Travel* offices around the city. You'll find events **listings** in Calgary's main dailies, the *Herald* and the *Sun*, with most coverage in the *Herald*'s Friday edition.

## Cafés and restaurants

**Bagels and Buns**, 17th Ave SW near 7th St. Informal and popular for breakfast and lunch.

**Bohemia Bistro**, 124–10th St NW off Kensington Rd (☎270-3116). Weird menu, strange building, but fine East European food. Closed Sun & Mon.

**Chianti Café and Restaurant**, 1438-17th Ave SW (☎229-1600). Dark, noisy, cheap and extremely popular – try to book – with pasta basics and the odd fancy dish.

**Entre Nous Café**, 2206-4th St SW (☎228-5525). Small, lively and congenial, big mirrors and burgundy decor giving a genuine bistro feel. Good French cooking; booking recommended.

**Hang Fung**, 119 3rd Ave SE. Cheap and authentic eatery in Calgary's modest Chinatown; lively on Sun afternoons.

**Kaos Café**, 718-17th Ave SW. Noted breakfasts, eclectic clientele; good for outside summer drinking. Live music Fri & Sat nights.

**Kensington Delicafé**, 1414 Kensington Rd NW. Casual and friendly, with a grown-up hippy feel. Varied menu features wholefood options, notorious desserts, huge portions and, by common consent, the best cheeseburger in Calgary. Also live music nightly and outdoor tables in summer.

**La Pentola**, 823-14th St NW (☎270-8343). Small, excellent Italian place, run by a Latin couple who do everything – cook, serve, sing and wash up.

**The Roasterie**, 314-10th St NW near Kensington Rd. Nice hang-out and café – no meals – newspapers, notice board and twenty kinds of coffee.

**Sara's Pyrohy Hut**, 1216-Centre St NE (☎277-2712). Calgary's only Ukrainian restaurant, with decor to match – upmarket farmyard look, rural antiques and wall hangings. Vast, solid portions, with good borsch and a sample of dishes called "Sara's Merry Mix". Book ahead.

**Sproutz**, 17th Ave SW between 3rd & 4th. Mexican food, including good vegetarian choices.

## Bars

**Dinero's**, 310 Stephen Avenue Mall. Favourite office-worker hang-out for an after-work drink and Tex-Mex food, but quiet the rest of the time.

**The Fox and Firkin**, 11th Ave SW between 5th & 6th. You may have to queue for one of the biggest and most popular of the numerous "Electric Avenue" bars which, like many Calgary bars, affects the atmosphere of a British pub – noisy, crowded, tatty and fun.

**O'Brien's Pub and Restaurant**, 636 Centre St S. Cheap and boisterous downtown bar with billiards and dancing.

**Rose and Crown** , 1503-4th St SW. Round the corner from *The Ship and Anchor*, the pub atmosphere here is more laboured and some of the clientele of the braying suit-and-tie type, but still a Calgary institution.

**St Louis Tavern**, 430 8th Ave SE. Cheaper drinks and more gritty ambience than bars a few blocks away on 11th Ave (closed Sun).

**The Ship and Anchor**, 17th Ave SW on the corner of 5th St. Genuine, friendly and laid-back "neighbourhood" pub, with special Anglo-Canadian connections, darts, fine music and excellent pub food.

**The Unicorn Pub**, 8th Ave SW (on the corner of 2nd St, downstairs in the mall). Well-known downtown pub whose cheap food brings in lunchtime punters.

## Live music venues

**Cover to Cover**, 738-11th Ave SW. Vies with *Sparkies* as Calgary's main music venue. Closed Mon.

**Kensington Delicafé**, 1414 Kensington Rd NW. Live music nightly in relaxed café/restaurant.

**The King Edward Hotel**, 438-9th Ave SE. Much-loved, down-at-heel location, with consistently good C&W and R&B bands.

**Marty's Café**, 338-17th Ave SW. One of Calgary's best spots, small, smoky, with peeling posters, junkshop memorabilia and a clientele from bikers to bankers; good food, too. Nightly music from 9.30pm: jazz at weekends, blues on Thurs. Outdoors in summer.

**Ranchman's Steak House**, 9615 Macleod Trail S. A classic honkytonk and institution, known throughout Canada, and often packed as a result. Live C&W and predictable – almost caricatured – atmosphere. Closed Sun.

**Sparkies**, 1006-11th Ave SW. Sunday-night jam sessions, "alternative" music on Tuesdays, bands and "variety" nights the rest of the week.

## Performing arts and cinema

The hub of the city's cultural endeavours is the new **Centre for the Performing Arts**, a dazzling new downtown complex with three performance spaces (9th Ave & 1st St SW, ☎294-7444) and the seat of the Calgary Philharmonic Orchestra. More modest **classical concerts** are the Music at Noon offerings in the Central Library (Sept–April), and the sessions – planned and impromptu – on the small stages in Devonian Gardens.

The Centre for the Performing Arts is also home base for **Theatre Calgary**, the city's premier professional company, and for the acclaimed *Alberta Theatre Project*, which produces five fairly avant-garde plays annually. The *Lunchbox Theatre* offers a popular and wildly varied programme aimed at downtown shoppers and passersby; performances are somewhat irregular, but tend to start at noon in the Bow Valley Square on the corner of 6th Avenue and 1st Street SW. Calgary's **ballet** world is dominated by the Alberta Ballet Company, a young and excellent troupe.

Daily papers give the lowdown on Calgary's many first-run **cinemas**, but for repertory, classic and foreign films try the *Plaza Theatre* at 1113 Kensington Road NW. For free lunchtime shows make for the *National Film Board Theatre*, 222-1st St SE. Movie diehards might also want to check out the **Museum of Movie Art**, home to the world's largest collection of cinema posters (4000 of them, dating back to 1920) at the University of Calgary, 9-3600-21st St NE (Tues–Sat 9.30am–5.30pm).

# Listings

**Airlines** *Air Canada*, 530-8th Ave SW (☎265-9555); *Canadian Airlines*, ☎235-1161 (Airbus to Edmonton, ☎235-8154; schedules & reservations ☎248-4888); *America West*, ☎1-800-247-5692; *Continental*, ☎1-800-525-0280; *Delta*, ☎265-7610; *Eastern*, ☎236-2833; *KLM*, ☎236-2600.

**Airport enquiries** ☎292-8400.

**American Express** 200 Centre St & 8th Ave SW (☎269-3757).

**Bike rental** *Abominable Sports*, 640-11th Ave SW (☎266-0899). Mountain bikes $15 per day; mopeds $20 per day.

**Books** *Canterbury's Bookshop*, 513-8th Ave SW, is the best general bookshop. For maps and travel books, *Map Town*, 640-6th Ave SW (☎266-2241).

Bus enquiries *Greyhound* (☎265-9111); *Airporter* (☎291-3848); *Brewster*, for airport/Banff/Jasper (☎260-0719); *Red Arrow Express*, for Edmonton (☎269-2884).
Car rental *Avis* (☎269-6166); *Budget* (☎263-0505); *Hertz* (☎221-1300); *Rent-a-Wreck*, 2339 Macleod Trail (☎237-7093); *Thrifty*, 117-5th Ave SE (☎262-4400).
Consulates *US*, 1000-615 Macleod Trail SE (☎266-8962).
Exchange *Calgary Foreign Exchange*, 307-4th Ave SW; *Royal Bank*, 339-8th Ave SW.
Hospital Calgary General Hospital, 841 Centre Ave E (☎268-9111).
Left luggage Facilities at the bus terminal, 850-16th St SW; $1 per 24hr.
Police 316-7th Ave SE (☎266-1234).
Post office 220-4th Ave SE.
Taxis *Associated* (☎276-5312); *Checker* (☎272-1111); *Red Top* (☎250-9222); *Yellow Cab* (☎250-8311).
Weather ☎263-3333.

# The Alberta Badlands

Formed by the meltwaters of the last ice age, the valley of the Red Deer River cuts a deep, eroded gash through the dulcet prairie about 140km east of Calgary, creating a surreal and anomalous landscape of bare, sun-baked hills and eerie lunar flats dotted with sagebrush and scrubby, tufted grass. On their own, the **Alberta Badlands** – this strangely alien patch of desert in the midst of lush grasslands – would be worth a visit, but they're made one of Alberta's most essential detours by the presence of the **Royal Tyrrell Museum of Palaeontology**, amongst the greatest museums of natural history in North America. The museum is located 8km outside the old coal-mining town of **Drumheller**, a dreary but obvious base if you're unable to fit the museum into a day trip from Calgary. Drumheller is also the main focus of the **Dinosaur Trail**, a road loop that explores the Red Deer Valley and surrounding badlands; you'll need wheels for this circuit, and for the trip to the **Dinosaur Provincial Park**, home to the Tyrrell Museum Field Station and the source of many of its fossils.

Drumheller is about ninety minutes' drive away from Calgary by **car**, and is best reached by taking Hwy 2 north towards Edmonton and branching east on Hwy 72 and Hwy 9. It's an easy day trip, and most people make straight for the Tyrrell Museum, which is signed from Drumheller on Hwy 838 (or "North Dinosaur Trail"). Coming out on one of the two Greyhound **buses** daily from Calgary to Drumheller makes a day-trip more of a squeeze. It's a touch too far to walk from Drumheller town centre to the museum, particularly on a hot day, but the local *Valley Taxi* (☎823-6333) will run you there from the bus depot for about $5.

## Drumheller

However you're getting around the area, you'll pass through **DRUMHELLER**, a moribund town which nonetheless has appeal by virtue of its extraordinary location and surroundings. Approaching from the west, nothing suggests the town's imminence until the appearance of a virulent red water tower and the road's sudden drop into a dark, hidden canyon and a gloomy, blasted landscape whose otherworldliness is heightened by its contrast to the vivid colours of the earlier wheat and grasslands. Drumheller sits at the base of the canyon, surrounded by the detritus and spoil heaps of its mining past – the Red Deer River having exposed not only dinosaur fossils but also valuable (and now exhausted) coal seams.

After taking in the initially enthralling setting, there's not much to do in Drumheller, despite the best efforts of its **tourist office** at 703-2nd Avenue W (May–Oct daily 9am–9pm; ☎823-7739). A limited and dog-eared selection of **accommodation** lies together a block from the bus terminal, the best of the downtown trio of hotels being the *Drumheller Travelodge* (☎823-3322) on Railway Avenue. At $70 a room it's overpriced, but preferable to the adjacent *Alexander Hotel* (☎823-2642) and *Waldorf Hotel* (☎823-2623), whose only advantage is on price, both with doubles from $30. The best central option is the *Rockhound Motor Inn*, South Railway Drive (☎823-5302), a big, modern motel on a bluff off the Hwy 56 approach from the west before it drops to the old town centre, with doubles for $80. If you've got a car, or don't mind walking, make for the still pleasanter *Badlands Motel* (☎823-5155), a brand-new collection of tasteful log cabins 1km out of town on Hwy 838, the road to the Tyrrell Museum.

The town's two **campgrounds** are close together and both nicely situated. The larger and better choice is probably the *Dinosaur Trailer Court* (April–Oct; ☎823-3291; $10), situated across the river north of downtown at the junction of Hwy 56 and Hwy 838. *Shady Grove Campground* (May–Oct; ☎823-2576; $10) is a few hundred metres south, on the other side of the bridge – less distant from the town's tatty confines but with boating and swimming possibilities. If you're driving, visit the tourist office for a full list of the many other private and provincial campgrounds up and down the valley.

You're as well to **eat** in the museum's good cafeteria, for little in town passes culinary muster. For picnic supplies, hit the tucked-away *All West* **supermarket** on 1st Street behind the main drag, and for cheap basic meals try the *Diana* on Main Street, a strange mix of diner, Chinese restaurant and local hang-out.

## The Royal Tyrrell Museum of Palaeontology

Packed with high-tech displays, housed in a sleek building and blended skilfully into the strange desolation of its surroundings, the **Royal Tyrrell Museum** is an object lesson in modern museum dynamics (May–Sept daily 9am–9pm; Oct–April Tues–Sun 10am–5pm; $4). It attracts half a million visitors a year, and its wide-ranging exhibits are likely to appeal to anyone with even a hint of scientific or natural curiosity. Although it claims the world's largest collection of complete dinosaur skeletons, the museum is far more than a collection of old bones, and as well as tracing the earth's history from the year dot to the present day, it's also a leading centre of study and academic research.

Laid out on different levels to suggest layers of geological time, the open-plan exhibit guides you effortlessly through a chronological progression, culminating in a huge central hall of over 200 dinosaur specimens – if there's a fault, it's that the hall is visible early on and tempts you to skip the lower-level displays. These place the dinosaurs in context, and provide what feels like a lifetime of biology and chemistry lessons rolled into one enjoyable morning, skilfully linking geology, fossils, plate tectonics, evolution and the like with Drumheller's own landscape. You also get a chance to peer into the **preparation lab** and watch scientists working on fossils – more interesting than it sounds – and see one of the world's best-equipped palaeontology centres in action.

By far the most impressive exhibits, naturally, are the **dinosaurs** themselves. Whole skeletons are immaculately displayed against three-dimensional backgrounds which persuasively depict the swamps of 60 million years ago and cleverly incorporate pictures of each specimen as it would have appeared in the flesh. Some are paired with full-size plastic dinosaurs, and it's a testimony to the ingenious presentation that these appear less macabre and menacing than the free-standing skeletons. Sheer size isn't the only fascination, either: *Xiphactinus*, for example, a four-metre specimen, is striking more for its delicate and beautiful tracery of bones. Elsewhere the emphasis is on the creatures' sheer diversity or on their staggeringly small brains – in one striking case, no larger than the eye of the animal in question.

The museum naturally also tackles the problem of the dinosaurs' **extinction**, placing the question neatly in context by pointing out that around ninety percent of all plant and animal species that have ever inhabited the earth have become extinct. Leave a few minutes for the **palaeoconservatory** off the dinosaur hall, a collection of living prehistoric plants, some unchanged in 180 million years, selected from fossil records to give an idea of the vegetation that would have typified Alberta in the dinosaur age.

## The Dinosaur Trail

The **Dinosaur Trail** is a catch-all circular road route of 51km embracing some of the viewpoints and lesser historic sights of the badlands and the Red Deer Valley area. The comprehensive *Visitor's Guide to the Drumheller Valley* lists thirty separate stop-offs, mostly on the plain above the valley, but you need only bother with the key stops: **Horsethief Canyon** and **Horseshoe Canyon**, two spectacular viewpoints of the wildly eroded valley; the **Hoodoos**, slender columns of wind-sculpted sandstone, topped with mushroom-like caps; the still largely undeveloped **Midland Provincial Park**, criss-crossed by badland trails and destined to document the area's mining heritage; and the **Atlas Coal Mine**, dominated by the teetering wooden "tipple", once used to sort ore and now a beautiful and rather wistful piece of industrial archaeology.

## Dinosaur Provincial Park

If you're driving you could feasibly fit in a trip to **Dinosaur Provincial Park** after the Tyrrell Museum, a 174-kilometre run, and then head back to Calgary on the Trans-Canada, which runs just south of the park. The nearest town is BROOKS on the Trans-Canada, 48km west of the **Field Station of the Tyrrell Museum**, the park's obvious hub (May–Sept daily 9am–9pm; Oct–April Sat & Sun 10am–5pm). There's an excellent provincial **campground** in the park which is open year-round, but only serviced from May to September ($6).

Nestled amongst some of the baddest of the badlands, this landscape is not only one of the most alien in Canada, but also one of the world's richest fossil beds and as a consequence a listed UN World Heritage Site. The field station has a few self-guided trails and a small museum that goes over the same ground as its parent in Drumheller, leaving the real meat of the visit to the **Badlands Bus Tour**, a guided tour of the otherwise out-of-bounds dinosaur dig near the centre of the park (10 tours daily May–Sept; $2). A few exposed skeletons have been left *in situ*, together with panels giving background information on the monsters.

# Highway 3 and the south

Most people travelling overland from Saskatchewan follow the Trans-Canada straight to Calgary; **Highway 3**, branching off at Medicine Hat, takes a more southerly course across the plains before finally breaching the Rockies at Crowsnest Pass. This is a quieter and less spectacular route into the mountains than the Trans-Canada, but it does offer a couple of worthwhile diversions along the way: the marvellously moni-kered **Head-Smashed-In Buffalo Jump**, a Native North American heritage site with an excellent interpretive centre, and **Waterton Lakes National Park**, a cross-border reserve that links with the United States' Glacier National Park.

## Medicine Hat

Though **MEDICINE HAT** is barely a hundred years old, the origin of its wonderful name has already been lost. The most likely story has to do with a Cree medicine man who lost his head-dress while fleeing a battle with the Blackfoot; his followers lost heart at the omen, surrendered, and were promptly massacred. These days you rarely see the town mentioned without the adage that it "has all hell for a basement", a quotation from Rudyard Kipling coined in response to the huge reserves of natural gas that lurk below the town. Discovered by railway engineers drilling for water in 1883 – when the place was merely a tent city around the Canadian Pacific station – the gas fields now feed a flourishing petrochemical industry which blots the otherwise park-studded downtown area on the banks of the South Saskatchewan River.

As an important junction on the Trans-Canada, Medicine Hat's main function is inevitably that of a glorified service station. **Motels** galore dot the town, many on the Trans-Canada or the 7th Street strip. The *Bel-Aire Motel*, 633-14th St (☎527-4421), is the cheapest with doubles starting at $24, and is conveniently situated at the junction of the Trans-Canada and Hwy 3. The most appealing of many options on the Trans-Canada is the *Best Western Inn*, 722 Redcliff Drive (☎527-3700), with doubles from $45.

# Lethbridge

Alberta's third city, **LETHBRIDGE** is booming on the back of oil, gas and some of the province's most productive agricultural land; none of which is of much consequence to people passing through, whom the city attempts to sidetrack with the **Nikka Yuko Centennial Gardens**(May–Oct daily 9am–5pm; $3) in its southeastern corner. Built in 1967 as a symbol of Japanese and Canadian amity, the gardens were perhaps a belated apology for the treatment of Japanese-Canadians during World War II, when 22,000 were interned – 6000 of them in Lethbridge. Five tranquil Japanese horticultural landscapes make up the gardens, along with a placid pavilion of cypress wood perpetually laid out for a tea ceremony.

Far removed from the gardens' decorum is **Fort Whoop-Up** (daily 10am–5pm), a modern reconstruction of the wild whiskey trading post set up in the 1870s by American desperadoes from Fort Benton, Montana. It was the most lucrative of the many similar forts which sprang up illegally all over the Canadian prairies and which led directly to the founding of the North West Mounted Police. Natives came from miles around to trade just about anything, including the clothes off their backs, for the lethal hootch, which was fortified by grain alcohol and supplemented by such ingredients as red peppers, dye and chewing tobacco.

Three *Greyhound* **buses** daily operate from Calgary to the Lethbridge bus terminal at 411-5th Street South. Most of the city's **accommodation** is on a single strip, Mayor Macgrath Drive, and there's little to choose between its rash of motels – almost all charge around $40 for a double. You might as well go for something upmarket like the *Sandman Inn*, 421 Mayor Macgrath Drive (☎328-1111) and pay $20 more, or the cheapest, the *Flagstone Motel*, 1124 Mayor Macgrath Drive (☎328-5591), with doubles from $32. Women alone should head for the *YWCA*, 604 8th St South (☎329-0088), a snug place with singles at $25. **Campers** can bed down at the *Henderson Lake Campgrounds* (☎328-5452; $7.50) near Henderson Lake alongside the Nikka Yuko Gardens.

# Fort Macleod and around

**FORT MACLEOD** catches traffic coming up from the States and down from Calgary on Hwy 2, which eases around the town centre via the rebuilt wooden palisade of the **Fort Museum** (May to mid-Oct daily; $3). One for real diehard Mountie fans only, this was the first fort established in Canada's Wild West by the North West Mounted Police, the Mounties' precursors. The NWMP had been dispatched to raid Fort Whoop-Up in Lethbridge but got lost, allowing the whiskey traders to flee; finding an empty fort, they continued west under the command of Colonel James Macleod to establish a permanent barracks on the river here.

Three daily **buses** serve the town from Lethbridge and three from Calgary, the latter continuing west to Cranbrook, Nelson and eventually to Vancouver in British Columbia. If you're stuck, the town has a brace of eight **motels**, the most central being the *Fort Motel* on Main Street (☎553-3606), with doubles from $35.

## Head-Smashed-In Buffalo Jump

While shots of Indians trailing lone buffalo with bow and arrow are Hollywood's idea of how Native North Americans foraged for food, the truth was often less romantic, but far more effective and spectacular. Over a period of more than 6000 years, Blackfoot hunters perfected a technique of luring buffalo herds into a shallow basin and stampeding them to their deaths over a broad cliff, where they were then butchered for meat, bone (for tools) and hide (for clothes and shelter). These jumps of mass slaughter existed all over North America, but the **Head-Smashed-In Buffalo Jump**, 18km west of Fort Macleod on Hwy 785, is the best preserved of any (daily May–Oct 9am–8pm, rest of year 9am–5pm; $5). Along with the Tyrrell Museum, the jump is the undoubted jewel in Alberta's crown of cultural attractions, and has been designated a UN World Heritage Site. Its name, which alone should be enough to whet your appetite, is a wonderfully literal description of how a nineteenth-century Blackfoot met his end after deciding the best spot to watch the jump was at the base of the cliff, apparently unaware he was about to be visited by some 500 plummeting buffalo.

The brand-new $10 million **interpretive centre**, a seven-storeyed architectural *tour de force*, is built into the 10-metre-high and 305-metre-wide cliff near the original jump. Below it stretches a ten-metre-deep bed of ash and bones accumulated from the millennia of successive stampedes, all protected by the threat of a $50,000 fine for anyone foolish enough to rummage for souvenirs. The facility delves deep into the history of the jump and into Native North American culture in general, the undoubted highlight being a film which attempts to recreate the thunderous death plunge using a herd of buffalo which were slaughtered, frozen and then somehow made to look like live bison hurtling to their deaths. Around the centre the jump is surrounded by a couple of kilometres of **trails**, the starting point for free tours conducted by native guides.

There is no public transport to the site, though taxis are available in Fort Macleod (about $20).

## Waterton Lakes National Park

**Waterton Lakes National Park**, about 55km south of Fort Macleod, is little more than an addendum to the much larger Glacier National Park to which it is joined across the United States border; still, despite its modest acreage, it contains scenery as stupendous as any of the bigger parks of the Canadian Rockies. Launched as an "International Peace Park" to symbolise the understated relationship between Canada and its neighbour, Waterton Lakes and Glacier remain separate national enclaves – to cross from one to the other by road you have to exit the park and pass through immigration controls, which are as stringent as any if you're not a national of either of the home countries. (Backpackers, on the other hand, can cross the border without formalities.) A park **entry permit** (also valid for all other national parks in the Canadian Rockies) costs $4.25 for one day, $9.50 for four days or $26 for a full year.

From Fort Macleod, access to **WATERTON** townsite, the park's only base and services centre, is either on Hwy 3 west and Hwy 6 south (via PINCHER CREEK) or on Hwy 2 south to CARDSTON and then west on Hwy 5. A special *Greyhound* **bus** service runs between Calgary and Waterton during the summer (daily; $15), otherwise your best bet if you're without wheels is to hitch out of Fort Macleod on Hwy 2. Two access roads from Waterton probe west into the park interior and provide the kick-off point for most trails: the **Akamina Parkway** follows the Cameron Creek valley for 20km to Cameron Lake, while the **Red Rock Canyon Parkway** weaves up Blakiston Creek for about 15km to the mouth of Red Rock Canyon. A good way of sampling the scenery lining both roads is to **rent a bike** from Waterton, one outlet being *Pat's Texaco and Cycle Rental*, Mount View Road (☎859-2266).

## HIKING IN WATERTON LAKES PARK

Waterton Lakes Park's 160km of **trails** have a reputation as not only the best constructed in the Canadian Rockies, but also among the most easily graded, well marked and scenically routed – all factors in making them some of the country's most heavily tramped paths. Most walks are day hikes, and most climax at small alpine lakes cradled in spectacular hanging valleys. Options for backpacking are necessarily limited by the park's size, though the 36-kilometre **Tamarack Trail**, following the crenellations of the Continental Divide between Cameron Lake and Red Rock Canyon, is rated as one of the Rockies' greatest highline treks (maximum elevation 2560m); the 20-kilometre **Carthew– Alderson Trail** from Cameron Lake to Waterton (max 2311m), a popular day's outing, can also be turned into a two-day trip by overnighting at the Alderson Lake campsite.

The single most popular day's walk is the **Bertha Lake Trail** from Waterton, 5.8km each way and about 460m of ascent (allow 3–4hr for the round trip): a short, steep hike to a busy but remarkably unsullied, mountain-ringed lake (1755m). Another superlative walk out of Waterton is the unique **Crypt Lake Trail**, which involves a boat trip to the trailhead across Waterton Lake and a crawl through a rock tunnel before the 8.7-kilometre hike (675m vertical ascent) to the great glacial amphitheatre containing Crypt Lake (1955m); rock walls tower 600m on three sides, casting a chill shadow that preserves small icebergs on the lake's surface throughout the summer. If you make the trip, allow time to catch the last boat back to Waterton, and if you plan on camping be aware that the site here is one of the most heavily used in the park's backcountry.

Of the several trails reached by access roads, the **Rowe Lake** (5.2km one way, 555m of ascent) and **Carthew Summit** (7.9km one way, 660m vertical) are the best of the Akamina Parkway routes (Rowe Lake has a designated campsite). The most exhilarating options from the head of the Red Rock Canyon road are the **Twin Lake Trail** (11km one way, 450m vertical) and the **Goat Lake Trail** (6.7km, 550m of ascent), both with campsites.

Waterton townsite offers the only indoor **accommodation** in the park, though its famous *Prince of Wales Hotel* (☎226-5551), at $100 for a double, might be out of your price range, and unless you have a prior booking it's likely to be full for its entire season (early June to mid-Sept). Otherwise you can try round the lake near Waterton at *Crandell Mountain Lodge* (April–Oct; ☎859-2288), with doubles from $30 to $60; *El-Cortez Motel* (☎859-2366), with doubles for $45; or *Northland Lodge* (mid-June to mid-Sept; ☎859-2353), with doubles at $55. You'd be advised to call and if possible book ahead for any of the town's overnight possibilities. The most central **campground** is located just at the southern edge of the townsite ($10). For help if you arrive roomless, or for details of the park or free backcountry use permits, call at the **Waterton Information Office** (☎859-2445), which is clearly marked on the road as you approach the town from the north.

## Crowsnest Pass

**Crowsnest Pass** is the most southerly of the three major routes into the Rockies and British Columbia from Alberta, and far less attractive than the Calgary and Edmonton approaches. In its early stages, however, as Hwy 3 pushes west out of Fort Macleod across glorious windblown prairie, it augurs well: the settlements are bleaker and more backwoods in appearance, and the vast views to the mountain-filled horizon, unbroken even by fence or telegraph pole, appear much as they must have to the first pioneers. As the road climbs towards the pass, however, the grime and melancholy of the area's derelict mining heritage increasingly make themselves felt. A century ago Crowsnest's vast coal deposits promised to make it the "Pittsburgh of Canada", an expectation dashed by a series of disasters and the local mines' rapid obsolescence.

You're unlikely to choose the Crowsnest route west in preference to the Calgary-to-Banff option, but it's still a direct route if you're hurrying to Vancouver or aim to explore the Kootenays in southern British Columbia. After breasting the pass, Hwy 3 drops into BC and follows the often spectacular Elk River Valley to join Hwy 95 at Cranbrook (covered in Chapter Seven).

## Bellevue and the Frank Slide

BELLEVUE is the first village worthy of the name after Fort Macleod; an oddball and close-knit spot with an old-world feel unusual in these parts. It's distinguished by a church the size of a dog kennel and a wooden tepee painted lemon yellow, as well as the claim to have "the best drinking water in Alberta" – a tame tourist lure from a sleepy place that clearly doesn't want visitors. Nonetheless, it supports a small **infocentre** and one of the pass's more commercial **campgrounds**, *Crowsnest Campground* (☎562-2932; $10), located just off the highway, with 110 sites, hot showers and a heated swimming pool.

Dominating the skyline behind the village are the crags and vast rockfall of the **Frank Slide**, a huge landslide that has quite obviously altered the contours of Turtle Mountain, once riddled with the galleries of local mines. In April 1903 some 100 million tons of rock on a front 1km long and 700m high trundled down the mountain to bury seventy people and their houses in less than two minutes. The morbidly interesting **Frank Slide Interpretive Centre** is just off the highway about 1km north of the village, and as well as looking at the circumstances of the disaster, it highlights European settlement in the area, the coming of the Canadian Pacific Railway to Alberta, and the technology, attitudes and lives of local miners (daily mid-May to early Sept 9am–8pm; rest of year 10am–4pm; free).

## Blairmore, Coleman and the Pass

BLAIRMORE, 2km beyond the slide, is a scrappy gridiron redeemed only by the walks and four winter ski runs on the hill above it. COLEMAN is the place to spend the night if you have to, especially if you've always wanted to be able to say you've seen "the biggest piggybank in the world". The town amounts to little – a single road, a strip of houses, three garages and a battered **motel**, the *Stop Inn* (☎562-7381; doubles from $35), a place favoured by loggers. Almost as knocked about is the *Grand Union International Hostel*, 7719-17th Ave (☎562-8254), with rooms from $15. More appealing is the dubiously named *Kozy Knest Kabins Triple K Motel* (☎563-5155), open only from May to October and situated 8km west of Coleman on Hwy 3 beside Crowsnest Lake.

The village is handy for the **Leitch Collieries Provincial Historic Site** just off the main road, a turn-of-the-century coal mine all but ruined and overgrown, but enthusiastically described to all comers by the interpretive staff who wander the site (mid-May to mid-Sept daily 9am–5pm; free).

Beyond Coleman the road climbs towards **Crowsnest Pass** (1382m) itself, and after a rash of sawmills – even a small oil and gas refinery – the natural scenery finally takes centre stage in a reassuring mix of lakes, mountains and trees protected by **Crowsnest Provincial Park**. There's a rustic provincial **campground** overlooking the lake at Crowsnest Creek, about 15km west of Coleman ($5).

# THE CANADIAN ROCKIES

Few of North America's terrains come loaded with as great a baggage of expectation as the **Canadian Rockies**, and it's a relief to find that the superlatives can scarcely do credit to the sheer immensity of this domain of forests, lakes, rivers and snow-capped mountains. Although most visitors confine themselves to a handful of **national parks**, the range spans almost 1500km to the Yukon border, forming the vast watershed of the Continental Divide, from which rivers flow to either the Pacific, Arctic or Atlantic ocean. Landscapes on such a scale makes a nonsense of artificial borderlines, and the major parks are national creations that span both Alberta and British Columbia. Four of the parks – Banff, Jasper, Yoho and Kootenay – share common boundaries, and it's these that receive the attention of most of the several million annual visitors to the Rockies.

You'll find little to choose between the parks in terms of scenery, and in any case attempting to plan an itinerary that takes them all in comfortably is a logistical impossibility. Most people start with **Banff National Park** – the Disneyland of the Canadian national park system – and then follow the otherworldly **Icefields Parkway** north to larger and much less busy **Jasper National Park**. From there it makes sense to head west to **Mount Robson Provincial Park**, effectively a continuation of Jasper, which protects the highest and most dramatic peak in the Canadian Rockies. Thereafter you're committed to leaving the Rockies unless you double back from Jasper to Banff – no hardship, given the scenery en route – where you can pick up the Trans-Canada Highway through the smaller **Yoho**, **Glacier** and **Revelstoke** national parks. Finally, **Kootenay National Park** is more easily explored than its neighbours, though you'll have to backtrack towards Banff or loop down from Yoho to pick up the road that provides its only access. (Waterton Lakes National Park, hugging the US border, is covered on p.423.)

Though you can get around all the parks by **bus** or hitching, travelling by **car** or **bike** is the obvious way to get the most out of the region. Once there, you'd be foolish not to tackle some of the 3000km of **trails** that criss-cross the mountains, all of which are well worn and well signed – the biggest problem is knowing which to choose. We've highlighted the best short walks and day hikes in any given area, but for more details you'll want to consult the **park visitor centres**, which sell 1:50,000 topographical maps and usually offer small libraries of trail books for reference; *The Canadian Rockies Trail Guide*, by Brian Patton and Bart Robinson, is an invaluable buy if you plan on doing any serious hiking or backpacking. Other activities – fishing, skiing, canoeing, whitewater rafting, cycling, horseriding, climbing and so on – are comprehensively dealt with in visitor centres and infocentres, and you can easily **hire equipment** or sign up for organised tours in the bigger national park towns.

A word of **warning**: don't underestimate the Rockies. Despite the summer throngs, excellent roads and sleek park facilities, the vast proportion of parkland is wilderness and should be respected as such. Be prepared for sudden weather changes – even in summer – and for encounters with wildlife such as bears (see p.442). Don't head into the backcountry without a map and the latest advice from the nearest visitor centre, and don't try to be a hero if you're inexperienced in the outdoors. Even if you're sticking to roads, it's important to realise the distances involved and the shortage of accommodation in this region.

---

### PARK PERMITS

Motorists and motorcyclists have to buy a **vehicle permit** to stay overnight in any of the national parks covered in this chapter, or to drive the Icefields Parkway. A one-day permit, valid for all parks, costs $4.25 per vehicle; a four-day permit is $9.50 and an annual permit (valid April & March) is $26.75. Note that cyclists, pedestrians and bus or train passengers don't have to pay. There's no fee to enter provincial parks. A separate **backcountry permit**, free at any park visitor centre or infocentre, is required for all overnight backcountry use.

## WINTER IN THE ROCKIES

Six major **winter resorts** are found in the Rockies – two in Kananaskis Country, two around Banff, and one each near Lake Louise and Jasper. These are by no means the only places to ski in Canada but, along with Whistler in British Columbia, they're amongst the best, the most popular and the fastest-growing areas in the country – and not only for downhill and cross-country but also for more esoteric activities like dog-sledding, ice climbing, skating, snowmobiling, snowshoeing, canyon crawling and ice fishing. At most resorts, the **season** runs from mid-December till the end of May; conditions are usually at their best in March, when the days are getting warmer and longer, and the snow is deepest. Resort **accommodation** is hardest to come by during Christmas week, the mid-February school holidays and at Easter – if you're planning to spend the night, make sure you've got reservations. **Equipment** can be rented locally by the day or by the week.

**Nakiska**, 25km south of the Trans-Canada Highway in Kananaskis Country, is Canada's newest resort. Developed for the 1988 Winter Olympics, it's one of the most user-friendly and state-of-the-art facilities on the continent, with snowmaking on all its varied terrain. Cross-country skiing is especially good here and throughout Kananaskis, with trails that take anything from twenty minutes to four days. **Fortress Mountain**, 15km south of Nakiska on Hwy 40, is a much smaller, homelier area where you're likely to share the slopes with school groups and families.

Banff's resorts are invariably the busiest and most expensive, and heavily patronised by foreigners (especially Japanese). **Mount Norquay** has long been known as an advanced downhill area – "steep and deep" in the local parlance – but has recently expanded its intermediate runs, and also boasts the Rockies' only night skiing. Higher and more exposed, **Sunshine Village** has even better scenery but few advanced runs; there's also a popular nordic centre where you can take lessons.

**Lake Louise**'s three big hills add up to Canada's most extensive resort, and one that's widely ranked amongst the best in North America. In addition to downhill skiing, a number of short and long cross-country trails criss-cross the valley and the lake area. Jasper's **Marmot Basin** is a more modest downhill area, but it's quieter and cheaper than those further south, and the park, particularly around Maligne Lake, has almost limitless cross-country skiing possibilities.

# Kananaskis Country

Most first-time visitors race straight up to Banff, ignoring the verdant foothill region southwest of Calgary. **Kananaskis Country**, a protected area created out of existing provincial parks to take some of the pressure off Banff, remains almost the exclusive preserve of locals in the know, most of whom come for skiing – many of the 1988 Olympic runs were in this area. Kananaskis embraces a huge tract of the Rockies and has all the mountain scenery and outdoor pursuit possibilities of the parks, but without the people or the commercialism. It is, however, an area without real focus, much of it remote wilderness; you'll need a bike or car, as nothing in the way of public transport moves out here; and the only fixed accommodation is in expensive, modern lodges – though it's idyllic camping country.

For **access**, it's possible to take minor roads from Calgary to some of the smaller foothill areas of the east – BRAGG CREEK being a particular Calgarian favourite – but the most obvious approach is to take Hwy 40, a major turn off the Trans-Canada Highway, which bisects Kananaskis's high mountain country from north to south and provides the ribbon to which most of the trails, campgrounds and scattered service centres cling.

About 3km down the highway is the **Barrier Lake Information Centre** (daily 9am–5pm), where you can get a full breakdown on any outdoor activity you care to indulge in. Another 40km south of the centre is a short spur off Hwy 40 to **Upper**

**Kananaskis Lake**, heart of Peter Lougheed Provincial Park, and probably the biggest concentration of accessible boating, fishing, camping and hiking possibilities in the region. The infocentre here advises on short trails, with the **Expedition Trail** (2.4km) one of the most popular. If you intend to get to grips with Kananaskis properly, however, it's worth buying the definitive *Kananaskis Country Trail Guide* by Gillean Daffern, widely available in Calgary.

---

The **telephone code** for Banff and Jasper parks is ☎403.

---

# Banff National Park

**Banff National Park** is the most famous of the Canadian Rockies' parks, which makes it Canada's leading tourist attraction – so be prepared for the crowds that throng its key centres, **Banff** and **Lake Louise**, as well as the best part of its 1500km of trails, most of which suffer a continual pounding during the summer months. That said, it's

worth putting up with every commercial indignity to enjoy the sublime scenery – and if you're camping or are prepared to walk, the worst of the park's excesses are fairly easily left behind.

Two popular highways offer magnificent vistas – the **Bow Valley Parkway** from Banff to Lake Louise, and the **Icefields Parkway** from Lake Louise to Jasper, transport links that have superseded the railway that first brought the park into being. The arrival of the **Canadian Pacific** at the end of the nineteenth century brought to an end some 10,000 years of native presence in the region – an epoch which previously had been disturbed only by trappers and the prodigious exploits of explorers like Mackenzie, Thompson and Fraser, who had sought to breach the Rockies with the help of native guides earlier in the century. Banff itself sprang to life in 1883 after three railway workers stumbled on the present town's Cave and Basin **hot springs**. Within two years of the discovery the government had set aside the Hot Springs Reserve as a protected area, and in 1887 enlarged it to form Canada's first national park, and only the third in the world.

## Banff Townsite

**BANFF TOWNSITE** (or just **BANFF**) is the unquestioned capital of the Canadian Rockies, and with its intense summer buzz it can be a fun and bustling base; if you've come for communion with nature, however, you'll want to get out as soon as possible. Although only a small resort by European standards, it still handles an immense amount of tourist traffic, much of it of the mega-coach-tour variety. Locals complain loudly that literally half the town is owned by the Japanese, and it's certainly one of the place's bigger surprises to find a huge number of Japanese signs and menus in shops and restaurants. Backpackers are also a massive presence in summer, and depending on your outlook you'll either enjoy the company – and the nightlife – or head straight for the mountains to escape the crowds. Either way you won't avoid some contact with the town, which contains essential shops and services that are almost impossible to come by elsewhere in the park.

### Arrival and information

Getting to Banff **by car** is almost too convenient, the town being just ninety minutes from Calgary on a fast, four-laned stretch of the Trans-Canada. The approach from the west is more winding, the total journey time from Vancouver being about twelve hours.

Six *Greyhound* **buses** run from Calgary daily, and five from Vancouver (via either Kamloops or Cranbrook), arriving at Banff's brand-new terminal at 100 Gopher Street (☎762-6767). Services between Banff and Jasper are provided by *Brewster Transportation*, which runs a single, heavily used bus daily in each direction for which it's well worth reserving a seat (late May to mid-Oct, weather permitting); they also run one service daily each way between Banff and Calgary International Airport. There's now no *VIA* **rail** passenger service through Banff – a private company runs luxury trains once a week between Calgary and Vancouver via Banff, but tickets are a prohibitive $400.

Banff's showpiece **infocentre**, at 224 Banff Ave (daily June–Sept 8am–10pm; Oct–May 10am–6pm; ☎762-3777), has information on almost any park-related subject you could name, including bear sightings, trails and the weather, as well as audio-visual displays. Among the many freebies available, pick up *Banff and Vicinity Drives and Walks* and *The Icefields Parkway* for maps of park facilities, the *Backcountry Visitors' Guide* for an invaluable overview of **backpacking** trails and campsites, and *Trail Bicycling in the National Parks* for conditions and full list of **mountain bike** trails in the parks. Staff will help with room-hunting, but aren't allowed to make specific recommendations – so it's often quicker to use the central reservation service (see next page).

For **bike rentals** go to *Spoke 'n' Edge*, 315 Banff Ave (☎762-2854); *Bactrax Rentals*, 339 Banff Ave (☎762-8177); or *Mountain Mopeds*, 451 Banff Ave, for mopeds. *Avis* has an office at 209 Bear St (☎762-3222) for **car hire**, with rates that start at about $50 a day with 100km free (IYHF discounts).

## Accommodation

It's almost impossible to turn up in Banff during July and August and hope to find a bed. Anything that can be booked has usually been snapped up, and many people are forced to backtrack to Canmore or even Calgary to find space. The **central reservation service** may be able to dig something out at short notice, for a fee (☎1-800-661-1676). Before turning to motels you could try **private rooms** and **bed and breakfasts** by asking for the *Private Home Accommodation List* at the infocentre, but don't expect too much – it rarely has more than about a dozen addresses. Most of the town's **motels** are on the spur from the Trans-Canada into town, and many charge uncommonly high rates for basic lodgings – typically around $100 and up for doubles.

**Campgrounds** may not be quite as bad, but even these generally fill up by 2 or 3pm in summer, so try to sound out all accommodation beforehand. Bear in mind that in addition to the places we've listed there are less-developed sites along both the Bow and Icefields parkways to the north. None of the government campgrounds takes reservations, and all are continually thronged in the summer. The *Banff International Youth Hostel* (see below) has a new system that allows you to book into any of southern Alberta's smaller hostels, which is advisable if you're heading east from here. Note that the *Spray River Hostel* is now closed, though it still appears in some literature.

### HOTELS, MOTELS AND B&B

**Blue Mountain Lodge**, 137 Muskrat St (☎762-5134). Nine rooms and a couple of cabins, $45–75 including light breakfast.

**Bow Valley Motor Lodge**, 228 Bow Ave (☎762-2261). Good views from some rooms; doubles $75–100, $6 for a third person in a double room.

**High Country Inn**, 419 Banff Ave (☎762-2236; ☎1-800-661-1244). Big, 70-room mid-range motel with doubles for $85, third bed for $10.

**Holiday Inn Lodge**, 311 Marten St (☎762-3648). Five rooms with full breakfast for $40–70 a night, three without breakfast at $20, and two cabins with cooking facilities for $65–80; open year-round.

**Irwin's Motor Inn**, 429 Banff Ave (☎762-4566 or ☎1-800-661-1721). Doubles at $72 put this motel in Banff's lower price bracket.

**King Edward Hotel**, corner of Banff Ave and Caribou (☎762-2251). Rooms are snapped up fast in this Banff institution, one of the town's liveliest spots. Both cheap and central, it's also got a good bar, great little diner, and plenty of locals. Doubles start at $35.

**Mrs Cowan's**, 118 Otter St (☎762-3696). Nine rooms, $20–50 a night with private or shared bathrooms and continental breakfast.

**Pension Tannehof**, 121 Cave Ave (☎762-4636). Contact Herbert Riedinger, who has 13 doubles from $65–85 including breakfast; off-season rates are $50.

**Red Carpet Inn**, 425 Banff Ave (☎762-4184). No-frills motel with doubles for $70.

**Spruce Grove Motel**, 545 Banff Ave (☎762-2112). The cheapest motel in town, with $55 doubles.

**Voyager Inn**, 555 Banff Ave (☎762-3301; ☎1-800-372-9288). Motel with swimming pool, sauna and doubles from $85.

### HOSTELS

**Banff International Youth Hostel**, Tunnel Mountain Rd (IYHF; ☎762-4122). A 3-km slog from downtown – take a *Happy Bus* from Banff Ave in summer – but a modern place with friendly staff and excellent facilities. The infoboard is a good source of advice, ride offers and so forth. Meals are available all day, and rooms are mainly four-bed dorms at $14 for members, $19 for non-members.

**Banff YWCA**, 102 Spray Ave (☎762-3560). More convenient than the youth hostel – cross the river south of town and it's the first building on the left. Open to men and women, with plenty of clinically

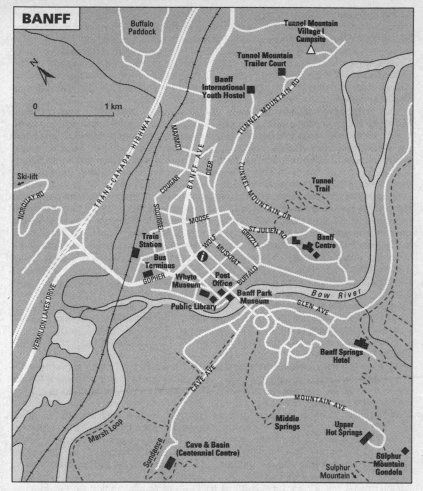

clean rooms, but they go quickly; singles $38, doubles $46, bunks $14 (bring your own sleeping bag, or hire blankets). Downstairs café has good, cheap food and entertainingly eccentric service.

## CAMPGROUNDS

**Tunnel Mountain Village I**, 1km beyond the hostel on Tunnel Mountain Rd. The nearest camp-ground to downtown – get there by *Happy Bus* from Banff Ave. A huge 622-pitch government-operated site, with electricity and showers; from $9.50. Nearby *Tunnel Mountain Trailer Court* is reserved for RVs. *Village I* closes on Oct 1, but the smaller *Tunnel Mountain Village II* then opens to provide unserviced winter camping. All three sites are set amidst trees, with lovely views, plenty of space and various short trails close at hand to escape fellow campers. Big-horn sheep, elk, and even the odd bear may drop in.

**Two Jack Main** and **Two Jack Lakeside**, 13km northeast of town. Both are only semi-serviced (flush toilets but no showers) and are open from early June to late September. $6.50 and $8.50 respectively.

## Gondola rides

Gondolas are what Canadians call cable-cars, of which the town has two prize examples. High-price tickets buy you crowds, great views and commercialised summits, but also the chance for some high-level hiking without the slog of an early-morning climb. They're also good for a quick glimpse of the remote high country if you're short of time or unable to walk the trails. The best times to take a ride are early morning or evening, when wildlife sightings are more likely, and when the play of light gives an added dimension to the views.

The **Sulphur Mountain Gondola** on Mountain Avenue has been trundling skywards for thirty years, pulling up at a stomach-churning 51 degrees to immense views and an ugly summit restaurant (year-round daily 9am–8pm; $7.50). It takes just eight minutes to reach the 2255-metre high point, though from the restaurant a one-kilometre path, the **Summit Ridge Trail**, has been blazed to take you a bit higher. Another short walk, the **Vista Trail**, leads to Sanson Peak, another viewpoint. Note that if you hike up from the car park (see box) you can ride the gondola down for free. The summit restaurant does some surprisingly good deals, especially on breakfasts; far too much of the food, unfortunately, ends up being eaten by bighorn sheep which, protected within the parks and unafraid of humans, gather here for handouts. Don't encourage them – feeding wildlife is against park regulations and can land you with a stiff fine.

The newer **Sunshine Gondola**, 18km southwest of town, whisks you 4km to the Sunshine Village Resort at 2215m and some staggering views (July & Aug Mon–Thurs 8.30am–7.30pm, Fri–Sun 8.30am–10.30pm; $12). At no extra cost, the **Standish Chairlift** takes you on from the resort to the Continental Divide (2430m) and a post marking the BC–Alberta border. Two gravel **trails** return from here to the resort, both by way of **Sunshine Meadows**, a beautiful and unusually large tract of alpine grassland. The shorter loop takes in Rock Isle Lake, while the longer tour (2hr) passes Grizzly and Lynx lakes before dropping to Sunshine Village.

## The hot springs

Once you've ridden a gondola, the next stop on the standard tourist itinerary is to plunge in one of the town's two **hot springs**. There are quieter places in western Canada to take the waters, but hot springs are always a mildly bizarre experience, and though the crowds are a pain, the prices are reasonable. The recently renovated **Cave and Basin Hot Springs**   (daily June–Sept 8.30am–11pm; $2) have a moderate (32°C) pool, although the original cave and spring that gave birth to the national park are now out of bounds to the hoi-polloi. The centre is southwest of downtown on Cave Avenue. If you're in this part of town, you could walk the **Sundance Canyon Trail** close to the springs, an easy ninety-minute climb with the aptly named Viewpoint Path the preferred descent.

At 40°C, the **Upper Hot Springs** (same details) on Mountain Avenue are a steamier alternative, but they receive a lot of traffic from people coming off the Sulphur Mountain Gondola. They also leave a more pungent sulphurous aftersmell. For an extra couple of dollars you can hire bathing suit, towel and locker.

## The museums

With some of the world's most spectacular mountains on your doorstep, sightseeing in Banff might seem an absurd undertaking, yet it's good to have some rainy-day options. The downtown **Park Museum** on Banff Avenue (daily 10am–6pm; free) bulges with two floors of stuffed animals, many of which are indigenous to the park. Hunting of game animals was banned in the park in 1890, but not before populations of moose, elk, sheep, goats and grizzlies had been severely depleted. Game wardens only arrived to enforce the injunction in 1913, and even then they didn't protect the "bad" animals – wolves, coyotes, foxes, cougars, lynx, eagles, owls and hawks – which were hunted until the 1930s as part of park's "predator-control program". Many of the formaldehyde victims in the museum date from this period. If it's bucketing down outside, the lovely wood-panelled **reading room** is a snug retreat, full of magazines and books on nature and wildlife and a perfect spot to while away a cold afternoon.

The nearby **Natural History Museum**, 112 Banff Ave (daily summer 10am–8pm; winter 10am–6pm; $2), concentrates on the Rockies' geological history, but throws in accounts of its forests, flowers and minerals. The main draw, however, is a completely irrelevant twenty-minute film on volcanoes (there are no volcanoes, extinct or otherwise, in these parts), and a po-faced account of the ludicrous legend of a giant Bigfoot Indian – there's a huge model on the way out by means of illustration. The **Whyte Museum of the Canadian Rockies** (daily 10am–6pm; $2) contents itself with a look at the Rockies' emergence as a tourist destination, and some of the early expeditions to explore and conquer the interior peaks.

## The Banff Springs Hotel

At $880 a night for a suite (plus $20 for any pets), the **Banff Springs Hotel** is probably out of your league, though you can't spend much time in town without coming across at least one mention of the place, and, it's difficult to miss its Gothic superstructure in the flesh. Built in 1888, the luxury hotel makes ends meet by soaking up and then disgorging coachloads of Japanese tourists. Tours of the building are organised, but unless you're a fan of Victorian hotel architecture and its allied knick-knacks you can easily give them a miss. It can be good for a voyeuristic hour or so, however, to take a coffee or beer in the second-floor café; prices on anything else are ludicrous.

### HIKING NEAR BANFF TOWNSITE

Banff Townsite is one of two obvious bases for walks in the park (the other is Lake Louise), and there are trails around the town to cater to all levels of fitness.

**Day hikes** from town are limited – in most cases you'll need to drive, hitch or taxi out a few kilometres along the Trans-Canada or to the Sunshine Village Gondola area to reach trailheads that leave the flat valley floor for the meat of the mountains. Only a couple of longish ones strike out directly from town: the **Spray River circuit**, a flat, 13-kilometre round trip past the Banff Springs Hotel up the Spray River; and the **Sulphur Mountain Trail**, a 5.5-kilometre switchback that climbs 655m under the gondola to its terminal at 2255m.

The most popular day hike in the area is probably the trail to **Cascade Amphitheatre** (2195m), which starts at Mount Norquay Ski Area, 6km north of the Trans-Canada up Mount Norquay Road. The trail offers a broad medley of landscapes, ranging from alpine meadows to deep, ice-scoured valleys and a close view of the knife-edge mountains that loom so tantalisingly above town. Allow about three hours for the 7.7-kilometre walk, which involves a respectable 610m of ascent. For the same amount of effort, you could tackle **Elk Lake** (2165m) from the ski area, though at 13.5km each way it's a long day's hike; some people turn it into an overnight by using the campsite 2.5km short of Elk Lake. Shorter, but harder on the lungs, is the third of Banff's trio of popular local walks, **C Level Cirque** (1920m), reached by a four-kilometre trail from the Upper Bankhead Picnic Area on the Lake Minnewanka road east of Banff. Elsewhere, the **Sunshine Meadows** area has five increasingly popular high trails of between 8km and 20km, all possible as day hikes and approached either from the Sunshine Gondola or its parking area, 18km southwest of Banff.

The best **backpacking** options lie in the **Egypt Lake** area west of Banff townsite, most of the longer trails radiating from the campsite at Egypt Lake itself. Once you're in the backcountry around Banff, however, the combination of trails is virtually limitless in whichever direction you care to explore. The keenest hikers tend to march the routes that lead from Banff to Lake Louise – the **Sawback Trail** and **Bow Valley Highline**, or the tracks in the Upper Spray and Bryant Creek Valley south of the townsite.

## Eating and drinking

Banff has any number of overpitched and often overpriced tourist **restaurants**, running the gamut from Japanese and other ethnic cuisines to nouvelle-frontier grub. If you haven't got unlimited funds, though, the *Banff Youth Hostel* and the *YWCA* cafeterias probably offer the best value for money. Cafés, snack places and the usual fast-food chains are also gentle on tight budgets; in general avoid the summer tables of Banff Avenue's cafés – *Café de Paris* is the favourite – which are crowded but pricey. Given Banff's huge number of summer travellers and large seasonal workforce, there are plenty of people around in summer looking for nighttime action. As a result, the town is surprisingly lively, and offers several drinking and dance outlets.

To stock up if you're camping, use the big *Safeway* supermarket at 318 Marten Street and Elk (daily 8am–10pm).

**Aardvarks**, 304 Wolf St. Popular pizza place that gets particularly frantic after the bars have closed (closed Sun).

**Balkan Village**, 120 Banff Ave. A popular Greek outlet, known for cheap, big portions and an atmospheric interior; belly dancing on Tues in the winter to whip things up, but in summer the place turns raucous on its own, with frequent impromptu navel displays from well-oiled customers.

**Barbary Coast**, upstairs at 119 Banff Ave. Popular bar, with long queues in summer. Closed Sun.

**Le Beaujolais**, corner of Banff Ave and Buffalo St (☎762-2712). One of western Canada's best and most expensive restaurants. Reservations recommended.

**Coffee Shop**, corner of the Wolf and Bear Mall. Best for coffee and cakes.

**Grizzley's**, Moose Street. Ecologically dubious caribou and bear specialities and, ironically, also vegetarian platters.

**Joe Btfspik's Diner**, 221 Banff Ave. Tries a touch too hard to evoke period feel – all red vinyl chairs and vivid black and white floors – but it still does excellent, if slightly overpriced, food; you may have to queue at peak times.

**Melissa's**, 218 Lynx St (next to the *Homestead Inn*). Set in an old log cabin, this is probably Banff's most popular daytime destination: big breakfasts, steaks, salads and burgers. However, you'll probably have to queue, and it's a quick turnover place – for a more leisurely drink try the upstairs bar, a favourite watering hole.

**Rose and Crown**, 202 Banff Ave. Part of a chain, but generates a moderately successful pub atmosphere (darts, mock-Victorian interior) and, away from the family-orientated restaurant, it can be a good drinking venue. Food is of the pub-lunch variety and you can also shake a leg in the adjoining nightclub and disco.

**Schultz's Grill**, downstairs in the *King Edward Hotel*, corner of Banff Ave and Caribou. One of the few places to escape the tourist throng, a spot in which rucksacks are banned and which is marked out firmly as locals' territory. Good bar, casual atmosphere, an excellent diner and live music nightly.

**Silver City**, 110 Banff Ave. Very popular bar, with live music on Friday and Saturday evenings.

# Highway 1 and the Bow Valley Parkway

Two roads run parallel through the Bow Valley from Banff to Lake Louise (60km). Faster is **Highway 1** (the Trans-Canada); quieter is the **Bow Valley Parkway**, on the other (north) side of the river, eleven years in the making and opened in 1989 as a special scenic route. After Banff, there's only one link between the two roads, at CASTLE JUNCTION, 30km from Lake Louise.

Both routes, needless to say, are staggeringly beautiful, as the mountains – which at Banff seem rather distant – begin to creep closer to the road. For the entire run the **Bow River**, broad and emerald green, crashes through rocks and forest, looking as close to one's image of a "mighty river" as it's possible to get. Despite the tarmac and heavy summer traffic, the surroundings are pristine and – if this is your introduction to the mountains – they begin to suggest the immensity of the wilderness to come. Sightings of elk and deer are common, particularly around dawn and sundown, and occasionally you'll spot moose.

## Highway 1

Most people either cruise this fast stretch of the Trans-Canada without stopping – knowing that the road north of Lake Louise is more spectacular still – or leap out at every trail and rest stop, overcome with the grandeur of it all. With a **car** you'll have the freedom of choice, though for the sake of wildlife try to stick to the 90kph speed limit; on *Greyhound* or *Brewster* **buses** you're whisked through to Lake Louise in about forty minutes. Hitching should be no problem, though in summer there's plenty of competition for lifts.

## The Bow Valley Parkway

The **Bow Valley Parkway** if anything rates a higher quotient of scenic grandeur than the Trans-Canada, and offers more in the way of distractions if you're taking your time: several trails, campgrounds, and a number of accommodation options. Everything of consequence on the road is well signed. The largest concentration of gawping trippers is likely to be found at the Merrent pull-off, which gives fantastic and often-photographed views of the Bow Valley and the railway winding through the mountains.

Three **lodges** are spaced equally en route, and though expensive, they may have room when Lake Louise's hotels are stretched. First is the *Johnson Canyon Resort*, 26km west of Banff (mid-May to late Sept; ☎762-2971), with a shop, garage, pool, and doubles from $58 to $86. Next comes *Castle Mountain Village*, 32km west of Banff near Castle Junction (year-round; ☎762-3868), chalets from $50 to $85, and finally *Baker Creek Chalets*, 12km east of Lake Louise (year-round; ☎522-3761), with log cabins from $60 to $100.

Far cheaper are the parkway's two charming **youth hostels**, starting with *Castle Mountain Hostel*, 1.5km east of Castle Junction (year-round; closed Wed; ☎762-2367; $9). Try to call, or better still book ahead through the hostel at Banff – even in winter, when the place fills up with skiers. *Corral Creek Hostel* is a cosy circle of cabins 5km east of Lake Louise (year-round; members $8; no phone); it's closed on Mondays, though in off-season you're unlikely to be turned away.

---

**BOW VALLEY TRAILS**

Five major trails branch off the **Bow Valley Parkway**. If you're just passing through and want a breath of air, the best short walk would be the **Johnston Canyon Trail** (2.7km each way), an incredibly engineered path to a series of spray-veiled waterfalls. From the upper falls you can continue on to the **Ink Pots**, a series of seven cold-water springs, for a total distance of 5.8km (215m of vertical) – about two hours of walking. Another short possibility is the **Castle Crags Trail** (3.7km each way; 520m gain) from the signed pull-off 5km west of Castle Junction. Short but steep, and above treeline, this walk offers superlative views as far as the eye can see across the Bow Valley and the mountains beyond. Allow ninety minutes one-way to take account of the stiff 520-metre climb.

The best day hike is to **Rockbound Lake** (8.4km each way), a steepish climb to 2210m with wild lakeland scenery at the end; allow at least two and a half hours one way, and be prepared for an appreciable 760-metre gain. The other trails – Baker Creek (20.3km) and Pulsatilla Pass (17.1km) – are backpacking numbers, linking with the thick network of paths in the Slate Range northeast of Lake Louise.

**Hwy 1** (the Trans-Canada) has numerous trails, amongst which two stand out. Proximity to Banff and superb walking make the trail to **Bourgeau Lake** (7.5km one way) a popular trek; allow two and a half to three hours for the 725-metre ascent, which starts from a parking area 10km west of Banff. **Shadow Lake** (14.3km each way) is manageable as a long day hike, though a campsite at the lake (1840m) occupies one of the Rockies' more impressive sub-alpine basins and gives access to a number of onward trails. The main trail starts from the Redearth Creek parking area 20km west of Banff; allow four hours for the 440-metre climb to the lake.

Three national park **campgrounds** provide excellent retreats if you're tenting: the first, *Johnston Canyon* (mid-May to mid-Sept; $5), is the best equipped, but still doesn't have showers; after that comes *Castle Mountain*, near Castle Junction (late June to early Sept; $5), and *Protection Mountain*, 5km north of Castle Junction (same details).

# Lake Louise

The Banff park's other main centre, **Lake Louise**, is a very different place from Banff – less a town than two distinct and artificial resorts. The first is a small mall of shops and hotels just off the Trans-Canada known as **Lake Louise Village**. The second is the lake itself, the self-proclaimed "gem of the Rockies" and – despite its crowds and monster hotel – a sight you have to see. The lake is 4.5km from the village on a winding road, Lake Louise Drive – or, if you're walking, 2.7km by Louise Creek Trail, 4.5km by the Tramline Trail. You're better off saving the walking for around the lake, however, and either hitch a ride up or take a shuttle **bus** (summer only; $4) from the village. Both areas, but the lake in particular, are desperately busy in summer, the road resounding to the crunching gears of a thousand tour buses. Winter isn't much better, when people pile in for what many claim is some of the best powder **skiing** in Canada.

Whether you'll stay, at least near the lake, is doubtful, though the mountains around are magnificent **hiking country** and the park's most popular day-use area. You'll have to weigh awesome scenery against crowds, however, for these are some of the most heavily used trails on the continent – 50,000-plus people in summer – though, as ever, longer backpacking routes lead quickly away from the herd.

### Lake Louise Village

**LAKE LOUISE VILLAGE** doesn't amount to much, but it's an essential supply stop, and has more or less everything you need in terms of food and shelter (at a price). Most of it centres round a single mall and car park, with a few outlying motels dotted along the service road to the north. First stop should be the brand-new **Lake Louise Information Centre**, a few steps from the car park, which offers not only information but also high-tech natural-history exhibits, toilets and telephones (mid-May to mid-Oct daily 8am–6pm; open till 10pm in high summer). Almost as useful is the excellent *Woodruff and Blum* bookshop in the mall, where there's a full range of **maps**, guides and background reading on the area. A couple of doors down, *Wilson Mountain Sports* is good for **bike and equipment hire**. The mall also has public washrooms and a launderette. The general store is good (and has a **money exchange**), as is the busy café opposite, *Laggan's Bakery*.

*Greyhound* **buses** stop in the car park (6 daily to Banff and Calgary; 3 to Vancouver and the west). In summer *Brewster* runs services to Jasper (2 daily), but make sure you aren't boarding one of the company's many coach tours. *Pacific Western Coaches* (☎762-4558) runs a daily service to Calgary airport in summer.

A short way from the village is the **Lake Louise Gondola**, which runs partway up Mount Whitehorn (2669m). To reach it return to and cross over the Trans-Canada, and follow the road towards the ski area; the gondola is signed left after about 1km (June–Sept daily 9am–6pm; $7 return, $5 one way). At the top (2034m) are the usual gasping views, self-service restaurant, and several trailheads.

### The lake

Before you see **Lake Louise** you see the hotel: *Chateau Lake Louise*, a 1924 monstrosity that would never have been given planning permission today. Yet, for all its powers of desecration, after a few minutes you find it fading into insignificance alongside the immense beauty of its surroundings. The lake is Kodachrome turquoise, the mountains sheer, the glaciers vast; the whole ensemble is utter natural perfection. Lake

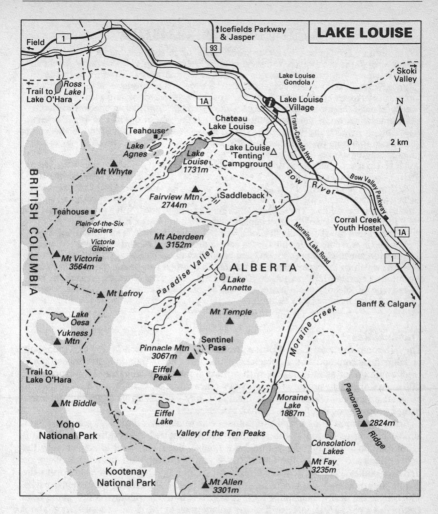

Louise was unknown to white Canadians until 1882, when Tom Wilson, an explorer and railway worker, was led to it by a local native. Wilson wrote soon after: "I never, in all my explorations of these five chains of mountains throughout western Canada, saw such a matchless scene ... I felt puny in body, but glorified in spirit and soul."

All the same, you'll wish you could have been Tom Wilson, and seen the spot unsullied by the hotel, the snap-happy tourists and the general clutter on its eastern shore. The waterfront is a two-minute walk from an over-large car park to the left of the hotel. Notice-boards here seem mainly concerned with the dispute over how the lake came by its name – was it named in honour of the governor's wife, or after the fourth daughter of Queen Victoria? It's hard to care either way. More interesting is the account of Hollywood's discovery of the lake in the 1920s, when it was used to suggest "exotic European locations".

## HIKES AROUND LAKE LOUISE

Trails in the Lake Louise area are invariably crawling in summer, but all are good for a short taste of the scenery, the two most popular walks ending at tea houses – mountain chalets where you can buy welcome snacks at inflated prices. The first is the **Lake Agnes Trail** (3.4km) which strikes off from the right (north) shore of the lake. It's a gradual, 400-metre climb, relieved by ever more magnificent views, and a tea house beautifully situated beside mountain-cradled Lake Agnes (2135m); allow one to two hours. Beyond the tea house you can continue on the right side of the lake to **Big Beehive** (2255m), a popular and incredible eyrie 1km beyond. Just as rewarding is the one-kilometre trail from the tea house to **Little Beehive**, a mite lower, but still privy to full-blown panoramas over the broad sweep of the Bow Valley.

If you're a stronger walker, or simply want to make a good day's trek, follow the steep trail down from the Big Beehive to the second tea house at the **Plain of the Six Glaciers** (2100m). Alternatively, you can follow the **Six Glaciers Trail** from the hotel along the lakeshore to the same point (5.3km to the tea house, 365m vertical gain), about ninety minutes' walking. The scenery is thrilling glaciated stuff, with a good viewpoint at the end, but this is one of the most popular walks in the whole park.

Slightly less travelled is the last local walk, the **Saddleback Trail** (3.7km one way), whose main attraction is that it provides access to **Fairview Mountain**, one of the area's finest viewpoints. Allow between one and two hours to Saddleback (2330m; an ascent of 595m), which as the name suggests is a saddle between two peaks; the trail on to the summit of Fairview (2745m) strikes off right from here. Even if you don't make the last push, the Saddleback views alone – across to the 1200-metre wall of Mount Temple (3544m) – are monumentally staggering.

## Practicalities

The 515-room **Chateau Lake Louise** (☎522-3511 or ☎1-800-268-9411) has a monopoly on lakeside accommodation: doubles here cost up to $550, though in low season (Oct–Dec) some go for as little as $95, with a third person only an extra $15. Surprisingly, this makes the chateau one of the cheaper places to stay, though you'd be advised to book ahead even in off-season. Look inside anyway – it's bizarrely appealing and horrifying by turns – and snaffle a free cup of glacier water.

Accommodation in or near Lake Louise Village is only a little less expensive, and almost certain to be full in the summer. Banff's **central reservations** (☎1-800-661-1676) can make bookings for you in Lake Louise, but if you want to stay cheaply the only options are canvas or the *Corral Creek* **youth hostel**, 5km east of the village on the Bow Valley Parkway (closed Mon; $8; no phone). You can hire bikes from the hostel "houseparent", the quaint term used for hostel wardens in the national parks. The best **hotel** deal you can hope for is to take one of the "economy rooms" at the *Lake Louise Inn* (☎522-3791), just north of the village mall to the right – these start at about $70, and if you club together with three other people you can take advantage of cheaper deals (if you've just come off the trail, try to look as presentable as possible at reception). Also try the *Mountaineer Lodge* (May–Oct; ☎522-3844), with doubles between $90 and $120, or one of the lodges on the road between the village and the lake: *Paradise Lodge* (☎522-3595), with doubles from $85 to $150, or *Deer Lodge* (☎522-3991), whose doubles go for around $120. The top-of-the-pile choice away from the lake is the village's *Post Hotel* (☎522-3989), with doubles from $150 to $250.

The park-run **campground**, *Lake Louise Tent*, is a lovely one close to the village – follow the signs off the road up to the lake – but it gets busy in summer and, with the railway close by, it can be awfully noisy (mid-May to early Oct; serviced, but no showers; $8.50). *Lake Louise Trailer*, an RV site a short distance beyond, is open to tents for winter camping (Oct–April).

## HIKING: PARADISE VALLEY, MORAINE LAKE, SKOKI VALLEY

Besides the trails near Lake Louise, further hiking possibilities abound in the two parallel tributary valleys to the south – Paradise and Moraine (Valley of the Ten Peaks) – and in the Skoki Valley/Boulder Pass area across the Bow Valley to the east.

### Paradise Valley

**Paradise Valley** was named in 1894 by the mountaineer Walter Wilcox, who could think of nothing more appropriate for "a valley of surpassing beauty, wide and beautiful, with alternating open meadows and rich forests". The trail starts from a parking area 3km up the Moraine Lake Road, which branches south off the road from Lake Louise Village to Lake Louise. The walk here is basically a straightforward hike up one side of the valley and down the other, a loop of 18km which inflicts on you a modest 385m of vertical gain. Most people take in the **Lake Annette** diversion for its unmatched view of Mount Temple's 1200-metre north face (unclimbed until 1966), and many overnight at the **campsite** at the head of the valley (9km from the parking area), though this is on record as one of the busiest sites in the park. Others toughen the walk by throwing in the climb up to Sentinel Pass (2605m) on the ridge south of the valley, which gives the option of continuing down the other side to connect with the Moraine Lake trails.

### Moraine Lake

Sister to Lake Louise and its scenic peer, **Moraine Lake** should look familiar: it graces the back of Canadian $20 bills, though the illustration naturally does little justice to the shimmering water and the jagged, snow-covered peaks that inspired the nickname Valley of the Ten Peaks. The area offers three basic routes, any one of them easily accomplished in a day, but each with sting-in-the-tail additions if you want added exertion; all start from the lake, which lies at the end of twelve-kilometre Moraine Lake Road.

The easiest is the 2.9-kilometre stroll to **Consolation Lakes**, an hour's trip that's often busy, but still a relief from the tourist madness that grips Moraine Lake itself. If you're tenting, fairly fit, or can arrange a pick-up, the highline Panorama Ridge Trail (2255m) branches off here to run 22km to the Banff–Radium highway 7km west of Castle Junction.

The most popular walk, and perhaps the busiest in the park, is the **Larch Valley–Sentinel Pass Trail**, though most people only walk the first 2.4km through the pastoral meadows and stands of larch immediately above Moraine Lake to Larch Valley. Views of the encircling peaks here are as majestic as any, but if you have the legs aim to push onto the Sentinel Pass, three hours and 720m above Moraine Lake – and, at 2605m, the highest point reached by a major trail in the Canadian Rockies. From here you could continue down into Paradise Valley and complete a superlative day's walk by picking up the valley loop (see above) back to the Moraine Lake Road.

The third option, the **Eiffel Lake–Wenkchemna Pass Trail**, follows the Larch Valley path before branching off for the stark, glaciated grandeur at the head of the Valley of the Ten Peaks. It's 5.6km to Eiffel Lake (2255m), and 720m of uphill slog, but if the weather and your lungs are holding out a rougher track continues to Wenkchemna Pass (2605m) 4km beyond to give views from the Divide over Banff, Yoho and Kootenay parks.

### The Skoki Valley

Day hikes in the **Skoki Valley** region east of Lake Louise are thinner on the ground than around Moraine Lake, and to enjoy this area you'll need a tent to overnight at any of the six campsites (or the luck and forethought to book into the *Skoki Lodge*, a dream accommodation in the midst of the mountains and 15km from the nearest road). The main access trail initially follows a gravel road forking off to the right of the Lake Louise Ski Area, off Hwy 1. Many people hike as far as **Boulder Pass** (2345m), 8.6 km and 640m ascent from the parking area, as a day-trip and return the same way instead of pushing on to the lodge, 8km beyond. From the lodge or the campsites you can thread together any number of trails, long or short, all well signposted and all documented in the *Canadian Rockies Trail Guide*.

Apart from snacks in Lake Louise Village, **eating** is confined to hotel dining rooms, most of them overpriced. Food at the *Post Hotel*'s downstairs bar is within the means of most travellers; for a real blowout you could tuck in at the formal restaurant upstairs, ranked as one of western Canada's top ten restaurants.

# The Icefields Parkway

The splendour of the **Icefields Parkway** (Hwy 93) can hardly be overstated: a 230-kilometre road from Lake Louise to Jasper through the heart of the Rockies, it is justifiably ranked as one of the world's ultimate drives. Its apparently unending succession of huge peaks, lakes and forests – capped by the stark grandeur of the Columbia Icefield – is overwhelming, and after two and half hours you're likely to find yourself saddled with a bad case of landscape fatigue. Fur traders and natives used the route as far back as 1800 and christened it the "Wonder Trail", though the present highway was only opened in 1940 as part of a Depression-era public works programme. Now about a million people a year make the journey to experience what the park blurb calls a "window on the wilderness", and yet, except for July, you can cruise serenely with no sense of the madding crowd.

At about its midway point the Icefields Parkway crosses from Banff into Jasper National Park, and though you might turn back here, the divide is almost completely arbitrary, and the parkway is impossible to treat as anything but a whole. For this reason we've followed the obvious itinerary – the one most people follow – in treating the road as a self-contained journey. Distances given in brackets are from Lake Louise, which is virtually the only way to locate places on the road, though everything mentioned is clearly marked off the highway by distinctive brown-green national park signs.

## Access, information and planning

**Driving** or **cycling** is the best way to do the parkway, but hitching is also a distinct possibility – though the word is that people, particularly in RVs, like to do their scenery-watching in private. *Brewster Transportation* runs several tours and a single scheduled **bus** daily in both directions between Banff and Jasper from late May to mid-October, though services at either end of the season are often weather-affected ($40 single).

Tourist literature often gives the misleading impression that the Icefields Parkway is highly developed. In fact, the wilderness is extreme – there are only two points for **services**, at Saskatchewan Crossing (77km from Lake Louise), where the David Thompson Highway (Hwy 11) branches off for RED DEER, and at the Columbia Icefield (127km). Saskatchewan Crossing is the only place campers can stock up with groceries.

Needless to say, you could spend days exploring the trails, long and short, off the road. Many are extremely short, however, and if you allow a day to drive the road, you'll have time to stop off at the half a dozen or so essential sights; ideally, though, you should give yourself at least three days to do the Icefields Parkway. Five **youth hostels** and twelve excellent park **campgrounds** are spaced along the parkway at regular intervals. Two of the campgrounds and four of the hostels are open year-round, though snow often closes the road from October onwards. If you demand more comfort, you'll have to overnight at Banff, Lake Louise or Jasper. The only **hotel** accommodation – which is invariably booked solid – is at Saskatchewan Crossing.

## Lake Louise to the Columbia Icefield

It's extremely hard to know what to see if you're short of time on the parkway, but the following are the must-sees and must-dos along the 122-kilometre stretch from Lake Louise to the Columbia Icefield: best view – Peyto Lake; best lake walk – Bow Lake; best waterfalls – Panther–Bridal Falls; best short walk – Parker Ridge. Temptations for longer walks are numerous, and the difficulty, as ever, is knowing which to choose.

We've listed only short strolls and day hikes here; for the backpacking options refer to *The Canadian Rockies Trail Guide*.

The first **youth hostel** north of Lake Louise is *Mosquito Creek* (24km), a single log cabin which sleeps 38 and has basic food supplies (year-round; closed Tues; no phone). Slightly beyond is the first **campground**, *Mosquito Creek* (mid-June to mid-Sept; $8) and one of the parkway's two winter campgrounds (walk-in only; free). Two hikes start from alongside the campground: **Molar Pass** (9.8km; 3hr; elevation gain 535m), a manageable day-trip with good views, and **Upper Fish Lake** (14.8km; 5hr; elevation gain 760m), which follows the Molar Pass trail for 7km before branching off and crossing the superb alpine meadows of North Molar Pass (2590m).

At the *Num-Ti-Jah Lodge* access road just beyond (37km) is the start of the trail to **Bow Lake** and **Bow Glacier Falls** (4.3km; 1–2hr; elevation gain 155m), a great short walk that takes in the flats around Bow Lake and then climbs to some immense cliffs and several huge waterfalls beyond. Another 3km up the road is the twenty-minute stroll to **Peyto Lake Lookout**, one of the finest vistas in the Rockies. The panorama only unfolds in the last few seconds, giving a genuinely breathtaking view of the vivid emerald lake far below; mountains and forest stretch away as far as you can see.

After 57km you reach the *Waterfowl Lake* **campground** (mid-June to mid-Sept; $8) and the **Chephren Lake Trail** (3.5km; 1hr; elevation gain 80m), which leads to quietly spectacular scenery with a minimum of effort. SASKATCHEWAN CROSSING (77km) has outrageously expensive food, petrol and *The Crossing* (early March to mid-Nov; ☎761-7000), a hotel/restaurant with doubles for $68. Eleven kilometres north are the *Rampart Creek* **youth hostel** (year-round; closed Wed; $8) and **campground** (late June to early Sept; $8). The last of the Banff National Park campgrounds is the tiny *Cirrus Mountain* site at the 103km mark (late June to early Sept; $8).

Shortly before **Panther Falls** (113.5km) the road makes a huge hairpin climb (the so-called "Big Hill") that opens up yet more panoramic angles on the vast mountain spine stretching back towards Lake Louise. The unmarked and very slippery trail to the falls, which are probably the most spectacular in the park, is 1km long and starts from the lower end of the second of two car parks on the right. Beyond it (117km) is the trailhead to **Parker Ridge** (2.4km one way), a spectacular short walk into the alpine zone (2130m) and commanding views from the summit ridge. Ideally placed for this area and the Columbia Icefield – and therefore invariably busy – is the *Hilda Creek* **youth hostel**, 1km beyond. The setting is stunning, and accommodation (for 21) is in cosy log cabins.

## The Columbia Icefield

Covering an area of 325 square kilometres, the **Columbia Icefield** is the largest collection of ice and snow in the entire Rockies, and the largest glacial area in the northern hemisphere south of the Arctic Circle. Meltwater flows from it into the Arctic, Atlantic and Pacific oceans, fed by six major glaciers, of which three – the Athabasca, Dome and Stutfield – are visible from the Icefields Parkway. The busy **Icefield Centre** (June–Sept) provides an eerie viewpoint for the most prominent of these, the Athabasca Glacier, as well as offering information and slide shows on the glaciers and the Castleguard Caves which honeycomb the ice – Canada's most extensive, but inaccessible to the public.

You can walk onto the **Athabasca Glacier**, but full-scale expeditions are the preserve of experts unless you join an organised trip. *Brewster*'s special "Snocoaches" run 75-minute trips over the glacier (early May to mid-Oct daily 9am–5pm; daily 10am–4pm; $17), but they're heavily subscribed, so aim to avoid the peak 11am–2.30pm rush. More dedicated types can sign up for the **Athabasca Glacier icewalks** (3-hr walks mid-June to early Sept daily at 12.30pm, $16; 5-hr walks Thurs & Sun 11.30am, $21), led by licensed guides. Call ☎852-4242 for details, or sign up on the spot at the front desk of the *Icefields Chalet* – be sure to bring warm clothes, boots and provisions.

## BEARS

Two types of **bears** roam the Rockies – black bears and grizzlies – and you don't want to meet either. They're not terribly common in these parts (sightings are all monitored and posted at park centres), but if you're camping or walking it's essential to know how to avoid dangerous encounters, and what to do if confronted or attacked. Popular misconceptions about bears abound – that they can't climb trees, for example (they can, and very quickly) – so it's worth picking up the parks service's pamphlet *You are in Bear Country*, which cuts through the confusion and lays out some occasionally eye-opening procedures. Be prepared, and if you don't want your scalp pulled off, follow the **cardinal rules**: don't approach bears, don't feed them, and don't run.

When **hiking**, walk in a group and make noise (many people carry a whistle), as bears are most threatened if surprised. Be alert when travelling into the wind, as your scent won't carry to warn bears of your approach, and stay away from dead animals and berry patches, which are important food sources. Watch for bear signs – tracks, diggings and droppings – and keep in the open as much as possible.

**Camp** away from rushing water, paths and animal trails, and keep the site scrupulously clean, leaving nothing hanging around in the open. Lock **food and rubbish** in a car, or hang it between two trees at least 4m above ground (many campgrounds have bear poles or steel food boxes). Take all rubbish away – don't bury it. Avoid smelly foods, fresh meat and fish, and don't cook or eat in or near the tent – lingering smells may invite unwanted nocturnal visits. Likewise, keep food off clothes and sleeping bags, and try to sleep in clean clothes at night. Bears have an acute sense of smell – avoid scented cosmetics – and may be attracted to women during menstruation, so dispose of tampons in an airtight container. They're also attracted by sex, so watch what you do in your tent if you don't want a rather drastic *coitus interruptus*.

Bears are unpredictable, and there's no guaranteed life-saving way of coping with an aggressive bear. **Calm behaviour**, however, has proved to be the most successful strategy. A bear moving towards you can be considered to have it in for you, other signs being whoofing noises, snapping jaws, and the head down and ears back. A bear raised on its hind legs and sniffing is trying to identify you: absurd as it sounds, stand still and start speaking to it in low tones. Ideally, you want to make a wide detour, leave the area or wait for the bear to do so – and always leave it an escape route. Whatever you do, **don't run** (a bear can outrun a racehorse), nor scream or make sudden movements (surprising the animal is the surest way to provoke an attack). Unfortunately bears often bluff, and will charge and veer at the last moment, so though it's a fairly tall order, resist the urge to turn and run – instead back away quietly. Don't throw anything and do everything as slowly and calmly as possible. If things look ominous, put your pack on the ground as a distraction. Forget about **trees**, as black bears can climb them better than you, though grizzlies may get bored after about 4m.

If you're **attacked** things are truly grim, and quack tactics are unlikely to help you. With grizzlies, playing dead – curling up in a ball, protecting face, neck and abdomen – may be effective. Fighting back will only increase the ferocity of a grizzly attack, but a good bop to the nose will sometimes send a black bear running: it's worth a try. As a last resort only, try to intimidate the bear with anything at hand. **Chemical repellents** are available, but of unproven efficacy.

The *Icefields Chalet* doesn't have accommodation, but you can get **food** at the cafeteria and restaurant. Two unserviced **campgrounds** are 2km and 3km south of the Icefield Centre respectively: *Columbia Icefield* is for tents only (mid-May to mid-Oct, or until the first snow; $8); *Wilcox Creek* takes tents and RVs (mid-June to mid-Sept; $8).

## Columbia Icefield to Jasper

If there's a change beyond the Columbia Icefield, it's a barely quantifiable lapse in the scenery's awe-inspiring intensity over the 108-kilometre stretch towards Jasper. As the road begins a gradual descent the peaks retreat slightly, taking on more alpine and less dramatic profiles in the process. Much of this scenic slackening, however, may be no more than your inability to take any more in, for the landscape, by any other standard, is still magnificent. Short trails are less frequent, but there are two key stop-offs at Sunwapta Falls and Athabasca Falls.

Seventeen kilometres beyond the icefield is the *Beauty Creek* **youth hostel** (May–Sept, closed Tues; groups only during winter; members $8). Nine kilometres further is the unserviced *Jonas Creek* **campground** (mid-May to first snowfall; $8).

**Sunwapta Falls** (175km) are fifteen minutes' walk through the woods from the road, and while not dramatic unless in spate, are interesting for the deep canyon they've cut through the surrounding valley. A short trail along the riverbank leads to more rapids and small falls downstream. If you want to put up nearby, the *Honeymoon Lake* **campground** is 4km further along the parkway (mid-June to mid-Oct; $8).

The last main stop before you're in striking distance of Jasper Townsite, **Athabasca Falls** are impressive enough, but the platforms and paths show the strain of handling thousands of feet, and it's hard to feel you're in the wilderness any longer. One kilometre away, however, is the excellent and relatively new *Athabasca Falls* **youth hostel** (year-round, closed Tues; members $8); the *Mount Kerkeslin* **campground**, 3km back down the road, spreads over a dulcet riverside site (mid-May to early Sept; $8). Branching off from the Icefields Parkway at Athabasca Falls is Highway 93A, a thirty-kilometre parallel stretch of quieter road where the chances of spotting wildlife are higher, but where the trees crowd in more and cut out most of the views.

# Jasper National Park

Always considered the second of the Rockies' big four parks, **Jasper National Park** covers an area greater than Banff, Yoho and Kootenay put together, and feels far wilder and less commercialised. Its backcountry is more extensive and less travelled, and **Jasper Townsite**, the only settlement, is far less of a resort than Banff. Most pursuits centre on Jasper and the **Maligne Lake** area about 50km southeast of the townsite. Other key zones are **Maligne Canyon**, a popular destination on the way to the eponymous lake, the **Icefields Parkway**, covered in the previous section, and finally – of course – the park's vast backcountry.

Jasper boasts 1000km of trails, but opportunities for day and half-day hikes are more limited and scattered than in other parks. Most shorter strolls start from the townsite, but are effectively only low-level walks to forest-circled lakes; the best of the more exciting **day hikes** (outlined on p.448) start from more remote points off the Maligne Lake road, Icefields Parkway (Hwy 93) and Yellowhead Highway (Hwy 16).

The park scores more highly with its system of **backpacking** trails and is rated as the leading area for backcountry hiking in North America. As in all the big national parks, if you're planning an overnight stay in the backcountry you're expected to pick up a free permit from the park information centre in Jasper Townsite or at the Columbia Icefield. Overnight hikes are beyond the scope of this book – again, get hold of a copy of *The Canadian Rockies Trail Guide* – but a few to look out for are Jonas Pass, Maligne Pass, the popular Skyline Trail, the Tonquin Valley area, and the long-distance North and South Boundary trails (the latter both over 160km ).

## Jasper Townsite

**JASPER**'s small-town feel comes as a relief after the razzmatazz of Banff. Named after a nineteenth-century trapper, its streets still have the windswept, open look of a frontier town, and though the mountains don't ring it with quite the same majesty as in Banff,

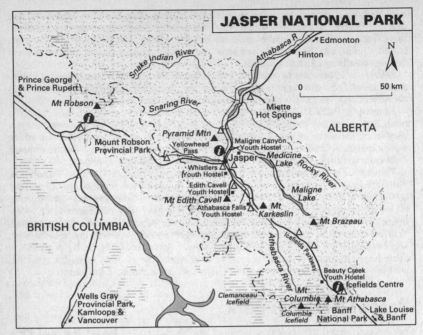

you'll probably feel the town better suits its wild surroundings. Apart from a cable-car, however, nothing here even pretends to be a tourist attraction; this is a place to sleep, eat and stock up. Though Jasper's tourist onslaught is no match for Banff's, you'll still be in competition with a horde of summer travellers, and accommodation, even if you're camping or hostelling, can be as tight as anywhere.

### Arrival, transport and information

Where Banff's strength is its convenience from Calgary, Jasper's is its ease of access from Edmonton, with plenty of transport options and approaches, as well as a wider range of onward destinations. *Greyhound* (☎852-3926) runs four **buses** daily from Edmonton along the Yellowhead Highway (Hwy 16), plus onward services to Kamloops/Vancouver (4 daily) and Prince George (2 daily). *Brewster Transportation* (☎852-3332) operates services to Banff (1 daily) and Calgary (1 daily), and also runs day-trips to Banff taking in sights on the Icefields Parkway ($49.50); note, however, that weather can play havoc with *Brewster*'s schedules between October and April. Both companies share the same **bus terminal**, located in the railway station building at 314 Connaught Drive.

*VIA* **trains** operate to Jasper from Edmonton and continue on to Vancouver (via Kamloops) or Prince Rupert (via Prince George). As this is now the only scheduled rail route through the Rockies, sightseers and transcontinental train buffs make summer places hard to come by, but at other times there's little need to book a seat. **Fares** are slightly more than those of buses on the equivalent routes, and journey times are considerably longer. Three trains operate on Tuesday, Friday and Sunday in each direction on each of three routes: Jasper–Edmonton, Jasper–Vancouver and Jasper–Prince Rupert. The **ticket office** is open on train days only (☎852-4102 or ☎1-800-561-8630).

To get around locally, the summer-only **Jasper Area Shuttle** makes runs from the offices of *Maligne Tours*, 626 Connaught Drive, out to the Jasper Tramway (via *Whistlers* campground and *Whistlers* hostel) and Maligne Lake (via the canyon, hostel and Skyline trailheads). The shuttle seems to have a local monopoly, however, and ticket prices are high for some trips. **Hiring a bike** is another excellent option, and you can rent wheels at the *Whistlers Youth Hostel*, at the *Sawridge Hotel*, 82 Connaught Drive, or downtown from *Freewheel Cycles* at the Husky Gas Station, 611 Patricia St. The last offers a one-way rental from Jasper to Banff with eighteen-speed touring bike and panniers to let you ride the Icefields Parkway. For a **taxi** call ☎852-3146 or ☎852-3600.

The main **Travel Alberta** office is at the western edge of town, 632 Connaught Drive (June–Sept daily 8am–8pm; May 9am–6pm; ☎852-4919). When this is shut, or for additional information, contact the **Chamber of Commerce** in the same building (Mon–Fri 9am–noon & 1–5pm; ☎852-3858). Neither office books accommodation, but ask for the *Approved Accommodation List*, which gives an extensive rundown of fifty or so addresses, and the *Summer Accommodation Rates* leaflet, a detailed list of campgrounds and more upmarket choices. The excellent **park information centre** is at 500 Connaught Avenue at the other end of town – 50m east of the station, set back from the road on the left (mid-June to early Sept daily 8am–8pm; rest of year 9am–5pm; ☎852-6176). It has all relevant information, **maps** for sale, and amiable staff willing and able to answer most questions.

## Accommodation

**Beds** in Jasper are never quite as expensive or elusive as in Banff, but accommodation is still almost unobtainable in July and August. If you arrive without a booking in this period, make for the Chamber of Commerce and ask if they'll call around some of the town's fifty or so private rooms, where you can expect to pay anything from $30 to $90

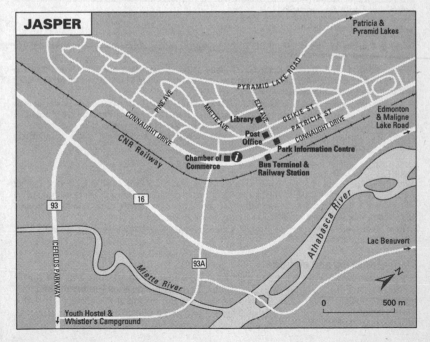

for a double, sometimes with breakfast thrown in. If you can afford more, or are desperate, the private *Jasper Central Reservations* (☎852-5656 or ☎852-5665) may come up with something – for a fee. Most **motels** are well spaced out along Connaught Drive on the eastern edge of town, and most charge well over $100 for double room, though prices and pressure on rooms drop sharply in off-season. There are **campgrounds** close to the townsite, but as with hotels they fill up promptly in summer.

### HOTELS, MOTELS AND CHALETS

**Alpine Village** (☎852-3285). Open May to mid-Oct and located 2.5km south of town on Hwy 93A; offers an assortment of cabins, from one-room to deluxe, for $50–130.

**Amethyst Motor Lodge**, 200 Connaught Drive (☎852-3394). Eastside motel with double rooms for $70–110; third bed $10.

**Astoria Hotel**, Patricia St (☎852-3351). Adequate central hotel, one block from the railway station and bus terminal, with doubles from $80–100.

**Athabasca Hotel**, 510 Patricia St (☎852-3386). Jasper's most central hotel, with typical bar downstairs, one block back from the station. Doubles $35–55.

**Bonhomme Bungalows**, 100 Bonhomme St (☎852-3209). Bungalows, chalet and lodge units in the townsite priced between $65–100.

**Chalet Patricia**, 310 Patricia St (☎852-5533). Three private rooms under one roof in the town centre from $45.

**Marmot Lodge**, 92 Connaught Drive (☎852-4471 or ☎1-800-661-6521). Cheapest of the east-end motels with doubles at $90.

**Sawridge Hotel Jasper**, 82 Connaught Drive (☎852-5111 or ☎1-800-661-6427). Large and plushly appointed hotel on the eastern edge of town with doubles for $110, $10 for an additional person.

**Tekarra Lodge** (☎852-3058). Cabins with wood-burning stoves open May–Oct, located 1km south of town on the Athabasca River off Hwy 93A; doubles $50–100.

**Whistlers Motor Hotel** (☎852-3361). Located directly opposite the station, this is the town's most central motel, with doubles at $89.

### HOSTELS

**Maligne Canyon Hostel** (IYHF; ☎852-3584). A group of cabins 11km east of town near Maligne Canyon (closed Wed).

**Mount Edith Cavell Hostel**, Edith Cavell Road 11km off Hwy 93A (IYHF). Cosier than the *Whistlers* hostel (see below); open mid-June to Oct every day except Thurs; opens up for any skier that makes it in during the winter.

**Whistlers Mountain Youth Hostel** (IYHF; ☎852-3215). Jasper's nearest youth hostel is 6km south of town on Whistlers Mountain Road, accessed from the Icefields Parkway (Hwy 93). The 4km uphill walk from Hwy 93 is a killer, but during the day in the summer take the *Jasper Area Shuttle* ($2). A modern place with a reputation for over-efficient management, it fills up quickly in summer, so arrive early or book. Members $12.

### CAMPGROUNDS

**Whistlers**, 3km south of town. Jasper's main campground, open early June to early Oct, with all facilities; from $12. If you're hitching in from Banff, watch out for the sign and ask to be dropped off – it saves the walk back from town; otherwise the *Jasper Area Shuttle* runs to the campground several times daily in summer ($2).

**Wapiti**, 1km south of *Whistlers* on Hwy 93. Caters more for RVs, but it's the only one in the park open year-round ($8).

## Eating, drinking and nightlife

Options for **eating out** are more restricted here than in Banff, but then the town's ambience isn't one that goes with fine dining. Perhaps the best spot in town – and definitely not posh – is *Mountain Foods Café*, opposite the station at 606 Connaught Drive (☎852-4050). The menu is cheap and varied (including plenty of vegetarian choices), the food is excellent, the staff friendly, and it's a good place to meet people; there's also a good wholefood shop at the back. Turn left after the station for the big and cheap *Smitty's Restaurant*, where you can drink coffee and write postcards all day; the non-smoking *Coco's Café* is also cheap and popular, though small. For something smarter, try the pink *Something Else* restaurant on Patricia Street – generally silly and over-priced, but okay for pizzas. *Dano's* nearby is good for ice cream and yoghurt.

Shopping for food, use *Nutters* at the west end of Patricia Street, a **supermarket** with a wholefood bias, or the bigger *IGA* on Connaught Drive.

Most **drinking** goes on in the *Athabasca Hotel* on Patricia Street, which also has a "nightclub" annex with dancing and **live music**. The *Astoria* on Connaught Drive attracts more of a thirtyish crowd, with music and darts in an unpretentious atmos-phere. For other evening entertainment there's the *Chaba Theatre*, a **cinema** directly opposite the station. Nightlife generally is low-key, however: with most of the camp-grounds and motels too far out of town for people to get in, the fun is generally of the make-your-own variety out at the hostel or campground.

## Jasper Tramway and the lakes

With little on offer in town, you'll need a bike or a car to get anything out of the area. The obvious trip is on the **Jasper Tramway**, 7km south of town on Whistlers Mountain Road, off the Icefields Parkway (mid-April to mid-Sept daily 8.30am–9.30pm; $8). The 2.5-kilometre cable-car ride takes seven minutes, and leaves you at an interpretive centre, expensive restaurant, and an excellent viewpoint (2285m) that allows you to take your bearings on much of the park. A steep trail ploughs up from there to The Whistlers summit (2470m), an hour's walk that requires warm clothes year-round and reveals even more stunning views. A tough ten-kilometre trail runs the route of the tramway from *Whistlers Mountain Youth Hostel*; if you walk up, you can ride back down for $3.50.

Two pairs of lakes are the town's other popular nearby targets. A winding road wends northwards to **Patricia** and **Pyramid lakes**, both about 5km from Jasper and racked full of rental facilities for riding, boating, canoeing, windsurfing and sailing. Food and drink is available locally, but the two lakefront lodges are usually heavily booked (the one at Pyramid Lake is open year-round). Most short trails around here are accessed from the approach road, the best taster being the **Patricia Lake Circle**, a 4.8km loop; you can also walk to these and several other smaller nearby lakes along an extensive network of trails from town. Slightly closer to town on the east side of the Athabasca River, **Lake Edith** and **Lake Annette** are both busy day-use areas – the water is surprisingly warm, and in summer you can lie out on sandy beaches or grassy areas. A clutch of picnic sites are the only development, and a wheelchair-accessible trail meanders around Lake Annette (2.4km).

Few other hikes from town are spectacular, but if you want a quick diversion the **Old Fort Point Loop** (6.5km round trip) is the most scenic. The **Valley of the Five Lakes** (4.6km) is an even better short walk, but the trail starts 10km south of town off the Icefields Parkway – worth it if you have a car or are willing to hitch, but not if you have to walk out on the road.

## Maligne Lake road

Bumper to bumper with cars, campers and tour buses in the summer, the **Maligne Lake road** runs east from Jasper for 48km, taking in a number of beautiful but busy and overdeveloped sights. If you have time to spare, and the transport, you could set aside day for the trip; if time is short, head elsewhere, or devote it to one of the trails above Maligne (pronounced Ma-*leen*) Lake itself. If you intend to do anything that requires hiring equipment (canoeing or fishing), reservations are essential in summer: contact *Maligne Tours*, 626 Connaught Drive, Jasper (☎852-3370).

Only 11km from Jasper, **Maligne Canyon** is the most heavily sold excursion from town, a place of whining children and aimless adults whose popularity is underlined by a rash of signs, an oversized car park, and a cheap and chintzy café/souvenir shop. Signs promise one of the Rockies' most spectacular gorges, which is an overpitched claim: the canyon is admirably deep (50m), but almost narrow enough to jump across – many people have tried and most have died in the attempt. In the end it's the geological rather than the scenic effect that's most interesting; the violent erosive forces responsible for the canyon are explained on the main trail loop, an easy twenty-minute amble that can be extended to 45 minutes, or even turned into a hike back to Jasper, though this would be a waste of a morning. In winter, licensed guides lead tours (more like crawls) through the frozen canyon – contact *Maligne Tours*.

Next stop is picture-perfect **Medicine Lake**, 32km from Jasper, which experiences intriguing fluctuations in level. The explanation is that underground springs feed the lake, while underwater sinks siphon the water off; when the springs freeze in winter the lake drains and sometimes disappears altogether, only to be replenished in the spring. Few people spend much time here, however, preferring to press on to Maligne Lake, which makes it a quietish spot to escape the headlong rush down the road.

Reached at the end of the road, 48km from Jasper, enormous **Maligne Lake** – 22km long and 92m deep – is a stunning place in its own right, surrounded by snow-covered mountains, most of which rear up over 3000m. The road peters out at a warden station,

---

### DAY HIKES IN JASPER

One of Jasper's best day hikes, the **Opal Hills Circuit** (8.2km round trip, 460m vertical ascent), starts from the picnic area to the left of the uppermost Maligne Lake car park, 48km east of Jasper. After a blood-pumping haul up the first steep slopes, the trail negotiates alpine meadows and offers sweeping views of the lake before reaching an elevation of 2160m; the trip takes about four hours, but you could easily spend all day loafing around the meadows. The **Bald Hills Trail** (5.2km one way, 480m vertical) starts with a monotonous plod along a fire road from the same car park, but ends with what Mary Schaffer, one of the area's first white explorers, described as "the finest view any of us had ever beheld in the Rockies"; allow four hours round trip, which goes as high as 2170m.

A superlative short, sharp walk – perhaps the park's best – starts from Miette Hot Springs, 58km northeast of Jasper. The **Sulphur Skyline** (4km one way, 700m vertical) offers exceptional views of knife-edged ridges, deep gorges, crags, and remote valleys. Be sure to take water with you, and allow two hours each way for the steep climb to 2070m. The trailhead is signed from the **Miette Hot Springs** complex, reached from Jasper by heading 41km east on Hwy 16 and then south 17km; the *Jasper Area Shuttle* makes the trip in summer ($5 one way). More soothing, and a good way to round off a day, are the springs themselves, the hottest in the Rockies – so hot they have to be cooled for swimming (mid-June to early Sept daily 8.30am–10.30pm; $2.50). You can hire suits, towels and lockers for an extra $2. Other trails from the springs make for the Fiddle River (4.3km one way, 275m vertical gain) and Mystery Lake (10.5km one way, 475m vertical).

To get to the trailhead for **Cavell Meadows** (3.8km one way, 370m vertical), drive 7.5km south on the Icefields Parkway, then 5km along Hwy 93A and finally 14km up Mount Edith Cavell Road; there's also a daily shuttle bus from Jasper and it takes bikes so you can ride back down. The scenery is mixed and magnificent – but the hike is popular, so don't expect solitude. As well as Cavell's alpine meadows, there are views of Angel Glacier and the dizzying north wall of Mount Edith Cavell (named after a British nurse who was executed for helping the Allies during World War I). Allow two hours round trip; the maximum elevation is 2135m.

three car parks and a restaurant flanked by a picnic area and the start of the short Lake Trail (3.2km). A small waterfront area is equipped with five berths for boats that run ninety-minute **cruises** on the lake – even if you normally disdain this sort of trip, it's worth doing for the incredible views (May 20–June 24 hourly 10am–4pm; June 25–Sept 4 10am–5pm; Sept 5–Sept 30 10am–3pm). The boats are small, however, and reservations are in order during peak times: again, contact *Maligne Tours*. Riding, fishing, rafting and guided hiking tours are also available. There's no accommodation or camping facilities here, although two backcountry **campgrounds** can be reached by canoe.

# Mount Robson Provincial Park

**Mount Robson** (3954m), the highest peak in the Canadian Rockies, is protected by an extensive provincial park bordering Jasper National Park to the west. The scenery here is the equal of anything anywhere else in the Rockies, and Mount Robson itself is one of the most staggering mountains you're likely to encounter; facilities are thin on the ground here, though, so it's essential to stock up on food and petrol before entering the park.

Both road and rail links from Jasper climb through **Yellowhead Pass** (1146m), one of the most important native and fur-trading routes across the Rockies for centuries. The pass, 20km west of Jasper Townsite, marks the boundary between Jasper and Mount Robson parks, Alberta and British Columbia, and Mountain and Pacific time zones (set your watch back one hour). This stretch of road is less dramatic than the Icefields Parkway, given over to more mixed woodland – birch interspersed with firs – and mountains that sit back from the road with less scenic effect. The railway meanders alongside the road most of the way, occasionally occupied by epic freight trains hundreds of wagons long – alien intrusions in a wilderness of rocks, river and forest. Just down from the pass, **Yellowhead Lake**, the park's first landmark, is mildly desecrated by a picnic spot but redeemed by its day-hiking potential. Look for moose around dawn and dusk at aptly named **Moose Lake**, another 20km further west.

---

The **telephone code** for the Mount Robson, Yoho, Glacier, Mount Revelstoke and Kootenay parks is ☎604.

---

## Mount Robson

If the first taste of the park is relatively tame, the first sight of **Mount Robson** is amongst the most breathtaking in the Rockies. The preceding ridges creep up in height and close back on the road, hiding the sudden view of one of North America's most massive peaks until the last moment. The British explorer WB Cheadle gave the first description of the mountain in 1863: "On every side the mighty heads of snowy hills crowded round, whilst, immediately behind us, a giant amongst giants, and immeasurably supreme, rose Robson's peak . . . We saw its upper portion dimmed by a necklace of light, feathery clouds, beyond which its pointed apex of ice, glittering in the morning sun, shot up far into the blue heaven above."

The overall impression is of immense size, thanks mainly to the colossal drop of Robson's sheer south face, and to the view from the road which frames the mountain as a single mass isolated from other peaks. The source of the name has never been agreed on, but local natives called it *Yuh-hai-has-hun* – the Mountain of the Spiral Road, an allusion to the clearly visible layers of rock that resemble a road winding to the

### HIKING IN MOUNT ROBSON PARK

Starting 2km from the park visitor centre, the **Berg Lake Trail** (22km each way, 795m ascent) is perhaps the most popular short backpacking trip in the Rockies, and the only trail that gets anywhere near Mount Robson. You can do the first third or so as a comfortable day walk, passing through forest to lovely glacier-fed Kinney Lake (6.7km). Trek the whole thing, however, and you traverse the stupendous **Valley of a Thousand Waterfalls** – the most notable being sixty-metre Emperor Falls (14.3km) – and eventually enjoy the phenomenal area around **Berg Lake** itself. Mount Robson rises an almost sheer 2400m from the lakeshore, its huge cliffs cradling two creaking rivers of ice, Mist Glacier and Berg Glacier – the latter, one of the Rockies' few "living" or advancing glaciers, is 1800m long by 800m wide and the source of the great icebergs that give the lake its name. Beyond the lake you can pursue the trail 2km further to Robson Pass (1652m) and another 1km to **Adolphus Lake** in Jasper National Park. The most popular campsites are between Berg Lake and the pass, but if you've got a Jasper backcountry permit you could press on to Adolphus where there's a less frequented site with more in the way of solitude. Once you're camped at Berg Lake, a popular day-trip is to **Toboggan Falls**, which starts from the campsite at the north end of the lake and climbs past a series of cascades and meadows to eventual views over the lake's entire hinterland.

Two other hikes start from Yellowhead Lake, at the other (eastern) end of the park. To get to the trailhead for **Yellowhead Mountain** (4.5km one way, 715m ascent), follow Hwy 16 9km down from the pass and then take a gravel road 1km on an isthmus across the lake. After a steep two-hour climb through forest, the trail levels out in open country at 1830m, offering sweeping views of the Yellowhead Pass area. The **Mount Fitzwilliam Trail** (13km, 945m ascent), which leaves Hwy 16 about 1km east of the Yellowhead Mountain Trail (but on the other side of the highway), is a more demanding walk, especially over its last half, but if you don't want to backpack to the endpoint – a truly spectacular basin of lakes and peaks – you could easily walk through the forest to the campground at **Rockingham Creek** (6km).

summit. Looking at the monolith, it's not surprising that this was one of the last major peaks in the Rockies to be climbed (1913) and is still considered a dangerous challenge.

## Practicalities

Trains don't stop anywhere in the park, but if you're travelling by bus you can ask to be let off at Yellowhead Pass or the **visitor centre** (May–Sept), located at the Mount Robson viewpoint near the western entrance to the park.

Most of the park's few other facilities are found near the visitor centre: a **café** and **garage** (May–Sept) and two commercial **campgrounds**, *Emperor Ridge* (June–Sept; ☎566-4714; $10), 300m north of Hwy 16 on Kinney Lake Road, and *Mount Robson Ranch* (June–Sept; ☎566-4370; $10), on Hargreaves Road south of the highway. The latter also has six **cabins** for rent ($70), though you'll be lucky to find space in high season. The only other beds in the park are the cabins belonging to *Mount Robson Adventure Holidays* (June–Sept; ☎566-4351), 16km east of the visitor centre (towards Jasper), though preference for these may go to people signed up for the company's canoeing and hiking day-trips. Outside the park, 5km west of the visitor centre on Hwy 16, are the jointly owned *Robson Meadows Campground* (May–Oct; ☎566-4821) and *Mount Robson Lodge*, the latter with eight cabins at $35 to $40 nightly.

If you're planning on **backpacking**, camping is only permitted at seven wilderness campsites in the park; to use these you have to register and pay an overnight fee at the visitor centre. *Mount Robson Adventure Holidays* **hires equipment** – complete outfits start at $22 a day.

# Yoho National Park

Wholly in British Columbia on the western side of the Continental Divide, **Yoho National Park**'s name derives from a Cree word meaning "awe" or "wonder" – a testament to its amazing mountains, lakes and waterfalls. The park's intimate scale has long ensured its popularity; climbers in particular rate the terrain highly. The Trans-Canada divides Yoho neatly in half, sharing the broad, glaciated valley bottom of the Kicking Horse River with the old Canadian Pacific Railway. The only centre of habitation in the park is **FIELD**: backed by an amphitheatre of sheer-dropped mountains and looking for all the world like a pioneer settlement, it amounts to no more than a few wooden houses; the nearest full-service towns are Lake Louise, 28km east, and Golden, 54km west.

The park's great appeal is the numerous well-maintained trails radiating from the central hubs of **Lake O'Hara**, the **Yoho Valley** and **Emerald Lake**. This makes these areas – rather than Field – the focal points of the park, and also busy places in summer. Side roads lead to Emerald Lake and the Yoho Valley, so if you choose you can drive in, do a hike, and then move on at night. Access to Lake O'Hara is by foot, or special bus for those with lodge or campground reservations. Note that the Trans-Canada also gives direct access to short but scenic trails, the most popular being Wapta Falls, Paget Lake and Sherbrooke Lake. These take only an hour or so, and are the best choice if you only want a quick taste of the park before moving on.

### Practicalities

Field is a flag stop for *Greyhound* **buses** (5 daily in each direction) – wave them down from the *Petro-Canada* just east of the turn-off from the highway to the village, though most stop anyway to drop parcels. Despite claims in some literature, there are no longer any passenger trains to Field.

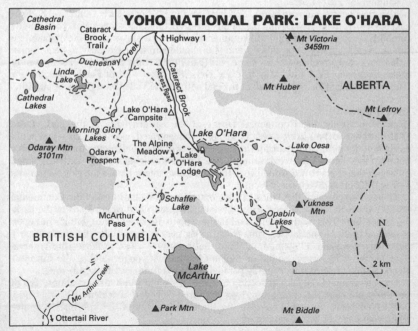

Yoho's **park information centre**, marked by a distinctive blue roof about 1km east of Field (daily summer 8am–9pm; winter 8.30am–4.30pm; ☎343-6433), has displays, lectures and slide shows (summer only), and advises on trail and climbing conditions. It also gives out a useful backcountry guide and sell a series of excellent 1:50,000 **maps** of the park. As ever, backcountry camping requires a permit, and if you intend to camp at Lake O'Hara it's essential to make **reservations** at the information centre (May–Sept).

Yoho's popularity and accessibility mean huge pressure on summer accommodation; outside late July and August, however, you should have few problems, and if you're really stuck, you can always make for one of the motels in Golden (see p.454). The only officially listed **rooms** near the main highway are at *Cathedral Mountain Chalets* (June–Sept; ☎343-6442), 4km east of Field, with double cabins for $40–60, though you may strike lucky with private rooms in Field itself (ask around or inquire at the information centre). The park's two **lodges** are likely to be too expensive for most budgets even if they have space. *Emerald Lake Lodge* (year-round; ☎343-632), built by the Canadian Pacific in 1902 as a spur to tourism, is a more tasteful version of *Chateau Lake Louise*, arranged as several wooden villas beside Emerald Lake; doubles are $100 to $210 off-season, twice that in high summer. *Lake O'Hara Lodge* (closed May & Oct–Dec; ☎343-6418) has a similar monopoly on the Lake O'Hara area, with doubles ranging between $105 and $208.

The best of the park's cheap lodging takes some effort to get to. The *Whiskey Jack* **youth hostel** (mid-June to mid-Sept; ☎283-5551), ideally placed about 500m south of Takakkaw Falls in the Yoho Valley, charges $8 for members. The *Alpine Club of Canada* operates a couple of cabins on Lake O'Hara ($15) and a hut 8.5km south of Takakkaw Falls by trail ($15), but reservations are required and you need to be a club member – write to Box 1026, Banff, Alberta TOL OCO, or call ☎403/762-4481. *Twin Falls Chalet* (☎269-1497), 8km south of Takakkaw Falls by trail, also offers a few beds in summer for $12 per person.

The most central **campground**, *Kicking Horse* (mid-May to early Oct; $11–15), 5km east of Field, is fully serviced and pleasingly forested, though it echoes with goods trains rumbling through day and night. In summer there's a separate overflow site at half price (no showers), but even this fills up and you should aim to arrive early in peak times. Other park campgrounds are *Hoodoo Creek* (late June to early Sept; $10), 23km west of Field; *Chancellor Peak* (mid-May to early Oct; $8), 28km west of Field; *Lake O'Hara* (June–Oct; $8) and *Takakkaw Falls* at the end of the Yoho Valley road (June–Sept; $10).

## Lake O'Hara

Backed up against the Continental Divide at the eastern edge of the park, **Lake O'Hara** is one of the Rockies' best bases for a concentrated hiking holiday – you could easily spend a fortnight exploring the huge variety of well-constructed trails that strike out from the central lodge and campground. The setting is matchless, the lake framed by two of the peaks that provide the setting for Lake Louise across the ridge – mounts Lefroy (3423m) and Victoria (3464m).

To get there, turn off the Trans-Canada onto Hwy 1A (3.2km west of the Continental Divide), cross the railway and turn right onto the gravel road which leads to the parking area (1km). This road continues all the way up to the lake (13km), but it's not open to general traffic. A special **bus** runs from the car park up to the lake (late June to early Sept daily at 8.30am, 11.30am & 4.30pm), but priority is given to those with reservations for the lodge, campground or Alpine Club huts. If you're walking, the **Cataract Brook Trail** (12.9km) runs roughly parallel to the road and is more picturesque.

Don't swan up to the lake expecting to spend the night without reservations. Ten of the thirty places at the campground are kept free daily and allocated on a first-come, first-served basis, but you'll have to get there early – ask at the information centre about your chances before setting off.

## Hikes from Lake O'Hara

For walking purposes the Lake O'Hara region divides into five basic zones, each of which fully deserves a day of exploration: Lake Oesa, the Opabin Plateau, Lake McArthur, the Odaray Plateau and the Duchesnay Basin.

If you have time to do only one day hike, the classic trail is probably the **Opabin Plateau Trail** (3.2km one way; 250m vertical) – despite its short length, you could spend hours wandering the plateau's tiny lakes and alpine meadows on the secondary trails which criss-cross the area. The path starts from the *Lake O'Hara Lodge* and finishes at Opabin Lake. Most people return to O'Hara via the East Circuit Trail, but to create a still more exhilarating hike – and a good day's outing – many walk the Yukness Ledge, a section of the Alpine Circuit (see below) which cuts up from the East Circuit just 400m after leaving Opabin Lake. This is a spectacular high-level route to **Lake Oesa**, from where it's just 3.2km down to Lake O'Hara. Oesa is one of many beautiful lakes in the region, and the **Lake Oesa Trail** (3.2km one way; 240m vertical) from Lake O'Hara is the single most walked of the paths in the O'Hara area.

The **Odaray Plateau Trail** (2.6km one way; 280m ascent) also rates high, but it too is popular. The longest and least-walked path is the **Linda Lake–Cathedral Basin** trip, a beautiful walk past several lakes to a great viewpoint at Cathedral Platform Prospect (7.4km one way; 305m ascent). The most challenging route is the **Alpine Circuit** (11.8km), a high-level route taking in Oesa, Opabin and Schaffer lakes. This is straightforward in fine weather, and when all the snow has melted; very fit and experienced walkers should have little trouble, though there's considerable exposure, and some scrambling is required. At other times it's best left to climbers, or left alone completely.

## Yoho Valley and Emerald Lake hikes

The most tramped path in the Yoho Valley is the **Twin Falls Trail** (8.5km one way; 290m elevation gain), starting from the Takakkaw Falls car park. This straightforward six-hour round trip has the reward of the Twin Falls cataract at the end – plus fine scenery and lesser waterfalls en route. If you're tenting – or very fit – you can combine Twin Falls with any of three other highly scenic walks: the Whaleback (4.5km one way; allow 1hr 30min), the Highline (24.4km back to Field, a two-day trek), and the Little Yoho Valley (5.3km one way; 2hr). The last is the principle goal of most backpackers in the Yoho Valley.

From Emerald Lake the best day-trip is the comparatively underused **Hamilton Lake Trail** (5.5km one way; 850m vertical; 2–3hr) which leaves from the parking area at the end of Emerald Lake Road. It's reasonably demanding and steep in places, and confined to forest for the first hour or so – thereafter it's magnificent. The more modest climb to **Emerald Basin** (4.3km one way; 300m vertical; 1–2hr) also gives relative peace and quiet, following the lakeshore (a popular stroll), climbing through forest, and ending in a small, rocky amphitheatre.

# The Yoho Valley and Emerald Lake

Less compact an area than Lake O'Hara, the **Yoho Valley** and nearby **Emerald Lake** together make up one of the Rockies' most important backpacking zones. Though popular and easily reached – access roads head north from the Trans-Canada up both the Emerald and Yoho valleys – the region is not, however, quite as beseiged as its counterpart to the south. The scenery is equally mesmerising, and if fewer of the trails are designed for day hikes, many of them interlock so that you can tailor walks to suit your schedule or fitness.

In centuries past, these side valleys are thought to have been used by the Cree to hide their women and children while the men crossed the mountains into Alberta to trade and hunt buffalo. The eradication of the buffalo herds, and the arrival of the railway in 1884, put paid to such ways.

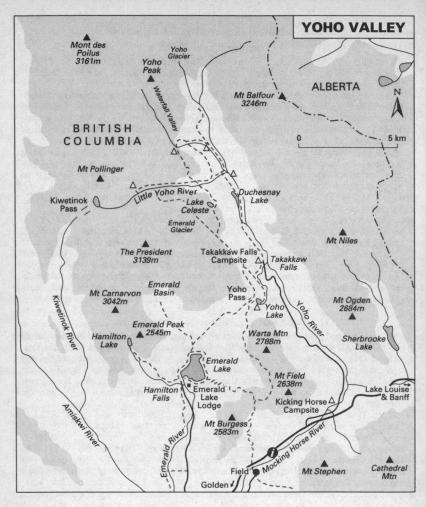

Most of the area's trails start from the end of the Yoho Valley Road at the **Takakkaw Falls** parking area (14km); the road leaves the Trans-Canada about 5km east of Field (signed from the *Kicking Horse* campground). The Emerald Lake road leaves the Trans-Canada about 2km west of Field and ends at the *Emerald Lake Lodge* (8km). The lodge has a **restaurant** where walking boots are certainly not in order, and a less hidebound **bar** for drinks and snacks.

## Golden

Fifty-four kilometres west of Field, **GOLDEN** is positioned roughly midway between Yoho and Glacier national parks and is the nearest town to either. If ever a name failed to conjure an accurate picture of a place it's Golden, which, despite a backdrop of mountains, amounts to little more than an ugly ribbon of motels and garages at the junction of Hwy 1 and Hwy 95. The town proper occupies a semi-scenic site down by the Columbia River, way below the highway strip, but unless you're using the municipal campground you'll have no call to do anything but look down on it from above.

A small **infocentre** sits at the strip's southern end disguised as a plastic and wood tepee (June–Sept). Two hundred metres north is the **bus terminal**, next to the *Golden Palace Restaurant*, a good spot for Chinese-Canadian **food** and, like several joints around, open 24 hours a day. The choice of **motels** is large, but all are much of a muchness, looking over the road or onto the backs of garages opposite; none has anything you could call a view of the mountains. The *Sportsman* (☎344-2915), however, is off the road, with doubles at $28 to $44 – the price range of most neighbouring establishments. You could also try the *Swiss Village* (☎344-2276) and the *Selkirk Inn* (☎344-6315).

**Campgrounds** have prettier settings, particularly the *KOA Campground* (☎344-6464; $12), 3km east of the strip on Hwy 1. The town's own site, the *Golden Municipal Campground* (☎344-5412; $5), is also well sited on the banks of the river on 10th Avenue, three blocks east of the main street.

# Glacier National Park

Strictly speaking, **Glacier National Park** is part of the Columbia Mountains rather than the Rockies, but on the ground little sets it apart from the magnificence of the other national parks, and all the park agencies include it on an equal footing with its larger neighbours. More so than elsewhere in the Rockies, however, the park is the domain of ice, rain and snow. As the name suggests, **glaciers** – 422 of them – form its dominant landscape, with fourteen percent of the region permanently blanketed with ice or snow. Scientists have identified 68 new glaciers forming on the sites of previously melted ice-sheets in the park – a highly uncommon phenomenon in the Rockies, and worldwide. The main ice-sheet, the still-growing **Illecillewaet Neve**, is easily seen from the Trans-Canada Highway or from the park visitor centre. Note, however, that Glacier falls within British Columbia's interior wet-belt: weather here is so atrocious that locals like to say that it rains or snows four days out of every three, and in truth, you can expect a soaking three days out of five.

The peaks of the Columbia range are every bit as imposing as those of the Rockies – Glacier's highest point, **Mount Dawson**, is 3390m tall – and historically they've presented as much of a barrier as their neighbours. Natives and then railwaymen shunned the icefields and the rugged interior for centuries until the discovery of **Rogers Pass** (1321m) in 1881 by Major AB Rogers, the chief engineer of the Canadian Pacific. After incredible hardships, navvies had driven the railway over the pass by 1885, paving the way for trains which, until 1916, were instrumental in opening up the region both to settlers and tourists. Despite the railway's best efforts, however, the pounding of repeated avalanches eventually forced the company to bore a tunnel under the pass, and the flow of visitors to the area fell to almost nothing.

In the 1950s the pass was chosen as the route for the Trans-Canada Highway, whose completion in 1962 once again made the area accessible. This time huge snowsheds were built, backed up by the world's largest **avalanche-control system**. Experts monitor the slopes year-round at critical points close to the highway, and at dangerous times they call in the army who blast howitzers into the mountains to dislodge potential slips.

Glacier is easy enough to get to, but it doesn't tie in well with a circuit of the other parks; many people end up traversing it at some point simply because the main route west passes this way, but even then comparatively few stop, preferring to admire the scenery from the road. The visitor centre is a flag stop for *Greyhound* **buses**, which zip through here seven times a day in each direction. Entering Glacier you pass from Mountain to Pacific time – remember to set your watch back an hour.

---

HIKING IN GLACIER

Glacier primarily has a reputation as a playground for serious climbers, but day-hikers and backpackers still have plenty of options. Some of the park's 21 **trails** (140km of walking in all) push close to glaciers for casual views of the ice – though only two spots are now safe at the toe of the Illecillewaet – and the backcountry here is noticeably less busy than in the Big Four parks to the east.

The easiest of the short strolls off the road are the **Abandoned Rails Trail** (30min), which starts from the visitor centre, and the **Meeting of the Water Trail** (30min) from the Illecillewaet campground, the hub of Glacier's trail network. Six manageable day hikes radiate from the campground, all giving superb views onto the park's main glaciers, particularly the **Avalanche Crest** and **Abbott's Ridge** trails. Other hikes include **Flat Creek** (9km) and **Bostock Creek** (9km), a pair of paths on the park's western edge heading north and south from the same point on the Trans-Canada. The single best long-haul trail,

Amongst the backpacking routes, the longest is the **Beaver River Trail** (30km-plus), which peels off from the highway at the Mount Shaughnessy picnic area on the park's eastern edge (this is also a favourite mountain bike route). The single best long-haul trail, however, is the **Copperstain Creek Trail** (16km), which leaves the Beaver River path after 3km, and climbs to meadows and bleak alpine tundra from where camping and onward walking options are almost endless.

## Practicalities

Information on the park is available at the **visitor centre** (mid-June to early Oct daily 9am–9pm; winter daily 9am–5pm), 1km west of Rogers Pass, which houses a variety of high-tech audio-visual aids, including a fun video on avalanche control called *Snow Wars*. In summer, staff run **guided walks** featuring flowers, wildlife and glaciers, some of them fairly strenuous and lasting up to five hours. If you're heading for the backcountry, pick up *Footloose in the Columbias*, a general hiker's guide to Glacier and Revelstoke national parks; you can also buy good walking maps of the park. Alongside the visitor centre is a **garage** and a **shop**, the only services on the Trans-Canada between Golden and Revelstoke.

Accommodation, for all intents and purposes, is only available in Golden (see p.454). The sole in-park **hotel** is the excellent *Best Western Glacier Park Lodge* (☎837-2126), located east of the visitor centre, but it's likely to be full in season; doubles start at $85 (less in off-season), extra beds $5.

The park **campgrounds** are *Illecillewaet* (mid-June to early Oct; $8), 3.4km west of the visitor centre just off the Trans-Canada, and *Loop Brook*, 2km further west (mid-June to early Sept; $8), which provides the luxuries of wood, water and flush toilets only. If you don't manage to get into these, or want more facilities, there are three commercial campgrounds west of the park on the Trans-Canada towards Revelstoke. Free wilderness camping is allowed anywhere if you register with the visitor centre and pitch more than 3km from the road.

# Mount Revelstoke National Park

Smallest of the national parks in this region, **Mount Revelstoke National Park** is an arbitrary creation, put together at the request of local people in 1914. In truth, the lines on the map mean little, for the superlative scenery in the 16km of no-man's-land between Glacier and Revelstoke is largely the same as that within the parks. The mountains here are especially steep, their slopes often scythed clear of trees by avalanches. As ever, you can see plenty of what matters from the Trans-Canada as it peeks out of countless tunnels – forests and snow-capped peaks aplenty, and far below, the railway and the Illecillewaet River as it crashes through a twisting, steep-sided gorge.

**REVELSTOKE**, the only community within striking range of the park, sits just outside the western boundary. Like many mountain towns, it's divided between a motel-and-garage strip along the Trans-Canada and a dispersed, frontier-type collection of houses to the rear. But while the strip is as much of an affront to the mountains as any, the river and rugged scenery roundabout are redeeming features; the downtown area also has a nice feel, having been spruced up as a placatory measure following the disaster at the dam site (see below), though if you're without transport it's a good twenty-minute walk from the strip.

The main access to the park interior is busy **Summit Road** (generally open June–Oct), which strikes north from the Trans-Canada at the town of Revelstoke and winds 26km through forest and alpine meadows to the top of Mount Revelstoke (1938m). You can also walk this stretch on the **Summit Trail** (10km one way; 4hr) from the car park at the base of Summit Road – preferably downhill. Most of the park's few long trails start from the parking lot at the summit, the most popular being the **Miller Lake Trail** (6km one way); the backpacking fraternity head to **Eagle Lake**, off Summit Road. Note that the *Footloose in the Columbias* booklet, available from Glacier's Rogers Pass visitor centre, has trail information for Revelstoke.

The most popular short walk in the park is the award-winning **Giant Cedars Trail**, a one-kilometre jaunt off the road on the park's eastern edge that negotiates a tract of ancient cedar forest. **Meadows in the Skies Trail** is a quick loop through alpine meadows at the top of Summit Road.

## Practicalities

*Greyhound* **buses** stop at the town of Revelstoke on their way between Kamloops and Calgary (7 daily in each direction); the terminal is at the west end of the strip, immediately after the big blue river bridge (☎837-5874 for information). The **infocentre** is 200m beyond on the left (July & Aug daily 8am–8pm, May & June daily 10am–6pm). For park information use the infocentre, or call in on the **Park Administration Office** in the post office building at 313 3rd St West (Mon–Fri 9am–5pm; ☎837-5155); the Rogers Pass visitor centre also has material on Revelstoke.

A far more amenable place to stay than Golden, the town of Revelstoke has plenty of **accommodation** – fifteen motels and half a dozen campgrounds – but if you're stopping over you need go no further than the *Frontier Motel* (☎837-5119), located immediately behind the infocentre and slap bang on the Trans-Canada. Doubles are only $35 and, in addition to a 24-hour shop and garage alongside, there's the adjoining *Frontier* **restaurant** – superior steak-and-salad fare, reasonable prices, friendly service and a genuine cowpoke atmosphere. In town, the *One-Twelve Restaurant* at 112 Victoria Road is a local favourite, featuring pub, dance floor and restaurant.

The best of the **campgrounds** is *KOA* (April–Oct; ☎837-2085; $12), 5km east of town on the Trans-Canada, though it's hardly as convenient as the *Lamplighter Campground* (April–Oct; ☎837-3385; $10), situated on the main road at the west side the bridge. Camping **in the park** is free, but isn't allowed in the Miller Lake area or anywhere within 2km of the Trans-Canada and Summit Road, and registration at the Park Administration Office is obligatory.

## Revelstoke Dam

It might sound dull, but the heavily promoted **Revelstoke Dam** – Canada's largest – makes an interesting outing (mid-March to late Oct daily 9am–5pm except mid-June to early Sept 8am–8pm; free). Located 4km north of the town on Hwy 23 and signed from the infocentre, the 175-metre-tall barrier holds back the waters of the Columbia River, one of North America's great rivers and here around 500km from its source. The **visitor centre** is a sleek, space-age affair, and offers a well-put-together self-guided tour which, however, omits to tell you that insufficient mapping during the construction caused a landslide into the dam that threatened to swamp Revelstoke: millions had to be spent or it would have been curtains for the town. The whole tour takes up to two hours, but the boring bits are easily skipped in favour of a lift to the top for a great view of the dam and surrounding valley.

# Kootenay National Park and Radium Hot Springs

**Kootenay National Park**, lying across the Continental Divide from Banff in British Columbia, is the least known of the four contiguous parks of the Rockies, and the one most easily missed out – many people prefer to follow the Trans-Canada through Yoho rather than commit themselves to the less enthralling westward journey on Hwy 3 imposed by Kootenay. The park's scenery, however, is on a par with its neighbours, and if you're not determined to head west you could follow a neat loop starting from Banff through Kootenay on Hwy 93 to Radium Hot Springs (the only town in this area), north on Hwy 95, and back on the Trans-Canada through Yoho to Lake Louise and Banff – a round trip you could drive in a day with a few short walks and a dip in **Radium**'s hot springs to boot.

Kootenay lends itself to admiration from a car, bus or bike – it is, after all, little more than a 100-kilometre ribbon of land on either side of Hwy 93 (here known as the **Banff–Windermere Parkway**). In many ways the mountains seem closer at hand and more spectacular than on the Icefields Parkway, partly because the road climbs higher over the Continental Divide, and partly because the park's origins guaranteed it an intimate link with the highway. In 1905 Randolph Bruce, a local businessman, persuaded the Canadian government and Canadian Pacific to push a road from Banff through the Rockies to connect the Prairies with western seaports. Previously the area had been the reserve of the Kootenai Indians and had been explored by David Thompson, but otherwise it was an all but inviolate mountain fastness. The project began in 1911 and produced 22km of road before the money ran out. To wangle more cash British Columbia was forced to cede 8km of land on each side of the highway to the government as a national park.

## Practicalities

Unless you involve yourself in superhuman backpacking exploits, the only access to Kootenay is on Hwy 93, a good road that leaves the Trans-Canada at Castle Junction (in Banff National Park), traverses Kootenay from north to south, and joins Hwy 95 at Radium Hot Springs at the park's southern entrance. Radium is a stop for the two daily *Greyhound* **buses** east and west on the southern British Columbia route between Cranbrook, Banff and Calgary; both buses also make flag stops at Vermillion Crossing, a summer-only huddle of shop, cabins and petrol station midway through the park.

If you're coming from the east you'll hit the **Marble Canyon Information Centre** about 15km from Castle Junction (mid-June to early Sept daily 8.30am–4.30pm, open till 8pm Fri–Mon); coming the other way, the **West Gate Information Centre**, park warden station and ticket booth are at the southern/western end of the highway close to Radium (late June to mid Sept daily 8am–8pm; late May–late June Sat & Sun only). The latter can sell you a topographical map of the park ($8.50), but both distribute the free *Backcountry Guide to Kootenay National Park*, which is all you need if you're not planning anything too ambitious.

Park staff are also on hand at the park's only two roadside serviced **campgrounds**: *McLeod Meadows*, 25km north of Radium, and *Marble Canyon*, near the Marble Canyon Information Centre (both mid-May to early Sept; $10). If you want more comforts and easier access use the big *Redstreak* campground, 3km north of Radium Hot Springs (May–Sept; ☎347-9567; $10–18); note that the turn-off for the site is a minor road signed off Hwy 95 from the village, by the RCMP station, and not off the main Hwy 93 which branches north 200m to the west for the hot springs and the park proper. A dozen or more **backcountry sites** with pit toilets and firewood are scattered around the park within easy backpacking range of the highway, but you have to pick up a free **permit** from the infocentres to overnight at any of these.

There is no indoor **accommodation** in Kootenay National Park – the nearest rooms are in Radium Hot Springs (see p.460).

## Vermillion Pass and Marble Canyon

**Vermillion Pass** (1637m) is the northern entrance to the park, the Great Divide's watershed and the border between Alberta and British Columbia, though little fanfare marks the transition – only the barren legacy of a huge forest fire which ravaged the area in 1968, leaving a blanket of stark, blackened trunks as far as the eye can see. It's worth taking the short **Fireweed Trail** (1km) through the apparent desolation from the pass car park to see how nature deals with such disasters, indeed how it seems to invite lightning fires to promote phoenix-like regeneration. Young plants and shrubs are pushing up into the clearings, attracting birds and small mammals to new food sources, and a broad carpet of lodgepole pines have taken root amongst the blasted remnants of the earlier forest – these are the first trees to colonise any such site, as they specifically require the heat of a fire to release their seeds.

**Marble Canyon**, 8km south of Vermillion Pass, provides a doddle of a trail that's probably the most heavily trafficked of Kootenay's shorter hikes. The one-kilometre track crosses a series of log bridges over Tokumm Creek, which has carved through a fault in the local limestone to produce a 37-metre-deep gorge. In cold weather this is a fantastic medley of ice and snow, but in summer the climax is the viewpoint from the top of the path onto a thundering waterfall as the creek pounds its way through the narrowest section of the gorge. The **Tokumm Creek Trail** (11km one way; 570m vertical gain) pushes on up to the head of the valley at Kaufmann Lake.

## The Paint Pots

You could extend the Marble Canyon walk by picking up the Paint Pots Trail south, which puts another 2.7km onto your walk, or drive 2km south and stroll 1km to reach the same destination. Either way you come to the **Paint Pots**, one of the Rockies' more magical spots: red, orange and mustard-coloured pools prefaced by damp, moss-clung forest and views across the whitewater of the Vermillion River to the snow-capped mountains beyond. Natives came from all over North America to these vivid ponds to collect **ochre**, which they added to animal fat or fish oil to use in rock or ceremonial body painting. Ochre has always had spiritual significance for Native Americans, who claim these oxide-stained pools and their yellow-edged surroundings were inhabited by animal and thunder spirits. Standing in the quiet, rather gloomy glade, particularly on overcast days, it's easy to see why – not that the atmosphere or sanctity of the place stopped European speculators in the 1920s from mining the ochre to ship to paint manufacturers in Calgary. Five longer trails branch onwards from the Paint Pots into the Ochre Creek Valley above, each served by campsites, the nearest of which is 4.4km from the pools at the junction of Ochre and Tumbling creeks.

## Vermillion Crossing and Kootenay Crossing

**Vermillion Crossing**, 20km south of the Paint Pots Trail, is gone in a flash, but it's the only place, in the summer at least, to pick up petrol and food in the park. It's also the trailhead for one of the Rockies' tougher walks, up over Honeymoon Pass and Redearth Pass to Egypt Lake and the Trans-Canada Highway in Banff National Park.

Just south of the crossing are equally demanding trails which provide the only west-side access into the wilderness of **Mount Assiniboine Provincial Park**. Sandwiched between Kootenay and Banff, the wilderness park was created, one feels, simply to do some sort of honour to Mount Assiniboine (3618m), a sabre-tooth-shaped mountain with one of the most dramatic profiles imaginable (the "Matterhorn of the Rockies"). The **Simpson Road Trail** (8.2km) leads to the park boundary, and then divides into two paths (20km & 32km) which lead to Lake Magog in the heart of Assiniboine.

**Kootenay Crossing** is no more than a ceremonial spot – it was where the ribbon was cut to open Hwy 93 in 1923 – though a clutch of short trails fan out from the park warden station here, and the nearby *Dolly Varden* campground is the only spot specifically set aside for winter camping in the park. **Wardle Creek** nearby is one of the best places to unpack a picnic if you're determined to stick to the road – many RV owners are, and you'll bump into more camera-wielding fanatics at the **Kootenay Valley Viewpoint**, arguably one of the broadest views and biggest lay-bys on the highway.

For its final rundown out of the park, the highway doglegs west through the **Sinclair Pass**, a red-cliffed gorge filled with the falling waters of Sinclair Creek and the start of the **Kindersley Pass Trail**, possibly the most scenic day hike in the park, and certainly its most strenuous. The 9.8-kilometre trail climbs 1055m to Kindersley Summit (2395m), which presents one of the Rockies' most sublime views: an endless succession of peaks fading to the horizon away to the northeast. Rather than drop back through the open tundra the way you've come, many people push on another 2km and contour around the head of the Sinclair Creek valley before dropping off the ridge (the Kindersley-Sinclair Coll) to follow the **Sinclair Creek Trail** (6.4km) back to meet the highway 1km from the starting point.

## Radium Hot Springs

**RADIUM HOT SPRINGS** is far less attractive than its evocative name suggests, but as the main service centre for Kootenay National Park, its tacky cluster of motels and garages are likely to claim some of your time and probably your money. The town spreads across the flats of the Columbia Valley, just 3km from the park's southern/western entrance at the junction of Hwy 93 and Hwy 95.

The **hot springs** themselves are off the Banff–Windermere Parkway (Hwy 93) 2km north of town, and are administered by the park authorities (May–Sept daily 8.30am–11pm; Oct–April Mon–Fri noon–9pm, Sat & Sun 9.30am–9pm; $2). Indians used the springs for centuries, and commercial white development started as early as 1890 when Roland Stuart bought the area for $160. Traces of supposedly therapeutic radium found in the water turned Stuart's investment into a recreational goldmine. When the government appropriated the springs for inclusion in the national park it paid him $40,000 – a small fortune, but considerably less than what they were worth, which at the time was estimated to be $500,000. The pools today are outdoors, but are serviced by a large, modern centre. In summer, 4000 people a day take the plunge into the odourless 45°C waters – enough to discourage any idea of a quiet swim, though in late evening or off-season (when the hot pool steams invitingly) you can escape the bedlam and pretend more easily that the water is having some sort of soothing effect. The radium traces sound a bit worrying, but 4000 Canadians can't be all wrong.

If you have the choice, aim to stay in one of the new **motels** creeping up the Sinclair Valley around the hot springs area away from downtown – they're more expensive, but far more attractively sited than the thirty-odd motels in town. Try the *Radium Hot Springs Lodge* (☎347-9622) on the bluff above the springs, with doubles from $50; *Addison's Bungalows* (April–Oct; ☎347-9545), a mix of motel and cabins next door, with doubles from $50; or the adjacent *Mount Farnham Bungalows* (☎347-9515), with doubles from $40. Almost alongside the park entrance are the *Alpen Motel* (☎347-9823), with doubles at $74, and the neighbouring *Kootenay* (☎347-9490) and *Crescent*

(☎347-9570) motels, both with doubles at $45 and $40–60 respectively. Most of the motels along the main drag in town are small places with doubles for around $45 – the cheapest are the *Tuk-In* (☎347-9464), with rooms from $36, and the *Sunset* (☎347-9863), with doubles from $28.

## travel details

### Trains

**From Edmonton** to Vancouver (3 weekly; 24hr); Prince Rupert via Jasper and Prince George (3 weekly; 30hr); Winnipeg via Saskatoon (3 weekly; 24hr).

**From Jasper** to Edmonton (3 weekly; 5hr 30min); Vancouver (daily Tues–Sun June–Oct; 17hr); Prince Rupert via Prince George (3 weekly; 20hr).

**From Calgary** to Vancouver with private *Rocky Mountain Railtours* (2 weekly July–Sept; $465 one way).

### Buses

**From Edmonton** to Calgary (14 daily; 3hr 30min); Vancouver (6 daily; 14hr); Jasper (6 daily; 4hr 30min); Grande Prairie (4 daily; 6hr); Peace River (3 daily; 6hr 30min); Hay River via Peace River (1 daily; 14hr 30min); Dawson Creek (2 daily; 7hr 15min); Fort St John (2 daily; 9hr 15min); Prince George (2 daily; 17hr); Whitehorse (1 daily mid-May to mid Oct; 3 weekly rest of the year; 28hr); Drumheller (1 daily; 4hr 45min); Saskatoon (4 daily; 5hr); Winnipeg (2 daily; 21 hr).

**From Calgary** to Edmonton (14 daily; 3hr 30min); Banff (5 daily; 1hr 40min); Lake Louise (4 daily; 2hr 35min); Vancouver via Kamloops (7 daily; 13hr); Vancouver via Vernon, Kelowna and Penticton (3 daily; 16hr); Vancouver via Fort Macleod, Cranbrook, Nelson, Osoyoos and Hope (2 daily; 24hr); Winnipeg via Lethbridge, Medicine Hat and Regina (2 daily; 24hr); Creston via Banff, Radium Hot Springs and Cranbrook (1 daily; 7hr 30min); Drumheller (2 daily; 1hr 50min); Saskatoon (2 daily; 9hr); Coutts (US; connections for Las Vegas and Los Angeles) via Fort Macleod and Lethbridge (1 daily; 4hr 30min).

### Flights

**From Edmonton** to Calgary (every 30min; 50min); Vancouver (every 30min; 1hr 25min); Toronto (10 daily; 4hr 10min); Montréal (9 daily; 5hr).

**From Calgary** to Edmonton (every 30min; 50min); Vancouver (every 30min; 1hr 20min); Toronto (14 daily; 4hr); Montréal (12 daily; 5hr).

# CHAPTER SEVEN

# SOUTHERN BRITISH COLUMBIA

T he often pristine scenery of **Southern British Columbia** more than lives up to most people's image of the wilds of Canada. What may come as a surprise, however, is the sheer natural diversity of the region: between the expected extremes of the mountainous, forested interior and the fjord-cut mountains of the coast lies a jigsaw of landscapes, including genteel farmland, ranching country, immense lakes and even a patch of real desert. British Columbia contains both Canada's wettest and its driest climates, and more species of flora and fauna than the rest of the country put together. The range of recreational possibilities is equally impressive: the country's biggest ski area, its warmest lakes and some of its best beaches are all here, not to mention hot springs, hiking, sailing and canoeing galore, and some of the best salmon fishing in the world.

Culturally and logistically, southern British Columbia stands apart from the northern half of the province, containing most of the roads, towns and accessible sights. Ninety-five percent of the population lives in the south, mainly in **Vancouver**, Canada's third largest city. A cosmopolitan, sophisticated and famously hedonistic place, Vancouver gives the lie to the stereotype of the Canadian West as an introverted, cultural wasteland, and its combination of glittering skyline and generous open spaces stands as a model of urban planning. The province's modest capital is **Victoria**, a vastly smaller city on the southern tip of Vancouver Island, which affects a somewhat English ambience to lure more tourists than it probably deserves.

If you're making a circuit of the **interior**, or even just cutting across it as part of a transcontinental route, you'll want to set aside time for the mountain-hemmed lakes and tidy mining towns of the **Kootenays** or – if you're into wine tasting or rowdy lakeside resorts – the **Okanagan**. For big wilderness and waterfalls, **Wells Gray Provincial Park** stands out, though exhilarating hikes and camping are possible in dozens of other parks. Variety is also the byword for **Vancouver Island**, by far the largest of an archipelago of islets off BC's coast, where in a short time you can move from wild seascapes and rainforest to jagged, glaciated peaks. Vancouver Island can also be used as a springboard for the ferry up the famed **Inside Passage** to Prince Rupert and beyond; inland, roads and rail lines converge to follow a single route north through the endless expanse of the **Cariboo** region of the interior plateau.

## Some history

Long before the coming of Europeans, British Columbia's coastal region supported five key **native peoples** – the Kwakiutl, Bella Coola, Nuu-chah-nulth, Haida and Tlingit – all of whom lived largely off the sea and developed a culture in many ways more sophisticated than that of the more nomadic and hunting-orientated tribes of the interior (see box on p.526). Although it's rare these days to come across native faces in interior southern BC, villages of living culture still exist on parts of Vancouver Island, and you can find examples of their totemic art in the excellent museum displays of Victoria and Vancouver.

The British explorer **Francis Drake** probably made the first sighting of the mainland by a European during his round-the-world voyage of 1579. Spanish explorers sailing from California and Russians from Alaska explored the coast almost two centuries later, though it was another Briton, **Captain Cook**, who made the first recorded landing in 1778. Following the **Nuu-chah-nulth Convention** of 1790 – a neat piece of colonial bluster which wrested from the Spanish all rights on the mainland as far as Alaska for the British – **Captain George Vancouver** first mapped the area in 1792–94.

Exploration of the interior came about in course of the search for an easier way to export furs westwards to the Pacific, instead of the arduous haul eastwards across the continent. **Alexander Mackenzie** of the North West Company made the first crossing of North America north of Mexico in 1793, followed by two further adventurers, **Simon Fraser** and **David Thompson**, whose names also resonate as sobriquets for rivers, shops, motels and streets across the region. For the first half of the nineteenth century most of western Canada was ruled as a virtual fiefdom by the **Hudson's Bay Company**, a monopoly which antagonised the Americans, which in turn persuaded Britain to formalise its claims to the region to forestall American expansion. The 49th Parallel was agreed as the national boundary, though Vancouver Island, which lies partly south of the line, remained wholly British and was officially designated a crown colony in 1849. The "Bay" still reigned in all but name, however, and took no particular interest in promoting immigration; as late as 1855 the island's white population was only 774, and the mainland remained virtually unknown except to trappers and the odd prospector.

The discovery of **gold** on the Fraser River in 1858, and in the Cariboo region three years later, changed everything, attracting some 25,000 people to the goldfields and creating a forward base on the mainland that was to become Vancouver. It also led to the building of the **Cariboo Road** (the present Highway 97) and the **Dewdney Trail** (Highway 3), which opened up the interior and helped attract the so-called **Overlanders** – a huge straggle of pioneers that tramped from Ontario and Québec in the summer of 1862. Britain declared mainland British Columbia a crown colony in 1858 to impose imperial authority on the region and, more importantly, to lay firm claim to the huge mineral wealth which was rightly believed to lie within it. When Canada's eastern colonies formed the Dominion in 1867, though, British Columbia dithered over joining until it received the promise of a railway to link it to the east in 1871 – though the Canadian Pacific didn't actually arrive for another fifteen years.

While British Columbia no longer dithers, it still tends to look to itself – and increasingly to the new economic markets of the Pacific Rim – rather than to the rest of Canada. The francophone concerns of the east are virtually nonexistent here – there is, for example, just one French school in the entire province. For the most part British Columbians are well off, both financially and in terms of quality of life, and demographically the province is one of Canada's youngest. If there are flies in the ointment, they're the **environmental pressures** thrown up by an economy which relies on primary resources for its dynamism: British Columbia supplies twenty-five percent of North America's commercial timber, and exports significant amounts of hydro-electric power, fish, zinc, silver, oil, coal and gypsum. Few of these can be exploited without exacting a toll on the province's natural beauty; British Columbians may be well-off, but they're increasingly aware of the environmental cost of their prosperity.

---

**TOLL-FREE INFORMATION NUMBER**

Tourism British Columbia ☎1-800-663-6000.

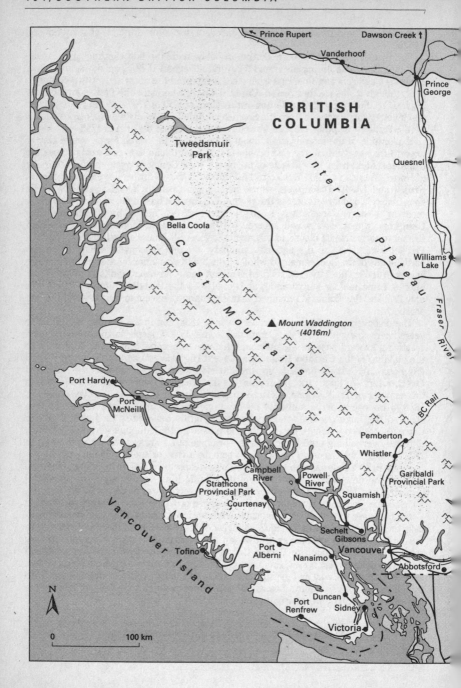

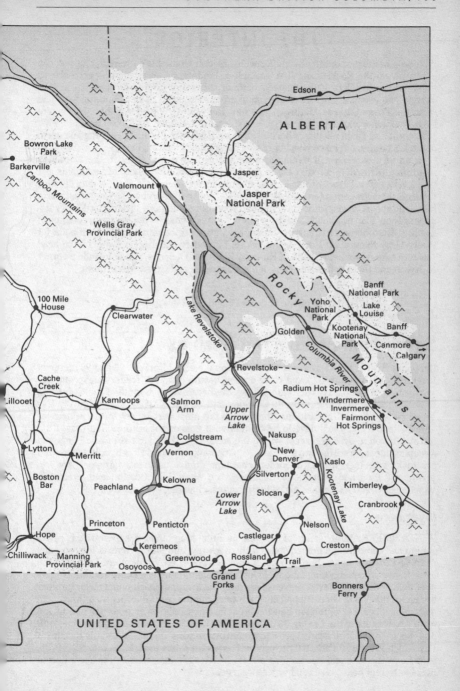

# THE INTERIOR

It says something about the magnificence of British Columbia's **interior** that you can enter it from the Rockies and find a clutch of landscapes every bit as spectacular as those you've just left. Unfortunately, both of the major routes through the region confine you to some of its least interesting areas. The most obvious and quickest line west, the **Trans-Canada Highway**, isn't one you want to consider at all unless you're keen to reach Vancouver in a hurry – little after Revelstoke really compares to what you might find further south or north. Nor does **Highway 3**, rumbling along just north of the US border, offer a convincing reason for sticking to it religiously.

In an ideal world you'd pursue a meandering course that takes in the **Kootenay** region in the province's southeastern corner – an idyllic assortment of mountains and lakes, and several towns that are fun to stay in for their own sake – and on west through the **Okanagan**, an almost Californian enclave of orchards, vineyards, warm lakes and resort towns, whose beaches and scorching summers suck in hordes of vacationers from all over Canada and the western United States. From here you could push north to **Kamloops**, the transport hub of the entire region and a jumping-off point for **Wells Gray Provincial Park** or the Yukon. The other major option would be to head south to take in the better parts of Highway 3 west of Osoyoos, which include a corner of **desert** and the spectacular ridges of the **Cascades** and **Coast Mountains**.

> The **telephone code** for British Columbia is ☎604.

## South from Radium Hot Springs

Dropping down from Kootenay and Yoho national parks, highways 93 and 95 merge at Radium Hot Springs (p.460) and carry on southwards through scenery as spectacular as anything in the parks. The route follows the broad valley bottom of the **Columbia River**, bordered on the east by the Rockies and on the west by the marginally less breathtaking **Purcell Mountains**, though for the most part access to the wilderness here is limited and you'll have to be content with enjoying it from the highway. It's a fast run if you're driving, except where the road hugs the river's dramatic bluffs and sweeping meanders. Highways 93 and 95 part company near **Cranbrook**, where you can make for either of two US border crossings, double back eastwards on Hwy 3 to Crowsnest Pass and Alberta, or head west on Hwy 3 to Creston and eventually Vancouver. *Greyhound* **buses** ply all these routes, changing at Cranbrook.

### Invermere

WINDERMERE, 13km south of Radium, is little more than a supermarket, petrol station and campground immediately off the highway, and hardly hints at the presence of **INVERMERE**, about 1km beyond. A summer resort on Windermere Lake with the usual range of aquatic temptations, Invermere makes a nicer **accommodation** prospect than Radium. However, droves of anglers, boaters and beach bums mean summer vacancies may be in short supply, in which case call the central **infocentre** (May–Sept daily 8am–8pm; 342-6316) for bed-and-breakfast possibilities or head for one of the town's four **motels**: the *Lee-Jay*, 1015-13th St (☎342-9227), is the most reasonable, with doubles from $32. The nearest provincial **campground** is 7km back towards Radium at Dry Gulch Provincial Park, but the private *Pantycelyn Campland* (May–Oct; ☎342-9736; $15) is on the lake and has its own private beach. Try the *Lakeside Inn* for a decent **meal** or to rent boats, bikes and watersports gear.

From Invermere a minor road climbs west into the mountains to the burgeoning **Panorama Ski Resort** (18km), whose slick facilities include only limited and expensive accommodation. In summer the chief recommendation of the area is hiking, particularly if you continue up the road to the less tainted **Purcell Wilderness Conservancy**, one of the few easily accessible parts of the Purcell Mountains. If you have a tent and robust hiking inclinations, you could tackle the 61-kilometre **trail** through the area to ARGENTA on the northern end of Kootenay Lake (see p.472), an excellent cross-country route that largely follows undemanding valleys except when crossing the Purcell watershed at Earl Grey Pass (2256m).

## Fairmont Hot Springs and beyond

**FAIRMONT HOT SPRINGS** spills over the Columbia's flat floodplain, less a settlement than an ugly modern upmarket resort that feeds off the appeal of the hot springs themselves. The pools were commandeered from the Kootenay natives in 1922 for exploitation as a tourist resource, the calcium springs (daily 8am–10pm; $4) being particularly prized by the whites for their freedom from the sulphurous stench of many BC hot dips. If you don't fancy coughing up around $130 to stay at the resort you could try the big **campground** one minute from the pools, though it's mainly geared for RVs (☎345-6311; $12–20), or the new *Spruce Grove Resort* 2km south of Fairmont, with rooms starting at $42 and a lovely riverside campground (March–Nov; ☎345-6561; $10–13).

South of Fairmont, the road curves around the **Dutch Creek Hoodoos**, fantastically eroded river bluffs, before coming to **Columbia Lake** – not one of the area's most picturesque patches of water, though the *Mountain Village*, a fine wooden **restaurant** crammed with hundreds of old bottles, makes a good meal stop just short of a colossal lumber yard that blights CANAL FLATS at the head of the lake. Just south of the mill is the turn-off for **Whiteswan Lake Provincial Park**, a handkerchief-sized piece of unbeatable scenery at the end of a twenty-kilometre gravel road; the park has several campgrounds but few trails, as its main emphasis is on boating and trout fishing. The same access road continues another 30km to **Top of the World Provincial Park**, a far wilder region where you need to be completely self-sufficient – the walk-in campsites offer only water and firewood. Hiking in the park is good, an obvious shortish jaunt being the trail from the parking area to Fish Lake (7km one way), where there's a small cabin (summer only; small charge) and an unserviced campsite.

Back on Hwy 93/95 south of Fairmont, the Columbia Valley's scenery begins to wane as the Rockies retreat and the almost pastoral openness of the river's meadows is replaced by a blanket of trees. SKOOKUMCHUCK, marked as a town on most maps, is in fact little more than a sawmill whose chimneys belch out toxins that ride the air for miles downwind.

## Kimberley

**KIMBERLEY**, a few kilometres from Skookumchuck on Hwy 95a, is British Columbia's highest town (1117m), and in many ways one of its silliest, thanks to a tourist-tempting ruse to transform itself into a Bavarian village after the imminent closure of the local mine in the 1970s threatened it with economic oblivion. The result is a masterpiece of kitsch that's almost irresistible: buildings have been given a plywood-thin veneer of authenticity, piped Bavarian music dribbles from shops with names like *The Yodelling Woodcarver*, and even the fire hydrants have been painted to look like miniature replicas of Happy Hans, Kimberley's lederhosened mascot. The ploy might seem absurd to many Europeans, but there's no doubting the energy and enthusiasm that have gone into it, nor the economic rewards that have accrued from the influx of tourists and European immigrants – Germans included – who've provided an authentic range of cafés and restaurants and a variety of family-orientated summer activities.

Most of the Teutonic gloss is around the **Bavarian Platzl** on Spokane Street in the small downtown area, whose fake houses compare poorly with the authentic wooden buildings and more alpine surroundings on the outskirts.

If nothing else, you can leave Kimberley safe in the knowledge that you have seen the **"World's Biggest Cuckoo Clock"**, a fraudulent affair which amounts to little more than a large wooden box that twitters inane and incessant music. The dreaded contraption performs on being fed 25¢, and people oblige often enough that Happy Hans (rather than a cuckoo) makes his noisy appearance almost continuously; when he doesn't, the council employs some unfortunate to play the accordion morning, noon and night to keep up the musical interludes.

Apart from the clock, and a small **museum** upstairs in the library just down the road, other minor local sights include the **Sullivan Mine**, pre-Bavarian Kimberley's main employer and one of the world's biggest lead and zinc mines, which is occasionally opened up in the summer (ask at the infocentre). At MARYSVILLE, a couple of kilometres south of town on Hwy 95A, you can take a twenty-minute amble to see the **Marysville Waterfalls**, a series of small falls in verdant surroundings.

If you need **accommodation**, try the central *Inn of the Rockies*, 300 Wallinger Ave (☎427-2266 or ☎1-800-661-7559), with doubles from $42, or the *North Star Motel* (☎427-5633) at the northern edge of town, where rooms are about $40. Drop into the twee but excellent *Chef Bernard* café and **restaurant** opposite the clock, where the owner – heartily sick of Bavaria – plays Irish fiddle music as a mark of defiance. He's also known as one of the best local chefs, and people come from miles for his special fondue evenings. Locals' favourite cheap eatery is *La Casa Amigos*, 290 Spokane St, just down from the post office on the main crossroads. For full details of Kimberley's many summer events call in on the **infocentre** (daily 9am–6pm) at 350 Ross St, just off the main crossroads past the *Inn of the Rockies*. The key draw is **Julyfest**, which concludes with a one-week beer festival and – almost inevitably – an international accordion championship.

## Fort Steele Heritage Town

If you stick to Hwy 93/95 rather than going through Kimberley, you'll come to **Fort Steele Heritage Town** (daily 9.30am–dusk; $6), an impressively reconstructed turn-of-the-century village in a superb mountain-ringed setting. It started life in the 1860s as a provisions stop and river crossing for gold prospectors heading east to the seams on Wildhorse Creek, 6km beyond the present town site, but by 1887 the Mounties had arrived to keep order, and they raised a fort under their commander, the eponymous Sam Steele. The discovery of lead and silver locally put the place on the map in its own right, but boom soon gave way to bust when the new railway ignored the town in favour of Cranbrook.

Staffed by volunteers in period dress, the town consists of sixty restored buildings, including such diversions as an old-time music hall, stage coaches, blacksmiths and bakers, all under the auspices of the province, which takes the edge off the commercial greed that usually characterises such places. In summer you can watch demonstrations of weaving, quilting, ice-cream making and the like.

## Cranbrook

The ex-mining town of **CRANBROOK**, despite a location that marks it out as a transport hub, is one of the most dismal in the province, its dreariness hardly redeemed by the surrounding high mountains. A long strip of motels, neon clutter and marshalling yards dominates a downtown area otherwise distinguished only by thrift shops and closing-down sales. Local lifeblood, such as it is, flows from the motels, this being an obvious place to eat, sleep and drive away from the next morning.

The only sight to speak of is the **Cranbrook Railway Museum**, a smallish affair that centres on the restored carriages of an old trans-Canada luxury train (May–Sept daily 9am–8pm; Oct–April noon–5pm). The period buildings pushed by the tourist office aren't enough to justify the trawl round the streets.

If you must stay in town – which you may have to do, as there's little in the way of accommodation on the roads north and south – the top of the range is the *Inn of the South* at 803 Cranbrook (☎489-4301), a large, modern motel on the main road with doubles from $64. Cheaper and friendlier is the *Heritage Estate Motel* (☎426-3862), near the southern edge of town and therefore removed from some of the bleaker corners, where rooms start at $35. The town has a municipal **campground** at Baker Park on 14th Ave and 1st St (May–Sept; ☎426-2162; $10–12), though it's a good deal less appealing than Jimsmith Lake Provincial Park, located 4km southwest of town (year-round; $10; no showers).

Next door to the *Heritage Estate Motel* is the *Heritage Rose Dining House*, an expensive and highly spoken-of **restaurant** whose fine veranda-fronted building is an architectural oasis in these dour surroundings; the other local choice is the *Apollo*, at 1012 Cranbrook St. Opposite the latter is the *Greyhound* **bus terminal** (☎426-3331), hidden in a jungle of neon behind *McDonald's* and the *Mohawk* petrol station. Bus services run east to Fernie, Sparwood and southern Alberta (2 daily); west to Nelson, Castlegar and Vancouver (3 daily); north to Kimberley, Radium, Banff and Calgary (1 daily); and south to Spokane in the US (1 daily).

## East from Cranbrook

Hwy 93 leaves Hwy 95 between Fort Steele and Cranbrook, following Hwy 3 as far as Elko before branching off south for the United States border (91km). An unsullied hamlet of around half a dozen homes, **ELKO** is gone in a flash, but you might stop to eat at *Wendy's Place*, a homely, backwoods spot, or to camp at the excellent *Koocanusa Lake Campground* (May–Oct; ☎529-7484; $12), signed off Hwy 93 3km west of town. Hwy 3 offers colossal views of the Rockies and the fast-flowing, ice-clear Elk River, before hitting **FERNIE**, 32km north of Elko, a pleasant place of tree-lined streets and small wooden houses, surrounded by a ring of knife-edged mountains. The *Cedar Lodge* (☎423-4622) is the place to stay here, and has rooms from $50 to $80, or failing that, the cheaper *Inn Towner Motel* (☎423-6308), at 601-2nd Ave, where doubles are $32. The **infocentre** (daily 9am–5pm) stands alongside a reconstructed wooden oil derrick 2km north of town on Hwy 3. **Fernie Snow Valley**, 5km west of town and 2km off the main highway, boasts what is reputedly the longest ski season in the BC Rockies (Nov–May); out of season, adjoining **Mount Fernie Provincial Park** has plenty of hiking trails, picnic areas and campgrounds.

Hwy 3 leaves the Elk Valley at **SPARWOOD**, 29km beyond Fernie, where signs of the area's coal-mining legacy begin to appear. Close to the town – but barely visible – is Canada's largest open-cast **coal mine**, a maw capable of disgorging up to 18,000 tonnes of coal daily. Tours of the mine (July & Aug weekdays at 1.30pm) leave from the local **infocentre** (daily 9am–6pm), at the junction of Hwy 3 and Aspen Drive – look for the big miner's statue. The town itself is surprisingly neat and clean, and the big *Black Nugget Motor Inn* (☎425-2236; doubles from $45) on Hwy 3 makes a convenient place to stay.

### Elkford

The remainder of Hwy 3 in British Columbia is despoiled by mining; the road crests the Continental Divide 19km east of Sparwood at **Crowsnest Pass** (see p.424). Far more scenic is the drive north from Sparwood on Hwy 43, which heads upstream beside the Elk River for 35km to **ELKFORD**. Nestled against a wall of mountains to the east and more gentle hills to the west, the village claims to be the "wilderness capital of British

Columbia" – a high-pitched punt, but close to the mark if you're prepared to carry on up one or other of two rough gravel roads to the north. The more easterly one follows the Elk a further 80km to **Elk Lakes Provincial Park** close to the Continental Divide, one of the wildest road-accessible spots in the province. The slightly better route to the west heads 55km into the heart of unbeatable scenery below 2792-metre **Mount Armstrong**. Both areas offer excellent chances of spotting wildlife like cougars, deer, moose, elk and members of North America's largest bighorn sheep population.

Before entering either area, however, it's essential to pick up maps and information at the Elkford **infocentre** (daily 9am–5pm), located at the junction of Hwy 43 and Michel Road. They'll also be able to give directions to nearby **Josephine Falls**, a few minutes' walk from the parking area on Fording Mine Road. Whether you're staying here or pushing on north, a tent is essential: the only accommodation options are Elkford's municipal **campground** (April–Oct; ☎865-2241; $10) and wilderness camp-sites around Elk Lakes.

## West from Cranbrook

Following westbound Hwy 3 (southbound Hwy 95) out of Cranbrook you first reach **MOYIE**, a tiny community on the edge of lovely **Moyie Lake**, a welcome visual relief after the unending tree-covered slopes hereabouts. Though there's no motel accommodation, there are three local **campgrounds**, including the excellent one at **Moyie Lake Provincial Park** – reach it by taking Munro Lake Road from the northernmost point of Moyie Lake. The private *Green River Campground* is on the lakeshore signed about 1km off Hwy 3/95 (May–Oct; ☎426-4154; $12).

A few kilometres beyond Moyie, buses drop off at the small *Shell* garage in unspoilt **YAHK**, no more than a few houses nestled amidst the trees but a quiet stopover none-theless, courtesy of the good single **motel**, *Bob's* (☎424-5581; doubles from $32). Hwy 95 branches off from Hwy 3 here and heads south for the US border (11km). Incidentally, the highway crosses a **time zone** between Moyie and Yahk – clocks go back one hour.

Don't stop in **CRESTON** unless you want a taste of the terminally bland or such sightseeing frippery as "Canada's best mural". The **infocentre** is in a log cabin (the town's only building of interest) on the east side of town at 1711 Canyon St: use it if by mischance you need **accommodation**, though with twenty or so motels and camp-grounds to choose from, chances are you won't be fighting for a bed. The cheapest and most central spot is the *Hotel Creston* (☎428-9321), with doubles at $29; motels on the town's fringes offer more salubrious, if slightly costlier alternatives. In addition to *Greyhounds* passing through here along Hwy 3, *Empire Bus Lines* runs an early-morning service from here to Spokane, WA (daily except Tues & Wed).

# The Kootenays

**The Kootenays** is one of the most attractive and unvisited parts of British Columbia, and one of the most loosely defined. It consists essentially of two major north–south valleys – the Kootenay and the Columbia, which are largely taken up by **Kootenay Lake** and **Upper** and **Lower Arrow Lakes** – and three intervening mountain ranges – the Purcells, Selkirks and Monashees, whose once-rich mineral deposits formed the kernel of the province's early mining industry. **Nelson** is the key town, slightly periph-eral to the Kootenays' rugged core, but a lovely place, and one of the few provincial towns that holds out real attractions in its own right. Scattered lakeside hamlets, nota-bly **Kaslo** and **Nakusp**, make excellent bases for excursions into mountain scenery which in the Kootenays has a pristine quality not found elsewhere. Watery activities – canoeing and fishing in particular – are excellent, and you can also explore the ramshackle mining heritage of near-ghost towns like **Sandon** and **New Denver**, or wallow in the hot springs at **Nakusp**.

**Getting around** the region is tricky if you're without transport, for there are next to no public services (see the "Nelson" section for details on buses), which is a shame because the roads here are amongst the most scenic in a province noted for its scenery. Even with your own car, there's no way to do the Kootenays justice without retracing your steps at times. You can dip in and out of the region from the Trans-Canada Highway (to the north) or Hwy 3 (to the south), but any trans-Kootenay route is more attractive than either of these main highways: the most **scenic routes** are Hwy 31A from Kaslo to New Denver, and Hwy 6 from New Denver to Vernon. Given no time constraints, your best strategy would be to enter from Creston and exit via Vernon, which sets you up for the Okanagan.

# Highway 3A to Kootenay Bay

Starting from just north of Creston, **Highway 3A** picks a slow, twisting course up the eastern shore of **Kootenay Lake** to the free car ferry at Kootenay Bay. Apart from the ample scenic rewards of the lake and the mountains beyond it, the highway is almost completely empty for all of its 79km, and none of the villages marked on maps amount to anything more than scattered houses hidden in the woods. The only noteworthy sight is the **Glass House**, midway up the lake at BOSWELL, which ranks highly in the list of Canada's more bizarre offerings. Constructed entirely from embalming bottles, the house was built by a Mr Brown after 35 years in the funeral business, "to indulge", so the wonderfully po-faced pamphlet tells you, "a whim of a peculiar nature". The retired mortician travelled widely visiting friends in the funeral profession until he'd collected 500,000 bottles – that's 250 tonnes worth – to build his lakeside retirement home. Nearby **accommodation** is provided by the *Heidelburg Inn* (☎223-8263), with doubles at $45 including a cooked breakfast, and the *Mountain Shores Resort* (☎223-8258), a combination of motel (doubles $50–75), cottages and **campground** (April–Oct; $12–15).

At **GRAY CREEK**, a few kilometres onward, check out the superb *Gray Creek Store*, which boasts the once-in-a-lifetime address of 1979 Chainsaw Avenue and claims, with some justification, to be "The Most Interesting Store You've Ever Seen". The shop basically *is* Gray Creek – it's the sort of place you go to get your chainsaw fixed and where real lumberjacks come for their red-checked shirts. There are two lakeside **campgrounds** nearby, the *Old Crow* (June–Sept; ☎227-9495; $10) and the *Lakeview* (year-round; ☎227-9367; $10).

**CRAWFORD BAY** and **KOOTENAY BAY** are names on the map that refer in the flesh to the most fleeting of settlements, the latter also being the **ferry terminal** for boats to Balfour on the west shore. As a place to stay, this side of the crossing is a touch brighter, and there's an **infocentre** just off the road at Crawford Bay if you need help finding some of the nicer accommodation tucked away in the woods nearby. The cheapest **motel** is the *Last Chance* (☎227-9477), near the ferry dock, with doubles at $32; nearby *Wedgewood Manor* (April–Nov; ☎227-9233) is upmarket and pleasantly plush, but doubles are $60 (breakfast included) and you'll have to book ahead to secure one of its four rooms. The better of two **campgrounds** here is the nicely wooded *Kokanee Springs Resort* on Hwy 3A (☎227-9292), but it's as well to know that Balfour has a greater choice of sites.

The thirty-minute **ferry crossing** – purportedly the longest free ferry crossing in the world – is beautiful. Free boats leave every fifty minutes from June to September, and every two hours the rest of the year, but it's a first-come, first-served affair, and in summer unless you're a pedestrian or bike passenger it can be a couple of sailings before your turn comes round.

## Balfour and Ainsworth Hot Springs

**BALFOUR** is less the fishing village it's billed as than a fairly shoddy and dispersed collection of motels, garages and cafés – albeit in verdant surroundings – designed to catch the traffic rolling on and off the Kootenay Lake ferry. RV **campgrounds** line the road to Nelson for about 2km, but the quietest are those furthest from the terminal, and much better still is Kokanee Creek Provincial Park, about 10km beyond. The handiest **motel** for the ferry is the *Balfour Beach Inn* (April–Nov; ☎229-4235), with doubles at $40, convenient for the small pebbly beach just north of the terminal.

About 15km north of Balfour on Hwy 31, **AINSWORTH HOT SPRINGS** is home to some 100 residents – a town by local standards. The tasteful *Ainsworth Hot Springs Resort* (☎229-4212) is ideal if you want to take in the scalding water of the **mineral springs** (daily 8.30am–9.30pm; $5), though at $75 a double the chalets are expensive, and local opinion rates the Nakusp hot springs (see p.475) far more highly. The nicest local **motel** is the *Mermaid Lodge* (☎229-4969), with doubles from $33. Spelunkers might want to take a tour ($10) of **Cody Caves Provincial Park**, 15km up a rough side road (well signed) above town.

A touch further up the increasingly beautiful Hwy 31 comes the self-contained **Woodbury Resort** (year-round; ☎353-7177), a collection of motel, cottages, campground (tents $12) and watersport facilities – pitched on the lakeshore with lovely views and a small beach, it makes an attractive long-term accommodation prospect if you're tenting. Directly opposite is the **Woodbury Mining Museum** (July–Sept daily 9–6; $4), a quaint pioneer building crammed with mining regalia and the entrance to a thirty-minute underground tour of the old lead, zinc and silver workings.

## Kaslo and around

**KASLO** must rate as one of British Columbia's most attractive and friendliest little villages. Huddled at the edge of Kootenay Lake and dwarfed by towering mountains, its half-dozen streets are lined with picture-perfect wooden homes and flower-filled gardens. It started life as a sawmill in 1889 and turned into a boomtown with the discovery of silver in 1893; diversification, and the steamers that plied the lakes, saved it from the cycle of boom and bust that ripped the heart out of so many similar towns. Kaslo remains an urbane and civilised community whose citizens work hard at keeping it that way, supporting a cultural centre, art galleries, rummage sales, even a concert society. Finding your way round is no problem, nor is finding information – everyone is disarmingly helpful – but there's an **infocentre** (April–Oct daily 9am–6pm) at the main crossroads if you need it.

The **town hall**, a distinctive green and white wooden building dating from 1898, is an architectural gem by any standards, as is the church opposite. Yet Kaslo's main attraction is the *SS Moyie*, the oldest surviving **paddle steamer** in North America, which ferried men, ore and supplies along the mining routes from 1897 until the advent of reliable roads in 1957. A museum of antiques, artefacts and photographs is due to open when its refurbishment is complete (daily 10am–4.30pm; $3). Look for the small hut alongside, the "world's smallest post office" (closed since 1970), and drop in on Kaslo's thriving **arts centre**, the *Langham Cultural Society*, for theatrical performances and art exhibitions.

Kaslo makes an ideal base for tackling two of the region's major parks – Kokanee Glacier Provincial Park and the Purcell Wilderness Conservancy – and for pottering around some of the charming lakeshore communities. People at the arts centre can advise on getting to **ARGENTA**, a refugee settlement of Quakers who came from the States to start a new life; it's also the western trailhead for the sixty-kilometre Earl Grey

Pass Trail over the Purcell Mountains to Invermere (p.466). This area, incidentally, offers a good chance of seeing **ospreys**: the Kootenays' 100 or so breeding pairs represent the largest concentration of the species in North America.

## Practicalities

For the practical side of things, by far the best thing to do is visit the town's social hub, the excellent **Treehouse Restaurant** on Front Street, a warm and wood-cosy place where you can eat superbly and easily strike up conversations. The nearby *Mariner Inn and Motel* has a beer hall, and is more of a lowlife hang-out.

The best central **accommodation** is the *Kaslo Motel* (☎353-2431), with doubles from $33 – for most other options head for the marina just north of the centre where the cheap A-frame cabins at *Sunny Bluffs Motel and Campground* (☎353-2277; doubles $38) and its nine camping pitches are idyllically set, and *Kaslo Marina* (☎353-7777) has waterfront doubles at $38. For **bed and breakfast** try the *Loki Lodge* (☎353-2684), run by an Edinburgh couple, with doubles from $45. More interesting accommodation possibilities are available further up the lake, most notably two rustic bed and breakfasts at Argenta – for details contact the Farleys at *Earl Grey Pass* (☎366-4472; from $20 per person), or the Pollards at *Place Cockaigne* (☎366-4394; from $30).

Kaslo has a free municipal **campground** on the flat ground by the lake at the end of Front Street, past the *SS Moyie* on the right. *Mirror Lake Campground* (mid-April to mid-Oct; ☎353-7102), beautifully situated 2km south of town on the main road to Ainsworth, has more facilities and charges $10 per site. Shopping in the village is best done at the old-style *Lakeview Store* at the top of Front Street, the likes of which has probably only been seen in *The Waltons*.

### Kokanee Glacier Provincial Park

Kaslo is the most sensible of several possible jumping-off points for **Kokanee Glacier Provincial Park**, straddling the Selkirk Mountains to the southwest, as the access road from here – signed off Hwy 31A 5km northwest of town – offers the best views and choice of trails. (Other approaches are from Ainsworth, Hwy 6 in the Slocan Valley, and Hwy 3A between Balfour and Nelson.) The 29-kilometre Kaslo road cuts to the heart of the park, reaching the Joker Millsite parking area set amidst spectacular glacier-ringed high country. Of the eleven trails in the area, the obvious **hike** from the car park runs up to Helen Deane and Kaslo lakes (8km round trip), an easy morning amble. If you're staying overnight you can pick from the usual undeveloped campsites (you're supposed to camp in designated sites only) and three basic summer-only **cabins** ($6 nightly; no cooking facilities) – the main one, *Slocan Chief*, is past Helen Deane Lake alongside a park ranger office.

## Highway 31A and the Slocan Valley

After Kaslo you can either rattle north over gravel road to link with the Trans-Canada Highway at Revelstoke, a wild and glorious 150-kilometre drive with a ferry crossing at GALENA BAY, or stay in the Kootenays and shuffle west on **Hwy 31A** through the Selkirk Mountains to the Slocan Valley. The latter road ascends from Kaslo alongside the Kaslo River, a crashing torrent choked with branches and fallen trees and hemmed in by high mountains and cliffs of dark rock that lend the drive a melancholy air. Even if you know nothing about geology, these crags' metallic sheen suggests the mineral potential that fired the early growth of so many of the settlements in the region. Near its high point the road passes a series of massively picturesque lakes: **Fish Lake** is deep green and has a nice picnic spot at one end; **Bear Lake** is equally pretty; and **Beaver Pond** is an amazing testament to the beaver's energy and ingenuity.

## Sandon

The ghost town of **SANDON** is located 13km south of Hwy 31A, up a signed gravel side road that climbs through scenery of the utmost grandeur. Unfortunately Sandon itself is too much ghost and not enough town to suggest how it might have looked in its silver-mining heyday when it had 24 hotels, 23 saloons, an opera house and 2000 inhabitants. That it's now dilapidated rather than evocative is due mainly to a flood which swept away the earlier boardwalk settlement in 1955, leaving a partly inhabited rump that clutters around a café and **infocentre** immediately past the salmon-pink wooden building at the top of the town.

The trip is redeemed, however, if you hike the **KNS Historic Trail** (6km each way) from the site, which follows the course of the 1895 Kaslo–Slocan ore-carrying railway, past old mine works and eventually to fine views of the New Denver Glacier across the Slocan Valley to the west. Coupled with leaflets from the infocentre, the walk vividly documents the area's wild-west mining history, harking back to an era when the district – known as "Silvery Slocan" – produced the lion's share of Canada's silver. "Silver, lead, and hell are raised in the Slocan," wrote one local newspaper in 1891, "and unless you can take a hand in producing these articles, your services are not required." The immense vein of silver-rich galena that started the boom was discovered by accident in 1891 by two colourful prospectors, Eli Carpenter and Jack Seaton, when they got lost on the ridges returning to Ainsworth from Slocan Lake. Back in the bar they fell out over the find, and each raced out with his own team to stake the claim. Seaton won, and was to become a vastly wealthy silver baron who travelled in his own train carriage across Canada, condemning Carpenter to return to his earlier profession as a tightrope walker and to an ultimately penurious death.

## New Denver and the Slocan Valley

After the Sandon turn-off Hwy 31A drops into the **Slocan Valley**, a minor but still spectacular lake-bottomed tributary between the main Kootenay and Columbia watersheds, and meets Hwy 6 at **NEW DENVER**. Born of the same silver-mining boom as Kaslo, and with a similar lakeside setting and genuine pioneer feel, New Denver is, if anything, quieter than its neighbour. The clapboard houses are in peeling, pastel-painted wood, and the tree-lined streets are mercifully free of neon, fast food and any evidence of tourist passage. As a stopover it's as good as Kaslo, for which purpose there's a single beach-hut-type **motel**, the *Lucerne* (☎358-2228; doubles $31), and the simple *New Denver Municipal Campground* (year-round; ☎358-2316; $10–12) on the south side of the village. For **food** try the *Apple Tree Sandwich Shop* on the main street. **Silvery Slocan Museum** is good for twenty minutes on the background and artefacts of the area's mining heritage. The central **infocentre** (summer only) is the place to pick up specific information on the surrounding valley.

Southbound out of New Denver, Hwy 6 follows the tight confines of the Slocan Valley for another 100km of ineffable mountain and lake landscapes. The 125,000-acre **Valhalla Provincial Park** wraps up the best of this on the eastern side of Slocan Lake; a wilderness area with no developed facilities, most of it is out of reach unless you can boat across the water, though there are two trails which penetrate it from the hamlet of **SLOCAN** at the south end of the lake. For a short taste of the local outdoors, the canter up the old railway bed from Slocan is a popular short hike, and there's more fresh air at the Mulvey Basin and Cove Creek **beaches**, each with small provincial campgrounds. Note, too, that gravel roads lead up from Hwy 6 to the more accessible heights of **Kokanee Glacier Provincial Park** to the east (p.473).

If you need to **stay** en route south there are about half a dozen options, all in rustic settings with great mountain or lake views. Try either *Lemon Creek Lodge* (☎355-2403), a motel-campground 7km south of Slocan, with doubles at $40, or the *Slocan Inn* (☎355-2230) in Slocan itself, with rooms at the same price. In addition to provincial

**campgrounds** at Mulvey Basin and Cove Creek (both May–Oct; $10), there's the commercial *Slocan City* (May–Oct; ☎355-2277; $10) and the unserviced *Silverton Municipal Campground* (May–Oct; free), just south of New Denver.

# Highway 6: Nakusp and onward

**Highway 6** may not be the most direct east–west route through British Columbia, but it's got to be one of the most dramatic. From New Denver it initially strikes north and after 30km passes **Summit Lake**, a perfect jewel of water, mountain and forest that's served by the *Three Islands* **campground** (May–Sept; ☎265-3023; $10). A rough road ("Take At Your Own Risk") runs south from here into the mountains and a small winter ski area.

Another 16km beyond, **NAKUSP** is, like Kaslo and Nelson, a rare thing in British Columbia: a town with enough charisma to make it worth visiting for its own sake. The setting is par for the course in the Kootenays, with a big lake – **Upper Arrow Lake**, part of the Columbia River system – and the snowcapped Selkirk Mountains to the east for a backdrop. The nearby hot springs are the main attraction, but you could happily wander the town for a morning, or boat or swim off the public **beach**. The only actual sight in town is the **Nakusp Museum** at 6th Avenue and 1st Street, full of the usual archive material and Victorian bric-a-brac (May–Sept; free). The helpful **infocentre**, based in the fake paddle-steamer building next door, can provide details on local fishing, boating and hiking possibilities, and – if you're driving onwards – timings for the Galena Bay and Fauquier ferries.

For a place to **stay** try the central *Leland Hotel* (☎265-4221), a rather rough-and-ready retreat built in 1892, featuring an interesting downstairs bar; the owner, Klaus, offers longer-term stays below the usual $20–30 room rates. The *Kuskanax Lodge* (☎265-3618 or ☎1-800-663-0100) is equally central but more upmarket, with doubles from $49, and also has a good **restaurant** – though not as good as the more expensive *Lord Minto*, Nakusp's top eatery.

If you're only going to try the hot springs experience once, **Nakusp Hot Springs**, a well-signposted complex 13km northeast of town, is the place to do it (June–Sept daily 9.30am–10pm, Oct–May 10.30am–9pm; $3.50). The manager, Stirling Mitchell, is friendly and energetic, and it's not unusual for late-night informal parties to develop around the two outdoor pools. Unlike many similar enterprises, the natural pools are cleaned each night and are backed up by nice changing facilities. The springs are popular in the summer, however, partly because there's a lovely **campground** alongside (☎352-4033; $6). The adjoining *Cedar Chalets* (☎352-4034) offers doubles at $49, but reservations are essential in summer.

## On from Nakusp

Highway 23, the lesser of two onward routes from Nakusp, heads north to Revelstoke (99km), a lonely and spectacular journey which involves a free ferry crossing halfway at GALENA BAY (hourly sailings each way). Highway 6, however, doglegs south from Nakusp for 57 delightful kilometres to the ferry crossing at **FAUQUIER**, a handful of buildings which include a garage, a store, the *Mushroom Addition* **café** for coffee and meals, and a potentially useful **motel** – the only one for miles – the *Alpine Lakes Motel and Restaurant* (☎269-7622; doubles from $36), bang on the lakeside near the ferry. There's a crude **campground** 2km back towards Nakusp, marked by two big arrrows sticking in the ground, and 3km beyond that the *Goose Downs* **bed and breakfast** is signed off the road to the west (from $50 per person).

The free **ferry** across Lower Arrow Lake takes about five minutes and departs half-hourly from 5.15am to 9.45pm and operates an intermittent shuttle throughout the night. NEEDLES amounts to no more than a ramp off the ferry on the other side.

There's an unofficial **campground** at Whatshan Lake, 3km off the highway just after Needles, but otherwise Highway 6 is a gloriously empty ribbon as it burrows through the staggering Monashee Mountains – though some of the time it's too hemmed in by forest for you to catch anything but billions of trees. After cresting Monashee Pass (1198m), the highway begins the long descent through the **Coldstream Valley** towards the Okanagan. Snow dusts the mountains here year round, crags loom above the meadows that increasingly break the forest cover, and beautiful flower-filled valleys wind down to the highway. The first sign of life in over 100km is the *Gold Panner* **campground**, a good spot to overnight or explore the utter wilderness of **Monashee Provincial Park** to the north. The park is reached by rough road from the hamlet of CHERRYVILLE, 10km further west, which despite its cartographic prominence is just three houses, a garage and *Frank's General Store*.

**LUMBY**, another 20km beyond, is scarcely more substantial, although the $42 **rooms** at the *Diamond Motor Inn* (☎547-9221) are worth considering if it's late, given that Okanagan lodgings on ahead could well be packed. The town also boasts a simple riverside **campground** run by the local Lions Club (May–Oct; ☎547-9504; $7). Beyond, the road glides through lovely pastoral country: orchards, verdant meadows, low, tree-covered hills, and fine wooden barns built to resemble inverted longboats.

# Nelson

**NELSON** is one of British Columbia's best towns, and one of the few interior settlements you could happily spend two or three days in – longer if you use it as a base for touring the Kootenays by car. It's home to more than its share of refugees from the Sixties, a hangover that's nurtured a friendly and close-knit community, a healthy cultural scene and a liveliness – manifest in alternative cafés, nightlife, secondhand clothes shops and the like – that you'll be hard pushed to find elsewhere in the province outside Vancouver. At the same time it's a young place that's permeated with immense civic pride, which was given a further boost by the filming here of *Roxanne*, Steve Martin's version of Cyrano de Bergerac (there's a *Roxanne* walk). Producers chose the town for its idyllic lakeside setting and 350-plus turn-of-the-century homes, factors which for once live up to the Canadian talent for hyperbole – in this case a claim to be "Queen of the Kootenays" and "Heritage Capital of Western Canada".

Located 34km west of Balfour on Hwy 3A, the town forms a tree-shaded grid of streets laid over the hilly slopes that edge down to the westernmost shores of Kootenay Lake. Most homes are immaculately kept and vividly painted, and even the commercial **buildings** along the parallel main streets – Baker and Vernon – owe more to the vintage architecture of Seattle and San Francisco than to the drab Victoriana of much of eastern Canada. If you want to add purpose to your wanderings, pick up the *Heritage Walking Tour* pamphlet from the **infocentre**, 225 Hall St (daily June–Aug 8am–8pm; Sept–May 9am–5pm), which takes you around the sort of houses that many Canadians dream of retiring to, and only occasionally oversells a place – notably when it lands you in front of the jam factory and the electricity substation. You could even go out of your way for some of the town's **shops**, particularly those of its many artists and craftspeople, who in summer club together to present **Artwalk**, a crawl round no fewer than sixteen galleries. Most of these have regular openings and wine-gorging receptions, making for numerous free-for-all parties. *Oliver's Books* on Baker Street is excellent for maps, guides and general reading, with a bias towards the sort of New Age topics that find a ready market here.

For the most part the area owes its development to the discovery of copper and silver ore on nearby Toad Mountain at the turn of the century, and though the mines declined fairly quickly, Nelson's diversification into gold and lumber, and its roads, railway and waterways, saved it from mining's usual downside. Today mining is back on the agenda as old claims are re-explored, and even if the idea of the town's **Museum of Mines** (daily 9am–5pm; free), next to the infocentre, leaves you cold, it's worth meeting the curator, an old prospector who talks at length – and interestingly – on the quest for silver, copper and gold, past and present.

It's probably less worthwhile to trek over to the **Nelson Museum**, about twenty minutes' walk from the centre, which offers a rather haphazard display that's obviously the work of enthusiastic amateurs (summer daily 1–6pm; closed Sun in winter; $1). There are, however, odd points of interest, notably a chronicle of the original 1886 Silver King Mine that brought the town to life, as well as tantalisingly scant details on the Doukhobor, a Russian religious sect whose members still live in self-contained communities around the Kootenays (see p.374).

## Practicalities

Nelson is served by *Greyhound* **buses** (☎352-3939) that run west to Penticton (for connections to Vancouver, the Okanagan and Kamloops) and east to Cranbrook (connections to Calgary via Banff or Fort Macleod). There are also infrequent minibus services to Kaslo (☎353-2492 for details) and Nakusp (☎265-3511). The depot is almost on the lakeshore, just below the town proper.

There's a reasonable spread of **accommodation**, and though all three downtown **hotels** are fairly down-at-heel, they're all cheap: the *Lord Nelson*, 616 Vernon St (☎352-7211), with doubles from $30, is marginally the best; the *Queen's*, 621 Baker St (☎352-5351), is the cheapest and dingiest with doubles from $26; the *Savoy*, 198 Baker St (☎352-7285), has doubles at $32. Most of the **motels** are on Hwy 31A at the north end of town or over the miniature Forth Road bridge on the north side of the lake. Here try the *Lakeside Motel*, 805 Nelson Ave (☎352-3185), with doubles from $38; the *Villa Motel*, 655 Hwy 3A (☎352-5515), with doubles starting at $40, including the use of an indoor pool; or the *North Short Inn*, 687 Hwy 3A (☎352-6606), where doubles are $50 with continental breakfast. The nearest **campground** is *City Tourist Park*, on the corner of High Street and Willow (mid-May to early Oct; ☎352-0169; from $8). If this is full, head east towards Balfour and the many sites near the ferry terminal.

The choice of **restaurants** is broad, and you can't go far wrong wandering and choosing something that looks tempting. *Stanley Baker's*, a locals' place on Baker Street next to the *Nelson Shopping Company* mall, is good for cappuccino, snacks and big, cheap breakfasts. For an alternative café and bookstore try the *Vienna*, just off Baker Street opposite the *Bank of Montreal*. For evening meals, downtown residents head for the *Main Street Diner*, 616 Baker St (closed Sun). *Bogart's*, at 198 Baker St (part of the *Savoy Hotel*), looks dubious from outside but cooks reliable pastas, ribs and seafood specials. The *Victoria Street Restaurant*, 408 Victoria St (closed Mon), has seafood, European and **vegetarian** leanings. If you're shopping for your own meals, the big **supermarkets** are in or near the mall alongside the bus depot.

# Highway 3: the border towns

Unless you plan to head south into the States, British Columbia's tawdry necklace of border towns on **Highway 3** is as good a reason as any for taking a more northerly route across the central part of the province. None amounts to much, and you'd be advised to whisk through by car or *Greyhound*; if you have to break the journey, aim to do it in **Salmo** or **Castlegar**, towns on which some of the Kootenays' charm has rubbed off. Things get more interesting again around **Osoyoos** and **Keremeos**, where the road enters a parched desert landscape, and then climbs into the gripping mountain scenery of the Coastal Ranges, passing through **Manning Provincial Park** before joining the Trans-Canada Highway.

If you're crossing over **the border** hereabouts, incidentally, don't be lulled by the remote customs posts into expecting an easy passage: if you don't hold a Canadian or US passport you can expect the sort of grilling you'd get at major entry points.

## Creston to Salmo

A classic stretch of Canadian blacktop, Hwy 3 climbs from the fruit-growing plains around Creston to **Kootenay Pass** (1774m) – though the views are less of spectacular mountains than of a pretty tracery of creeks and rivers crashing down through forest on all sides. This is one of the highest main roads in the country – it's frequently closed by bad weather – and it has no services for 70km after Creston, so check your petrol before setting out. If you're cycling, brace yourself for a fifty-kilometre uphill slog, but the reward is an unexpected and stunning lake at the pass, where there's a pull-off, picnic area and views of high peaks in the far distance.

Despite the large volume of traffic converging on it along Hwy 3 and Hwy 6, tiny **SALMO** somehow manages to retain a pioneer feel: most of its tidy wooden buildings are fronted by verandas, and in summer they're decked out with baskets of flowers. The **infocentre** (mid-June to mid-Sept) is on the corner of Hwy 6 and 4th Street, but it doesn't have a lot to promote apart from the "world's smallest telephone box", next to the *Salcrest Motel* on the south side of town, and the **museum** (May–Sept Mon–Fri 10am–4pm), a more credible attraction housed in a picturesque white-painted building at 4th Street and Railway Avenue, which charts the vicissitudes of pioneer life and also hosts occasional travelling exhibitions. In winter there's **skiing** at the Salmo ski area just 2km east of town.

**Buses** pull in here for a long rest stop at the terminal by the *Petro-Canada* garage on the north side of the village. If you need to overnight, use either of the two central motels: the *Reno* (☎357-9937; doubles $34), one block east of the bus terminal, or the *Salcrest* (☎357-9557; doubles from $30), at the junction of highways 3 and 6. The nearest **campground** is the *Hidden Creek Guest Ranch* (May–Oct; ☎357-2266; $7–12), 6km north of town on Hwy 6. For **food** try *Charlie's Pizza and Spaghetti House*, an old-style diner on 4th Street. Just up the road, the *Silver Dollar Pub* is the town's favourite **bar**, with pool tables, a jukebox and lots of good ol' boys in an atmospheric wooden interior. *Salmo Foods*, opposite the bar, is the best supermarket for stocking up.

## Castlegar

**CASTELGAR** is a strange, diffuse place with no obvious centre, probably because roads and rivers – this is where the Kootenay meets the Columbia – make it more a transport hub than a community. In its time it was famous for its immigrant **Doukhobor** population, members of a Russian sect who fled religious persecution in 1899 and brought their pacifist-agrarian lifestyle to western Canada. Although their way of life waned after the death of their leader Peter Verigin in 1924, the Doukhobors' considerable industry and agricultural expertise transformed the Castlegar area; many locals still practise the old beliefs, and Russian is still taught in local schools.

Much of the community's heritage has been collected in the **Doukhobor Village Museum** (Wed–Sun 9am–5pm; $3), just off the main road on the right after you cross the big suspension bridge over the Kootenay River. A Doukhobor descendant is on hand to take you through the museum, which houses a winsome display of farm machinery, handmade tools and traditional Russian clothing that's intriguing as much for its alien context as for its content. As interesting as the museum, and highly recommended if you've built up a massive appetite, is the Doukhobor **restaurant** alongside. The ambience is bizarrely austere – the walls are bare but for a few crafts and jumble-sale notices – and the menu an exercise in straight-laced cuisine: Doukhobor chefs face something of a daily creative challenge, given that they can't use meat, fish or alcohol in the cooking. To meet it they produce just two set dinners daily: one brings you borsch, bread, tart and coffee; the other delivers things called *varenyky*, *galoopsie*, *pyrogy* and *nalesnici*, all tasty and shudderingly stodgy.

Castlegar's **infocentre** is off the main road as you leave town for Grand Forks over the Columbia bridge. The best **motel** – small, and with a nice view – is the *Cozy Pines* on Hwy 3 on the west edge of town (☎365-5613; doubles $34). Closer in, the modern and attractive *Fireside* (☎365-2128) has doubles for $46. Three kilometres out of town to the west is the *Hislop's Hiway Campsite*, 1725 Mannix Rd (May–Oct; ☎365-2337; $10–12).

## Rossland

TRAIL is home to the world's largest lead and zinc smelter, a vast industrial complex whose chimneys cast a dismal shadow over the village's few houses. **ROSSLAND**, 10km away, also has a mining foundation – gold this time, some $125 million worth of which ($2 billion at today's prices) was gouged from the surrounding hills around the turn of the century. If you're into mining heritage, a tour of the **Le Roi Gold Mine** – once one of the world's largest, with 100km of tunnels – and the adjoining **Rossland Historical Museum** will stuff you with fascinating technical and geological background (mid-May to mid-Sept daily 9am–5pm; $5, or $2.50 for museum only). The **infocentre** (May–Oct 9am–8pm), at the junction of the town's two main roads, is most useful for details of the **Nancy Greene Recreation Area** northwest of town. Though the recreation area is best known for its world-class skiing – its **Red Mountain Ski Area** is a training ground for members of the Canadian national team – it's also excellent for hiking, an outdoor commodity that isn't easy to come by in these parts. There's no camping, however.

## Grand Forks, Greenwood and Midway

**GRAND FORKS** is not grand at all – it's very small and very dull and little more than a perfunctory transit settlement built on a river flat. Several *Greyhound* **buses** drop in daily, probably the biggest thing to happen to the place, stopping at *Stanley's*, which is the spot for sustenance unless you shop at the big *Overwaitea* supermarket alongside. The small **museum** by the traffic lights is the standard small-town model and can be seen in about the time it takes for the lights to change. Just north of town, **Christina Lake** is a modestly unspoilt summer resort with lots of swimming, boating and camping opportunities. A dozen or so motels and campgrounds sprout along its shore, with about the same number in and around the town itself, but it's hard to see how you'd want to use them except in an emergency.

West out of town, however, the scenery along Hwy 3 begins to change from bland meandering hills to a flatter, drier landscape of bleached grass and sagebrush that anticipates the deserts to the west and the mild Okanagan to the northwest. In the long climb to **GREENWOOD**, however, the pines reappear, heralding a wild, battered brute of a village which has suffered from the closure of its mines and can't muster much more than a couple of old buildings and some old workings. The all but redundant **infocentre** is housed in the town museum on the main road (May–Sept). You're pretty sure of a welcome in any of the local **motels**, cheapest of which is the *Evening Star* (☎445-6733) with doubles from $28.

After the long scenic drudgery of Hwy 3, the landscape beyond Greenwood starts to change dramatically; by **MIDWAY**, just a few kilometres west, the hills are strange, broad whalebacks cut by open valleys and covered in coarse scrub and brown-baked grass. The hamlet's handful of scattered homes are like a windblown and wistful ghost town, making an evocative backdrop for the overgrown train tracks and tiny **railway museum** housed alongside a rusted minuscule steam engine.

## Osoyoos

Beyond Midway the road climbs steeply to Anikas Pass (1234m) and suddenly unfolds a dramatic view, far below, of **OSOYOOS** and a sizeable lake surrounded by bare, ochre hills. Descending, you enter one of Canada's strangest landscapes – a bona fide desert of half-bare, scrub-covered hills, sand, lizards, cactus, snakes, and Canada's lowest average rainfall (around 25cm per year). Temperatures here are regularly 10°C higher than in Nelson, less than a morning's drive away, enabling exotic fruit like bananas and pomegranates to be grown and prompting Osoyoos to declare itself the "Spanish Capital of Canada". The houses here are supposed to have been restyled to give the place an Iberian flavour to match its climate, but on the ground it's almost impossible to find any trace of the conversion.

The town is otherwise distinguished only by its position beside **Lake Osoyoos** in the Okanagan Valley – Hwy 97, which passes through the town, is the main route into the Okanagan region. In summer the place comes alive with swimmers and boaters, drawn to the warmest water of any lake in Canada, and with streams of American RVs slow-tailing their way northwards to where the real action is. The relative lack of crowds and strange scenery might persuade you to do your beach-bumming in Osoyoos, though even here you'll be pushed to find space in any of the town's twenty **hotels** and **motels** during high season; one of the cheapest and most central is the *Rialto* (☎495-6022), with good views over the lake and doubles ranging from $18 to $35. Most of the motels are across the causeway on the southeastern shore of the lake, alongside the **bus stop** and the vivid pink *Pay 'n' Save*. For more choice and help, contact the **infocentre** at the junction of Hwy 3 and Hwy 97. You're more likely to get a place in one of the half-dozen local **campgrounds** – try the *Cabana Beach* (April–Oct; ☎495-7705; $12–21) at 55 East Lakeshore Drive or *Van Acres* (May–Sept; ☎495-6912; $14–20) at 7004-67th St.

**Moving on** from Osoyoos involves a major decision if you're travelling by car or bike, the choices being to continue west on Hwy 3 towards Vancouver, or to strike north on Hwy 97 through the Okanagan to the Trans-Canada Highway. If you're on a *Greyhound*, the bus heads north and the decision can be deferred until Penticton, the major parting of the ways for services in this part of BC.

## Keremeos

Even if your destination is the Okanagan, it's well worth taking the long way round from Osoyoos on highways 3 and 3A via **KEREMEOS**. After the desert of Osoyoos, the landscape lurches suddenly into a more rural mode, thanks mainly to a climate which blesses the region with the longest growing season in the country – hence the tag, "Fruit Stand Capital of Canada". Arguably the most nicely situated town this side of Nelson, Keremeos spreads over a dried-up lake bed, with hills rising up from the narrow plain on all sides. Lush, irrigated orchards surround the town, offset in spring by huge swathes of flowers across the valley floor, and depending on the season you can pick up fruit and veg from stands dotted more or less everywhere: cherries, apricots, peaches, pears, apples, plums – even grapes – all grow in abundance, and if you're not taken with the food there's the chance of **wine tastings** at the *St Laszio Vineyards*, 1km east of town on Hwy 3.

Keremeos itself is a rustic, two-street affair that's almost unspoilt by neon or urban clutter. A few shopfronts are oldish, and several make a stab at being heritage houses – the *Old Fish and Chipper* on Main Street, for example – and though there's little to see or do, it's a pleasant spot to spend the night. There are about half a dozen **motels** locally: the nicest is the *Similkameen* (☎499-5984), about 1km west of the centre in open country surrounded by lawns and orchards; doubles from $25. For the best of the **campgrounds**, press on 13km west on Hwy 3 to the *Lucky R* (May–Oct; ☎499-2065; $10–12.50), solitary and set amidst trees and lawns on the river.

## On to Princeton

West of Keremeos, Hwy 3 retraces the historic **Dewdney Trail**, a 468-kilometre mule track used in the 1860s to link Hope (p.494) with the Kootenay goldfields. Another of British Columbia's extremely picturesque patches of road, for much of the way it follows the ever-narrowing Similkameen Valley, backed by ranks of pines and white-topped mountains. To explore some of the backcountry off the highway, take the 21-kilometre gravel road (signed just west of Keremeos) south into the heart of **Cathedral Provincial Park**, a spectacular upland enclave with an unserviced campground and 32km of marked trails.

**HEDLEY**, an old gold-mining hamlet 25km west of Keremeos, is these days just a single street with great scenery and a couple of motels. Try the *Corona Motel and Campground* (April–Oct; ☎242-8302), with doubles from $35 and tent sites from $10. Beyond Hedley, off the highway, lies **Bromley Rock**, a lovely if oversanitised picnic stop looking down on the whitewater of the Similkameen River.

Lacklustre low hills ripple around **PRINCETON**'s dispersed collection of drab, rather jerry-built houses. The **motels** – of which there are plenty – group around a large and grim lumber mill on the east side of town, but you're better off hanging on for Hope, another 131km on. If circumstances dump you in town overnight, try the *Riverside Motel* (☎295-6232) on Thomas Street, three blocks north of the town centre, where individual log cabins start at $30. The **bus depot** is at the west end of things at the *Village Kitchen Restaurant*, not so far from the all but redundant **infocentre**, which is housed in an old Canadian Pacific rail wagon.

## Manning Provincial Park

One of the few parks in the Canada's Coast and Cascade ranges, **Manning Provincial Park** parcels up a typical assortment of mountain, lake and forest scenery about 60km south of Princeton and is conveniently bisected by Hwy 3. Even if you're just passing through it's an idea to walk at least one of the short **trails** off the road, the best of which is the flower-festooned Rhododendron Flats path at the park's western edge. The most popular drive within the park is the fifteen-kilometre side road to **Cascade Lookout**, a viewpoint over the Similkameen Valley and its amphitheatre of mountains; a gravel road carries on another 6km from here to **Blackwall Peak**, the starting point for the **Heather Trail** (10km one way), renowned for its swathes of summer wildflowers. Other manageable day hikes leave the south side of the main highway, the majority accessed from a rough road to Lightning Lake just west of the park visitor centre.

**Accommodation** at the *Manning Park Resort* (☎840-8836), on Hwy 3 almost exactly midway between Princeton and Hope, runs to cabins and chalets, but all these go quickly in summer; expect to pay between $55 and $80 for any rooms that are available. There are also several provincial **campgrounds** on and off the highway, the best on the road being *Hampton* and *Mule Deer*, 4km and 8km east of the visitor centre respectively ($10). The **park visitor centre**, 1km east of the resort (May–Sept 9am–8pm), is good for trail leaflets and has history and natural history exhibitions.

# The Okanagan

The vine- and orchard-covered hills and warm-water lakes of the **Okanagan** are in marked contrast to the rugged beauty of British Columbia's more mountainous interior, and have made the region not only Canada's most favoured fruit-growing area but also one of its most popular summer holiday destinations. However, unless you want rowdy beach life or specifically enjoy mixing it with Canadian and American families on their annual vacation, you'll probably want to ignore the area altogether, despite its high word-of-mouth reputation. Few things can be as disorientating as stumbling onto one of the brash towns of the Okanagan after lazing through BC's mountain emptiness. Three main centres – **Penticton**, **Kelowna** and **Vernon**, ranging from north to south along 100-kilometre **Okanagan Lake** – together contain the lion's share of the province's interior population, and all lay on an array of accommodation and mostly tacky attractions for the summer hordes.

On the plus side, the almost year-round Californian lushness that makes this "the land of beaches, peaches, sunshine and wine" means that, in the relative peace of **off-season**, you can begin to experience the region's potential charms: fruit trees in blossom, quiet lakeside villages and free wine tastings in local vineyards. Not only that, you can also expect room rates to be up to fifty percent less in off-season. Kelowna is the biggest and probably best overall base at any time of the year, but local **buses** link all the towns and *Greyhounds* ply Hwy 97 on their way between Osoyoos and Kamloops or Salmon Arm.

## Penticton

**PENTICTON** is a corruption of the Salish phrase *pen tak tin* – "a place to stay forever" – but this is not a sobriquet the most southerly of the Okanagan's big towns even remotely deserves. Its summer daily average of ten hours of sunshine ranks it higher than Honolulu, making tourism its biggest industry after fruit (this is "Peach City"). That, along with Penticton's proximity to Vancouver and the States, keeps prices well over the odds and ensures that the town and beaches are swarming with watersports jocks, cross-country travellers, RV skippers and lots of happy families. Off the beaches there's some festival or other playing virtually every day of the year to keep the punters entertained, the key ones being the spring-celebrating **Blossom Festival** in April and the **Peach Festival** at the end of July.

Most leisure pastimes in Penticton – water-orientated ones in particular – take place on or near Okanagan Lake, just ten blocks from the town centre. **Okanagan Beach** is the closest sand to downtown and is usually covered in oiled bodies (not to mention liberal amounts of clogging guano) for most of its one-kilometre stretch; **Skaha Beach**, 4km south of town on Skaha Lake, is a touch quieter and trendier; both close at midnight, and sleeping on them is virtually out of the question. If you don't want to crash out on the beaches, you can take your sun from a cruise on the lake aboard the *Casabella Princess* which departs from 45 E Lakeshore Drive by the *Delta Hotel* (call ☎493-5551 for times; $8.50).

If you're determined to sightsee, the **museum** at 785 Main St has a panoply of predictable Canadiana (Mon–Fri 10am–5pm; donation). Just off Main Street there's the **South Okanagan Art Gallery**, which often carries high-quality shows, and – it *would* have to be the "world's something" – also qualifies as the "world's first solar-powered art gallery" (Tues–Sun 10am–5pm). More tempting perhaps, and an ideal part of a day's stopover – possibly to fit in before a sprawl on the beach – is a trip to the **Casobello Wines Vineyard**, 2km south of town off Hwy 97 on Skaha Lake Road, which has tours and free tastings every half hour (July & Aug Mon–Fri 10am–4pm). Otherwise, Penticton's main diversions are that curse of Canadian tourist towns – the waterslides.

## Practicalities

Arriving by *Greyhound*, you'll pull into the **bus depot** just off Main Street between Robinson and Ellis streets (☎493-4101); Penticton is a major intersection of routes, with buses bound for Vancouver (5 daily), Kamloops (2 daily), Nelson and points east (2 daily), and Wenatchee/Spokane (WA) in the States (1 daily; change at Osoyoos). The downtown area is small and easy to negotiate, particularly after a visit to the big **info-centre** at 185 Lakeside Drive (daily 9am–5pm, longer in summer); if it's shut there's a big map and notice-board outside, plus smaller summer offices north and south of town on Hwy 97. All three concentrate on recreational pursuits, and dozens of specialist shops around town hire out equipment for every conceivable activity. For **bikes**, look up *Riverside Bike Rental* at 75 Riverside Drive on the west side of the lakefront (May–Sept daily).

Although Penticton boasts a brimful of **accommodation**, it doesn't make digging out a room in summer any easier. In high season it's best to head straight for the infocentre and ask for help, and if this fails there are so many **motels** you can easily walk from one to the next in the hope of striking lucky; most of the cheaper fall-backs line the messy southern approach to the town along Hwy 97. One of the best and more central choices is the *Ti-ke Shores Motel* on the lake at 914 Lakeshore Drive (☎492-8769), with luxurious doubles from $49 ($25 off-season). Still central, but cheaper, is the friendly *Peach Bowl Motel*, two blocks from the beach at 1078 Burnaby Ave (☎492-8946; doubles $35). Try also the *Kozy Guest House*, 1000 Lakeshore Drive (☎493-8400; doubles $40), or the *Three Gables Hotel*, 353 Main St (☎492-3933; doubles $50).

Most **campgrounds** have their full-up signs out continuously in summer, and you'll have trouble if you arrive without a reservation. The best and therefore busiest sites are along the lake, and the bulk of the second-rank spots near the highway on the southern approaches. Recommended are *South Beach Gardens*, 3815 Skaha Lake Rd (May–Oct; ☎492-0628; $15–20), or *Wright's Beach Camp*, south of town on Hwy 97 on Lake Skaha (May–Sept; ☎492-7120; $17–24).

Budget **eating** choices don't extend much beyond the fast-food joints and cafés bunched largely around Main Street: try *Taco Grande*, 452 Main St, for Mexican and cheap breakfasts; *Elite*, 340 Main St, the best overall for basic burgers, soup and salads; or *Theo's*, at 687 Main St, a friendly, crowded Greek place that does big portions. Somewhat pricier but ever popular is *Angelini's* across from the Skaha Centre on Skaha Lake Road, which also has a Greek emphasis. For something different and more upmarket, search out *Salty's Beach House*, 988 Lakeshore Dr, a restaurant that's eccentric in all departments – setting, service and menu – but delivers excellent food.

# Kelowna

If you want a summer suntan and cheek-by-jowl nightlife – neither of which you'd readily associate with the British Columbian interior – then **KELOWNA** ("grizzly bear" in the Salish dialect) – is probably the place to come. People had such a good time here in the summer of 1988 that the annual Kelowna Regatta turned into a full-blown and very un-Canadian riot in which the police were forced to wade in with truncheons and tear gas. The following year people from as far away as Vancouver responded to invitations to a showdown in similar vein, arriving with truckloads of rocks to hurl at the enemy; the main event has since been cancelled, but the beach and downtown bars are as busy as ever. That this modest city should have fostered such an urban-style melée isn't all that surprising. Compared to other interior towns, Kelowna (pop. 70,000) is a sprawling metropolis, and to the unsuspecting tourist its approaches come as an unpleasant surprise – particularly the appalling conglomeration of motels, garages and fast-food joints on Hwy 97 at the north end of town.

That said, the lakefront and beaches, though heavily developed, aren't too bad, and in off-season Kelowna can make a good couple of days' respite from mountains and forests. Main attractions are the public beach off **City Park**, a lovely green space that fronts downtown, and the strips along Lakeshore Road south of Kelowna's famed pontoon bridge, which tend to attract a younger, trendier crowd – **Rotary Beach** here is the windsurfers' hang-out, and **Boyce Gyro Park**, just north, is where the town's teenagers practise their preening and petting. Across the bridge and 2km up the lake's west bank, **Bear Creek Provincial Park** is a lovely spot with another great beach and campground, but it's also horrendously popular.

Kelowna owes its prosperity primarily to one man, Father Pandosy, a French priest who founded a mission here in 1859 and planted a couple of apple trees two years later. Much of Canada's **fruit** is now grown in the area – including virtually all the apricots, half the pears and plums, and thirty percent of the apples. The infocentre can point you to dozens of juice, fruit, food and forestry tours, but if you feel like sampling the more hedonistic fruits of Father Pandosy's labours, consider visiting one of the local **vineyards**, all of them known for their open-handed generosity with free samples after a tour of the premises. **Calona Wines** is Canada's second biggest winery, and it's just six blocks off Hwy 97 at 1125 Richter (summer daily 9am–4pm; tours every 30min), but the infocentre can provide a full run-down of smaller and more far-flung estates. All of them join together in early October to lay on the region's annual **wine festival**.

Getting away from Kelowna's crowds isn't easy, but the closest you come to shaking them off is by climbing **Knox Mountain**, the high knoll that overlooks the city to the north, just five minutes' drive (or thirty minutes' walk) from downtown. It offers lovely views over the lake and town, particularly at sunset, and there's a wooden observation tower to make the most of the panorama. RVs are kept out of the area by a barrier dropped at dusk, but if you took a sleeping bag up there – though not a tent – you might get away with an undisturbed night.

## Practicalities

The **bus terminal** is at the east end of town at 2366 Leckie Road on the corner of Harvey (Hwy 97), and sees off two buses daily to Calgary, Banff, Cache Creek and Kamloops respectively (☎860-3835). The **infocentre** (daily June–Aug 8am–8pm; Sept–May 9am–5pm), five blocks back from the lake at 544 Harvey, is full of all the information you could possibly need. To **rent a bike** go to *Sports Rent*, 3000 Pandosy St.

**Accommodation** can be a major headache in the height of summer unless you can get to one of the **motels** on northbound Hwy 97 early in the morning; you'll probably find a bed here, but in a neon- and traffic-infested area well away from downtown and the lake (prices drop the further out you go). Remarkably, there's only one downtown **hotel**, the perfectly placed and very comfortable *Willow Inn* at 235 Queensway (☎762-2122), with doubles at $45 – ring or book very early for summer vacancies, and don't be deterred by the adjoining bar which appears to be the headquarters of the Kelowna chapter of the Hell's Angels. The newly opened *Kelowna Backpackers Hostel*, 2343 Pandosy St (☎763-6024), slightly relieves the pressure on cheap rooms, but its downtown location means it fills up quickly; shared rooms are $10 each, doubles from $30.

If you're camping and want to stay close to the action, three **campgrounds** conveniently back onto Lakeshore Road: *Tiny Town* at Boyce Gyro Park (April–Oct; ☎762-6302; $15–20), and *Hiawatha* (year-round; ☎862-8222; $20–23) and *Lakeside* (year-round; ☎860-4072; $19–27) at Rotary Beach. Arrive early at Bear Creek Provincial Park to be sure of camping space (May–Sept; $14). Most of the other campgrounds are on the other side of the lake at Westbank, a left turn off Hwy 97 on Boucherie Road just over the pontoon bridge (probably too far out if you haven't got a car) – try *West Bay Beach* (March–Oct; ☎768-3004; $17.50–21).

Most **eating** places are crammed into the small downtown area. The variety is large, and a short walk should offer something to suit most tastes and budgets. Most travellers and young locals head for *Jonathan L Seagull* on Bernard Street, opposite the Paramount cinema, which has a relaxed bar atmosphere and live music most nights – usually a singer and guitar. Despite its slick cocktail-lounge ambience, *Earl's Hollywood on Top*, 211 Bernard Ave at the corner of Abbott (☎763-2777), is good for ribs, seafood and steaks; go early to get a table on the upstairs patio. For sheer value, however, *Poor Boys' Restaurant* at 450 Bernard St is unbeatable: portions are huge, the decor minimal, and prices absurdly low. At the other extreme, you could splurge on seafood at *Le Papillon*, 375 Leon Ave, one of the region's top restaurants (☎763-3833; closed Sun).

# Vernon

If you're continuing north from Kelowna, be sure to take the minor road on the western shore of Okanagan Lake – a quiet detour that offers something of the beauty for which the area is frequently praised but which is pretty hard to find amongst the commercialism of towns to the south. From the road, weaving in and out of woods and small bays, the lake looks enchanting in the right light. The shore is often steep and there are few places to get down to the water – though you might squeeze a tent between the trees for some unofficial camping.

The beach scene is less frenetic in **VERNON** than elsewhere in the Okanagan. Located at the junction of highways 6 and 97 near the northern edge of Okanagan Lake, the town attracts fewer of the bucket-and-spade brigade, though the emphasis on fruit and the great outdoors is as strong as ever, and the main highway through town is bumper to bumper with motels, fast-food outlets and ever more garish neon entreaties. On the whole you'll find it easier to find a place to stay here than in Kelowna – but there are fewer reasons for wanting to do so.

Downtown Vernon centres on 32nd Avenue (Hwy 97) and leaves a far more gracious impression than the town's outskirts by virtue of its elegant tree-lined streets and 500 listed buildings. The locals are an amenable and cosmopolitan bunch made up of British, Germans, Chinese and Salish, plus an abnormally large number of Jehovah's Witnesses, whose churches seem to have a monopoly on religious observance in the town. The local **museum**, by the clock tower at 3009 32nd Ave, does the usual job on local history (Mon–Sat 10am–5.30pm; free). At the southern entrance to town, **Polson Park** makes a green sanctuary from the crowds, but for beaches you have to head further afield to **Kalamalka Beach** on Kalamalka Lake, south of Vernon, or to **Kin Beach** on Okanagan Lake west on Okanagan Landing Road – both places with adjoining campgrounds.

Other outdoor recreation (but not camping) is on hand at **Silver Star Recreation Area**, a steep 22-kilometre drive to the northeast on 48th Avenue off Hwy 97, where in summer a **ski lift** (July–Sept daily 10am–4pm; $5) trundles to the top of Silver Star Mountain (1915m) for wide views and meadow-walking opportunities; the most used trail wends from the summit back to the base area. Three kilometres from the *Silver Star* complex are the **Cedar Springs Public Hot Springs** (daily noon–11pm; $5).

## Practicalities

Vernon's **infocentre** is at 3700 33rd Street, one block west of Hwy 97 (daily June–Aug 8am–8pm; Sept–May 9am–5pm), along with seasonal offices north and south of town on the main highway. The **Greyhound station** is on the corner of 30th Street and 31st Avenue (☎545-0527). Local motels may well have **rooms** when nearby towns are full, and if your preference is for cheap but dingy head first for the central *National Hotel*, 2922-30th Ave (☎545-0731), where doubles start at $26. The *Polson Park Motel* (☎549-

2231), opposite the eponymous park on 24th Avenue, has nicer doubles from $28. The more upmarket *Schell Motel*, 35th St and 30th Ave (☎545-1351; doubles from $35), tempts clients with a pool and sauna. **Campgrounds** near town all get busy, and you may have to trek along the lakeshore for some way to strike lucky; try *Dutch's Tent and Trailer Court* (May–Sept; ☎545-1023; $15) at 15408 Kalamalka Rd, 3km south of Vernon near Kalamalka Beach. Much more rural are the pitches at *Cedar Falls Campground* (May–Sept; ☎545-2888; $12) near Cedar Springs Public Hot Springs (see previous page), and at Ellison Provincial Park, 25km off to the southwest on Okanagan Lake.

In the **food** department, there's plenty of cosmopolitan choice, especially amongst the many cafés and sandwich places. Try *Jackie's*, a local favourite on 30th Avenue at 34th Street, or *Little Hobo* on 30th Avenue at 31st Street – or for something more special, throw money away at Vernon's top restaurant, *Café Campeache*, 3202-31st Ave (☎542-1518; closed Sun & Mon).

## Highway 97: Vernon to Westwold

Passing through landscapes of edenic clarity, **Highway 97** is a far better exit from (or entrance to) the Okanagan than the dreary road to Salmon Arm (see opposite). The grass-green meadows, grazing cattle and low wooded hills here are the sort of scenery pioneers must have dreamed of; most of the little hamlets en route make charming spots to stay, and if you have time and transport any number of minor roads lead off to small lakes, each with modest recreational facilities.

Twelve kilometres north of Vernon, near the junction with the west-side Okanagan Lake road, stands the **O'Keefe Ranch**, a collection of early pioneer buildings and a tidy little museum that's well worth a half-hour's pause (May–Oct daily 9am–5pm; extended hours July & Aug; $4). In addition to a proficient summary of nineteenth-century frontier life, the museum contains an interesting section on Native Canadians' role in the two world wars, when some 25 percent of eligible men immediately volunteered for service – a tour of duty that did little to resolve their national dilemma, which the museum sums up pithily with the observation that they belong to that "unhappy group who lost the old but are unable to obtain the new". Outside, a complete period street includes a persuasively detailed general store where you can buy oddments from staff in old-time dress – a twee conceit, but one that fails to take the edge off the place's surprisingly successful evocation of an era. You feel the past most strongly in the church and graveyard, where the lovely building and its poignant handful of graves – three generations of O'Keefes, who first settled here in 1867 – capture the isolation and closeknit hardship of pioneer life. All the grandchildren died within a few years of each other in the 1980s.

The first settlement along the way, **FALKLAND** is a tidy, unassuming place whose two **motels** blend easily into its rustic village atmosphere. The nicer of the pair is the *Highland* (☎379-2249), with doubles at $32, but you might also drop into the infant info-centre (summer only) for lists of local bed and breakfasts. There are also a couple of quiet campgrounds. Country lanes lead north and east from here to **Bolean Lake** (10km), served by a small lodge and campground (May–Oct; no phone; rooms $25, tents $10); to **Pillar Lake** (13km) and the *Pillar Lake Resort* (May–Oct; ☎379-2623), which provides cabins from $28 to $60 and campsites from $12; and to **Pinaus Lake** (10km) and its adjacent campground (April–Oct; no phone; $12).

**WESTWOLD**, 13km beyond, is a dispersed ranching community of clean, old wooden houses and large pastures that present a picture of almost idyllic rural life. Beyond it lies **Monte Lake**, served by the excellent *Heritage Campground and RV Park* (April–Oct; ☎375-2478; $10) and the equally well-tended and unspoilt public campground at **Monte Lake Provincial Park**. Both places make good spots to overnight before hitting the more uncompromising scenery beyond MONTE CREEK, where Hwy 97 meets the Trans-Canada Highway.

# Salmon Arm and the Shuswap

Given the variety of routes across southern BC there's no knowing quite when you'll find yourself in **SALMON ARM**, but that's not something that need concern you in planning an itinerary because the town – the largest of the bland resorts spread along Shuswap Lake's 1000km of navigable waterways – has little to recommend it other than sublime views across an arm of the lake. It's a much smaller place than its heavy bold label on most maps would suggest – and you know you're in trouble when you see signs proclaiming it "Home of the World Famous Non-Irrigated Macintosh Apple". The town is oddly dispersed and has a scrappy and haphazard appearance, but if you're driving it makes a natural break along one of the Trans-Canada's more monotonous stretches. To get anything out of it you'll have to pull off the main drag, which is formed by the Trans-Canada itself, and head one block south to the lakeside which, barring a huge sawmill and plywood works, is a pleasant open area with a view of distant hazy hills.

The lake and the surrounding region take their name from the Shuswap natives, the northernmost of the great Salishan family and the largest single tribe in British Columbia. The name of the town harks back to a time when it was possible to spear salmon straight from the lake, and fish were so plentiful that they were shovelled onto the land as fertiliser. Shuswap still provides an important sanctuary for hatched salmon fry before they make their long journey down the Thompson and Fraser rivers to the sea; the abundance of such lakes, together with ideal water temperatures, free-flowing, well-oxygenated and silt-free tributaries, and plenty of sand and gravel beds for egg-laying, make the Fraser River system the continent's greatest salmon habitat.

One of the few reasons you might make a special journey to the Salmon Arm area is to watch the huge migrations of **spawning salmon** that take place around October. Anything up to two million fish brave the run from the Pacific up to their birthplace in the Adams River – one of the most famous spawning grounds in the province – which during the peak week of the run attracts around 250,000 visitors. This short stretch of river is protected by **Roderick Haig-Brown Provincial Park**, reached from Salmon Arm by driving 46km west on the Trans-Canada to SQUILAX and then 5km north on a side road. If you're thinking of dangling a line, pick up the *Fishing in Shuswap* leaflet from the infocentre in Salmon Arm, and don't forget to pick up a licence at the same time.

The best chance of a leg-stretch around here is at **Herald Provincial Park** on the shore opposite Salmon Arm (turn right off Hwy 1 at TAPPEN, 6km west of town). There's good swimming from a sandy beach, a provincial **campground**, and a lovely fifteen-minute walk culminating at Margaret Falls.

## Practicalities

*Greyhound* **buses** serve Salmon Arm from Vancouver and Calgary (5 daily in each direction) and Kelowna, Vernon and Penticton (2 daily). The bus terminal is at the West Village Mall on Hwy 1, and the infocentre (year-round Mon–Sat 8.30am–5.30pm) is nearby at 70 Hudson Avenue NE.

The most convenient of Salmon Arm's many **motels** is the *Village Motel* (☎832-3955), plumb in the town centre with doubles from $30 to $48. Of several **campgrounds**, the obvious first choice is the *Salmon Arm KOA*, 3km east of town in a big wooded site, whose excellent facilities include a heated swimming pool (May–Oct; ☎832-6489; $16–20). For beds or tent space, the *Salmon River Motel and Campground*, 1km west of downtown at 90-40th St (year-round; ☎832-3065), is also good; rooms are $43, tent pitches $12. For posh **food**, locals splash out at the *Orchard House* on 22nd Street on the east side of town. For cheaper soup, salads and sandwiches, try the central *Eatery* on Alexander Street or the *Brass Kettle* out west on the Trans-Canada.

### SALMON

At times it seems impossible to escape the **salmon** in British Columbia. Whether it's on restaurant menus, in rivers, or in the photographs of grinning fishermen clutching their catch, the fish is almost as much a symbol of the region as its mountains and forests. Five different species inhabit the rivers and lakes of western Canada: **pink, coho, chum, chinook** and, most important of all, the **sockeye**.

Though they start and finish their lives in fresh water, salmon spend about four years in the open sea between times. Mature male and female fish make their epic migrations from the Pacific to **spawn** in the BC rivers of their birth between June and November, swimming about 30km a day; some chinook travel over 1400km up the Fraser beyond Prince George, which means almost fifty days' continuous swimming upstream. Though the female lays as many as 4000 eggs, only about six percent of the offspring survive: on the Adams River near Salmon Arm, for example, it's estimated that of 4 billion sockeye eggs laid in a typical year, 1 billion survive to become fry (hatched fish about three-quarters of an inch long), of which 75 percent are eaten by predators before becoming smolts (year-old fish), and only five percent of these then make it to the ocean. In effect each pair of spawners produces about ten mature fish; of these, eight are caught by commercial fisheries and only two return to reproduce.

These are returns which clearly put the salmon's survival and British Columbia's lucrative **fishing industry** on a knife-edge. Caught, canned and exported, salmon accounts for two thirds of BC's $1 billion annual revenues from fishing – the largest of any Canadian province, and its third-ranking money-earner after forestry and energy products. Commercial fishing suffered its first setback in British Columbia as long ago as 1913, when large rock slides at Hell's Gate in the Fraser Canyon disrupted many of the spawning runs. Although fish runs were painstakingly constructed to bypass the slides, new pressures have subsequently been heaped on the salmon by mining, logging, urban and agricultural development, and the dumping of industrial and municipal wastes. An increasingly important line of defence, **hatcheries** have been built on rivers on the mainland and Vancouver Island to increase the percentage of eggs and fry that successfully mature. Meanwhile overfishing, as the above figures suggest, remains a major concern, particularly as the **drift nets** of Japanese and Korean fleets (intended for neon squid) over the past decade have taken numerous non-target species, including BC and Yukon salmon. Under intense lobbying from Canada and the US, both nations have agreed to a moratorium on large-scale drift nets from June 30, 1992.

For a decidedly alternative form of accommodation head east along the Trans-Canada to SICAMOUS, a pleasant but very busy waterfront village which, though crammed with motels and campgrounds, is better known for its many **houseboats**. A few rent by the night, but most tend to be let weekly by about half a dozen local agencies scattered around the village.

# Kamloops

Almost any trip in southern British Columbia brings you sooner or later to **KAMLOOPS**, a town which has been a transport centre from time immemorial – its name derives from the Shuswap word for "meeting of the rivers" – and which today marks the meeting point of the Trans-Canada and Yellowhead (South) highways, the country's principle transcontinental roads, as well as the junction of the Canadian Pacific and Canadian National railways. The largest interior town in southern British Columbia (pop. 75,000), it's a fairly unobjectionable place, except when the wind blows from the uptown sawmills – when it smells as if something's been dead for a week – but there's no need to hop off a bus or train to spend any time here. If you're camping or driving, however, it makes a convenient provisions stop, especially if you're heading north on Hwy 5 or south on the Coquihalla Highway, neither of which has much in the way of facilities.

Kamloops is determinedly functional and not a place to spend a happy day wandering, but all the same the **Kamloops Museum** (July–Sept Tues–Sat 10am–9pm, Oct–June 10am–4pm; free) is one of the more interesting provincial offerings, with illuminating archive photographs – especially the one of the railway running down the centre of the main street – artefacts, bric-a-brac, period set pieces and an especially well done section on the Shuswap Indians. The stuffed-animal display, without which no BC museum is complete, has a fascinating little piece on the life cycle of the tick presented without any noticeable irony. For a more complete picture of local native history and traditions, call at the **Secwepemec Museum**, just over the bridge on Hwy 5 (Mon–Fri 8.30am–4.30pm; donation).

Perhaps the most interesting thing about Kamloops is its surroundings, dominated by strange, bare-earthed brown hills that locals like to say represent the northernmost point of the Mohave Desert. There's no doubting the almost surreal touches of near-desert, which are particularly marked in the bare rock and clay outcrops above the bilious waters of the Thompson River and in the bleached scrub and failing stands of pines that spot the barren hills. Most scenic diversions lie a short drive out of town, and the infocentre has full details of every last local bolthole, with a special bias towards the 200 or so trout-stuffed lakes that dot the hinterland. The nearest and most popular on a hot summer's day is **Paul Lake Provincial Park**, 17km northeast of town on a good paved road, with swimming and a provincial campground.

## Practicalities

The **infocentre** is a little out of downtown on 10th Avenue – to reach it, follow River Street immediately next to the main bridge over the Thompson River (June–Sept daily 8am–8pm, Oct–May Mon–Fri 9am–5pm). They have full accommodation and recreational details for the town and much of the province, and a particularly useful book of bed and breakfasts. They're also keen to emphasise that Kamloops has *no fort*, this for some reason being something most people come expecting to see.

The **Greyhound terminal** (☎374-1212) is in the Aberdeen Mall, off Hwy 1 a good 6km west of the centre, and is a crucial interchange for buses to all parts of the province; the #3 local bus into town leaves from immediately outside. Kamloops is also served by three weekly **trains** in each direction to Edmonton (via Jasper) and Vancouver. The *VIA rail* office is at 95 3rd Avenue, behind Landsdowne Street, but is open only on days trains are running (☎372-5858).

Kamloops's huge volume of accommodation is aimed fair and square at the motorist and consists of thick clusters of **motels**, most of which blanket the town's eastern margins on Hwy 1 (called "Valleyview" in the *BC Accommodation Guide*) or out on Columbia Street West. The *Thrift Inn* (☎374-2488) is the cheapest of all, with doubles from $30, but it's about the last building on eastbound Hwy 1 out of town. You pay a premium for central beds, most of which are on Columbia Street: the *Whistler Inn Apartment Hotel* is about as central as you can get, at 375 5th Ave (☎828-1322), with doubles from $30 to $55; or try the *Fountain Motel*, 506 Columbia (☎374-4451), with doubles at $48. There's also a clutch of places around the bus terminal, in case you arrive late and have no need to drop into town.

The nearest **campground** is the *Silver Sage Tent and Trailer Park* at 771 East Athabasca (☎372-9644; $12–16), but if you've got a car aim for the far more scenic facilities at Paul Lake Provincial Park (see above).

Snack **food** is cheap and served in generous portions at the popular *Steiger's Swiss Café*, 359 Victoria St, which really is run by Swiss and does good muesli, cappuccino (a change from the usual watery rubbish), lots of sticky buns, and excellent bread. If you're on a rock-bottom budget, head for *Barnsey's*, "home of the 50¢ cup of coffee": it's at the back of *Bob's PX Store* at 246 Victoria St. For supermarket stock-ups, the *Safeway* is on the corner of Seymour and 5th Avenue. If you're splashing out on a proper meal, on the other hand, the best restaurant is the well-known *Fat Mel's* on Kamloops Square off Seymour and 3rd Avenue – despite some dubiously silly signs on the door, it's a good mix of Tex-Mex, Cajun and Italian food, and the atmosphere's lively and friendly.

# Highway 5: Clearwater and Wells Gray Park

Northbound **Highway 5** (here known as the Yellowhead South Highway) heads upstream along the broad North Thompson River as it courses through high hills and rolling pasture between Kamloops and **Clearwater**, and beyond, in one of the most astounding road routes in the country, follows the river as it carves through the Monashee Mountains from its source near VALEMOUNT, finally meeting the main Yellowhead Highway (Hwy 16) at TETE JAUNE CACHE, a total distance of 338km. The entire latter half of the journey is spent side-stepping the immense **Wells Gray Provincial Park**, one of the finest protected areas in British Columbia.

*Greyhound* **buses** cover the route on their run between Kamloops and Prince George via Clearwater (2 daily in each direction), as do *VIA* **trains**, which connect Kamloops with Jasper via Clearwater (3 weekly). To get into Wells Gray without your own transport, however, you'd have to hitch from Clearwater up the 63-kilometre main access road – a feasible proposition at the height of summer, but highly unlikely at any other time. Note that there are other, far less travelled gravel roads into other sectors of the park from BLUE RIVER, 112 km north of Clearwater on Hwy 5, and from 100 MILE HOUSE, on Hwy 97 west of the park.

## Clearwater

**CLEARWATER** is a dispersed farming community that's invisible from Hwy 5, and unless you arrive by rail there's no need to drop down to it at all. Everything you need apart from the odd shop is on or just off the junction between the highway and the slip road to the village, including the **bus stop** and the excellent **infocentre** (daily June–Aug 8am–8pm; Sept–May 9am–5pm), a model of the genre which has immensely useful information on all aspects of Wells Gray Provincial Park. If you're planning on staying locally or doing any walking or canoeing, take time to flick through the reference books devoted to accommodation, trails and paddling routes.

Clearwater is the only realistic place to stay along Hwy 5 if you're planning on doing Wells Gray. By far the best prospect, thanks to its lovely views over Dutch Lake, is *Jasper Way Inn* (☎674-3345), 1km off the highway to the west and well signed from the infocentre; doubles, some with cooking facilities, cost $45 to $50. If it's full try the big *Wells Gray Inn* (☎674-2214), close by on the main road; the $60 doubles here are more comfortable, but lack the view. The latter is virtually the only place to **eat** locally. Three **campgrounds** lie within walking distance of the infocentre: the best – again, on the lake – is the *Dutch Lake Resort* (May–Oct; ☎674-3351; $12–15).

## Wells Gray Provincial Park

**Wells Gray Provincial Park** is the equal of any of the Rocky Mountain national parks to the east – it's so untamed that many of its peaks remain unclimbed and unnamed. Wildlife sightings are common throughout the park – especially if you tramp some of the wilder trails, where encounters with black bears, grizzlies and mountain goats are a possibility, not to mention glimpses of smaller mammals such as timber wolves, coyotes, weasels, martens, minks, wolverines and beavers.

With some 250km of maintained trails and dozens of other lesser routes, the park is superb for **hiking**. Short walks and day hikes from the park access road are described below, but serious backpackers can easily spend a week or more tramping the Murtle River (14km) and Kostal Lake (26km) trails, among others. Make sure to pick up a free *BC Parks* map-pamphlet at the Clearwater infocentre, and if you're thinking of doing any backcountry exploration you'll want to invest in their more detailed topo maps and guides. **Cross-country skiing** is also possible, but there are only a few groomed routes in the park: details from the infocentre.

Another of the park's big attractions is **canoeing** on Clearwater and Azure lakes, which can be linked with a short portage to make a 100-plus-kilometre dream trip for paddlers; you can rent canoes for long- or short-haul trips from *Clearwater Lake Tours* (☎674-3052). Whitewater rafting down the Clearwater River is also popular, and half-day to full-week tours can be arranged through the Clearwater infocentre or the two accommodation options below. Several local operators run shorter commercial boat trips around Clearwater Lake, as well as full-scale **tours** featuring horse riding, camping, trekking, fishing, boating, even float-plane excursions around the park – the Clearwater infocentre has the inside story on all of these.

The only indoor **accommodation** in or near the park is at the *Wells Gray Ranch* (May–Oct; ☎674-2792) just before the park entrance, which offers four cabins at $60 a night, and at the slightly larger but equally lonely *Helmcken Falls Lodge* (Jan–March & May–Oct; ☎674-3657) at the entrance itself, which offers similar facilities at about the same price. You'll be lucky to find vacancies in summer, however. Both of these also have a few pitches for tents, but there's far better roadside **camping** along the park access road at Spahats Creek and in the park at Dawson Falls (just 10 pitches) and Clearwater Lake (35 pitches) – these last two fill up promptly in summer, however. Many backpackers' campsites dot the shores of the park's major lakes; *Clearwater Lake Tours* operates a water-taxi service which can drop you off at any site on Clearwater Lake and pick you up at a pre-arranged time.

## Sights and hikes along the access road

Even if you're not geared up for the backcountry, the access road to the park from Clearwater opens up a medley of waterfalls, walks and viewpoints that make a day or more's detour extremely worthwhile. It's paved for the first 30km to the park boundary, but the remaining 33km to Clearwater Lake are gravel.

About 8km north of Clearwater, a short walk from the car park at **Spahats Creek Provincial Park** brings you to 61-metre Spahats Falls, the first of several mighty cascades along this route. You can watch the waters crashing down through layers of pinky-red volcanic rock from a pair of observation platforms, which also provide an impressive and unexpected view of the Clearwater Valley way down below. A few hundred metres further up the road, a fifteen-kilometre gravel lane peels off into the **Wells Gray Recreation Area**; a single trail from the end of the road strikes off into alpine meadows, feeding four shorter day trails into an area particularly known for its bears. This is also the site of a juvenile correction centre, which must rank as possibly the most beautiful but godforsaken spot to do time in North America. About 15km further up the main access road, a second four-wheel-drive track branches east to reach the trailhead for **Battle Mountain** (2369m; 19km), with the option of several shorter hikes like the Mount Philip Trail (5km) en route.

**Green Mountain Lookout**, reached by a rough, winding road to the left just after the park entrance, offers one of the most enormous roadside panoramas in British Columbia, and it's a sight that will help you grasp the sheer extent of the Canadian wilderness: as far as you can see, there's nothing but an almighty emptiness of primal forest and mountains. Various landscape features are picked out on plaques, and the immediate area is a likely place to spot moose.

Next essential stop is **Dawson Falls**, a broad, powerful cascade (91m wide and 18m high) just five minutes' walk from the road – signed "Viewpoint". Beyond, the road crosses an ugly iron bridge and shortly after meets the start of the **Murtle River Trail** (14km one way), a particularly good walk if you want more spectacular waterfalls.

Immediately afterwards, a dead-end side road is signed to **Helmcken Falls**, the park's undisputed highlight. They're heavily visited, and it's not unknown for wedding parties to come up here to get dramatic matrimonial photos backed by the luminous arc of water plunging into a black, carved bowl fringed with vivid carpets of lichen and splintered trees, the whole ensemble framed by huge plumes of spray wafting up on all sides. At 137m, the falls are two and a half times the height of Niagara – or, in the infoboards' incongruous comparison, approximately the same height as the Vancouver skyline.

Continuing north, the park access road rejoins the jade-green Clearwater River, passing tastefully engineered picnic spots and short trails that wend down to the bank for close-up views of one of the province's best whitewater rafting stretches. The last sight before the end of the road is **Ray Farm**, home to John Bunyon Ray, who in 1912 was the first man to homestead this area. Though it's not much to look at, the farm offers a sobering insight into the pioneer mentality – Ray's struggle to scrape a living and raise a family in this harsh environment beggars belief – and the wooden shacks are scattered in picturesque ruin in a lovely, lush clearing. The park road ends at **Clearwater Lake**, where there are a couple of boat launches, a provincial campground and a series of short trails clearly marked from the roadhead.

# Kamloops to Vancouver

Two major routes connect Kamloops and Vancouver. These days most cars, buses and anyone in any sort of hurry take the **Coquihalla Highway** (Hwy 5), a four-lane super-highway opened in 1987 that has lopped hours off the time it takes to get across British Columbia. The scenery is unexceptional in the early going, dominated by grazing land and endless lines of arid, half-wooded hills, but things look up considerably after Coquihalla Pass (1244m), when forests, mountains and crashing rivers make a dramatic reappearance – compromised somewhat by old mines, clearcuts and recent road-building scars. There's only a single exit, at the supremely missable town of MERRITT, and literally no services for the entire 182km from Kamloops to Hope, where the Coquihalla joins the Trans-Canada for the home stretch into Vancouver. Come stocked up with petrol and food, and be prepared to pay a toll (about $12) at the top of the pass – a wind- and snow-whipped spot that must offer amongst the loneliest employment opportunities in the province.

The older, slower (and more scenic) route to Vancouver is on the **Trans-Canada Highway** or **VIA rail**, which both follow a more meandering course along the Thompson River and then the lower reaches of the Fraser River. The remainder of this section details this route.

## Cache Creek

Heading west out of Kamloops, the Trans-Canada shadows Kamloops Lake and churns sluggishly through a broad, arid valley of scrub and semi-derelict irrigation schemes that do little to soften the rock-strewn bare hills. Beyond the end of the lake the high-way makes a brief detour from the Thompson Valley to **CACHE CREEK**, which has a reputation as a hitch-hiker's black hole and indeed is the sort of sleepy place you could get stuck in for days. Locals also say it didn't help that an escaped child murderer,

Charles Olsen, was recaptured nearby in 1985 – since when they've been understandably wary of picking up strangers. The town's name is accounted for by a variety of legends in a similar vein, the most romantic version concerning a couple of prospectors who buried a hoard of gold and never returned to pick it up. Sadly, it's likelier to derive from early trappers' more prosaic habit of leaving a cache of supplies at points on a trail to be used later.

Cache Creek is known as the "Arizona of Canada" for its baking summer climate, which settles a heat-wasted somnolence on its dusty streets. The parched, windswept mountains roundabout are anomalous volcanic intrusions in the regional geology, producing a legacy of hard rock and semi-precious stones – including jade – that attract climbers and rockhounds. There's not much else to do here, but for local insights visit the **infocentre** on the northwest side of town near the main road junction (summer 9am–6pm). If you're stranded or struck by the hitch-hikers' curse, there are about half a dozen **motels**, of which the best is the bizarrely built *Castle Inn* (☎457-9547), with doubles from $40 to $48. The nearest **campground** is the *Brookside* (May–Oct; ☎457-6633; $10), east of town on the main highway.

# The Fraser Canyon

Veering south from Cache Creek, the Trans-Canada resumes its run down the Thompson Valley to LYTTON, where it joins the Fraser River, squeezed here by the high ridges of the Cascade and Coast ranges into one of British Columbia's grandest waterways. Though it's now a clear-cut transport corridor – the Canadian Pacific Railway also passes this way – the **Fraser Canyon** was long regarded as impassable; to negotiate it, the Trans-Canada is forced to push through tunnels, hug the Fraser's banks, and at times cling perilously to rock ledges hundreds of metres above the swirling waters.

The river is named after **Simon Fraser**, one of Canada's remarkable early explorers, who as an employee of the North West Company travelled its entire 1300-kilometre length in 1808 under the mistaken impression he was following the Columbia. "We had to pass where no man should venture", he wrote, and made most of the journey on foot guided by local natives, pushing forward using ladders, ropes and improvised platforms to bypass rapids too treacherous to breach by boat. Few people, needless to say, felt the need to follow Fraser's example until the discovery of **gold** near Yale in 1858; prospectors promptly waded in and panned every tributary of the lower Fraser until new strikes tempted them north to the Cariboo.

BOSTON BAR, 45km south of Lytton, boasts about four motels and is also a centre for **whitewater** raft trips down the Fraser as far as Yale. Various companies run several trips a week from May to August; contact *Frontier River Adventure* for details (☎867-9244). Ten kilometres south of Boston Bar is the famous **Hell's Gate**, where – in a gorge almost 180m deep – the huge swell of the Fraser is squeezed into a 38-metre channel of foaming water that crashes through the rocks with awe-inspiring ferocity. The water here is up to 60m deep and as fast-flowing (8m a second) as any you're likely to see, but to get down to the river there's a certain amount of resort-like commercialism to negotiate and an "Air-Tram" to pay for (March–Oct daily; $8). Close by there are also displays on the various provisions made to help migrating salmon complete their journeys, which have been interrrupted over the years by the coming of the road and railway beside the Fraser. The river is one of the key runs for Pacific salmon, and every summer and autumn they fill the river as they head for tributaries and upstream lakes to spawn (see p.488).

YALE, 20km south of the rapids, closes the teeth of the canyon with a ring of plunging cliffs. Sitting at the river's navigable limit, it was once the largest city in North

America west of Chicago and north of San Francisco: during the 1858 gold rush its population mushroomed to over 20,000, a growth only tempered by the end of the boom and the completion of the Canadian Pacific. Today it's a small lumber town of about 250, though a visit to the **Yale Museum** on Douglas Street (summer daily 9am–6pm) offers an exhaustive account of the town's golden age. The **infocentre** is also on Douglas. For **rooms** you can't do much better than *Fort Yale Motel* (☎863-2216), with doubles from $30.

# Hope

Reputedly christened by prospectors with a grounding in Dante, **HOPE** – as in "Abandon all hope . . ." – is a pleasant mountain-ringed town and the last port of call before all scenic splendour is abandoned in the flat run of meadows and small towns en route for Vancouver. It's also achieved a certain fame as the town wasted in spectacular fashion by Sylvester Stallone at the end of *First Blood*, the first Rambo movie. Despite the number of roads that converge here – the Trans-Canada, Hwy 3 and the Coquihalla – it remains a remarkably unspoilt stopover.

The **infocentre** (daily 9am–5pm, 8am–8pm in summer) is the building next to the artfully dumped pile of antique farm machinery at 919 Water Avenue The town **museum** is in the same building, and offers the usual hand-me-downs of Hope's erstwhile old-timers. Across the road, the lovely view across the Fraser as it funnels out of the mountains is one of the town's best moments. Fishing, canoeing, even gold-panning are all popular time-wasters around the hundreds of local lakes, rivers and creeks, details of which are available from the infocentre, which also prints a summary of local hikes. Of these, the **Rotary Trail** (3km) to the confluence of the Fraser and Coquihalla rivers is popular, as is the more demanding clamber over gravel paths to the top of **Thacker Mountain** (5km). Another walking expedition worth pursuing is the dark jaunt through the **tunnels** of the abandoned Vancouver–Nelson railway, reached by a short trail from the **Coquihalla Canyon Provincial Park**, 6km northeast of town off Coquihalla Highway. This was one of the backcountry locations used during the filming of *First Blood*, and offers spectacular views over the cliffs and huge sandbars of the Coquihalla Gorge. **Kawkawa Lake Provincial Park**, 3km northeast of Hope off Hwy 3, is another popular mountain retreat, endowed with plenty of hiking, relaxing and swimming opportunities.

### Practicalities

Most of what happens in Hope happens on its single main street, Water Avenue. The *Greyhound* **bus terminal** is here, a critical juncture if you're on the bus because you'll have to transfer depending on whether you're going west to Vancouver, north to Kamloops or east to Penticton and the Okanagan. Cheap **motels** proliferate along Hwy 3 as you leave town heading east, and though most are much of a muchness, the *Flamingo* (☎869-9610), last on the strip, has a nice piney setting with doubles from $25. Closer in on the same road, the *Heritage* (☎869-7166), a lovely grey-wood building smothered in flowers, is also excellent, but slightly more expensive with doubles from $35 to $48. **Campgrounds**, too, are numerous, but most are some way from downtown. The municipal site is at *Coquihalla Park* (year-round; ☎869-5671; $10), off Hwy 3 and reached via 7th Avenue. The top-of-the pile *KOA Campground* is 5km west of town (March–Oct; ☎869-9857; $15–20).

**Food** facilities and late-night entertainment are extremely limited in what is, despite Vancouver's proximity, still a small-time Canadian town. For snacks try the bakery on the main street, or the rock-bottom café in the *Greyhound* station. For more ambitious fare try the *Hope Hotel* and *Lee's Kettle Valley Restaurant*, both on Wallace Street.

# VANCOUVER

**VANCOUVER** is rightly preceded by a reputation as one of the world's most beautiful and laid-back cities. Cradled between the ocean and snow-capped mountains, its dazzling downtown district fills a narrow peninsula bounded by Burrard Inlet to the north, English Bay to the west and False Creek to the south, with greater Vancouver sprawling south to the Fraser River. Edged around its idyllic waterfront are fine beaches, a dynamic port and a magnificent swathe of parkland, not to mention the mirror-fronted ranks of skyscrapers that look across Burrard Inlet to the residential districts of North and West Vancouver. Beyond these comfortable suburbs, the Coast Mountains rise in steep, forested slopes to form a dramatic counterpoint to the downtown skyline – and the most stunning of the city's many outdoor playgrounds.

The city's 1.3 million residents exploit their spectacular natural setting to the hilt. Whether it's sailing, swimming, fishing, hiking, skiing, golf or tennis, locals barely have to move to indulge in a plethora of **recreational** whims. Summer and winter the city oozes hedonism and healthy living, typically West Coast obsessions that spill over into its sophisticated **arts and culture**. Vancouver claims a world-class museum and symphony orchestra, as well as opera, theatre and dance companies at the cutting edge of contemporary arts. Festivals proliferate throughout its mild, if occasionally rain-soaked summer, and numerous music venues provide a hotbed for up-and-coming rock bands and a burgeoning jazz scene.

Vancouver is not all pleasure, however. Business continues apace in Canada's third largest and fastest-growing city, much of its prosperity stemming from a **port** so laden with the raw materials of the Canadian interior – lumber, wheat, minerals – that it now outranks New York as North America's largest port, and handles more dry tonnage than the West Coast ports of Seattle, Tacoma, Portland, San Francisco and San Diego put together. The port in turn owes its prominence to Vancouver's much-trumpeted position as a **gateway to the Far East**, and its increasingly pivotal role in the new global market of the Pacific Rim. This lucrative realignment is strengthened by a two-way flow in traffic: in the past decade Vancouver has been inundated with Hong Kong Chinese (the so-called "yacht people"), an influx which has pushed up property prices and strained the city's reputation as an ethnically integrated metropolis.

Much of the new immigration has focused on Vancouver's extraordinary **Chinatown**, just one of a number of ethnic enclaves – Italian, Greek, Indian and Japanese in particular – which lend the city a refreshingly gritty quality that belies its sleek, modern reputation. So too do the city's semi-derelict areas, whose worldly low-life characters seem at odds with the glitzy lifestyles pursued in the lush residential neighbourhoods. Low rents and Vancouver's cosmopolitan young have also nurtured an unexpected **counterculture**, distinguished by varied restaurants, secondhand shops, avant-garde galleries and one-off clubs and bars – spots where you'll probably have more fun than in many a Canadian city.

## A brief history of Vancouver

**Coast Salish** natives inhabited about ten villages on the shores of Burrard Inlet before the coming of white people. A highly developed culture, they were skilled carpenters, canoe makers and artists, though little in the present city – outside its museums – pays anything but lip service to their existence. Vancouver Island is the best bet if you're in search of latter-day tokens of Salish culture.

Europeans appeared on the scene in the eighteenth century when **Spanish** explorers charted the waters along what is now southwestern British Columbia. In 1778 **Captain James Cook** reached nearby Nootka Sound while searching for the Northwest Passage, launching a British interest in the area and leading to wrangles

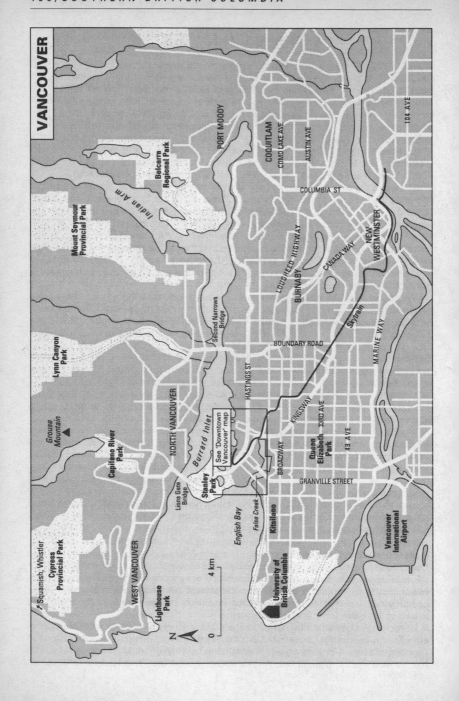

VANCOUVER

Squamish, Whistler

Cypress
Provincial Park

Lighthouse
Park

WEST VANCOUVER

Grouse
Mountain

Capilano River
Park

NORTH VANCOUVER

Lynn Canyon
Park

Mount Seymour
Provincial Park

Indian Arm

Belcarra
Regional Park

PORT MOODY

COQUITLAM

COMO LAKE AVE

AUSTIN AVE

104 AVE

COLUMBIA ST

NEW
WESTMINSTER

LOUGHEED HIGHWAY

BURNABY

CANADA WAY

Skytrain

MARINE WAY

Second Narrows
Bridge

BOUNDARY ROAD

HASTINGS ST

KINGSWAY

3RD AVE

49 AVE

Lions Gate
Bridge

Stanley
Park

Burrard Inlet

See 'Downtown
Vancouver' map

BROADWAY

Queen
Elizabeth
Park

GRANVILLE STREET

English Bay

False Creek

Kitsilano

University of
British Columbia

Vancouver
International
Airport

N

0        4 km

with the Spanish, though these were quickly settled in Britain's favour when Spain became embroiled in the aftermath of the French Revolution. **Captain George Vancouver** officially claimed the land for Britain in 1792, but stayed only a day in the area – scant homage to a place that was to be named after him a century later.

In 1827 the Hudson's Bay Company set up a fur-trading post at **Fort Langley**, 48km east of the present city; the first white settlement on the mainland, it was nonetheless kept free of homesteaders, who would have scared off the furry creatures. Major colonisation of the area only came after the Fraser River and Cariboo gold rushes in 1858, when **New Westminster** (now a southern suburb of Vancouver) became the mainland's chief port. In 1862, three British prospectors, unable to find gold, bought a strip of land on the southern shore of Burrard Inlet and – shortsightedly, given the amount of lumber around – started a brickworks; this soon gave way to the Hastings Sawmill and a shantytown of bars which by 1867 had taken the name of **Gastown**. Two years later Gastown became incorporated as the town of **Granville** and prospered on the back of its timber and small coal deposits.

The birth of the present city, though, dates to 1884, when the **Canadian Pacific Railway** decided to make it the terminus of its transcontinental railway. In 1886, on a whim of the CPR president, Granville was renamed Vancouver – only to destroyed on June 13 that year when fire razed all but half a dozen buildings. This proved a short-lived setback, however, and since the arrival of the first train from Montréal in 1887 the city has never looked back.

# Arrival, information and city transport

**Vancouver International Airport**, Canada's second busiest, is situated on Sea Island, 13km south of the centre. International flights arrive at the main terminal, domestic flights at the smaller south terminal. You'll find a **tourist information** booth on Level 2 of the main terminal (daily 6am–midnight) and **foreign exchange** facilities on each level, along with free phone lines to the upmarket hotels. The best way to get into Vancouver is on the private **Airport Express Bus** (6.15am–12.30am; $6.75), known as the "Hustle Bus", which leaves every fifteen minutes from Level 2, stopping at downtown hotels and the bus terminal. (When flying out of Vancouver, note that the Express Bus departs from Bay 20 of the bus terminal between 6.25am and 10.40pm; it also calls at the Hyatt Regency Hotel, and can be flagged down at the corner of Broadway and Granville). **Taxis** into town cost about $20. **Public transport** is cheaper ($1.35) but slower (1hr) and involves a change of bus – take the Metro Transit bus #100 to the corner of 71st and Granville, then change to the #21 which drops off downtown in Granville Street.

Vancouver's **bus terminal** is at 150 Dunsmuir Street and Hamilton; to get to downtown, leave by the main entrance and turn left uphill (a 10-min walk), or hop on the SkyTrain (see "Transport", next page) at Stadium station across the road. There are **left luggage** facilities here and a very useful **hotel board**, whose free phone line connects to some of the city's genuine cheapies – some of whom will deduct the taxi fare from the terminal from your first night's bill.

The skeletal **VIA train** services operate out of a terminal at 1150 Station Sreet; they run to and from Edmonton and the east via Jasper (3 weekly) and to Seattle making connections with the US *Amtrak* network (daily). A second station, belonging to the private freight-based **BC Rail** – serving Lillooet (daily) and Prince George (3 weekly) – is located in semi-industrial wasteland at 1311 W 1st Street, in North Vancouver. Trains arrive late at night, so your best bet for getting into the city is a taxi, unless you can cope with walking the length of Pemberton Avenue – about twenty minutes – to catch a #239 bus to connect with the SeaBus; for early-morning departures there's a connecting bus from the bus terminal at 6.20am.

## Information

The **Vancouver Travel Infocentre** is at Pavilion Plaza, 4 Bentall Centre, 1055 Dunsmuir Street, near the junction with Burrard (daily 8am–6pm; ☎683-2772 or ☎1-800-888-8835). Besides information on the city and much of southeastern British Columbia, the office provides **foreign exchange** facilities, *BC Transit* tickets, and tickets to sports and entertainment events. It's also got one of the most comprehensive **accommodation services** imaginable, backed up by bulging photo albums of hotel rooms and B&Bs, though staff steadfastly refuse to make recommendations. A smaller kiosk is open during the summer outside *Eaton's Department Store* on the corner of Georgia and Granville (daily 9.30am–5.30pm, open till 9pm Thurs & Fri).

## Transport

Vancouver's **public transport** system is an efficient, integrated network of bus, light-rail and ferry services operated by *BC Transit* (☎261-5100). Tickets generally cost $1.35 ($1.85 for longer journeys and the SeaBus during peak hours) and are valid for transfers throughout the system for ninety minutes from the time of issue; day passes, valid only after 9.30am, cost $3.50. You can buy tickets at stations or any shop displaying a blue and red *BC Transit* sticker (so-called "Faredealer" outlets).

The invaluable *BC Transit Guide* ($1.25) is available from the infocentre and Faredealer shops, while free **bus** timetables can be found at the infocentre, *7–11* stores and the central library. You can buy tickets on the bus, but make sure you have the right change to shovel into the box by the driver; you have to ask specially for transfer tickets. Normal buses stop running around midnight, when a patchy "Night Owl" service comes into effect on major routes until about 4am.

**SeaBus** ferries ply between downtown and North Vancouver, a ride definitely worth taking for its own sake: the views of the mountains across Burrard Inlet, the port and the downtown skyline are superb. Two 400-seat catamarans make the crossing every quarter- or half-hour (6.15am–1am), taking about thirteen minutes. Departures are from a terminal housed in the old Canadian Pacific station at the bottom of Seymour Street, downtown, and from Lonsdale Quay in North Van. Bicycles can cross only on weekends and holidays, and you need an extra ticket for them.

Vancouver's single light-rail line – **SkyTrain** – is a model of its type: driverless, completely computerised and magnetically propelled half underground and half on raised track, it covers 22km between the downtown Waterfront station (housed in the CPR building with the SeaBus terminal) and the southeastern suburb of New

---

### BUS ROUTES

Some of the more important Vancouver **bus routes** are:

**#1** – Gastown–English Bay loop.
**#3 & #8** – Gastown–Downtown–Marine Drive.
**#4 & #10** – Granville Street–University of British Columbia.
**#50** – Gastown–False Creek–Broadway.

**#51** – SeaBus Terminal–Downtown–Granville Island.
**#19** – Pender Street (Downtown)–Stanley Park.
**#20 & #17** – Downtown–Marine Drive; transfer to #100 for the airport.

Some **scenic routes** are worth travelling for their own sakes:

**#250** – Georgia Street (Downtown)–North Van–West Van–Horseshoe Bay.
**#52** – "Around the Park" service through Stanley Park (April–Oct Sat & Sun only); board at Lost Lagoon or Denman Street.

**#351** – Howe Street–White Rock–Crescent Beach (1hr each way).
**#210** – Pender Street–Phibbs Exchange; change there for the #211 (mountain route) or #212 (ocean views) to Deep Cove.

Westminster. Only the first three or four stations are of any practical use to the casual visitor, but the 27-minute trip is worth taking if only to see how the Canadians do these things – spotless interiors, teutonic punctuality and fully carpeted carriages.

# Accommodation

Vancouver has a surprisingly large number of **cheap hotels**, but some – mainly in the area east of downtown – are of a dinginess at odds with the city's slick and efficient image. Gastown, Chinatown and the area between them hold the cheaper places, usually on top of a bar where live bands and late-night drinking will keep you awake till the small hours. You're a bit better off in the lower price bracket in one of the faintly pleasanter hotels north of the Granville Street Bridge, a tame but central red-light area. **Midrange hotels** are still reasonable ($65–90), but Vancouver is a tourist city and things can get tight in summer – book ahead for the more popular places. A lot of the nicer options are in the West End, a quiet residential area bordering Vancouver's wonderful Stanley Park, five or ten minutes' walk from downtown. Out of season, hotels in all categories drop their prices, and you can reckon on thirty-percent discounts on the prices given below.

Bed-and-breakfast accommodation can be booked through agencies, but most of them operate as a phone service only and require two days' notice – in the first resort, use the infocentre's accommodation service. Though seldom central or cheap – reckon on $50 for a double – B&Bs are likely to be relaxed and friendly, and if you choose well you can have beaches, gardens, barbecues and as little or as much privacy as you want.

In addition to the **hostels**, budget accommodation is available in summer at the **University of British Columbia**, though this is a long way from downtown, and most rooms go to convention visitors – inquire at the Walter Gage Residence in the Student Union Mall (☎228-2963). Vancouver is not a camper's city – the majority of the in-city **campgrounds** are for RVs only and will turn you away if you've only got a tent. We've listed the few places that won't.

## Hotels

**Abbotsford Hotel**, 921 W Pender and Burrard (☎681-4335). Something of a city institution, this old seven-storey block in the middle of the financial district has more character than most and lots of original Art Deco touches. Doubles from $85.

**Austin Motor Inn**, 1221 Granville (☎685-7235). Cheap and reasonably cheerful, given the tacky locale. Singles $32–42; doubles and triples $42–52.

**Barclay Hotel**, 1348 Robson and Jervis (☎688-8850). Converted to evoke a chintzy French rustic ambience, but one of the nicer of several hotels at the north end of Robson, and rated one of the city's bargains. Singles $65–75; doubles $79; triples $89.

**Buchan Hotel**, 1906 Haro, near Robson and Denman (☎685-5354). Rooms are small and past their best, but still a genuine bargain given the peaceful downtown location near Stanley Park and English Bay Beach. Doubles from $60; weekly rates available.

**Burrard Motor Inn**, 1100 Burrard near Helmcken (☎663-0366). A city-centre motel with standard fittings, but all rooms look onto a pleasant garden courtyard, and some have kitchens. Singles $52–64; doubles $62–74; triples $76–82.

**Cecil Hotel**, 1336 Granville near Burrard Bridge (☎683-8505). The best of the dowdy cluster of hotels at the bottom of Granville Street, most of which have tatty bars promising "exotic dancers"; noisy but convenient. Singles and doubles $35–45.

**Hotel California**, 1176 Granville St (☎688-8701). It looks like a last-hoper from the outside, but it's nicer than it looks; rooms have been recently refurbished to block out the rock'n'roll from below. Singles from $30; doubles from $40.

**Dominion Hotel**, 210 Abbott and Water (☎681-6666). A nice, newly decorated old building on the edge of Gastown – ask for one of the new rooms with private bathrooms, preferably away from the thundering live music. Singles and doubles $35–55.

**Kingston Hotel**, 757 Richards and Robson (☎684-9024). A well-known bargain two blocks from the bus terminal, its clean and well-decorated interior affecting the spirit of a "European-style" hotel. Book ahead. Singles $30–45; doubles $50–65 (includes small breakfast). Long-stay terms available.

**Nelson Place Hotel**, 1006 Granville (☎681-6341). Small but reasonably cosy rooms, though the live music and strippers downstairs aren't marks in its favour. Singles and doubles $45-55.

**Niagara Hotel**, 435 W Pender (☎688-7574). A couple of blocks from the bus station and advertised by an extraordinary neon waterfall, this is a grim-fronted hotel with small rooms (some with private baths) and very low prices – singles $25–40, doubles $30–42.

**Patricia Hotel**, 403 E Hastings (☎255-4301). Big, well-known and widely advertised budget choice, but rather far from downtown in the heart of Chinatown: an exciting or grim location, depending on your point of view. Clean and newly renovated, it's the best of the many in this area. Singles $32–49; doubles $39–59; triples $43–59.

**Sandman Inn**, 180 W Georgia and Homer (☎681-2211). Flagship of a chain with hotels all over western Canada; rooms are only adequate for the price, but it's a big place with good chance of space, and ideally placed next to the bus terminal. Singles and doubles from $85.

**Shatto Inn at Stanley Park**, 1825 Comox St (☎681-8920). A small, quiet, family-run place two blocks from the park and the beach; some rooms have balconies and/or kitchen units. Singles $50–70; doubles $60–80; triples $70–95.

**Sunset Inn Apartment Hotel**, 1111 Burnaby between Davie and Thurlow (☎684-8763). One of the best West End "apartment" hotels and a good spot for a longer stay – spacious rooms (all with kitchens and balconies), laundry, nearby shops. Ten minutes' walk to downtown. Singles/doubles $65–100; triples $68–108.

**Sylvia Hotel**, 1154 Gilford St (☎681-9321). A local landmark located in a "heritage" building, this is a popular place with a high word-of-mouth reputation – reservations recommended. It's only two blocks from Stanley Park, and its snug bar, quiet, old-world charm and sea views make it as good as you'll get in Vancouver. Singles $50–70; doubles and triples $55–80.

**West End Guest House**, 1362 Haro near Jervis (☎681-2889). A wonderful small guesthouse with an old-time parlour and bright rooms, each with private bathroom; book well in advance. No smoking. Singles and doubles $80–150; triples $150 (full breakfast included).

## Bed-and-breakfast agencies

**A Home Away from Home**, ☎873-4888.

**Best Canadian**, ☎738-7207.

**Born Free**, ☎298-8815.

**Canada West Accommodations**, ☎987-9338.

**Town and Country**, ☎731-5942.

## Hostels

**Globetrotter's Inn**, 170 W Esplanade, North Vancouver (☎988-5141). Less convenient than the central hostels, though it's still only five minutes from Lonsdale Quay and the SeaBus terminal. Dorm $12; single $25; double $30.

**Vincent's Backpacker's Hostel**, 927 Main St (☎682-2441). Friendly, with colourful charm and no curfew, but not as clean or well organised as the youth hostel (below). Convenient for bus, train and SkyTrain stations; book or arrive early (office open 8am–midnight). Dorm $8; single $16; double $20.

**Vancouver International Hostel (IYHF)**, 1515 Discovery St (☎224-3208). Canada's biggest youth hostel (350 beds) has a superb position by Jericho Beach south of the city – take bus #4 from Granville Street to the Jericho Park stop on 4th Avenue. It fills up quickly, occasionally leading to a three-day limit in summer; open all day, with an excellent cafeteria, but the 2am curfew and lights-out are rigidly enforced. Dorm only: $8 members, $10 non-members.

**YMCA**, 955 Burrard St, between Smithe and Nelson (☎681-0221). Less exalted than the *YWCA*, but newly renovated and central. Shared bathrooms, cafeteria, pool and sports facilities. Singles $40; doubles $50; long-term rates available in winter.

**YWCA**, 580 Burrard and Dunsmuir (☎662-8188 or ☎1-800-663-1424). A hotel in all but name, with the best value at this price and central location; sports and cooking facilities, cheap cafeteria. Men allowed only with women partners or family. Singles from $40; doubles from $52; triples $60; long-term rates available in winter.

## Camping

**Burnaby Cariboo RV Park**, 8765 Cariboo Place, Burnaby (☎420-1722). Has an excellent reputation for its luxurious facilities (indoor pool, jacuzzi, laundry, free showers). Take Cariboo exit from Hwy 1. Shuttle bus to various sights. $25.

**Capilano Mobile Park**, 295 Tomahawk, West Vancouver (☎987-4722). The most central site for trailers and tents, beneath the north foot of the Lion's Gate Bridge. Reservations (with deposit) essential June–Aug. $20.

**Mount Seymour Provincial Park**, North Vancouver (☎986-2261). Lovely spot, but only a few tent sites alongside car parks #2 and #3. Full facilities but open July–Sept only. $12.

**Richmond RV Park**, Hollybridge and River Rd, Richmond (☎270-7878). The best of the year-round outfits, with the usual facilities; take Hwy 99 to the Westminster Highway and follow signs. Open April 15–Oct 15. $16–18.

# The City

Vancouver is not a city which offers or requires relentless sightseeing. Its breathtaking physical beauty makes it a place where often it's enough just to wander and watch the world go by – "the sort of town", wrote Jan Morris, "nearly everyone would want to live in." In summer you'll probably end up doing what the locals do, if not actually sailing, hiking, skiing, fishing or whatever, then certainly on a beach, lounging in one of the parks or spending time in waterfront cafés.

In addition to the myriad leisure activities, however, there are a handful of sights which make worthwhile viewing by any standards. You'll inevitably spend a good deal of time in the **downtown** area and its Victorian-era equivalent, **Gastown**, now a renovated and less than convincing pastiche of its past. **Chinatown**, too, could easily absorb a morning, and contains more than its share of interesting shops, restaurants and rumbustiously busy streets. For a taste of the city's hedonistic side, hit **Stanley Park**, a huge area of semi-wild parkland and beaches that crowns the northern tip of the downtown peninsula, or **Granville Island**, by far the city's most tempting spot for wandering and people-watching. If you prefer a cultural slant on things, hit the formidable **Museum of Anthropology** or the other museums of the Vanier Park complex.

At a push, you could cram the city's essentials into a couple of days. If you're here for a longer stay, though, you'll want to venture further out from the centre: trips across Burrard Inlet to **North Vancouver** lend a different panoramic perspective of the city, and easily lead into the mountains and forests that lend Vancouver its tremendous setting.

## Downtown

You soon get the hang of Vancouver's **downtown** district, an arena of streets and shopping malls centred on **Robson Street**, which on hot summer evenings is like a latter-day vision of *la dolce vita* – a dynamic meeting place crammed with cafés, restaurants, late-night stores, and plenty of bronzed hunks and lean-limbed blondes cruising in open-topped cars. At other times a more sedate class hangs out on the steps of the Vancouver Art Gallery or glides in and out of the two big department stores, *Eaton's* and *The Bay*, all downtown landmarks.

For a suitable introduction to Vancouver, you could do worse than walk down to the waterfront and **Canada Place**, the Canadian pavilion for Expo '86 and now an architectural overkill which houses a luxury hotel, cruise ship terminal and two glitzy convention centres. It was opened by Charles and Di – it's that sort of place. For all its excess, however, it makes a superb viewpoint, with stunning vistas of mountains, sea and buzzing boats, helicopters and float planes. In its design and the manner in which it juts into the port, the place is meant to suggest a ship, and you can walk the building's perime-

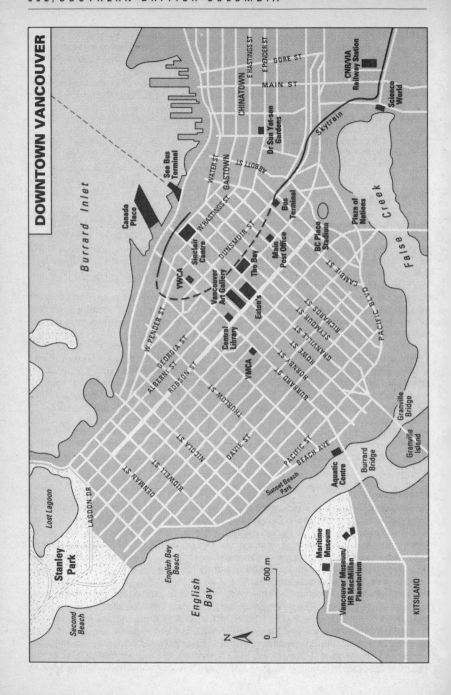

ter as if "on deck", stopping to read the boards that describe the immediate cityscape and the appropriate pages of its history. Inside are expensive shops, a restaurant, and an *IMAX* cinema (daily noon–9pm; $6); most of the films shown – on boats and obscure wildlife – are a waste of a good screen.

Most of the **Expo site** here and to the east has been levelled or is undergoing rigorous redevelopment. The geodesic dome survives, however, and has become a striking city landmark – but the museum it now houses, **Science World**, is a disappointment (daily 10am–5pm; $6). Only children, at whom the place seems largely aimed, will be satisfied by the few high-tech, hands-on displays, which include the opportunity to make thunderous amounts of noise on electronic instruments and drum machines. The best things are the building itself and the vast screen of the Omnimax Cinema at the top of the dome. Another remnant of Expo is the 60,000-seat **BC Place Stadium** at 1 Robson Street, the world's largest air-inflated dome (tours daily at 11am, 1pm & 3pm; $3.50); unless you're there for a sporting event, the "mushroom in bondage" of popular parlance isn't worth the bother.

An alternative to Canada Place's vantage point, the **Harbour Centre Building** at 555 W Hastings is one of the city's tallest structures, and is known by locals either as the "urinal" or, more affectionately, the "hamburger" after its bulging upper storeys. On a fine day it's worth paying to ride the stomach-churning, all-glass elevators that run up the side of the tower to the fortieth-storey observation deck (March–Sept daily 10am–9pm; $4); admission also buys you the viewing of a gung-ho promotional film, the *Vancouver Discovery Show.*

## THE VANCOUVER ART GALLERY

Centrally located in the imposing old city courthouse, the **Vancouver Art Gallery** at the corner of Howe and Robson (Mon, Wed, Fri & Sat 10am–5pm; Thurs 10am–9pm; Sun noon–5pm; $3.50; free Thurs 5–9pm) looks as if it ought to contain a treasure trove of art, but too much space is given to dud Canadian works of the sort that give modern art a bad name. What redeems the place are the powerful and almost surreal works of Emily Carr, who was born on Vancouver Island in 1871 and whose paintings – characterised by deep greens and blues – evoke something of the scale and intensity of the West Coast and its native peoples. A sparse international collection offers Warhol and Lichtenstein, with token rooms of half a dozen Italian, Flemish and British paintings. The gallery café is excellent.

## Gastown

An easy walk east of downtown – five minutes from Canada Place and centred largely on Water Street – **Gastown** is a determined piece of city rejuvenation aimed fair and square at the tourist, distinguished by new cobbles, fake gas lamps, *Ye Olde English Tea Room* and generally overpolished patina. The name derives from "Gassy" Jack Leighton, a retired sailor turned publican who opened a bar in 1867 to service the nearby lumber mills, whose bosses banned drinking on or near the yards. Trade was brisk, and a second bar opened, soon followed by a village of sorts – "Gassy's Town" – which, though swept away by fire in 1886, formed in effect the birthplace of modern Vancouver. Over the years, the downtown focus moved west and something of Gastown's boozy beginnings returned to haunt it, as its cheap hotels and warehouses turned into a skid row for junkies and alcoholics. By the 1970s the area was declared an historic site – the buildings are the still the city's oldest – and an enthusiastic beautification programme set in motion.

The end product never quite became the dynamic, city-integrated spot the planners had hoped, but it's worth a stroll for its buskers, Sunday crowds and occasional points of interest. These do not include the hype-laden **steam–powered clock**, the world's first and hopefully last, at the west end of Water Street. It's invariably surrounded by tourists armed with cocked cameras, all awaiting the miniature Big Ben's toots and whistles every fifteen minutes, and bellowing performances on the hour that seem to presage imminent explosion. The steam comes from an underground system that also heats surrounding buildings.

Nearby you'll find the *Town Pump*, one of the city's top music venues (see "Nightlife"), and the **Inuit Gallery**, a large commercial showcase of Inuit art at 345 Water Street (Mon–Sat 9.30am–5.30pm). Interesting and informative is the **Western Canadian Wilderness Committee** shop and office, 20 Water St – if you thought BC was people, trees and nature in peace and harmony, this leading conservation group will soon disabuse you.

Probably the most surprising aspect of Gastown, however, is the contrast between its manicured pavements and the down-at-heel streets immediately to the south and east. The bustling hub of **alternative Vancouver**, the area between Gastown and Chinatown is a mecca of secondhand clothes shops, bookshops, galleries, new designers and cheap five-and-dimes. In places, however, this area recalls Gastown's bad old days: unpleasantly seedy, pocked with the dingiest of dingy bars and hotels, and inhabited by characters to match.

## Chinatown

Vancouver's vibrant **Chinatown** – centred on Pender Street from Carrall to Gore and on Keefer Street from Main to Gore (#22 bus from Burrard) – is a city apart. Vancouver's 100,000 Chinese are expected soon to surpass San Francisco's as the largest Chinese community outside the Far East and are the city's oldest and largest ethnic group after the British-descended majority. Many crossed the Pacific in 1858 to join the Fraser Valley gold rush; others followed under contract to help build the Canadian Pacific Railway. Most stayed, and found themselves treated appallingly. Denied citizenship and legal rights until as late as 1947, they sought safety and familiarity in a ghetto of their own, where clan associations and societies provided for new arrivals and the local poor – and helped build the distinctive houses of recessed balconies and ornamental roofs that have made the area a protected historic site.

Unlike Gastown's gimmickry, Chinatown is all genuine – shops, cheap hotels, markets, tiny restaurants and dim alleys vie for attention amidst an incessant hustle of jammed pavements and buzz of Chinese conversation. Virtually every building replicates an Eastern model without a trace of self-consciousness, and written Chinese characters feature everywhere in preference to English. Striking and unexpected after downtown's high-rise glitz, the district brings you face to face with Vancouver's oft-touted multi-culturalism, and helps explain why Hong Kong immigrants continue to be attracted to the city. There's an edge to Chinatown, however, especially at night, and though central districts are fine, lone tourists are better off avoiding Hastings and the back streets.

Apart from the obvious culinary temptations (see "Eating and drinking"), Chinatown's main points of reference are its **markets**. One of the best is *Yuen Fong* at 242 E Pender, where you can be sure to find fearsome butchery displays and such edibles as live eels, flattened ducks, hundred-year-old eggs and other stuff you'll be happy not to identify. Keefer Street is **bakery** row, with lots of tempting stickies on offer like moon cakes and *bao*, steamed buns with a meat or sweet bean filling. On the corner of Keefer and Main is the *Ten Ren Tea and Ginseng Company*, with a vast range of teas, many promising cures for a variety of ailments (free tastings). In a similar vein, it's worth dropping into one of the local **herbalists** to browse amongst their panaceas: snake skins, reindeer antlers, buffalo tongues, dried seahorses and bears' testicles are all available if you're feeling under the weather. *Ming Wo*, at 23 E Pender, is a fantastic cookware shop, with probably every utensil ever devised, while *China West*, 41 E Pender, is packed with slippers, jackets, pens, cheap toys and the like.

Chinatown's chief cultural attraction is the **Dr Sun Yat-sen Garden**, at 578 Carrall Street near Pender, a 2.5-acre park billed as the first classical Chinese garden ever built outside China (May–Sept 10am–8pm, Oct–April 10am–4.30pm; $3). Named after the founder of the first Chinese Republic, who was a frequent visitor to Vancouver, the park was created for the '86 Expo and cost $5.3 million, half a million dollars of which came from the People's Republic accompanied by 52 artisans and 950 crates of materials. The horticultural emissaries, following traditional methods which didn't allow use of a single power tool, spent thirteen months replicating a fourteenth-century Ming garden to achieve a subtle balance of *yin* and *yang*: small and large, soft and hard, flowing and immovable, light and dark. Regular free guided tours explain the Taoist philosophy behind the carefully placed elements.

Alongside the entrance to the gardens, the **Chinese Cultural Centre**, Chinatown's community centre and a sponsor of New Year festivities, offers classes and hosts changing exhibitions. Nearby is a small Dr Sun Yat-sen Park (free) which, though less worked than the Dr Sun Yat-sen Garden, is still a pleasant place to take a time-out from Chinatown. Hours are the same as for the garden, and there's an alternative entrance on Columbia Street and Keefer.

## Stanley Park

One of the world's great urban spaces, **Stanley Park** is Vancouver's green heart, and one of the things that makes the city the place it is. At nearly 1000 acres, it's the largest urban park in North America – less a tame collection of lawns and elms than a semi-wilderness of dense rainforest, marshland and beaches. Ocean surrounds it on three sides, with a road and parallel cycleway/pedestrian promenade following the seawall right the way round the peninsula for a total of 10.5km. Away from the coastal trail network and two big draws – the aquarium and the zoo – the interior is nearly impenetrable scrub and forest, with few paths and few people.

The peninsula was partially logged in the 1860s, when Vancouver was still a twinkle in "Gassy" Jack Leighton's eye, but in 1886 the newly formed city council – showing typically Canadian foresight and an admirable sense of priorities – moved to make what had become a military reserve into a permanent park. Thus its remaining first-growth forest of cedar, hemlock and Douglas fir, and the swamp now known as Lost Lagoon, were saved for posterity in the name of Lord Stanley, Canada's Governor General from 1888 to 1893.

The park is a simple walk from most of downtown, if a fairly lengthy one from eastern districts. Beach Avenue and Alberni Street are the best entrances if you're on foot, leading to the southern start of the seawall; Georgia Street takes you to the northern entrance. Bus #19 runs to the foot of Alberni Street from points along Pender Street, while the special "Around the Park" service (bus #52) carries on from there hourly at weekends and on holidays (April–Oct), but it doesn't run if it's raining. Driving is foolish, especially at weekends, when parking is just about impossible.

**Walking** around the park, especially on a busy Sunday, gives a fair taste of what it means to live in Vancouver. The first thing you see is the **Lost Lagoon**, a fair-sized lake that started life as a tidal inlet, and got its name because its water all but disappeared at low tide. Dozens of waterfowl species inhabit its shoreline, and odd little sights dot the promenade, all signed and explained, the most famous being the *Girl in a Wetsuit* statue, a lascivious update of Copenhagen's *Little Mermaid*.

If you want a more focused walk, the **Cathedral Trail**, northwest of the Lost Lagoon, takes you past some big first-growth cedars. **Prospect Point**, on the park's northern tip, is a busy spot but worth braving for its beautiful view of the city and the mountains rising behind West Vancouver across the water. Guided **nature walks** depart every Tuesday from the Alberni Street bus stop (May, June & Sept at 10am) and from Lumberman's Arch Water Park (July & Aug at 10am & 7pm).

Given the park's size, a **bicycle** affords more flexibility than walking – see "Listings" at the end of the Vancouver section for rental outlets. You can pick up a free cycling map of the park from *Stanley Park Rentals* at 676 Chilco and Alberni (just across from the Alberni Street bus stop). Though people do swim in the sea, most bathers prefer to dip in the **swimming pool** next to Second Beach (see box). Facilities of all sorts – cafés, playgrounds, golf, outdoor dancing – proliferate near the downtown margins.

## THE CHILDREN'S ZOO AND VANCOUVER AQUARIUM

The small **Children's Zoo** north of Lost Lagoon is the most-visited place in the park, with farm and other animals, many allowed to wander in a special open area (daily 10am–5pm; free). The main zoo nearby is far less attractive, and there are repeated calls for its closure on the grounds of cruelty – one look at the obviously distressed and unbelievably mangy polar bears will convince you. The neighbouring **Vancouver Aquarium** is a more full-blown affair, its 6000 marine species making it Canada's largest (summer daily 9.30am–8pm; winter 10am–5.30pm; $6). Certain parts are interesting, even for non-fish enthusiasts – especially the salmon section – but the aquarium, too, has been targeted by animal-rights campaigns for its treatment of performing beluga and killer whales (not to mention cooped-up seals and otters); given the aquarium's reputation as a tourist attraction, however, the campaigners have a long, uphill battle yet.

### VANCOUVER'S BEACHES

Though most of the sand comes from Japan in container ships, Vancouver's **beaches** feel like the real thing. All are clean and well-kept – the clarity of the water is remarkable, given the size of the city's port – and the majority have lifeguards during the summer months. The best beaches face each other across False Creek and English Bay, starting with Stanley Park's three adjacent strands: **English Bay Beach**, along Beach Avenue; **Second Beach**, to the north, which also features a shallow onshore swimming pool; and **Third Beach**, further north still, the least crowded of the three and the one with the best views of West Vancouver and the mountains.

Across the water to the south and west of the Burrard Bridge, **Kitsilano Beach**, or "Kits", is a city favourite, especially with the university crowd and well-heeled locals. An old hippy and alternative-lifestyle redoubt, it still betrays shades of its past, and there's always plenty going on; nearby you can retreat to a heated saltwater pool (summer only). **Jericho Beach**, west of Kits and handy for the youth hostel, is a touch quieter and serves as a hang-out for the windsurfing crowd. Still further west, **Spanish Banks** is the least crowded of all, and marks the start of a fringe of sand and parkland that continues round to the UBC campus. Clothing-optional **Wreck Beach** is just off the campus area – ask any student to point you towards the half-hidden access paths.

Finally, **Ambleside**, west of the Park Royal Mall, is the most accessible beach if you're in North or West Vancouver.

## Granville Island

**Granville Island**, huddled under the Granville Street Bridge south of downtown, is the city's most enticing "people's place" – the title it likes for itself – and almost lives up to its claim to be the "heart of Vancouver". Friendly, easy-going and popular, its shops, markets, galleries, marina and open spaces are juxtaposed with a light-industrial setting whose faint whiff of warehouse squalor saves the area from being precious. The island was reclaimed from swampland in 1917 as an ironworks and shipbuilding centre, but by the 1960s the yards were derelict and the place had become a rat-infested dumping ground for the city's rubbish. In 1972 the federal government agreed to bankroll a programme of residential, commercial and industrial redevelopment that retained the old false-fronted buildings, tin-shack homes, seawall and rail sidings. The best part of the job had been finished by 1979 – and was immediately successful – but work continues unobtrusively today, the various building projects only adding to the area's sense of change and dynamism.

The most direct approach is to take **bus** #50 from Gastown or Granville Street. Alternatively, bathtub-sized private **ferries** ply back and forth almost continuously between the island and the Aquatic Centre at the foot of Thurlow Street (daily summer 7.30am–10pm; winter 7.30am–8pm; $1), and also connect to Vanier Park (see below). The walk down Granville Street and across the bridge is deceptively long, and probably only worthwhile on a fine day.

Virtually the first building you see on the island augurs well: the **Granville Island Brewery**, a small outfit run by a German brewmaster, offers guided tours that include free tastings of its additive-free beers (tours June–Sept regularly 9am–5pm; Oct–May 2pm only; free). Dominant amongst the maze of shops, galleries and businesses, the **Granville Island Public Market** (Mon–Sat 9am–6pm) is the undisputed highlight of the area. On summer weekends it's Vancouver's place to be, playing host to the city's muesli set, numerous arts-and-crafts types, and a phalanx of dreadful but harmless buskers. The quality and variety of **food** is staggering, with dozens of kiosks and cafés selling ready-made titbits and potential picnic ingredients. Parks, patios and walkways nearby provide lively areas to eat and take everything in. Other spots to look out for include *Blackberry Books* (one of the city's best bookshops), the Water Park (a kids-only playground with hoses to repel intruders) and the *Bridges* pub/restaurant/wine bar, which has a nice outdoor drinking area. You can also rent **canoes** for safe and straightforward paddling in False Creek and English Bay from *Ecomarine Ocean Kayak*, 1688 Duranleau.

## Vanier Park museum complex

A little to the west of Granville Island, **Vanier Park** conveniently collects all but one of the city's main museums: the **Vancouver Museum**, the **Macmillan Planetarium** and the **Maritime Museum**. The complex sits on the waterfront at the west end of the Burrard Bridge, near Kitsilano Beach and the residential-entertainment centres of Kitsilano and West 4th Avenue, and Vanier Park itself is a fine spot to while away a summer afternoon. You could easily incorporate a visit to the museums with a trip to Granville Island using the **ferry** (see above). Coming from downtown, take the #22 **bus** from anywhere on Burrard or West Pender – get off at the first stop after the bridge and walk down Chester Street to the park.

### THE VANCOUVER MUSEUM

Canada's largest civic museum, the **Vancouver Museum**, 1100 Chestnut St (Tues–Sun 10am–5pm; open daily July & Aug; $4), traces the history of the city and the lower British Columbian mainland, and invokes the area's past in its very form – the flying-saucer shape is a nod to the conical cedar-bark hats of the Northwest Coast Indians, former inhabitants of the area. The fountain outside, looking like a crab on a bidet, recalls the animal of Indian legend which guards the harbour entrance.

Though it's the main focus of interest at Vanier Park, the museum is not as captivating as you'd expect from a city like Vancouver. It claims 300,000 exhibits, but it's hard to know where they all are, and a visit needn't take more than an hour or so. A patchy collection of baskets, tools, clothes and miscellaneous artefacts of native peoples – including a huge whaling canoe, the only museum example in existence – homes in on the 8000 years before the coming of white settlers. After that, the main collection, weaving in and out of Vancouver's history up to World War I, is full of offbeat and occasionally memorable insights if you have the patience to read the material – notably the accounts of early explorers' often extraordinary exploits, the immigration section (which re-creates what it felt like to travel steerage) and the forestry displays. The twentieth-century section is disappointing, most of the time looking more like an antique shop than a museum.

### THE PLANETARIUM AND OBSERVATORY
The **Macmillan Planetarium**, downstairs from the museum, ranks as one of North America's best (Tues–Sun up to 4 star shows daily; $5–6.50), though its rock and laser extravaganzas (most evenings at 8.30pm) are for fans of the genre only. Also on display – and accorded almost the status of a national shrine – is the favourite piano of Glenn Gould (see p.228). The **Gordon Southam Observatory**, next door, is open for public star-gazing on clear nights; astronomers are on hand to show you the ropes and help you position your camera for a "Shoot the Moon" photography session of the heavens (summer daily 7–11pm; winter Fri–Sun; free).

### THE MARITIME MUSEUM
The **Maritime Museum** (daily 10am–5pm; $3), a short walk from the Vancouver Museum, features lovely early photographs evoking turn-of-the-century Vancouver, though the rest of the presentation hardly does justice to the status of the city as one of the world's leading ports. The shabbier displays, however, are redeemed by the renovated *St Roch*, a two-masted schooner that was the first vessel to navigate the famed Northwest Passage in a single season (see p.605); it now sits impressively in its own wing of the museum, where it can be viewed by guided tour only. Special summer shows spice things up a little, with such dubious activities as hornpipe dancing and shanty-song singalongs (Wed 5–9pm; free) and an annual mid-July open period. Outside the museum on **Heritage Harbour** you can clamber (free of charge) over more restored vessels.

## The Museum of Anthropology
Located well out of downtown on the University of British Columbia campus, the **Museum of Anthropology** is far and away Vancouver's most important museum (Tues 11am–9pm, Wed–Sun 11am–5pm; $4, free on Tues). Emphasising the art and culture of the natives of the Pacific Northwest, and the Haida in particular, its collection of carvings, totem poles and artefacts is unequalled in North America.

To **get there** by bus, catch the #10 from Granville and stay on until the end of the line. The campus is huge and disorientating – to find the museum, turn right from the bus stop, walk along the tree-lined East Mall to the very bottom (10min), then make a left on NW Marine Drive and walk till you see the museum on the right (another 5min). In the foyer pick up a free mini-guide or the larger booklet for $1 – a worthwhile investment, given the exhibits' almost total lack of labelling, but still pretty thin.

Much is made of the museum's award-winning layout, a cool and spacious collection of halls designed by Arthur Erikson, and the huge **Great Hall**, inspired by native cedar houses, makes as perfect an artificial setting for its thirty-odd **totem poles** as you could ask for. Huge windows look out to more poles and Haida houses, which you're free to wander around, backed by Burrard Inlet and the distant mountains. Most of the poles and monolithic carvings indoors and out are taken from the coastal tribes of the Haida, Salish, Tsimshian and Kwakiutl, all of which share cultural elements. The suspicion – though it's never confessed – is that scholars really don't know terribly much of the arcane mythology behind the carvings, but the best guess as to their meaning is that the various animals correspond to different clans or the creatures after which the clans were named. To delve deeper into the complexities, it's worth joining an hour-long **guided walk**.

One of the museum's great virtues is that none of its displays is hidden away in basements or back rooms; instead they're jammed in overwhelming numbers into drawers and cases in the galleries to the right of the Great Hall. Most of the permanent collection revolves around **Canadian Pacific** cultures, but the **Inuit** and **Far North** exhibits are also outstanding. So, too, are the jewellery, masks and baskets of Northwest native tribes, all markedly delicate after the blunt-nosed carvings of the Great Hall. Look out especially for the *argillite* sculptures, made from a jet-black slate found only on BC's Queen Charlotte Islands. The **African** and **Asian** collections are also pretty comprehensive, if smaller, but appear as something of an afterthought alongside the indigenous artefacts. A small, technical archaeological section rounds off the smaller galleries, and a new wing designed to house the Koerner Collection, 600 European ceramics dating from the fifteenth century onwards, is due to open soon.

The museum saves its best for last. Housed in a separate rotunda, **The Raven and the Beast**, a modern sculpture designed by Haida artist Bill Reid, is the museum's pride and joy and has achieved almost iconographic status in the city. Carved from a 4.5-ton block of cedar and requiring the labour of five people over three years, it describes the Haida legend of human evolution with stunning virtuosity, depicting terrified figures squirming from a half-open clam shell, overseen by an enormous and stern-faced raven. However, beautiful as the work is, its rotunda setting makes it seem oddly out of place – almost like a corporate piece of art.

### AROUND THE MUSEUM

There are any number of odds and ends dotted around the museum, but they amount to little of real interest. Turn right out the front entrance and a five-minute walk leads to the **Nitobe Memorial Garden**, a small Japanese garden that might be good for a few minutes of peace and quiet (April–Sept 10am–6pm, Oct–March 10am–3pm; $2). Beyond is the greater area of the university's **botanical garden**, whose only points of interest for non-gardeners are the macabre poisonous plants of the "Physick" Garden and the swathes of shrubs and huge trees in the Asian Garden. While you're out here, you might also take advantage of the **University Endowment Lands**, on the opposite, west side of the museum. A huge tract of wild parkland – as large as Stanley Park, but used by a fraction of the number of people – the endowment lands boast 48km of trails and abundant wildlife (blacktail deer, otters, foxes and bald eagles). Best of all, there are few human touches – no benches or snack bars, and only the occasional signpost.

The best way to round off a visit, and to meet students and take the place's social pulse, is a trip to the **Pit Pub** in the UBC Student Union Building near the bus stop.

## North Vancouver

Perhaps the most compelling reason to visit **North Vancouver** is the trip itself – preferably by *SeaBus* – which provides views of not only the downtown skyline but also the teeming port area, a side of the city that's otherwise easily missed. Most of North Van itself is residential, as is neighbouring West Vancouver, whose cosseted citizens boast the highest per capita income in Canada. You'll probably cross to the north shore less for these leafy suburbs than to sample the outstanding areas of natural beauty here: **Lynn Canyon**, **Grouse Mountain**, **Capilano Gorge**, **Mount Seymour** and **Lighthouse Park**. All nestle in the mountains that rear up dramatically almost from the waterfront – the proximity of Vancouver's residential areas to genuine wilderness being one of the most remarkable aspects of the city.

Most of North Vancouver is within a single bus ride of **Lonsdale Quay**, the north shore's *SeaBus* terminal. **Buses** to all points leave from two parallel bays immediately in front of you as you leave the boat – blue West Van buses are run by an independent company but accept *BCTransit* tickets.

The **Lonsdale Quay Market**, to the right of the buses, is worth making the crossing for whether or not you intend to explore further. While not as vibrant as Granville Island Market, it's still an appealing place, with great food stalls and takeaways, plus walkways looking out over the port, tugs and moored fishing boats.

## LYNN CANYON PARK

The easiest target for a quick taste of backwoods Vancouver is **Lynn Canyon Park**, a quiet, forested area with a modest ravine which, unlike the more popular Capilano Gorge (see below), you don't have to pay to cross. Several walks of up to ninety minutes take you through fine scenery – cliffs, rapids, waterfalls and an eighty-metre-high bridge over Lynn Creek – all just twenty minutes from Lonsdale Quay. Take bus #228 from the quay to its penultimate stop at Peters Street, from where it's a ten-minute walk to the gorge; alternatively, take the #239 to Phibbs Exchange and then the less frequent #229, which drops you about five minutes closer. Before entering the gorge, it's worth popping into the **Ecology Centre**, a friendly and informative place where you can pick up maps and pamphlets on park trails and wildlife (daily 10am–5pm).

## GROUSE MOUNTAIN

The trip to **Grouse Mountain** is a popular one, thanks mainly to the Swiss-built **cable-car** that runs almost to its 1250-metre summit (daily 10am–9pm; $8.50). A favourite among people learning to **ski** after work, the mountain's brightly illuminated slopes are a North Vancouver landmark on winter evenings. In summer, the cable-car is an expensive way of getting to the top – which with a couple of restaurants and allied tourist paraphernalia is anything but wild – but the views are stunning. Another chairlift takes you (for $2) the remaining 120m to the summit. Fortunately there's plenty of space to escape the hordes, and several **trails**, long and short, set off from the top of the cable-car and the summit. Arguably the best hike is to Grouse Lake (1hr); more rugged paths lead into the mountains of the West Coast Range.

To get to the base station from Lonsdale Quay, take a special #232 **bus** (25min); off-season, when the #232 is less frequent, you could take the #246 and change to the #232 at EDGEMOUNT VILLAGE. From Georgia Street downtown catch the West Van #247, which goes direct to the cable-car terminal.

## CAPILANO RIVER PARK

Lying just off the approach road to Grouse Mountain, **Capilano River Park**'s most publicised attraction is a seventy-metre-high **suspension bridge** over the vertiginous Capilano Gorge. Though part of the park, the turn-of-the-century footbridge is privately run as a money-making scam – stick to the paths and avoid the $5 pedestrian toll. More interesting is the **salmon hatchery** just upstream (daily 9am–5pm; free), a provincial outfit designed to help salmon spawn and thus combat declining stocks: it nurtures some two million fish a year. The building is well designed and the information plaques interesting, but it's a prime stop on city coach tours, so the place can often be packed.

Capilano is probably best visited on the way back from Grouse Mountain – from the cable-car station it's an easy downhill walk (1km) to the north end of the park, below the Cleveland Reservoir, source of Vancouver's disconcertingly brown drinking water, and from there marked trails follow the eastern side of the gorge to the hatchery (2km). The area below the hatchery is worth exploring, especially the Dog's Leg Pool (1km) along a swirling reach of the Capilano River, and if you really want to stretch your legs you could follow the river the full 7km to its mouth on the Burrard Inlet. Alternatively, you could ride the #232 bus to the Cleveland Dam or the main park entrance – the hatchery is reached by a side road (or the Pipeline Trail) from the main entrance.

## MOUNT SEYMOUR PROVINCIAL PARK

**Mount Seymour Provincial Park** is the most easterly of the North Vancouver parks, the biggest (8668 acres), and the one that comes closest to the flavour of high mountain scenery. To get there by bus, take the #239 from Lonsdale Quay to Phibbs

Exchange and then the #215 to the Mount Seymour Parkway (1hr) – from there you'll have to walk, cycle or hitch up the thirteen-kilometre road to the heart of the park. The road climbs to over 1000m and ends at a car park where boards spell out clearly the trails and mountaineering options available. There's also a café, toilets, a small infocentre (summer only) and a **chairlift** that takes you up to 1200m (July–Aug daily 11am–5pm; Sept–Oct Sat & Sun only, weather allowing; $3). In winter this is the most popular family and learners' **ski area** near Vancouver.

Many **trails** here are manageable in a day, but be aware that conditions can change rapidly and snow lingers as late as June. One hike goes to the summit of Mount Seymour itself (1453m), and other recommended hikes take you to Dog Mountain and Mystery Lake, both about three easy hours' round trip, or Goldie Lake, a half-hour stroll. Views are immense on good days, particularly from the popular **Vancouver Lookout** on the parkway approach road, where a map identifies the city landmarks below.

### LIGHTHOUSE PARK

**Lighthouse Park** offers a seascape wilderness at the extreme western tip of the north shore, 8km from the Lion's Gate Bridge. Smooth granite rocks and low cliffs line the shore, backed by huge Douglas firs up to 1500 years old, some of the best virgin forest in southern BC. The rocks make fine sunbeds, though the water out here is colder than around the city beaches. A map at the car park shows the two trails to the **lighthouse** itself – you can take one out and the other back, a round trip of about 5km which involves about two hours' walking. Although the park has its secluded corners, it can be disconcertingly busy during summer weekends. The West Van #250 bus makes the journey from Georgia Street in downtown.

# Eating and drinking

Vancouver's ethnic restaurants are some of Canada's finest, and span the price spectrum from budget to blowout. **Chinese** and **Japanese** cuisines have the highest profile (though the latter tend to be expensive), followed by **Italian**, **Greek** and other European imports; **Vietnamese** and **Thai** are recent arrivals on the scene. Specialist seafood restaurants are surprisingly thin on the ground, but those that exist are of high quality and often remarkably cheap, and at any rate seafood crops up on most menus – salmon is ubiquitous in all its forms. **Vegetarians** are well served by a number of specialist places, though less so by the trendy, overpriced and generally forgettable restaurants serving so-called Californian ("New American") cuisine, which has replaced Japanese as Vancouver's flavour of the month.

**Restaurants** are spread around the city, with perhaps only North and West Vancouver rating as relative culinary deserts. Places in the West End and Gastown are generally tourist- and expense-account orientated, in marked contrast to Chinatown's bewildering plethora of genuine and cheap options. Downtown also offers plenty of choice, as do Kitsilano (W 4th Ave) and neighbouring West Broadway. **Cafés**, found mainly around the beaches, in parks, along downtown streets, and especially on Granville Island, are at their best in summer.

The city also has a commendable assortment of **bars**, many a good cut above the functional dives and sham pubs found elsewhere in BC. Note, however, that the definitions of bar, café, restaurant and nightclub can be considerably blurred: food in some form – usually substantial – is available in most places, while daytime cafés and restaurants also operate happily as nighttime bars. In this section we've highlighted places whose main emphasis is food and drink; entertainment venues are listed in the next section.

## Cafés and snacks

**Alma Street Café**, 2505 Alma and Broadway. Cheap and very popular (weekend breakfast queues). Menu changes daily, with emphasis on salads, fish and pasta. Open till 11pm; live jazz on Fri & Sat evenings.

**Benny's Bagel and Pretzel Works**, 1090 Robson. 24-hour snacks.

**Café Luxy**, 1235 Davie St. Pleasant, easy-going atmosphere. Open until 4am at weekends.

**Café S'il Vous Plaît**, 500 Robson and Richards. Young, casual and vaguely alternative with good sandwiches, basic home-cooking and local art displays. Open till 10pm.

**City Picnics Café**, 475 W Hastings. Basic breakfasts at $2.99.

**Did's Place**, 823 Granville. Popular post-drinking hang-out. Good pizza, loud music. Open till 3am.

**Doll and Penny's**, 1167 Davie. Fun place with big servings, daily drinks specials. Open 24hr.

**Elbow Room**, 720 Jervis and Alberni. A clean greasy spoon: by general consent, the best basic breakfasts (and pancakes) in the city. Packed at weekends. Daytime only, breakfasts until mid-afternoon.

**Gallery Café**, Vancouver Art Gallery, 750 Hornby. Relaxed, stylish and pleasantly arty for coffee, good lunches and healthy, high-quality food (especially desserts); also has a popular summer patio. No admission to museum required.

**Hamburger Mary's**, 1202 Davie. Best burgers in the city. Open all night.

**Isadora's**, 1540 Old Bridge, Granville Island. Good breakfasts, weekend brunches (frequent queues) and light, creative meals with good veg/wholefood options. Lots of outdoor seating. Open till 10pm.

**Joe's Café**, 1150 Commercial Drive and William. Lively hang-out, popular with students, artists and local bohos. Open till midnight.

**Marine View Coffee Shop**, 19-975 Centennial. A cheap fisherman's eating spot near the docks and canneries; hard to find, but worth the trek if you want seafood – take the Heatley overpass from Powell Street. Closes 4pm.

**The Only Café**, 20 E Hastings and Carrall. People in Vancouver cite this institution, founded in 1912, when they want to prove the city has character. Seafood (the best in town) and potatoes are the only menu items at this very cheap edge-of-Chinatown greasy spoon; counter seating, no toilets, no credit cards, no licence, and no messing with the tough service. Closed Sun.

**Starbucks**, 1100 Robson and Thurlow, 815 Hornby near Robson, and at the *SeaBus* terminal. Hip and sleek espresso bars with downtown's best cup of coffee.

**Taf's Café**, 829 Granville. Popular alternative spot that attracts punks-and-their-dogs clientele; okay food, juke-box and displays of local art. Open till the small hours.

---

### VANCOUVER'S CHINESE CUISINES

**Chinese restaurants** dominate Vancouver's culinary horizon, but with hundreds to choose from, each with hundreds of menu items, it's easy to be intimidated.

The majority of places serve **Cantonese** food, most of the city's Chinese population having their roots in Canton Province. This food should be fairly familiar – stir fries, simple sauces, chop suey, chow mein – but other provincial cooking may be more bewildering. **Szechuan** restaurants, of which there are many, tend to the spicy and peppery, with wanton use of chillies. **Shanghai** dishes are more highly flavoured than Cantonese, less so than Szechuan, making use of wine, sugar, salt and soya sauce. **Mandarin** (or Peking) cuisine is delicate but flavourful, and – as rice isn't grown in that part of China – dumplings, buns or noodles are often served as an accompaniment. For lunch or a snack, **noodle houses** are amongst the cheapest of what are already some of the cheapest restaurants in the city.

The restaurants listed here will point you in the right direction, but it's often enough to wander around Chinatown and look for the busiest places as a reliable guide of quality. Few places, however, offer much in the way of English menus. The best time for a meal is on Sundays, when Chinese families eat out, **dim sum** being as much of an institution in Vancouver as it is elsewhere. During the week most restaurants close at 10pm, so visit for lunch or between 6 and 8pm; few take bookings.

## Chinese restaurants

**Grand Garden**, 608 Main and Keefer (☎681-4721). Best for lunchtime or late-night noodles – a quick, filling meal for $4. Try the barbecue pork, duck, wonton or fishball noodles in soup.

**The Green Door**, 111 E Pender and Columbia (☎685-4194). Average Cantonese fare, but a legendary city institution whose perfect and seedy atmosphere is redolent of Chinatown in the 1940s. Open Oct–May; unlicensed.

**Hon's Wun Tun House**, 524 Main and Pender (☎688-7018). Cheap, basic and popular for the house speciality, "potstickers" – fried meat-filled dumplings.

**Ming's**, 147 E Pender and Main (☎683-4722). Huge, fancy place which has been the most popular *dim sum* spot for years. Queues start at 11am at weekends; leave your name with host at the top of the stairs and wait for number to be called.

**New Diamond**, 555 Gore and Pender. For quiet *dim sum*.

**On On Tea Garden**, 214 Keefer. A fairly ordinary place with cheap, basic food, but for years this was Chinatown's most famous restaurant – it was here that Pierre Trudeau conducted much of his secret courtship of Margaret.

**Yang's**, 4186 Main and 26th (☎873-2116). A friendly, family-run Mandarin place, this is probably Vancouver's best Chinese (and pricier than most); great Peking duck, some very fiery dishes, plus a noted noodle lunch on Saturdays. Follow the advice of staff when ordering. Dinner daily except Wed; lunch Sat & Sun only.

## Italian restaurants

**Fettucini's**, 1179 Commercial Drive. Good selection of pasta, fish and chicken dishes.

**Gallo D'Oro**, 1800 Renfrew and 2nd Ave. Home-cooking and massive portions. Closed Sun.

**Nick's Spaghetti House**, 631 Commercial Drive. New management after 30 years in the same family, but still sound food and fun atmosphere. In the heart of Vancouver's small Italian district – take bus #20 from downtown.

**The Old Spaghetti Factory**, 55 Water St. Part of a popular nationwide chain and better than the tourist trap it appears from outside, with a spacious 1920s Tiffany interior.

**Orlando's Fresh Pasta Bar**, 220 Abbott. Probably Vancouver's cheapest pasta.

**Piccolo Mondo**, 850 Thurlow and Smithe (☎688-1633). Pricey but excellent food: expense accounts at lunch, smoochy couples in the evenings.

## Greek restaurants

**Orestes**, 3116 W Broadway. Good, basic Greek food.

**Souvlaki Place**, 1807 Morton near Denman. A few tables with a lovely view of English Bay. Take-out service available: buy your *falafel* or *souvlaki*, cross to the beach and watch the sun go down. Handy for Stanley Park.

**Vassilis**, 2884 W Broadway near Macdonald (☎733-3231). Family-run outfit with a high reputation; serves a mean roast chicken. Closed weekend lunchtimes.

## Other ethnic restaurants

**Dar Lebanon**, 678 W Broadway and Heather, 1961 W 4th and Maple, and 2807 W Broadway and Macdonald. Reasonably cheap Lebanese food.

**Kamei-Sushi**, 813 Thurlow and Robson (☎684-4823). Superlative sushi, but at stratospheric prices. Closed weekends.

**Momiji**, 3550 Fraser near 19th Ave (☎872-2027). Slow service, over-bright lighting, but excellent Japanese food at very low prices. Closed Mon.

**Quilicum**, 1724 Davie near Denman (☎681-7044). The city's only restaurant offering genuine native American cuisine – seaweed, roast caribou, alder-barbecued oysters, barbecued juniper duck with wild rice. Quite expensive. Dinner only.

**The Sitar**, 564 W Broadway. Cheap, reliable Indian.

**A Taste of Jamaica**, 941 Davie St. Cheap and authentic Jamaican food, with reggae accompaniment and red-gold-green decor. Closed Sun lunchtime.

**Topanga**, 2904 W 4th Ave (☎733-3713). An extremely popular Mexican restaurant.

**Vina Vietnamese Cuisine**, 851 Denman and Haro. Go for the crab or combo plates.

## Vegetarian restaurants

**Buddhist Vegetarian**, 363 E Hastings. The city's only Chinese vegetarian restaurant.

**Concept 2**, 724 Nelson St. Organically grown ingredients in West Coast cooking; relaxed atmosphere with live jazz.

**The Naam**, 2724 W 4th Ave near Stephens. Hippy hangover, but still the oldest, best and most popular health-food and vegetarian restaurant in the city. Folk music some evenings, outside eating in summer. Open 24hr.

**Ruffage**, 1280 W Pender. Healthy food; no smoking.

**Sweet Cherubim**, 3629 W Broadway, 4242 Main St and 1105 Commercial Drive. Good organic and vegetarian restaurant/shop .

## Pubs and bars

**The Arts Club**, 1585 Johnston on Granville Island, and 1181 Seymour and Davie. Both are quietish bars; the former, which is part of the theatre complex, has a waterfront view and puts on blues and jazz after Fri & Sat shows.

**Bimini's**, 2010 W 4th Ave and Maple. Nice, relaxed pub with occasional live music – Kits Beach's best for a drink.

**Blarney Stone**, 216 Carrall. Gastown location for a lively Irish pub with a genuine feel. Restaurant, live Irish music and dance floor. Closed Sun.

**Darby D Dawes**, 2001 Macdonald St and 4th Ave. A pub handy for Kits Beach and the youth hostel, occasionally playing host to the area's more monied locals. Meals served 11.30am–7pm, snacks till 10pm; live music Fri and Sat evenings, jam sessions on Sat afternoons.

**English Bay Café**, 1795 Beach and Denman. Good for sunset views of English Bay – the downstairs bistro, not the expensive restaurant upstairs.

**La Bodega**, 1277 Howe near Davie. One of the city's best and most popular places, with tapas and excellent main courses, but more dedicated to lively drinking. It's packed later on, so try to arrive before 8pm. Closed Sun.

**Rose and Thorne**, 757 Richards near Georgia. Popular, comfortable and very close to the look and feel of an English pub.

**Sylvia Hotel**, 1154 Gilford and Beach. Nondescript but easy-going hotel bar, popular for quiet drinks and superlative waterfront views.

**Unicorn Pub**, 770 Pacific Blvd and Robson. Live music (often of the sing-along variety), pub food and many different beers, plus a large, popular summer patio.

# Nightlife and entertainment

Vancouver gives you plenty to do come sundown, laying on a varied and cosmopolitan blend of **live music** and comedy. Clubs are more adventurous than in many a Canadian city, particularly the fly-by-night alternative dives in the Italian quarter on Commercial Drive and in the backstreets off Gastown and Chinatown. There's also a choice of smarter and more conventional clubs, a handful of discos and a smattering of **gay** and **lesbian** clubs and bars. Summer nightlife often takes to the streets in West Coast fashion, with outdoor bars, and to a certain extent beaches, becoming venues in their own right. Fine weather also allows the city to host a range of **festivals**, from jazz to theatre, and the **performing arts** are as widely available as you'd expect in a city as culturally self-conscious as Vancouver.

The most comprehensive **listings** guide to all the goings-on is *Georgia Straight*, a free weekly published on Fridays; the monthly *Night Moves* concentrates more on live music. For detailed information on **gay and lesbian** events, check out *Angles*, a free monthly magazine aimed specifically at the gay and lesbian community, which is available at clubs, bookshops and many of the *Georgia Straight* distribution points. **Tickets** for many major events are sold through *Ticket-Master*, based at 1304 Hornby Street and with forty outlets round the city (☎280-4444); they'll sometimes unload discounted tickets for midweek and matinee performances.

# Live music, discos and clubs

Vancouver's live-music venues showcase a variety of local bands. Mainstream **rock** groups which have made it nationally from the city – and still play to home fans – include No Means No, Roots Roundup and Bob's Your Uncle; others hoping to follow them to fame and fortune are Strange But True, Second Nature, Green House, Audio Graffiti, Melancholy Dream and Free-Water Knockout – none of them likely to make it on the strength of their names. (For some reason the city is also a fertile breeding ground for **heavy metal** bands, and the fans here are particularly vocal.) **Jazz** is currently hot news in Vancouver, with a dozen spots specialising in the genre (ring the Jazz Line at ☎873-8999 for current and upcoming events). And while Vancouver isn't as cowpoke as, say, Calgary, it does have several clubs dedicated to **country and western**, though many are in the outer suburbs.

Many venues also double as clubs and discos, and as in any city with a healthy alternative scene there are also plenty of fun, one-off clubs that have an irritating habit of cropping up and disappearing at speed. Cover charges are usually nominal, and tickets are often available (sometimes free) at record shops. At the other end of the spectrum, the 60,000-seat *Pacific Coliseum* is on the touring itinerary of most international acts.

## Rock venues

**Club Soda**, 1055 Homer and Nelson. Large club aimed at the twenties age-group, with theatre-style seating, a big dance floor and high-tech video systems. Features an eclectic line-up of local Top 40 bands and lesser-known live shows on Sun, Mon & Wed nights; Monday is heavy metal night.

**Commodore Ballroom**, 870 Granville and Smithe. Recently given a $1 million facelift – but retaining its renowned 1929 sprung dance floor – the city's best midsized venue (room for 1200) has an adventurous music policy, regularly attracting top national and international names; club nights feature a new DJ every 2–3 weeks.

**86 Street Music Hall**, 750 Pacific Blvd and Cambie. Local Top 40 bands and big-name international gigs.

**Metro**, 1136 W Georgia and Thurlow. Vast, raucous and busy club that hosts local and touring bands. Dubious cabaret features events like "Mr Nude Rock 'n' Roll – a hen-night favourite. Closed Sun.

**Railway Club**, 579 Dunsmuir and Seymour. Long-established favourite with a reputation for excellent bookings and casual atmosphere. Has a separate "conversation" lounge, so it's ideal for a drink (and weekday lunches); watch for the Sat jazz sessions (3–7pm). Arrive before 10pm at weekends – the place is tiny.

**Roxy**, 932 Granville and Nelson. Nightly live bands with emphasis on retro 1950s, 1960s and 1970s music. Casual, fun angle with weekly theme parties, old films, comedy turns and a Wednesday "Student Night".

**Town Pump**, 66 Water and Abbott. Vancouver's best-known music venue, offering a wide range of solid and reliable bands nightly. Convenient mid-Gastown location attracts a varied clientele – it's known as something of a pick-up spot. Bar food and piano lounge until 9pm, when the band strikes up.

**Waterfront**, 686 Powell. Indie, alternative, rock and jazz bands nightly.

## Jazz and blues

**Alma Street Café**, 2505 Alma St at W 10th Ave. Wed–Sat sessions feature some of the city's best modern jazz, including top names from the States.

**Arts Club Theatre Backstage Lounge**, 1585 Johnston, Granville Island. The theatre-goers' lounge is a nice spot to hear R&B, jazz and blues, or watch the boats and sunset on False Creek.

**Carnegie's**, 1619 W Broadway near Fir. Popular bar and grill with top local and imported jazz bands in an upmarket and fake British pub atmosphere. Closed Sun.

**Classical Joint Coffee House**, 231 Carrall near Water. Intimate and low-key, the city's oldest coffee house is something of a staid home to the local jazz scene, though it also hosts folk and classical events. No alcohol – only chess games as a diversion.

**Eldorado**, at *Mulhern's Pub*, 2330 Kingsway. Big dance floor, local bands playing R&B, blues and early rock.

**Fairview**, 898 W Broadway. Local blues and 1950s rock 'n' roll in a pub atmosphere (snacks during the day, good-value evening meals).

**Glass Slipper**, 185 E 11th Ave at Main. Home of the Coastal Jazz and Blues Society, and so a more lively headquarters for the city's jazz culture than the *Classical*. Lots of contemporary and improvised sessions, often from the house band, the New Orchestra Workshop. Fri, Sat & Sun only.

**Hogan's Alley** (in *Puccini's Restaurant*), 730 Main St near E Georgia. Local jazz, and some blues and R&B in an intimate spot near Chinatown; good Italian food, too. Music Thurs, Fri & Sat.

**Hot Jazz Club**, 2120 Main St and 5th. Oldest and most established jazz club in the city. Mainly trad – swing, Dixieland and New Orleans, both local and imported. Good dance floor and big bar. Wednesday is jam night; closed Sun & Mon.

**Jake O'Grady's**, 3684 E Hastings. Live blues nightly.

**Lamplighters Pub**, 210 Abbott St. Blues every night.

**Landmark Jazz Bar**, *Sheraton-Landmark Hotel*, 1400 Robson and Nicola. Large club whose jazz emphasis is shifting slightly to R&B; atmosphere is Bavarian beer-cellar (good, solid food). Live music and dancing Wed–Sat.

**Yale Hotel**, 1300 Granville and Drake. Seedy neighbourhood, but an outstanding venue dedicated exclusively to hard-core blues and R&B. Relaxed air, big dance floor and outstanding local and international names. Noted jam sessions with up to 50 players at a time on Sat (3–8pm) and Sun (3pm–midnight). Closed Mon & Tues.

## Country and western

**Boone County Cabaret**, 801 Brunette Ave, Coquitlam. Just off the Trans-Canada – take bus #151 – this is suburbia's favourite C&W club. No cover Mon–Thurs, and free dance lessons on Mon, Tues & Thurs at 8pm. Closed Sun.

**Cheyenne Social Club**, Lynnwood Hotel, 1515 Barrow St, North Vancouver. Local C&W Thurs, Fri & Sat.

**JR Country Club**, Sandman Inn, 180 W Georgia near Cambie. Downtown's main C&W venue highlights top Canadian bands in fake Old West setting; no cover Mon–Thurs. Closed Sun.

## Discos and clubs

**Amnesia**, 99 Powell St at Columbia. Big, multi-level Gastown disco playing Top 40 music, crammed with bars, video screens and theatrical lighting. Closed Tues & Sun.

**Graceland**, 1250 Richards between Davie and Drake. Bizarre spot for art and fashion crowd. Very loud current dance music, occasional live shows and local avant-garde art on the walls. Closed Sun.

**Luv-A-Fair**, 1275 Seymour and Davie. Madcap eclectic crowd ranging from punks to drag queens. Boasts excellent dance floor and sound system, plenty of imported videos and Euro-disco, and occasional theme nights and live bands. Closed Sun.

**Richard's on Richards**, 1036 Richards and Nelson. Probably the city's best-known club/disco, but aimed foursquare at the BMW set.

**Shampers**, Coast Plaza at Stanley Park, 1733 Comox St and Denman. The West End's most popular dance floor; also open for lunch, with piano bar music till 9pm.

**Sneakey's**, 595 Hornby and Dunsmuir. Long-established fifth-storey hideaway for late-twenties and thirties age-group.

**Soft Rock Café**, W 4th Ave and Cypress. Well-heeled, mainstream dancing, live music and full meals. Popular, with frequent queues. Closed Mon.

**Systems**, 350 Richards and Hastings. Dedicated dancers, glitzy set-up, big sound and light systems; Top 40 and AOR. Closed Sun.

## Comedy clubs

**Punchlines Comedy Theatre**, 15 Water and Carrall. Gastown breeding ground of new talent. "Amateur Night" on Mon, "Comedy Jams" Tues–Thurs. Shows at 9.30pm & 11.30pm; closed Sun.

**Yuk Yuk's Komedy Kabaret**, Plaza of Nations, 750 Pacific Blvd and Cambie. Hosts top US and Canadian stand-up acts; amateur night on Wed. Shows at 9pm, plus 11.30pm on Sat & Sun. Closed Mon & Tues.

## Gay clubs and venues

**Castle Pub**, 750 Granville. Quiet gay pub. Closed Sun.

**Celebrities Night Club**, 1022 Davie and Burrard. Big disco for men and women.

**Gandydancer**, 1222 Hamilton and Davie. Trendiest and most innovative of the gay clubs. Tues & Wed are contest and cabaret nights; Fri men only.

**Heritage House Hotel**, 455 Abbott and Pender. Main-floor lounge and pub for men and women open nightly; downstairs is known as a lesbian bar (Tues–Sat; women only Fri & Sat).

**Numbers Cabaret**, 1042 Davie and Burrard. Disco for men only upstairs, mixed downstairs.

**Odyssey**, 1251 Howe near Davie. Live music Tues and Wed, disco the rest of the week. Men only on Fri.

**Shaggy Horse**, 818 Richards and Robson. Gay club patronised by an older crowd.

# Performing arts and cinema

Vancouver serves up enough highbrow culture to suit the whole spectrum of its cosmopolitan population, with plenty of unusual and avant-garde performances to spice up the more mainstream fare you'd expect of a major North American city. The focus of the city's performing arts is the **Queen Elizabeth Theatre** (☎873-3311), near the bus station at 649 Cambie and Dunsmuir, which plays host to a steady procession of visiting theatre, opera and dance troupes, and even the occasional big rock band. For information on the Vancouver arts scene call the Arts Hotline (☎684-ARTS) or visit their office at 884 Granville near Smithe, in the Granville entrance of the *Orpheum Theatre*. There's a special line for information relating to dance (☎872-0432).

The western capital of Canada's film industry, Vancouver is also increasingly favoured by Hollywood studios in their pursuit of cheaper locations and production deals. It's no surprise, then, that the spread of **cinemas** is so good. Home-produced and Hollywood first-run films play in the downtown cinemas on "Theatre Row" – the two blocks of Granville between Robson and Nelson – and other big complexes, and there's no shortage of houses for more esoteric productions.

## Theatre

**Arts Club Theatre** (☎687-1644). A leading light in the city's theatre scene, performing at three venues: the main stage, at 1585 Johnston St on Granville Island, offers mainstream drama, comedies and musicals; the next-door bar presents small-scale revues and cabarets; and a third stage, at 1181 Seymour and Davie, focuses on avant-garde plays and Canadian dramatists – a launching pad for the likes of Michael J Fox.

**Back Alley Theatre**, 751 Thurlow near Robson (☎688-7013). In addition to its quality shows (mainly comedies), this intimate venue has achieved a cult status for its "theatresports", a quirky set-up in which teams of actors compete for applause – improvisation and audience participation are the order of the day.

**Firehall Arts Centre**, 280 E Cordova and Gore (☎689-0926). Stationed in the alternative and multi-ethnic heart of the city, this is the leader of Vancouver's community and avant-garde theatre pack, and also presents mime, music, video and visual arts.

**Vancouver East Cultural Centre**, 1895 Venables and Victoria (☎254-9578). Renowned performance space housed in an old church, utilised by a highly eclectic mix of theatre, dance, mime and musical groups.

**Waterfront Theatre**, 1405 Anderson St (☎685-6217). Home to three resident companies; also holds workshops and readings.

**Theatre under the Stars**, Malkin Bowl, Stanley Park (☎687-0174). Summer productions here are generally fun and lightweight, but occasionally suffer from being staged in Canada's rainiest city.

## Dance and opera

**Anna Wyman Dance Theatre** (☎662-8846). Although their repertoire runs the balletic gamut, this group is chiefly dedicated to contemporary dance; in addition to their theatre shows, they occasionally put on free outdoor performances at Granville Island and at Robson Square near the Art Gallery.

**Ballet British Columbia** (☎669-5954). The province's top company, performing – with major visiting companies – at the *Queen Elizabeth Theatre.*

**Vancouver Opera** (☎682-2871). Lays on four lavish productions between October and May at the *Queen Elizabeth Theatre.*

## Cinema

**Cineplex**, in the lower level of the Royal Centre at Georgia and Burrard. Ten-screen complex – the biggest first-run venue in town.

**Pacific Cinematheque**, 1131 Howe near Helmcken. Best of the art houses; programmes may not be to all tastes, but any film buff will find something to tempt.

**Paradise**, 919 Granville. The best bargain for first runs.

**Ridge Theatre**, 3131 Arbutus and 16th Ave. New releases, European films and classic reruns.

**Vancouver East Cinema**, 2290 Commercial and 7th. Affiliated to the *Ridge*, with similar fare.

# Festivals

Warm summers, outdoor venues and a culture-hungry population combine to make Vancouver an important festival city. Recognised as one of the leading beanos of its kind, Vancouver's annual **International Jazz Festival** (late June to early July) is organised by the enthusiastic Coastal Jazz and Blues Society. Past line-ups have featured such luminaries as Wynton Marsalis, Youssou n'Dour, Ornette Coleman, Carla Bley and John Zorn. In all, some 400 international musicians congregate annually, many offering workshops and free concerts in addition to paid-admission events. Other music festivals include the **North Vancouver Folk Festival**, a bevy of international acts centred on the *Centennial Theatre* in mid-June and, further afield in Whistler (see p.559), a **Country & Bluegrass Festival** in mid-July.

Theatre festivals come thick and fast, particularly in the summer. The chief event – and one that's growing in size and reputation – is the **Fringe Festival**, modelled on the Edinburgh equivalent. It currently runs to 550 shows, staged by ninety companies at ten venues. There's also an annual **Shakespeare Festival** (June–Aug) in Vanier Park and an **International Comedy Festival** in early August on Granville Island. Many of the city's art-house cinemas join forces to host the **Vancouver International Film Festival**, an annual showcase for over 150 films running from late September to mid-October. Canada's largest independent dance festival, **Dancing on the Edge**, runs for ten days in September at the *Firehall Arts Centre*, featuring the work of fifty of the country's hottest (and weirdest) choreographers.

# Listings

**Airlines** *Air Canada*, ☎688-5515; *American Airlines*, ☎222-2532; *British Airways*, ☎270-8131; *Canadian Airlines*, ☎682-1411.

**American Express** 1040 W Georgia near Burrard (☎669-2813) is open Mon–Fri 8.30am–5.30pm, Sat 10am–4pm. Another office on the fourth floor of the *The Bay* department store, Granville & Georgia, is open Mon–Fri 9.30am–5pm.

**Bike rental** *Stanley Park Rentals*, 676 Chilco & Alberni (☎681-5581); *Bayshore/West Point Cycles*, 1876 W Georgia near Denman (☎688-2453); and *Robson Cycles*, 1463 Robson near Broughton (☎687-2777).

**Books** *Duthie Books*, 919 Robson St, is the best mainstream bookshop. *World Wide Books and Maps*, 1247 Granville St, is adequate for maps, guides and travel.

**Buses** For long-haul destinations, *Greyhound* (☎662-3222); for Vancouver Island, *Pacific Coach Lines* (☎662-8074); for the Sunshine Coast, Powell River, Whistler, Pemberton and Nanaimo on Vancouver Island, *Maverick Coach Lines* (☎662-8051 or ☎1-800-972-6300). Note that only *Greyhound* accepts credit cards.

**Car rental** *Rent-A-Wreck*, 1015 Burrard St (☎688-0001) and 1085 Kingsway near Glen (☎876-5629); *Hertz*, 666 Seymour St (☎688-2411); *Budget*, 450 W Georgia St (☎685-0536).

**Consulates** *Great Britain*, 800-1111 Melville (☎683-4421); *US*, 1075 W Georgia (☎685-4311).

**Doctors** The College of Physicians will provide the names of three doctors closest to you (☎733-7758). For the nearest dentist, call ☎736-3621.

**Exchange** *International Securities Exchange*, 1169 Robson near Thurlow; *Deak International*, 617 Granville near Dunsmuir.

**Ferries** *BC Ferries* for services to Vancouver Island, the Gulf Islands, the Sunshine Coast, Prince Rupert, the Inside Passage and the Queen Charlotte Islands; recorded information on ☎669-1211/685-1021.

**Gay and lesbian switchboard** 1-1170 Bute St ☎684-6869.

**Hospitals** *St Paul's Hospital* is the closest to downtown at 1081 Burrard St (☎682-2344). The city hospital is *Vancouver General* at 855 W 12th near Oak, just south of Broadway (☎875-4111).

**Left luggage** At the bus station ($1 per 24hr).

**Library** 750 Robson and Burrard; open Mon–Thurs 9.30am–9.30pm, Fri & Sat 9.30am–6pm. An excellent source of books and free literature on Vancouver, BC and Canada.

**Lost property** *BC Transit*, ☎682-7887; police (☎665-2232).

**Newspapers and magazines** UK and US editions at *Manhattan Books and Magazines*, 1089 Robson near Thurlow, and *European News Import*, 1136 Robson.

**Parking** Main downtown garages are at *The Bay* (entrance on Richards near Dunsmuir), Robson Square (on Smithe and Howe), and the Pacific Centre (on Howe and Dunsmuir) – all are expensive and fill up quickly. A better idea might be to leave your car at the free *Park'n'Ride* in New Westminster (off Hwy 1).

**Pharmacies** *Shopper's Drug Mart*, 1125 Davie and Thurlow, has the longest hours of any downtown pharmacy – Mon–Sat 9am–midnight, Sun 9am–9pm. *Carson Midnite Drug Store*, 6517 Main at 49th, is open daily until midnight.

**Post office** Main office at 349 W Georgia and Homer; branches in *The Bay* and *Eaton's* department stores.

**Taxis** *Yellow Cab* (☎681-3311); *Vancouver Taxi* (☎255-5111).

**Train enquiries** *VIA* (☎1-800-665-8630); *BC Rail* (☎631-3500).

**Weather** ☎666-1087.

**Women's Resource Centre** 1144 Robson near Thurlow (☎685-3934); open Mon–Fri 10am–2pm.

# VANCOUVER ISLAND

**Vancouver Island's** proximity to Vancouver makes it one of western Canada's premier tourist destinations, though its popularity is out of all proportion to what is, in most cases, a pale shadow of the scenery on offer on the mainland. The largest of North America's west coast islands, it stretches almost 500km from north to south, but has a population of around only 500,000, mostly concentrated around **Victoria**, whose small-town feel belies its role as British Columbia's second metropolis and provincial capital. It is also the most British of Canadian cities in feel and appearance, something it shame-lessly plays up to attract its two million – largely American – visitors annually. While Victoria makes a convenient base for touring the island – and, thanks mainly to its super-lative museum, it merits a couple of days in its own right – little else here, or for that matter in any of the island's other sizeable towns, is enough to justify an overnight stop.

For most visitors Vancouver Island's main attraction is the great outdoors. The island is a mosaic of landscapes, principally defined by a central spine of snow-capped mountains which divide it decisively between the rugged and sparsely populated wilderness of the west coast and the more sheltered lowlands of the east. Rippling hills characterise the northern and southern tips, and few areas are free of the lush forest mantle that supports one of BC's most lucrative logging industries. Apart from three minor east–west roads, all the urban centres are linked by a single highway running almost the entire length of the east coast.

Once beyond the main centres of **Duncan** and **Nanaimo**, the northern two-thirds of the island is distinctly underpopulated. Locals and tourists alike are lured by the beaches at **Parksville** and **Qualicum**, while the stunning seascapes of **Pacific Rim National Park**, protecting the central portion of the island's west coast, and **Strathcona Provincial Park**, which embraces the heart of the island's mountain fastness, are the main destinations for most visitors. Both offer the usual panoply of outdoor activities, hikers being particularly well served by the national park's **West Coast Trail**, a tough and increasingly popular long-distance path.

For a large number of travellers, however, the island is little more than a necessary way-station on a longer journey north. Thousands annually make the trip to **Port Hardy** at the northern tip to pick up the ferry that follows the so-called **Inside Passage**, a breathtaking trip up the British Columbia coast to Prince Rupert. You'll probably meet more backpackers plying this route than anywhere else in western Canada, many of them en route to the far north on the ferries that continue on from Prince Rupert to Skagway and Alaska.

## Getting to Vancouver Island

There are three ways to reach Vancouver Island – by bus and ferry, car and ferry, or air. Most people travelling under their own steam from Vancouver go the first route, which is a simple matter of buying an all-inclusive through ticket to Victoria. More involved crossings to other points on the island, however, are worth considering if you wish to skip Victoria and head as quickly as possible to Port Hardy for the Inside Passage ferry connections, or to Strathcona or Pacific Rim parks.

### By bus and ferry

If you're travelling without transport, the most most painless way to Victoria is to buy a **Pacific Coach Lines** (*PCL*) ticket at the Vancouver bus terminal, which takes you, inclusive of the ferry crossing, to Victoria's central bus station. Buses leave hourly in the summer, every two hours in the winter: total journey time is about three and a half hours and a single ticket costs $19.50. The ferry crossing takes 95 minutes, and offers some stunning views as the boat navigates the narrow channels between the Gulf Islands en route. Be sure to keep your ticket stub for reboarding the bus after the crossing. It's also worth stocking up on food on board, as subsidised ferry meals are famously cheap (queues form instantly). You can save yourself about $10 by using public transport at each end and buying a ferry ticket ($5.75) separately, but for the extra hassle and time involved it hardly seems worth it.

### Other ferries

Crossings are a good deal less straightforward for **motorists**, especially during the busy summer months. Pick up the widely available *BC Ferries* timetables and make a reservation, or be prepared for some long queues.

*BC Ferries* (☎386-3431) operates four routes to the island across the Strait of Georgia from mainland British Columbia. The most direct and heavily used by Victoria–Vancouver passengers is the **Tsawwassen to Swartz Bay** connection, the

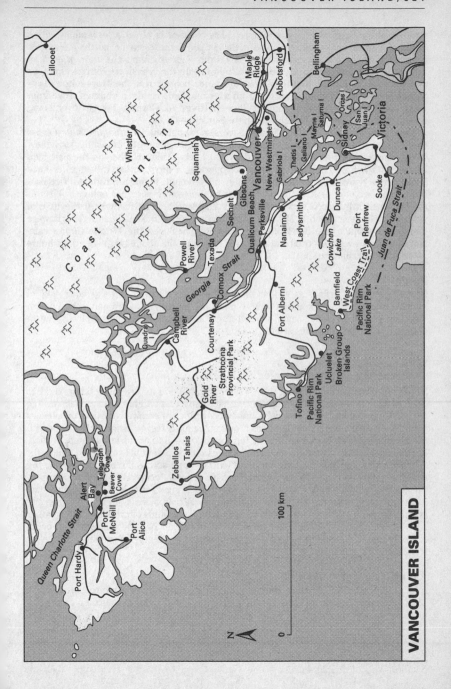

**VANCOUVER ISLAND**

route used by *Pacific Coach Lines*' buses. Tsawwassen is about a forty-minute drive south of downtown Vancouver; Swartz Bay is the same distance north of Victoria. Ferries ply the route almost continuously from 7am to 9pm. The new *Mid-Island Express* from **Tsawwassen to Nanaimo**, midway up the island, as yet has only four departures daily for the two-hour crossing. More boats cover the **Horseshoe Bay–Nanaimo** route, a 95-minute journey from a terminal about fifteen minutes' drive from West Vancouver. The fourth route is **Powell River to Comox**, Powell River being some 160km northwest of Vancouver on the Sunshine Coast.

Travellers **from the United States** have several options. *Washington State Ferries* (☎381-1551) runs ferries **from Anacortes**, ninety minutes north of Seattle, to Sidney, thirty minutes north of Victoria (1–2 daily; 3hr), via Friday Harbor on the San Juan Islands. *Black Ball Transport* (☎386-2202) operates a ferry across the Juan de Fuca Strait between **Port Angeles** on Washington's Olympic Peninsula right to Victoria's Inner Harbour (1–4 daily; 95min). For foot passengers, a speedier option is *Victoria Rapid Transit*'s hydrofoil service from Port Angeles (1 daily; 55min). At the time of writing the long-established *BC Stena Line* ferries between **Seattle** and Victoria were threatened with closure. For foot passengers only, however, the *Victoria Clipper* catamaran makes two daily trips between the two cities in about two and a half hours (☎206/448-5000 in Seattle).

## By air

Several provincial airlines as well as the big two – *Air Canada* and *Canadian* – fly to Victoria, though it's an expensive way to make the journey if you're only coming from Vancouver or Washington state. Open return fares from Vancouver typically run to around $115, excursion fares around $75.

# Victoria

**VICTORIA** has decided it's not named after a queen and an era for nothing, and has gone to town in serving up lashings of fake Victoriana and chintzy commercialism – tea rooms, Union Jacks, bagpipers, pubs and ersatz echoes of empire confront you at every turn. Much of the waterfront area has a quaint, English feel – "Brighton Pavilion with the Himalayas for a backdrop", as Kipling remarked – and Victoria has more British-born residents than anywhere in Canada, but its tourist potential is exploited chiefly for American visitors who make the short sea journey from across the border. Despite the seasonal influx and the sometimes atrocious attractions designed to part tourists from their money, it's a small, relaxed place, worth lingering in if only for its inspirational museum – and with the Commonwealth Games taking place here in 1994, the city should be getting livelier with each passing month. Though often damp, the weather here is extremely mild: Victoria's meteorological station has the distinction of being the only one in Canada to record a winter in which the temperature never fell below freezing.

## A brief history of Victoria

Inhabited originally by **Salish natives**, Victoria received its first **white colonists** in 1843 when the Hudson's Bay Company chose the island's southeastern tip as the site of a new fur-trading post (Fort Victoria). British pioneers were brought in to settle the land by a Bay subsidiary, the Puget Sound Agricultural Company, which quickly built several large company farms as a focus for immigration. In time, the harbour became a major port for the British navy's Pacific fleet, a role it still fulfills for the bulk of Canada's present navy.

Boomtime came in the 1850s following the mainland gold strikes, when Victoria's port became an essential stop-off and supplies centre for prospectors heading across the water and into the interior. Military and bureaucratic personnel moved in to ensure order, bringing Victorian morals and manners with them. Alongside there grew a rumbustious shanty town of shops, bars and brothels, one run by "Gassy" Jack Leighton, soon to become one of Vancouver's unwitting founders.

Though the gold-rush bubble soon burst, Victoria carried on as a military, economic and political centre, becoming capital of the newly created British Columbia in 1866 – years before the foundation of Vancouver. British values were cemented in stone by the Canadian Pacific Railway, which built the *Empress Hotel* in 1908 in place of a proposed railway link that never came. Victoria's planned role as Canada's western rail terminus was surrendered to Vancouver, and with it any chance of realistic growth or industrial development. These days the town survives almost entirely on the backs of tourists, the civil service bureaucracy, and – shades of the home country – retirees in search of a mild-weathered retreat.

## Arrival and information

**Victoria International Airport** is 20km north of the city centre on Hwy 17. The *Airporter* shuttle bus heads downtown every half-hour between 8.15am and 11.45pm; single fare for the thirty-minute journey is $9. The **bus terminal** is downtown at 700 Douglas and Belleville, close to the Royal British Columbia Museum; the central *VIA* **train station** is at 450 Pandora Street, about seven blocks north of the *Empress Hotel*, but you'll only arrive there if you've managed to get a seat on the lone daily train from Courtenay and Nanaimo.

Victoria's **infocentre**, at 812 Wharf Street, almost in front of the *Empress Hotel* on the harbour (daily May–Sept 9am–8pm; Oct–April 9am–5pm; ☎382-2127), can probably claim to be the world's best-stocked tourist office. Its huge range of information – on both Victoria and Vancouver Island as a whole – makes as good a reason as any for starting a tour of the island from the city.

You're unlikely to need to take a local **bus** anywhere, but if you do, most services run from the corner of Douglas and Yates. The fare within the large central zone is $1 – tickets and day passes are sold at the infocentre and marked outlets, or you can pay on board if you have the exact fare.

## Accommodation

Victoria fills up quickly in the summer, and most of its budget accommodation is well known and heavily patronised. Top-price hotels cluster around the Inner Harbour area; **hostels** and more downmarket alternatives are scattered all over, though the largest concentration of cheap **hotels** and **motels** is around the Gorge Road and Douglas Street areas northwest of downtown. Reservations are virtually obligatory in all categories, though the infocentre's accommodation service will root out a room if you're stuck (☎382-1131 or ☎1-800-663-3883). They are more than likely to offer you **bed and breakfast**, of which the town has a vast selection; many owners of the more far-flung places will pick you up from downtown. It's also worth consulting one of the specialist B&B agencies: *All-Season* (☎595-2337), *Canada-West* (☎388-4620) or *Garden City* (☎479-9999).

Victoria's commercial **campgrounds** are full to bursting in summer, with most space given over to RVs. Few of these are convenient for the city centre anyway – given that you'll have to travel, you might as well head for one of the more scenic provincial park sites. Most are on the Trans-Canada Highway to the north, or on Hwy 14 east of Victoria.

## Hotels and motels

**Cherry Bank Hotel**, 825 Burdett St (☎385-5380). Deservedly popular budget hotel, marked by dubious red decor and a rotating plastic mermaid on the roof, but excellent rooms and a good breakfast included in the price. Singles start at $35, doubles at $45; reservations essential.

**Hotel Douglas**, 1450 Douglas and Pandora (☎383-4157). Clean, no-frills and slightly rough-edged hotel. Opposite city hall on bus routes #1, 6, 14 and 30. Singles from $30 with shared bath, doubles from $45.

**Helm's Inn**, 668 Superior St (☎385-5767). Popular if gaudily decorated hotel just half a block from the Royal BC Museum. Singles and doubles start at $75; off-season rooms from $50.

**James Bay Inn**, 270 Government and Toronto (☎384-7151). Vying with the *Cherry Bank* as Victoria's best budget option, this old Edwardian building was the last home of painter Emily Carr. Simple but adequate rooms, restaurant and *Unwinder* pub in the basement. Located two blocks south of the Government Buildings (buses #5 or 30 to Government and Superior Street). Wide variety of rooms with singles from $25, doubles from $30.

**Maple Leaf Inn**, 120 Gorge Rd (☎388-9901). Alpine chalet ambience with sauna and swimming pools. Free coffee and coin-operated laundry. Singles from $40, doubles from $45; rooms with kitchen for a $10 supplement.

**Mayfair Motel**, 650 Speed Ave and Douglas (☎388-7337). Small motel 2km north of downtown. Doubles $50–60.

**Oak Beach Hotel**, 1175 Beach Dr (☎598-4556). Upmarket, mock-Elizabethan hotel on Haro Strait, 6km east of downtown, with good sea and island views. The most basic rooms cost $65–100 from May–Sept, with ten percent discounts off-season. Bus #2.

**Strathcona**, 919 Douglas St (☎383-7137). Large, modern downtown hotel, rooms with baths and TVs. Singles from $40, doubles from $45.

**Sussex Apartment Hotel**, 1001 Douglas and Broughton (☎386-3441). Choice of old-fashioned studio rooms or small apartments with kitchenettes. Take bus #1, 4, 5 or 30. Singles $40–50, doubles $50–60; weekly and monthly rates available except May 15–Aug 31.

## Bed and breakfast

**Battery Street Guest House**, 670 Battery St (☎385-4632). Central location between Douglas and Government streets, one block from the sea; singles from $35, doubles from $55.

**Bryn Gwyn Guest House**, 809 Burdett St (☎383-1878). Very central location. Singles from $40, doubles from $60.

**Craigmyle Guest House**, 1037 Craigmyle Rd (☎595-5411). Comfortable, friendly antique-furnished home 1.5km walk from downtown; buses #11 or 14 to the corner of Fort Street and Joan Crescent; singles from $40, doubles from $60.

**Glyn House**, 154 Robertson St (☎598-0064). Southeast of the city on the marine drive and 3min walk from Gonzales Beach. Period decor in 1912 home and rooms with private bathrooms, also available for weekly and monthly rentals; doubles from $70.

**Heritage House**, 3308 Heritage Lane (☎479-0892). Popular mansion-sized spot in a quiet residential area northwest of the centre. Bus #22 to Grange Road. Singles from $55; reservations essential in summer.

**Seaside Cottage**, 157 Robertson St (☎595-1047). Overlooking the ocean southeast of the centre; singles from $45.

## Hostels and student accommodation

**Salvation Army Men's Hostel**, 525 Johnson St (☎384-3396). Better than it sounds, being clean and modern, but for men only. Rooms are given on a first-come, first-served basis, with doors open at 4pm. Dorm beds are $10, private rooms $20.

**University of Victoria** (☎721-8395). From May to September you can take rooms at the university's nicely situated campus, 20min from downtown on buses #7 or 14. By phone ask for the University Housing and Conference Services, or register on-site at the Housing Office, near the campus Coffee Gardens. Private rooms with shared bath from $25 for singles, $40 for doubles, including breakfast.

**Victoria Backpackers' Hostel**, 1418 Fernwood Rd (☎386-4471). Less convenient than the youth hostel: take bus #1, 10, 11, 14, 27 or 28 to Fernwood. Dorm beds are $10; private singles $20, doubles $30. No curfew.

**Victoria Youth Hostel**, 516 Yates and Wharf (☎385-4511). A large, modern and well-run place just a few blocks north of the Inner Harbour. Open Mon–Thurs 7.30am to midnight, Fri–Sun 7am–2am. Members $10. Bus #23 or #24 from the Johnson Street Bridge.

**YWCA**, 880 Courtney and Quadra (☎386-7511). Shared cafeteria and sporting facilities, including swimming pool, but rooms for women only. Located a short stroll from downtown and on the #1 bus route. Singles are $25, doubles $40; discounts Sept–May.

## Campgrounds

**Fort Victoria Camping**, 340 Island Hwy 1A (☎479-8112). Closest site to downtown, located 6km north of Victoria off the Trans-Canada.

**Goldstream Provincial Park**, 2930 Trans-Canada Highway (☎387-4363). 20km north of the city, but Victoria's best camping option, with plenty of hiking, swimming and fishing opportunities.

**Thetis Lake**, 1938 Trans-Canada Highway (☎478-3845). Runs a close second to Goldstream Park for the pleasantness of its setting, and is only 10km north of downtown.

**McDonald Provincial Park**. A government site with limited facilities 32km from Victoria, but only 3km from the Swartz Bay Ferry Terminal if you've just come off the boat or have a ferry to catch the next morning.

**Weir's Beach Resort**, 5191 Williams Head Rd (☎478-3323). Enticing beach front location 24km east of Victoria on Hwy 14.

# The City

The Victoria that's worth bothering with is very small: almost everything worth seeing, as well as the best shops and restaurants, is within walking distance in the **Inner Harbour** area and the Old Town district behind it. Foremost amongst its diversions are the Royal British Columbia Museum and the *Empress Hotel*. Most of the other trumpeted attractions are dreadful, and many charge entry fees out of all proportion to what's on show. If you're tempted by the Royal London Wax Museum, Sea World (caged killer whales), Undersea Gardens, Miniature World, English Village, Anne Hathaway's Cottage, the Olde English Inn or any of Victoria's other dubious commercial propositions, details are available from the infocentre.

The best of the area's beaches are well out of town on Hwy 14 and Hwy 1 (see p.536), but for some local swimming head to **Willows Beach** on the Esplanade in Oak Bay, 2km east of Victoria.

## The Royal British Columbia Museum

The **Royal British Columbia Museum**, 675 Belleville St (May–Sept daily 9.30am–7pm; Oct–April Tues–Sun 10am–5.30pm; $5), is perhaps the best museum in Canada, and certainly one of North America's top ten. All conceivable aspects of the province are examined, but the **native peoples** section is probably the definitive collection of a much-covered genre, while the natural history sections – huge re-creations of natural habitats, complete with sights, sounds and smells – are mind-boggling in scope and imagination. Allow at least two trips to take it all in; the entry ticket is valid for 48 hours.

From the word go – a huge stuffed mammoth and sculpture of a tweedy Brit and his chiffon-swathed wife taking tea – you can tell that thought, humour and a lot of money have gone into the museum. Much of the cash must have been sunk into its most popular display, the **Open Ocean**, a self-contained, in-depth look at the sea and the deep-level ocean. Groups of ten are admitted into a series of tunnels, dark rooms, lifts and mock-ups of submarines at thirty-minute intervals. You take a time-coded ticket and wait your turn, so either arrive early or reckon on seeing the rest of the museum first. Though rather heavy-handed in its we're-all-part-of-the-cosmic-soup message, it's still an object lesson in presentation and state-of-the-art museum dynamics. It's also designed to be dark and enclosed, and signs wisely warn you to stay out if you suffer even a twinge of claustrophobia.

The first floor contains **dioramas**, full-scale reconstructions of some of the many natural habitats found in British Columbia. The idea of re-creating shorelines, coastal rainforests and Fraser Delta landscapes may sound far-fetched, yet all are incredibly realistic, down to dripping water and cool, dank atmospheres. Audio-visual displays and a tumult of information accompany the exhibits (the beaver film is worth hunting down), most of which focus attention on the province's 25,600km of coastline, a side of the island usually overlooked in favour of its interior forests and mountains.

Upstairs on the second floor is the mother of all the tiny museums of bric-a-brac and pioneer memorabilia in BC. Arranged eccentrically from the present day backwards, it explores every aspect of the province's **social history** over two centuries in nit-picking detail. Prominently featured are the best part of an early-twentieth-century town, complete with cinema and silent films, plus comprehensive displays on logging, mining, the gold rush, farming, fishing and lesser domestic details, all the artefacts and accompanying information being presented with impeccable finesse.

Up on the mezzanine third floor is a superb collection of **Native American art, culture and history** (see box below). It's presented in gloomy light, against sombre wood walls and brown carpet: precautions intended to protect the fragile exhibits, but which also create a solemn atmosphere in keeping with the tragic nature of many of

## THE NATIVE CULTURES OF THE NORTHWEST COAST

Of all of Canada's native peoples the numerous linguistic groups that inhabit the northwest coast of British Columbia have the most sophisticated art tradition and the most lavish of ceremonials. Traditionally their social organisation stemmed from a belief in a mythical time when humans and animals were essentially the same: each tribe was divided into **kin-groups** who were linked by a common supernatural animal ancestor and shared the same names, ritual dances, songs and regalia. Seniority within each kin group was held by a rank of chiefs and nobles, who controlled the resources of private property such as house sites, stands of cedar, and fishing, gathering and hunting territories.

Such privileges, almost unique among Canadian native groups, led to the accumulation of private wealth, and thus great emphasis was placed on their inheritance. Central to the power structure was the ceremonial **potlatch**, which was held in the winter-village, a seasonal resting place for these otherwise nomadic people, located where the supernatural forces were believed to be most accessible. The potlatch marked every significant occasion from the birth of an heir to the raising of a carved pole, and underscored an individual's right to his or her inherited status. Taking its name from the Chinook word for "gift", the potlatch also had the function of **redistributing wealth**. All the guests at the potlatch acted as witnesses to whatever event or object was being validated, and were repaid for their services with gifts from the host chief. Though these gifts often temporarily bankrupted the host, they heightened his prestige and ensured that he would be repaid in kind at a subsequent potlatch.

The most important element of potlatches were the **masked dances** that re-enacted ancestral encounters with supernatural beings, and were the principal means of perpetuating the history and heritage of each kin-group. Created by artists whose innovative ideas were eagerly sought by chiefs in order to impress their guests, the dramatic masks were often elaborate mechanisms that could burst open to reveal the wearer or – like the well-known Cannibal Bird – could produce loud and disconcerting noises.

The **Kwakiutl** produced the most developed potlatches, featuring highly ranked dances like the *hamatsa* or **"cannibal dance"**, whose performers had served a long apprenticeship as participants in less exalted dances. Before the *hamatsa* the initiate was sent to the "Cannibal at the North End of the World", a long period of seclusion and instruction in the snow-bound woods. On returning to the village he would seem to be in a complete cannibalistic frenzy and would rush around biting members of the audience. These apparent victims were all paid for their role, which usually involved cutting them-the displays. The collection divides into two epochs – before and after the coming of Europeans – tellingly linked by a single native carving of a white man, starkly and brilliantly capturing the initial wonder and weirdness of the new arrivals. Alongside are shamanic displays and carvings of previously taboo subjects, subtly illustrating the first breakdown of the old ways. The whole collection reflects this thoughtful and oblique approach, taking you to the point where smallpox virtually wiped out in one year a culture which was eight millennia in the making. A section on land and reservations is left for last – the issues are contentious even today – and even if you're succumbing to museum-fatigue, the arrogance and duplicity of the documents on display will make you gasp. The highlights in this section are many, but try to make a point of seeing the short film footage *In the Land of the War Canoes* (1914), the **Bighouse** and its chants, and the audio-visual display on native myths and superstition. Outside the museum, there's also **Thunderbird Park**, a strip of grass with a handful of totem poles.

## Helmcken House

**Helmcken House** (Tues–Sun 10am–5pm) stands in Thunderbird Park adjacent to the museum, a predictable heritage offering that showcases the home (built in 1852), furnishings and embroidery talents of the Helmcken family. Dr John Helmcken was

---

selves with knives to draw a flow of blood – and the *hamatsa* would burst blood-filled bladders in his mouth to add to the carnage, while relatives shook rattles and sang to tame him. A fantastic finale came with the arrival of the loudly clacking "Cannibal Birds", dancers dressed in long strips of cedar bark and huge masks, of which the most fearsome was the "Cannibal Raven", whose long straight beak could crush a human skull. The *hamatsa* would then return in ceremonial finery completely restored to his human state.

As elsewhere in Canada, **European contact** was disastrous for the coastal peoples. The establishment of fur-trading posts in the early nineteenth century led to the abandonment of traditional economic cycles, the loss of their creative skills through reliance on readily available European goods, the debilitation of alcohol and internecine wars. Though most of BC remains non-treaty, lands on Vancouver Island were surrendered to become the "Entire property of the White people forever" in return for small payments – the entire Victoria area was obtained for 371 blankets. Infectious disease, the greatest of all threats, reached its peak with the 1862 smallpox epidemic, which spread from Victoria along the entire coast and far into the interior, killing probably a third of BC's native population.

In this period of decline, potlatches assumed an increased significance as virtually the only medium of cultural continuity, with rival chiefs asserting their status through ever more extravagant displays – even going as far as to burn slaves who had been captured in battle. Excesses such as these and the newly adopted "whiskey feasts" were seen by the **missionaries** as a confirmation that these peoples were enveloped in the "dark mantle of degrading superstition". With BC's entry into confederation the responsibility for the natives fell to the federal government in faraway Ottawa, much of whose knowledge of the indigenous peoples came from the missionaries – the subsequent **Indian Act**, passed in 1884, prohibited the potlatch ceremony.

For a while the defiant native groups managed to evade detection by holding potlatches at fishing camps rather than the winter-villages, and there were few successful prosecutions until the 1920s. Things came to a head in 1922 with the conviction of 34 Kwakiutl from Alert Bay – all were sentenced to jail terms but a deal was struck whereby all those who surrendered their potlatch regalia were freed. Thirty years later, when potlatching was relegalised, native pressure began to mount for return of these treasures from the collections into which they had been dispersed, but it took a further twenty years for the federal government to agree to return the goods on condition that they be put on public display. Though the masks totally lose their dramatic emphasis in static exhibitions, many of the more local museums have a dual function as community centres, and as such are vital to the preservation of a dynamic native culture.

Fort Victoria's doctor and local political bigwig, and his house is a typical monument to Victoria values. It's probably only of interest if you've so far managed to avoid any of Canada's many thousands of similar houses. Nonetheless it's free, and the staff are friendly. Just behind there's another old building, the **St Anne's Schoolhouse** ($2).

## The Parliament Buildings

Impressive by Canadian standards, the huge Victorian pile of the **Parliament Buildings**, at 501 Belleville St, is old and imposing in the manner of a large British town hall. Beautifully lit at night (though locals grumble about the cost), the domed building is fronted by the sea and well-kept gardens – a pleasant enough ensemble, though it doesn't warrant the manic enthusiasm visited on it by hordes of summer tourists. Designed by Francis Rattenbury, who was also responsible for the *Empress Hotel* opposite, it was completed in 1898. Figures from Victoria's grey bureaucratic past are duly celebrated, the main door guarded by statues of Sir James Douglas, who chose the site of the city, and Sir Matthew Baillie Begbie (aka the "Hanging Judge"), responsible for law and order during the heady days of gold fever. Sir George Vancouver keeps an eye on proceedings from the top of the dome. Free tours start from the main steps daily in summer every twenty minutes (precise timings depend on the political business of the moment). Look out for the dagger which killed Captain Cook, and the gold-plated dome, painted with scenes from Canadian history.

## Beacon Hill Park

The best park within walking distance of the town centre is **Beacon Hill Park**, south of the Inner Harbour behind the museum. Victoria's biggest green space, it has lots of paths and quiet corners, and plenty of views over the water to the distant mountains (especially on its southern side). It also claims the world's tallest totem pole, Mile Zero of the Trans-Canada Highway, and – that ultimate emblem of Englishness – a cricket pitch. Some of the trees are massive old-growth timbers that you'd normally only see on the island's west coast.

## Crystal Gardens and Butchart Gardens

The heavily advertised **Crystal Gardens**, behind the bus terminal at 713 Douglas St (daily 10am–5pm; $5.50), was designed on the model of London's destroyed Crystal Palace and was billed on opening in 1925 as housing the "Largest Saltwater Swimming Pool in the British Empire". Now much restored, the greenery-, monkey- and bird-filled greenhouse makes for an unaccountably popular tourist spot; only the exterior has any claims to architectural sophistication, and much of its effect is spoilt by the souvenir shops on its ground-floor arcade. Once the meeting place of the town's tea-sipping elite, it still plays host to events such as the *Jive and Ballroom Dance Club* and the *People Meeting People Dance*. The daytime draws are the conservatory-type tea room and tropical gardens.

If you're really into things horticultural you'll want to make a trek out to the **Butchart Gardens**, 22km north of Victoria on Hwy 17 towards the Swartz Bay ferry terminal (daily 8am–sunset; $10; $1 for readmission within 24hr; bus #74 from downtown). Internationally renowned, they were started in 1904 by the wife of a mine owner to landscape one of her husband's quarries, and now cover fifty acres, comprising rose, Japanese and Italian gardens and lots of decorative details. About half a million visitors a year tramp through the foliage, which includes over a million plants and 700 different species.

## The Empress Hotel

A town is usually desperate when one of its key attractions is a hotel, but in the case of Victoria the **Empress Hotel**, 721 Government St, is so physically overbearing and plays such a part in the town's tourist appeal that it demands some sort of attention. You're unlikely to be staying here – rooms start at around $200 and are largely snapped up by Japanese visitors – but it's well worth wandering through the huge lobbies and palatial dining areas for a glimpse of well-restored colonial splendour. In a couple of lounges there's a fairly limp dress code – no trainers, dirty jeans or backpacks – but elsewhere you can wander at will.

The hotel's **Crystal Lounge** and its lovely Tiffany-glass dome forms the most opulent part of the hotel on view, but the marginally less ornate entrance lounge is *the* place for the charade of afternoon tea, and indulging can be a bit of a laugh. There's also a reasonable bar downstairs, the **Garden Café**, and the so-called **Bengal Lounge** where you can have a curry and all the trimmings for about $10 (the hotel also boasts Victoria's best-appointed toilets). For a splurge try the London clubland surroundings – chesterfields and aspidistras – and the champagne-and-chocolate-cake special ($8.50) on offer in the lounge to the left of the entrance lobby.

### The rest of the city

Outside the Inner Harbour Victoria has a scattering of minor attractions that don't fit into any logical tour of the city – and at any rate are only short-stop diversions. Most have a pioneer slant (Regent's Park House, Snooke Regional Museum, Sidney Museum), though if you want old buildings the best is **Craigdarroch Castle**, 1050 Joan Crescent (daily summer 9am–7.30pm; winter 10am–5pm; $4; bus #11 or #14 from downtown). It was built by Robert Dunsmuir, a caricature Victorian politician and coal tycoon who was forced to put up this gaunt Gothic pastiche to lure his wife away from Scotland. There's the usual clutter of Victoriana and period detail, in particular some impressive woodwork and stained glass.

Much the same goes for **Point Ellice House**, 2616 Pleasant St (July–Sept Thurs–Mon 10am–5pm; free), less enticing because of its shabby surroundings, and for the nearby **Craigflower Heritage Site** on Admiral's Road (Wed–Sun 10am–4pm; free). In its day the latter was the first of Victoria's farming homesteads, marking the town's transition from trading post to permanent community. It was built in 1856 to remind owner Kenneth McKenzie of Scotland, and soon became the foremost social centre in the fledgling village – mainly visited by officers because McKenzie's daughters were virtually the only white women on the island.

The **Maritime Museum** at 28 Bastion Square (Mon–Sat 10am–4pm, Sun noon–4pm; $4) is of interest mainly for the lovely chocolate-and-vanilla-coloured building, and for the tiny square itself, the restored heart of Fort Victoria. A minute away is the **Emily Carr Gallery**, 1107 Wharf St (Mon–Sat 10am–5pm; free), home to numerous paintings by the province's favourite daughter. The works are an almost surreal amalgam of landscape and native culture, an attempt to preserve "art treasures of a passing race". The **Art Gallery of Greater Victoria**, 1040 Moss St (Mon–Wed & Fri–Sat 10am–5pm, Thurs 10am–9pm, Sun 1–5pm; $3), is of little interest unless you're up for contemporary Canadian paintings and the country's best collection of Japanese art.

## Eating and drinking

Although firmly in Vancouver's culinary shadow, Victoria still has a plethora of **restaurants** offering greater variety – and higher prices – than you'll find in most other BC towns. **Pubs** tend to be plastic mock-ups of their British equivalents, with one or two worthy exceptions, as do the various **cafés** that pander to Victoria's self-conscious afternoon tea ritual. Good snacks and pastry shops abound, while at the other extreme there are budget-busting establishments if you want a one-off treat or a change from the standard Canadian menus that await you on the rest of the island – the exception being Sooke, which might merit its own gastronomic excursion (see p.535).

## Cafés, tea and snacks

**Barb's Fish and Chips**, Fisherman's Wharf off Kingston. Classic home-cut chips and fish straight off the boat.

**Blethering Place**, 2250 Oak Bay Ave. A local institution and the place to come if you must indulge in the tea-taking ritual. Scones, cakes and dainty sandwiches served up against the background of hundreds of Toby Jugs and Royal Family memorabilia.

**C'est Bon Croissant**, 10 Bastion Square. Plain and filled croissants to eat in or take away.

**Demitasse Coffee Bar**, 1320 Blanshard St near Pandora. Popular hole-in-the-wall café with excellent coffee, salads, bagels, lunchtime snacks, and an open fire at the back.

**Dutch Bakery**, 718 Fort St. Pastries and chocolate to take away, or to eat in the popular coffeeshop at the back.

**Empress Hotel**, 721 Government St. Tea in the lobby here is worth it just once. Tourists and locals alike on their best behaviour amidst the chintz and potted plants. No jeans or anoraks.

**Goodies**, 1005 Broad St (upstairs). Good day or night spot, and handy if you fail to find a table at the nearby *Pagliacci's*. Famed for huge breakfasts, eccentric omelettes and an array of Canadian, Californian and Mexican dishes.

**John's Place**, 723 Pandora Ave near Douglas. Quick and comprehensive breakfasts until 3pm, cheap basic lunches, free newspapers, great juke-box and occasional live music and dancing at weekends. Draws an interesting clientele from punks to business types.

**386-Deli**, 1012 Blanshard St. Lunches only (except Fri dinner) with imaginative soup, pasta and dessert menu which changes daily.

## Restaurants

**Chez Pierre**, 512 Yates St (☎388-7711). Long-established, reliable and expensive French restaurant.

**Da Tandoor**, 1010 Fort St. Tandoori specialist that shares honours with the *Taj Mahal* as the best of Victoria's half-dozen or so Indian restaurants; overlong menu, however, and over-the-top interior.

**Flying Rhino**, 1219 Wharf St. Organic vegetarian restaurant with friendly and vaguely alternative feel, New Age notice-board and wholefood shop. Mon–Fri 8am–8pm, weekends 10am–6pm.

**Foo Hong's**, 564 Fisgard St. Plain but popular joint, and probably the city's best Chinese restaurant, though any in Victoria's tiny Chinatown pales beside its Vancouver equivalent.

**Grand Central Café**, 555 Johnson St (passageway). Smooth, laid-back ambience and beautiful summer patio provides the setting for modern cuisine with a Cajun and Creole twist.

**La Petite Columbe**, 604 Broughton St (☎383-3234). Romantic and intimate French restaurant for a splurge at dinner (lunches are more reasonable).

**Metropolitan Diner**, 1715 Government St. More upmarket than the "diner" tag suggests, and offers a wildly eclectic menu that blends Californian, French and Far Eastern cuisine in a *nouvelle* mix.

**Pagliacci's**, 1011 Broad St between Fort and Broughton. Best restaurant in Victoria if you want fast, furious atmosphere, live music, good Italian food and excellent desserts. A rowdy throng begins to queue almost from the moment the doors are open.

**Periklis**, 531 Yates St. Greek restaurant with belly dancers, plate-spinning and the like.

**Scott's Restaurant**, 650 Yates St near Douglas. Genuine diner, cheap breakfast and dinner specials, open 24 hours.

**Taj Mahal**, 679 Herald St. Good Indian fare with chicken, lamb and tandoori specialities.

**Wah Lai Yuen**, 560 Fisgard St. Cheap and cheerful Chinese with good food, formica tables, open kitchen and plenty of locals.

## Bars

**Big Bad John's**, next to the *Strathcona Hotel* at 919 Douglas St. Victoria's most atmospheric bar by far: bare boards, a fug of smoke, and authentic old banknotes and IOUs pasted to the walls.

**Pig and Whistle**, 634 Humboldt St. One of several hideously mocked-up British pubs complete with English "bobby" and Pearly King and Queen.

**Spinnakers Brew Pub**, 308 Catherine St near Esquimalt Rd. Thirty different beers, including several home-brewed options (occasional tours of the brewery possible). Restaurant, live music and good harbour views draw mixed and relaxed clientele. Take bus #23 to Esquimalt Road.

**Swan's Pub**, 506 Pandora Ave at Store St. A highly popular hotel-café-brewery housed in a 1913 warehouse, this is the place to come and watch Victoria's young, successful professionals at play. Several foreign and six home-brewed beers on tap.

# Nightlife

Nocturnal diversions in Victoria are tame compared to Vancouver's, but there's more to the town than its tea rooms and chintzy shops initially suggest. Highbrow tastes are surprisingly well catered for, and there's a smattering of **live-music** venues and **discos** to keep you happy for the limited time you're likely to spend in the city. Jazz is particularly easy to come by – for information on the city's jazz underground, contact the *Victoria Jazz Society* (☎388-4423).

**Listings** appear in the two main daily newspapers, the *Daily Colonist* and the *Victoria Times*; in the *Monday Magazine*, a weekly tabloid printed on Thursday despite its title; and in the fortnightly *Arts Victoria*. **Tickets** for most offerings are available from the city's main performance space, the *McPherson Playhouse*, 3 Centennial Square, Pandora and Government (☎386-6121).

Summer brings out the buskers and **free entertainment** in the city's people-places – James Bay, Market Square and Beacon Hill Park in particular. A string of summer festivals offer further cut-price possibilities, most notably two jazz jamborees: the **Dixieland Jazz Festival**, held over four days in April, highlights about a dozen top international bands; and June's **Jazz Fest** features some 150 less-well-known and inevitably more varied bands who perform in Market Square. Others include the arts-orientated **Victoria International Festival** in July and August and the more avant-garde **Fringe Festival** in September.

## Clubs and live music

**Banana Moon Nite Club**, 770 Yates and Blanshard. Rock and "boogie" bands nightly, with a jam session on Sundays.

**Esquimalt Inn**, 856 Esquimalt Rd. C&W seven nights a week, with 3pm jam session each Saturday and Sunday. Take the #23 bus.

**The Forge**, 919 Douglas St. Biggest, best and noisest of the hard-rock venues, this club occupies the garish, neon-lit basement of the *Strathcona Hotel*. Music and dancing nightly.

**Harpo's**, 15 Bastion Square. Easily the best of Victoria's live-music venues, an intimate space which has hosted an eclectic mix of names that have included Robert Cray, Billy Bragg and the Wailers. Cover from $5; closed Sun.

**Hermann's Dixieland Inn**, 753 View St. Dimly lit club thick with Fifties atmosphere which specialises in Dixieland but has occasional excursions into fusion and blues. Mon–Fri 11.30am–2am, Sat 3pm–2am.

**La Bohème**, 537 Johnson St, opposite Market Square. Occasionally precious coffee bar (downstairs) and restaurant that also hosts wide-ranging live music Tues–Sat.

**Pagliacci's**, 1011 Broad St. Potpourri of live music starting at 9pm Tues–Sat, in packed and popular restaurant.

**The Rail**, 2852 Douglas St. Pub-style rock venue located in the *Colony Motor Inn*.

**Rumors**, 1325 Government St. Gay and lesbian club. Closed Sun.

**Victoria Folk Music Society**, Norway House, 1110 Hillside Ave. Hosts weekly acoustic sets at 8pm.

## Discos

**Club California**, 1318 Broad St. Large upstairs dance floor, lots of big rock video screens, plenty of theme nights.

**Julie's Cabaret**, 603 Pandora Ave. Standard disco housed in *Monty's Pub* in the Victoria Plaza. Nightly; $3 cover.

**Merlin's**, 1208 Wharf St. Central waterfront club that attracts early-twenties crowd. Theme nights include a Thurs women's night with male dancers. $3 cover charge after 9.30pm at weekends.

**Pier 42**, 1605 Store St at Pandora. You may well have to queue to join the slightly older crew who frequent the basement disco of the *Swan Pub*. Musical emphasis is on Sixties and Seventies classics and current Top 40 fodder. Tues–Sat.

**Spinners**, 858 Yates St near Quadra. Expensive club frequented by the 14–19 age-group. Wed–Sat till midnight.

**Sweetwaters Niteclub**, Market Square off Store St (☎383-7844). Central, upmarket and elegant spot with queues seven days a week and a reputation as a singles club.

## Theatre

**Belfry Theatre**, 1291 Gladstone St and Fernwood (☎385-6815). Foremost of Victoria's several highly active companies. Its five-play season in its own theatre is nationally renowned, and though the programme concentrates on contemporary Canadian dramatists, the repertoire runs the gamut of twentieth-century theatre.

**Intrepid Theatre Company**, 620 View St (☎383-2663). Responsible for the nine-day September Fringe Festival, featuring some 200 highly varied shows.

**Kaleidoscope Theatre**, 715 Yates St (☎383-8124). Internationally renowned troupe known particularly for its work with young audiences.

**Victoria Theatre Guild**, 805 Langham Court Rd (☎384-2142). Lightweight musicals, dramas and comedies.

## Classical music, opera and dance

**Pacific Opera Victoria** (☎386-6121). Highly acclaimed company which produces three operas yearly in Feb, April and Sept at the *McPherson Playhouse*.

**Victoria Operatic Society**, 798 Fairview Rd (☎381-1021). Year-round performances of lightweight operatic fare.

**Victoria Symphony Orchestra**, 846 Broughton Rd (☎385-6515). Numerous concerts annually, usually performed at the nearby *Royal Theatre*.

## Listings

**Airlines** *Air BC* (☎382-9242); *Canadian Airlines* (☎382-6111).

**Bike rental** *Budget Cycle Time*, 327 Belleville St and 727 Courtney St;   *Explore Victoria*, 1007 Langley St; *Harbour Scooters*, 843 Douglas St and 1223 Wharf St.

**Bus information** For services to Vancouver, *Pacific Coast Lines* (☎385-4417); for services on the island, *Island Coach Lines* (☎385-4411) – both at 700 Douglas and Belleville.

**Camping supplies** *Jeune Brothers*, 570 Johnson St.

**Car rental** *Budget Discount Car Rentals*, 727 Courtney St (☎388-7874); *Budget*, 843 Douglas St (☎388-5525); *Hertz*, 901 Douglas St (☎388-4411); *Rent-A-Used-Car*, 752 Caledonian Ave (☎388-6230).

**Exchange** *The Victoria Conference Centre Currency Exchange*, 724 Douglas St (Mon–Sat 10am–6pm).

**Ferries** *BC Ferries* (☎386-3431); *Black Ball Transport* (☎386-2202); *Victoria Clipper* (☎382-8100); *Victoria Rapid Transit* (☎361-9144); *Washington State Ferries* (☎381-1551 or ☎1-800-542-7052).

**Gay and lesbian information** ☎361-4900.

**Hospital** *Fairfield Health Centre*, 841 Fairfield Rd (☎389-6300), is three blocks from the *Empress Hotel*; *Victoria General Hospital*, 35 Helmcken Rd (☎727-4212).

**Laundry** 812 Wharf St, below the infocentre.

**Left luggage** At bus terminal; $1.25 per 24hr.

**Lost property** Contact Victoria police (☎384-4111) or *BC Transit*'s lost-and-found line (☎382-6161).

**Pharmacy** *Shopper's Drug Mart*, 1222 Douglas St, open daily 8am–9pm.

**Post office** 1230 Government and Yates (☎388-3575). Open weekdays 8.30am–5pm.

**Royal Canadian Mounted Police** 625 Fisgard and Government (☎384-4111).

**Taxis** *Blue Bird Cabs* (☎382-4235); *Crown Taxi* (☎381-2242); *Victoria Taxi* (☎383-7111).

**Train information** *VIA rail*, 450 Pandora St (☎383-4324 or ☎1-800-665-8630).

**Weather** ☎656-3978.

# The Southern Gulf Islands

Scattered between Vancouver Island and the mainland lie several hundred tiny islands, most no more than lumps of rock, a few large enough to hold permanent populations and warrant a regular ferry service. Two main clusters are accessible from Victoria: the **Southern Gulf Islands** and the San Juan Islands, both part of the same archipelago, except that the San Juan group is in the United States.

You get a good look at the Southern Gulf Islands on the ferry from Tsawwassen – twisting and threading through their coves and channels, the ride sometimes seems even a bit too close for comfort. The coastline makes for superb **sailing**, and an armada of small boats criss-cross between the islands for most of the year. Hikers and campers are also well served, and **fishing**, too, is good, with some of the world's biggest salmon having met their doom in the surrounding waters. The climate is mild, though hardly "Mediterranean" as claimed in the tourist blurbs, and the vegetation is particularly lush. There's also an abundance of marine wildlife (sea lions, orcas, seals, bald eagles, herons, cormorants). All this has made the Gulf Islands the dream idyll of many Canadians, whether they're artists, writers, pensioners or drop-outs from the mainstream. For full details of what they're all up to, grab a copy of the local listings, the *Gulf Islander*, distributed on the islands and the ferries.

### Getting to the islands

*BC Ferries* sails to five of the Southern Gulf Islands – **Saltspring**, **Pender**, **Saturna**, **Mayne** and **Galiano** – from SWARTZ BAY, 33km north of Victoria on Hwy 17 (a few others can be reached from Chemainus and Nanaimo, for which see those sections on p.538 and p.540). Reckon on at least two crossings to each daily, but be prepared for all boats to be jammed solid during the summer. Pick up the company's *Southern Gulf Islands* timetable, widely available on boats and in the mainland infocentres, which is invaluable if you aim to exploit the many inter-island connections. If you just want a quick, cheap cruise, *BC Ferries* runs a daily four-hour jaunt from Swartz Bay around several of the islands. All the ferries take cars, bikes and motorbikes, though with a car you'll need to make a reservation (in Vancouver ☎669-1211; in Victoria ☎386-3431). Bear in mind that there's next to no public transport on the islands, so what few taxis there are can charge more or less what they wish.

For the San Juans you obviously have to pass through US immigration, but you can get good stopover deals on ferries between SIDNEY on Vancouver Island and ANACORTES on the Washington mainland, and foot passengers travel free between the four main islands.

Aim to have your **accommodation** worked out well in advance in summer. **Campers** should have few problems finding a site, most of which are located in the islands' many provincial parks, though at peak times you'll want to arrive before noon to ensure a pitch – there are no reservations. For help, use the *BC Accommodations* guide, or contact the Victoria infocentre.

### Saltspring Island

SALTSPRING (pop. 5000), the biggest of the islands, is served by three ferry terminals; FULFORD and VESUVIUS BAY provide links to Vancouver Island, LONG HARBOUR to points on the BC mainland via other islands. Locals are a particularly cosmopolitan bunch, the island having been colonised not by whites but by pioneer black settlers seeking refuge from prejudice in the US. If you're here to slum it on a **beach**, the best strips are on the island's more sheltered west side (Beddis Beach, off the Fulford–Ganges road), at Vesuvius Bay and at Drummond Park near Fulford.

The main village is GANGES, close to Long Harbour, armed with a small **infocentre** (May–Sept daily 8am–6pm) and a rapidly proliferating assortment of galleries, tourist shops and holiday homes. Community spirit reaches a climax during the annual **Artcraft**, a summer crafts fair that showcases the talents of the island's many dab-handed creatives.

Ganges' infocentre is the place to check out the island's relatively plentiful **accommodation**, whether it's a bed and breakfast (owners can arrange to pick you up from the ferry) or one of the so-called "resorts" dotted round the island – usually a handful of houses with camping, a few rooms to rent, and little else. Each of the ferry terminals also has a range of mid-price motels. Some of the nicer spots include the *Arbutus Court Motel* on Vesuvius Bay Road at Vesuvius Bay (☎537-5415; doubles \$55–80); the *Spindrift Resort* at Wellbury Point (☎537-5311; cottages \$75–135), overlooking Long Harbour ferry terminal; and the *Booth Bay Resort*, 375 Baker Rd, Ganges (☎537-5651; cottages \$70–90). One of the island's better-known **eateries** is *The Inn at Vesuvius* alongside the ferry at Vesuvius Bay, favoured with live music nightly and a great **bar** deck overlooking the harbour.

The island's best hiking and its top **campground** centre on Ruckle Provincial Park, along with further walking and good views on and around Mount Maxwell.

### Galiano Island

Long and finger-shaped, **GALIANO** (pop. 700) is one of the more promising islands to visit if you want variety and a realistic chance of finding somewhere to stay. There are two ferry terminals: STURDIES BAY, which takes boats from the mainland, and MONTAGUE HARBOUR, which handles the Vancouver Island crossings. The **infocentre** is in the latter (May–Sept daily 8am–6pm), which also has bike, boat and canoe hire, motels, bed and breakfasts, and an excellent **campground** at nearby Montague Harbour Provincial Park.

*Galiano Gables* operates as a **mini hostel** (☎539-2594; non-IYHF) and is located on Warbler Road, 3.5km from Sturdies Bay; turn left up Burrill Road off the main road after the *Burrill Bros* store. For a pub with **rooms**, try the *Hummingbird Inn* (☎539-5472), the island's only pub, conveniently close to the ferry on Sturdies Road (a bus meets boats and also runs out to the provincial park); doubles start at \$60 including breakfast. **Food** is reasonable at the *Hummingbird*, likewise at *La Berengerie*, on the corner of Montague and Clanton Road (☎539-5392), a genteel restaurant which also has a few bed-and-breakfast rooms upstairs. For a downy and comfortable stay in peaceful surroundings try the *Woodstone Country Inn* (☎539-2022; doubles from \$75) on Georgeson Bay Road close to Montague Harbour Provincial Park. The best choice on the island's quieter northern end are the log cabins of the *Bodega Resort*, Porlier Pass Drive–Cook Drive (☎539-2677; doubles from \$65), set in acres of woods and meadows and with sea views.

If you're **canoeing**, stick to the calmer waters, cliffs and coves of the west coast. **Hikers** can walk almost the entire length of the east coast, or climb Mount Sutil (323m) or Mount Galiano (342m) for views of the mainland mountains. Locals' favourite **beach** is at Coon Bay at the island's northern tip.

### North and South Pender

The bridge-linked islands of **NORTH** and **SOUTH PENDER** can muster about 1000 people between them, most of whom will try to entice you into their studios to buy arts and crafts. The **infocentre** is at the ferry terminal in OTTER BAY (May–Sept daily 8am–6pm) on North Pender, home of the *Otter Bay Marina*, where you can rent **bikes** and buy maps for a tour of the islands' rolling, hilly interior. The best **beaches** are at Hamilton (North Pender) and Mortimer Spit (South Pender). **Accommodation**-wise there's plenty of bed and breakfasts, and a wooded **campground** at Prior Centennial Provincial Park. For more upmarket rooms, try the rural *Eastridge Chalets* near Prior Park on Canal Road, North Pender (☎629-3353; doubles from \$55), or *Pender Lodge*, MacKinnon Road, North Pender (☎629-3221; doubles from \$65).

## Mayne and Saturna islands

**MAYNE** is the first island to your left if you're crossing from Tsawwassen to Swartz Bay – which is perhaps as close as you'll get, since it's the quietest and most difficult to reach of the islands served by ferries, with very few places to stay. That may be as good a reason as any for heading out here, however, particularly if you have a bike to explore miles of quiet country roads. Best of several **beaches** is Bennett Bay, a sheltered strip with warm water and good sand. It's reached by heading east from Miner's Bay (5min from the ferry terminal at VILLAGE BAY) to the end of Fernhill Road and then turning left onto Wilks Road. Village Bay has a summer-only **infocentre** (daily 8am–6pm) which should be able to fill you in on the limited but expanding number of **bed-and-breakfast** possibilities – though the island is small enough to explore as a day trip – or on the *BlueVista Resort*, a few cabins overlooking Bennett Bay on Arbutus Drive (☎539-2463; doubles from $45). The *Tinker's Retreat* on Georgia Point Road operates as a private **mini-hostel** and is open in summer only (☎539-2280).

**SATURNA**, to the south, is another bed-and-breakfast hideaway: try *Boot Cove Lodge* a couple of miles from the ferry at SATURNA POINT, home to a pub, a shop and the **infocentre** (May–Sept daily 8am–6pm) which will rent you boats and bicycles. The best local **beach** is at Winter Cove Marine Park (no campground) and there's walking, wildlife and good views to the mainland from Mount Warburton Pike.

# Highway 14: Victoria to Port Renfrew

**Highway 14** runs west from Victoria to Port Renfrew, lined with numerous beaches and provincial parks, most – especially those close to the city – heavily populated during the summer months. The 107-kilometre route is covered in summer by the *Port Renfrew Connector* (☎361-9080), a twice-daily private bus service intended for hikers walking the West Coast Trail (see p.549), but popular for the ride alone. Victoria city buses go as far as **SOOKE** (38km; take #50 to Western Exchange and transfer to a #61), best known for its **All Sooke Day** in mid-July, when lumberjacks from all over the island compete in various tests of forestry expertise. The **infocentre** lies across the Sooke River Bridge at 2070 Phillips and Sooke (daily 10am–6pm). This is the last place of any size, so stock up on supplies if you're continuing west. Check out the small **Sooke Region Museum** (daily 10am–5pm) if you want to bone up on the largely logging-dominated local history. Quite a few people make the trip here just for the **food** at *Sooke Harbour House*, 1528 Whiffen Spit (☎642-3421), one of the finest restaurants on the West Coast and frequently lauded as the best in Canada; it's expensive, but has a surprisingly casual atmosphere.

Beaches beyond Sooke are largely grey pebble and driftwood, the first key stop being **French Beach Provincial Park**, 20km from Sooke. An infoboard here fills in the natural history background, and there are maps of trails and the highlights on the road further west. There's good walking on the fairly wild and windswept beach, and camping on the grass immediately away from the shore. Sandy, signposted trails lead off the road to beaches over the next 12km to **JORDAN RIVER**, a one-shop, one-hamburger-stall town known for its good surf. Just beyond is the best of the beaches on this coast, part of **China Beach Provincial Park**, reached after a fifteen-minute walk from the road through rainforest.

There's a campground if you're staying over; otherwise you can push on – the road is gravel from here on – past Mystic and Sombrio beaches to **PORT RENFREW**, a logging community that's gained recently from being the western starting point of the West Coast Trail. Accommodation, however, is still limited to *Gallaugher's West Coast Fish Camp* on Beach Road (☎647-5535; cottages $60) and the *Port Renfrew RV Park and Marina* on Parkinson Road (☎647-5430; from $9). South of the village on a logging road

(6km) is **Botanical Beach**, a sandstone shelf and tidal pool area that reveals a wealth of marine life at low tide.

If you're driving and don't want to retrace your steps, think about taking the gravel logging roads from the village on the north side of the San Juan River to either Shawnigan Lake or the Cowichan Valley. They're marked on most maps, but it's worth picking up the detailed map of local roads put out by the *Sooke Combined Fire Organization* (ask at the Victoria infocentre); heed all warnings about logging trucks.

# Highway 1: Victoria to Nanaimo

If you leave Victoria with high hopes of Vancouver Island's lauded scenery, **Highway 1** – the final western leg of the Trans-Canada – will come as a disappointing introduction to what you can expect along most of the island's southeast coast. After a lengthy sprawl of suburbs, blighted by more billboards than you'd see in supposedly less scenic cities, the landscape becomes suddenly wooded and immensely lush; unfortunately the beauty is constantly interrupted by bursts of dismal motels, highway junk, and huge swathes of destruction where the road is being widened into a dual carriageway. **Buses** operated by *Island Coach Lines* make the trip between Victoria and Nanaimo (6 daily). One **train** a day also covers this route, and beyond to Courtenay, but it's a single-carriage job and gets booked solid in summer; it stops at every stump.

**Thetis Lake Park**, appearing on the right at 10km, is good for swimming; there's a busy beach near the car park, but it's quieter round the shore, or beyond at the bottom of the hill at Prior Lake. Prettier still is **Goldstream Provincial Park**, 5km beyond LANGFORD, where you'll find a good **campground** (busy in summer) and a network of marked **trails** designed for anything between five minutes and an hour's walking. Try the paths to Mount Finlayson for views of the ocean – views you also get if you carry on up the highway, which soon meets Saanich Inlet, a bay with a lovely panorama of wooded ridges across the water. To **stay**, the *Malahat Mountain Oceanview Motel* (☎478-9231), 35km north of Victoria, is best sited to catch the sea and island vistas; doubles start at $45.

A marginally more scenic diversion off the main road takes you to **Shawnigan Lake**, fringed by a couple of provincial parks. If you're biking or are prepared to rough it, note the logging road that links the north end of the lake to Port Renfrew on the west coast.

## Duncan

**DUNCAN**, 60km north of Victoria, begins inauspiciously, with a particularly scrappy section of highway spoiling what would otherwise be an exquisitely pastoral patch of country. Still, the town's Native Heritage Centre merits a stop – unlike the Glass Castle, a messy affair made from glass bottles off the road to the south, and the even sillier "World's Largest Hockey Stick", arranged as a triumphal arch into the town centre. It was won at auction by Duncan, in competition with dozens of other cities.

Duncan's **infocentre** is opposite the *Overwaitea* supermarket on the main road (Mon–Fri 8.30–5pm), close to the **bus station**, which has six daily connections to and from Victoria (1hr 10min away). Duncan is not a place you want even to start thinking of staying in, but for **meals** you could try *Arbutus*, 195 Kenneth St and Jubilee, much-favoured by locals, or the *White Hart Tea Shop* on Station Street. Three kilometres south of town on Hwy 1, the *Pioneer House Restaurant* has a rustic log-cabin feel helped by a genuine saloon bar transplanted from a period building in Montana. Alternatively, head 10km north of Duncan to the *Red Rooster Diner* (by the *Mount Sicker* petrol station), reputed to be the greasy spoon immortalised by Jack Nicholson in *Five Easy Pieces*. It's still a classic – good, cheap food, vinyl booths and all the authentic tacky trimmings you'd expect.

### The Native Heritage Centre

The first real reason to pull over out of Victoria is Duncan's brand-new **Native Heritage Centre**, 200 Cowichan Way (May–Sept daily 10am–6pm), on your left off the highway in the unmissable wooden buildings next to Malaspina College.

Duncan has long been the self-proclaimed "City of Totems", reference to a rather paltry collection of poles – arranged mostly alongside the main road – that belong to the local Cowichan tribes, historically British Columbia's largest native group. The tribes still preserve certain traditions, and it's been their energy – along with cash from white civic authorities, attuned as ever in Canada to potentially lucrative tourist attractions – that have put up the poles and pulled the centre together. Much of the emphasis is on shifting native crafts, especially the ubiquitous lumpy jumpers for which the area is famous, but you can usually expect to find historical displays and demonstrations of dancing, knitting, carving, weaving and even native cooking.

### British Columbia Forest Museum Park

Vancouver Island is one of the most heavily logged areas in Canada, and the **British Columbia Forest Museum Park**, located 1km north of town on Hwy 1, is run by the province to preserve artefacts from its lumbering heritage; but with industry bigwigs as museum trustees, you can't help feeling it's designed to be something of a palliative in the increasingly ferocious controversy between loggers and environmentalists (May–Sept daily 9am–7pm; $4). Nonetheless, it does a thorough job on trees, and if the forestry displays in Victoria's museum have whetted your appetite, you'll have a good couple of hours rounding off your arboreal education. The entrance is marked by a small black steam engine and a massive piece of yellow logging machinery.

Ranged over a hundred-acre site next to a scenic lake, the well-presented displays tell everything you want to know about trees and how to cut them down. The steam train round the park is a bit gimmicky, but a good way of getting around; check out the forest dioramas and the artefacts and archive material in the **Log Museum** in particular. There's also the usual array of working blacksmiths, sawmills, a farmstead, an old logging camp, and a few as-yet undeforested patches where you can take time out.

The complex forms part of the **Cowichan and Chemainus Ecomuseum**, a vaguely defined park that takes in much of the surrounding area intended to preserve the logging heritage of the area – a curiously ill-defined concept that appears to be largely a PR excercise on the part of the logging companies. Ask for details of tours and maps from the Duncan infocentre, or the Ecomuseum office, 160 Jubilee St.

## The Cowichan Valley

Striking west into the hills from Hwy 1 north of Duncan, Hwy 18 enters the **Cowichan Valley** and fetches up at Cowichan Lake, the largest freshwater lake on the island. Rather than drive, however, the nicest way up the valley is to walk the eighteen-kilometre **Cowichan Valley Footpath**, following the river from GLENORA (a hamlet southwest of Duncan at the end of Robertson Road) to LAKE COWICHAN VILLAGE on the lake's eastern shore. You could do the trip in a day, camp en route, or turn around at SKUTZ FALLS and climb up to the Riverbottom Road to return to Duncan.

A road, rough in parts, circles **Cowichan Lake** (allow 2hr to drive it) and offers access to a gamut of outdoor pursuits, most notably fishing – the area is touted, with typical Canadian hyperbole, as the "Fly-fishing Capital of the World". The water gets warm enough for summer swimming, and there's also ample hiking in the wilder country above. At YOUBOU on the north shore you can visit the **Pletcher Challenge Heritage Mill**, a working sawmill (tours May–Sept): this area boasts some of the most productive forest in Canada, thanks to the lake's mild microclimate, and lumber is the obvious mainstay of the local economy. On the road up to the lake from Duncan you

## OLD-GROWTH FORESTS: GOING, GOING, GONE

While Vancouver Island isn't the only place in Canada where environmentalists and the forestry industry are at loggerheads, some of the most bitter and high-profile confrontations have taken place here. The island's wet climate is particularly favourable to the growth of thick **temperate rainforest**, part of a belt that once stretched from Alaska to northern California. The most productive ecosystem on the planet, **old-growth** virgin Pacific rainforest contains up to ten times more biomass per acre than its more famous tropical counterpart – and, though it covers a much smaller area, it is being felled at a greater rate and with considerably less media outrage. Environmentalists estimate that British Columbia's portion of the Pacific rainforest has already been reduced by two thirds; all significant areas will have been felled, they predict, within fifteen years. The powerful logging industry claims two thirds survive, but even the Canadian government – largely in thrall to and supportive of the industry – concedes that a mere 3.5 percent of the BC rainforest is currently protected.

What is clear is that the government wants a very firm lid kept on the whole affair. In 1990 it commissioned a report into **public opinion** on the issue in the United Kingdom, which takes half of all British Columbia's plywood exports, three-quarters of all its lumber shipments to Europe, and a third of all Canada's paper pulp output. It observed that "UK public opinion appears to be highly uncritical of Canadian forestry, largely because awareness of the subject is low . . . [there is] a reassuringly romantic and simplistic image of Canadian forestry based on a lumberjack in a checked shirt, felling a single tree." The report concluded that "media attention and coverage of Canadian forestry management issues should not be sought."

No such apathy exists in British Columbia, however. The controversy over logging often pits neighbour against neighbour, for 270,000 in the province depend directly or

pass the **Valley Demonstration Forest**, another link in the industry's public-relations armoury, with signs and scenic lookouts explaining the intricacies of forest management.

For details of the area's many tours, trails and outfitters contact the **infocentre** at Lake Cowichan village (May–Sept daily 9am–8pm). Good, cheap **campgrounds** line the shore, which despite minimal facilities can be quite busy in summer – don't expect to have the place to yourself. The biggest and best is at Gordon Bay Provincial Park on the south shore, a popular family place but with a quiet atmosphere and a good sandy **beach**. There are also plenty of hotels, motels and the like in all the lakeside settlements.

## Chemainus

**CHEMAINUS** is the "Little Town That Did", as the billboards for miles around never stop telling you. Its mysterious achievement was the creation of its own tourist attraction, realised when the closure of the local sawmill – once amongst the world's largest – threatened the place with almost overnight extinction. In 1983 the town's worthies commissioned an artist to paint a huge mural recording the area's local history. This proved so successful that more panels quickly followed, drawing visitors to admire the artwork and tempting them to spend money in local businesses as they did. As murals go these are surprisingly good, and if you're driving it's worth the short, well-signed diversion off Hwy 1.

**Buses** also detour here on the run up to Nanaimo (☎246-3354 for details), and the train drops you slap bang next to a mural. You can also pick up a ferry from Chemainus to the small islands of **Kuper** and **Thetis**. There's a summer-only **infocentre** in town (May–Sept daily 9am–6pm), and if you fancy **staying** – the homely waterside setting is indirectly on the industry, and multinationals like McMillan Bloedel and Fletcher Challenge dominate the scene. **Employment** is a major rallying cry here, and the prospect of job losses through industry regulation is usually enough to override objections. The trend towards **automation** only adds fuel to the argument: by volume of wood cut, the BC forestry industry provides only half as many jobs as in the rest of Canada, which means, in effect, that twice as many trees have to be cut down in BC to provide the same number of jobs.

Some **environmental groups** have resorted to such tactics as fixing huge nails in trees at random – these ruin chainsaws and lumber mill machinery, but also endanger lives. In the autumn of 1991, 200 people were arrested on the island for obstructing logging operations. The most level-headed and impressive of the conservation groups, the **Western Canada Wilderness Committee** (WCWC), condemns these acts of environmental vandalism, and instead devotes its energies to alerting the public to the landslide damage and destruction of salmon habitats caused by logging, and the dioxin pollution from pulp mills that has closed 220,000 acres of offshore waters to fishing for shellfish. They point out that the battle is over what they call "the last cookies in the jar", for only eight of the island's 91 watersheds over 12,000 acres have escaped logging; the old-growth bonanza is nearly over, they argue, and the industry might as well wean itself over to sustainable practices now, before it's too late.

In the meantime, however, ninety percent of timber is still lifted from the rainforest instead of from managed stands, clear-cutting of old-growth timber is blithely described by McMillan as "a form of harvesting", and independent audits suggest that companies are failing to observe either their cutting or replanting quotas. Things may change following the election of a new centrist provincial government in October 1991, which has pledged to improve forestry practices and protect at least twelve percent of the province within reserves.

nicer than either Duncan or Nanaimo – try the *Horseshoe Bay Inn*, 9576 Chemainus Rd (☎246-3425), with doubles from $45. There's also a **mini youth hostel** open year-round at 3040 Henry Road (☎246-4407), about 2km north of town off the Ladysmith road (the wardens, Robert and Vi Matula, can pick you up from the village). Rooms start at $12; there's a kitchen and showers, but you're supposed to bring your own sleeping bag. The best choice for **food** is the *Upstairs Downstairs Café*, 9745 Willow St, with cheap, varied dishes including several good vegetarian options.

## Ladysmith

**LADYSMITH**'s claim to fame is based solely on an accident of geography, as it straddles the 49th Parallel, the latitude that divides mainland Canada and the US. Canada held onto Vancouver Island only after some hard bargaining, even though the boundary's logic ought to put much of it in the States. There's little to the place other than the usual motels and garages, though a recent attempt to spruce up the older buildings won it a Western Canada Award of Excellence. Ladysmith's scenic profile, it has to be said, would be considerably higher were it not for a huge sawmill and a waterfront hopelessly jammed with lumber. The **infocentre** at the Black Nugget Museum, 12 Gatacre St, has walking maps of the "heritage centre". The **museum** itself (daily noon–4pm; $2) is a restored 1906 hotel stuffed with predictable memorabilia. If you stop off, check out **Transfer Beach Park**, where the water's said to be the warmest in the Pacific north of San Francisco.

For **accommodation**, there's the *Inn of the Sea*, 3600 Yellow Point Rd (☎245-2211), out of town on the seafront and a popular bolt-hole for weekending Victorians; doubles start at $75. For **food** call in at the oldest "English-style pub" in BC, the *Crow and Gate* just off the the main road 19km north of the town.

# Nanaimo

With a population of about 50,000, **NANAIMO** is Vancouver Island's second biggest city, the terminal for ferries from Horseshoe Bay and Tsawwassen on the mainland, and a watershed between the island's populated southeastern tip and its wilder, more sparsely peopled countryside to the north and west. The town itself is unexceptional, though the setting, as ever in BC, is eye-catching – particularly around the harbour, which bobs with yachts and rusty fishing boats, and (assuming you're coming from Victoria) allows the first views across to the big mountains on the mainland.

Coal first brought white settlers to the region, many of whom made their fortunes here, including the Victorian magnate Robert Dunsmuir, who was given £750,000 and almost half the island in return for building the Victoria–Nanaimo railway – an indication of the benefits that could accrue from the British government to those with the pioneering spirit. Five bands of Salish natives originally lived on the site, which they called **Sney-ne-mous**, or "meeting place", and it was they who innocently showed the local black rock to Hudson's Bay agents in 1852.

The old mines are closed, and the town's pockets are now padded by forestry, deep-sea fishing and tourism – it's largely in the pursuit of the latter that Nanaimo lays on the annual **Bathtub Race** and **Silly Boat Race**, in which bathtubs are raced (and sunk, mostly) across the 55km to Vancouver. The winner takes the silver Plunger Trophy from the Loyal Nanaimo Bathtub Society. It's all part of the Marine Festival held in the second week of July. More highbrow is the May to June **Nanaimo Festival**, a cultural jamboree that takes place in and around Malaspina College, 900 Fifth St. The town's other minor claim to fame is the Nanaimo bar, a glutinous chocolate confection made to varying recipes and on sale everywhere.

The town's twenty-five or so gardens and small parks, many of them hugging the shore, are perfectly aligned for a seafront breath of air. **Piper's Lagoon Park** offers a windblown, grassy spit, with lots of trails, flowers, rocky bluffs and good sea views: it's off Hammond Bay Road north of the city centre. For beaches you could head for **Departure Bay**, again north of the centre off Stewart Avenue, which is the main summer hang-out for the day-glo and ghetto-blaster crowd. Plenty of local shops hire out a range of marine gear, as well as bikes and boats.

For the wildest of the local parks, head due west of town to **Westwood Lake Park**, good for a couple of hours' lonely hiking and some fine swimming. Tongue-twisting **Petroglyph Provincial Park**, off Hwy 1 well to the south of downtown, showcases Native American carvings of the sort found all over BC (particularly along coastal waterways), many of them thousands of years old. Often their meaning is vague, but they appear to record important rituals and events. There are plenty of figures – real and mythological – carved into the local sandstone here, though their potential to inspire wonder is somewhat spoilt by more recent graffitti and the first thin edge of Nanaimo's urban sprawl.

In Nanaimo itself, only two other sights warrant the considerable amount of energy used to promote them. The **Centennial Museum**, just off the main harbour area at 100 Cameron Street (daily 10am–5pm), houses a collection that runs the usual historical gamut of pioneer, logging, mining, native peoples and natural history displays. The best features are the reconstructed coal mine and the interesting insights into the town's cosmopolitan population – a mix of Polish, Chinese, Welsh, Native and English citizens who see themselves today as some of the island's "friendliest folk". The **Bastion**, close by, is a wood-planked tower built by the Hudson's Bay Company in 1853 as a store and a stronghold against native attack, though in the event it was never used in anger. It's the oldest (perhaps the only) such building in the west. These days it houses a small museum of Hudson's Bay memorabilia (daily 10am–5pm); its silly tourist stunt, without which no BC town would be complete, is "the only ceremonial cannon firing west of Ontario" (daily at noon, summer only). This is marginally more impressive than the town's claim to have the most retail shopping space per capita in the country.

## Practicalities

Nanaimo's dingy **bus terminal** (☎753-4371) is some way from the harbour on the corner of Comox and Terminal (behind the *Tally-Ho Inn*), with six daily runs to Victoria, two to Port Hardy and three to Port Alberni, for connections to Tofino and Ucluelet. **BC Ferries** (☎753-1261) sails from Departure Bay, 2km north of downtown (bus #2 to the north end of Stewart Ave), to Horseshoe Bay on the mainland (7am–9pm, hourly in summer, every two hours off-season; foot passengers $4.75 one way).

You'll find a typically overstocked **infocentre** on the main highway north of downtown at 266 Bryden St (May–Sept daily 8am–8pm; Oct–April Mon–Fri 9am–5pm; ☎754-8474). They'll phone around and help with accommodation referrals, and shower you with pamphlets on the town and the island as a whole. There are also the usual details of the many boat rides and tours you can make to local sawmills, canneries, nature reserves, fishing research stations and so on.

Nanaimo's cheapest beds are at the **IYHF youth hostel**, known as the *Thompson*, 1660 Cedar Hwy, 10km south of town (☎722-2251) – take bus #11, or the free hourly shuttle from the bus terminal (2–9pm). The hostel only sleeps twelve, so call ahead during peak periods, or take advantage of the adjoining campground. There's also a central private ten-bed **mini-hostel**, the *Nicol Street Hostel*, 65 Nicol St (May to early Sept; ☎753-1188), located seven blocks south of the bus terminal and one block south of the Harbour Park Shopping Centre off Hwy 1. A handful of camping spots are also available, plus bike rental. Both hostels charge $10 for members, $15 for non-members.

Numerous **motels** are clustered on the city limits, the best-known cheapies being the *Colonial*, 950 Terminal Ave on Hwy 1 (☎754-4415), and the *Big 7*, 736 Nicol St (☎754-2328) in the downtown area. Both have doubles at around $40. For more tasteful lodgings, try the *Tally Ho Inn*, 1 Terminal Ave (☎753-2241), with doubles from $60, or the *Schooner Cover Resort* (☎468-7691), 26km north of town near NANOOSE BAY; doubles start at $75.

If you're **camping**, by far the best choice is Newcastle Island Provincial Park (see below), which has the only pitches within walking distance of town. Other sites are spread along the main road to the north and south. The best of these – a rural, watery retreat – is the *Brennan Lake Campground*, 6km north of the ferry terminal off Hwy 19 at 4228 Biggs Rd (☎756-0404; from $12).

Where **eating** is concerned, have your obligatory Nanaimo bar or other cheap edibles at the food stands in the **Public Market**, handy for the ferry terminal on Stewart Avenue (daily 9am–9pm). The big *Overwaitea* supermarket is 2km north of town on Hwy 19. For meals try *Gina's*, 47 Skinner St, an unmissable Mexican outfit perched on the edge of a cliff and painted bright pink with an electric blue roof. The town's best **seafood** choice is the *Bluenose Chowder House*, 1340 Stewart Ave (closed Mon), also party to a nice outside terrace. Up the road near the BC Ferry terminal, *The Grotto*, 1511 Stewart Ave, is another reliable choice (closed Sun & Mon).

## Newcastle and Gabriola islands

Barely a stone's throw offshore from Nanaimo lies **Newcastle Island**, and beyond it the larger bulk of **Gabriola Island**, both incongruously graced with palm trees: they're beneficiaries of what is supposedly Canada's mildest climate.

Ferries make the crossing every hour on the hour (10am–9pm; $4 round trip) from Maffeo-Sutton Park to Newcastle Island Provincial Park, which has a fine stretch of sand, tame wildlife, no cars, and lots of walking and picnic possibilities. By contrast, there are about fifteen crossings to Gabriola Island (20min), a much quieter place that's home to about 2000 people, many of them artists and writers. The latter offers several beaches – the best are Gabriola Sands and Drumbeg Provincial Park – and lots of scope for scuba-diving, beachcombing and easy walking, plus the added curiosity of the **Malaspina Galleries**, a series of caves and bluffs sculpted by wind and surf. Both islands have numerous **B&Bs** and several **campgrounds**, though if you're thinking of staying the night it's as well to check first with the Nanaimo infocentre.

# From Nanaimo to Pacific Rim National Park

North of Nanaimo Highway 1 is replaced by **Highway 19**, a messy stretch of road spotted with billboards and a rash of motels, marinas and clapboard houses. Almost every last inch of the coast is privately owned, this being the chosen site of what appears to be every British Columbian's dream holiday home. Don't expect, therefore, to be able to weave through the houses, wooden huts and boat launches to reach the tempting beaches that flash past below the highway. For sea and sand you have to hang on for **Parksville**, 37km north of Nanaimo, and its quieter near neighbour **Qualicum Beach**.

Parksville marks a major parting of the ways: while Hwy 19 continues up the eastern coast to Port Hardy, **Highway 4**, the principle trans-island route, pushes west to **Port Alberni** and on through the tremendously scenic Mackenzie Mountains to **Pacific Rim National Park**. *Island Coach Lines* (☎385-4411) runs three **buses** daily from Nanaimo to Port Alberni, where there are connecting services for **Ucluelet** and **Tofino**, though you should have few problems hitching this stretch of highway.

## Parksville

The approach to Parksville from the south is promising, heralded by a lonely **infocentre** 6km south of town alongside the entrance to *Craig's Camping*. Thereafter the road takes you through lovely wooded dunes, with lanes striking off eastwards to hidden beaches and a half-dozen secluded **campgrounds**. Four kilometres on is the best of the beaches, stretched along **Rathtrevor Beach Provincial Park**. In summer this area is madness – there's more beach action here than just about anywhere in the country, and if you want to lay claim to some of the park's camping space expect to start queueing first thing in the morning. The public sand here stretches for 2km and sports all the usual civilised facilities of Canada's tamed outdoors: cooking shelters, picnic spots and walking trails.

The dross starts beyond the orange bridge into **PARKSVILLE** and its eight blocks of motels and garages. The worst of the development has been kept off the promenade, however, which fronts **Parksville Beach**, whose annual **Sandfest** draws 30,000 visitors a day in July to watch the World Sandcastle Competition. The beach offers lovely views across to the mainland and boasts Canada's warmest seawater – 21°C in summer. Though busy, it's as immaculately kept as the rest of the town – a tidiness that bears witness to the reactionary civic pride of Parksville's largely retired permanent population. You'll see some of these worthy burghers at play during August when the town hosts the World Croquet Championships.

For local **information**, Parksville's Chamber of Commerce is clearly signed off the highway in downtown (May–Sept daily 8am–6pm). Ask especially for details of the many **hiking** areas and other nearby refuges from the beaches' summer maelstrom, and **fishing**, which is naturally another of the region's big draws.

If you must **stay**, camping offers the best locations. There are a multitude of **motels** in town and "resort complexes" out along the beaches, though summer vacancies are few and far between. South of Rathtrevor Beach Provincial Park try a pair of cottage resorts which look onto the sea: *Tigh-Na-Mara*, 1095 East Island Hwy (☎248-2072; $75–130), and *Graycrest on the Sea*, 1115 East Island Hwy (☎248-6513; $77–145). A touch more upmarket is *Beach Acres*, 1015 East Island Hwy (☎248-3424), with its own pool, sandy beach, and cabins from $125. At the same sort of price, the *Island Hall Resort Hotel*, 181 West Island Hwy (☎248-3225), is one of the smarter and better-known downtown establishments, though you'd be just as well off in the neighbouring *Sea Edge Motel* (☎248-8377), which shares the *Island Hall*'s beach and has doubles from $70.

## Qualicum Beach

QUALICUM BEACH, says its Chamber of Commerce, "is to the artist of today what Stratford-on-Avon was to the era of Shakespeare" – a bohemian enclave of West Coast artists and writers that has also been dubbed the "Carmel of the North". Both estimations pitch things ridiculously high, but compared to Parksville the area has more greenery and charm, and it's infinitely less commercialised, even though it probably has just as many summer visitors.

More a collection of dispersed houses than a town, Qualicum's seafront is correspondingly wilder and more picturesque, skirted by the road and interrupted only by an **infocentre** (the obvious white building midway on the strand), and a couple of well-sited **hotels**: the *Sand Pebble Inn* (☎752-6974; $55–75) and the *Captain's Inn* (☎752-6743; $55–85). A cluster of motels sit at its northern end, where the road swings inland, the best being the *Shorewater* (☎752-6901; $72–98). Keep heading north and the road becomes quieter and is edged with occasional **campgrounds**, amongst which the *Qualicum Bay* and *Spider Lake Provincial Park* sites stand out (both from $8).

Twenty-four kilometres north of the Qualicum is the area's only half-decent sight, the **Big Qualicum River Fish Hatchery**, a so-called "enhancement centre" which encourages salmon to spawn and thus bolster dwindling stocks. A tour of the government-run concern will fill you in on as much as you ever wanted to know about salmon.

## Highway 4 to Port Alberni

If you've not yet ventured off the coastal road from Victoria, the short stretch of Hwy 4 to Port Alberni offers the first real taste of the island's beauty. The cheapest place to stay along here is the log-cabin-style **mini hostel** (☎248-5694; $10) at 2400 Hwy 4 in COOMBS, about 10km west of Parksville – take the third entrance past the school on the south side of the main road. Buses will stop here on request, but there are only half a dozen beds – and no cooking facilities – so call in advance.

The first worthwhile stop is **Englishman River Falls Provincial Park**, 3km west of Parksville and then another 9km off the highway. Named after an early immigrant who drowned here, the park wraps around the Englishman River, which tumbles over two main sets of waterfalls. A thirty-minute trail takes in both falls, with plenty of swimming and fishing pools en route. The popular year-round campground is on the left off the approach road before the river, nestled amongst cedars, dogwoods – BC's provincial tree – and lush ferns.

Back on the main highway, a further 8km brings you to **Little Qualicum Hatchery**, given over to chum, trout and chinook salmon, and just beyond it a right turn for **Little Qualicum Falls Provincial Park**, claimed by some to be the island's loveliest small park. A magnificent forest trail follows the river as it drops several hundred metres through a series of gorges and foaming waterfalls. A half-hour stroll gives you views of the main falls, but for a longer **hike** try the five-hour Wesley Ridge Trail. There's a sheltered **campground** by the river and a recognised **swimming area** on the river at its southern end.

Midway to Port Alberni, the road passes **Cameron Lake** and then a belt of old-growth forest. At the lake's western end, it's well worth walking ten minutes into **MacMillan Provincial Park** (no campground) to reach the famous **Cathedral Grove**, a beautiful group of huge Douglas firs, some of them reaching 70m tall, 2m thick and up to 1000 years old. The park is the gift of the vast McMillan timber concern, whose agents have been responsible for felling similar trees with no compunction over the years. Wandering the grove will take only a few minutes, but just to the east, at the Cameron Lake picnic site, is the start of the area's main **hike**. The well-maintained trail was marked out by railway crews in 1908 and climbs to the summit of **Mount Arrowsmith** (1817m), a long, gentle twenty-kilometre pull through alpine meadows that takes between six and nine hours. The mountain is also one of the island's newer and fast-developing ski areas.

# Port Alberni

Self-proclaimed "Gateway to the Pacific" and (along with half of Vancouver Island) "Salmon Capital of the World", **PORT ALBERNI** is an ugly town dominated by the sights and smells of its huge lumber mills. It's also a busy fishing port, but its main interest to travellers is as a forward base for Pacific Rim National Park. If you've ever wanted to hook a salmon, this is probably one of the easier places to do so – there are any number of boats and guides ready to help out.

The only conventional sight is the **Alberni Valley Museum**, 4255 Wallace St and 10th Ave, home to a predictable but above-average logging and Native American collection (daily 10am–5pm; free). For hot-weather swimming, locals head out to **Sproat Lake Provincial Park**, 8km north of town on Hwy 4. It's a hectic scene in summer, thanks to a fine beach, picnic area, and a pair of good campgrounds – one on the lake, the other north of the highway about 1km away. Of peripheral interest, you can take a guided tour of the world's largest fire-fighting planes or follow the short trails that lead to a few ancient petroglyphs on the park's eastern tip.

Sproat Lake marks the start of the superb scenery that unfolds over the 100km of Hwy 4 west of the town. Only heavily logged areas detract from the grandeur of the Mackenzie Range and the majestic interplay of trees and water. Ride out prepared, however, as there's no petrol or shop for about two hours of driving.

### Practicalities

*Island Coach Lines* (☎724-1266) runs three **buses** daily to and from Nanaimo, with the terminal on Victoria Quay at 5065 Southgate. Jump off at the *7–11*, one stop earlier, to be nearer the centre of town. *Orient Stage Lines* (☎723-6924) runs one connection daily from here on to Ucluelet and Tofino in Pacific Rim National Park. For help and information on fishing charters, hiking options, minor summer events, or tours of the two local pulp mills, call in at the **infocentre** (daily 9am–6pm) off Hwy 4 east of town – look out for the big yellow mural.

For **accommodation** there are the usual motel choices, though for a good central hotel you might be better off with the *Barclay*, 4277 Stamp Ave (☎724-7171), with doubles from $70. *Hospitality Inn*, 3835 Redford St (☎723-8111), is another reliable choice, with rooms starting at $70. Cheaper, and in more salubrious surroundings 14km west of town on Hwy 4, is the *Westbay* (☎723-2811), with doubles from about $30. The infocentre has a list of the constantly changing **bed and breakfast** outlets. For **camping** you can try the small *Dry Creek Public Campground*, 4850 Argyle St and 3rd Ave (May–Sept; ☎723-6011), or, further afield, the nicer *China Creek Marina and Campground* (☎723-2657), 15km south of the town on Alberni Inlet, which has a wooded, waterside location and sandy, log-strewn beach. Camping at Sproat Lake (see above) is excellent, but busy in the summer.

Eating possibilities are numerous. For good **seafood** try the waterfront *Four Winds*, Harbour Quay (☎723-2333). The *Canal*, 5093 Johnson St, serves good Greek food, and for cheap lunches there's the *Paradise Café*, 4505 Gertrude St, and several deli-bakeries, of which the best are probably the *Mountain View*, 3727 10th Ave, and the *Yvette Deli*, 4926 Argyle St.

## The MV Lady Rose

The single best thing you can do in Port Alberni is to leave it, preferably on the **MV Lady Rose**, a small boat that plies between Kildonan, Bamfield, Ucluelet and the Broken Group Islands (see p.549). Primarily a conduit for freight and mail, it also takes up to 100 passengers, many of whom use it as a drop-off for canoe trips or the West Coast Trail at Bamfield. You could easily ride it simply for the exceptional scenery – huge cliffs and tree-covered mountains – and for the abundant wildlife (sea lions, whales, eagles and the like, depending on the time of year).

The boat leaves early every morning from the Argyle Street dock, following a different itinerary on different days of the week, and is back in port by the middle of the afternoon. Tickets cost $20 to $30, depending how far west you're travelling, and are quickly snapped up in the summer (☎723-8313 for information and reservations).

## Pacific Rim National Park

**Pacific Rim National Park** is the single best reason to visit Vancouver Island, a stunning amalgam of mountains, coastal rainforest, wild beaches, and unkempt marine landscapes that stretches intermittently for 130km between the towns of Tofino in the north and Port Renfrew to the south. It divides into three distinct areas: **Long Beach**, which is the most popular; the **Broken Group Islands**, hundreds of islets only really accessible to sailors and canoeists; and the **West Coast Trail**, a tough but increasingly popular long-distance footpath. The whole area has also become a mecca for **whale-watching**, and dozens of small companies run charters out from the main centres to view the migrating mammals.

Lying at the north end of Long Beach, **Tofino** is still essentially a fishing village and the best base for general exploration. **Ucluelet** to the south is comparatively less attractive, but more geared to accommodating the park's many thousands of annual visitors. **Bamfield**, a tiny and picturesque community still further south, is known mainly as the northern endpoint of the West Coast Trail and as a marine research and whale-watching centre.

**Weather** in the park is an important consideration, because it has a well-deserved reputation for being appallingly wet, cold and windy – and that's the good days. An average of 300cm of rain falls annually, and in some places it buckets down almost 700cm, well over ten times what falls on Victoria. So don't count on doing much swimming or sunbathing: think more in terms of spending your time admiring crashing Pacific breakers, hiking the backcountry and maybe doing a spot of beachcombing.

### Tofino

**TOFINO**, most travellers' target base in the park, is beginning to show the first adverse effects of its tourist influx, but it clearly realises it has a vested interest in preserving the salty, waterfront charm that brings people here in the first place. Crowning a narrow spit, the village is bounded on three sides by tree-covered islands and water, gracing it with magnificent views and plenty of what the tourist literature refers to as "aquaculture". As a service centre it fulfills most functions, offering food, accommodation and a wide variety of boat and seaplane tours (most with a whale-spotting dimension). It's easily reached from Port Alberni by the once-daily *Orient Coach Lines* connection.

Sleepy in off-season, the place erupts into a commercial frenzy during the summer, though there's little to do in town other than walk its few streets and soak up the atmosphere. Thereafter, most people head south to explore Long Beach, or put themselves at the mercy of the boat and plane operators. If you don't go for a general cruise round the coast (about 3hr), the best trip is out to **Meares Island** (15min by boat), a beautiful island swathed in lush temperate rainforest. The marked **Tribal Park** trail (2hr 30min) meanders among some of the biggest trees you'll ever see, many of them over 1000 years old and up to six metres across – big enough to put a tunnel through. Incredibly, there are plans to log the island, a move which has hit national headlines and, needless to say, given rise to considerable opposition and bad feeling.

The other popular trip is to **Hotsprings Cove** (1hr by boat, 15min by float plane), Vancouver Island's only hot springs. A thirty-minute trek from the landing stage, they consist of a small waterfall and four pools, becoming progressively cooler towards the sea. Be prepared for a crowd in summer. Rough camping is possible, but not encouraged, and a new motel is set to open near the quay.

The relatively quiet **Chesterman's Beach**, by contrast, is walkable from the village, and beyond it – accessible at low tide – lies **Frank Island**, a good spot for some free camping. For the best (unmarked) local beach, however, turn right just past the *Dolphin Motel* as you leave Tofino to the south, then drop down from the small car park.

*PRACTICALITIES*

The **infocentre** at 315 Campbell St (May–Sept daily 9am–8pm) can give you the exhaustive lowdown on all the logistics of boat and plane tours. They may also be able to get you into one of the village's ever-expanding roster of **bed and breakfasts**, should you be so unwise as to turn up in Tofino without reservations in high summer. Otherwise try the private **youth hostel**, *Tinwas Guest House*, 2km from the harbour at 1119 Pacific Rim Highway (☎725-3402), which has a wide variety of bunks and rooms, with and without bedding and washrooms, from $20 to $75 (no cooking facilities or meals). You can also camp here (from $12), with washing facilities and the possibility of beach barbecues for outdoor cooking.

The main concentration of **motels**, "cottage resorts" and campgrounds is south of the village, where you can try the excellent *Tofino Swell Lodge*, 340 Olsen Rd (☎725-3274), with rooms from $30 to $80 depending on season, or the *Dolphin Motel* (☎725-3377), with doubles from $40 to $60. For a bit more class, head for the *Ocean Village Beach Resort*, just north of Long Beach on the main road; "cottage" doubles start at $80. More central options, all with sea views, are: the *Schooner Motel*, 311 Campbell St (☎725-3478; doubles $67–85); *Maquinna Lodge Hotel*, 120 1st St (☎725-3261; doubles from $70); *Pacific Breeze Motel*, 760 Campbell St (☎725-3269; doubles $55–95); and the *Duffin Cove Resort Motel*, 215 Campbell St (☎725-3448; rooms $85–110).

Besides the youth hostel, **camping** options include *Bella Pacifica Resort and Campground* (☎725-3400; from $17, with free hot showers), and *Crystal Cove Beach Resort* (☎725-4213; from $14) – both are by the water about 3km south of Tofino.

For **food**, right-on environmentalists cluster at the *Common Loaf Bake Shop*, 131 1st St, a good choice for coffee and snacks. The *Crab Bar*, 601 Campbell St, sells only crab, beer and bread (plus some imaginative salads), though the best all-round restaurant is *The Loft*, 346 Campbell St, good for breakfast, lunch or dinner with friendly atmosphere and outdoor eating in the summer.

## Long Beach

The most easily reached and developed of the park's components, **Long Beach** is just what it says, a long tract of wild, windswept sand and rocky points stretching for about 16km from Tofino to Ucluelet. The snow-covered peaks of the Mackenzie Range rise up over 1200m as a scenic backdrop, and behind the beach grows a thick, lush canopy

## WHALES

Pacific Rim National Park is amongst the world's best areas for whale-watching, thanks to its location on the main migration routes, food-rich waters and numerous sheltered bays. People come from five continents for the spectacle, and it's easy to find a boat going out from Tofino, Ucluelet or Banfield, most charging around $30 a head for the trip. Regulations prohibit approaching within 100m of an animal but, though few locals will admit it, there's no doubt that the recent huge upsurge in boat tours has begun to disrupt the **migrations**. The whales' 8000-kilometre journey – the longest known migration of any mammal – takes them from their breeding and calfing lagoons in Baja, Mexico, to summer feeding grounds in the Bering and Chukchi Seas off Siberia. The northbound migration takes from February to May, with the peak period of passage between March and April. A few dozen animals occasionally abort their trip and stop off the Canadian coast for summer feeding (notably at Maquinna Marine Park, 20min by boat from Tofino). The return journey starts in August, hitting Tofino and Ucluelet in late September and early October. **Mating** takes place in Mexico during December, after which the males turn immediately northwards, to be followed by females and their young in February.

Although killer whales (orcas) are occasionally seen, the most commonly spotted type are **grey whales**, of which some 19,000 specimens are thought to make the journey annually. Averaging 14m in length and weighing 35 to 50 tonnes, they're distinguished by the absence of a dorsal fin, a ridge of lumps on the back, and a mottled blue-grey colour. Females have only one offspring yearly, following a gestation period of thirteen months, and, like the males, cruise at only two to four knots – perfect for viewing, and, sadly, for capture.

Even if you don't take a boat trip, you stand a faint chance of seeing whales from the coast as they dive, when you can locate their tails, or during fluking, when the animals surface and "blow" three or four times before making another five-minute dive. There are telescopes at various points along Long Beach, the best known viewpoints being Schooner Cove, Radar Hill, Quistis Point and Combers Beach near Sea Lion Rocks.

of coastal rainforest. The white-packed sand itself is the sort of primal seascape that is all but extinct in Europe, littered with beautiful, sea-sculpted driftwood, smashed by surf, broken by crags, and dotted with islets and rock pools oozing with marine life.

As this is a national park, it's all been slightly tamed for human consumption, but in the most discreet and tasteful manner. The best way to get a taste of the area is to walk the beach itself, or to follow any of nine well-maintained **hiking trails**. Most are quite short, though the Half Moon Bay and Shorepine Bog trails are 8km and 10km respectively. Try the South Beach Trail (#4; 1.5km) for admiring the surf, and Half Moon Bay (#2; 10km) for a quieter, sandy bay. All the paths are clearly marked from Hwy 4, but it's still worth picking up a *Hiker's Guide* from the infocentre.

Scenery aside, Long Beach is noted for its **wildlife**, the BC coastline reputedly having more marine species than any other temperate area in the world. As well as the smaller stuff in tidal pools – starfish, anemones, snails, sponges and suchlike – there are large mammals like whales and sea lions, as well as thousands of migrating birds (especially in Oct–Nov), notably pintails, mallards, black brants and Canada geese. Better weather brings out lots of beachcombers (Japanese glass fishing floats are highly coveted), clam diggers, anglers, canoeists, windsurfers and divers, though the water is usually too cold to venture in without a wet suit, and rip currents make swimming dangerous.

### PRACTICALITIES

Long Beach's **infocentre**, on Hwy 4 3km north of the T-junction for Tofino and Ucluelet, can provide a wealth of material on all aspects of the park, and in summer staff offer guided walks and interpretative programmes (mid-March to early Oct daily

9am–7pm). For more Long Beach information and lots of well-presented displays, head for the **Wickaninnish Interpretive Centre** (mid-March to early Oct daily 10am–5pm), on your left towards the beach after the infocentre.

There are two park **campgrounds**, the best being that at *Greenpoint*, set on a lovely bluff overlooking the beach (washrooms but no showers; firewood available). However, it's likely to be full every day in July and August, and it's first come, first served, so you may have to turn up for several days before getting a spot. The other site – more primitive, but equally lovely and popular – is at the northern end of the beach at *Schooner Cove* (outhouses only). The thirty-minute walk from the nearest car park reduces demand a little, and also means it tends to be more of a backpackers' hang-out. The nearest commercial sites and conventional accommodation are in Tofino and Ucluelet.

## Ucluelet

**UCLUELET** means "People of the Sheltered Bay" and was named by the Nuu-chah-nulth natives who lived here for centuries to exploit some of the world's richest fishing grounds immediately offshore. Today the port is still the third largest in BC by volume of fish landed, a trade that gives the town an industrial fringe – mainly lumber and canning concerns – and makes it a less appealing, if nonetheless popular base for anglers, whale-watchers and tourists headed for Long Beach to the north.

**Buses** and **boats** call here from Port Alberni – *Orient Coach Lines* makes the road trip once a day, and the *MV Lady Rose* docks here three days a week (see p.545). There's plenty of **accommodation**, much of it spread along Peninsula Road, the main approach to town from Hwy 4. For full details visit the **infocentre**, 1620 Peninsula Rd (May–Sept daily 9am–6pm). Reasonable lodgings include the *Canadian Princess* (☎726-7771), a hotel in an old steamer moored in the harbour, with doubles starting at $50; *Burley's*, 1078 Helen Rd (☎726-4444), a waterfront house with doubles from $35; and the *West Coast Motel*, 247 Hemlock (☎726-7732), with doubles from $50. The **public campground** (☎726-4355; $14) overlooks the harbour. **Seafood** here is as fresh as it comes, and is best sampled at *Smiley's* just across from the *Canadian Princess* on Peninsula Road, a no-frills, no-decor diner popular with locals. For fish with a Chinese slant, try the *Peninsula Café*, 1648 Peninsula Rd. For walking and wildlife, the nearest trails are at **Terrace Beach**, just north of the town.

---

### NUU-CHAH-NULTH WHALE HUNTS

All the peoples of the Northwest coast are famed for their skilfully constructed canoes, but only the **Nuu-chah-nulth** – whose name translates roughly as "all along the mountains" – used these fragile cedar crafts to pursue whales, an activity that was accompanied by elaborate ritual. Before embarking on a whaling expedition the whalers had not only to be trained in the art of capturing these mighty animals but also had to be purified through a rigorous programme of fasting, sexual abstinence and bathing. Whalers also visited forest shrines made up of a whale image surrounded by human skulls or corpses and carved wooden representations of deceased whalers – the dead were thought to aid the novice in his task and to bring about the beaching of dead whales near the village.

When the whaler was on the chase, his wife would lie motionless in her bed; it was thought that the whale would become equally docile. His crew propelled the canoe in total silence until the moment of the harpooning, whereupon they frantically back-paddled to escape the animal's violent death throes as it attempted to dive, only to be thwarted by a long line of floats made from inflated sea lion skins. After exhausting itself, the floating whale was finally killed and boated back to the village, where its meat would be eaten and its blubber processed for its highly prized oil.

## The Broken Group Islands

The only way for the ordinary traveller to approach these 100 or so islands, speckled across Barkley Sound between Ucluelet and Bamfield, is by seaplane, chartered boat or the *MV Lady Rose* (see p.545). Boats dock at Gibraltar Island. Immensely wild and beautiful, the islands have the reputation for the best **canoeing** in North America, and for some of the continent's finest **scuba-diving**. You can hire canoes and gear (contact the *Lady Rose* office), and then take them on board the *Lady Rose* to be dropped off en route. You need to know what you're doing, however – there's plenty of dangerous water – and should pick up the relevant marine chart (*Broken Group* 3670; $9), available locally. Divers can choose from among fifty shipwrecks claimed by the reefs, rough waters and heavy fogs that beset the aptly named islands.

Eight rough **campgrounds** serve the group, but water is hard to come by: pick up the park leaflet on camping and freshwater locations. A park warden patrols the region from Nettle Island; otherwise the islands are as pristine as the day they rose from the sea.

## The West Coast Trail

One of North America's classic walks, the **West Coast Trail** starts 5km south of Bamfield (see next page) and traverses exceptional coastal scenery for 77km to Port Renfrew. It's no stroll, and though it's becoming very popular – too popular, say many – it still requires experience, equipment and a fair degree of fitness. Many people, however, do the first easy stage as a day-trip taster from Bamfield. Reckon on five to eight days for the full trip; carry all your own food, camp where you can, and be prepared for rain, landslips, treacherous stretches, thick, soaking forest, and almost utter isolation.

As originally conceived, the trail had nothing to do with promoting the great outdoors. Mariners long ago dubbed this area of coastline the "graveyard of the Pacific", and when the *SS Valencia* went down with all hands here in 1906 the government was persuaded that constructing a trail would at least give stranded sailors a chance to walk to safety along the coast (trying to penetrate the interior's rainforest was out of the question). The path followed a basic telegraph route that linked Victoria with outlying towns and lighthouses, and was kept open by linesmen and lighthouse keepers until the 1960s, when it fell into disrepair. Early backpackers re-blazed the old trail; some 4000 now make the trip annually, and the numbers are rising.

**Weather** is a key factor in planning any trip; the trail is really only passable between June and September (July is the driest month), which is also the only period when it's patrolled by wardens and the only time locals are on hand to ferry you (for a fee) across some of the wider rivers en route. However, you should be prepared for dreadful weather and poor trail conditions at all times. Take cash with you to pay for ferries and nominal fees for camping on native land.

An increasing amount of literature and route guides are appearing on the trail every year (available in most BC bookshops), but for **maps** and **information** visit the main infocentres at Port Alberni (very knowledgeable staff) or Long Beach. The recommended trail map is the 1:50,000 *West Coast Trail, Port Renfrew–Bamfield*, available from the Ministry of the Environment, 553 Superior St, Victoria (☎387-1441). Current trail conditions, information and emergency cover are available at Bamfield/Pachena Bay (May–Sept; ☎728-3234) and Port Renfrew (☎647-5434).

**Access** is also an important consideration. For the northern trailhead at Bamfield take the *MV Lady Rose* from Port Alberni (call ☎723-8313 for current schedule; $20 one way). In addition, *Pachena Bay Express* runs a summer-only bus service along the 100-kilometre gravel road from Port Alberni to Bamfield (☎728-3448 for times). The southern trailhead is near Port Renfrew (see p.535).

## Bamfield

**BAMFIELD** is a quaint spot, half-raised above the ocean on a wooden boardwalk, but it has only limited and mainly expensive **accommodation**, so many walkers plan on hitting the trail straight off the bus or boat. If you think you'll need a bed, try to make reservations, especially at the *Sea Beam Fishing Resort* (☎728-3286) – call anyway for directions or for a taxi pick-up. The setting is tranquil, and it has a small kitchen, common room with open fire and sixteen beds arranged as one-, two- or three-bed dorms from $15: **camping** space is also available for $12. Otherwise call the *Bamfield Trails Motel* (☎728-3231), *Aguilar House* (☎728-3323), *Bamfield Inn* (☎728-3354) or *Captain's Landing* (☎728-3383), all heavily in demand and costing $50 to $80. More places, particularly bed-and-breakfast options, are opening each year.

If you just want to tackle the first stage of the West Coast Trail and return to Bamfield in a day, you can walk the 11km to the **Pachena Lighthouse**, starting from the Ross Bible Camp on the Ohiaht Indian campground at Pachena Beach. After that, the route becomes the real thing.

# North Vancouver Island

It's a moot point where the north of Vancouver Island starts, but if you're travelling on Hwy 19 the landscape's sudden lurch into more unspoilt wilderness after Qualicum Beach makes as good a watershed as any. Few of the towns amount to much, and you could bus, drive or hitch the length of the island to Port Hardy and take the **Inside Passage** ferry up to Prince Rupert – the obvious and most tantalising itinerary – without missing a lot. Alternatively, you could follow the main highway only as far as **Courtenay**, and from there catch a ferry across to the mainland. If you have the means, however, try to get into the wild, central interior, much of it contained within **Strathcona Provincial Park**.

## Denham Island, Hornby Island and Courtenay

North of Qualicum Beach the scenery is uneventful but restful on the eye, graced with ever-improving views of the mainland. Hwy 19 is interrupted by one hamlet, BUCKLEY BAY, which consists of a single bed and breakfast and the ferry terminal to **Denham** and **Hornby islands** (18 sailings daily; $8 single) – two outposts described, with some justification, as the "undiscovered Gulf Islands". You'll need a car or bike (the latter can be hired on the islands) to explore them in any depth: highlights are the unspoilt hill country, the beach at Hornby's Tribune Bay, and the laid-back (if wary) population, a mishmash of alternative types including refugee draft-dodger hippies from the Vietnam War. There are plenty of small **hotels** and **campgrounds**: contact the Denham **tourist centre** (☎335-2293) or the hub of Hornby life, the *Hornby Island Co-op* (☎335-1121).

Beyond Buckley Bay is a short stretch of wild, pebbly beach, and then the **Comox Valley**, open rural country that's not as captivating as the brochures might lead you to expect. Of three settlements here – COMOX, CUMBERLAND and **COURTENAY** – only the last is of interest, and only then as a ferry link to Powell River on the mainland. The terminal is a good twenty minutes' drive from the town down backroads – hitching is almost impossible, so you have to take a taxi or hold out for the minibus shuttle that leaves the bus depot twice on Tuesday and Friday to connect with sailings. Courtenay is connected to Nanaimo and Victoria by **bus** (4 daily), and is the terminus for **trains** from Victoria (1 daily). If you get stranded in town, there are plenty of **motels** along the strip on the southern approach, close to the **infocentre** at 2040 Cliffe Ave (daily 9am–5pm; longer hours in summer). The best **camping** is 20km north of Courtenay at Miracle Beach Provincial Park – a vast, but very popular, tract of sand.

The **Comox Valley** scores higher inland, on the eastern fringes of Strathcona Provincial Park (see next page) and the new **skiing** areas of Forbidden Plateau and Mount Washington. There's plenty of **hiking** in summer, when the Forbidden Plateau lifts operate at weekends from 11am to 3pm. A great day hike on Mount Washington is the five-hour walk on well-marked trails from the ski area across Paradise Meadows to Moat Lake or Circlet Lake. For details of tougher walks (Battleship Lake, Lady Lake), ask at the infocentre. Access to the trailheads is by minor road from Courtenay.

# Campbell River

Of the hundred or so Canadian towns that claim to be "Salmon Capital of the World," **CAMPBELL RIVER**, 46km north of Courtenay, is probably the one that comes closest to justifying the boast. Fish and fishing dominate the place to a ludicrous degree, and you'll soon be heartily sick of pictures of grinning anglers holding impossibly huge chinook salmon. Massive shoals of these monsters are forced into the three-kilometre channel between the town and the mainland, making the job of catching them little more than a formality. The town grew to accommodate fishermen from the outset, centred on a hotel built in 1904 after word spread of the colossal fish that local Cape Mudge natives were able to pluck from the sea. Today about sixty percent of all visitors come to dangle a line in the water. Others come for the scuba-diving (once described by *National Geographic* as the second best in the world). For the casual visitor, the place serves as the main road access to the wilds of Strathcona Provincial Park.

If you want to **fish**, hundreds of shops and guides are on hand to help out and hire equipment. It'll cost about $15 a day for the full kit, and about $50 for a morning's guidance. Huge numbers of people, however, fish from the new 200-metre **Discovery Pier**, Canada's first saltwater fishing pier ($1). **Diving** rentals come more expensive; try *Beaver Aquatics* near the Quadra ferry dock in Discovery Bay Marina (☎287-7652). If you merely want to know something about salmon before they end up on a plate, drop in on the **Quinsam Salmon Hatchery**, 5km west of town on the road to Gold River (daily 8am–4pm).

Campbell River's well-stocked **infocentre** is at 923 Island Highway (daily 9am–6pm). Four *Island Coachlines* **buses** daily run to Victoria, but there's only one a day north to Port Hardy and towns en route. The **bus terminal** is on the corner of Cedar and 13th near the Royal Bank (☎287-7151). **Accommodation** is no problem, Campbell River being a resort first and foremost: try the *Super 8 Motel* on the main road south of town (☎286-6622), or the carving-stuffed *Campbell River Lodge*, 1760 North Island Hwy (☎287-7446), with doubles from $60. You won't be able to escape the fishing clutter common to all hotels unless you head for a **bed and breakfast**. Contact the infocentre for listings, or try *Pier's House B&B*, 670 Island Hwy (☎287-2943; doubles $45). For nice wooded **camping** use the *Parkside Campground*, 5km west of town on Hwy 28 (☎287-3113; from $12).

Cheap **eateries** abound, mainly of the fast-food variety, and in the pricier restaurants there's no prize for spotting the main culinary emphasis. Best burger place is *Del's Drive-In & Diner*, 1423 Island Hwy, known as a place with plenty of local colour. For beer and snacks try the *Royal Coachman*, 84 Dogwood St. For a seafood treat head for *Shagpokes* at the *Anchor Inn*, 261 Island Hwy (good views), or the *Gourmet by the Sea* on the main road about 15km south of town at Bennett's Point.

## Quadra Island

**Quadra Island** is fifteen minutes away from Campbell River and makes a nice respite from the fish. Ferries run roughly hourly from the well-signed terminal out of town. The main excuse for the crossing is the **Kwagiulth Museum and Cultural Centre**, home to one of the country's most noted collections of potlatch regalia (daily 10am–

4.30pm; closed Sun & Mon off-season; $2). As elsewhere in Canada, the masks, costumes and ritual objects were confiscated by the government in an attempt to stamp out one of the natives' most potent ceremonies, and only came back on condition they would be locked up in a museum (see p.526).

While on the island you could also walk its coastal **trails**, or climb Chinese Mountain for some cracking views. There's swimming off a rocky beach at **Rebecca Spit Provincial Park**, but the water's warmer and there's a bit of sand at the more distant **Village Bay Park**. There's **accommodation** at the *Heriot Bay Inn* on Heriot Bay Rd (☎285-3322; doubles $60–150; camping from $14) and *Whiskey Point Lodge*, by the ferry dock at 725 Quathioski Cove Rd (☎285-2201; doubles $50–60).

# Strathcona Provincial Park

Vancouver Island's largest protected area, and the oldest park in British Columbia, **Strathcona Provincial Park** is one of the few places on the island where the scenery approaches the grandeur of the mainland mountains. Only two areas have any sort of facilities for the visitor – **Forbidden Plateau**, approached from Courtenay, and the more popular **Buttle Lake** region, accessible from Campbell River via Hwy 28. The *Gold River Minibus* will drop you at the head of Buttle Lake, about 40km west of Campbell River (Sun, Tues & Thurs). The rest of the park is unsullied wilderness, but fully open to backpackers and hardier walkers. Be sure to pick up the blue *BC Parks* pamphlet (available from the infocentre at Campbell River and elsewhere): it has a good general map and gives lots of information, such as the comforting fact that there are no grizzly bears in the park.

You'll see numerous pictures of **Della Falls** around Campbell River, which at 440m are amongst the world's highest, though unfortunately it's a two-day trek with a canoe passage thrown in if you're going to see them.

The approach to the park along Hwy 28 is worth taking for the scenery alone; numerous short trails and nature walks are signposted from rest stops, most no more than twenty minutes' stroll from the car. **Elk Falls Provincial Park** is the first stop, ten minutes out of Campbell River, noted for its gorge and waterfall.

### Park practicalities

The **park centre** is located at the junction of Hwy 28 and the Buttle Lake road (May–Sept only); fifteen information shelters around the lake also provide some trail and

---

### HIKING IN STRATHCONA

**Hiking**, it hardly needs saying, is superb in Strathcona, with a jaw-dropping scenic combination of jagged mountains – including Golden Hinde (2220m), the island's highest point – lakes, rivers, waterfalls and all the trees you could possibly want. Seven marked **trails** fan out from the Buttle Lake area, together with six shorter nature walks, most less than 2km long, amongst which the Lady Falls and Lupin Falls trails stand out for their waterfall and forest views. All the longer trails can be tramped in a day, though the most popular, the **Elk River Trail** (10km), which starts from Drum Lake on Hwy 28, lends itself to an overnight stop. Popular with backpackers because of its gentle grade, the path ends up at Landslide Lake, an idyllic camping spot. The other highly regarded trail is the **Flower Ridge** walk, which starts at the southern end of Buttle Lake. Backcountry camping is allowed throughout the park, and the backpacking is great once you've hauled up onto the summit ridges above treeline. For serious exploration buy the relevant topographic maps at MAPS BC, Ministry of Environment and Parks, Parliament Buildings, Victoria.

wildlife information. Buttle Lake has two provincial **campgrounds** with facilities, one alongside the park centre, the other at Ralph River on the extreme southern end of Buttle Lake, accessed by the road along the lake's eastern shore. Both have good **swimming** areas nearby.

The park's only commercial **accommodation** is provided by the *Strathcona Park Lodge* (☎286-2008 or ☎286-3122), just outside the Buttle Lake entrance, a weird mixture of hotel, outdoor pursuits centre, hostel and campground. For the **hostel** you'll need your own sleeping bag and you must call in advance (pick-ups from Campbell River are sometimes available); rates are about $15 per person, with use of a kitchen. Hotel rooms are $40 to $75 for doubles. You can also hire canoes, bikes and other outdoor equipment, and sign up for any number of organised tours and activities.

## Gold River and Tahsis

There's not a lot happening at **GOLD RIVER,** a tiny logging community 89km west of Campbell River – founded in 1965, the place only has one hotel and a couple of shops – but the ride over on Hwy 28 is superb, and there's the chance to explore the coastline by boat. Every Thursday, year-round, the **Uchuck III**, a converted World War II minesweeper, takes mail, cargo and passengers up the coast to Tahsis from the dock at the end of Hwy 28, about 15km southwest of Gold River, returning early evening. It's a lovely trip, with great sea views, tree-covered mountains, and several drop-offs at obscure villages en route. Additional sailings are laid on for tourists in July and August (☎283-2325 for information).

One of the area's two minor attractions is **Quatsino Cave**, the deepest vertical cave in North America, parts of which are open to the public – for details ask at the infocentre on Village Square Plaza (May–Sept daily 9am–7pm); the other is the **Big Drop**, a stretch of Gold River whitewater known to kayakers worldwide. **Accommodation** is expensive at the *Gold River Chalet* (☎283-2244; doubles from $107), and the *Ridgeview Motel*, in a panoramic spot above the village at 395 Donner Court (☎283-2277; rooms $90) – but the *Peppercorn Trail Motel and Campground* on Mill Road (☎283-2443) has rooms for $40 and will let you **camp** for $15. There's also a basic campground run by the local Lions Club.

Note that there are also two beautiful roads north from Gold River, both rough, but worth the jolts for the scenery. One provides an alternative approach to **TAHSIS**, which has a couple of motels if you need to break your journey: the cheaper of the pair is the *Tahsis Motel*, Head Bay Rd (☎934-6318), with rooms for $60.

## North to Port McNeill, Telegraph Cove and Alert Bay

The main highway north of Campbell River cuts inland and climbs through increasingly rugged and deserted country, particularly after SAYWARD, the one main community en route. Near Sayward is the marvellously oddball **Valley of a Thousand Faces**: 1400 famous faces painted onto cedar logs, the work of a Dutch artist, a labour which is more interesting than it sounds (May–Aug daily 10am–4pm; donation). Almost alongside is an RV and tent **campground**, the *White River Court* (☎282-3265; from $10). With a car, you could strike off south from here for 62km to **Schoen Lake Provincial Park**, featuring a couple of forest trails and a well-kept campground.

**PORT McNEILL**, 180km north of Campbell River and the first real town along Hwy 19, is merely a motel and logging centre and devoid of interest. By contrast, **TELEGRAPH COVE**, reached by a rough side road just to the east, is an immensely likeable place and the best of BC's so-called "boardwalk villages": the whole community is raised on wooden stilts over the water, a sight that's becoming ever more popular with tourists. As an added bonus, the village has become one of the island's premier **whale-watching** spots, the main attraction here being the "pods" of orcas (killer whales) that calve locally. Some nineteen "families" live at nearby Robson Bight, established as an ecological reserve in 1982. The best outfit for a trip to see them is *Stubbs Island Charters* (☎928-3185), but their daily sailings (June–Oct) are popular, so call well in advance to be sure of a place.

In summer you can buy food at a small café, but otherwise the only provision for visitors is an incongruous new building with shop, ice-cream counter and coffee bar. The only **accommodation** is the *Telegraph Cove Resorts Campground*, a short walk from the village and one of the best-located sites on Vancouver Island, a reputation which makes reservations essential in summer (May–Sept; ☎928-3131; from $10).

The breezy fishing village of **ALERT BAY**, on Cormorant Island, is reached by numerous daily ferries from Port McNeill. The fifty-minute crossing sets you back only $2 and in season provides a good chance of seeing whales en route. Despite the predominance of the non-native industries (fish processing), half the population of the island is of native Namgis stock. The **infocentre** is immediately to your right as you come off the ferry. Bear left out of the main part of the village to reach the excellent **U'Mista Cultural Centre** (Mon–Sat 9am–5pm; $3), which houses a collection of potlatch items and artefacts returned by the government and shows a couple of award-winning films; you might also come across local kids being taught native languages, songs and dances. The village also claims the world's tallest fully carved **totem pole** (other contenders, say villagers, are mostly pole and not much carving). Also worth a look is the wildlife and weird swamp habitat at **Gator Gardens** behind the bay. Most people come over for the day, but **accommodation** options include *Ocean View Accommodations*, 390 Poplar St, 1km from the ferry terminal (☎974-5457; doubles $50); *Bayside Inn Hotel*, overlooking the harbour at 81 First St (☎974-5857; doubles $45); and *Oceanview Camping* on Alder Rd (☎974-5213; $10).

## Port Hardy

Dominated by big-time copper mining, a large fishing fleet and the usual logging concerns, **PORT HARDY** is best known among travellers as the departure point for ships plying the famous **Inside Passage** to Prince Rupert.

If possible, time your arrival to coincide with one of the sailings which leave every other day in summer and twice weekly in winter. **Bus** services are scheduled to do this for you. A daily *Island Coach Lines* bus (☎949-7532 in Port Hardy, ☎385-4411 in Victoria) leaves Victoria early in the morning with a change in Nanaimo, arriving at the Port Hardy ferry terminal in late afternoon; between June and September an extra service operates over the same route on even-numbered dates, departing at noon. *Maverick Coach Lines* (☎753-4371 in Nanaimo, ☎662-3222 in Vancouver) runs an early-morning bus from Vancouver to Nanaimo (inclusive of ferry), connecting with the daily *ICL* bus to Port Hardy. You can **fly** direct from Vancouver International Airport to Port Hardy with *Time Air* (☎279-6611 in Vancouver) or *Air BC* (☎278-3800 in Vancouver).

The Port Hardy **ferry terminal** is actually well away from the town itself at Bear Cove, where buses stop before carrying on to stop opposite the **infocentre**, 7250 Market St (daily 9am–6pm). If you stay overnight, leave plenty of time to reach the terminal – sailings are usually around 7.30am. Many travellers to Port Hardy are in RVs, but there's still some pressure on hotel **accommodation** in summer, and it's as well to call ahead if you're not coinciding with one of the ferry sailings. The cheapest rooms are out of town at the *Airport Inn* (☎949-9424), with doubles from $48, but you'd be better off in one of the more central choices like the *North Shore Inn*, 7370 Market

St (☎949-8500), with nice views of the harbour, nightly live music and doubles from $65; more upmarket is the *Best Western Port Hardy Inn*, 9040 Granville St (☎949-8525), doubles from $70. Five minutes south of town is the *Pioneer Inn* (☎949-7271), with doubles from $48. The *Wildwoods* **campground** (☎949-6753) is the perfect tenting option, being within easy walking distance of the ferry. The *Quatse River Campground* (☎949-2395; $12) is at 5050 Hardy Road opposite the *Pioneer Inn*.

**Food** is nothing special, but there's a bevy of budget outlets, so you should be able to fill up for well under $10. Granville and Market streets have the main restaurant concentrations: try *Snuggles*, next to the *Pioneer Inn*, which aims at a cosy English pub atmosphere with live music, theatre (Fri nights) and steaks, salads and salmon grilled over an open fire.

The infocentre can give you all the details about Port Hardy's tiny but free **museum**, and the immense wilderness of **Cape Scott Provincial Park**, which is accessible only by foot and is supposed to have some of the most consistently bad weather in the world.

---

### THE INSIDE PASSAGE

One of Canada's great trips, the **Inside Passage** aboard *BC Ferries' Queen of the North*, between Port Hardy and Prince Rupert on the British Columbia mainland, is a cheap way of getting what people on the big cruise ships are getting: mountains, islands, waterfalls, glaciers, sea lions, whales, eagles and some of the grandest coastal scenery on the continent. By linking up with the *Greyhound* bus network or the *VIA* rail terminal at Prince Rupert, it also makes a good leg in any number of convenient itineraries around British Columbia. Other travellers will want to press on from Prince Rupert to Skagway by boat and then head north into Alaska and the Yukon (see p.570 for details on the *Alaska Marine* ferries). It's a good way of meeting fellow travellers, particularly if you pitch a tent in the boat's gymnasium, which is set aside for the purpose.

The sea passage takes twenty hours, with one stop at BELLA BELLA. Be aware that from October 5 to May 25 the sailings in both directions are predominantly at night, which rather defeats the object of the trip. The cost is about $80 single for a foot passenger, $155 for a car; reservations are **essential** throughout the summer season if you're taking a car or want a cabin. Make bookings by phone (☎386-3431 in Victoria; ☎669-1211 in Vancouver), fax (☎381-5452 in Victoria) or post (BC Ferry Corporation, 1112 Fort St, Victoria, BC). Include name and address; number in party; length, height and type of car; choice of day-room or cabin; and preferred date of departure and alternatives. Full payment is required up front. Cabins can be reserved by foot passengers, and range from $27 (2-berth, lower deck) to $65 on the boat deck. If you're making a round trip and want to leave your car behind, there are several supervised lock-ups in Port Hardy: try *Daze Parking* (☎949-7792).

---

# NORTH OF VANCOUVER

Apart from Vancouver Island, two other excursions from Vancouver stand out, each of which can easily be extended to embrace longer itineraries out of the city. The first is the 150-kilometre **Sunshine Coast**, the only stretch of accessible coastline on mainland British Columbia, and a possible springboard to Vancouver Island and the Inside Passage ferry to Prince Rupert. The second is the inland route to **Garibaldi Provincial Park**, containing by far the best scenery and hiking country within striking distance of Vancouver, and the high-profile ski resort of **Whistler**; the road becomes a summer-only route beyond Whistler, but train passengers can forge on through wilder parts all the way to Prince George.

# The Sunshine Coast

A mild-weathered stretch of sandy beaches, rugged headlands and quiet lagoons backed by forested hills, the **Sunshine Coast** receives heavy promotion – and heavy tourist traffic as a result – though the scenic rewards here are slim compared to the interior. In summer, however, this area offers what are reputedly some of Canada's best diving, boating and fishing opportunities, all of which stoke a string of busy villages eager to provide accommodation, run tours and rent anything from bikes to full-sized cruisers.

**Highway 101** runs the length of the coast, but it's interrupted at two points by size-able inlets that entail lengthy ferry crossings. Motorists face enormous queues to get on the boats in summer (reservations aren't possible), but the crossings present no problems for bus or foot passengers – indeed, they're the best bits of the trip. Given that the area is hardly worth full-scale exploration by car anyway, you might as well go by **bus**; it's perfectly feasible to get to Powell River and back in a day. *Maverick Coach Lines* (☎662-3222) runs two buses daily to Powell River (5hr; $25) and a third as far as Sechelt (2hr; $12); the same number make the return trip.

## Along Highway 101

Soon reached and well signposted from North Vancouver, **HORSESHOE BAY** is the departure point for the first of the Hwy 101 **ferry** crossings, a half-hour passage through the islands of fjord-like Howe Sound (regular sailings year-round). Ferries also ply from here to Nanaimo on Vancouver Island, with hourly sailings in summer and every other hour in off-season. For information on either of these services contact *BC Ferries* in Vancouver (☎669-1211 or ☎685-1021), or pick up a timetable from the Vancouver infocentre.

**GIBSONS**, the terminal on the other side of Howe Sound, is a scrappy place spread widely over a wooded hillside – the nicest area is around the busy marina, where you'll find the **infocentre** at 417 Lower Marine Drive (daily 9am–6pm). Motels abound, but for decent camping hold out for **Roberts Creek Provincial Park**, 8km northwest of the terminal on Hwy 101. Beyond, the service and supplies centre of **SECHELT** panders to tourists less than Gibsons, and ongoing development lends the town a messy air which isn't helped by its drab, flat location. Just 4km north, however, **Porpoise Bay Provincial Park** has a campground, a sandy beach, good swimming and a few short woodland trails. The main road beyond Sechelt is very pretty, and offers occasional views to the sea when it's not trapped in the trees. Pender Harbour comprises a collection of small communities of which **MADEIRA PARK** is the most substantial; whales occasionally pass this section of coast – which, sadly, is the source of most of the whales in the world's aquariums – but the main draws are fishing and boating.

**EARL'S COVE** is nothing but the departure ramp of the second **ferry** en route, a longer crossing (45min) which again offers fantastic views of sheer mountains plunging into the sea. A short trail (4km) from the adjacent car park leads to a viewpoint for the **Skookumchuck Narrows**, where the Sechelt Inlet constricts to produce boiling rapids at the turn of each tide. On board the ferry, look north beyond the low wooded hills – devoid of all human trace – to the immense waterfall which drops off a Lost World-type plateau into the sea.

From JERVIS BAY, the opposite landing stage, the country is comparatively less travelled. A couple of kilometres up the road is the best of all the provincial parks in this region, **Saltery Bay Provincial Park**. Everything here is discreetly hidden in the trees between the road and the coast, and the campground – beautifully sited – is connected by short trails to a couple of swimming beaches. The main road beyond is largely enclosed by trees, so there's little to see of the coast, though various **camp-**

**grounds** give onto the sea, notably the big *Oceanside* site, 4km short of Powell River, which sits on a superb piece of shoreline (☎485-2435; $10). Although it's given over mainly to RVs, there are a few sites for tents.

## Powell River and beyond

Given its seafront location, **POWELL RIVER** inevitably has its scenic side, but like many a BC town its unfocused sprawl and nearby sawmill dampen the overall appeal. The main road cruises past almost 4km of box-like retirement bungalows before reaching the town centre, which, despite the promises of the local tourist trade, is no edenic resort. If you're catching the **ferry** to Courtenay on Vancouver Island (4 daily; 75min), you might not even see the townsite, as the terminal is 2km to the east at WESTVIEW, and some of the **buses** from Vancouver are timed to coincide with the boats; if your bus doesn't connect, you can either walk or call a taxi (☎483-3666). The local **infocentre** (daily 9am–5pm), which is immediately at the end of the wooden ferry pier, can supply a visitor's map with detailed coverage of the many trails leading inland from the coast hereabouts; they can also advise on boat trips on Powell Lake, immediately inland, and tours to Desolation Sound, further up the coast.

In the event of having to stay overnight locally, you can choose from a dozen or so **motels** in town and two at the terminal itself. Of the latter, the new *Marina Motel* (☎485-4242), on the left as you look at the ferry, is immensely preferable to the bar and strip-joint opposite. Doubles come at $36, and there's a good little diner downstairs. For other **food**, try the fish-and-chip shop on the left just beyond the dingier motel, or the *Seaview* immediately above the terminal. For pricier seafood specials the popular choice is the *Beach Gardens Resort Hotel*, 7074 Westminster St, at the extreme eastern edge of Powell River. The most central of several **campgrounds** is the *Willingdon Beach* on the seafront off Marine Avenue (☎485-2242; $8.50–13.50).

The northern endpoint of Hwy 101 – which, incidentally, starts in Mexico City, making it one of North America's longest continuous routes – is the hamlet of LUND, 28km up the coast from Powell River. **Desolation Sound Marine Provincial Park**, about 10km north of Lund, offers some of Canada's best boating and scuba-diving, plus fishing, canoeing and kayaking. There's no road access to the park, but a number of outfitters in Powell River run tours to it and can hire all the equipment you could possibly need – try *Westview Live Bait Ltd*, 4527 Marine Ave, for **canoes**; *Coulter's Diving*, 4557 Willingdon Ave, for **scuba gear**; and *Spokes*, 4710 Marine Drive, for **bicycles**. The more modest **Okeover Provincial Park**, immediately north of Lund, has an unserviced campground.

# The Sea to Sky Highway

A fancy name for Highway 99 between North Vancouver and Whistler, the **Sea to Sky Highway** has a slightly better reputation than it deserves, mainly because Vancouver's weekend hordes need to reassure themselves of the grandeur of the scenery at their doorstep. Where it undoubtedly scores is in its early coastal stretch, where the road clings perilously to an almost sheer cliff and mountains come dramatically into view on both sides of Howe Sound. Views here are better than along the Sunshine Coast, though plenty of campgrounds, motels and minor roadside distractions fill the route until the mountains of the Coast Range rear up beyond Squamish for the rest of the way to Whistler.

If you've a **car** you're better off driving the highway only as far as Garibaldi Provincial Park – the summer-only section between Pemberton and Lillooet is very slow going. Six daily *Maverick Coach Lines* **buses** (☎662-3222) connect Vancouver and

Whistler ($18; 3 daily continue to Pemberton), which you can easily manage as a day trip, though a far more interesting and popular way of covering this ground is by **train**. *BC Rail* operates a daily passenger service between North Vancouver and Lillooet, calling at Whistler and other minor stations; the train arrives in Lillooet at 1pm and sets off back for Vancouver at 3.30pm, making for an excellent day-trip ($27 return to Whistler, $50.50 return to Lillooet). Another train continues on to Prince George daily between mid-June and late September, and on Sunday, Wednesday and Friday the rest of the year ($130 one way) – a better way to make this journey than by bus via Hope and Cache Creek. Reservations are required if you're travelling beyond Lillooet (☎631-3500).

## North Vancouver to Squamish

Road and rail lines meet with some squalor at **BRITTANIA BEACH**, whose **BC Museum of Mining** is the first reason to take time out from admiring the views (May–Aug Wed–Sun 10am–4pm; Sept Sat & Sun only; $5). Centring around what was, in the 1930s, the largest producer of copper in the British empire, the museum is housed in a huge, derelict-looking white building on the hillside and is chock-full of hands-on displays, original working machinery and archive photographs.

Beyond Brittania Beach a huge, chimney-surrounded lumber mill hoves into view across Howe Sound to spoil the scenic wonder along this stretch, though **Petgill Lake** makes a nice picnic spot. This is but one of several small coastal reserves, the most striking of which is **Shannon Falls Provincial Park**, signed right off the road and worth a stop for its spectacular 335-metre **waterfall** (5min walk from the road) – though the proximity of the road, plus some commercial fuss and bother, detract a touch.

The sea views and coastal drama end at **SQUAMISH**, not a pretty place, whose houses spread out over a flat plain amidst warehouses, logging waste and old machinery. All the town has by way of fame is the rock literally overshadowing it, which is puzzlingly claimed to be the world's "second biggest rock". It's certainly big. If you must be here, come in August when the town holds what it deems to be the World Lumberjack Competition; at all other times this is a pit stop only. Most of the relevant parts of the town are concentrated on Cleveland Avenue, including the **infocentre** (daily 9am–6pm; longer hours in summer), the big *Overwaitea* supermarket and the most central **accommodation**, the drab *Chieftan Hotel* (☎892-5222; doubles from $36).

The road north of Squamish continues to be a mess, but after about 5km begins to enter the classic river, mountain and forest country redolent of the BC interior. The journey thereafter is a joy, with only the march of electricity pylons and big road-widening schemes to take the edge off an idyllic drive.

## Garibaldi Provincial Park

Unless you're skiing, **Garibaldi Provincial Park** is the main incentive for heading this way. As you'd expect, it's a huge and unspoilt area which combines all the usual breathtaking ingredients of lakes, rivers, forests, glaciers and the peaks of the Coast Mountains (Wedge Mountain, at 2891m, is the park's highest point). Four rough roads access the park from points along the highway between Squamish and Whistler, but you'll need transport, or a lot of luck hitching, to reach the trailheads at the end of them. Pick up the excellent *BC Parks* pamphlet for Garibaldi from the Vancouver tourist office for a comprehensive run-down on all trails, campsites and the like. Unless you're camping, the only accommodation close to the park is at Whistler, though with an early start from Vancouver you could feasibly enjoy a good walk and return the same day.

There are five main areas with trails, of which the **Black Tusk/Garibaldi Lake** region is the most popular and probably most beautiful. Try the trail from the parking area at Rubble Creek to Garibaldi Lake (9km; 3hr one way) or to Taylor Meadows (7km; 2hr 30min). Further trails then fan out from Garibaldi Lake, including one to the huge basalt outcrop of **Black Tusk** (2316m), a rare opportunity to reach an alpine summit without any rock climbing. The other hiking areas from south to north are **Diamond Head, Cheakamus Lake, Singing Pass** and **Wedgemount Lake**. Access to each is clearly signed from the highway, and all have wilderness campsites and are explored by several trails of varying lengths. Outside these small defined areas, however, the park is untrammelled wilderness. Bear in mind there are also hiking possibilities outside the park from Whistler (see below), where in summer you can get a head start on hikes by riding up the ski lifts.

## Whistler

**WHISTLER** is less a town than a full-blown resort. **Whistler Village** is the centre, a brand-new and characterless conglomeration of hotels, mountain-gear shops and more loud people in nasty fluorescent clothes than are healthy in one place at the same time. To confuse things, however, a string of smaller resorts straggle a good 6km along Hwy 99 south of the "village", culminating in **Whistler Creek**, home to the main **infocentre** (daily 9am–5pm; longer hours in summer; ☎932-5528) but not terribly useful as a base unless you're skiing. But **skiing**, of course, is what most people are here for, eager to indulge at one of the world's top-ranked resorts, home to the longest vertical run in North America (2100m) and, since 1988, the best summer skiing in the northern hemisphere. If you're not on skis, however, you can still ride one of the two lifts from the village up **Blackcomb Mountain**, where's there's an expensive café, great views and several trailheads. If you're walking, pick up the duplicated sheet of trails from the infocentre or from the smaller kiosks in the village, or better yet buy the 1:50,000 *Whistler and Garibaldi Region* map. The two most popular short walks are the **Rainbow Falls** and **Singing Pass** trails.

### Practicalities

Soulless and appallingly planned it may be, but Whistler Village has all the facilities of any normal village, with the difference that they all charge many more times what you'd pay anywhere else. If money's no object the **infocentre** (see above) will direct you to masses of comfortable chalet accommodation; otherwise call **Whistler Central Reservations** (☎932-4222), who can help find room for you in an appropriate price bracket. Remember that chalets can put extra beds in double rooms at nominal rates – a cost-cutting tactic if there are several in your group. Otherwise, there are several budget options; none is convenient for the village, but that's not necessarily a hardship.

First choice must be the **youth hostel** on Alta Lake, one of the nicest hostels in BC (☎932-5492), a signposted forty-minute walk from the infocentre; note that *BC Rail* trains will stop alongside the hostel if you ask the conductor. As it's popular year-round, it's worth reserving space by sending the first night's money as a deposit, or at least calling ahead. All beds are in shared rooms and cost $10 for members. A little closer to Hwy 99 (behind the *Husky* garage) is the *Backpacker's Guest House*, 2124 Lake Placid Rd (☎932-1177), with private or shared rooms from $15. Also cheap are *Seppo's Log Cabin*, 7114 Nestor's Rd (☎932-6696), with beds for $25, and the *Fireside Lodge* (☎932-4545) at Nordic Estates, 3km south of the village, with beds at $15. Finally, you could try the *Whistler Lodge* (☎228-5851), also in Nordic Estates, which is owned by the University of British Columbia but lets non-students stay for $15; check-in time is from 4pm to 10pm. Best of the **campgrounds** is the *Whistler KOA*, 1km north of the village off Hwy 99 to the right (☎932-5181; $15).

If you're up for **drinking** and **nightlife**, Whistler certainly has plenty of both in winter – and increasingly in summer. People come up for seasonal work from Vancouver, and get together in places like *Tapley's Neighborhood Pub* next to the conference centre and the big bar at the main gondola terminal. **Food** is expensive unless you buy your own at the shops in less flashy Whistler Creek: in the village the best place for **snacks** is *Ingrid's Cork and Cheddar* in the "Village Square" opposite the *Alexis Restaurant*, which has many claims to being Canada's most kitsch restaurant. *Bart's* restaurant and pub, at the top end of the village, and *The Keg*, in Sundial Place, are reliable steak, salad and salmon type places.

## North of Whistler

Hwy 99 funnels down to two slow lanes at PEMBERTON, and beyond, whether you're travelling by road or rail, you're treated to some wonderfully wild country in which Vancouver and even Whistler seem a long way away. Patches of forest poke through rugged mountainsides and scree slopes, and a succession of glorious lakes culminate in Sefton Lake, whose hydro-electric schemes feed power into the grid as far south as Arizona, accounting for the pylons south of Whistler.

At the lumber town of **LILLOOET** the railway meets the Fraser River (p.561), which marks a turning point in the scenery as denuded crags and hillsides increasingly hint at the High Noon-type ranching country to come. In July and August, the rocky banks and bars of the sluggish, mud-coloured river immediately north of town are dotted with vivid orange and blue tepees and tarpaulins. These belong to Native North Americans who still come to catch, dry and smoke salmon as the fish make their way upriver to spawn – one of the few places where this tradition is continued, and well worth stopping to watch. The town boasts four central **motels** if you need to stay: best are the *Mile 0 Motel*, 616 Main St (☎256-7511; rooms from $30), and the *4 Pines Motel* on the corner of 8th Avenue and Russell Street (☎256-4247; rooms from $32).

Over the next 100km the **Fraser Valley** is more than enough to justify the price of a train ticket to Prince George. The alpine profile of the Coast Range flattens out into the high, table-topped ridges of the Cariboo Plateau, and the railway looks down to the dry, dustbowl gullies and cliffs of the vast canyon from a vantage point some 1000m above the river. The views are some of the grandest and strangest in the province, taking in huge horizons of bleached ochre soil and deserts of lonely scrubby pasture that belonged once to the so-called **"remittance men"**: the off-beam, half-mad or just plain dangerous sons of nineteenth-century English aristocrats dispatched here on a monthly remittance, or allowance, and encouraged not to get in touch. There were many such errant offspring locally, and several ranches here – some of the biggest in Canada – were long owned by Britons, amongst them the ranch bought in 1912 by the Marquis of Exeter and run by his son, Lord Martin Cecil, who used it as a base for the Emissaries of Divine Light, a religious group, until his recent death.

# The Cariboo

**The Cariboo** is the name given to the broad, rolling ranching country and immense forests of British Columbia's interior plateau, which extend north of Lillooet between the Coast Mountains to the west and Cariboo Mountains to the east. The region contains by far the dullest scenery in the province, and what little interest it offers – aside from fishing and boating on thousands of remote lakes – comes from its **gold-mining** heritage. Initially exploited by fur traders to a small degree, the region was fully opened up following the discovery of gold in 1858 in the lower Fraser Valley by prospectors who had made their way north from the Californian goldfields. The building of the **Cariboo Wagon Road**, a stagecoach route north out of Lillooet, spread gold fever right up the Fraser watershed as men leapfrogged from creek to creek, culminating in the big finds at Williams Creek in 1861 and Barkerville a year later.

Much of the old Wagon Road is today retraced by lonely **Highway 97** – the Cariboo Highway – and **VIA rail**, which run in tandem through hour after hour of straggling pine forests and past the occasional ranch and small, marsh-edged lake – scenery which strikes you as pristine and pastoral for a while but which soon leaves you in a tree-weary stupor. If you're forced to stop over there are innumerable lodges, ranches and motels on or just off the highway, and you can pick up copious material on the region at the Vancouver tourist office or infocentres en route.

A compact little village surrounded by green pastures and tree-covered hills, **CLINTON** – named after a British duke – marks the start of the heart of Cariboo country. The town has a couple of motels, the most central being the *Nomad* (☎459-2214), with rooms from $28, and the in-town *Gold Trail RV Park and Campground* (☎459-2519; pitches $9–13). The three tiny settlements beyond Clinton at 70, 100, and 150 MILE HOUSE are echoes of the old roadhouses built by men who were paid by the mile to blaze the Cariboo Wagon Road – which is doubtless why 100 Mile House is well short of a 100 miles from the start of the road. **WILLIAMS LAKE**, a busy and drab transport centre, huddles in the lee of a vast crag on terraces above the lake of the same name, with plenty of motels, boat launches and swimming spots south of the town – but hardly a place you'd want to spend any time in unless you're around on the first weekend in July for its famous **rodeo**.

Highway 20 branches west here, a part-paved, part-gravel road that runs 455km to **BELLA COOLA**. Most of the way is through the interminable forest of the Cariboo Plateau, but the last 100km or so traverses the high peaks of the Coast Mountains. *Chilcotin Stage Lines*, based at 27-7th Ave in Williams Lake (☎392-6170), runs buses all the way to Bella Coola, where there are a few hotels but no onward sea route: unless you fly out, you'll have to head back the way you came.

North of Williams Lake on Hwy 97, the **Fraser River** re-enters the scenic picture, and after a dramatic stretch of canyon, reinstates more compelling hills and snatches of river meadows. This also marks the start, however, of some of the most concerted **logging operations** in all British Columbia, presaged by increasing numbers of crude pepper-pot kilns used to burn off waste wood. By **QUESNEL**, home of the "world's largest plywood plant", you're greeted with scenes out of an environmentalist's nightmare: whole mountainsides cleared of trees, piles of sawdust the size of small hills, and unbelievably large lumber mills surrounded by stacks of logs and finished timber which stretch literally as far as the eye can see.

Most people who take the trouble to drive this route detour from Quesnel to **Barkerville Provincial Historic Park**, 90km to the east in the heart of the Cariboo Mountains, the site of the Cariboo's biggest gold strike and an invigorating spot in its own right, providing a much-needed jolt to the senses after the sleepy scenery to the south (June–Sept daily 9am–6pm; Oct–May Mon–Fri; $6). In 1862 a Cornishman named Billy Barker idly staked a claim here and after digging down a few feet was about to pack up and head north. Urged on by his mates, however, he dug another couple of spadefuls and turned up a cluster of nuggets worth $600,000. Within months Barkersville, as it was later dubbed, had become the largest city in the region, and rode the boom for a decade until the gold finally played out. Today numerous buildings have been restored, and the main administrative building has displays on mining methods and the gold rush, together with propaganda on their importance to the province.

If you want to **stay** up here there are just two options, both at WELLS, 8km west of the park: *Hubs Motel* (☎994-3313), with doubles at $34, and the *White Cap Motor Inn* (☎994-3489), with rooms at $40 and a few camping spaces for $13.50.

## travel details

### Trains

**From Vancouver** to Jasper (June–Sept daily except Wed; Oct–May 3 weekly; 19hr); Edmonton (3 weekly; 25hr); Prince George (June 15–Oct 1 daily; rest of year 3 weekly; 13hr 30min); Lillooet (June 15–Oct 1 daily; rest of year 4 weekly; 5hr 30min); Winnipeg via Edmonton and Saskatoon (3 weekly; 40hr).

**From Victoria** to Courtenay via Nanaimo (1 daily; 4hr 35min).

### Buses

**From Vancouver** to Calgary via Kamloops (6 daily; 13hr); Calgary via Princeton and Kelowna (2 daily; 18hr); Calgary via Penticton, Nelson and Cranbrook (2 daily; 24hr); Edmonton via Jasper (3 daily; 16hr 30min); Vernon (6 daily; 6hr); Prince George via Cache Creek and Williams Lake (2 daily; 13hr); Powell River (2 daily; 5hr 10min); Whistler (6 daily; 2hr 30min); Pemberton (3 daily; 3hr 10min); Victoria (8 daily; 5hr); Nanaimo (8 daily; 5hr).

**From Penticton** to Prince George via Kamloops and Cache Creek (2 daily; 13hr).

**From Victoria** to Vancouver (8 daily; 5hr); to Nanaimo (7 daily; 2hr 20min); Campbell River (5 daily; 5hr); Port Hardy (1 daily; 9hr 45min); Port Renfrew (2 daily; 2hr 30min).

**From Nanaimo** to Victoria (7 daily; 2hr 20min); to Port Alberni (4 daily; 1hr 20min).

**From Port Alberni** to Tofino via Ucluelet (1–2 daily; 5hr 30min); Nanaimo (4 daily; 1hr 20min).

### Flights

**From Vancouver** to Victoria (14 daily; 25min); Calgary (20 daily; 1hr 15min); Edmonton (14 daily; 1hr 30min); Winnipeg (8 daily; 2hr 40min); Ottawa (10 daily; 4hr 40min); Toronto (15 daily; 4hr 55min); Montréal (8 daily; 5hr 35min).

**From Victoria** to Vancouver (14 daily; 25min); Calgary (4 daily; 1hr 40min).

### Ferries

**From Vancouver** to Victoria (hourly 7am–9pm; 1hr 35min); Nanaimo (16 daily; 1hr 35min–2hr).

**From Powell River** to Courtenay (4 daily; 1hr 15min).

**From Victoria** to Vancouver (hourly 7am–10pm; 1hr 35min); Anacortes and San Juan Islands, USA (1–2 daily; 2hr 30min); Seattle, USA (1–2 daily; 2hr 30min).

**From Courtenay** to Powell River (4 daily; 1hr 15min).

# CHAPTER EIGHT

# THE NORTH

C anada's **north**, the counterbalance to the country's traditional tendency to look to Europe or the US, exists in the popular imagination as a perpetually frozen wasteland blasted by ferocious gloomy winters and inhabited – if at all – by a tribe of hardened characters beyond the reach of civilisation. In truth, it's a region whose months of summer sunshine offer almost limitless opportunities for outdoor activities and an incredible profusion of flora and fauna, a country within a country whose settlements have a distinct character that's often been forged by the mingling of white settlers and **native peoples**. The indigenous hunters of the north are as varied as in the more hospitable lands of the south, but two groups predominate: the **Dene**, people of the northern forests who traditionally occupied the Mackenzie River region from the Albertan border to the river's delta at the Beaufort Sea; and the arctic **Inuit** (literally "the people"), once known as the Eskimos or "fish eaters", a Dene coinage picked up by early European settlers and now discouraged. Of all of Canada's first peoples, the remoter Inuit communities are the ones who have most fully preserved the integrity of their culture.

The **north** is as much a state of mind as a place. People "north of 60" – north of the 60th Parallel – claim the right to be called **northerners**, but those north of the Arctic Circle look with light-hearted disdain on these "southerners". All mock the inhabitants of the northernmost corners of Alberta and Manitoba, who, after all, live with the luxury of being able to get around their regions by road. Yet in the eyes of any outsider, in terms of landscape and spirit of place the north begins well to the south of the 60th Parallel, which is why this chapter includes not just the provinces of the "true north" – **Yukon Territory** and the **Northwest Territories** – but also **northern British Columbia**, a region more stark and extreme than BC's southern reaches.

## Northern British Columbia

The two roads into the Yukon strike through northern British Columbia: the **Alaska Highway**, connecting Dawson Creek to Fairbanks in Alaska, and the **Cassiar Highway**, running from near Prince Rupert to Watson Lake, on the Yukon border. The Cassiar's passage through the Coast Mountains offers the best landscapes, but it's the Alaska Highway – serviced by daily *Greyhound* buses and plentiful motels and campgrounds – that is more travelled, starting in the rolling wheatlands of the Peace River country before curving into the spruce forests and sawtooth ridges of the northern Rockies. Most towns on both roads are battered and perfunctory places built around lumber mills, oil and gas plants and mining camps, though increasingly they are spawning motels and restaurants to serve the now powerful surge of summer visitors out to capture the thrill of driving the frontier highways. Equally popular are the **sea journeys** offered by northern British Columbia, among the most breathtaking trips in all Canada. **Prince Rupert**, linked by ferry to Vancouver Island, is the springboard for boats to the magnificent **Queen Charlotte Islands** – home of the Haida people – and up to Alaska.

---

**TOLL-FREE INFORMATION NUMBERS**

Tourism British Columbia ☎1-800-663-6000.
TravelArctic (NWT & Yukon) ☎1-800-661-0788.

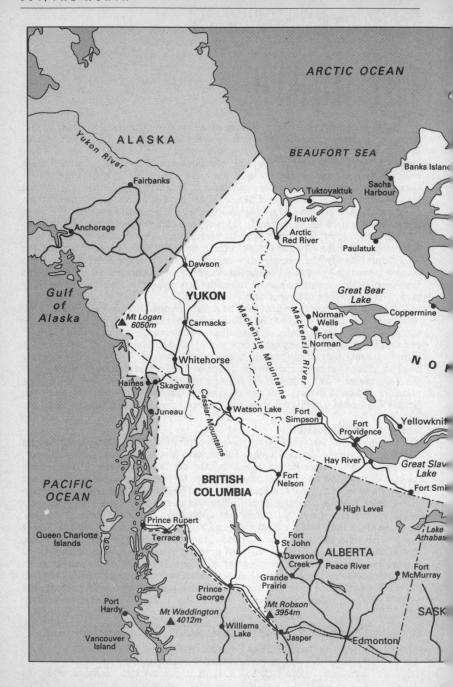

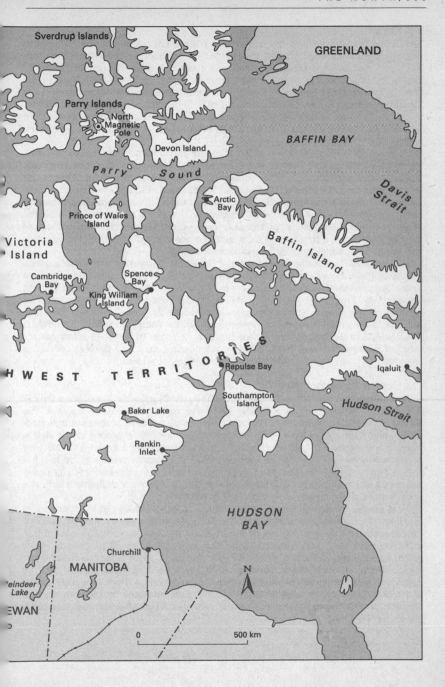

## The Yukon

The Cassiar and Alaska highways converge at Watson Lake, a weather-beaten junction that straddles the sixtieth parallel and marks the entrance to the **Yukon Territory** (YT), perhaps the most exhilarating and varied destination in this part of the world. Taking its name from a Dene native word meaning "great", it boasts the highest mountains in Canada, wild sweeps of forest and tundra, and **Dawson City**, focus of the Klondike goldrush and now a fascinating nineteenth-century relic. Dawson was also for a time the territory's capital, a role that has now shifted south to **Whitehorse**, a town booming on tourism and the ever-increasing exploitation of the Yukon's vast mineral resources.

Road access is easier than you might think, for in addition to the Alaska Highway, which runs through the Yukon's southern reaches, there's the **Klondike Highway**, which strikes north to link Whitehorse with Dawson City. North of Dawson the recently completed **Dempster Highway** is the only road in Canada to cross the Arctic Circle, offering an unparalleled direct approach to the northern tundra and to several remote communities in the Northwest Territories. The Yukon's other major road is the short spur linking the Alaskan port of Skagway to Whitehorse, a road which shadows the **Chilkoot Trail**, a treacherous track taken by the poorest of the 1898 prospectors and now an increasingly popular long-distance footpath.

The Chilkoot Trail forms a link in one of the finest **itineraries** that Canada offers. Following the old goldrush trail, the route begins at Skagway – reached by ferry from Prince Rupert – then follows the Chilkoot to Whitehorse, from where it heads north to Dawson City. From there you could continue up the Dempster Highway, or travel on the **Top of the World**, an equally majestic road into the heart of Alaska. However, many people up from Skagway or plying the mainland routes from British Columbia head to Alaska directly on the Alaska Highway, a route which gives extraordinary views of **Kluane National Park**, a largely inaccessible mountain fastness containing the country's highest peaks and its most extensive glacial wilderness.

## The Northwest Territories

If the Yukon is the far north at its most accessible, the **Northwest Territories** (NWT) is Canada at its most uncompromising. Just three roads nibble at the edges of this almost unimaginably vast area, a region which occupies a third of the country's landmass – about the size of India – but which contains only 60,000 people, almost half of whom live in or around **Yellowknife**, the territories' peculiarly overblown capital. Few people would dispute that it's the least congenial of Canada's provincial capitals, but unless you're taking the Dempster Highway to **Inuvik**, Yellowknife will probably feature on any visit to the NWT, for this is the hub of a network of flights which, at a price, service all the area's widely dispersed communities.

Most people are here to fish or canoe, to hunt or watch wildlife, or to experience at first hand the **Inuit** native cultures and ethereal landscapes unique to the region. More for convenience than any political or geographical reasons, the NWT is divided into **eight regions**, each with a tourist association responsible for its promotion. We've given the addresses of these regional offices in the guide, and we recommend that you contact them whatever you're planning. At the very least obtain a copy of the free *Explorers' Guide*, which summarises accommodation options, airline connections, many of the available tours – costing anything from $50 to $5000 – and the plethora of outfitters who provide the equipment and back-up essential for any but the most superficial trip to the NWT.

---

The telephone code for British Columbia is ☎604.

# Prince George

Outsiders rate **PRINCE GEORGE** so low that they call it "The Pig". A rough-edged place carved from the forest, it's British Columbia's third largest city and operates fair and square as the region's services and transport centre, making it highly likely you'll have more than a passing acquaintance with its dispersed and half-deserted downtown streets. Forestry forms the core of its industrial landscape and pulp mills, kilns, planers, plywood plants and allied chemical works are the images you'll take from here – if you ever wanted the inside story on the lumber business, this is the place to find it.

Prince George started life in about 1805 when Simon Fraser established a North West Trading Company post here and named the place **Fort George** in honour of the reigning George III. As a commercial nexus it quickly altered the lives of the local **Carrier Sekani** natives, who abandoned their semi-nomadic migration from winter to summer villages in favour of a permanent settlement alongside the fort. Little changed until 1914 when the Grand Trunk Railway – later the Canadian National – rolled into town and spawned an influx of pioneers and loggers. The town was connected by road to Dawson Creek and the north as late as 1951, and saw the arrival of the Pacific Great Eastern Railway in 1958 – two developments that give some idea of how recent the opening up of the Canadian north has been.

The town is a disorienting open-plan network of roads and sporadic houses between Hwy 97 and a sprawling downtown area at the junction of the Fraser and Nechako rivers. As far as things to see are concerned you might as well stick to what the town does best and take the free **tours** around some of its big mills and processing plants. *Tourism Prince George* coordinate the trips, and to book a place on these surprisingly popular tours you have to contact one of the town's two **infocentres**: one is at the junction of Hwy 97 and Hwy 16 to Prince Rupert (May–Sept daily 9am–8pm; ☎563-5493), and the other is opposite the bus terminal at 1198 Victoria St and 15th Ave (daily 9am–5pm; longer hours in summer; ☎562-3700). Company buses pick up from the centres and deliver you to one of several firms, the biggest being **Northwood Pulp and Timber**, where you are shown thousands of seedlings being grown in controlled conditions, the sawmills, and one of the continent's largest pulp mills. Outside, in a graphic illustration of the scale of Canadian forestry, logs, planks and piles of sawdust the size of small hills stretch almost as far as the eye can see.

## Practicalities

The *Greyhound* **bus terminal** is well south of downtown at 1566 12th Ave (☎564-5454), but close to a handful of hotels that remove the need to have further dealings with the place. Only **VIA rail** drops you downtown at 1300 1st Ave (☎564-5223); if you're heading for motels or the bus terminal it's worth using a taxi; try *Prince George Taxi* (☎564-4444) or *Emerald Taxi Ltd* (☎563-3333). The **BC Rail** trains arrive 5km south of downtown on Hwy 97 at the end of Terminal Boulevard, but there's a free connecting bus service to various points, including the motels at the bus terminal and on Hwy 97 for a quick getaway the following day.

The best choice among the **motels** on the Hwy 97 strip is the *Spruceland Inn* (☎563-0102; doubles around $55) at the junction of Hwy 97 and 15th Ave. In the same range is the nearby *Esther's Inn* (☎562-4131), one block off the highway at 10th Ave where the price includes the use of extras like swimming pool and jacuzzi. Closer to downtown make for the *Downtown Motel*, 650 Dominion St (☎563-9241; rooms $38–44); the *Holiday Inn*, 444 George Street (☎563-0055; doubles $86–107); or the *Connaught Motor Inn* (☎562-4441; rooms $45–53), directly opposite the bus terminal. All the **campgrounds** are some way out of town, the best being the *KOA Prince George* about 5km west on Hwy 16 (April–Oct; ☎964-7272; $14); the fee includes extras like free hot showers and a heated outdoor pool.

With **food** don't expect much in the way of culinary sophistication and stick to good chains like *Earl's*, 15th Ave and Central St; the 1950s-style *Niners Diner* on the corner of 5th and George; or the costlier *Cariboo Steak and Seafood Restaurant* on 5th Ave between George and Dominion streets. To cheer up a night in a motel, venture out to **bars** like *Steamers*, 2595 Queensway; *JJ's*, 3601 Massey; or the *Rockpit Club*, 1380 2nd Ave where there's live music – usually a local heavy metal band going through its paces.

**Moving on**, there are three *VIA rail* connections weekly to Prince Rupert and to Edmonton via Jasper; *BC Rail* run daily trains to Vancouver in summer (3 weekly in winter) and it's well worth making a reservation on what is one of the more scenic of Canada's rail journeys (☎561-4033). *Greyhound* run one bus daily to Whitehorse in the Yukon, three daily to Vancouver, and two daily to Prince Rupert.

# Prince George to Prince Rupert

There are two ways to make the 735km journey west from Prince George to **Prince Rupert**: using Highway 16 or the parallel *VIA* railway, neither of them terribly scenic until they reach the glorious river and mountain landscapes of the **Skeena Valley** 150km before Prince Rupert. Most people make this trip as a link in a much longer journey, either to reach Prince Rupert to pick up **ferries** north to Alaska or south to Port Hardy on Vancouver Island, or to pick up the start of the Cassiar Highway, a rough wilderness road that cuts north from the Skeena Valley to meet the Alaska Highway at Watson Lake over the Yukon border. It's also the only way to reach the Queen Charlotte Islands, accessible by ferry from Prince Rupert.

### Vanderhoof to Smithers

Riding out of Prince George you're confronted quickly with the relentless monotony of the Interior Plateau's rolling forests, an arboreal grind broken only by the occasional lake and the grey silhouettes of distant low-hilled horizons. At **VANDERHOOF**, 98km down the highway, gentler patches of pasture begin to poke through the tree cover, but these do little to soften the impact of the town itself. An abrupt grid of garages and motels, it's best known for its annual July air show and the more graceful aerial dynamics of thousands of Canadian geese at the nearby **Nechako Bird Sanctuary**. Before pushing on, make a point of grabbing a coffee at the *OK Café*, part of a fine collection of half-wood heritage houses at the town's western end.

Beyond here the ride becomes more verdant still, making the **accommodation** possibilities of **FORT FRASER**, 50km beyond, more attractive than those of Vanderhoof itself; try the quaint-looking wooden cabins of the *Northgate Motel* (☎690-7414) on the hamlet's eastern edge. If you're **camping** hold out for the *Piper's Glen Campsite* ($8) 5km to the west, whose meadow site shelves gently to the lake.

Beyond BURN'S LAKE the scenery picks up still more, as if preparing for the mountains in the distance, though the run of villages continue to offer little but places to fill up either the tank or the stomach. If you're going as far as to **stay** in this region aim for the unspoilt hamlet of **TELKWA**, where the excellent new *Douglas Motel* (☎846-5679), just 150m out of the village on the banks of the Bulkley River, has doubles from $47. Next day give a few minutes to a stroll up the riverfront street of heritage buildings and its handsome brown and white wood-planked **pioneer museum**.

**SMITHERS**, the largest place after Prince George (370km to the east), is focused on a crossroads, with an infocentre on one corner and a big *Super-Valu* **supermarket** for supplies on the other. If you're overnighting here ignore the brace of motels on the road and settle for the big white-timbered *Hudson Bay Lodge* (☎847-4581) outside the village as you enter from the east – doubles are $67. If this is too much, try the *Florence Motel* (☎847-2678) on the west side of town, where doubles start at $35.

## The Skeena Valley

Hard on the heels of industrial TERRACE, the **Skeena River** (the "River of the Mists") carves a beautiful valley through the Coast Mountains, an important trade route for natives and sternwheelers before the coming of the railway in 1912. For a couple of hours the road and railway run past a huge backdrop of snow-capped peaks half reflected in the mist-wraithed estuary. Out on the water there's a good chance of seeing the ripples of beavers and sea otters, not to mention bald eagles perched on the river's immense log jams. Dark valleys peel off the main river's majestic course, suggestive of a deep, untrodden wilderness and repeatedly pierced by delicate threads of waterfalls half-visible though the trees.

Shortly after Hwy 16 meets the river crashing down from the north, a couple of minor roads strike off to four nearby **Gitksan native villages** where something of the culture of the area's indigenous Gitksan native tribes has been preserved. **KSAN** and KISPIOX, home to the best totems and long houses, are a few kilometres off Hwy 16 on a minor road out of NEW HAZLETON; just north of Ksan a road links to KITWANGA and KITWANCOOL. The most easterly of the Northwest Coast tribes, the Gitksan traditionally lived off fish and game rather than agriculture, and were consummate artists and carvers. Many of their traditions were eroded by the coming of whites, and by missionaries in particular, but in the 1950s the tribe's elders made a determined decision to resurrect as much of their dying culture as possible, and re-created an entire 1870 settlement at Ksan. Although there's a good deal of commercialism, this is the village to concentrate on – native women act as guides around several long houses, giving a commentary on the carvings, clothes, buildings and masks on show, as well as offering accounts of local history (tours daily mid-May to mid-Oct 9am–5pm; $6).

# Prince Rupert

There's a bracing tang of salt and fish on the air in **PRINCE RUPERT**, a distinctive port which comes as an invigorating relief after the run of characterless villages out of Prince George. A good-looking place, it resembles a Scottish fishing town, looking out over an archipelago of islands and ringed by mountains which tumble to the sea along a beautiful fjord-cut coastline. A crowd of cars, backpackers and RVs washes daily through its streets off the **Alaska and Port Hardy ferries**, complementing the seafront's vibrant activity, and adding to the coffers of a town that's quite clearly on the up and up. There's nothing much to do, but if you're waiting for a boat it's an amiable enough spot and you'll probably bump into more fellow travellers here than almost anywhere else in northern BC.

Although you wouldn't know to look at it, the harbour's one of the world's largest deep-water ports, and handles a huge volume of trade (grain, coal and fish in particular) – one reason why the old Hudson's Bay post was chosen as the terminus of Canada's second **transcontinental rail link**. The Grand Trunk Railway chairman, Charles M Hays, hoped to turn Prince Rupert into a port to rival Vancouver. In 1912 he set off for Britain to raise stock for the venture, but unfortunately chose to book a return passage on the *Titanic*. Although he went down, the railway was finished two years later – too late, in the event, to steal a march on Vancouver.

Around town, make for the excellent little **Museum of Northern British Columbia** (May–Sept Mon–Sat 9am–9pm, Sun 9am–5pm; Oct–April Mon–Sat 10am–5pm; free), annexed to the infocentre (same hours; ☎624-5637) on 1st Ave and McBride St at the northern end to the town's tight downtown zone. It's particularly strong on the culture and history of the local **Tsimshian** natives, and has a clutch of wonderful silent archive films on a variety of topics from fishing to the building of the railway – ideal ways to whittle away a wet afternoon, of which Prince Rupert has plenty.

There's also a small art gallery with a few native works, and a well-stocked bookshop, a good complement to the infocentre, which also has a useful Alaskan section. While you're here it's worth seeing if any of the local tours or boat trips appeal, many of which are inexpensive and make a good way to see the offshore islands and wildlife.

Beyond the museum there's little else to see, though a little out of town the gondola ride to **Mount Hays** gives a bird's-eye view of the harbour and the chance to spot bald eagles – to reach it take the Wantage Road turnoff by the *McDonald's* on Hwy 16.

## Practicalities

The **Greyhound station** is in the centre of town at 822 3rd Ave and 8th St and handles two buses in and out of town to Prince George daily (about $70 one way). The **VIA railway station** is on the waterfront at 1st Ave and 2nd St, with trains to Prince George on Monday, Wednesday and Friday. If you want to get in or out of town quickly note that *Canadian* (☎624-9181) and *BC Air* (☎624-4554) both have local offices and fly to many BC destinations, including three scheduled **flights** daily to Vancouver ($250 single).

Finding a place to **stay** shouldn't present problems outside July and August, and in desperation you can always backtrack along Hwy 16 to the villages beyond the Skeena Valley. The town's one decent budget choice, the *Pioneer Rooms* at 167 3rd Ave (☎624-2334), has doubles from $15–35. Both the *Oceanview Hotel*, 950 1st Ave (☎624-6259), and the *Commercial*, 901 1st Ave (☎624-6142), have doubles from $25, but they're pretty much redknecked places of dubious repute. The cheapest of the many mid-range places is the *Aleeda*, 900 3rd Ave (☎627-1367; doubles from $55), followed by the nice *Prince Rupert Motor Inn*, 720 1st Ave, many of whose $60 doubles have fine sea views. Also try the *Slumber Lodge Motor Inn*, 909 3rd Ave (☎627-1711), and the *Parkside Resort*, 101 11th Ave (☎624-9131), a smart lurid green complex about a kilometre out of town and more likely to have room when downtown places are full; doubles at both start at $60. The

---

### FERRIES FROM PRINCE RUPERT

Ferry terminals for both **BC Ferries** (for Port Hardy and the Queen Charlotte Islands) and the **Alaska Marine Highway** (for Skagway and Alaska Panhandle ports) are at FAIRVIEW DOCK 2km southwest of town at the end of Hwy 16. Walk-on tickets for foot passengers are rarely a problem at either terminal, but advance reservations are essential if you're taking a car or want a cabin for any summer crossing. A town bus meets all incoming sailings, but for outbound sailings it's probably best to grab a taxi from downtown. Both operators sometimes allow backpackers to put a tent in their boats' gym or solariums.

**BC Ferries** operate the *MV Queen of Prince Rupert* to **Skidegate** on the Queen Charlotte Islands six times weekly in summer, less frequently in winter, a crossing which takes about 6hr 30min and costs $16 (plus $61 for cars). For booking or timetable information contact Prince Rupert's infocentre or *BC Ferries* direct on ☎624-9627. Ferries **to Port Hardy** leave four times weekly in summer and once weekly in winter for a stunning 15hr cruise that costs around $80 single for walk-on passengers. To take on a car ($165) you'll need to have made a booking at least two months in advance.

The **Alaska Marine Highway** (☎624-1744) ferries run to **Skagway** almost daily in July and August, four times weekly for the rest of the summer and in spring and autumn, and twice weekly in winter (US$115; US$278–331 per car). They stop frequently en route, with the chance to go ashore for a short time, though longer stopovers must be arranged when buying a through ticket. For all Alaskan sailings turn up at least an hour before departure to go through US customs and immigration procedures, and note that though the journey takes two days there are various restrictions on the fresh food you can take on board. You can't make telephone or credit card bookings, and have to pay in person for tickets at the terminal ticket office (May–Sept daily 5am–noon; on days of sailings the rest of the year).

only big local **campground** is the *Park Avenue Campground*, 1750 Park Ave (year-round; ☎624-5861; $9–15), west of town just 2km from the ferry terminals. Otherwise the *Parkside Resort* has fourteen sites ($15) which few people know about, and there's also the rural *Prudhomme Lake* provincial site (April–Nov; $8), 16km east on Hwy 16.

Fresh **fish** is the obvious thing to **eat** locally, preferably at the *Green Apple*, a homely shack and town institution that serves a mean halibut and chips for $6; it's at 301 McBride just before Hwy 16 turns into town. For something a touch more upmarket locals flock to the *Smile's Seafood Café* which has been doing a roaring trade since 1934 at 113 George Hills Way, about 300m north of the infocentre; the *Breakers Pub* next door is also a popular hostelry. *Bogey's* under the *Prince Rupert* high-rise hotel on 2nd Ave, between 6th and 7th streets, is another leading **bar**; it also does decent food, and seems to be one of the few places prepared to open for breakfast.

# The Queen Charlotte Islands

Ranged some 130km off the Prince Rupert coast, the **Queen Charlotte Islands** are an archipelago of about 150 islets which have become something of a cult amongst travellers and western Canadians – partly for their scenery and almost legendary remoteness from the mainstream, but also because they've achieved a high profile in the battle between the forestry industry and ecology activists. At the forefront of the battle are **Haida**, widely acknowledged as Canada's most advanced native group before the arrival of whites, and who have made the islands their home for over 10,000 years (see box overleaf). Their culture and their many deserted villages form part of the Charlottes' attraction, but many people come here to sample the islands' immensely rich **flora and fauna**, a natural profusion that's earned them the title of the "Canadian Galapagos".

The Queen Charlottes were one of only two areas in western Canada to escape the last ice age, which left many so-called **relic species** in place – elsewhere the coming of the ice altered the evolutionary progress. Unique species not found elsewhere in the country include a fine yellow daisy, the world's largest **black bears**, and subspecies of pine-marten, deer mouse, hairy woodpecker, saw-whet owl and Stellar's jay. There are also more **eagles** here than anywhere else in Canada, as well as the world's largest population of Peale's peregrine falcons and the elusive **black-footed albatross** – whose wingspan exceeds that of the largest eagles. Fish, too, are immensely plentiful, and there's a good chance of spotting a profusion of whales, otters, sea-lions and other aquatic mammals.

Plenty of people head out here by ferry from Prince Rupert, which docks near **Queen Charlotte City** on **Graham Island**, the northern of the group's two main collections of islands. Most of the Charlottes' 6000 inhabitants live either here or at **Masset** to the north, leaving the southern islands – known for convenience as **Moresby Island** – an all but deserted primal wilderness. Public transport on the islands is non-existent, hitching is difficult, and car rental rates rank as some of the world's highest. Unless you have a car, bike or canoe, you could have a long and expensive trip that shows you very little of what you came for.

## Graham Island

Most casual visitors stick to **Graham Island** as it has the bulk of the islands' roads and accommodation, both of which are concentrated along the eastern side of the island between **Queen Charlotte City** in the south and **Masset** to the north. These settlements and the villages in between – Skidegate, Tlell and Port Clements – shelter in the lee of the islands, away from an indented west coast which has the highest combined seismic, wind and tidal energy of any North American coastline, producing treacherous

### THE HAIDA

The **Haida** are widely considered to have the most highly developed culture and most sophisticated art tradition of British Columbia's indigenous peoples. Extending from the Queen Charlotte Islands to south Alaska, their lands included major stands of red cedar, the raw material for their huge dugout **canoes**, intricate **carvings** and refined **architecture**. Haida trade links were built on the reputation of their skill, other BC tribes considering the ownership of an Haida canoe, for example, as a major status symbol. Renowned as traders and artists, the Haida were also feared **warriors**, paddling into rival villages and returning with canoes laden with goods, slaves and the severed heads of anyone who had tried to resist. This success at warfare was due, in part, to their use of wooden slat armour, which included a protective face visor and helmets topped with terrifying images.

Socially the Haida divided themselves into two main groups, the **Eagles** and the **Ravens**, which were further divided into hereditary kin-groups named after their original village location. Marriage within each major group – or *moiety* – was considered incestuous, so Eagles would always seek Raven mates and vice versa. Furthermore, descent was traced through the **female line**, which meant that a chief could not pass his property on to his sons because they would belong to a different *moiety* – instead his inheritance passed to his sister's sons. Equally, young men might have to leave their childhood village to claim their inheritance from their maternal uncles.

Haida **villages** were an impressive sight, their vast cedar-plank houses dominated by fifteen-metre totem poles which displayed the kin-group's unique animal crest or other mythical creatures, all carved in elegantly fluid lines. Entrance to each house was through the gaping mouth of a massive carved figure; inside, supporting posts were carved into the forms of the crest animals and most household objects were similarly decorative. Equal elaboration attended the many Haida ceremonies, of which one of the most important was the **mortuary potlatch**, which served as a memorial service to a dead chief and the validation of the heir's right to succession. The dead individual was laid out at the top of a carved pole near the village entrance, past which the visiting chiefs would walk wearing robes of finely woven and patterned mountain-goat wool and immense head-dresses fringed with long sea-lion whiskers and ermine skins. A hollow at the top of each head-dress was filled with eagle feathers which floated down onto the witnesses as the chiefs sedately danced.

After **European contact** the Haida population was devastated by smallpox epidemics, their numbers reduced from 6000 in 1835 to 588 by 1915. Consequently they were forced to abandon their traditional villages and gather at two sites, Masset and Skidegate. At other locations the homes and totems fell into disrepair, and only at **Ninstints**, a remote village at the southern tip of the Queen Charlottes, has an attempt been made to preserve an original Haida settlement; it has now been declared a World Heritage Site by UNESCO.

These days the Haida number around 2000, and are highly regarded in the Canadian art world; Bill Reid, Freda Diesing and Robert Davidson are amongst the best-known **figures**, and scores of other Haida craftspeople produce a mass of carvings and jewellery for the tourist market.

---

seas and a tidal range of eight metres. Much of the east coast is full of sandy beaches and a string of provincial parks where you can appreciate the milder climes produced by the Pacific's Japanese Current, a warming stream that contributes to the islands' lush canopy of 1000-year-old spruce and cedar rainforests. On the downside, though, it drenches both sides of the islands with endless rainstorms, even in summer.

## Queen Charlotte City

It would be hard to imagine anywhere less like a city than **QUEEN CHARLOTTE CITY**, a picturesque fishing village about 5km west of the SKIDEGATE terminal for ferries to and from Prince Rupert. Most of its residents squeeze a living from the McMillan Bloedel timber giant, whose felling exploits have cleared most of the hills around the port, and who have a veto on access to many of the backcountry logging roads. For a fine overview of the place try the stroll to the top of **Sleeping Beauty Mountain**, which is reached by rough track from Crown Forest Roads near Honna Road. The village **dump** south of the houses rates as another sight for the black bears and bald and golden eagles that gather there at dusk. Otherwise if you've the cash you can sign up for any number of fishing, canoeing or boating **tours** by contacting the **infocentre** at *Joy's Island Jewellers Store* (June–Sept daily 8am–6pm; Oct–May Mon–Fri 9am–5pm; ☎559-4742), about a kilometre east of town on 3rd Ave. The staff are incredibly knowledgeable, and there's a good selection of detailed guides and maps to the area: Joy herself may let you camp on her lawn if you arrive late with nowhere to stay. There's also a **Parks Canada** office for information on Moresby Island (see next page), west of town along Hwy 33 (Mon–Fri 8am–4.30pm; ☎559-8818).

**Accommodation** is scarce and demand high in summer so try to call ahead at the *Premier Hotel*, 3101 3rd Ave (☎559-8451), which has doubles from $40; *Gracie's Place*, 3113 3rd Ave (559-4262), with homely ocean-view rooms at $50; and the *Spruce Point Lodging* (☎559-8234; dorm beds $15, double rooms $55), opposite the Chevron garage at the west end of town. The *Hecate Inn* (☎559-4543), on the corner of 3rd Ave and 4th St, has doubles from around $60.

## Skidegate, Tlell and Port Clements

Ferries dock here, but there's not much doing at **SKIDEGATE**, though you could catch up on more accessible aspects of the Haida culture at the **Queen Charlotte Islands Museum**, just north of the terminal (Tues–Sat 9am–5pm; $2). Check out, too, the **carving shed** just up the road, home to the *Loo Taas* ("Wave Eater") canoe when it's not out on hire to rich tourists – for a mere $1500 you could take a six-hour tour in the 80-metre vessel. Here or at the nearby **Skidegate Mission** is the place to inquire about permits to visit some of the 500 or more abandoned tribal villages and sites on the southern islands. In summer the Mission's also the scene of a 6pm Thursday **seafood feast** open to all-comers for $20.

Moving up the east coast, the ranching community of **TLELL** 42km north is gone in the blink of an eye, but there's a **hostel** here, the *Bellis Lodge* (☎557-4434; $17), and the tiny nearby *Weavers Inn Motel* (☎557-4491), in a lovely rural setting, has doubles for $50 including coffee and breakfast.

As the road cuts inland for **PORT CLEMENTS**, 20km to the northwest, it forms the southern border of the **Naikoon Provincial Park**, an enclave which extends over Graham Island's northeast corner and is designed to protect fine beach, dune and dwarf woodland habitats. There's a small **park centre** on the road 2km north of Tlell, together with a provincial **campground** (May–Oct; $8). About 8km beyond look out for the picnic site and trails at the southern tip of **Mayer Lake**, one of the nicer spots to pull over. Port Clements itself has a small museum of forestry and pioneer-related offerings, but is most famous for the world's only **Golden Spruce** tree, a 300-year-old bleached albino tree which puzzles foresters by refusing to produce anything but ordinary green-leafed saplings. It's 6km south of the village signed off the logging road to JUSKATLA, a timber camp established in World War II to supply Queen Charlotte spruce for war planes.

## Masset

**Masset** is the biggest place on the islands, a town of 1600 people, half of whom are employed by a military base built in 1971, the other half by fishing and crab canning. Most visitors are here to **birdwatch** at the **Delkatla Wildlife Sanctuary**, a saltwater marsh north of the village which supports 113 bird species, or to wander the neighbouring village of Haida, or "Old Masset", where some 600 natives still live and work. Many are involved in carving knick-knacks for tourists, or organising wilderness tours, but a few are restoring and adding to the few totems still standing locally.

The **infocentre** (June–Oct daily 9am–5pm) is on Tow Hill Road, the main road into Masset, and has full details of birdwatching possibilities. They can't do much about the village's limited **accommodation** prospects other than point you to the *Naikoon Park Motel* on Tow Hill Rd (☎626-5187; doubles $35); the *Singing Surf Inn*, 1504 Old Beach Rd (☎626-3318; rooms $76); or to a handful of bed and breakfasts like the *Alaska View Lodge* (☎626-3333) which you soon find wandering the streets. The only **campground** around is the *Masset-Haida Lions Campground* ($8) on Tow Hill Rd, 2km north of town alongside the wildlife sanctuary.

## Moresby Island

**Moresby Island** is all but free of human contamination except for deserted Haida villages (one of which has the world's largest stand of totems), forestry roads and the small logging community of **SANDSPIT**, some 15km from the ALLIFORD BAY terminal for the *Interisland Ferry* link with Skidegate (12 daily; $2). Most locals here and on Graham Island work in Moresby's forests, and the **forestry issue** has divided the community between the Haida and ecologists – "hippies" in the local parlance – and the lumber workers (the "rednecks"). At stake are the islands' temperate rainforests and the traditional sites of the Haida, politically shrewd media manipulators who've sent representatives to Brazil to advise local tribes with their own rainforest programmes. They've also occasionally provided the muscle to halt logging on the islands, and to prove a point sometimes block access to HOTSPRING ISLAND, whose thermal pools are a favourite target of visiting tourists. On the other hand the forests provide jobs and some of the world's most lucrative timber – a single good sitka trunk can be worth up to $60,000. At the time of writing most of Moresby has been declared a National Park Reserve, though stiff lobbying from the logging companies leaves its position perilous.

If you're determined enough you can canoe, mountain bike or backpack the interior, but you need to know what you're doing and be prepared to lug plenty of supplies. There's a *Parks Canada* office at Sandspit (May–Sept daily 8.30am–6pm; ☎637-5362) and at Queen Charlotte City (see above) for information on the reserve, and the Sandspit's **infocentre** on Beach Rd (June–Sept daily 9am–6pm; ☎637-5436) has details on tours and the limited facilities on the whole southern half of the archipelago. Sandspit's only **accommodation** apart from a couple of bed and breakfasts are the *Sandspit Inn* near the airstrip (☎637-5334; doubles from $70), and the *Moresby Island Guest House* (☎637-5305; rooms from $50).

# The Cassiar Highway

The 733km of the **Cassiar Highway** (Hwy 37) from the Skeena Valley east of Prince Rupert to Watson Lake just inside Yukon Territory are some of the wildest and most beautiful on any British Columbian road. Still less famous than the Alaska Highway, the road is increasingly travelled by those who want to capture some of the adventure that accompanied the wilder reaches of its better-known neighbour in the Fifties and Sixties. Long stretches are still gravel, however, and the petrol and repair facilities, let alone food and lodgings, are extremely patchy: you shouldn't contemplate the journey unless your motor's in top condition, has two spare tyres, and spare fuel containers. The longest stretch without petrol is the 240km between MEZIADIN LAKE and EDDONTENOJON, but you should really fill up at every opportunity. The road also provides a shorter route from Prince George to the Yukon than the Alaska Highway, and as more of it is paved the number of big trucks and logging vehicles using it is on the rise – creating more potential hazards. British Columbia's *North by Northwest Tourist Association* puts out several complete lists of facilities, all vital accompaniments to any journey, and all available from infocentres in Prince Rupert and Terrace.

If you're ready to drive the distances involved, you'll also probably be prepared to explore the highway's two main side roads to **Stewart** and to **Telegraph Creek**, and possibly the rough roads and trails that lead into two wilderness parks midway up the highway – the **Mount Edziza Provincial Park** and the **Spatsizi Plateau Wilderness Park**. If you can't face the road's entire length, the trip to Terrace – an easy section to hitch – offers exceptional sea and mountain **scenery**, as well as the chance to cross into Alaska at **Hyder** to indulge in its vaunted alcoholic border initiation.

## To Stewart

The Cassiar starts near Kitwanga, one of four native villages off Hwy 16 (see p.569), and a crossroads of the old "grease trail", named after the candlefish oil which was traded between Coast and Interior tribes. Almost immediately the road pitches into the mesmerising high scenery of the Coast Ranges, a mountain, lake and forest medley that reaches a crescendo after about 100km and the side turn to STEWART. Here a series of immense glaciers culminates in the dramatic appearance of **Bear Glacier**, a vast sky-blue mass of ice that comes down virtually to the highway and has the strange ability to glow in the dark. Stewart itself is a shrivelled mining centre that sits at the end of the Portland Canal, the world's fourth longest fjord, a natural boundary between Canada and Alaska that lends the town a superb peak-ringed location. Dominating its rocky amphitheatre is **Mount Rainey**, whose cliffs represent one of the greatest vertical rises from sea level in the world.

The **infocentre** is housed with the local museum in the City and Fire Hall between 6th and 7th streets (daily May–Oct 9am–8pm). If you want to sleep over, there are two co-owned **hotels**: the *King Edward*, 5th and Columbia (☎636-2244), and the Alpine (☎636-2445), both with doubles from $40. The *King Edward*, bar one Chinese spot, is the town's only **pub** and **restaurant**. The nearest **campground** is the *Stewart Lions Campground* on 8th Ave (May–Oct; $9–12). In summer Stewart is added to the itinerary of the Friday sailings of the *Alaska Marine Highway* ferry, enabling you to ride a boat to KETCHIKAN and thence to either Skagway or Prince Rupert, completing a neat circular itinerary.

## Hyder

Most people come to **HYDER**, population 70, simply to drink in one or both of its two bars. It's a ramshackle place 3km from Stewart on a road that crosses the **border into Alaska** with none of the usual formalities – there being nothing beyond the end of the road but 800km of wilderness. At the *Glacier Inn* the tradition is to pin a dollar to the wall in case you return broke and need a drink, and then toss back a shot of hard liquor in one and receive an "I've Been Hyderized" card. It sounds a bit of a tourist carry-on, but if you arrive out of season there's a genuine amiability about the place that warrants its claims to be the "The Friendliest Ghost Town in Alaska". The bars are open 23 hours a day and a couple of **motels** are on hand if you want to keep on drinking: the *Sealaska Inn*, Premier Ave (☎636-9001), and the *The Grand View Inn*, (☎636-9174), both with rooms around $60.

## Dease Lake

For several hundred kilometres beyond the Stewart junction there's nothing on the Cassiar other than the odd garage, campground, trailhead and patches of burnt or clear-cut forest etched into the Cassiar and Skeena mountains. In places, though, you can still see traces of the incredible 1900-mile Dominion Telegraph line that used to link the Dawson City goldfields with Vancouver, and of a proposed railway extension out of Prince George that was abandoned as late as 1977.

**DEASE LAKE**, the first place of any size, is close to **ISKUT**, a native village which offers tours into the neighbouring wilderness parks, which are also accessible by float plane from Dease Lake itself. The road itself, however, is wild and beautiful enough round here, and the 240km up to the Yukon border from Dease Lake are some of the most miraculous of what is already a superb journey. Much of this area was swamped with gold-hungry pioneers during the **Cassiar Gold Rush** of 1872–80, the period when the region got its name – possibly from a white prospector's corruption of *kaskamet*, the dried beaver meat eaten by local Kaska tribes. In 1877 one Alfred Freedman plucked one of the world's largest pure gold nuggets – a 72-ounce monster – from a creek east of present-day **CASSIAR**, though these days the mining has a less romantic allure, being centred on an open-pit **asbestos mine** 5km from the village. Most of the world's high-grade asbestos comes from here, and has left poisonous-looking piles of green chrysotile asbestos tailings for miles around.

### Telegraph Creek

For a taste of what is possibly a more remarkable landscape than you see on the Cassiar, it's worth driving the potentially treacherous 75-kilometre side road from Dease Lake to **TELEGRAPH CREEK**, a place whose look and feel can scarcely have changed since the turn of the century, when it was a major telegraph station and trading post for the gold rush towns to the north. The road navigates some incredible gradients and bends, twisting past canyons, old lava beds and touching on several **native villages**, notably at TAHLTAN RIVER where salmon are caught and cured in traditional smokehouses and sold to passing tourists. If you're lucky you might see a Tahtlan Bear dog, a species now virtually extinct. Only about ankle high, and weighing less than a stone, these tiny animals were able to keep a bear cornered by barking and darting around until a hunter came to finish it off. Telegraph Creek itself is an object lesson in how latter-day pioneers live on Canada's last frontiers: it's home to a friendly mixture of city exiles, hunters, trappers and ranchers, but also a cloistered bunch of **religious fundamentalists** who've eschewed the decadent mainstream for wilderness purity. Such groups are growing in outback Canada, an as-yet undocumented phenomenon that's creating friction with the easy-going types who first settled the backwoods.

Much of the village revolves around the *General Delivery* – a combined café, grocery and garage – and small adjoining **motel**, the *Stikine River Song Lodge* (☎235-3196), whose eight doubles include kitchenettes and go for $45–55. No one here, except perhaps the Bible brigade, should mind if you pitch a tent – but ask around first.

# Prince George to Dawson Creek

**Dawson Creek** is the launching pad for the Alaska Highway, and though not somewhere you'd otherwise stop, it's almost impossible to avoid a night here whether you're approaching from Edmonton and the east or **from Prince George** on the scenically more uplifting **John Hart Highway** (Hwy 97). Named after a former BC premier, this seemingly innocuous road is one of the north's most vital highways. Completed in 1952, it linked at a stroke the road network of the Pacific Coast with that of the northern interior, cutting 800km off the journey from Seattle to Alaska, for example, a trip which previously had to take in a vast inland loop to Calgary. The route leads you out of British Columbia's upland interior to the so-called Peace River Country, a region of slightly ridged land which belongs in look and spirit to the Albertan prairies. There's some 409km of driving, and two daily *Greyhound* **buses** make the journey.

Out of Prince George the road bends through mildly dipping hills and mixed woodland, passing small lakes and offering views to the Rockies, whose distant jagged skyline keeps up the spirits as you drive through an otherwise unbroken tunnel of conifers. About 70km on, **Bear Lake** and the **Crooked River Provincial Park** entice just off the road, and it's well worth taking the small lane just west of the park entrance for an idyllic patch of water fringed on its far shore by a fine sickle of sand. There's a free provincial **campground** at the park, and the *Grizzly Inn* **motel** just beyond (☎972-4436), with rooms from $50 and the road's first services after Prince George.

MACKENZIE JUNCTION, 152km from Prince George, and MACKENZIE, 29km off the highway, are scrappy, unpleasant places easily avoided and soon forgotten as the road climbs to **Pine Pass** (933m), one of the lower road routes over the Rockies, but spectacular all the same. The **Bijoux Falls Provincial Park**, just before it, is good for a picnic near the eponymous falls, and if you want to **camp** make sure to plump for the *Pine Valley Park Lodge* (May–Oct; $8), an immensely scenic lakeside spot that looks up to crags of massively stratified and contorted rock just below the pass. Thereafter the road drops steeply through CHETWYND to the increasingly flatter country that heralds Dawson Creek.

## Dawson Creek

Arrive in **DAWSON CREEK** late and leave early: except a small museum next to the town's eye-catching red grain hopper, and the obligatory photograph of the cairn marking **Mile Zero** of the Alaska Highway, there's nothing to do here except eat and sleep. Contact the **infocentre** at the museum, 900 Alaska Ave (daily 9am–6pm; longer in summer; ☎782-9595), for details of the **motels** – and there are plenty of them, mostly concentrated on the Alaska Highway northeast of town. If you've climbed off a *Greyhound* at the **bus terminal**, 1201 Alaska Ave, try the new *Econo-Motel* (☎782-9181; doubles from $36) beyond the Co-op Mall east of the Mile Zero cairn. None of the three local **campsites** are places you'd want to linger, but the most attractive is the *Mile 0 City Campground* (May–Aug; ☎782-2590; $8.50–14), about a kilometre west of the town's main spread opposite 20th St on the Alaska Highway. For something to **eat** call at the excellent *Alaska Café* on 10th St, an attractive old wooden building completely at odds with the rest of the town. The food and ambience are good – though prices aren't the cheapest – and the bar's not bad cither.

# Dawson Creek to Whitehorse

Well over a half of the **Alaska Highway** – a distance of about 1500km – winds through northern British Columbia from Dawson Creek to Whitehorse, the capital of the Yukon. Don't be fooled by the string of villages emblazoned across the area's maps, for there are only two towns worthy of the name en route, **Fort St John** and **Fort Nelson** – the rest are no more than a garage, a store and perhaps a motel. **Watson Lake**, on the Yukon border, is the largest of these lesser spots, and also marks the junction of the Alaska and Cassiar highways. All the way down the road, though, it's vital to book accommodation during July and August.

**Driving** the Alaska Highway is no longer the adventure of days past – that's now provided by the Cassiar and Dempster highways. Food, petrol and lodgings are found at between 40- and 80-kilometre intervals, though cars still need to be in good shape. You should drive with headlights on at all times, and take care when passing or being passed by heavy trucks. It also goes without saying that wilderness – anything up to 800km of it to each side – begins at the edge of the highway and unless you're very experienced you shouldn't contemplate any off-road exploration. Any number of guides and pamphlets are available to take you through to Fairbanks, but *The Milepost*, the road's bible, now almost in its 50th edition, is for all its mind-numbing detail the only one you need buy.

From mid-May to mid-October daily (except Sun) a **Greyhound** bus leaves Dawson Creek in the morning and plies the road all the way to Whitehorse; it runs on Tuesday, Thursday and Saturday the rest of the year. The twenty-hour trip finishes at 5am, with only occasional half-hour meal stops, but covers the road's best scenery in daylight.

### THE ALASKA HIGHWAY

The **Alaska Highway** runs northeast from Mile Zero at Dawson Creek through the Yukon Territory to Mile 1520 in Fairbanks, Alaska. Built as a military road, it's now an all-weather highway travelled by daily bus services and thousands of tourists out to recapture the thrill of the days when it was known as the "junkyard of the American automobile". It's no longer a driver's Calvary, but the scenery and the sense of pushing through wilderness on one of the continent's last frontiers are still as alluring as ever.

As recently as 1940 there was no direct land route to the Yukon or Alaska other than trails passable only to experienced trappers. When the Japanese invaded the Aleutian Islands during World War II, however, they both threatened the traditional sea routes to the north and seemed ready for an attack on mainland Alaska – the signal for the building of the joint US–Canadian road to the north. A proposed coastal route from Hazelton in British Columbia was deemed too susceptible to enemy attack (it's since been built as the Cassiar Hwy). A possible inland route which bypassed Whitehorse and followed the Rockies would have taken five years to build. This left the so-called **Prairie Route**, which had the advantage of following a line of airbases through Canada into Alaska, a chain known as the **Northwest Staging Route**. In the course of the war, some 8000 planes were ferried from Montana to Edmonton and then to Fairbanks on this route, where they were picked up by Soviet pilots and flown into action on the Siberian front.

Construction of the highway began on **March 9, 1942**, the start of months of misery for most of the 20,000 mainly US soldiers shanghaied to ram a road through mountains, mud, mosquito-ridden bog, icy rivers and forest during some of the harshest extremes of weather imaginable. Incredibly, crews working on the eastern and western sections met at

## Dawson Creek to Fort Nelson

You need to adapt to a different notion of distance on a 2500-kilometre drive: on the Alaska Highway points of interest are a long way apart, and pleasure comes in broad changes in scenery, in the sighting of a solitary moose, or in the passing excitement of a lonely bar. Thus it's forty minutes before the benign ridged prairies around Dawson Creek prompt attention by dropping suddenly into the broad, flat-bottomed valley of the Peace River, a canyon whose walls are scalloped with creeks, gulches and deep muddy scars. Soon after comes **FORT ST JOHN**, which until the coming of the highway – when it was the field headquarters of the road's eastern construction gangs – was a trading post for local Sikanni and Beaver natives which had remained little changed since its predecessor had sunk into the mud of the Peace River. The ensuing shanty town received a boost when the province's largest oil field was discovered nearby in 1955, and it's now a functional settlement with all the services you need – though at just 75km into the highway it's unlikely you'll be ready to stop. If you are, there are a dozen **motels**: solid choices are the *Alexander Mackenzie Inn*, 9223 100th St (☎785-8364 or ☎1-800-663-8313; $50–70), and the *Four Seasons Motor Inn*, 9810 100th St (☎785-6647; $60).

The next stop is **WONOWON**, 161km from Dawson, typical of the bleak settlements all the way up the road: wooden shacks and corrugated iron, a few wires strung between poles, rusting oil and gas storage tanks, and concrete blocks laid out as a nominal attempt at a kerb, as if to impose some civic order on the wilderness. **PINK MOUNTAIN** (226km) is much the same, and has a restaurant favoured by truckers (but run by hatchet-faced staff), and a reasonable **campsite** across the road (☎772-3226; May–Oct $8–20) – though thirty kilometres on is one of the better of the campgrounds on this section of the road, the *Sikanni River Lodge* (☎773-6531; $10). Thereafter the road offers immense **views** of utter wilderness in all directions, the trees as dense as ever, but noticeably more stunted than further south and nearing the limit of commercial viability. Look out for the bright "New Forest Planted" signs everywhere, presumably just a riposte from the loggers to the ecology lobby, as they are invariably backed by a graveyard of sickly looking trees.

Contact Creek, British Columbia, in September 1942, and completed the last leg to Fairbanks in October – an engineering triumph which had taken less than a year but cost around $140 million. The first full convoy of trucks to make Fairbanks managed an average 25 kph in one of the worst winters in memory.

By 1943 the highway already needed virtual rebuilding, and for seven years workers widened the road, raised bridges, reduced gradients, bypassed swampy ground and started to remove some of the vast bends that are still being ironed out – one reason why it's now only 1488 miles, for example, to the old Mile 1520 post in Fairbanks. All sorts of ideas have been put forward as reasons for the numerous curves – that they were to stop Japanese planes using the road as a landing strip, that they simply went where bulldozers could go at the time, or even at one point that they followed the trail of a rutting moose. Probably the chief reason is that the surveying often amounted to no more than a pointed finger aimed at the next horizon.

Although the road is widely celebrated there are sides to the story that are still glossed over. Many of its toughest sections, for example, were given to black GIs, few of whom have received credit for their part in building the highway – you'll look in vain for black faces amongst the white officers in the archive photos of ribbon-cutting ceremonies. Another tale is the road's effect on natives on the route, scores of whom died from epidemics brought in by the workers. Yet another was the building of the controversial "Canadian Oil" or **Canol pipeline** in conjunction with the road, together with huge dumps of poisonous waste and construction junk. Wildlife en route was also devastated by trigger-happy GIs taking recreational potshots as they worked: the virtual eradication of several species was part of the reason for the creation of the Kluane Game Sanctuary, the forerunner of the Yukon's Kluane National Park.

## Fort Nelson

One of the highway's key centres, **FORT NELSON** greets you with a large poster proclaiming "Jail is only the beginning – don't drink and drive", a sobering sign that hints at the sort of extremes to which people hereabouts might go to relieve the tedium of winter's long semi-twilight. Everything in town except a small **museum** devoted to the highway's construction speaks of a frontier supplies depot, the last in a long line of trading posts attracted to a site which is fed by four major rivers and stands in the lee of the Rockies. Dour buildings stand in a battered sprawl around a windswept grid, only a single notch up civilisation's ladder from the time in the late Fifties when this was still a community without power, phones, running water or doctors. Life's clearly too tough here to be geared to anything but pragmatic survival and exploitation of its huge natural gas deposits – the town has the world's second largest gas-processing plant and the huge storage tanks to prove it. Natives and white trappers live as they have for centuries, hunting beaver, wolf, wolverine, fox, lynx and mink, as well as the ubiquitous moose, which is still an important food source for many natives.

The town's many **motels** are much of muchness and you'll be paying the same rates – about $60 for doubles worth half that – which characterise the north. The *Motor Hotel* (☎774-6971) and *Pioneer Motel* (☎774-6459) are both central – though location's not terribly important here – and on the town's southern approaches to the town the *Blue Bell Motel* (☎774-6961) is better looking than many of the run-of-the-mill places.

## Fort Nelson to Liard Hot Springs

Landscapes divide markedly around Fort Nelson, where the highway arches west from the flatter hills of the Peace River country to meet the **northern Rockies** above the plains and plateau of the Liard River. Within a few kilometres – once the road has picked up the river's headwaters – you're in some of the most grandiose scenery in British Columbia. The services and motels become scarcer, but those that exist – though often beaten-up looking places – make atmospheric and often unforgettable places to stop. The *Summit Lake Motel*, 250km west of Fort Nelson, is one such, near the highway's highest point (1295m); the *Rocky Mountain Lodge* (☎232-5000), 15km on, is if anything more dilapidated, but has an astounding position and an adjacent campground ($10).

**TOAD RIVER**, 60km beyond, has perhaps the best motel of all on this lonely stretch, the *Toad River Lodge* (☎232-5401; doubles $50), thanks to its superlative views of thickly forested and deeply cleft mountains on all sides. Two kilometres to its north is the *Poplars Campground* (☎232-5465; $12), an equally attractive spot despite its offputting claims to be "Home of the Foot-Long Hot Dog".

**Muncho Lake**, the next big natural feature, sits at the heart of a large provincial park whose ranks of bare mountains foretell the barren tundra of the far north. There's a small motel and campsite at the lake's southern end, but it's worth hanging on for the Strawberry Flats provincial campground ($8) midway up the lake or the fine *Highland Glen Lodge and Campground* (☎776-3481) for a choice of log cabin motel rooms ($65) or camping sites ($9–16).

About 70km beyond the lake is the excellent *Liard River Lodge* (☎776-3341), a wonderfully cosy and friendly spot for food or a $60 room. (*Liard* comes from the French for poplar, a ubiquitous tree in these parts.) It's also close to one of the most popular spots on the entire Alaska Highway, the **Liard Hot Springs**, whose two thermal pools are amongst the best and hottest in BC. They're reached by a short wooden walkway across steaming marsh, and are otherwise unspoilt apart from a wooden changing room and the big high-season crowds. As the marsh never freezes, it attracts moose and grizzlies down to drink and graze and some 250 plant species grow in the mild microhabitat nearby, including fourteen species of orchid, lobelias, ostrich ferns and other rare boreal forest plants. The nearby provincial campground is one of the region's most popular, and fills up early in July and August (May–Oct; $10).

---

The telephone code for all the Yukon and NWT, unless stated otherwise, is ☎403.

---

## Watson Lake to Whitehorse

Beyond Liard Hot Springs the road follows the Liard River, settling into about 135km of unexceptional scenery before **WATSON LAKE**, just over the Yukon border. Created by the coming of the highway, it's neither an attractive nor terribly big place, but shops, motels and garages have sprung up here to service the traffic congregating off the Cassiar and Campbell highways to the north and south. If you're just passing through it's worth pulling off to look at the **Alaska Highway Interpretive Centre** (daily May–Sept 9am–9pm; ☎536-7469), which as well as providing information on the Yukon also describes the highway's construction through archive photos and audiovisual displays. It's located on the highway next to the *Chevron* garage close to the famous **Sign Post Forest**. This bit of tourist gimmickry was started by a homesick GI in 1942 who erected a sign pointing the way and stating the mileage to his home in Danville, Illinois. Since then the signs have just kept on coming, and at last count numbered over 10,000.

It's still 441km from Watson Lake to Whitehorse, so you may well decide to stay in town. The cheapest spot is the *Alcan Motel* (☎536-7774), with doubles from $42. Close behind is the *Cedar Lodge Motel* (☎536-7406), with rooms at $55. Both places are small, however, and you may have to plump for one of the bigger hotels, all which have rooms around $90 – the best is the *Belvedere Hotel* (☎536-7712). The nearest campground is the rustic Yukon government site, 4km west of the sign forest (May–Oct; $5), but for full services use the *Gateway to Yukon RV Park and Campground* near the *Husky* garage (year-round; ☎536-7448; $8).

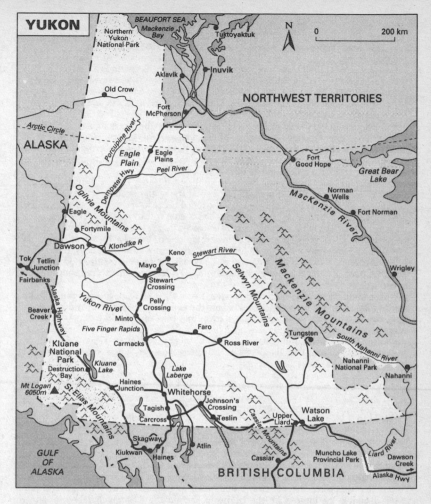

West of Watson Lake the road picks up more fine mountain scenery, running for hour after hour past apparently identical combinations of snow-capped peaks and thick forest. Unlovely **TESLIN**, 263km to the west, was founded as a trading post in 1903 and now has one of the Yukon's largest Native Canadian populations. Many still live by hunting and fishing and the **George Johnston Museum** (daily June–Sept 9am–7pm; $2) on the right on the way into the village has a good collection of local Tlingit arte-facts and the photos of the eponymous Johnston, a Tlingit who recorded his culture on film between 1910 and 1940. If you do get stuck overnight – it's 179km to Whitehorse – there are three **motels**: the *Northlake Motel* (☎390-2571; $40) is cheapest; the *Yukon Motel* (☎390-2575) has rooms from $45–60 and unserviced **campground** ($10); and *Teslin Lake Resort* (May–Sept; ☎390-2608), just out of the village, has a few rooms at $45 and a good **campground**.

## THE CHILKOOT TRAIL

No single image better conjures the human drama of the 1898 gold rush than the lines of prospectors struggling over the **Chilkoot Trail**, a 53-kilometre path over the Coast Mountains between **Dyea**, north of Skagway in Alaska, and **Bennett Lake** on the British Columbian border south of Whitehorse. Before the rush Dyea was a small village belonging to the Chilkat Tlingit natives, a tribe who made annual trade runs over the trail to barter fish oil, clam shells and dried fish with the Tutchone, Tagish and other interior Dene tribes in exchange for animal hides, skin clothing and copper. The Chilkat jealously guarded access to the **Chilkoot Pass** (1122m), the key to the trail and one of only three glacier-free routes through the Coast Mountains west of Juneau. Sheer weight of numbers and a show of force from a US gunboat, however, opened the trail to stampeders who used it as a link between the ferries from the Pacific Coast ports and the Yukon River, which they then rode to the goldfields at Dawson City.

For much of 1897 the pass and border were disputed by the US and Canada until the Canadian NWMP established a storm-battered shack at the summit and enforced the fateful "ton of goods" entry requirement. Introduced because of chronic shortages in the goldfields, this obliged every man entering the Yukon to carry a ton of provisions – a condition which was to have appalling consequences for the stampeders. Weather conditions and the trail's fifty-degree slopes proved too severe even for horses or mules, so that men had to carry supplies on their backs over as many as fifty journeys. Many died in avalanches or lost everything during a winter when temperatures dropped to -51°C and 25 metres of snow fell. Even so, the lure of gold was enough to drag some 22,000 over the pass.

These days most people off the **ferries from Prince Rupert and the Alaska Panhandle** make the fantastic journey across the mountains by car or *Gray Line* bus on Hwy 2 from **Skagway to Whitehorse**, a route that parallels the old trail at a distance. More affluent tourists take the restored *White Pass & Yukon Railroad*, originally built to supercede the Chilkoot Trail (twice daily May 18–Sept 24; Skagway–White Pass by train then connecting bus to Whitehorse; $89). Increasing numbers, however, are walking the old trail, which has been laid out and preserved by *Parks Canada* as a **long-distance footpath**. Its great appeal lies not only in the scenery and natural habitats – which embrace coastal rainforest, tundra and subalpine boreal woodland – but also in the numerous artefacts like old huts, rotting boots, mugs and broken bottles still scattered where they were left by the prospectors.

The trail is well marked, regularly patrolled and generally fit to walk between about June and September. Although it takes only about four days you shouldn't launch into it lightly. There are dangers from bears, avalanches, drastic changes of weather and from exhaustion – there's one twelve-kilometre stretch, for example, for which you have to allow twelve hours. Excellent maps, guides and information are available from Skagway's Visitor Information Bureau and at the *Parks Canada* office in Whitehorse.

If, like most people, you're walking the path from south to north, you must first pre-clear **Canadian customs** at Fraser on Hwy 2, 25km north of Skagway. This you can do by phone, however, by calling ☎821-4111. They give you a time limit to complete the trail, after which you must report to the Customs and Immigration Office in Whitehorse at 101 Main St (daily 8.30am–4.30pm; ☎667-6471).

Walk or taxi the 15km from Skagway to the trailhead at Dyea to start the walk, and then be prepared to camp, for though there are three cabins on the trail, the chances of finding space are almost zero. There are eight approved **campgrounds** at intervals along the trail, but these too become busy, though it's unlikely you'll be turned away. Note that no rough camping is allowed. At Bennett Lake at the end of the trail you can either take a **boat** to Carcross and pick up a *Gray Line* bus to Whitehorse, or take a minibus to **Log Cabin** on Hwy 2 136km south of Whitehorse and pick up buses to either Whitehorse or Skagway. For a short taste of the *White Pass* railway you could also take the train from Bennett Lake to Fraser, 8km south of Log Cabin ($14), and catch the *Gray Line* buses from there.

# Whitehorse

**WHITEHORSE** is the Yukon's capital, the centre of its mining and forestry industries, and a stop-off for thousands of summer visitors. But whereas roads bring in today's business, the town owes its existence to the **Yukon River**, a 3000-kilometre artery that rises in BC's Coast Mountains and flows through the heart of the Yukon and Alaska to the Bering Sea. The floodplain and strange escarpment above the present town were long a resting point for Dene Natives, but the spot burgeoned into a full-blown city with the arrival of thousands of stampeders in the spring of 1898. Having braved the Chilkoot Pass (see box) to meet the Yukon's upper reaches, men and supplies then had to navigate the **Miles Canyon** and White Horse rapids southeast of the town. After the first few boats through had been reduced to matchwood, the prospectors constructed a tramway around the rapids, and in time raised a shanty town at the canyon's northern head to catch their breath before the river journey to Dawson City.

The completion of the White Pass and Yukon Railway to Whitehorse (newly named after the rapids) put the tentative settlement on a firmer footing – almost at the same time as the gold rush petered out. In the early years of this century the town's population dwindled quickly from about 10,000 to about 400; for forty years the place slumbered, barely sustained by copper mining and the paddle wheelers which plied the river carrying freight and the occasional tourist. Boom for the second time arrived with the building of the Alaska Highway, when the town's population swelled from 800 to 40,000, a kickstart which has stood it in good stead ever since.

### Arrival and information

Whitehorse's **airport** is on the bluff above the town, about 5km from downtown; shuttle buses and taxis connect with downtown. The *Greyhound* **bus terminal** is at 3211 3rd Ave at the extreme eastern end of downtown some ten minutes' walk from Main Street – you turn left out of the terminal for the town centre, something it's as well to know if you stagger off the daily *Greyhound* from Dawson Creek, which arrives at 5am.

Whitehorse's **Visitor Information Centre** is a block east of Main St at 302 Steele St (daily May–Sept 8am–8pm; ☎667-2915). Its staff are friendly and have built up an unusual **comments book**, filled with enlightening complaints and up-to-date tips from travellers coming from Alaska and the north. The *Parks Canada* information office alongside the *SS Klondike* (May–Sept daily 9am–6pm; ☎667-4511) is the place to pick up information on the Chilkoot Trail. Almost as useful as these is *Books on Main*, 203 Main St, which has a full range of Yukon books, guides and pamphlets you won't find elsewhere. For an outstanding selection of **maps** visit *Jim's Toy and Gifts*, 208 Main St.

### Accommodation

It's as well to call ahead in summer to reserve **accommodation**, especially at the excellent **youth hostel**, the *Fourth Avenue Residence*, 4051 4th Ave (☎667-4471); note that it's at the far western end of 4th Avenue, a good ten-minute walk from downtown. More a hotel than a hostel, it offers a wide variety of room deals and weekly rates ranging from shared dorms at $18–25 daily to private doubles with TV from $45.

The cheapest listed **hotel** is the *Chilkoot Trail Motel*, 4190 4th Ave (☎668-4190), but see the information centre's complaints book for some inspired vitriol on the place. Cheap, fairly grim and with live bands to serenade you through the small hours, is the *98 Hotel*, 110 Wood St (☎667-2641), with doubles at $35. Slightly better is the *Fort Yukon Hotel*, about 200m west of the bus terminal at 2163 2nd Ave (☎667-2595), with doubles at $40. The *Stratford Motel*, 401 Jarvis St (☎667-4243), is spotlessly clean, boasts a friendly staff and has doubles at $70. At the top of the range there are two comfortable hotels belonging to *Westmark*, a northern chain; the *Klondike Inn*, 2288 2nd Ave (☎668-4747), and the *Whitehorse Hotel*, 2nd Ave and Wood St, both with doubles at $140.

Ask at the information centre for their **bed and breakfast** list, or call the long-established *Baker's Bed and Breakfast*, 84 11th Ave (☎633-2308), where singles are $45 and doubles $55. The *Robert Service* **campground** has been set out specifically for tents and backpackers about fifteen minutes' walk down South Access Road (mid-May to mid-Sept; ☎668-3721; $5). The heavily advertised *Trail of 98 RV and Campground* on the road between the Alaska Highway and downtown is as bleak as a car park and no good for tents.

## The town

Although greater Whitehorse spills along the Alaska Highway for several kilometres, the old **downtown** core is a forty-block grid centred on Main Street and mostly sandwiched between Second and Fourth avenues. Now graced only with a handful of pioneer buildings, the place still retains the dour integrity of a frontier town, and at night the baying of timber wolves and coyotes is a reminder of the wilderness immediately beyond the city limits. Nonetheless, the tourist influx provides a fair amount of action in the bars and cafés, and the streets are more appealing than in many northern towns.

The main thing to see is the **SS Klondike** (daily May–Sept 9am–6pm; free), one of only two surviving paddle-steamers in the Yukon, now rather sadly beached at the western end of 2nd Avenue, though it has been beautifully restored to the glory of its 1930s heyday. More than 250 stern-wheelers once plied the river, taking 36 hours to make the 700-kilometre journey to Dawson City, and five days to make the return trip against the current. The *SS Klondike* laboured against the river until 1955, ferrying 300 tons of cargo a trip, until an inexperienced pilot ran her aground and condemned her to museum status. The boat has the status of a National Historic Site, and so visits are by guided tour only.

Elsewhere in town you could pop into the **MacBride Museum** at 1st Ave and Wood St (daily May–Oct 9am–6pm; $3) for the usual zoo of stuffed animals, pioneer and gold-rush memorabilia, as well as **archive photos** and a display on the Asiatic tribes who drifted across the Bering Straits to inhabit the Americas. It's as well to resist the widely touted **stage shows**, however – a pair of expensive and tourist-orientated vaudeville acts of the banjo-plucking and frilly-knickered dancing variety.

Your money's better spent taking one of the **river tours** that shoot the **Miles Canyon** 9km south of the town, otherwise reached off the Alaska Highway, or from the South Access Road which hugs the river edge beyond the *SS Klondike*. The building of a hydro-electric dam has tamed the rapids' violence and replaced them with **Schwatka Lake**, but the two-hour trip on the *MV Schwatka* (2pm & 7pm daily June–Sept; $15) gives a better view of the river's potential ferocity and of the canyon's sheer walls than from the viewpoints off the road. Book tickets through *Atlas Tours* in town at the Westmark Hotel Mall (☎668-3161), or go straight to the dock above the dam about 3km down Canyon Road. If you fancy a walk or a site for a picnic, you might stroll from the main canyon car park some of the 11km to Canyon City, the all-but-vanished site of the initial stage of the stampeder's tramway.

## Eating

Of several friendly laid-back **eating** places the best overall is the *Talisman Café*, 2112 2nd Ave (daily 6am–11pm; closed Sun), which serves a range of full meals, and is also a spot where you might while away time with a cup of coffee. Slightly more expensive and twee, but still popular, is *The Bistro* at 205 Main St, known for its huge breakfasts, proper *cappuccino*, and calorie-stuffed desserts. The *No Pop Sandwich Shop*, 2112 2nd Ave, is altogether less cosy, but it's popular all the same and the food's good. Next door there's an excellent if rather hippy bakery often crammed with campers, *The Alpine*

*Bakery*, 4123 2nd Ave (Thurs–Sat 10am–5.30pm), whose counter greets you with the Shakespearian sentiment "one feast, one house, one mutual happiness".

### Onward from Whitehorse

Whitehorse provides the main **transport** links not only to most other points in the territory, but also to Alaska and the Northwest Territories. There are twice-daily *Canadian* **flights** to Calgary ($450), Edmonton ($400) and Vancouver ($400), and the airline has an office at 4th Ave and Elliot (☎668-3535). In this part of the world, however, it's also well worth knowing the various smaller airline options. *Air North* (☎668-2228) operates alarmingly old-fashioned planes between Whitehorse, Dawson City, Old Crow, Juneau and Fairbanks and issues a 21-day pass ($550) for travel between all five destinations. *Alkan Air* (☎668-6616) offers flights to Dawson City ($240), Faro, Mayo, Old Crow, Watson Lake, a handful of BC destinations, and to Norman Wells and Inuvik in the NWT ($390). The one and only connection to Yellowknife, a potentially vital link in any northern itinerary, is with *Delta Air* (☎668-6804; $360).

This is the end of the line for *Greyhound* **buses** in Canada (☎667-2223). For **Alaska and Yukon stops west of Whitehorse**, the expensive *Gray Lines*' **Alaskon Express** (☎667-2223) runs from Skagway to Whitehorse (daily late May to mid Sept; US$60) and then on to Anchorage (Tues, Fri & Sat only; US$150) and Fairbanks (Tues, Fri & Sun only; US$135); note, however, that the bus sometimes stops overnight at BEAVER CREEK (YT), so you may have to find the price of accommodation for certain long-haul routes into Alaska. At the time of writing a more ramshackle and much cheaper service in an old army bus operated to Alaska from the *Fourth Avenue Residence* (see "Accommodation").

*Norline* buses (☎668-3355) operate out of the main bus terminal and run **to Dawson City** (summer Mon, Wed & Fri; Sept–Oct and March–April Tues & Thurs; weekly in winter; $80). *North West Stage Lines* (☎668-6975) run irregular services in old school buses **to Beaver Creek** and over gravel roads **to Faro and Ross River** about 200km northeast of Whitehorse – a journey that's particularly popular with (mainly German) canoeists headed for the South Macmillan River, one of Canada's best river trips.

For **car rental** try *Hertz*, 4158 4th Ave (☎667-2505), *Budget Car and Truck*, 4178 4th Ave (☎667-6200) or *Norcan*, Mile 917 Alaska Highway – which unlike its competitors might rent you a car or truck suitable for gravel roads like the Dempster and Cassiar highways.

# Kluane Country

**Kluane Country** is the pocket of southwest Yukon on and around the 491-kilometre stretch of the Alaska Highway from Whitehorse to **Beaver Creek** at the border with Alaska. "Kluane" comes from the Southern Tutchone native word meaning a "place of fishing" after the area's teeming waters, and of **Kluane Lake** in particular, the Yukon's highest and largest sheet of water. These days, though, the name's associated more with the all but impenetrable wilderness of the **Kluane National Park** – a region that contains Canada's highest mountains, the most extensive non-polar icefields in the world, and the greatest diversity of plant and animal species in the far north. The park's main centre is **Haine's Junction** at the intersection of the Alaska Highway and the Haines Road. Although motels and campgrounds regularly dot the Alaska Highway, the region's only other places of any size are **Destruction Bay** and **Burwash Landing** on Kluane Lake. *Gray Line*'s **Alaskon Express** buses ply the length of the Alaska Highway, and it's also a heavily hitched section of road.

## Haines Junction

A blunt and modern place with a fine mountain-circled setting, **HAINES JUNCTION** mushroomed into life in 1942 during the building of the Alaska Highway as a base for the construction of the Haines Road – a highway which connects with Skagway's sister port at Haines, 174km to the southeast. Today it's most useful as the biggest service centre between Whitehorse and Tok in Alaska and as the eastern headquarters of the Kluane National Park – though the park covers a vast tract west of the Alaska Highway well to the north and south of the village. The combined *Canada Parks* and Yukon government **Visitor Reception Centre** is on Logan Street just off the north side of the Alaska Highway (daily May–Sept 8.30am–9pm; Oct–April 9am–5pm). If you want to stay the cheapest of the motels is the *Gateway* (☎634-2371) on the junction of Haines Road and the Alaska Highway; it has rooms from $45 as well as a few serviced **camp-sites** to the rear. *Mother's Cozy Corner* (☎634-2511), just down the Alaska Highway on the corner of Bates Road, has doubles from $60. The simple *Pine Lake* **campground** (May–Oct; $5) is 4km west of the village signed off the Alaska Highway, or there's the bigger and more central *Kluane RV Kampground* in town (May-Sept; ☎634-2691; $8). The best place to eat is the *Village Bakery* alongside the reception centre.

## Kluane National Park

Created in 1972 using land from the earlier Kluane Game Sanctuary, the **Kluane National Park** contains some of the country's greatest but most inaccessible scenery, and for the most part you must be resigned to seeing and walking its easterly margins from points along the Alaska Highway. Together with the neighbouring Wrangell-St Elias National Park in Alaska the park protects the **St Elias Mountains**, though from the highway the peaks you see rearing up to the south are part of the subsidiary Kluane Range. Beyond them, and largely invisible from the road, are St Elias' **Icefield Ranges** which contain Mount St Elias (5488m), **Mount Logan** (5950m) – Canada's highest point – and Mount McKinley (6193m) in Alaska, the highest point in North America. Below them, and covering half the park, is a huge base of mile-deep glaciers and icefields, home to just one permanent resident, the legendary iceworm. Unless you're prepared for full-scale expeditions, this interior is off limits, though from as little as $60 you can take plane **tours** over the area with *Glacier Air Tours* at Burwash Landing (☎841-5171; May 24–Sept 1); details of this and other guided tours are available from the Haines Junction reception centre.

---

### WALKING IN KLUANE NATIONAL PARK

Kluane's **trail system** is still in its infancy, though for experienced walkers there are wilderness routes totalling about 250km which largely follow old mining roads or creek beds and require overnight rough camping. The few more manageable walks start from seven distinct trailheads, each mapped on pamphlets from Haines's reception centre, which also organises popular guided day walks during the summer.

Three trails start from points along a 20-kilometre stretch of Haines Road immediately south of Haines Junction. The path nearest to the town, and the most popular walk, is the 19km round trip **Auriol Trail**; the nearby **Rock Glacier Trail** is a quick one-kilometre jaunt to St Elias Lake; the third and longest is the **Mush Lake Road** route (21.6km one way). North of Haines Junction most people walk all or part of two paths which strike out from the Sheep Mountain information kiosk on Kluane Lake – either the **Sheep Mountain Ridge** (11.5km), with good chances of seeing the area's Dall sheep, or the longer **Slim's River West Trail** (28.4km) which offers a relatively easy way of seeing the edges of the park's icefield interior.

On the drier, warmer ranges at the edge of the icefields a green belt of meadow, marsh, forest and fen provides sanctuary for a huge variety of **wildlife** such as grizzlies, moose, mountain goats, and a 4000-strong herd of white **Dall sheep** – the animals the park originally set out to protect. These margins also support the widest spectrum of **birds** in the far north, some 150 species, including easily seen raptors like peregrine falcons, bald eagles, golden eagles and smaller birds like arctic terns, mountain bluebirds, tattlers and hawk owls.

Limited **trails** (see box opposite) offer the chance to see some of these creatures, but the only **campground** within the park is the site at *Kathleen Lake*, on the Haines Road 16km southeast of Haines Junction ($6) – though there is plenty of hotel and camping accommodation along the Alaska Highway.

## Kluane Lake

The Kluane region might keep its greatest mountains out of sight, but it makes amends by laying on the stunning **Kluane Lake** along some 60km of the Alaska Highway. About 75km northwest of Haines Junction, and hot on the heels of some magnificent views of the St Elias Mountains, the huge lake (some 400 square kilometres) is framed on all sides by snow-covered peaks whose glaciers feed its ice-blue waters. Although it's not part of the national park, there's a second park centre at its southern tip, the **Sheep Mountain Information Kiosk** (mid-May to mid-Sept daily 10am–6pm; July & Aug 9am–7pm).

If you want to boat or fish there are rental facilities at the two main settlements along the shores, Destruction Bay and Burwash Landing, each of which also has a small selection of **accommodation** to supplement the odd lodges and campgrounds along the Alaska Highway. In the smaller **DESTRUCTION BAY** (pop. 44) use the *Talbot Arm Motel* behind the Chevron garage (☎841-4461), which has double rooms at $80 and a partly serviced **campground** ($10).

At **BURWASH LANDING**, 15km beyond, there's the *Burwash Landing Resort* (☎841-4441) with doubles from $50 and a big unserviced campsite (May–Oct; free). The best overall **campground** is the lovely Yukon government *Congdon Creek* site off the Alaska Highway, 12km south of Destruction Bay.

## Beaver Creek

**BEAVER CREEK** is Canada's westernmost settlement and the last stop before Alaska. Following concerted lobbying from its one hundred inhabitants, however, it no longer houses the customs post – this has been moved a couple of kilometres up the road in response to complaints from the locals about the flashing lights and sirens that used to erupt whenever a tourist forgot to stop. The border is open twenty-four hours a day, but there's a high chance you may have to stay here, particularly if you're catching the *Alaskon* **bus** service from Skagway and Whitehorse, which stops overnight at Beaver Creek on some trans-Alaskan routes. The bus company can arrange to book you into the expensive *Westmark Inn* (May–Sept; ☎258-0560), where doubles cost $130 a time: if that's too steep you've got the choice of booking yourself in at the eccentric *Ida's Motel* (☎862-7223) or failing that, into *Marvin's Inn* (no phone), both of which have doubles at $50.

The *Westmark* does have a large serviced **campground** ($18), though they're happier to see RVs than backpackers. There's a good Yukon government site 10km south at *Snag Junction* (May–Oct; $5). Also be warned that if US Customs take against you or your rucksack, they can insist on seeing at least $400 cash, and won't be swayed by any number of credit cards. For full details on border crossing and what to expect on the other side, visit the Yukon **visitor information centre** (May–Sept daily 9am–9pm).

# Dawson City

Few episodes in Canadian history have caught the imagination like the **Klondike gold rush**, and few places have remained as evocative of their past as **DAWSON CITY**, the stampede's epicentre. For a few months in 1898 this former patch of moose pasture became one of the richest and most famous places on earth, as something like 100,000 people struggled across huge tracts of wilderness to seek their fortunes in the richest goldfield of all time. Most people approach the town on the Klondike Highway from Whitehorse, a wonderful road running through almost utter wilderness, and knowing the background to the place it's hard not to near the road's end without high expectations.

## THE KLONDIKE GOLD RUSH

Gold rushes in North America during the nineteenth century were nothing new, but none generated quite the delirium of the **Klondike gold rush** in 1898. Over a million people are estimated to have left home for the Yukon goldfields, the largest single one-year mass movement of people in the century. Of these about 100,000 made it to the Yukon, about 20,000 panned the creeks, 4000 found something and a couple of dozen made – and invariably lost – huge fortunes.

The **discovery of gold in 1896** on the Klondike, a tributary of the Yukon River, was the culmination of twenty years of prospecting in the Yukon and Alaska. A Hudson's Bay fur trader first noticed gold colours in 1842, and the first substantial report was made by an English missionary in 1863, but as the exploitation of gold was deemed bad for trade in both furs and religion neither report was followed up. The first mining on any scale took place in 1883 and gradually small camps sprang up along almost 2000 miles of river at places like Forty Mile, Sixty Mile and Circle City. All were established before the Klondike strike, but were home to only a few hundred men, hardened types reared on the earlier Californian and British Columbian gold rushes.

The discovery of the gold that started the stampede is inevitably shrouded in myth and countermyth. The first man to prospect near the Klondike River was **Robert Henderson**, a dour Nova Scotian and the very embodiment of the lone pioneer. In early 1896 he found eight cents' worth of gold in a pan scooped from a creek in the hills above present-day Dawson City. This was considered an excellent return at the time, and a sign to Henderson that the creek would make worthwhile yields. He panned out about $750 with four companions and then returned downriver to pick up supplies.

Henderson then set about finding a route up the Klondike to meet the creek he'd prospected, and at the mouth of the Klondike met **George Washington Carmack** and a couple of his native friends, Skookum Jim and Tagish Charley. Henderson told Carmack of his hopes for the area, and then – with a glance at the natives – uttered the phrase that probably cost him a fortune, "There's a chance for you George, but I don't want any damn Siwashes [natives] staking on that creek." Henderson wandered off into the hills, leaving Carmack, rankled by the remark, to prospect a different set of creeks – the right ones, as it turned out. On the eve of August 16 Skookum Jim found $4 of gold in a pan on Bonanza Creek, a virtually unprecedented amount at the time. Next day Carmack staked the first claim, and rushed off to register the find leaving Henderson prospecting almost barren ground on the other side of the hills.

By the end of August all of Bonanza had been staked by a hundred or so old-timers from camps up and down the Yukon. Almost all the real fortunes had been secured by the winter of 1896 when the snows and frozen river effectively sealed the region from the outside world. The **second phase** occurred after the thaw when a thousand or so miners from the West Coast arrived drawn by vague rumours emanating from the north of a big find. The headlong rush that was to make the Klondike unique, however, followed the

Little at first, however, distinguishes its surroundings. Some 500km from Whitehorse the road wanders through low but steeply sided hills covered in spruce, aspen and dwarf firs, and then picks up a small ice-clear river – the **Klondike**. Gradually the first small spoil heaps appear on the hills to the south, and then suddenly the entire valley bottom turns into a devastated landscape of vast boulders and abandoned workings. The desolate tailings continue for several kilometres until the Klondike flows into the much broader **Yukon** and the town, previously hidden by hills, comes suddenly into view.

A good many tourists and backpackers come up here, many drawn by the boardwalks, rutted dirt streets and dozens of false-fronted wooden houses, others to canoe the Yukon or ride the Dempster or Top of the World highways into Alaska and the

docking in **July 1897** of the *Excelsior* in San Francisco and the *Portland* in Seattle. Few sights could have been as stirring a proof of the riches up for grabs as the battered Yukon miners who came down the gangplanks dragging bags, boxes and sacks literally bursting with gold. The press were waiting for the *Portland*, which docked with two tons of gold on board, all taken by hand from the Klondike creeks by just a few miners. The rush was now on in earnest.

Whipped up by the media and the outfitters of Seattle and San Francisco, thousands embarked on trips that were to claim the lives of hundreds. The most common route – the "poor man's route" – was to take a boat from a west coast port to Skagway and then climb the dreaded **Chilkoot Pass** to pick up the Yukon River at Whitehorse, then boat the last 500 miles to Dawson City. The easiest and most expensive route lay by boat upstream from the mouth of the Yukon in western Alaska. The most dangerous and most bogus were the "All Canadian Route" from Edmonton and overland trails through the northern wilderness.

The largest single influx came with the melting of the ice on the Yukon in May 1898 – 21 months after the first claim – when a vast makeshift armada drifted down the river. When they docked at Dawson City, the boats nestled six deep along a two-mile stretch of the waterfront. For most it was to have been a fruitless journey – every inch of the creeks having long been staked – yet in most accounts of the stampede it is clear that this was a rite of passage as much as a quest for wealth. Pierre Berton observed that "there were large numbers who spent only a few days in Dawson and did not even bother to visit the hypnotic creeks that had tugged at them all winter long. They turned their faces home again, their adventure over . . . It was as if they had, without quite knowing it, completed the job they had set out to do and had come to understand that it was not the gold they were seeking after all."

As for the gold, it's the smaller details that hint at the scale of the Klondike. The miner's wife, for example, who could wander the creek by her cabin picking nuggets from the stream bed as she waited for her husband to come home; or the destitutes during the Great Depression who could pan $40 a day from the dirt under Dawson's boardwalks; or the $1000 panned during rebuilding of the *Orpheum Theatre* in the Forties, all taken in a morning from under the floorboards where it had drifted from miners' pockets half a century before; or the $200 worth of dust panned nightly from the beermats of a Dawson saloon during 1897.

By about 1899 the rush was over, not because the gold had run out, but because the most easily accessible gold had been taken from the creeks. It had been the making of Alaska; Tacoma, Portland, Victoria and San Francisco all felt its impact; Edmonton sprang from almost nothing; and Vancouver's population doubled in year. It was also the first of a string of mineral discoveries in the Yukon and the far north, a region whose vast and untapped natural resources are increasingly the subject of attention from multinationals as rapacious and determined as their grizzled predecessors.

Northwest Territories. After decades of decline *Parks Canada* is restoring the town, now a deserved National Historic Site, a process which is bringing about increased commercialism, new hotels and a sense that something may be about to be lost in the place. This said, in a spot where permafrost buckles buildings, it snows in August, and temperatures reach -60°C during winters of almost perpetual gloom, there's little real chance of Dawson losing the gritty, weather-battered feel of a true frontier town. More to the point, small-time prospecting still goes on, and there are one or two rough-and-ready bars whose hardened locals take a dim view of sharing their beers, let alone their gold, with coachloads of tourists.

You could easily spend a couple of days here, one exploring the town, the other touring the old Klondike creeks to the east. If at all possible prime yourself with background beforehand to one of the most colourful chapters in Canada's history: Pierre Berton's widely available bestseller, *Klondike – The Last Great Gold Rush 1896–1899*, is a superbly written introduction both to the period and to the place.

## The Town

You should start any wander on **Front Street**, the leading edge of a street grid that runs parallel to the Yukon River and which is home to the impressive **Visitor Reception Centre** (daily May–Sept 9am–9pm; ☎993-5566). Loaded with a huge amount of material, the place also shows good introductory archive and contemporary films throughout the day, as well as organising free tours of the town's **heritage buildings** – though these are easily seen on your own, as are the cabins which belonged to two chroniclers of the gold rush, poet **Robert Service** and the better-known **Jack London**. The local **museum** is also good for an hour, but when all's said and done it's the atmospheric streets of Dawson that are most compelling.

### The Heritage Buildings

Fuelled by limitless avarice, Dawson between 1898 and 1900 exploded into a full-blown metropolis of 30,000 people – the largest city in the Canadian west and the equal of places like Seattle and San Francisco in its opportunities for vice, decadence and good living. There were opera houses, theatres, cinemas (at a time when motion-picture houses were just three years old), steam heating, three hospitals, restaurants with French chefs, and bars, brothels and dance halls which generated phenomenal business – one Charlie Kimball took $300,000 dollars in a month from his club, and spent the lot within days. Rules of supply and demand made Dawson an expensive town, with a single two-metre frontage fetching as much in rent in a month as a four-bedroom apartment in New York cost for two years.

Only a few of the many intact **heritage buildings** around the town date from the earliest days of the rush, dozens having been lost to fire and to permafrost, whose effects are seen in some of the most appealing of the older buildings: higgledy-piggledy collapsing ruins of rotting wood, weeds and rusting corrugated iron. Elsewhere restoration projects are in full flow, and have saved wonderful wooden buildings like the **Palace Grand Theatre** on King Street (1899), where you can also watch the wistful award-winning black and white film, *City of Gold*, a documentary which first drew the attention of the federal government to Dawson's decline in the Fifties (daily 2.30pm; free). Nearby there's the working **Post Office** (1901), and the **Anglican Church**, a cream and brown clapboard building built in 1902 with money collected from the miners. On Queen Street is **Diamond Tooth Gertie's Gambling House**, founded by one of the town's more notorious characters, and still operating as the only legal **casino** in Canada (July–Sept Mon–Sat 8pm–2am; $5); all proceeds go to the restoration of Dawson.

## The museum

Dawson has scope for a full-blown and fully integrated museum on its past, but at present the job's done reasonably well by the **Dawson City Museum**, 5th and Church St (daily June–Sept 10am–6pm; $4). There's an adequate historical run-through of the gold rush from the first finds, though you get more out of the displays if you have some background to the period. Some of the most fascinating material is in the old diaries and newspaper cuttings which vividly document the minutiae of pioneer life and events such as the big winter freeze of 1897–88 when temperatures reputedly touched -86°C, and of the summer heat wave of 1898 when the sun shone unbroken for almost 23 hours daily, bringing temperatures in the upper thirties. The museum also shows some of the hundreds of old films that were discovered under some Dawson floorboards a few years back, and holds interesting touring exhibitions in the wood-framed rooms upstairs that once housed the council offices.

## The Robert Service and Jack London cabins

The cabins of Dawson's two literary lions are only about a hundred metres apart on 8th Avenue, about ten minutes' walk from Front Street. Most Canadians hold **Robert Service** in such high esteem that it comes as a shock actually to hear famous verses like *Songs of Sourdough* and *The Shooting of Dan McGrew*, though they do sometimes achieve a sort of inspired awfulness. Born in Preston, England, in 1874, the poet wrote most of his gold-rush verse before he'd even set foot in the Yukon – he was posted by his bank employers to Whitehorse in 1904 and only made Dawson in 1908. He retired a rich man on the proceeds of his writing, spending his last years mainly in France, where he died in 1958. His **cabin** (June–Sept daily 10am–5pm) is probably cosier and better decorated than it was almost a century ago, but it still gives an idea of how most people must have lived once Dawson was reasonably established. During the summer people flock here to hear poetry recitals in front of the cabin from a bearded eccentric dressed and mannered as the "Bard of the Yukon" (daily July & Aug at 10am & 3pm; free).

**Jack London's Cabin** was home to a more convincing writer, but is a less persuasive piece of reconstruction, being little more than a bleak, blank-walled and incomplete hut. London knew far more than Service of the real rigours of northern life, however, having spent time in 1897 as a ferryman on Whitehorse's Mile's Canyon before moving north to spend about a year holed up on Henderson's Creek above the Klondike River. He returned home to California penniless, but loaded with a fund of material that was to find expression in books like *The Call of the Wild*, *White Fang* and *A Daughter of the Snows*. Alongside the hut there's a good little museum of pictures and memorabilia, presided over by an amiable and knowledgeable curator, an author in his own right (hut and museum daily June 1 to Sept 15 10am–noon & 1–6pm; free).

# Around Dawson

While in Dawson make a point of seeing the two creeks where it all started and where most of the gold was mined – **Bonanza and Eldorado**, both over 20km away from the townsite along rough roads to the southeast. These days there's no working mine left in the region, though most of the claims are still owned and definitely out of bounds to amateurs. However, it's still possible to see some of the huge dredges that replaced individual endeavour once the easily reached gold had been taken out. Another popular local excursion is to **Midnight Dome**, the gouged-out hill behind the town, while further afield numerous RVs, cyclists and hitch-hikers follow the **Top of the World Highway** which runs on beyond the Alaskan border to link with the Alaska Highway at Tetlin Junction.

## Bonanza and Eldorado creeks

To reach **Bonanza Creek** follow the Klondike Highway – the continuation of Front Street – for 4km to the junction with Bonanza Creek Road. The road threads through scenes of apocalyptic piles of boulders and river gravel for some 12km until it comes to a simple cairn marking **Discovery Claim**, the spot staked by George Carmack after pulling out a nugget the size of his thumb, or so the story goes. Every 150 metres along the length of the creek in front of you – the width of a claim – was to yield some 3000kg of gold, or about $25 million worth at 1900 prices. Exact amounts of gold taken out are difficult to establish because it was in miners' interests to undervalue their takings to the authorities, but most estimates suggest that around $600 million worth left the creeks between 1897 and 1904. Given a claim's huge value they were often subdivided and sold as "fractions": one miner pulled out over 100kg of gold in eight hours from a fraction – almost $1 million worth.

At Discovery Claim the road forks again, one spur running east up Eldorado Creek, if anything richer than Bonanza, the other following Upper Bonanza Road to the summit of **King Solomon's Dome**, where you can look down over smaller scarred rivulets like Hunker and Dominion Creek, before returning in a loop to the Klondike Highway via Hunker Road.

As time went by and the easily reached gold was exploited, miners increasingly consolidated claims, or sold out to large companies who installed dredges capable of clawing out the bedrock and gravel. Numerous examples of these industrial dinosaurs litter the creeks, but the largest and most famous is the **No. 4 Dredge** at Claim 17 BD ("Below Discovery") off Bonanza Creek Road, which from the start of operations in 1913 was able to take as much as a 25kg of gold daily. Modern mines are lucky to produce a quarter of that amount in a week.

Without a car you'll have to rent a bike or join up with one of the various **goldfield tours** run by *Gold City Tours*, Front St (☎993-5175), either to see the dredges and creeks, or to **pan for gold** yourself, at a price. Only three small fractions on Claim 6 can currently be panned free of charge – inquire at the reception centre for latest locations.

## Midnight Dome and Top of the World Highway

The **Midnight Dome** is the distinctive hill that rears up behind Dawson City, half-covered in stunted pines and half-eaten away by land slips. It's named because from its summit at midnight on June 21 you can watch the sun dip to the horizon before rising again straight away – Dawson being only 300km south of the Arctic Circle. The Midnight Dome Road runs 8km to its summit (884m) from the Klondike Highway just out of the town proper. It's an extremely steep haul, but more than worth the slog for the massive views over Dawson, the goldfields, the Yukon's broad meanders and the ranks of mountains stretching away in all directions. At the solstice there's a race to the top and lots of drink-sodden and fancy dress festivities down in Dawson. *Gold City Tours* also run regular daytime and evening tours up here.

You can snatch further broad vistas from the **Top of the World Highway** (Hwy 9), a summer-only gravel road reached by ferry from Front Street across the Yukon (daily every 45min; free). After only 5km the road unfolds a great panorama over the area, and after 14km another **viewpoint** looks out over the Yukon valley and the **Ogilvie Mountains** straddling the Arctic Circle. Thereafter the road runs above the tree-line as a massive belvedere and can be seen switch-backing over barren ridges way into the distance. It hits the **Alaska border** 108km from Dawson, where you can cross only when the customs post is open (May–Oct 9am–9pm). Unlike the Dempster Highway (see next page) there's no **bus** on this route, but you should be able to hitch easily in summer because it's much travelled as a neat way of linking with the Alaska Highway at TOK for the roads to Fairbanks and Anchorage or the loop back to Whitehorse. Be prepared to make only about 50kph, and inquire about local difficulties and petrol availability at the Dawson visitor reception centre.

## Practicalities

Dawson City's **airport** is 19km southeast of the town on the Klondike Highway, and is used by *Alkan Air* (☎668-6616) scheduled services to Inuvik (NWT), Old Crow, Mayo and Whitehorse, and by *Air North* (☎993-5110) services to Fairbanks, Whitehorse, Watson Lake and Juneau. *Norline* **buses** (☎993-5331) from Whitehorse arrive at *Arctic Drugs* on Front Street (3 weekly in summer; 2 weekly in winter). Tickets for all air services, Alaska and BC ferries, and for the Dempster Highway **bus** to Inuvik, can be arranged at *Gold City Travel* on Front Street.

More and more places to **stay** are opening up in town, but the increased competition isn't bringing prices down. The cheapest deal around, particularly if you round up a group of people, are the four-berth cabins at the *Trail of '98 Mini Golf* (☎993-6101; $40 per cabin), but they're 5km out of town at the junction of the Klondike Highway and Bonanza Creek Road. There's no power or running water but washrooms are available nearby. The cheapest place in town is *Mary's Rooms* at 3rd Ave and Harper (May–Sept; ☎993-6013), a ramshackle collection of spartan rooms with doubles at $45. At the time of writing a hostel-type place, *McLondon's Bunkhouse*, was due to open at 2nd Ave and Princess (☎993-5538) with "no-nonsense rooms at no-nonsense prices" – $45 with shared bathroom. *Klondike Kate's Motel* (June 1 to Sept 3; ☎993-5491) at 3rd and King has nine individual cabins from $65. Somewhat less appealing despite the false-fronted exterior are the $60 doubles at the *Westminster Hotel*, 3rd and Queen (☎993-6013; April–Sept), a rough-house spot where the miners come in to drink long and noisily into the night. In the lower range it might be a better idea to go for one of a handful of **bed and breakfast** options around $65 for a double: look for the pink house at 7th and Harper for the *White Ram B&B* (☎993-5772); the *5th Ave B&B* is next to the museum (☎993-5941); *Dawson City B&B* (☎993-5649) is at the junction of the Yukon and Klondike rivers.

Cheap places go quickly, however, and you may have to move up a price bracket, where there's a wider choice of wooden-fronted and fairly plush **hotels**. The *Downtown Hotel*, 2nd Ave and Queen (☎993-5346), and the *Eldorado Hotel*, 3rd Ave and Princess (☎993-5451), are both open year-round and have rooms from $110. The *Triple J*, 5th and Queen (☎993-5323), and the *Midnight Sun Hotel* are about the same price, but open only between May and October. Top of the range is the swish *Westmark*, 5th and Harper (☎993-5542), with doubles at $150, though they run frequent promotions to fill empty rooms at $69.

The main town **campground** for tents is the government *Yukon River Campground* ($5), which is on the west bank of the Yukon immediately right after the ferry crossing from the top of Front Street. The *Gold Rush Campground* in town at 5th Ave and York is a bleak but busy place designed mainly for RVs (May–Sept; ☎993-5247; $18).

For **eating** there are a couple of good snack places on Front Street – the *98 Drive In* and rather austere *Nancy's*. *Klondike Kate's* at 3rd and King is the friendliest and most laid-back for staples like cheap breakfasts and straightforward dinners; the popular *Marina's*, 5th and Harper (☎993-6800), is the best place for something a touch more special, with pizzas and excellent dinners up to about $25.

**Nightlife** revolves around drinking in the main hotel bars, or an hour or so at *Diamond Tooth Gertie's* at 4th and Queen, Canada's only legal **gambling** hall. You can also catch the almost equally touristy period-costume melodramas and vaudeville acts held at the *Palace Grand Theatre* (June–Sept nightly except Tues at 8pm; $12).

# The Dempster Highway

Begun in 1959 to service the northern oil fields, and completed in 1988 – by when the accessible oil had been siphoned off – the 740-kilometre **Dempster Highway** between Dawson City and Inuvik in the Northwest Territories is the only road in Canada to cross the **Arctic Circle**, offering a tremendous journey through a superb spectrum of landscapes. An increasingly travelled route – which locals say means four cars an hour – it crosses the **Ogilvie Mountains** just north of Dawson before dropping down to **Eagle Plains** and almost unparalleled access to the sub-arctic tundra. Shortly before meeting the NWT border after 470km it rises through the **Richardson Mountains** and then drops to the drab low hills and plain of the Peel Plateau and Mackenzie River. For much of its course the road follows the path of the dog patrols operated by the Mounties in the first half of the century, taking its name from a Corporal WJD Dempster, who in March 1922 was sent to look for a patrol lost between **Fort Macpherson** (NWT) and Dawson. He found their frozen bodies just 26 miles from where they had set off.

## Practicalities

The Dempster is a gravel road and the journey by **car** takes anything between twelve and fifteen hours in good conditions. If you're **cycling** or motorbiking, both increasingly popular ways of doing the trip, you need to be prepared for rough camping, and should call at the **NWT Information Centre** on Front Street in Dawson City (May–Sept 9am–7pm; ☎1-800-661-0752) for practical as well as invaluable anecdotal information from the staff. If you're without transport you might pick up a **lift** here, or take the **Dempster Highway Bus Service** run by *Gold City Tours*. Departures leave from Dawson at 8am on Monday and Friday between June 14 and September 2, with an additional Wednesday service between June 26 and August 14. **Tickets** cost $198 one way to Inuvik ($350 return) and $99 to Eagle Plains/Arctic Circle ($175 same day return).

In the Dempster's Yukon section there are **facilities only** at **Eagle Plains Hotel** (☎979-4187; doubles $100, camping $7), 363km to the north. There are also three rudimentary Yukon government **campgrounds** at *Tombstone Mountain*, 72km north of Dawson; at *Engineer Creek* (194km); and at *Cornwall River* (447km). In July and August there's a trailer information centre at Tombstone Mountain with details of good trails from the campsite.

The only other **hotel** is the small *Tetlit Service Co-op* (☎952-2339; $100) in the NWT at the tiny Dene village of **Fort Macpherson** 115km south of Inuvik. There's also petrol here and the unserviced NWT government *Nutuiluie Campground and Information Centre* 3km south of the settlement (June–Sept; $5). The even tinier **Arctic Red River**, 80km south of Inuvik, also has petrol and two rooms at $75 each (☎953-3003).

## Dawson City to the Arctic Circle

Having come this far north it's hard to resist the temptation of crossing the **Arctic Circle** 403km north of Dawson City, a journey that takes you over the most captivating stretch of the highway. At the very least you should take a short ride out of the mixed deciduous spruce woods of Canada's boreal forests for a look at the tundra which starts beyond the **North Fork Pass** (1370m), just 79km north of Dawson. All distances given below are from Dawson City, almost the only way to locate things on the road.

After the millions of lodgepole pines in northern Canada, it's almost time for a celebration when you pass what are on record as the country's most northerly pines (8km). Beyond them you'll see occasional trapper's cabins: the hunting of mink, wolverine and lynx is still lucrative, providing the Yukon's 700 or so full-time trappers with a $1.5

million annual income. At **Hart River** (80km) you should see part of the 1200-strong Hart River Woodland **caribou herd**; unlike the barren-ground herds further north these caribou have sufficient fodder to graze a single area instead of making seasonal migrations. **Golden eagles** and **ptarmigan** are also common on willow-lined streams like Blackstone River (93km), as are **tundra birds** like Lapland longspurs, lesser golden plovers, mew gulls and long-tailed jaegers. At Moose Lake (105km) **moose**, needless to say, can often be seen feeding, along with numerous species of waterfowl like northern shoveller, American widgeon and the **arctic tern**, whose Arctic to Antarctic migration is the longest of any bird.

**Chapman Lake** (120km) marks the start of the northern Ogilvie Mountains, a region which has never been glaciated and so preserves numerous relic species of plant and insect, as well as providing an important early wintering range for the **Porcupine Caribou Herd**; as many as 40,000 caribou cross the highway in mid-October – and they have right of way. Unique **butterfly** species breed at Butterfly Ridge (155km), close to some of the more obvious caribou trails which cross the region, and it should also be easy to spot Dall sheep, cliff swallows and bald eagles.

The **Arctic Circle** (403km) is marked by a battered cairn on the Dempster and the summer home to one of the country's premier eccentrics, one Harry Waldron, the self-proclaimed "Keeper of the Arctic Circle". In his late sixties, Harry sits in a rocking chair in a tuxedo with a glass of champagne and regales all comers with snippets of Robert Service, facts about the Arctic and some fairly unimpeachable views on the environment. An ex-highway worker, he started his act of his own accord, but proved so popular that he's now paid by the Yukon government to sit and do his spiel. After Harry's rocking chair the road climbs into the Richardson Mountains to meet the border of the NWT (470km) before the less arresting flats of the Mackenzie River and the run to Inuvik.

---

## NUNAVUT

"Apparently we have administered these vast territories in an almost continuous state of absence of mind."

Prime Minister Louis S St Laurent to the Canadian parliament in 1953.

Long an amorphous political entity administered not as a semi-autonomous province but by central government, the **Northwest Territories** are set to be superseded by a land treaty which will divide the territories in two and create a new eastern Arctic territory called **Nunavut**. The new $1.15 billion land deal – the largest in Canadian history – will return a homeland to the Inuit, who in return will give up their claim to the remainder of the NWT, which will probably be renamed. The territory will cover a fifth of Canada's land surface – an area five times the size of California – and be home to some 17,500 Inuit, about eighty percent of the new region's population. The deal follows fifteen years of talks, but at the time of writing was still to be ratified by a plebiscite of natives which will in turn have to pass through the Canadian parliament – a process which could take a further six months.

The outcome of the deal hangs in the balance. **Ovide Mercredi**, grand chief of the Assembly of First Nations, representing 500,000 natives, is on record as saying the Inuit are giving away too much and receiving too little. He seems to have a point. Of the 136,000 square miles in question, the Inuit have mineral rights to only 14,000, though they now have unrestricted rights to hunt, fish and trap over a far greater area. More crucially, however, the region will still have a centrally appointed government along the lines of the present Yukon and NWT administrations, and this lack of native self-government may well provide a stumbling block to the deal's ratification.

# Delta-Beaufort

The **Delta-Beaufort** region centres on **Inuvik** and embraces the mighty delta of the **Mackenzie River**, which reaches across the Beaufort Sea to Banks Island, the most westerly of Canada's arctic islands. The delta ranks as one of the country's great **bird** habitats, with swans, cranes and big raptors amongst the many hundreds of species which either nest or overfly the region during spring and autumn migration cycles. It also offers the chance of seeing pods of **beluga whales** and other big sea mammals, while native guides on Banks Island give you the chance of sighting musk-ox, white fox and polar bears.

After Inuvik and the two villages on the short NWT section of the Dempster – Fort McPherson and Arctic Red River – the area's other four settlements are **fly-in communities** reached from Inuvik. Two of them, **Aklavik** and **Tuktoyaktuk**, are close by NWT standards, and are the places to fly out to if you want a comparatively accessible taste of aboriginal northern culture. **Sachs Harbour** (on Banks Island) and **Paulatuk** lie much further afield, and are forward bases for more arduous tours into the delta and arctic tundra.

## Inuvik

**INUVIK** (pop. 3500), the furthest north you can drive on a public highway in North America, was built as a planned town in 1954 to replace Aklavik, a settlement wrongly thought to be doomed to envelopment by the Mackenzie's swirling waters and shifting mud flats. It's a strange melting pot, with native Dene, Métis and Inuvialuit living alongside the trappers, pilots, scientists and frontier entrepreneurs drawn here in the Seventies when boom followed the **oil exploration** in the delta. Falling oil prices and the rising expense of exploitation, however, soon toppled the delta's vast rigs and it seems that the oil is likely to remain largely untapped until the next century.

Wandering the town is an eye-opening introduction to the vagaries of northern life, from the strange stilted buildings built to prevent their heat melting the permafrost, to the all too visible signs of the **alcholism** that affects this and many northern communities – a problem rarely alluded to outside them, partly because it's the region's native groups that seem most afflicted. Suicides here are four times the national average for Native Canadians. On a happier note, the influence of Inuvialuit people in local political and economic life has increased, to the extent that the **Western Claims Settlement Act** of 1984 saw the government cede titles to various lands in the area, returning control that had been lost to the fur trade, the church, oil companies and southern government. A potent symbol of the church's local role in particular resides in the town's most photographed building, the **Igloo Church**, a rather incongruous yoking of a native icon and foreign religion.

### Practicalities

*Canadian Airlines* have scheduled **flights** daily to Inuvik from Edmonton, usually via Yellowknife, Fort Smith or Hay River (☎979-2951), and several regional companies run regular services from Whitehorse, Dawson City and numerous smaller destinations in the NWT. In summer a **bus** service operates from Dawson (see p.593); the **Dempster Highway** is open year-round except for brief periods during the November freeze and April thaw.

For **information** on Inuvik and the region generally contact the *Delta-Beaufort Tourism Association* on Mackenzie Road, a continuation of the Dempster Highway and Inuvik's main street (daily June–Sept 10am–6pm; ☎979-4321). There are only three **hotels** in town, all charging from $115 for doubles: the *Eskimo Inn* (☎979-2801), in central downtown; the *Finto Motor Inn* (☎979-2647), between the airstrip and down-town; and the central *Mackenzie* (☎979-2861), probably the smartest of the three. *Robertson's Bed and Breakfast*, 48 Mackenzie Rd (☎979-3111), has doubles from $70 which need to be booked up to three weeks in advance during summer, as does the beautifully situated *Outlook Bed and Breakfast* (☎979-3789; doubles $70–90), just out of town at Boot Lake. **Eating** possibilities are largely confined to the expensive hotel dining rooms – where at a price you can gorge on char, caribou and musk-ox – unless you make for the *Sunriser Coffee Shop*, 185 Mackenzie Rd, which serves snacks and breakfasts that won't break the bank.

Inuvik may be the best place to **hire a car** for the NWT, because southern firms tend not to rent vehicles for rough roads, and make hefty charges if you return a car that's obviously been over gravel: the *Budget* (☎979-2888) and *Tilden* (☎979-3383) outlets rent out suitably robust trucks and pick-ups. The two big **tour operators** in town are both worth investigating, as each runs a selection of affordable daily boat and plane tours as well as full-blown two-week expeditions; contact the *Arctic Tour Company* (☎979-2054), opposite the Igloo Church at 175 Mackenzie Rd, and *Midnight Express Tours*, 105 Mackenzie Rd (☎979-3068).

# The fly-in communities

Accessible only by air except in winter, when incredible snow roads are ploughed across the frozen delta, Delta-Beaufort's four fly-in communities are closer to more fascinating arctic landscapes and cultures than the similarly remote spots around Yellowknife. All are accessible by *Aklak Air*, Box 1190, Inuvik (☎979-3377), and all have shops, though their prices make it wise to take in your own supplies.

**AKLAVIK** (pop. 800), some 50km west of Inuvik on the western bank of the Mackenzie delta, means the "Place of the Barren Lands Grizzly Bear". For generations it has been the home of Inuvialuit families who once traded and frequently clashed with the Gwich'in of Alaska and the Yukon. Today both live together in a town which mixes modern and traditional, and whose inhabitants are proud not to have jumped ship when they were invited to leave their sinking town for Inuvik in the Fifties. Most are happy to regale you with stories of the "Mad Trapper of Rat River", a crazed drifter who reputedly killed trappers for the gold in their teeth. After allegedly shooting a Mountie, he grabbed world headlines briefly in 1931 as he managed to elude capture for forty days in the dead of a brutal winter. He was eventually shot on the Eagle River and is buried in town in unconsecrated ground. There's no restaurant and only one shop, but two places to **stay**: the *Daadzaii Lodge* (☎978-2252) and *Bessie's Boarding and Room Rentals* (☎978-2215), both with rooms from $75. **Flights** from Inuvik operate daily except Sunday ($60 single).

**TUKTOYAKTUK**, or simply Tuk (pop. 1000), sits on a sandspit on the Beaufort coast about 137km north of Inuvik, and acts as a springboard both for oil workers and for tourists, outsiders who have diluted the traditional ways of the whale-hunting Karngmalit (or Mackenzie Inuit). Most casual visitors come to see pods of beluga and great bowhead whales, or to look at the world's largest concentration of **pingoes**, 1400 volcano-like hills thrown up by frost heaves across the delta's otherwise treeless flats. Tuk's only **hotels**, the *Hotel Tuk Inn* (☎977-2381) and the *Pingo Park Lodge* (☎977-2155), both charge from $120 for rooms. **Flights** from Inuvik operate daily ($100 single).

**PAULATUK** (pop. 250), 400km east of Inuvik, is amongst the NWT's smallest permanent communities, and was started by the Roman Catholic Mission in 1935 as a communal focus for the semi-nomadic Karngmalit, who despite such paternalism have fought off the adverse effects of missionaries and trader-introduced alcoholism to hang on to some of their old ways. Hunting, fishing and trapping still provide their economic staples, along with handicrafts aimed at the tourists who are out here mainly for the chance to watch or hunt big game. The *Paulatuk Hotel* has **accommodation** for twelve people (☎580-3027) at $180 a room. **Flights** operate twice weekly from Inuvik ($230 single).

The only settlement on Bank's Island, **SACH'S HARBOUR** (pop. 150) supports a handful of self-sufficient Inuit families who survive largely by outfitting hunters and trapping musk-ox for food and underfur (*qiviut*), which is spun and woven into clothes on sale locally. About $175 gets you a **room** at the Icicle Inn (☎690-4444). There are two **flights** from Inuvik weekly (from $250 single).

# Sahtu

The **Sahtu** embraces the Mackenzie River south of its delta as far as Fort Norman and the tranche of land across to and including **Great Bear Lake** to the east, the world's eighth largest lake. There's no year-round road access: you either fly in here, canoe the Mackenzie – no mean feat – or sign up with fishing and hunting charters that boat or fly you into the backcountry. Most tours operate out of the area's nominal capital at **Norman Wells**, or its near neighbour **Fort Norman**, both on the Mackenzie in the lee of the Franklin Mountains, which separate the river and Great Bear Lake. The area has just three other lonely communities: **Fort Good Hope** on the Mackenzie north of Norman Wells; **Fort Franklin** on Great Bear Lake, a self-sufficient Dene community of hunters and trappers; and **Colville Lake**, north of Great Bear Lake, a spot which amounts to little more than a few log cabins in the woods.

*Canadian Airlines* fly daily to Norman Wells from Inuvik and Edmonton, and within the area *North-Wright Air* link all five communities from Norman Wells (☎587-2288). For general information on the area write to or call *Sahtu Tourism Association*, Box 115, Norman Wells, NWT (☎873-2122).

### Norman Wells and Fort Norman

**NORMAN WELLS** thrives on oil, first noticed as a yellow liquid seeping from the rocks by the explorer Alexander Mackenzie as early as 1789, but only exploited in 1919 after Dene natives had led geologists to the same spot. Production was boosted during World War II when the American government sponsored the building of the **Canol Pipeline** to supply the Alaska Highway – now long abandoned, though the town continues to pump about 30,000 barrels a day through a pipeline to Zama, Alberta. These days the Canol's old route is becoming an increasingly popular **long-distance footpath**, a tough 372-kilometre wilderness trail from Norman Wells to the Canol Road above Ross River (YT). The mountains east of town contain some of the NWT's bleaker and more spectacular ranges, but good outdoor skills are a must unless you sign up for a tour. If you want to spend time on the river, *Mountain River Outfitters* (☎587-2324) runs days trips to Fort Good Hope and the Arctic Circle (June 15–Sept 15) and also **rents canoes**. There are three **hotels** in town, each charging upwards of $90 for rooms: the *Mackenzie* (☎587-2511); the *Norman Wells Inn* (☎587-2744); and the *Rayuka Inn* (☎587-2354).

**FORT NORMAN**, some 60km to the south, owes its longer history to a strategic site at the junction of the Mackenzie and Great Bear rivers. Long a Dene native settlement, it's now an ethnically mixed community that looks to trapping and the oilfield for its livelihood. Most visitors use it to outfit canoe and boat trips downstream to Norman Wells, with the *Fort Norman Lodge* (☎588-4311; rooms $65) as a base; reservations are essential.

# Nahanni-Ram

The **Nahanni-Ram** area in the southwestern corner of the NWT centres on **Fort Simpson**, which is accessible by two long gravel roads: from the west, the **Liard Highway** follows the Liard Valley from close to Fort Nelson (BC) on the Alaska Highway; from the east the **Mackenzie Highway** follows the Mackenzie valley from close to Fort Providence and Hay River. Both roads offer drives through a fairly mundane wilderness of boreal forest and muskeg bog, and neither penetrates beyond Fort Simpson to offer ordinary travellers access to the **Nahanni National Park**, the area's jewel. **Air** access into the region is with *Simpson Air* (☎695-2505), who fly daily to Fort Simpson from Fort Smith, Fort Nelson (BC) and Fort St John (BC), and between the region's tiny outlying settlements at Nahanni Butte, Wrigley and Jean Marie River. For more information on the area write or call the *Nahaani-Ram Tourism Association*, Box 177, Fort Simpson (☎695-3182).

## Nahanni National Park and Fort Simpson

With gorges deeper than the Grand Canyon and waterfalls twice the height of Niagara, the **Nahanni National Park** ranks as one of the finest wilderness parks in North America. Located close to the Yukon border in the heart of the Mackenzie Mountains, it clasps around the **South Nahanni River**, a renowned 322-kilometre stretch of water whose whitewater torrents, pristine mountains and 1200-metre deep canyons have attracted the world's most eminent explorers and the ultimate thrill-seeking canoeists. Unless you fit one of these categories, however, or can afford to fork out for guided boat trips or sightseeing by air, there's no way of getting close to the best areas, even by backpacking.

All means of access and facilities for the park reside in **FORT SIMPSON**, 150km to the east, a spot inhabited for 9000 years by the Slavey native peoples and their ancestors – the longest continually inhabited region in the NWT. A fur post in 1804, and later a big staging point for boats heading down the Mackenzie, the place is now best known as the spot to **hire camping equipment** or book onto **tours and charter flights** to the interior. For sightseeing flights use *Deh Cho Air* (☎770-4103), and for canoe and raft rentals contact *North Nahaani Tours* (☎695-3601) or *Simpson Air* (☎695-2505), who can also arrange for canoe drop-offs within the park. Most of the town's other operators are into full-scale expeditions that run into thousands of dollars. For park information visit the **Information Centre** on Main St (July & Aug daily 8.30am–5pm; Sept–June Mon–Fri same hours) or contact the park superintendent (☎695-3151).

If you're hoping to **stay** in town be sure to book ahead for either the small *Maroda Motel* (☎695-2602; doubles from $80), or the larger *Nahanni Inn* (☎695-2201; rooms from $100).

# Big River

**Big River** covers the country stretching north from Alberta to the south shore of the Great Slave Lake, and embraces not one but several rivers, including large parts of the the Mackenzie and Slave watersheds, and several of the territories' most accessible towns. **Hay River**, near the head of the Mackenzie Highway from Alberta, is the area's hub and provides a gateway both to the **Great Slave Lake**, the third largest in North America, and to Fort Smith and the upper reaches of the mainly Albertan Wood Buffalo National Park (see p.406). Unless you're headed for the park, however, or are prepared to drive east to **Fort Resolution** to see one of the most southerly examples of living Dene culture, most of this region and its seemingly limitless ridges of boreal forest is not the most rewarding zone of the north. This said, just when it's not necessary, it's relatively easy to get around under your own steam: *Greyhound* **buses** run daily to ENTERPRISE just south of Hay River, where they connect three times weekly with *Arctic Frontier Carriers* (☎873-4892) buses to **Fort Providence** and Yellowknife, and with three weekly *North of 60* (☎874-6411) services to Fort Smith and Fort Resolution. For more information on the whole area contact the *Big River Tourism Association*, Box 185, Hay River (☎874-2422).

## Hay River

**HAY RIVER** (pop. 3000) is a typical no-nonsense northern town designed for practicalities rather than sightseeing self-indulgence. Long a strategic site, it's been inhabited for thousands of years by Slavey Dene natives attracted by its position on Great Slave Lake at the mouth of the Hay River. White settlers had put it on the map by 1854, but the inevitable Hudson's Bay trading post arrived only in 1868, and it wasn't until recently – with the completion of the Mackenzie Highway, oil and gas exploration, and the arrival of a railway to carry zinc ore from local mines – that the town became an important transportation centre. It's now also one of the most important **ports** in the north, shipping freight up the Mackenzie in huge barges to provide a precarious lifeline for High Arctic communities as far away as Inuvik and Tuktoyaktuk. If you're stuck in town, the best way to kill time is to wander the wharves where piles of supplies compete for space with tugs, barges, huge dredges and the town's big fishing fleet.

There's ample **accommodation** here, much of it a good deal cheaper than elsewhere in the north. Most reasonable is the *Cedar Rest Motel* (☎874-3732; doubles from $40) on the main road close to the bus terminal, followed by the *Migrator Motel* (☎874-6792; rooms from $55). The best if you want comfort after a long haul is downtown's *Ptarmigan Inn* (☎874-6781; doubles from $90).

# The Northern Frontier

The **Northern Frontier** is the broad sweep of lake-spotted barren land between the Great Slave and Great Bear lakes, and is largely the playground of canoeists and naturalists, or of hunters on the trail of the region's 400,000-strong caribou herd. At its heart lies **Yellowknife**, Canada's most northerly big town and for the time being also the capital of the NWT (see "Nunavut" box, p.595). Despite its surreal inappropriateness in a region of virtual wilderness, it's not worth making a special point to see – but you may have to see it anyway, as this is the main hub of transport throughout the territories. **Buses** run here from Edmonton via Hay River, and there are regular *Canadian* and *NWT Air* (*Air Canada*) **flights** from all major Canadian cities, as well as numerous smaller airline connections from most NWT destinations. For **information** on the region contact the *Northern Frontier Visitors Association*, Box 1107, Yellowknife (☎873-3131 or ☎1-800-661-0788).

## Yellowknife

Nothing about **YELLOWKNIFE** – named after the copper knives of the Slavey natives – can hide the fact that it's a city that shouldn't really be here. Its high-rise core of offices and government buildings exists to administer the NWT and support a workforce whose service needs keep a population of 14,000 occupied in a region whose resources should by rights support only a small town. Even the Hudson's Bay Company closed down their trading post here as early as 1823 on the grounds of economics, and except for traces of gold found by prospectors on the way to the Klondike in 1898, the spot was a forgotten backwater until the advent of commercial gold and uranium mining in the Thirties. This prompted the growth of the **Old Town** on an island and rocky peninsula on Great Slave Lake, and in turn of the **New Town** on the sandy plain behind it. In 1967 Yellowknife replaced Ottawa as the seat of government for the NWT, and oiled by bureaucratic profligacy ever since, the city has blossomed, if that's the word for so unprepossessing a place.

Visitors are steered carefully to quaint Old Town cabins such as the still-operating **Wildcat Café** (daily June–Sept) and a few battered buildings on the aptly named Ragged Ass Road, more or less the only memorials to the old ways – though if you venture to the outskirts you'll find native shanty settlements and scenes of poverty that take the lustre off the high-rises of the city centre. The **Northern Heritage Centre** (summer daily 9am–5pm; closed Mon in winter; free), three blocks off downtown on Frame Lake, peddles a more sanitised view of native culture, offering extensive displays of northern artefacts, Inuit carvings and persuasive dioramas of local wildlife and habitats. Shops around town also sell a variety of northern native crafts, all cheaper than you'll find in southerly cities, but still expensive if beautiful products of a living culture – even if it's not at its healthiest in the city itself.

Otherwise the only things to do close to town are to look round Canada's largest **gold mine** (details ☎873-6301), or drive out on the **Ingraham Trail**, an 81-kilometre highway that was to be the start of a major NWT "Road to Resources" but which was abandoned in the Sixties. There are plenty of boat launches, picnic sites and campgrounds en route, as well as short walking trails like the **Cameron River Falls** (48km from Yellowknife), and lakeside beaches where the hardier of the city's population brave the water.

### Practicalities

The **Yellowknife Tourist Information Cabin** is at 52nd St and 49th Ave (daily 10am–6pm mid-June to late Aug). **Hotels** in the city have plenty of rooms, but prices are high, and it can be worth looking up one of the dozen or so **bed and breakfasts** if you're on a tight budget: try the Old Town's *Arctic House B&B* near the *Wildcat Café* at 20 Hearne Hill Drive (☎873-6238), or the *Blue Raven B&B*, 37 Otto Drive (☎873-7259), both of which do half-board deals for around $60. The **YWCA** two blocks from downtown at 50004 54th St (☎920-2777) takes men and women and has doubles from $75. The *Twin Pine Motor Inn* (☎873-8511) on Franklin Ave between the Old Town and downtown is the cheapest of the hotels proper, with doubles from $90, but for something more salubrious you're looking at $130 and over for rooms in the top spots – the *Discovery Inn*, 4701 Franklin Ave (☎873-4151); the *Explorer*, 49th Ave-48th St (☎873-3531); and the *Yellowknife Inn*, 50th St-49th St (☎873-2601).

For **eating**, the *Lunchbox*, a basement cafeteria in the Yellowknife Centre Mall, is a cheap, plastic and popular place for office workers at breakfast and lunch. *Mr Mike's* downstairs in the Scotia Mall is big and busy, and has a good salad bar and plenty of steak and burger basics. Most of the hotels have good dining rooms, and much of the nightlife revolves around their lounges, notably the plush *Polaris Lounge* nightclub at the *Explorer* – though you'll meet more interesting types at the *Miner's Mess*, a cosmopolitan bar at the *Yellowknife Inn* downtown on Franklin Ave.

# Keewatin

The **Keewatin** stretches west from Hudson Bay into the great so-called "Barrenlands" of the NWT interior. Along with the arctic islands to the north it's likely to form the bulk of **Nunavut**, Canada's new territory, belated recognition for a region that contains the majority of NWT's indigenous Inuit. Most of the region's communities lie on the arc of Hudson Bay's western coast, from **Arviat** in the south through **Whale Cove**, **Rankin Inlet**, the area's main centre, to **Chesterfield** and **Coral Harbour** in the north. In all of these you will find an almost unchanged way of life – the local arts and handicrafts are outstanding, and in places you can hear the old drummers and "throat singers" traditionally responsible for handing down the stories and myths of the Inuit. **Baker Lake** is the Arctic's only inland Inuit community and marks both Canada's geographic centre and a way of getting into the **tundra** that characterises the vast proportion of the region. This is a subtle landscape that's worth more than its "Barrenland" label suggests, particularly in summer, when the thaw brings to life thousands of tiny streams and lakes, and some 300 species of wildflowers amidst the lichens and grasses that provide fodder for huge herds of musk-ox and caribou. Millions of wildfowl can also be seen, and the huge skies and flat horizons are also one of the best places in Canada to see the **aurora borealis** (see box overleaf).

For more **information** on the district contact *Travel Keewatin*, Dept Eg, Box 328, Rankin Inlet (☎645-2618). *First Air* (☎1-800-267-1st AIR) have direct **flights** to Rankin

---

### THE INUIT

"They be like to Tartars, with long blacke haire, broad faces, and flatte noses, and tawnie in colour, wearing Seale skinnes . . .The women are marked in the faces with blewe streakes downe the cheekes, and round about the eies".

An officer on Frobisher's 1576 search for the Northwest Passage

Distinct from all other Canadian natives by virtue of their culture, language and Asiatic physical features, the **Inuit** are the dominant people of a **territory** that extends all the way from northern Alaska to Greenland. Nowadays increasingly confined to reserves, they once led a **nomadic** existence in one of the most hostile environments on earth, dwelling in domed **igloos** during the winter and **skin tents** in the summer, and moving around using **kayaks** (*umiaks*) or **dog sleds** (*komatik*). The latter were examples of typical Inuit adaptability – the runners were sometimes made from frozen fish wrapped in sealskin, and in the absence of wood, caribou bones were used for crossbars.

Their prey – caribou, musk-ox, seals, walruses, narwhals, beluga whales, polar bears, birds and fish – provided oil for heating and cooking, hides for clothing and tents, harpoon lines, ivory and dog harnesses. Using harpoons, bows and arrows and spears, ingenious hunting methods were devised: to catch caribou, for example, huge **inuksuits**, piles of rocks that resembled the human form, were used to steer the herd into a line of armed hunters.

The Inuit **diet** was composed totally of flesh, and every part of the animal was eaten, usually raw, from eyeballs to the heart. Delicacies included the plaited and dried intestines of seals and whole sealskins stuffed with small birds and left to putrefy until the contents had turned to the consistency of cheese. All food was **shared** and the successful hunter had to watch his catch being distributed amongst other families in the group, in accordance with specific relationships, before his own kin were allowed the smallest portion. **Starvation** was common – it was not unusual for whole villages to perish in the winter – and consequently **infanticide**, particularly of females, was employed to keep population sizes down. Elderly people who could not keep up with the travelling group were abandoned, a fate that also befell some **offenders** against the social code, though the usual way of resolving conflict was the **song-duel**, whereby the aggrieved would publicly ridicule the behaviour of the other, who was expected to accept the insults with good grace.

Making **clothes**, most often of caribou hide, was a task assigned to **women** and was as essential to survival as a man's ability to hunt. Older women also **tattooed** the faces of the younger ones by threading a sinew darkened with soot through the face to make lines that radiated from the nose and mouth. Women were usually betrothed at birth and married at puberty, and both polygamy and polyandry were frequent – though female infanticide made it rare for a man to have more than two spouses.

Inlet from Yellowknife, and connecting services from Ottawa and Montréal via Iqualuit on Baffin Island. Within the area *Calm Air* (☎645-2746) fly scheduled services from Churchill in Manitoba to all the Keewatin villages. Outfitters and small charter firms in all the communities are available to fly or guide you into the interior or out into Hudson Bay for fishing and naturalist trips.

All the villages also have **hotels**, though they're mostly small and reservations are essential year-round. In **Rankin Inlet** there are three possibilities: the big *Siniktarvik Hotel* (☎819/645-2807) with doubles from $130, and the *Nanuq Inn* (☎819/645-2839) and *Keewatin Guest House* (☎819/645-2839), both with rooms from $100. At **Baker Lake** use the *Iglu Hotel* (☎819/793-2801) or *Baker Lake Lodge* (☎819/793-2965), both with doubles from $100. **Coral Harbour** has *Leonie's Place* (☎819/925-9751) and the *Esunquaq Motel* (☎819/925-9969), with doubles from $150. **Arviat** possesses only the *Padlei Inn* (☎819/857-2919), with rooms from $125.

Communion with supernatural spirits was maintained by a **shaman** or *angakok*, who was often a woman, and the deity who features most regularly in Inuit myth is a goddess called **Sedna**, who was mutilated by her father. Her severed fingers became seals and walruses and her hands became whales, while Sedna lived on as the mother and protector of all sea-life, capable of withholding her bounty if strict **taboos** were not adhered to. These taboos included keeping land and sea products totally separate – and so seals could never be eaten with caribou and all caribou clothing had to be made before the winter seal hunt.

Although sporadic **European contact** dates back to the Norse settlement of Greenland and some Inuit were visited by early missionaries, it wasn't until the early nineteenth century that the two cultures met in earnest. By 1860 commercial **whalers** had begun wintering around the north of Hudson Bay, employing Inuit as crew members and hunters for their food in return for European goods. Even then, the impact on the Inuit was not really deleterious until the arrival of **American whalers** in Canadian waters in 1890, when the liberal dispensing of alcohol and diseases such as smallpox and VD led to a drastic **decline in population**.

By the early decades of this century **fur traders** were encouraging the Inuit to stop hunting off the coast and turn inland using firearms and traps. The accompanying **missionaries** brought welcome medical help and schools, but put an end to multiple marriages, shamanism and other traditional practices. More changes came when Inuits were employed to build roads, airfields and other military facilities during World War II and to construct the line of radar installations known as Distant Early Warning during the Cold War era. As well as bringing **new jobs**, this also focused **government attention** on the plight of the Inuit.

The consequent largesse was not wholly beneficial: subsidised housing and welfare payments led many Inuit to abandon their hunting camps and settle in **permanent communities**, usually located in places strategic to Canada's sovereignty in the Arctic. Without knowledge of the English and French languages, these Inuit were left out of all decision-making and often lived in a totally separate part of towns that were administered by outsiders. Old values and beliefs were all but eroded by television and radio, and high levels of depression, alcoholism and violence became the norm. The 1982 ban on European imports of sealskins created mass **unemployment**, and although hunting still provides the basics of subsistence, the high cost of ammunition and fuel makes commercial-scale hunting uneconomical.

All is not gloom, however. Inuit cooperatives are increasingly successful and the production of **soapstone carvings** – admittedly a commercial adulteration of traditional Inuit ivory art – is very profitable. Having organised themselves into politically active groups and secured such **land claims** as Nunavut, the Inuit are slowly rebuilding an ancient culture that was shattered in under half a century.

The **aurora borealis**, or "Northern Lights", is a beautiful and ethereal display of light in the upper atmosphere that can be seen over large parts of northern Canada. The night sky appears to shimmer with dancing curtains of colour, ranging from luminescent monotones – most commonly green or a dark red – to fantastic veils that run the full spectrum. The display becomes more animated as it proceeds, twisting and turning in patterns called "rayed bands", and as a finale a corona sometimes appears in which rays seem to flare in all directions from a central point.

Named after the Roman goddess of dawn, the aurora was long thought to be produced by sunlight reflected from polar snow and ice, or refracted light produced in the manner of a rainbow. Research still continues into the phenomenon, but it seems the aurora is caused by **radiation** emitted as light from atoms in the upper atmosphere as they are hit by fast-moving electrons and protons. The earth's geomagnetic field certainly plays some part in the creation of the aurora, but its source would appear to lie with the **sun** – auroras become more distinct and are seen spread over a larger area two days after intense solar activity, the time it takes the "solar wind" to arrive.

You should see the northern lights as far south as Prince George in British Columbia, and over much of the Northwest Territories and northern Manitoba. They are at their most dazzling from **December to March** when nights are longest and the sky darkest, though they are potentially visible year-round.

# The Arctic Coast

Canada's last frontier, the **Arctic Coast** encompasses the country's northern mainland coast from the Mackenzie to Baffin Island and – as "coast" is a relative term in a region where the sea is often frozen – numerous islands too, most notably Victoria and King William Island. This region is home to **Inuit** who as recently as fifty years ago had known little or no contact with the outside world. Few explorers ever encountered them, and even the most determined of western agencies – the church and the trading companies – failed to compromise a people who are still extraordinarily isolated by climate, distance and culture. Today, however, few of the native Inuit live according to the ways of popular myth. Except on the odd trapping party, for example, igloos have been replaced by government-built homes, and the bone tools, sledges and kayaks of a generation ago have been superseded by rifles, snow bikes and light aircraft.

You still have to be fairly determined, however, to reach any of the region's **eight communities** (five on the coast, three on islands), let alone explore the hauntingly beautiful icefields and tundra. People up here are usually looking to spot wildlife, fish, or, more dubiously, to hunt for musk-ox, caribou and – shamefully – for polar bears, a practice the government defends by claiming "it's done the Inuit way, using dog teams, on a demanding safari over land and sea ice". Most visitors base themselves either at **Coppermine**, or at Victoria Island's **Cambridge Bay**, the transport and service capital.

The region's main **tourist office** is the *Arctic Coast Tourism Association*, Box 91, Cambridge Bay (☎983-2224). Cambridge Bay is served by *Canadian Airlines* scheduled **flights** from Calgary and Edmonton, along with *Aklak Air* (☎979-3777) from Inuvik and Delta-Beaufort towns and *First Air* (☎873-6884) from Yellowknife and Baffin Island. Within the Arctic Coast area itself, *First Air* fly between all the settlements except Bathurst Inlet and Umingmaktok, which can be reached by charter aircraft only.

Each community, remarkably, has **accommodation**, but reservations are vital and prices steep. At **Cambridge Bay** there's the *Ikaluktutiak Hotel* (☎983-2215), where rooms cost from $130, and meals – which you're almost bound to have to buy – around

$50 a head. The smaller *Enokhok Inn* (☎983-2444) offers almost identical rates, but provides deals on longer stays. At **Coppermine**, the *Coppermine Inn* (☎982-3333) is the sole option with just eleven rooms at $120 a time. One of the most northerly communities, **Holman**, across Victoria Island from Cambridge Bay, has the *Arctic Char Inn* (☎396-3501), whose eight rooms start at $120.

# Baffin Island

Baffin Island comprises half a million square kilometres of arctic vastness, whose main attraction is **Auyuittuq National Park** on the Cumberland Peninsula, Canada's northernmost accessible national park. With a treeless landscape, mountains towering over 5000 feet, icy glacial streams and 24-hour daylight from May to July, hiking in Auyuittuq offers one of the most majestic experiences in Canada. However, with temperatures rising to a mere 6°C from June to August, it's a brutal environment that will appeal only to the truly adventurous; expensive though they are, package tours are definitely recommended if this is your first venture into such a forbidding place. Be sure to bring all necessary gear with you, as the island supplies arrive just once a year.

## THE NORTHWEST PASSAGE

Traversed in its entirety fewer than fifty times, the fabled **Northwest Passage** around the American continent exerts a continuing romantic allure – and, in the wake of oil discoveries in the far north, an increasingly economic attraction too. The world's severest maritime challenge, it involves a 1500-kilometre traverse from north of Baffin Island to the Beaufort Sea above Alaska. Some 50,000 icebergs constantly line the eastern approaches and thick pack ice covers the route for nine months of the year, with temperatures rising above freezing only in July and August. Perpetual darkness reigns for four months of the year, and thick fog and blizzards can obscure visibility for the remaining eight months. Even with modern technology navigation is almost impossible: the magnetic compass is useless as the magnetic north lies in the passage, and the gyro compass is unreliable at high latitudes; little is know of arctic tides and currents; sonar is confused by submerged ice; and the featureless tundra of the arctic islands provide few points of visual or radar reference.

**John Cabot** can hardly have been happy with his order from Henry VII in **1497** to blaze the northwest trail, the first recorded instance of such an attempt. The elusive passage subsequently excited the imagination of the world's greatest adventurers, men such as Sir Francis Drake, Jacques Cartier, Sir Martin Frobisher, James Cook and **Henry Hudson** – cast adrift by his mutinous crew in 1611 when the Hudson Bay turned out to be an icebound trap rather than the passage.

Details of a possible route were pieced together over the centuries, though many paid with their lives in the process, most famously **Sir John Franklin**, who vanished into the ice with 129 men in 1845. Many rescue parties set out to find Franklin's vessels, *HMS Erebus* and *HMS Terror*, and it was one searcher, **Robert McClure**, who – in the broadest sense – made the first northwest passage in 1854. Entering the passage from the west, he was trapped for two winters, and then sledged to meet a rescue boat coming from the east. The **first sea crossing**, however, was achieved by the Norwegian **Roald Amundsen**, his success in 1906 coming after a three-year voyage. The first single-season traverse was made by a Canadian Mountie, **Henry Larsen**, in 1944 – his schooner, the *St Roch*, is now enshrined in Vancouver's Maritime Museum. More recently huge icebreakers have explored the potential of cracking a commercial route through the ice mainly for the export of oil from the Alaskan and new Beaufort finds and for the exploitation of minerals in Canada's arctic north.

The main gateway to Baffin Island is **Iqaluit** (formerly Frobisher Bay), whose population of 3300 is dominated by Inuits, many of whom exist on welfare payments since the 1982 Greenpeace campaign against seal products wiped out the basis of their export economy.

## Practicalities

**Getting to Baffin Island** is only feasible by **air**. *First Air/Bradley Air Service* (☎1- 800-267-1247 or ☎613/839-3340) and *Canadian Airlines* (☎1-800-665-1430 or ☎819/979-5331) make the trip from Montréal (1–2 daily; 3hr) and from Ottawa (4 weekly; 4hr). Ticket prices can get as low as $400 return, but are usually in the region of $700. *First Air* and *Northwest Territorial Airways* (☎403/920-2500) also link Yellowknife to Iqaluit (5 weekly; 3hr 50min) for around $650 return.

Within the island, there is a daily one-hour *First Air* flight during the summer from Iqaluit to **Pangnirtung**, the gateway to Auyuittuq National Park, which costs $238 for a return. There are also scheduled flights to the various small communities and chartered sightseeing flights: contact *Air Baffin* (☎819/979-4018) for details.

*INFORMATION*
Useful information on outfitters, guides and accommodation can be obtained from *The Baffin Island Tourism Association*, Iqaluit, NWT (☎819/979-6551). However, hiking maps should be bought in advance from *The Canada Map Office*, 615 Booth St, Ottawa, Ontario K1A 0E9. Information on the Auyuittuq park is available from Auyuittuq National Park Reserve, Pangnirtung, NWT XOA 0R0 (☎819/473-8828).

*ACCOMMODATION*
In summer the Inuit families of **Iqaluit** abandon their homes in favour of tents, and your best accommodation option is to join them – there are no fixed campgrounds. Iqaluit's four **motels** charge in the region of $150 for a double: *The Navigator* (☎819/979-6201); *Discovery Lodge* (☎819/979-4433); *Frobisher Inn* (☎819/979-5241); and *Bayshore Inn* (☎819/979-6733). In **Pangnirtung** there is an established free campground, *Pisuktinee Tungavik*, and a church which will let you sleep on the floor for a donation if you are desperate. The only commercial accommodation is the *Auyuittuq Lodge* with doubles for $220 (☎819/473 8955). The lodge has good but expensive meals and they allow exhausted hikers to use their showers for $10 or so.

---

### SPECIALIST OPERATORS

**Adventure Canada**, Worldwide Adventures, 1159 West Broadway Ave, Vancouver (☎604/736-7447). Five- to seven-day dogsled ventures during May and June.

**Adventure Playground Tours**, 130 Albert St, Ottawa (☎613/238-2058). Weekend trips from Ottawa during July and August.

**Blackfeather Wilderness Adventures**, 1341 Wellington St West, Ottawa (☎613/722- 9717). Two weeks in Auyuittuq National Park in July. $2495 all inclusive from Ottawa.

**Canada North Outfitting Inc**, Box 1300, 87 Mills St, Almonte, Ontario (☎613/256-4057). Ten-day trips around Baffin from Ottawa in August from $5765. Backpacking trips in Auyuittuq National Park for eleven days in July, from $1965, all inclusive from Ottawa.

**Goligers**, Box 478, Iqaluit, NWT (☎819/979-5338). Individual tours around Baffin.

**Sobek Expeditions Inc**, 159 Main St, Unionville, Ontario (☎416/479-2600). Six- to eighteen-day tours by sea-kayak, voyageur canoe or tandem canoe.

## Auyuittuq National Park Reserve

Straddling the Arctic Circle in the northeast of Baffin Island, **Auyuittuq National Park Reserve** is one of the most spectacular destinations in the Canadian north. The heart of the park is the massive **Penney Ice Cap**, a remnant of the ice sheet which extended over most of Canada east of the Rockies about 18,000 years ago, and the major **hiking route** is the 110-kilometre Pangnirtung/Aksayuk Pass, which cuts through the mountains between Cumberland Sound and the Davis Strait. Auyuittuq is Inuit for "the land that never melts", but despite the unrelenting cold there is abundant life here: in summer the sparse tundra plants burst into green and the wildflowers are blooming, and the amazing array of wildlife includes lemmings, polar bears, caribou, arctic hares and foxes, snow geese, peregrines, narwhals, walruses, bowhead and beluga whales, as well as harp, ringed and bearded seals.

The only transport for the 25km from Pangnirtung to the south entrance of the park is by **freighter canoe**, which the Inuit also charter for fishing, whale-watching and sightseeing trips. The rates on these "canoes" – which are like small fishing boats with outboard motors – are set by the Inuit cooperative, and work out at $90 for two people one way, plus $25 for each additional person. The boats can only pass through the Pangnirtung Fjord after the ice break-up in July – at other times you have to walk. Arrangements for a canoe pick-up should be possible by radio from the few emergency shelters in the park, but be warned that last summer all the batteries were stolen, so you may have to arrange your pick-up before being dropped off.

Services within the park are extremely limited and the weather is highly unpredictable. Snowstorms, high wind and rain occur frequently, and deaths from hypothermia have been known even in the height of summer. All-weather hiking gear is essential, and a walking stick or ski pole is required to assist you with the ice-cold stream crossings that occur every 200–300 metres and which are can still be waist-high in July. There is no wood for fuel as the park is located miles north of the treeline, so a camping stove is also essential.

## travel details

### Trains

**From Prince George** to Vancouver (June 15–Oct 1 daily; rest of year 3 weekly; 13hr 30min); Prince Rupert (3 weekly; 13hr); Edmonton via Jasper (3 weekly; 8hr 15min).

### Buses

**From Prince George** to Prince Rupert (2 daily; 11hr); Edmonton via Jasper (2 daily; 9hr 45min); Dawson Creek (2 daily; 6hr 30min); Vancouver via Williams Lake and Cache Creek (2 daily; 13hr).

**From Dawson Creek** to Prince George (2 daily; 6hr 30min); Edmonton (2 daily; 9hr); Whitehorse (mid-May to mid-Oct 1 daily except Sun; rest of year 3 weekly; 21hr).

**From Whitehorse** to Dawson Creek (mid-May to mid-Oct 1 daily except Sun; rest of year 3 weekly; 21hr); Dawson City (June–Sept 3 weekly; Oct & March–June 2 weekly; rest of year 1 weekly; 7hr 30min); Skagway (mid-May to mid-June 1 daily except Wed & Sun; 4hr).

**From Dawson City** to Whitehorse (June–Sept 3 weekly; Oct & March–June 2 weekly; rest of year 1 weekly; 7hr 30min); Inuvik (mid-June to early Sept 2–3 weekly; 12hr).

**From Hay River** to Yellowknife (3 weekly; 12hr); Fort Smith (weekdays; 7hr); Fort Resolution (3 weekly; 6hr); Peace River (daily except Mon; connections for Edmonton and Grande Prairie; 8hr).

### Flights

*Listed below are only the main direct scheduled flights operated by the big carriers; for details on the vast range of small provincial companies operating within the north, see the town entries in the guide.*

**To Whitehorse** from Vancouver (3 daily; 2hr 20min).

**To Yellowknife** from Edmonton (3 daily; 1hr 35min); Inuvik (1 daily; 2hr 35min); Fort Smith (1 daily; 1hr 30min); Norman Wells (1 daily; 1hr 15min); Resolute (2 weekly; 3hr 20min); Cambridge Bay (1 weekly; 1hr 30min).

**To Inuvik** from Yellowknife (1 daily; 2hr 35min).

**To Iqaluit** from Montréal (1–2 daily; 3hr); Ottawa (4 weekly; 4hr); Yellowknife (5 weekly; 3hr 50min).

# PART THREE
## THE
# CONTEXTS

# THE HISTORICAL FRAMEWORK

Fully unified only since 1949, and now facing disintegration in the face of Québec's impulse towards independence, Canada is a country of intertwining histories rather than a single national evolution. Not only does each of its provinces maintain a high degree of autonomy, but each grouping of native peoples can claim a heritage that cannot be fully integrated into the story of white Canada. Therefore, what follows can do no more than trace the outline of a subject that can be pursued more thoroughly through some of the books recommended later.

## THE BEGINNINGS

The ancestors of the **native peoples** of North America first entered the continent around **twenty-five thousand years** ago, when vast glaciers covered most of the northern continents, keeping the sea level far beneath that of today. It seems likely that the continent's first human inhabitants crossed the land bridge linking Asia with present-day Alaska – they were probably Siberian hunter-nomads travelling in pursuit of mammoths, hairy rhinos, bison, wild horses and sloths, the ice-age animals that made up their diet. These people left very little to mark their passing, apart from some simple graves and the grooved, chipped stone spearheads which earnt them the name **Fluted Point People**. In successive waves the Fluted Point People moved down through North America, across the isthmus of Panama, until they reached the southernmost tip of South America. As they settled, so they slowly developed distinctive cultures and languages, whose degree of elaboration depended on the resources of their environment.

About **five thousand years** ago another wave of migration passed over from Asia to North America. This wave was made up of the first group of **Inuit** migrants who – because the sea level had risen and submerged the land bridge under the waters of today's Bering Strait – made their crossings either in skin-covered boats or on foot over the winter ice. Within the next thousand years the Inuit occupied the entire northern zone of the continent, moving east as far as Greenland and displacing the earlier occupants. These first Inuits – called the **Dorset Culture** after Cape Dorset in NWT, where archaeologists first identified its remains in the 1920s – were assimilated or wiped out by the next wave of Inuit, who, crossing into the continent three thousand years ago, created the **Thule** culture – so-called after the Greek word for the world's northern extremity. The Thule people were the direct ancestors of today's Inuit.

## THE NATIVE PEOPLES

Before the Europeans arrived, the native peoples – numbering around 300,000 – were divided into three main language groups, Algonquian, Athapascan (principally in the North and West) and Inuktitut (Inuit). Within these groups existed a multitude of cultures. None of these people had a written language, the wheel was unknown to them and their largest draught animal, prior to the introduction of the horse, was the dog. However, over the centuries, each of the tribes developed techniques that enabled them to cope with the problems of survival posed by their environments.

### THE NORTHERN PEOPLES

Immediately prior to the arrival of the Europeans, Canada was divided into a number of cultural zones. In the extreme north lived the nomadic **Inuit** (see. p.602), whose basic unit was the family group, small enough to survive in the precarious conditions. The necessarily small-scale nature of Inuit life meant that they developed no political structures and gathered together in larger groups only if the supply of food required it – when, for example, the Arctic char were running upriver from the sea to spawn, or the caribou were migrating.

Immediately to the south of the Inuit, in a zone stretching from the Labrador coast across the Canadian Shield to northern British Columbia, lived the tribes of the **northern forests**. This was a harsh environment too, and consequently these peoples spent most of their time in small nomadic bands following the game on which they depended. Indeed, variations between the tribes largely resulted from the type of game they pursued: the **Naskapi** fished and hunted seals on the Labrador coast; the **Chipewyan**, occupying the border country between the tundra and forest to the west of Hudson Bay, mainly hunted caribou; the **Wood Cree**, to the south of the Chipewyan, along the Churchill River, hunted deer and moose; and the **Tahltan** of British Columbia combined hunting with seasonal fishing. Like the Inuit, the political structures of these tribes were rudimentary and, although older men enjoyed a certain respect, there were no "chiefs" in any European sense of the term. In fact, decisions were generally made collectively with the opinions of successful hunters – the guarantors of survival – carrying great weight, as did those of their shaman, whose main function was to satisfy the spirits that they believed inhabited every animate and inanimate object around them.

### THE IROQUOIS

The southern zone of Canada, stretching from the St Lawrence along the northern shores of the Great Lakes to southern British Columbia was climatically much kinder, and it's in this region that Canada's native peoples developed their most sophisticated cultures. Here, along the banks of the St Lawrence and the shores of the Great Lakes, lived the **Iroquois-speaking** peoples, divided into three tribal confederacies: the **Five Nations**, the **Huron** (see p.263) and the **Neutrals**. All three groups cultivated maize, beans and squash in an agricultural system that enabled them to lead a settled life – often in communities of several hundreds. Iroquois society was divided into matriarchal clans, whose affairs would be governed by a female elder. The clan shared a longhouse and when a man married (always outside of his own clan), he would go to live in the longhouse of

his wife. Tribal chiefs (*sachems*) were male, but they were selected by the female elders of the tribe and they also had to belong to a lineage through which the rank of sachem descended. Once selected a Sachem had to have his rank confirmed by the federal council of the inter-tribal league: in the case of the Five Nations this consisted of *sachems* from the Seneca, Cayuga, Onondaga, Onieda and Mohawk tribes. Iroquoian society had its nastier side too. An assured winter supply of food enabled the Iroquois to indulge in protracted inter-tribal warfare: in particular, the Five Nations were almost always at war with the Hurons.

### THE OJIBWA AND BLACKFOOT PEOPLES

To the west of the Iroquois, between lakes Superior and Winnipeg, lived the **Ojibwa**, forest hunters who learned to cultivate maize from the Iroquois. and also harvested the wild rice that grew on the fringes of the region's lakes. Further west still, on the prairies, lived the peoples of the **Blackfoot Confederation**: the **Piegan**, **Blackfoot** and **Blood** tribes. The economy of this grouping was based on the bison: its flesh was eaten; its hide provided clothes and shelter; its bones were made into tools; its sinews provided bow strings; and its hooves were melted down to provide glue. In the late seventeenth century, the hunting techniques of these prairie peoples were transformed by the arrival of the horse, which had made its way – either wild or by trade – from Mexico, where it had been introduced by the Spanish conquistadors. The horse made the bison easy prey and, as with the Iroquois, a ready food supply spawned the development of a militaristic culture centred on the prowess of the tribes' young braves.

### THE PACIFIC PEOPLES

On the **Pacific coast**, tribes such as the **Tlingit** and **Salish** were dependent on the ocean, which provided them with a plentiful supply of food. There was little cohesion within tribes and people from different villages – even though of the same tribe – would at times be in conflict with each other. Yet these had a rich ceremonial and cultural life, as exemplified by the excellence of their wood-carvings, whose most conspicuous manifestations were the totem poles, which reached colossal sizes in the nineteenth century.

## THE COMING OF THE EUROPEANS

The first recorded contact between Europeans and the native peoples of North America occurred in 1000 AD, when a **Norse** expedition sailing from Greenland landed somewhere on the Atlantic seaboard. It was a fairly short-lived stay – according to the Icelandic sagas, the Norse were forced by the hostility of the aboriginals to abandon the colonies in the area they called Vinland.

In 1492 Ferdinand and Isabella of Spain were finally persuaded to underwrite **Christopher Columbus**'s expedition in search of the westward route to Asia. Columbus bumped into the West Indies instead, but his "discovery" of islands that were presumed to lie off India encouraged other European monarchs to sponsor expeditions of their own. In 1497 **John Cabot**, supported by the English king Henry VII, sailed west and sighted Newfoundland and Cape Breton. On his return, Cabot reported seeing multitudes of cod off Newfoundland and his comments effectively started the **Newfoundland** cod fishery. In less than sixty years up to four hundred **fishing** vessels, from Britain, France and Spain, were making annual voyages to the Grand Banks fishing grounds around the island. Soon some of the fishermen established shore bases to cure their catch in the sun, and, when they started to over-winter here, the settlement of the island began. By the end of the sixteenth century the cod trade was largely controlled by the British and French, and Newfoundland became an early cockpit of English-French rivalries, a colonial conflict that continued until England secured control of the island in the 1713 Treaty of Utrecht.

## NEW FRANCE

Meanwhile, in 1535 **Jacques Cartier**, on a voyage paid for by the French crown, made his way down the St Lawrence, also hoping to find Asia. Instead he stumbled upon the Iroquois, first at Stadacona, on the site of Québec, and later at Hochelaga, today's Montréal. At both places the Frenchman had a friendly reception, but the Iroquois attitude changed after Cartier seized one of their *sachems* and took him to France. For a time the Iroquois were a barrier to further exploration up the St Lawrence, but subsequently they abandoned their riverside villages, enabling French traders to move up the river buying **furs**, an enterprise pioneered by seasonal fishermen.

The development of this trade aroused the interest of the French king, who in 1603 commissioned **Samuel de Champlain** to chart the St Lawrence. Two years later Champlain founded **Port Royal** in today's Nova Scotia, which became the capital of **Acadie** (Acadia), a colony whose agricultural preoccupations were soon far removed from the main thrust of French colonialism along the St Lawrence. It was here, on a subsequent expedition in 1608, that Champlain established the settlement of Québec at the heart of **New France**, and, to stimulate the fur trade, allied the French with those tribes he identified as likely to be his principal suppliers. In practice this meant siding with the Huron against the Five Nations, a decision that intensified their traditional hostility. Furthermore, the fur trade destroyed the balance of power between the tribes: first one and then another would receive, in return for their pelts, the latest type of musket as well as iron axes and knives, forcing enemies back to the fur trade to redress the military balance. One terrible consequence of such European intervention was the **extermination of the Huron people** in 1648 by the Five Nations, armed by the Dutch merchants of the Hudson River.

As pandemonium reigned among the native peoples, the pattern of life in **New France** was becoming well established. On the farmlands of the St Lawrence a New World feudalism was practised by the land-owning seigneurs and their *habitant* tenants, while the fur territories – entered at Montréal – were spreading into the interior. Many of the fur traders adopted native dress, learnt aboriginal languages, and took wives from the tribes through which they passed, bringing into existence the mixed-race people known as the **Metis**. The furs they brought back to Montréal were shipped down river to Québec whence they were shipped to France. But a consequence of the domination of the labour-extensive fur trade was that the white population in the French colony remained relatively small – there were only 18,000 New French in 1713. In the context of a growing British presence, it represented a dangerous weakness.

## THE RISE OF THE BRITISH

In 1670 Charles II of England had established the **Hudson's Bay Company** and given it control of a million and a half square miles adjacent to the Bay, a territory called Rupert's Land, after the king's uncle. Four years later the British captured the Dutch possessions of the Hudson River Valley: thus New France was trapped. Slowly the British closed the net: in 1713, they took control of Acadia, renaming it Nova Scotia (New Scotland), and in 1755 they deported its French-speaking farmers. When the Seven Years' War broke out in 1758 the French attempted to outflank the British by using the Great Lakes route to occupy the area to the west of the British colonies and then, with the help of their native allies, pin them to the coast. In the event the British won the war by exploiting their naval superiority. A large force under the command of **General Wolfe** sailed up the St Lawrence and, against all expectations, successfully scaled the Heights of Abraham, to capture Québec city. Montréal was captured later on in 1760 – at that point the French North American empire was finished.

For the native peoples the ending of the Anglo-French conflict was a mixed blessing. If the war had turned the tribes into sought-after allies, it had also destroyed the traditional inter-tribal balance of power and subordinated native to European interests. A recognition of the change wrought by the end of the war inspired the uprising of the Ottawas in 1763, when **Pontiac**, their chief, led an unsuccessful assault on Detroit, hoping to restore the French position and halt the progress of the English settlers.

Moved largely by a desire for a stable economy, the response of the British Crown was to issue a proclamation which confirmed the legal right of the natives to their lands and set aside the territory to the west of the Appalachian Mountains and the Great Lakes as "**Indian Territory**". Although colonial governors were given instructions to remove trespassers on "Indian Land", in reality the proclamation had little practical effect until the twentieth century, when it became a cornerstone of the native peoples' attempts to seek compensation for the illegal confiscation of their land.

The other great problem the British faced in the 1760s was how to deal with the French-speaking **Canadiens** of the defunct New France – the term *Canadiens* used to distinguish local settlers from those born in France, most of whom left the colony after the British conquest. Initially the British government hoped to anglicise the province, swamping the French-speaking population with English-speaking Protestants. In the event large-scale migration failed to materialise immediately, and the second English governor of Québec, **Sir Guy Carleton**, realised that – as discontent grew in the American colonies – the loyalty of the *Canadiens* was of vital importance.

Carleton's plan to achieve this was embodied in the 1774 **Quebec Act**, which made a number of concessions to the region's French speakers: Catholics were permitted to hold civil appointments; the seigneurial system was maintained; and the Roman Catholic Church allowed to collect tithes. Remarkably, all these concessions were made at a time when Catholics in Britain were not politically emancipated.

## THE MIGRATIONS

The success of this policy was seen during the **American War of Independence** and the Anglo-American War of 1812: the *Canadiens* refused to volunteer for the armed forces of the Crown, but equally they failed to respond to the appeals of the Americans – no doubt calculating that their survival as a distinctive cultural group was more likely under the British than in an English-speaking United States.

In the immediate aftermath of the American War of Independence, the population of what was left of British North America expanded rapidly, both in "Canada" – which then covered the present-day provinces of Québec and Ontario – and in the separate colonies of New Brunswick, Nova Scotia, Prince Edward Island and Newfoundland. The first large wave of migration came from the United States as 40,000 **United Empire Loyalists** made their way north to stay within British jurisdiction. Of these, all but 8000 moved to Nova Scotia and New Brunswick, the rest going to the western edge of Québec, where they laid the foundations of the future province of Ontario. Between 1783 and 1812 the population of Canada, as defined at the time, trebled to 330,000, with a large part of the increase being the product of *revanche du berceau* (revenge of the cradle) – an attempt, encouraged by the Catholic clergy, to out-breed the ever increasing English-speaking population.

However, tensions between Britain and the United States still deterred potential colonists, a problem resolved by the **War of 1812**. Neither side was strong enough to win, but by the Treaty of Ghent in 1814, the Americans recognised the legitimacy of British North America, whose border was established along the **49th parallel** west from Lake of the Woods to the Rockies. Immigration now boomed, especially in the 1840s, when economic crises and shortages in Great Britain, including the Irish famine, pushed it up to levels that not even the fertile *Canadiens* could match. Between 1815 and 1850 800,000 immigrants entered British North America, with most heading for "Upper Canada", later Ontario, which received 66,000 in the single year of 1832.

Frenetically the surveyors charted new townships, but could not keep pace with demand. The result was that many native peoples were dispossessed in direct contravention of the 1763 proclamation. By 1806 the region's native peoples had lost 4.5 million acres.

## THE DIVISION AND UNION OF CANADA

During this period economic expansion was principally generated by the English-speaking merchants who now controlled the Montréal-based fur trade, organised as the **North-West Company**. Seeking political changes that would enhance their economic power, they wanted their own legislative assembly and the universal application of English law, which of course would not have been acceptable to the French-speakers.

In 1791, through the **Canada Act**, the British government imposed a compromise, dividing the region into **Upper** and **Lower Canada**, which broadly separated the ethnic groups along the line of the Ottawa River. In Lower Canada, the French-based legal system was retained, as was the right of the Catholic Church to collect tithes, while in Upper Canada, English common law was introduced. Each of the new provinces had an elective assembly, though these shared their limited powers with an appointed assembly, whilst the executive council of each province was responsible to the appointed governor, not the elected assembly.

This arrangement allowed the assemblies to become the focal points for vocal opposition, but ultimately condemned them to impotence. At the same time, the plutocrats built up chains of influence and power around the appointed provincial governments: in Upper Canada this grouping was called the "**Family Compact**", in Lower Canada the "**Château Clique**".

By the late 1830s considerable opposition had developed to these cliques. In Upper Canada the **Reform Movement** led by **William Lyon Mackenzie** demanded a government accountable to a broad electorate, and the expansion of credit facilities for small farmers. In 1837, both Mackenzie and **Louis-Joseph Papineau**, the reform leader in Lower Canada, were sufficiently frustrated to attempt open rebellion. Neither was successful and both were forced into exile in the United States, but the rebellions did bring home to the British Government the need for effective reform, prompting the **Act of Union** of 1840, which united Lower and Upper Canada with a single assembly.

The rationale for this arrangement was the racist belief that the French-Canadians were incapable of handling elective government without Anglo-Saxon guidance. Nevertheless, the assembly provided equal representation for Canada East and West – in effect the old Lower and Upper Canadas. A few years later, this new assembly achieved **responsible government** almost accidentally. In 1849, the Reform Party, who had a majority of the seats, passed an Act compensating those involved in the 1837 rebellions. The Governor-General, Lord Elgin, disapproved, but he didn't exercise his veto – so, for the first time, a Canadian administration acted on the vote of an elected assembly, rather than imperial sanction.

The Reform Party, who pushed through the compensation scheme, included both French- and English-speakers and mainly represented small farmers and businessmen opposed to the power of the cliques. In the 1850s it became the Canadian **Liberal Party**, but this French-English coalition fell apart with the emergence of "Clear Grit" Liberals in Canada West in the 1860s. This group argued for "Representation by Population" – in other words, instead of equal representation for the two halves of Canada, they wanted constituencies based on the total population. As the English-speakers outnumbered the French, the "Rep by Poppers" rhetoric seemed a direct threat to many of the institutions of French Canada. As a consequence many French-Canadians transferred their support to the **Conservative Party**, while the radicals of Canada East, the **Rouges**, developed a nationalist creed.

The Conservative Party represented the fusion of a number of elements, including the rump of the business cliques who had been so infuriated by their loss of control that they burnt the Montréal parliament building to the ground in 1849. Some of this group campaigned to break the imperial tie and join the United States, but, when the party fully emerged in 1854, the old "Compact Tories" were much less influential than a younger generation of moderate conservatives, like **John A. Macdonald**. Such moderates sought, by overcoming the democratic excesses of the "Grits" and the nationalism of the "Rouges", to weld together an economic and political state that would not be absorbed by the increasingly powerful United States.

## CONFEDERATION

In the mid-1860s "Canada" had achieved responsible party government, but British North America was still a collection of **self-governing colonies**. In the east, Newfoundland was almost entirely dependent on its cod fishery; Prince Edward Island had a prosperous agricultural economy, and both Nova Scotia and New Brunswick had boomed on the backs of the shipbuilding industry. Far to the west, on the Pacific coast, lay fur-trading British Columbia, which had just beaten off American attempts to annex the region during the Oregon crisis, finally resolved in 1846, when the international frontier was fixed along a westward extension of the original 49th parallel. Not that this was the end of British Columbia's problems: in 1858 gold was discovered beside the Fraser River and, in response to the influx of American prospectors, British Columbia was hastily designated a Crown Colony – a process that was repeated in 1895 when gold was discovered in the Yukon's Klondike. Between Canada West and British Columbia stretched thousands of miles of prairie and forest, the old Rupert's Land that was still under the extremely loose authority of the Hudson's Bay Company.

The American Civil War raised fears of a US invasion of the incoherently structured British North America, at the same time as "Rep by Poppers" agitations were making problematic the status of the French-speaking minority. These issues prompted a series of conferences to discuss the issue of **Confederation**, and after three years of debate the British Parliament passed the British North America Act of 1867. In effect this was a constitution for the new **Dominion of Canada**, providing for a federal parliament to be established at Ottawa; for Canada East and West to become the provinces of Québec and Ontario respectively; and for each province to retain a regional government and assembly. All of the existing colonies joined the Confederation except British Columbia, which waited until 1871, Prince Edward Island, till 1873, and Newfoundland, which remained independent until 1949.

## THE CONSOLIDATION OF THE WEST

Having apparently settled the question of a constitution, the Dominion turned its attention to the west. In 1869, the territory of the Hudson's Bay Company was bought for £300,000; the **North-West Territories**, as the area then became known, reverted to the Crown until Canada was ready to administer them, irrespective of the wishes of its population, the Plains Indians and the 7000-odd settlers, of whom 5000 were **Metis**. The Metis, whose main settlement was near the site of modern-day Winnipeg, were already alarmed by the arrival of Ontario expansionists and were even more alarmed when government land surveyors arrived to divide the land into lots that cut right across their holdings. Fearful of their land rights, the Metis formed a provisional government under the leadership of **Louis Riel** and prepared to resist the federal authorities.

In the course of the rebellion, Riel executed a troublesome Ontario Orangeman by the name of Thomas Scott, an action which created uproar in Ontario. Despite this, the federal government negotiated with a Metis delegation and appeared to meet all their demands, although Riel was obliged to go into exile in the States. As a result of the negotiations, Ottawa created the new province of **Manitoba** to the west of Ontario in 1870, and set aside 140 acres per person for the Metis — though land speculators and lawyers ensured that fewer than twenty percent of those eligible actually got their land.

Dispossession was also the fate of the **Plains Indians**. From 1871 onwards a series of treaties were negotiated, offering native families 160-acre plots and a whole range of goods and services if they signed. By 1877 seven treaties had been agreed (eventually there were eleven), handing over to the government all of the southern prairies. However, the promised aid did not materialise; instead the native peoples found themselves confined to small, infertile reservations.

The federal government's increased interest in the area — spurred by the **Cypress Hills Massacre** of Assiniboine natives in 1873 — was underlined by the arrival in 1874 of the first 275 members of the newly formed North-West Mounted Police: the **Mounties**. One of their first actions was to expel the American whisky traders who had earned the region the nickname Whoop-up Country. Once the police had assumed command, Ottawa passed the **Indian Act** of 1880, making a Minister of Indian Affairs responsible for the native peoples. The minister and his superintendents exercised a near dictatorial control, so that almost any action that a native person might wish to take, from building a house to making a visit off the reservation, had to be approved by the local official, and often the ministry in Ottawa too. The Act laid down that an applicant for "enfranchisement" as an ordinary Canadian citizen had to pass through a three-year probation period and was to be examined to see if the applicant had attained a sufficient level of "civilisation". If "enfranchised", such people became so-called "non-status Indians", as opposed to the "status Indians" of the reservations.

Meanwhile, during the 1870s, most of the **Metis** had moved west into the territory that would become the province of **Saskatchewan** in 1905. Here they congregated along the Saskatchewan River in the vicinity of Batoche, but once again federal surveyors caught up with them and, in the 1880s, began to divide the land into the familiar gridiron pattern. In 1885, the Metis again rose in **revolt** and, after the return of Riel, formed a provisional govern-

ment. In March they successfully beat off a detachment of Mounted Police, encouraging the neighbouring Cree people to raid a Hudson's Bay Company Store. It seemed that a general native insurrection might follow, born of the desperation that accompanied the treaty system, the starvation which went with the disappearance of the bison, and the ravages of smallpox. The government dispatched a force of 7000 with Gatling guns and an armed steamer, and after two preliminary skirmishes the Metis and the Cree were crushed. Riel, despite his obvious insanity, was found guilty of treason and hanged in November 1885.

The defeat of the Metis opened a new phase in the development of the west. In 1886 the **first train ran from Montréal to Vancouver** and settlers swarmed onto the prairies, pushing the population up from 250,000 in 1890 to 1,300,000 in 1911. Clifford Sifton, Minister of the Interior, encouraged the large-scale immigration from Eastern Europe of what he called "stalwart peasants in sheepskin coats". These Ukrainians, Poles, Czechs and Hungarians ploughed up the grasslands and turned central Canada into a vast granary, leading the Dominion into the "wheat boom" of the early twentieth century.

## NATIVE PEOPLES IN THE TWENTIETH CENTURY

For the **native peoples** the opening of the twentieth century ushered in a far from happy time. Herded onto small reservations under the authoritarian paternalism of the ministry, they were subjected to a concerted campaign of Europeanisation — ceremonies such as the sun dance and the potlatch were banned, and they were obliged to send their children to boarding schools for ten months of the year. Deprived of their traditions and independence, they lapsed into poverty, alcoholism and apathy. In the late 1940s, the academic Frederick Tisdall estimated that no fewer than 65,000 reservation aboriginals were "chronically sick" from starvation. The Inuit were drawn into increasing dependence on the Hudson's Bay Company, who encouraged them to concentrate on hunting for furs rather than food, while the twin agencies of the Christian missions and the Royal Canadian Mounted Police worked to incorporate the Inuit into white culture. All over Canada, a major consequence of the disruption of the traditional way of life was the spread of disease, especially TB, which was fifteen to twenty times more prevalent amongst the aboriginal population than amongst whites.

In 1951 a new **Indian Act** increased the autonomy of tribal bands, but despite this and increased federal expenditure, aboriginal people remained well behind the rest of Canadian society: in 1969 the average income of a Canadian family was $8874, whilst eighty-eight percent of aboriginal families earned $3000 or less, with fifty percent earning less than $1000.

In recent years, however, native peoples have begun to assert their identity. "Status Indians" are now represented by the **Assembly of First Nations** (AFN), who have sponsored a number of legal actions over treaty rights, many of the cases being based on breaches of the 1763 proclamation, which stated that native land rights could only be taken away by direct negotiation with the Crown. The Chief of the AFN, **Ovide Mercredi** – a lawyer and former human rights commissioner – has announced that the objective of the AFN is to secure an equal status with the provincial governments, a stance indicative of the growth in native self-confidence over the last twenty years, despite the continuing impoverishment of the reservations. The political weight of the AFN has been made clear in the constitutional talks over the **Inuit homeland** in the Northwest Territories, but not all of Canada's natives see negotiation as their salvation – the action of armed Mohawks to prevent a golf course being built on tribal burial grounds at **Oka** in Québec displayed an almost uncontainable anger against the dominant whites, and has divided sympathies across the country.

## QUÉBEC AND THE FUTURE OF CANADA

Just as Canada's native peoples drew inspiration from the national liberation movements of the late 1950s and 1960s, so too did the **Québécois**. Ever since the conquest of 1760, Francophones had been deeply concerned about *la survivance*, the continuation of their language and culture. Over the years there had been periods of tension between Francophones and Anglophones, notably during both world wars, when the Québécois opposed the introduction of conscription because it seemed to subordinate their interests to those of Britain. Nevertheless, despite these difficulties, the essentially conservative political-religious establishment usually recommended the accommodation of the British and later the federal authorities. This same establishment upheld the traditional values of Catholic rural New France, a consequence of which was that Québec's industry and commerce developed under Anglophone control. Thus, in early twentieth-century Montréal, a Francophone proletariat worked in the factories of Anglophone owners, an Anglophone dominance that was compounded by the indifference of Canada's other provinces to French-Canadian interests, spurring the development of a new generation of Québec **separatists**.

**Expo '67**, held in Montréal, was meant to be a confirmation of Canada's arrival as an industrial power of the first rank, but when president de Gaulle of France used the event as a platform to announce his advocacy of a "free Québec", it turned into the catalyst for a political row that has dominated the country ever since. The following year, **René Lévesque** – creator of the slogan *Maitres chez Nous* (masters in our own house) – formed the **Parti Québécois**, with the ultimate goal of full independence. The same year saw the election as prime minister of **Pierre Trudeau**, a French-Canadian politician dedicated to the maintenance of the federation, highlighting the increasing polarisation of Francophone opinion.

The PQ represented the constitutional wing of a social movement which at its most militant extreme embraced the activities of the short-lived **Front de la Libération du Québec** (FLQ). In 1970 the FLQ kidnapped and murdered Pierre Laporte, the province's Minister of Labour, an action which provoked Trudeau into putting the troops onto the streets of Montréal. This reaction was to benefit the PQ, a modernising party of the social-democratic left, which came to power in 1976 and set about using state resources to develop economic interests such as the Québec hydroelectric plant on James Bay. It also reformed education – including controversial legislation to make Québec unilingual – and pressed ahead with plans for a referendum on secession. But when the referendum came, in 1980, sixty percent of

Québec's electorate voted "non" to separation, partly because the 1970s had witnessed a closing of the opportunity gap between the Francophone and Anglophone communities.

In 1985, the PQ were defeated by **Robert Bourassa**'s Liberals, perhaps reflecting a shift in Francophone feeling, but in the last few years the belief that *la survivance* depends on full independence has revived – Bourassa remains in power largely by espousing much of the nationalist agenda. Since the failure in 1990 of the **Meech Lake** conference, which was called to draw up a new de-centralised constitution, support for Québec separatism has been running at 70 percent in the province, and the forthcoming referendum seems certain to reverse the 1980 result.

The future of the federation is the most fractious political issue in present-day Canada, but Québécois discontent is not the only problem to have dogged the premiership of the Conservative **Brian Mulroney**, who succeeded to office in 1984. The free trade agreement (FTA) between the US and Canada, which Mulroney pushed through parliament in 1989, has destroyed his country's protective tariffs, exposing its industries to undercutting and causing the loss of thousands of jobs; the collapse of the North Atlantic cod fishery has brought Nova Scotia and Newfoundland to the brink of economic ruin; and the wheat-producing areas of the west complain that Ottawa fails to secure adequate prices for its produce. These issues, and Mulroney's deep unpopularity amongst the majority of Canadians, threaten to tear the country apart: it remains to be seen how, or if, federal and provincial forces can be reconciled.

# CANADIAN WILDLIFE

Canada has just about every natural habitat going, from ice-bound polar islands in the far north to sun-drilled pockets of desert along the United States border. Between these extremes the country's mountains, forests and grasslands support an incredible variety and profusion of wildlife – any brief account can only scratch the surface of what it's possible to see. National and provincial parks offer the best starting places, and we've listed some of the outstanding sites for spotting particular species. However, don't expect to see the big attractions like bears and wolves easily – despite the enthusiasm of guides and tourist offices, these are encountered only rarely.

## EASTERN FORESTS

Canada's **eastern forests** divide into two main groups – the Carolinian forest of southwestern Ontario, and the Great Lakes–St Lawrence forest extending from the edge of the Carolinian forest to Lake Superior and the Gulf of St Lawrence.

### CAROLINIAN FOREST

The **Carolinian forest** forms a narrow belt of largely deciduous hardwood trees similar to the broadleaved woodlands found over much of the eastern United States. Trees are often typical of more southerly climes – Kentucky coffee tree, tulip tree, sassafras, sycamore, chinquapin oak, shagbark hickory and more ordinary staples like beech, sugar maple, basswood and swamp oak. None of these is rare in the States, but in Canada they grow only here, thanks to the region's rich soils and relatively warm, sheltered climate.

A good deal of the Carolinian flora and fauna is coming under increasing threat from southern Ontario's urban and agricultural sprawl. These days much of the original forest has shrunk to a mosaic of fragments protected by national and provincial parks. The forests are most often visited by tourists for the astounding October colours, but if you're looking for wildlife you might also catch Canada's only marsupial, the **opossum**, or other southern species like the **fox squirrel** (introduced on Lake Erie's Pelee Island), the **eastern mole**, which occurs only in Essex County on Lake Erie's north shore, and the **eastern vole**, found only in a narrow band around Lake Erie.

Naturalists are equally drawn here for the **birds**, many of which are found nowhere else in Canada, especially during seasonal migrations, when up to 100 species can easily be seen in a day. Most noteworthy of the more unusual species is the golden swamp warbler, a bird of almost unnaturally colourful plumage. More common visitors are hooded and Kentucky warblers, blue-winged and golden-winged warblers, gnatcatchers and virtually every species of eastern North American hawk. Sharp-shin hawks are common, and during autumn migrations up to 70,000 broad-winged hawks might be seen in a single day near Port Stanley on Lake Erie's north shore.

In the wetlands bordering the forests, particularly at Long Point on Lake Erie, you can search out **reptiles** found nowhere else in the country. Most impressive is the water-loving fox snake, a harmless animal that reaches often well over a metre in length, but often killed because of its resemblance to the rattlesnake and venomous copperhead – neither of which is found in the region. Also present, but in marked decline, are several **turtle** species, especially Blanding's, wood, spotted and spiny softshell.

## GREAT LAKES–ST LAWRENCE FOREST

Occurring in one of the most densely populated parts of Canada, the mixed conifer forests of the **Great Lakes–St Lawrence** area have been heavily logged and severely affected by urbanisation. Most of the trees are southern species – beech and sugar maple, red and white pines – but are mixed with eastern hemlock, spruce, jack pine, paper birch and balsam fir typical of more northerly forests.

Ironically, widespread human disturbance has, if anything, created a greater diversity of forest types, which makes this region second only to southern British Columbia in the number of bird species it supports. It also provides for large numbers of **white-tailed deer**, a rare beneficiary of logging as it prefers to browse along the edges of clearings. In the evergreen stands on the north shore of the St Lawrence there are also large numbers of Canada's smallest mammal, the **pygmy shrew**. These tiny animals must eat their own weight in food daily and can't rest for more than an hour or so – they'd starve to death if they tried to sleep through the night.

## GRASSLANDS

Contrary to the popular image of Canada's interior as a huge prairie of waving wheat, true grassland covers only ten percent of the country. Most is concentrated in the southernmost reaches of Alberta and Saskatchewan, with tiny spillovers in Manitoba and British Columbia – areas which lie in the Rockies' rain shadow and are too dry to support forest.

Two grassland belts once thrived in the region, tallgrass prairie in the north and short-

---

## WILDLIFE CHECKLIST

This is by no means an exhaustive list of all Canada's wildlife species and their habitats – it should be treated simply as an indication of the places and the times that you are most likely to see certain species and types of wildlife.

**Beluga, fin, humpback, blue** and **minke whales**: near Tadoussac, north of Québec City; summer.

**Bison**: Wood Buffalo National Park (Alberta).

**Black bears**: Glacier National Park (BC); Banff and Jasper national parks (BC); Kananaskis Country (Alberta); summer.

**Butterfly migrations**: Point Pelee and Long Point, Lake Erie (Ontario); spring and autumn.

**Caribou**: Dempster Highway north of Dawson City (Yukon); autumn.

**Cranes and pelicans**: Last Mountain Lake, north-west of Regina (Saskatchewan); late August.

**Dall's sheep**: Sheep Mountain, Kluane National Park (Yukon); summer.

**Desert species**: Cacti, sagebrush, rattlesnakes and kangaroo rats around Osoyoos (BC); summer.

**Eagles and owls** Boundary Bay, 20km south of Vancouver (BC); winter.

**Elk**: Banff and Jasper national parks (BC); Kananaskis Country (Alberta); summer.

**Grey whales**: Pacific Rim National Park, Vancouver Island (BC); spring and summer.

**Grizzly bears**: Glacier National Park and at Khutzeymateen Estuary, north of Prince Rupert (BC); August.

**Killer whales**: Robson Bight in Johnstone Strait, Vancouver Island (BC); summer.

**Orchids**: Bruce Peninsula National Park (Ontario); spring and summer.

**Polar bears**: near Churchill, Manitoba; autumn.

**Prairie species**: Hawks, coyotes and rattle-snakes in the Milk River region (Alberta); May–June.

**Salmon**: Adams River sockeye salmon run near Salmon Arm (BC); October.

**Seabirds**: Gannets, murres and black kittiwakes around Cape St Mary's (Newfoundland); waterfowl, seabirds and seals in the Queen Charlotte Islands (BC); northern gannets on Bonaventure Island, Gaspé Peninsula (Québec); June–July.

**Sea otters and sea lions**: off Pacific Rim National Park, Vancouver Island (BC); spring and summer.

**Snow geese**: Cap-Tourmente, north of Québec City; autumn.

**Wildflowers** Numerous woodland species on Vancouver Island and the Gulf Islands, and at Mount Revelstoke National Park (BC); late spring to summer.

grass in the south. Farming has now not only put large areas of each under crops, but also decimated most of the large mammals that roamed the range – pronghorns, mule deer, white-tailed deer and elk – not to mention their predators like wolves, grizzlies, coyotes, foxes, bobcats and cougars.

The most dramatic loss from the grasslands, though, has been the **bison** (or buffalo), the continent's largest land mammal. Once numbering an estimated 45 million, bison are now limited to just a few free-roaming herds in Canada (see p.402). They're extraordinarily impressive animals – the average bull stands six feet at the shoulder and weighs over a ton – and early prairie settlers were so struck with their size that they believed bison, not the climate, had been responsible for clearing the grasslands.

Once almost as prevalent as the bison, but now almost as rare, is the **pronghorn**, a beautiful tawny-gold antelope species. Capable of speeds of over 100kph, it's the continent's swiftest land mammal, so you'll generally see nothing but distinctive white rump disappearing at speed. Uniquely adapted for speed and stamina, the pronghorn has long legs, a heart twice the size of similar-sized animals, and an astonishingly wide windpipe. It also complements its respiratory machinery by running with its mouth open to gulp maximum amounts of air. Though only the size of a large dog, it has larger eyes than those of a horse, a refinement that spots predators several kilometres away. These days, however, wolves and coyotes are more likely to be after the prairie's new masters – countless small rodents like gophers, ground squirrels and jackrabbits.

**Birds** have had to adapt not only to the prairie's dryness but also, of course, to the lack of extensive tree cover, and most species nest on the ground; many are also able to survive on reduced amounts of water and rely on seed-centred diets. Others confine themselves to occasional ponds, lakes and "sloughs", which are important breeding grounds for ducks, grebes, herons, pelicans, rails and many more. Other birds typical of the grassland in its natural state are the marbled godwit, the curlew, and raptors such as the **prairie falcon**, a close relation of the peregrine falcon that's capable of diving speeds of up to 290kph.

## BOREAL FOREST

The **boreal forest** is Canada's largest single ecosystem, bigger than all the others combined. Stretching in a broad belt from Newfoundland to the Yukon, it fills the area between the eastern forests, grasslands and the northern tundra, occupying a good slice of every province except British Columbia. Only certain **trees** thrive in this zone of long, cold winters, short summers and acidic soils: although the cover is not identical countrywide, expect to see billions of white and black spruce (plus red spruce in the east), balsam fir, tamarack (larch) and jack pine, as well as such deciduous species as birch, poplar and aspen – all of which are ideal for wood pulp, making the boreal forest the staple resource of the country's **lumber industry**.

If you spend any time in the backcountry you'll also come across **muskeg**: neither land nor water, this porridge-like bog is the breeding ground of choice for Canada's pestilential hordes of mosquitoes and blackflies – and Canada has 1.3 million square kilometres of it. It also harbours mosses, scrub willow, pitcher plant, leatherleaf, sundew, cranberry and even the occasional orchid.

The boreal forest supports just about every animal recognised as distinctively Canadian: moose, beaver, black bear, wolf and lynx, plus a broad cross-section of small mammals and creatures like deer, caribou and coyote from transitional forest-tundra and aspen-parkland habitats to the north and south.

**Wolves** are still numerous in Canada, but hunting and harassment has pushed them to the northernmost parts of the boreal forest. Their supposed ferocity is more myth than truth; intelligent and elusive creatures, they rarely harm humans, and it's unlikely you'll see any – though you may well hear their howling if you're out in the sticks.

**Lynx** are even more elusive. One of the northern forest's most elegant animals, this big cat requires a 150- to 200-square-kilometre range, making Canada's northern wilderness one of the world's few regions capable of sustaining a viable population. Nocturnal hunters, lynx feed on deer and moose but favour the hare, a common boreal creature that is to the forest's predators what the lemming is to the carnivores of the tundra.

**Beavers**, on the other hand, are commonly seen all over Canada. You may catch them at dawn or dusk, heads just above the water as they glide across lakes and rivers. Signs of their legendary activity include log jams across streams and ponds, stumps of felled saplings resembling sharpened pencils, and dens which look like domed piles of mud and sticks.

Lakes, streams and marshy muskeg margins are all favoured by **moose**. A lumbering animal with magnificent spreading antlers, it is the largest member of the deer family and is found over most of Canada, but especially near swampy ground, where it likes to graze on mosses and lichens. It's also a favourite with hunters, and few northern bars are without their moose head – perhaps the only place you'll see this solitary and reclusive species.

Forest wetlands also offer refuge for **ducks and geese**, with loons, grebes and songbirds attracted to their surrounding undergrowth. Canada's three species of ptarmigan – willow, rock and white-tailed – are also common, and you'll see plenty of big **raptors**, including the great grey owl, Canada's largest owl. Many boreal birds migrate, and even those that don't, such as hawks, jays, ravens and grouse, tend to move a little way south, sometimes breaking out into southern Canada in mass movements known as "irruptions". Smaller birds like chickadees, waxwings and finches are particularly fond of these sporadic forays.

## MOUNTAIN FORESTS

Mountain forests cover much of western Canada and, depending on location and elevation, divide into four types: West Coast, Columbia, montane and sub-alpine.

### WEST COAST FOREST

The **West Coast**'s torrential rainfall, mild maritime climate, deep soils and long growing season produce Canada's most impressive forests and its biggest trees. Swathes of luxuriant temperate **rainforest** cover much of Vancouver Island and the Pacific coast, dominated by Sitka spruce, western red cedar, Pacific silver fir, western hemlock, western yew and, biggest of all, **Douglas fir**, some of which tower 90m and are 1200 years old. However, these conifers make valuable timber, and much of this forest is under severe threat from logging. Some of the best stands – a fraction of the original – have been preserved on the Queen Charlotte Islands and in Vancouver Island's Pacific Rim National Park.

Below the luxuriant, dripping canopy of the big trees lies an **undergrowth** teeming with life. Shrubs and bushes like salal, huckleberry, bunchberry, salmonberry and twinberry thrive alongside mosses, ferns, lichens, liverworts, skunk cabbage and orchids. All sorts of animals can be found here, most notably the **cougar** and its main prey, the Columbian blacktail **deer**, a subspecies of the mule deer. **Birds** are legion, and include a wealth of woodland species such as the Townsend's warbler, Wilson's warbler, orange-crowned warbler, junco, Swainson's thrush and golden-crowned kinglet. Rarer birds include the rufous **hummingbird**, which migrates from its wintering grounds in Mexico to feed on the forest's numerous nectar-bearing flowers.

### COLUMBIA FOREST

The **Columbia forest** covers the lower slopes (400–1400m) of British Columbia's interior mountains and much of the Rockies. **Trees** here are similar to those of the West Coast's warmer and wetter rainforest – western red cedar, western hemlock and Douglas fir – with Sitka spruce, which rarely thrives away from the coast, the notable exception. The undercover, too, is similar, with lots of devil's club (a particularly vicious thorn), azaleas, black and red twinberry, salmonberry and redberry alder. Mountain lily, columbine, bunchberry and heartleaf arnica are among the common flowers.

Few mammals live exclusively in the forests with the exception of the **red squirrel**, which makes a meal of conifer seeds, and is in turn preyed on by hawks, owls, coyotes and weasels, among others. Bigger predators roam the mountain forest, however, most notably the **brown bear**, a western variant of the ubiquitous **black bear**. Aside from the coyote, the tough, agile black bear is one of the continent's most successful carnivores and the one you're most likely to see around campgrounds and rubbish dumps. Black bears have adapted to a wide range of habitats and food sources, and their only natural enemies – save wolves, which may attack young cubs – are hunters, who bag some 30,000 annually in North America.

Scarcer but still hunted is the famous **grizzly bear**, a far larger and potentially dangerous creature distinguished by its brownish fur and the ridged hump on its back. Now extinct in many of its original habitats, the grizzly is largely confined to the remoter slopes of the Rockies and West Coast ranges, where it feeds mainly on berries and salmon. Like other bears, grizzlies are unpredictable and readily provoked – see p.442 for tips on minimising unpleasant encounters.

## MONTANE FOREST

**Montane forest** covers the more southerly and sheltered reaches of the Rockies and the dry plateaux of interior British Columbia, where spindly Douglas fir, western larch, ponderosa pine and the **lodgepole pine** predominate. Like its eastern counterpart, the jack pine, the lodgepole requires intense heat before opening and releasing its seeds, and huge stands of these trees grew in the aftermath of the forest fires which accompanied the building and running of the railways.

Plentiful voles and small rodents attract **coyotes**, whose yapping – an announcement of territorial claims – you'll often hear at nights close to small towns. Coyotes are spreading northwards into the Yukon and Northwest Territories and eastwards into Ontario and Québec, a proliferation that continues despite massive extermination campaigns, prompted by the coyotes' taste for livestock.

Few predators have the speed to keep up with coyotes – only the stealthy **cougar**, or wolves hunting in tandem, can successfully bring them down. Cougars are now severely depleted in Canada, and the British Columbia interior and Vancouver Island are the only regions where they survive in significant numbers. Among the biggest and most beautiful of the carnivores, they seem to arouse the greatest bloodlust in hunters.

Ponderosa and lodgepole pines provide fine cover for **birds** like goshawks, Swainson's hawks and lesser species like ruby-crowned kinglets, warblers, pileated woodpeckers, nuthatches and chickadees. In the forest's lowest reaches the vegetation and birds are those of the southern prairies – semi-arid regions of sagebrush, prickly pear and bunch grasses, dotted with lakes full of common **ducks** like mallard, shoveler and widgeon. You might also see the cinnamon teal, a red version of the more common green-wing teal, a bird whose limited distribution draws birdwatchers to British Columbia on its own account.

## SUB-ALPINE FOREST

**Sub-alpine forests** cover mountain slopes from 1300m to 2200m throughout the Rockies and much of British Columbia, supporting lodgepole, whitebark and limber pines, alpine fir and Engelmann spruce. It also contains a preponderance of **alpine larch**, a deciduous conifer whose vivid autumnal yellows dot the mountainsides to beautiful effect.

One of the more common animals of this zone is the **elk**, or **wapiti**, a powerful member of the deer family which can often be seen summering in large herds above treeline. Elk court and mate during the autumn, making a thin nasal sound called "bugling". Respect their privacy, as rutting elk have notoriously unpredictable temperaments.

Small herds of **mule deer** migrate between forests and alpine meadows, using small glands between their hooves to leave a scent for other herd members to follow. They're named after their distinctive ears, designed to provide early warning of predators. Other smaller animals which are also attracted to the sub-alpine forest include the golden-mantled ground squirrel, and birds such as Clark's nutcracker, both tame and curious creatures which often gather around campgrounds in search of scraps.

## ALPINE ZONES

**Alpine zones** occur in mountains above the treeline, which in Canada means parts of the Rockies, much of British Columbia and large areas of the Yukon. Plant and animal life varies hugely between summer and winter, and according to terrain and exposure to the elements – sometimes it resembles that of the tundra, at others it recalls the profile of lower forest habitats.

In spring, alpine meadows are carpeted with breathtaking displays of **wildflowers**: clumps of Parnassus grass, lilies, anemones, Indian paintbrushes, lupins and a wealth of yellow flowers such as arnica, cinquefoil, glacier lily and wood betony. These meadows make excellent pasture, attracting elk and mule deer in summer, as well as full-time residents like **Dall's sheep**, the related **bighorn** and the incredible **mountain goat**, perhaps the hardiest of Canada's bigger mammals. Staying close to the roughest terrain possible, mountain goats are equipped with short, stolid legs, flexible toes and non-skid soles, all designed for clambering over near-vertical slopes, grazing well out of reach of their less agile predators.

**Marmots**, resembling hugely overstuffed squirrels, take things easier and hibernate through the worst of the winter and beyond. In a good year they can sleep for eight months, prey only to grizzly bears, which are strong enough and have the claws to dig down into their dens. In their waking periods they can be tame and friendly, often nibbling contentedly in the sunnier corners of campgrounds. When threatened, however, they produce a piercing and unearthly whistle. (They can also do a lot of damage: some specialise in chewing the radiator hoses of parked cars.) The strange little **pika**, a relative of the rabbit, is more elusive but keeps itself busy throughout the year, living off a miniature haystack of fodder which it builds up during the summer.

**Birds** are numerous in summer, and include rosy finches, pipits and blue grouse, but few manage to live in the alpine zone year-round. One which does is the white-tailed **ptarmigan**, a plump, partridge-like bird which, thanks to its heavily feathered feet and legs, is able to snowshoe around deep drifts of snow; its white winter plumage provides camouflage. Unfortunately, ptarmigans can be as slow-moving and stupid as barnyard chickens, making them easy targets for hunters and predators.

## COASTLINES

Canada has three coastlines: the Atlantic, the Pacific and the Arctic (dealt with under "Tundra"). Each boasts a profusion of maritime, dunal and intertidal life; the Pacific coast, warmed by the Japanese current, actually has the greatest number of species of any temperate shore. Few people are very interested in the small fry, however – most come for the big mammals, and **whales** in particular.

**Grey whales** are most common in the Pacific, and are often easily spotted from mainland headlands in the February to May and September to October periods as they migrate between the Arctic and their breeding grounds off Mexico. Once hunted close to the point of extinction, they've now returned in large numbers, and most West Coast harbours have charter companies offering whale-watching tours.

**Humpback whales** are another favourite, largely because they're curious and follow sightseeing boats, but also because of their surface acrobatics and long, haunting "songs". They too were hunted to near-extinction, and though protected by international agreement since 1966 they still number less than ten percent of their original population.

Vancouver Island's inner coast supports one of the world's most concentrated populations of **killer whales** or **orcas**. These are often seen in family groups or "pods" travelling close to shore, usually on the trail of large fish – which on the West Coast means **salmon**. The orca, however, is the only whale whose diet also runs to warm-blooded animals – hence the "killer" tag – and it will gorge on walrus, seal and even minke, grey and beluga whales.

Another West Coast inhabitant, the **sea otter** differs from most marine mammals in that they keep themselves warm with a thick soft coat of fur rather than with blubber. This brought them to the attention of early Russian and British fur traders, and by the beginning of this century they were virtually extinct. Reintroduced in 1969 to Vancouver Island's northwest coast, they are now breeding successfully at the heart of their original range. With binoculars, it's often easy to spot these charming creatures lolling on their backs, cracking open sea urchins or mussels with a rock and using their stomachs as anvils; they often lie bobbing asleep, entwined in kelp to stop them floating away.

Northern **fur seals** breed on Alaska's Pribilof Islands but are often seen off the British Columbian coast during their migrations. Like their cousin, the northern **sea lion**, a year-round resident, they are "eared seals", who can manage rudimentary shuffling on land thanks to short rear limbs which can be rotated for forward movement. They also swim with strokes from front flippers, as opposed to the slithering, fishlike action of true seals.

The **Atlantic**'s colder waters nurture fewer overall species than the Pacific coast, but many birds and larger mammals – especially **whales** – are common to both. One of the Atlantic region's more distinctive creatures is the **harp seal** (or saddleback), a true seal species that migrates in late winter to breeding grounds off Newfoundland and in the Greenland and White seas. Most pups are born on the pack-ice, and for about two weeks sport fluffy white coats that have been highly prized by the fur trade for centuries. Until the late-1960s tens of thousands of young seals died annually in an unsupervised slaughter whose methods – clubbing and skinning alive – brought about outrage on an international scale (see p.98).

## TUNDRA

**Tundra** extends over much of northern Yukon and the Northwest Territories, stretching between the boreal forest and the polar seas. Part grassland and part wasteland, it's a region distinguished by high winds, bitter cold and **permafrost**, a layer of perpetually frozen subsoil which covers over thirty percent of Canada. The tundra is not only the domain of ice and emptiness, however: long hours of summer sunshine and the melting of topsoil nurture a carpet of wildflowers and many species of birds and mammals have adapted to the vagaries of climate and terrain.

Vegetation is uniformly stunted by poor drainage, acidic soils and permafrost, which prevents the formation of deep roots and locks nutrients in the ice. **Trees** like birch and willow can grow, but they spread their branches over a wide area, rarely rising over 1m in height. Over ninety-nine percent of the remaining vegetation consists of perennials like **grasses** and sedges, small flowering annuals, mosses, lichens and shrubs. Most have evolved ingenious ways of protecting themselves against the elements: arctic cotton grass, for example, grows in large insulated hummocks in which the interior temperature is higher than the air outside; others have large, waxy leaves to conserve moisture or catch as much sunlight as possible. **Wildflowers** during the short, intense spring can be superlative, covering seemingly inert ground in a carpet of purple mountain saxifrage, yellow arctic poppy, indigo clusters of arctic forget-me-not and the pink buds of Jacob's ladder.

Tundra grasses provide some of the first links in the food chain, nourishing mammals such as white **arctic ground squirrels**, also known as parkas, as their fur is used by the Inuit to make parka jackets. Vegetation also provides the staple diet of **lemmings**, amongst

the most remarkable of the arctic fauna. Instead of hibernating these creatures live under the snow, busily tucking away on shoots in order to double their weight daily – the intake they need merely to survive. They also breed almost continuously, which is just as well for they are the mainstay of a long list of predators. Chief of these are **arctic white foxes**, ermines and weasels, though birds, bears and arctic wolves may also hunt them in preference to larger prey. Because they provide a staple diet to so many, lemming populations have a marked effect on the life cycles of numerous creatures.

A notable exception is the **caribou**, a member of the reindeer family and the most populous of the big tundra mammals. Caribou are known above all for their epic migrations, frequently involving thousands of animals, which start in March when the herds leave their wintering grounds on the fringes of the boreal forest for calving grounds to the north. The exact purpose of these migrations is still a matter of conjecture. They certainly prevent the overgrazing of the tundra's fragile mosses and lichens, and probably also enable the caribou to shake off some of the wolves that would otherwise shadow the herd (wolves have to find southerly dens at this time to bear their own pups). The timing of treks also means that calving takes place before the arrival of biting insects, which can claim as many calves as predators – an adult caribou can lose as much as a litre of blood a week to insects.

The tundra's other large mammal is the **musk ox**, a vast, shaggy herbivore and close cousin of the bison. The musk ox's Achilles' heel is a tendency to form lines or circles when threatened – a perfect defence against wolves, but not against rifle-toting hunters, who until the introduction of conservation measures threatened to be their undoing. Canada now has some of the world's largest free-roaming herds, although – like the caribou – they're still hunted for food and fur by the Inuit.

Tundra **birds** number about 100 species and are mostly migratory. Three-quarters of these are waterfowl, which arrive first to take advantage of streams, marshes and small lakes created by surface meltwater: arctic wetlands provide nesting grounds for numerous swans, geese and ducks, as well as the loon, which is immortalised on the back of the Canadian dollar coin. The red-necked **phalarope** is a particularly specialised visitor, able to feed on aquatic insects and plankton, though not as impressive in its abilities as the migratory **arctic tern**, whose 32,000-kilometre round trip from the Antarctic is the longest annual migration of any creature on the planet. The handful of non-migratory birds tend to be scavengers like the raven, or predators like the **gyrfalcon**, the world's largest falcon, which preys on arctic hares and ptarmigan. Jaegers, gulls, hawks and owls largely depend on the lemming: the snowy owl, for example, synchronises its returns to southern Canada with four-year dips in the lemming population.

Fauna on the arctic **coast** has a food chain that starts with plankton and algae, ranging up through tiny crustaceans, clams and mussels, sea cucumbers and sea urchins, cod, ringed and bearded seals, to beluga whales and **polar bears** – perhaps the most evocative of all tundra creatures, but still being killed in their hundreds for "sport" despite almost thirty years of hunting restrictions. Migrating **birds** are especially common here, notably near Nunaluk Spit on the Yukon coast, which is used as a corridor and stopover by millions of loons, swans, geese, plovers, sandpipers, dowitchers, eagles, hawks, guillemots and assorted songbirds.

# BOOKS

Most of the following books should be readily available in the UK, US or Canada. We have given publishers and prices for each title that's in print; the currency indicates in which countries the book is published – all dollar prices are US dollars unless designated as Can$. Note that virtually all the listed books published in the US will be stocked by major Canadian bookshops. Where a dollar price appears without a publisher, this means that the book is produced by the same publisher as in the UK.

## TRAVEL

**Hugh Brody** *Maps and Dreams* (Faber, o/p; Pantheon, $10.95). Brilliantly written account of the lives and lands of the Beaver natives of northwest Canada. For further acute insights into the ways of the far north see also the same author's *Living Arctic* (Faber, £4.95; University of Washington Press, $14.95) and *The People's Land: Eskimos and Whites in the Eastern Arctic* ($3.95).

**Stephen Brook** *Maple Leaf Rag: Travels Across Canada* (Picador, o/p; Random $7.95). Humorous but at times embarrassingly contrived account of a journey to "admire the quirky but genuine receptivity of the country's liberal-minded citizens".

**P Browning** *The Last Wilderness* (Great West Books, Can$9.95). An engrossing description of a harsh and lonely canoe journey through the Northwest Territories.

**Ranulph Fiennes** *The Headless Valley* (Hodder & Stoughton, o/p in UK). Tales of derring-do from noted adventurer, whitewater rafting down the South Nahanni and Fraser rivers of British Columbia and the NWT.

**Barry Lopez** *Arctic Dreams: Imagination and Desire in Northern Landscape* (Pan, £6.99; Bantam, $9.95). Extraordinary award-winning book combining natural history, physics, poetry, earth sciences and philosophy in a dazzling portrait of the far north.

**Duncan Pryde** *Nununga: Ten Years of Eskimo Life* (Eland, £7.99; Hippocrene $12.95). Less a travel book than a social document from a Glaswegian who left home at 18 to spend ten years with the Inuit.

**Gary and Joannie McGuffin** *Canoeing Across Canada* (Diadem £5.95; Stone Wall $8.95). Reflections on a 6000-mile journey through the country's rivers and backwaters.

**Susanna Moodie** *Roughing it in the Bush: Or Forest Life in Canada* (Virago, £7.50; Beacon, $14.95). Wonderful narrative written in 1852, describing an English couple's slow ruin as they attempt to create a new life in southeastern Ontario.

## CULTURE AND SOCIETY

**Beatrice Culleton** *April Raintree* (Pemmican, Can$10). Heart-rending account of the enforced fostering of Metis children in Manitoba during the 1950s.

**Don Dumond** *The Eskimos and Aleuts* (Thames & Hudson, £7.95; $11.95). Anthropological and archaeological tour-de-force on the prehistory, history and culture of northern peoples: backed up with fine maps, drawings and photographs.

**Paula Fleming** *The North American Indians in Early Photographs* (Phaidon, £14.95). Stylised poses don't detract from a plaintive record of a way of life that has all but vanished.

**Allan Gregg and Michael Posner** *The Big Picture* (MacFarlane, Walter & Ross, $19.95). A contemporary survey on what Canadians think of everything from sex to politics.

**Richard Gwyn** *Smallwood: The Unlikely Revolutionary* (McClelland & Stewart; Can$10). Detailed biography of Joey Smallwood, the Newfoundland premier who pushed his island into Confederation in 1949. Gwyn's exploration of island corruption and incompetence is incisive and intriguing in equal measure.

**Paul Kane** *Wanderings of An Artist among the Indians of North America* (Charles E Tuttle, o/p). Kane, one of Canada's better known landscape artists, spent three years travelling from Toronto to the Pacific Coast and back in the 1840s. His witty account of his wanderings makes a delightful read – any major Canadian secondhand bookshop should have it.

**Alan B Macmillan** *Native Peoples and Cultures of Canada* (Douglas & McIntyre, Can$19.95). Excellent anthology on Canada's native groups from prehistory to current issues of self-government and land claims. Well-written and illustrated throughout.

**Dennis Reid** *A Concise History of Canadian Painting* (Oxford University Press, £14.95; $17.95). Not especially concise, but a thorough-trawl through Canada's leading artists, with bags of biographical detail and lots of black and white illustrations of major works.

**Mordecai Richler** *Oh Canada! Oh Québec!* (Chatto, £14.95; Knopf, $18.95). A satirical chronicle of the hysteria, zeal and chicanery surrounding Québec's independence movement.

**Mordecai Richler** *Home Sweet Home* (Triad Grafton, o/p in UK; $6.95). Entertaining but occasionally whingeing anecdotes from all corners of the country.

**The True North – Canadian Landscape Painting 1896–1939** (Lund Humphries, £15). A fascinating and well-illustrated book exploring how Canadian artists have treated the country' challenging landscapes.

## HISTORY

**Owen Beattie and John Geiger** *The Fate of the Franklin Expedition 1845–48* (Bloomsbury, £8.95; NAL Dutton, $9.95). An account both of the doomed expedition to find the Northwest Passage and the discovery of artifacts and bodies still frozen in the northern ice; worth buying for the extraordinary photos.

**Pierre Berton** *Klondike: The Last Great Goldrush 1896–1899* ($5.95). Exceptionally readable account from one of Canada's finest writers of the characters and epic episodes of the Yukon gold rush.

**Pierre Berton** *The Arctic Grail* ($5.95). Another Berton blockbuster, this time on the quest for the North Pole and the Northwest Passage from 1818 to 1919. All the author's other books are well worth reading; see also *The Last Spike*, an account of the history and

building of the transcontinental railway; *The Mysterious North: Enconters with the Canadian Frontier 1947–1954; Flames across the Frontier*, episodes from the often uneasy relationship between Canada and the US; and *Vimy*, an account of the World War I battle fought mainly by Canadians which Berton sees as a turning point in the nation's history.

**Gerald Friesen** *The Canadian Prairies: A History* (University of Toronto, Can$20). Stunningly well researched and detailed account of the development of Central Canada. A surprisingly entertaining book that's particularly good on the culture of the Metis and Plains Indians.

**Kenneth McNaught** *The Penguin History of Canada* (Penguin, £7.99). Recently revised and concise analysis of the country's economic, social and political history.

**Peter Neary and Patrick O'Flaherty** *Part of the Main: an Illustrated History of Newfoundland and Labrador* (Breakwater, Can$10). Lively text and excellent illustrations make this the best account of the province's history, though it's short of contemporary information.

**Peter C Newman** *Caesars of the Wilderness* ($8.95). Highly acclaimed and readable account of the rise and fall of the Hudson's Bay Company.

**George Woodcock** *A Social History of Canada* (Penguin, $13.95; Can$14.95). Erudite yet readable book about the peoples of Canada and the changes in lifestyle from wilderness to city.

## NATURAL HISTORY

**Richard Chandler** *The Macmillan Field Guide to North Atlantic Shorebirds* (Macmillan, £12.95). Well-illustrated and comprehensive handbook.

**Tim Fitzharris and John Livingston** *Canada: A Natural History* (Viking Studio, £20; $40). The text is prone to purple fits, but the luscious photographs make this a book to savour.

**The Pocket Guide Series** (Dragon's World, £6.95 each). Clearly laid out and well illustrated, the Pocket Book series are excellent basic handbooks for general locations of species identification and background. Individual titles are: *The Pocket Guide to*

*Mammals of North America* (John Burton); *The Pocket Guide to Birds of Prey of North America* (Philip Burton); *The Pocket Guide to Wild Flowers of North America* (Pamela Forey); *The Pocket Guide to Trees of North America* (Alan Mitchell); *The Pocket Guide to Birds of Western North America* (Frank Shaw).

**Paul Thomas** *Fur Seal Island* (Souvenir Press, £12.95; Souvenir, $25). The North Pacific seals' battle for survival.

**Lyall Watson** *Whales of the World* (Hutchinson, £11.95; NAl Dutton, $31.00). Encyclopaedic and lavishly illustrated guide to the biggest sea mammals.

## LITERATURE

**Anahareo** *Grey Owl and I: A New Autobiography* (Davies, Can$7). The story of Grey Owl's Iroquois wife, their fight to save the beaver from extinction and her shock at discovering that her husband was in fact an Englishman. Good insights into the changing life of Canada's natives in this century.

**Margaret Atwood** *Surfacing* (Virago £4.99; Fawcett, $4.95). Canada's most eminent novelist is not always easy reading, but her analysis, particularly of women and society, is invariably witty and penetrating. *Surfacing,* the tale of a young divorcee who returns to a remote part of northern Québec to investigate the disappearance of her father, is perhaps the best of her novels with a Canadian setting – the surroundings become instrumental in an extreme voyage of self-discovery that'll leave you unable to look at the Canadian wilderness in quite the same way again. *Cat's Eye* (Virago £5.99; Bantam, $5.95) deals with a painter returning to Toronto to find herself overwhelmed by the past, a theme also explored in *Lady Oracle* (Virago, £5.99; Bantam, $5.95) the account of a poet confused by a life divided between London and Toronto, who plans a new life in Italy after faking her death. *Wilderness Tips* (Bloomsbury, £14.95; Doubleday, $20), is her latest collection of short stories and is mainly about women looking back over the bastards in their lives.

**Elizabeth Bishop** *The Complete Poems* (Chatto, £10.99). Though American by birth, Bishop spent much of her youth in Nova Scotia. Many of her early poems feed off her Canadian childhood and a fascination with the rough landscapes of the northeast.

**Leonard Cohen** *Poems:1956–1968* (Cape, £5.95). A fine collection from a Sixties survivor who enjoyed high critical acclaim as a poet before emerging as a husky-throated crooner of bedsit ballards. See also his recently reissued *Beautiful Losers,* one of the most aggressively experimental Canadian novels of the Sixties (Blackspring, £5.95; $4.95).

**Robertson Davies** *The Cornish Trilogy* (Penguin, £9.99; $8.95) and *The Deptford Trilogy* (Penguin, £8.99; $8.95). Davies' big, dark and complicated upmarket soap operas are partly set in the semi-rural Canada of his youth, though earlier books such as *Tempest-Tost* and *Fifth Business* ($4.95 each) make more of their Canadian locales.

**Lovat Dickson** *Wilderness Man* (Macmillan, $5.95; Can$5.95). The fascinating story of Archie Belaney, the Englishman who became famous as his adopted persona, Grey Owl. Written by his English publisher and friend, who was one of many that did not discover the charade until after Grey Owl's death.

**Rita Donovan** *Dark Jewels* (University of Toronto Press, o/p). A novel about the trials and tribulations of miners during the 1920s in Sydney, Cape Breton.

**Timothy Findley** *The Wars* (Penguin, $6.95; $5.95) and *Famous Last Words* (Penguin, $6.95; $5.95). Two novels dealing with the waste and dehumanisation of war – the former set in World War I, the latter in World War II. Findley's latest, *Inside Memory: Pages from a Writer's Notebook* (Harper Collins, $27.95) is a collection of sometimes painful reminiscences, addressing his homosexuality, his lapses into alcoholism and his careers in fiction, acting and screenwriting.

**Grey Owl** *The Men of the Last Frontier; Pilgrims of the Wild; The Adventures of Sajo and Her Beaver People; Tales of an Empty Cabin* (all Macmillan $9; Bishopgate Can$10). First published in the 1930s, these books romantically describe life in the wilds of Canada at the time when exploitation was changing the land forever. His love of animals and the wilderness are inspiring and his forward-thinking ecological views are particularly startling.

**Hammond Innes** *Campbell's Kingdom* (Fontana, £2.99; Carroll & Graf, $3.50). A melodrama of love and oil-drilling in the Canadian Rockies – though the landscape's less well evoked than in *The Land God Gave Cain* (Fontana, £2.99; Carroll & Graf, $3.50), the story of one man's search for "gold and truth" in Labrador.

**Margaret Laurence** *A Jest of God* (Virago, £4.99). Manitoba-born Laurence epitomised the new vigour that swept through the country's literature during the Sixties – though the best of her fiction was written in England. Most of her books are set in the fictional prairie backwater of Manawaka, and most explore the loneliness and frustration of women within an environment of stifling small-town conventionality. Always highly revered at home, Laurence's reputation is on the increase abroad; most of her books are now published in the UK by Virago – see also *The Stone Angel* and *The Diviners*.

**Stephen Leacock** *Sunshine Sketches of a Little Town* (McClelland & Stewart, Can$4). Whimsical tale of Ontario small-town life; the best of a series based on the author's summertime stays in Orillia.

**Jack London** *Call of the Wild, White Fang and Other Stories* (Penguin, £4.99; $5.95). London spent over a year in the Yukon goldfields during the Klondike gold rush. Many of his experiences found their way into his vivid if sometimes overwrought tales of the northern wilderness.

**Malcolm Lowry** *Hear Us O Lord from Heaven thy Dwelling Place* (Picador, £7.99; Carroll & Graf, $9.95). Lowry spent almost half his writing life (1939–54) in log cabins and beach houses he built for himself around Vancouver. *Hear Us O Lord* is a difficult read to say the least: a fragmentary novella which amongst other things describes a disturbing sojourn on Canada's wild Pacific coast.

**W O Mitchell** *Who Has Seen the Wind* (Macmillan, $12). Canada's equivalent of *Huckleberry Finn* is a folksy story of a young boy coming of age in small-town Saskatchewan, with great off-beat characters and fine evocations of Prairie life. Mitchell's *The Vanishing Point* (Macmillan $12.95), though witty and fun to read, is a moving testimony to the complexities of native assimilation in a country dominated by "immigrants".

**Brian Moore** *Black Robe* (Pan, £4.99; Fawcett, $3.95). Moore emigrated to Canada from Ireland in 1948 and stayed long enough to gain citizenship before moving on to California. *Black Robe* – the story of a missionary's jour-

ney into native territory – is typical of the author's preoccupations with Catholicism, repression and redemption.

**L M Montgomery** *Anne of Green Gables* (Harrap, £5.95; Bantam, $8.85). Growing pains and bucolic bliss in a cloying children's classic from 1908.

**Alice Munro** *Lives of Girls and Women* (Penguin, £5.99; $6.95); *The Progress of Love* (Flamingo, £4.99; $5.95); *Dance of the Happy Shades* (Penguin £5.99; $6.95); *The Beggar Maid* (Penguin; £5.99; $6.95); *Friend of my Youth* (Vintage, £5.99; $6.95). Amongst the world's finest living short-story writers, Munro deals primarily with the lives of women in the semirural and Protestant backcountry of southwest Ontario.

**New Oxford Book of Canadian Verse** (ed. Margaret Atwood, OUP, £12.95 ). Canadian poets are increasingly finding a distinctive voice, but few except this collection's editor have made much impact outside their native country. Atwood's own sharp, witty examinations of nationality and gender, are among the best in this anthology – more of her verse is published in the UK by Virago.

**Oxford Book of Canadian Ghost Stories** (OUP, £9.95; $8.95). Over twenty stories, including W P Kinsella's *Shoeless Joe Jackson Comes to Iowa* – the inspiration for the fey *Field of Dreams*.

**Oxford Book of Canadian Short Stories in English** (ed. Margaret Atwood, OUP, £12.95; $27.95). A broad selection which delves beyond the better known names of Alice Munro and Margaret Atwood.

**Oxford Companion to Canadian Literature** (OUP, £35). At almost 900 pages, this is the last word on the subject, though it's more useful as a work of reference than as a primer for the country's literature.

**Mordecai Richler** *The Apprenticeship of Duddy Kravitz* (Penguin, £5.99; $9.95). Richler uses his early experiences of Montréal's working-class Jewish ghetto in many of his novels, especially in this, his best known work, an acerbic and slick cross-cultural romance built around the ambivalent but brilliantly drawn figure of Kravitz. Richler's pushy and ironic prose is not to all tastes, but you might also try *Solomon Gursky Was Here* (Penguin, £6.99; $9.95).

**Robert Service** *The Best of Robert Service* (Running Press, £14.95; Putnam, $7.95). Service's Victorian ballads of pioneer and gold-rush life have a certain period charm, but generally make unintentionally hilarious reading.

**Elizabeth Smart** *By Grand Central Station I Sat Down and Wept* (Paladin, £3.99). A cult masterpiece which lyrically details the writer's love affair with the English poet George Barker. See also the less well-known *The Assumption of Rogues and Rascals* (Paladin, £3.99) and the acclaimed *Collected Poems* (Paladin, £4.99).

**Audrey Thomas** *The Wild Blue Yonder* (Fourth Estate, £13.99). A collection of witty tales about male-female relationships by renowned Canadian short-story writer.

**John Wyndham** *The Crysalids* (Penguin, £3.99; Ballantine, $4.95). A science-fiction classic built around a group of telepathic children and their adventures in post-holocaust Labrador.

### SPECIALIST GUIDES

**Don Beers** *The Wonder of Yoho* (Rocky Mountain Books, Can$14.95). Good photos and solid text extolling the delights of Yoho National Park in the Rockies.

**Darryl Bray** *Kluane National Park Hiking Guide* (Travel Vision, Can$12.95). A much-needed guide to long and short walks in a park where the trail network is still in its infancy.

**Castleman, Pitcher & Stanley** *The Alaska-Yukon Handbook* (Moon £9.99; $11.95; Can$12.95). Only sixteen of this book's 300 pages refer directly to the Yukon, but it contains some useful background and introductory material, and is good if you're combining a trip to both places.

**Ron Dalby** *The Alaska Highway: An Insider's Guide* (Fulcrum, Can$14.95). Less detailed but less dry than its main competitor, the better-known and encyclopaedic *Milepost* (Northwest Books, $14.95).

**Neil G Carey** *A Guide to the Queen Charlotte Islands* (Northwest Books, $12.65). An authoritative guide to islands which are difficult to explore and ill-served by back-up literature.

**Daniel Desjjrdins** (editor) *Montréal Night and Day* (Ulysse, Can$11.95). Trendy, up-front guide to the hippest and most sophisticated sides of Montréal.

**John Dodd and Gail Helgason** *The Canadian Rockies Access Guide* (Lone Pine, Can$15.95). Descriptions of 115 day hikes, with degrees of difficulties, time needed, sketch maps of routes, wildlife descriptions and numerous photos.

**David Dunbar** *The Outdoor Traveller's Guide to Canada* (Stewart, Tabori & Chang, £12.99; $17.95; Can$18.95). Too bulky to be a useful guide in the field, but a lavishly illustrated introduction to the outdoor pursuits, wildlife and geology of 37 of the country's best national and provincial parks.

**Ben Gadd** *A Handbook of the Canadian Rockies* (Corax, Can$25). Widely available in western Canada's larger bookshops, this is a lovingly produced and painstakingly detailed account of walks, flora, fauna, geology and anything else remotely connected with the Rockies.

**Suzy Gresham and Judith Thomas** *Born to Shop Canada* (Bantam, $8.95; Can$9.95). One of an excellent American series – pocket-size but with comprehensive details of finding the best of Canada's products from clothes designers to Inuit crafts.

**Anne Hardy** *Where to Eat in Canada* (Oberon, Can$11.95). The only coast-to-coast Canadian guide covering eateries from the smallest greasy spoon to haute-cuisine. Very subjective, but excellent details on specialities, opening hours and prices.

**Ed and Lynn Henderson** *Adventure Guide to the Alaska Highway* (Moorland, £11.99; Hunter, Can$13.95) A reasonable though not terribly penetrating guide to the highway, how to prepare for it and what to see.

**Jane King** *The British Columbia Handbook* (Moon, £10.95; $11.95; Can$12.95). A comprehensive but dated and uncritical look at the province.

**The Lost Moose Catalogue** (Lost Moose Publishing, Can$19.95). Highly entertaining and iconoclastic magazine-style guide and commentary on the contemporary mores of the Yukon and far north.

**Teri Lydiard** *The British Columbia Bicycling Guide* (Gordon Soules, Can$9.95). Small but extremely detailed pointer to some tempting routes, backed up with good maps.

**Janice E Macdonald** *Canoeing Alberta* (Macdonald, Can$12.95). A canoeist's Bible, with many detailed accounts of the province's waterways, and especially good on routes in the Rockies.

**Ken Madsen and Graham Wilson** *Rivers of the Yukon* (Primrose Publishing, Can$12.95). An invaluable guide to some of the country's best canoeing rivers.

**Linda Moyer and Burl Willes** *Unexplored Islands of the US and Canadian West Coast* (John Muir, £8.99; Can$12.95). A generous portion of the guide is devoted to an intimate but rather homely run through some of British Columbia's lesser known islands.

**Betty Pratt-Johnson** series (Adventure Publishing; Can$8.95 each). The author has produced five separate books whose 157 canoeing routes provide the definitive account of how and where to canoe the lakes and rivers of British Columbia.

**Bruce Obee** *The Gulf Islands Explorer* (Whitecap, Can$12.95). Also useful in the same series is Eliane Jones' *The Northern Gulf Islands Explorer.*

**Bruce Obee** *The Pacific Rim Explorer* (Whitecap, Can$12.95). A good overall summary of the walks, wildlife and social history of the Pacific Rim National Park and its nearby towns.

**Gerda Pantel** *The Canadian Bed and Breakfast Guide* (Fitzhenry & Whiteside, Can$10). Over a thousand B&B listings (all written by the hosts) from across the country. Useful pointers as to proximity of public transport and local sights.

**Brian Patton and Bart Robinson** *The Canadian Rockies Trail Guide* (Summerthought, £12.95; Can$14.95). An absolutely essential guide for anyone wishing to do more than simply scratch the surface of the Rockies' walking possibilities.

**Doug Robertson** *The Best Hiking in Ontario* (Hurtig, Can$12.95). Covering nearly all of Ontario's hiking areas, but sketchy in parts and rather out of date.

**Archie Shutterfield** *The Chilkoot Trail: A Hiker's Historical Guide* (Alaska Northwest Books, Can$10.95). An pithy accompaniment to the Chilkoot Trail that should be read in conjunction with Pierre Berton's *Klondike.*

**Sierra Club of West Canada** *The West Coast Trail* (Douglas & McIntyre, Can$8.99). Now in its sixth edition, this is probably the best of several guides to Vancouver Island's popular but demanding long-distance footpath.

# LANGUAGE

Canada has two official languages – **English** and **French** – but there are numerous native tongues as well. Tensions between the two main groups play a prominent part in the politics of Canada, but the native languages are more or less ignored except in areas such as the Northwest Territories, where **Inuktitut**, the language of the Inuit, is spoken widely. The Inuit are the only native population with their own language TV channel; the only group afforded even comparable attention are the Montagnais – Montagnais-Naskapi translations appear in northern Québec and Labrador official publications. In a brief glossary such as this there is no space to get to grips with the complexities of native Canadian languages, and very few travellers would have any need of an overview anyway – due to the suppression of their mother tongues through the years, most natives (including those in Québec) have a good knowledge of English, especially if they deal with tourists in any capacity.

## FRENCH IN QUÉBEC

Québec's official language differs from its European source only as far as North American English differs from British English. Yet while the Québécois French vocabulary, grammar and syntax may not constitute a separate language, the speech of Québec can pose a few problems. Tracing its roots back to seventeenth-century popular French, the Québécois language has obviously come under English influence, producing a dialect that's a source of amusement to most French people and bafflement for Anglophones who thought they were familiar with the French language. Within Québec itself there are marked regional differences of pronunciation, so much so that Montréalers find it hard to understand northern Québécois.

However, Québécois are extremely sympathetic when visiting English-speakers make the effort to speak French – and most Québécois are much more forthcoming with their knowledge of English when talking to a Briton or American than to a Canadian. Similarly easygoing is the attitude towards the formal *vous* (you), which is used less often in Québec – you may even be corrected when saying *S'il vous plaît* to saying *S'il te plaît*. Another popular phrase that you are likely to come across is *pas de tout* (not at all) which in Québec is pronounced *pan toot*, completely different from the French *pa de too*. The same goes for *c'est tout?* ("is that all?", pronounced *say toot*), which you'll hear every time you buy something in a shop.

With **pronunciation** there's little point trying to mimic the local dialect – generally, just stick to the classic French rules. Consonants at the ends of words are usually silent and at other times are much as in English, except that **ch** is always sh, **ç** is s, **h** is silent, **th** is the same as t, **ll** is like the y in yes and **r** is growled. One major way Québécois pronunciation differs is that the v is pronounced, unlike in France where it is pronounced as a w.

## FRENCH WORDS AND PHRASES

### Basics

| | | | |
|---|---|---|---|
| Good morning/afternoon/Hello | Bonjour | Tomorrow | Demain |
| Good evening | Bonsoir | Day after tomorrow | Aprés-demain |
| Good night | Bonne nuit | Yesterday | Hier |
| Goodbye | Au revoir | Now | Maintenant |
| Yes | Oui | Later | Plus tard |
| No | Non | Wait a minute! | Un instant! |
| Please | S'il vous/te plaît | In the morning | Le matin |
| Thank you (very much) | Merci (beaucoup) | In the afternoon | L'après-midi |
| You're welcome | Bienvenue/de rien/Je vous en prie | In the evening | Le soir |
| | | Here/there | Ici/Là |
| OK | D'accord | Good/bad | Bon/mauvais |
| How are you? | Comment allez-vous? / Ça va? | Big/small | Grand/petit |
| | | Cheap/expensive | Bon marché/cher |
| Fine, thanks | Très bien, merci | Early/late | Tôt/Tard |
| Do you speak English? | Parlez-vous anglais? | Hot/cold | Chaud/froid |
| I don't understand | Je ne comprends pas | Near/far | Près (pas loin)/loin |
| I don't know | Je ne sais pas | Vacant/occupied | Libre/occupé |
| Excuse me | Je m'excuse | Quickly/slowly | Vite/lentement |
| Excuse me (in a crowd) | Excusez-moi | Loudly/quietly | Bruyant/tranquille |
| Sorry | Pardon/désolé(e) | With/without | Avec/sans |
| I'm English/Scottish/Welsh/Irish/American | Je suis anglais(e)/écossais(e)/gallois(e)/irlandais(e)/américain(e) | More/less | Plus/moins |
| | | Enough/no more | Assez/ça suffit |
| | | Mr | Monseiur |
| I live in . . . | Je demeure à | Mrs | Madame |
| Today | Aujourd'hui | Miss | Mademoiselle |

### Questions and Directions

| | | | |
|---|---|---|---|
| Where? | Où? | Can you give me a lift to . . . ? | Pouvez-vous me conduire jusqu'à . . . ? |
| When? | Quand? | | |
| What? (what is it?) | Quoi? (qu'est-ce que c'est?) | Can you tell me when to get off? | Pouvez-vous me dire quand descendre? |
| How much/many? | Combien? | What time is it? | Quelle heure est-il? |
| Why? | Pourquoi? | What time does it open? | A quelle heure ca ouvre? |
| It is/there is (is it/is there . . ?) | C'est/Il y a (est-ce/Y a-t-il . . .?) | How much does it cost | Combien çela coûte-t-il? |
| How do I get to . . . ? | Où se trouve . . . ? | How do you say it in French? | Comment ça se dit en francais? |
| How far is it to . . . ? | A quelle distance est-il à . . . ? | | |

### Numbers

| | | | | | | | |
|---|---|---|---|---|---|---|---|
| 1 | un/une | 11 | onze | 21 | vingt-et-un | 101 | cent-et-un |
| 2 | deux | 12 | douze | 22 | vingt-deux | 110 | cent-dix |
| 3 | trois | 13 | trieze | 30 | trente | 200 | deux cents |
| 4 | quatre | 14 | quatorze | 40 | quarante | 500 | cinq cents |
| 5 | cinq | 15 | quinze | 50 | cinquante | 1000 | mille |
| 6 | six | 16 | seize | 60 | soixante | 2000 | deux milles |
| 7 | sept | 17 | dix-sept | 70 | soixante-dix | 1,000,000 | un million |
| 8 | huit | 18 | dix-huit | 80 | quatre-vingts | | |
| 9 | neuf | 19 | dix-neuf | 90 | quatre-vingt-dix | | |
| 10 | dix | 20 | vingt | 100 | cent | | |

## Accommodation

| | | | |
|---|---|---|---|
| Hotel | *Hôtel* | Do you have anything cheaper? | *Avez-vous quelque chose de meilleur marché?* |
| Is there a room nearby? | *Y a-t-il une chambre près d'ici?* | Full board | *Tout compris* |
| Do you have a room . . . | *Avez-vous une chambre . . .* | Can I see the room? | *Je peux voir la chambre?* |
| for one/two/three people | *pour une/deux/trois personne(s)* | I'll take this one | *Je vais prendre celle-ci* |
| for one/two/three nights | *pour une/deux/trois nuit(s)* | I'd like to book a room | *J'aimerais reserver une chambre* |
| for one/two weeks | *pour une/deux semaine(s)* | I have a booking | *J'ai une réservation* |
| with a double bed | *avec un lit double* | Can we camp here? | *Pouvons-nous camper ici?* |
| with a shower/bath | *avec douche/salle de bain* | Is there a campsite nearby? | *Y a-t-il un camping près d'ici?* |
| hot/cold water | *eau chaude/froide* | Tent | *Tente* |
| How much is it? | *C'est combien?* | Cabin | *Chalet* |
| It's expensive | *C'est chère* | Youth hostel | *Auberge de jeunesse* |
| Is breakfast included? | *Est-ce que le petit déjeuner est compris?* | | |

## Travelling

| | | | |
|---|---|---|---|
| Aeroplane | *Avion* | One way/return | *Aller simple/aller-retour* |
| Bus | *Autobus* | Can I book a seat? | *Puis-je réserver un siège* |
| Train | *Train* | What time does it leave? | *Il part à quelle heure?* |
| Car | *Voiture* | When is the next bus/ train/ferry to . . . | *Quand est le prochain bus/train/traversée pour . . . .* |
| Taxi | *Taxi* | | |
| Bicycle | *Velo* | | |
| Ferry | *Traverse* | Do I have to change? | *Ai-je à transférer?* |
| Ship | *Bâteau* | Where does it leave from? | *D'où est-ce qu'il part?* |
| Hitch-hiking | *Faire du pouce* | | |
| On foot | *À pied* | How many kilometres? | *Combien de kilometres?* |
| Bus station | *Gare routière/gare des autobuses* | How many hours? | *Combien d'heures?* |
| Railway station | *Gare centrale* | What number bus is it to . . .? | *Quel autobus dois-je prendre pour aller à/au* |
| Ferry terminal | *Terminus* | Where's the road to . . . ? | *Où est la route pour . . .?* |
| Port | *Port* | Next stop, please | *Le prochain arrêt, s'il plaît* |
| A ticket to . . . | *Un billet pour . . .* | | |

## Some signs

| | | | |
|---|---|---|---|
| Entrance/Exit | *Entrée/Sortie* | Platform | *Voie* |
| Free entrance | *Entrée Libre* | Cash desk | *Caisse* |
| Gentlemen/Ladies | *Messieurs/Dames* | Go/Walk | *Marchez* |
| WC | *Toilette* | Stop | *Arretez* |
| Vacant/Engaged | *Libre/Occupé* | Customs | *Douanes* |
| Open/Closed | *Ouvert/Fermé* | Do not touch | *Defense de toucher* |
| Arrivals/Departures | *Arrivées/Departs* | Danger | *Danger* |
| Closed for holidays | *Fermé pour les vacances* | Beware | *Attention* |
| Pull/Push | *Tirez/Poussez* | First aid | *Premiers soins* |
| Out of order | *Hors d'usage/Brisé* | Ring the bell | *Sonnez* |
| To let | *A loué* | No smoking | *Defense de fumer* |

## Driving

| | | | |
|---|---|---|---|
| Left/right | *Gauche/droite* | No through road | *Cul-de-sac* |
| Straight ahead | *Tout droit* | No overtaking | *Défenser de dépasser* |
| Turn to the left/right | *Tournez à gauche/droite* | Passing lane only | *Voie reservée au* |
| Car park | *Le terrain de* | | *depassement* |
| | *stationnement* | Speed | *Vitesse* |
| No parking | *Défense de stationner/* | Self-service | *Libre service* |
| | *stationnement interdit* | Full service | *Sevice complet* |
| Tow-away zone | *Zone de Remorquage* | Fill the tank with regular | *Faites le plein avec de* |
| Cars towed at owners | *Remorquage à vos frais* | . . . super . . . unleaded | *l'essence ordinaire . . .* |
| expense | | | *du super . . . du sans* |
| One way street | *Sens unique* | | *plomb* |
| No entry | *Défenser de entrer* | Please check the oil . . . | *Vérifiez l'huile . . . la* |
| Slow down | *Ralentir* | battery . . . radiator . . . | *batterie . . . le radiateur* |
| Proceed on flashing | *Attendez sur le feu vert* | tire pressure . . . plugs | *. . . pression des pneus/* |
| green light | *clignotant* | | *tires . . . bougies* |
| Turn on headlights | *Allumez vos phares* | Blow up the tyres | *Souffler les tires* |

# INDEX

## HELP US UPDATE

We've gone to a lot of effort to make sure that the **Rough Guide to Canada** is thoroughly up-to-date and accurate. However things do change, and we'd very much appreciate any comments, corrections or additions for the next edition of the book. For the best letters, we'll send a copy of the new edition or any other Rough Guide. Please mark letters "Rough Guide Canada Update" and send to:
Rough Guides, 1 Mercer Street, London WC2H 9QJ
or
Rough Guides, 375 Hudson Street, 4th Floor, New York NY10014

# DIRECT ORDERS IN THE UK

| Title | ISBN | Price |
|---|---|---|
| Amsterdam | 1858280060 | £7.99 |
| Australia | 1858280354 | £12.99 |
| Barcelona & Catalunya | 1858280486 | £7.99 |
| Berlin | 1858280338 | £8.99 |
| Brazil | 0747101272 | £7.95 |
| Brittany & Normandy | 1858280192 | £7.99 |
| Bulgaria | 1858280478 | £8.99 |
| California | 1858280575 | £9.99 |
| Canada | 185828001X | £10.99 |
| Crete | 1858280494 | £6.99 |
| Cyprus | 185828032X | £8.99 |
| Czech & Slovak Republics | 185828029X | £8.99 |
| Egypt | 1858280753 | £10.99 |
| England | 1858280788 | £9.99 |
| Europe | 185828077X | £14.99 |
| Florida | 1858280109 | £8.99 |
| France | 1858280508 | £9.99 |
| Germany | 1858280257 | £11.99 |
| Greece | 1858280206 | £9.99 |
| Guatemala & Belize | 1858280451 | £9.99 |
| Holland, Belgium & Luxembourg | 1858280036 | £8.99 |
| Hong Kong & Macau | 1858280664 | £8.99 |
| Hungary | 1858280214 | £7.99 |
| Ireland | 1858280516 | £8.99 |
| Italy | 1858280311 | £12.99 |
| Kenya | 1858280435 | £9.99 |
| Mediterranean Wildlife | 0747100993 | £7.95 |
| Morocco | 1858280400 | £9.99 |
| Nepal | 185828046X | £8.99 |
| New York | 1858280583 | £8.99 |
| Nothing Ventured | 0747102082 | £7.99 |
| Paris | 1858280389 | £7.99 |
| Peru | 0747102546 | £7.95 |
| Poland | 1858280346 | £9.99 |
| Portugal | 1858280842 | £9.99 |
| Prague | 185828015X | £7.99 |
| Provence & the Côte d'Azur | 1858280230 | £8.99 |
| Pyrenees | 1858280524 | £7.99 |
| St Petersburg | 1858280303 | £8.99 |
| San Francisco | 1858280826 | £8.99 |
| Scandinavia | 1858280397 | £10.99 |
| Scotland | 1858280834 | £8.99 |
| Sicily | 1858280370 | £8.99 |
| Spain | 1858280079 | £8.99 |
| Thailand | 1858280168 | £8.99 |
| Tunisia | 1858280656 | £8.99 |
| Turkey | 1858280133 | £8.99 |
| Tuscany & Umbria | 1858280559 | £8.99 |
| USA | 185828080X | £12.99 |
| Venice | 1858280362 | £8.99 |
| West Africa | 1858280141 | £12.99 |
| Women Travel | 1858280710 | £7.99 |
| Zimbabwe & Botswana | 1858280419 | £10.99 |

# DIRECT ORDERS IN THE USA

| Title | ISBN | Price |
|---|---|---|
| Able to Travel | 1858281105 | $19.95 |
| Amsterdam | 1858280869 | $13.95 |
| Australia | 1858280354 | $18.95 |
| Berlin | 1858280338 | $13.99 |
| Brittany & Normandy | 1858280192 | $14.95 |
| Bulgaria | 1858280478 | $14.99 |
| Canada | 185828001X | $14.95 |
| Crete | 1858280494 | $14.95 |
| Cyprus | 185828032X | $13.99 |
| Czech & Slovak Republics | 185828029X | $14.95 |
| Egypt | 1858280753 | $17.95 |
| England | 1858280788 | $16.95 |
| Europe | 185828077X | $18.95 |
| Florida | 1858280109 | $14.95 |
| France | 1858280508 | $16.95 |
| Germany | 1858280257 | $17.95 |
| Greece | 1858280206 | $16.95 |
| Guatemala & Belize | 1858280451 | $14.95 |
| Holland, Belgium & Luxembourg | 1858280877 | $15.95 |
| Hong Kong & Macau | 1858280664 | $13.95 |
| Hungary | 1858280214 | $13.95 |
| Italy | 1858280311 | $17.95 |
| Kenya | 1858280435 | $15.95 |
| Mediterranean Wildlife | 1858280699 | $15.95 |
| Morocco | 1858280400 | $16.95 |
| Nepal | 185828046X | $13.95 |
| New York | 1858280583 | $13.95 |
| Paris | 1858280389 | $13.95 |
| Poland | 1858280346 | $16.95 |
| Portugal | 1858280842 | $15.95 |
| Prague | 185828015X | $14.95 |
| Provence & the Côte d'Azur | 1858280230 | $14.95 |
| St Petersburg | 1858280303 | $14.95 |
| San Francisco | 1858280826 | $13.95 |
| Scandinavia | 1858280397 | $16.99 |
| Scotland | 1858280834 | $14.95 |
| Sicily | 1858280370 | $14.99 |
| Thailand | 1858280168 | $15.95 |
| Tunisia | 1858280656 | $15.95 |
| USA | 185828080X | $18.95 |
| Venice | 1858280362 | $13.99 |
| Women Travel | 1858280710 | $12.95 |
| Zimbabwe & Botswana | 1858280419 | $16.95 |

Rough Guides are available from all good bookstores, but can be obtained directly in the USA and Worldwide (except the UK*) from Penguin:

Charge your order by Master Card or Visa (US$15.00 minimum order): call 1-800-255-6476; or send orders, with complete name, address and zip code, and list price, plus $2.00 shipping and handling per order to: Consumer Sales, Penguin USA, PO Box 999 – Dept #17109, Bergenfield, NJ 07621. No COD. Prepay foreign orders by international money order, a cheque drawn on a US bank, or US currency. No postage stamps are accepted. All orders are subject to stock availability at the time they are processed. Refunds will be made for books not available at that time. Please allow a minimum of four weeks for delivery.

The availability and published prices quoted are correct at the time of going to press but are subject to alteration without prior notice. Titles currently not available outside the UK will be available by January 1995. Call to check.

* For UK orders, see separate price list

Train     110 or 66   R̄
                    130 ⇒ 220

393 7411

T ⇒ Quebec     173.34
                    ~~166.13~~

~~Tour pass~~ ~~$115(?)~~
          Route pass $189

              Transfer      M        Arrw

sunday  T̄                           7 or 8
      12 15 night      6.55         = 3 hrs
                                    10 or 11

Voyage Colonial.

                                   97.37

      9.00              8.55       45 +
                                   3 hrs.

  arrive Monday am

97 37        132
66.
————————————
168 32

Muse de la civil
10 - 7

Anglican Ch, 9 - 5

Musée du feu   10 - 5.30 closed
                            today
Citadelle   9am - 7pm.

Museu de Quebec.

10 - 5.45 pm

① 

Monday ⇒ Tues　Wednes　Thurs　Friday　Sat　Sun
　 ⎵ 　　　　Rachel　Toronto　cottage　cottage　Toronto
　Quebec　　　　　boat　　　　cottage　　Tom?

② 

Mon　　Tues　Wednes　Thurs　Friday　Sat　Sun
　　　　　　Toronto　Toronto　cottage　cottage　island
Quebec　⎵　　Trevor　boat　　　　cottage

Q.

416 266 2853

Boat (?)

# You are
## A STUDENT

# You travel
## THE WORLD

# You want
## TO SAVE MONEY

# Here's how

The International Student Identity Card

Entitles you to discounts and special services worldwide.

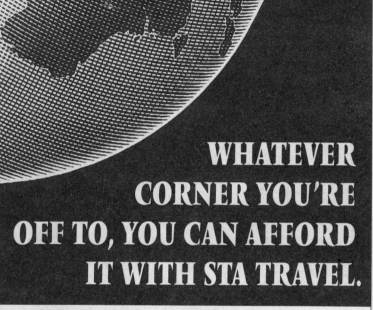

# WHATEVER CORNER YOU'RE OFF TO, YOU CAN AFFORD IT WITH STA TRAVEL.

At STA Travel we're all seasoned travellers, so wherever you're bound, we're bound to have been. We offer the best deals on fares with the flexibility to change your mind as you go. There are even better deals for students.

Call 071-937 1221 for your free copy of The STA Travel Guide.
117 Euston Road, NW1. 86 Old Brompton Road, SW7.
North America 071-937 9971, Europe 071-937 9921, Long Haul 071-937 9962,
Round the World 071-937 1733, or 061-834 0668 (Manchester).
USA freephone 1-800-777-0112.
Manchester, Leeds, Cambridge, Bristol, Oxford, London.

ABTA (99209) IATA

**WHEREVER YOU'RE BOUND, WE'RE BOUND TO HAVE BEEN.**

**STA TRAVEL**